Worldmark Encyclopedia of U.S. and Canadian Environmental Issues

Worldmark Encyclopedia of U.S. and Canadian Environmental Issues

Susan Bevan Gall and Margaret K. Antone,

EDITORS

GALE
CENGAGE Learning·

Detroit • New York • San Francisco • New Haven, Conn • Waterville, Maine • London

Worldmark Encyclopedia of U.S. and Canadian Environmental Issues

Susan Bevan Gall and Margaret K. Antone, Editors

Project Editor: Kimberley A. McGrath

Managing Editor: Debra Kirby

Rights Acquisition and Management: Robyn V. Young

Imaging and Multimedia: John L. Watkins

Manufacturing: Wendy Blurton, Dorothy Maki

Product Managers: Douglas A. Dentino

Product Design: Kristine A. Julien

For product information and technology assistance, contact us at
Gale Customer Support, 1-800-877-4253.
For permission to use material from this text or product,
submit all requests online at www.cengage.com/permissions.
Further permissions questions can be emailed to
permissionrequest@cengage.com

Cover and banner photographs: Hand in oil copyright Julie Dermansky/Corbis, 2011; Geese over water image copyright Marty Ellis/ShutterStock.com, 2011; Industrial garbage dumped image copyright Daniel Dempster Photography/Alamy, 2011; Banner image Canadian Rockies copyright Lowell R. Laudon/JLM Visuals. Reproduced by permission.

While every effort has been made to ensure the reliability of the information presented in this publication, Gale, a part of Cengage Learning, does not guarantee the accuracy of the data contained herein. Gale accepts no payment for listing; and inclusion in the publication of any organization, agency, institution, publication, service, or individual does not imply endorsement of the editors or publisher. Errors brought to the attention of the publisher and verified to the satisfaction of the publisher will be corrected in future editions.

LIBRARY OF CONGRESS CATALOGING-IN-PUBLICATION DATA

Worldmark encyclopedia of U.S. and Canadian environmental issues / Susan Bevan Gall and Margaret K. Antone, editors.
    p. cm.
    Includes bibliographical references and index.
    ISBN 978-1-4144-9088-5 (hardcover) – ISBN 1-4144-9088-7 (hardcover) – ISBN 978-1-4144-9089-2 (e-book) – ISBN 1-4144-9089-5 (e-book)
    1. Environmentalism–United States–Encyclopedias. 2. Environmentalism–Canada–Encyclopedias. 3. United States–Environmental conditions–Encyclopedias. 4. Canada–Environmental conditions–Encyclopedias. I. Gall, Susan B. II. Antone, Margaret K.

GE197.W67 2012
304.20973'03–dc23   2011049277

Gale
27500 Drake Rd.
Farmington Hills, MI, 48331-3535

ISBN-13: 978-1-4144-9088-5   ISBN-10: 1-4144-9088-7

This title is also available as an e-book.
ISBN-13: 978-1-4144-9089-2 ISBN-10: 1-4144-9089-5
Contact your Gale, a part of Cengage Learning sales representative for ordering information.

Printed in China
1 2 3 4 5 6 7 16 15 14 13 12

Contents

Contents

Contributors and Reviewers

While compiling the *Worldmark Encyclopedia of U.S. and Canadian Environmental Issues*, the editors relied upon the expertise and contributions of the following scientists, scholars, and researchers, who served as contributors and/or reviewers for the encyclopedia.

Lilian Alessa, PhD
Assistant Professor of Biological Sciences
University of Alaska Anchorage

Nathaniel Baer
Energy Program Director
Iowa Environmental Council

Jack N. Barkenbus, PhD
Associate Director
Climate Change Research Network/Vanderbilt Institute for Energy and Environment

Florence Bocquet, PhD
Managing Director, Center for Research and Education in Wind (CREW)
University of Colorado at Boulder

Mark Brohman
Executive Director
The Nebraska Environmental Trust

Dennis Burton
Executive Director
Schuylkill Center

John Colton, PhD
Environment and Sustainability Studies
Acadia University

Sarah Cottrell
Deputy Secretary
New Mexico Environment Department

John Cusick, PhD
Environmental Studies Program Advisor
University of Hawaii

Dorothy Daley, PhD
Associate Professor, Political Science & Environmental Studies
University of Kansas

James E. Deacon, PhD
Distinguished Professor of Environmental Studies, Retired
University of Nevada Las Vegas

Merrily A. Enquist
Oregon State University Extension Service

Alan Fryar, PhD
Associate Professor and Director of Graduate Studies, Earth & Environmental Sciences
University of Kentucky

Gwendolyn Geidel, PhD
Assistant Director, School of the Environment
University of South Carolina

Marian Riggs Gelb
Executive Director
Iowa Environmental Council

Stephen W. Golladay, PhD
Joseph W. Jones Ecological Research Center at Ichauway

Guy A. Hanley
Curator of Collections, Cyril Moore Science Center
Minot State University

Joyce Hardin, PhD
Environmental Studies Chair
Hendrix College

Timothy H. Heaton, PhD
Professor of Earth Sciences
University of South Dakota

Donata Henry, PhD
Ecology & Evolutionary Biology
Tulane University

Chris Hoagstrom, PhD
Assistant Professor, Department of Zoology
Weber University

Steven Hollenhorst, PhD
Associate Dean, College of Natural Resources
University of Idaho

Nadine Johnson
Arizona Association of Environmental Education

Pauline Johnson, PhD
University of Alabama

Pawan Kahol, PhD
Professor and Associate Dean, College of Natural and Applied Science
Missouri State University

James Kotcon, PhD
West Virginia University

Laura Lemmens
Head Librarian
Great West Life Site Library, Alberta

Dan Lucas
Senior Planner
Tallahassee-Leon County Planning Department

Peter Marx
Senior Policy Advisor–Choose Clean Water Coalition, Chesapeake Mid-Atlantic Regional Center
National Wildlife Federation

Jen Mihills
National Wildlife Federation

Robert W. Nairn, PhD
Director, Center for Restoration of Ecosystems and Watersheds, School of Civil Engineering and Environmental Science
University of Oklahoma

Michael Nardolilli
President
Northern Virginia Conservation Trust

Kathleen Nuckolls, PhD
Lecturer, Environmental Studies
University of Kansas

Richard M. Petrone, PhD
Associate Professor, Department of Geography & Environmental Studies, Director, Cold Regions Research Centre
Wilfrid Laurier University

Robert Pitt, PhD
Professor and Environmental Institute Director
University of Alabama

Rick Reibstein
Adjunct Professor, Geography and Environment and Center for Energy and Environmental Studies, Department of Geography and Environment
Boston University

Roy Rich, PhD
Center for International Energy, Environment, and Policy (CIEEP), Jackson School of Geosciences
University of Texas, Austin

Celeste Royer
Director of Environmental Education
San Luis Obispo County Office of Education

Robert Sanford, PhD
Professor and Chair, Department of Environmental Science
University of Southern Maine

Kathleen Saul
Evergreen State College

John Tanaka, PhD
Renewable Resources Department Head
University of Wyoming

Stephanie Tatham
Attorney, Kaplan Kirsch & Rockwell
Denver, Colorado

Reader's Guide

The *Worldmark Encyclopedia of U.S. and Canadian Environmental Issues* (WEUSCEI) addresses issues of increasing interest in the twenty-first century: environmental preservation, energy resources, climate change, and careers and business initiatives—categorized as green jobs or green business—that prioritize environmental concerns. WEUSCEI also explores the economic and political forces that prioritize other factors over the environment and, as a result, may be resistant to pursuing a green agenda. WEUSCEI's articles explore the state of the natural environment, renewable energy resources, and green business activities, and other forces that influence them, in each of the 50 U.S. states and 13 Canadian provinces and territories.

Overview essays on the United States and Canada present a snapshot of the situation as of 2011, with a view to future trends. The U.S. overview was prepared by Richard Reibstein, an attorney and adjunct professor in environmental law at Suffolk University and Boston University. Canada's overview was prepared by Laura Lemmens, Head Librarian, Great West Life Site Library, Alberta.

❧ Profile Features

In WEUSCEI each state, province, and territory has an article devoted to its unique environment as well as the local initiatives to protect, preserve, and use its natural resources. The overview strives to include in each section the current thinking on environmental issues and forces at play and how the state/provincial/territorial outlook on these environmental issues has evolved over time. Overviews were developed in consultation with, and reviewed by, subject-matter experts. Sources used and resources for further study are cited at the end of each article.

The overviews are organized according to standard headings, which facilitate comparison among the states, provinces, and territories. Each overview begins with an introduction presenting a general review of the natural features of the state, province, or territory. The general climate is also described, with historical patterns reviewed and notable dramatic weather events highlighted. In addition, the government's actions on climate change and response to federal climate change initiatives are discussed.

Following the introduction is a section on natural resources, water, and agriculture. Readers will learn about the principal natural resources, along with the major challenges to the natural environment being faced. Where appropriate, these descriptions may be presented according to region. Special attention is focused on natural resources with economic impact, such as fishing, minerals, and water resources that support notable shipping and/or recreation. This section includes a brief summary of the parks, forests, and protected areas, as well as indigenous wildlife and plant life, noting any problems being caused by invasive nonnative species. Also included is a description of the prevailing agricultural practices in the state, province, or territory, along with a summary of organic farming efforts. Water resources and issues are presented, along with political activities related to them. Any other major issues pertaining to natural resources and agriculture are discussed as appropriate.

The next section deals with energy resources. The major energy sources of the state, province, or territory are summarized, with news or facts about the use of coal, natural gas, nuclear power, and renewable energy resources. Energy issues specific to the state, province, or territory are presented, along with analysis of historically entrenched energy sectors and related political debates. Where applicable, the section includes information on local energy plans and goals, including the status of the Renewal Energy Portfolio strategies.

The initiatives supporting sustainable business practices (known as green business), support for sustainable (or green) building practices, and efforts to grow this sector of the economy by supporting green jobs are the subject of the next section. It describes where these initiatives stand as of 2011, and where they appear to be headed. The focus of economic development and other government initiatives are outlined, notable green building projects, and entrenched practices that are resistant to change are highlighted. In this section, too, buildings that have received certification under the Green Building Council's Leadership in Energy and Environmental Design (LEED) program are mentioned.

The final section of each entry focuses on a single issue that is unique to the state, province, or territory. Examples of topics covered in this section are the proposed wind farm for Nantucket Sound (Massachusetts), invasive species (Asian carp) in Lake Michigan (Michigan), water resources (Nevada), mining of oil sands (Alberta), biomass energy debate (Nova Scotia), and ecotourism (Yukon).

Maps and Profile Tables

Each state, province, and territory article is accompanied by a map created specifically for WEUSCEI. The maps illustrate (by county for the United States) pollution density in color coding. Icons are used on the maps to indicate each state's main energy sources, locations of power plants, and major mineral deposits. In addition, every map provides the locations of national parks and the highest and lowest points within the state, province, or territory. For the U.S. state maps, major state parks are also featured.

Also accompanying the entries is a profile in table format. The profile provides information on the physical characteristics of the state, province, or territory (such as national forest lands and parks) and statistics on production of renewable energy, oil and gas reserves, and soil and air pollution.

❧ Other Features

Completing the work are: a chronology of environmental history, for both the United States and Canada; a glossary of special terms; a section listing major environmental protection and advocacy organizations in the United States and Canada, with contact and Web site information; a general bibliography, with books, periodicals, and Web sites, for further study; and a general index.

❧ Sources

Many sources were consulted in the preparation of the state, province, and territory profiles appearing in WEUSCEI. Sources are listed at the end of each article.

❧ Acknowledgments

The editors and contributors acknowledge with gratitude the support of the thirty-nine subject-matter experts, listed elsewhere in the front matter, who provided invaluable assistance in the development and review of the state, province, and territory profiles.

Glossary of Special Terms

A

ABIOTIC: A term used to describe the portion of an ecosystem that is not living, such as water or soil.

ABLATION (GLACIAL): The erosive reduction of ice or snow from the surface of a mass of ice.

ACID: A substance that when dissolved in water is capable of reacting with a base to form a salt.

ACID MINE DRAINAGE (AMD): Water that is polluted from contact with products or processes associated with mining, usually coal mining.

ACID RUNOFF: A substance that when dissolved in water is capable of reacting with a base to form a salt.

ACTIVE FAULT: A fault where movement has been known to occur in recent geologic time.

ADAPTATION: Adjustment in a system found in nature to a new environment or a change to an existing environment.

AFFORESTATION: Planting trees on land that was not formerly forested.

AEROSOL: Liquid droplets or minute particles suspended in air.

AFTERSHOCK: A subsequent earthquake (usually smaller in magnitude) following a powerful earthquake that originates at or near the same place.

AGRICULTURE: Replacement of a natural ecosystem with animals and plants chosen by people.

AIR POLLUTION: The existence in the air of substances in concentrations that are determined unacceptable. Contaminants in the air we breathe come mainly from manufacturing industries, electric power plants, automobiles, buses, and trucks.

ALBEDO: A numerical expression describing the ability of an object or planet to reflect light.

ALFISOIL: Rich soil formed under deciduous forest.

ALGAE: Single-celled or multicellular plants or plantlike organisms that contain chlorophyll, thus making their own food through photosynthesis.

ALGAL BLOOM: Sudden reproductive explosion of algae (single-celled aquatic green plants) in a large, natural body of water such as a lake or sea. Blooms near coasts are sometimes called red tides.

ALTERNATIVE ENERGY: An energy source that is used as an alternative to fossil fuels. Solar, wind, and geothermal power are examples of alternative energies.

AMBIENT: Existing condition.

AMOSITE: The brown form of asbestos.

ANABOLISM: The process by which energy is used to build up complex molecules.

ANAEROBIC: Pertaining to the absence of oxygen.

ANAEROBIC BACTERIA: Bacteria that grow without oxygen, also called anaerobes.

ANNEX I COUNTRIES/PARTIES: Term used to describe a group of countries in documents related to the United Nations Framework Convention on Climate Change. The group includes all the countries in the Organization of Economic Cooperation and Development (OECD). Annex I countries made a commitment to return individually or jointly to their 1990 levels of greenhouse gas emissions by the year 2000.

ANTARCTIC TREATY: A 1959 series of agreements regulating international relations in Antarctica, establishing the area as a demilitarized zone to promote open scientific research.

ANTHROPOGENIC: Made by humans or resulting from human activities.

ANTHROPOGENIC SOURCES: Sources that are due to human activity. An example of anthropogenic air pollution is the burning of wood for fuel.

AQUACULTURE: The farming of fish or shellfish in freshwater or saltwater.

AQUIFER: Rock, soil, or sand that is able to hold and transmit water.

ARIDOSOL: Type of soil found in arid environments.

ARTESIAN SPRING OR WELL: Groundwater that flows from the aquifer to the surface without the need for a pump.

ASBESTOS: An incombustible fibrous mineral once commonly used for fireproofing and electrical insulation.

ASPHYXIATES: Compounds that cause a shortage of oxygen.

ATMOSPHERE: The air surrounding the Earth, described as a series of layers of different characteristics. The atmosphere, composed mainly of nitrogen and oxygen with traces of carbon dioxide, water vapor, and other gases, acts as a buffer between Earth and the sun.

ATOMIC BOMB: A highly destructive weapon that derives its explosive power from the fission of atomic nuclei.

ATOMIC NUCLEUS: The small, dense, positively charged central region of an atom, composed of protons and neutrons.

ATV: Abbreviation for "all-terrain vehicle," a four-wheeled vehicle designed for off-road use that is straddled like a motorcycle and steered with handlebars.

AVIAN INFLUENZA: Also known as bird flu, it is a respiratory disease caused by the H5N1 virus that is thought to have originated in Asian poultry factory farms. The disease, which is lethal when passed from bird-to-bird, is evolving to be capable of person-to-person transmission.

B

BASEL CONVENTION: A 1992 global treaty designed to restrict the movement of hazardous waste between nations, especially from developed to less-developed countries.

BASELINE POWER: The amount of steady, non-intermittent electric power that is constantly being produced by a power source.

BATTERY: Device that can easily convert stored energy in the chemical bonds of an electrolyte into electrical energy.

BEDROCK: Solid layer of rock lying beneath Earth's surface.

BENTHIC: Living on, or associated with, the ocean floor.

BIOAUGMENTATION: The introduction of specific strains of microorganisms to break down pollutants in contaminated soil or water.

BIOCHEMICAL OXYGEN DEMAND: The amount of oxygen required by decomposing microorganisms in a water sample and an important measure of water pollution.

BIODEGRADABLE: Capable of being degraded in the environment by the actions of microorganisms.

BIODIESEL: A fuel made from a combination of plant and animal fat. It can be safely mixed with petro diesel.

BIODIVERSITY: Literally, "life diversity": the wide range of plants and animals that exist within any given geographical region.

BIOENGINEERED CROP: Herbicide or insect-resistant plants developed through genetic engineering.

BIOFUEL: A fuel derived directly by human effort from living things, such as plants or bacteria. A biofuel can be burned or oxidized in a fuel cell to release useful energy.

BIOGEOCHEMICAL CYCLE: The chemical interactions that take place among the atmosphere, biosphere, hydrosphere, and geosphere.

BIOLOGICAL MAGNIFICATION: An increase in the concentration of toxins as they pass up the food chain.

BIOMASS: The sum total of living and once-living matter contained within a given geographic area; or, organic matter that can be converted to fuel and is regarded as a potential energy source.

BIOME: A well-defined terrestrial environment (e.g., desert, tundra, or tropical forest) and the complex of living organisms found in that region.

BIOREMEDIATION: The use of living organisms to help repair damage such as that caused by oil spills.

BIOSPHERE: All life forms on Earth and the interactions among those life forms.

BOG: Area of wet, spongy ground consisting of decayed plant matter.

BOILING CRYOGEN: Low-temperature liquid at its bubble point; the temperature and pressure at which evaporation begins.

BOOM: A physical barrier placed around an oil spill to contain it.

BOREAL FORESTS: A forest biome of coniferous trees running across northern North America and Eurasia; its high northern latitudes are often referred to as taiga.

BOREHOLE: Exploratory hole drilled for the purposes of gathering data.

BOTTOM TRAWLING: An industrial fishing practice in which large, heavy nets are dragged across the sea floor.

BREVETOXIN: Any of a class of neurotoxins produced by the algae that cause red tide (coastal algae blooms). Brevetoxins can be concentrated by shellfish and poisonous to humans who eat the shellfish.

BROWNFIELD SITE: A site contaminated with hazardous waste.

BYCATCH: Non-target species killed in the process of fishing.

C

CALVING: Process of iceberg formation in which huge chunks of ice break free from glaciers, ice shelves, or ice sheets due to stress, pressure, or the forces of waves and tides.

CAP-AND-TRADE PROGRAM: An emissions trading program designed to control industrial pollution by providing economic incentives.

CAPTIVE BREEDING: A wildlife conservation method in which rare or endangered species are bred in restricted environments such as zoos or wildlife preserves.

CAPTURE FISHERY: The harvesting of fish stocks occurring naturally in a body of water.

CARBON BANKING: Form of accounting that tracks the carbon emissions, reductions, and offsets of a client in a way that is analogous to the treatment of money in ordinary banking. A helpful adjunct to emissions trading schemes.

CARBON CREDITS: Units of permission or value, similar to monetary units such as dollars or euros, that entitle their owner to emit one metric ton of carbon dioxide (CO_2) into the atmosphere per credit.

CARBON CYCLE: The circulation of carbon (C) atoms through natural processes such as photosynthesis.

CARBON DIOXIDE: An odorless, colorless, non-poisonous gas, with the chemical formula CO_2, that is released by natural processes and by burning fossil fuels. The increased amounts of CO_2 in the atmosphere enhance the greenhouse effect, blocking heat from escaping into space and contributing to the warming of Earth's lower atmosphere.

CARBON FOOTPRINT: The amount of carbon dioxide (or of any other greenhouse gas, counted in terms of the greenhouse-equivalent amount of CO_2) emitted to supply the energy and materials consumed by a person, product, or event.

CARBON SEQUESTERING: Storage or fixation of carbon in such a way that it is isolated from the atmosphere and cannot contribute to climate change.

CARBON SEQUESTRATION: The uptake and storage of carbon (C) from the atmosphere into carbon sinks (such as oceans, forests, or soils).

CARBON SINK: A forest or other ecosystem that absorbs and stores more carbon than it releases.

CARCINOGEN: A cancer-causing agent, such as a chemical or virus.

CARRYING CAPACITY: The population of a species that an ecosystem can support with food, water, and other resources.

CARTOGRAPHY: The science of mapmaking.

CATABOLISM: The process by which large molecules are broken down into smaller ones with the release of energy.

CAVE, CAVERN: Naturally occurring underground chamber usually formed by the dissolution of rock.

CELLULOSIC FERMENTATION: Digestion of high-cellulose plant materials (e.g., wood chips, grasses) by bacteria that have been bred or genetically engineered for that purpose. The useful product is ethanol, which can be burned as a fuel.

CHANNEL: A water-filled path which connects mudflats and salt marshes to the ocean in an estuary.

CHLOROFLUOROCARBONS (CFCs): A family of chemical compounds consisting of carbon, fluorine, and chlorine that were once used widely as propellants in commercial sprays but regulated in the United States since 1987 because of their harmful environmental effects.

CHRYSOTILE: The white form of asbestos, which is less deadly than the blue or brown form.

CIRRUS CLOUD: A thin cloud of tiny ice crystals forming at 20,000 feet (6 km) or higher; reflects sunlight from Earth and also reflects infrared (heat) radiation back at the ground.

CLAY: The portion of soil comprising the smallest particles, resulting from the weathering and breakdown of rocks and minerals.

CLEAN DEVELOPMENT MECHANISM: One of the three mechanisms set up by the Kyoto Protocol of 2007 to, in theory, allow reductions in greenhouse-gas emissions to be implemented where they are most economical. Under the Clean Development Mechanism, polluters in wealthy countries can obtain carbon credits (greenhouse pollution rights) by funding reductions in greenhouse emissions in developing countries.

CLEAR-CUT: A parcel of forest in which all trees have been removed for harvesting.

CLEAR-CUTTING: A forestry practice involving the harvesting of all trees of economic value at one time.

CLIMATE: A term used to describe the average weather, in lay terms, or the mean and variability of climate factors over a period of time. The World Meteorological Organization (WMO) describes climate as the range over three decades of temperature, precipitation, and wind.

CLIMATE CHANGE: A significant change in one or more of the factors that may be classified as contributing to climate, namely temperature, precipitation, and wind. Climate change may result from natural factors or human activities that change the atmosphere's composition or the Earth's surface.

CLIMATE MODEL: A quantitative method of simulating the interactions of the atmosphere, oceans, land surface, and ice. Models can range from relatively simple to quite comprehensive.

CLIMATE NEUTRAL: The process of reducing greenhouse emissions so as to create a neutral impact on climate change.

CLIMATE SYSTEM: Also described as the Earth system, the components of the environment on Earth that affect climate—atmosphere, hydrosphere, cryosphere, lithosphere, and biosphere.

CLOUD: A patch of condensed water or ice droplets.

CO-GENERATION: The simultaneous generation of both heat and electricity at one facility.

COLD WAR: A term describing the ideological, political, economic, and military tensions and struggles between the two dominant superpowers of the era, the United States and the former Union of Soviet Socialist Republics (USSR) between 1945 (the end of the World War II) and the collapse of the Soviet Union in 1991.

COLIFORM: Bacteria present in the environment and in the feces of all warm-blooded animals and humans; useful for measuring water quality.

COLONIZATION: The process by which a species populates a new area.

COMBUSTION: The process of burning a material.

COMMUNITY: All of the populations of species living in a certain environment.

COMPOSTING: Breakdown of organic material by microorganisms.

CONDENSATION: The coalescence of water molecules from the vapor to the liquid or solid phase.

CONFERENCE OF PARTIES (COP): Term used to describe the meeting of the countries (parties) participating in any one of the programs undertaken under the sponsorship of the United Nations. However, it is most frequently used to refer to the parties participating in the United Nations Framework Convention on Climate Change (UNFCCC).

CONSERVATION: The act of using natural resources in a way that ensures that they will be available to future generations.

CONTIGUOUS ZONE: A maritime zone extending 24 nautical miles (44 km) from the outer edge of the territorial sea, in which a coastal state can exert limited control of its laws.

CONTINENTAL DRIFT: A theory that explains the relative positions and shapes of the continents and other geologic phenomena by lateral movement of the continents. This was the precursor to plate tectonic theory.

CONTINENTAL SHELF: A gently sloping, submerged ledge of a continent.

CONTRAIL: A high-altitude cloud formed by the passage of an aircraft.

CONTROLLED BURN: A forest management technique in which small, controlled fires are set to clear brush and prevent larger wildfires in the future.

COPENHAGEN ACCORD: Document produced at the fifteenth session of the Conference of Parties (COP) to the United Nations Framework Convention on Climate Change in December 2009.

CORAL: Invertebrate organisms in the phylum *Cnidaria* that form reefs in tropical ocean waters.

CORAL ATOLL: A low tropical island, often roughly ring-shaped, formed by coral reefs growing on top of a subsiding island. The rocky base of the atoll may be hundreds of feet below present-day sea level.

CORAL BLEACHING: Decoloration or whitening of coral from the loss, temporary or permanent, of symbiotic algae (zooxanthellae) living in the coral.

CORAL POLYP: A living organism that, as part of a colony, builds the rocky calcium carbonate ($CACO_3$) skeleton that forms the physical structure of a coral reef.

CORE: The central region of a star, where thermonuclear fusion reactions take place to produce the energy necessary for the star to support itself against its own gravity.

CORIOLIS EFFECT: A force exemplified by a moving object appearing to travel in a curved path over the surface of a spinning body.

CORIOLIS FORCE: The apparent tendency of a freely moving particle to swing to one side when its motion is referred to a set of axes that is itself rotating in space, such as Earth. Winds are affected by rotation of the Earth so that instead of a wind blowing in the direction it starts, it turns to the right of that direction in the Northern Hemisphere, and left in the Southern Hemisphere.

CRIMINALIZATION: The social or legal process by which a certain behavior comes to be redefined as a crime.

CROCIDOLITE: The blue form of asbestos.

CROP: Plants grown for food, energy, or some other human need.

CRUST: The hard, outer shell of Earth that floats upon the softer, denser mantle.

CRYOSPHERE: One of the components that makes up the Earth's climate system, cryosphere is made up of snow, permanently frozen ground (or permafrost), floating ice, and glaciers. Changes in the cryosphere cause changes in ocean levels.

CULL: The selection, often for destruction, of a part of an animal population.

CYANOBACTERIA: Photosynthetic bacteria, commonly known as blue-green algae.

CYCLONE: A large-scale system of low pressure in which circular winds blow counterclockwise in the Northern Hemisphere and clockwise in the Southern Hemisphere.

D

DDT: One of the earliest insecticides, dichlorodiphenyltrichloroethane, used until banned by many countries in the 1960s after bird populations were decimated by the substance, and other negative environmental consequences were recognized.

DEAD ZONE: An area of ocean in which nothing can live except bacteria that flourish on fertilizer from agricultural runoff.

DEBRIS: The remains of anything broken down or destroyed.

DECIDUOUS: Plants that shed leaves or other foliage after their growing season.

DEEP SEA MINING: The extraction of valuable mineral deposits from the ocean floor; not yet practiced due to legal, environmental, and monetary concerns.

DEFORESTATION: A reduction in the area of a forest resulting from human activity.

DEGRADATION: The microbial breakdown of a complex compound into simpler compounds with the release of energy.

DEGRADED WATER: Water that has been reduced in quality through industrial use.

DEMANUFACTURING: The disassembly, sorting, and recovering of valuable or toxic materials from electronic products such as televisions and computers.

DENDROARCHAEOLOGY: The analysis of wooden material from archaeological sites using the techniques of dendrochronology.

DENDROCLIMATOLOGY: The study of past climates using the techniques of dendrochronology.

DEPLETED URANIUM (DU): A byproduct of spent nuclear fuel, DU is a dense metal with a variety of civilian and military uses. It is often used to enhance the armor piercing qualities of munitions, although its deployment is riddled with controversy and it has been linked to increased incidence of cancer rates and birth defects.

DEPTH HOAR: Brittle, loosely arranged crystals at the base of a snowpack.

DESALINATION: Removal of salt from salt water to produce fresh water.

DESERT: A land area so dry that little or no plant or animal life can survive.

DESERTIFICATION: Transformation of arid or semi-arid productive land into desert.

DETRITUS: Matter produced by decay or disintegration of living material.

DEVELOPING NATION: A country that is relatively poor, with a low level of industrialization and relatively high rates of illiteracy and poverty.

DEVELOPMENT: The process by which a multicellular organism is produced from a single cell.

DINOFLAGELLATE: Small organisms with both plant-like and animal-like characteristics, usually classified as algae (plants). They take their name from their twirling motion and their whiplike flagella.

DIRECT ACTION TACTICS: Methods of political or social activism involving immediate, confrontative demand for change, such as strikes, sit-ins, and boycotts.

DISTILLATION: The process of purifying a liquid by successive evaporation and condensation.

DISTURBANCE SEVERITY: The amount of vegetation killed by fire or tree cutting activity, and the type of growing space made available for new plants.

DIURNAL: Performed in twenty-four hours, such as the diurnal rotation of Earth; also refers to animals and plants that are active during the day.

DOMOIC ACID: A neurotoxin produced by the algae that cause red tide (coastal algae blooms). Domoic acid can be concentrated by shellfish and poisonous to humans who eat the shellfish.

DREDGING: The excavation of sediment from the bottom of a body of water.

DRIP IRRIGATION: Slow, localized application of water just above the soil surface.

DRY SPELL: A short period of drought, usually lasting fewer than 14 days.

DRYLAND: Land where freshwater supplies are limited.

DUCKS UNLIMITED: An international nonprofit organization founded in Canada in the 1940s to preserve and protect wetlands.

E

ECOLOGICAL: Having to do with interactions among organisms.

ECOLOGICAL NICHE: The sum of the environmental requirements necessary for an individual to survive and reproduce.

ECOLOGICAL SERVICES: The benefits to human communities that stem from healthy forest ecosystems, such as clean water, stable soil, and clean air.

ECOLOGY: The branch of science dealing with the interrelationship of organisms and their environments.

ECOSYSTEM: A system of living organisms interacting with each other and their physical environment.

ECOSYSTEM PROCESSES: The dynamic interrelationships among and between living organisms and their particular habitat elements.

ECOSYSTEM SERVICES: Services that a natural or restored ecosystem provides to human communities, including improving water quality, reducing soil erosion, flooding, and landslides and increasing carbon sequestration.

ECO-TERRORISM: Criminal sabotage against persons or property carried out by an environmentally oriented group for symbolic purposes.

ECO-TOURISM: Environmentally responsible travel to natural areas that promotes conservation, has a low visitor impact, and provides for beneficially active socio-economic involvement of local peoples.

ECOZONE: A broad section of Earth's surface that features distinct climate patterns, ocean conditions, types of landscapes, and species of plants and animals.

EFFLUENTS: Waste materials, often as outflow from septic or water treatment systems, that are discharged into the environment.

EL NIÑO/SOUTHERN OSCILLATION: A global climate cycle that arises from interaction of ocean and atmospheric circulations. Every two to seven years, westward-blowing winds over the Pacific subside, allowing warm water to migrate across the Pacific from west to east. This suppresses normal upwelling of cold, nutrient-rich waters in the eastern Pacific, shrinking fish populations and changing weather patterns around the world.

ELECTRICAL GRID: Network of power lines that carry electricity from the source of generation to where the power can be used.

ELECTROMAGNETIC ENERGY: Energy conveyed by electromagnetic waves, which are paired electric and magnetic fields propagating together through space. X-rays, visible light, and radio waves are all electromagnetic waves.

EMBRYOLOGY: The study of early development in living things.

EMISSIONS: Release of a substance into the atmosphere; emissions are almost always gases.

ENDANGERED SPECIES: A species that is vulnerable to extinction.

ENDEMIC SPECIES: A species that is exclusively native to a certain area.

ENERGY INTENSITY: Ratio of the energy consumption to a factor related to the energy demand, such as square footage of floor space, number of employees, etc.

ENERGY RECOVERY: Incineration of solid waste to produce energy.

ENVIRONMENTAL DEGRADATION: The overall deterioration of environmental quality due to a range of issues, such as deforestation, desertification, pollution, and climate change.

ENVIRONMENTAL ESTROGEN: Compounds in toxic waste that mimic estrogen in their effect on humans and other animals.

ENVIRONMENTAL IMPACT STATEMENT: A document outlining the potential environmental impact of any new federal project, required by the U.S. National Environmental Policy Act.

ENVIRONMENTAL INVESTIGATION AGENCY (EIA): An independent, international campaigning organization that investigates and exposes environmental crime.

ENVIRONMENTAL MOVEMENT: A diverse social, political, and scientific movement revolving around the preservation of Earth's environment.

ENVIRONMENTAL PROTECTION AGENCY: An agency of the United States government since 1970, charged with protecting human health and the environment through research, regulation, and education.

ENZYME: A protein that catalyzes a chemical reaction, usually by lowering the energy at which the reaction can occur, without itself being changed by the reaction.

EPIFAUNA: Animals that live attached to the surface of a substrate such as rocks or pilings.

EQUINOX: Either of the two times during the year when the sun crosses the plane of Earth's equator, making night and day of approximately equal length.

EROSION: The wearing away of soil or rock over time by the action of water, glaciers, or wind.

ESTUARY: Lower end of a river where ocean tides meet the river's current.

ETHANOL: A compound of carbon, hydrogen, and oxygen (CH_3CH_2OH) that is a clear liquid at room temperature; also known as drinking alcohol or ethyl alcohol.

EUPHOTIC ZONE: The uppermost layer of a body of water in which the level of sunlight is sufficient for photosynthesis to occur.

EUSTATIC SEA LEVEL: Change in global average sea level caused by increased volume of the ocean (caused both by thermal expansion of warming water and by the addition of water from melting glaciers). Often contrasted to relative sea level rise, which is a local increase of sea level relative to the shore.

EUTROPHICATION: The process whereby a body of water becomes rich in dissolved nutrients through natural or human-made processes. This often results in a deficiency of dissolved oxygen, producing an environment that favors plant over animal life.

EVAPORITES: Salts deposited by the evaporation of aqueous solutions.

EVAPOTRANSPIRATION: The sum of evaporation and plant transpiration. Potential evapotranspiration is the amount of water that could be evaporated or transpired at a given temperature and humidity, if there was plenty of water available. Actual evapotranspiration cannot be any greater than precipitation, and will usually be less because some water will run off into rivers and flow to the oceans.

EVERGREEN: Bearing green leaves throughout the entire year.

E-WASTE: A term describing electronic equipment at the end of its useful life. E-waste is the fastest-growing type of waste in the world.

EXCLUSION ZONE: A zone established by a sanctioning body to prohibit specific activities in a specific geographic area.

EXCLUSIVE ECONOMIC ZONE (EEZ): A maritime zone extending 200 nautical miles (370 km) from the outer edge of the territorial sea, in which a coastal state has special rights over the exploration and use of marine resources.

EXTINCT: No longer in existence. In geology, it can be used to mean a process or structure that is permanently inactive (e.g., an extinct volcano).

EXTINCTION: The total disappearance of a species or the disappearance of a species from a given area.

EXXON VALDEZ: An oil tanker that spilled millions of gallons of oil in Prince William Sound, Alaska, beginning on March 24, 1989.

F

FACTORY FARMS: Enclosed or open-air facilities that house thousands to tens of thousands of poultry, swine, or cattle.

FAULT: A fracture in the continuity of a rock formation resulting from tectonic movement.

FAUNA: The animal life existing in a defined area.

FEEDSTOCK: Raw material required for an industrial process.

FELONY: A crime that is considered serious and is punishable by a more stringent sentence than what is given for a misdemeanor.

FEMA: The United States Federal Emergency Management Agency, founded in 1979 as an agency of the Department of Homeland Security, is responsible for coordinating responses to disasters taking place within the United States.

FERMENTATION: A chemical reaction in which enzymes break down complex organic compounds (for example, carbohydrates and sugars) into simpler ones (for example, ethyl alcohol).

FILTER FEEDERS: Animals that obtain their food from filtering passing water.

FIREBREAK: A strip of cleared or plowed land that acts as a barrier to slow or stop the progress of a wildfire.

FISH FARMING: The commercial production of fish in tanks or enclosures, usually for food; also known as aquaculture.

FISHERY: An industry devoted to the harvesting and selling of fish, shellfish, or other aquatic animals.

FISHING STOCK: A subpopulation of fish occupying a certain area that is in reproductive isolation from the rest of its species.

FISSION: A process in which the nucleus of an atom splits, usually into two daughter nuclei, with the transformation of tremendous levels of nuclear energy into heat and light.

FLOOD IRRIGATION: Irrigation carried out by flooding a crop with water.

FLORA: The plant life of an area.

FLUOROCARBONS: Compounds of carbon (C) and fluorine (f) that often contain other elements.

FLYWAY: A flying route regularly taken by migratory birds.

FODDER: Food for grazing animals.

FOLIAR: Pertaining to the leaf.

FOOD CHAIN: A sequence of organisms, each of which uses the next lower member of the sequence as a food source.

FOOD WEB: An interconnected set of all the food chains in the same ecosystem.

FORAMINIFERA: Single-celled marine organisms that inhabit small shells and float free in ocean surface waters. The shells of dead foraminifera sink to the sea bottom as sediment, forming thick deposits over geological time. Because the numbers and types of foraminifera are climate-sensitive, analysis of these sediments gives data on ancient climate changes.

FORESHOCK: A tremor that precedes a much larger earthquake.

FOREST MONOCULTURE: The development of a forest that is dominated by a single species of tree and which lacks the ecological diversity to withstand disease and parasites over the long term.

FOSSIL: A remnant of a past geological age that was embedded and has been preserved in Earth's crust.

FOSSIL FUELS: Nonrenewable fuels formed by biological processes and transformed into solid or fluid minerals over geologic time. Fossil fuels include coal, petroleum, and natural gas.

FOSSIL RECORD: The time-ordered mass of fossils that is found in the sedimentary rocks of Earth. The fossil record is one of the primary sources of knowledge about evolution and is also used to date rock layers.

FRAGMENTATION: Breakup of a continuous habitat into several smaller areas.

FREEDOM-OF-THE-SEAS DOCTRINE: An eighteenth-century agreement establishing the right of neutral shipping in international waters.

FRESHWATER: Water containing less than one gram per liter of dissolved solids.

G

GAIA HYPOTHESIS: The hypothesis that Earth's atmosphere, biosphere, and its living organisms behave as a single system striving to maintain a stability that is conductive to the existence of life.

GAMMA RAYS: Streams of high-energy electromagnetic radiation given off by an atomic nucleus undergoing radioactive decay.

GENE PLUNDER: Exploiting genetic diversity without compensating the country of origin.

GENETIC: Having to do with the genetic material, or DNA, in an organism.

GENETICALLY-MODIFIED (GM): Organism containing a gene transferred from another organism.

GENOME: The total content of genetic material in organisms.

GEOCODING: In geographic information systems, the assignment of geological data to particular features on maps or to other data records, such as photographs.

GEOGRAPHIC INFORMATION SYSTEMS (GIS): A set of computer-based tools that collects, analyzes, and maps spatial data.

GEOLOGICAL TIME: The period of time extending from the formation of the Earth to the present.

GEOLOGIST: A person who studies the origin, history, and structure of Earth.

GEO-REFERENCING: The process used for referring information to a geographic region.

GEOSPATIAL INFORMATION: The combination of a huge range of information taken from various sources and referenced by a geographic region.

GEOSPHERE: Soil, sediment, and rock layers that make up the Earth's crust.

GIGAWATT: A unit of power that is equal to one billion watts.

GLACIAL: Pertaining to glaciers or ice sheets.

GLACIER: A large mass of ice slowly moving over a land mass, resulting from a multi-year surplus accumulation of snowfall in excess of snowmelt.

GLOBAL POSITIONING SYSTEM (GPS): A system consisting of 25 satellites used to provide highly precise position, velocity, and time information to users anywhere on Earth or in its neighborhood at any time.

GLOBAL SOUTH: Academic term referring to under-developed countries.

GLOBAL WARMING: Warming of Earth's atmosphere that results from an increase in the concentration of gases that store heat, such as carbon dioxide (CO_2).

GLOBALIZATION: The integration of national and local systems into a global economy through increased trade, manufacturing, communications, and migration.

GRAFTING: Uniting a shoot or bud with a growing plant.

GRAVEL: The most coarse particles in soil.

GRAVITY: An attractive force that exists between all mass in the universe such as the moon and Earth.

GRAZING CAPACITY: The number of animals that a given area of land can support.

GREEN: Environmentally friendly or safe; nonpolluting or not adding to global warming.

GREEN CHEMISTRY: An approach to chemical manufacturing that reduces its negative impact on the environment.

GREEN MOVEMENT: A social ideology focused on environmental and quality-of-life issues, promoting values such as global responsibility, community-based economics, and sustainability.

GREEN PARTIES: Values-oriented political parties based on the environmental and social principles of the green movement.

GREENHOUSE EFFECT: The warming of Earth's atmosphere due to water vapor, carbon dioxide (CO_2), and other gases in the atmosphere that trap heat radiated from Earth's surface.

GREENHOUSE GASES (GHGs): Gases that accumulate in the atmosphere and absorb infrared radiation, contributing to the greenhouse effect.

GREENHOUSE-GAS EMISSIONS: Releases of greenhouses gases into the atmosphere.

GROUNDWATER: Fresh water that is present in an underground location.

GULF STREAM: A warm, swift ocean current that flows along the coast of the eastern United States and extends northward toward Europe.

GYRE: A zone of spirally circulating oceanic water that tends to retain floating materials, as in the Sargasso Sea of the Atlantic Ocean.

H

HABITABILITY: The degree to which a given environment can be lived in by human beings. Highly habitable environments can support higher population densities, that is, more people per square mile or kilometer.

HABITAT: The location and accompanying conditions where a plant or animal lives.

HALF-LIFE: The amount of time it takes for half an initial amount to disintegrate.

HEAT ISLAND: An urban area with significantly higher air and surface temperatures than surrounding areas. Occurs because pavement and buildings absorb solar energy while being little cooled by evaporation compared to vegetation-covered ground.

HERBICIDE: A chemical substance used to destroy or inhibit plant growth.

HERBICIDE SELECTIVITY: The ability to kill weeds while leaving a crop unharmed.

HERBIVORE: A plant-eating organism.

HOLDING POND: A reservoir used to hold polluted or sediment-laden water until it can be treated or recycled.

HOT SPRING: A spring produced by superheated water emerging from Earth's crust.

HOTSPOTS: Locations that are at high risk from natural hazards.

HUNTER-GATHERERS: Human groups that subsist on game and gathered vegetation.

HURRICANE KATRINA: A Category 3 hurricane that caused over 1,800 deaths and catastrophic damage to the Gulf Coast region of the United States in August 2005.

HYDROCARBONS: Molecules composed solely of hydrogen and carbon atoms.

HYDROELECTRICITY: Electricity generated by causing water to flow downhill through turbines, which are fanlike devices that turn when fluid flows through them. The rotary mechanical motion of each turbine is used to turn an electrical generator.

HYDROFLUOROCARBONS: Gaseous compounds consisting of hydrogen, fluorine, and carbon that have no ozone depletion potential; a suggested replacement for chlorofluorocarbons (CFCs).

HYDROGEN: The simplest and most abundant element in the universe, which is being investigated as a fuel source.

HYDROLOGIC CYCLE: The overall process of evaporation, vertical and horizontal transport of vapor, condensation, precipitation, and the flow of water from continents to oceans.

HYDROLOGY: The study of the distribution, movement, and physical-chemical properties of water in Earth's atmosphere, surface, and near-surface crust.

HYDROPHOBIC: Compounds do not dissolve easily in water, and are usually nonpolar. Oils and other long hydrocarbons are hydrophobic.

HYDROSPHERE: The total amount of liquid, solid, and gaseous water present on Earth.

HYDROTHERMAL VENTS: Underground jets of mineral-rich hot water.

HYPOXIA: A condition in which cells of the body are deprived of oxygen.

I

ICE AGE: Period of glacial advance.

ICE CORE: A cylindrical section of ice removed from a glacier or ice sheet in order to study climate patterns of the past.

ICE CRYSTALS: An arrangement of water molecules in which motion among the molecules slows and the structure takes on a rigid shape, as a consequence of temperatures near freezing. Crystals often form around particulate matter (dust, pollutants, etc.).

ICE JAM: An stationary accumulation of river ice that restricts water flow and increases the risk of flooding.

ICE SHEET: Glacial ice that covers at least 19,500 square miles (50,000 sq km) of land and that flows in all directions, covering and obscuring the landscape below it.

ICE SHELF: Section of an ice sheet that extends into the sea a considerable distance and that may be partially afloat.

IMMUNOSUPPRESSANT: Something used to reduce the immune system's ability to function, like certain drugs or radiation.

IMPERVIOUS SURFACES: Land surfaces created by human construction that do not allow rainfall to penetrate into the soil and down to aquifers.

IN SITU REMEDIATION: A procedure in which decontamination of a polluted area is performed onsite by using or simulating natural processes.

INCINERATION: The burning of solid waste as a disposal method.

INDIGENOUS PEOPLES: Human populations that migrated to their traditional area of residence sometime in the relatively distant past, e.g., before the period of global colonization that began in the late 1400s.

INDIGENOUS SPECIES: A species that is native to its region, but may occur in other regions as well.

INDUSTRIAL REVOLUTION: The period, beginning about the middle of the eighteenth century, during which humans began to use steam engines as a major source of power.

INERTIA: The tendency of an object to continue in its state of motion.

INFAUNA: Animals living within the material, such as mud or sand, at the bottom of an ocean or sea, or on the beach.

INFRARED RADIATION: Electromagnetic radiation of a wavelength shorter than radio waves but longer than visible light that takes the form of heat.

INNOCENT PASSAGE: The right of all ships to pass through the territorial waters of another state subject to certain restrictions.

INSECTICIDE: A chemical substance used to kill insects.

INSOLATION: Solar radiation received at Earth's surface.

INTEGRATED PEST MANAGEMENT: An ecological pest-control strategy involving minimal application of pesticides.

INTERGLACIAL: Occurring between periods of glacial action.

INTERGLACIAL PERIOD: A geological time period between glacial periods, which are periods when ice masses grow in the polar regions and at high elevations.

INTERGOVERNMENTAL PANEL ON CLIMATE CHANGE (IPCC): The Intergovernmental Panel on Climate Change (IPCC) was established by the World Meteorological Organisation (WMO) and the United Nations Environment Programme (UNEP) in 1988 to assess the science, technology, and socioeconomic information needed to understand the risk of human-induced climate change.

INTERNAL COMBUSTION ENGINE: An engine that relies on the chemical energy released during the combustion of a fuel to create power.

INTERNATIONAL UNION OF GEOLOGICAL SCIENCES (IUGS): Nongovernmental group of geologists founded in 1961 and headquartered in Trondheim, Norway. The group fosters international cooperation on geological research of a transnational or global nature.

INTERNATIONAL WHALING COMMISSION: An international body established ICRW to provide for the proper conservation of whale stocks and make possible the orderly development of the whaling industry.

INTERSPECIFIC COMPETITION: The competition between individuals of different species for the same limited resource.

INTERTROPICAL: Pertaining to a narrow belt along the equator where convergence of air masses of the northern and southern hemispheres produces a low-pressure atmospheric condition.

INTRASPECIFIC COMPETITION: The competition among members of the same species for the same limited resource.

INVASIVE SPECIES: A nonnative species whose introduction causes, or is likely to cause, economic or environmental harm or harm to human health.

INVERSION: A type of chromosomal defect in which a broken segment of a chromosome attaches to the same chromosome, but in reverse position.

IONIZING RADIATION: Any electromagnetic or particulate radiation capable of direct or indirect ion production in its passage through matter. In general use: Radiation that can cause tissue damage or death.

IRON FERTILIZATION: The process of seeding the ocean with iron to stimulate the growth of microorganisms, in an effort to trap carbon and lessen the release of carbon dioxide to the atmosphere.

ISOBAR: A line on a map connecting points at which the barometric pressure is the same at a specified moment.

ISOTOPE: A form of a chemical element distinguished by the number of neutrons in its nucleus.

J

JET STREAM: Currents of high-speed air in the atmosphere. Jet streams form along the boundaries of global air masses where there is a significant difference in atmospheric temperature.

K

KARST: Type of terrain created when soluble rocks, such as limestone and dolomite, dissolve. Karst terrain features unique hydrology, including springs, caves, and sinkholes, and productive aquifers. About 40 percent of U.S. groundwater comes from karst aquifers.

KEELING CURVE: Plot of data showing the steady rise of atmospheric carbon dioxide from 1958 to the present, overlaid with annual sawtooth variations due to the growth of northern hemisphere plants in summer.

KEPONE: A carcinogenic pesticide, banned in the United States in 1975, that caused a 1970s environmental disaster in Hopewell, Virginia.

KEYSTONE SPECIES: A species whose impact on its environment has a disproportionately large effect relative to its abundance.

KRILL: Small marine crustaceans of the order Euphausiacea, which are consumed as food by certain whales.

KYOTO PROTOCOL: Extension in 1997 of the 1992 United Nations Framework Convention on Climate Change (UNFCCC), an international treaty signed by almost all member countries with the goal of mitigating climate change.

L

LA NIÑA: A cycle of cooling in the equatorial Pacific that causes a disruption of global weather patterns; the opposite of El Niño.

LAND DEGRADATION: Gradual land impoverishment caused primarily by human activities such as agriculture.

LANDFILL: A low-lying area in which solid refuse is buried between layers of dirt.

LANDFILL SITE: Solid waste disposal site consisting of a lined, covered hole in the ground.

LANDMINE: A bomb planted on or near the surface of the ground that is triggered by something passing over it.

LEGISLATION: The making or enacting of laws.

LENTIC: The vertically layered nature of a lake.

LEVEE: A raised embankment designed to prevent a river from overflowing.

LIGHT POLLUTION: Also known as photopollution and luminous pollution, refers to the presence of excessive amounts of light in the atmosphere.

LIQUEFACTION: The process of changing the state of something to a liquid.

LITHOSPHERE: Outermost layer of Earth's surface.

LITTLE ICE AGE: A cold period lasting from approximately 1550–1850 in Europe, North America, and Asia, marked by rapid expansion of mountain glaciers.

LITTORAL: The region of a lake near the shore.

LOTIC: Flowing water, as in rivers and streams

M

MAGMA: Molten rock formed in the interior of Earth.

MALARIA: A group of parasitic diseases common in tropical and subtropical areas, characterized by attacks of chills, fever, and sweating.

MANTLE: The thick, dense layer of rock that underlies Earth's crust and overlies the core.

MAP SCALE: Portrays the relationship between a distance/size on map and the corresponding distance/size on the land.

MARIANAS TRENCH: A canyon almost 36,000 feet (11,000 m) in depth located in the floor of the Pacific Ocean; it is the deepest part of the world's oceans.

MARINE: Living in, or associated with, the sea.

MASS BALANCE (GLACIAL): The difference between the accumulation and ablation (reduction) of ice mass over a period of time.

MASS EXTINCTION: An extinction event characterized by high levels (or rates) of species extinction in a geologically short period of time.

MESOSPHERE: The third layer of the atmosphere, extending from the stratosphere to about 50 miles (80 km) above Earth.

METHANE: An odorless, colorless, flammable gas, with the formula CH_4, that is the simplest hydrocarbon compound and the major constituent of natural gas.

METHYL ISOCYANATE: A toxic chemical used in the manufacture of pesticides, which caused a disastrous 1984 chemical leak in Bhopal, India.

MICROCOSM: A miniature representation of a system that is used to model the system and study interactions.

MICROFINANCING: An economic development strategy in which small loans (microcredit) and other financial services are provided to very low-income individuals.

MIGRATORY: Traveling from one place to another at regular times of year, often over long distances.

MILANKOVITCH CYCLES: Regularly-repeating variations in Earth's climate caused by shifts in its orbit around the sun and its orientation (i.e., tilt) with respect to the sun.

MISDEMEANOR: A criminal offense that is considered minor and is punishable by a much lesser sentence than a felony.

MODEM: A device that permits information from a computer to be transmitted over a telephone line or cable.

MODIFIED MERCALLI SCALE: A scale used to compare earthquakes based on the effects they cause.

MOLLISOL: Rich soil formed under grasslands.

MONOCULTURE: A single species.

MONSOON: An annual shift in the direction of the prevailing wind that brings on a rainy season and affects large parts of Asia and Africa.

MUDFLAT: An area of low-lying muddy land that is covered at high tide and exposed at low tide.

MUNICIPAL WASTE: Waste that comes from households or is similar to household waste.

N

NATO: The North Atlantic Treaty Organization is a military alliance comprising the United States and 25 other members states, along with 14 major allies. It was involved in the bombing of Serbia in 1999 and, most recently, in Afghanistan.

NATURAL GAS: Deposits of gas, consisting of 50–90 percent methane (CH_4) and small amounts of other compounds, such as propane (C_3H_8) and butane (C_4H_{10}), found underground.

NATURAL SELECTION: Also known as "survival of the fittest"; the natural process by which those organisms best adapted to their environment survive and pass their traits to offspring.

NATURALIST: One who studies or is an expert in natural history, especially in zoology or botany.

NEUROTOXIN: A poison that interferes with nerve function, usually by affecting the flow of ions through the cell membrane.

NICHE: A term describing a species' habitat, range of physical and biological conditions, and relationships within its ecosystem.

NITROGEN CYCLE: Biochemical cycling of nitrogen by plants, animals, and soil bacteria.

NITROGEN FIXATION: Conversion of atmospheric nitrogen into nitrate by the roots of leguminous plants.

NITROGEN OXIDES: Compounds of nitrogen (N) and oxygen (O) such as those that collectively form from burning fossil fuels in vehicles.

NONGOVERNMENTAL ORGANIZATION (NGO): A voluntary organization that is not part of any government; often organized to address a specific issue or perform a humanitarian function.

NONPOINT SOURCE POLLUTANTS: Pollutants that come from a wide range of sources.

NONRENEWABLE RESOURCE: A natural resource of finite supply that cannot be regenerated.

NUCLEAR WASTE: Material left over from nuclear processes that is often radioactive or contaminated by radioactive elements.

NUCLEAR WEAPON: A military device whose explosive power is derived from nuclear fission or fusion.

NUCLIDE: A type of atom having a specific number of protons and neutrons in its nucleus.

O

OCEAN HEAT TRANSPORT: Movement by ocean currents of warm water from the tropics toward the poles, effectively transporting heat energy toward the poles where it is more quickly radiated into space.

OIL: Liquid petroleum.

OIL SLICK: A layer of oil floating on the surface of water.

OPPORTUNITY COST: The total cost incurred by choosing one option over another.

ORE: Rock containing a significant amount of minerals.

ORGANIC FARMING: Farming that uses no artificial chemicals or genetically engineered plants or animals.

ORGANIC WATER POLLUTANT: Organic materials from farm or food waste that increase the nutrient content of water.

OVERFISHING: Overharvesting applied to fish.

OVERGRAZING: The grazing of land over extended periods of time or without sufficient recovery periods, to the detriment of vegetation and soil quality.

OVERHARVESTING: Harvesting so much of a resource that its economic value declines and/or its existence is threatened.

OZONE: An almost colorless, gaseous form of oxygen, with an odor similar to weak chlorine, that is produced when an electric spark or ultraviolet light is passed through air or oxygen.

OZONE-DEPLETING SUBSTANCE (ODS): Human-made compounds that have been shown to deplete stratospheric ozone. These include chlorofluorocarbons (CFCs), bromofluorocarbons (halons), and others.

OZONE HOLE: A term invented to describe a region of very low ozone concentration above the Antarctic that appears and disappears with each austral (Southern Hemisphere) summer.

OZONE LAYER: The layer of ozone that begins approximately 9 miles (15 km) above Earth and thins to an almost negligible amount at about 31 miles (50 km), and which shields Earth from harmful ultraviolet radiation from the sun. The highest natural concentration of ozone (approximately 10 parts per million by volume) occurs in the stratosphere at approximately 16 miles (25 km) above Earth. The stratospheric ozone concentration changes throughout the year as stratospheric circulation changes with the seasons. Natural events such as volcano eruptions and solar flares can produce changes in ozone concentration, but human-made changes are of the greatest concern.

P

PACK ICE: Floating sea ice that has been driven together into a single large mass.

PALEOCLIMATE: The climate of a given period of time in the geologic past.

PALEOCLIMATOLOGY: The study of past climates throughout geological history, and the causes of variations among those climates.

PALEONTOLOGY: The study of life in past geologic time.

PARASITE: An organism that lives on or in another organism, and which harms the host.

PARTICULATE MATTER (PM): Very small pieces of matter, such as in soot, fumes, or mists.

PASTURE: Low-growing plants suitable for grazing livestock, or land containing such plants.

PEAT: Partially carbonized vegetable matter that can be cut and dried for use as fuel.

PEER REVIEW: The standard process in science for reducing the chances that faulty or fraudulent claims will be published in scientific journals. Before publication of an article, scientists with expertise in the article's subject area review the manuscript, usually anonymously, and provide feedback/criticisms that may lead to revision or rejection of the article.

PELAGIC: Living in, or associated with, open areas of ocean away from the bottom.

PERMAFROST: Perennially frozen ground that occurs wherever the temperature remains below 32°F (0°C) for several years.

PERSONAL WATERCRAFT: Small boats, steered by handlebars and propelled by a jet of water. Often known under the trade name "Jet Ski."

PESTICIDE: Substances used to reduce the abundance of pests or any living thing that causes injury or disease to crops.

PETROLEUM: A deposit formed from the action of high pressure and temperature on the buried remains of organisms from millions of years ago.

pH: The measure of the amount of dissolved hydrogen ions in solution.

PHASE: In the study of waves, a repeating or periodic wave's phase is the relationship of its pattern of peaks and valleys to a fixed reference (such as time).

PHOCOMELIA: A birth defect in which the upper portion of a limb is absent or poorly developed, so that the hand or foot attaches to the body by a short, flipperlike stump.

PHOTOCHEMICAL SMOG: A type of smog created by the action of sunlight on pollutants.

PHOTOSYNTHESIS: The process by which plants convert carbon dioxide (CO_2) to carbohydrates (energy) using sunlight and chlorophyll.

PHOTOVOLTAIC (PV): Described as the process by which light is converted into electricity. This is the process on which solar energy generation is based. Some materials have a property known as the photoelectric effect, which causes them to absorb photons of light and release electrons. The free electrons are captured and an electric current is produced.

PHYLUM (PLURAL, PHYLA): A biological classification group ranked between kingdom and class.

PHYTOPLANKTON: Microscopic marine organisms (mostly algae and diatoms) that are responsible for most of the photosynthetic activity in the oceans.

PLANKTON: Floating animal and plant life.

PLEISTOCENE EPOCH: The geologic period characterized by ice ages in the Northern Hemisphere, from 1.8 million to 10,000 years ago.

POACHING: Illegal hunting.

POINT SOURCE POLLUTANT: A pollutant that enters the environment from a single point of entry.

POINT SOURCE POLLUTION: Pollution arising from a fixed source, such as a pipe.

POLAR CELLS: Part of a group of atmospheric air circulation patterns occurring at the Earth's poles.

POLLUTION: Physical, chemical, or biological changes that adversely affect the environment.

POLLUTION CREDIT: A credit allowing the holder to legally emit a certain amount of pollutants, and which can be bought and sold as part of a cap-and-trade emissions program.

POPULATION MODEL: A mathematical model that can project the demographic consequences to a species as a result of certain changes to its environment.

PRECESSION: The comparatively slow torquing of the orbital planes of all satellites with respect to Earth's axis, due to the bulge of Earth at the equator which distorts Earth's gravitational field. Precession is manifest by the slow rotation of the line of nodes of the orbit (westward for inclinations less than 90 degrees and eastward for inclinations greater than 90 degrees).

PRECIPITATION: Moisture that falls from clouds as a result of condensation in the atmosphere.

PREDATOR-PREY MODEL: A mathematical model used to analyze interaction between two species in an ecosystem.

PRIMARY ENERGY SUPPLY: The total amount of available energy embodied in natural resources (such as coal) that has not been subjected to any conversion or transformation processes.

PRIMARY POLLUTANT: Any pollutant released directly from a source to the atmosphere.

R

RADIATION: Energy transfer mechanism whereby electromagnetic waves release energy when absorbed by another object.

RADIATIVE FORCING: A change in the balance between incoming solar radiation and outgoing infrared radiation, resulting in warming or cooling of Earth's surface.

RADIOACTIVE: Containing an element that decays, emitting radiation.

RADIOACTIVITY: The property possessed by some elements of spontaneously emitting energy in the form of particles or waves by disintegration of their atomic nuclei.

RADIOLARIA: Single-celled animals with silica skeletons.

RADIOMETRIC AGE: The age of an object as determined by the levels of certain radioactive substances present in that object.

RADIOMETRIC DATING: Use of naturally occurring radioactive elements and their decay products to determine the absolute age of the rocks containing those elements.

RADIOSONDES: Set of instruments carried into the atmosphere by weather balloons to measure temperature, humidity, and air pressure at various altitudes.

RECHARGE: Replenishment of an aquifer by the movement of water from the surface into the underground reservoir.

RECLAMATION: The act of restoring to use.

RECYCLING: The act of processing waste materials into new products or to be reused. The goals of recycling may include reducing waste and conserving raw materials.

REFORESTATION: The replanting of a forest that had been cleared by fire or harvesting.

REFUSE-DERIVED FUEL: Solid waste from which unburnable materials have been removed.

RELATIVE HUMIDITY: The amount of water vapor in the air compared to the maximum amount it could hold at that temperature.

RELATIVE SEA LEVEL: Sea level compared to land level in a given locality. Relative sea level may change because land is locally sinking or rising, not because the sea itself is sinking or rising (eustatic sea level change).

REMEDIATION: A remedy. In the case of the environment, remediation seeks to restore an area to its unpolluted condition, or at least to remove the contaminants from the soil and/or water.

REMOTE SENSING: The acquisition of data about an object or area without coming into contact with it.

RENEWABLE ENERGY: Energy that can be naturally replenished. In contrast, fossil fuel energy is nonrenewable.

RENEWABLE ENERGY SOURCE: An energy resource that is naturally replenished, such as sunlight, wind, or geothermal heat.

RENEWABLE RESOURCE: Any resource that is renewed or replaced fairly rapidly (on human historical time-scales) by natural or managed processes.

RESERVOIR: The collection of naturally occurring fluids in the porosity of a subsurface rock formation.

RESIDENCE TIME: For a greenhouse gas, the average amount of time a given amount of the gas stays in the atmosphere before being absorbed or chemically altered.

RESOLUTION: Pixels per square inch on a computer-generated display or photograph.

RESPIRATION: The process by which animals use up stored foods (by combustion with oxygen) to produce energy.

RETURN INTERVAL: The average time between occurrences of disturbances in a given stand of trees.

REWILDING: The restoration of a plant or animal to its historic habitat.

RICHTER SCALE: A scale used to compare earthquakes based on the energy released by the earthquake.

RUNOFF: Water that falls as precipitation and then runs over the surface of the land rather than sinking into the ground.

RUN-UP HEIGHT: The vertical distance between the mean-sea-level surface and the maximum point attained on the coast.

S

SABOTAGE: The deliberate act of interference, disruption, or destruction of an opponent's operations as part of a dispute.

SALINITY: Measurement of the amount of sodium chloride (NaCl) in a given volume of water.

SALINIZATION: An increase in salt content. The term is often applied to increased salt content of soils due to irrigation; salts in irrigation water tend to concentrate in surface soils as the water quickly evaporates rather than sinking down into the ground.

SALT MARSH: Wetland which is sometimes flooded with seawater.

SALTATION: The intermittent, leaping movement of small particles due to the force of wind or running water.

SATURATION POINT: The maximum concentration of water vapor that the air can hold at a given temperature.

SAVANNA: A flat, open grassland ecosystem found in tropical or subtropical regions.

SAXITOXIN: A neurotoxin found in a variety of dinoflagellates. If ingested, it may cause respiratory failure and cardiac arrest.

SCORCHED EARTH: A military policy involving widespread destruction of property and resources, especially by burning, so that an advancing enemy cannot use them.

SEA LICE: A type of crustacean that is a parasite of farmed fish including salmon and rainbow trout.

SEA SEDIMENT CORE: A cylindrical, solid sample of a layered deposit of sediment on the ocean floor that can provide information about past climate changes.

SEA SHEPHERD CONSERVATION SOCIETY: An international, nonprofit marine wildlife conservation group known for its radical direct-action tactics.

SEDIMENT: Solid unconsolidated rock and mineral fragments that come from the weathering of rocks and are transported by water, air, or ice and form layers on Earth's surface. Sediments can also result from chemical precipitation or secretion by organisms.

SEDIMENT LOADING: Presence of moving mineral particles in rivers or streams. Faster-moving water can carry more sediment. Erosion increases sediment loading, limited by stream capacity for increased sediment loading.

SEDIMENTARY ROCK: Rock formed from compressed and solidified layers of organic or inorganic matter.

SEISMIC WAVE: A wave of energy that travels through Earth as the result of an earthquake or explosion.

SELECTION PRESSURE: Factors that influence the evolution of an organism. An example is the overuse of antibiotics, which provides a selection pressure for the development of antibiotic resistance in bacteria.

SEMIARID: Receiving very little annual rainfall, roughly 10–20 inches (25–50 cm), and characterized by short grasses and shrubs.

SENSOR: A device to detect or measure a parameter as it is occurring.

SESSILE: Any animal that is rooted to one place. Barnacles, for example, have a mobile larval stage of life and a sessile adult stage of life.

1750 VALUE: Refers to pre-industrial greenhouse gas levels. The 2001 Intergovernmental Panel on Climate Change (IPCC) determined that greenhouse gas concentrations prior to 1750 were uninfluenced by human activity.

SEWAGE: Waste and wastewater discharged from domestic and commercial premises.

SHALLOW-WATER WAVES: Waves that have a greater wavelength and in which the ratio between the depth of water and the wavelength is very small.

SHARPS WOUNDS: Wounds caused by discarded medical instruments including hypodermic needles and, scalpels (knives) and other sharp objects potentially contaminated by human contact.

SHOALING EFFECT: Transformation that takes place when a wave travels from deep water to shallow water resulting in the decrease in wavelength and increase in the height of the wave.

SHORT TON: Measurement of weight equaling 2,000 pounds, used in the United States.

SIERRA CLUB: An environmental organization founded in 1892 by American naturalist John Muir (1838–1914), whose mandate includes the protection and, when needed, restoration, of natural environments.

SILENT SPRING: A seminal 1962 book, written by Rachel Carson (1907–1964), that is credited with inspiring widespread public interest in pollution and the environment.

SILVICULTURE: Management of the development, composition, and long-term health of a forest ecosystem. The objective is often to allow logging of the forest over many years.

SLUDGE: Semisolid material formed as a result of wastewater treatment or industrial processes.

SMOG: A mixture of smoke or other atmospheric pollutants combined with fog.

SNOW PACK: An area of naturally formed, packed winter snow that accumulates in mountain or upland regions.

SOFTWARE: Computer programs or data.

SOIL: Unconsolidated materials above bedrock.

SOLAR RADIATION: Radiation, which has a specific range of wavelengths, emitted by Earth's sun.

SOOT: A black, powdery, carbonaceous substance produced by the incomplete combustion of coal, oil, wood, or other fuels.

SPECIATION: The evolutionary development of new biological species.

SPECIES: A biological classification group ranked below genus, consisting of related organisms capable of interbreeding.

SPECIES DIVERSITY: The number of different species living in a particular place.

SPECTRAL: Relating to a spectrum, which is an ordered range of possible vibrational frequencies for a type of wave. The spectrum of visible light, for example, orders colors from red (slowest vibrations visible) to violet (fastest vibrations visible) and is itself a small segment of the much larger electromagnetic spectrum.

SPODOSOL: Acidic soil formed under pine forests.

SPRAWL: The unregulated and unplanned spread of urban and suburban development in a metropolitan region.

SPRING: The emergence of an aquifer at the surface, which produces a flow of water.

STAKEHOLDERS: A group of people holding investments, shares, or interest in a commercial enterprise.

STEPPE: Grasslands that occur in places with cold winters and warm summers.

STORM SURGE: Rise of the sea at a coastline due to the effect of storm winds.

STORM WATER: Water that flows over the ground when it rains or when snow melts.

STRATA: A bed or layer of sedimentary rock in which composition is usually the same throughout.

STRATIGRAPHY: The branch of geology that deals with the layers of rocks or the objects embedded within those layers.

STRATOSPHERE: The region of Earth's atmosphere ranging between about 9 and 30 miles (15–50 km) above Earth's surface.

STRATOSPHERIC OZONE LAYER: Layer of Earth's atmosphere from about 9 and 22 miles (15–35 km) above the surface in which the compound ozone (O_3) is relatively abundant.

STRICT LIABILITY: Liability that is imposed without a finding of fault, such as negligence or intent.

STRIP MINING: A method for removing coal from seams located near Earth's surface.

SUBMARINE SLIDES: Marine landslides that can transport subsurface rock and sediment down the continental slope.

SUBMERGED SHORELINE: A shoreline formed by the submergence of a landmass, characterized by bays, promontories, and other minor features.

SUBSIDENCE: A sinking or lowering of a part of Earth's surface.

SUBSISTENCE: Having secured enough provisions to cover basic needs.

SUBSISTENCE FARMER: A farmer whose products are intended to provide for his/her own basic needs, with little or no profit.

SUCCESSION: Regrowth of forest following its disturbance by deforestation.

SUPERFUND: Legislation that authorizes funds to clean up abandoned, contaminated sites.

SUPERFUND SITE: A Superfund site is a location contaminated by hazardous waste that has been designated by the United States Environmental Protection Agency (EPA) for management and cleanup.

SURFACE WATER: Water collecting on the ground or in a stream, river, lake, wetland, or ocean, as opposed to groundwater.

SUSTAINABILITY: Practices that preserve the balance between human needs and the environment, as well as between current and future human requirements.

SUSTAINABLE: Capable of being sustained or continued for an indefinite period without exhausting necessary resources or otherwise self-destructing: often applied to human activities such as farming, energy generation, or the maintenance of a society as a whole.

SUSTAINABLE AGRICULTURE: Agricultural use that meets the needs and aspirations of the present generation without compromising those of future ones.

SUSTAINABLE DEVELOPMENT: Development (i.e., increased or intensified economic activity; sometimes used as a synonym for industrialization) that meets the cultural and physical needs of the present generation of persons without damaging the ability of future generations to meet their own needs.

SUSTAINABLE RESOURCE: A resource that can be renewed or maintained indefinitely.

SUSTAINABLE WHALING: The process by which a limited number of whales from thriving species, such as the minke, are culled each year.

SYMBIOSIS: A pattern in which two or more organisms of different species live in close connection with one another, often to the benefit of both or all organisms.

SYMBIOTIC: Describes a relationship in which two or more organisms of different species live in close connection with one another, often to the benefit of both or all organisms.

T

TAIGA: The part of the boreal forest occurring in high northern latitudes, consisting of open woodland of coniferous trees growing in a rich floor of lichen.

TECTONIC PLATES: Thick crustal blocks that move relative to one another on the outer surface of Earth, causing continents to shift.

TEMPERATE: Pertaining to a region located between 30 and 60 degrees latitude in both hemispheres in which the climate undergoes seasonal change in temperature and moisture.

TERATOGENIC EFFECT: The combined consequences of the consumption of a harmful substance on a developing fetus.

TERRITORIAL WATER: A maritime zone of coastal waters extending up to 12 nautical miles (22 km) from the baseline of a coastal state, within which a state can exert control of its laws and regulations.

THERMAL PLUME: A discharge of heated waste water into the water supply.

THERMAL POLLUTION: Industrial discharge of heated water into a river or lake, creating a rise in temperature that is injurious to aquatic life.

THERMOHALINE CIRCULATION: Large-scale circulation of the world ocean that exchanges warm, low-density surface waters with cooler, higher-density deep waters; also termed meridional overturning circulation.

THERMOSTERIC EXPANSION: Expansion as a response to a change in temperature, also called thermal expansion.

THREATENED SPECIES: A species that is likely to become an endangered species over all or much of its range.

THROUGHFLOW: The horizontal flow of water through soil.

TIDE: The changing surface level of a large body of water such as the ocean or a lake that results from changes in the gravitational pull on the water by the moon and the sun.

TIDE CYCLE: A period that includes a complete set of tide conditions or characteristics, such as a tidal day or a lunar month.

TIDE GAUGE: A device, usually stationed along a coast, that measures sea level continuously. Measurements from tide gauges were the main source of sea-level data prior to the beginning of satellite measurements in the 1970s.

TOPOGRAPHY: The surface features of an area, such as hills or valleys.

TOXIN: A poisonous substance produced by living cells or organisms.

TRACE GAS: Term used to describe gases that are less abundant in Earth's atmosphere. These include ammonia, ozone, methane, and water vapor. While the volumes of these gases are small, they exert effects on Earth's weather.

TRADE WINDS: Surface air from the horse latitudes that moves back toward the equator and is deflected by the Coriolis force, causing the winds to blow from the northeast in the Northern Hemisphere and from the southeast in the Southern Hemisphere.

TRANSCENDENTALISM: A literary and philosophical movement asserting the existence of an ideal spiritual reality that transcends the empirical and scientific and is knowable through intuition.

TRANSIT PASSAGE: The right of free navigation and overflight for the purpose of continuous transit through a strait between one part of the high seas and another.

TRANSPIRATION: Loss of water taken in by roots from leaves through evaporation.

TREE RINGS: Marks left in the trunks of woody plants by the annual growth of a new coat or sheath of material. Tree rings provide a straightforward way of dating organic material stored in a tree trunk.

TROPICAL: The area between 23.5 degrees north and south of the equator. This region has small daily and seasonal changes in temperature, but great seasonal changes in precipitation.

TROPICAL DEPRESSION: A rotating system of thunderstorms with low atmospheric pressure in the center and maximum windspeed less than 39 mph (63 km/h).

TROPICAL STORM: A low-pressure storm system that forms over warm tropical waters, with winds ranging from 30 to 75 mph (48 to 121 km/h).

TROPOSPHERE: The lowest layer of Earth's atmosphere, ranging to an altitude of about 9 miles (15 km) above Earth's surface.

TSUNAMI: A series of ocean waves resulting from an undersea disturbance, such as an earthquake.

TUNDRA: A type of ecosystem dominated by lichens, mosses, grasses, and woody plants. It is found at high latitudes (arctic tundra) and high altitudes (alpine tundra). Arctic tundra is underlain by permafrost and is usually very wet.

TURBIDITY: A measure of the degree to which water loses its clarity due to the presence of suspended particles.

TURBINE: An engine that moves in a circular motion when force, such as moving water, is applied to its series of baffles (thin plates or screens) radiating from a central shaft.

U

ULTRAVIOLET RADIATION (UV): Energy range beyond the violet of the visible spectrum. UV radiation represents only about five percent of the total energy emitted by the Sun, but UV is a major energy source for the stratosphere.

UNITED NATIONS FRAMEWORK CONVENTION ON CLIMATE CHANGE (UNFCCC): The Convention on

Climate Change sets an overall framework for intergovernmental efforts to tackle the challenge posed by climate change. As of 2011, some 189 countries having ratified it. The Convention entered into force on 21 March 1994.

UPWELLING: The vertical motion of water in the ocean by which subsurface water of lower temperature and greater density moves toward the surface of the ocean.

URBAN HEAT ISLAND EFFECT: Warming of atmosphere in and immediately around a built-up area. Occurs because pavement and buildings absorb solar energy while being little cooled by evaporation compared to vegetation-covered ground.

V

VAPORIZATION: The conversion of a solid or liquid into a gas.

VARVE: An annual layer or series of layers of sediment deposited in a body of still water.

VELD: An area of elevated open grassland, characteristic of parts of southern Africa.

VORTEX: A rotating column of a fluid such as air or water.

W

WASTE TRANSFER STATION: A structure in which wastes are temporarily held and sorted before being transferred to larger facilities.

WASTEWATER: Water that carries away the waste products of personal, municipal, and industrial operations.

WATER CONSUMPTION: Use of water in such a way that it cannot be reused.

WATER FOOTPRINT: The total volume of water used to produce goods and services consumed by an individual, business or nation.

WATER INTENSITY: The amount of water used to produce specific goods or services.

WATER STRESS: Inability to provide enough water to meet basic needs.

WATER TABLE: The level of the aquifer under the ground.

WATER VAPOR: The most abundant greenhouse gas, it is the water present in the atmosphere in gaseous form. Water vapor is an important part of the natural greenhouse effect. While humans are not significantly increasing its concentration, it contributes to the enhanced greenhouse effect because the warming influence of greenhouse gases leads to a positive water vapor feedback. In addition to its role as a natural greenhouse gas, water vapor plays an important role in regulating the temperature of the planet because clouds form when excess water vapor in the atmosphere condenses to form ice and water droplets and precipitation.

WATER WITHDRAWAL: Removal of water from a water supply, some of which will later be returned.

WATERSHED: The expanse of terrain from which water flows into a wetland, water body, or stream.

WEATHER: Conditions experienced at a particular moment in time and place, measured in terms of such factors as temperature, wind velocity, humidity, precipitation, and cloud cover.

WEATHERING: The natural processes by which the actions of atmospheric and other environmental agents, such as wind, rain, and temperature changes, result in the physical disintegration and chemical decomposition of rocks and earth materials in place, with little or no transport of the loosened or altered material.

WETLAND: A shallow ecosystem where the land is submerged for at least part of the year.

WHALE OIL: Oil rendered from the blubber of a whale.

WILDLAND FIRE USE: A fire-management technique that uses naturally ignited fires to benefit natural resources.

WIND: A natural motion of the air, especially a noticeable current of air moving in the atmosphere parallel to Earth's surface, caused by unequal heating and cooling of Earth and its atmosphere.

WIND CELLS: Vertical structures of moving air formed by warm (less-dense) air welling up in the center and cooler (more-dense) air sinking around the perimeter; also called convective or convection cells.

WIND SHEAR: Variation in wind speed within a current of wind: that is, when wind shear is present, part of a wind current is moving at one speed while another, nearby part of the current, moving parallel to the first, is moving at a different speed.

WOOD PULP: A suspension of wood tissue in water that is often used to make paper.

WORLD BANK: International bank formed in 1944 to aid in reconstruction of Europe after World War II, now officially devoted to the eradication of world poverty through funding of development projects.

X

XENOBIOTICS: Synthetic organic compounds that are hard to break down in the environment.

Z

ZOONOSIS (ZOONOTIC DISEASE): Any disease that can be transmitted from animals to humans.

ZOOPLANKTON: Small, herbivorous animal plankton that float or drift near the surface of aquatic systems and that feed on plant plankton (phytoplankton and nanoplankton).

ZOOXANTHELLAE: Algae that live in the tissues of coral polyps and, through photosynthesis, supply them with most of their food.

Chronology

This section outlines key events in environmental history in both the United States and Canada.

UNITED STATES

1750–1799

1775   On June 16 George Washington (1732–1799) appoints the first engineer officers in the army, setting the stage for the creation of the U.S. Army Corps of Engineers.

1800–1859

1802   On March 16, the U.S. Army Corps of Engineers is established as a separate, permanent branch of the U.S. Army. The Corps of Engineers is given the task of establishing and operating the U.S. Military Academy at West Point.

1807   President Thomas Jefferson (1743–1826) signs a bill establishing the U.S. Coast and Geodetic Survey to conduct a survey of the country's coasts.

1838–1863

The Corps of Topographical Engineers is established to conduct engineering surveys for military purposes and to explore possible routes for movement of troops. Working with the Corps of Engineers, the Corps of Topographical Engineers engages in 25 years of surveying and mapping the West, the Great Lakes region, and elsewhere, and in the construction of lighthouses in coastal areas. The Corps of Topographical Engineers is abolished in 1863, and their functions are assumed by the Corps of Engineers.

1849   The Smithsonian Institution provides weather instruments to telegraph companies and establishes and weather observation network. Some 150 volunteers throughout the United States report weather observations to the Smithsonian, where weather maps are created.

1860–1869

1864   On June 30, President Abraham Lincoln (1809–1865) signs a bill granting the Yosemite Valley and the Mariposa Grove to the State of California.

1867   On March 30, U.S. Secretary of State William H. Seward (1801–1872) and Russian minister to the United States Eduard de Stoeckl (1804–1892) complete negotiations for the U.S. purchase of nearly 600,000 square miles (1,560,000 sq km) of Alaska territory. The United States pays Russia $7.2 million, or about two cents per acre, for the land.

1870–1879

1870   On February 9, President Ulysses S. Grant (1822–1885) signs into law an act to create the U.S. Weather Bureau. The Weather Bureau will make meteorological observations at military stations and elsewhere and prepare forecasts and warnings about weather. General Albert J. Meyer (1828–1880) serves as the first director.

1871   The U.S. Bureau of Commercial Fisheries is formed.

1872 Yellowstone National Park Act is passed; it is the first time public lands are preserved for public enjoyment anywhere in the world.

1878 Reflecting the expansion of its duties to include surveying interior land areas, the U.S. Coast Survey becomes the U.S. Coast and Geodetic Survey (USC&GS).

1880–1889

1889 On May 30, an earthen dam near Johnstown, Pennsylvania, breaks. Some 2,209 die and 1,880 homes and businesses are destroyed in the flood that results.

1890–1899

1890 On October 1, Yosemite National Park and General Grant National Park, both in California, are authorized by the U.S. Congress. Under the terms of the act the Yosemite National Park was constituted from territory surrounding Yosemite Valley. The Yosemite Valley itself remained under management of the State of California

1891 The Forest Reserve Act is passed by the U.S. Congress. Under the act, more than 17.5 million acres of forest are set aside by 1893.

The U.S. Secretary of Agriculture directs scientists to conduct rain-making experiments by setting off explosions from balloons in the air.

1892 On June 4, the Sierra Club is established by John Muir (1838–1914), Robert Underwood Johnson (1853–1937), and William Colby (1875–1964).

1895 The American Scenic and Historic Preservation Society is founded in New York City with the intent to preserve historic buildings, parks, monuments, and other public art.

1897 The Forest Management Act, also known as the Organic Act, is passed by the U.S. Congress. The act stipulates that the regulated harvesting of timber, mining of mineral resources, and use of water on forest reservations may be permitted by the Secretary of the Interior.

1899 On March 3, the Rivers and Harbors Act (also called the Refuse Act) passes the U.S. Congress. The act preserves navigable waters and makes it unlawful to throw garbage and refuse into navigable waters, except with a Corps of Engineers permit.

1900–1909

1900 On May 25, the Lacey Act becomes the first federal law to regulate commercial animal markets. It prohibits interstate commerce of animals killed in violation of state games laws. The act covers all fish and wildlife and their parts or products, as well as plants.

1903 On March 14, President Theodore Roosevelt (1858–1919) creates the first National Bird Preserve (the beginning of the Wildlife Refuge system) on Pelican Island, Florida.

Newspaper publisher E. W. Scripps (1854–1926) and biologist William Ritter (1856–1944) establish the Scripps Institute of Oceanography.

1905 On January 24, Congress establishes the country's first game preserve in Wichita, Kansas.

On February 1, the Bureau of Forestry becomes the U.S. Forest Service.

On March 3, the California state legislature acts to give control of the Yosemite Valley to the federal government. A joint resolution of the U.S. Congress on June 11 accepts jurisdiction over Yosemite Valley and consolidates it with the national park lands of Yosemite National Park.

The National Audubon Society is organized by George Bird Grinnell (1849–1938) to promote wildlife conservation. The society is named in honor of wildlife painter John James Audubon (1785–1850).

1906 On June 29, the U.S. Congress passes the Burton Act, making diversion of water for power supplies subordinate to preservation of Niagara Falls.

1908 On May 23, the National Bison Range is established on Flathead Indian Reservation in Montana. The range will provide a sanctuary for the American bison.

1909 By this year the administration of President Theodore Roosevelt (1858–1919) has created 42 million acres of national forests, 53 national wildlife refuges, and 18 areas of "special interest," including the Grand Canyon.

1910–1919

1910 The Corps of Engineers refers to the Rivers and Harbors Act of 1899 in issuing its objection to a proposed sewer city for New York City. A judge ruled that pollution control was an issue under state, not federal control.

1913 The National Council for Industrial Safety (now called the National Safety Council) is established with the goal to prevent injuries and deaths in the workplace, homes, communities, and on roadways.

William T. Hornaday (1854–1937), head of the New York Zoological Society, writes *Our Vanishing Wildlife, Its Extermination and*

Preservation. By 1914, he helps establish the Permanent Wildlife Protection Fund with grants from Andrew Carnegie (1835–1919), Henry Ford (1863–1947), and George Eastman (1854–1932).

1916   The Fire Weather Service is established, with district forecast centers established to issue fire weather forecasts.

On August 25, President Woodrow Wilson (1856–1924) approved legislation to create the National Park Service. Stephen T. Mather (1867–1930) becomes the first director, a post he holds until January 8, 1929.

1918   The Save the Redwoods League is founded by Frederick Russell Burnham (1861–1947), Madison Grant (1865–1937), John C. Merriam (1869–1945), and Henry Fairfield Osborn (1857–1935). The goal of the organization is to protect the remaining coast redwood trees in California.

The Migratory Bird Treaty Act is established to regulate hunting. Spring hunting and the marketing of hunted birds is now prohibited. The act also prohibits the importation of wild bird feathers for women's fashion into the United States.

Clare Marie Hodges is hired as a park ranger at Yosemite National Park, becoming the first female park ranger in the National Park Service.

1920–1929

1920   The Mineral Leasing Act of 1920 establishes the rules and regulations that allow for the leasing of federal lands for the purpose of mineral exploration, drilling, and mining.

The Federal Water Power Act is enacted to promote the development of hydroelectric projects in the United States. The act establishes the Federal Power Commission as the licensing authority.

1922   On August 11, the National Coast Anti-Pollution League is formed by municipal officials from Atlantic City to Maine who are concerned about oil and sewage pollution detracting from tourism. Led by Gifford Pinchot (1865–1946), Theodore Roosevelt's forester, the league succeeds in getting an international oil dumping treaty passed by the U.S. Congress in 1924.

1927   Flooding of the Mississippi River and its tributaries results in the worst flood in the history of the Lower Mississippi Valley. More than 200 people die in the floods, and more than 600,000 are displaced. There is extensive damage to homes, businesses, farms, and local infrastructure. The event is soon known as the Great Mississippi Flood of 1927.

1928   Congress authorizes construction of the Boulder Canyon Project with the intent to build a massive dam along the Colorado River. One year later, President Herbert Hoover (1874–1964) changes the location of the dam from Boulder Canyon to Black Canyon. The project is known as Boulder Dam until it is rededicated as the Hoover Dam.

In response to the Great Mississippi Flood of 1927, Congress passes the Flood Control Act of 1928 authorizing the U.S. Army Corps of Engineers to design and build a major flood control system, which soon becomes known as the Mississippi River and Tributaries Project. This is the first comprehensive flood control and navigation act for the nation.

1929   The Migratory Bird Conservation Act passes. It provides for the creation of sanctuaries where migratory birds can live. It also creates the Migratory Bird Conservation Commission, which approves the purchase or rental of areas of land or water as sanctuaries for migratory birds and water fowl, upon the recommendation of the secretary of the Department of the Interior.

1930–1939
1930–1936

A prolonged period of drought is accompanied by frequent and severe dust storms in several of the Great Plains states as high winds strip tons of topsoil from the barren farmland creating "black blizzards." As millions of acres of farmland became unusable, thousands of people from the "Dust Bowl," an area that included the panhandle regions of Oklahoma and Texas and neighboring parts of New Mexico, Colorado, and Kansas, are forced to leave their family farms and seek employment elsewhere.

The Civilian Conservation Corps (CCC) is formed as a public work relief program for unemployed, unmarried men from relief families. A part of the New Deal of President Franklin D. Roosevelt (1882–1945), the CCC provides unskilled manual labor jobs related to the conservation and development of natural resources in rural lands owned by federal, state, and local governments.

1934   On May 30, the U.S. Congress passes an act authorizing a park to be established in Florida's Everglades, with land to be acquired through public donations. According to the act, Everglades National Park was to be 'wilderness, (where) no development . . . or plan for the entertainment of visitors shall be undertaken which will interfere with the preservation intact of the unique flora and fauna of historic values the essential primitive natural conditions now prevailing in this area.'

1935   A hurricane warning service is established in the United States, under the Weather Bureau. The Smithsonian Institution begins making long-range weather forecasts based on solar cycles; floating automatic weather instruments mounted on buoys begin collecting marine weather data.

On September 30, President Franklin D. Roosevelt dedicates the Hoover Dam. The dam is completed two years ahead of schedule. The U.S. Congress had authorized its construction, the largest federal project undertaken at that time, in 1928.

The Federal Water Power Act of 1920 is amended to give the Federal Power Commission authority over all interstate electric power transmissions and projects and electric sales rates. The amended act is now known as the Federal Power Act.

1936   Congress passes the Flood Control Act of 1936, making flood control, including the design, construction, and operation of dams and reservoirs, a formal duty of the U.S. Army Corps of Engineers.

The National Wildlife Federation is founded by Jay Norwood "Ding" Darling (1876–1962). Darling is a Pulitzer Prize-winning cartoonist and chief of the U.S. Bureau of Biological Survey.

1937   Glen Thomas Trewartha (1896–1984), a geographer and professor at the University of Wisconsin, publishes a textbook entitled *An Introduction to Weather and Climate*, in which he introduces the term "greenhouse effect" by comparing the atmosphere as a "plane of glass," similar to that found in a greenhouse, which helps maintain higher surface temperatures.

1940–1949

1940   The U.S. Fish and Wildlife Service is created, as the Department of the Interior combines the Bureau of Fisheries with the Bureau of Biological Survey. Field biologist and longtime conservationist Ira Gabrielson (1889–1977) takes the post as the first chief of the bureau.

On June 8, the Bald Eagle Protection Act is passed by the U.S. Congress. The act protects the bald eagle and the golden eagle by prohibiting the capture, possession, or commerce of the birds.

1947   On October 14, the Los Angeles Air Pollution Control District is created. This is the first air pollution agency in the United States.

Marjory Stoneman Douglas (1890–1998) publishes *The Everglades: River of Grass*, which redefines the public's conception of the Everglades as an area in need of protection. This same year on December 6, President Harry S. Truman (1884–1972) dedicates Everglades National Park in a ceremony in Everglades City.

1948   On June 30, the Federal Water Pollution Control Act authorizes the Surgeon General of the Public Health Service to prepare comprehensive programs for eliminating or reducing the pollution of interstate waters and tributaries and improving the sanitary condition of surface and underground waters.

In October, a dense fog of air pollution form over the industrial town of Donora, Pennsylvania, and lingers for five days, killing 20 people and causing sickness in 6,000 of the town's 14,000 people. This is one of the first recorded incidents of deadly air pollution in the United States.

1949   November 10–11, the first National Air Pollution Symposium in the United States is held in Los Angeles, California.

1950–1959

1951   The Severe Weather Warning Center begins operation at Tinker Air Force Base, Oklahoma. It is the forerunner of the National Severe Storms Center.

On October 22, The Nature Conservancy is established in the District of Columbia.

1955   From March 1–2, the First International Congress on Air Pollution is held in New York City. It is sponsored by the American Society of Mechanical Engineers, and discusses "management, administrative, engineering, meteorological, biological, and health problems" related to air pollution.

On July 14, the National Air Pollution Control Act is passed, becoming the first federal air pollution law. It mandates federal research programs to investigate the health and welfare effects of air pollution.

1960–1969

1960   The first fully commercial nuclear power plant, the 250MW Yankee Nuclear Power Station (YNPS), popularly known as Yankee Rowe, designed by Westinghouse Corporation, begins operation in Rowe, Massachusetts. The plant was permanently shut down on October 1, 1991.

1962   On September 27, Rachel Carson's (1907–1964) *Silent Spring* is published. The strong reaction to the book opens up a dialogue about the relationship between people and nature, and contributes to the push to ban of the pesticide DDT, which occurred in 1972.

1963   On December 17, the Clean Air Act is created, and is the first federal legislation regarding air pollution control. The act establishes a federal program within the U.S. Public Health Service and authorizes research into techniques for monitoring and controlling air pollution.

1964   On September 3, the Wilderness Act creates the legal definition of wilderness in the United States, and protects some 9 million acres (36,000 sq km) of federal land.

1965   The Coast and Geodetic Survey becomes part of the Environmental Sciences Services Administration (ESSA).

The National Emissions Standards Act, an amendment to the Clean Air Act, creates federal automobile emissions standards. The standards created are reductions from 1963 emissions, with a 72 percent reduction for hydrocarbons, a 56 percent reduction for carbon monoxide, and a 100 percent reduction for crankcase hydrocarbons.

The Solid Waste Disposal Act passes intending to address the nation's solid waste problems through a series of research projects, investigations, experiments, training, demonstrations, surveys, and studies.

1966   The National Historic Preservation Act authorizes the National Register to coordinate and support public and private efforts to identify, evaluate, and protect historic and archeological resources in the United States.

On October 15, the Endangered Species Preservation Act authorizes the Secretary of the Interior to list endangered fish and wildlife and allows the U.S. Fish and Wildlife Service to spend up to $15 million per year to buy habitat for listed species. It also directs federal land agencies to preserve habitat for these species on their lands. This act is the predecessor to the Endangered Species Act of 1973.

1967   The first list of endangered species under the Endangered Species Preservation Act is issued in March. The list includes 36 birds, 22 fish, 14 mammals, and 6 reptiles and amphibians.

On November 21, the Air Quality Act (amendment to the Clean Air Act) establishes a framework for defining air quality control regions based on meteorological and topographical factors of air pollution. Responsibility for issuing air pollution advisories is assigned to the Weather Bureau's National Meteorological Center.

1968   On October 2, Congress passes the Wild and Scenic Rivers Act to preserve certain rivers with notable natural, cultural, and recreational value. Rivers may be classified as wild, scenic, or recreational at the time they are added the National System of Wild and Scenic Rivers. As of July 2011, the system included 203 rivers in 38 states and Puerto Rico, representing about one-quarter of one percent of the country's rivers.

1969   Congress passes the National Environmental Policy Act (NEPA), one of the first laws written to establish a broad national framework for environmental protection. NEPA's basic policy is to assure that all branches of government give proper consideration to the environment prior to undertaking any major federal action. The Act takes effect on January 1, 1970.

On June 22, oil and chemicals in the Cuyahoga River in Cleveland, Ohio, catch fire, with flames reaching five stories in height. This incident helped lead to the passage of the Clean Water Act in 1972.

On November 26, the UNESCO conference on Man and His Environment takes place in San Francisco, sparking hope for international cooperation on environmental issues. Peace activist John McConnell (1915–) presents the concept of Earth Day.

On December 30, the Federal Coal Mine Health and Safety Act creates the Mining Enforcement and Safety Administration (MESA), later renamed the Mine Safety and Health Administration (MSHA), within the Department of Interior. Its responsibilities parallel those of Occupational Safety and Health Administration (OSHA) but address underground and surface mining of coal. The Coal Act requires two annual inspections of every surface coal mine and four at every underground coal mine, and dramatically increases federal enforcement powers in coal mines.

1970–1979

1970   A major rewrite of the Clean Air Act sets National Ambient Air Quality Standards (NAAQS), New Source Performance Standards (NSPS), Hazardous Air Pollutant standards, and auto emissions tailpipe standards.

The Natural Resources Defense Council (NRDC), a nonprofit organization based in New York, is founded by a group of concerned law students and attorneys involved in environmental law. The NRDC lobbies Congress and state and local governments on such issues as habitat protection, pollution, and renewable energy.

On January 1, the National Environmental Policy Act (NEPA) is signed into law. Title I of

NEPA contains a Declaration of National Environmental Policy, which requires the federal government to try to protect the environment while allowing necessary development. Section 102 requires federal agencies to incorporate environmental considerations in their planning and decision-making and to prepare environmental impact statements (EISs), which should provide an assessment of the environmental impact of federal actions. Title II of the Act establishes the Council on Environmental Quality (CEQ).

On April 3, the Environmental Quality Improvement Act amends the National Environmental Policy Act of 1969 and assigns additional responsibilities to the Council on Environmental Quality.

On April 22, the first national Earth Day celebration creates a national political presence for environmental concerns.

On August 18, the General Authorities Act combines all areas administered by the National Park Service into one National Park System.

On October 3, the National Oceanic and Atmospheric Administration (NOAA) is formed, bringing together the U.S. Coast and Geodetic Survey (formed in 1807), the Weather Bureau (formed in 1870), and the Bureau of Commercial Fisheries (formed in 1871).

On December 2, Reorganization Plan No. 3 creates the Environmental Protection Agency (EPA) by Presidential Executive Order. The formation of the EPA marks a dramatic change in national policy regarding the control of air pollution. Whereas previous federal involvement had been mostly in advisory and educational roles, the new EPA emphasizes stringent enforcement of air pollution laws.

On December 30, the Occupational Health and Safety Administration (OSHA) is formed within the Department of Labor. Responsibilities include setting standards for employee exposure to hazardous substances.

1971 On January 13, the Lead-Based Paint Poisoning Prevention Act passes Congress, limiting lead content in paint and authorized funds for cleanup.

1972 On October 18, in a major rewrite to previous legislation, the amendments to the Federal Water Pollution Control Act (FWPCA) introduce a two-phase program to eliminate the discharge of pollutants into water systems by 1985.

On October 21, amendments to the Federal Insecticide, Fungicide, and Rodenticide Act transfer responsibility for the 1947 act from the USDA to the EPA. New provisions require

that pesticides developed after 1972 must be proven to have no unreasonable adverse effects on public health or the environment before being commercially produced or sold for the U.S. market. The widely used pesticide DDT is banned under these amendments.

On October 23, the Marine Protection, Research, and Sanctuaries Act, also known as the Ocean Dumping Act, is passed by the Congress. It authorizes the EPA to regulate ocean dumping of industrial waste, sewage sludge, biological agents, radioactive waste, and other wastes into the territorial waters of the United States through a permit program. A prohibition on medical waste is enacted in 1988.

1973 American Rivers, a nonprofit organization dedicated to preserving river habitats in the United States, is founded.

On December 28, Congress passes the Endangered Species Act. It is designed to protect critically imperiled species from extinction and the ecosystems upon which they depend.

1974 On December 16, the Safe Drinking Water Act passes, requiring the EPA to establish National Primary Drinking Water Regulations (NPDWRs) for contaminants that may cause adverse public health effects. This is the main federal law dealing with the quality of drinking water in the United States.

1975 The Hazardous Materials Transportation Act passes with the intent to provide protection against risks in the transportation of hazardous material.

1976 On June 22, the Resource Conservation and Recovery Act (RCRA) gives the EPA the authority to control hazardous waste from its generation to its transportation, treatment, storage, and disposal. The RCRA also sets forth a framework for the management of non-hazardous solid wastes.

1976 On October 11, the Toxic Substances Control Act (TSCA) passes Congress, regulating the introduction of new or already existing chemicals.

1977 On August 3, the Surface Mining Control and Reclamation Act becomes the primary federal law that regulates the environmental effects of coal mining in the United States. It creates two programs: one for regulating active coal mines and a second for reclaiming abandoned mine lands.

On December 27, amendments to the Clean Water Act require review of all National Ambient Air Quality Standards by 1980. Congress also adds additional protection for Class I National Park and Wilderness air quality.

1978   On November 9, the National Energy Conservation Policy Act is enacted as part of the National Energy Act. The Act requires utilities to provide residential consumers with energy conservation audits and other services to encourage slower growth of electricity demand.

     Residents in Love Canal, a working-class community in upstate New York, sell their houses to the federal government and evacuate the area. The town sits atop 21,000 tons of toxic industrial waste that had begun to bubble up into backyards and cellars. The disaster led to the formation of the Superfund program in 1980.

1979   On March 28, the Three Mile Island nuclear reactor near Harrisburg, Pennsylvania, partially melted down. While there were no fatalities and the facility continued to operate, the incident sparked national awareness about the dangers of nuclear power accidents. The incident led to new regulations in the nuclear industry, and contributed to the continued decline of new reactor construction.

1980–1989

1980   On September 29, the Fish and Wildlife Conservation Act authorizes financial and technical assistance to states for the development, revision, and implementation of conservation plans and programs for nongame fish and wildlife.

     On December 2, the Alaska National Interest Lands Conservation Act passes Congress and sets aside over 100 million acres for conservation and 26 new rivers in the Wild and Scenic Rivers System.

     On December 11, the Superfund program is created when the Comprehensive Environmental Response, Compensation, and Liability Act (CERCLA) is passed. This program directs the EPA to clean up abandoned toxic waste dumps.

1982   The Nuclear Waste Policy Act (enacted on January 7, 1983) is passed by Congress. The Act creates a timetable and procedure for establishing a permanent, underground repository for high-level radioactive waste by the mid-1990s. It also provides for some temporary federal storage of waste, including spent fuel from civilian nuclear reactors.

1983   The Defense Environmental Restoration Program is funded by an act of Congress. The program enlarges the scope of the Army Corps of Engineers' environmental work to include removal of hazardous materials at military installations. The Corps of Engineers was already providing engineering assistance to the EPA for toxic waste removal at civilian sites, under the Superfund program enacted at the end of 1980. By 1984, the Corps of Engineers is responsible for environmental restoration programs at all former military sites.

1986   The Water Resources Development Act of 1986, more simply called WRDA 86, is passed by Congress. This law signifies a major shift in water resources planning, shifting responsibility for financial support and management of water resources away from the federal government. The law authorizes about $16.23 billion in spending for water projects, of which the federal government commits about $12 billion with the remainder to come from states, port authorities, commercial navigation companies, and local communities. There are 377 new Corps of Engineers' water projects authorized for construction or study under the Act.

     On June 19, amendments to the Safe Drinking Water Act (originally passed in 1974) set standards for 83 contaminants, wellhead protection, new monitoring for certain substances, filtration for certain surface water systems, disinfection for certain groundwater systems, restriction on lead in solder and plumbing, and more enforcement powers.

     On October 17, the Emergency Planning and Community Right-to-Know Act (EPCRKA) requires manufacturers to report releases and transfers of 330 toxic chemicals to the EPA for entry into a public database.

     On October 17, the Superfund Amendments and Reauthorization Act (SARA) amends the Comprehensive Environmental Response, Compensation, and Liability Act (CERCLA) passed in 1980. The amendments stress the importance of permanent remedies in cleaning up hazardous waste sites, by requiring Superfund actions to consider the standards and requirements found in other state and federal environmental laws and regulations. The amendments also provide new enforcement authorities and settlement tools, increase state involvement in every phase of the Superfund program, increase the focus on human health problems posed by hazardous waste sites, encourage greater citizen participation in making decisions on how sites should be cleaned up, and increase the size of the trust fund to $8.5 billion.

1987   On February 4, the Water Quality Act amends the Federal Water Pollution Control Act of 1972. The new Act requires that industrial stormwater dischargers and municipal separate storm sewer systems (often called "MS4") obtain National Pollutant Discharge Elimination System (NPDES) permits by specific deadlines.

On September 16, Montreal Protocol on Substances That Deplete the Ozone Layer is adopted. The Montreal Protocol marks the first step in international efforts to protect stratospheric ozone. Later amended four times, this treaty provides the basis for part of the 1990 Clean Air Act.

1989   The Montreal Protocol on Substances That Deplete the Ozone Layer, signed in 1987, enters into force. It is an international treaty designed to protect the ozone layer by phasing out the production of ozone-depleting chemicals.

A February broadcast on CBS's television program *60 Minutes* highlights a Natural Resources Defense Council report that cites health risks connected with Alar, a pesticide widely used on apples. While the EPA had classified Alar as a probable human carcinogen, it was not until after the broadcast that the EPA decided to issue a ban. Before the ban took effect, in June Uniroyal, Alar's manufacturer, voluntarily removed the product from the U.S. market. Some scientists described the Alar episode as a "scare", citing that it is likely that large amounts of Alar would need to be ingested for it to be dangerous.

On March 24, the *Exxon Valdez* oil tanker runs aground on a reef in Prince William Sound in Alaska, dumping 10.8 million gallons of oil into the water. The oil slick eventually spreads 500 mi (800 km) from the site of the accident and pollutes thousands of miles of coastline. Despite cleanup efforts, hundreds of thousands of animals perish due to the oil.

1990–1999

1990   On January 29, the Nonindigenous Aquatic Nuisance Prevention and Control Act establishes a federal program to prevent the introduction and to control the spread of introduced aquatic nuisance species and the brown tree snake. Under this act, the U.S. Fish and Wildlife Service Branch of Invasive Species also manages the Aquatic Nuisance Species Task Force and the Aquatic Nuisance Species Program.

On November 15, the Clean Air Act Amendments of 1990 set provisions for implementing the Montreal Protocol in the United States. They set new standards for automobile emissions, mandated low-sulfur gasoline, required Best Available Control Technology

(BACT) for toxins, and mandated a reduction in chlorofluorocarbons (CFCs).

On August 18, the Oil Pollution Act passes Congress to mitigate and prevent civil liability for future oil spills off the coast of the United States.

1992   On October 6, the Alien Species Prevention and Enforcement Act makes it illegal to ship plants or animals that are covered under the Lacey Act or the Plant Protection Act through the U.S. mail.

1993   The National Environmental Trust (originally Environmental Information Center) is founded with funding by Pew Charitable Trusts.

The nonprofit organization, U.S. Green Building Council, is founded. The organization began planning for the Leadership in Energy and Environmental Design (LEED) program soon after.

1994   On February 11, President Bill Clinton (1946–) signs Executive Order 12898 on Environmental Justice, directing federal agencies to identify and address disproportionately high adverse effects on human health or the environment of activities affecting minority and low-income populations.

1994   The Northwest Forest Plan is adopted. The plan is a series of federal policies and guidelines governing land use on federal lands in the Pacific Northwest. Parts of the plan involve restricting logging in old-growth forests and protecting critical habitat for the northern spotted owl.

1996   On May 13, the Mercury-Containing and Rechargeable Battery Management Act is signed into law. The purpose of the act is to phase out the use of mercury in batteries and to provide efficient and cost-effective collection, recycling, and/or proper disposal of used nickel-cadmium batteries, small sealed lead-acid batteries, and certain other batteries.

On August 3, the Food Quality Protection Act standardizes the way the EPA will manage the use of pesticides and amends the Federal Insecticide, Fungicide, and Rodenticide Act and the Federal Food Drug and Cosmetic Act.

On August 6, amendments to the Safe Drinking Water Act provide new and stronger approaches to prevent the contamination of drinking water, better information for consumers, regulatory improvements, and new funding for states and communities through the Drinking Water State Revolving Fund.

1997   On December 11, the Kyoto Protocol is adopted by the United States and 121 other nations, but is not ratified by U.S. Congress.

1999   On February 3, Executive Order 13112 is signed establishing the National Invasive Species

Council. The Council ensures that Federal programs and activities to prevent and control invasive species are coordinated, effective, and efficient.

2000–2011

In March, the U.S. Green Building Council (USGBC) introduces the Leadership in Energy and Environmental Design (LEED) program to provide building owners and operators with a framework for "a framework for identifying and implementing practical and measurable green building design, construction, operations and maintenance solutions."

On June 20, the Plant Protection Act consolidates and updates all major statutes pertaining to plant protection and quarantine and permits the Animal and Plant Health Inspection Service (APHIS) to address all weed issues. It also permits the APHIS to take emergency actions to address incursions of noxious weeds.

On October 11, a Massey Energy Company impoundment dam collapses near Inez, Kentucky. More than 300 million gallons of thick, black coal slurry sludge is released into the Big Sandy River's Tug Fork and its tributaries, destroying 100 miles (160 km) of streams and killing millions of fish. Massey Energy Co. reported spending about $77.9 million on cleanup and paid $3.25 million in fines to the state of Kentucky. Massey Energy Co. subsidiaries Omar Mining and Independence Coal paid $400,000 in fines after pleading guilty to criminal Clean Water Act violations.

2001   The Natural Resource Defense Council (NRDC) launches the BioGems Initiative, which is structured to mobilize concerned citizen volunteers to use the power of the Internet to take action on issues of environmental concern, particularly in situations where habitats, environments, and species are threatened by development.

On December 12, a Unites States National Research Council report, *Abrupt Climate Change: Inevitable Surprises*, suggests that climate change may arrive very quickly, causing sudden and catastrophic damage to people, property, and natural ecosystems.

2002   On January 11, the Small Business Liability Relief and Brownfields Revitalization Act amends the Comprehensive Environmental Response, Compensation, and Liability Act (CERCLA or Superfund) by providing funds to assess and clean up brownfields, clarifying CERCLA liability protections, and providing funds to enhance state and tribal response programs.

In March, the U.S. wind energy industry wins passage of an extended production tax credit for electricity generated by wind power.

2003   On January 29, the U.S. Court of Appeals for the 4th Circuit rules in favor of mining companies, allowing them to continue mountaintop mining practices that dump tons of rock and dirt into valleys and streams.

On April 23, the Nutria Eradication and Control Act authorizes the Secretary of the Interior to financially support a program to create measures to eradicate or control nutria and to restore marshland damaged by nutria.

On December 25, 12 eastern U.S. states file suit to prevent the Environmental Protection Agency (EPA) from making changes that threaten to destroy the New Source Review (NSR) section of the federal Clean Air Act. The suit challenges new rules that will allow major polluters to significantly increase emissions without installing additional pollution control equipment.

2004   On October 6, Forest Service regulations preserving viable populations of wildlife in national forests are relaxed when evaluating road-building, logging or other forest proposals. The change is part of a campaign to give timber companies more access to national forests.

On October 30, the Brown Tree Snake Control and Eradication Act provides for the control and eradication of the brown tree snake on the island of Guam. It also provides for the prevention of the introduction of the species into other areas of the United States.

2005   In March, Congress votes to open the Alaska National Wildlife Refuge to oil drilling, but the vote is stopped in late November as public opinion turns against the idea that the amount of oil in the refuge justifies the environmental costs.

On June 5, World Environment Day is held in San Francisco. This is the first time the event has been held in the United States in 30 years.

On August 8, the Energy Policy Act of 2005 changes U.S. energy policy by providing tax incentives and loan guarantees for energy production of various types.

2006   In June, former U.S. vice president Al Gore (1948–) releases *An Inconvenient Truth*, a documentary that describes global warming.

On August 3, the EPA recommends new limits on the use of thousands of pesticides due to their ill effects on human health following a congressionally mandated 10-year review of more than 230 chemicals. The first to be banned is lindane, a toxic insecticide used for agricultural purposes.

On September 26, James Hansen (1941–) of the National Aeronautics and Space Administration (NASA) announces that Earth's overall temperature reaches its highest level in 12,000 years.

On September 27, California imposes a cap on greenhouse gas emissions, the first U.S. state to do so.

2007 On April 2, the United States Supreme Court rules that states may regulate "greenhouse" gases in *Massachusetts v. EPA*.

On August 24, the U.S. Interior Department's Office of Surface Mining Reclamation and Enforcement proposes easing environmental requirements for mountaintop removal mining. The proposals outraged many people in Appalachia, leading in part to the West Virginia Council of Churches statement against mountaintop removal mining.

On October 12, former U.S. vice president Al Gore is awarded the Nobel Peace Prize (jointly with the Intergovernmental Panel for Climate Change) for the documentary film, *An Inconvenient Truth*, and related climate change efforts.

On December 30, the U.S. Climate Data Center announces that 2007 was the warmest year on record.

2008 On March 11, the U.S. National Research Council reports that rising sea levels threaten key infrastructure in the United States.

On December 22, more than a billion gallons of coal fly ash sludge spills out of a holding dam at the Tennessee Valley Authority (TVA) Kingston Fossil Plant in Tennessee. The fly ash slurry contains significant amounts of arsenic, beryllium, boron, cadmium, chromium, chromium VI, cobalt, lead, manganese, mercury, molybdenum, selenium, strontium, thallium, and vanadium, along with dioxins and PAH compounds. TVA misleads residents of the region about the safety of the spill materials, leading to a significant media uproar and a federal investigation by the spring of 2009.

2009 On January 15, the U.S. Climate Action Partnership presents a plan to reduce the country's greenhouse gas emissions to 20 percent of 2005 levels by 2050 through a cap and trade system. The business-backed plan is seen as a method to cushion the impact of climate legislation that will be taken up in Congress.

On March 30, President Barack Obama (1961–) signs the largest wilderness protection bill in 15 years, protecting two million acres in nine states.

On April 17, the EPA rules that emissions of six greenhouse gases, including carbon dioxide, are a danger to public and should be regulated.

On May 11, the EPA takes charge of the toxic coal ash spill that occurred in 2008 at the Kingston Fossil power plant in Tennessee

On September 30, the EPA announces new Clean Air Act regulations to reduce greenhouse gas emissions from electric power plants.

2010 On April 20, an explosion on the Deepwater Horizon offshore drilling rig in the Gulf of Mexico kills eleven and badly injures nine more workers. About 206 million gallons of oil spill as a result and coastal environments from Louisiana to Florida are affected. The gushing well is finally plugged on September 19, 2010. The dangers and costs of recovering oil at extreme ocean depths were highlighted by this incident in the Gulf of Mexico.

On April 22, the EPA issues rules on automotive fuel efficiency and, for the first time, regulates greenhouse gas emissions. New regulations for coal-fired power plants follow.

On April 28, U.S. Secretary of Interior Ken Salazar (1955–) announces approval of the controversial Cape Wind project, which will install 130 wind turbines on Horseshoe Shoal in Nantucket Sound off the coast of Massachusetts. The installation will be miles away from shore and is projected to produce up to 420 megawatts of energy from wind.

2011 On January 13, the EPA vetoes a water permit for the massive Spruce No. 1, a mountaintop removal coal mining site in West Virginia. The veto is a major victory for environmentalists, but it sparks a strong negative response from the coal industry.

On January 15, the EPA approves the use of auto fuel made of 15 percent ethanol blended with gasoline. This sparks renewed debate over environmental benefits and drawbacks of ethanol produced from corn.

On June 20, the U.S. Supreme Court rejects a nuisance suit and rules that the EPA has the authority to regulate greenhouse gas emissions. The suit was filed in 2004 by states and environmental groups against American Electric Power in the hope of holding utilities accountable under the common nuisance law. The court said that the litigation was superseded by the Clean Air Act.

CANADA

1840–1899

1842 The Geological Survey of Canada (GSC) is founded on April 14. It is mandated to create an inventory of the mineral, soil, and water resources of Canada, made up of southern Ontario and Quebec. The GSC is the first agency to conduct forest research. Sir William Logan (1798–1875) is the founding director; his is knighted by Britain's Queen Victoria (1837–1901) in 1851. Canada's highest mountain, Mount Logan, is later named for the GSC's founding director.

1885 The reserve that will later become Banff National Park is created. This is Canada's first national park.

1887 The first statistical report on the country's mineral resources, entitled *Statistical Report on the Production, Value, Exports, and Imports of Minerals in Canada* is issued.

1899 The Federal Forestry Service is created within the Department of the Interior. The annual budget for the Forestry Service is C$1,000.00

1900–1909

1907 The Department of Mines is created by an act of parliament. Its mandate is to "map the forest areas of Canada, and to make and report upon the investigations useful to the preservation of the forest resources of Canada."

1908 The GSC establishes a Topographical Division to create maps of the country.

1909 The United Kingdom, on behalf of Canada, signs the Boundary Waters Treaty with the United States to prevent disputes over shared waters. This leads to the formation of the International Joint Commission, which oversees shared interests on the use of the Great Lakes, which form part of the border between the United States and Canada.

1910–1919

1911 On May 19, Parks Canada is formed as the Dominion Parks Branch under the Department of the Interior, becoming the world's first national park service. Its name has changed a number of times, known variously as the Dominion Parks Branch, National Parks Branch, Parks Canada, and the Canadian Parks Service, before a return to Parks Canada in 1998.

1917 The Migratory Birds Convention Act passes to protect migratory birds, their eggs, and their nests from hunting, trafficking, and commercialization. A permit is required to engage in any of these activities.

1918 The first International Joint Commission report describes major water pollution in parts of the Great Lakes.

1920–1929

1921 Lake of the Woods Control Board (LWCB) Act provides statutory establishment of the LWCB, defines its jurisdiction and powers, and provides for board members to be appointed by Canada and Ontario. These acts gave the LWCB jurisdiction over Lac Seul and the English and Winnipeg Rivers as well as over Lake of the Woods, which borders the provinces of Ontario and Manitoba and the U.S. state of Minnesota.

1928 The Lac Seul Conservation Act provides for the construction of a dam on Lac Seul in order to create a hydropower reservoir. Lac Seul, a crescent-shaped lake in northwestern Ontario, is approximately 150 miles (241 km) long and is the second largest body of water lying entirely within Ontario's borders.

1930–1939

1930 On May 30, the Canada National Parks Act passes, enabling Parks Canada to designate and maintain national parks and national parks reserves.

1940–1949

1947 On April 18, National Wildlife Week Act is established as a yearly memorial to conservationist Jack (John Thomas) Miner (1865–1944). In the early twentieth century, Miner established a bird sanctuary on his family's land, and the tagging of the ducks in his sanctuary constituted the first complete banding record.

1949 The Canada Forestry Act grants the Canadian Forest Service legal authority to enter into forest resource agreements with provinces.

1950–1959

1955 International River Improvements Act ensures that Canada's water resources in international river basins are developed and used in the best national interest.

1960–1969

1963 Canadian Parks and Wilderness society is formed to protect Canada's public lands and water.

1965 The International Joint Commission directs Canada and the United States to reduce phosphorus discharges into the Great Lakes in order to control eutrophication. Eutrophication, or overfertilization, can cause massive blooms of algae. When the algae die, their decomposition process used all of the oxygen in the water, creating dead zones on the bottom of the body of water. This is especially a problem in Lake Erie.

1969 Pollution Probe is created by a group of University of Toronto students and faculty. A charitable organization that researches and advocates for environmental solutions, Pollution Probe draws widespread support by acting as a focal point for growing public concern about the environment.

1970–1979

1970 Dangerous levels of mercury are found in Ontario fish, leading to bans on consumption of some fish.

The Canadian Environmental Law Association and the Canadian Environmental Law and Research Foundation (CELRF) are founded.

On February 4, the Liberian tanker *Arrow* runs aground in Chedabucto Bay, Nova Scotia, during heavy rains. The tanker spills heavy bunker C oil, which contaminates 190 mi (304 km) of shoreline.

On September 30, the Canada Water Act provides the framework for cooperation with provinces and territories in the conservation, development, and utilization of Canada's water resources.

The Arctic Waters Pollution Prevention Act forbids ships from dumping solid or liquid waste into Canada's Arctic waters, and requires them to notify Canadian officials in the event of an oil spill.

1971 The nongovernmental environmental organization Greenpeace is founded in Vancouver, British Columbia.

In March, the Canadian Environment Week Act establishes Canadian Environment Week as a time for grassroots action to help preserve, protect, and restore the environment. This annual event coincides with the United Nations World Environment Day on June 5.

On June 11, Environment Canada is created to be the federal agency in Canada responsible for the preservation and enhancement of the quality of the natural environment.

1972 Canadian Maurice Strong (1929–) heads the Stockholm Conference on the Human Environment. The conference draws worldwide attention to environmental issues and leads to the creation of environment departments by governments around the world.

On April 15 Canada and the United States sign the first Great Lakes Water Quality Agreement, which aims to control sewage and phosphorus discharges.

1973 The Canada Wildlife Act allows for the creation, management, and protection of wildlife areas for research activities, conservation, or interpretation of wildlife.

1974 Dichlorodiphenyltrichloroethane (DDT) use is restricted in Canada.

The Mackenzie Valley Pipeline Inquiry is commissioned by the government on March 21 to investigate the impacts of pipeline proposed to be built through the Northwest Territories, in the Yukon and Mackenzie River valley.

1976 The Environmental Assessment Act passes in Ontario, the first province to require environmental assessments in the planning and approval of certain projects.

From May 31 to June 11, Canada hosts the first United Nations Conference on Human Settlements (Habitat) in Vancouver, British Columbia. The conference focuses on rapid global urbanization.

On July 23, Canada signs the World Heritage Convention. Nahanni National Park in Northwest Territories is designated as the world's first natural World Heritage Site by UNESCO (United Nations Educational, Scientific, and Cultural Organization).

1977 On June 9, report of the Mackenzie Valley Pipeline Inquiry, titled *Northern Frontier, Northern Homeland*, states that an oil and gas pipeline in the Mackenzie River valley of northwestern Canada should only be built in an environmentally sound manner and only after native land claims are settled. Canadian Justice Thomas Berger (1933–) recommends a ten-year moratorium on construction. The inquiry was initiated in 1974 and cost approximately C$5.3 million. Berger headed the inquiry; during the investigation he heard testimony from interested groups and visited some 35 communities that would be affected by the pipeline project.

1978 Canada and the United States sign the second Great Lakes Water Quality Agreement. This agreement introduces the concept of protecting the entire ecosystem of the lakes, zero discharge of persistent toxic substances to the lakes, and the elimination of toxic substances that build up in the food chain.

The United States raises concerns about transboundary acid rain with Canada. This ignites a decade-long struggle between the countries to understand and deal with the corrosive air pollution issue.

In April, the Northern Pipeline Act creates the Northern Pipeline Agency to oversee the planning and construction of the Canadian section of the Alaska Highway Gas Pipeline Project. The pipeline will transmit natural gas from Alaska and Northern Canada into Alberta.

1979 The National Parks Policy is revised to make preserving ecological integrity the priority in Canadian Parks.

1980–1989

1980 Provinces begin to introduce curbside recycling, which will be implemented over the course of the decade.

On August 5, Canada and the United States sign a memorandum of intent to curb acid rain and other air pollution problems, but it will take most of the decade to reach a formal agreement.

Canada—along with the United States, Sweden, and Norway—bans most aerosol uses of chlorofluorocarbons (CFCs).

1981 The Canadian Coalition on Acid Rain is formed to lead a campaign to get controls on acid rain. It is the largest environmental group in Canada for the majority of the decade.

There are rising concerns that chemicals from leaking Niagara River chemical dumps and industrial discharges are a threat to drinking water drawn from the river and from Lake Ontario.

1984 Seven eastern Canadian provinces agree with the federal government on a 50 percent cut in the emissions of sulphur dioxide, which causes acid rain. This will require major cuts by nickel and copper smelters and by coal-burning power plants.

The Environmental Assessment and Review Process Guidelines Order formalizes federal environmental assessments.

Ivvavik National Park becomes Canada's first national park established through a land claim agreement with the country's native people.

1985 The Department of the Environment Act legally incorporates Environment Canada as the Department of the Environment.

The Fisheries Act prevents the further depletion of fish through unregulated fishing practices. This act establishes controls for fisheries as a means to protect crustaceans, shellfish, fish, and marine mammals.

The Canada Oil and Gas Operations Act passes to promote safety, environmental protection, conservation of oil and gas resources, and joint production arrangements. The act is jointly administered by the Department of Natural Resources and Indian Affairs and Northern Development Canada.

The remaining uses of DDT in Canada are further limited, with a four-year phase out.

On April 13, a spill of polychlorinated biphenyls (PCBs) from a transport truck in northern Ontario becomes a flashpoint in a provincial election as people worry about the threat to health.

On November 1, a "blob" of perchloroethylene (dry cleaning fluid) from a chemical spill is found on the bottom of the St. Clair River in Sarnia, Ontario. This raises fears of possible widespread leaks of toxic chemicals in that region, known as Canada's chemical valley. Public concern helps push the chemical industry to even greater efforts at reducing spills and emissions.

1986 Canada releases its first national State of the Environment report.

The Canadian Council of Resource and Environment Ministers establishes the National Task Force on Environment and Economy, which recommends setting up round tables to discuss environment and economy at national, provincial, and local levels.

The Canadian Chemical Producers' Association, reacting to growing concerns about the safety of chemicals, launches the Responsible Care program, in which the industry group sets rules to reduce its risks and impacts. The organization sets guiding principles to which companies must adhere as a condition of membership. This model is adopted by chemical industry groups in a number of countries.

1987 The National Task Force on Environment and Economy establishes the Round Table on Environment and Economy, and reports on what Canada needs to do to move toward sustainable development. The task force makes 40 recommendations focusing on how to create a more sustainable economy and educating students about the environment.

Canada and the United States sign a Protocol to the Great Lakes Water Quality Agreement, broadening its scope.

On April 4, the Canada–Newfoundland Atlantic Accord Implementation Act between the government of Canada and the government of Newfoundland and Labrador is implemented. The Act deals with offshore petroleum resource management and revenue sharing.

1988 The National Parks Act is amended, formalizing the principle of ecological integrity in the park system.

In June, Canada holds the World Conference on the Changing Atmosphere (the Toronto Atmosphere Conference) publicizing the issue of climate change and bringing calls for major cuts in the emissions of greenhouse gases, such as carbon dioxide. The meeting recommends a 20 percent initial cut by 2005. This conference is held at the start of a heat wave, drought, and smog crisis that affects several parts of the world. The Mississippi River drops to its lowest recorded level, leading to calls for water diversions from the Great Lakes.

On June 30, Canada adopts a new Environmental Protection Act.

On August 23, a fire in a warehouse containing PCBs at St. Basile-le-Grand, Quebec, forces the evacuation of more than 3,300 people for three weeks and provokes debate over how to safely dispose of these hazardous chemicals.

1989   In August, PCBs, including from some from the St. Basile-le-Grand fire, are shipped from Quebec to Wales for incineration. The ship carrying the PCBs is turned back at UK ports by protests, and the wastes are returned to Canada.

Canada's energy ministers meet, but fail to agree on a way to reduce carbon dioxide emissions by 20 percent by 2005. The ministers endorse the 20 percent target, however, which was recommend by the Toronto Atmosphere Conference.

The Endangered Spaces campaign is launched by the Canadian Parks and Wilderness Society and World Wildlife Canada to encourage the completion of the national parks system. The goal of the campaign is to establish parks and protected areas that represent each of the country's approximately 350 natural regions.

Systematic overfishing has devastated the centuries-old cod fishery off eastern Canada, forcing the Canadian government to cut fishing quotas. Tens of thousands lose their jobs, fish packing plants close and many people emigrate, particularly from hard-hit Newfoundland. The fishery crisis drains communities of their people and causes long-term social and economic dislocations. It is one of the starkest examples of the results of the unsustainable use of natural resources.

1990–1999

1990   The Canadian and Manitoba governments establish the International Institute for Sustainable Development in Winnipeg as a global centre of expertise.

The first GLOBE conference (Global Opportunities for Business and the Environment), an international environment industry trade fair and conference, is held in Vancouver, British Columbia. It becomes a biennial event.

The Canadian government promises to stabilize the country's emissions of greenhouse gases at 1990 levels by the year 2000.

The North American Wetlands Conservation Council is created to implement the North American Waterfowl Management Plan, to take a leadership role in wetlands policy and awareness, and to provide leadership to the Canadian Habitat and Species Joint Ventures.

From February 12 to 28, a fire in a pile of 14 million tires near the town of Hagersville, Ontario, provokes a debate on how to safely dispose of wastes.

On December 11, the federal government releases an ambitious Green Plan for the country, promising billions of dollars in spending. It includes smog controls, a safe drinking water act, the virtual elimination of toxic wastes, cleaning up the Great Lakes, a 50 percent cut in garbage, a packaging act. The act also includes plans for the completion of a national parks system by 2000.

1991   A group of youth, educators, business and government leaders, and community members establish Learning for a Sustainable Future (LSF), a non-profit organization that integrates sustainability education into Canada's education system.

Signed on March 13, the Canada–United States Air Quality Accord resolves the transboundary dispute over acid rain after more than a decade of negotiations. The accord establishes a framework for addressing shared concerns relating to air pollution. In the first annex to the agreement, it also sets out objectives for each country to reduce emissions that lead to acid rain.

1992   Canada's fisheries minister John Crosbie (1931–) places a moratorium on the northern cod fishery off Newfoundland, which had collapsed due to overfishing and mismanagement. The ministry also stops the sockeye salmon fishery in the Fraser River for the rest of the year because of fish shortages.

The Canadian Environmental Assessment Act requires federal departments, agencies, and Crown corporations to conduct environmental assessments for proposed projects where the federal government is the proponent or where the project involves federal funding, permit, or license.

The Energy Efficiency Act comes into effect, providing Natural Resources Canada with the authority to promote energy efficiency and alternative energy sources.

The Wild Animal and Plant Protection and Regulation of International and Interprovincial Trade Act forbids the import, export, and interprovincial transportation of certain animal and plant species, unless the specimens are accompanied by the appropriate documents (licenses and/or permits). In all cases, the Act applies to the plant or animal, alive or dead, as well as to its parts and any derived products. Forbidden species include: species that appear on the Convention on International Trade in Endangered Species of Wild Fauna and Flora (CITES) control list; foreign species whose capture, possession, and export are prohibited or regulated by laws in their country of origin; Canadian species whose capture, possession, and transportation are regulated by provincial or territorial laws; and species whose introduction into Canadian ecosystems could endanger Canadian species.

Saskatchewan teacher and activist Elizabeth Dowdeswell is named the third head of the United Nations Environment Programme.

On October 17, ECO-ED, the World Congress for Education and Communication on Environment and Development, draws more than 2,000 to Toronto, Ontario, in the first major conference to be held since the Earth Summit in Rio de Janeiro, Brazil, in June 1992.

1993   British Columbia is hit by major protests against logging in old-growth forests. Protestors try to get purchasers to boycott products from such forests. The province will see both violent protests and agreements on sustainable forestry involving loggers, environmental groups, citizens, native peoples and governments.

The federal government closes most of remaining Atlantic cod fishery and some other fisheries to conserve dwindling stocks. About 40,000 people are out of work as a result and struggle to find other sources of income. Some turn to other fisheries, such as crab, while others are forced to leave the region to seek employment elsewhere.

1994   On January 1, Canada, the United States, and Mexico sign the North American Free Trade Agreement (NAFTA), lowering tariff barriers. They also sign an environmental side agreement, the North American Agreement for Environmental Cooperation. This leads to the creation of the Commission for Environmental Cooperation, based in Montreal, Quebec. The environmental agreement and commission provide tools for collaboration among the three nations on environmental and sustainable development issues, and provide a forum for citizens from the countries to hold governments accountable for the enforcement of environmental laws.

1995   On January 12, the Department of Natural Resources Act comes into force, creating Natural Resources Canada from the Department of Energy, Mines, and Resources and the Department of Forestry.

On January 19, the Canadian Environmental Assessment Act comes into force with a goal of promoting environmental assessment as a planning tool to protect and sustain a healthy environment. It requires environmental assessments of projects involving the federal government.

Canada creates the office of the Commissioner of the Environment and Sustainable Development under the Office of the Auditor General, with a mandate to produce an annual "green" report on the federal government. At the same time, federal departments and some agencies are required to prepare sustainable development strategies and action plans.

1996   On July 19 and 20, torrential floods kill ten people and drive thousands from their homes in the Saguenay region of Quebec. Parts of Alberta, Manitoba, and Ontario are struck by floods, hail, and tornadoes, which cause widespread damage.

1997   On March 20, the Nuclear Safety and Control act is assented to, overseeing the health, safety, environment, and security aspects of the long-term management of nuclear fuel waste.

On April 29, Canada signs the Kyoto Protocol, committing to cut their emissions by 6 per cent from 1990 levels by the period 2008–2012.

On July 9, the Plastimet recycling plant in Hamilton catches fire, burning at least 441 tons (400 t) of polyvinyl chloride plastic (PVC) plastic over four days. Huge clouds of black smoke containing dangerous chemicals roll over the region, provoking health concerns among residents and firefighters. It raises questions about the safe handling of recycled materials.

1999   The Canadian government increases spending for the environment department for the first time in five years.

On November 15, the Canadian Environmental Protection Act (CEPA) passes to contribute to sustainable development through pollution prevention and to protect the environment, human life, and health from the risks associated with toxic substances. It establishes the CEPA Environmental Registry, where industries, individuals, interest groups, and others can find information about environmental planning within Canada.

2000–2011

2000   Starting on May 15, heavy rainfalls carry *Escherichia coli* (*E. coli*) bacteria from farm wastes into a poorly protected drinking water well in the small, rural town of Walkerton, Ontario. The resulting outbreak of illnesses kills seven people and leaves more 2,500 ill. This triggers more concern about drinking water safety in Canada and raises concerns about the ability of governments to protect water quality.

2001   On February 19, the Canada National Parks Act passes, setting new standards for park management plans, requiring legal designation of wilderness areas, limiting commercial development in national park communities, and establishing seven new national parks and one national park reserve.

On April 25, the protozoan *Cryptosporidium parvum* is found in the drinking water of North Battleford, Saskatchewan. Some 5,800 people become ill as a result of drinking contaminated water, raising questions about drinking water protection.

2002   The government of Canada announces its "Action Plan to Protect Canada's Natural Heritage." This is the government's most ambitious expansion of national parks and marine conservation areas in more than 100 years. Under the plan, ten new parks will be established, and existing national parks will receive government investment to restore environmental health.

On November 15, the Nuclear Fuel Waste Act comes into force, ensuring that the long-term management of nuclear fuel waste will be carried out in a comprehensive, integrated, and economically sound manner.

On December 12, the Species at Risk Act passes to protect endangered or threatened organisms and their habitats, and to manage species which are not yet threatened, but whose existence or habitat is in jeopardy.

On March 22, the Canada Foundation for Sustainable Development Technology Act establishes a foundation to fund projects to develop and demonstrate new technologies to promote sustainable development, including technologies to address climate change and air quality issues.

2003   Two new national parks—Gulf Islands National Park Reserve in British Columbia and Ukkusiksalik National Park in Nunavut—are the first to be created under the Action Plan to Protect Canada's Natural Heritage.

In May Gulf Islands National Park Reserve (GINPR) is established by agreement between the governments of Canada and British Columbia. GINPR is located between southern Vancouver Island and mainland British Columbia. Included within the reserve are islands, islets, and reefs in the southern Strait of Georgia, Boundary Pass, and Haro Strait. The

reserve protects examples of rare ecosystems, including the endangered Garry Oak ecosystems, and some of the world's largest marine mammals, including sea lions and endangered orca whales.

On August 23 Ukkusiksalik National Park is declared a national park, becoming Canada's forty-first national park. The park surrounds Wager Bay, a 80-mile (100-km) long saltwater inlet on the northwest coast of Hudson Bay in Nunavut. Ukkusiksalik takes its name from the soapstone found within its boundaries.

2004   On November 8, it is reported that rapid climate change is occurring in the Arctic, according to 300 scientists who worked for four years on the international Arctic Council. The scientists conclude that sea ice in the Arctic covers 10 percent less surface area than it had 30 years earlier, and is only about half as thick.

2005   On January 22, the Labrador Inuit Park Impacts and Benefits Agreement, along with a Memorandum of Agreement for a National Park Reserve in the Torngat Mountains with the Government of Newfoundland and Labrador, leads to the formal establishment of the Torngat Mountains National Park Reserve of Canada.

Learning for a Sustainable Future (LSF) partners with Environment Canada and Manitoba Education, Citizenship and Youth (MECY) to undertake five initiatives to support the U.N. Decade for Education for Sustainable Development. These initiatives include establishing Provincial/Territorial Education for Sustainable Development Working Groups; forming a National Education for Sustainable Development Expert Council (now called ESD Canada); undertaking the Canadian Sustainability Curriculum Review Initiative; launching the ESD Resource Database; and holding Youth Taking Action Forums.

2006   On February 7, some five million acres (2,023,436 ha) of the Great Bear rain forest in British Columbia are saved from logging, and another ten million acres (4,046,873 ha) will be logged under strict protocols following an agreement between provincial and national governments.

2009   On May 14, Ontario, Canada passes the Green Energy Act providing "feed in tariffs" designed to accelerate the use of wind and solar energy. It is patterned after existing investment plans in Denmark, Germany, and other European nations.

2010   On June 23, the government announces intentions to pass legislation to reduce greenhouse gas emissions from electricity generation in its effort to achieve a 17 percent reduction over 2005 greenhouse gas emissions in the country overall by 2025. Regulations will be published in 2012 and are scheduled to take effect July 15, 2015.

On October 13, Canada puts bisphenol A (BPA) on the toxic substances list. BPA is a common additive in plastics.

2011   On January 21, Canada issues regulations concerning the use of phthalates, a category of chemicals used to soften plastics.

The National Parks Project is commissioned by Primitive Entertainment and Discovery World HD to create a series of documentary films about some of the country's national parks to mark the one-hundredth anniversary of the national parks system.

In December, Environment Minister Peter Kent announced that Canada would be formally withdrawing from the Kyoto Protocol, indicating, "Kyoto is not the path forward for a global solution for climate change."

List of Conversions

Measurements and Conversions

Length

1 centimeter	0.3937 inch
1 centimeter	0.03280833 foot
1 meter (100 centimeters)	3.280833 feet
1 meter	1.093611 US yards
1 kilometer (1,000 meters)	0.62137 statute mile
1 kilometer	0.539957 nautical mile
1 inch	2.540005 centimeters
1 foot (12 inches)	30.4801 centimeters
1 US yard (3 feet)	0.914402 meter
1 statute mile (5,280 feet; 1,760 yards)	1.609347 kilometers
1 British mile	1.609344 kilometers

Area

1 sq centimeter	0.154999 sq inch
1 sq meter (10,000 sq centimeters)	10.76387 sq feet
1 sq meter	1.1959585 sq yards
1 hectare (10,000 sq meters)	2.47104 acres
1 sq kilometer (100 hectares)	0.386101 sq mile
1 sq inch	6.451626 sq centimeters
1 sq foot (144 sq inches)	0.092903 sq meter
1 sq yard (9 sq feet)	0.836131 sq meter
1 acre (4,840 sq yards)	0.404687 hectare
1 sq mile (640 acres)	2.589998 sq kilometers

Volume

1 cubic centimeter	0.061023 cubic inch
1 cubic meter (1,000,000 cubic centimeters)	35.31445 cubic feet
1 cubic meter	1.307943 cubic yards
1 cubic inch	16.387162 cubic centimeters
1 cubic foot (1,728 cubic inches)	0.028317 cubic meter
1 cubic yard (27 cubic feet)	0.764559 cubic meter

Liquid Measure

1 liter	0.8799 imperial quart
1 liter	1.05671 US quarts
1 hectoliter	21.9975 imperial gallons
1 hectoliter	26.4178 US gallons
1 imperial quart	1.136491 liters
1 US quart	0.946333 liter
1 imperial gallon	0.04546 hectoliter
1 US gallon	0.037853 hectoliter

Weight

1 kilogram (1,000 grams)	35.27396 avoirdupois ounces
1 kilogram	2.204622 avoirdupois pounds
1 quintal (100 kg)	220.4622 avoirdupois pounds
1 quintal	1.9684125 hundredweights
1 tonne (metric ton, 1,000 kg)	1.102311 short tons
1 metric ton	0.984206 long ton
1 avoirdupois ounce	0.0283495 kilogram
1 troy ounce	0.0311035 kilogram
1 avoirdupois pound	0.453592 kilogram
1 avoirdupois pound	0.00453592 quintal
1 hundred weight (cwt., 112 lb)	0.50802 quintal
1 short ton (2,000 lb)	0.907185 metric ton or 907.185 kg
1 long ton (2,240 lb)	1.016047 metric tons or 1,1016 kg

Electric Energy

1 horsepower (hp)	0.7457 kilowatt
1 kilowatt (kW)	1.34102 horsepower
1 megawatt (MW)	1,000 kilowatts
1 gigawatt (GW)	1,000 megawatts

Temperature

Celsius (C)	Fahrenheit-32 X 5/9
Fahrenheit (F)	9/5 Celsius + 32

Petroleum

One barrel = 42 US gallons = 34.97 imperial gallons = 158.99 liters = 0.15899 cubic meter (or 1 cubic meter = 6.2898 barrels).

Overview of Current Environmental Issues, United States

♣ Introduction

In 2011, environmentalists in the United States and around the world were talking about climate change, renewable energy, sustainability, and recycling. Finding the best policies to deal with these broad topics challenged leaders in both the public and private sectors. At the United Nations-sponsored talks on climate change held in Cancun, Mexico, and attended by representatives of 190 nations in late 2010, delegates agreed to a plan to curtail climate change that included establishing a fund to help developing countries participate. The 2010 conference was the sixteenth meeting convened by the UN. When the meeting adjourned, commentators observed that the compromise agreements fell short of the broad changes that activists and scientists had hoped for.

By the beginning of the second decade of the twenty-first century, most scientists agreed that the surface temperature of planet Earth had increased by almost 1°C (1.5°F) since the late 1800s, and that human activity was the primary cause of the warming. The dramatic worldwide increase in the number of heat waves, droughts, flooding, hurricanes, tornados, dust storms, and other extreme weather events follows the general predictions made by climate change scientists. Tying a particular weather event to climate change is impossible, but the pattern of increase appeared to confirm the theory.

Inspiring legislatures and government agencies to respond to the pattern is not simple, however. The 112th U.S. Congress (January 2011–2013) attempted to prevent the Environmental Protection Agency (EPA) from taking action, particularly on greenhouse gas (GHG) emissions. Energy Committee chairman Fred Upton, Republican from Michigan, put forth H.R. Bill 910, which was passed by the House of Representatives in April 2011. (As of late 2011, the Senate version of the bill had not made it to a vote.) If enacted, the bill would prohibit the EPA from addressing carbon emissions; in addition, a spending bill passed by the House in February of 2011 would cut off relevant funds.

Meanwhile, the human population continues to increase and engage in activities that affect the environment. The U.S. Census Bureau reported that the U.S. population grew nearly 10 percent from 2000 to 2009, exceeding 300 million. Environmental problems are escalating, too. More than half of America's waters are in poor condition, groundwater supplies are being depleted, cleanup still has not been completed at hundreds of priority contaminated sites (known by the EPA as Superfund sites), and about 127 million people live in counties with polluted air. Upon taking office in 2009, EPA administrator Lisa Jackson set forth a clear agenda: addressing climate change, improving air quality, assuring the safety of chemicals, cleaning up communities, protecting America's waters, expanding the conversation on environmentalism and working for environmental justice, and building strong state and tribal partnerships. However, she was challenged to implement this ambitious agenda with an EPA budget that was cut by 16 percent from the year before.

Former interior secretary Bruce Babbitt, in a speech at the National Press Club in June 2011, observed that "Congress, led by the House of Representatives, has declared war on our land, water, and natural resources."

The range of environmental problems includes:

1. Loss of wildlife habitat

2. Real and threatened species extinctions

3. Actual and prospective water shortages

4. Food quality and security concerns

5. Wetlands and coastal ecological impacts

6. Air and water pollution

7. Pesticides

8. Toxics in products

9. Threats to national parks

10. Unanswered questions about the safety of nanotechnology

11. Genetically modified organisms

12. Asthmagens and sensitizers

13. Endocrine disruptors

14. Pharmaceuticals and personal care products discharged into our waters

Environmental problems have mounted in number, intensity, and complexity.

Although the weakening of the EPA stems from a belief that its regulations hobble business, there are proponents of the idea that environmental regulations benefit industry indirectly while benefitting society as a whole. A June 2011 Office of Management and Budget (OMB) review found that EPA's regulations, which may not benefit industry directly, have benefits for society that far outweigh their costs. The OMB report stated that "32 major EPA rules together will ultimately yield estimated annual benefits between $82 billion and $551 billion in 2001 dollars, with annual costs in the $23 billion to $29 billion range."

Many U.S. corporations claim to be environmentally responsible. To help assess these claims, the Global Reporting Initiative (GRI), founded in 1997, provides a mechanism for standardized reporting of corporate social and environmental responsibility. As of 2010, GRI listed more than 1,850 organizations submitting reports on activities in these areas. It has become common for companies to reference GRI's guidelines in their reports to shareholders and the public on corporate initiatives for sustainability.

James Gustave Speth, former administrator of the United Nations Development Programme (UNDP), founder and president of the World Resources Institute, and chair of the U.S. Council on Environmental Quality, spoke to the National Council on Science and Environment in 2010. On that occasion he said, "If we look at real world conditions and trends, we see that we are winning victories but losing the planet, to the point that a ruined world looms as a real prospect for our children and grandchildren." However, Speth is hopeful, and, in concert with many others, he is articulating a vision for a changed economic system. Combined with the potential for a green economy, responsible business management, green chemistry, cleaner production, and rising consumer interest in green products and lifestyles, a new environmental agenda encompasses economic and technological change.

⚜ What Are the Solutions?

There are many available technical fixes for environmental problems. "An incomplete list," writes Harold Latin of Rutgers University, "would include at least a half-dozen different types of solar energy processes, wind turbines, wave power and tidal power generators, geothermal energy, increased hydropower generation, nuclear energy, hydrogen fuel cells, plasma gasification (a thermal chemical process to convert garbage and industrial wastes into biofuels), methane combustion from waste disposal sites and feed lots, and diverse biofuels made from nearly every biological material." New technologies lead to new business opportunities and new job opportunities, and changes in economic and consumption patterns. Some of the technologies make energy generation possible on a community or individual household basis, providing the chance for what German solar pioneer Herman Scheer has called "energy autonomy," from which communities can gain independence from centralized systems. A Brookings Institute report found that "The clean economy offers more opportunities and better pay for low- and middle-skilled workers than the national economy as a whole."

A new, holistic strategy of embracing all the connections inherent in the changes needed to solve environmental problems has the chance of changing our history of "siloed" issues, where one group focuses on air, another on water, and neither group works with a vision shared by other political groups. Ecological concepts of dynamic systems, promoted by mid-twentieth century environmental thinkers, are gaining ground, applied now to economics by ecological economists; to building by contractors, architects, and designers employing design for recycling, greenbuilding, biomimicry, and biophilia; and to policy, business, and living by practitioners of life-cycle perspectives and advocates of product stewardship. In 1972, the Stockholm Conference on Human Environment (Earth Summit I), the first UN conference on the environment, introduced the world to the term "interdependency." The 2012 Earth Summit (Rio Plus 20) uses the themes of vision, cooperation, and transformation to establish a framework for sustainable economies that are not just green but that also address poverty. Surveying the environmental landscape reveals ever more troubling indicators of a deteriorating planet, but also movement toward new environmental politics to address the underlying causes of the impacts we see.

⚜ Status Report: Climate Change

Varying sources have reported on the weather change. A 2011 National Academy of Sciences (NAS) report stated "Climate change is occurring, is very likely caused primarily by the emission of greenhouse gases from human activities, and poses significant risks for a range of human and natural systems. . . . [the impacts] of most concern to the United States include more intense and frequent heat waves, risks to coastal communities from sea level rise, greater drying of the arid Southwest, and increased public health risks." In June 2011, more than

4,000 daily high temperature records in the United States were tied or broken. In addition, nearly 160 places reported the record high monthly temperatures for June and 42 reported the all-time record highest temperature ever. Droughts occurred in the Southwest and Southeast, bringing dust storms in Arizona and the driest October-to-June period in Texas since the state began keeping rainfall records in 1895. An extreme heat wave covered large portions of the United States from mid-July, increasing heat-related visits to hospital emergency rooms, and 141 million Americans were under heat advisories by July 22. Examining tree rings, USGS scientists found snowpack declines over recent decades in the Rocky Mountains, in a study released in June of 2011.

The NAS report stated that impacts will linger for hundreds or even thousands of years, and that "Because of time-lags inherent in the Earth's climate, the observed climate changes as greenhouse gas emissions increase reflect only about half of the eventual total warming that would occur for stabilization at the same concentrations." The NAS report noted, however, that "many of the actions that could be taken to reduce vulnerability to climate change impacts are common sense investments that will offer protection against natural climate variations and extreme events."

The Obama administration has proposed legislation and regulation to limit greenhouse gas emissions and cited the value of investments that will create green jobs and international economic competitiveness. Secretary of energy Steven Chu, a Physics Nobel Prize winner, said better electricity infrastructure for renewable energy and energy efficiency will "lay the foundation for sustained, long-term economic expansion." The U.S. military stepped up its assessment of climate change as a national security threat and developed roadmaps for adaptation.

🍂 Activism and Results

A decade of mounting activism peaked with the passage of the American Clean Energy & Security Act in June of 2009 by the House of Representatives, which set mandatory limits on 87 percent of greenhouse gas emissions. The bill did not become law. But on January 1, 2009, mindful of the Supreme Court's decision in the 2007 *Massachusetts v. EPA* that such gases qualify as air pollutants under the Clean Air Act, EPA initiated new GHG-permitting procedures for new large emitters already required to report under other Clean Air Act provisions. In July, the permitting requirement was extended to more large carbon emitters, and although efforts to improve the efficiency of commercial and industrial boilers were stalled for major sources, they did come into force for smaller "area" sources. Resistance mounted to the 2007 Federal Energy Independence and Security Act requirements banning the manufacture of incandescent lighting, beginning in 2012, but House repeal efforts failed.

Despite the opposition in the Republican-controlled House to action on climate change, by 2011 most states had passed laws to promote clean energy. The U.S. Conference of Mayors had called on the federal government to enact greenhouse gas reduction legislation (130 cities competed to win the Mayor's Climate Protection awards; Houston, Texas and Evanston, Illinois won). Major businesses united with environmental organizations to form the U.S. Climate Action Partnership, calling on the federal government "to quickly enact strong national legislation to require significant reductions of greenhouse gas emissions." Also, more than 600 universities and colleges had submitted reports to the American College and University Presidents Climate Commitment, in furtherance of the association's 2007 climate pledge.

🍂 Natural Resources, Water, and Agriculture

In the United States, 620 animal species and 796 plant species are currently listed as threatened or endangered, 149 animal species, and 121 plant species are candidates for listing, and 22 animal species and 3 plant species are proposed for listing. Critical habitat has been designated for only 601 species in all; 1,072 habitat conservation plans have been approved, and 1,137 species have approved recovery plans. Wildlife news included the passing of the last Eastern jaguar, the impact of the Deepwater oil spill on Gulf biota (including the effect of oil dispersants), and the worldwide decline of predatory species, seen as causing the swelling of prey populations, throwing food chains out of balance.

According to the U.S. Geological Survey (USGS) "more than 6,500 nonindigenous species are now established in the United States, posing risks to native species, valued ecosystems, and human and wildlife health" and costing an estimated $120 billion a year.

The most recent USGS State of the Birds report of the U.S. Geological Survey's (USGS) Gap Analysis describes the dependency on public lands of more than 1,000 species, many in decline. Public lands have competing uses, such as resource extraction, energy development, (and) recreation. Grassland birds are "among our nation's fastest declining species, yet only a small amount—13 percent—of grassland is publicly owned and an even smaller percentage is managed primarily for conservation. All of the nation's 40 waterfowl species and many other wetland-associated bird species depend on the network of National Wildlife Refuges and other publicly protected wetlands." Stewardship of public wetlands demonstrates what works and it "has resulted in remarkable recovery of waterfowl and water bird populations."

On June 30, 2011, the FWS's listing of the polar bear as endangered due to global warming, challenged by the state of Alaska and others, was upheld by a U.S. District Court in Washington D.C. *© Wild Arctic Pictures/Shutterstock.com*

A ten-year effort to add strength to the protections of the Endangered Species Act (ESA) culminated in a July 2011 settlement between the U.S. Fisheries and Wildlife Service (FWS) of the Interior Department and the Center for Biological Diversity. The agreement states that the FWS will make decisions on whether to add hundreds of species to the endangered list, including the walrus, wolverine, Mexican grey wolf, and the New England cottontail rabbit. The future of wolf management is in transition as a U.S. district court rejected an attempt to return responsibility to the states of Idaho and Montana (for inconsistency with ESA). The Defenders of Wildlife, which believes that conflicts with humans is the main threat to the 5,000 wolves in the lower 48 states (and perhaps more than 10,000 wolves in Alaska), has created the Wolf Coexistence Partnership. The partnership promotes nonlethal ways of protecting livestock from wolf predation and increases acceptance of carnivores. On June 30, 2011, the FWS's listing of the polar bear as endangered due to global warming, which had been challenged by the state of Alaska (and hunters), was upheld by a U.S. District Court in Washington, D.C. On July 18, 2011, the FWS listed the whitebark pine as threatened or endangered, due to climate change. According to the Natural Resources Defense Council, which petitioned for the listing in 2008, "This is the first time that the federal government has declared a widespread tree species in danger of imminent extinction because of climate change."

According to the National Resource Conservation Service of the U.S. Department of Agriculture (USDA), soil erosion was reduced by about 40 percent between 1985 and 1995 by a Conservation Reserve program, which pays farmers to convert highly erodible cropland to vegetative cover. But according to the Earth Island Institute, the recent high prices for crops raised for biofuels has led to the plowing up of 12 million acres (4,856,247 ha) by 2007, and the fact that half of all U.S. farmland is rented also

reduces the incentive for continued conservation. In July 2011, the professional association for soil experts, the Soil and Water Conservation Society, issued a statement warning that climate change is exacerbated by current agricultural practices, and presents a threat to future agricultural productivity, "due to accelerated erosion" and "water use exceeding water storage replacement." The statement recommended maintaining vegetative cover, using only perennial crops for biofuels, the use of agroforestry to provide windbreaks, and communication of the importance of the fact that soil "serves as a sponge capturing carbon from the atmosphere." Attention to the loss of phosphates increased, as phosphates are necessary for growing food, and soil replenishment is not keeping pace with erosive loss.

The USDA's National Water Management Center (NWMC) reports that agricultural irrigation is now 65 percent of U.S. ground water use, reaching a peak of 83 billion gallons per day in 1980, exceeding safe yield in many areas. "Some aquifers have been permanently damaged because full recharge of depleted aquifer storage will not be possible where compaction and subsidence have occurred." Texas has lost 1.435 million acres (580,000 ha) of irrigated cultivated cropland, mostly due to dwindling ground-water supplies. South-central Arizona has seen water table declines of 200 feet (60 m), and in some areas near Phoenix, land subsidence caused by aquifer depletion has reached 18 feet (5.5 m), "indicating considerable and potentially irreversible impacts on aquifer storage and conductivity." States thought of as water-rich resources are also experiencing ground water shortages, including Arkansas and Rhode Island. NWMC points to the necessity for good aquifer assessments, safe yield measurement, and drought action plans. USDA provided $60 million in fiscal year 2010 for agricultural water conservation, funding drip irrigation and satellite and Internet technology to allow farmers to monitor water-use data in real time, helping them to decide how much water to use on their crops, and when to apply it.

According to the National Summary of State Information on Surface Waters maintained by the U.S. Environmental Protection Agency, the U.S. has more polluted water than clean water. Only about six million acres (2.4 million ha) of lakes and ponds are in good condition, compared with about 11.6 million acres (4.7 million ha) that are impaired. Nearly seven million square miles (18.2 sq km) of bays and estuaries are good, and about 11.7 million square miles (30.4 million sq km) are impaired. About one million square miles (2.6 million sq km) of ocean and "near coastal" waters are good, while about 4.8 million square miles (12.5 million sq km) are impaired. Of coastal shoreline miles, about 1,600,000 (2,600,000 km) are good, and about 902 miles (1,450 km) are impaired, and about 1.3 million acres (526,000 ha) of wetlands are in good condition, compared with about 750,000 acres (304,000 ha) that are impaired. Of

USDA's National Water Management Center (NWMC) reports that agricultural irrigation is now 65 percent of U.S. ground water use, exceeding safe yield in many areas. © *ilFede/ShutterStock.com*

935 million miles (1.5 billion km) of rivers and streams, about half are in good condition, and half are impaired. Only 26.5 percent of rivers, 42.2 percent of lakes, 21 percent of bays, 11 percent of ocean and near coastal areas, 1.9 percent of wetlands, and 4.2 percent of coastal shorelines have been assessed.

The types and causes of pollution differ for each resource, but the most important threats are pathogens, sediment, nutrients and oxygen depletion, PCBs, mercury, and other metals. The most important "probable source groups" are agriculture, atmospheric deposition, municipal discharges, unspecified nonpoint sources, and "unknown."

Trees are at risk, according to a 2009 article in *Science*, based on a USGS survey that found that "background (noncatastrophic) mortality rates have increased rapidly in recent decades, with doubling periods ranging from 17 to 29 years among regions. Increases were also pervasive across elevations, tree sizes, dominant genera, and past fire histories." Regional warming and water deficits were identified as likely contributors.

Although it has been known since 1977 that gas leaks could produce "sudden death" in nearby vegetation, the effect became news in 2010 when Jan Schlichtmann, the attorney portrayed in *A Civil Action*, founded the Massachusetts Shade Tree Trust to receive compensation from gas companies for trees killed or damaged by gas leaks. In June 2011, the *New York Times* reported that a recently approved pesticide, Imprelis, used by lawn care specialists, was the leading suspect in the deaths of thousands of trees on golf courses and lawns across the country.

The probable causes of bee colony collapse disorder, affecting some 30 percent of managed U.S. hives, have been identified as parasites, fungi, and pesticides, with viruses emerging as highly significant, though some have conjectured that the underlying cause is stress from transport and handling for commercial uses. It is estimated that white-nose syndrome has killed more than a million bats since it was first discovered in New York in 2006. Bat Conservation International reported in June 2011 that it has been found in Canada, Kentucky, and Ohio. Forty fish stocks are subject to overfishing in U.S. waters, including cod, red snapper, and two species of flounder, according to the National Atmospheric and Oceanic Administration. Stocks of 21 fishes—including haddock, pollock, and spiny dogfish—have rebounded to healthy levels.

🍁 Food Supply Effects on the Environment

The problems of "factory" farms (termed CAFOs Concentrated [or Confined] Animal Feeding Operations) include overuse of antibiotics, creating resistant strains of microorganisms, massive concentrated quantities of animal waste leading to nutrient overloading and ammonia emissions, crowded conditions and other inhumane treatment of animals, and inequities for contract farmers. According to the USDA, during the period 1987–2002, cattle farms doubled in size, dairy by 240 percent, chicken production farms increased in size by 60 percent, and hog farms by 2,000 percent. Production has continued to shift to larger operations since 2002. A 2010 study by the National Association of Local Boards of Health noted that "Large farms can produce more waste than some U.S. cities—a feeding operation with 800,000 pigs could produce over 1.6 million tons of waste a year. ...Annually, it is estimated that livestock animals in the United States produce each year somewhere between 3 and 20 times more manure than people in the United States produce, or as much as 1.2–1.37 billion tons of waste (EPA, 2005). Though sewage treatment plants are required for human waste, no such treatment facility exists for livestock waste." EPA recently agreed to collect information to finalize its proposed rule to control discharges from CAFOs.

Organic food, since 2000 certified as such by the USDA, grew from a $1 billion annual market in 1990 to nearly $25 billion in 2010. Environmentally aware consumers now frequently request locally produced food as well, to reduce greenhouse gas emissions from transportation. They also request humanely raised livestock. A new food movement has been growing to patronize local, organic, family-owned farms, rather than large-scale industrial agriculture, as a means of fostering a lower impact agriculture. In January 2011, agriculture secretary Tom Vilsack's approval of genetically modified alfalfa angered organic growers, as it followed public discussion of the concept known as "co-existence", in which genetically modified organisms (GMOs) are limited to ensure that they are contained. Organic crops subject to pollen drift can show detectable traces of GMOs, which will render them unmarketable where GMOs are forbidden.

❧ Effects of Energy Generation on the Environment

In 2009 (the latest year of annual trend reports available from the U.S. Energy Information Agency [EIA] in late 2011), the United States used 94.6 quadrillion Btus of energy, up from 32 in 1949, but down from 100.5 in 2005. (One "quad" is 172 million barrels of oil—8 to 9 days of U.S. oil use, 50 million tons of coal—enough to generate about 2 percent of annual U.S. electricity use, or 1 trillion cubic feet of natural gas–about 4 percent of annual U.S. natural gas use). Fossil fuels provided 78 quadrillion Btus, nuclear power provided 8.3 quads, and renewables supplied 7.7. Of the fossil fuels, 19.7 quads came from coal, 23.4 came from natural gas, and 35.3 came from petroleum. Of the renewables, 2.7 came from hydroelectric, 0.4 came from geothermal, 0.1 came from solar, 0.7 came from wind, and 3.9 came from biomass.

According to the most recent monthly energy review of the U.S. Energy Information Administration (EIA), domestic renewable energy production is now greater than that of nuclear power. Production of renewable energy, including hydropower, increased by 15.07 percent compared to the first quarter of 2010. Coal consumption dropped 12 percent, due to the number of coal-fired power plants in the United States declining from 645 coal-fired power plants in 2001 to 594 in 2009.

Most of our transportation (94 percent) is powered by oil, which supplies only 1 percent of the energy used to generate electrical power. Ninety-three percent of coal is used for generating electrical power. About a third each of natural gas is used for generating power, heating homes, and in industrial processes, with 3 percent used in transportation.

After the earthquake and tsunami at Japan's Fukushima nuclear facilities in April 2011, the U.S. Nuclear Regulatory Commission convened a task force that recommended enhancements to reactor safety at the "more than 100 nuclear power plants (likely to be) operating throughout the United States for decades to come." By late spring of 2011, public support for nuclear power had declined significantly, according to polls by the Pew Trust and the Civil Society Institute, among others.

Xcel Energy Inc. was scheduled to receive (and states it will return to ratepayers) more than $100 million from the federal government, due to the government's failure to remove nuclear waste, stored in wet pools and dry storage casks at two of the Minnesota utility's reactors by a 1998 deadline. There are 74 lawsuits filed by utilities against the federal government for similar waste storage issues at nuclear power plants stemming from the 1982 Nuclear Waste Act. The Department of Energy (DOE) signed contracts with the companies to remove high-level radioactive waste and store it in a permanent repository, and utilities paid into a fund to finance the program, but the DOE failed to take the waste.

In July 2011, according to a spokesman for the National Oceanic and Atmospheric Administration (NOAA), nearly 500 miles (800 km) of Gulf Coast were still contaminated with oil from the Deepwater Horizon oil well blowout, and oil is still washing up ashore. More than 1,000 people continue with cleanup efforts. A June report by the National Research Council to the new Bureau of Ocean Energy Management (formed in response to the gulf disaster), recommended an aggressive use of several regulatory tools to strengthen the regulation of offshore drilling. A ruptured pipeline beneath the Yellowstone River that leaked about 42,000 gallons (158,987 l) of oil in early July of 2011, was found to have carried crude oil from the oil sands of Alberta, Canada, which is "more corrosive and more abrasive than the Wyoming oil that the pipeline was supposed be carrying, potentially leading to increased wear and tear on the pipe." In August 2011, author and advocate Bill McKibben and other environmental figures were arrested for blocking the sidewalk in front of the White House in protest of the Keystone XL pipeline (which was intended to carry tar sand oil from Alberta to refineries in the United States). McKibben stated that the tar sands are "the second biggest pool of carbon on the Earth. If we start burning them it's essentially game over for the climate."

EPA's new Clean Air Mercury and Clean Air Interstate rules require significant reductions in sulfur dioxide, nitrous oxide, and mercury. Several "Clean Coal" projects, by which government financing assists in the development of new technologies to reduce carbon, sulfur, nitrogen, and mercury emissions, have been withdrawn. However, the Great River Energy, in Maple

Total installed grid capacity of solar photovoltaic (PV) in the United States came to 2.15 GW in 2010, with more than 50,000 installations, almost doubling the rate from 2009 to 2010. Of the 2010 installations, 374 MW were commercial, 384 MW were by utilities, and 262 MW were residential. © *topseller/ShutterStock.com*

Grove, Minnesota, has successfully tested "dry fining," a system that uses a plant's waste heat and a fluidized-bed drying process to remove moisture and impurities from "low-rank" coals, such as lignite. This method reduces sulfur dioxide and mercury an estimated 40 percent, nitrogen oxide by 20 percent, and carbon dioxide by 4 percent. Progress had stalled on the FutureGen project for carbon sequestration, though drilling is now scheduled for FutureGen 2.0, in Meredosia, Illinois, which projects 90 percent capture of the plant's carbon emissions. Neighbors have expressed concerns about migration of the carbon dioxide into the aquifer, releases of gas into the atmosphere, and compensation for effects on their land.

On July 28, 2011, a settlement was reached between a Massey Coal subsidiary and plaintiffs complaining that their residential water wells had been poisoned by leaks from coal slurry that had been injected into abandoned wells. An investigation by a West Virginia state commission into an explosion at a Massey mine on April 5, 2010, led to a finding that the company "made life difficult" for miners who tried to address safety and built "a culture in which wrongdoing became acceptable." In response to

the 2008 coal ash disaster at the Tennessee Valley Authority's Kingston plant, the TVA inspector general reviewed coal ash storage practices, finding contamination issues related to several sites. The Institute for Southern Studies noted that the EPA had already documented 137 sites of concern in 34 states "where coal ash has contaminated water supplies with arsenic and other toxic metals." A "recent EPA risk assessment found that people who live near coal ash impoundments and drink from wells have as much as a 1 in 50 chance of getting cancer due to arsenic contamination." New information also came out about the health impacts of mountain-top removal, a method for mining coal that produces large areas of devastated landscape, including links to significantly higher prevalence rates for birth defects in children born to nearby families.

Concerns about natural gas drilling have involved the contaminated waters released from hydrofracturing operations ("fracking," which uses water, chemicals, and sand to break apart underground rock), and the inefficient capture of gases, seen as polluting both underground water sources and an exacerbation of climate change (methane has about 24 times the greenhouse gas effect than carbon dioxide). Environmental advocates seek a reversal of a 2005 exemption from the Safe Drinking Water Act, stricter regulation of discharges under the Clean Water Act, and stricter oversight of drilling operations. Attention to the issue was greatly enhanced when the film "Gasland" won the 2010 Sundance Film Festival documentary prize.

Total installed grid capacity of solar photovoltaic (PV) in the United States came to 2.15 GW in 2010, with more than 50,000 installations, almost doubling the rate from 2009 to 2010. Of the 2010 installations, 374 MW were commercial, 384 MW were by utilities, and 262 MW were residential. An additional 814 MW in thermal equivalents were added for heating. The Interstate Renewable Energy Council (IREC) gave credit to stable state and federal incentives, federal stimulus funding, improved capital markets, state renewable portfolio standards (RPS), and PV module price decline. Less dramatic growth was seen in solar heating (6 percent from 2009 to 2010), due to "unstable" and small incentives, and competition with inexpensive natural gas. IREC notes the coming expiration of the U.S. Treasury Grant in Lieu of the Investment Tax Credit Program (ITC) (known as the Treasury Cash Grant program, which provides commercial installations with the alternative of a cash grant instead of a tax credit).

At least thirty states now have renewable portfolio standards (laws requiring utilities to use renewable sources to meet a portion of electrical demand, on varying increasing schedules), and at least twenty states now have laws requiring utilities to help customers achieve better energy efficiency. Based on the experience with these kinds of statutes, the American Council for an Energy-Efficient Economy estimates that a comparable federal law would save almost $170 billion, create more than 220,000 jobs, eliminate the need to build 390 power plants, and reduce greenhouse gas emissions by four percent. Forty-two states and Washington, D.C., now also have net-metering laws, which require that customers be allowed to place their excess energy (typically, from PV or wind turbines) on the grid, and that they be paid for it if they feed in more than they use. Craig Lewis, executive director of the CLEAN coalition (Clean Local Energy Accessible Now), which advocates for policies that pay for selling your excess power to the grid (known in Europe as "feed-in tariffs"), claims that interconnection by many small sources, rather than a central station approach, would achieve three times more job creation. Lewis also notes that a virtually ignored market with powerful potential is wholesale distributed generation, typically 20 megawatts or smaller, which is between small net-metering at the residential level, and large centralized stations. With this model, a building owner can put panels on the roof, take care of the interconnection, and then distribute to tenants. Another new model is being demonstrated by San Francisco's

Solar@Work, a group purchase program for small and mid-size businesses, which plans to purchase 2 megawatts and save members hundreds of thousands of dollars over the lifetimes of the systems.

Experts see more complications for the future development of biofuels, although U.S. production increased to 13 billion gallons in 2010, (from 50 million in 1979), with the help of subsidies of more than $5.68 billion in 2010 alone. Production used 40 percent of the country's corn crop, and played a major role in food price increases. The Congressional Research Service estimated in October 2011 that if the entire U.S. corn crop were devoted to fuel, only 18 percent of U.S. gasoline consumption would be replaced. Heavy fertilizer use contributes to the marine dead zone in the Gulf, and the global warming reduction benefits of biofuels have been questioned, due to the heavy use of machinery in corn production and refining. EPA has downgraded its goal of producing 100 million gallons of cellulosic (nonfood) ethanol by end of 2011, to 6.5 million gallons, as cost-effective processes for converting lignin and hemicellulose have not yet been developed. The business prospects for algae are also mixed, with major companies (BP, Valero) remaining invested, and others (Shell) withdrawing. Predictions state that algae biofuel will not be ready as quickly as hoped. However, algae does not compete with food and can be used to absorb carbon dioxide emissions.

Tax credits of up to 30 percent of construction costs for wind energy production, which spurred growth in wind farms, making that sector the second-fastest growing source of new electricity after natural gas, expire in 2012. Tax credits for solar energy production expire in 2016. The American Wind Energy Association and the American Council on Renewable Energy are lobbying for the right to form "master limited partnerships," which are tax constructs used by the oil and gas industry to shift tax burdens to investors.

Secretary of the Interior Ken Salazar announced two large-scale solar developments in California, a wind energy project in Oregon, and a transmission line in Southern California, which are projected to create more than 1,300 construction jobs and provide a combined 550 megawatts of electricity (enough to power 185,000 to 380,000 homes). At the end of July 2011 President Obama and thirteen auto executives agreed to an increase in fleet-wide fuel economy standards from 35.5 miles per gallon (mpg) in 2012 to 54.5 miles per gallon for cars and light trucks to be sold in 2025.

Other areas of focus for clean energy development include:

1. Storage (with batteries, flywheels, compressed air, pumped water) at facilities and for efficient movement of electricity on the grid

2. Smart grid technologies to allow for distributed generation and information feedback

3. Demand response programs that help utilities to avoid brownouts due to failure to meet peak load requirements

4. Energy efficient appliances and vehicles (including new mileage-per-gallon standards, hybrid vehicles, and all-electric vehicles and charging stations)

5. Tapping the energy of the earth (geothermal or ground-source heat pumps) at individual homes and buildings or centralized power stations

6. Concentrated solar power, which uses mirrors to generate great heat

7. Efficient insulation of buildings and efficient heating and cooling technologies

8. Efficient lighting

9. Nuclear fusion

10. Financing, training, and technical assistance to promote the adoption of these and other practices

11. Methane generation from biodigestion

12. Low-smoke cooking for less developed regions, and research and development of new technologies

13. Education of a new generation of clean energy specialists

Toxics and Pollution

In early May 2010, the president's Cancer Panel, charged since 1971 with annual reports to the president on reducing cancer, released a 240-page report that focused for the first time on environmental causes of cancer. It stated that "the true burden of environmentally induced cancers has been grossly underestimated" and urged the president to use his powers to "remove the carcinogens and other toxins from our food, water, and air that needlessly increase health care costs, cripple our nation's productivity, and devastate American lives." Referring to the 300 contaminants that have been found in umbilical cord blood of newborn babies, the report commented that "to a disturbing extent, babies are born 'pre-polluted.'"

In an interview pertaining to the Mossville, Louisiana, appeal to the Inter-American Commission on Human Rights, an EPA administrator commented that the petitioners "basically make a case that the laws of this country do not provide them an opportunity for redress. And it is true that at this point there are no environmental justice laws—there's nothing on the books that gives us the ability to do it." (Mossville is near 14 chemical plants and residents receive large amounts of pollutants.) However, on August 4, 2011, heads of 17 federal agencies signed a memorandum of understanding on implementing President Obama's Executive Order 12898 on Environmental Justice,

Evidence of acid rain. © *Mary Terriberry/ShutterStock.com*

formalizing commitments previously made and providing a way for agencies to better coordinate efforts. (An Executive Order does not confer new powers on agencies, but only directs how they implement the mandates of Congress.)

The six criteria air pollutants, the focus of ambient air pollution monitoring, have been significantly reduced since 1990. Ground-level ozone, measured by eight-hour averages, is down by 14 percent. Particle pollution less than 2.5 microns in size (PM2.5) is down by 19 percent. Particles of 10 microns in size or less (PM10, one-seventh the size of a human hair) are down by 31 percent, lead by 78 percent, nitrogen dioxide (NO2) by 35 percent, carbon monoxide (CO) by 68 percent, and sulfur dioxide (SO2) by 59 percent. About 127 million people, however, live in counties that still have air below quality standards. EPA regulatory development to further improve air quality includes addressing emissions from locomotive and marine engines, and gasoline and diesel vehicles, including non-road vehicles.

There are 1,627 sites still listed on the National Priorities List of most seriously contaminated sites (NPL). The final remedy has been completed at 1,098 sites and 475 of the sites are "ready for anticipated use." A little less than a third of the listed sites still need to be cleaned up.

An NAS review of the EPA's assessment of the risks of formaldehyde generated further discussion. The NAS study upheld some of the EPA's findings but criticized the Integrated Risk Information System (IRIS). To industry complaints that EPA had unfairly "demonized" chemicals such as arsenic, dioxin, and formaldehyde, EPA experts responded that "endless efforts to deconstruct individual studies should not obscure [a] trend" of chemicals in fact being found, in time, to be more hazardous than originally assessed.

In March 2010, the EPA announced a new drinking water strategy that involves grouping drinking water contaminants rather than listing them individually, partnering with states to improve monitoring, developing new treatment technologies, and using the authority of multiple statutes (such as the Federal Insecticide, Fungicide, and Rodenticide Act), to protect water sources. As part of this effort, the EPA also identified 134 chemicals as priorities as part of its endocrine disruptor screening program, mandated by Congress in 1996 to cover chemicals similar to female hormones, and expanded by the EPA to include those with androgenic (male hormone) effects, and to include effects on fish and wildlife as well as public health.

As part of Administrator Jackson's chemicals policy reform, by June 8, 2011, the EPA had declassified the identities of more than 150 chemicals that had formerly been claimed as confidential, including nonylphenol and perfluorinated compounds used in nonstick and stain-resistant materials, fire-resistant materials, air fresheners, and dispersants.

The EPA's 2011 green chemistry awards, which recognized work on producing basic chemicals from renewable feedstocks, water-based paints, and substitutions for organic solvents, brought the total to 82 award winners since the program began in 1996. The EPA estimates that winning technologies alone, not counting 1,400 nominees, have reduced the use or generation of more than 199 million pounds of hazardous chemicals, saved 21 billion gallons of water, and eliminated 57 million pounds of carbon dioxide releases. Michigan has been pursuing a green chemistry initiative since 2006, and California since 2007. The New England regional administrator of EPA in 2010 convened diverse stakeholders to launch a green chemistry effort in the region. Several states have passed laws to limit toxics in products. Examples include Maine's 2008 law restricting chemicals of high concern in children's toys and Washington's Children's Safe Products Act. The Lowell, Massachusetts, Center for Sustainable Production is maintaining a database of state chemicals policies and hosting meetings to coordinate policy discussions.

The Great Lakes Clean Water Organization (GLCW) has coordinated the Yellow Jug Old Drugs program, a collection method to prevent water pollution by pharmaceuticals. Begun in May 2009, there are 215 participating pharmacies, and the program is now expanding. Individuals can bring unused/unwanted/expired drugs to participating pharmacies, and the drugs go to a Waste to Energy facility, which is preferable to flushing them down the toilet or putting them in landfills.

In January 2011, Earthjustice, California Rural Legal Assistance, Inc., and others sued the state of California for approving the use of the carcinogenic strawberry pesticide methyl iodide, which is used instead of methyl bromide. Although France, Germany, and Italy acted to suspend the use of neonicotinoid pesticides, suspected of causing bee colony collapse disorder (CCD), the EPA states that it has found no evidence "that an EPA-approved pesticide used according to the label instructions has caused CCD."

❧ Green Business, Green Building, Green Jobs

The Brookings Institution defines the green (or clean) economy as "the sector of the economy that produces goods and services with an environmental benefit." In a July 2011 report, the Brookings Institution estimated that the green sector of the economy provides 2.7 million jobs, many of which are in mature sectors, with newer "clean-tech" sectors (including solar photovoltaic [PV], wind, fuel cell, smart grid, biofuel, and battery industries) providing strong jobs growth. The report said that green or clean activities and jobs related to environmental aims pervade all sectors of the U.S. economy, and a quarter are in manufacturing establishments (such as electric vehicles, green chemical products, and lighting), which is much higher than the 9 percent average for the overall economy. Clean economy jobs also provide strong exports, such as biofuels, green chemicals, and electric vehicles. The report noted that stronger growth has occurred where establishments have clustered (similar companies located near each other), such as professional environmental services in Houston, solar photovoltaic in Los Angeles, fuel cells in Boston, and wind in Chicago. The report noted that "significant policy uncertainties and gaps are weakening market demand for clean economy goods and services, chilling finance, and raising questions about the clean innovation pipeline reinforces the need for engagement and reform." Other countries are moving to capture world demand for clean products and the related jobs they represent. The report observed that "vigorous private sector-led growth needs to be co-promoted through complementary engagements by all levels of the nation's federal system to ensure the existence of well-structured markets, a favorable investment climate, and a rich stock of cutting-edge technology." Clean economy investment would create "3.2 times more jobs overall than fossil-fuel investments," according to a 2009 study by the Political Economy Research Institute at the University of Massachusetts, Amherst.

By March 2011, some 51,700 green jobs had been created by American Recovery and Reinvestment Act (popularly referred to as the "stimulus package") and President Obama had instituted a Race to the Green program to continue the effort. One of the first federal efforts was Recovery Through Retrofit, to encourage nationwide weatherization of homes and "help people earn money, as home retrofit workers, while also helping them save money, by lowering their utility bills." A 2009 report by the Council on Environmental Quality, Middle Class Task Force, noted that the country has almost

130 million homes, which combined generate more than 20 percent of our carbon dioxide emissions, and "existing techniques and technologies in energy efficiency retrofitting can reduce home energy use by up to 40 percent per home and lower associated greenhouse gas emissions by up to 160 million metric tons annually by the year 2020."

A July 2011 report by the Environmental Defense Fund (EDF) found that energy efficiency in general represents a "significant largely untapped opportunity for meeting the dual goals of financial return and environmental protection." The EDF noted that high capital and development costs, long payback periods, limited capital availability, uncertainties, and split incentives (such as when the costs and opportunities of energy are divided between tenants and landlords) are stalling the development of this market sector. The report recommended aggregating projects so that many small sources can be grouped into one effort, developing a secondary market so that project values can be traded (and investors have a means of exit other than waiting for project completion), and establishing the connection between energy efficiency investments and the increased value of properties.

In testimony before the U.S. House Energy & Commerce Subcommittee on Commerce, Manufacturing, and Trade on March 3, 2011, Rhone Resch, president and CEO of the Solar Energy Industries Association, pointed out that the U.S. solar industry had expanded at a consistent 50 percent annual growth rate over the last four years. In the last year alone, it grew from $3.6 billion to $6.0 billion, during a time when other industries contracted. However, Resch said, "China, Germany, Italy, and Japan are investing heavily in solar and they are beating us." Resch recommended continuing the Section 1603 Treasury program (known as Treasury grants, in which tax deductions can be converted to immediate grant funding). He also recommended restoring incentives for solar manufacturing, "policies that facilitate financing for clean energy technologies that cannot obtain financing in the commercial market place" and restoring funding to the Department of Energy's loan guarantee program. A Clean Energy Development Administration (CEDA), proposed by House Democrats in 2009 and also supported in 2011 by the U.S. Chamber of Commerce, would provide financial services such as loans and loan guarantees to help inject capital into clean energy projects. At the time, however, House bill H.R. 1 eliminated all such funding in 2011.

In November 2010, the U.S. construction market was visibly turning green, according to a McGraw-Hill report entitled *Green Outlook 2011: Green Trends Driving Growth*. Green building construction starts were up 50 percent from 2008 to 2010 in value, and represented "25 percent of all new construction activity in 2010. According to projections, the green building market size is expected to reach $135 billion by 2015."

The green building market has already provided significant benefits, according to the 2010 Green Building Market Report by GreenBiz, which estimated that "the current annual CO_2 savings from LEED buildings is approximately 8 million tons from energy efficiency and renewables." Total water savings from LEED (Leadership in Energy and Environmental Design, the widely accepted greenbuilding standard) through 2010 is 33 billion gallons, comprising 0.5 percent of annual non-residential water use. The report projected that employment in green building will approach 5 million by 2020, and almost 17 million by 2030, and that "the productivity benefits from LEED buildings to date are estimated at $6.4 billion and we expect this number to exceed $22 billion by 2020, and nearly reach $75 billion by 2030."

A culture of greening has been growing, bringing with it a host of advisors on how to be green, such as the *Good Guide, or Degrees of Green*, electronic publications such as *The Daily Green, Grist,* or *Environmental Leader,* and eco-certifications such as *Green Seal, Ecologo,* or the U.S. Environmental Protection Agency's *Energy Star or Design for the Environment* labels. All of these provide guidance on how to be green. Although much corporate and some third-party "greenwashing" is suspected, the mass of information provides a sense that there are solutions to environmental problems.

Another notable development is the greening of academia. More universities have adopted green agendas, climate action plans, and hired sustainability coordinators. The STARS rating method (Sustainability Tracking, Assessment, and Rating System) promoted by the Association for the Advancement of Sustainability in Higher Education gained its one-hundredth participant, with 22 institutions earning a gold rating. For a university report to be accepted, the report must be affirmed by the institution's highest ranking executive.

What Americans really think about the environment remains a primary question. A 2010 study by Stanford professor Jon Krosnick showed that most polls are misreading public sentiment. When a poll asks what people think is the most important problem, few people reply that it is the environment. However, when asked what is the most serious problem facing the world in the future if nothing is done to stop it, more people say "the environment", than the economy or unemployment. Although the House actively stalled environmental progress in 2011, the supply of political means and will shifts unpredictably. The growing need to act on environmental matters, indications that citizens do care about it, and the chance to reap financial gains from green investment, provide hopes for renewed environmental commitment. Environmentalism may again find expression in concerted political action, given the array of issues to address, and the growing sense of how environmental problems may be solved.

BIBLIOGRAPHY

Books

Scheer, Hermann. *Energy Autonomy: The Economic, Social and Technological Case for Renewable Energy.* Exford, UK: Earthscan/James & James, 2006.

Periodicals

Bello, David. "The False Promise of Biofuels," *Scientific American*, August 2011.

Dernbach, John C. "Creating the Law of Environmentally Sustainable Economic Development," *Pace Environmental Law Review* 28 (3) Spring 2011.

Estes, J. A., et al. "Trophic Downgrading of Planet Earth", *Science* 333 (6040) (July 15, 2011): 301–306.

Van Mantgem, P. J., et al. "Widespread Increase of Tree Mortality Rates in the Western United States," *Science* 323 (5913) (January 2009): 521–524.

Web Sites

ACUPCC Reporting System. American College & University Presidents' Climate Commitment. Available at http://rs.acupcc.org/stats/

"American College & University Presidents' Climate Commitment." Available from http://www2.presidentsclimatecommitment.org/html/commitment.pdf

America's Climate Choices. National Academy of Sciences National Research Council, Division on Earth and Life Studies. Available from http://americasclimatechoices.org/ACC_Final_Report_Brief04.pdf

"CAFO Rule History." National Pollutant Discharge Elimination System (NPDES). Available from http://cfpub.epa.gov/npdes/afo/aforule.cfm

"Candidate Species." U.S. Fish & Wildlife Service. Available from http://www.fws.gov/endangered/esa-library/pdf/candidate_species.pdf

Clayton, Mark. "Nuclear Power in US: Public Support Plummets in Wake of Fukushima Crisis." March 22, 2011. *Christian Science Monitor.* Available from http://www.csmonitor.com/USA/2011/0322/Nuclear-power-in-US-public-support-plummets-in-wake-of-Fukushima-crisis

Clean Coal Technology & The Clean Coal Power Initiative. U.S. Department of Energy. Available from http://www.fossil.energy.gov/programs/powersystems/cleancoal/

"Climate Change: Regulatory Initiatives." U.S. Environmental Protection Agency. Available from http://www.epa.gov/climatechange/initiatives/index.html

Connors, Fred. "Coal Slurry Settlement Is Reached." July 28, 2011. *The Intelligencer Wheeling News-Register.* Available from, http://www.theintelligencer.net/page/content.detail/id/557464/Coal-Slurry-Settlement–Is-Reached.html?nav=515

Cunningham, Wayne. "New CAFE Rules Nearly Double Fuel Economy by 2025." July 29, 2011. CNET.com Available from http://reviews.cnet.com/8301-13746_7-20085539-48/new-cafe-rules-nearly-double-fuel-economy-by-2025/

Davis, Spencer. "The Effect of Natural Gas on Trees and Other Vegetation." *Journal of Arboriculture.* Available from http://joa.isa-arbor.com/request.asp?JournalID=1&ArticleID=1460&Type=2

Dettro, Chris. "Landowner opposition scuttles Morgan County FutureGen Site." January 5, 2011. *The State Journal-Register.* Available from http://www.sj-r.com/top-stories/x1458591834/Landowner-opposition-scuttles-Morgan-County-FutureGen-site

Dolak, Devin, and Enjoli Francis. "Extreme Heat: Emergency Rooms Report Increase in Patients." July 21, 2011. ABC World News. Available from http://abcnews.go.com/US/extreme-heat-emergency-rooms-report-increase-patients/story?id=14122090#.TsVPD1bperg

Earth Charter. Available from http://www.earthcharterinaction.org/content/

Earth Summit 2012. Available from http://www.earthsummit2012.org/

Ecosystems: Invasive Species Program. U.S. Geological Survey. Available from http://ecosystems.usgs.gov/invasive/

Endocrine Disrupter Screening Program (EDSP). U.S. Environmental Protection Agency. Available from http://www.epa.gov/endo/

Executive Summary: Sizing the Clean Economy: A National and Regional Green Jobs Assessment, Brookings Institution, July 13, 2011. Available from http://www.brookings.edu/~/media/Files/Programs/Metro/clean_economy/0713_exec_summary.pdf

"Existing U.S. Coal Plants." 2009. Sourcewatch, a project of the Center for Media and Democracy. Available from http://www.sourcewatch.org/index.php?title=Existing_U.S._Coal_Plants

Federal Interagency Working Group on Environmental Justice, U.S. Environmental Protection Agency. Available from http://www.epa.gov/environmentaljustice/interagency/index.html

"Fisheries: Overfishing continues in 40 U.S. fish stocks, NOAA says." July 15, 2011. *Greenwire>*, 7/15/11.

Gasland. Available from http://www.gaslandthemovie.com/whats-fracking

Global Climate Change Impacts in the US (2009) :Unites States Global Change Research Program. Available from http://www.globalchange.gov/what-we-do/ assessment/previous-assessments/global-climate-change-impacts-in-the-us-2009

Goldenberg, Suzanne. "Pentagon to Rank Global Warming as Destabilising Force." January 31, 2010. theguardian.co.uk. Available from http://www. guardian.co.uk/world/2010/jan/31/pentagon-ranks-global-warming-destabilising-force

"Gray Wolf." Defenders of Wildlife. Available from http://www.defenders.org/wildlife_and_habitat/ wildlife/wolf,_gray.php

"Green Building Market Grows 50% in Two Years Despite Recession, Says McGraw-Hill Construction Report." PR Newswire. Available from http://www. prnewswire.com/news-releases/green-building-market-grows-50-in-two-years-despite-recession-says-mcgraw-hill-construction-report-107547978. html

Green Building Market and Impact Report 2010. November 17, 2010. GreenBiz.com. Available from http://www.greenbiz.com/business/research/ report/2010/11/17/green-building-market-and-impact-report-2010

Green Chemistry Award Winners: 2011 Award Recipients. U.S. Environmental Protection Agency. Available from http://www.epa.gov/opptintr/green-chemistry/pubs/pgcc/past.html

"Green Jobs Created or Saved in the Final Quarter of the Recovery Act", March 10, 2011.Council of State Governments, Knowledge Center. Available from http://knowledgecenter.csg.org/kc/content/ green-jobs-created-or-saved-final-quarter-recovery-act

Healthy Child, Healthy World. Available from http:// healthychild.org/

Hribar, Carrie. *Understanding Concentrated Animal Feeding Operations and Their Impact on Communities*. 2010. National Association of Local Boards of Health. Available from http://www.cdc.gov/nceh/ ehs/Docs/Understanding_CAFOs_NALBOH.pdf

Imhoff, Daniel. *CAFO: The Tragedy of Industrial Animal Factories*. San Rafael, CA: Earth Aware Editions, 2010.

"Implementation of Agenda 21, the Programme for the Further Implementation of Agenda 21 and the Outcomes of the World Summit on Sustainable Development." United Nations General Assembly. Available from http://css.escwa.org.lb/GARes/ 64-236.pdf

"In U.S. Domestic Renewable Energy Production Surpasses Nuclear and Closes in on Oil," July 18,

2011. *Clean Edge News*. Available from http:// cleanedge.com/news/story.php?nID=7714

"The Issues: Factory Farming." Sustainable Table: Serving Up Healthy Food Choices. Available from http://www.sustainabletable.org/issues/factory-farming/

Kristof, Nicholas. "New Alarm Bells about Chemicals and Cancer", *The New York Times*, May 5, 2011. Available from http://www.nytimes.com/2010/ 05/06/opinion/06kristof.html

"Landmark Agreement Moves 757 Species toward Federal Protection." Center for Biological Diversity. Available from http://www.biologicaldiversity.org/ programs/biodiversity/species_agreement/index. html

Leahy, Stephen. "Peak Soil: The Silent Global Crisis." Spring 2008. *Earth Island Journal*. Available http:// www.earthisland.org/journal/index.php/eij/ article/peak_soil/

MacDonald, James M., and William D. McBride. *The Transformation of U.S. Livestock Agriculture*. January 2009. U.S. Department of Agriculture. Available from http://www.ers.usda.gov/Publications/ EIB43/EIB43.pdf

"Mandatory Reporting of Greenhouse Gases Rule (74 Federal Register 5620)." Available from http:// www.epa.gov/climatechange/emissions/ghgrule-making.html

"Memorandum of Understanding on Environmental Justice and Executive Order 12898. U.S. Environmental Protection Agency." Available from http://epa.gov/environmentaljustice/ resources/publications/interagency/ej-mou-2011-08.pdf

"Mountaintop Removal Linked to Birth Defects in Appalachia's Coal Country." June 21, 2011. *Living on Earth*. Public Radio International. Available from http://www.loe.org/blog/blogs.html?serie-sID=1&blogID=12

National Water Management Center. U.S. Department of Agriculture, Natural Resources Conservation Service. Available from http://www.nrcs.usda.gov/ wps/portal/nrcs/main/national/nwmc

"A New Approach to Protecting Drinking Water and Public Health." U.S. Environmental Protection Agency. Available from http://water.epa.gov/ lawsregs/rulesregs/sdwa/dwstrategy/upload/ Drinking_Water_Strategyfs.pdf

Northey, Hannah. "Nuclear Waste: DOE to pay Xcel $100M to Settle Storage Lawsuits." July 11, 2011. News on Green: On Green Issues, the Environment, Conservation, and Nature. Available from http://

newsongreen.org/nuclear-waste-doe-to-pay-xcel-100m-to-settle-storage-lawsuits/

The Office of Solid Waste and Emergency Response Fiscal Year 2010 End of the Year Report. U.S. Environmental Protection Agency. Available from http://www.epa.gov/oswer/docs/oswer_eoy_2010.pdf

Our Nation's Air, 2010. U.S. Environmental Protection Agency. Available from http://www.epa.gov/airtrends/2010/report/highlights.pdf

Parker, Brock. "For Trees, Death by Gas Leak Is Out of the Shadoes." June 27, 2010. Boston.com. Available from http://www.boston.com/news/local/articles/2010/06/27/for_trees_death_by_gas_leak_is_out_of_the_shadows/

Pearson, Sophia. "Polar Bear's Listing as Threatened Species Upheld by Judge." Bloomberg.com Business Exchange. Available from http://www.businessweek.com/news/2011-06-30/polar-bear-s-listing-as-threatened-species-upheld-by-judge.html

"Pesticide issues in the works: Honeybee colony collapse disorder." February 18, 2011. U.S. Environmental Protection Agency: About Pesticides. Available from http://www.epa.gov/opp00001/about/intheworks/honeybee.htm

Pollack, Andrew. "U.S. Approves Genetically Modified Alfalfa." *The New York Times.* January 27, 2011. Available from http://www.nytimes.com/2011/01/28/business/28alfalfa.html

Pollin, Robert et al. *Green Prosperity: How Clean-Energy Policies Can Fight Poverty and Raise Living Standards in the United States.* June 2009. Department of Economics and Political Economy Research Institute, University of Massachusetts Amherst, 6/2009. Available from http://www.peri.umass.edu/fileadmin/pdf/other_publication_types/green_economics/green_prosperity/Green_Prosperity.pdf

"Position Statement on Climate Change and Soil Water Conservation." Soil and Water Conservation Society: Healthy Land Clean Water for Life. Available from http://www.swcs.org/documents/filelibrary/climate/SWCS_Climate_Position_Statement_751_46C025478C4CA.pdf

"Pressure Builds on Pipeline Decision." July 29, 2011. *Living on Earth.* Public Radio International. Available from http://www.loe.org/shows/segments.html?programID=11-P13-00030&segmentID=3

Product Stewardship Institute. Available from http://www.productstewardship.us/

Putting Meat on the Table, A Report of the Pew Commission. 2008. Available from http://www.ncifap.org/bin/e/j/PCIFAPFin.pdf

Recommendations for Enhancing Reactor Safety in the 21st Century, The Near-Term Task Force Review of Insights from the Fukushima Da-Ichi Accident. July 12, 2011. U.S. Nuclear Regulatory Commission. Available from http://pbadupws.nrc.gov/docs/ML1118/ML111861807.pdf

Recovery Through Retrofit, October 2009. Council on Environmental Quality, Middle Class Task Force: Available from http://www.whitehouse.gov/assets/documents/Recovery_Through_Retrofit_Final_Report.pdf

Reducing Environmental Cancer Risk 2008–2009 Annual Report. National Cancer Institute. Available from http://deainfo.nci.nih.gov/advisory/pcp/annualReports/pcp08-09rpt/PCP_Report_08-09_508.pdf

"Report: Green jobs increase as ARRA funding ends," March 14, 2011. American City & County. Available from http://americancityandcounty.com/admin/economic_dev/green-jobs-arra-20110314/

"Reports: Academies' Findings, Climate Change." National Academies, Division of Earth and Life Studies. Available from http://dels.nas.edu/Climate/Climate-Change/Reports-Academies-Findings

Robbins, Jim. "New Herbicide Suspected in Tree Deaths." July 14, 2011. *The New York Times.* Available http://www.nytimes.com/2011/07/15/science/earth/15herbicide.html?pagewanted=all

Romm, Joseph. "Opinion polls underestimate Americans' concern about the environment and global warming," May 13, 2010. Climate Progress. Available from http://thinkprogress.org/romm/2010/05/13/206000/opinion-polls-underestimate-americans-concern-about-the-environment-and-global-warming/

Runyon, Jennifer. "CLEAN is a Better FIT for the USA." July 14, 2011. Renewable Energy World. Available from http://www.renewableenergyworld.com/rea/blog/post/2011/07/clean-is-a-better-fit-for-the-usa

Schwartz, Ariel. "Shell Ditches Algae Biofuel." February 2, 2011. Fast Company. Available from http://www.fastcompany.com/1723391/shell-ditches-algae-biofuel-during-year-of-choices

"SEIA President Rhone Resch's Testimony before the U. S. House Energy & Commerce Subcommittee on Commerce, Manufacturing and Trade." March 3, 2011. Solar Energy Industries Association. Available from http://www.seia.org/cs/news_detail?pressrelease.id=128

"Sizing the Clean Economy: A National and regional Green Jobs Assessment." July 13, 2011. Brookings Institution. Available from http://www.brookings. edu/reports/2011/0713_clean_economy.aspx

"Snowpack Declines in Rockies Unusual Compared to Past." June 9, 2011. University of Arizona. Available from http://uanews.org/node/40236

The State of the Birds 2011. Available from http://www. stateofthebirds.org/

"State of the Climate National Overview, October 2011." National Oceanic and Atmospheric Administration. Available from http://www.ncdc.noaa. gov/sotc/national/

"Table 1.1 Primary Energy Overview, 1949–2010." U.S. Energy Information Administration. Available from http://www.eia.gov/totalenergy/data/annual/ txt/ptb0101.html

"Table 1.3 Primary Energy Consumption Estimates by Source, 1949–2010." U.S. Energy Information Administration. Available from http://www.eia. gov/totalenergy/data/annual/txt/ptb0103.html

Tavernise, Sabrina. "Report Faults Mine Owner." May 19, 2011. *The New York Times.* Available from http://www.nytimes.com/2011/05/20/us/ 20mine.html?pagewanted=all

Teitell, Beth. "Dim View of Lighting Law." August 4, 2011. *Boston Globe* Available from http://articles. boston.com/2011-08-04/lifestyle/29851339_1_ 60-and-40-watt-bulbs-energy-efficient-compact-fluorescent-lights-energy-independence

"Testimony of Rena Steinzor, Professor, University of Maryland School of Law and President, Center for Progressive Reform before the U.S. House of Representatives Committee on Science, Space, and Technology, Subcommittee on Investigations and Oversight." July 14, 2011. Center for Progressive Reform. Available from://www.progressivereform. org/articles/IRIS_Testimony_Steinzor_071411.pdf

"Texas Drought: Cooler Weather Brings No Drought Relief." Lower Colorado River Authority. Available from http://www.lcra.org/water/drought/index.html

"Timeline of EPA Action on Greenhouse Gases." July 2011. Environmental and Energy Study Institute. Available from http://files.eesi.org/epa_ghg_ timeline_070711.pdf

TSCA Submissions with Newly Declassified Claims for Confidential Business Information (CBI). March and June 2011. U.S. Environmental Protection Agency Available from http://www.epa.gov/oppt/ existingchemicals/pubs/declassified/declassified_ claims.html

"Update: Human Rights in Cancer Alley." July 22, 2011. Planet Harmony. Available from http:// myplanetharmony.com/update-human-rights-cancer-alley

USCAP (United States Climate Action Partnership. Available from http://www.us-cap.org/

USGS Gap Analysis Program. U.S. Geological Survey. Available from http://gapanalysis.usgs.gov/

The U.S. Mayors Climate Protection Agreement. Available from http://www.usmayors.org/climateprotec-tion/documents/mcpAgreement.pdf

U.S. *Solar Market Trends 2010* Interstate Renewable Energy Council. Available from http://irecusa. org/wp-content/uploads/2011/06/IREC-Solar-Market-Trends-Report-June-2011-web.pdf

U.S. State Chemicals Policy. Chemicals Policy & Science Initiative, Lowell Center for Sustainable Production, University of Massachusetts Lowell. Available from http://www.chemicalspolicy.org/chemicalspolicy. us.state.database.php

vanEngelsdorp, Dennis, et al. "Preliminary Results: Honey Bee Colony Losses in the U.S., Winter 2010–2011." Cooperative Extension Service. Available from http://www.extension.org/pages/58013/ honey-bee-winter-loss-survey

"Watershed Assessment, Tracking & Environmental Results." U.S. Environmental Protection Agency. Available from http://iaspub.epa.gov/waters10/ attains_nation_cy.control#wqs

"What are the major sources and users of energy in the United States?" October 25, 2011. U.S. Energy Information Administration. Available from http:// www.eia.gov/energy_in_brief/major_energy_ sources_and_users.cfm

"What We Do/White-nose Syndrome." Bat Conservation International. Available from http://www. batcon.org/index.php/what-we-do/white-nose-syndrome.html

"Wind Power Wants U.S. Oil Tax Break Used by KKR, Blackstone." July 19, 2011. *San Francisco Chronicle.* Available from http://www.sfgate.com/cgi-bin/ article.cgi?f=/g/a/2011/07/19/bloomberg1376-LOMXK60UQVI901-1Q0MUIBI21QJT4-CRIPG708V6S0.DTL

Zuckerman, Laura. "Montana Spill Pipeline May Have Carried Oil Sands Crude." July 14, 2011. Reuters. com. Available from http://www.reuters.com/ article/2011/07/15/us-oil-spill-montana-idUSTRE76E0OJ20110715

Alabama

Nicknamed the "Yellowhammer State" after its state bird, the southeastern state of Alabama was primarily an agricultural state until the 1960s. During the next decade, Alabama attracted heavy manufacturing and mineral extraction enterprises in an effort to boost the economy. Turning away from its dependence on agriculture was not without consequences, however. Heavy industry, auto assembly plants, and power plants brought air and water pollution along with higher-paying jobs. The state has continued to suffer from poor air quality for decades, particularly around the metropolitan area of Birmingham, the state's most populous city. However, efforts to improve air quality have been picking up speed in recent years. Alabama leaders also continue to work on recovery efforts to restore the coastal environment and local economy after the 2010 Deepwater Horizon Gulf oil spill.

Climate

Alabama's three climatic divisions are the lower coastal plain, largely subtropical and strongly influenced by the Gulf of Mexico; the northern plateau, marked by occasional snowfall in winter; and the Black Belt and upper coastal plain, lying between the two extremes. Mobile is one of the rainiest cities in the United States, recording an average precipitation of 66.3 inches (168 cm) a year between 1971 and 2000. Its location on the Gulf of Mexico leaves the coastal region open to the effects of hurricanes. In August 2005, Hurricane Katrina, one of the deadliest hurricanes in U.S. history, swept through the region, causing two deaths in Mobile, extensive flooding, and power outages for over 300,000 people in Alabama. In April 2011, a series of tornados stormed through the state leaving 131 dead and causing major destruction, with neighborhoods in Tuscaloosa reporting some of the worst damage.

According to the National Wildlife Federation, average temperatures in Alabama could increase by 5.85°F (3.25°C) if climate change continues unabated. Such conditions could cause both increased rainfall and flooding, and also more severe drought conditions. The sea level along Alabama's coast could also rise up to 15 inches (38 cm) over the course of the century, causing coastal erosion and the loss of wetlands. Higher than average temperatures can also aid in the proliferation of invasive species such as the water hyacinth, blue tilapia, and Brazilian pepper. These species crowd out native species and could therefore drastically alter the region's ecosystems.

Alabama does not have an official Climate Change Action Plan, but in 1997, researchers from the University of Alabama released a report called *Policy Planning to Reduce Greenhouse Gas Emissions in Alabama*. This report summarized some of the best options and strategies for the mitigation of greenhouse gas emissions in six categories: Energy Efficiency, Waste Reduction and Recycling, Methane/Natural Gas, Transportation, Sequestration, and Other General Recommendations. The recommendations included increased building efficiency standards in the commercial sector, the development and implementation of a state recycling and waste reduction plan, and more public transportation. Information provided in the report on the potential effects of climate change for Alabama has become outdated, since greenhouse gas projections were included only through 2010 and several mitigating actions occurred before the end of that year. In August 2010, the Climate Action Reserve (CAR), a private nonprofit organization that hosts the largest carbon offset registry in North America, ranked Alabama as fifth in the nation for reduction of greenhouse gas emissions through registered carbon offset projects. According to the CAR, on an annual basis, the amount of greenhouse gases reduced by Alabama's carbon offset projects is equal to the amount that would be saved by removing 39,518 passenger vehicles from the road for one year.

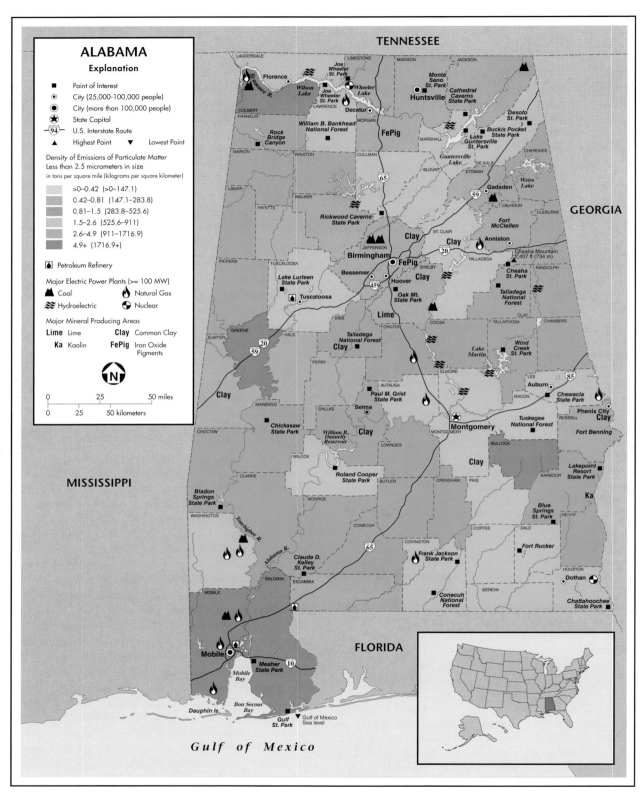

SOURCES: "County Emissions Map: Criteria Air Pollutants." *AirData*. U.S. Environmental Protection Agency. Available from http://www. epa.gov/air/data/geosel.html; *Energy Maps*. U.S. Energy Information Administration. Available from http://www.eia.gov/state; *Highest and Lowest Elevations*. U.S. Geological Survey. Available from http://egsc.usgs.gov/isb/pubs/booklets/elvadist/elvadist.html#Highest; *2007 Minerals Yearbook*. U.S. Geological Survey. Available from http://minerals.usgs.gov/minerals/pubs/state. © 2011 Cengage Learning.

🌿 Natural Resources, Water, and Agriculture

Natural Resources

The state of Alabama has 22.6 million acres (9.1 million ha) of forest which make up 71 percent of the state's area. Alabama's timberlands are a diverse mix of timber types with 45 percent in hardwoods, 41 percent pine, and 14 percent mixed pine and hardwoods. The state has an abundance of poplar, cypress, hickory, oak, and various gum trees. Red cedar grows throughout the state; southern white cedar is found in the southwest, hemlock in the north. Other native trees include hackberry, ash, and holly, with species of palmetto and palm in the Gulf Coast region.

According to the Alabama Forestry Association, the forest industry produces more than $15 billion in products per year. The industry also directly employs approximately 70,000 residents with an annual payroll of $2.2 billion. Another 100,000 workers are indirectly employed by forestry. In all, forestry employs about 12 percent of Alabama's total work force either directly or indirectly. There are 850 forestry companies in Alabama, including more than 100 sawmills, 14 pulp and paper mills, 28 veneer and/or panel plants, and approximately 700 secondary wood processing operations.

Mammals found in the state include the white-tailed deer, Florida panther, bobcat, beaver, muskrat, and most species of weasel. The fairly common raccoon, opossum, rabbit, squirrel, and red and gray foxes are also native, while nutria and armadillo have been introduced to the state. Alabama's birds include golden and bald eagles, osprey and various other hawks, yellowhammers or flickers (the state bird), and black and white warblers; game birds include quail, duck, wild turkey, and geese. Hunting is big business for the state, with approximately 391,000 hunters having a direct economic impact of $840 million annually and providing more than 17,500 jobs.

According to the U.S. Fish and Wildlife Service, a total of 104 animal and 19 plant species were listed as threatened or endangered in 2011. Animal species included the Alabama beach mouse, gray bat, Alabama red-belly turtle, finback and humpback whales, and wood stork. American chaffseed, Alabama leather flower, and the Alabama canebrake pitcher-plant were among the endangered plant species. Alabama's biodiversity is unmatched anywhere else in the United States, especially when it comes to freshwater aquatic species such as mussels, snails, crayfish, fish, and amphibians. This abundance of species contributes to the fact that it is home to 67 species out of 120 freshwater aquatic species listed as threatened or endangered. Overall, the state considers 219 species as being a conservation concern.

The highest production of non-fuel minerals in Alabama is of limestone, sand and gravel, sand and clay, and granite. According to the U.S. Geological Survey, in 2010 the state ranked first in the nation for common clays, second in the nation for lime and iron-oxide-pigment, and third in the nation for kaolin clay. Other minerals that are mined in the state include dolomite, marble, sandstone, shale, and quartzite. The state was ranked twenty-first in the nation in total nonfuel mineral production in 2010 with a value $1 billion.

Alabama State Profile

Physical Characteristics

Land area	50,644 square miles (131,167 sq km)
Inland water area	1,057 square miles (2,738 sq km)
Coastal area	518 square miles (834 sq km)
Highest point	Cheaha Mountain 2,407 feet (734 m)
National Forest System lands (2010)	670,000 acres (271,000 ha)
State parks (2011)	22

Energy Statistics

Total energy production (2009)	1,600 trillion Btu
State ranking in total energy production (2009)	13
Renewable energy net generation total (2009)	15.6 million megawatt hours
Hydroelectric energy generation (2009)	12.5 million megawatt hours
Biomass energy generation (2009)	14,000 megawatt hours
Wind energy generation (2009)	NA
Wood and derived fuel energy generation (2009)	3 million megawatt hours
Crude oil reserves (2009)	37 million barrels (5.9 million cu m)
Natural gas reserves (2009)	2,871 billion cubic feet (81.3 billion cu m)
Natural gas liquids (2008)	55 million barrels (8.7 million cu m)

Pollution Statistics

Carbon output (2005)	136.0 million tons of CO_2 (123.4 million t)
Superfund sites (2008)	13
Particulate matter (less than 2.5 micrometers) emissions (2002)	36,391 tons per year (33,013 t/yr)
Toxic chemical releases (2009)	91.1 million pounds (41.3 million kg)
Generated hazardous waste (2009)	2 million tons (1.8 million t)

SOURCES: AirData. U.S. Environmental Protection Agency. Available from http://www.epa.gov/air/data; *Energy Maps, Facts, and Data of the U.S. States.* U.S. Energy Information Administration. Available from http://www.eia.gov/state; *The 2012 Statistical Abstract.* U.S. Census Bureau. Available from http://www.census.gov/compendia/statab; *United States Energy Usage.* eRedux. Available from http://www.eredux.net/states.

Water

The largest lake wholly within Alabama is Guntersville Lake, covering about 108 square miles (280 sq km) and formed during the development of the Tennessee River region by the Tennessee Valley Authority (TVA). The TVA lakes—also including Wheeler, Pickwick, and Wilson—are all long and narrow, fanning outward along a line that runs from the northeast corner of the state westward to Florence. Wetlands cover about ten percent of the state.

The longest rivers are the Alabama, extending from the mid-central region to the Mobile River for a distance of about 160 miles (257 km); the Tennessee, which flows across northern Alabama for about the same distance; and the Tombigbee, which flows south from north central Alabama for over 150 miles (241 km). The Alabama and Tombigbee rivers, which come together to form the Mobile River, and the Tensaw River flow into Mobile Bay, an arm of the Gulf of Mexico. The Mobile River, which has its source in Tickanetley Creek, Georgia, has a total length of 774 miles (1,246 km) and is the twentieth longest river in the country. There have been concerns for the state's rivers, as 61 percent of them are at risk of losing their Clean Water Act protections due to decisions made by the U.S. Supreme Court. Already, more than 2.5 million residents get their drinking water from sources fed by streams and rivers that are no longer protected.

A report from the Alabama Rivers Alliance and the Southern Environmental Law Center that called for updated water pollution rules was released in 2011. The *Alabama Water Agenda* promotes updates to water protection laws, and calls for increased water pollution inspections and tougher penalties for polluters. According to the report, less than one-tenth of the state's waterways have been inspected by environmental officials, and the state spends less per capita on water protection than most other states. Members of the Alabama Rivers Alliance stated that the major problem in the state is a lack of a comprehensive water policy. They are pushing for a policy that changes how the state approaches water regulation and pays more attention to how farmers and industry use ground and surface water. Such a policy would do much to improve the state's water quality. One of the major roadblocks in monitoring water quality in Alabama is a lack of funding. The Alabama Department of Environmental Management's (ADEM) budget has not been increased since the 1990s, but its responsibilities have continued to expand. Environmental groups involved in the creation of the agenda are also pushing for ways to fund the ADEM, such as having money generated from pollution penalties going directly into the state's general fund.

Despite the challenges confronting the state's waterways, there was still significant fishing activity in Alabama. In 2008, the U.S. Fish & Wildlife Service issued a report, *2006 National Survey of Fishing, Hunting, and Wildlife-Associated Recreation*. The survey, which is conducted every five years in the fifty states, reported that there were 806,000 anglers in Alabama in 2006, and retail sales from fishing generated $1.7 billion in economic activity for the state. Freshwater fish such as bream, shad, bass, and sucker are common. Along the Gulf Coast there are seasonal runs of tarpon (the state fish), pompano, redfish, and bonito.

In 2010, Alabama's commercial fish catch had an estimated value of $27.2 million, down from more than $40 million in 2009—shrimp and blue crab the most valuable catches. The principal fishing port is Bayou La Batre. As of 2003, there were 69 processing and 26 wholesaling plants in the state, with a combined total of about 1,649 employees. The commercial fishing fleet had about 1,775 boats and vessels in 2001.

The 2010 Deepwater Horizon Gulf Oil Spill had a significant immediate impact on the fishing and tourist industries of the entire region, as temporary fishing bans were put in place and local beaches were closed to the public. While research continues on the potential long-term effects, reports issued around the time of the one-year anniversary of the spill indicated that the Gulf of Mexico may be showing signs of a quicker-than-anticipated recovery. A biologist from the Alabama Division of Marine Resources reported that shrimp, crabs, and fish appeared to be developing normally, despite fears that the oil and dispersants used during clean-up would threaten the next harvest.

As for tourism, the beaches of Baldwin County were reportedly clear and inviting once again, well in advance of the 2011 summer season. Some researchers, however, were quick to point out that the spill may have affected the Gulf ecosystem in ways that are not yet clearly detectable. For instance, it is difficult to know exactly how the dolphin and sea turtle populations have been affected, since there could have been more fatalities than those that have washed ashore. There has also been a dramatic decrease in the abundance of zooplankton in the waters of the Gulf and an increase in the abundance of oil-consuming bacteria. The presence of the bacteria can lead to a decrease in oxygen levels in the water. In terms of the economy, some leaders worry that adverse public perceptions could affect the seafood and tourist industries for some time, if potential consumers and visitors worry about the safety of the food and beaches.

The state of Alabama has chosen to respond to the spill with a call to action. Noting the challenges of the Gulf spill, former governor Bob Riley issued Executive Order 52 in September 2010 to create the Coastal Recovery Commission of Alabama. The

The safety of offshore supplies has also come into question after the April 2010 Deepwater Horizon oil spill in the Gulf of Mexico. Clean-up from the spill continued for months after the incident. © *Danny E Hooks/ShutterStock.com*

commission was charged with developing a plan for the restoration of the environment, the economy, and public health in southern Alabama. The commission's final report, *A Roadmap to Resilience: Towards a Healthier Environment, Society and Economy for Coastal Alabama*, was released in December 2010. It goes beyond the consideration of immediate recovery needs to include recommendations on ways to prepare the region for future disasters, including hurricanes and floods. Environmental recommendations include the restoration of the barrier islands and beaches, the creation of a world-class marine and coastal institution that focuses on the Gulf, and the creation of a Coastal Environmental Management Council to advise leaders on developments that affect the coastal environment. The Coastal Alabama Leadership Council was incorporated in April 2011 as the permanent successor to the commission, with a charge to implement the oil spill recovery plan and to provide leadership for the collaborative efforts of local public and private organizations. The council is expected to have a strong role in allocating funds received from BP as part of the recovery effort.

Agriculture

In 2009, Alabama had more than 48,000 farms on 9 million acres (3.6 million ha) of land. According to the U.S. Department of Agriculture, the state ranked third in the nation in producing chickens for meat, quail, and peanuts. The state also ranked fourth in production of poultry and eggs, sixth in aquaculture, and eighth in cotton production. The highest valued crops in production dollars were field and miscellaneous crops, followed by soybeans and hay.

The Alabama Sustainable Agriculture Network (ASAN), based in Birmingham, is a network of farmers and consumers who seek to promote sustainable agriculture in the state. ASAN sponsors or co-sponsors a variety of workshops and programs to support sustainable agriculture practices in the state. In 2008, Alabama was home to only eight certified organic farming operations on 305 acres (141.6 ha) of land. However, there could be many more operations that are not certified. The majority of this production is in organic vegetables, fruit, greenhouse herbs, and fallow. The Georgia Crop Improvement Association and Quality Certification

Services in Florida serve as certifying agents for Alabama's organic farmers.

⚘ Energy

Alabama has reserves of natural crude oil, mainly in the Black Warrior Basin in the north and the Gulf Coast in the south. The state has three refineries, one near Mobile, one near Tuscaloosa, and one in Atmore. Petroleum products made at Alabama's refineries are delivered to local and regional markets and also shipped via pipeline to states in the northeast. Alabama markets receive additional finished petroleum products from Texas and Louisiana through the Colonial and Plantation pipelines.

Natural gas production in the state accounts for more than one percent of the United States' total output. Half of this production comes from onshore wells, while two-fifths come from coalbed methane deposits. Alabama purchases additional supplies of natural gas transported by pipeline mainly from the Gulf of Mexico, Louisiana, and Texas. The Southeast Supply Header pipeline, transporting natural gas from the Perryville Hub in Texas to southern Alabama, came online in September 2008. This pipeline has a capacity of 1 billion cubic feet (28 million cu m) per day and is intended to give Alabama consumers an alternative to offshore supply, which may be vulnerable to weather-related disruptions. The safety of offshore supplies has also come into question after the April 2010 Deepwater Horizon oil spill in the Gulf of Mexico. Officials have had to worry about how to balance economics and the environment: how to continue to receive resources from the Gulf without further damaging our environment. A moratorium on offshore drilling was lifted in October 2010, and the Coastal Recovery Commission of Alabama's December 2010 report outlines a recovery plan and recommendations to prepare for future disasters.

Alabama has substantial deposits of coal, mostly in the northern part of the state. The dominant fuel for electric power generation, additional coal is shipped in from other states, primarily Wyoming, Kentucky, and West Virginia. There are nine coal power plants in the state. Another one-fourth of the state's electricity generation comes from its two nuclear power plants: Browns Ferry and Joseph M. Farley.

One-fourth of Alabama's electricity generation comes from its two nuclear power plants: Browns Ferry and Joseph M. Farley. *©iStockPhoto.com/toddmedia*

Renewable Energy Sources

With more than two dozen hydroelectric dams, Alabama is one of the top producers of hydroelectric power east of the Rocky Mountains. Hydroelectric power typically supplies at least five percent of state electricity generation. The state has 12 hydroelectric plants, located mainly along the Alabama and Coosa Rivers.

Alabama ranks among the top states in net summer capacity for generation from wood and wood waste. The state also contains one of the world's largest solid biofuel plants—Dixie Pellets, LLC—designed to produce 520,000 metric tons of wood pellets each year, the majority of which is shipped to Europe. Dixie Pellets, LLC, is built on a 25-acre (10 ha) parcel on the Alabama River that was once a state docks grain facility.

As of 2010, Alabama was one of a group of states that do not have a Renewable Portfolio Standard.

🌿 Green Business, Green Building, Green Jobs

Green Business

According to a 2009 report by the National Governors Association Center for Best Practices on Alabama's green economy, the state has a diverse array of green businesses with different levels of specialization. Areas of particular strength and growth in the state are water and wastewater, and transportation. Companies in the water and wastewater segment include Solen Inc., Veolia Water, Tri Aqua LLC, McWane, and Pure Water. These companies provide services and water treatment equipment. The state's transportation sector is primarily made up of firms producing biofuels such as Alabama Biodiesel Corp., Allied Renewable Energy, and Enersight Fuels, Inc. It should be noted that there have been issues with companies such as Alabama Biodiesel Corp. and pollution from their refinery. The scientific and regulatory communities are divided on the toxicity of biodiesel products. A number of pollutants have been found in Alabama rivers near biodiesel refineries, and despite the divide in opinion on these pollutants, there have been calls for these companies to take more responsibility for their waste products.

Alabama offers some green incentives to businesses that wish to switch to more sustainable energy sources. One such program is the Biomass Energy Program, which aids businesses in installing biomass energy systems. Program participants can receive up to $75,000 in interest subsidy payments to help defray the interest expense on loans to install approved biomass projects. Technical assistance is also available through the program. Landfill gas is considered as a potential source of energy in the program for industrial processes and other uses. Several landfill waste disposal facilities across Alabama have been identified as prime candidates for landfill gas recovery and utilization.

Tennessee Valley Authority offers an incentive program for Valley residents in Alabama. Called Generation Partners, the program offers a production-based incentive to Valley businesses for the installation of renewable generation systems using solar, wind, low-impact hydropower, and biomass. All new Generation Partners participants will receive a $1,000 incentive to help offset start-up costs, then TVA will purchase all of the green energy output as a premium payment above the retail rate and any fuel cost adjustments. The participating power company will then provide monthly statements showing the energy used and any credit due, and power bills will be reconciled by the company either monthly or annually. Energy consumed at the business, whether it is generated at the site or delivered over the local power distribution system, is billed at the standard rate.

Green Building

Alabama does not have a required state building energy code, but did adopt the voluntary Residential Energy Code for Alabama (RECA) in 2004, a state-developed code equivalent to the 2000 International Energy Conservation Code (IECC). After an attempt in the state legislature to require the 2006 IECC for commercial buildings failed in the state Senate, a joint resolution established the 2006 IECC as the recommended, voluntary code for the state of Alabama. As of December 1, 2008, all new construction of state-funded buildings is subject to the 2006 IECC, though residential and commercial construction is not yet required to comply.

The United States Green Building Council Alabama Chapter has four divisions in the state: North, Birmingham, Central, and Gulf Coast. The chapter aids with LEED projects throughout the state, and provides networking, educational programs and opportunities for those who want to learn more about green building and sustainability options. One of the projects that the Central Alabama division has been working on is the "City of Progress" Enterprise, which is a group of LEED-certified homes located in the Turtleback Subdivision of Birmingham. Home buyers and builders can receive federal tax credits for buying or building a green home there, and the homes generally use 40 percent less energy and 50 percent less water.

In 2009, the Birmingham Charter Movement was begun, with the aim of completing a full Birmingham Charter, or a plan for the sustainable development of the city. This charter will create a new set of protocols for sustainable development worldwide, and will discard wasteful, environmentally destructive modes and patterns of urban development left over from the twentieth century, with Birmingham as its model city.

Green Jobs

According to the Pew Charitable Trusts, in 2007 Alabama had more than 7,800 clean energy jobs in 799 businesses. About 85 percent of these jobs were in conservation and pollution mitigation. A 2009 report from the National Governors Association Center for Best Practices on Alabama's Green economy states that with more than 2,500 jobs, recycling and waste is the largest of the state's green segments. Following this is air and environment with 2,250 jobs, and water and wastewater with 1,900 jobs.

In 2010, the Alabama Department of Economic and Community Affairs received grant funds from the U.S. Department of Labor to establish the Alabama Center for Renewable Energy Sector Training. This center will prepare individuals for careers in five "Energy Efficiency and Renewable Energy (EERE)" industries. 1,350 participants are expected to earn a degree or a certificate. Certificates will include the Photovoltaic Entry Level Certificate of Knowledge by the North American Board of Certified Energy Practitioners, Entry Level Solar Certification by the Electronics Technicians Associates, Entry Level Geothermal Professional Certificate from the HeatSpring Learning Institute, and LEED Accredited Professional Training.

❧ Air Quality in Birmingham: A Continuing Problem

In the American Lung Association's 2010 State of the Air report, Birmingham, Alabama ranked fifth among the nation's worst places for particle pollution, and nineteenth for ozone pollution. While problem air days have decreased across the United States due to new pollution controls on coal-fired power plants and cleaner burning fuels and vehicles, Birmingham's ranking has relatively stayed the same since 2006. The city's concentration of heavy industry, topography, weather, and proximity to three large coal-fired power plants has contributed to its poor air quality for many years. Particle pollution can cause early death, heart attacks, inflammation of lung tissue, and asthma attacks, while ozone can also lead to early death, cause shortness of breath, chest pain, asthma, and pulmonary inflammation.

The adverse health and economic effects of Birmingham's air quality have shown themselves quite dramatically in recent years. In *Clean Air for the Birmingham Area*, a 2009 report from the Southern Environmental Law Center, over 17 percent of Alabama teens between the ages of 15 and 18 and seven percent of adults are asthmatics, a condition sometimes caused by and worsened by ozone and soot pollution. As a result, asthma cost the state about $100 million in direct costs of medicines and healthcare services, and about $76 million in indirect costs. Asthma rates have continued to rise despite these costs. Mercury from power plants that has ended up in rivers and estuaries has caused the Alabama health department to impose fish consumption restrictions due to the high mercury levels found in 36 bodies of water. The polluted air has also resulted in lost opportunities for economic investment. About $5 billion was lost and 15 major manufacturing projects had to be turned down due to poor air quality.

What Is Causing the Air Pollution?

The primary sources of Birmingham's air pollution are three coal-fired power plants: Gaston, Gorgas, and Miller. These plants release sulfur dioxide and nitrogen oxides, which form soot pollution, and are also the primary source of the nitrogen oxides that make ozone. On top of that, the three plants are also the leading cause of mercury emissions, with the Miller plant ranking first in the country for mercury in 2007. The Miller plant also ranks second nationally for power plant carbon emissions. This, coupled with the fact that the state emits more carbon dioxide than any other, has raised further concerns about climate change and the effects it could have on the state.

The Need for Action

Despite ranking in the top ten for air pollution for years, action has been slow to improve Birmingham's air quality. The Southern Environmental Law Center's report suggests seven solutions that will help the city achieve better air quality:

- Place stringent limits on nitrogen oxides and sulfur dioxide at the Gorgas, Gaston, and Miller power plants, and make sure that the company follows through on installing and operating control devices to maximize emissions reductions throughout the year.

- Require concrete reductions in the mercury emissions of the Miller, Gaston, and Gorgas plants, along with other coal-fired power plants in the state.

- Expand Alabama Department of Environmental Management's (ADEM) proposed boundary for nonattainment of the new ozone standard from Jefferson and Shelby Counties to include Bibb, Blount, Chilton, Cullman, St. Clair, and Walker Counties. Generally, counties should be excluded only if ADEM can clearly show that they are not contributing to the Birmingham area's ozone pollution.

- Pass legislation mandating cuts in power plant emissions as other states have done.

- Create a long-range transportation plan that boosts mass transit and recognizes the link between land use and transportation.

- Reduce particle pollution from heavy-duty diesel engines and reduce the economic and public health burden of diesel pollution.

- Make energy efficiency and renewable energy higher priorities.

Recent changes along these lines have begun to be implemented that will begin to make Birmingham's air healthier. In August 2010, new air pollution rules were put in place for 100 cement kilns across the country, which should result in significant reductions in mercury and fine particle pollution from the cement manufacturing industry. The plants that will be affected in Alabama include National Cement Co. of Alabama, Inc., Holcim, Inc. (located in Birmingham), and Cemex, Inc. The kilns will be modernized with technologies such as scrubbers and activated carbon injection. Such updates will aid in cutting about 92 percent of mercury, 92 percent of particulate matter, 97 percent of hydrogen chloride, and 83 percent of total hydrocarbons that are normally released from these kilns. This could result in up to 2,500 premature deaths avoided each year once the rules go into effect in 2013.

Legislation was also underway in 2011 for Birmingham to be redesignated from a Nonattainment Area (NAA)—meaning that in 2005 the city did not meet requirements for the 24-hour National Ambient Air Quality Standard (NAAQS) for fine particulate matter (PM2.5)—to attainment status. Air monitoring data from 2008 through 2010 demonstrated that all monitors in the Birmingham NAA met the air quality standards required, and based on this data the Department of Environmental Management is requested that Birmingham be given attainment status. Attainment status was granted for the 1997 Annual Fine Particulate Standard and became effective on July 29, 2011.

As new strategies are enacted to improve Birmingham and Alabama's air quality, Birmingham's air quality will continue to improve, granting better quality of life to its citizens.

BIBLIOGRAPHY

Books

Canney, Donald L. *In Katrina's Wake: The U.S. Coast Guard and the Gulf Coast Hurricanes of 2005.* Gainesville, FL: University Press of Florida, 2010.

Love, Dennis. *My City Was Gone: One American Town's Toxic Secret, Its Angry Band of Locals, and a $700 Million Day in Court.* New York: Harper Perennial, 2007.

Melosi, Artin, ed. *Environment, vol. 8 of The New Encyclopedia of Southern Culture.* Chapel Hill, NC: University of North Carolina Press, 2007.

Pasquill, Robert G. *The Civilian Conservation Corps in Alabama, 1933-1942: A Great and Lasting Good.* Tuscaloosa, AL: University of Alabama Press, 2008.

Pasquill, Robert G. *Planting Hope on Worn-out Land: The History of the Tuskegee Land Utilization Project: Macon County, Alabama, 1935-1959.* Montgomery, AL: New South Books, 2008.

Perez, Karni R. *Fishing for Gold: The Story of Alabama's Catfish Industry.* Tuscaloosa, AL: Fire Ant Books, 2006.

Randolph, John. *The Battle for Alabama's Wilderness: Saving the Great Gymnasiums of Nature.* Tuscaloosa, AL: Fire Ant Books, 2005.

Strutin, Michal, and Tony Arruza. *The Smithsonian Guides to Natural America: The Southeast–South Carolina, Georgia, Alabama, Florida.* Washington, DC: Smithsonian Books, 1996.

Walker, Sue. *In the Realm of Rivers: Alabama's Mobile-Tensaw Delta.* Montgomery, AL: New South Books, 2005.

Young, Beth Maynor, and John C. Hall. *Headwaters: A Journey on Alabama Rivers.* Tuscaloosa, AL: University of Alabama Press, 2009.

Web Sites

Alabama Department of Environmental Management. Available from http://adem.alabama.gov/default.cnt

Alabama Forest Facts. Alabama Forestry Association. Available from http://www.alaforestry.org

Alabama Forestry Association. Available from http://www.alaforestry.org/

"Alabama Hunter's Fact Sheet." Outdoor Alabama. Available from http://www.outdooralabama.com/hunting/HunterFactSheet.pdf

Alabama: Profile of the Green Economy. NGA Center for Best Practices. Available from http://www.nga.org/Files/pdf/09GREENPROFILEAL.PDF

"Alabama State Energy Code for Buildings." Alabama Incentives/Policies for Renewables & Efficiency. Available from http://www.dsireusa.org/incentives/incentive.cfm?Incentive_Code=AL01R&re=1&ee=1

Alabama Sustainable Agriculture Network. Available from http://www.asanonline.org/future_events.html

Alabama State Parks. Available from http://www.alapark.com/

"American Recovery and Reinvestment Act of 2009: State Energy Sector Partnership (SESP) and Training Grants." U.S. Department of Labor Employment and Training Administration. Available from http://

www.doleta.gov/pdf/SESP_Summaries_FINAL_02042010.pdf

Annual Report Statistical Supplement of the Department of Industrial Relations Mining and Reclamation Division Mine Safety and Inspection Section for the Fiscal Year Ending September 30, 2009. State of Alabama Department of Industrial Relations. Available from http://dir.alabama.gov/mr/2009_ANNUAL.pdf

Approval and Promulgation of Implementation Plans and Designations of Areas for Air Quality Planning Purposes; Alabama: Birmingham; Determination of Attaining Data for the 1997 Annual Fine Particulate Standard. Environmental Protection Agency. Available from http://www.federalregister.gov/articles/2011/06/29/2011-16378/approval-and-promulgation-of-implementation-plans-and-designations-of-areas-for-air-quality-planning

Approval and Promulgation of Implementation Plans and Designations of Areas for Air Quality Planning Purposes; Alabama: Birmingham; Determination of Attaining Data for the 2006 24-Hour Fine Particulate Standard. Environmental Protection Agency. Available from http://www.federalregister.gov/articles/2010/09/20/2010-23318/approval-and-promulgation-of-implementation-plans-and-designations-of-areas-for-air-quality-planning#p-9

"Biomass Energy Program." Alabama Incentives/Policies for Renewables & Efficiency. Available from http://dsireusa.org/incentives/incentive.cfm?Incentive_Code=AL02F&re=1&ee=1

Clean Air for the Birmingham Area. Southern Environmental Law Center. Available from http://www.southernenvironment.org/uploads/publications/BAR_0909_Final.pdf

"The Clean Energy Economy: Alabama." The Pew Charitable Trusts. Available from http://www.pewcenteronthestates.org/uploadedFiles/wwwpewcenteronthestatesorg/Fact_Sheets/Clean_Economy_Factsheet_Alabama.pdf

Coastal Recovery Commission of Alabama. Available from http://crcalabama.org

Ferrara, David. "1 year later, few signs of oil spill on Orange Beach." *Mobile Press-Register.* April 20, 2011. Available from http://blog.al.com/live/2011/04/1_year_later_few_signs_of_oil.html

"Five states top the list in reducing greenhouse gas emissions." Climate Action Reserve. August 24, 2010. Available from http://www.climateactionreserve.org/2010/08/24/five-states-top-the-list-in-reducing-greenhouse-gas-emissions

"Global Warming and Alabama." National Wildlife Federation. Available from http://www.nwf.org/~/media/PDFs/Global%20Warming/Global%20Warming%20State%20Fact%20Sheets/Alabama.ashx

Griffin, Robert A., Gunther, William D., and William J. Herz. *Policy Planning to Reduce Greenhouse Gas Emissions in Alabama.* The University of Alabama. Available from http://www.epa.gov/statelocalclimate/documents/pdf/Alabama_action_plan.pdf

"How the Birmingham Charter could change the world." *Birmingham Weekly.* October 1, 2009. Available from http://bhamweekly.com/birmingham/article-1151-how-the-birmingham-charter-could-change-the-world.html

"Listings and Occurrences for Alabama." U.S. Fish and Wildlife Service. Avaialable from http://ecos.fws.gov/tess_public/pub/stateListingAndOccurrenceIndividual.jsp?state=AL&s8-fid=112761032792&s8fid=112762573902&s8-fid=24012856065172

McCary, Jennifer. "Green Energy Taking Root in Alabama: Easing out of post-startup phase." *Wood Bioenergy.* Available from http://www.woodbioenergymagazine.com/magazine/2009/summer/article-dixie-pellets.html

National Emission Standards for Hazardous Air Pollutants From the Portland Cement Manufacturing Industry and Standards of Performance for Portland Cement Plants. 40 CFR Parts 60 and 63. Environmental Protection Agency. Available from http://www.epa.gov/ttn/oarpg/t1/fr_notices/portland_cement_fr_080910.pdf

NOAA Fisheries, Office of Science & Technology, Fisheries Statistics, Commercial Fisheries. Available from http://www.st.nmfs.noaa.gov/pls/webpls/MF_ANNUAL_LANDINGS.RESULTS

Raines, Ben. "Alabama's lax laws leave rivers unprotected; groups want new water laws." *Mobile Press-Register.* July 23, 2011. Available from http://blog.al.com/live/2011/07/state_groups_want_new_water_la.html

Raines, Ben. "Scientists surprised, cautious over environment's apparent post-oil spill recovery." *Mobile Press-Register.* April 21, 2011. Available from http://blog.al.com/live/2011/04/scientists_optimistic_but_caut.html

A Roadmap to Resilience: Towards a Healthier Environment, Society and Economy for Coastal Alabama. Coastal Recovery Commission of Alabama. Available from http://crcalabama.org/wp-content/uploads/2011/02/CRC-Report-02-2011.pdf

Smith, Sarah. "Pollution Violations May Test Public Support for Biodiesel." *Biodiesel Magazine.* June

2008. Available from http://www.biodieselmaga-zine.com/article.jsp?article_id=2383&q=&page=all

Spencer, Thomas. "Alabama's unmatched aquatic biodiversity." Al.com. November 8, 2010. Available from http://blog.al.com/birmingham-news-stor-ies/2010/11/alabamas_unmatched_aquatic_bio.html

Sportfishing in America. American Sportfishing Associa-tion. Available from http://www.asafishing.org/images/statistics/resources/Sportfishing%20in%20America%20Rev.%207%2008.pdf

State of Alabama Ambient Air Monitoring 2010 Consol-idated Network Review. Alabama Department of Environmental Management. Available from

http://www.adem.state.al.us/programs/air/airqu-ality/2010AmbientAirPlan.pdf

"Top Ten Frightening Facts about Alabama's Rivers." Alabama Rivers Alliance. Available from http://www.alabamarivers.org/press-room/headlines/top-ten-frightening-facts-about-alaba-ma2019s-rivers

2006 National Survey of Fishing, Hunting, and Wildlife-Associated Recreation—Alabama>. U.S. Fish & Wildlife Service. Available from http://www.census.gov/prod/2008pubs/fhw06-al.pdf

United States Green Building Council of Alabama. Available from http://www.usgbcofal.org/index.php

Alaska

❧ Alaska: Vast and Beautiful

Alaska, the largest, most northern state in the United States, has a land area spanning approximately 571,951 square miles (1,481,346 sq km). In a relative sense, Alaska is more than twice the size of the second largest U.S. state, Texas, and represents a full 16 percent of total U.S. land area. The eleven highest mountains in the United States and the highest mountain in North America—Mount McKinley—are found in Alaska, as are half of the world's glaciers.

Topographically, Alaska can be divided into six distinct regions. The coastal panhandle is a highly mountainous region of southeastern Alaska largely separate from the mainland. It sits adjacent to British Columbia. Northwest of the coastal panhandle is south-central Alaska, which stretches along the Gulf of Alaska and includes the Kenai Peninsula and Cook Inlet—an arm of the Pacific Ocean that penetrates inland hundreds of miles to Anchorage. Farther west is the southwestern region, which contains the Alaska Peninsula and the 1,700-mile-long (2,736-km) Aleutian Island chain—a sweep of barren, volcanic islands that extend westward into the Pacific. North of the southwestern region is western Alaska, a large, lake infused tundra extending from Bristol Bay to the Seward Peninsula and containing the deltas of the Yukon and Kuskokwim rivers—the two longest rivers in the state. Interior Alaska comes next, spanning over the heart of the state, north of the Alaska Range and south of the Brooks Range. Finally, the Arctic region constitutes the northern slice of the state, extending from Kotzebue to Canada north of the Seward Peninsula.

Alaska's Quickly Changing Climate

As a sprawling, topographically diverse state, Alaska's climate varies considerably. While in the far north, in the Arctic region, winter temperatures can average −20°F (−29°C), other areas of Alaska, such as the interior, have seen temperatures as high as 90°F (32°C) in summer.

According to the Nature Conservancy, a U.S.-based conservation organization, climate change will impact Alaska more immediately and more intensely than any of the lower forty-eight U.S. states. By 2100, global temperatures in Alaska are projected to rise by 5 to 18°F (3 to 10°C), which could threaten Alaska's coasts (as sea levels rise), its forests and fisheries (as invasive species from warmer climates invade), and its economy (as climate change disrupts traditional infrastructure and industries). Other organizations, including the U.S. Geological Survey (USGS), have recognized that there will be both "winners" and "losers" with climate change, and have noted, along with the unwanted effects, some "positive" impacts of the warming climate. According to the USGS, possible positive effects include an extended growing season for forestry and agriculture, fewer construction problems in places where permafrost has melted, and possible increases in salmon catches, as happened in the Bering Sea after 1977, when the waters warmed significantly.

The effects of climate change were visible during the summer of 2011, when thousands of Pacific walruses pulled themselves onto the beaches of northwest Alaska three weeks earlier than the year before. Normally, walrus mothers and pups would pull themselves onto sea ice and use it as a platform from which to dive for food in shallower waters. But the ice has melted so much since 2007 that the only ice left was too far out to sea, and over waters that are too deep to provide food. The walruses are therefore forced to crowd the beaches, where stampedes can crush pups. The U.S. Geological Survey Alaska Science Center Pacific Walrus Research Program has collected data on walrus behavior and movements in the area both when sea ice was present and when it was absent. It was observed that in 2011 sea ice was at its lowest since 2007.

Undoubtedly, climate change promises to be deeply disruptive to the state. In light of this, then-Alaska governor Sarah Palin in 2007 signed Administrative Order 238, which created the Alaska Climate Change

Half of the world's glaciers are found in Alaska, including these in the Harriman Fiord, Prince William Sound. © *Robert Fried/Alamy*

Sub-Cabinet. In January 2009, the sub-cabinet revealed its climate change strategy for the state. The sub-cabinet focused on a wide range of issues—from addressing public infrastructure issues to emphasizing how a warming climate could impact human health and disease. The sub-cabinet had formed an Immediate Action Work Group, which identified six communities—Kivalina, Koyukuk, Newtok, Shaktoolik, Shishmaref, and Unalakleet—that were most likely to be seriously affected by climate change. While no specific action plans had been implemented as of late 2011. Since its creation in 2009, the Work Group has met regularly to consider the needs of these communities and develop strategies to prevent or mitigate the effects of natural disasters such as floods and fires.

❧ Natural Resources, Water, and Agriculture

Huge State; Huge Resources

Unprecedented in its size and scope, Alaska is a state of many natural resources. Forests cover about 35 percent of the state's total land area. Of this, the federal government owns more than 63 percent and the state owns a little over 24 percent. The forests are divided into three management regions. The coastal rainforest of the southern coast features stands of western hemlock, Sitka spruce, yellow cedar, and red cedar. The transitional forest region further north features paper birch, aspen, white and black spruce, and black cottonwood. The interior forest, which covers most of the central portion of the state, is part of the boreal forest ecosystem and also features stands of birch and aspen.

Forest product industries are still important in the state, though many of the large-scale mills of the mid-1900s have been replaced by smaller, more localized operations into the 2000s. Commercial timber production is a major activity at each of the three state forests. Haines and Tanana Valley were designated in 1982 and 1983 respectively. The newest, Southeast State Forest, was designated in 2010, specifically to create and sustain jobs in the timber industry. The initial area of the park was set at 25,291 acres (10,235 ha). However, in 2011, the state legislature passed House Bill 105 to expand the forest by adding another 23,181 acres (9,381 ha). Timber management is allowed on about one-third of the total land area of Southeast State Forest.

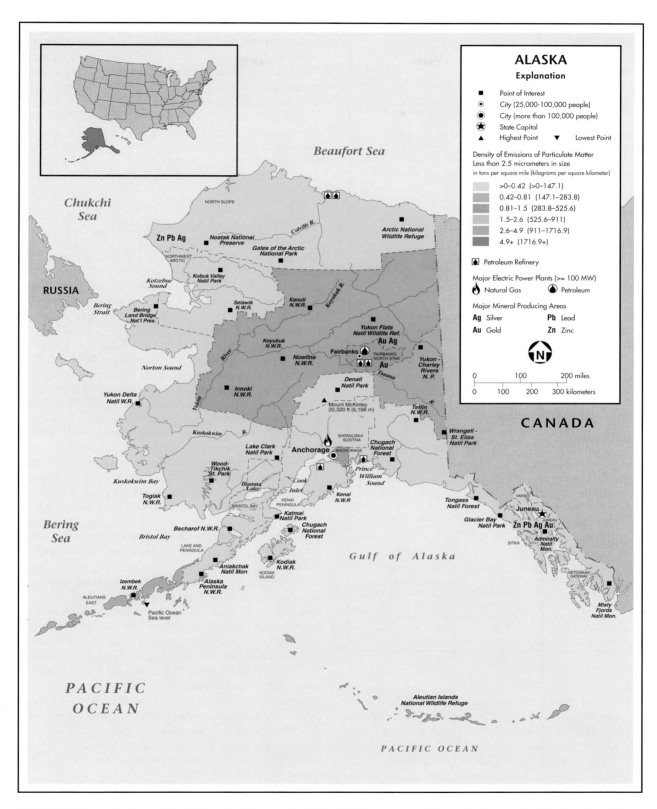

SOURCES: "County Emissions Map: Criteria Air Pollutants." *AirData*. U.S. Environmental Protection Agency. Available from http://www.epa.gov/air/data/geosel.html; *Energy Maps*. U.S. Energy Information Administration. Available from http://www.eia.gov/state; *Highest and Lowest Elevations*. U.S. Geological Survey. Available from http://egsc.usgs.gov/isb/pubs/booklets/elvadist/elvadist.html#Highest; *2007 Minerals Yearbook*. U.S. Geological Survey. Available from http://minerals.usgs.gov/minerals/pubs/state.   © 2011 Cengage Learning.

Alaska State Profile

Physical Characteristics

Land area	570,665 square miles (1,478,016 sq km)
Inland water area	20,028 square square miles (51,872 sq km)
Coastal area	28,162 miles (45,322 sq km)
Highest point	Mount McKinley 20,320 feet (6,194 m)
National Forest System lands (2010)	21.9 million acres (8.9 million ha)
State parks (2011)	123

Energy Statistics

Total energy production (2009)	1,900 trillion Btu
State ranking in total energy production (2009)	12
Renewable energy net generation total (2009)	1.3 million megawatt hours
Hydroelectric energy generation (2009)	1.3 million megawatt hours
Biomass energy generation (2009)	7,000 megawatt hours
Wind energy generation (2009)	7,000 megawatt hours
Wood and derived fuel energy generation (2009)	NA
Crude oil reserves (2009)	3.5 billion barrels (566.9 million cu m)
Natural gas reserves (2009)	9,101 billion cubic feet (257.7 billion cu m)
Natural gas liquids (2008)	299 million barrels (47.5 million cu m)

Pollution Statistics

Carbon output (2005)	44.8 million tons of CO_2 (40.6 million t)
Superfund sites (2008)	6
Particulate matter (less than 2.5 micrometers) emissions (2002)	1,613 tons per year (1,463 t/yr)
Toxic chemical releases (2009)	699.1 million pounds (317.1 million kg)
Generated hazardous waste (2009)	1,900 tons (1,700 t)

SOURCES: AirData. U.S. Environmental Protection Agency. Available from http://www.epa.gov/air/data; *Energy Maps, Facts, and Data of the U.S. States.* U.S. Energy Information Administration. Available from http://www.eia.gov/state; *The 2012 Statistical Abstract.* U.S. Census Bureau. Available from http://www.census.gov/compendia/statab; *United States Energy Usage.* eRedux. Available from http://www.eredux.net/states.

Two of the largest national forests in the United States are found in Alaska—the Tongass National Forest and the Chugach National Forest. Together, these forests span nearly 23 million acres (9.3 million ha). The state park system covers more than 3.2 million acres (1.3 million ha), ranking as the largest park system in the nation by land area. There are also twenty-three national parks, reserves, and sites.

Much of Alaska's ecosystem remains intact, due in part to extensive federal protection. Federal and state governments own nearly 80 percent of Alaska's territory and nearly one-fifth the state's wilderness is protected under national park or federal and state wilderness and preserve designations, providing extensive protection. These vast, unspoiled lands allow several species of large mammals, including the caribou, brown bear, and mountain goat, to flourish in Alaska.

The U.S. Fish and Wildlife Service (USFWS) lists sixteen animal and one plant species in Alaska as either threatened or endangered. Endangered species include five species of whale, the stellar sea lion, and the Canada wood bison. The sole endangered plant species is the Aleutian shield fern.

The Endangered Species Act on Thin Ice

The plight of the polar bear has been a controversial one within the state since 2008, when the USFWS listed it as threatened species under the federal Endangered Species Act. In November 2010 the USFWS also took the step of designating a stretch of Arctic land off the coast of Alaska (187,157-sq mi [484,734-sq km]) as a critical habitat for the polar bears. Polar bears have been considered by some to be uniquely vulnerable to the effects of climate change and the melting of the sea ice in the Arctic that serves as their natural habitat. In August 2008, the Alaska state government, then under the administration of Governor Sarah Palin, filed a lawsuit against USFWS to contest the listing. The state has argued that the decision was not based on the best available scientific and commercial data, and that the polar bear population as a whole stable is stable, due to substantial protection and conservation efforts that are already in place. The suit was consolidated with ten similar suits, including one filed by the American Petroleum Institute, in the U.S. District Court for the District of Columbia.

Governor Sean Parnell was an adamant opponent of the designation and has been quite vocal in opposition to what he and other Alaskans view as inappropriate federal regulation over the state's natural resources. In his 2010 State of the State address, Parnell stated that the federal government has misused the Endangered Species Act as a regulatory weapon to delay the development of Alaska's resources. The designation of land as a critical habitat could block future development projects within the area, since federal officials will be required to consider whether or not each project will have an adverse affect on the polar bear habitat and population conservation and recovery efforts.

In response, the state of Alaska filed another lawsuit against the USFWS in March 2011, claiming that there is insufficient evidence that the designated areas are essential to existing polar bear conservation efforts. The Alaska Oil and Gas Association filed a similar suit

Despite lawsuits filed by the state of Alaska against the U.S. Fish and Wildlife Service, the polar bear maintains its federally threatened species status. © *Yvonne Pijnenburg-Schonewille/ShutterStock.com*

the same month, claiming that the designation will pose a serious threat to the growth of the economy, resulting in the loss of billions of dollars, while providing little improvement in conservation efforts. On the other side, at least three conservation groups, Greenpeace, Defenders of Wildlife, and the Center for Biological Diversity, have stepped forward to offer official support for the measure. In fact, the Center for Biological Diversity, which has a field office in Anchorage, was instrumental in petitioning the government to place the polar bears on the endangered species list, though they had hoped to have the bears listed as "endangered" and not simply "threatened." The organization has also petitioned to place the Pacific walrus on the list, and has threatened to sue the USFWS for their decision to preclude the species from the list. Ultimately, the decision to list the polar bear as a federally threatened species was upheld in June 2011.

In addition to huge energy reserves—oil, natural gas, and coal—Alaska also enjoys tremendous mineral and biological resources. Metallic minerals, such as zinc, lead, gold, and silver, represent important resources in Alaska. In 2007, the state ranked as first in the nation for production of silver and zinc, second for lead, and third

for gold. The Red Dog Mine near Kotzebue produced nearly 70 percent of the total value of Alaskan minerals in 2007, primarily through lead, silver and zinc production. The Fort Knox mine and Pogo Mine are the primary gold producers. The state also produces a significant quantity of sand and gravel and crushed stone. With a value of $3.2 billion, the state's nonfuel mineral production ranked fifth in the nation in 2010.

Water Galore

With several major rivers and more than three million lakes larger than 20 acres (8 ha), Alaska contains more than one-quarter of the total inland water of the United States. The largest lake in the state is Lake Iliamna, which is located just west of the Cook Inlet. Lake Iliamna spans more than 1,000 square miles (2,600 sq km) and represents the second largest freshwater lake lying entirely within the United States (Lake Michigan is the largest). The Yukon River, which flows west from Canada to the Norton Sound, is the longest river in the state and the third longest in the United States. Alaska's rivers and lakes are vital to the state's robust salmon and fishing industry, which is one of the most important in the United States. The rivers and lakes also provide wonderful opportunities for other forms of recreation.

Alaska's coastal waters provide a wide array of valuable resources. The Chukchi and Bering Seas are believed to hold rich reserves of oil and gas. The Port of Valdez lies at the southern terminus of the trans-Alaska oil pipeline, providing easy transport for both oil and cargo to and from markets in the U.S. Pacific Northwest. The Port of Anchorage is the largest cargo port in the state, handling more than 90 percent of the consumer goods moving in and out of the state. It is also listed as one of the 19 National Strategic Ports. Commercial fishing operations are important at both of these ports as well. The fishing port of Dutch Harbor-Unalaska has frequently ranked as first in the nation for landings and among the top five for value. In 2008, Dutch Harbor ranked first in landings and second in value, while the port of Kodiak ranked fifth in landings and third in value. Salmon, pollock, Pacific cod, sea herring, and Dungeness crab are among the most valuable species of the Alaskan catch.

The Alaska Department of Fish and Game sponsors a number of programs to protect the native marine wildlife of the state, including those for harbor seals, ice seals, stellar sea lions, and beluga whales. Round Island along the north shore of Bristol Bay is well known for its walrus rookery. Izembek Lagoon, a part of the Izembek National Wildlife Refuge, contains what is considered to be one of the most extensive eelgrass meadows in the world. The refuge is a nesting ground for hundreds of thousands of migratory birds and ducks.

Cold Climate, Short Growing Season Stunts Agriculture

According to the U.S. Department of Agriculture, the size of the average Alaskan farm has decreased consistently since 1978, whereas the number of farms in the state has grown. In 2007, there were 686 farms in Alaska spanning 1,377 square miles (3,566 sq km). Alaska's climate affords state farmers a brief but intense summer growing season. Hay, potatoes, lettuce, cabbage, carrots, beef, pork, and greenhouse and nursery products are staples of the Alaskan agricultural sector. That Alaska lacks critical export infrastructure, however, such as roads and highways, stunts the growth of Alaskan agriculture.

The growth of agriculture is limited by weather, climate and fertilizer options. Recently, the use of fish (salmon) fertilizer has seen an increase in small farms in villages outside of Alaska's "usual" agricultural belt (the Matanuska Susitna Valley and Tanana Valley). Roads and highways connect the major growing regions of the state. Alaska ranks last in agricultural productivity in the United States.

Like the conventional agricultural sector, organic farming in Alaska remains a small industry. In 2007, Alaska had just sixteen certified organic or exempt farms—fewer than any state other than Delaware. The average Alaskan organic farm extended 27.5 acres (11 ha) and generated $29,500 per year in sales.

❧ Energy: Oil, Gas, Reserves Energize Debate

On a per capita basis, Alaska competes with Wyoming for the title of the largest electricity consumer in the nation; Alaska regularly consumes more than three times the national average. In an absolute sense, however, Alaska remains in the lower third of energy consumers, with only twelve states consuming less total energy than Alaska. Energy demand in Alaska is driven by the robust gas and petroleum sectors, which dominate the state's economy. Refining and extraction—two staple industries in Alaska—demand considerable resources. Interestingly, of the marketed natural gas produced in Alaska, only about one-quarter actually reaches consumers; the vast majority is consumed on the production site, as lease or plant fuel.

Major Oil Producer

Alaska serves as the second largest oil producing state in the nation, behind Texas. The Alaskan North Slope (ANS), where a majority of Alaska's oil operations are centered, contains an incredible amount of oil and is home to the country's largest oil field, Prudhoe Bay. But despite the region's vast oil deposits, production in ANS has been in decline in recent years. According to the U.S. Department of Energy, the ANS was producing 2.2 million barrels of oil a day in 1988, or 25 percent of total U.S. production. By 2007, ANS production had declined to 720,000 barrels, or 14 percent of U.S. totals. This decline has fueled the contentious debate over whether to open the Arctic National Wildlife Refuge (ANWR) to drilling. ANWR sits within the ANS and is known to hold tremendous oil reserves. However, environmentalists lament this discussion, as ANWR is a protected region home to an array of animals and wildlife, which could be perversely affected by drilling and related activity.

An example of the fight between environmentalists and oil companies is illustrated by the Trans Alaska Pipeline System. Completed in 1977, the pipeline system was the most costly private construction project of its time, and has since moved over 15 million barrels of oil from the North Slope of Alaska to the northern most ice-free port in Valdez. The pipeline has aroused controversy since its construction over concerns that it would be detrimental to the environment. In fact, in January 2011, a small oil leak at the Prudhoe Bay intake station caused the pipeline to be shut down. Operators worked quickly to ensure the pipeline would not be down for more than a day or two at a time, as long delays could cause a rise in oil prices for consumers. Fortunately, this leak caused little to no environmental damage. However, there have been repeated leaks and spills in the pipeline network over the last several years, the most serious occurring in 2006. That spill was one of several costly accidents for BP (owner of the largest share of the consortium that runs the pipeline) before the blowout of their well in the Gulf of Mexico in 2010. Balancing their oil industry while keeping their environment pristine has been a continuing struggle for the state of Alaska.

Renewable Potential

Alaska's extensive network of rivers offers it massive hydroelectric potential, larger than most U.S. states. Alaska already obtains a considerable percentage of its power from hydroelectric sources (one-fifth), but the state's electric grid continues to be dominated by natural gas, which produces about 60 percent of the state's electricity. Biomass also represents a huge renewable energy resource in Alaska, and rural communities in interior Alaska, in particular, are increasingly turning to biomass (wood products) for energy.

However, for largely economic reasons, Alaska has been slow to adopt the progressive energy standards that are growing in popularity among other U.S. states. In 2009, former Alaska governor Sarah Palin rejected $29 million in federal stimulus funds, because the acceptance of those funds would have required Alaska to put forth a statewide energy code. She was the only governor in the United States to do so. On June 16, 2010, however, Palin's successor, Governor Sean Parnell, signed House Bill 306, which established a statewide energy policy for Alaska. The bill envisioned Alaska producing 50 percent of its electricity from renewable resources by

Pipeline carrying oil from the north slope of Alaska to Valdez, Alaska. © *iStockPhoto.com/Jonathan Nafzger*

2025—primarily through hydroelectric projects—and set a goal of increasing energy efficiency by 20 percent by 2020. The July 2010 report *Alaska Energy Pathway* details the actions that will be taken to reach the 20 percent goal, some of which include continuing public education and outreach to educate Alaskans about how to improve energy efficiency at home and work; to continue developing an electrical efficiency program for residential buildings; to support retrofitting of public buildings; and to develop innovative approaches to improving efficiency in colder climates. The report goes on to list more strategies to meet both the 20 percent and 50 percent goals, which include programs to improve energy security; support economic development, education, and workforce development; and to invest in technological innovations tailored for Alaska's environment. If these actions are followed, the state could see a reduction of up to 77 percent of greenhouse gas emissions and a significant lowering of the use of fossil fuels.

Although environmentalists generally welcome the prospect of harnessing renewable energy, some of the hydroelectric energy proposals have incited a backlash in Alaska, as the proposed rivers support Alaska's rich salmon populations and other economically, culturally, and biologically important species.

🍁 Green Business, Green Building, Green Jobs

Coal Gasification Plans Stir Optimism in the Cook Inlet

Cook Inlet Region, Incorporated (CIRI) is an Alaska Native corporation based in Anchorage that is heavily invested in the green and alternative energy sector. One CIRI project that has generated national and international interest is an underground coal gasification (UCG) project proposed on the west side of the Cook Inlet, across from Anchorage. The project, which was gaining momentum in 2009 and 2010, was planned to power a 100 mega-watt power station using the cutting edge UCG process. UCG is a growing alternative energy technology that allows companies to harvest coal seams, deep underground, with minimal surface disruption and no ecologically damaging mining. Two holes are drilled deep into the earth into naturally forming coal seams, located significantly beneath the water table. Well operators pump a pressurized oxidant, such as air, down through one of the drill holes to start a fire in the coal seam. Heat and pressure convert the coal seam into gas, which then flows to the surface through the second hole, where it is processed into syngas, an energy-rich gas that can be handled and used like natural gas.

Advocates hail the UCG technology as a way to reduce greenhouse gas emissions, and coupling UCG with carbon capture and sequestration—a process CIRI plans to implement—would further reduce the carbon footprint of the process. Carbon capture and sequestration would allow CIRI to capture carbon emissions from the syngas production, compress it, transport it, and inject it into deep subsurface geologic structures that advocates say would hold the carbon gas indefinitely. Unlike traditional coal mines, no surface water is spoiled by the UCG process and the gas that flows up from the coal seam burns considerably cleaner than traditional coal. At the same time, some worry about potential disruptions to the water table, as UCG requires boring through the water table to reach the underground coal seams. Still, many environmentalists look to UCG with cautious optimism, as it appears to be a far greener way to harvest coal energy than conventional mining and burning. CIRI's Cook Inlet UCG plant could be operational by 2014.

Alaska Pioneers Green Building Standards

Alaska's cold climate makes efficient building an essential part of reducing energy expenditures, and Alaska has taken a number of steps to encourage the development of green building. The Alaska Housing Finance Corporation (AHFC) represents one state organization that runs several programs that incentivize this field in Alaska. In 1985, more than a decade before the U.S. Green Building Council developed its LEED standard, AHFC piloted the Alaska Building Energy Efficiency Standard (BEES), which set standards for thermal resistance, air leakage, moisture protection, and ventilation for homes and buildings in the state. AHFC required that all residential or community-owned properties, constructed after January 1, 1992, meet BEES standards if they were to receive any state financial assistance. In addition to withholding financing to homes that fail to meet BEES standards, AHFC offers substantial cash rebates and incentives to individuals who purchase new green built homes, make energy efficiency modifications, or who weatherize their homes.

Accelerating Effort to Grow Green Jobs

According to the Pew Charitable Trusts, Alaska is one of the few states in the nation where green jobs grew at a slower rate (9.4 percent) than conventional jobs (15.7 percent) from 1998 to 2007. Of the green jobs generated over that period, more than 75 percent were in the conservation and pollution mitigation sector, as opposed to the clean energy sector. However, Alaska appears to be increasingly moving towards the clean energy field. In 2009, the American Recovery and Reinvestment Act diverted $18 million to Alaska for weatherization assistance, and on June 16, 2010, Alaskan governor Sean Parnell signed House Bill 306, which expanded funding for workforce training and development in energy conservation, efficiency, and availability. House Bill 306 promised investments in state university programs that would help Alaska achieve reductions in energy costs and would help attract clean energy businesses to the state.

Exxon Valdez: A Touchstone for Today

In 2010, the worst oil spill in U.S. history rattled the Gulf of Mexico. For months, immense plumes of thick oil surged from a deep water British Petroleum (BP) oil well in the Gulf of Mexico, marring beaches, killing wildlife, and severely disrupting economic activity across several states in the region. As BP began to contain the oil leak in July 2010, all eyes focused forward: How long would it take to truly clean up this mess and restore the Gulf of Mexico, people wondered? But perhaps the most instructive lesson in American oil cleanup and recovery could be gleaned not from the Gulf of Mexico, but rather close to the Gulf of Alaska. For it was in the Prince William Sound that the second worst oil spill in U.S. history occurred—the 1989 *Exxon Valdez* oil spill—one that, with the benefits of hindsight, has given us insights into the potential and limits of environmental remediation and policy.

The story behind the *Exxon Valdez* disaster is well known: A large oil tanker (the *Exxon Valdez*) deviated from the prescribed shipping lane in Prince William Sound, Alaska, and ran aground on a nearby and well-known reef. Roughly 37,000 tons (10.9 million gallons) of Alaska North Slope (ANS) crude oil spilled into Prince William Sound as a result of the grounding and 16 percent (486 miles [782 km]) of the total shoreline of the sound was oiled to some degree. A massive cleanup effort was launched immediately, and more than 11,000 people were involved in the cleanup in the opening months of the spill, a moment captured dramatically by the media. However, the *Exxon Valdez* cleanup effort and related scientific studies lasted for years after the 1989 spill and long after the television cameras departed. Scientists, local governments, and Exxon Mobile—the oil company responsible for the disaster—remained active in the region for several years after the spill, even beyond the June 1992 pronouncement by federal and state government officials that no additional cleanup of the shoreline was warranted.

The shoreline ecology program (SEP), which began in 1990 and continued throughout the decade, represented one of the longer-range programs assessing the recovery of the biological communities in the spill zone. One of the principle challenges for scientists studying the spill zone was to effectively define "recovery" in Prince William Sound. Biological systems are defined by constant change, and scientists knew that it would be a mistake to base the "recovery" of Prince William Sound on pre-spill conditions. Even if the *Exxon Valdez* had never ran aground, scientists asserted, the biology of Prince William Sound could be dramatically different in 2010 than it was 1985. Natural fluctuations in water temperature and salinity, for example, can have huge ecological effects. Thus, scientists were careful when assigning causality to ecological change in the region.

This fact added complexity to many observable ecological trends in the sound. Huge schools of whirling herring, which were staples of the pre-spill marine ecosystem in Prince William Sound, no longer flooded the area. In 1993, authorities declared the Prince William Sound herring fishery collapsed, as only 25 percent of the expected adults returned that year to spawn. Meanwhile, other species, such as the pink salmon, rebounded strongly in the region, at times above pre-spill levels. Scientists were at a loss to explain these trends. Was the herring's disappearance due to the oil spill or something else? Evidence was inconclusive. In 2008, the Exxon Valdez Oil Spill Trustee Council, a government created monitor, launched the Prince William Sound Integrated Herring Restoration Plan to determine what, if anything, could be done to restore the Pacific herring in Prince William Sound—a species on which local communities and larger ocean predators had depended for years. In July 2010, a draft of the Integrated Herring Restoration Plan was released. The report outlines nine restoration activities for consideration, and outlines scientific and procedural preparations that need to take place before any restoration activity can be implemented. The report then concludes with a restoration plan that is split into three phases over time, with the final phase concluding in 2022.

Scientists were less challenged to establish causality with other pieces of evidence, such as the presence of weathered (diluted) and unweathered (undiluted) oil. Even a decade after the spill, several locations in Prince William Sound had isolated deposits of weathered oil from the spill. A 2001 Environmental Protection Agency study, which surveyed ninety-one sites along Prince William Sound, found that more than half—fifty-three sites—still contained oil. The casual observer gazing across Prince William Sound in 2010 might be struck by how pristine and healthy the beaches and water look. But in less visible places, such as deep subsurface reservoirs under gravel beaches, significant deposits of oil remained. The *Exxon Valdez* Oil Spill Trustee Council concluded that it could take "decades and possibly centuries" for the remaining oil, which was estimated in 2003 at 21,000 gallons (79,500 l), to disappear entirely.

Positive Effects

One positive development of the *Exxon Valdez* oil spill was the surge in common sense regulations that made oversea oil transport much safer. In 1990, in direct response to the *Valdez* disaster, U.S. Congress established the Oil Pollution Act (OPA), which required all single-hulled oil tankers operating in U.S. waters to be phased out by 2010 (the *Exxon Valdez* was a single-hulled tanker). OPA additionally set up a liability fund for oil spills, called for more comprehensive spill disaster plans, and supported citizen-led oversight committees that wished to police safety claims by shippers. Today, special tug vessels must accompany all tankers in and out of Prince William Sound, and advanced monitoring devices must now be affixed to oil tankers, allowing the U.S. Coast Guard to track their movement through the sound. Almost fifty miles of containment boom sit ready for use along Prince William Sound, more than ten times the amount available at the time of the *Exxon Valdez* disaster, and mandated drills are held each year in Prince William Sound to prepare response teams for spills significantly larger than the *Exxon Valdez* oil spill.

Local communities have also mobilized in the wake of the disaster. In 1994, the *Exxon Valdez* Oil Spill Trustee Council consulted with twenty-two communities affected by the spill area to create the Exxon Valdez Oil Spill Restoration Plan. Through the plan, hundreds of millions of dollars were allocated to research, habitat protection, science management, and restoration. This money has contributed directly to our understanding of the oil spills and the best ways to address them—a mission that, if applied, will certainly help the communities in the Gulf of Mexico move forward with their own disaster recovery.

The War Against Offshore Drilling in the Chukchi Sea

In May 2011 Shell Oil presented a proposal to the federal government seeking permission to drill ten exploratory oil wells in Alaska's Arctic waters. Shell executives visited Native Alaskans in their remote communities to attempt to win their support for the venture, and to attempt to convince residents that Shell is as concerned with the environment as they are. Many Native Alaskan communities on the Chukchi Sea depend upon marine mammals for their livelihood, and are worried that drilling operations would disrupt the migrating patterns of walruses and whales. Shell has begun gathering data and conducting research to determine if their actions would disrupt wildlife, and if it does if they can find a solution. One of the many issues is noise. Noise from drilling, seismic surveys, and shipping could threaten migratory and feeding patterns of sea mammals. The results from tests of seismic surveys, recorded on acoustic listening devices, were mixed. While bowhead and beluga whales seemed unaffected, walrus calls in the vicinity stopped. Walruses rely on their calls to stay in touch with their pups and herds when separated, so seismic tests could compromise herd integrity and the mother-pup bond. Shell has responded by studying how to muffle the noise from drilling operations, and to map migration patterns to attempt to minimize their impact.

One of the most difficult hurdles Shell faces is convincing both locals and the government that they can protect the area from a devastating spill. Environmentalists point out that cleaning up a spill in the Arctic would be far more difficult than in the Gulf of Mexico, due to high winds, high seas, and the frigid cold and ice. For eight months of the year, the Chukchi Sea is almost completely iced over, which could both cause damage to a drilling platform as well as make it difficult to detect a spill. The ice and the ever-changing arctic landscape also makes the construction of transporting oil via a pipeline problematic. Shell has been working with soil experts and oceanographers to study the land and currents.

BIBLIOGRAPHY

Books

Arnold, David F. *The Fisherman's Frontier: People and Salmon in Southeast Alaska.* Seattle, WA: University of Washington Press, 2008.

Barth, Steve, Richard A. Cooke, and Kim Heaco. *The Smithsonian Guides to Natural America: The Pacific–Hawaii, Alaska.* Washington, DC: Smithsonian Books, 1995.

Brinkley, Douglas. *The Quiet World: Saving Alaska's Wilderness Kingdom, 1879–1960.* New York, NY: Harper, 2011.

Haycock, Stephen W. *Frigid Embrace: Politics, Economics, and the Environment in Alaska.* Corvallis, OR: Oregon State University Press, 2002.

Kollin, Susan. *Nature's State: Imagining Alaska as the Last Frontier.* Chapel Hill, NC: University of North Carolina Press, 2001.

Lourie, Peter. *Arctic Thaw: The People of the Whale in a Changing Climate.* Honesdale, PA: Boyds Mills Press, 2007.

Morse, Kathryn Taylor. *The Nature of Gold: An Environmental History of the Klondike Gold Rush.* Seattle, WA: University of Washington Press, 2003.

Nagle, John Copeland. *Law's Environment: How the Law Shapes the Places We Live.* New Haven, CT: Yale University Press, 2010.

Rennicke, Jeff. *Treasures of Alaska: Last Great American Wilderness.* Washington, DC: National Geographic Society, 2010.

Ross, Ken. *Environmental Conflict in Alaska.* Boulder, CO: University Press of Colorado, 2000.

Willis, Roxanne. *Alaska's Place in the West: From the Last Frontier to the Last Great Wilderness.* Lawrence, KS: University Press of Kansas, 2010.

Web Sites

"Administrative Order 238." Available from http://gov.state.ak.us/admin-orders/238.html

"Alaska Agricultural Census: Historical Highlights." United States Department of Agriculture. Available from http://www.agcensus.usda.gov/Publications/2007/Full_Report/Volume_1,_Chapter_1_State_Level/Alaska/st02_1_001_001.pdf

Alaska Energy Pathway. Alaska Energy Authority. Available from ftp://ftp.aidea.org/AlaskaEnergyPathway/2010EnergyPathway8-12Press.pdf

"Alaska North Slope: A Promising Future or an Area in Decline?" Available from http://www.netl.doe.gov/technologies/oil-gas/publications/AEO/ANS_Potential.pdf

"Alaska Quick Facts." U.S. Energy Information Administration. U.S. Department of Energy. Available from http://tonto.eia.doe.gov/state/state_energy_profiles.cfm?sid=AK

"Alaska's Climate Change Strategy: Addressing Impacts in Alaska." Available from http://www.climate-change.alaska.gov/aag/docs/aag_ES_27Jan10.pdf

"Alaska's State Forests." Alaska Department of Natural Resources, Division of Forestry. Available from http://forestry.alaska.gov/stateforests.htm#sesf

"American Recovery and Reinvestment Act: Alaska." Democratic Policy Committee. Available from http://dpc.senate.gov/docs/fs-111-1-24-states/ak.pdf

Anderson, James J. "Review of the Influence of Climate on Salmon." School of Fisheries. University of Washington. Available from http://www.cbr.washington.edu/papers/jim/climate.html

"Carbon Capture and Sequestration." World Resources Institute. Available from http://www.wri.org/project/carbon-capture-sequestration

"Clean Energy Economy: Alaska." Pew Charitable Trusts. Available from http://www.pewcenter-onthestates.org/uploadedFiles/wwwpewcenter-onthestatesorg/Fact_Sheets/Clean_Economy_Factsheet_Alaska.pdf

"Climate Change's Impacts in Alaska." The Nature Conservancy. Available from http://www.nature.org/initiatives/climatechange/files/alaskafacts3.pdf

"Climate Change's Impacts in Alaska." U.S. Geological Survey. Available from http://esp.cr.usgs.gov/info/assessment/alaska.html

"Climate Change Sub-Cabinet." Available from http://www.climatechange.alaska.gov/docs/govrpt_jul08.pdf

Doremus, Holly. "Court upholds polar bear 'threatened' status." Legal Planet. July 1, 2011. Available from http://legalplanet.wordpress.com/2011/07/01/court-upholds-polar-bear-threatened-status/

Draft Integrated Herring Restoration Plan. Exxon Valdez Oil Spill Trustee Council. Available from http://www.evostc.state.ak.us/Universal/Documents/Publications/IHRP%20DRAFT%20-%20July%202010.pdf

"Energy Rebates, Loans, and Weatherization Programs." Alaska Housing Finance Corporation. Available from http://www.ahfc.state.ak.us/energy/weatherization_rebates.cfm

"*Exxon Valdez*: Long Term Effects From Residual Oil." Environmental Protection Agency. Available from http://www.epa.gov/oem/docs/oil/fss/fss02/ricepresent.pdf

"The Exxon Valdez Oil Spill: A Report to the President." Environmental Protection Agency. Available from http://www.epa.gov/history/topics/valdez/04.htm

"*Exxon Valdez* Oil Spill Restoration Plan." Exxon Valdez Oil Spill Trustee Council. Available from http://www.evostc.state.ak.us/Universal/Documents/Restoration/1994RestorationPlan.pdf

"*Exxon Valdez* Oil Spill Trustee Council." Available from http://www.evostc.state.ak.us/

"Fisheries of the United States–2009." NOAA Fisheries. Available from http://www.st.nmfs.noaa.gov/st1/fus/fus09/index.html

Fresco, Nancy, and F. Stuart Chapin III. "Assessing the Potential for Conversion to Biomass Fuels in Interior Alaska." United States Department of Agriculture. Available from http://www.fs.fed.us/pnw/pubs/pnw_rp579.pdf

"Governor Sarah Palin Rejects Federal Funding For Renewable Energy." Environmental News Network. Available from http://www.enn.com/energy/article/39834

Graham, Sarah. "Environmental Impacts of *Exxon Valdez* Spill Still Being Felt." *Scientific American*. Available from http://www.scientificamerican.com/article.cfm?id=environmental-effects-of

"House Bill 306." Alaska State Legislature. Available from http://www.legis.state.ak.us/basis/get_bill_text.asp?hsid=HB0306A&session=26

Krauss, Clifford. "Shell Tries to Calm Fears on Drilling in Alaska." *The New York Times*. May 1, 2011. Available from http://www.nytimes.com/2011/05/02/business/energy-environment/02shell.html

Krauss, Clifford. "Small Leak Shuts Down Oil Pipeline in Alaska." January 9, 2011. *New York Times* Available from http://www.nytimes.com/2011/01/10/business/energy-environment/10oil.html?scp=1&sq=january%209%20small%20leak%20shuts%20down%20oil%20pipeline%20in%20alaska&st=cse

Joling, Dan. "Alaska files suit against feds over polar bear habitat status." *Anchorage Daily News*. March 10, 2011. Available from http://www.adn.com/2011/03/09/1746219/alaska-files-lawsuit-over-designation.html

Joling, Dan. "Environmental group plans lawsuit to protect walrus." *Anchorage Daily News*. April 22, 2011. Available from http://www.adn.com/2011/04/21/1821781/environmental-group-plans-lawsuit.html

Lydersen, Kari. "Oil Group Joins Alaska in Suing To Overturn Polar Bear Protection." *The Washington Post*. August 31, 2008. Available from http://www.washingtonpost.com/wp-dyn/content/article/2008/08/30/AR2008083001538.html

"Minerals in Alaska." Alaska Public Lands and Information Center. Available from http://www.alaskacenters.gov/minerals.cfm

Mufson, Steven. "Proposed oil drilling off Alaska coast prompts studies of environmental impact." *The Washington Post*. August 22, 2011. Available from http://www.washingtonpost.com/business/economy/proposed-oil-drilling-off-alaska-coast-prompts-studies-of-environmental-impact/2011/08/02/gIQAO6vsWJ_story.html

"Oil Pollution Act of 1990." United States Senate. Available from http://epw.senate.gov/opa90.pdf

"Pipeline in Alaska to Restart Soon." January 16, 2011. *New York Times* Available from http://www.nytimes.com/2011/01/17/business/energy-environment/17pipeline.html?scp=1&sq=pipeline%20in%20alaska%20to%20restart%20soon&st=Search

"Species." Alaska Department of Fish and Game. Available from http://www.adfg.alaska.gov/index.cfm?adfg=species.main

State of Alaska: Statewide Assessment of Forest Resources. Alaska Department of Natural Resources: Division of Forestry. Available from http://forestry.alaska.gov/pdfs/2010AlaskaStatewideAssessment.pdf

Struck, Doug. "Twenty Years Later, Impacts of the Exxon Valdez Linger." Yale University. Available from http://e360.yale.edu/content/feature.msp?id=2133

"Summary Points: 10 Years of Intertidal Monitoring After the Exxon Valdez Spill." National Oceanic and Atmospheric Administration. Available from http://response.restoration.noaa.gov/topic_subtopic_entry.php?RECORD_KEY%28entry_subtopic_topic%29=entry_id,subtopic_id,topic_id&entry_id%28entry_subtopic_topic%29=254&subtopic_id%28entry_subtopic_topic%29=13&topic_id%28entry_subtopic_topic%29=1

"Syngas with Carbon Capture at Cook Inlet." *New York Times.* Available from http://green.blogs.nytimes.com/2009/11/06/syngas-with-carbon-capture-at-cook-inlet/#more-30877

"2007 Minerals Yearbook: Alaska." United States Geological Survey. Available from http://minerals.usgs.gov/minerals/pubs/state/2007/myb2-2007-ak.pdf

"2007 Agricultural Census: Area Summary Highlights." United States Department of Agriculture. Available from http://www.agcensus.usda.gov/Publications/2007/Full_Report/Volume_1,_Chapter_2_County_Level/Alaska/st02_2_001_001.pdf

"2009 Status Report." Exxon Valdez Oil Spill Trustee Council. Available from http://www.evostc.state.ak.us/Universal/Documents/Publications/20th%20Anniversary%20Report/2009%20Status%20Report%20%28Low-Res%29.pdf

"Underground Coal Gasification: Coal Energy without Mining." Available from http://www.cirienergy.com/

Weise, Elizabeth. "Walruses haul-out three weeks early, global warming blamed." *USA Today.* August 19, 2011. Available from http://content.usatoday.com/communities/sciencefair/post/2011/08/walrus-haul-out-three-weeks-early-global-warming-blamed/1

Arizona

Home to the Grand Canyon National Park, the Petrified Forest, the Red Rock Country of Sedona, and a wide stretch of the Sonoran Desert, Arizona presents a rich tapestry of natural landscapes, which in turn support a wonderful diversity of wildlife. Those landscapes, however, and everywhere in between, face ongoing environmental challenges, requiring continual attention and action on behalf of residents and government officials alike. The most pressing challenge involves ongoing efforts to secure an adequate and sustainable water supply in a state where a desert climate limits the supply of this precious resource. One of the most recent efforts toward conservation and sustainable water management includes the establishment of a Blue Ribbon Panel on Water Sustainability, which aims to promote the use of reclaimed (recycled) water for agricultural and industrial use. Since the potential effects of climate change could exacerbate the existing problems, the state is currently working on the recommendations in their climate action plan to reduce greenhouse gas emissions. With an eye toward cleaner air and sustainable energy, the state is set to build the first refinery in the United States that is specifically designed to produce clean petroleum fuels and is considering ways to revive its forest systems through a management process that could also boost the development of green building and biomass energy businesses.

Climate: Addressing the Challenge of Climate Change

While the climate in Arizona is generally dry, average temperatures do vary by topography. The interior uplands experience seasonal temperature changes with cool winters and warm, sunny summers, while the desert regions typically feature higher temperatures year-round.

Arid conditions lead to a number of natural hazards, including droughts and forest fires. Some state officials and environmentalists are concerned that these hazards may increase and intensify if temperatures rise as a result of global climate change. According to the National Wildlife Federation, rising temperatures in the state could drastically alter habitats for the state's diverse wildlife species. Warmer stream temperatures would put many of the state's already threatened fish species in danger, and the decades-long drought the state has experienced has depleted water sources, a trend that will continue if action isn't taken to stop these patterns.

To address these and other related issues, the state legislature is currently considering the recommendations of the Climate Change Action Plan (2006), submitted by the Climate Change Advisory Group pursuant to Executive Order 2005-02. According to data compiled as part of a preliminary inventory and forecast report, greenhouse gas (GHG) emissions in Arizona increased by nearly 56 percent between 1990 and 2005 and are projected to increase by 148 percent through 2020, if no reductive actions are taken. The overall recommendation of the action plan is to set a state goal for the reduction of GHG emissions to 2000 levels by 2020 and to 50 percent below 2000 levels by 2040.

Arizona and the Western Climate Initiative

In 2007, Arizona became a founding member of the Western Climate Initiative (WCI), a regional action group committed to developing a joint strategy for the reduction of GHG emissions. In 2008, the WCI announced the development of a GHG cap-and-trade program that is expected to take effect in participating states and Canadian provinces beginning January 2012. In February 2010, Arizona governor Janice Brewer announced by Executive Order 2010-06 that the state would not participate in the WCI cap-and-trade program, but would continue its membership within the organization. Some state officials believe that the cap-and-trade program would lead to greater job loss and a decrease in business investment at a time when the economy is already struggling. Brewer also noted that the state is already making positive advances in the reduction of

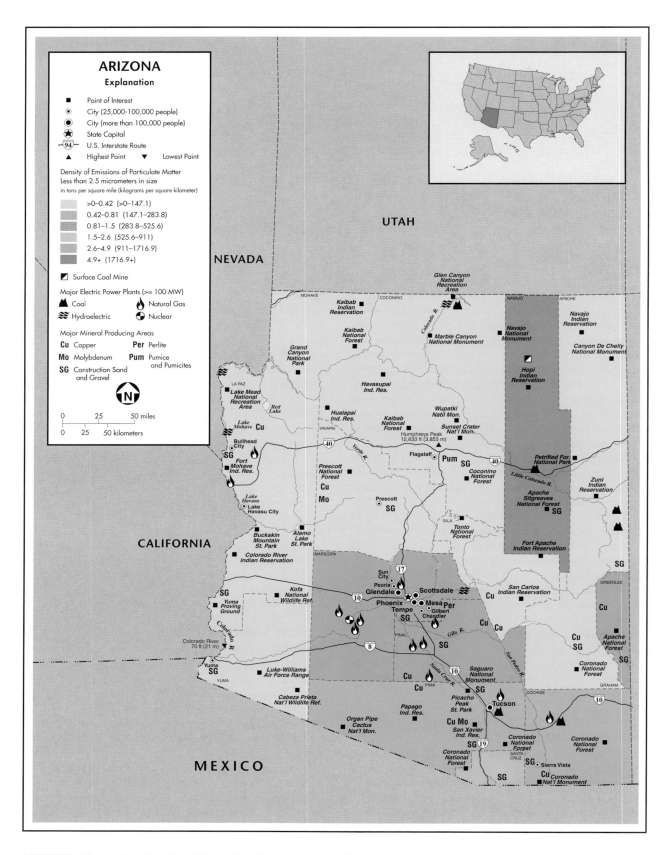

ARIZONA
Explanation

■ Point of Interest
⊙ City (25,000-100,000 people)
◉ City (more than 100,000 people)
★ State Capital
⊸94⊸ U.S. Interstate Route
▲ Highest Point   ▼ Lowest Point

Density of Emissions of Particulate Matter
Less than 2.5 micrometers in size
in tons per square mile (kilograms per square kilometer)

>0–0.42 (>0–147.1)
0.42–0.81 (147.1–283.8)
0.81–1.5 (283.8–525.6)
1.5–2.6 (525.6–911)
2.6–4.9 (911–1716.9)
4.9+ (1716.9+)

▨ Surface Coal Mine

Major Electric Power Plants (>= 100 MW)
▲ Coal   ♦ Natural Gas
≈ Hydroelectric   ◓ Nuclear

Major Mineral Producing Areas
Cu Copper   Per Perlite
Mo Molybdenum   Pum Pumice and Pumicites
SG Construction Sand and Gravel

Ⓝ

0   25   50 miles
0   25   50 kilometers

UTAH

NEVADA

CALIFORNIA

MEXICO

SOURCES: "County Emissions Map: Criteria Air Pollutants." *AirData*. U.S. Environmental Protection Agency. Available from http://www.epa.gov/air/data/geosel.html; *Energy Maps*. U.S. Energy Information Administration. Available from http://www.eia.gov/state; *Highest and Lowest Elevations*. U.S. Geological Survey. Available from http://egsc.usgs.gov/isb/pubs/booklets/elvadist/elvadist.html#Highest; *2007 Minerals Yearbook*. U.S. Geological Survey. Available from http://minerals.usgs.gov/minerals/pubs/state.   © 2011 Cengage Learning.

GHG emissions through the implementation of renewable portfolio standards and the development of solar energy and other energy-efficiency programs throughout the state. The governor established a Climate Change Oversight group to monitor the work of the WCI and offer recommendations as to the state's actions or response towards future developments in the initiative.

❧ Natural Resources, Water, and Agriculture

Natural Resources: Saving the Forest by Cutting Down Trees

With many of the state's most spectacular forest areas protected within national and state parks, the wood and forest product industry of the state is relatively small. However, efforts to protect and conserve these natural resources may actually boost forest-related industries within the next decade. The mature ponderosa pine and mixed conifer forests that Arizona is known for have dwindled considerably, as old growth trees have died at a greater rate than they have been replaced. Aggressive fire suppression policies have led to conditions that encourage the growth of younger pines, providing an overabundance of small diameter trees that are commonly known as "ladder fuel" by those involved in forest protection efforts. In the event of a wildfire, these smaller trees can catch and spread fire very quickly, putting the forest as a whole at greater risk. To address the situation, the state government has introduced a forestry action plan through which small diameter trees might be responsibly harvested to reduce fuel loads, while also providing materials for green building and biomass energy plans.

In May 2011, Arizona experienced the largest wildfire in the state's history. Called the Wallow Fire, after the Bear Wallow Wilderness in which it began. The Bear Wallow Wilderness is located in the Apache and Sitgreaves National Forests in east-central Arizona. The fire is believed to have been caused by a camp fire gone out of control on or around May 29. It ended up burning more than 469,000 acres (189,798 ha) and destroying more than 30 homes. The fire has sent plumes of smoke that affected air quality from Arizona and New Mexico to as far away as east of the Rocky Mountains.

The state's twenty-two national parks and monuments, including the Grand Canyon National Park and the Petrified Forest, draw more than one million tourists each year and serve as habitats for a variety of animal species, ranging from mountain lions, coyotes, and black and brown bears, to black-tail jackrabbits, kangaroo rats, and Gunnison's prairie dog. There are numerous rattlesnakes in the state and many species of lizards can be found in the desert areas. Various species of cacti are harvested for commercial use, particularly as souvenirs for tourists.

Arizona State Profile

Physical Characteristics

Land area	113,595 square miles (294,210 sq km)
Inland water area	396 square miles (1,026 sq km)
Coastal area	NA
Highest point	Humphreys Peak 12,633 feet (3,851 m)
National Forest System lands (2010)	11.2 million acres (4.6 million ha)
State parks (2011)	30

Energy Statistics

Total energy production (2009)	580 trillion Btu
State ranking in total energy production (2009)	27
Renewable energy net generation total (2009)	6.6 million megawatt hours
Hydroelectric energy generation (2009)	6.4 million megawatt hours
Biomass energy generation (2009)	22,000 megawatt hours
Wind energy generation (2009)	30,000 megawatt hours
Wood and derived fuel energy generation (2009)	137 million megawatt hours
Crude oil reserves (2009)	NA
Natural gas reserves (2009)	NA
Natural gas liquids (2008)	NA

Pollution Statistics

Carbon output (2005)	88.8 million tons of CO_2 (80.5 million t)
Superfund sites (2008)	9
Particulate matter (less than 2.5 micrometers) emissions (2002)	11,009 tons per year (9,987 t/yr)
Toxic chemical releases (2009)	60.9 million pounds (27.6 million kg)
Generated hazardous waste (2009)	31,100 tons (19,100 t)

SOURCES: AirData. U.S. Environmental Protection Agency. Available from http://www.epa.gov/air/data; *Energy Maps, Facts, and Data of the U.S. States.* U.S. Energy Information Administration. Available from http://www.eia.gov/state; *The 2012 Statistical Abstract.* U.S. Census Bureau. Available from http://www.census.gov/compendia/statab; *United States Energy Usage.* eRedux. Available from http://www.eredux.net/states.

© 2011 Cengage Learning.

According to the U.S. Fish and Wildlife Service, Arizona is home to 41 animal and 18 plant species that are either threatened or endangered as of 2011. Endangered animals include the California condor, the black-footed ferret, and the Mount Graham red squirrel. Endangered and threatened plant species include seven varieties of cacti, Kearney's blue star, and the Arizona cliff rose.

Arizona was ranked first in the nation for copper production in 2007, providing about 60 percent of the U.S. supply. The state has also been among the top five for the production of molybdenum, perlite, sand and gravel, silver, pumices, and zeolites. Zinc, lead, uranium, and tungsten are mined within the state as well. In 2010, Arizona ranked second in the nation with a production value of $6.7 billion for nonfuel minerals.

Uranium mining around the Grand Canyon area has continued to be a point of contention in the state. In 2009 Secretary of the Interior Ken Salazar announced a two-year ban on new mining on federal land around Grand Canyon National Park. Although the ban is on all mining, the main effect is on exploration and development of breccia-pipe uranium deposits. During the two-year ban the Department of the Interior studied a proposed 20-year ban on new mining in the area. Lawmakers have gone back and forth over the issue, with some wanting to protect the area from the environmental consequences of mining, while others push for it because mining will create jobs and stimulate the economy. Salazar extended the two-year ban in June 2011 and announced his intention to continue pushing for a 20-year mining ban in the area in lieu of an environmental impact statement.

Rosemont Copper

The proposed opening of the Rosemont Copper mine in the Santa Rita mountains has led to a great deal of controversy from local authorities and environmental activists. The primary concerns involve the use of nearly 30,000 acres (12,140 ha) of land in or adjacent to the Coronado National Forest in Pima County. Opponents state that the proposed open-pit mining operations in this area would have a significant adverse affect on the environment, particularly in soil, air, and groundwater contamination. The use of public lands for mining operations will also decrease or eliminate the recreational opportunities available in the area for the public. However, Rosemont Copper reports that all of the preliminary land purchases and permits have been in full compliance with the regulations of the U.S Forest Service and Bureau of Land Management. Rosemont Copper also states that water conservation and other environmental issues are being fully addressed by in the development of an operation plan for the mine. According to a 2009 economic impact assessment conducted by Arizona State University, the mine project will translate into more than $19 million annually in local tax revenues, supporting about 2,100 local jobs each year. The U.S. Forest Service was expected to release a draft environmental impact statement concerning the Rosemont project in the fourth quarter of 2011, and to publish a decision in January 2012.

Water: The Mighty Colorado and the Central Arizona Project

The Colorado River and its two major tributaries, the Little Colorado and the Gila, form the major river system in the state. Eighteen fish species in the rivers and streams of Arizona are listed as threatened or endangered. These

There are very few natural lakes in Arizona, but there are several large reservoirs formed by dams. These include Lake Powell which is formed by Glen Canyon Dam on the Colorado River. © *artconcept/ ShutterStock.com*

include the desert pupfish, razorback sucker, Gila chub, and the Little Colorado River spinedace. Nonnative species, such as rainbow, brown, and brook trout, have been stocked for sports fishing through the efforts of the Alchesay-Williams Creek National Fish Hatchery, located on the Fort Apache Indian reservation, and the Willow Beach National Hatchery, downriver from Hoover Dam. The Colorado River provides water for more than 4 million people and 300,000 acres (121,400 ha) of farmland through the Central Arizona Project (CAP), which consists of a 336-mile (541-km) canal that extends from the Colorado River through central and southern Arizona to a terminus in Tucson. With a complex series of tunnels, pumping stations, aqueducts, and pipelines, the CAP is the largest water storage and distribution system in the state.

There are very few natural lakes in the state, but there are several large reservoirs formed by dams. These include Lake Mead (formed by Hoover Dam), Lake Powell (formed by Glen Canyon Dam), Lake Mohave, Lake Havasu, Roosevelt Lake, and San Carlos Lake. The Hoover, Glen Canyon, and Theodore Roosevelt dams all serve as sources of hydroelectric power and provide water for irrigation systems. There is no commercial fishing industry in Arizona. Sport fishing is popular, however, with state fish hatcheries stocking more than three million fish in Arizona's lakes, rivers, and streams each year. In 2006, sport fishing brought the state more than $1.3 billion.

The Arizona Department of Environmental Quality announced a streamlined general air quality control permit process for the operation of wastewater treatment plants in August 2011. As of that date, permits could be obtained more quickly and at a lower cost while still maintaining the same level of environmental protection. The permits cover wastewater treatment activities that pertain to air quality, such as odor controls, fuel burning boilers, and fuel burning generators.

Agriculture: Sustainable Practices in Agriculture Maximize Water Use

Dairy products and cattle are the top agricultural commodities in the state, representing more than 40 percent of total farm receipts. In crops, Arizona ranks among the top five states in the nation for the production of lettuce, cantaloupe and honeydew melons, spinach, broccoli, and lemons. In cotton production, the state ranks among the top ten. Hay, wheat, barley, and other citrus fruits are also important crops. Organic products must be certified under the USDA National Organics program, since the state does not sponsor a separate program.

With a generally dry climate, a majority of the farmland in the state is linked to irrigation systems. With water a scarce commodity, it is no surprise that research in sustainable practices in agriculture has focused on water use. Water saving subsurface drip irrigation and gravity-flow nonpressurized drip systems are both being utilized in some areas. Low-thirst barley varieties have also been studied and introduced, in part, through the efforts of the Sustainable Agriculture program at the University of Arizona's Cooperative Extension. As of 2011, the state had 110 certified organic operations.

⚜ Energy

Arizona's First Refinery Will Produce Clean Burning Gasoline

Arizona has very little crude oil and, as of 2010, no refineries. However, Arizona Clean Fuels Yuma is set to build the first refinery in the United States that is specifically designed to produce clean petroleum fuels. Arizona Clean Burning Gasoline (Arizona CBG), an

Arizona Clean Burning Gasoline (Arizona CBG), an oxygenated and reformulated blend of gasoline, was introduced for year-round use in Maricopa County, which includes the Phoenix metropolitan area, in 1997. According to estimates from state agencies, the use of this blend has reduced the amount of ground-level ozone pollutants in the area by about 12 percent, carbon monoxide by 10 percent, and other toxic air pollutants by 15 percent. © Buddy Mays/Alamy

oxygenated and reformulated blend of gasoline, was introduced for year-round use in Maricopa County, which includes the Phoenix metropolitan area, in 1997. According to estimates from state agencies, the use of this low-sulfur blend has reduced the amount of ground-level ozone pollutants in the area by about 12 percent, carbon monoxide by 10 percent, and other toxic air pollutants by 15 percent. A special oxygenated blend of gasoline is used in the Tucson area during the winter months. The refinery was expected to be operational in 2012 and would be located in a remote area of the Mohawk Valley about 48 miles (77 km) east of Yuma and 100 miles (161 km) southwest of Phoenix. When completed in 2014, the facility will have the capacity to produce 6 million gallons (22.7 million liters) of gasoline per day, including Arizona CBG, CARB 3 (a reformulated diesel specified for use in California), and other low-sulfur gasoline products.

Electricity

About 40 percent of the state's electricity supply comes from coal-fired plants. Most of the coal supply comes from mines in the Black Mesa Basin of the state, with additional supplies from New Mexico. Twenty-five percent of the state's electricity is supplied by the Palo Verde nuclear power plant, which is the largest nuclear plant in the country. While imported natural gas is used to produce much of the remaining demand for electricity, some supply comes from hydroelectric power plants at the Glen Canyon and Hoover dams of the Colorado River. About 50 percent of all residents use electricity as a primary source for home heating, with an additional 40 percent relying on natural gas.

Cashing in on Sunny Days

The wide, sun-drenched Arizona deserts present great potential for the development of solar energy. In 2007, the Arizona Department of Commerce published the *Arizona Solar Electric Roadmap Study*, which found that up to 1,000 megawatts of solar electricity could be added to the state by 2020, accompanied by the creation of 3,000 new jobs. To encourage the switch to solar energy, a number of industrial, commercial, and residential tax incentives are available for the use of solar power. If all goes well, the state will welcome one of the world's largest solar plants in 2013. The project, which was approved in 2008 and originally scheduled for completion in 2011, was held up by financial concerns at the onset of the recession. In July 2010, President Obama announced the pledge of a $1.45 billion conditional commitment loan to Abengoa Solar, the chosen developer of the Solana project. This Recovery Act funding guaranteed that the project continued as scheduled. Construction began at the end of 2010 and the plant was scheduled to begin operation in 2013. When completed, the 1,900-acre

(769-ha) Solana Generating Station, located 70 miles (113 km) southwest of Phoenix, will produce enough energy to supply 70,000 Arizona homes. Abengoa expects to support 1,600 jobs during the construction phase of the project and anticipates the creation of 85 permanent jobs for operations. In addition, two assembly facilities will be constructed on the Solana site to facilitate construction, along with a mirror manufacturing facility that will provide the more than 900,000 mirrors necessary for the project. These facilities are expected to provide an additional 150 jobs.

Renewable Portfolio Standards and Distributed Renewable Energy

Arizona's renewable portfolio standard, adopted in 2006, requires all electric utilities to provide 15 percent of their electricity from renewable sources by 2025. Of that percentage, 30 percent must come from distributed renewable energy (DRE) resources by 2012. DRE resources are small-scale generation operations that are located at or very near the premises of the consumer, such as solar panels installed on the roof of a home. According to the statute, half of the DRE requirements must be fulfilled through residential installations and half from nonresidential, nonutility installations (AAC R14-2-1801).

❧ Green Business, Green Building, Green Jobs

Building Green

By executive order, all newly constructed state-funded buildings must meet the requirements for silver-level certification under the U.S. Green Building Council Leadership in Energy & Environmental Design (LEED) program. They must also be designed to derive at least 10 percent of their energy from renewable resources. In 2010, Governor Jan Brewer announced that more than $12 million from the state's share of American Recovery and Reinvestment Act funds would be used for energy efficiency projects in twenty-five local school districts. Several schools have already received funding through the School Facilities Board for solar energy projects, which will aid in reaching both green building and distributed renewable energy goals.

Community colleges in Arizona are working to fulfill the state's commitment to green building. In 2010, the Maricopa Community College district of ten schools signed the American College and University Presidents Climate Commitment to reduce greenhouse gases. The Mesa Community College Physical Science Building, which is expected to realize annual energy cost savings of $52,000, received LEED Gold certification. Another LEED Gold building, Mariposa Hall at Estrella Mountain Community College, which opened in 2010,

featured such innovative building practices as the use of local and recycled building materials, water and energy conservation systems, and a rainwater harvesting system. In 2011, the Arizona Association for Environmental Education began a pilot project to offer the state's first certification program for environmental education.

In April 2011, Del Webb—a builder of new homes, townhomes, and condominiums in Arizona—announced that they would be featuring solar and other energy-efficient features in two of its new retirement communities in the Phoenix area. Sun City Festival in Buckeye and Sun City Anthem in Florence will have approximately 11,200 new homes combined. This means that these communities will be the largest in Arizona and among the largest in the nation that offer solar power as standard to buyers. The solar-electric power systems will be integrated into the roofs of the homes. The 1.8 kW systems supplement the energy needs of each home and feeds back into the grid any surplus energy that is generated. The homes will also feature high-efficiency heating and cooling systems and low water use plumbing fixtures.

Clean Energy Sector Leads in Green Business

According to surveys conducted by the National Governors Association Center for Best Practices and the Pew Charitable Trusts, Arizona's green economy clearly centers on clean energy, with subsets in generation, storage, and efficiency systems. From 1998 to 2007, jobs in the clean energy sector increased by 43 percent. Into 2010, the push for the development of solar energy at industrial, commercial, and residential levels may prove to be a major driving force in boosting the state's green economy. Green building design and materials, along with sustainable agriculture services, are considered to be growing segments of the green economy as well.

The Arizona Green Chamber of Commerce, the first state-level green chamber of commerce in the nation, launched its first local chapter in Phoenix in November 2008. The chamber provides and promotes a wide range of resources and events for business leaders committed to creating a new green economy and implementing environmentally responsible business practices.

The Arizona Department of Environmental Quality (ADEQ) has begun taking efforts to help make transportation greener for businesses that ship goods across the border between Mexico and Arizona. Using federal grant money, the agency offers to pay Mexican truck owners to replace old mufflers with new catalytic converters that reduce harmful emissions up to 30 percent. Similar converters are already required for U.S. trucks, which prompted the ADEQ to urge Mexican trucking companies that travel across the border to take part in this project. Focusing on the twin communities of Nogales, Arizona and Nogales, Sonora, Mexico, the

Phoenix-based company Auto Safety House performs the replacements with the help of a Nogales business-man with contacts on the Mexican side of the border. Working from a lot just a few hundred yards from the border crossing, the process takes two to three hours to complete at a cost of $1,600. Fifty-five trucks had new converters installed in 2010, and the replacements were continued into 2011. Trucking companies in Nogales, Mexico, are jumping at the opportunity, since concerns have been rising in the country in recent years over the high level of air pollution. Mexican authorities have installed air monitors on both sides of the border to help pinpoint pollution sources more accurately, while the catalytic converters help to improve the situation in the meantime.

The Green Skills Pipeline and the School of Sustainability

The state of Arizona has received $500 million in grants for employment and training programs through the American Recovery and Reinvestment Act. Included in that total is the 2009 award of $5 million to the Arizona Department of Economic Security for the development of the Green Skills Pipeline to a Clean Energy Economy project, which will provide training in jobs for about 1,500 workers interested in green building and energy efficiency careers.

Arizona students interested in professional careers in the new green economy have an excellent resource in the School of Sustainability at Arizona State University. Established in 2007, the school is partnered with the Global Institute of Sustainability to provide a transdisciplinary curriculum that covers environmental issues from local and global perspectives. As the first of its kind in the nation, the school serves not only its students, but also local industry and business leaders who contact faculty members for information on sustainability and environmental responsibility.

GateWay Community College (GWC), which is part of the Maricopa Community Colleges network, provides solar installation training courses and water and hydrologic studies programs. GWC is the sole state proctor for the Arizona Department of Environmental Quality (ADEQ) Water Quality Operator Certification required to work in water careers across the state. The Maricopa Community Colleges also offer various other programs in sustainability and green technologies.

❧ The Never-Ending Story of Water Sustainability in Arizona

The desert climate that affects most of the state places the issues of water use, conservation, and sustainability as ongoing priorities for state and local government. While water is a generally scarce commodity everywhere, some areas of the state experience prolonged seasons of drought that only exacerbate the situation. Concerns over water availability and sustainability have also heightened in recent years as Arizona has become the second fastest growing state in the nation. For 2009, the estimated population of Arizona was about 6.6 million. That figure is expected to increase to more than 11 million by 2030. A majority of the population lives in the greater Phoenix and Tucson areas, which are part of the Sonoran Desert. With the increase in population comes an increased demand for water, not only at the municipal level, but at agricultural and industrial levels as well, with increased needs for businesses and food production. Approximately 70 percent of the state's water supply is consumed by agriculture, 22 percent is used by municipalities, and 8 percent is used by industry. Add the potential effects of climate change, specifically higher temperatures and increased evaporation of lakes and streams, and it is easy to see why Arizona state officials are actively seeking solutions for water sustainability.

In August 2009, Governor Jan Brewer announced the formation of the Blue Ribbon Panel on Water Sustainability. The panel was co-chaired by officials from the Arizona Department of Water Resources, the Arizona Corporation Commission, and the Arizona Department of Environmental Quality and charged with the task of indentifying and suggesting ways to overcome any obstacles to increased water sustainability. Their primary focus was on considering new strategies for the use of reclaimed, or recycled, water, which is the only water source in the state that shows major potential for increased development. Reclaimed water involves the treatment of wastewater for reuse in agriculture, industry, and landscaping projects, the latter of which include maintenance of golf courses, parks, and wildlife areas. The main obstacle to development of this source is public perception, as residents are often hesitant to consider local applications of treated wastewater. As the panel began a schedule of regular meetings in 2010, a special working committee was established within the panel to conduct public meetings that provided educational resources on the benefits of and necessity for the use of reclaimed water.

The panel's final report, issued in November 2010, included eighteen sets of recommendations in five categories: education/outreach, standards, information development and research agenda, regulatory improvements, and incentives. Under the category of education, the panel called for increased efforts to educate the public on the potential benefits of water reuse programs and to encourage public and private water agencies to implement reuse programs by 2012. The development of a specific reclaimed water distribution system operator training program and associated certification was also recommended. The panel suggested amendments to the tax codes to allow incentives for capital investments in reclaimed water infrastructure projects. They also suggested that there should be some incentives to encourage the increased use of alternative water supplies where it may be appropriate. Under the category of research, the panel recommended the development of a strategic research plan to address questions concerning the human health effects of reclaimed water. One of the known questions involves the presence of trace amounts of prescription or over-the-counter pharmaceuticals in the wastewater, caused primarily by consumer disposal of unused or expired medications. The panel suggests that pharmacies should be required to post information on the proper disposal of medications and perhaps initiate pharmaceutical take-back programs for consumers. The overall goal is to increase the use of reclaimed and recycled water by 40 percent by 2030. These recommendations from the panel have been submitted to the governor, the state legislature, and related state agencies for review and further action.

This is not the first or only active water conservation program supported by the state. The 1980 Groundwater Management Code represents an early landmark effort for the state, in recognition of the need to aggressively manage the state's finite groundwater resources. About 43 percent of the state's water supply comes from groundwater. But through the last century, water has been pumped out more quickly than it has replenished, creating a condition known as overdraft. Five Active Management Areas (AMAs) were established under the code, coinciding with the major geographic areas of Prescott, Phoenix, Pinal, Tucson, and Santa Cruz. Each AMA has a set of conservation goals that incorporate the needs and resources of the area. The Phoenix, Prescott, and Tucson AMAs are currently working toward a primary goal of reaching a safe-yield point by 2025. Safe yield refers to the condition when the amount of groundwater being withdrawn each year is not greater than the amount that is being replenished.

The code also established three Irrigation Non-Expansion Areas (INAs): Joseph City, Harquahala, and Douglas. INAs are subject to restrictions that generally prohibit the increase of irrigated acres of land. Within these areas and throughout the state, the Arizona Department of Water Resources has established a number of best practices in agriculture that promote a number of irrigation and farming techniques to optimize the use of limited water resources. These include techniques such as drip (or trickle) irrigation, which uses low-volume, low-pressure water emitters that can deliver water to precise locations.

Though it was developed thirty years ago, the Groundwater Management Code has been kept current and active through management plan evaluations that have so far been adjusted at ten-year intervals, with each new plan presenting more rigorous requirements for agricultural, municipal, and industrial water users.–

BIBLIOGRAPHY

Books

August, Jack L. *Dividing Western Waters: Mark Wilmer and Arizona V. California*. Fort Worth, TX: Texas Christian University Press, 2007.

Clements, Eric L. *After the Boom in Tombstone and Jerome, Arizona: Decline in Western Resource Towns*. Reno, NV: University of Nevada Press, 2003.

Felger, Richard Stephen, and Bill Broyles, eds. *Dry Borders: Great Natural Reserves of the Sonoran Desert*. Salt Lake City: University of Utah Press, 2007.

Folliott, Peter F., and Owen K. Davis, eds. *Natural Environments of Arizona: From Deserts to Mountains*. Tucson: The University of Arizona Press, 2008.

Kupei, Douglas E. *Fuel for Growth: Water and Arizona's Urban Environment*. Tucson: The University of Arizona Press, 2003.

Logan, Michael F. *Desert Cities: The Environmental History of Phoenix and Tucson*. Pittsburgh, PA: University of Pittsburgh Press, 2006.

Mays, Larry W., ed. *Water Resources Sustainability*. New York: McGraw-Hill Professional, 2006.

Page, Jake, and George H. H. Huey. *The Smithsonian Guides to Natural America: The Southwest–New Mexico, Arizona*. Washington, DC: Smithsonian Books, 1995.

Price, Jay M. *Gateways to the Southwest: The Story of Arizona State Parks*. Tucson: The University of Arizona Press, 2004.

Schipper, Janine. *Disappearing Desert: The Growth of Phoenix and the Culture of Sprawl*. Norman: University of Oklahoma Press, 2008.

Web Sites

"Active Management Areas & Irrigation Non-Expansion Areas." Arizona Department of Water Resources. Available from http://www.azwater.gov/AzDWR/WaterManagement/AMAs/default.htm

"ADEQ offers new air quality control permit." *Arizona Range News*. August 10, 2011. Available from http://www.willcoxrangenews.com/articles/2011/08/10/news/news17.txt

American Recovery and Reinvestment Act of 2009: State Energy Sector Partnership (SESP) and Training Grants. (Arizona, p. 4) U.S. Department of Labor. Available from http://www.doleta.gov/pdf/SESP_Summaries_FINAL_02042010.pdf

Arizona Blue Ribbon Panel on Water Sustainability Final Report. Available from http://www.adwr.state.az.

us/AzDWR/waterManagement/documents/
BRP_Final_Report-12-1-10.pdf

Arizona Administrative Code. "Corporation Commission
Fixed Utilities, 14-2-1801 (renewable portfolio
standards)." Available from http://www.azsos.gov/
PUBLIC_SERVICES/Title_14/14-02.htm

Arizona Clean Fuels Yuma. Available from http://www.
arizonacleanfuels.com

Arizona Climate Change Advisory Group. *Arizona
Climate Change Action Plan.* Available from
http://www.azclimatechange.gov/download/
O40F9347.pdf

Arizona Climate Change Initiative. Available from
http://www.azclimatechange.gov/index.html

Arizona Department of Commerce. *Arizona Solar
Electric Roadmap Study.* Available from http://
www.azcommerce.com/doclib/energy/az_solar_
electric_roadmap_study_full_report.pdf

Arizona Department of Commerce. *Frequently Asked
Questions About Gasoline.* Available from http://
www.azcommerce.com/doclib/ENERGY/Revised-
FAQs053106.pdf

Arizona Department of Water Resources. *Arizona's
Water Supplies and Water Demands.* Available from
http://www.azwater.gov/AzDWR/PublicInforma-
tionOfficer/documents/supplydemand.pdf

Arizona Department of Water Resources. *Overview of the
Arizona Groundwater Management Code.* Available
from http://www.azwater.gov/AzDWR/Water-
Management/documents/Groundwater_Code.pdf

Arizona: Profile of the Green Economy. National Governors Association, Center for Best Practices. Available
from http://www.nga.org/Files/pdf/09GREEN-
PROFILEAZ.PDF

*An Assessment of the Economic Impacts of the Rosemont
Copper Projecton the Economies of the Cochise/Pima/
Santa Cruz Counties Study Area,the State of
Arizona, and the United States.* Arizona Department
of Mines and Mineral Resources. Available from
http://www.rosemontcopper.com/assets/files/
reports/ASU%20Final%20Report11-09.pdf

"Arizona's fish stocking program, native fish conservation." March 10, 2011. *Sonoran News.* Available from http://www.sonorannews.com/archives/
2011/110309/frontpage-fish.html

Blue Ribbon Panel on Water Sustainability, Arizona
Department of Water Resources. Available from
http://www.azwater.gov/AzDWR/water
Management/BlueRibbonPanel.htm

Central Arizona Project. Available from http://www.
cap-az.com/about-cap

Clean Energy Economy. Pew Charitable Trusts. Available
from http://www.pewcenteronthestates.org/
uploadedfiles/clean_economy_report_web.pdf

DuHamel, Jonathan. "Rosemont copper mine would
benefit economy and community but is buried in
bureaucracy." April 14, 2011. *Tucson Citizen.*
Available from http://tucsoncitizen.com/wryheat/
2011/04/14/rosemont-copper-mine-would-bene-
fit-economy-and-community-but-is-buried-
in-bureaucracy/

"Energy Efficiency & Renewable Energy in Schools."
Arizona Department of Commerce. Available from
http://www.azcommerce.com/Energy/EE-
Renewable??Schools.htm

"Forest Fires–Arizona 2011 (Wallow Fire)." *The New
York Times.* Available from http://topics.nytimes.
com/top/news/science/topics/forest_and_brush_-
fires/index.html?scp=1&sq=arizona%20wildfir-
e&st=cse

"Global Warming and Arizona." National Wildlife
Federation. Available from http://www.nwf.org/
Global-Warming/In-Your-State.aspx

Governor's Forest Health Advisory and Oversight
Councils. *Statewide Strategy for Restoring Arizona's
Forests: Sustainable Forests, Communities & Economies.* June 2007. Available from http://azgovernor.
gov/fhc/documents/ForestStatewideStrategy.pdf

McKinnon, Shaun. "U.S. funds, Arizona effort help
Mexico trucks pollute less." April 11, 2011.
AZCentral.com. Available from http://www.azcen-
tral.com/community/pinal/articles/2011/04/11/
20110411arizona-mexico-truck-pollution-
regulation.html

Niemuth, Nyal J. *Arizona's Metallic Resources: Trends
and Opportunities.* Arizona Department of Mines
and Mineral Resources, February 2008. Available
from http://www.admmr.state.az.us/Publications/
ofr08-26.pdf

Phoenix Green Chamber of Commerce. Available from
http://www.arizonagreenchamber.org/Phoenix

"President Obama Touts Nearly $2 Billion in New
Investments to Help Build a Clean Energy Economy." The White House, Office of the Press
Secretary. July 3, 2010. Available from http://www.
whitehouse.gov/the-press-office/weekly-address-
president-obama-touts-nearly-2-billion-new-
investments-help-build-a-

"Program Funding." Governor Brewer's Office of
Economy Recovery. Available from http://az.gov/
recovery/programs-labor-federal.html

Quinones, Manuel. "Fight Over Mining Near Grand
Canyon, Other Riders Will Return After Recess."
The New York Times. August 9, 2011. Available from

http://www.nytimes.com/gwire/2011/08/09/09greenwire-fight-over-mining-near-grand-canyon-other-ride-22281.html?scp=2&sq=arizona%%20environment&st=cse

"Renewable Energy." Arizona Department of Commerce. Available from http://www.azcommerce.com/Energy/Renewable

Rosemont Copper. Available from http://www.rosemontcopper.com/index.html

Save the Scenic Santa Ritas. Available from http://www.scenicsantaritas.org

"Solana Generating Station." Arizona Public Services. Available from http://www.aps.com/main/green/Solana/About.html

"Solar Included on All New Sun City Homes in Arizona." April 12, 2011. Yahoo! News. Available from http://finance.yahoo.com/news/Solar-Included-on-All-New-Sun-bw-3419800083.html?x=0&.v=1

"State Energy Profiles: Arizona." U. S. Energy Information Administration. Available from http://tonto.eia.doe.gov/state/state_energy_profiles.cfm?sid=AZ

State of Arizona, Office of the Governor. *Executive Order 2005-05: Implementing Renewable Energy and Energy Efficiency in New State Buildings.* http://www.governor.state.az.us/eo/2005_05.pdf

State of Arizona, Office of the Governor. *Executive Order 2010-06: Governor's Policy on Climate Change.* Available from http://www.azclimatechange.gov/download/eo-2010-06.pdf

"Sustainable Agriculture in Arizona." Arizona Cooperative Extension. Available from http://cals.arizona.edu/extension/sustainableag/index.html

U.S. Fish and Wildlife Service Species Reports. "Listings and Occurrences for Arizona." Available from http://ecos.fws.gov/tess_public/pub/stateListingAndOccurrenceIndividual.jsp?state=AZ

"Water Quality: Safe Drinking Water: Operator Certification." Arizona Department of Environmental Quality (ADEQ). Available from http://www.azdeq.gov/environ/water/dw/opcert.html

Western Climate Initiative. Available from http://www.westernclimateinitiative.org./

Arkansas

Arkansas, the Natural State, lives up to its nickname with the wealth of natural resources found throughout the state. Agriculture and aquaculture are significant industries for the state, which ranks as a leading national producer for rice, poultry, and catfish. Underground, the Fayetteville shale formation of the Arkoma basin is regarded by the oil and gas industry as the second most productive shale play in the United States. (In the oil and gas industry, the term "play" refers to a geographic region where an economic quantity of oil or gas is likely to be found.) The state also has relatively significant sources of nonfuel minerals, including bromine, silica stone, and bauxite. Currently, the state relies heavily on fossil fuels to meet its energy needs; however, recent legislation promoting energy efficiency programs and development in alternative energy sources may open the door for a greener, cleaner energy future for the state.

Climate

Arkansas has a temperate climate with temperatures that generally average between 58°F (14°C) and 65°F (18°C) throughout the year. The southern lowlands experience warmer, more humid conditions than the mountain regions. Average rainfall is between 45 and 55 inches (114 and 139 cm) annually, with the most rain found in the delta region along the eastern edge of the state.

Climate change has already had an effect on the environment of Arkansas. According to a report from the National Wildlife Federation, warmer air and water temperatures have resulted in a significant reduction in the number of waterfowl migrating to the state during the winter seasons. Since migratory bird hunting contributes more than $110 million to the state's economy each year, such a trend could have a significant economic impact within a relatively short period of time. Additionally, warmer temperatures in Arkansas could lead to dwindling forest resources, which would

have an effect on the timber and outdoor recreation industries.

According to *Arkansas Greenhouse Gas Inventory and Reference Case Projections, 1990–2025*, published by the Center for Climate Strategies, the amount of greenhouse gas emissions in Arkansas increased by 30 percent from 1990 through 2005. This rate of change was much faster than the national average of 16 percent during the same period. If greenhouse gas emissions continue unabated, levels could increase to 74 percent over 1990 levels by 2025. While the state has not yet passed specific legislation concerning climate change mitigation, the Arkansas Governor's Commission on Global Warming completed a report in 2008 that offers a comprehensive set of fifty-four policy recommendations directed toward the reduction of greenhouse gas emissions and the development of new energy strategies. The final report from the commission also recommended a target goal to reduce greenhouse gas emissions by 20 percent of 2000 levels by 2020 and by 50 percent by 2035. As of 2011, however, the state did not have an official climate change action plan.

🍂 Natural Resources, Water, and Agriculture

Natural Resources

About 54 percent of the state's land area is covered in forest, according to the 2007 Forest Survey/Forest Inventory and Analysis completed by the Arkansas Forestry Commission and reported on the Arkansas Forestry Association's Web site. However, the forest industry accounts for only 22 percent of the forest, with the majority (58 percent) under private control. The state's forests are oak-hickory (42 percent), pine (29 percent), bottomland hardwood (16 percent) and oak-pine (11 percent). In 2009, the state's forest industries contributed about $2.83 billion to the Arkansas economy.

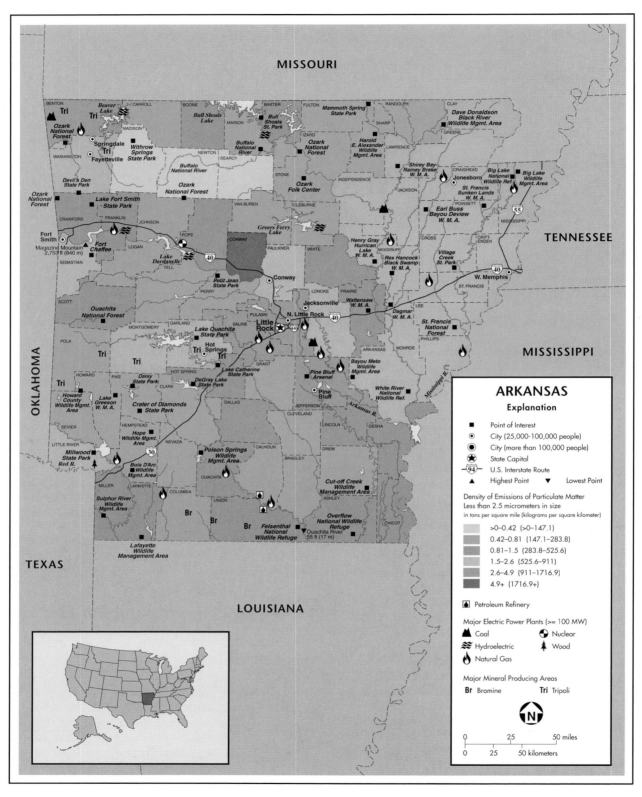

SOURCES: "County Emissions Map: Criteria Air Pollutants." *AirData*. U.S. Environmental Protection Agency. Available from http://www. epa.gov/air/data/geosel.html; *Energy Maps*. U.S. Energy Information Administration. Available from http://www.eia.gov/state; *Highest and Lowest Elevations*. U.S. Geological Survey. Available from http://egsc.usgs.gov/isb/pubs/booklets/elvadist/elvadist.html#Highest; *2007 Minerals Yearbook*. U.S. Geological Survey. Available from http://minerals.usgs.gov/minerals/pubs/state. © 2011 *Cengage Learning*.

Arkansas is home to fifty-two state parks, five national parks, and three national forests. These natural habitats are home to a wide variety of wildlife species, including beaver, black-tailed jackrabbit, bobcat, coyote, gray fox, and nine-banded armadillo. Black bear, deer, elk, squirrel, rabbit, quail, turkey, American alligator, and feral hogs are all hunted in season. The state's native reptiles include the venomous copperhead and cottonmouth snakes and the western diamondback and western pygmy rattlesnakes. In 2011, the U.S. Fish & Wildlife Service listed twenty-six animal and six plant species as threatened or endangered, including the Ozark cavefish, cave crayfish, Arkansas River shiner, and running buffalo clover.

Minerals

Arkansas is the only state in the nation that produces bromine, which is used primarily in the manufacture of other chemicals, and silica stone, which is a natural abrasive. The state is also a leading producer of bauxite, gypsum, and ranks among the top producers in the nation of tripoli (an abrasive. Crater of Diamonds State Park in Murfreesboro is the site of the only public diamond mine in the world. In 2010 the state was ranked thirty-first in nonfuel mineral production with a value of $630 million.

Rivers, Springs, and Wetlands

The primary rivers are the Mississippi, Arkansas, Red, White, Ouachita, and St. Francis. Hydroelectric plants along the White, Arkansas, and Ouachita rivers generated about 9 percent of the state's power in 1985, which was the peak. By 2006, hydroelectric power was contributing about 30.8 trillion Btus, or 7 percent, to the state's supply of electricity. The Buffalo River, designated as a national river, flows through northern Arkansas. Numerous springs are found in Arkansas, of which the best known is Mammoth Spring, with a flow rate averaging nine million gallons an hour. There are forty-seven springs at the base of Hot Springs Mountain in Hot Springs National Park.

Arkansas's largest lake is the artificial Lake Ouachita, which was formed through the construction of the Blakely Mountain Dam on the Ouachita River. Lake Chicot is the state's largest natural lake and the largest oxbow lake in North America.

About 8 percent of the state is covered in wetlands. The wetlands of the Cache-Lower White River were designated as Ramsar Wetlands of International Importance in 1989. The site includes two national wildlife refuges and three state-managed wildlife areas.

Aquaculture and Asian Carp

Arkansas is a national leader in aquaculture, with catfish and baitfish among the top products. The world's largest baitfish and goldfish farms are found in Lonoke County.

Commercial hatcheries also raise hybrid bass, Asian carp (also called Chinese carp), and a variety of sport fish, such as bluegill, crappie, and yellow perch. Freshwater prawn, marine shrimp, and crawfish are all raised and sold in the state as well. Five species of trout, four species of lampreys, and more than twenty species of perch are found in Arkansas's waters, along with dozens of other species.

The introduction of nonnative Asian carp species has become controversial, both locally and in the northern Great Lakes states. Four species of Asian carp—bighead, silver, grass, and black—were first imported into the United States in the 1960s and 1970s by Southern catfish farmers who used the fish to naturally remove algae and other matter from their farm ponds. Recent reports revealed that the U.S. Fish & Wildlife Service was also responsible for some fish imports, as the silver and bighead carp were studied for potential use in environmental cleanup projects. Bighead carp have also been farm raised for sale as a food fish that is particularly popular among Asian communities within the United States. However, some carp were accidently released into local waterways of the Mississippi River basin in the 1990s, when major flooding caused the catfish farm ponds to overflow into river areas. Since then, the carp have been steadily making their way upriver toward the Great Lakes. The Asian carp can be quite large, weighing as much as one hundred pounds. They are extremely prolific and eat large quantities of food.

The greatest concern over the migration of Asian carp species into the Great Lakes is that, once there, they will disrupt the food chain by consuming large amounts of food on which other native fish rely, thereby becoming a dominating species in a relatively short amount of time. Federal and state officials from the Mississippi River and Great Lakes states have initiated a number of measures in efforts to prevent the spread of the Asian carp to the Great Lakes. One of the most recent is the Asian Carp Prevention and Control Act (S 1421—111th Congress), which was passed by the U.S. Congress and was signed into law on December 14, 2010. The law adds the bighead carp species of Asian carp to the list of injurious species that are prohibited from being imported or transported across state lines under the Lacey Act. The final rule was published in March 2011. The new law has affected Arkansas fish farmers, who are now prohibited from selling their bighead fish crops outside of the state. (The black and silver carp had been listed as injurious species previously under the Lacey Act in 2007.)

Another invasive species, the northern snakehead fish has become yet another threat to the Mississippi River basin. The northern snakehead has been spreading through the waterways of Arkansas, and has been found in states as far away as California. What makes the snakehead difficult to control is the fact that they are able to survive out of water for up to several days if they stay

Arkansas State Profile

Physical Characteristics

Land area	52,030 square miles (134,757 sq km)
Inland water area	1,149 square miles (2,976 sq km)
Coastal area	NA
Highest point	Magazine Mountain 2,753 feet (839 m)
National Forest System lands (2010)	2.6 million acres (1.0 million ha)
State parks (2011)	52

Energy Statistics

Total energy production (2009)	760 trillion Btu
State ranking in total energy production (2009)	19
Renewable energy net generation total (2009)	5.8 million megawatt hours
Hydroelectric energy generation (2009)	4.2 million megawatt hours
Biomass energy generation (2009)	57,000 megawatt hours
Wind energy generation (2009)	NA
Wood and derived fuel energy generation (2009)	1.5 million megawatt hours
Crude oil reserves (2009)	28.0 million barrels (4.5 million cu m)
Natural gas reserves (2009)	10,869 billion cubic feet (307.8 billion cu m)
Natural gas liquids (2008)	2 million barrels (300,000 cu m)

Pollution Statistics

Carbon output (2005)	62.4 million tons of CO_2 (56.6 million t)
Superfund sites (2008)	8
Particulate matter (less than 2.5 micrometers) emissions (2002)	11,344 tons per year (10,291 t/yr)
Toxic chemical releases (2009)	34.0 million pounds (15.4 million kg)
Generated hazardous waste (2009)	273,200 tons (247,800 t)

SOURCES: AirData. U.S. Environmental Protection Agency. Available from http://www.epa.gov/air/data; *Energy Maps, Facts, and Data of the U.S. States.* U.S. Energy Information Administration. Available from http://www.eia.gov/state; *The 2012 Statistical Abstract.* U.S. Census Bureau. Available from http://www.census.gov/compendia/statab; *United States Energy Usage.* eRedux. Available from http://www.eredux.net/states.

© 2011 Cengage Learning.

moist; they are able to wiggle and flop for short distances to new bodies of water. The snakehead eats other fish and has few predators, and could therefore wipe out native species. The discovery of snakeheads in Arkansas led to a 2009 operation to attempt to eradicate the fish. Biologists used the fish poison rotenone on 400 miles (644 km) of local waterways. While they removed more than 700 snakeheads during that operation, they have since found more than 50 specimens in areas that they previously poisoned. Officials stated that the examples of the snakehead and Asian carp call for stricter animal control laws in the United States. Thus far, a draft national control and management plan for the northern snakehead has been drawn up at the request of Congress, which recommends compiling research on snakeheads to better predict where they might become established; making anti-invasive species laws consistent and clear and establishing tough penalties; urging states to develop rapid response plans and containment procedures; evaluating eradication methods; and creating a National Northern Snakehead Web site to disseminate information.

Agriculture

Agriculture is the state's leading industry, accounting for about 12 percent of gross domestic product. Arkansas is ranked as first in the nation for the production of rice and second for production of poultry and eggs. The state has generally ranked within the top five for production of cotton, turkeys, and sweet potatoes.

While the Arkansas State Plant Board provides assistance in some activities associated with organic farming, the state does not have its own organic certification program. Organic certification is available through Indiana Certified Organic, the Oklahoma Department of Agriculture, and Oregon Tilth.

The 2011 Mississippi River floods had a significant impact on the state's agricultural sector. A total of sixty-three counties were declared disaster areas as a result of the flooding, with more than one million acres (0.4 million ha) of cropland affected. According to the Arkansas Farm Board, damages were expected to top $500 million, not including repair to infrastructure, farm equipment, loss of grain in storage, or repairs to farmland. The loss in rice production alone was expected to result in damages of $300 million. Cotton and forage crops also suffered heavy losses, with preliminary damage estimates at $66 million and $37 million respectively.

⚜ Energy

Oil and Natural Gas

Small oil reserves are found in the Arkoma basin of the western region and in the Gulf Coastal Plain of the south. While the state has two oil refineries, additional petroleum products are supplied from Texas and Louisiana. Arkansas is one of the few states that allow the statewide use of conventional gasoline, rather than a reformulated blend.

Arkansas has substantial natural gas reserves located in the Arkoma basin and the Gulf Coastal Plain. Along with conventional production, some natural gas has been produced from coal bed methane deposits. Since the early 2000s, the Fayetteville shale formation, also in the Arkoma basin, has become the second most productive shale play in the United States. Total natural gas production in Arkansas accounts for about 1 percent of the total U.S. annual production. The state's industrial sector is the largest consumer of natural gas. About 49 percent of all households rely on natural gas for home heating.

The Arkansas pipeline (shown is the 2008 groundbreaking ceremony) moves natural gas from the Fayetteville Shale formation to states in the Northeast, Southeast and upper Midwest.
© AP Images/Mike Wintroath

Fracking and the Guy-Greenbrier Earthquake Swarm

In early 2011, oil and gas companies using the hydraulic fracturing method, commonly referred to as fracking, were brought under scrutiny by the Arkansas Oil & Gas Commission as some experts claimed there was a connection between drilling activities and the 2010–2011 Guy-Greenbrier earthquake swarm. In September–October 2010 through March 2011, nearly 800 earthquakes were recorded in this area of north-central Arkansas. The strongest quake, measured at 4.7 magnitude, occurred on February 27, 2011, near the town of Greenbrier. It was followed by dozens of smaller aftershocks, including one at 3.8 magnitude and another at 3.4 magnitude.

A number of media sources published reports linking the swarm to fracking operations, or more specifically, the disposal of fracking wastewater in injection wells. In the fracking process, large amounts of water, sand, and chemicals are pumped into the underground shale at extremely high pressure in order to fracture the rocks below, thereby releasing the natural gas within. The resulting water is then pumped back up to the surface. One method of disposal is to create an injection well, which essentially involves injecting the wastewater back into an area of rocky ground. Some experts have said that the wastewater can lubricate the surrounding rock, creating potential for an earthquake. They also note that there seems to have been an increase in seismic activity within the Guy-Greenbrier area since injection wells were first employed in April 2009.

Other experts have pointed out that the increase in seismic activity could very well be attributed to other natural causes. Earthquake swarms are not new to northern Arkansas. The Enola area experienced earthquake swarms in 1982 (with the strongest at 4.5 magnitude) and in 2001 (with the strongest at 4.4). Most earthquakes throughout the northern regions are micro-quakes, rated at very low magnitudes and causing no structural damages to buildings.

Following the February 2011 quake, the Arkansas Oil & Gas Commission (AOGC) imposed an emergency moratorium on the drilling of new injection wells in the area while the commission held hearings on the matter. The initial moratorium extended through July 2011 as hearings continued. According to a public announcement released in March 2011, the Arkansas Geological Survey (AGS) and the AOGC found no correlation between seismic activity and the drilling of injection or production wells in the area. However, at least one researcher from the Center for Earthquake Research and Information (CERI) at the University of Memphis has noted concern over the number of quakes that have occurred within close proximity to the disposal injection wells. CERI and AGS have been working together to deploy a local seismic array in the Greenbrier-Enola areas to monitor the situation.

Ultimately, the Arkansas Oil and Gas Commission voted to ban wells for the disposal of natural gas drilling fluids in July 2011. Officials stated the ban is necessary to avoid a possible catastrophe. Four disposal wells were closed after the vote, and the drilling of new wells was banned over a 1,150-square-mile (2,978-sq-km) segment of the shale in central Arkansas north of Conway. The drilling of new natural gas wells would remain unaffected; however, the method of fluid disposal will be altered, with companies having to truck the fluids to injection wells elsewhere in Arkansas or in Oklahoma or Texas.

A series of class action lawsuits were also filed against local drilling companies as a result of the quakes. In May 2011, three families filed suit against six gas companies over claims that drilling activities have polluted water wells near their homes with natural gas. The same month, a lawyer from the group Stop Arkansas Fracking filed a class action suit against BHP Billiton Petroleum and Clarita Operating, alleging that the injection wells were, in fact, the cause of the earthquakes, and that the quakes

In early 2011, oil and gas companies using the hydraulic fracturing method, commonly referred to as fracking, were brought under scrutiny. © *Cernan Elias/Alamy*

resulted in property damage, loss of fair market value in real estate, and emotional distress for his clients.

Electricity

Coal-fired plants generated about 45.9 percent of the state's supply of electricity in 2007, with coal supplies imported from Wyoming. Another 29.1 percent of the electric supply is generated by the Arkansas Nuclear One Plant in Russellville and 11.4 percent is produced by natural gas-fired plants. About 33 percent of all households rely on electricity as a source for home heating.

Renewables

Hydroelectric power is Arkansas's primary renewable energy source, with hydroelectric plants along the White, Arkansas, and Ouachita rivers generating about 7.3 percent of the state's supply of electricity.

The state has not adopted an official renewable portfolio standard. However, in 2009 the state legislature created the Arkansas Alternative Energy Commission (Act 1301) with a mandate to study the needs and impacts of various forms of alternative energy on the economic future of the state. The commission, with members representing utility companies, consumers, and the state, will be studying alternatives such as bioenergy (biomass), solar, wind, and more to determine ways in which the state might promote and develop renewable energy sources.

❧ Green Business, Green Building, Green Jobs

Green Business

Clean energy and energy efficiency projects have created a strong foundation for the growth of the green economy

in Arkansas, and the potential for further development in these sectors is just as strong. According to a report from The Pew Charitable Trusts, jobs in the state's clean economy increased at more than twice the rate of total jobs between 1998 and 2007. The Arkansas Alternative Fuels Development Act of 2007 (Act 873) represents one major initiative designed to further promote the growth and development of clean energy technologies. Through the act, grant incentives are provided for producers, distributers, and processors of alternative fuel and feedstocks.

In a 2010 study from Georgia Institute of Technology and Duke University entitled *Energy Efficiency in the South*, it was estimated that new developments in energy efficiency could translate into 8,700 new jobs for Arkansas by 2020, increasing to 11,700 by 2030.

Moving Forward with Green Job Training

In February 2010, the state received a grant of $7.4 million from the U.S. Department of Energy to launch three new green job training centers in the state. The centers will be located at NorthWest Arkansas Community College, the North Little Rock campus of Pulaski Technical College, and the Stuttgart campus of Phillips Community College of the University of Arkansas. However, part of the funding will be used to develop mobile training units to be dispatched to other community colleges throughout the state. From 2010 through 2013, the state hopes to offer a minimum of sixty courses through the centers to benefit at least six hundred workers. Additionally, the newly created Arkansas Energy Sector Partnership received a $4.8 million grant from the American Recovery and Reinvestment Act Funds to provide green jobs training for workers in the energy efficiency assessments, renewable electric power, and energy efficient building, construction, and retrofitting. Courses will be offered through community colleges and other training centers from 2010 through 2013. Recruiters will make a particular effort to attract high school dropouts, unemployed workers, former prison inmates, and other at-risk individuals.

Green Building: Legislation for a Strong Foundation

The state government has issued several forms of legislation to promote greater energy efficiency and sustainable practices in public buildings. The Arkansas Energy and Natural Resources Conservation Act of 2005 encouraged state agencies and institutes of higher education to seek certification from the U.S. Green Building Council Leadership in Energy and Environmental Design (LEED) program or the Green Globes program in public building projects. Under Title 22 of the Arkansas Code of 1987, additional state-specific provisions apply for those seeking such certification in that credits are given for projects that employ practices such as carbon sequestering and the use of bio-based materials from certified sources.

In 2009, the governor issued an executive order (EO 09-07) directing all executive branch agencies to submit strategic energy plans that incorporate energy saving measures for the agency. These plans went into effect in October 2009. Other state agencies were also encouraged to develop similar strategic energy plans. Also in 2009, the state legislature approved Act 1494, which amended Title 22 to require the Arkansas Energy Office to develop a plan for reducing energy use in all existing state buildings by 20 percent by 2014 and by 30 percent by 2017. Within the general assembly, the Legislative Task Force on Sustainable Building Design and Practices (Act 1336 2009) works to develop goals and strategies to promote energy efficiency in state buildings.

Poultry Waste Contamination of the Illinois River: The Legal Case of *Oklahoma v. Tyson Foods, Inc. et al*

While eleven Arkansas poultry companies and the state of Oklahoma await the final decision of U.S. District Court Judge Gregory K. Frizzell concerning the matter of poultry litter pollution in the Illinois River, it seems as if local farmers and landowners may have already solved much of the problem out of court.

The case of the *Attorney General of the State of Oklahoma et al v. Tyson Foods, Inc. et al* was filed in 2005 through the efforts of Oklahoma's attorney general, Drew Edmondson. In the suit, Edmondson alleged that the improper use of poultry litter as a fertilizer on farms throughout the Illinois River watershed has led to contamination of the Illinois River (shared by Arkansas and Oklahoma) and Lake Tenkiller in Oklahoma. Specifically, high levels of phosphorus were noted along the river by sampling and through the increased presence of algae bloom, which leaves the water a greenish color and can reduce oxygen levels in the water to a point that fish cannot survive. The suit places fault on eleven major poultry producing companies in Arkansas, including Tyson Poultry and Cal-Maine Farms, since these companies are responsible for the production of hundreds of thousands of tons of poultry waste each year. The court has been asked to hold these companies responsible for cleanup efforts and for tighter regulations on the use of poultry litter, in part by defining it as solid waste.

Poultry litter is a mixture of manure from chickens and turkeys and other materials, such as bedding or feathers. Farmers in both Arkansas and Oklahoma use this litter as a low cost, high quality fertilizer for crops and pastures. In handling the litter, poultry growers in both states are required to adhere to detailed animal waste management plans and farmers must follow specific regulations concerning the use of fertilizers of any type in watershed areas. Such regulations generally prohibit the use of poultry litter on erodible soil areas or within about 300 feet (91 m) of streams.

The case was heard before the Oklahoma Northern District Court beginning in September 2009, with closing arguments in February 2010. As of 2011, Judge Gregory K. Frizzell had not issued a final ruling in the case.

The case has raised many questions and concerns over the issue, with the most immediate being whether or not the poultry companies are really the responsible parties. Attorneys for the poultry companies have argued that the poultry farmers with whom the companies have contracts are the owners of the litter and are therefore responsible for its use and/or disposal. They have also argued that these farmers have generally complied with state-imposed standards and regulations concerning the use of the litter as fertilizer. Therefore, if these standards have proven to be too lenient, it is the state's responsibility to impose stricter standards, rather than expecting poultry companies to regulate the use of litter or bear the responsibility for any alleged misuse.

During the course of the trial, the court dismissed the claim that poultry litter should be considered as hazardous waste or solid waste. This was a major relief for farmers who use the manure for fertilizer. If the waste had been defined as hazardous, local farmers would have lost more than just an inexpensive soil supplement. The cost to dispose of hazardous waste is much higher, since there are tighter regulations. Many poultry farmers would find themselves out of business if they had to meet the higher costs of waste disposal.

As the closing arguments began in February 2010, the state of Oklahoma filed an amendment to the suit asking the court to consider an application limit of 65 pounds (29 kg) of poultry litter per acre (0.4 ha). The possibility of such a limit has been an additional cause of concern for farmers, since many claim that this amount would be far too low to be effective. If poultry litter is banned or limited to such a small amount, farmers could be forced to rely on far more expensive commercial fertilizers. The application of poultry litter costs about $26 per ton. Application of commercial fertilizers can cost as much as $300 per ton.

While the court deliberates and the litigants wait, it seems as if the farmers and state farm agencies have already taken effective actions to address the heart of the problem, mainly the higher levels of phosphorous found in the Illinois River. In September 2010, an Associated Press report noted that the level of phosphorous released into the river from wastewater treatment plants had dropped from 125,000 pounds (57 kg) in 2003 to 68,300 pounds (31 kg) in 2007. Just as important, local boaters and campers claim to be enjoying a clean, clear river. Some claim that the improvements are a direct result of the lawsuit, since the publicity for the suit did much to raise awareness of the problem and forced state agencies to act. However, some reports indicate that the farmers themselves have been concerned about the situation for a number of years, and with the help of state agencies, have steadily taken measures to reduce the level of contaminants to the watershed, while continuing to employ responsible practices in the use of poultry litter for fertilizer. In any case, both the Illinois River and Lake Tenkiller appear to be improving, even without the direct involvement of federal courts.

BIBLIOGRAPHY

Books

Compton, Neil. *The Battle for the Buffalo River: The Story of America's First National River.* Jonesboro, AR: Ozark Society Foundation, 2010.

Johnson, Ben F. *Arkansas in Modern America, 1930–1999.* Fayetteville, AR: University of Arkansas Press, 2000.

McNeilly, Donald P. *The Old South Frontier: Cotton Plantations and the Formation of Arkansas Society, 1819–1861.* Fayetteville, AR: University of Arkansas Press, 2000.

Melosi, Artin, ed. *Environment, vol. 8 of The New Encyclopedia of Southern Culture.* Chapel Hill, NC: University of North Carolina Press, 2007.

Smith, Kenneth L. *Buffalo River Handbook.* Jonesboro, AR: Ozark Society Foundation, 2004.

Steward, Dana F., ed. *A Rough Sort of Beauty: Reflections on the Natural Heritage of Arkansas.* Fayetteville, AR: University of Arkansas Press, 2002.

Sutton, Keith B., ed. *Arkansas Wildlife: A History.* Fayetteville, AR: University of Arkansas Press, 1998.

Trauth, Joy, and Aldemaro Romero, eds. *Adventures in the Wild: Tales from Biologists of the Natural State.* Fayetteville, AR: University of Arkansas Press, 2008.

Whayne, Jeannie. Delta Empire: *Lee Wilson and the Transformation of Agriculture in the New South.* Louisiana State University Press, 2011.

White, Mel, Tria Giovan, and Jim Bones. *The Smithsonian Guides to Natural America: The South Central States–Texas, Oklahoma, Arkansas, Louisiana, Mississippi.* Washington, DC: Smithsonian Books, 1996.

Web Sites

Act 873 (2007): Arkansas Alternative Fuels Development Act of 2007. Arkansas General Assembly. Available from http://www.arkleg.state.ar.us/assembly/2007/R/Acts/Act873.pdf

Act 1301 (2009): An Act to Create the Arkansas Alternative Energy Commission. Arkansas General Assembly. Available from http://green.arkansas.gov/Documents/Act1301.pdf

Act 1336 (2009): An Act to Extend the Legislative Task Force on Sustainable Building Design and Practices. Arkansas General Assembly. Available from http://green.arkansas.gov/Documents/Act1336.pdf

Act 1494 (2009): An Act to Promote the Conservation of Energy and Natural Resources in Buildings Owned by Public Agencies and Institutions of Higher Education. Arkansas General Assembly. Available from http://green.arkansas.gov/Documents/Act1494.pdf

Arkansas Agriculture Department. Available from http://aad.arkansas.gov/Pages/default.aspx

Arkansas Alternative Energy Commission. Available from http://www.aaec.arkansas.gov/Pages/default.aspx

Arkansas Code of 1987: Title 22—Public Property. State of Arkansas. Available from http://www.arkleg.state.ar.us/bureau/Publications/Arkansas%20Code/Title%2022.pdf

Arkansas Energy and Natural Resources Conservation Act. Arkansas General Assembly. Available from http://www.arkansas.gov/lobbyist/arliab/src/public/bills/2005/html/HB2445.html

"Arkansas Energy Facts." Institute for Energy Research. Available from http://www.instituteforenergyresearch.org/state-regs/pdf/Arkansas.pdf

Arkansas Forestry Association. Available from http://arkforests.org/index.html

Arkansas Game and Fish Commission. Available from http://www.agfc.com/Pages/default.aspx

Arkansas Geological Survey. Available from http://www.geology.arkansas.gov/geohazards/earthquakes.htm

Arkansas Governor's Commission on Global Warming: Final Report. Available from http://www.arclimatechange.us/ewebeditpro/items/O94F20338.pdf

Arkansas Greenhouse Gas Inventory and Reference Case Projections, 1990–2025. Center for Climate Strategies. Available from http://www.arclimatechange.us/ewebeditpro/items/O94F20076.pdf

Arkansas Grown. Available at http://www.arkansasgrown.org/Pages/default.aspx

Arkansas Oil & Gas Commission. Available from http://www.aogc.state.ar.us

Arkansas Parks. Available from http://www.arkansas.com/state-federal-parks

Arkansas Statewide Forest Resource Assessment. Available from http://www.arkansasforestry.org/ArkansasForestryCommAssessment-FINAL.pdf

Arkansas 2007 Minerals Yearbook. United States Geological Survey. Available from http://minerals.usgs.gov/minerals/pubs/state/2007/myb2-2007-ar.pdf

ARRA Green Jobs Training: Arkansas Energy Sector Partnership and Training Grant. Available from http://winrockusprograms.org/public/files/pdfs/Arkansas-Energy-Sector-Partnership-Grant.pdf

Associated Press. "Illinois river quality appears to improve after lawsuit." NewsOK. September 28, 2010. Available from http://newsok.com/illinois-river-quality-rises-as-federal-suit-continues/article/3499127

"Bighead Carp Added to Federal List of Injurious Wildlife." U.S. Fish & Wildlife Service. March 21, 2011. Available from http://www.fws.gov/midwest/news/release.cfm?rid=369

"The Clean Energy Economy: Arkansas." The Pew Charitable Trusts. Available from http://www.pewcenteronthestates.org/uploadedFiles/wwwpewcenteronthestatesorg/Fact_Sheets/Clean_Economy_Factsheet_Arkansas.pdf

Descant, Skip. "Northwest Arkansas Lands Green Jobs Training Center." *Northwest Arkansas Times.* February 27, 2010. Available from http://nwa-working-families.blogspot.com/2010/02/nwa-green-jobs-training-center.html

Electric Power and Renewable Energy in Arkansas. U.S. Department of Energy, Energy Efficiency & Renewable Energy. http://apps1.eere.energy.gov/states/electricity.cfm?state=AR#fuel

Energy Efficient in the South: State Profiles of Energy Efficiency Opportunities in the South—Arkansas. Available from http://www.seealliance.org/se_efficiency_study/arkansas_efficiency_in_the_south.pdf

EO 09-07: To Encourage the Reduction of Energy Consumption by State Agencies and the Environmental Impact of State Agency Operations. Office of the Governor, State of Arkansas. Available from http://governor.arkansas.gov/newsroom/files/eo_0907.pdf

"Fayetteville Shale Natural Gas." University of Arkansas. Available from http://lingo.cast.uark.edu/LINGOPUBLIC/index.htm

"A Few Interesting Facts about Arkansas." Arkansas: The Natural State. http://www.arkansas.com/things-to-do/history-heritage/facts.aspx

"Flooding's cost to Arkansas agriculture could top $500 million." Arkansas Farm Bureau. May 10, 2011. Available from http://www.arfb.com/news_information/press_releases/2011/051011.aspx

Flynn, Dan. "Poultry Litter Limits Offered by OK." *Food Safety News.* Available from http://www.foodsafetynews.com/2010/02/poultry-litter-limits-offered-by-ok

"Global Warming and Arkansas." National Wildlife Federation. Available from http://www.nwf.org/Global-Warming/~/media/PDFs/Global%20Warming/Global%20Warming%20State%20Fact%20Sheets/Arkansas.ashx

"Illinois River quality appears to improve after lawsuit." Associated Press. Available from http://newsok.com/illinois-river-quality-rises-as-federal-suit-continues/article/3499127

Johnson, Katherine. "Class action lawsuits filed against six natural gas companies." Fox 16 News. May 18, 2011. Available from http://www.fox16.com/news/local/story/Class-action-lawsuits-filed-against-six-natual/qsuFUKeZq0aKHO6iPN-WFA.cspx

Johnson, Katherine. "Natural gas companies face another lawsuit." Fox 16 News. May 20, 2011. Available from http://www.fox16.com/news/story/Natural-gas-companies-face-another-lawsuit/W9jnxdKqE0CvFWXRFM0y3g.cspx

Lam, Tina. "Snakeheads can move on land, eat other fish—and could be another threat to Great Lakes." *Detroit Free Press.* August 6, 2011. Available from http://www.freep.com/article/20110807/NEWS05/108070504/Snakeheads-can-move-land-eat-other-fish-could-another-threat-Great-Lakes

Liu, Alec & Jeremy A. Kaplan. "Earthquakes in Arkansas May Be Man-Made Experts Warn." Fox News. March 1, 2011. Available from http://www.foxnews.com/scitech/2011/03/01/fracking-earthquakes-arkansas-man-experts-warn

Martin, Linda. "Update on the poultry litigation in Oklahoma." American College of Environmental Lawyers. February 26, 2010. Available from http://www.acoel.org/2010/02/articles/water/update-on-the-poultry-litigation-in-oklahoma-poultry-litter-is-not-a-solid-waste-under-rcra

Maxwell, Sally. "The Good, the Bad, and the Chicken Litter." *Sequoyah Country Times.* May 19, 2006. Available from http://www.sequoyahcountytimes.com/view/full_story/688130/article-The-Good–The-Bad–And-The-Chicken-Litter

National Control and Management Plan for the Northern Snakehead. U.S. Fish & Wildlife Service. Available from http://www.fws.gov/northeast/

marylandfisheries/reports/National%20Manage-
ment%20Plan%20for%20the%20Northern%20
Snakehead.pdf

"Natural Gas: Arkansas Commission Votes To Shut
Down Wells." The Huffington Post. July 27, 2011.
Available from http://www.huffingtonpost.com/
2011/07/27/natural-gas-arkansas-commission-
shut-down-wells_n_911541.html

"Poster of 2010–2011 Arkansas Earthquake Swarm."
United States Geological Survey. Available from
http://earthquake.usgs.gov/earthquakes/
eqarchives/poster/2011/20110228.php

"State Energy Profiles: Arkansas." U.S. Energy Information Administration. Available from http://
tonto.eia.doe.gov/state/state_energy_profiles.cfm?
sid=AR

Stop Arkansas Fracking. Available from http://www.
stoparkansasfracking.org

Svoboda, Sandra. "Fishing for truth: Did government
agencies help create the Asian carp crisis?" *Metro
Times*. April 19, 2010. Available from http://www.
mlive.com/news/detroit/index.ssf/2010/04/
fishing_for_truth_did_governme.html

California

While the Golden State may be best known as a land of sun, sand, and man-made glitz and glamour, the third-largest state in the union is a wonder of natural extremes. From the forests of the snow-capped Sierra Nevada to the scorching hot desert landscapes of Death Valley, the state is home to amazingly diverse plants and wildlife, as well as having the largest population of humans in the nation. However, the state faces many challenges in maintaining a sustainable environment for all its inhabitants. Water is scarce in many regions, making the maintenance of an adequate water supply even more difficult in the summer drought seasons. Furthermore, air pollution and greenhouse gas emissions in urban areas are notoriously high, a fact that has prompted some of the nation's most aggressive legislative measures towards emissions reduction and adaptation to climate change. The search for alternative fuel sources, including solar and biofuel energy, is well underway, but continued progress may be hampered by controversies surrounding the protection of natural landscapes and the fear that too much change too soon will lead to a greater slump in an already strained economy.

Climate

Average temperatures and rainfall throughout the state can vary dramatically from one region to another, with heavy winter snowfalls in the Sierra Nevada and extreme desert heat in the Imperial Valley. The highest recorded temperature in the United States was registered at Death Valley on July 10, 1913, when the summer heat reached 134°F (57°C). Between the extremes, most of the state experiences two general seasons: long, dry summers and mild, rainy winters. Summer droughts are common in many areas of the state, with several areas prone to destructive and deadly wildfires. Tropical rainstorms along the coast often occur during the winter months.

The California Climate Adaption Strategy

Since 2008, the California Climate Change Center, an agency of the California Energy Commission, has conducted a number of studies concerning the impact of climate change on the state. These studies indicate that sea levels along the California coastline have risen by nearly 8 inches (20 cm) in the past century. Projections indicate a potential rise of about 16 inches (41 cm) above 2000 levels by 2050 and between 3.3 feet (1 m) and 4.75 feet (1.4 m) above 2000 levels by 2100. Such a change could put 480,000 people at risk and threaten $100 billion in property and infrastructure. The rise would cause significant saltwater contamination to the state's water supply. Likewise, rising temperatures can affect the water supply as sources such as the Sierra snowpack melt at accelerated rates. The reports also indicate that the state's timber industry could decline anywhere between 4.9 percent and 8.5 percent in value by 2100 as climate change makes forests more vulnerable to destruction by fires and pests.

The government of California has taken several bold measures in facing the challenges of climate change. In 2006, Governor Arnold Schwarzenegger signed the Global Warming Solutions Act (AB 32), which calls for the reduction of greenhouse gasses to 1990 levels by the year 2020, representing an overall reduction of about 30 percent from current projections. Some of the adopted reduction measures went into effect by the end of 2010, with the full set of measures set to be implemented in 2012. In 2008, the governor called for the development of a more comprehensive adaptation strategy to prepare for the expected and unexpected impact of climate change on the state (Executive Order S-13-08). The result was the *2009 California Climate Adaptation Strategy*, which is meant to serve as a comprehensive guide for legislators as they develop the necessary policies to protect the environment and natural resources of the state in the years to come.

California air pollution and greenhouse gas emissions in urban areas, such as Los Angeles, are notoriously high, which has prompted some of the nation's most aggressive legislative measures towards emissions reduction and adaptation to climate change. © *Jens Peermann/ShutterStock.com*

🌿 Natural Resources, Water, and Agriculture

National Forests and Valuable Timber

California has a long history of conservation efforts in wilderness areas. As a result, nearly half of the state's forests—which cover about 40 percent of the total land area of the state—are protected at the state or national level. These include the popular Sequoia and Yosemite National Parks, which were formed in part through the efforts the Sierra Club, founded in California in 1892 by naturalist John Muir. While the protected giant sequoias—some of which are believed to be more than 3,000 years old—are a major attraction for park visitors, softwoods such as fir, pine, and cedar attribute to a thriving commercial lumber industry. The state's forest resources may also serve as a valuable source for biofuel stock, as some reports estimate that biofuels from wood could generate up to 4 percent of the state's total supply of electricity.

The state's forests are also home to an amazing variety of animals, including Columbian black-tailed deer, Roosevelt elk, gray fox, bobcat, and black bear.

Coyote, mountain lion, and mule deer can be found in several areas of the state. Bighorn sheep can be spotted in some of the mountain regions, while the kangaroo rat, desert tortoise, roadrunner, and numerous species of reptiles can be found in the desert regions. Garter snakes, rattlesnakes, and numerous species of salamander make their homes in the state as well. More than 600 species of birds can be found in California, including Anna's hummingbird and red-winged blackbird, along with the endangered California condor. The U.S. Fish and Wildlife service lists 128 animal and 183 plant species as either threatened or endangered. The bald eagle was removed from the list of endangered species in 2007.

With 278 parks, California has the largest state park system in the nation. An $11 million cut in the annual funding for parks resulted in the May 13, 2011, announcement by the Department of Parks and Recreation that up to 70 of the state's parks would be closed by July 2012. In identifying which parks should be designated for closure, Parks and Recreation sought to minimize the effect on attendance and revenue. According to the Department's press release, the closures will result in an estimated 8 percent reduction in attendance and a 6 percent reduction in revenue.

The new Van Sickle CA/NV Bi-State Park was opened in July 2011, although budget stresses in both states had threatened to delay the official opening. Located on the California-Nevada boundary in South Lake Tahoe, it is the only bi-state park in the United States with a single entrance that provides access to both sides of the state line. The park contains land donated to the Nevada Division of State Parks by Jack Van Sickle in 1988 and additional land purchased by the California Tahoe Conservancy.

Rich in Gold and Gravel

The state that was born on the heels of the Gold Rush of 1849 continues to produce significant quantities of the precious metal. In fact, the Golden State has seen a dramatic increase in gold production with the reopening of the Mesquite Mine in 2008 and of the Briggs Gold Mine in 2009. Silver is produced in the state as a byproduct of gold production. The production of nonfuel industrial minerals is just as important to the economy as production in precious metals, as the state is ranked first in the production of construction sand and gravel, diatomite, pumice, and pumicite. California is the only state that produces boron and rare earth minerals. The state was ranked sixth in the nation for nonfuel mineral production in 2010 with a value of $2.7 billion.

Water

The longest rivers in the state, the Sacramento and San Joaquin, are both fed by snowmelt from the Sierra Nevada. There are several smaller mountain rivers and

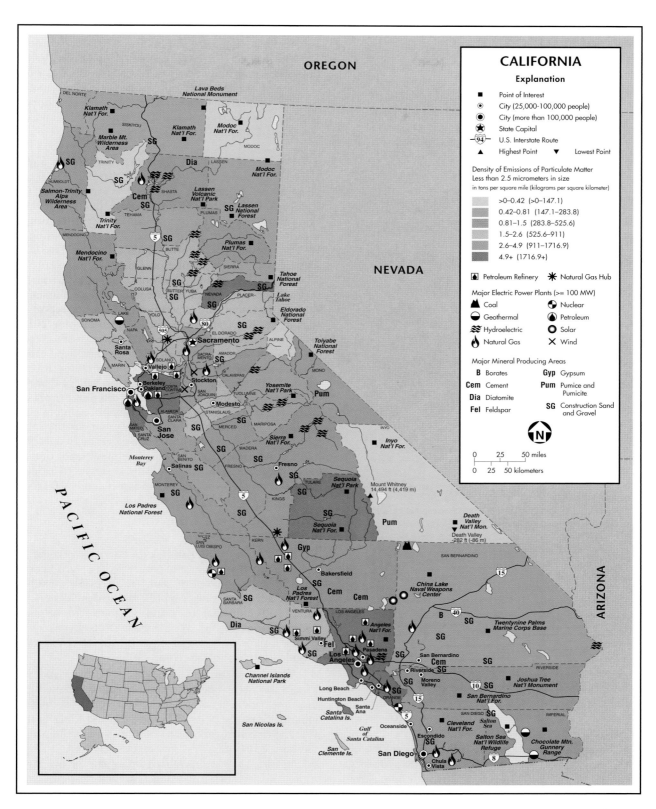

SOURCES: "County Emissions Map: Criteria Air Pollutants." *AirData*. U.S. Environmental Protection Agency. Available from http://www.epa.gov/air/data/geosel.html; *Energy Maps*. U.S. Energy Information Administration. Available from http://www.eia.gov/state; *Highest and Lowest Elevations*. U.S. Geological Survey. Available from http://egsc.usgs.gov/isb/pubs/booklets/elvadist/elvadist.html#Highest; *2007 Minerals Yearbook*. U.S. Geological Survey. Available from http://minerals.usgs.gov/minerals/pubs/state. © 2011 Cengage Learning.

California State Profile

Physical Characteristics

Land area	155,766 square miles (403,432 sq km)
Inland water area	2,842 square miles (7,361 sq km)
Coastal area	222 square miles (357 sq km)
Highest point	Mount Whitney 14,494 feet (4,418 m)
National Forest System lands (2010)	20.8 million acres (8.4 million ha)
State parks (2011)	270

Energy Statistics

Total energy production (2009)	2,800 trillion Btu
State ranking in total energy production (2009)	7
Renewable energy net generation total (2009)	53.4 million megawatt hours
Hydroelectric energy generation (2009)	27.8 million megawatt hours
Biomass energy generation (2009)	2.5 million megawatt hours
Wind energy generation (2009)	5.8 million megawatt hours
Wood and derived fuel energy generation (2009)	3.7 million megawatt hours
Crude oil reserves (2009)	2.8 billion barrels (450.7 million cu m)
Natural gas reserves (2009)	2.7 trillion cubic feet (78.5 billion cu m)
Natural gas liquids (2008)	129.0 million barrels (20.5 million cu m)

Pollution Statistics

Carbon output (2005)	389.0 million tons of CO_2 (352.8 million t)
Superfund sites (2008)	94
Particulate matter (less than 2.5 micrometers) emissions (2002)	19,118 tons per year (17,343 t/yr)
Toxic chemical releases (2009)	36.7 million pounds (16.6 million kg)
Generated hazardous waste (2009)	699,600 tons (634,700 t)

SOURCES: AirData. U.S. Environmental Protection Agency. Available from http://www.epa.gov/air/data; *Energy Maps, Facts, and Data of the U.S. States.* U.S. Energy Information Administration. Available from http://www.eia.gov/state; *The 2012 Statistical Abstract.* U.S. Census Bureau. Available from http://www.census.gov/compendia/statab; *United States Energy Usage.* eRedux. Available from http://www.eredux.net/states.

© 2011 Cengage Learning.

streams, many of which are popular trout fishing spots. Many of the rivers in the southern part of the state are seasonal, filling up during the spring floods and evaporating under the summer sun.

The largest lake in the state is the saline sink known as the Salton Sea. Officially designated as a drainage reservoir, nearly 90 percent of inflow comes from agricultural runoff from the Imperial, Coachella, and Mexicali Valleys. The unique mixture of nutrients provided by this runoff supports an amazing variety of fish and bird life. Lake Tahoe in the Sierra Nevada is the largest freshwater alpine lake in North America.

California is home to five Ramsar Wetlands of International Importance: Bolinas Lagoon, Tomales Bay, the Grassland Ecological Area in the Central Valley of the San Joaquin River basin, the Laguna de Santa Rosa Wetland Complex, and the Tijuana River National Estuarine Research Reserve. These sites serve as homes to numerous species of migratory and native birds and are rich in plant species.

Diverting Water for Agribusiness: Is it Safe?

Officials announced in August 2011 that they had taken steps toward obtaining a sustainable water supply for California and the Sacramento–San Joaquin River Delta ecosystem. The water supply would be obtained through a peripheral canal to export water to corporate agribusiness and southern California water agencies. The U.S. Department of the Interior, U.S. Department of Commerce, and the California Natural Resources Agency agreed to complete a combined environmental impact statement and environmental impact report as part of the Bay Delta Conservation Plan by June 2012. Part of this agreement was for the agencies to also come up with a number of alternatives to the peripheral canal. The canal was opposed by environmentalists, fishing groups, farmers, and Indian tribes, who believe that the project would result in the extinction of a number of fish, including Sacramento River Chinook salmon and Central Valley steelhead. Diverting water for the canal would not only put fish species in danger, but would also take some of the region's agricultural land out of production, since water would be diverted to irrigate farmland on the west side of the San Joaquin Valley.

Power and Profit from California Waters

There are nearly 1,400 dams and reservoirs in California, with about 200 under federal jurisdiction. Such a large number of dams is necessary, first, to provide adequate water supplies for residential, agricultural, and industrial use, and secondly, to produce hydroelectric power. With nearly 400 hydropower plants, California is one of the top hydroelectric power producing states in the nation.

The natural harbors of San Francisco Bay and San Diego Bay were once the most important centers for maritime trade, but have since been eclipsed in commercial importance by the ports of Los Angeles and Long Beach. Commercial fishing in coastal waters is an important part of the state economy, with Los Angeles serving as a major fishing port. The state has ranked among the top five in the nation in landings of Dungeness crab, squid, chub mackerel, and salmon. Deep-sea fishermen are drawn to the coastal waters for catches of giant sea bass, California halibut, white catfish, and sturgeon. Whales, sea lions, seals, and a wide variety of shorebirds can be found along the California coast as well.

Terraced vineyard in Sonoma, California, exemplifies biodynamic agricultural techniques.
© Ron Kacmarcik/ShutterStock.com

A Toast to California Wines—and More

For some tourists, a trip to a California winery is more enticing than a day at the beach. California ranks first in the nation in wine production, creating 90 percent of all U.S. wines. As a wine-producing region, the state ranks fourth in the world, following France, Italy, and Spain. Furthermore, the wine industry generates $61.5 billion for the state economy and draws 20.7 million tourists each year, particularly to the vineyards of Sonoma and Napa Valley.

California is the nation's sole producer (99 percent or more) of grapes, raisins, and several other specialty crops, including almonds, artichokes, figs, kiwifruit, olives, pomegranates, and walnuts. The state ranks first in the nation in the production of milk, cream, and vegetables, with lettuce, tomatoes, broccoli, carrots, and celery among the top vegetable commodities. Strawberries, oranges, and lemons are also among the top 20 commodities. California's farmland only accounts for about 4 percent of the national total, but with such a wide variety of produce, California ranks first in the nation in the total value of agricultural products.

The state's first organic agriculture program was established in 1990 through the California Product Act. This was replaced by the California Organic Products Act of 2003, which placed the program in line with the National Organic Standards. Certified cattle and poultry are among the top organic commodities of the state, with gross sales of over $100 million per year. Salad mix, carrots, strawberries, and tomatoes are also top sellers in the state's organic market.

Problems with Pesticide

In January 2011, a coalition of farm workers and environmental activists announced that they had filed a lawsuit against the state to prevent the use of the carcinogenic strawberry pesticide methyl iodide. The suit claims that the decision of the Californian Department of Pesticide Regulations (CDPR) that approved the use of the pesticide violates the California Environmental Quality Act, the California Birth Defects Prevention Act, and the Pesticide Contamination Prevention Act (a groundwater protection act). Methyl iodide is a known carcinogen that is used to create cancer cells in some lab situations. In use as a pesticide, it is injected into the soil before planting to eradicate weed seeds and plant diseases.

The CDPR stated that the use of methyl iodide is meant to replace that of methyl bromide, a substance that is known to deplete ozone. The U.S. EPA has approved the use of methyl iodide as a federally restricted pesticide and the CDPR maintains that the use of the pesticide is still subject to several tight restrictions. However, activists and farm workers contend that the decision of the CDPR was made against the advice of the state Scientific Review Committee. They claim that the use of the pesticide could lead to serious groundwater contamination problems as well a health problem for those on the front lines, namely those workers involved in strawberry planting and harvest. The suit was filed in the Alameda Superior Court by Earthjustice and California Rural Legal Assistance, Inc. The list of plaintiffs includes the United Farm Workers of America and Pesticide Action Network North America.

Two significant out-of-court developments occurred in March 2011. First, the U.S. EPA announced that it would accept public comments through April 30, 2011, relating to a petition from Earthjustice and U.S. Senator Dianne Feinstein (D-Calif.) to reconsider the federal approval of methyl iodide. Based on the results of this comment period, the EPA could decide to reconsider its own recommendations concerning the chemical. California governor Jerry Brown also announced that he would take a "fresh look" at the state's own decision of approval. The governor's announcement came about one week after the Department of Pesticide Regulation director, Mary-Ann Warmerdam, issued her intent to resign by the end of March. Warmerdam, who was appointed under former governor Arnold Schwarzenegger, was the one responsible for issuing the decision of approval in December 2010. She has taken a job in the private sector. Environmentalists and farmers are asking Governor Brown to reopen the process of reviewing the use of methyl iodide once a new director is appointed. As of late 2011, methyl iodide was still being used in the state.

Energy

Oil

California ranks third in the nation (following Texas and Alaska) for the production of crude oil, producing more than 10 percent of the national supply. The primary drilling sites are located in Kern County (in the south central region of the state) and the Los Angeles basin. The state is home to 17 of the 100 largest oil fields in the nation, including the South Belridge oil field in the San Joaquin Valley (Kern County), which ranks as the third largest in the contiguous states. A moratorium on offshore oil and gas leasing in the federally administered Outer Continental Shelf was lifted in 2008. However, California's own U.S. Representative John Garamendi introduced the West Coast Ocean Protection Act of 2010 (HR 5213) to the House on May 5, 2010. The bill calls for an amendment to the Outer Continental Shelf Lands Acts that would permanently prohibit offshore drilling along the coast of California, Oregon, and Washington. It comes as a direct response to the 2010 BP Deepwater Horizon Oil Spill. The bill has been referred to the Subcommittee on Energy and Mineral Resources.

Cleaner-Burning Gasoline

The state ranks third in the nation for petroleum refining capacity, producing more than 11 percent of the national total of refined petroleum. These refineries are among the most sophisticated in the world and are specifically designed to produce cleaner fuels, such as low-sulfur diesel and reformulated gasoline, often referred to as cleaner burning gasoline. Since 1996, all gasoline sold in the state has been a reformulated blend known as the

California Cleaner Burning Gasoline (CA CBG), which offers lower emissions of sulfur dioxide, carbon monoxide, and nitrogen oxide. Since the state requires such a specific motor fuel blend, motorists sometimes experience short-term increases in the cost of fuel when demand is particularly high and supplies are low.

Natural gas production within the state accounts for less than 2 percent of the national supply and covers only 20 percent of statewide demand.

Electricity

More than 45 percent of the state's supply of electricity is produced in natural gas–fired plants. Another 12 percent is produced by hydroelectric power and 14 percent comes from two nuclear plants. California is one of the top hydroelectric power–producing states in the nation, generating a little more than 5 percent of the nation's supply through nearly 400 hydropower plants, many of which are located in the eastern mountain ranges. State emission laws limit the use of coal-fired plants within the state; however, some of the electricity imported into California is produced by coal-fired plants across the state's border. For instance, the Los Angeles Department of Water and Power operates the Intermountain coal-fired plant in Utah.

Renewable Energy Sources

California ranks first in the nation for the production of electricity through non-hydroelectric renewable energy sources. More than 15 percent of the national total and 10 percent of the state supply of electricity is produced through renewable energy sources, including wind, solar, geothermal, and biomass energies. The Geysers facility in the Mayacamas Mountains north of San Francisco is the world's largest geothermal power plant, with a net generating capacity of 725 megawatts. The state is also a leading producer of wind energy, with more than 13,000 operational wind turbines representing nearly 10 percent of the nation's capacity.

The Ivanpah Project

The California Mojave Desert is an ideal site for large solar power facilities; however, some recently proposed projects have been challenged by environmental groups arguing that the facilities disturb the natural habitat's rare plants and animals and mar the natural beauty of the desert landscape. The Ivanpah Solar Electric Generating System, for example, was first proposed by BrightSource Energy in 2007, but did not begin to receive necessary approvals until August 2010. At the beginning of that month, the U.S. Bureau of Land Management (BLM) issued its final environmental impact statement (FEIS), which essentially marked federal approval for the chosen design of the project.

BrightSource intends to use its proprietary Luz Power Tower technology, which is a low-impact environmental design that involves the use of mirrors mounted on individual poles that are placed directly into the ground. This allows the solar field to be built along the existing natural contours of the landscape and can be placed away from areas of sensitive vegetation. Other technologies involve land grading and the construction of concrete pads that are more permanently damaging to the landscape. The Ivanpah project will also employ an air-cooling system that converts steam back into water in a closed-loop cycle, thus conserving water. Construction began on the project in October 2010. When completed, it will be the largest solar plant in the world, with the capacity to generate enough electricity to power more than 140,000 homes. The new source of energy could also reduce carbon dioxide emissions by more than 400,000 tons annually. The project is expected is expected to provide $300 million in local and state tax revenues over the same period.

California Solar Initiative

The move toward solar energy is promoted on a smaller scale through the California Solar Initiative (CSI), which provides rebates and other financial incentives for the installation of solar energy systems in existing homes and new and existing commercial buildings. Also known as the Million Solar Roofs Initiative, the goal of the CSI is to have one million solar roofs in operation by 2018, enough to generate 3,000 megawatts of clean energy.

Leading by example, AT&T activated the first of six solar power installations for California-based offices in August 2010. The 296-kilowatt rooftop solar power installation at the Trade Street site in San Diego generated 420,000 kilowatt hours of energy during its first full year of operation. Additional installations were added at sites in Dunnigan, Commerce, Mojave, Santa Ana, and West Sacramento in 2011. These projects are facilitated through contracts with SunEdison, which is responsible for construction, monitoring, and maintenance of the installations. In return, AT&T will purchase the energy produced to offset their grid demand. SunEdison had estimated that all six systems, once activated, will generate more than 3.2 million kilowatt hours of energy within the first year of combined operations. The projects are also expected to avoid about 62 million pounds of carbon dioxide emission over the first twenty years of operation.

Meeting the Demand for Clean Energy

Ranking first in the nation in population, California comes in second (after Texas) in total energy demand. However, the state also has one of the lowest per capita consumption rates in the country. The success of statewide energy-efficiency programs is noted as one major contributing factor to lower consumption. A mild climate may also contribute to a lower demand for energy related to heating and cooling systems.

The state's first Renewable Portfolio Standards were adopted in 2002, with a mandate to public utilities to produce at least 20 percent of all electricity through renewable energy sources by 2017 (Senate Bill 1078). An amendment was made to the standards in 2006 that changed the 20 percent deadline to December 31, 2010 (Senate Bill 107). Governor Arnold Schwarzenegger raised the bar yet again in 2008 by issuing an executive order that placed the goal at 33 percent by 2020 (Executive Order S-14-08). On February 24, 2011, the state legislature passed a bill placing this 33 percent goal within the state law (SB 2x), thereby creating one of the most ambitious renewable energy standards in the country. Governor Brown signed the bill on April 12, 2011, despite opposition from some major business groups. On May 5, 2011, the California Public Utilities Commission (CPUC) issued a new Renewable Portfolio Standards (RPS) Rulemaking 11-05-005 to implement amendments associated with the bill.

✿ Green Business, Green Building, Green Jobs

Green Business

The development and growth of green business is easily attributed to the government's proactive approach to meeting environmental challenges through legislation that also promotes the establishment of green industries. The adoption of energy efficiency standards, for instance, has forced a change in operations for a number of businesses and inspired growth and development within the clean energy sector. According to a 2008 report of the California Economic Strategy Panel, energy generation and energy efficiency building standards and renewable energy accounted for about 74 percent of the entire green economy. Overall, the state is home to more than 10,000 clean tech companies.

Some cities in the state are encouraging their local businesses to take steps to reduce unnecessary waste, such as eliminating single-use plastic bags. In July 2011, a proposed ban on single-use plastic bags in Manhattan Beach was upheld. A group called Save the Plastic Bag Coalition had fought the ban, arguing that it would degrade the environment because paper bags take more energy to produce than plastic bags. The judge dismissed the group's argument, stating that the town's population was too small to require analyzing such effects. The ban was scheduled to go into effect in January 2012, and bans are also pending in other California towns, including Monterey, Oakland, and Sunnyvale. Long Beach passed a ban on plastic bags in large food stores in August 2011. Larger jurisdictions have considered charging 5 to 25 cents on single-use plastic bags to discourage wholesale switching to paper bags, which also have environmental issues.

Green Building

The California Green Building Standards Code became effective in August 2009. The code calls for the implementation of green building practices on all new and existing state-owned buildings, with an added directive to reduce electricity consumption in state buildings by 20 percent by 2015. New construction projects are expected to meet the Leadership in Energy and Environmental Design (LEED) standards from the United States Green Building Council at a rating of Certified or above. Buildings of more than 100,000 square feet (9,290 sq m) must meet the LEED Silver rating. The state also hopes to move toward LEED certification for existing buildings. The Audubon Center at Debs Park in Los Angeles is an example of a Platinum-rated new construction project. The National Resources Defense Council–Robert Redford Building in Santa Monica stands as an example of a Platinum-level renovation.

Green Jobs: Many Shades of Green

The most recent comprehensive information on the green jobs climate for the state was published in December 2009 through the efforts of Collaborative Economics and Next 10. *Many Shades of Green: Diversity and Distribution of California's Green Jobs* provides statistical information on the number of green jobs available throughout the state from 1995 through 2008. According to this report, green business increased by 45 percent during this period. This led to a 36 percent increase in the number of green jobs during the same period, while total jobs in the state grew by 13 percent. As of 2008, services accounted for 45 percent of all California green jobs, while manufacturing accounted for 21 percent. Employment in green transportation increased by 152 percent from 1995 to 2008, while the energy generation and energy efficiency sectors each saw an increase of employment of more than 60 percent in the same period. In a regional context, the Sacramento area saw the greatest growth in green jobs with an increase of about 87 percent. The core green employment figure was estimated at 159,000 jobs in 2008.

Green Collar Jobs Act

In recent years, the state government has approved a number of initiatives aimed at increasing the number of green jobs. In 2008, the legislature passed the Green Collar Jobs Act (AB 3018), which established the Green Collar Jobs Council with a mission to develop a comprehensive strategy to prepare workers for the growth of the green economy. In 2009, the governor launched the California Green Corp, a program designed to provide training opportunities in green collar jobs for at-risk youth.

The Ivanpah Solar Electric Generating System, which has been under construction since October 2010, is expected to create one thousand union jobs during the construction phase, pursuant to the contract made between BrightSource and the engineering and construction firm Bechtel. The project is expected to contribute $650 million in wages over the first thirty years of operation.

🍂 Global Warming Solutions Act Prompts Heated Debate

In 2006, then-Governor Arnold Schwarzenegger signed the Global Warming Solutions Act (AB 32), which calls for the reduction of greenhouse gases to 1990 levels by the year 2020, representing an overall reduction of about 30 percent from current projections. At the time, the state of California was hailed by many for adopting the most aggressive climate change legislation in the nation; but in 2010, as the measures leading to full implementation of the act were beginning to take shape, AB 32 became a controversial topic.

In order to present the most efficient model possible for implementation of the AB 32 measures, the California Air Resources Board revealed its Climate Change Scoping Plan in 2008, which details the necessary steps and strategies for reaching the 2020 emission reduction goal. These include an expansion of existing energy efficiency programs, setting new targets for transportation-related emissions, and introducing new incentives to support and encourage the necessary transitions. A cap-and-trade program will also be established, which will establish a cap (or limit) on the amount of greenhouse gas emissions allowed for certain companies, and will allow these companies to trade permits (or allowances) in order to stay within target. While some of the adopted reduction measures were set to go into effect by the end of 2010, the final set of measures is not scheduled to be implemented until 2012. With the current state of the economy, an increasing number of people are saying it's too much, too soon.

The state has already seen an increase in the number of green jobs and green businesses, primarily as a result of legislation concerning energy efficiency standards and renewable energy source goals. Government supporters of AB 32 regard the act as a substantial commitment to both the preservation of the environment and the growth of the economy. While most opponents appreciate the spirit of the act, they argue that the cost of implementing the full measures of the act as scheduled will lead to a greater economic deficit, making things much worse before they get any better.

Leading to the elections of November 2010, they called for a suspension of the act until the economy has stabilized.

The primary campaign against AB 32 was known as the California Jobs Initiative (CJI). The initiative was sponsored by a coalition of companies, organizations, and individuals, including U.S. Representative Tom McClintock (Republican). Facts compiled on the CJI website indicated that AB 32 would lead to the loss of more than 1.1 million jobs, an increase in retail electricity rates by up to 60 percent, and substantial increases in the cost of transportation fuels and natural gas. Opponents of the act believe that many existing businesses will be forced to close as their costs increase, and that major investors will steer clear of California to find a more welcome home in states with less restrictive standards. Some opponents have also argued that AB 32 effectively usurps the powers of local government by placing such matters as land use, waste management, building codes, and transportation under state control, rather than with municipal leaders who understand the needs and resources of their communities.

The CJI-proposed solution involved the suspension of full implementation of the act until such time that the unemployment rate in California has dropped to 5.5 percent for four consecutive calendar quarters. In June 2010, the unemployment rate in California was estimated by the California Employment Development Department at 12.4 percent for May 2010. In support of this cause, CJI solicited more than 800,000 signatures to place the matter in the hands of the voters as Proposition 23 at the November 2010 ballot.

On the other side of the fence, the California Air Resources Board released a detailed economic analysis of the AB 32 Scoping Plan in March 2010. The study compared the costs and results of doing nothing with that of implementing the plan. According to the report, if AB 32 is not fully implemented, the state economy is projected to expand by an average annual rate of 2.4 percent between 2006 and 2020, with fuel costs increasing at an annual rate of 1.7 percent. If the act is implemented as scheduled, the overall growth rate is projected to remain the same, but the cost of fuel expenditures would reduce by 4.9 percent over the same period of time. State officials argue that the plan will lead to the creation of new jobs, as the state stays ahead of national trends in developing a green economy. Supporters also believe that the implementation of energy efficiency standards will save consumers money in the long run. In the wake of the spring 2010 BP Deepwater Horizon oil spill in the Gulf of Mexico, the California Jobs Initiative faced additional attacks from environmental groups and clean-tech companies alike, related to the fact that two of the largest industrial supporters of this initiative are the Texas-based Valero and Tesoro oil companies.

People recycling aluminum cans in Madera, California.
© Bill Bachmann/Alamy

At the November 2010 ballot, Proposition 23 was defeated by 61 percent of California voters, meaning that AB 32 would not be suspended. Since then, the California Air Resources Board has continued to move forward in the process of implementing several key programs included in the measures, in part by conducting public workshops on topics such as the mandatory commercial recycling regulation.

However, the battle has not ended. After the November vote, six local environmental groups, including the Association of Irritated Residents (AIR) and the Coalition for a Safe Environment, joined forces to file suit against the Air Resources Board. The plaintiffs claimed that the board did not meet the mandatory statutory requirements in approving the AB 32 Scoping Plan by failing to fully evaluate alternatives to the proposed cap-and-trade program. The plaintiffs represent a number of low-income communities. They argue that the cap-and-trade system, with a measure that allows companies to buy carbon credits from other companies as one way to meet their obligations to lower greenhouse gas emissions, would essentially allow some of the worst polluters to avoid cutting back on pollutants, particularly at large facilities located in poorer neighborhoods. The owners could simply buy enough credits to continue business as usual. More specifically, the plaintiffs balked at the lack of attention given to the idea of a carbon tax or carbon fees in place of cap-and-trade.

On March 18, 2011, Judge Ernest H. Goldsmith of the San Francisco superior court agreed that the Air Resources Board failed to fully evaluate the alternatives. The judge also ruled that the board failed to fully consider the public comments on the plan before its adoption. This decision could bring a halt to all of the measures outlined in AB 32, including those relating to energy efficiency programs, until the board completes a second environmental assessment. The board intends to appeal the decision, but more immediately planned to meet with the plaintiff groups to negotiate for a limited injunction that would delay progress on the cap-and-trade measure while allowing work on other, less controversial measures to move forward.

In the meantime, some of those responsible for the successful defeat of Proposition 23 in November have banded together once again to continue a campaign of support for the progress of AB 32. The nonpartisan group, known as Californians for Clean Energy and Jobs, represents a partnership of various business and environmental groups, including the Silicon Valley Leadership Group, the California League of Conservation Voters, and the Natural Resources Defense Council.

BIBLIOGRAPHY

Books

August, Jack L. *Dividing Western Waters: Mark Wilmer and Arizona V. California*. Fort Worth, TX: Texas Christian University Press, 2007.

Asmus, Peter. *Introduction to Energy in California*. Berkeley, CA: University of California Press, 2009.

Beidleman, Richard G. *California's Frontier Naturalists*. Berkeley, CA: University of California Press, 2006.

Donahue, Debra L. *The Western Range Revisited: Removing Livestock from Public Lands to Conserve Native Biodiversity*. Norman, OK: University of Oklahoma Press, 2000.

Elkind, Sarah S. *How Local Politics Shape Federal Policy: Business, Power, and the Environment in Twentieth-Century Los Angeles*. Chapel Hill, NC: The University of North Carolina Press, 2011.

Gottlieb, Robert. *Reinventing Los Angeles: Nature and Community in the Global City*. Cambridge, MA: MIT Press, 2007.

Green, Dorothy. *Managing Water: Avoiding Crisis in California*. Berkeley, CA: University of California Press, 2007.

Holing, Dwight. *The Smithsonian Guides to Natural America: The Far West–California, Nevada*. Washington, DC: Smithsonian Books, 1996.

Huntley, Jen A. *The Making of Yosemite: James Mason Hutchings and the Origin of America's Most Popular National Park*. Lawrence, KS: University Press of Kansas, 2011.

Lightfoot, Kent G. and Otis Parrish. *California Indians and Their Environment: An Introduction*. Berkeley, CA: University of California Press, 2009.

Orsi, Jared. *Hazardous Metropolis: Flooding and Urban Ecology in Los Angeles*. Berkeley, CA: University of California Press, 2004.

Palumbi, Stephen R. and Carolyn Sotka. *The Death and Life of Monterey Bay: A Story of Revival*. Washington, DC: Island Press, 2011.

Rothman, Hal. *The New Urban Park: Golden Gate National Recreation Area and Civic Environmentalism*. Lawrence, KS: University Press of Kansas, 2004.

Web Sites

"AB 32 Scoping Plan." California Environmental Protection Agency Air Resources Board. Available from http://www.arb.ca.gov/cc/scopingplan/scoping-plan.htm

Air Resources Board. "Update on Litigation Challenging Scoping Plan for the Global Warming Solutions Act, AB32." March 24, 2011. Available from http://docs.nrdc.org/air/files/air_11032501a.pdf

"AT&T Activates First of Six Solar Power Installations Planned for California." Environmental Leader. August 24, 2010. Available from http://www.environmentalleader.com/2010/08/24/att-activates-first-of-six-solar-power-installations-planned-for-california

Bacher, Dan. "It's full speed ahead for California's great water rip-off." Red, Green, and Blue. August 14, 2011. Available from http://redgreenandblue.org/2011/08/14/its-full-speed-ahead-for-californias-great-water-rip-off/

BrightSource Energy: Ivanpah Project. Available from http://www.brightsourceenergy.com/projects/ivanpah

"BrightSource Energy Breaks Ground on Ivanpah Solar Electric Generating System." BrightSource Energy. October 27, 2010. Available from http://www.brightsourceenergy.com/images/uploads/press_releases/Ivanpah_Groundbreaking_Press_Release.pdf

"California Agricultural Resource Directory 2010." California Department of Food and Agriculture. Available from http://www.cdfa.ca.gov/Statistics

California Geological Survey—Mineral Resources. State of California, Department of Conservation. Available from http://www.consrv.ca.gov/cgs/geologic_resources/mineral_resource_mapping/Pages/Index.aspx

California Jobs Initiative. Available from http://www.yeson23.com/

California Natural Resources Agency. *2009 California Climate Adaptation Strategy.* Available from http://www.energy.ca.gov/2009publications/CNRA-1000-2009-027/CNRA-1000-2009-027-F.PDF

"California Reformulated Gasoline Program." Air Resources Board, California Environmental Protection Agency. Available from http://www.arb.ca.gov/fuels/gasoline/gasoline.htm

California State Legislature. *Assembly Bill 32: California Global Warming Solutions Act of 2006.* Available from http://www.leginfo.ca.gov/pub/05-06/bill/asm/ab_0001-0050/ab_32_bill_20060927_chaptered.pdf

California State Legislature. *Assembly Bill 3018: California Green Collar Jobs Act.* Available from http://info.sen.ca.gov/pub/07-08/bill/asm/ab_3001-3050/ab_3018_bill_20080222_introduced.pdf

California State Legislature. *Senate Bill 2X: Renewable Energy Sources.* Available from http://www.leginfo.ca.gov/pub/11-12/bill/sen/sb_0001-0050/sbx1_2_bill_20110201_introduced.pdf

California State Legislature. *Senate Bill 107: Public Interest Energy Research, Demonstration, and Development Program.* Available from http://www.energy.ca.gov/portfolio/documents/sb_107_bill_20060926_chaptered.pdf

California State Legislature. *Senate Bill 1078: California Renewable Portfolio Standard Program.* Available from http://www.energy.ca.gov/portfolio/documents/SB1078.PDF

"California Sued to Block Strawberry Fumigant Methyl Iodide." Environment News Service. January 5, 2011. Available from http://www.ens-newswire.com/ens/jan2011/2011-01-05-091.html

"California's Unemployment Rate Decreases to 12.4 Percent Nonfarm Payroll Jobs Increase by 28,300." California Employment Development Department. Available from http://www.edd.ca.gov/About_EDD/pdf/urate201006.pdf

The Clean Energy Economy: California. The Pew Charitable Trusts. Available from http://www.pewcenteronthestates.org/uploadedFiles/wwwpewcenteronthestatesorg/Fact_Sheets/Clean_Economy_Factsheet_California.pdf

Clean Technology and the Green Economy: Growing Products, Services, Businesses, and Jobs in California's Value Network. Collaborative Economics. Available from http://www.coecon.com/Reports/GREEN/FINAL_Green_Economy_March_2008.pdf

"H.R. 5213: West Coast Ocean Protection Act of 2010." Govtrack.us. Available from http://www.govtrack.us/congress/bill.xpd?bill=h111-5213

Heberger, Matthew, et al. *The Impacts of Sea-Level Rise on the California Coast. California Climate Change Center.* Available from http://www.energy.ca.gov/2009publications/CEC-500-2009-024/CEC-500-2009-024-D.PDF

Herdt, Timm. "Brown will take a 'fresh look' at methyl iodide decision." M.vcstar.com. March 23, 2011. Available from http://m.vcstar.com/news/2011/mar/23/brown-will-take-a-145fresh-look-at-methyl-iodide

"Ivanpah Solar Electric Generating System." California Energy Commission. Available from http://www.energy.ca.gov/sitingcases/ivanpah/index.html

Jones, Donna. "Pesticide foes look to new governor for help: Methyl iodide faces court and political challenge." *Mercury News.* January 3, 2011. Available from http://www.mercurynews.com/breaking-news/ci_17001230

Kahn, Debra. "Plastic Bag Decision in Calif. Court Sets CEQA Precedent." *The New York Times.* August 2, 2011. Available from http://www.nytimes.com/gwire/2011/08/02/02greenwire-plastic-bag-decision-in-calif-court-sets-ceqa-44970.html?scp=5&sq=california%20environment%202011&st=cse

Kapnick, Sarah, and Alex Hall. *Observed Changes in the Sierra Nevada Snowpack: Potential Causes and Concerns.* California Climate Change Center. Available from http://www.energy.ca.gov/2009publications/CEC-500-2009-016/CEC-500-2009-016-D.PDF

McGreevy, Patrick. "California Assembly OKs increased renewable energy requirement." *Los Angeles Times.* March 30, 2011. Available from http://www.latimes.com/news/local/la-me-energy-20110330,0,818402.story

Mieszkowski, Katharine. "Prop., 23 Goes Up in Smoke." *The Bay Citizen.* November 2, 2010. Available from http://www.baycitizen.org/elections-2010/story/prop-23-goes-smoke

Moser, Susan, et al. *The Future Is Now: An Update on Climate Change Science Impacts and Response Options for California.* California Climate Change Center. Available from http://www.energy.ca.gov/2008publications/CEC-500-2008-071/CEC-500-2008-071.PDF

Office of the Governor, State of California. *Executive Order S-13-08.* Available from http://gov.ca.gov/executive-order/11036

Office of the Governor, State of California. *Executive Order S-14-08.* Available from http://gov.ca.gov/executive-order/11072

"Park Closure List, May 2010." California Department of Parks and Recreation. Available from http://www.parks.ca.gov/?page_id=26685

Roosevelt, Margot. "Bid to suspend California's global warming law qualifies for November ballot." *Los Angeles Times*, June 23, 2010. Available from http://articles.latimes.com/2010/jun/23/local/la-me-climate-initiative-20100623

Roosevelt, Margot. "California's bid to curb global warming could soon get back on track." *Los Angeles Times.* March 23, 2011. Available from http://www.latimes.com/business/la-fi-climate-court-20110323,0,2026986.story

Roosevelt, Margot. "Effort underway to suspend California's global-warning law." *Los Angeles Times*, February 6, 2010. Available from http://articles.

latimes.com/2010/feb/06/local/la-me-ballot-warming6-2010feb06

Roosevelt, Margot. "Judge places California's global warming program on hold." *Los Angeles Times.* March 21, 2011. Available from http://latimes-blogs.latimes.com/greenspace/2011/03/california-global-warming-program-put-on-hold/comments/page/6/

Standen, Amy. "EPA opens public comment period on strawberry pesticide." California Watch. March 22, 2011. Available from http://californiawatch.org/dailyreport/epa-opens-public-comment-period-strawberry-pesticide-9361

"State Energy Profiles: California." United States Energy Information Administration. Available from http://tonto.eia.doe.gov/state/state_energy_profiles.cfm?sid=CA#

Woody, Todd. "Major California Solar Project Moves Ahead." *The New York Times*, March 17, 2010. Available from http://greeninc.blogs.nytimes.com/2010/03/17/major-california-solar-project-advances

Colorado

With a mean average elevation of 6,800 feet (2,074 m), Colorado is the highest state in the nation. However, some of the state's most precious resources are found underground. Colorado is one of the nation's top producers of marketed natural gas, 40 percent of which is produced from coalbed methane (produced from coal seams). The Piceance Basin in the northwestern part of the state is part of the larger tri-state Green River Formation, which covers parts of Colorado, Wyoming, and Utah. The Green River Formation contains what are believed to be the largest oil shale deposits in the world. In addition, the state has ranked among the top five in the nation for the production of gold and is the leading producer of molybdenum. Above ground, the mountains and mesas of the state have their own potential as well, particularly in the development of wind and geothermal power from sources in the Rocky Mountains. The pine forests along the north central portion of the state are currently threatened by an epidemic of native mountain pine beetles, but forest management officials are hopeful that in their aftermath a new and better forest environment will grow, one that will perhaps support a sustainable wood products and biomass energy industry.

Climate

Colorado features a highland continental climate with abundant sunshine and generally low humidity. Winters are cold and snowy, especially in the higher elevations of the Rocky Mountains, while summers bring warm, dry days and cool nights.

According to state government reports, greenhouse gas emissions in Colorado soared from 1990 to 2005 with an increase of 35 percent. That climb has been projected to reach 81 percent by 2020 if no decisive actions are taken to reduce and control emissions. According to the National Wildlife Foundation, temperatures in Colorado could rise by about 6.75°F (3.75°C) by 2100 if steps aren't taken to mitigate global warming. This increase in temperature would cause hotter and drier summers, which would result in more wildfires and severe droughts. In turn, when rains do come, they will likely be heavier and more severe, causing flash flooding. Rising temperatures will change the makeup of entire ecosystems in the state, threatening at-risk species and their habitats. The loss of wildlife and habitat would also cause a steep loss of tourism dollars, which the state relies on heavily.

The first steps toward changing that forecast were taken in 2007 through the introduction of the Colorado Climate Action Plan, which calls for the reduction of greenhouse gas emissions by 20 percent of 2005 levels by 2020 and by 80 percent by 2050. The primary strategies for achieving this goal include the development of a New Energy Economy that focuses on energy efficiency and alternative energy sources, along with educational and incentive programs to encourage residents and businesses alike to adopt green practices.

Natural Resources, Water, and Agriculture

Great Outdoors Colorado

Colorado has nearly 24 million acres (9.7 million ha) of forests and woodlands, accounting for more than one-third of the state's land area. Only about 6 million acres (2.4 million ha) are privately owned and two-thirds of Colorado's forests are under protection by federal land management agencies. As a result, the state's forest industries are relatively small.

Quaking aspen, Rocky Mountain juniper, Colorado blue spruce, and various species of pine and fir are among the most common tree species. The Colorado pines, however, have been threatened in recent years through epidemic infestations of bark beetles (including the mountain pine beetle and spruce beetle) and the western spruce budworm. By feeding on foliage or burrowing into the barks of the trees, these pests have killed entire large sections of forest throughout the state. The mountain pine beetle epidemic that began in 1996 has led to the destruction of nearly 1.02 million acres (0.4 million ha) of the state's 1.5 million acres (0.6 million ha) of lodgepole pines. The spruce beetle epidemic, affecting high-elevation Engelmann spruce forests, began in 2002. In 2009, a total of 114,000 acres (46,130 ha) of native spruce beetle infestations were mapped in Colorado alone. An additional 150,000 new acres (60,700 ha) were mapped in Colorado and southern Wyoming in 2010. The western spruce budworm is primarily active in southern Colorado. In 2010, the budworm affected a total of 216,000 acres (87,410 ha) of forest, but this figure represented a decline in the number of acres affected during 2009, which stood at more than 360,000 acres (145,690 ha). Besides the loss of trees and decline in forest habitat that resulted from these infestations, the remaining dead wood poses an additional threat by providing quick burning fuel for wildfires. The Colorado State Forest Service has developed a number of strategies to address the challenges affecting the state's forests. One option under consideration is the development of a wood utilization and marketing program that would focus on a responsible harvest of dead trees to be converted into products such as pet bedding, landscaping mulch, and biomass fuel.

In April 2011, nine Colorado environmental groups united against a government plan to open up roadless national forest land to drilling and mining operations. Coal companies on Colorado's Western Slope would be allowed to make temporary roads for drilling and maintaining methane gas vents. These nine environmental groups have rejected the draft plan. If the courts favor the new plan over the national rule, then individual forest managers will decide how many new roads will be allowed for drilling, logging, and other activities based on local plans. By July 2011, another draft regarding the roadless rule had received more than 50,000 comments from stakeholders and from the public. The U.S. Forest Service and the state of Colorado planned to analyze the comments and formulate a response in the Final Environmental Impact Statement, expected in late 2011.

In 1992, Colorado voters approved the creation of the Great Outdoors Colorado (GOCO) Trust Fund, which receives 50 percent of the proceeds from the state lottery for projects that benefit the state's parks, rivers, and wildlife.

Colorado is home to forty-two state parks. However, at least four of these are in jeopardy of closing due to major cuts in the latest five-year financial plan from the State Parks Board. The recession has translated into major decreases in funding for the parks. In fiscal year 2008/2009, the parks received $6.7 million from the state's General Fund. For fiscal year 2010/2011, however,

funding dropped to $2.6 million. According to reports from the State Parks Board, there may be no contributions available from the General Fund for fiscal year 2011/2012. The board has already initiated layoffs of both full-time and seasonal employees and has cut salaries across the board for permanent positions. Camping and boating fees have been raised and lottery funds for capital projects have been redirected to cover operating costs. The five-year plan for fiscal years 2010/2011–2014/2015 anticipates the closure of one park (Bonny Lake) and proposes closure of three more parks (Sweitzer Lake, Harvey Gap, and Paonia). The plan also presents the option of selling oil and gas mineral leases in some park areas. In addition, the board hopes to find ways to expand private funding through the Foundation for State Parks and to make administrative changes that would streamline operations or share responsibilities with other state agencies.

There are four national parks in Colorado, including Rocky Mountain National Park, which is known for its habitats for elk and bighorn sheep. While common mammals such as cottontails, badgers, ground squirrels, and deer can be found in most areas, species such as mountain lions, black bear, moose, and bison are generally found only in protected areas. A variety of bluebirds, plovers, chickadees, and owls are found throughout the state. The whooping crane, piping plover, Mexican spotted owl, and the gray wolf are among the seventeen animals listed as threatened or endangered by the U.S. Fish and Wildlife Service (USFWS). The USFWS also lists sixteen plant species as threatened or endangered, which include three varieties of cacti and two varieties of milk-vetch (small shrubs).

In early 2011, the Colorado Division of Wildlife began reintroducing bighorn sheep into the mountains southwest of Denver. Wild bighorn sheep had not been seen in the area since the mid-1960s, but have flourished elsewhere. The Hayman wildfire of 2002 created an ideal habitat for the sheep: treeless and rocky. Twelve sheep were released in January 2010, and another twelve in February. Bighorn sheep got a boost in July 2011 when the Rocky Mountain Bighorn Society donated almost $150,000 to aid research, transplants, and habitat improvements. The funds will go to eleven projects for bighorn sheep preservation, including several prescribed burns conducted by the U.S. Forest Service, vaccine research, and additional transplants in the Sangre de Cristo Mountains and Dolores River areas.

The Colorado Division of Reclamation Mining & Safety reports that there are over 1,700 active mineral operations in Colorado, with metals such as gold, silver, and molybdenum being the most important to the local economy. The state has ranked among the top five in the nation for the production of gold and is the leading producer of molybdenum, which is used as an alloy

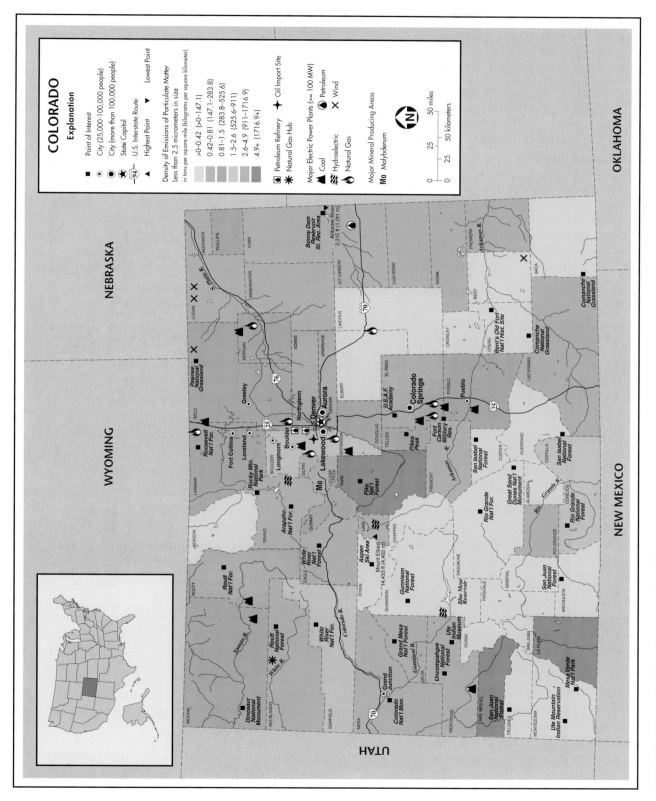

SOURCES: "County Emissions Map: Criteria Air Pollutants." *AirData*. U.S. Environmental Protection Agency. Available from http://www.epa.gov/air/data/geosel.html; *Energy Maps*. U.S. Energy Information Administration. Available from http://www.cia.gov/state; *Highest and Lowest Elevations*. U.S. Geological Survey. Available from http://egsc.usgs. gov/isb/pubs/booklets/elvadist/elvadist.html#Highest; *2007 Minerals Yearbook*. U.S. Geological Survey. Available from http://minerals.usgs.gov/minerals/pubs/state. © 2011 Cengage Learning.

agent in stainless steel and cast iron to increase strength and resist corrosion. Uranium and vanadium can also be found in Colorado, but very little has been mined in recent years. The state also produces industrial minerals such as sand and gravel, clay, stone, gypsum, and cement. In 2010, the state was ranked eleventh in the nation in non-fuel mineral production with a value of $1.9 billion.

Canyons, Caves, and the Continental Divide

The Continental Divide, the natural hydrological divide of the Americas that separates the waters that flow into the Pacific and those that flow into the Atlantic, stretches in a north-south line through the Rocky Mountains just to the west of Colorado's geographic center. The major rivers in the state include the Colorado, South Platte, North Platte, Rio Grande, and Arkansas. The Gunnison is a tributary of the Colorado River. There are a number of dams along these rivers that provide irrigation for farmland and water supplies for municipalities. Rivers running through the western region of the states have formed deep ravines and gorges among the broad, flat plateaus that characterize the area. The Royal Gorge of the Arkansas River is one of the deepest canyons in the state. A number of subterranean caves created by the rivers can be found throughout the area as well. The Colorado and Yampa Rivers are among the most popular for whitewater rafters.

While there is no significant commercial fishing in the state, sportfishing in lakes, rivers, and streams is very popular, with perch, trout, and black bass serving as popular catches. The Blue Mesa Reservoir, created by a dam along the Gunnison River, is Colorado's largest lake and the largest Kokanee salmon fishery in the nation. The Hotchkiss National Fishery produces rainbow trout for stocking reservoirs in Colorado and New Mexico.

Part of Colorado great outdoors are also hot springs and glaciers. There are several hot springs still active in Colorado, with one of the largest at Pagosa Springs in the San Juan Forest of southwestern Colorado. Several glaciers, including Arapahoe, St. Mary's, Andrews, and Taylor, are located on peaks at or near the Continental Divide.

Agriculture: Colorado Proud

In agriculture, Colorado ranks first in the nation for the production of proso millet (a common feed grain), providing more than half of the U.S. supply. The state comes in at second in the nation for sheep and goats and among the top five for cattle and calves, which are the state's top commodity. Colorado is among the top five producers of sunflowers for seeds and oil. Dairy products, wheat, corn, hay, and potatoes are also important state commodities. About 80 percent of all farms and ranches are family-owned. An estimated

Colorado State Profile	
Physical Characteristics	
Land area	103,641 square miles (268,429 sq km)
Inland water area	454 square miles (1,176 sq km)
Coastal area	NA
Highest point	Mt. Elbert 14,433 feet (4,399 m)
National Forest System lands (2010)	14.5 million acres (5.9 million ha)
State parks (2011)	42
Energy Statistics	
Total energy production (2009)	2,400 trillion Btu
State ranking in total energy production (2009)	9
Renewable energy net generation total (2009)	5.1 million megawatt hours
Hydroelectric energy generation (2009)	1.9 million megawatt hours
Biomass energy generation (2009)	56,000 megawatt hours
Wind energy generation (2009)	3.2 million megawatt hours
Wood and derived fuel energy generation (2009)	NA
Crude oil reserves (2009)	279 million barrels (44.4 million cu m)
Natural gas reserves (2009)	23,058 billion cubic feet (652.9 billion cu m)
Natural gas liquids (2008)	722 million barrels (114.8 million cu m)
Pollution Statistics	
Carbon output (2005)	89.7 million tons of CO_2 (81.4 million t)
Superfund sites (2008)	18
Particulate matter (less than 2.5 micrometers) emissions (2002)	13,766 tons per year (12,488 t/yr)
Toxic chemical releases (2009)	20.2 million pounds (9.2 million kg)
Generated hazardous waste (2009)	41,500 tons (37,700 t)

SOURCES: AirData. U.S. Environmental Protection Agency. Available from http://www.epa.gov/air/data; *Energy Maps, Facts, and Data of the U.S. States*. U.S. Energy Information Administration. Available from http://www.eia.gov/state; *The 2012 Statistical Abstract*. U.S. Census Bureau. Available from http://www.census.gov/compendia/statab; *United States Energy Usage*. eRedux. Available from http://www.eredux.net/states.

© 2011 Cengage Learning.

9,000 migrant and H2A certified workers (temporary or seasonal foreign workers who are not seeking immigration) are employed at Colorado farms and ranches each year.

The Colorado Department of Agriculture (CDA) is accredited by the U.S. Department of Agriculture as an organic state certifier under the National Organic Program. To promote local foods for local consumers, the CDA sponsors the Colorado Proud program, which partners local farmers and ranchers with local grocery stores and restaurants. According to the USDA, there are 327 certified organic operations in Colorado.

⚘ Energy

Oil and the Green River Formation

Oil production in Colorado accounts for about 1 percent of the national total, and proven crude oil reserves provide an equal percentage. Most oil is produced from the Denver and Piceance basins, the latter of which is also part of the larger Green River Formation that extends through portions of Colorado, Utah, and Wyoming. The Green River Formation contains what are believed to be the largest known oil shale deposits in the world. Oil shale is a type of sedimentary rock containing bituminous materials that can be mined and processed to generate oil. The federally owned Green River Formation contains an estimated total of 1 trillion barrels of oil. Conservative estimates indicate that only about 800 billion barrels are recoverable, an amount that is three times greater than the proven oil reserves of Saudi Arabia. However, the recovery process has thus far proven to be too complex and too expensive to be an economically feasible option for oil production.

While Colorado has two oil refineries in Commerce City, additional petroleum products are imported by pipeline from Wyoming, Texas, and Oklahoma. An oxygenated blend of motor gasoline is required for use in the Denver-Boulder and Fort Collins areas, but the rest of the state uses conventional gasoline.

ConocoPhillips announced plans in 2011 to start oil exploration in four counties around metropolitan Denver. About 46,000 acres (18,616 ha) of the Niobrara formation will be explored near the old Lowry bombing range in Arapahoe County. The formation is 6,000–8,000 feet (1,829–2,438 m) below the surface and stretches from Wyoming to New Mexico. As of August 2011, officials were in an investigative phase, studying possible impacts of exploration—particularly its effects on aquifers—and how to manage those impacts. Another important issue is whether or not ConocoPhillips can profitably produce oil from the formation. Officials remain hopeful that oil exploration in the area will bring economic benefits.

Natural Gas and the Rockies Express Pipeline

Colorado is one of the nation's top producers of marketed natural gas, with production that accounts for about 5 percent of the national total. More than 40 percent of Colorado's natural gas is produced from coalbed methane (produced from coal seams), which accounts for nearly 30 percent of the national total. While the San Juan and Raton basins are the primary sources of coalbed methane, further development is underway in the Piceance basin, which contains the second-largest proved reserves in the nation. Only about 40 percent of the state's natural gas is used locally, and the remainder is exported to markets in the West and Midwest. The Rockies Express Pipeline, which became fully operational in November 2009, is one of the largest pipelines in the country. It extends for 1,679 miles (2,700 km) from the Piceance basin (northwestern Colorado) to eastern Ohio with a capacity of 1.8 billion cubic feet of natural gas per day.

About 75 percent of all households use natural gas as their primary source for home heating.

Nearly 70 percent of the electricity generated in the state is from coal-fired plants. Some coal is produced locally from underground and surface mining in the western basins of the state, with bituminous, subbituminous, and lignite coal available in large supply. Additional supplies are imported from Wyoming. About 25 percent of all electricity is produced from natural-gas fired plants. Some is produced through hydroelectric power.

Energy from Beer and Pine

The state has great potential for the development of renewable energy sources, particularly in wind and geothermal power from sources in the Rocky Mountains. There are some corn-fed ethanol plants in the state, primarily in the northeast. One notable, but small, plant is attached to the Molson Coors brewery in Golden, which uses waste beer to produce ethanol. The Hayden Cary & King Company applied for a $26-million grant from the U.S. Department of Energy for the construction of a biomass plant in Vail. This biomass plant would use trees that have been destroyed by the recent pine bark beetle epidemic as fuel for a high-heat wood gasification operation to power hot water boilers to supply local lodges, hotels, public buildings, and snow-melt systems beneath streets and sidewalks. The company did not receive the grant money in July 2010, but began looking for other funding opportunities immediately after. Whether or not they will be able to fund the plant remains to be seen. A bill supporting the development of biomass energy through tax incentives (Senate Bill 10-177) was signed by the governor in June 2010.

The U.S. National Renewable Energy Laboratory (NREL) has a major research facility located in Golden, Colorado. NREL is dedicated to renewable energy and energy efficiency technology research and development (R&D). NREL's research covers a both land-based and offshore wind energy engineering disciplines.

Renewable Portfolio Standard

In 2004, Colorado became the first state to adopt a renewable portfolio standard by ballot initiative, producing a standard that required large utilities to generate or purchase at least 10 percent of their retail electric sales from renewable sources. That original standard was updated twice, with the most recent change in March 2010 through the passage of House Bill 10-1001, which

Hallett Peak from Nymph Lake, Rocky Mountain National Park.
© *iStockPhoto.com/sherwoodimagery*

requires investor-owned utilities to produce up to 30 percent of retail electric sales from renewable sources by 2020. The new law also requires utilities to produce 3 percent of retail sales through distributed generation by 2020. Distributed generation relates to small-scale generation systems located on-site at a customer's facility or home, such as solar panels installed on a local business.

❧ Green Business, Green Building, Green Jobs

Green Business Start-Ups Abound

Colorado's green economy is relatively small, but growing at an impressive pace. In a recent report published by the nonprofit research group, Headwaters Economics, Colorado was noted for gaining more than $796 million in green economy venture capital investments and nearly $300 million in energy-related federal stimulus in the past decade. Various financial incentives have been set in place to attract companies such as Vestas

Americas, which has wind-turbine factories in Windsor and Brighton.

Colorado State University, which has become well-known for research and advances in clean energy technology, has aided in the launch of several new businesses through its Green University Business Start-up program. One such company, Abound Solar, opened its first production facility in Longmont in 2009. The company produces low-cost, high-efficiency solar panels.

Colorado State's Engines and Energy Conversion Laboratory (EECL) was named one of *Popular Science* magazine's 25 Most Awesome College Labs in 2011. The EECL is one of the nation's largest independent energy laboratories, and develops large-scale solutions to global energy problems with a focus on engine technology, smart electric grids, advanced biofuels, and energy technology. The goal of the laboratory is to prepare students for the workforce through hands-on learning. More than sixty students work at the EECL regularly, on projects varying from improving the efficiency of natural gas compression engines to building cleaner cookstoves. One of the projects that the lab has been involved in is a collegiate competition to reengineer the GM Chevrolet Malibu. Students from the EECL and the university's Motorsports Engineering Research Center will convert the Malibu into a hybrid/electric or fuel-cell vehicle to reduce its environmental impact. Called "EcoCAR 2: Plugging into the Future," the lab's team is one of 16 teams chosen to take part in the competition by General Motors and the U.S. Department of Energy.

Former Governor Bill Ritter exercised tremendous support for the further development of what was termed the "New Energy Economy" in the state. (In fact, after leaving office, Ritter became head of the Center for the New Energy Economy at Colorado State University.) Some of that encouragement was shown through the passage of multiple legislative acts and executive orders that support the use of clean energy, such as updates to the renewable portfolio standards or enactment of a clean energy technologies bill (SB10-177), which promotes the use of biomass energy through incentives. According to state reports, the number of clean energy businesses has grown 18 percent since 2004, making it the fastest-growing economic sector.

The New Energy Jobs Creation Act 2010

The development of new green businesses requires improved workforce training programs that are adequately designed to support those businesses. According to the Headwaters Economics report, the number of green jobs in Colorado increased by 30 percent from 2005 to 2007. Much of that growth has been attributed to statewide clean energy initiatives, as the state reports that Colorado has the fourth-highest concentration of clean-energy

Solar panels at the base of the Rocky Mountains, Colorado.
© iStockPhoto.com/David Parsons

all state agencies to meet a specific set of reduction goals by June 30, 2012. These include the reduction of energy use by 20 percent, of paper use by 20 percent, of water consumption by 10 percent, and of state vehicle petroleum consumption by 25 percent. Executive Order D2010-006 issued in 2010 added a mandate for the diversion of 75 percent of waste materials from landfills and the adoption of a zero-waste policy by 2012. The Byron G. Rogers Courthouse in Denver is an example of a gold-level LEED certified building. The NREL Science & Technology Facility in Golden is a Platinum-level LEED certified building.

Mountain Pine Beetle

The growing, destructive presence of an invasive non-native insect species can be the worst nightmare for forest management and conservation workers. But what happens when the native species begin to wreak havoc on the environment? This is the situation that has faced the Colorado State Forest Service since 1996 as the native mountain pine beetles (*Dendroctonusponderosae*) have been emerging each year in epidemic numbers, with devastating effects on the state's lodgepole and ponderosa pine stands.

The mountain pine beetle, also known as the Rocky Mountain pine beetle or Black Hills beetle, is native to pine forests in western North America. The beetles have a one-year life cycle, beginning as eggs deposited under the bark of pine trees in the fall. Larvae that survive through winter temperatures begin to feed on the trees in early spring. From mid-June through September, adult beetles emerge from the trees to seek mates and find other trees in which to lay eggs. Each adult female can lay about 75 eggs, which are deposited in a vertical tunnel under the bark that is known as an egg gallery. The trees species most affected are lodgepole and ponderosa pines, though Scotch, limber, bristlecone, and piñon pines have been attacked as well. Adult females typically seek out older, larger trees that are already under some type of stress, such as injury, fire damage, overcrowding, or disease. However, when a larger than average outbreak occurs, the beetles will turn to large healthy trees first, then younger trees as well.

The Colorado epidemic has primarily affected trees in the north-central region of the state, with the lodgepole forests on the western slopes of the Continental Divide suffering heavy losses since 1998. By 2007, the infestation had spread to the Front Range in Boulder and Larimer counties. Lodgepole forests are located at high elevations, where cold winter temperatures would normally kill off much of the beetle larvae. Forests at high elevations have not historically been at risk for major outbreaks of beetles, but warmer winters and seasons of drought are the most likely causes for the recent epidemic.

workers in the country. To keep that trend going, in June 2010 the governor signed a series of New Energy Economy bills designed to support the revolution in clean-energy use and technology throughout the state and, consequently, create new energy jobs in the process. One of the bills, now known as the New Energy Jobs Creation Act 2010 (House Bill 10-1328), creates a statewide New Energy Improvement District, which will serve as a financing program to allow homeowners to install clean-energy technologies. This act is expected to create at least 3,000 new jobs. At the same time, House Bill 10-1333 was signed into law to create the Green Jobs Colorado Training Program and Training Fund, which will provide grants to community colleges, vocational schools, and other training providers in the development of clean-energy job skills programs.

To introduce job seekers to the world of the green economy, the Governor's Energy Office (GEO) has collaborated with the Environmental Defense Fund to produce a guidebook for green jobs entitled *Careers for Colorado's New Energy Economy*. The book explores careers in energy efficiency, wind, solar, recycling, waste management, and other related industries.

Green Building: Greening Government Initiative

The Greening Government Initiative for energy-efficiency and waste reduction in state-buildings was created in April 2007 through the enactment of Senate Bill 07-51 and Executive Orders D0011-07 and D0012-07. Senate Bill 07-51 established mandatory sustainability requirements for the design and construction of state-owned or state-assisted buildings. Under the law, all state-sponsored new construction and renovation projects over 5,000 square feet must meet the gold-level certification standards established through the U.S. Green Building Council's Leadership in Energy and Environmental Design (LEED) program. The executive orders require

The beetles burrow into the trees leaving behind a resin-like substance known as a pitch tube, the presence of which is the first indication that a tree has been infested. Once under the bark, they chew away at the tree forming long channels and depositing traces of blue stain fungi, so named because it leaves a blue-gray stain on the sapwood of the tree. The growth combines with the burrowing of numerous insects to kill the tree. It is estimated that the beetles born from one tree can kill two trees within a year.

Unfortunately, there is very little that can be done to stop or slow an infestation. A number of chemical sprays and applications have been used by homeowners in an attempt to repel the beetles from their trees, but such measures are only effective if the proper dosage is used at the proper time, and the entire tree must be dosed. Once an infested tree has been discovered, a number of methods have proven nonetheless successful in killing off the beetles and larvae within the tree to prevent future generations. Burning, scorching, and chipping the wood will usually kill existing larvae. Extreme cold and heat can kill the larvae during the winter or early spring, when it is at its most vulnerable. But such methods are typically only feasible for a small number of trees.

Throughout 2009, the intensity of infestations increased in the forests east of the Continental Divide, with some areas suffering attacks of at least ten trees per acre. Throughout 2010, the hardest hit areas were noted along the northern Front Range west of Boulder and Fort Collins and in southwestern Colorado. For forests at large, waiting out the storm is about all that can be done. An aerial survey conducted in 2008 found that there are 1.16 million impacted acres (0.47 million ha) of lodgepole pines affected in Colorado, which brings the cumulative number of affected acres to 1.9 million (0.77 million ha). Since other species of pine have been affected as well, an estimated 2.9 million acres (1.17 million ha) of forest have thus been distressed throughout the epidemic. The good news is that the epidemic does seem to be running its course. The bad news is that the latest decline in the number of beetles is most likely linked to the death of the trees that are the primary nesting spot for the beetles.

With an eye toward restoration and the prevention of future epidemics, the Colorado Forest Service launched a new forest management strategy in June 2010. *The Colorado Statewide Forest Resource Strategy* contains a number of options for responsible planning and management of all forest and woodland areas. One option involves the harvest of dead and dying trees for conversion into products such as pet bedding, landscaping mulch, and biomass fuel. This includes the development of a marketing plan to support a well-managed and sustainable wood products and timber supply industry. In areas with high volumes of trees, smaller trees can be harvested, which will ensure the health of others. Other options involve harvesting and planting programs specifically established to produce areas with a number of different tree species and with stands of differing ages. Since the beetles normally look for mature pine trees to nest in, creating a more diverse structure of ages and species of trees will likely lead to smaller outbreaks in the future. Several of these measures may also help to prevent the spread of wildfires, which are highly destructive in particular in overcrowded areas of dead or young trees.

Throughout 2010, the forest service selectively cleared trees from about 12,000 acres (4,856 ha) of land, but this action was controversial, as a number of environmental groups argued that clearing dead trees can increase the spreads of invasive plant species. There is also a concern that removal of the trees could lead to a decline in soil nutrients necessary for forests to recover on their own.

A 2011 report from Colorado State University's Forest Restoration Institute found that in areas of infestation that were untreated, the lodgepole pine will likely be naturally replaced by subalpine fir stands. Subalpine fir will take over in areas where there was more variety of tree species, but in areas where lodgepole pines were dominant there has been little sign of new growth. The report also predicted that the forest structure should return to its pre-outbreak conditions in 80 to 120 years in both treated and untreated areas.

While the final result will take many years to assess, forest workers seem optimistic that this current epidemic is only one small part of the natural process of what will continue to be a healthy forest environment for years to come.

BIBLIOGRAPHY

Books

Benedict, Audrey Delella. *The Naturalist's Guide to the Southern Rockies: Colorado, Southern Wyoming, and Northern New Mexico.* Golden, CO: Fulcrum Publishing, 2008.

Bronsan, Kathleen A. *Uniting Mountain and Plain: Cities, Law, and Environmental Change along the Front Range.* University of New Mexico Press, 2002.

Donahue, Debra L. *The Western Range Revisited: Removing Livestock from Public Lands to Conserve Native Biodiversity.* Norman, OK: University of Oklahoma Press, 2000.

Lamb, Susan, and Tom Bean. *The Smithsonian Guides to Natural America: The Southern Rockies–Colorado, Utah.* Washington, DC: Smithsonian Books, 1996.

Park, Lisa, and David Pellow. *The Slums of Aspen: Immigrants vs. the Environment in America's Eden.* New York, NYY: NYU Press, 2011.

Paulson, Deborah D., and William L Baker. *The Nature of Southwestern Colorado: Recognizing Human*

Legacies and Restoring Natural Places. Boulder, CO: University Press of Colorado, 2006.

Scamehorn, H. Lee. *High Altitude Energy: A History of Fossil Fuels in Colorado.* Boulder, CO: University Press of Colorado, 2002.

Tyler, Daniel. *Silver Fox of the Rockies: Delphus E. Carpenter and Western Water Compacts.* Norman, OK: University of Oklahoma Press, 2003.

Wohl, Ellen E. *Virtual Rivers: Lessons from the Mountain Rivers of the Colorado Front Range.* New Haven, CT: Yale University Press, 2001.

Wolf, David A. *Industrializing the Rockies: Growth, Competition, and Turmoil in the Coalfields of Colorado and Wyoming, 1868-1914.* Boulder, CO: University Press of Colorado, 2003.

Web Sites

"About Oil Shale." Oil Shale & Tar Sands Programmatic EIS, U.S. Department of the Interior, Bureau of Land Management. Available from http://ostseis.anl.gov/guide/oilshale/index.cfm

Associated Press. "Colorado may close state parks, lease for drilling." *The Denver Post.* January 1, 2011. Available from http://www.denverpost.com/commented/ci_16987843?source=commented-/

Berwyn, Bob. "Colorado: Beetle-kill a catalyst for dramatic forest changes." March 15, 2011. *Summit County Citizens Voice.* Available from http://summitcountyvoice.com/2011/03/15/colorado-beetle-kill-a-catalyst-for-dramatic-forest-changes/

Berwyn, Bob. "Colorado: Roadless rule elicits more than 50,000 comments." Summit Voice.July 15, 2011. Available from http://summitcountyvoice.com/2011/07/15/colorado-draft-roadless-rule-elicits-more-than-50000-comments/

"Bighorn Sheep." Colorado Department of Natural Resources. Available from http://wildlife.state.co.us/WildlifeSpecies/Profiles/Mammals/Pages/BighornSheep.aspx

Colorado Climate Center. Available from http://ccc.atmos.colostate.edu

Colorado Department of Agriculture. Available from http://www.colorado.gov/cs/Satellite/Agriculture-Main/CDAG/1165692857739

Colorado Division of Reclamation Mining & Safety. Available from http://mining.state.co.us/About%20DMG.htm

Colorado Division of Water Resources. Available from http://www.dwr.state.co.us/SurfaceWater/Default.aspx

Colorado General Assembly. *House Bill 10-1328. New Energy Jobs Creation Act of 2010.* Available from http://www.leg.state.co.us/CLICS/CLICS2010A/csl.nsf/fsbillcont3/CFC9C14941AD7A8E872576BF005A7C63?Open&file=1328_01.pdf

Colorado General Assembly. *House Bill 10-1333: Concerning the Creation of the Green Jobs Colorado Training Program.* Available from http://www.leg.state.co.us/CLICS/CLICS2010A/csl.nsf/fsbillcont3/EF619483FD7DC170872576A80027B7F3?Open&file=1333_01.pdf

Colorado General Assembly. *House Bill 1001 (2010): Renewable Portfolio Standards.* Available from http://www.leg.state.co.us/clics/clics2010a/csl.nsf/fsbillcont3/47C157B801F26204872576AA00697A3F?open&file=1001_enr.pdf

Colorado General Assembly. *Senate Bill 07-51: Concerning a Requirement for Increased Resource Efficiency for State-Assisted Buildings.* Available from http://www.leg.state.co.us/clics/clics2007a/csl.nsf/fsbillcont3/8EFE2CB5022F6CF687257251007C22D3?Open&file=051_enr.pdf

Colorado General Assembly. *Senate Bill 10-177: Concerning the Promotion of Clean Energy Technologies.* Available from http://www.leg.state.co.us/clics/clics2010a/csl.nsf/fsbillcont3/97C0229ED33B43B1872576D600543865?open&file=177_enr.pdf

Colorado Geological Survey. Available from http://geosurvey.state.co.us/Default.aspx?tabid=106

Colorado Proud. Available from http://www.colorado.gov/cs/Satellite/Agriculture-Main/CDAG/1167928162081

Colorado State Forest Service. *Colorado Statewide Forest Resource Strategy.* Available from http://csfs.colostate.edu/pdfs/assessmentstrategysmall.pdf

"Ethanol from Waste Beer." Molson Coors. Available from http://www.molsoncoors.com/responsibility/environmental-responsibility/energy/from-grains-to-gas

Finley, Bruce. "Environmental groups, sportsmen blast plan that weakens forest protections." April 15, 2011. *The Denver Post.* Available from http://www.denverpost.com/news/ci_17851179

Finley, Bruce. "Northern Front Range forests among prime beetle-kill areas in 2010." *The Denver Post.* January 22, 2011. Available from http://www.denverpost.com/news/ci_17163793

"Fishing." Colorado Division of Wildlife. Available from http://wildlife.state.co.us/fishing

Five-Year Financial Plan: FY 10/11–FY 14–15. Colorado State Parks Board. Available from http://parks.state.co.us/SiteCollectionImages/parks/Shared Documents/FINAL_CSP_FINANCIAL_PLAN_Web.pdf

"Forest Health Aerial Survey Highlights for 2010." USDA Forest Service. Available from http://www.fs.usda.gov/wps/portal/fsinternet/!ut/p/c5/04_SB8K8xLLM9MSSzPy8xBz9CP0os3gjAwhwtDDw9_AI8zPyhQoYAOUjMeXDfODy-HWHg-zDrx8kb4ADOBro-3nk56bqF-RGGGSZOCoCAPi8eX8!/dl3/d3/L2dJQSEvUUt3QS9ZQnZ3LzZfMjAwMDAwMDBBODBBPSEhWTjJNMDAwMDAwMDA!/?navtype=BROWSEBYSUBJECT&cid=stelprdb5253133&navid=091000000000000&pnavid=null&ss=1102&position=Not%20Yet%20Determined.Html&ttype=detail&pname=Region%202-%20Home

"Glaciers of Colorado." Glaciers of the American West. Available from http://glaciers.research.pdx.edu/Glaciers-Colorado

"Global Warming and Colorado." National Wildlife Federation. Available from http://www.nwf.org/Global-Warming/In-Your-State.aspx

Governor's Energy Office, Colorado, and the Environmental Defense Fund. *Careers for Colorado's New Energy Economy.* Available from http://rechargecolorado.com/images/uploads/pdfs/careers_for_colorado_09.pdf

Great Outdoors Colorado. Available from http://goco.org.s57353.gridserver.com

"The Green University." Colorado State University. Available from http://www.green.colostate.edu/index.aspx

Hartman, Todd. "Death of Trees catastrophic: Lodgepole die-off imperils recreation, supplies of water" *Rocky Mountain Times.* January 15, 2008. Available from http://www.rockymountainnews.com/news/2008/jan/15/beetle-infestation-get-much-worse

Headwaters Economics. *Clean Energy Leadership in the Rockies: Competitive Positioning in the Emerging Green Economy.* Available from http://www.headwaterseconomics.org/greeneconomy/CleanEnergyLeadership.pdf

Hoban, Erin. "Biomass plant gets warm, cautious reception from Vail." *Vail Mountaineer.* May 20, 2010. Available from http://www.vailmountaineer.com/News/NewsArticles/ArticleView/tabid/83/ArticleId/10/Biomass-plant-gets-warm-cautious-reception-from-Vail.aspx

Johnson, Kirk. "A Homecoming for Bighorn Sheep in Colorado." February 18, 2011. *The New York Times.* Available from http://www.nytimes.com/2011/02/19/us/19bighorn.html

Leaherman, D.; A, I Aguyao; and T. M. Nehall. "Mountain Pine Beetle." *Insect Series: Trees and Shrubs.* Colorado State University Extension.

Available from http://www.ext.colostate.edu/pubs/insect/05528.pdf

"Mountain Pine Beetle." Colorado Forest Service. Available from http://csfs.colostate.edu/pages/mountain-pine-beetle.html

"Mountain Pine Beetle News." March 25, 2011. Mountain Pine Beetle Treatment. Available from http://www.mountainpinebeetletreatment.com/

National Renewable Energy Laboratory. Available from http://www.nrel.gov

Office of the Governor, State of Colorado. *Colorado Climate Action Plan: A Strategy to Address Global Warming.* Available from http://www.colorado.gov/cs/Satellite?blobcol=urldata&blobheader=application%2Fpdf&blobkey=id&blobtable=MungoBlobs&blobwhere=1228626349291&ssbinary=true

Office of the Governor, State of Colorado. *Colorado's New Energy Economy.* Available from http://www.colorado.gov/cs/Satellite?blobcol=urldata&blobheader=application%2Fpdf&blobkey=id&blobtable=MungoBlobs&blobwhere=1251636882611&ssbinary=true

Office of the Governor, State of Colorado. *Executive Order D0011 07: Greening of State Government—Goals and Objectives.* Available from http://www.colorado.gov/governor/press/pdf/executive-orders/2007/ExecutiveOrder-Greening-State-Government-GoalsObjectives.pdf

Office of the Governor, State of Colorado. *Executive Order D0012 07: Greening of State Government—Detailed Implementation.* Available from http://www.colorado.gov/governor/press/pdf/executive-orders/2007/ExecutiveOrder-Greening-Government-ImplementationMeasures.pdf

Office of the Governor, State of Colorado. *Executive Order D2010-006: Greening of the States Government—Earth Day 2010.* Available from http://www.colorado.gov/cs/Satellite?blobcol=urldata&blobheader=application%2Fpdf&blobheadername1=Content-Disposition&blobheadername2=MDT-Type&blobheadervalue1=inline%3B+filename%3D683%2F123%2FD+2010-006+%28Greening+2010%29+2.pdf&blobheadervalue2=abinary%3B+charset%3DUTF-8&blobkey=id&blobtable=MungoBlobs&blobwhere=1251624454444&ssbinary=true

Pankratz, Howard. "ConocoPhillips to begin oil exploration near metro Denver." *The Denver Post.* July 30, 2011. Available from http://www.denverpost.com/business/ci_18582568

"Popular Science Lists Colorado State University Engines and Energy Conversion Laboratory One of Nation's

Top 25 Academic Laboratories." Colorado State University. August 16, 2011. Available from http://www.news.colostate.edu/Release/5840

Recharge Colorado: Greening of State. Available from http://www.rechargecolorado.com/index.php/programs_overview/greening_government

"Rockies Express Pipeline." Kinder Morgan. Available from http://www.kindermorgan.com/business/gas%5Fpipelines/rockies%5Fexpress

Rosenberry, Dena. "Efforts to assist bighorn sheep get financial boost." Out There Colorado. August 12, 2011. Available from http://www.outtherecolorado.com/blogs/efforts-to-assist-bighorn-sheep-get-financial-boost.html

Royal Gorge Bridge and Park. Available from http://www.royalgorgebridge.com

"State Energy Profiles: Colorado." U.S. Energy Information Administration. Available from http://tonto.eia.doe.gov/state/state_energy_profiles.cfm?sid=CO

2009 Report on the Health of Colorado Forests: Threats to Colorado's Current and Future Forest Resources. Colorado State Forest Service. Available from http://csfs.colostate.edu/pdfs/105504_CSFS_09-Forest-Health_www.pdf

Whaley, Monte. "Cash-strapped Colo. state parks may open up to more oil, gas drilling." *The Denver Post.* November 16, 2010. Available from http://www.denverpost.com/news/ci_16623845

"Wildlife Profiles and Information." Colorado Division of Wildlife. Available from http://wildlife.state.co.us/WildlifeSpecies/Profiles

Connecticut

Connecticut is one of the smallest, but more densely populated states in the United States. Cities are located primarily along the coast and the center of the state, with smaller towns scattered along some of Connecticut's smaller rivers and lakes. About two-thirds of the land in the state is undeveloped.

Early Adopters of the Climate Change Action Plan

Connecticut's climate is relatively mild, considering the cooler climates of its neighboring northern New England states. The four seasons are distinct and the state receives a generous amount of precipitation each year. Average temperatures during months or seasons can vary greatly from one year to the next, making predictability difficult, though typically the northwest region experiences cooler temperatures than other parts of the state, and the southwest coastal area is, on average, warmer.

Global climate change could have a variety of adverse effects on the environment, wildlife, and human population of the state. According to a report from Environmental Defense Fund, warmer water temperatures in the Long Island Sound have contributed to a decline in the local lobster population. Rising sea levels in this area could lead to further losses of wildlife habitats. Rising temperatures and increased precipitation in this region could also lead to a higher incidence rate of respiratory ailments and heat-related illnesses. A series of factsheets published by the Connecticut Department of Environment Protection under the title *Facing Our Future* provides more detailed information on the anticipated effects of climate change on fisheries, forestry, infrastructure, water resources, biodiversity, and more.

A greenhouse gas (GHG) emissions inventory completed by the Northeast States for Coordinated Air Use Management (NESCAUM) in 2009 indicated that the leading culprit for GHG emissions in Connecticut (as elsewhere) is the carbon dioxide emissions related to the use of fossil fuels, accounting for more than 90 percent of all GHG emissions throughout the state in 2007. About 43 percent of this total came from the transportation sector, followed by electric power generation at 22 percent and residential activity (primarily the use of heating fuels) at 21 percent.

Recognizing the need to take action, Connecticut became one of the first states to implement a comprehensive climate change action plan, which was released in 2005. The plan included fifty-five recommendations from five main focus areas: transportation and land use; residential, commercial, and industrial; agriculture, forestry, and waste; electricity generation; and education and outreach. Some of the initiatives born from the plan include: the Connecticut Clean Energy Options program, a renewable portfolio standard, and the Connecticut Global Warming Solutions Act (2008 Public Act. No. 08-98), which ordered GHG emissions to be reduced to 10 percent below what they were in 1990 by 2020 and 80 percent below what they were in 2001, by 2050. Additionally, Connecticut is one of thirteen states to have adopted California's low emission vehicle standards.

Connecticut is a member of the Regional Greenhouse Gas Initiative (RGGI), a cooperative cap-and-trade program involving ten Northeastern and Mid-Atlantic states. The program is designed with the goal to reduce power sector carbon dioxide emissions by 10 percent by 2018. To that end, the regional cap established by the group was set at 188 million short tons of carbon dioxide per year from 2009 to 2014. Starting in 2015 the cap will decrease by 2.5 percent each year. Carbon dioxide allowances for power plants can be obtained or traded in quarterly auctions. Each state may then reinvest its auction proceeds in programs that support the growth of a clean energy economy.

In 2010 alone, the RGGI in Connecticut oversaw $29.6 million invested in energy efficiency programs. These programs, overseen by the Energy Conservation Management Board, provided energy efficiency services to more than one million households and 7,700 businesses. This resulted in a 6.3 billion kilowatt hour lifetime savings, which is equivalent to reducing energy costs by $1.3 billion and avoiding the emission of 4.3 million tons of carbon dioxide. Also in 2010, $4.78 million was approved for solar photovoltaic (PV) energy systems on municipal buildings.

In Connecticut, 69.5 percent of the state's auction proceeds are used to support energy efficiency programs administered by leading utility companies and regulated by the Energy Conservation Management Board. Another 23 percent support renewable energy programs administered through the Connecticut Clean Energy fund. The first three-year control (or compliance) period began on January 1, 2009 and was set to end on December 31, 2011. At that time, each regulated power plant must submit one allowance for each ton of carbon dioxide emitted during the control period. The RGGI represents the first mandatory, market-based carbon dioxide emissions program in the United States.

🌿 Natural Resources, Water, and Agriculture

Defining Boundaries

The four major geographic regions of the state are defined by the Connecticut and Quinnipiac rivers, the southern coastal area, and the northern region, containing the uplands. Situated in the western highlands in the northwesternmost corner of the state is the 2,454-foot (748-m) Mount Frissell, the point of highest altitude and part of the Green Mountain range of the Appalachian Mountains. Referred to as the coastal lowlands, the area along the Atlantic coast is mostly flat. The valleys around the Quinnipiac River and the Connecticut River form the state's central lowlands, where the state's population is densest and industrial activity is greatest.

Forests and Parks

About 60 percent of the state's land area is covered with forest, with the uplands being the most heavily forested region. Nearly 85 percent is under private ownership. The most common tree species include red maples, northern red oaks, and eastern white pines, with other significant species being the black oak, sweet birch, eastern hemlock, white ash, sugar maple, scarlet oak, and white oak (the official state tree). The oak/hickory forest type is the most common in the state, accounting for more than 70 percent of the total forest area. The state lost about 20 percent of its trees in the hurricane of 1938, with the greatest losses seen in the eastern portion of the state. The existing mature forests in the state are primarily made up of those that survived this and subsequent natural disasters and wildfires. According to the most recent forest inventory (published in 2010), about 68

percent of the forest stands are between 60 and 99 years old. The relative absence of forest stands in the younger and older age ranges poses a challenge both for sustainable management of wildlife habitats and the timber industry, as both need a wider range of ages for optimal health and productivity. The sale of private forestlands for commercial or industrial development is also a concern.

Flowers and plants in the uplands include the mountain laurel (state flower), pink azalea, trailing arbutus, Solomon's seal, and Queen Anne's lace. The U.S. Fish and Wildlife Service lists the sandplain gerardia and the American chaffseed as endangered plants in the state, and the small whorled pogonia as threatened.

There are more than sixty state parks, forests, and reserves, and three areas maintained by the National Park Service: the Weir Farm National Historic Site, the Quinebaug & Shetucket Rivers Valley National Heritage Corridor, and part of the Appalachian National Scenic trail.

More Aggressive Preservation Efforts Needed

Wildlife inhabiting Connecticut's forests include: the black bear, coyote, bobcat, flying squirrel, striped skunk, white-tailed deer, fisher, and beaver, among others. Common birds found across the state include: the American crow, brown-headed cowbird, osprey, American woodcock, bobwhite, and mute swan. The U.S. Fish and Wildlife Service lists eighteen animal species in Connecticut as either endangered or threatened, including five species of sea turtles.

The Connecticut Audubon Society has taken a leading role in the advocacy and protection of the state's wildlife. Of the 19 wildlife sanctuaries in the state owned and managed by the Connecticut Audubon Society, the largest are the Bafflin Sanctuary at Pomfret Farms, and the Richard G. Croft Memorial Preserve in Goshen. Nearly all 700 acres (283 ha) of the preserve remain undeveloped. Additionally, the Stewart B. McKinney National Wildlife Refuge has ten different divisions that extend along the shores.

Despite the land and wildlife protection efforts of organizations like the Connecticut Audubon Society, the state is not on track to meet the goals of the conservation plan established in 1997 (CGS 23-8(b)). According to the Council on Environmental Quality 2008 Annual Report, in order to meet the total preservation goal for 2023 (more than 670,000 acres [271,140 ha]) the state must preserve more than 11,000 acres (4,450 ha) of land each year. In 2007 and again in 2008, only 3,000 acres (1,210 ha) were preserved, putting the state in an even more difficult position to meet goals in subsequent years.

This is not to say that no significant action is being or has been taken. On July 28, 2009, the Connecticut Department of Environmental Protection (DEP), the

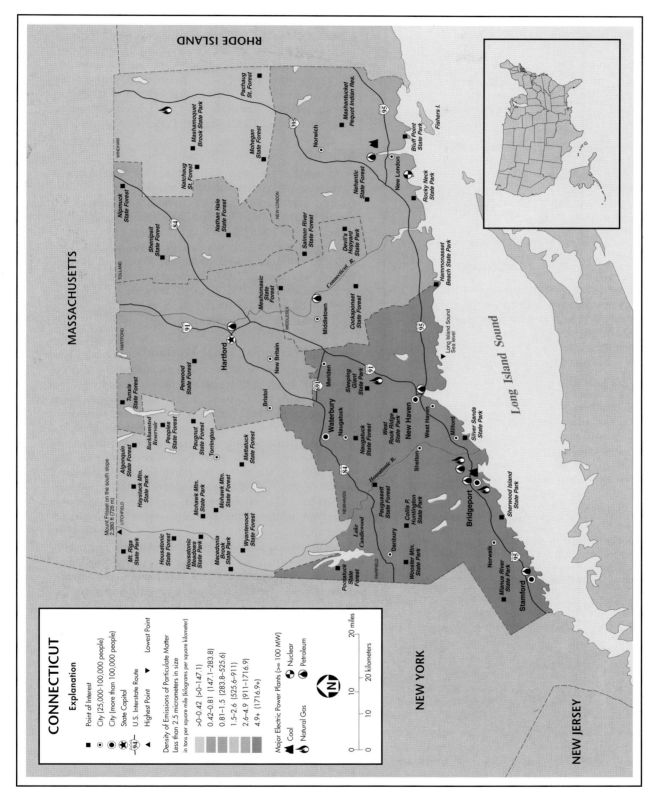

SOURCES: "County Emissions Map: Criteria Air Pollutants." *AirData.* U.S. Environmental Protection Agency. Available from http://www.epa.gov/air/data/geosel.html; *Energy Maps.* U.S. Energy Information Administration. Available from http://www.eia.gov/state; *Highest and Lowest Elevations.* U.S. Geological Survey. Available from http:// egsc.usgs.gov/isb/pubs/booklets/elvadist/elvadist.html#Highest; *2007 Minerals Yearbook.* U.S. Geological Survey. Available from http://minerals.usgs.gov/minerals/pubs/ state. © 2011 *Cengage Learning.*

Connecticut State Profile

Physical Characteristics

Land area	4,840 square miles (12,536 sq km)
Inland water area	164 square miles (425 sq km)
Coastal area	539 square miles (867 sq km)
Highest point	Mt. Frissell on south slope 2,380 feet (725 m)
National Forest System lands (2010)	24,000 acres (10,000 ha)
State parks (2011)	72

Energy Statistics

Total energy production (2009)	190 trillion Btu
State ranking in total energy production (2009)	40
Renewable energy net generation total (2009)	1.3 million megawatt hours
Hydroelectric energy generation (2009)	510,000 megawatt hours
Biomass energy generation (2009)	758,000 megawatt hours
Wind energy generation (2009)	NA
Wood and derived fuel energy generation (2009)	1,000 megawatt hours
Crude oil reserves (2009)	NA
Natural gas reserves (2009)	NA
Natural gas liquids (2008)	NA

Pollution Statistics

Carbon output (2005)	42.4 million tons of CO_2 (38.4 million t)
Superfund sites (2008)	14
Particulate matter (less than 2.5 micrometers) emissions (2002)	1,201 tons per year (1,089 t/yr)
Toxic chemical releases (2009)	3.3 million pounds (1.5 million kg)
Generated hazardous waste (2009)	21,100 tons (19,200 t)

SOURCES: AirData. U.S. Environmental Protection Agency. Available from http://www.epa.gov/air/data; *Energy Maps, Facts, and Data of the U.S. States.* U.S. Energy Information Administration. Available from http://www.eia.gov/state; *The 2012 Statistical Abstract.* U.S. Census Bureau. Available from http://www.census.gov/compendia/statab; *United States Energy Usage.* eRedux. Available from http://www.eredux.net/states.

© 2011 Cengage Learning.

United States Fish and Wildlife Service (USFWS), and the National Oceanic and Atmospheric Administration (NOAA) announced that the final Housatonic River Basin Natural Resource Restoration Plan was adopted by the Natural Resource Trustee SubCouncil. This plan resulted from an agreement reached between the states of Connecticut and Massachusetts and the General Electric Company (GE). GE, which had released polychlorinated biphenyls (PCBs) from its Pittsfield, Massachusetts, plant into the Housatonic, agreed to provide funding to clean up the Housatonic River.

In addition, under the Comprehensive Environmental Response, Compensation, and Liability Act (CERCLA, popularly referred to as the SuperFund Act), the U.S. Environmental Protection Agency provided funding for other natural resource restoration projects in Connecticut. All together, more than $7 million funded some 27 projects, sponsored by local and state government and nonprofit organizations. These projects include the Blackberry River Fish Passage Restoration, Trout Unlimited's Salmon Kill Restoration and Enhancement, Wetland Habitat Restoration on the Lower Housatonic River, and Indian Fields Wildlife Preserve.

Minerals

Few minerals of significant value are produced in Connecticut. Primary nonfuel mineral production is crushed stone and construction sand and gravel, and the production value of these minerals has seen an annual decrease since 2005. According to a report from the U.S. Geological Survey, the nonfuel production value from 2005 to 2006 decreased by almost 9 percent, or $14 million, and again in 2007, decreasing another 5 percent, or $9 million from 2006. In 2010, the state ranked forty-third in the nation for total nonfuel mineral production, with a value of $141 million.

Inland Wetlands, Tidal Wetlands

Water is one of the state's most abundant resources. There are nearly 6,000 miles (9,660 km) of rivers and streams, and more than 2,000 lakes, ponds, and reservoirs. The largest river is the Connecticut River, flowing south through the center of the state, emptying into Long Island Sound, an estuary of the Atlantic Ocean that is bordered on the north by Connecticut's southern coast and on the south by Long Island. The largest bodies of water—both humanmade—are the 5,000-acre (2,020-ha) Lake Candlewood and the Barkhamsted Reservoir, which is the source of most of Hartford's water supply.

The coastal lowlands along the Atlantic are mostly flat and are rich with salt grasses, glasswort, purple gerardia, and sea lavender. Just inland, black grass, switch grass, marsh elder and sea myrtle are abundant. The marsh areas are home to diverse fern species, cattails, cranberry, spicebush, and sweet pepperbush, to name a few. The Atlantic waters are home to five species of sea turtles and two species of whale, all of which are listed as endangered or threatened by the federal government. The least tern, oystercatcher, piping plover, osprey, and double-crested cormorant are among the birds that can be found along coastal areas.

Wetlands protection in Connecticut is the responsibility of the municipalities, which issue about 4,500 decisions per year. The state provides training and oversight for wetlands preservation. The number of wetland acres that have been disturbed or destroyed has decreased each year since 2002. However, in October 2008, the Connecticut Council on Environmental Quality published a special report, *Swamped: Cities, Towns, the Connecticut DEP and the Conservation of*

The marsh areas of Connecticut are home to diverse fern species, such as cattails, cranberry, spicebush, and sweet pepperbush.
© Marianne A. Campolongo/Alamy

Inland Wetlands, that found variability in the effectiveness of enforcement by municipalities and recommended that the state Department of Environmental Protection increase training to improve consistency in wetlands protection across the state.

Protection of these areas was in part established through by the *Tidal Wetlands Act* (CGS sections 22a-28 through 22a-35) and the Connecticut Coastal Management Act. Additionally, the Connecticut River Estuary and Tidal River Wetlands Complex have been identified and listed in the Ramsar List of Wetlands of International Importance.

The commercial fishing industry has weakened significantly due to coastal water pollution, which affects the supply of both freshwater fish and shellfish in the Long Island Sound. State agencies, such as the Connecticut River Atlantic Salmon Commission, are making efforts to manage and restore the population of Atlantic salmon to the Connecticut River. Other restoration projects, led by organizations such as the Connecticut River Watershed Council, will benefit a variety of species.

Restoration efforts in the Mattabesset and Scantic rivers focus on dam removal to allow migratory aquatic species access to their habitats. There are more than 70,000 acres (28,330 ha) of shellfish farms in the state's coastal waters, with farm-gate sales of shellfish at more than $30 million annually. The American shad and sea lamprey are the most abundant fish in Connecticut's rivers and are commonly caught by recreational fishers.

In August 2011 the Long Island Sound Study Citizens Action Committee (CAC) unveiled their SoundVision Action Plan. The plan will continue the work of the CAC in healing the Long Island Sound. It has four major components: Protecting clean water; creating safe places for all animals of the sound; building Long Island Sound communities that work; and investing economically in the Sound. One of the steps the plan recommends is to find funding for upgrades to wastewater treatment centers in New York City and the Connecticut cities of Bridgeport, New Haven, and Hartford. These cities dump the bulk of their sewage into the Sound, and the group hopes upgrades to treatment plants would lower the amount of nitrogen in the sound that can cause dead zones. The SoundVision Action Plan aims to achieve its goals over a two-year period. Save the Sound, along with Congresswoman Rosa DeLauro, went on a month-long SoundVision schooner tour of the Sound in August 2011, stopping in five ports in Connecticut and three in New York in order to engage the public and inform them of the action plan.

Increased Support for Small-Scale Farms

With less than 15 percent of the state being utilized for agricultural production, agriculture does not account for much of the state's economic output. But having a fairly long growing season (mid-April through mid-October) continues to benefit the small farms in operation. Greenhouse and nursery products (primarily produced for landscaping) account for about 45 percent of total farm receipts. The dairy industry is important to the state, which is home to more than 150 active dairy farms, supplying products that include ice cream, cheese, butter, and yogurt, as well as milk. Dairy livestock and poultry (also important) are raised primarily in the uplands region. Forage crops and corn for silage are the primary field crops, though a variety of vegetables are also produced. Shade tobacco was once a highly prosperous specialty crop, but production is on the decline. In 2007, the state ranked seventh in the nation for overall production of tobacco.

The growing interest in the local food movement, and increasing desire of consumers to know where their food comes from and to eat more healthfully and organically, has prompted the state's Department of Agriculture to create programs such as the Farm-to-Chef Program, Farm-to-School Program, and the CT Grown program. Small-scale farming projects have seen a great increase in support from the community, from CSAs and farmers' markets to community and urban farming projects, managed by a local organization, on land owned by the city or town.

Organic farmers gain certification through the USDA National Organic Program accredited Baystate Organic Certifiers. Support for local organic farmers is provided in part through the Connecticut Chapter of the Northeast Organic Farming Association CTNOFA, which maintains an annual list of certified organic farms throughout the state. The CTNOFA guide also includes notations for those that have signed the Farmers Pledge, which involves a voluntary commitment to farming, marketing, and farm management in accordance with sound ecological and economic principles. While farmers must provide a signed copy of the pledge to be added to the guide, there is no formal inspection process to guarantee compliance with the pledge standards, which include a promise to steer away from the use of synthetic insecticides and fertilizers, and from the use of genetically modified or chemically treated seeds. The pledge also calls on farm owners to use ethical business practices that include provisions for paying a living wage to workers and ensuring workers rights to collective bargaining. According to data available from the USDA, there were 82 certified organic farms in Connecticut in 2009, with organic product sales estimated at $5.2 million.

❧ Energy: Nuclear-Powered, Solar Potential

Having no petroleum or natural gas resources of its own, Connecticut relies on imported oil. There are no refineries in the state. Groton and New Haven are home to two of only three oil reserve sites in the northeastern part of the country. About half of all households use fuel oil to heat their homes. The state receives natural gas through an interstate pipeline.

Connecticut's electricity prices are among the highest in the United States. However, consumption is relatively low because the state's mild summers don't generate heavy demand for air conditioning, and heating is generally nonelectric.

Approximately half of the state's electric power comes from nuclear sources. Millstone Nuclear Power plant in Waterford, owned by Dominion Generation, is the state's only nuclear power facility. Roughly 17 percent of the state's electricity comes from natural gas plants, 14 percent from coal-fired plants, 7 percent from petroleum-fired plants, and 5 percent from other renewable sources (which includes landfill gas, municipal solid waste, hydroelectric power, and solar radiation).

The Millstone Nuclear Power Station, a combination of three nuclear reactors, began construction in 1966. It is located at Millstone Point on the north shore of Long Island Sound. *© Roger Ressmeyer/CORBIS*

Although not in the forefront of renewable energy resource development, the state does have potential for wind power development and was ranked among the top ten states for solar power capacity in 2008. Changes in state regulations have pushed forward the research and development of renewable resource potential.

Originally established in 1998, the state's renewable portfolio standard has gone through many revisions since its initial inception. It currently mandates that 27 percent of electrical power be generated from renewable sources by 2020. Additionally, companies supplying electricity must obtain a minimum of 23 percent renewable energy and 4 percent combined heat and power systems by 2020. Eligible renewable sources include solar thermal electric, photovoltaics, landfill gas, wind, biomass, hydroelectric, fuel cells, municipal solid waste, CHP/cogeneration (combined heat and power), tidal energy, wave energy, and ocean thermal energy.

❧ Green Business, Green Building, Green Jobs

Green Economic Growth: What Sectors Will Benefit Most?

Recent government-funded initiatives providing green jobs training programs for Connecticut residents indicate an increase in the need for skilled workers in those areas. Part of the trouble in measuring green economic growth is that there is not a standardized definition for green jobs. The Connecticut state departments of labor and economic and community development report that the sectors seeing the biggest growth in green jobs in 2009 were customer service and laborers. Connecticut is preparing for growth in green jobs by implementing job training programs and education incentives.

In the 2009 *Sustainability and Connecticut Business Survey*, more than 70 percent of small businesses surveyed in the state were engaging in some sustainable/green business practices, about a 25 percent increase from 2007. Leaders in green business development practices—spanning all sectors—are recognized through programs such as the Connecticut Green Business Awards, which identifies businesses with innovative programs in such areas as renovation, recycling, and solar energy.

Award-Winning Sustainable Design

The city of New Haven has produced many inspiring sustainable design projects in recent years. The American Institute of Architects (AIA) Committee on the Environment awards the top ten green building projects (listed as the AIA/COTE award) annually. In 2007, the New Haven Whitney Water Purification Facility, designed by Steven Holl Architects, was the winner. The facility boasts innovative green design concepts and watershed management practices. The Yale Sculpture Building and Gallery, designed by Kieran Timberlake Associates, LLP, took an award in 2008. The building includes bike stalls and showers to encourage cycling and the use of public transportation, and is within walking distance of five bus lines. Also notable was the use of collected rainwater to flush toilets in the facility. In 2010 the award went to Kroon Hall, the new Yale School of Forestry and Environmental Studies, designed by Hopkins Architects and Centerbrook Architects and Planners.

As a result of a number of green initiatives begun during Governor Jodi Rell's administration, (2004–11), she earned a spot on Greenopia's "top ten most environmentally responsible governors" list in 2009. (Greenopia is an organization that seeks to create directories of local resources for citizens interested in supporting businesses dedicated to green and sustainable practices.) These initiatives included green building, green jobs, and green transportation planning.

Connecticut's state building code incorporates the 2006 International Energy Conservation Code, which mandated energy efficiency requirements for new construction and major renovations. Regulations require at least a Silver LEED (the Leadership in Energy and Environmental Design standard of the US Green Building Council) rating, and apply to new construction projects of $5 million or greater and renovations budgeted at more than $2 million.

In addition to the state's efforts to legislate and incentivize green building practices, organizations like the Connecticut Green Building Council (CGBC), a chapter of the United States Green Building Council, play an integral role in statewide awareness. The CGBC promotes and advocates for highly efficient construction through educational programs, and has a design awards program for institutional, commercial and residential green design/construction projects.

Leading Legislation on Green Collar Initiatives

In May 2010, the state enacted a law (sHB No. 5435) that will forgive student loan debt to students earning a bachelor's degree (up to $10,000) or an associate's degree (up to $5,000) in a green field from an educational institution in Connecticut.

Several nonprofit organizations have launched programs to create jobs and raise awareness of sustainable business and building practices. One such organization, Groundwork Bridgeport, was launched in 1998 to convert blighted areas of the city into parks and to develop environmental education and job training to accomplish the conversion. Groundwork Bridgeport was one of the original trusts in the Groundwork USA Network, which was modeled after a successful program in the United Kingdom. Groundwork USA started as a collaborative effort between the Environmental Protection Agency (EPA) and the National Park Service (NPS). Initial funding for Groundwork Bridgeport came from those organizations and the city of Bridgeport.

Much of the "green" work in Connecticut is in home improvement, some of which is funded by the weatherization projects. Greater Bridgeport Community Enterprise, Inc. has provided a significant amount of this work through its Green Team program, which is aimed at increasing the energy efficiency of residential dwellings. Greater Bridgeport Community Enterprise was one of several organizations that received funding from the U.S. Department of Labor to create green job programs. Since November 2009, they have received approximately $4 million to develop green job training programs.

To assist job seekers with entrance into the green workforce, the Green Job Bank was established in 2009. Funding was awarded to a consortium (made up of Connecticut and seven other northeast states) through the American Recovery and Reinvestment Act of 2009. This funding led to the establishment of Connecticut's Green Collar Jobs Council, a cooperative venture of several state departments and chaired by the Connecticut Employment and Training Commission.

State Faces Scrutiny Over Vetoed Energy Bill

In 2006, Governor Jodi Rell issued Executive Order 15, which created an Office of Responsible Growth to balance economic growth with the preservation of the state's natural environment and resources. Reducing energy demands and supporting renewable sources were objectives included in Executive Order 15. But in May 2010, Governor Rell vetoed an energy reform bill (Bill 493: An Act Reducing Electricity Costs and Promoting Renewable Energy), causing much controversy and public debate. Governor Rell claimed that the bill would actually raise utility rates for customers. She explained the veto, stating that the bill was hastily thrown together and passed without critical review or public input. Among those disappointed by Rell's veto were John W. Fonfara, state senator and co-chair of the General Assembly's Energy and Technology Committee, and Richard Blumenthal, Connecticut's attorney general. Fonfara disputed Rell's claim that the bill lacked public input, stating that it was based on input from renewable energy experts and based on earlier legislation.

After the veto of Bill 493, the state was further scrutinized for its underutilization of available funds from the American Recovery and Reinvestment Act (ARRA, federal stimulus program) of 2009. Connecticut was allocated close to $170 million to develop programs to boost the state's renewable energy industry. As of August 2010, less than 12 percent of the funds had been spent, but some initiatives had made significant progress. The Connecticut Clean Energy Fund and the Home Energy Solutions Program have invested approximately 23 percent of their ARRA allocation, primarily to fund installations of geothermal and solar thermal projects.

The state has also updated its "Green Plan" regarding land acquisition and protection (pursuant to EO 15), reviewed funding and transportation policies and projects, increased housing opportunities, and created economic incentives for individuals and businesses, agencies, and organizations. An important component is the Landscape Stewardship Initiative, which specifically addresses the need for coordinated efforts between the state's various environmental protection, conservation, land use, and development programs in order to reach goals more efficiently. Rell's Executive Order 23 called for the labor commission to establish a 21st Century Green Jobs Training Initiative, the commissioner of education to establish a Green Collar Corps, and the office of workforce competitiveness to establish a Green Science and Engineering Advisory Group.

In July 2011, Senate Bill 1243: An Act Concerning the Establishment of the Department of Energy and Environmental Protection and Planning for Connecticut's Energy Future was passed. The Department of Energy and Environmental Protection (DEEP) is formed through this act by merging the departments of Environmental Protection and Public Utility Control. The clean energy and efficiency financing and investment programs in the bill will help to cut the energy bills of residents. It also has measures supporting everything from energy efficiency retrofits to clean energy installations and construction of infrastructure for electric vehicles. Some of the bill's key clean energy provisions include: Creating a renewable energy credit incentive program supporting construction of hundreds of megawatts of larger scale zero-emission distributed renewable energy systems like solar and wind; requiring the new

Clean Energy Finance and Investment Authority to create a residential solar rebate program to install at least 30 megawatts of new residential solar systems; requiring state buildings to reduce energy use 10 percent by 2013 and another 10 percent by 2018; and authorizing the new Clean Energy Finance and Investment Authority to invest in energy efficiency retrofits, renewable energy systems, as well as electric and alternative vehicle infrastructure.

BIBLIOGRAPHY

Books

Cumbler, John T. *Reasonable Use: The People, the Environment, and the State, New England 1790-1930.* New York, NY: Oxford University Press, 2001.

Finch, Robert, and Jonathan Wallen. *The Smithsonian Guides to Natural America: Southern New England–Connecticut, Rhode Island, Massachusetts.* Washington, DC: Smithsonian Books, 1996.

Hammerson, Geoffrey A. *Connecticut Wildlife: Biodiversity, Natural History and Conservation.* Lebanon, NH: University Press of New England, 2004.

Kershner, Bruce, and Robert T. Leverett. *The Sierra Club Guide to the Ancient Forests of the Northeast.* San Francisco, CA: Sierra Club Books, 2004.

Lomuscio, James. *Village of the Dammed: The Fight for Open Space and the Flooding of a Connecticut Town.* Lebanon, NH: University Press of New England, 2005.

Weingold, Marilyn. *The Long Island Sound: A History of Its People, Places, and Environment.* New York, NY: NYU Press, 2004.

Web Sites

"About Connecticut." State of Connecticut web site. Available from http://www.ct.gov/ctportal/cwp/view.asp?a=843&q=246434#LAND

"Bracing for Climate Change in the Constitution State: What Connecticut Could Face." Environmental Defense. Available from http://www.edf.org/documents/3504_ct-climate_09_view.pdf

Cartledge, James. "Connecticut Governor Vetoes Clean Energy Reforms." BrighterEnergy.org. Available from http://www.brighterenergy.org/11018/news/legislation/connecticut-governor-vetoes-clean-energy-reforms/

"Connecticut Career Resource Network Update." Connecticut Department of Labor Office of Research. Available from http://www1.ctdol.state.ct.us/lmi/pubs/ccrn_spring09.pdf

Connecticut Chapter of the Northeast Organic Farming Association. Available from http://www.ctnofa.org/index.htm

Connecticut Climate Change Action Plan. Available from http://ctclimatechange.com/wp-content/uploads/2009/03/CT_Climate_Change_Action_Plan_2005.pdf

The Connecticut Economic Digest. Connecticut Department of Labor Office of Research. September 2010 issue. Vol. 15, No. 9. Available from http://www1.ctdol.state.ct.us/lmi/digest/pdfs/cedsep10.pdf

"Connecticut: Incentives/Policies for Renewables and Efficiency." DSIRE. Available from http://www.dsireusa.org/incentives/incentive.cfm?Incentive_Code=CT04R&state

"Connecticut." Institute for Energy Research. Available from http://www.instituteforenergyresearch.org/states/connecticut/

"Connecticut May Forgive Student Loans for Green Jobs." May 1, 2010 newsbrief from *Environmental Building News.* Available from http://www.buildinggreen.com/auth/article.cfm/2010/5/1/Connecticut-May-Forgive-Student-Loans-for-Green-Jobs/

Connecticut's Forest Resource Assessment and Strategy, 2010. Connecticut Department of Environmental Protection, Division of Forestry. Available from http://www.ct.gov/dep/cwp/view.asp?a=2697&q=454164&depNav_GID=1631

"Current Habitat Restoration Projects." Connecticut River Watershed Council. Available from http://www.ctriver.org/programs/restoration/current_projects/index.html

"DEP, USFWS, and NOAA Announce Final Fund Allocation for 27 Projects Approved for the Housatonic River Basin Natural Resource Restoration Plan." Connecticut Department of Environmental Protection. Available from http://www.ct.gov/Dep/cwp/view.asp?A=3605&Q=444288

"Endangered and Threatened Species Fact Sheets." Connecticut Department of Environmental Protection. Available from http://www.ct.gov/dep/cwp/view.asp?a=2723&q=326210

"Environmental Quality in Connecticut." State of Connecticut. Available from http://www.ct.gov/ceq/cwp/view.asp?a=3718&Q=435666

"Executive Order No. 15." State of Connecticut Governor's web site. Available from http://www.ct.gov/governorrell/cwp/view.asp?A=1719&Q=320908

Facing Our Future: Adapting to Connecticut's Changing Climate. Connecticut Department of Environment Protection. Available from http://www.ct.gov/dep/lib/dep/air/climatechange/adaptation/090320facingourfuture.pdf

"Forestry." Connecticut Department of Environmental Protection. Available from http://www.ct.gov/dep/cwp/view.asp?a=2697&q=322792&depNav_GID=1631%20

"Governor Rell: State Awarded Stimulus Funds to Identify Green Jobs, Training Opportunities." M. Jodi Rell, Governor of Connecticut. Available from http://www.ct.gov/recovery/cwp/view.asp?A=3711&Q=451018

"Governor Rell's Executive Order No. 23 Establishes Blueprint for Green Collar Job Creation." M. Jodi Rell, Governor of Connecticut. Available from http://www.ct.gov/governorrell/cwp/view.asp?A=3675&Q=433280

Groundwork Bridgeport. Available from http://www.groundworkbridgeport.org/

Hanle, Juliana. "Connecticut forests hit by economic crisis." *Yale News.* February 17, 2011. Available from http://www.yaledailynews.com/news/2011/feb/17/connecticut-forests-hit-by-economic-crisis

"Informational Series Fact Sheets." Connecticut Department of Environmental Protection. Available from http://www.ct.gov/dep/cwp/view.asp?a=2723&q=326214&depNav_GID=1655

"January 2010 Connecticut Green Business Awards." Available from http://www.americantowns.com/ct/newhaven/news/january-2010-connecticut-green-business-awards-255287

Kane, Brad. "State Lags in Spending Energy Cash." *Hartford Business Journal* online. Available from http://www.hartfordbusiness.com/article.php?RF_ITEM[]=Article$0@14472;Article&css_display=print

New England Agricultural Statistics, 2009. United States Department of Agriculture. Available from http://www.nass.usda.gov/Statistics_by_State/New_England_includes/Publications/Annual_Statistical_Bulletin/09start.htm

"Overview of Climate in Connecticut." Connecticut State Climate Center. Available from http://www.canr.uconn.edu/nrme/cscc/CTweatherstationintroduction/CONNCTICUTINTRODUCTION.HTM

Regional Greenhouse Gas Initiative: Connecticut State Investment Plan. Available from http://www.rggi.org/rggi_benefits/program_investments/Connecticut

Senate Bill 1243: An Act Concerning the Establishment of the Department of Energy and Environmental Protection and Planning for Connecticut's Energy Future. Connecticut General Assembly. Available from http://www.cga.ct.gov/2011/ACT/PA/2011PA-00080-R00SB-01243-PA.htm

SoundVision: Long Island Sound Water Conservation. Available from http://www.lisoundvision.org//index.cfm

"Species Reports." U.S. Fish & Wildlife Service. Available from http://ecos.fws.gov/tess_public/pub/stateListingAndOccurrenceIndividual.jsp?state=CT

State of Connecticut Department of Environmental Protection home page. Available from http://www.ct.gov/dep/site/default.asp

"State Fact Sheet: Protecting and Restoring Natural Resources in Connecticut." National Oceanic and Atmospheric Administration (NOAA) Damage Assessment, Remediation and Restoration Program (DARRP). Available from http://www.darrp.noaa.gov/factsheet/pdf/Connecticut/DARRP_State_Factsheets_Connecticut.pdf

"State Water Allocation Report." State of Connecticut Department of Environmental Protection. Available from http://www.ct.gov/dep/lib/dep/water_inland/diversions/water_alloc_rpt/uses.pdf

"Swamped: Cities, Towns, the Connecticut DEP and the Conservation of Inland Wetlands." Connecticut Council on Environmental Quality. Available from http://www.ct.gov/ceq/lib/ceq/swamped_with_links.pdf

"Top 40 Environmental Accomplishments of the Past 40 Years." Connecticut Department of Environmental Protection. Available from http://www.ct.gov/dep/cwp/view.asp?a=2688&Q=456184&depNav_GID=1511

2009 Connecticut GHG Inventory Update. Connecticut Department of Environmental Protection. Available from http://www.ct.gov/dep/lib/dep/air/climatechange/inventory/2009_ghg_update_final_-_070110_edit.pdf

Varnon, Rob. "It Isn't Easy Being a Green Economy." ctpost.com. April 23, 2010. http://www.ctpost.com/local/article/It-isn-t-easy-being-a-green-economy-460965.php

Delaware

Delaware boasts a diversity of habitats and natural resources. The northern region of the state is part of the Appalachian piedmont with rolling hills and steep stream valleys. The southern portion of the state is classified as Atlantic Coastal Plain with flat sandy ground and marshy regions, including the Cypress Swamp. Plentiful water resources are valued by local residents and those of the greater Mid-Atlantic region of the United States. The state is the home to more than 800 different species of wildlife, providing habitat for a wide variety of species along coastal beaches, tidal marshlands, and mixed forests. Despite its small size, the state has taken big steps to protect and conserve its natural land, and has made noticeable efforts to reduce the overall energy demand of the state.

Effects of Climate Change

The climate in Delaware is temperate and humid. Fahrenheit temperatures range from low twenties in the winter to high eighties in the summer.

According to data supplied through the Center for Energy and Environmental Policy (CEEP) at the University of Delaware, global climate change could have significant effects for the state. With its low elevation, Delaware's shoreline and coastal environment are particularly at risk from rising sea levels caused by a rise in temperature. Temperatures across the state could increase by 3 to 4°F (1.7 to 2.2° C) by 2100, resulting in hotter and longer summer seasons and increases in precipitation of 15 percent to 40 percent under the highest emissions scenario. (Under the lower emissions scenario, precipitation increases are predicted to increase in the range of 7–9 percent.) In addition, the already high rates of ground level ozone could worsen through the change in temperature and other weather patterns.

In an effort to protect the land and future of the state's environment and diverse species, the CEEP, the Delaware Energy Office, and the Delaware Climate Change Consortium (DCCC) worked together to create the Delaware Climate Change Action Plan in 2000, which outlined policy options to reduce greenhouse gas emissions by 25 percent by 2010.

Delaware is a member of the Regional Greenhouse Gas Initiative (RGGI), a cooperative cap-and-trade program involving ten Northeastern and Mid-Atlantic states. The program is designed with the goal to reduce power sector carbon dioxide emissions by 10 percent by 2018. To that end, the regional cap established by the group was set at 188 million short tons of carbon dioxide per year from 2009 to 2014. Starting in 2015 the cap will decrease by 2.5 percent each year. Carbon dioxide allowances for power plants can be obtained or traded in quarterly auctions. Each state may then reinvest its auction proceeds in programs that support the growth of a clean energy economy.

In Delaware, 65 percent of the state's auction proceeds are earmarked for the Sustainable Energy Utility, which offers energy efficiency and renewable energy programs for residents and business owners. Another 15 percent is used to support programs for low income consumers, such as the Low Income Home Energy Assistance Program and home weatherization projects. Carbon dioxide allowances can also be obtained through the Chicago Climate Futures Exchange and the Green Exchange. The first three-year control (or compliance) period began on January 1, 2009 and ended on December 31, 2011. At that time, each regulated power plant submitted one allowance for each ton of carbon dioxide emitted during the control period. The RGGI represents the first mandatory, market-based carbon dioxide emissions program in the United States.

❧ Natural Resources, Water, and Agriculture

Natural Resources

Forests cover about 30 percent of the state, with about half consisting of the oak/hickory forest type and one-quarter of the pine or pine/oak types. The most common tree species include red and white oak, hickory, loblolly pine, yellow-poplar, maples, and sweet gum. Black walnut, ash, tupelo, bald cypress, and Atlantic white cedar are also found. About 85 percent of the forestland is under private ownership and more than 25 percent of the forests are protected from development through a variety of initiatives. The forest product industry employs more than 2,600 people with an annual payroll of nearly $100 million.

There are fifteen state parks and preserves—totaling more than 20,000 acres (8,090 ha) of land—that are managed by the Division of Parks and Recreation, which provides land protection services as well as educational and recreational programs for visitors. Delaware's senator Tom Carper has put forth a proposal in Congress to establish the First State National Park in Delaware. The park would commemorate early American Dutch, Swedish, and English settlements and Delaware's role in the events leading up to the signing of our Constitution. As of 2011 Delaware was the only state without a designated national park.

Home to more than 800 species of wildlife, native mammals of the state include the white-tailed deer, gray fox, muskrat, raccoon, eastern gray squirrel, and common cottontail. Common birds include the robin and cardinal. The U.S. Fish and Wildlife Service lists sixteen animal and seven plant species in the state as either threatened or endangered, including the leatherback sea turtle, Delmarva fox squirrel, and Canby's dropwort. The Delaware Natural Heritage and Endangered Species Program (DE NHESP) studies and provides relevant information on the state's native flora and fauna.

Nonfuel mineral production in 2008 was valued at more than $20.6 million, representing a 22 percent decrease in value from 2007. However, this data provided by the U.S. Geological Survey did not include the production of magnesium compounds. In 2008, Delaware ranked fourth among the five states in the nation that produce magnesium compounds. The state produces these compounds for use in chemical and pharmaceutical manufacturing. Delaware's leading nonfuel minerals include construction sand and gravel. In 2010, the state was ranked fiftieth in the nation in nonfuel mineral production with a value of $12.7 million.

Delaware Waters in Danger

Water is one of the state's most valued resources, with dozens of freshwater lakes, ponds, rivers, streams, and wetlands.

The most prominent rivers include the Nanticoke, Mispillion, Christina, St. Johns, Leipsic, and Murderkill. The Delaware River at the northern border empties into Delaware Bay. The Delaware River Basin, which covers more than 13,500 square miles (34,965 sq km) in New Jersey, Pennsylvania, New York, and Delaware, serves as a major resource for more than 15 million people, providing water for drinking, agricultural, and industrial use. This important resource is managed primarily through the work of the Delaware River Basin Commission (DRBC). The commission was established in 1961 through the passage of concurrent legislation in the four basin states and with the accompanying signature of President John F. Kennedy. The compact that formed the commission created the first regional body to share equal authority with the federal government in the management of a river system. Since then, the commission has been instrumental in providing programs for water quality protection, supply allocation, conservation efforts, drought and flood management, watershed planning, and recreation. The commissioners include the governors of New Jersey, New York, Pennsylvania, and Delaware, and a federal representative; each commissioner has one vote, and all votes are of equal power.

The Port of Wilmington, at the confluence of the Delaware and Christian Rivers, is the busiest terminal on the Delaware River and serves as a major Mid-Atlantic trade gateway. The ports of Wilmington and New Castle both rank within the top fifty in the nation for foreign trade cargo volume.

There are more than 350,000 acres (141,640 ha) of wetlands alone, providing an area rich with environmental diversity and function. Delaware includes a portion of three major estuaries, the Chesapeake Bay, Inland Bays, and the Delaware Bay estuary, with the Delaware Bay being the largest portion. The Delaware Bay estuary, shared with New Jersey, is also a Ramsar Wetland of International Importance. The commercial fishing industry is still active, though no longer thriving as it once was. Blue crab is by far the most valuable catch, followed by striped bass, eastern oyster, knobbed whelk, and sea scallops. There are numerous recreational and sport fishing programs for residents and visitors. Among the most popular sport fish species are striped bass, trout, black drum, black sea bass, and summer flounder.

Despite their great quantity of freshwater sources, Delaware waters may be in danger. Because global warming has created a rise in sea levels, and this along with poorer water quality in general, both threaten the natural habitat, and the risk of saltwater contamination becomes more apparent. The Delaware Water Resources Center was established in 1965 through the University of Delaware and works with local and state government to provide research, planning, and policy assistance to maintain and preserve clean water supplies.

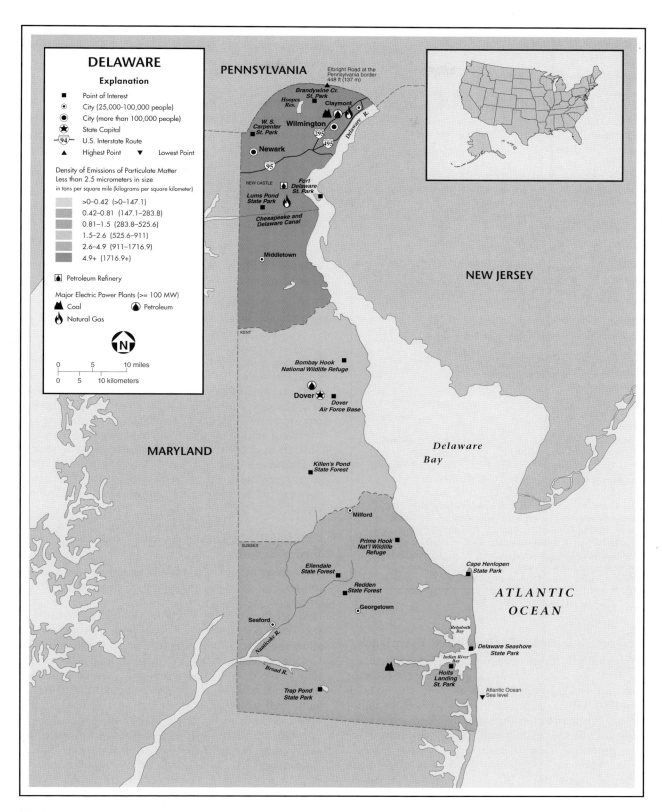

SOURCES: "County Emissions Map: Criteria Air Pollutants." *AirData*. U.S. Environmental Protection Agency. Available from http://www. epa.gov/air/data/geosel.html; *Energy Maps*. U.S. Energy Information Administration. Available from http://www.eia.gov/state; *Highest and Lowest Elevations*. U.S. Geological Survey. Available from http://egsc.usgs.gov/isb/pubs/booklets/elvadist/elvadist.html#Highest; *2007 Minerals Yearbook*. U.S. Geological Survey. Available from http://minerals.usgs.gov/minerals/pubs/state. © 2011 Cengage Learning.

Delaware State Profile

Physical Characteristics

Land area	1,949 square miles (5,048 sq km)
Inland water area	74 square miles (192 sq km)
Coastal area	372 square miles (599 sq km)
Highest point	Ebright Road 448 feet (137 m)
National Forest System lands (2010)	NA
State parks (2011)	17

Energy Statistics

Total energy production (2009)	4 trillion Btu
State ranking in total energy production (2009)	48
Renewable energy net generation total (2009)	126,000 megawatt hours
Hydroelectric energy generation (2009)	NA
Biomass energy generation (2009)	126,000 megawatt hours
Wind energy generation (2009)	NA
Wood and derived fuel energy generation (2009)	NA
Crude oil reserves (2009)	NA
Natural gas reserves (2009)	NA
Natural gas liquids (2008)	NA

Pollution Statistics

Carbon output (2005)	17.2 million tons of CO_2 (15.6 million t)
Superfund sites (2008)	14
Particulate matter (less than 2.5 micrometers) emissions (2002)	2,476 tons per year (2,246 t/yr)
Toxic chemical releases (2009)	8.1 million pounds (3.7 million kg)
Generated hazardous waste (2009)	19,800 tons (18,000 t)

SOURCES: AirData. U.S. Environmental Protection Agency. Available from http://www.epa.gov/air/data; *Energy Maps, Facts, and Data of the U.S. States.* U.S. Energy Information Administration. Available from http://www.eia.gov/state; *The 2012 Statistical Abstract.* U.S. Census Bureau. Available from http://www.census.gov/compendia/statab; *United States Energy Usage.* eRedux. Available from http://www.eredux.net/states.

© 2011 Cengage Learning.

Productive Farmlands, Protected Farmlands

Although Delaware is the second smallest state in the nation, its farms are impressively productive for both the state's size and growing season. With more than 500,000 acres (202,340 ha) of farmland, farms account for almost half of the total land in the state. The egg and poultry industries are the leading agricultural products in the state, producing more in sales than any other product farmed. The state's two primary field crops are corn and soybeans, accounting for more than 300,000 acres (121,410 ha) of production. Other noteworthy crops, though not nearly as largely farmed, are wheat, vegetables, and barley.

Pressures to develop farmland and the increasing power of factory farms have led to the sale of tens of thousands of acres of farmland since the 1990s. The Delaware Agricultural Lands Preservation Foundation was formed in 1991 to offer protection to farmers. In 2011, there were more than 100,000 acres (40,470 ha) of farmland protected. The state has more protected farmland per capita than any other state.

In spite of the growing demand for organic food and produce, Delaware has not yet demonstrated a shift to organic food production. According to a USDA Economic Research Service report, in 2008 Delaware had 164 acres (66 ha) of land dedicated to organic farming, and there were a total of four certified organic operations in the state. Organizations such as the Delaware Organic Food and Farming Association (DOFFA) work to raise awareness in local communities and provide educational workshops to those interested in transitioning to organic farming or beginning a new organic farm.

Energy

Every five years the Governor's Energy Task Force in Delaware must submit an updated energy plan for the state, according to a statute popularly known as the Delaware Energy Act (Delaware Code, 29 Del.C. Subch. II). The task force's March 2009 energy plan update reported heavy per capita energy use. The state ranked twentieth among the fifty states in per capita energy use. The report noted that total energy use across all sectors of Delaware's economy was 301 trillion Btus in 2006, with a per capita use of 353 million Btus, which was above the U.S. average that year of 333 million Btus per capita.

Crude Oil, Natural Gas and Coal: Finite Resources

The state is limited in its potential for energy production, as it has no ability to produce crude oil or natural gas, and there are no coal reserves. Although lacking the means to produce energy resources, the state does operate several power plants, which allow the state to process and distribute power locally. Coal-fired plants make up roughly three-fifths of the state's electricity generation and natural gas-fired power plants account for about one-fifth, with petroleum-fired plants making up around one-tenth of the state's electricity generation.

The Delaware City Refinery—which was the single oil refinery in the state—was shut down by Valero Corporation in November 2009 because of the economic downturn. It has since been purchased by a group of investors, who reopened the refinery in July 2011.

Producing no natural gas, the state relies primarily on supplies from Eastern Shore Natural Gas, one of two major suppliers that deliver the gas via an interstate natural gas pipeline system. Without coal reserves, Delaware receives its supplies by rail from West Virginia, Kentucky, Colorado, and Virginia.

Wind Power: Clean Energy Potential

Offshore wind power may be the state's best opportunity for alternative energy development. In response to a 2006 request for proposals from the state, the offshore wind developer Bluewater Wind proposed a 450-mega-watt capacity wind park, which would include 49 large turbines and 150 smaller ones located about 13 miles (21 km) off the coast. The proposal received initial acceptance in 2008 following the negotiation and approval of a 25-year power purchase agreement between Bluewater Wind and Delmarva Power for up to 200 megawatts of energy.

An additional boost for the project came in March 2011 when the federal Bureau of Ocean Energy Management, Regulation, and Enforcement (BOEMRE) announced an agreement that gives Bluewater Wind exclusive rights to negotiate a commercial lease with the government under the "Smart from the Start" Atlantic Offshore Wind program. The "Smart from the Start" program was launched in November 2010 as a way to accelerate and simplify the leasing process for wind energy facilities along the Atlantic Outer Continental Shelf. The non-competitive lease agreement was granted after Bluewater Wind was the only qualified organization that responded to the bureau's two requests for interest issued in April 2010 and again in January 2011. This led the BOEMRE to conclude that there was no other competitive interest for wind energy development in the federal waters of offshore Delaware. The non-competitive lease agreement was the first issued under the "Smart from the Start" program. "Smart from the Start" is expected to result in an expedited leasing process, but it does not guarantee that projects will be approved. The developer must still submit to the required environmental reviews and consultations with federal, state, and local authorities. If all goes well, the Bluewater Wind facility is expected to be operational no later than 2016. Momentum for the project slowed in mid-2011 due to financing issues. However, officials are hoping that the passage of the Incentivizing Offshore Wind Power Act, introduced in the Senate in July 2011 (and was referred to the House Committee on Ways and Means in October 2011), will give the project the financial boost that it needs. The legislation will secure investment tax credits for the first 3,000 MW of off-shore wind facilities placed into service in the US. In addition to wind power being a green, renewable resource that reduces dependence on finite resources, the use of this alternative energy source is expected to have a positive impact on the local economy, stabilizing energy costs for consumers.

Delaware residents are also taking advantage of federal subsidies and purchasing their own small wind turbines. In the northeast grid prices are high, so having a small turbine can be particularly helpful for people in rural areas. The Delaware Center for the Inland Bays and the state parks service both utilize Skystream 3.7 turbines. Skystream 3.7s are made by Southwest Power, a Flagstaff, Arizona-based company that is working with Delaware to move its headquarters to the state. Small-scale wind power can make a huge difference in a company or organization's electric bill. The Delaware Center for the Inland Bays states that with its wind turbine and solar panels combined, the energy generated took care of 85 percent of their electric bill in 2010.

The Delaware Department of Natural Resources and Environmental Control (DNREC) Energy Office has established ongoing workgroups to review energy policies and report back to the Governor's Energy Advisory Council, providing recommendations that support Delaware's energy goals. Recommendations have been made to reduce overall energy consumption, to be achieved in part by revising codes in residential and commercial building, establishing standards for new state-funded and public facilities, and providing weatherization assistance programs to qualifying home-owners.

Legislative Changes

A renewable portfolio standard (RPS) was developed in 2005 (Senate Bill 74). It requires that 10 percent of the electricity in Delaware come from renewable sources by the compliance year, which is 2019/20. (The compliance year runs from June to May.) In 2007 a new bill was introduced (Senate Bill 19) that increased the RPS target from 10 percent to 20 percent, doubling the target for the use of renewable energy, and introducing a 2.005 percent photovoltaic energy source requirement. In July 2010, the bill (SB 1 for SB 119) was revised again, increasing the target to 25 percent by compliance year 2025/26, with a minimum of 3.5 percent from photovoltaic sources. With the passage of Senate Bill 124 in July 2011, energy output from a qualified fuel cell provider can now help fulfill a portion of the requirements. The bill also requires Delmarva Power & Light to take responsibility for the RPS obligations of its customers, and also creates a regulatory framework through which the Delaware Public Service Commission will review a tariff to be filed by Delmarva deploying Delaware-manufactured fuel cells as part of a 30MW project.

❧ Green Business, Green Building, Green Jobs

Businesses Invest in Green Future

Tapping into the green market may require businesses to take risks, think differently, or change standard practices. Science-based products and services company DuPont, headquartered in Wilmington, implemented aggressive changes in its energy consumption, making modifications one facility at a time. DuPont also opened an $8-million photovoltaic research facility in Wilmington in June 2010. No less important, smaller-scale ways for local businesses to invest in a greener future are to participate in the state's Green Industries Program, where qualifying businesses are eligible for tax incentives and/or financial assistance. The program seeks to reduce the amount of waste businesses produce by encouraging the purchase of recycled materials whenever possible, and the recycling of new waste.

Green Building: New Energy Efficiency Standards Affect Change

Delaware has taken a leading role in energy conservation with its Weatherization Assistance Program, making residential updates to conserve energy that include improvements to or replacement of inefficient heating systems or hot water tanks, replacement or addition of insulation, and weatherstripping and caulking to seal air leaks. Since the program began, Delaware has completed more than one-third of all planned weatherization projects, allowing residents to save an average of 20 percent on home energy costs.

Delaware's Sustainable Energy Utility (SEU), a nonprofit corporation with $35 million from a state bond, was created in 2007, with programming beginning spring 2010. The SEU will develop markets for energy efficiency and conservation, customer-sited renewable energy, and affordable energy services for low and moderate income families. The concept of an SEU is illustrated by this example, cited in a February 2010 article in *The New York Times*. The SEU would pay to have solar panels, for example, installed on a school. Then it would arrange a contract to sell power to the school district over a decade or two, usually for the same price as electricity off the grid, until the cost of the system was paid off.

The SEU will get its first $35 million from a Delaware state bond, and the fund will be replenished—and the bonds repaid—as the school districts and other projects save energy. An independent auditor will routinely check the buildings to make sure their equipment is working properly, allowing the SEU to guarantee savings over the life of its contracts.

More recent local and state efforts to promote renewable energy include projects such as Energize Delaware Now (EDEN), a grassroots organization that provides educational programs on sustainability, green economics and renewable resources.

Revisions in building codes have increased standards for both existing structures and new construction throughout the state. In July 2009 SB 59 was signed, mandating that residential dwellings (three or less stories) built after July 1, 2010, must comply with the 2009 International Energy Conservation Code (IECC). All other new construction has to meet the American Society of Heating, Refrigerating, and Air Conditioning Engineers (ASHRAE) Standard 90.1-2007. Furthermore, residential building constructed after December 31, 2025, and commercial structures built after December 31, 2030, are required to be zero net energy capable, meaning the building would be efficient enough that it if the builder wanted to use on-site power generation, the building would consume zero energy.

Clean Energy Jobs Act, Green Collar Promise

In March 2010 the Delaware Clean Energy Jobs Act was introduced by Governor Jack Markell. Working in conjunction with the state's renewable portfolio standard, which requires that at least 25 percent of Delaware's energy consumption be from renewable sources by the year 2026, the Clean Energy Jobs Act is expected to facilitate the creation of hundreds of jobs with the anticipated wind power and solar photovoltaic projects. Four renewable energy bills, signed in July 2010, make up the Clean Energy Jobs package: SB 1 for SB 119, which further expanded the state's Renewable Portfolio Standard; SB 266, which updated the Green Energy Fund; SB 267, allowing customers to sell more energy back to suppliers; and SB 316, providing residential homeowners the ability to install ground-mounted solar energy systems without restrictions.

❧ Horseshoe Crab Population Declines, Migratory Shorebirds at Risk

The Delaware Bay hosts the largest spawning concentration of horseshoe crabs of anywhere. In May and June each year, full and new moons and high tides bring out the crabs, and the females lay their eggs along the coastal bay. Horseshoe crab eggs are a critical food source for migratory shorebirds, including the red knot, that use the Delaware Bay as a stopover; these eggs play an essential role in the successful migration of more than a half million shorebirds each year.

For decades, the population of horseshoe crabs has been sharply declining, and in turn, the migratory shorebird population has also begun to drop. The decline in the number of red knot bird species has specifically been studied; a study of red knot birds in South America, their winter habitat, recorded a drop in their numbers during the period 2000–2006. A principal cause of the decline in the red knot birds is the decrease in horseshoe crab eggs.

The migratory birds, traveling from wintering sites in Central and South America, can fly for several days at a

The Delaware River at the northern border empties into Delaware Bay. © 2011 Fuse/Jupiterimages Corporation

time, covering several thousand miles, before they make a stop. The stopovers they make are vital to their survival, and must provide an abundant supply of food with little interference. There are very few areas that meet these specific conditions, and the birds have long depended on the Delaware Bay.

Human interference is primarily responsible for this crisis. The crabs have seen a severe decline because they have been overharvested to provide bait for eel and conch fishers. Some bait alternatives are under development to reduce demand for crabs, but the damage to the population accounted for the loss of millions of crabs.

Chemical pollution is another possible influencing factor on the crab population decline. Methoprene, a mosquito larvicide used in Delaware, has been found to impair the crab's ability to molt, or shed its outer layer, preventing it from growing and maturing.

Additionally, adult crabs are used for medical research and by the biomedical and pharmaceutical products industries for eye research, surgical suture manufacturing, and wound dressing development for burn victims. Crabs are also used for their blood, which contains limulus amebocyte lysate (LAL), a component useful for the detection of bacterial endotoxins in drugs.

Although the crabs are released after one-third of their blood is collected, studies have indicated some 10——15 percent of the crabs do not survive after the bleeding procedure.

Conservation efforts by nonprofit and government organizations have led to the creation of protection programs and sanctuaries, but there has been no indication that the horseshoe crab population is recovering. U.S. Geological Survey research indicates the shrinking horseshoe crab population also parallels climate change. Rising sea levels and fluctuating water temperatures can have an adverse effect on the crab's ability to breed successfully.

Environmentalists have petitioned the U.S. Fish and Wildlife Service (FWS), asking that the red knot bird be listed under the Endangered Species Act. In response, in December 2008, the FWS elevated the bird's status to the highest level possible for a subpopulation, and acknowledged that the threat to the red knot bird's survival from declining horseshoe crab populations is ongoing and serious.

Collaboration among local and national government, wildlife protection, and scientific research communities is necessary to implement the critical steps to avoid future destruction of the critical Delaware Bay habitat.

BIBLIOGRAPHY

Books

Crenson, Victoria. *Horseshoe Crabs and Shorebirds: the Story of a Food Web*. New York: Cavendish, 2003.

Hickman, R. Edward. *Pesticide Compounds in stream-water in the Delaware River Basin, December 1998-August 2001*. Reston, VA: U.S. Department of the Interior, 2004.

Ross, John, and Bates Littlehales. *The Smithsonian Guides to Natural America: The Atlantic Coast and Blue Ridge– Maryland, District of Columbia, Delaware, Virginia, North Carolina*. Washington, DC: Smithsonian Books, 1995.

Web Sites

"Climate Change and the Delaware Action Plan." Center for Energy and Environmental Policy, University of Delaware. Available from http://www.udel.edu/ceep/publications/energy/reports/energy_delaware_climate_change_action_plan/factsheet.pdf

"Climate Change: Delaware's Water Resources." State of Delaware, Department of Natural Resources and Environmental Control. Available at http://www.dnrec.delaware.gov/ClimateChange/Pages/ClimateChangeDelawarewaterresources.aspx

"Climate Change: Global Challenges." State of Delaware: The Official Website of the First State. Available from http://www.dnrec.delaware.gov/ClimateChange/Pages/Climate%20change%20and%20Delaware.aspx

"Climate Change Implicated in Decline of Horseshoe Crabs." ScienceDaily. Available through http://www.sciencedaily.com/releases/2010/08/100830131344.htm

Craig, Lauren. "Offshore Wind Power Bill Offers Tax Credits." Earth Techling. August 1, 2011. Available from http://www.earthtechling.com/2011/08/offshore-wind-power-bill-offers-tax-credits/

"Delaware Bay Shorebirds." NJ Division of Fish and Wildlife. Available through http://www.state.nj.us/dep/fgw/ensp/shorebird_info.htm

"Delaware Climate Change Action Plan." University of DelawareCenter for Energy and Environmental Policy. January, 2000. Available at http://ceep.udel.edu/publications/globalenvironments/reports/deccap/fullreport.pdf

"Delaware Energy Plan." State of Delaware: The Official Website of the First State. Available from http://www.dnrec.delaware.gov/energy/information/Pages/DelawareEnergyPlan.aspx

Delaware Forest Resource Assessment. Delaware Forest Service. Available from http://dda.delaware.gov/forestry/061810_DFS_ResourceAssessment.pdf

"Delaware Governor Markell Introduces Clean Energy Jobs Act." SustainableBusiness.com, News. March 12, 2010. Available from http://www.sustainable-business.com/index.cfm/go/news.display/id/19927

"Delaware: Incentives/Policies for Renewables and Efficiency." DSIRE: Database of State Incentives for Renewables & Efficiency. Available from http://dsireusa.org/incentives/incentive.cfm?Incentive_Code=DE06R&re=1&ee=1

"Delaware Project Facts." NRG BluewaterWind LLC (2010). Available from http://www.bluewaterwind.com/de_overview.htm

Delaware State Building Energy Code. Database of State Incentives for Renewables and Efficiency. Available from http://www.dsireusa.org/incentives/incentive.cfm?Incentive_Code=DE08R&re=1&ee=1

Delaware Sustainable Energy Utility Oversight Board. Available from http://www.seu-de.org/index.html

Delaware Valley Green Building Council. Available from http://www.dvgbc.org/faq#faq1

"Delaware Water Resources Center." College of Agriculture & Natural Resources, University of Delaware. August, 2010. Available at http://ag.udel.edu/dwrc/

"Delaware Weatherization Assistance Program, American Recovery and Reinvestment Act (ARRA)." Delaware Department of Health and Social Services. Available from http://dhss.delaware.gov/dssc/files/att_001_weatherization.pdf

Dey, Amanda, Lawrence J. Niles, et al. "Update to the Status of the Red Knoot *Calidris canutus* in the Western Hemisphere, April 2011." Manomet. Available from http://www.manomet.org/sites/manomet.org/files/scidocs-pdfs/Red%20Knot%20status%20update%202011%20Dey%20et%20al%20%2011%2005-22.pdf

"Ecological Importance of the Horseshoe Crab." The Ecological Research & Development Group. Available from http://www.horseshoecrab.org/con/con.html

EDEN Program Overview. Delmarva Community Wellnet. Available from http://thewellnet.org/eden.html

Fact Sheet: Delaware Clean Energy Jobs Act. Governor Jack Markell, State of Delaware. Available from http://governor.delaware.gov/docs/clean-energy-jobs-act-summary.pdf

"Fisheries Section." Delaware Department of Natural Resources and Environmental Control, Division of Fish and Wildlife. Available at http://www.fw.delaware.gov/Fisheries/Pages/Fisheries.aspx

"Global Warming and Delaware." National Wildlife Federation. Available from http://www.nwf.org/Global-Warming/~/media/PDFs/Global%20Warming/Global%20Warming%20State%20Fact%20Sheets/Delaware.ashx

The Governor's Energy Advisory Council. "Delaware Energy Plan: 2009–2014." Available from http://www.dnrec.delaware.gov/energy/Documents/Energy%20Plan%20Council%20report%20-%20Final.pdf

The Governor's Energy Advisory Council. "Energy Plan Summary of Recommendations." Available from http://www.dnrec.delaware.gov/energy/information/Documents/Energy%20Plan%20Summary%20of%20Recommendations%20022609.pdf

"Green Industries Program." Delaware Economic Development Office. Available from http://dedo.delaware.gov/business/green_industries/index.shtml

Hattery, David. "NRG Bluewater Wind Sings Non-Competitive Agreement for Delaware Offshore Wind." *Renewable + Law.* April 4, 2011. Available from http://www.lawofrenewableenergy.com/2011/04/articles/wind-energy/nrg-bluewater-wind-signs-noncompetitive-agreement-for-delaware-offshore-wind

"Horseshoe Crab Decline Threatens Shorebird Species." ScienceDaily. Available through http://www.sciencedaily.com/releases/2006/02/060221235120.htm

"Interior Initiates Process for First 'Smart from the Start' Lease for Commercial Wind Power Offshore Delaware." U.S. Department of the Interior. March 24, 2011. Available from http://www.doi.gov/news/pressreleases/Interior-Initiates-Process-for-First-Smart-from-the-Start-Lease-for-Commercial-Wind-Power-Offshore-Delaware.cfm

McGurty, Janet. "UPDATE 1 – Conoco cuts trainer rates due to leak-source." Thomson Reuters: August 17, 2010. Available from http://www.reuters.com/article/idUSN1715196120100817

Nathans, Aaron. "DELAWARE: Big ideas for small wind turbines in rural areas." Delmarva Now. August 22, 2011. Available from http://www.delmarvanow.com/article/20110822/NEWS01/110822018

"The Natural Heritage and Endangered Species Program." Delaware Department of Natural Resources and Environmental Control, Division of Fish and Wildlife. Available at http://www.dnrec.state.de.us/nhp/default.shtml

Rahim, Saqib. "State and Local Governments Innovate to Cut Energy Waste." *The New York Times*, February 11, 2010. Available from http://www.nytimes.com/cwire/2010/02/11/11climatewire-state-and-local-governments-innovate-to-cut-92596.html

Regional Greenhouse Gas Initiative: Delaware State Investment Plan. Available from http://www.rggi.org/rggi_benefits/program_investments/Delaware

Schulte, Bret. "Q&A with Linda Fisher: DuPont Saves $3 Billion By Going Green." *U.S. News & World Report.* September 26, 2006. http://www.usnews.com/usnews/news/articles/060926/26fisher.htm

Seba, Erwin. "UPDATE 1-PBF says Delaware City refinery up and running." Reuters. July 15, 2011. Available from http://www.reuters.com/article/2011/07/15/refinery-operations-pbf-delawarecity-idUSN1E76E1T020110715

Senate Bill No. 19. Delaware State Senate: 144th General Assembly. Available from http://legis.delaware.gov/LIS/lis144.nsf/vwLegislation/SB+19/$file/legis.html?open

Senate Bill No. 59. Delaware State Senate: 145th General Assembly. Available from http://legis.delaware.gov/LIS/lis145.nsf/vwLegislation/SB+59/$file/legis.html?open

Senate Bill No. 74. Delaware State Senate: 143rd General Assembly. Available from http://depsc.delaware.gov/electric/rpsact.pdf

Senate Bill No. 124. Delaware State Senate: 146th General Assembly. Available from http://www.legis.delaware.gov/LIS/lis146.nsf/vwLegislation/SB+124/$file/legis.html?open

Senate Bill No. 266. Delaware State Senate: 145th General Assembly. Available from http://www.legis.delaware.gov/LIS/lis145.nsf/vwLegislation/SB+266/$file/legis.html?open

Senate Bill No. 267. Delaware State Senate: 145th General Assembly. Available from http://legis.delaware.gov/LIS/lis145.nsf/vwLegislation/SB+267/$file/legis.html?open

Senate Bill No. 316. Delaware State Senate: 145th General Assembly. Available from http://legis.delaware.gov/LIS/lis145.nsf/vwLegislation/SB+316/$file/legis.html?open

Senate Substitute No. 1 for Senate Bill No. 119. Delaware State Senate: 145th General Assembly. Available from http://legis.delaware.gov/LIS/lis145.nsf/vwLegislation/SS+1+for+SB+119/$file/legis.html?open

"Special Report: Progress in Implementing the Department of Energy's Weatherization Assistance Program Under the American Recovery and Investment Act." U.S. Department of

Energy. Available at http://ltgov.delaware.gov/documents/20100304-Weatherization ImplemenationReport.pdf

"Species Reports: Listings and Occurrences for Each State." U.S. Fish and Wildlife Service. Available at http://ecos.fws.gov/tess_public/StateListing AndOccurrence.do?state=DE

Starkey, Jonathan. "DuPont sales soar across the board: Electronics, photovoltaics lead year-to-year earnings leap." *The News Journal.* July 28, 2010. Available from http://www.delawareonline.com/article/20100728/BUSINESS/7280328/DuPont-sales-soar-across-the-board

"State Fact Sheets: Delaware." USDA, Economics Research Service. Available at http://www.ers.usda.gov/statefacts/de.htm#ORG

"Supporting Sustainable Agriculture in Delaware." Delaware Organic Food and Farming Association. http://www.delawareorganics.com/home.html

"2007 Census of Agriculture Data Released: Statistics for Delaware's $1 Billion Agricultural Industry Updated." Delaware Department of Agriculture. Available at http://dda.delaware.gov/pressrel/2009/020509_2007%20Census.pdf

"2009 State Agriculture Overview: Delaware." National Agricultural Statistics Service, United States Department of Agriculture. Available from http://www.nass.usda.gov/Statistics_by_State/Ag_Overview/AgOverview_DE.pdf

"Water Resources Agency: Introduction." Institute for Public Administration, University of Delaware. Available from http://www.ipa.udel.edu/wra/

Florida

Florida spans nearly 54,000 square miles (139,860 sq km) of land and ranks twenty-sixth in size among the 50 states in area. The land area is flat, and the southern end of the state is covered by the Everglades, the world's largest saw grass swamp. The Florida Panhandle, located in the northwest, contains gently rolling country, which merges and blends seamlessly into the scenery of Georgia and Alabama. Offshore islands include the Florida Keys, which extend southwest into the Gulf of Mexico.

Climate

The climate for most of Florida is humid subtropical, with the southernmost region of the state in the tropical zone. The relatively mild winter temperatures make the state a favorite destination for many tourists and retirees, but summer days can be challenging for residents. Florida's proximity to the Atlantic and the Gulf of Mexico opens the state to high levels of humidity and generally abundant rainfall. At the height of summer, relative humidity throughout the state can average between 50 percent and 80 percent throughout a single day. When temperatures hover around 90°F (low 09s) (32 to 34°C), the humidity creates a heat index of about 10°F (5.5°C) higher. The state experiences abundant rainfall, but there can be rather extreme fluctuations in the amount of precipitation from year to year, leaving agricultural lands vulnerable to droughts and floods. Florida's location in "Hurricane Alley" makes the state particularly vulnerable to severe storms. Sea breezes converge and produce rising air masses that result in frequent thunderstorms. Florida has the highest frequency and the most lightning strikes in the United States, with the highest concentration of cloud-to-ground lightning occurring between Tampa and Orlando.

Feeling the Heat in Florida

Scientists widely agree that climate change will have a profound impact on Florida's environment—perhaps more than any other state. The biggest concern stems from Florida's geographic proximity to the Atlantic Ocean and the Gulf of Mexico. According to the 2001 report from the Natural Resources Defense Council, *Feeling the Heat in Florida: Global Warming on the Local Level*, sea levels could rise by more than 16 inches (40 cm) by 2100, which could result in an inflow of water by as much as 400 feet (122 m) inland, thus devastating Florida's low-lying coastal areas and threatening the people, plants, and animals that live there. Warmer ocean waters cause greater hurricane intensity, as hotter ocean water more easily evaporates into the storms, feeding and increasing their strength.

An Unexpected Freeze

In 2010, however, it was colder than average temperatures that left a mark on the environment. According to the State of the Climate December 2010 report from the National Oceanic and Atmospheric Administration, Florida recorded its coldest December temperatures on record in 2010, with average statewide temperatures for the month at more than 9°F (5°C) below the twentieth-century average. The average temperature for the entire year was noted as the seventh coldest in 116 years, at about 1.3°F (0.72°C) below normal. The state experienced periods of low precipitation during the year as well. October through December 2010 was noted as the driest on record with precipitation at 5.15 inches (13.1 cm) below normal. The colder temperatures and drier conditions disrupted the winter vegetable planting season for some areas and led to the declaration of a state of emergency in December 2010 (EO 10-262) due to the threat of freezing temperatures. That state of emergency was extended three times (EO 10-275, EO 10-283, EO 11-06) leading into January 2011 as freezing temperatures persisted. The state of emergency allowed for the temporary suspension of some transportation regulations that could have hindered the export of harvested crops (i.e., weight restrictions on commercial vehicles).

Dry conditions in the state led to a different state of emergency in June 2011, when a summer drought caused 420 brush fires that charred more than 115,000 acres (46,539 ha). Many of the fires were started by lightning strikes, which did not have enough accompanying rainfall to quell the wildfires. Smoke from the fire caused visibility issues, even canceling and delaying flights from Daytona International Airport. Jacksonville had issued six air quality advisories by June 2011. There was a lull in the fires by July, after burning thousands of acres and causing the deaths of two firefighters. More fires caught in August 2011 in Volusia and Flagler counties.

Florida's Energy and Climate Change Action Plan

Aware of the need to act boldly and swiftly to address the threats associated with climate change, Florida governor Charlie Crist signed Executive Order 07-128 in 2007 to establish the Action Team on Energy and Climate Change. The action team was charged with creating a roadmap for how to address climate change in the state, and in 2008, the team completed the 608-page Florida Energy and Climate Change Action Plan. Included within the plan are more than fifty policy recommendations, ranging from a cap-and-trade program to massive investments in clean energy. If the plan is implemented in full, the action team reports, Florida would be on track to exceed the governor's target of reducing emissions by 40 percent by 2025 (EO 07-126), as well as saving the state more than $28 billion from 2009 to 2025.

❧ Natural Resources, Water, and Agriculture

Natural Resources: Forests

About 50 percent of Florida's land area (around 16.3 million acres; 6.6 million ha) is covered in forest, with more than 90 percent of this total area classified as timberland. The northern portion of the state is the most heavily forested area, with more than 80 percent of the state's timberland located in this region. The most common tree species are pines, including longleaf, slash, loblolly, shortleaf, sand, and pond varieties. Several types of oak (white, southern red, scrub, live) can be found in the northern forests as well, while trees such as red maple, beech, sweetgum, cypress, willow, and swamp chestnut oak are found among the floodplains. Tropical palms such as coconut and royal are common in many areas. About 60 percent of the timber harvested within the state is used to produce wood pulp for paper and paper products. About 80 percent of the forest land is under private ownership.

Natural Resources: Parks and Wildlife

Florida is home to 160 state parks covering more than 700,000 acres (283,280 ha). These are all under the management of the Florida Park Service, which is the first two-time winner of the National Gold Medal Award for Excellence in Park Recreation Management, which is presented by the American Academy for Park and Recreation Administration in partnership with the National Recreation and Park Association. In addition, the state hosts five national parks and preserves, including the popular Everglades National Park, and two national seashore areas—Canaveral National Seashore and the Gulf Islands National Seashore (shared with Mississippi).

In January 2011, the U.S. Secretary of the Interior Ken Salazar announced plans to create a new 150,000-acre (60,700-ha) reserve to be known as the Everglades Headwaters National Wildlife Refuge. The refuge would serve to protect the wildlife and habitats of the Kissimmee River valley, covering lands between Orlando and Lake Okeechobee. Under the preliminary plan, the government is expected to purchase about 50,000 acres (20,230 ha), while the remaining area would be protected through agreements made with private landowners.

Florida is home to more than 700 terrestrial animals and numerous aquatic and marine vertebrates. The white-tailed deer, wild hog, and gray fox can still be found in the wild. Small mammals, such as the raccoon, eastern gray and fox squirrels, and cottontail and swamp rabbits also remain common in the state. Managed species in the state include the alligator, black bear, gopher tortoise, bald eagle, panther, sea turtles, and manatee. The Florida Everglades serve as a bastion of biodiversity—with thousands of plants and animals, more than 360 species of birds, and upwards of 60 unique reptile species found in this region.

One of the most significant conservation challenges in Florida involves balancing human population growth with the state's conservation needs. Roads, houses, shopping complexes, and office buildings tremendously alter the natural environment and eliminate wildlife habitat across the state. Since 1972, the Environmental Land and Water Management Act has regulated growth management in Florida. In 1972 the Florida Legislature also created the first Environmental Land Management Study (ELMS) Committee, which sponsored proposals intended to manage development of the state such as the Local Government Comprehensive Planning Act of 1975. Substantial growth management revisions were also made in 1985, 1991, and 2005 to increase the role of state oversight. During the 2011 legislative session, vast changes to Florida's growth management laws were enacted, increasing the discretion afforded to local governments in creating and implementing growth

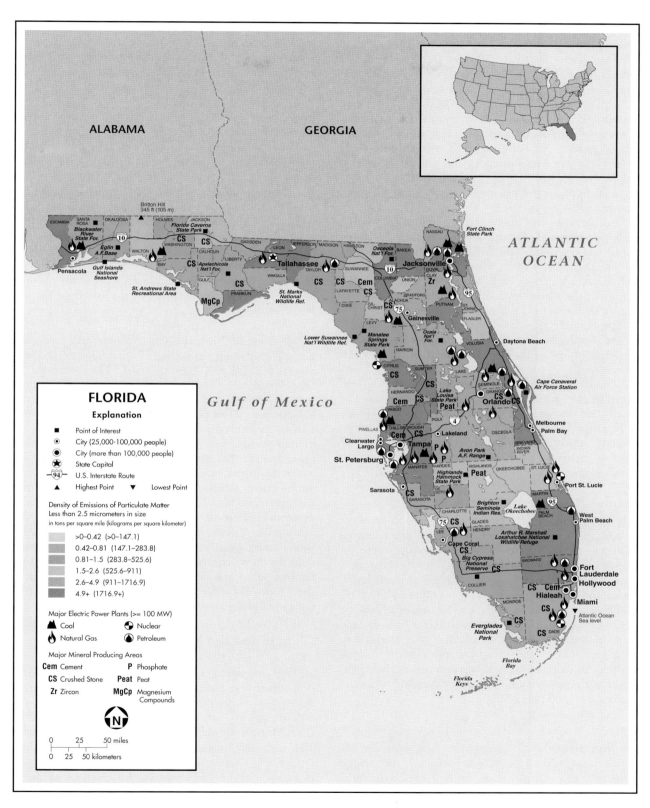

SOURCES: "County Emissions Map: Criteria Air Pollutants." *AirData*. U.S. Environmental Protection Agency. Available from http://www.epa.gov/air/data/geosel.html; *Energy Maps*. U.S. Energy Information Administration. Available from http://www.eia.gov/state; *Highest and Lowest Elevations*. U.S. Geological Survey. Available from http://egsc.usgs.gov/isb/pubs/booklets/elvadist/elvadist.html#Highest; *2007 Minerals Yearbook*. U.S. Geological Survey. Available from http://minerals.usgs.gov/minerals/pubs/state.   © 2011 Cengage Learning.

management policies and the local government comprehensive planning process.

The Areas of Critical State Concern Program protects resources and public facilities of major statewide significance. Designated Areas of Critical State Concern are: City of Apalachicola (Franklin County), City of Key West and the Florida Keys (Monroe County), the Green Swamp (portions of Polk and Lake counties), and the Big Cypress Swamp (Collier County). Large-scale developments affecting the environment and habitats have been regulated since the 1970s by the Developments of Regional Impact program, involving regional and state oversight.

Recognizing the need to address the wildlife challenges in the state, the Florida Fish and Wildlife Conservation Commission released in 2005 the Florida Wildlife Legacy Initiative, which essentially serves as a wildlife action plan for the state. The initiative identified the most pressing challenges facing the wildlife in the state. Almost all of these threats were directly or indirectly related to increased human activity in the state (habitat loss, fire suppression, water degradation, and artificial management of the physical environment).

The U.S. Fish and Wildlife Service lists 116 plant and animal species found in Florida as federally threatened or endangered. Among the animals listed are the Florida panther, the West Indian manatee, and the Key Largo woodrat. Among the endangered plant species is the Key tree cactus—a large, rare cactus found only in the Florida Keys.

Natural Resources: Minerals

Although Florida has few energy resources outside of the oil and gas sector, the state is rich in other natural resources. According to the U.S. Geological Survey, Florida's nonfuel mineral sector is more robust than nearly 90 percent of U.S. states, ranked at ninth in the nation and bringing in more than $2 billion in 2010. Florida leads the nation in the production of phosphate rock, a hyper valuable mineral essential for farming, and produces roughly 70 percent of total U.S. production. Phosphate rock is the most valuable nonfuel mineral produced in Florida The state was also ranked first in the nation in the production of masonry cement, zirconium concentrates, and peat in 2007.

Water

Approximately 30,000 lakes, ponds, and sinks dot the Florida landscape. Lake Okeechobee is the largest freshwater lake in the state, with 700 square miles (1,800 sq km) of surface area. Like all of Florida's lakes, Lake Okeechobee is extremely shallow, with a maximum depth of only 15 feet (5 m). As many as 10,000 springs may exist in Florida, but only around 700 have been mapped. Most of Florida's springs are located in the

region stretching from Hillsborough, Orange, Seminole, and Volusia counties north and west to Walton County. Silver Springs, near Ocala in north-central Florida, has the largest average flow of all inland springs, pumping 823 cubic feet (23 cu m) of water per second.

Florida has more than 1,700 rivers, streams, and creeks, with the longest being St. Johns River, which empties into the Atlantic Ocean. Other major rivers are the Suwannee, which flows south from Georgia through Florida and empties into the Gulf of Mexico; and the Apalachicola.

Florida's coastal waters are home to numerous species, including a variety of sharks, stingrays, and sturgeon; hawksbill, leatherback, and green sea turtles; North Atlantic right whale, several species of dolphin, and numerous varieties of finfish. More than 200 species of fish and invertebrates are harvested in commercial fishing ventures. The most important catches in terms of value include several species of shrimp, spiny lobster, stone and blue crab, king mackerel, and several varieties of grouper and snapper.

In August 2011 the first documented case of a human pathogen infecting a marine species was reported along the Florida coast. Elkhorn coral in Floridian and Caribbean waters had drastically declined between 2000 and 2010. A study identified the bacterium in white pox disease, known as *Serratiamarcescens*, as the culprit. The pathogen is common in human sewage, but can also be found in the waste of other animals. Researchers analyzed samples from waste water treatment facilities and compared them to waste samples from native animal species. While the pathogen was found in both sample types, the genetic analysis determined that the strain from human sewage was causing the disease in the corals. The study reveals a new disease pathway, from humans to wildlife rather than the more common reverse. Researchers state that the best solution is better wastewater treatment, both in the Florida Keys and in island nations that still lack sewage treatment systems.

Climate and the Manatee

Throughout 2010, the state experienced colder than average temperatures, particularly in the winter months of January and December. As a result, 279 manatees were reported dead from "cold-stress," according to the official reports of the Florida Fish and Wildlife Conservation Commission (FWC). Of these deaths, 151 occurred in January 2010 and 35 occurred in December. These cold-weather deaths pushed the total mortality rate to 767 manatees for the year, a figure that was nearly double the yearly average of the past five years. Officials from the FWC noted that finding natural warm water sites for the rescue of manatee in distress is already a concern under the manatee conservation plan.

Florida State Profile

Physical Characteristics

Land area	53,603 square miles (138,831 sq km)
Inland water area	5,373 square miles (13,916 sq km)
Coastal area	1,128 square miles (1,815 sq km)
Highest point	Britton Hill 345 feet (105 m)
National Forest System lands (2010)	1.1 million acres (476,000 ha)
State parks (2011)	160

Energy Statistics

Total energy production (2009)	560 trillion Btu
State ranking in total energy production (2009)	30
Renewable energy net generation total (2009)	4.5 million megawatt hours
Hydroelectric energy generation (2009)	208,000 megawatt hours
Biomass energy generation (2009)	2.3 million megawatt hours
Wind energy generation (2009)	NA
Wood and derived fuel energy generation (2009)	2.0 million megawatt hours
Crude oil reserves (2009)	9.0 million barrels (1.4 million cu m)
Natural gas reserves (2009)	7.0 billion cubic feet (200 million cu m)
Natural gas liquids (2008)	NA

Pollution Statistics

Carbon output (2005)	243.9 million tons of CO_2 (221.3 million t)
Superfund sites (2008)	54
Particulate matter (less than 2.5 micrometers) emissions (2002)	51,926 tons per year (47,106 t/yr)
Toxic chemical releases (2009)	85 million pounds (38.6 million kg)
Generated hazardous waste (2009)	168,900 tons (153,200 t)

SOURCES: AirData. U.S. Environmental Protection Agency. Available from http://www.epa.gov/air/data; *Energy Maps, Facts, and Data of the U.S. States.* U.S. Energy Information Administration. Available from http://www.eia.gov/state; *The 2012 Statistical Abstract.* U.S. Census Bureau. Available from http://www.census.gov/compendia/statab; *United States Energy Usage.* eRedux. Available from http://www.eredux.net/states.

© 2011 Cengage Learning.

Lake Apopka

In early 2011, below-average levels of precipitation led to concerns over the already precarious ecosystem of Lake Apopka. From October through December 2010, precipitation throughout the state was recorded at 5.15 inches (13.1 cm) below normal. With lower levels of precipitation anticipated for early 2011 as well, local officials decided to temporarily close a dam that stops the flow of water from Lake Apopka (on the borders of Orange and Lake Counties) through the Apopka-Beauclair Canal. This measure was meant to prevent the development of algae bloom and the resulting increase in plant and fish deaths that typically occur when water levels are low. However, the restricted water flow affects water levels in the Harris Chain of Lakes downstream, which are popular boating and fishing sites during the winter and spring months. In 2010, officials had closed the dam for five months to measure the effects of reducing discharge.

Agriculture: Citrus Fruits

Florida's most important agricultural products are its citrus fruits, accounting for about 70 percent of annual U.S. production. The state generally ranks within the top five nationally for production of oranges, grapefruits, and tangerines. Florida continues to supply most of the orange juice consumed in the United States, with at least 95 percent of the oranges harvested in the state being processed into juice. The state also ranks in the top five for sugarcane, squash, watermelon, sweet corn, snap beans, strawberries, and bell peppers. Florida greenhouse and nursery products are also important in the national market. Production of beef cattle and dairy products is fairly important, with the state often ranking within the top twenty nationally for these commodities. Florida is home to about 600 thoroughbred horse farms and training centers, which have produced forty-seven National Champions and six Kentucky Derby winners, along with other prize winners.

The value of Florida's crops alone exceeds $6.2 billion, with the state generally ranking within the top ten in the nation for agricultural value. Total agricultural revenue for the state is greater than $7.7 billion. In 2010, the state had roughly 47,500 farms, covering some 9.25 million acres (3.74 million ha). These farms represent nearly 30 percent of the state's entire land area.

Rapidly Growing Organic Farming Industry

Organic farming represents one of the fastest-growing segments of agriculture in Florida. Several organizations in the state, such as Florida Organic Growers, help farmers make the transition from conventional to organic farming, providing certification, inspections, and a host of valuable information on the topic.

Energy: Turning Orange Peels Into Biofuels

Florida consumes more residential energy per capita than the vast majority of other states in the nation, yet its total per capita energy consumption remains less than most other states. Economists attribute the high residential per capita energy demand to Florida's hot and humid climate and the year-round air conditioning that accompanies it. The relatively low overall per capita energy consumption is explained by the size of Florida's industrial sector, which relative to population size is very small.

Natural gas and coal constitute the two primary power-generating sources in Florida. Together, these two sources make up 70 percent of Florida's total power generation, 40 percent and 30 percent respectively. Because there are no coal mines in Florida, most of the fuel for the Florida's coal-fired plants is imported from Kentucky, Illinois, and West Virginia via railroads and barges. Nuclear power and petroleum-fired plants make up the bulk of the remaining energy production in the state, and Florida has more petroleum-fired electricity generation capacity than any state in the nation.

Geologists believe that sizable oil and gas reserves are locked, untapped, off the west coast of Florida in the Gulf of Mexico, particularly in the area which is part of the federally administered Outer Continental Shelf. Before the 2010 explosion of the Deepwater Horizon offshore oil rig in the Gulf of Mexico, which led to the worst oil spill in American waters, Governor Crist had softened his initial opposition to offshore drilling; after the spill, Crist discussed a state ban on all offshore drilling and proposed incentives to stimulate investment in renewable energy instead.

In early 2011, a bipartisan group of state legislators sponsored a bill to place the issue of offshore drilling on the 2012 ballot. Specifically, House Joint Resolution 383 proposed a referendum on a constitutional amendment that would permanently ban near-shore drilling off the Florida coast. The idea of a referendum garnered support from several environmental organizations in the state, some of which hadalready begun sponsoring petition campaigns to get the matter placed on the ballot, since the house resolution did not pass in 2011.

Outside of its oil and gas reserves, Florida has few energy resources. The state has plenty of oranges, though, and an interesting energy trend in Florida merges the respective scarcity and abundance of those resources. Researchers and entrepreneurs in Florida have planned since 2007 to open the world's first ethanol plant to make fuel from citrus waste. The planned facility, which will be located in Hendry County, Florida, will produce up to eight million gallons of ethanol per year from citrus peel waste and create an estimated 380 new jobs. U.S. Secretary of Agriculture Tom Vilsack announced in August 2011 a $75 million loan guarantee for the facility. Organizers also hope to use the plant to experiment with sugar cane stock as a way to produce ethanol as well, because Hendry County sits adjacent to the heart of Florida's sugar cane industry.

🌿 Green Business, Green Building, Green Jobs

Green Business: Sleeping Green to Rest Easy

Florida's Department of Environmental Protection (DEP) launched in 2004 the "Green Lodging Program," which recognizes lodging facilities that make a commitment to conserve and protect Florida's natural resources. The Green Lodging Program operates on a completely voluntary basis, but many hotels and lodges participate because the conservation aspect of the initiative saves money, while the DEP accreditation offers marketing opportunities.

In order for a business to qualify, owners must subject their business to a thorough property assessment, where they demonstrate strong environmental practices in six areas: communication and education to customers, employees, and the public; waste reduction, reuse, and recycling; water conservation; energy efficiency; indoor air quality; and transportation. In January 2008 Governor Crist showed support for the program by issuing a mandate to prohibit all state agencies and departments from contracting meeting or conferences spaces at any facilities that have not achieved DEP Green Lodging certification (EO 07-126). This requirement may be waived, however, with significant proof that an appropriate certified space is not available.

Green Building: Florida Green Homes are the Standard-Bearers of Marketing Success

The Florida Green Building Coalition (FGBC) is a Florida-based nonprofit organization dedicated to creating statewide green building programs that benefit both the environment and the economy. The coalition aims to educate all parties involved in the building and construction industry in Florida—from homebuilders to local governments to developers to consumers. In the process, the organization encourages informed consumption. With the help of FGBC, people buying homes in Florida can have an answer to their question: "is the city I am thinking of moving into committed environmentally friendly development?" Or, "Was the home I am considering buying built or renovated with green practices in mind?"

FGBC accomplishes these objectives by setting "green" standards for homes, buildings, and developments in Florida. Similar to the way the U.S. Green Building Council works to get green built properties certified under the Leadership in Energy and Efficiency Design (LEED), FGBC partners with the Florida Home Builder's Association and Enterprise Foundation to create a framework for rating new and existing homes under the Florida Green Home Standard. To achieve an FGBC certification, projects are rated in eight categories and must receive a collective score of one hundred.

Homeowners have an incentive to get their house Florida Green Home Standard certified because the program increases resale values and helps to reduce the costs of basic operation. Developers enjoy the certification because it serves as a marketing opportunity for their development and a way to stand out from the competition. And FGBC certifications positively affect communities because they increase efficient allocation of finite resources. The Florida Green Home Standard has been supported by the U.S. Department of Energy and since its inception in 2001 has certified over 1,500 homes across Florida.

At the state level, a number of green building and energy efficiency standards have been adopted for public buildings. Under the authority of HB 7135/Chapter 2008-227, enacted in June 2008), all new buildings constructed and financed by the state must be designed and built to meet the standards set by either the Florida Green Building Coalition, LEED, the Green Building Initiative Green Globes rating system, or some other nationally recognized high-performance rating system. Under Executive Order 07-126, the Florida Department of Management Service (DMS) has been directed to adopt LEED certification standards for all new buildings, with a goal to strive for Platinum certification in all projects. The mandate charges the DMS to implement measures that would bring all existing buildings into compliance with LEED standards as well, whenever and wherever it is economically feasible to do so. It is further mandated that all office spaces leased by the state must meet Energy Star building standards. A number of other conservation and energy efficiency standards for state buildings were included in this order.

In 2009, the state amended the educational building code so that all new educational facilities must include passive design elements and low energy usage features and that schools with hot water demands exceeding 1,000 gallons (3,785) per day must utilize a solar heating system that provides at least 65 percent of those needs, as long as this is economically feasible (Section 1013.44-2009).

Florida Legislature Supports Models of Efficiency

In 2008, the Florida Legislature enacted House Bill 697, establishing new local planning requirements relating to energy efficient land use patterns, transportation strategies to address greenhouse gas reductions, energy conservation, and energy efficient housing. Over 40 percent of Florida's greenhouse gas emissions are produced by the transportation sector, with 80 percent coming from vehicular travel. Therefore, in order to reduce greenhouse emissions from the transportation sector, the state advocates policies to reduce vehicle miles traveled. In 2009, the Florida Legislature established the Energy Economic Zone Pilot Program to address economic development and the creation of energy-efficient land use patterns. Two drastically different areas were selected as models for the program: the City of Miami Beach, a densely populated urban area, and Sarasota County, a county with significant portions of undeveloped land. As such, these two places were asked to develop strategies to reduce greenhouse gas emissions,

cultivate green economic development, encourage renewable electric energy generation, and promote product manufacturing that contributes to energy conservation and green jobs.

Green Jobs: Intellectual Collaboration Creates Clean-Energy Jobs

According to a 2009 Pew Charitable Trusts report, Florida ranked as one of the top ten states in terms of jobs in the green energy economy, securing more than 30,000 positions in the related fields. In addition, the state's economy attracted nearly $60 million in venture capital for green energy fields in the three years leading up to the report's publication—nearly half of total venture capital pouring into the state. While the state lacks some of the blockbuster legislative measures present in other states, such as renewable portfolio standards, which mandate that a certain percentage a state's energy come from renewable sources, Florida has taken strides towards a greener future. The Energy Systems Consortium represents an example of one statewide initiative that aims to achieve this. Florida governor Charlie Crist signed the bill creating the Energy Systems Consortium in 2008, with a stated goal of bolstering university-to-university cooperation on emerging energy technologies.

Workforce Florida Inc, the statewide workforce investment board charged with policy and oversight of all aspects of the state's workforce, has also taken steps to promote the development of a green economy for the state. Perhaps the most significant step was to develop a standard working definition of green jobs. In the June 2009 report, *Defining Green Jobs for Florida*, the Sustainability and Infrastructure Committee of Workforce Florida defined green jobs as those that "increase the conservation and sustainability of natural resources for the benefit of Floridians." This definition is noted as including those jobs that reduce energy use, lower carbon emissions, and/or protect natural resources. With this working definition in place, the promotion of green industries has been added as a goal in *Creating the Strategy for Today's Needs and Tomorrow's Talent: The 2010–2015 Strategic Plan for Workforce Development.*

❧ Thirst for Water, Hunger for Land Strains Florida's Resources

With an average of over 54 inches (137 cm) of rainfall per year, 7,700 lakes, 50,000 miles (80,467 km) of rivers and streams, and over 700 springs, Florida seems flush with water. Seasonal rainfall can widely fluctuate—major statewide or regional droughts occurred in the early 1970s, the early 1980s, 1989–1990, and 1999–2001.

The concentration of springs found in Florida does not occur anywhere else in the world. Most Florida springs exist where the limestone of the Floridan aquifer is exposed at the surface and groundwater is forced out from underground. This type of landscape is known as karst. The entire state of Florida is a karst region, resting on a limestone plateau. The state's population has nearly doubled since 1980 to around 18 million today, and is projected to double again by 2060. So as Florida grows, its need for clean water also grows.

Since 1975, Florida has relied more heavily on fresh groundwater than surface water to meet water supply needs. In 2005, groundwater withdrawals accounted for about 62 percent of all fresh water withdrawals in the state. Supplies of fresh, inexpensively treated groundwater are increasingly limited. In recent years, southeastern Florida communities have also realized they cannot rely on their traditional supply, the Biscayne Aquifer. Too much reliance on groundwater results in a system that is not drought resistant and can lead to water shortages and environmental damage. Because of their widespread use in Florida and high-volume discharges, septic systems have the cumulative potential to pollute ground water and springs if improperly sited, poorly maintained, or too densely concentrated. Agricultural irrigation is the largest user of fresh water in the state; however, public water supply is projected to soon overtake agriculture for the majority of water consumption. Nearly half of all water withdrawn for public supply in Florida is used to water lawns and landscaping. By 2025, demands in public water supply are projected to account for 43 percent of the total estimated use of 8.7 billion gallons (32.9 million l) per day.

Reclaimed water is an alternative water source that has received at least secondary treatment and is reused after being discharged from a wastewater treatment plant. Reclaimed water is not drinkable, but it can be reused for lawn irrigation, agricultural irrigation, groundwater recharge, and industrial processes. Reuse of reclaimed water reduces the demand for water from traditional sources by saving potable water for drinking and other needs. Two facilities in Orlando help the city recycle 100 percent of its wastewater, treated to irrigate more than 2,900 acres (1,172 ha) of citrus, 1,400 acres (567 ha) of golf courses, 2,100 acres (850 ha) of parks, and more than 3,600 residential lawns. Reclaimed water is only used in some areas and is underused in large parts of the state. South Florida alone sends 300 million gallons (1.1 billion l) per day of treated wastewater into the sea—water that could be put to use as reclaimed water.

Desalination removes salt from seawater or brackish water to produce drinking water. By using seawater from the Gulf of Mexico, desalination reduces the need for groundwater pumping and provides a reliable alternative water source. Obstacles to seawater desalination have been the high cost of production and environmental concerns over the disposal of the concentrated salt byproduct. The largest desalination plant in North America is the Tampa Bay Seawater Desalination Project, with a capacity to produce 25 million gallons (94.6 million l) per day, 10 percent of the Tampa Bay region's water supply needs. However, the plant cost $50 million more than estimated and undesired consequence of its operation have been enormous energy demands and carbon emissions.

Since the 1800s, Florida has lost 9.3 million acres (3.8 million ha) of wetlands. From the 1880s through the 1940s the state encouraged removal of wetlands, believing the policy would enhance public health and safety by controlling flooding and restraining transmission of disease. Draining wetlands was once politically popular, as it increased the amount of land available for agriculture and urbanization at a time when few industries existed in Florida. In 1904, Napoleon Bonaparte Broward was elected governor by promising to drain the Everglades. Drainage projects around Lake Okeechobee encouraged settlement and development of agriculture. At the time, there was general misunderstanding regarding the ecological value of the Everglades and wetlands in general.

The Florida Everglades: A Unique Ecosystem Threatened

The Everglades are the largest remaining subtropical wilderness in the contiguous United States. They extend from just south of Orlando to the southern tip of the state, and represent a 2 million acre (0.8 million ha) wetland ecosystem. Both fresh and saltwater areas are found in the expansive Florida Everglades. Prairies, pine rocklands, tropical hardwood forests, offshore coral reefs, and mangrove forests are also dotted throughout these famous Florida wetlands. The great spectrum of environments within the Everglades makes the area home to various species of aquatic birds, mammals, reptiles, and amphibians.

But the Florida Everglades are a threatened natural treasure, and some fifty-six species within the region are either threatened or endangered. Among the threatened species is the famous Florida panther, of which fewer than one hundred are believed to be living in the wild. The Florida Everglades faces several other critical threats. One of the biggest dangers to these wetlands comes from the population growth of south Florida. Since the early 1900s, the Everglades has shrunk in size by nearly half, from 4 million to 2 million acres (1.6 million to 0.8 million ha). Much of this shrinkage has been the result of residential and farming communities encroaching on the Everglades. Serious disruptions to the Everglades' ecology and water supply have been the result, and fertilizer runoff from regional farms has compounded these effects.

Invasive and introduced plant and animal species also threaten the Everglades' ecosystem. Non-native plants

The Florida Everglades serve as a bastion of biodiversity—with thousands of plants and animals, more than 360 species of birds, and upwards of 60 unique reptile species found in this region. © *Tomasz Szymanski/ShutterStock.com*

restore the Everglades and provide water for people and the environment. Congress authorized the first ten projects in the plan. The CERP focuses on preserving the natural water resources in central and south Florida, including the area of the Everglades. The plan has been described as the world's largest ecosystem restoration effort. Advocates of CERP base their efforts on the notion that the biggest challenge to rebuilding the Florida Everglades is the water supply. Florida residents demand consistent access to fresh water and flood protection for their homes. The Everglades—which are a source of fresh water and remains vulnerable to flooding—suffer as a result of these two human demands. How can Florida and the federal government balance the interest of citizens and residents with those of a unique, national treasure? That question is at the heart of the effort.

and animals disrupt the natural food chain and threaten the sustainability of the Everglades. Introduced and invasive species enter the Everglades from other parts of the world and, as a result, lack the predators of their old environment. Sometimes, similar predators do not exist at all in the Everglades, and consequently, the new species can quickly reproduce. In such environments, resources become severely strained and indigenous plants and animals—which have natural predators and competitors in the Everglades—have a hard time competing with the invasive or introduced species.

The destruction of Hurricane Andrew in 1992 caused thousands of captive exotic animals to escape into the Everglades, including many Burmese pythons. This environmental problem has been exacerbated by irresponsible pet owners who released pet Burmese pythons into the ecosystem when the snakes become too large to care for. The U.S. Fish and Wildlife Service wants to designate the snakes as "injurious species," a label that will prohibit interstate transactions. According to the U.S. International Trade Commission, about 832,000 live reptiles were brought into the United States in 2010. That same year, Florida banned the in-state sale of seven types of constrictors as pets. Owners could keep their snakes as long as they implanted identifier microchips into the animal and paid $100 annually for a permit. In Florida, Burmese pythons are a threat to the endangered Key Largo woodrat and the wood stork, and compete with the threatened eastern indigo snake for food and habitat.

Everglades Restoration: Planning for Success

Several organizations and state and federally funded programs exist to address these problems. In 1999, The U.S. Congress approved the Comprehensive Everglades Restoration Plan (CERP), a joint federal-state plan to

The Gulf of Mexico Oil Spill and Florida

The April 2010 Gulf of Mexico oil spill threatened the entire Gulf coastal environment, including Florida. In early May, Florida took action by declaring a state of emergency in twenty-six counties in the Panhandle and along the state's west coast. Health advisories (all of which were rescinded by mid-August) were issued for the counties of Escambia, Okaloosa, and Walton. The spill also affected local tourism, as many vacationers opted to stay away from Florida's beaches during the height of the spill. BP was committed to a continued cleanup and will maintain personnel to handle any further oiling. A deep cleaning effort throughout the winter months using heavy equipment was successful in removing tons of oil each day. This effort concluded prior to spring tourism, bird nesting, and turtle nesting seasons. More than 200 miles (320 km) of Florida's coastline were affected.

The Loop Current in the Gulf of Mexico is a warm ocean current that flows north through the Yucatan Strait into the Gulf of Mexico and then loops west toward the Florida Strait. It threatened to push surface oil from the spill toward the Florida Keys and beyond to the Atlantic Ocean and the east coast of Florida. Weather conditions and other currents pushed oil towards the coast of the Panhandle, where beaches were impacted by the spill mostly in the form of tar balls. There were reports that oil had indeed entered the Loop Current, as tar balls were found on beaches in the lower Keys. However, analysis of the tar proved that not all of the tar balls could be traced to the current spill. In addition, there were reports of a brown film on a beach, an orange substance found in sea foam, oiled fish, and an oily sheen on the water.

Florida is in a transition from response to recovery. By September 2010, more than 11,000 pounds (4,990 kg) of tar balls had been manually collected and more

Oil workers continue to clean at Pensacola Beach (July 7, 2010) after the spring 2010 explosion of the Deepwater Horizon oil rig.
© Lorraine Kourafas/ShutterStock.com

than 8,900 pounds (4,037 kg) had been mechanically collected along the beaches of Florida. By late June, commercial fishing was prohibited in the affected area, with sections beginning to be reopened to anglers in late July. One year after the oil spill, as of April 11, 2011, 2,497,515 pounds (1,132,854 kg) of oil had been removed from Florida's coastline, 98 percent of which came from Escambia and Santa Rosa counties.

The spill impacted Florida in a variety of areas. As stated above, beach habitats were affected by the presence of tar balls and oil. Dunes and coastal vegetation were also disturbed by oil spill response efforts, either by vehicles, the presence of responders, or their cleanup activities. (For example, seagrass beds were compromised by the installation of booms.) In response to the threat to the environment of coastal wildlife, including shorebirds and sea turtles, an effort was organized by federal wildlife agencies to move sea turtle hatchlings from the Panhandle to the Atlantic coast, to keep them from the oil.

On April 21, 2011, an agreement was announced by the Natural Resource Trustees for the Deepwater Horizon oil spill. BP agreed to provide $1 billion toward early restoration projects in the Gulf of Mexico to address injuries to natural resources caused by the spill. The selection of early restoration projects for all the Gulf states follows a public process, and is overseen by the Deepwater Horizon Trustee Council. Restoration projects must qualify under the Oil Pollution Act of 1990 and must include the rebuilding of coastal marshes, replenishment of damaged beaches, conservation of sensitive areas for ocean habitat for injured wildlife, and restoration of barrier islands and wetlands that provide natural protection from storms.

Cleanup efforts are ongoing, and along with it plenty of new research into how the spill will affect the Gulf of Mexico in the long term. The Florida Institute of Oceanography received a $10 million grant from BP to fund research relating to the spill. The Florida Institute of Oceanography is part of the Oil Spill Academic Task Force, which consists of both public and private Florida universities. The institutions that make up the Task Force are working together to gather information and data for researchers, government officials, and the public to help them understand the impact of the nation's largest environmental disaster.

BIBLIOGRAPHY

Books

Barnes, Jay. *Florida's Hurricane History.* Chapel Hill, NC: University of North Carolina Press, 2007.

Emison, Gerald, and John C. Morris, eds. *Speaking Green with A Southern Accent: Environmental Management and Innovation in the South.* Lanham, MD: Lexington Books, 2010.

Strutin, Michal, and Tony Arruza. *The Smithsonian Guides to Natural America: The Southeast–South Carolina, Georgia, Alabama, Florida.* Washington, DC: Smithsonian Books, 1996.

Web Sites

An act relating to energy (HB 7135/Chapter 2008-227). Florida State Legislature. Available from http://laws.flrules.org/files/Ch_2008-227.pdf

Associated Press. "Interior Chief Announces Everglades Headwaters Refuge." *First Coast News.* January 7, 2011. Available from http://www.firstcoastnews.com/news/florida/news-article.aspx?storyid=185410

Comas, Martin E. "Closing dam on Lake Apopka opens floodgates of criticism downstream." *Orlando Sentinel.* January 9, 2011. Available from http://articles.orlandosentinel.com/2011-01-09/news/os-lake-apopka-dam-lakes-20110109_1_lake-apopka-apopka-beauclair-canal-lake-beauclair

Cornelius, Andra, and Deborah McMullian. *Defining Green Jobs for Florida.* Workforce Florida, Inc. June 2009. Available from http://www.workforceflorida.com/Publications/docs/GreenJobsReport_6-17-09_ExComApproved.pdf

"Commercial Fisheries Landings in Florida." Florida Fish and Wildlife Conservation Commission. Available from http://myfwc.com/research/saltwater/fish-stats/commercial-fisheries/landings-in-florida

Creating the Strategy for Today's Needs and Tomorrow's Talent: 2010–2015 Strategic Plan for Workforce Development. Workforce Florida, Inc. Available from http://www.workforceflorida.com/Media/Media-Kit/WFIStrategicPlan2010_2015_Web.pdf

"Emergency Management/Freezing Temperatures Third Extended Emergency Order." Florida Department of Transportation. January 7, 2011. Available http://www.fdotmaint.com/PermitNew/Freeze/ Emergency%20Order%20(11-06).pdf

"Energy Economic Zone Pilot Program." Florida Department of Community Affairs. Available from http://www.dca.state.fl.us/fdcp/dcp/energyez/ index.cfm

Executive Order 07-126: Establishing Climate Change Leadership By Example (EO 07-126). State of Florida, Office of the Governor. Available from http:// edocs.dlis.state.fl.us/fldocs/governor/orders/ 2007/07-126-actions.pdf

Executive Order 07-128: Establishing the Florida Governor's Action Team on Energy and Climate Change. State of Florida Office of the Governor. Available from http://www.flclimatechange.us/ewebedit-pro/items/O12F15075.pdf

Feeling the Heat in Florida: Global Warming on the Local Level. Natural Resources Defense Council. Available from http://www.nrdc.org/globalwarming/florida/florida.pdf

Florida Climate Center. Available from http://www. coaps.fsu.edu/climate_center/index.shtml

"Florida Energy Systems Consortium." University of Florida. Available from http://www.floridaenergy. ufl.edu/

"The Florida Environmental Land and Water Management Act." Florida Statutes Title XXVII, Section 380. Florida State Legislature. Available from http://www.leg.state.fl.us/statutes/index.cfm? App_mode=Display_Statute&URL=0300-0399/ 0380/0380PartIContentsIndex.html&Statute Year=2010&Title=-%3E2010-%3EChapter% 20380-%3EPart%20I

"Florida Green Building Coalition." Available from http://floridagreenbuilding.org/

"Florida Manatee." *Florida Fish and Wildlife Research Institute.* Available from http://research.myfwc. com/features/default.asp?id=1001

"Florida Organic Growers." Available from http:// foginfo.org/

"Florida's Energy and Climate Change Action Plan." 2008. Center for Climate Strategies. Available from http://www.flclimatechange.us/ewebeditpro/ items/O12F20128.PDF

"Florida's Wildlife Legacy Initiative." Florida Fish and Wildlife Conservation Commission. Available from http://myfwc.com/docs/WildlifeHabitats/ Legacy_Strategy.pdf

"House Bill 697 (2008). Building Code Standards." Florida State Legislature. Available from http:// www.myfloridahouse.gov/Sections/Bills/billsdetail. aspx?BillId=38094&SessionId=57

House Joint Resolution 383 (2011). Florida House of Representatives. Available from http://www. myfloridahouse.gov/Sections/Documents/load-doc.aspx?FileName=_h0383__.docx&Document Type=Bill&BillNumber=0383&Session=2011

"The Journey to Restore America's Everglades: The Comprehensive Everglades Restoration Plan." Available from http://www.evergladesplan.org/ index.aspx

Katsvairo, Tawainga W., Jim J. Marois, Pawel P. Wiatrak, and David L. Wright. 2006. "Making the Transition from Conventional to Organic Farming Using Conservation Tillage in Florida." University of Florida. Available from http://edis.ifas.ufl.edu/ pdffiles/AG/AG24600.pdf

"Last year brutal for manatees." *Orlando Sentinel.* January 5, 2011. Available from http://blogs. orlandosentinel.com/news-environment-planet florida/2011/01/05/last-year-brutal-for-manatees

"Manatee Mortality Statistics." Florida Fish and Wildlife Research Institute. Available from http://research. myfwc.com/features/category_sub.asp?id=2241

"Overview of Florida Agriculture." Florida Department of Agriculture and Consumer Services. Available from http://www.florida-agriculture.com/agfacts. htm

Present Condition of Florida's Forest Resources: An Assessment 2005. Florida Division of Forestry. Available from http://www.fl-dof.com/plans_ support/ps_pdfs/resource_plan2030.pdf

Robertson, Campbell, James C. McKinley Jr., Shaila Dewan, and Damien Cave. "A Daunting Start of Summer for 5 Gulf State Governors." *The New York Times.* May 28, 2010. Available from http://www. nytimes.com/2010/05/29/us/29govintro.html

Skirble, Rosanne. "Human Waste Killing Caribbean Coral." Voice of America. August 19, 2011. Available from http://www.voanews.com/english/news/ usa/places/Human-Waste-Killing-Caribbean-Coral-128080723.html

Snyder, Jim. "Snakes Get Lobbyists in Fight OverBoa Ban." Bloomberg. August 5, 2011. Available from http://www.bloomberg.com/news/2011-08-05/ snakes-get-lobbyists-too-as-breeders-charm-congress-to-fight-u-s-boa-ban.html

"Species Report: Florida." U.S. Fish and Wildlife Service. Available from http://ecos.fws.gov/tess_public/ pub/stateListingAndOccurrenceIndividual.jsp? state=FL&s8fid=112761032792&s8fid=11276257 3902&s8fid=24012821595643

"State of Florida Executive Order Number 07–128." Available from http://myfloridaclimate.com/

2007_climate_summit/executive_orders_partnership_agreements/executive_order_07_128

"State of the Climate: National Overview for December 2010." NOAA National Climatic Data Center. Available from http://www.ncdc.noaa.gov/sotc/2010/12

Taylor, Gary. "As drought worsens, more than 420 wildfires burn across Florida." *The Orlando Sentinel.* June 16, 2011. Available from http://www.orlandosentinel.com/news/local/os-wildfires-florida-weather-orlando-20110616,0,5895997.story

"2007 Minerals Yearbook: Florida." U.S. Geological Survey. Available from http://minerals.usgs.gov/minerals/pubs/state/2007/myb2-2007-fl.pdf

Wheeler, Jason. "Offshore drilling ban gets big push from Charlie Crist and Alex Sink." Central Florida News 13. February 9, 2011. Available from http://www.cfnews13.com/article/news/2011/february/205871/Offshore-drilling-could-appear-on-2012-Florida-ballot

"Wildlife and Habitats." Florida Fish and Wildlife Conservation Commission. Available from http://myfwc.com/wildlifehabitats

Zimmerman, Cindy. "USDA Guarantees Loan for Florida Biofuels Plant."Domestic Fuel. Available from http://domesticfuel.com/2011/08/18/usda-guarentees-loan-for-florida-biofuels-plant/

Georgia

Georgia has long been known by its nickname, the Peach State. In 1996, the state government made the peach the official state fruit. Georgia ranks twenty-first in size—but ninth in population and fourth in population growth—among the fifty states. The state's population keeps growing. The population increased by more than 20 percent from 2000 to 2009. As the population has grown, particularly in the state capital of Atlanta and its surrounding suburbs, water sources were challenged to the demands for water. This put a strain on the state government, as a legal ruling (which has since been overturned) stated that Lake Lanier—Atlanta's primary water source—was never licensed as a water supply. Alabama and Florida have also claimed that, by withdrawing water from Lake Lanier, Georgia was compromising their water supply, which is downstream from the lake.

Climate

Georgia experiences mild winters, with the mountain region to the north averaging colder temperatures than the rest of the state. Summers are hot in the piedmont and on the coastal plain. Humidity is high, ranging from 82 percent in the morning to 56 percent in the afternoon in Atlanta. Rainfall varies considerably from year to year but averages 50 inches (127 cm) annually in the lowlands, increasing to 75 inches (191 cm) in the mountains; snow falls occasionally in central Georgia and the northern mountains. Tornadoes are an annual threat in the state, and coastal areas are subject to hurricane landfall and storm tides. The growing season is approximately 185 days in the mountains and a generous 300 days in southern Georgia.

Climate Change Impact

According to estimates by the U.S. Environmental Protection Agency (EPA), average summer temperatures in Georgia could increase by about 2°F (1.1°C) by 2100 as a result of global climate change. Average winter and spring temperatures could increase by about 3°F (1.7°C), with fall temperatures up by 4°F (2.2°C). In some parts of the state, average precipitation has already increased by about 10 percent during the last century. Some reports predict that summer and fall precipitation could increase by another 15 percent or more by 2100. Rising temperatures and changes in precipitation could have serious affects on agriculture and wildlife. Such changing climate patterns could also lead to more frequent occurrences of severe weather, such as droughts or destructive storms.

In addition, higher temperatures create stagnant weather patterns, which allow ozone to accumulate, decreasing air quality. Sea level rise is also a concern for the state. The EPA reports that the sea level at Fort Polaski is rising by a rate of about 13 inches (33 cm) per century. By 2100, the sea level could rise by another 25 inches (63.5 cm), if no mitigating measures are taken. Increasing sea levels are caused by warming of polar regions and loss of ice cover. This places the barrier islands, coastal ports, wetlands, and coastal developments at risk.

Georgia does not have a Climate Change Action Plan. However the city of Atlanta released a Sustainability Report in 2009, which stated that a task force will be assembled to develop city ordinances to reduce greenhouse gas emissions. According to Sustainable Atlanta, the city making progress in reducing its emissions by the 7 percent required by the U.S. Mayor's Climate Protection Agreement through development of the Atlanta Climate Action Plan. The Climate Action Plan will guide all city departments so that current initiatives and near-term objectives are aligned with achieving the 2012 emissions reduction goal.

❧ Natural Resources, Water, and Agriculture

Natural Resources

Georgia's forests cover 66 percent of the state at 24.8 million acres (10 million ha). Most of the forest land is owned by non-industrial private landowners, followed by the forest industry. Georgia has some 250 species of trees, most of which are of commercial importance. White and scrub pines, chestnut, northern red oak, and buckeye cover the mountain zone, while loblolly and shortleaf (yellow) pines and whiteback maple are found throughout the piedmont. White oak and cypress are plentiful in the eastern part of the state, and pecan trees—while not native to Georgia—are grown in orchards or planted as ornamental trees. Trees found throughout the state include red cedar, scaly-bark and white hickories, red maple, sycamore, yellow poplar, sassafras, sweet and black gums, dogwoods, and various magnolias.

The native forest of southern Georgia is longleaf pine (a yellow pine) and its associated wiregrass groundcover. This was largely eliminated by settlement and conversion to agriculture (only about 3 percent remains). This forest type is considered globally imperiled and is noted for its plant diversity. River bottoms in southern Georgia tend to be flood tolerant hardwood forests.

Georgia's forest industry has a direct economic impact of $16 billion and provides 154,000 jobs. According to the Georgia Forestry Commission, as of January 2009 there were 172 primary wood product manufacturing facilities that include 12 pulp mills, 9 engineered-wood product mills, and 93 saw mills. Additionally, there are more than 1,200 secondary manufacturers that convert manufactured wood products into value-added products such as furniture, cabinetry, and paper products.

Prominent among Georgia wildlife are the white-tailed deer, black bear, muskrat, raccoon, opossum, mink, common cottontail, and three species of squirrel—fox, gray, and flying. No fewer than 160 bird species breed in Georgia, among them the mockingbird, brown thrasher (the state bird), and numerous sparrows; the Okefenokee Swamp, a large wetland complex in southeastern Georgia, is home to the sandhill piper, snowy egret, and white ibis. The bobwhite quail is the most popular game bird. There are 79 species of reptiles, including venomous rattlesnakes (three species—canebrake, eastern diamondback, and pigmy), copperhead, coral snakes, and cottonmouth moccasin. The state's 63 amphibian species consist mainly of various salamanders, frogs, and toads. Outdoor recreation is very popular in the state, with more than 90 wildlife management areas available for hunters, along with extensive state and federal lands available for hiking, camping, boating and other outdoor activities.

In 2011, 77 species in Georgia were on the threatened and endangered species list of the U.S. Fish and Wildlife Service. Endangered animals include the West Indian manatee, three species of moccasinshell mussels, three species of sea turtle, the wood stork, three species of whale, the red-cockaded woodpecker, and shortnose sturgeon.

Protecting Sea Turtles The Tybee Island Marine Science Center, the Georgia Department of Natural Resources, and the Tybee Island city sea turtle program have been working together to protect the island's nesting loggerhead sea turtles. While acknowledging that Tybee Island is not the preferred nesting spot for the threatened loggerheads—due to its artificial white lighting and the lack of a natural beach—researchers and scientists do their best to protect the nests they have. In 2010, Tybee had ten sea turtle nests. Once scientists find a nest, they mark it with small wooden stakes and a Department of Natural Resources sign warning people to keep their distance. People generally respect the nests—it is predators such as raccoons, wild hogs, and armadillos that cause the most destruction to turtle nests. The Tybee Island Marine Science Center also works to educate the public about this threatened species. In 2011, the Center had a loggerhead, Salty, in residence. Salty is used as an educational and public relations tool, to help get visitors excited about protecting loggerheads. Plans are to release Salty into the wild when it reaches 20 inches (50 cm) in diameter, which is the Department of Natural Resource's limit for captive sea turtles. Having grown to that considerable size, Salty will have a better chance of survival and nesting than if it had left as a hatchling, thus its time as a sea turtle ambassador is not merely symbolic.

Georgia is the leading clay-producing state in the nation, and according to the U.S. Geological Survey, in 2007 its clay production accounted for 23.6 percent of the nation's total. Kaolin clay is the state's principal nonfuel raw mineral commodity. Kaolin clay is followed by crushed stone, portland cement, fuller's earth, construction sand and gravel, and masonry cement. The state is also ranked second in the nation for barite production and third for mica production. The northeastern portion of the state is noted for semi-precious gems. In 2010 the state was ranked fourteenth for overall nonfuel mineral production with a value of $1.5 billion.

Water

Fourteen major river basins occur in Georgia. Two great rivers originate in the state's northeast: the Savannah, which forms part of the border with South Carolina, and the Chattahoochee, which flows across the state to become the western boundary. The Flint joins the Chattahoochee at the southwestern corner of Georgia to form the Apalachicola, which flows through Florida into the Gulf of Mexico. The two largest rivers of central Georgia, the Ocmulgee and Oconee, flow together to

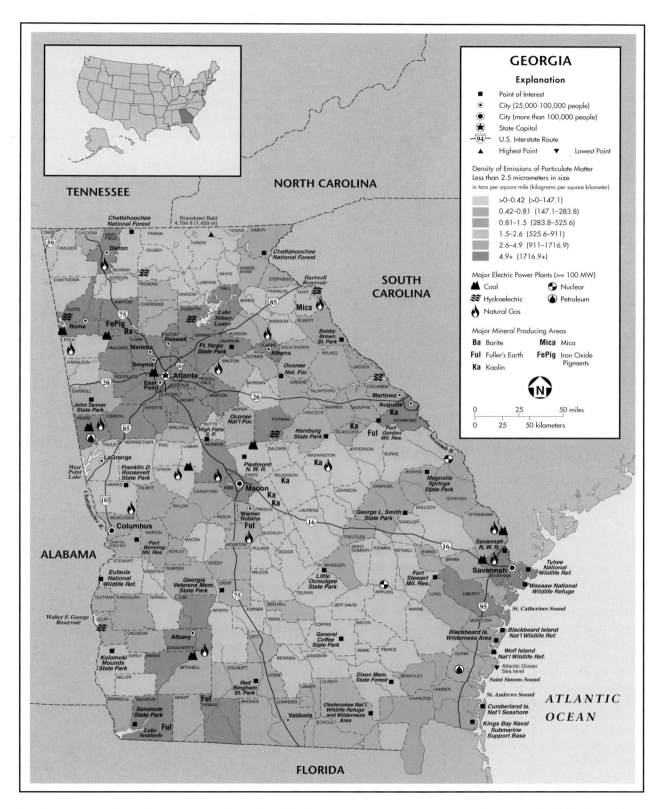

SOURCES: "County Emissions Map: Criteria Air Pollutants." *AirData*. U.S. Environmental Protection Agency. Available from http://www. epa.gov/air/data/geosel.html; *Energy Maps*. U.S. Energy Information Administration. Available from http://www.eia.gov/state; *Highest and Lowest Elevations*. U.S. Geological Survey. Available from http://egsc.usgs.gov/isb/pubs/booklets/elvadist/elvadist.html#Highest; *2007 Minerals Yearbook*. U.S. Geological Survey. Available from http://minerals.usgs.gov/minerals/pubs/state. © *2011 Cengage Learning.*

Bald cypress trees and bullhead lilies on the Suwannee River of Georgia's Okefenokee Swamp. © *Brian Lasenby/ShutterStock.com*

form the Altamaha, which then flows eastward to the Atlantic. Perhaps the best-known Georgia river, though smaller than those above, is the Suwannee, flowing southwest through the Okefenokee Swamp, across Florida and into the Gulf of Mexico, and famous for its evocation in the song "Old Folks at Home" by Stephen Foster. Huge reservoirs created by dams on the Savannah River are Clark Hill Reservoir and Hartwell Lake; reservoirs on the Chattahoochee River include Lake Seminole, Walter F. George Reservoir, Lake Harding, West Point Reservoir, and Lake Sidney Lanier. The most popular freshwater game fish are trout, bream, bass, and catfish, all but the last of which are produced in state hatcheries for restocking. Dolphins, porpoises, shrimp, oysters, and blue crabs are found along the Georgia coast. Commercial fish landings for 2008 were valued at more than $13 million, with shrimp and blue crab being the most valuable catches.

The Port of Savannah is ranked as one of the top twenty-five ports in the nation for overall cargo volume, and among the top fifteen for foreign trade volume. The Port of Brunswick has become one of the most productive ports on the East Coast for the transport of automobiles and heavy machinery. Port Bainbridge and Port Columbus are located along the Apalachicola-Chattahoochee-Flint (ACF) Waterway, also referred to as the Tri-Rivers Waterway. Both serve as cargo transit points with access to the Gulf of Mexico. Port Columbus is a dedicated bulk liquid facility.

Agriculture

According to the U.S. Department of Agriculture's 2007 census, Georgia s home to more than 47,000 farms totaling over 10 million acres (4 million ha). (The USDA conducts its census every five years.) The USDA also reported that, in 2008, Georgia was ranked first in production of broilers (chickens for meat), peanuts, pecans, rye, and spring onions; second in production of cotton, fresh market cucumbers, and snap beans; and third in production of cantaloupes and fresh market sweet corn.

More than forty varieties of peaches are grown in Georgia, and the state produces more than 130 million pounds (59 million kg) of the fruit annually. The state is also known for the production of the Vidalia onion, a sweet onion that is produced in 13 of the state's 159 counties.

Also in 2008, Georgia had 67 certified organic producers on 4,341 acres (1,757 ha) of land. Certified organic crops produced in the state are vegetables, tree nuts, grapes, berries, peanuts, and fallow. The Georgia Crop Improvement Association serves as the USDA-accredited certifying agent for organic producers.

🍁 Energy

Georgia ranks among the top ten in per capita energy consumption among the 50 states. According to the U.S. Energy Administration, Georgia mainly uses coal (63 percent) and nuclear power (26.8 percent) for its electricity generation. The remainder is supplied by a combination of hydropower, natural gas, and other sources. As there are no fossil fuel resources in the state, Georgia receives coal from Wyoming, Kentucky, and Virginia. Petroleum is also imported to the state, mainly from pipelines originating in the Gulf Coast region.

Georgia purchases its natural gas from other states and from abroad, including Trinidad and Tobago, Egypt, and states on the Gulf Coast. More than two-thirds of the natural gas that comes into the state goes on to South Carolina, and minimal amounts go to Florida and Tennessee. Georgia also imports international supplies at a liquefied natural gas (LNG) terminal located on Elba Island, at the mouth of the Savannah River. The Elba Island facility, which is one of nine existing LNG import sites in the United States, receives LNG by tanker from Trinidad and Tobago. An expansion of this facility was completed in 2010, raising the total send-out capacity

Georgia State Profile

Physical Characteristics

Land area	57,501 square miles (148,927 sq km)
Inland water area	1,420 square miles (3,678 sq km)
Coastal area	49 square miles (79 sq km)
Highest point	Brasstown Bald 4,784 feet (1,458 m)
National Forest System lands (2010)	867,000 acres (351,000 ha)
State parks (2011)	63

Energy Statistics

Total energy production (2009)	510 trillion Btu
State ranking in total energy production (2009)	31
Renewable energy net generation total (2009)	6.1 million megawatt hours
Hydroelectric energy generation (2009)	3.3 million megawatt hours
Biomass energy generation (2009)	80,000 megawatt hours
Wind energy generation (2009)	NA
Wood and derived fuel energy generation (2009)	2.7 million megawatt hours
Crude oil reserves (2009)	NA
Natural gas reserves (2009)	NA
Natural gas liquids (2008)	NA

Pollution Statistics

Carbon output (2005)	167.9 million tons of CO_2 (152.4 million t)
Superfund sites (2008)	14
Particulate matter (less than 2.5 micrometers) emissions (2002)	41,112 tons per year (37,296 t/yr)
Toxic chemical releases (2009)	80.2 million pounds (36.4 million kg)
Generated hazardous waste (2009)	4 million tons (3.7 million t)

SOURCES: AirData. U.S. Environmental Protection Agency. Available from http://www.epa.gov/air/data; *Energy Maps, Facts, and Data of the U.S. States.* U.S. Energy Information Administration. Available from http://www.eia.gov/state; *The 2012 Statistical Abstract.* U.S. Census Bureau. Available from http://www.census.gov/compendia/statab; *United States Energy Usage.* eRedux. Available from http://www.eredux.net/states.

© 2011 Cengage Learning.

from 1.2 billion cubic feet (bcf) (34 million cu m) of natural gas per day to 1.75 bcfd (50 million cu m). The expansion also included a 4.2 bcf (119 million cu m) storage tank and the new 190-mile (306-km) Elba Express Pipeline, which provides a transport capacity of 945 million cubic feet (27 million cu m) per day to markets in the southeast and eastern United States. The industrial, electric power, and residential sectors are Georgia's largest consumers of natural gas. Nearly one-half of all Georgia households use natural gas as their main energy source for home heating.

When it comes to renewable energy sources, Georgia is one of the top hydroelectric power producers east of the Rocky Mountains, and one of the nation's top producers of power from wood and wood waste, with just over 9 percent of the nation's capacity. Georgia Power has 20 hydroelectric dams and two nuclear power plants in the state.

In January 2011, the Environmental Protection Agency granted Georgia wood-fired power plants and biomass incinerator burners a three-year exemption from carbon dioxide pollution limits under the Clean Air Act. Conservation groups in the state filed a lawsuit in August 2011 that challenged the EPA's exemption. Groups are concerned that an increased demand for wood fuel from existing and proposed plants would use up supplies of wood waste, leading to deforestation. Incinerating trees releases carbon dioxide at a much faster rate than the tree's natural biodegradation, which could undermine efforts to curb emissions. Environmentalists have also argued that the EPA has no right to waive the Clean Air Act to benefit politically favored industries. Members of the National Alliance of Forest Owners (NAFO)—a group representing private forest owners—have staunchly backed the exemption. NAFO members include timber giants such as Plum Creek Timber and Weyerhauser. These companies spent more than $850,000 in lobbying during the 2010 election cycle alone.

Georgia does not have a renewable portfolio standard. However, the state adopted a net metering policy to credit customers' utility bills for electricity they provide to the grid generated from renewable sources.

☙ Green Business, Green Building, Green Jobs

Green Business

The state of Georgia has some tax credits, incentives, and rebates available for businesses that want to be more energy efficient. One such program is the Clean Energy Tax Credit. Established in 2008, this legislation established corporate tax credits (personal credits are also available) for renewable energy equipment and certain energy-efficient equipment installed in commercial settings. For renewable energy property, the tax credit is equal to 35 percent of the cost of the system (including installation).

The state is also home to the Georgia Green Loan program. Georgia Green Loans is a non-profit microlending agency that offers two incentives to green businesses. They are using their funding for the "Save & Sustain" program to subsidize commercial energy audits for Georgia small businesses and commercial property owners and are also providing low-interest loans for energy efficient improvements. Georgia Green Loans will cover most of the costs for commercial energy audits through a select group of energy auditing partners, allowing businesses to inform decisions on energy efficiency improvements. Loans can be used for a variety of technologies, including HVAC systems, insulation, and Energy Star appliances. Loans are available to renewable energy and energy efficiency businesses, in addition to other types of "green" businesses. Example loans include a family farm that grows organic vegetables, a restaurant that serves only locally-grown produce, a distributor of homemade jellies and sauces, an installer of solar panels or home insulation products, a manufacturer of biofuels, and a renewable energy entrepreneur.

Green Building

In 2008, as part of the Conserve Georgia campaign, then-state Governor G. E. "Sonny" Perdue initiated the Governor's Energy Challenge 2020. The initiative requires state government agencies and departments to reduce energy consumption by 15 percent by 2020. Reductions in energy use must come from energy efficiency measures and from renewable energy development. Funding from the American Recovery and Reinvestment Act of 2009 (ARRA) is being used by the Georgia Environmental Finance Authority (GEFA) to fund state agency retrofit projects. These projects will help meet the goal set by the Governor's Energy Challenge. The challenge is mandatory for state entities, but local governments, schools, businesses, and individuals have been encouraged to participate.

On the municipal level, in August of 2010, the city of Atlanta opened the Sustainable Home Initiative for a New Economy (SHINE) Program. This pilot program offers rebates for energy efficiency improvements to residents of Atlanta. A rebate worth 25 percent of the cost of installation—up to $2,000—is available during the pilot phase of the program. In order to qualify, a home must be assessed by a "Home Performance with ENERGY STAR" contractor. Energy efficiency improvements that are eligible for incentives include building insulation, programmable thermostats, duct and air sealing, and equipment insulation.

The University of Georgia Cooperative Extension's web site for family and consumer sciences provides links for homeowners to information regarding buying an energy efficient home, saving energy in an older home, how renters can save energy, and more energy efficient heating and cooling systems. There is also information about energy programs, such as the Energy Star Extension Network and Energy Efficiency for Residential Structures in Rural Georgia, and external links are provided to energy partners and other assistance programs.

Green Jobs

According to the Pew Charitable Trusts, in 2007 Georgia had more than 16,000 clean energy jobs in more than 1,800 businesses. A majority of these jobs were concentrated in the conservation and pollution mitigation sector, with jobs in energy efficiency coming in second.

Increasingly, Georgia colleges and universities are adding renewable energy training programs. For example, Lanier Technical College in Oakwood, Georgia offers an entry-level certificate of knowledge in photovoltaics. The course will familiarize students with photovoltaic systems and enable students to demonstrate knowledge, comprehension, and application of terms and concepts of system operations. Savannah Technical College also offers a photovoltaic systems installation and repair technician certificate. This program provides students with the opportunity to enter the workforce specialized in installing, inspection, and repairing solar panels in the electrical construction industry.

The Georgia Institute of Technology has a center for energy research that includes solar, wind, hydrogen, and bioenergy focuses. Both undergraduate and graduate students have opportunities to take classes and conduct research in renewable energy subjects. Georgia Tech is also home to the University Center for Excellence in Photovoltaics. Established in part by the Department of Energy, the center works to improve the fundamental understanding of advanced photovoltaic devices, to fabricate high efficiency solar cells, and to provide training and research opportunities for students.

🍀 The Fight for Water in Atlanta

Normally, the Atlanta area receives enough annual rainfall to meet the metropolitan area's water supply needs. However, the area's rivers and reservoirs have limited storage, so when a major drought occurs, like the one from 1998 to 2002, water becomes a limited resource. The year 2007 was one of the state's driest years of recent record, and despite recovering a bit in 2008 and 2009, drought once again returned to the state, especially affecting southern Georgia, in 2010. During these years, the state has run into conflicts over the Atlanta area's use of local reservoirs during droughts, and the city has been forced to look into alternate sources and conservation methods to supply water to its ever-growing population.

Ninety-eight percent of metro Atlanta's water comes from surface water, but the area's rivers are small, and there are limited opportunities for more reservoirs in the region. The area relies on existing reservoirs and six different water basins, and distribution of withdrawals between these basins is a necessity. Metropolitan Atlanta depends on the reservoirs of Lake Lanier and Lake Allatoona for 75 percent of its water supply. During times of drought, lake levels can be severely depleted. The Metropolitan North Georgia Water Planning District, comprised of Atlanta and ninety other municipalities, implemented three plans in 2003 in order to better manage water in the district. These plans include the

Metropolitan Atlanta depends on the reservoirs of Lake Lanier (shown here) and Lake Allatoona for 75 percent of its water supply. © *Tony Cunningham/Alamy*

District-wide Watershed Management Plan, the Long-term Wastewater Management Plan, and the Water Supply and Water Conservation Management Plan.

Some strategies that the Conservation Management plan has outlined for the region include the reallocation of the water in Lakes Lanier and Allatoona from power generation to water supply; building new reservoirs (such as the South Fulton reservoir, which was authorized in 2010); aggressive water conservation, which involves retrofitting old, inefficient plumbing fixtures; repairing and upgrading municipal distribution systems, and distributing water within the region between basins to serve households and businesses.

A Hitch in the Plan

Despite the positive changes that the Conservation Management plan would implement, along with a water conservation law that was passed in 2010, Georgia lawmakers are scrambling to save one of metro Atlanta's primary water sources: Lake Sidney Lanier.

Lake Lanier, a reservoir that is part of the Apalachicola-Chattahoochee-Flint (ACF) river basin in the northern part of the state, was created by the U.S. Army Corps of Engineers (USACE) through the construction of the Buford Dam on the Chattahoochee River in 1956. The authorized purpose for the lake was to provide flood control and hydropower. However, in 1989, the USACE recommended that a portion of the water supply could be reallocated to serve the growing demands of the Atlanta region. This decision set off an immediate legal challenge from Alabama and Florida, which also rely on waters from the ACF basin. They argue that an increase in water use by Atlanta would lead to serious shortages downstream, affecting commercial fisheries, wetland habitats, and the drinking water supplies of their own states. And so began what has become known as the Tri-State Water Wars.

In 1997, the states agreed to put their official lawsuits on hold by accepting the terms of the ACF Compact, which was ratified by the U.S. Congress. It provides a framework for the states to use in developing a joint water management plan for the basin. (A second compact was written for the Alabama-Coosa-Tallapoosa river basins, which are also an area of concern for all three states.) However, the compact expired in 2003 without a resolution. As a result, the lawsuits filed by Alabama and Florida against the state of Georgia and the USACE proceeded through the courts.

In 2009, U.S. District Judge Paul Magnuson ruled that virtually all water withdrawals from Lake Lanier were illegal, stating that the lake was never authorized to be used as a water supply, but for hydroelectric power and flood control. Georgia was given three years to petition the U.S. Congress for the official authorization to allow the water from the lake to be used for water supply, or to come to an agreement with Florida and Alabama. If approval is not obtained, withdrawals will be cut to 1970s levels, when the city of Atlanta and its water needs were much smaller. Losing the rights to draw water from Lake Lanier, without sufficient alternate water sources, would cut off the water supply for 3 million of the Atlanta area's residents. The state of Georgia has filed an appeal.

Meanwhile, by late 2010, Georgia, Alabama, and Florida had not yet to come to an agreement, and the governors of all three states were coming to the end of their terms. The year 2011 brought three new governors, with limited time left before the 2012 deadline. Georgia governor Nathan Deal allowed his state's appeal to continue into circuit court, with the case heard in March 2011. However, the three new governors have also refocused some of their efforts on continuing to negotiate a fair and sound agreement.

In June 2011, a three-judge panel overturned Judge Magnuson's 2009 ruling that would limit Georgia's access to the lake for water supply. The panel gave the Army Corps of Engineers one year to reevaluate Georgia's request and stated that water supply is a permissible use of the dam. Florida and Alabama appealed the ruling in August 2011, claiming that the panel failed to show that Congress allowed the Army Corps to earmark water for Atlanta's use, but in September, an 11th Circuit Court of Appeals panel, made up of ten judges (including three from Florida and two from Alabama), unanimously voted to refuse to hear the appeal. Alabama governor Robert Bentley responded that the two states would appeal to the U.S. Supreme Court, but Georgia governor Nathan Deal pledged to move forward with negotiations with the other two states.

Throughout this time, Georgia lawmakers continued to work on additional measures to assure an adequate water supply for years to come. In 2010, the state passed the most far-reaching water conservation law in its history. Senate Bill 370 requires the installation of low-flow plumbing fixtures in all new buildings, "submetering" in new multi-tenant buildings to allow each tenant's water use to be measured. It also requires local water systems to perform audits to pinpoint leaks and establishes a ban on outdoor watering between 10 a. m. and 4 p.m. While the bill takes positive steps, it likely will not be enough to eliminate the state's need for water from reservoirs such as Lake Lanier. The bill's requirements only apply new buildings and delay other mandates until 2012. The state hopes that while it won't entirely solve the issues at hand, the bill will send a positive message to other states that it is making changes, which it hopes will therefore influence the future decision about Lake Lanier.

While the debate rages on, Georgia has also been considering alternatives such as inter-basin transfers from basins outside of the metropolitan Atlanta region. However, this idea is causing concern among residents, who believe that this solution effectively steals from the water supply of others and would require legislative action. Other alternatives include building more reservoirs and raising the level of Buford Dam. However, each of these issues, like Lake Lanier, face challenges, so only time will tell how metro Atlanta will supply its growing population with enough water to meet its needs.

BIBLIOGRAPHY

Books

Melosi, Artin, ed. *Environment, vol. 8 of The New Encyclopedia of Southern Culture.* Chapel Hill, NC: University of North Carolina Press, 2007.

Nash, Steve. *Blue Ridge 2020: An Owner's Manual.* Chapel Hill, NC: University of North Carolina Press, 1999.

Strutin, Michal, and Tony Arruza. *The Smithsonian Guides to Natural America: The Southeast–South Carolina, Georgia, Alabama, Florida.* Washington, DC: Smithsonian Books, 1996.

Web Sites

2007 Minerals Yearbook: Georgia. U.S. Geological Survey. Available from http://minerals.usgs.gov/minerals/pubs/state/2007/myb2-2007-ga.pdf

Bluestein, Greg, and Ben Evans. "3-year countdown begins for Atlanta's water future." *Associated Press.* July 21, 2009. Available from http://www.signonsandiego.com/news/2009/jul/21/us-water-wars-072109/

"The Clean Energy Economy: Georgia." The Pew Charitable Trusts. Available from http://www.pewcenteronthestates.org/uploadedFiles/wwwpewcenteronthestatesorg/Fact_Sheets/Clean_Economy_Factsheet_Georgia.pdf

"Climate Change and Georgia." United States Environmental Protection Agency. Available from http://www.epa.gov/climatechange/effects/downloads/ga_impct.pdf

"Commercial Landings Data." Georgia Department of Natural Resources, Coastal Resources Division

Conserve Georgia. Available from http://www.conservegeorgia.org/

DeYoung, Bill. "Turtle tracking." Connect Savannah. August 9, 2011. Available from http://www.connectsavannah.com/news/article/104667/

"Forest Industry in Georgia—Industry Overview." Georgia Forestry Commission. Available from http://www.gfc.state.ga.us/ForestMarketing/IndustryOverview.cfm

"Georgia: 2007 Census of Agriculture-State Data." U.S. Department of Agriculture. Available from http://www.agcensus.usda.gov/Publications/2007/Full_Report/Volume_1,_Chapter_1_State_Level/Georgia/st13_1_009_010.pdf

"Georgia Agricultural Facts." U.S. Department of Agriculture. Available from http://www.nass.usda.gov/Statistics_by_State/Georgia/Publications/QuickFactSheet.pdf

Georgia Department of Natural Resources Wildlife Resources Division. Available from http://www.georgiawildlife.com/

Georgia Green Loans. Available from http://www.georgiagreenloans.org/

Georgia Ports Authority. Available from http://www.gaports.com/Home.aspx

Georgia Power: Generating Plants. Available from http://www.georgiapower.com/about/plants.asp

Georgia. U.S. Energy and Information Administration. Available from http://www.eia.doe.gov/state/state_energy_profiles.cfm?sid=GA

Henry, Ray. "Ala., Fla. Appeal ruling in water feud with Ga." *The Miami Herald.* August 12, 2011. Available from http://www.miamiherald.com/2011/08/12/2355889/appeals-due-in-tri-state-water.html

Henry, Ray. "Appeals court to consider tri-state water dispute." *Gwinnett Daily Post.* March 7, 2011. Available from http://www.gwinnettdailypost.com/home/headlines/Appeals_court_to_consider_tri-state_water_dispute_117550843.html

"How Atlanta is Working to Green Itself." Sustainable Atlanta. Available from http://www.sustainable-atlanta.org/pdf/Franklin%27s%20Presentation%20to%20Emory%20Students.pdf

Joyner, Chris, and Patrick Fox. "Appeals court refuses to rehear tri-state water case." AJC (Atlanta Journal Constitution online). Available from http://www.ajc.com/news/appeals-court-refuses-to-1184485.html

Metropolitan North Georgia Water Planning District. Available from http://www.northgeorgiawater.com/html/88.htm

Our Path to Sustainability: 2008–2009 Sustainability Report for Atlanta. Sustainable Atlanta. Available from http://www.sustainableatlanta.org/report/Sustainability%20Report.pdf

"Photovoltaic Entry Level Certificate of Knowledge Program." Lanier Technical College. Available from http://www.laniertech.edu/economic-development_/photovoltaic.asp

"Photovoltaic Systems Installation & Repair Technician Certificate." Savannah Technical College. Available from http://www.savannahtech.edu/cwo/Industrial_Technology/Photovatic_Systems_Installation_&_Repair_Technician

SB 370—Water; examine practices, programs, policies; develop programs for voluntary water conservation; reports of measurable progress. Georgia General Assembly. Available from http://www.legis.state.ga.us/legis/2009_10/sum/sb370.htm

State of the Forest: A Report on Georgia Forests 2007. Georgia Forestry Association. Available from http://www.gfagrow.org/PDF/07%20state%20of%20forest.pdf

Sturgis, Sue. "Lawsuit targets carbon-pollution exemption for wood-burning power plants." Facing South. August 16, 2011. Available from http://www.southernstudies.org/2011/08/lawsuit-targets-carbon-pollution-exemption-for-wood-burning-power-plants.html

"Tri-State Water Wars." Atlanta Regional Commission. Available from http://www.atlantaregional.com/environment/tri-state-water-wars

University Center of Excellence for Photovoltaics Research and Education (UCEP). Georgia Institute of Technology. Available from http://www.ece.gatech.edu/research/UCEP/ucephome.htm

"Water, Energy, Waste." Family and Consumer Sciences. The University of Georgia Cooperative Extension. Available from http://www.fcs.uga.edu/ext/housing/wew.php

"Water Wars Background." Alabama Rivers Alliance. Available from http://www.alabamarivers.org/current-work/water-wars

Williams, Dave. "Atlanta's running out of water, and time." *Atlanta Business Chronicle.* July 2, 2010. Available from http://atlanta.bizjournals.com/atlanta/stories/2010/07/05/story1.html?q=new%20reservoirs%20atlanta

Williams, Dave. "Candidates discuss Atlanta's water needs." *Atlanta Business Chronicle.* July 2, 2010. Available from http://atlanta.bizjournals.com/atlanta/stories/2010/07/05/story2.html?q=new%20reservoirs%20atlanta

Williams, Dave. "River groups call for new water plan." *Atlanta Business Chronicle.* July 15, 2010. Available from http://atlanta.bizjournals.com/atlanta/stories/2010/07/12/daily54.html?q=new%20reservoirs%20atlanta

Williams, Dave. "Senate panel OKs South Fulton reservoir." *Atlanta Business Chronicle.* April 20, 2010. Available from http://atlanta.bizjournals.com/atlanta/stories/2010/04/19/daily20.html

Hawaii

The state of Hawaii lies 2,100 mi (3,380 km) southwest of California and 3,019 mi (4,859 km) south of Alaska. It is the only U.S. state located entirely in the tropics. The state is made up of eight major islands: Kauai, Oahu, Molokai, Lanai, Maui, Hawaii, Niihau, and the uninhabited island of Kahoolawe. In addition, there are ten islands referred to as the Northwest Hawaiian Islands. Together, the islands constitute the Hawaiian Archipelago which stretches across 1,500 miles (2,400 km) of the Pacific Ocean. The island of Hawaii is the largest and is often referred to as "the Big Island." Since Hawaii became a state in 1959, tourism has been its largest industry. In recent years efforts have been made to make tourism more sustainable and environmentally friendly, as increasing numbers of visitors to the islands exacerbate environmental concerns.

Climate

Hawaii's tropical climate can be generalized as summer, from May to October, and winter from October to April. The state receives most of its precipitation during the winter months. Because the state lies within such a narrow latitude band between 19 and 24°N, temperatures vary little over the course of the year, and rarely go above 90°F (32°C) or below 60°F (15°C). The ocean water temperature around the islands is relatively mild, which make the consistent northwest tradewinds blowing onto land equally mild. The varied topography of the islands significantly influences local weather patterns due to orographic lifting of air masses. Windward (upwind) coasts tend to have more clouds and rainfall, while leeward (downwind) coasts are generally sunny and dry. Hawaii's landforms experience an ecological zonation from the subtropics to subalpine conditions on the highest mountains of the island of Hawaii and Maui, since temperature decreases with elevation by about 3°F per thousand feet.

The National Wildlife Federation warns that if measures are not taken to mitigate global warming, rising temperatures will further environmental degradation in the islands. Rising sea levels would destroy habitats for animals such as the endangered Hawaiian monk seal, while causing significant financial losses to coastal properties. Climate change could also lead to the destruction of the state's coral reefs, which serve as critical habitat for threatened and endangered marine life, while protecting coastlines from further erosion. In 1998, Hawaii released its Climate Change Action Plan. The purpose of the plan is to develop consensus as to Hawaii's goals for greenhouse gas emission reductions. The plan discusses the potential impacts that climate change could have on the state, lists past greenhouse gas emissions, and forecasts greenhouse gas emissions for 2020. It also provides recommendations for how greenhouse gas emissions goals should be set. In 2007, Hawaii passed the Global Warming Solutions Act that mandates the state reduce its greenhouse gas emissions to 1990 levels by 2020.

Mauna Loa Observatory: Hawaii's Contribution to Climate Change Science

Since the 1950s, instruments at the Mauna Loa Observatory have been measuring the level of carbon dioxide in Earth's atmosphere. Dr. Charles Keeling developed the first instrument to measure carbon dioxide in atmospheric samples and established a field station on the summit of the Big Island's Mauna Loa. He chose this spot because of its remote location. A tall metal tower reaching 11,135 feet (3,394 m) above sea level takes in air samples through hoses. The carbon dioxide levels in the samples are then measured. Carbon dioxide measurements are made with a nondispersive infrared sensor, a type of infrared spectrophotometer. Another instrument measures atmospheric particles by projecting a laser beam into the atmosphere nearby.

Keeling's continuous measurements led to the discovery that carbon dioxide in the atmosphere has been increasing at a dramatic rate. The first measurement he made in the 1950s was 310 parts per million (ppm); the level had risen to 380 ppm by the time of Keeling's death in 2005. The graph that illustrated the rising carbon dioxide levels came to be known as the Keeling Curve.

Keeling's work contributed to the world's awareness that consumption of fossil fuels is a factor in climate change. Former vice president Al Gore attended a class where the Keeling Curve was presented, which inspired him to begin a campaign to inform the world of the impact of human reliance on fossil fuels. Gore, along with the Intergovernmental Panel on Climate Change (IPCC), would go on to jointly win the Nobel Peace Prize for their work on the book and movie *An Inconvenient Truth*, which brought the climate change issue to wider public attention. Keeling's work continues at Mauna Loa, where hoses attached to a tower continuously measure samples and provide hourly calculations. Keeling's son, Ralph Keeling, has predicted that carbon dioxide levels could surpass 400 ppm by May 2014.

❧ Natural Resources, Water, and Agriculture

Natural Resources

Numerous animal and plant species have been introduced to the islands since Polynesian voyagers first settled these volcanic islands, causing many native and endemic species to become extinct or driven near extinction due to habitat loss. The only land mammal native to the Hawaiian Islands is the Hawaiian hoary bat. Some of the introduced mammals include dogs, cats, Indian mongoose, the chital axis deer, black-tail deer, the Norway rat, and the brush-tailed rock wallaby. Some of Hawaii's native birds are the Nene goose, Hawaiian duck, Laysan duck, Hawaiian petrel, Newell's Shearwater, Hawaiian hawk, the Oma'o, and the Nihoa finch, most of which are threatened by habitat loss and competition for food and shelter with non-native species.

Hawaii's native species and fragile ecosystem can be threatened by invasive species, that is, plants and animals that have been imported. To protect and support its native species, Hawaii has declared the importation and possession of snakes and certain lizards to be illegal. The state has been largely successful in keeping invasive snakes from the island. If they were to be introduced, they would not have any natural predators and would become a danger to birds and plants. The number of captured illegally held snakes, including those that have escaped into the wild, is alarming to wildlife officials, who are afraid that Hawaii could suffer the same fate as the island of Guam. After World War II, brown tree snakes overran Guam, wiping out almost all of the island's birds. There are

34 species of endangered forest birds in Hawaii, which risk being wiped out if nonnative snakes are allowed to reproduce. The fine for keeping a snake can be as high as $200,000; individuals who willingly surrender their snakes are granted amnesty by the Department of Agriculture. Still, the keeping of illegal snakes, and the possibility of snakes invading the islands through cargo ships and airplanes, remains a threat. Five snakes and eight illegal lizards were caught during the month of July 2011 alone.

According to the U.S. Fish and Wildlife Service, Hawaii was home to 62 threatened or endangered animal species and 320 threatened or endangered plant species in 2011. Endangered animal species include the Hawaiian hoary bat, the Maui parrotbill, and the Hawaiian monk seal. Endangered plants include 16 varieties of Alani, Clay's hibiscus, and Hawaiian vetch.

About 1.4 million acres (570,000 ha) of the Hawaiian Islands are forested. Hawaii's state forest is the eleventh largest in the nation at about 1.2 million acres (490,000 ha). Most of Hawaii's endemic tree species are hardwoods. Native species include kamani, koa, and ohia. About half of the state's plant species are native, and the other half have been introduced, with many of the introduced species becoming invasive. Hapuu (tree), Aiakanene (shrub), hinahina (or silver geranium), and Mamane (tree) are some of the state's endemic plant species. Revenues from the state's forest industry were $30.7 million in 2001 and the industry employed more than 900 people.

According to the U.S. Geological Survey, preliminary reports stated that nonfuel mineral production in Hawaii in 2009 was valued at $134 million. Hawaii mainly produces crushed stone, sand, and gravel for the construction industry. Significant amounts of black coral and precious coral gemstones are also produced. There were 63 mining operations in the state in 2007, which employed 3,380 people.

Water

Halulu Lake, on the island of Nihau, is the largest natural lake in Hawaii (182 acres/74 ha). The largest artificial lake, Waiia Reservoir (422 acres/171 ha), is found on Kauai. The state's longest rivers are Kaukonahua Stream (33 mi/53 km) found on Oahu and the Wailuku River (32 mi/51 km) on the island of Hawaii. Oahu, Molokai, Lanai, and Maui are situated on a submarine bank of less than 2,400 feet (730 m) deep, with the rest of the Pacific Ocean surrounding the state up to 20,000 feet (6,100 m) deep.

Hawaii's fishing industry is centered in the Port of Honolulu, which receives over 70 percent of its fish landings. Seafood species from Hawaiian waters include yellowfin tuna, blue marlin, sickle pomfret, and red snapper. Honolulu ranked twenty-ninth in the nation for fish landings by volume in 2008, and fifth in the nation in

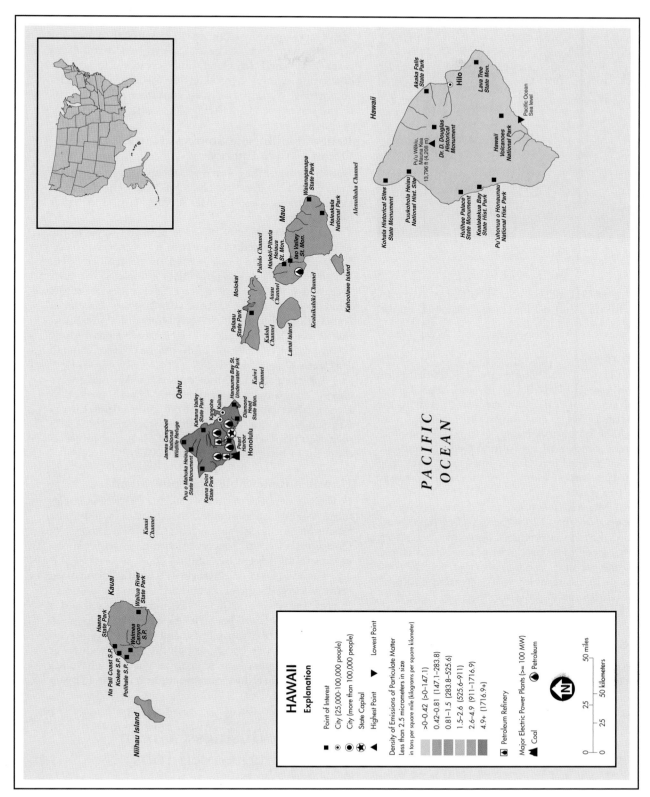

SOURCES: "County Emissions Map: Criteria Air Pollutants." *AirData.* U.S. Environmental Protection Agency. Available from http://www.epa.gov/air/data/geosel.html; *Energy Maps.* U.S. Energy Information Administration. Available from http://www.eia.gov/state; *Highest and Lowest Elevations.* U.S. Geological Survey. Available from http://egsc.usgs.gov/isb/pubs/booklets/elvadist/elvadist.html#Highest; *2007 Minerals Yearbook.* U.S. Geological Survey. Available from http://minerals.usgs.gov/minerals/pubs/state. © 2011 Cengage Learning.

Mauna Loa Observatory. © Loic Bernard/ShutterStock.com

landed value ($73.3 million). Sport fishing is extremely popular, with tuna and marlin among the most sought-after species.

Agriculture

In 2010, Hawaii was home to 7,500 farms on 1.1 million acres (450,000 ha) of land. The state is the top producer of coffee and macadamia nuts in the United States, and ranks fourth in production of sugarcane. The state's top five agricultural commodities in 2009 were commercial agricultural seeds, greenhouse products, sugarcane, macadamia nuts, and cattle and calves. The state's top exports from that same year were fruits and tree nuts.

In 2008, the state was home to 152 certified organic operations on more than 12,000 acres (4,860 ha) of land. Hawaii's organic farmers produced beef cows, vegetables, fruits, herbs, greenhouse products, potatoes, and fallow. Much of the organic produce is sold to the best restaurants in the state as part of increasing efforts to eat local products and improve food security.

❧ Energy

Hawaii does not have any reserves of oil or natural gas. Almost all of the energy consumed in Hawaii is produced with petroleum that is shipped to the state from Alaska and foreign countries. Petroleum-fired power plants supply three-fourths of the state's electricity generation, and the state has two petroleum refineries in Honolulu and Ewa Beach. Hawaii requires the use of oxygenated motor gasoline in vehicles statewide. After petroleum, coal and several renewable energy sources, including wind, solar, biodiesel and geothermal, contribute modestly to the rest of the state's energy needs.

Most homes don't require heating in Hawaii due to the state's mild tropical climate, therefore Hawaii is the lowest consumer of natural gas in the United States. However, it is one of three states that produce synthetic natural gas. The state's synthetic natural gas plant is located in Oahu, and creates the gas by converting refinery byproducts or waste products. The commercial sector is the main consumer of natural gas in the state.

Renewable Energy Sources: Harnessing the Ocean's Wave Energy

Hawaii is one of the top ten producers of solar energy in the United States. It also produces energy from hydroelectricity, geothermal, landfill gas, and other biomass sources.

Hawaii has some of the most powerful waves in the world, which has led to numerous wave energy projects being proposed and implemented. In September 2010, Ocean Power Technologies (OPT) completed the first-ever grid connection of a wave energy device in the United States at the Marine Corps Base Hawaii in conjunction with the U.S. Navy. Called a PowerBuoy, the device's deployment site is located approximately three-quarters of a mile (1.2 km) off the coast of Oahu in 100 feet (30 m) of water.

Another project from Oceanlinx, an Australian wave energy company, became the first Hawaii project to receive a preliminary permit from the Federal Energy Regulatory Commission in 2009 with plans for a 2.7-megawatt plant off the north coast of Maui. The project is expected to be operational by mid-2012.

Hawaii's Renewable Portfolio Standard

Hawaii's renewable portfolio standard (RPS) was implemented in 2003, and significantly expanded in 2009. The expansion included an increase in the amount of renewable electrical energy generation required by utilities to 40 percent by 2030.

The expansion of Hawaii's RPS in 2009 formalized many of the goals already established by the Hawaii Clean Energy Initiative in 2008. This initiative established a goal to help Hawaii increase its renewable and clean energy production capabilities, and to transition exclusively to renewable energy use on the islands with fewer human inhabitants. If these goals are met, they have the potential to help reduce oil consumption in Hawaii by up to 72 percent.

❧ Green Business, Green Building, Green Jobs

Green Building

In October 2009, Hawaii adopted the 2006 IECC as its statewide building code, but with state-specific amendments. Some of the state amendments include options for roof insulation, including cool roofs, advanced

Hawaii State Profile

Physical Characteristics

Land area	6,428 square miles (16,648 sq km)
Inland water area	40 square miles (104 sq km)
Coastal area	NA
Highest point	Pu'u Wekiu, Mauna Kea 13,796 feet (4,205 m)
National Forest System lands (2010)	1,000 acres (405 ha)
State parks (2011)	53

Energy Statistics

Total energy production (2009)	20 trillion Btu
State ranking in total energy production (2009)	47
Renewable energy net generation total (2009)	817,000 megawatt hours
Hydroelectric energy generation (2009)	113,000 megawatt hours
Biomass energy generation (2009)	284,000 megawatt hours
Wind energy generation (2009)	251,000 megawatt hours
Wood and derived fuel energy generation (2009)	NA
Crude oil reserves (2009)	NA
Natural gas reserves (2009)	NA
Natural gas liquids (2008)	NA

Pollution Statistics

Carbon output (2005)	21.5 million tons of CO_2 (19.5 million t)
Superfund sites (2008)	3
Particulate matter (less than 2.5 micrometers) emissions (2002)	2,344 tons per year (2,126 t/yr)
Toxic chemical releases (2009)	2.9 million pounds (1.3 million kg)
Generated hazardous waste (2009)	1,000 tons (900 t)

SOURCES: AirData. U.S. Environmental Protection Agency. Available from http://www.epa.gov/air/data; *Energy Maps, Facts, and Data of the U.S. States.* U.S. Energy Information Administration. Available from http://www.eia.gov/state; *The 2012 Statistical Abstract.* U.S. Census Bureau. Available from http://www.census.gov/compendia/statab; *United States Energy Usage.* eRedux. Available from http://www.eredux.net/states.

© 2011 Cengage Learning.

ventilation, and low-emittance roofs. The code also has more strict requirements for swimming pools as well as mandatory HVAC and other system commissioning.

A requirement was enacted in 2008 by Senate Bill 644, which stated solar-water heating (SWH) systems must be installed on all single-family new home construction, with a few exceptions. The legislation became effective in January 2010, and from that point building permits will only be given if a SWH is included. Exceptions can be made, but only if installing a SWH is found to be impractical, cost-prohibitive, another renewable energy technology is being used for heating water, or a demand water heater device is installed (a demand water heater does not use a gas tank and provides hot water only as needed using propane).

The state offers a number of incentives and tax credits for builders that make their structures more energy efficient. Tax credits are available for residential and commercial properties that install solar and wind energy systems. Hawaii also requires that building, construction, and development permits that incorporate energy and environmental design standards be given priority processing. On the municipal and county levels, loans are available in Honolulu and Maui counties for residents that install solar roofs. Honolulu also offers a real property tax exemption for buildings that incorporate alternative energy improvements. Properties that install these improvements are exempt from property taxes for 25 years.

Two announcements in July 2011 serve as a reminder that Hawaii is at the forefront of solar power production. SunPower Corporation and Citi announced a new fund of $105 million in residential solar lease projects. The fund extends the SunPower Lease to customers in Hawaii and seven other states. This expands their financing options for homeowners interested in their solar power systems. Customers would also be able to obtain SunPower systems through a cash purchase or through one of the company's many low-interest loans, making solar power more available to homeowners in Hawaii. That same month, SunRun and REC Solar announced a partnership to provide solar power for the West Hawaii Civic Center on the Big Island of Hawaii. This project will not only help the county achieve LEED Silver certification for the center, but will also save taxpayers a projected $500,000 over the next 20 years. The installation will generate more than 400,000 kilowatt hours of electricity per year; 770 barrels of oil would be required to produce an equivalent amount of electricity. Taxpayer savings from the project's first year alone will amount to around $46,000.

Green Business and Green Jobs

Companies like Hoku Corporation and Sopogy have created green businesses in Hawaii, with both of these companies developing solar technologies. The state government also has the Green Business Program, which supports businesses that decide to go green. The program helps businesses find ways to conserve energy, water, and other resources, and to reduce pollution and waste. It also provides an avenue for industry members to share information on practices that they have implemented to save money and conserve resources. The program originally focused on the hotel industry, since large numbers of visitors come to the state and strain its resources, but it looks to expand and include other businesses.

According to the Pew Charitable Trusts, Hawaii's clean energy economy grew by 43.6 percent between 1998 and 2007. The state was home to more than 2,700 clean energy jobs in 356 businesses in 2007. The majority

Hawaii is one of the top ten producers of solar energy in the United States. © *Mana Photo/ShutterStock.com*

of these jobs were in conservation and pollution mitigation, followed by training and support, energy efficiency, and clean energy. A report from the National Governor's Association Center for Best Practices stated that Hawaii's largest green economic segment in 2009 was air and environment, which made up over 43 percent of the state's green jobs. Between 2006 and 2008, over $12 million in green technology venture capital funds were brought into the state to support clean energy generation.

Hawaii's institutions of higher education and organizations offer many options for training and certification for green careers. The Building Industry Association of Hawaii offers courses for the Certified Green Professional (CGP) Designation program. The program offers builders the opportunity to expand their knowledge and client base by learning the principles of energy, water and resource efficiency. Hawaii Community College offers a certificate of achievement and an applied science degree in Tropical Forest Ecosystem and Agroforestry Management. Students in the program learn to manage Hawaii's threatened forests and work to regenerate its ecosystems. Students also have the opportunity for internships with organizations such as the National Park Service and the state Department of

Land and Natural Resources. The University of Hawaii System of campuses also offers certificate and degree programs in Sustainable Construction Technology and Sustainable Tourism.

❧ Sustainable Tourism: Welcoming Visitors While Maintaining Hawaii's Fragile Ecosystem

Every year, about 7.5 million people visit the state of Hawaii. Adding that number of short-term visitors to the resident population of over one million burdens the state with high energy costs, limited water resources, and the destruction of the state's natural habitats. Tourists can inadvertently bring seeds of invasive species that can cause environmental degradation, which is why there are efforts made to check all incoming cargo and passengers. The development of infrastructure for hotels has caused the destruction of native habitats with an increase in energy use in order to sustain this development. As a result of this constant growth, about 60 percent of Hawaii's animal and plant species are now considered endangered. It should also be noted that tourism also impacts Native Hawaiian cultural resources and practices.

Efforts by the government have begun to implement sustainable tourism and ecotourism practices. This will allow the economy to continue to benefit from tourism while maintaining and restoring island ecosystems. It is important to note that sustainable tourism and ecotourism are two separate entities. Sustainable tourism focuses on finding a balance between the environment, economy, and the socio-cultural aspects of development. Ecotourism is more focused and is considered a subset of sustainable tourism. Ecotourism includes travel to natural areas with minimal impacts while respecting local cultures and providing financial benefits for conservation and local communities.

Hawaii's Department of Business, Economic Development, and Tourism began the Sustainable Tourism Project in 2001, when the legislature authorized the department to conduct a study on Hawaii's capacity to sustain future growth in tourism. The study had two goals: to develop a tool to evaluate the impacts of tourism growth on economic sectors and infrastructure elements; and to examine the effects of visitors on the economy, physical infrastructure, natural environment, and socio-cultural aspects. The first goal was met by the development of the *Hawaii Sustainable Tourism Modeling System*. This tool allows the state to estimate the impact of various tourism growth scenarios on aspects of Hawaii's economy. Another accomplishment of the project was a vision for Sustainable Tourism in Hawaii, which is comprised of six goals agreed upon by stakeholders. The goals are that sustainable tourism will reflect the state's values, provide jobs, operate in harmony with the state's ecosystems, perpetuate the customs of Hawaii's native cultures, reinforce the state's heritage of aloha (a Hawaiian word meaning love, peace, and compassion) and tolerance of cultural diversity, and protect communities' sense of place. These goals were expanded upon and were incorporated into the Hawaii Tourism Authority's Strategic Plan for 2005 to 2015. This is a comprehensive plan that addresses the needs and responsibilities of Hawaii's tourism industry stakeholders.

While the government of Hawaii works to meet the goals of the Sustainable Tourism Project, other organizations and business owners are working to make tourism more sustainable and to promote eco-friendly vacations. The Hawaii Ecotourism Association is made up of members who support the goals of ecotourism, while there are a number of non-member tourism operators that commit to sustainable best practices. Visitors have opportunities to volunteer with a number of different organizations as a means of giving back to their destination of choice through beach clean ups, wildlife surveys, trail maintenance, and ecological restoration on public and private lands.

The State of Hawaii government continues to work toward its goals and to research the impacts of a development model based on continued consumption of limited resources. Their efforts, along with those of numerous organizations that promote alternatives to mass tourism, will contribute to preserving Hawaii's fragile ecosystems.

BIBLIOGRAPHY

Books

Barth, Steve, Richard A. Cooke, and Kim Heaco. *The Smithsonian Guides to Natural America: The Pacific–Hawaii, Alaska*. Washington, DC: Smithsonian Books, 1995.

Callies, David L. *Regulating Paradise: Land Use Controls in Hawaii*, 2nd ed. Honolulu, HI: University of Hawaii Press, 2010.

Culliney, John L. *Islands in a Far Sea: The Fate of Nature in Hawaii*, Rev. ed. Honolulu, HI: University of Hawaii Press, 2006.

Fletcher, Charles, et al. *Living on the Shores of Hawaii: Natural Hazards, the Environment, and Our Communities*. Honolulu, HI: University of Hawaii Press, 2010.

Grabowsky, Gail L. *50 Simple Things You Can Do to Save Hawaii*. Honolulu, HI: Bess Press, 2007.

Littschwager, David. *Remains of a Rainbow: Rare Plants and Animals of Hawaii*. Washington, DC: National Geographic Society, 2003.

Miike, Lawrence H. *Water and the Law in Hawai'i*. Honolulu, HI: University of Hawaii Press, 2004.

Okihiri, Gary Y. *Pineapple Culture: A History of the Tropical and temperate Zones*. Berkeley, CA: University of California Press, 2009.

Stephen, Lau L. *Hydrology of the Hawaiian Islands*. Honolulu, HI: University of Hawaii Press, 2006.

Whitton, Kevin. *Green Hawaii: A Guide to a Sustainable and Energy Efficient Home*. Honolulu, HI: Mutual Publishing, LLC, 2008.

Ziegler, Alan C. *Hawaiian Natural History, Ecology, and Evolution*. Honolulu, HI: University of Hawaii Press, 2002.

Web Sites

Certified Green Professional Designation. Building Industry Association of Hawaii. Available from http://www.biah.affiniscape.com/displaycommon.cfm?an=1&subarticlenbr=380

"The Clean Energy Economy: Hawaii." The Pew Charitable Trusts. Available from http://www.pewcenteronthestates.org/uploadedFiles/

wwwpewcenteronthestatesorg/Fact_Sheets/
Clean_Economy_Factsheet_Hawaii.pdf

"Climate of Hawaii." National Weather Service Forecast
Office. Available from http://www.prh.noaa.gov/
hnl/pages/climate_summary.php

The Forest TEAM Program. Hawaii Community College. Available from http://hawaii.hawaii.edu/for-
estteam/

Gillis, Justin. "A Scientist, His Work and a Climate
Reckoning." *The New York Times.* December 21,
2010. Available from http://www.nytimes.com/
2010/12/22/science/earth/22carbon.html

"Global Warming and Hawai'i." National Wildlife
Federation. Available from http://www.nwf.org/
Global-Warming/~/media/PDFs/Global%
20Warming/Global%20Warming%20State%20Fact%
20Sheets/Hawaii.ashx

Green Business Program. Department of Business,
Economic Development & Tourism. State of
Hawaii. Available from http://hawaii.gov/dbedt/
info/energy/resource/greenbusiness

Hale Ho'okipa Inn Bed and Breakfast. Available from
http://maui-bed-and-breakfast.com/

"Hawaii." *2007 Minerals Yearbook.* U.S. Geological
Survey. Available from http://minerals.usgs.gov/
minerals/pubs/state/2007/myb2-2007-hi.pdf

"Hawaii Building Energy Code." Hawaii Incentives/
Policies for Renewables & Efficiency. DSIRE.
Available from http://dsireusa.org/incentives/
incentive.cfm?Incentive_Code=HI11R&re=1&ee=1

Hawaii Climate Change Action Plan 1998. Department
of Business, Economic Development & Tourism,
Energy, Resources, and Technology Division and
Department of Health. State of Hawaii. Available
from http://hawaii.gov/dbedt/info/energy/publi-
cations/ccap.pdf

"Hawaii Fact Sheet." Economic Research Service. U.S.
Department of Agriculture. Available from http://
www.ers.usda.gov/StateFacts/HI.htm#TCEC

"Hawaii Fishing Industry." Hawaii Seafood. Available
from http://www.hawaii-seafood.org/hawaii-fish-
auction/

Hawaii Forest Industry Association. Available from
http://www.hawaiiforest.org/

"Hawaii: Profile of the Green Economy." The National
Governors Association Center for Best Practices.
Available from http://www.nga.org/Files/pdf/
09GREENPROFILEHI.PDF

Hawaii State Energy Profile. U.S. Energy Information
Administration. Available from http://www.eia.doe.
gov/state/state-energy-profiles.cfm?sid=HI

Hawaii Tourism Strategic Plan 2005-2015. Hawaii
Tourism Authority. Available from http://www.
hawaiitourismauthority.org/pdf/
tsp2005_2015_final.pdf

Hawaii Wildlife Fund. Available from http://wildhawaii.
org/

Hawaii's Comprehensive Wildlife Conservation Strategy.
State Department of Fish and Wildlife. Available
from http://www.state.hi.us/dlnr/dofaw/cwcs/
index.html

"Honolulu—Real Property Tax Exemption for
Alternative Energy Improvements." Hawaii
Incentives/Policies for Renewables & Efficiency.
DSIRE. Available from http://dsireusa.org/
incentives/incentive.cfm?Incentive_Code=HI28F&
re=1&ee=1

"Honolulu—Solar Roofs Initiative Loan Program."
Hawaii Incentives/Policies for Renewables & Efficiency. DSIRE. Available from http://dsireusa.org/
incentives/incentive.cfm?Incentive_Code=HI15F
&re=1&ee=1

Hoku Scientific. Available from http://www.hokuscien-
tific.com/

"Kaneohe Bay, Oahu, Hawaii—Project at Marine Corps
Base Hawaii (MCBH)." Ocean Power Technologies.
Available from http://www.oceanpowertechnolo-
gies.com/projects.htm

Kinsey, Beth. "Wildlife of Hawaii." Available from
http://wildlifeofhawaii.com/

"Listings and Occurrences for Hawaii." Species Reports.
U.S. Department of Fish and Wildlife. Available from
http://ecos.fws.gov/tess_public/pub/stateListin-
gAndOccurrenceIndividual.jsp?state=HI&s8-
fid=112761032792&s8fid=112762573902&s8-
fid=24012977843962

"Mining in Hawaii, 2007." National Mining Association.
Available from http://www.prh.noaa.gov/hnl/
pages/climate_summary.php

Niesse, Mark. "Snakes threaten Hawaii's ecosystem."
Associated Press. July 24, 2011. Available from
http://detnews.com/article/20110724/
NATION/107240306/Snakes-threaten-Hawaii%
E2%80%99s-ecosystem

"Ocean Energy." Hawaii's Energy Future. Available from
http://www.hawaiisenergyfuture.com/articles/
Ocean_Energy.html

"Organic Production." Economic Research Service. U.S.
Department of Agriculture. Available from http://
www.ers.usda.gov/Data/Organic/

Renewable Portfolio Standard, Hawaii Revised Statutes.
269 (2003): 91. Available from http://www.capitol.

hawaii.gov/hrscurrent/Vol05_Ch0261-0319/
HRS0269/HRS_0269-0091.HTM

School of Travel Industry Management. University of
Hawaii at Manoa. Available from http://www.tim.
hawaii.edu/default.aspx

"Solar and Wind Energy Credit (Corporate)." Hawaii
Incentives/Policies for Renewables & Efficiency.
DSIRE. Available from http://dsireusa.org/incen-
tives/incentive.cfm?Incentive_Code=HI02F&re=
1&ee=1

Sopogy MicroCSP. Available from http://sopogy.com/

*State of Hawaii Energy Resources Coordinator Annual
Report 2009.* Department of Business, Economic
Development & Tourism. State of Hawaii. Available
from http://hawaii.gov/dbedt/info/energy/publi-
cations/erc09.pdf

"SunPower and Citi Team to Finance $105 Million in
Residential Solar Lease Projects." PR Newswire. July
28, 2011. Available from http://www.prnewswire.
com/news-releases/sunpower-and-citi-team-to-
finance-105-million-in-residential-solar-lease-pro-
jects-126314183.html

"2009 State Agricultural Overview: Hawaii." U.S.
Department of Agriculture. Available from http://
www.nass.usda.gov/Statistics_by_State/Ag_Over-
view/AgOverview_HI.pdf

Volunteer on Vacation in Hawaii. Available from http://
volunteer-on-vacation-hawaii.com/

"West Hawaii Civic Center Solar System to Save
Taxpayers over $500,000." *The Sacramento Bee* July
26, 2011. Available from http://www.sacbee.com/
2011/07/26/3795873/west-hawaii-civic-center-
solar.html

Idaho

Idaho is the fourteenth largest state in the nation. Idaho is mostly mountainous, although the Snake River Plain is extensive and the Palouse region, which features low rolling hills, stretches along the state's northwestern border. Virtually the entire state is located in the Upper Columbia River basin, which includes major tributary rivers like the Snake, Salmon, and Clearwater.

It is also home, at Lewiston, to the farthest-inland seaport west of the Continental Divide. This port was made possible by a series of dams along the Columbia and Snake Rivers, which has resulted in the drastic decline of native salmon and other fish species that used the upper portions of the river as spawning grounds. Conflict exists between advocates of salmon recovery who want to remove the dams and proponents of the dams in the shipping, agribusiness, aluminum, and hydropower industries.

Idaho also has some of the largest unspoiled natural areas in the United States, including the Frank Church River of No Return Wilderness, the Selway Bitterroot Wilderness, and the Awtooth Wilderness.

Climate

Idaho has four distinct seasons, which are experienced on slightly different schedules by different parts of the state. Across the state, climatic conditions vary with the elevation. Boise and Lewiston, which are at lower elevation and protected from severe weather by nearby mountains, experience spring earlier and winter later. In eastern Idaho, the climate is continental with colder winter temperatures and less precipitation. Average temperatures in Boise range from 29°F (–2°C) in January to 74°F (23°C) in July.

In general, humidity is low in Idaho. Precipitation in southern Idaho averages 13 inches (33 cm) per year; in the northern part of the state, it is significantly greater, with the average annual precipitation at more than 30 inches (76 cm). Average annual precipitation at Boise is about 11.8 inches (29 cm), with more than 20 inches (53 cm) of snow. Much greater accumulations of snow are experienced in the mountains.

According to the National Wildlife Federation, if climate change continues unabated, temperatures in Idaho could rise 6.75°F (3.75°C) by 2100. Higher than average temperatures could significantly reduce snowpack in the Rocky Mountains, leading to warmer stream temperatures and altered flows. These could be harmful to the state's salmon, steelhead, and other cold-water fish. Idaho's alpine ecosystems could be drastically altered by warmer temperatures as well, leaving many species that depend on these ecosystems with nowhere to go. Vegetation could also change, leading forested areas to become more arid grasslands and sagebrush systems.

As of 2011, Idaho did not have a Climate Change Action Plan. However, the Idaho Department of Fish and Game will be incorporating climate change adaptation information into their revised Idaho Comprehensive Wildlife Conservation Strategy (CWCS). Potential impacts of climate change on threatened and endangered species and their habitats will be discussed. Strategies for adapting to climate change will also be covered in the CWCS.

⚘ Natural Resources, Water, and Agriculture

Natural Resources

Idaho has about 3,000 native plant species. Douglas fir, oak/mountain mahogany, juniper/piñxon, ponderosa pine, lodgepole pine, and spruce/fir make up the main forest types. A species of Syringa (*Philadelphus lewisii*—Lewis's Mock-orange) is the state flower. Five plant species were listed as threatened in 2011, which include Spalding's catchfly and the water howellia.

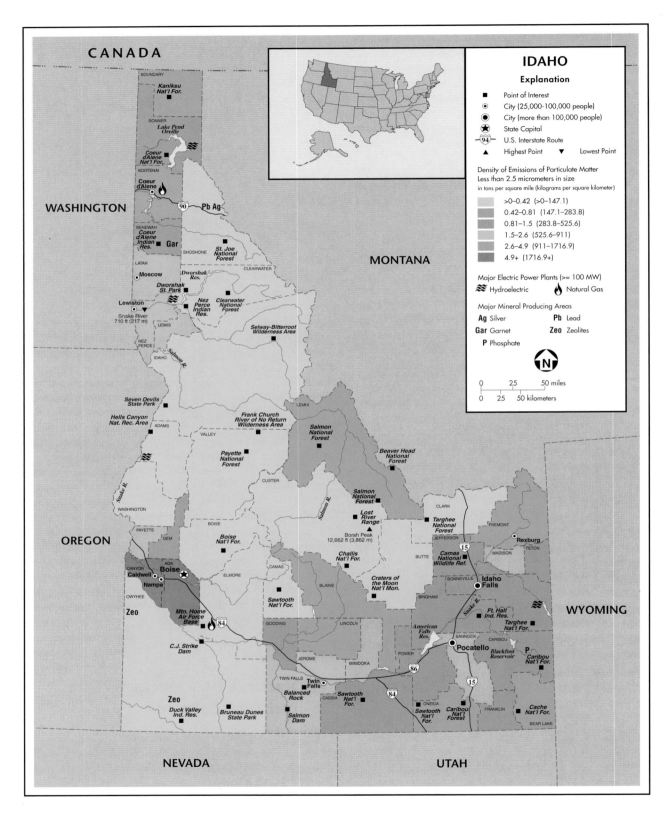

CANADA

WASHINGTON

MONTANA

OREGON

WYOMING

NEVADA

UTAH

IDAHO

Explanation

■ Point of Interest
◉ City (25,000–100,000 people)
◎ City (more than 100,000 people)
★ State Capital
─〔94〕─ U.S. Interstate Route
▲ Highest Point ▼ Lowest Point

Density of Emissions of Particulate Matter
Less than 2.5 micrometers in size
in tons per square mile (kilograms per square kilometer)

>0–0.42 (>0–147.1)
0.42–0.81 (147.1–283.8)
0.81–1.5 (283.8–525.6)
1.5–2.6 (525.6–911)
2.6–4.9 (911–1716.9)
4.9+ (1716.9+)

Major Electric Power Plants (>= 100 MW)
≈ Hydroelectric ♨ Natural Gas

Major Mineral Producing Areas

Ag Silver **Pb** Lead
Gar Garnet **Zeo** Zeolites
P Phosphate

0   25   50 miles
0   25   50 kilometers

SOURCES: "County Emissions Map: Criteria Air Pollutants." *AirData*. U.S. Environmental Protection Agency. Available from http://www.epa.gov/air/data/geosel.html; *Energy Maps*. U.S. Energy Information Administration. Available from http://www.eia.gov/state; *Highest and Lowest Elevations*. U.S. Geological Survey. Available from http://egsc.usgs.gov/isb/pubs/booklets/elvadist/elvadist.html#Highest; *2007 Minerals Yearbook*. U.S. Geological Survey. Available from http://minerals.usgs.gov/minerals/pubs/state. © *2011 Cengage Learning.*

The state of Idaho now holds authority over its wolf populations and set wolf hunting rules in July 2011. © *Photri Images/Alamy*

In 2009, a total of 109 primary forest products plants operated in Idaho. These plants employed 13,500 people directly and another 27,000 indirectly. Total sales value for Idaho's primary forest products is close to $2 billion annually. The majority of product sales, excluding residue-related products, are to markets outside of Idaho.

The state's game animals include elk, moose, white-tailed deer, pronghorn antelope, bighorn sheep, mountain goat, and cottontail rabbit. Game birds include several varieties of pheasant, partridge, quail, grouse, and waterfowl. A total of 16 animal species were listed as threatened or endangered as of 2011, including the woodland caribou, the northern Idaho ground squirrel, and three species of salmon. The Idaho Department of Fish and Game has management plans in place for the grizzly bear and bighorn sheep, along with the Idaho Comprehensive Wildlife Conservation Strategy.

The gray wolf was delisted as an endangered species in 2009. Responsibility for management of the animal's population was taken over by state authorities. That same year, a coalition of thirteen environmental groups challenged the wolf's delisting in a U.S. District Court. Their challenge was based on the fact that the wolf was delisted in Idaho and Montana, but not in Wyoming, when all three states were considered part of the wolf's range. The gray wolf was successfully relisted in Montana in August 2010, and on October 18, 2010, Idaho Governor C.L. "Butch" Otter reversed the earlier decision and returned responsibility for wolf management to the U.S. Fish and Wildlife Service.

This did not last long, however, and in April 2011 Congress attached a rider to a federal appropriations bill that once again delisted wolves in Montana and Idaho. The rider also states that the rule will not be subject to judicial review. Environmental groups argued in court in July 2011 that Congress overstepped its authority with the rider. They claim the rider is unconstitutional because the wolf case was being appealed with a decision pending, and it therefore interfered with the judicial branch. Legal experts disagree, stating that the environmental groups face difficult odds, since Congress is in full rights to order a rule exempt from judicial review if it has authored all rules involved.

The state of Idaho now holds authority over its wolf populations and set wolf hunting rules in July 2011. These rules include elevated kill limits in hunting zones in eastern Idaho and extending the hunting season in two northern hunting zones where the predators are blamed by outdoorsman for reducing elk populations. The rules generally means that the wolf hunting season will have no quotas in about three-quarters of the territory now occupied by wolves. Officials say Idaho will manage wolves and the hunt so that their population remains above 150 animals and 15 breeding pairs, but far below the current number of 1,000 animals estimated by state wildlife officials.

Idaho is home to 30 state parks, which include Ponderosa State Park, Harriman State Park, and the Trail of the Coeur d'Alenes.

Mining in Idaho

In 2010, total nonfuel mineral production in Idaho was valued at $1.2 billion. Over 50 percent of this production was in molybdenum (a metallic element used in strengthening steel) and silver. Idaho produces the most newly mined silver in the United States. Silver and molybdenum were followed by phosphate, sand and gravel, lead, zinc, copper, and building stone. Employment in the mining industry increased every year from 2003, with about 4,500 employees in 2008. Idaho does not have any known commercial deposits of oil and gas, although there has been some industry interest in natural gas fracking in Western Idaho.

Settlers were initially drawn to Idaho by the discovery of gold, but the mining of other minerals has overshadowed gold mining. However, the U.S. Bureau of Mines states that Idaho has more mineable gold than any other state. In recent years, as the price of gold has risen, many old mines have been reopened and the value of gold produced in Idaho has grown steadily. The state is also one of only two places in the world where star garnets can be found.

Water

The largest lakes in Idaho are Pend Oreille (180 square miles/466 sq km), Coeur d'Alene, Priest in the panhandle, and Bear on the Utah border. The Snake River is one of the longest in the United States, extending 1,038 miles (1,671 km) across Wyoming, Idaho, and Washington. It dominates the southern part of the state and at Hell's Canyon in the northernmost part of Adams County, it cuts the deepest gorge in North America at 7,913 feet (2,412 m) deep. The Salmon River—also known as the "River of No Return"—is a salmon-spawning stream that

Idaho State Profile

Physical Characteristics

Land area	82,643 square miles (214,044 sq km)
Inland water area	926 square miles (2,398 sq km)
Coastal area	NA
Highest point	Borah Peak 12,662 feet (3,859 m)
National Forest System lands (2010)	20.5 million acres (8.3 million ha)
State parks (2011)	30

Energy Statistics

Total energy production (2009)	130 trillion Btu
State ranking in total energy production (2009)	42
Renewable energy net generation total (2009)	11.3 million megawatt hours
Hydroelectric energy generation (2009)	10.4 million megawatt hours
Biomass energy generation (2009)	NA
Wind energy generation (2009)	313,000 megawatt hours
Wood and derived fuel energy generation (2009)	478,000 megawatt hours
Crude oil reserves (2009)	NA
Natural gas reserves (2009)	NA
Natural gas liquids (2008)	NA

Pollution Statistics

Carbon output (2005)	14.2 million tons of CO_2 (12.9 million t)
Superfund sites (2008)	6
Particulate matter (less than 2.5 micrometers) emissions (2002)	2,543 tons per year (2,307 t/yr)
Toxic chemical releases (2009)	47.9 million pounds (21.7 million kg)
Generated hazardous waste (2009)	4,800 tons (4,400 t)

SOURCES: AirData. U.S. Environmental Protection Agency. Available from http://www.epa.gov/air/data; *Energy Maps, Facts, and Data of the U.S. States.* U.S. Energy Information Administration. Available from http://www.eia.gov/state; *The 2012 Statistical Abstract.* U.S. Census Bureau. Available from http://www.census.gov/compendia/statab; *United States Energy Usage.* eRedux. Available from http://www.eredux.net/states.

© 2011 Cengage Learning.

separates northern from southern Idaho. Other major rivers include the Clearwater, Kootenai, Bear, Boise, and Payette. There are numerous trout, salmon, bass, and whitefish species in Idaho's lakes and streams.

The state is known for sportfishing and is home to more than ten world-class blue-ribbon wild trout streams. The Idaho Department of Fish and Game receives about $10.8 million annually from the sale of fishing licenses. Idaho is the only inland western state with ocean-run salmon and steelhead (the ocean-going form of rainbow trout).

Agriculture

Idaho is home to 25,500 farms on 11.4 million acres (4.6 million ha) of land. Potatoes are the state's most famous and valuable crop, with 320,000 acres (129,500 ha) of land planted in 2009 and production worth more than $750 million that same year. Other top crops include wheat, hay, soybeans, corn, sugarbeets, peas, and lentils. Top livestock items in 2009 were cattle and calves, followed by sheep, lambs, and mink.

The state also has a thriving aquaculture industry. It is the largest producer of farm-raised trout and the largest commercial producer of rainbow trout in the United States. The industry ranks as the third-largest food-animal industry in Idaho. The aquaculture industry, including support industries such as veterinary services and feed production, employs approximately 800 people in Idaho. Both cold- and warm-water facilities raise trout, steelhead, salmon, and sturgeon, and catfish, tilapia, and tropical fish, respectively.

As of 2010, there were 203 certified organic operations in the state. Organic foods grown in the state include potatoes, sweet corn, squash, onions, oyster mushrooms, beans, carrots, and apples.

⚘ Energy

Idaho does not produce any oil, but receives its petroleum supply via two pipelines from Montana and Utah. Total petroleum consumption in the state is low, and Idaho is one of the few states that uses conventional motor gasoline statewide (most states require specific gasoline blends in areas where air quality is a concern).

Almost one-half of Idaho households use natural gas for heat. Idaho receives natural gas from two systems: the Gas Transmission Northwest Co. pipeline system and the smaller Northwest Pipeline system. The first pipeline is from Alberta and enters the United States at Idaho's Kingsgate Center before flowing south to California markets. The Northwest Pipeline system supplies Idaho with gas from Canada via Washington state and if necessary, from Wyoming via Utah.

Idaho is connected to other western power grids, allowing the state to purchase large amounts of electricity from neighboring states. About one-third of Idaho households use electricity as their primary energy source for home heating.

Renewable Energy Sources

Despite having few fossil fuel reserves, Idaho is rich in renewable energy sources. Four-fifths of the state's electricity is supplied by hydroelectric power plants. The rest is supplied by natural gas fired power plants, coal- and wood-fired generation, biomass, solar, and wind turbines. Biomass has supplies approximately 9 percent of the total energy used in the state.

Idaho is home to the nation's largest privately owned hydroelectric power complex. The 450-megawatt Hells Canyon Complex is located on the Snake River. There are dozens more privately-owned hydroelectric power projects in the state. Overall, six of the state's ten largest generating facilities run on hydroelectric power. After a two-year moratorium on proposals for new coal-fired power plants expired in 2008, all proposals for coal-fired plants have been rejected. While this may seem like good news for the environment, much has also been lost due to hydropower in terms of endangered species, habitat, recreation and sports fisheries, and cultural value. As a result, the tradeoff between coal-fired power and hydroelectric power may not be the best in the end.

Idaho is also home to the first geothermal power plant in the Pacific Northwest. The U.S. Geothermal Raft River Facility began operating in 2008. The project has a 20-year contract with the Idaho Power company to sell 10 megawatts of electricity from the Raft River Unit 1 power plant.

As of 2011, Idaho does not have a renewable portfolio standard. However, in 2007 the Idaho Legislative Council Interim Committee on Energy, Environment, and Technology released the *2007 Idaho Energy Plan*. The plan did not recommend major changes to the structure of the state's energy industry and instead reaffirmed many initiatives already in place. The plan's aim is to ensure a reliable, low-cost energy supply, protect the environment, and promote economic growth by increasing investments in energy conservation and in-state renewable resources. The plan offers a number of recommendations to fulfill its objectives. These recommendations are split into policies and actions under the following categories: Electricity, Natural Gas, Energy Facility Siting, and Implementation.

❧ Green Business, Green Building, Green Jobs

Green Business

According to a profile on Idaho's green economy from the National Governors Association Center for Best Practices, the state has strong concentrations of green business activity in agriculture, air and environment, and water and wastewater. The air and environment segment accounts for the largest employment, with around 2,400 jobs. There are also roughly 800 jobs in the water and wastewater segment, and 200 in both agriculture and recycling and waste. In 2007, the state attracted nearly $20 million in clean technology venture capital. According to the Pew Charitable Trusts Clean Energy Economy report, Idaho has more wind power potential than Oregon and Washington combined.

Idaho offers a wide range of financial incentives and tax credits for businesses that want to become more energy efficient. The Idaho Business Advantage Program offers companies that invest a minimum of $500,000 in new facilities and create at least ten new jobs an enhanced tax credit of 62.5 percent of tax liability in any one year, a new jobs tax credit of up to $3,000 per job, a 2.5 percent real property improvement tax credit, and a 25 percent sales tax rebate on construction materials for the new facilities. In addition, respective county commissioners may also authorize a full or partial property tax exemption.

The Idaho Office of Energy Resources also offers the Idaho Bioenergy Program. This program helps both people and companies take advantage of and make better use of their locally grown, renewable biomass energy resources. It does this by providing technical assistance, offering educational workshops, and sharing costs for demonstration projects.

Green Building

Idaho uses the 2009 International Energy Conservation Code (IECC) as the mandatory building code statewide. Also, in May 2008, Idaho enacted House Bill 422 (the Energy Efficient State Building Act) to reduce the amount of energy consumed by state-owned buildings. Under this bill, all major facility projects must be designed, constructed, and certified to meet a target of at least 10 percent to 30 percent better efficiency than a comparable building on a similar site. A major facility includes projects that are larger than 5,000 square feet (465 sq m). Also included in the definition are building renovation projects greater than 5,000 square feet (465 sq m) with a project cost greater than 50 percent of the assessed value of the existing building.

On the municipal level, the city of Boise adopted a resolution in 2005 that requires consideration of green building standards in all new construction and remodels of city-owned facilities. The Foothills Learning Center, completed in 2005, is one of the city's early examples of green building design. The Learning Center has incorporated photovoltaic solar and hydrogen fuel cells for power as well as some water-permeable areas on patios, paths, and parking lots. Another green building project includes the WaterShed Environmental Education Center, finished in 2008. The Center was constructed at the West Boise Wastewater Treatment Plant, and serves as a teaching tool about sustainability. The Center received a Gold-Level Leadership in Energy and Environmental Design (LEED) rating.

The Banner Bank building in Boise was certified as LEED Platinum in 2006. The building uses 65 percent less energy and 80 percent less water than standard office buildings. Less water is used through an innovative system that captures stormwater from downtown Boise streets and parking lots. The stormwater, along with reused graywater from the building itself, is used to flush all the low-flush toilets and urinals at the site. Energy was saved by using a geothermal heating system, "smart" lighting, and underfloor air vents.

Green Jobs

In January 2010, the state was awarded $6 million in funding for green jobs training from the U.S. Department of Labor. The funding will be used to strengthen the state's offerings in renewable energy technologies, as well as studies in energy efficiencies. The funds will also be used to enhance dual-enrollment sustainable growth training programs, which allow high school students to garner college or professional-technical credits while still in high school.

The state of Idaho offers new business owners the Workforce Development Training Fund. The fund provides eligible Idaho companies with up to $2,000 per employee for job skill training. It can provide training for new employees of companies expanding in Idaho and skill upgrade training of current workers who are at risk of being permanently laid off. Idaho's technical colleges are willing to customize training suited to the specific needs of each company that is accepted.

In an effort to boost green energy training, Idaho State University began offering an Energy Systems Renewable Energy Technology program in 2011. The program is offered through the university's Energy Systems Technology and Education Center (ESTEC), and features a variety of renewable energy technologies such as wind, hydro, solar, and geothermal power. Courses are offered for the program online in an effort to include students from all parts of the state.

❧ Dam Removal on the Snake River

In 1945, Congress authorized the construction of four federal dams on the lower Snake River. The dams would create a river seaport and booming industrial hub at Lewiston, in northwest Idaho. Ice Harbor dam was completed in 1961, Lower Monumental in 1969, Little Goose in 1970, and Lower Granite in 1975. Three more dams were planned upstream; however, vocal opposition from fish and wildlife agencies, fishermen, and tribes over Ice Harbor and Lower Granite prevented those dams from being built. Even in 1950 fisheries biologists warned the dams would be catastrophic for wild salmon.

These unheeded warnings came to fruition when the Snake River salmon population declined by 90 percent after the Lower Granite dam was completed. Various fish species and varieties of salmon declined or disappeared in the years between 1987 and 1997. The important ecological function of healthy wild salmon has also been broken, from impacts to Puget Sound orcas that rely on Columbia-Snake Chinook as a primary food source, to decimating the health of streams and ecosystems throughout the basin that depend upon returning salmon to provide critical nutrients.

Deep in Hell's Canyon National Recreation Area is this dam in the Snake River. © *Jeffrey T. Kreulen/ShutterStock.com*

Along with environmental impacts, the local economy has been negatively affected as well. The loss of commercial and recreational fishing has cost the region jobs as well as revenue. The Lower Granite dam, while allowing the city of Lewiston to act as a major seaport, is now threatening to flood the city. As silt has piled up behind the dam, the water level has risen. This city will need to raise its levees, which will result in high construction fees.

Removing the Dams: The Best Solution?

Scientists have agreed that the best way to restore fish populations to the Snake River and its tributaries would be to remove these four dams. However, there are those who think otherwise. Some worry that removing the dams would harm the region's energy supply, since the dams generate electricity for many in the region. Another issue is grain transportation. Much of the grain produced in the region is transported in barges on the Snake River, and this method of transport was made possible by the lock and dam system. Also, many of the fields that produce the grain and other crops are irrigated by water from the dam system.

The problem is that no one knows exactly how much the economy will be impacted by the removal of the dams, and legislators and experts have been slow to calculate this. It is far more expensive to upgrade and maintain a dam than to take it down, but these costs have to be weighed against what will need to be done to replace the energy, transportation, and irrigation that the dams provide.

Many argue, however, that replacing the energy generated by the dams with renewable energy sources will not harm the economy. A 2002 study from the RAND Corporation states that this could create as many as 15,000 new jobs, and new, renewable power sources could generate even more power than the dams created.

The transportation issue could also be dealt with by public investment in improving the state's rail system. While only one of the reservoirs behind the lower Snake River dams provides irrigation, this irrigation will be able to continue once the dam is removed, according to the organization American Rivers. This could be done by extending water intake pipes to a free-flowing Snake River. While these steps would require significant investment, any negative effects to the economy would hopefully be in the short term, because they would allow economic activities to continue, with the added benefit of allowing salmon and other species to recover and access river.

In June 2011, the Western Division of the American Fisheries Society passed a resolution calling for the federal government to be more proactive about removing dams. The resolution came about after research performed by the society's scientists which demonstrated that a free-flowing Snake River would be vital to the recovery of fish populations. The resolution also supports the development of plans to help compensate those that would be negatively affected financially if the dams are removed. In the meantime, recent observations of the positive effects of dam removal on other rivers are helping to promote the removal of the lower Snake River dams. The removal of dams on the Rogue River in Oregon has led to the reappearance of a significant number of salmon nests. There has also been an increase in recreational activities, something that could also bring capital to the region if the Snake River dams are removed. As officials observe these positive outcomes, they may be motivated to take action for Snake River salmon.

BIBLIOGRAPHY

Books

Brooks, Karl Boyd. *Public Power, Private Dams: The Hells Canyon High Dam Controversy.* Seattle, WA: University of Washington Press, 2006.

Donahue, Debra L. *The Western Range Revisited: Removing Livestock from Public Lands to Conserve Native Biodiversity.* Norman, OK: University of Oklahoma Press, 2000.

Duffin, Andrew P. *Plowed Under: Agriculture & Environment in the Palouse.* Seattle, WA: University of Washington Press, 2007.

Eagan, Timothy. *The Big Burn: Teddy Roosevelt and the Fire that Saved America.* Boston, MA: Houghton Mifflin Harcourt, 2009.

Fiege, Mark. *Irrigated Eden: The Making of An Agricultural Landscape in the American West.* Seattle, WA: University of Washington Press, 1999.

Johnson, Jerry. *Knowing Yellowstone: Science in America's First National Park.* Lanham, MD: Taylor Trade Publishing, 2010.

Neil, J. Meredith. *To the White Clouds: Idaho's Conservation Saga, 1900–1970.* Pullman, WA: Washington State University Press.

Ritter, Sharon. *Lewis and Clark's Mountain Wilds: A Site Guide to the Plants and Animals They Encountered in the Bitterroots.* Moscow, ID: University of Idaho Press, 2002.

Schmidt, Jeremy and Thomas Schmidt. *The Smithsonian Guides to Natural America: The Northern Rockies–Idaho, Montana, Wyoming.* Washington, DC: Smithsonian Books, 1995.

Web Sites

An Act Relating to Energy Efficient State Buildings (HB 422). Legislature of the State of Idaho. Available from http://www3.state.id.us/oasis/2008/H0422.html#engr

Aquaculture in Idaho. Idaho Department of Environmental Quality. Available from http://www.deq.idaho.gov/water-quality/wastewater/aquaculture.aspx

"Banner Bank Building Boise, Idaho." Idaho Chapter, U. S. Green Building Council. Available from http://www.usgbcidaho.org/wp-content/uploads/2009/10/Banner-Bank-Profile1.pdf

Chasan, Daniel Jack. "Let's really talk about taking down those Snake River dams." June 7, 2010. Crosscut.com. Available from http://crosscut.com/2010/06/07/environment/19868/Let-s-really-talk-about-taking-down-those-Snake-River-dams/

"The Economics of Lower Snake River Dam Removal." American Rivers. Available from http://www.americanrivers.org/assets/pdfs/dam-removal-docs/lower_snake_econ_factsheet_06-05.pdf

"Fast Facts About the Idaho Forest." Idaho Forest Products Commission. Available from http://www.idahoforests.org/factfram.htm

"Global Warming and Idaho." National Wildlife Federation. Available from http://www.nwf.org/Global-Warming/In-Your-State.aspx

Green Building Practices. City of Boise. Available from http://www.cityofboise.org/Departments/Public_Works/EnvironmentalResourceCenter/SustainableandLivableBoise/page17468.aspx

Hurst, Dustin. "Idaho awarded $6 million in funding for green jobs training." Idaho Reporter.com. January 28, 2010. Available from http://www.idahoreporter.com/2010/idaho-awarded-6-million-in-funding-for-green-jobs-training/

Idaho Building Code. Online Code Environment & Advocacy Network. Available from http://bcap-ocean.org/code-information/idaho-building-code

Idaho Fish and Game: Fishing. Available from http://fishandgame.idaho.gov/cms/fish/

Idaho Fish and Game: Wildlife. Available from http://fishandgame.idaho.gov/cms/wildlife/

"Idaho Mining Industry." Idaho Mining Association. Available from http://www.idahomining.org/ima/idmining.html

Idaho Quick Facts. U.S. Energy Information Administration. Available from http://www.eia.doe.gov/state/state_energy_profiles.cfm?sid=ID

"Idaho-Montana wolf issues head back to court on Tuesday." The Spokesman-Review. July 25, 2011. Available from http://www.spokesman.com/blogs/outdoors/2011/jul/25/idaho-montana-wolf-issues-head-back-court-tuesday/

Idaho State Parks and Recreation. Available from http://parksandrecreation.idaho.gov/

"Idaho State University College of Technology to offer renewable energy technology program beginning March 2011." Idaho State University. Available from http://www2.isu.edu/headlines/?p=2827

"Idaho Wolf Management." Idaho Fish and Game. Available from http://fishandgame.idaho.gov/cms/wildlife/wolves/

Incentives: Idaho Department of Commerce. Available from http://www.commerce.idaho.gov/business/incentives-/

Learn, Scott. "After dam removals, Oregon's Rogue River shows promising signs for salmon." OregonLive.com. October 28, 2010. Available from http://www.oregonlive.com/environment/index.ssf/2010/10/early_signs_good_for_dam_remov.html

"Listings and occurrences for Idaho." U.S. Fish and Wildlife Service Species Reports. Available from http://ecos.fws.gov/tess_public/pub/stateListingAndOccurrenceIndividual.jsp?state=ID&s8fid=112761032792&s8fid=112762573902&s8fid=24012898508561

Morgan, Todd A., et al. *Idaho's Forest Products Industry: A Descriptive Analysis.* Forest Service, U.S. Department of Agriculture. December 2004. Available from http://www.idahoforests.org/img/pdf/rmrs_rb004.pdf

"Organic/Sustainable Farming." Idaho OnePlan. Available from http://www.oneplan.org/Crop/OrganicFarming.asp#foods

Pernin, Christopher G., et al. *Generating Electric Power in the Pacific Northwest: Implications of Alternative Technologies.* RAND Science and Technology. Available from http://www.wildsalmon.org/images/stories/sos/PDFs/randstudy.pdf

Save Our Wild Salmon. Available from http://www.wildsalmon.org/

2007 Idaho Energy Plan. Idaho Legislative Council Interim Committee on Energy, Environment and Technology. Idaho Office of Energy Resources. Available from http://www.energy.idaho.gov/informationresources/d/energy_plan_2007.pdf

"2009 State Agricultural Overview: Idaho." U.S. Department of Agriculture. Available from http://www.nass.usda.gov/Statistics_by_State/Ag_Overview/AgOverview_ID.pdf

U.S. Army Corps of Engineers. *Lower Snake River Juvenile Salmon Migration Feasibility Study.* Walla Walla District. Available from http://www.nww.usace.army.mil/lsr/

Working Snake River for Washington. Available from http://workingsnakeriver.org/

Wutz, Katherine. "'Free-flowing' river crucial to fish, society says." *Idaho Mountain Express.* July 1, 2011. Available from http://www.mtexpress.com/index2.php?ID=2005137351

Illinois

The wealth of resources in Illinois places the state as a leader in agriculture, industry, and energy. Being a leader sometimes comes with major challenges, however. For instance, Illinois is one of the top energy-producing states in the country and is a net exporter of energy, but also carries the burden of being one of the top energy-consuming states in the nation. Switching from reliance on coal and nuclear energy to renewable sources will take effort, but the state has set a goal to produce at least 25 percent of its energy from renewable resources by 2025. In 2010, Illinois also began work on a federally sponsored high-speed rail network, which would provide a major boost to the local clean tech transportation sector while also helping the state meet its ambitious greenhouse gas reduction goals.

However, as Illinois explores opening new transportation routes, the state was forced to deal with a threat to its river systems. The major rivers of the state provide much-used avenues for agricultural and industrial trade and a major canal system links the Mississippi River to the Great Lakes. But, in 2010, that vital link was the focus of several lawsuits filed in federal courts by neighboring states to force Illinois to close the waterway in an effort to protect Lake Michigan from the invasive Asian carp. Working with the U.S. Army Corps of Engineers, the state took action and installed a barrier system near Chicago. By March 2011, a research report was released by the Corps of Engineers, indicating that the barrier system seemed to be preventing carp from entering the Great Lakes.

Climate

Illinois's temperate climate produces cold, snowy winters and hot, wet summers. The state's fertile soils (over 600 types), high summer precipitation, and generally flat topography allow farms to flourish statewide. Chicago, located on the banks of Lake Michigan, is one the country's major metropolises. Chicago's reputation as the Windy City owes more to politics than weather; but with an average wind speed of 10.4 mph (16.7 km/h),

Chicago residents know their gusty days. Tornado activity is also relatively common in Illinois.

How global climate change will affect Illinois remains unclear. Climate data shows that Illinois is actually cooler and wetter today than it was a half-century ago. Still, Illinois has taken steps to establish concrete climate change policies. In 2006, Illinois governor Rod Blagojevich established the Illinois Climate Change Advisory Group, which he charged with developing climate change policy recommendations. In September 2007, that group outlined a set of policy options for the governor. Included in the advisory group's recommendations were, among other things, the adoption of renewable energy portfolio standards and upgrades to the passenger and freight rail system of Illinois. Then-Governor Blagojevich also independently announced a goal of reducing the state's production of greenhouse gasses to 1990 levels by 2020, and 60 percent below those levels by 2050.

Natural Resources, Water, and Agriculture

Natural Resources: Industrialization Causes Great Change

Illinois's landscape and natural resources have changed dramatically since European settlement. Urbanization and industrialization have taken a tremendous environmental toll as resources have been exploited and transformed for economic profit. Roughly 90 percent of the original hickory and oak forests in the state have been cut down; only 10 percent of the state's original wetlands remain; just one-tenth of one percent of Illinois's original prairie still exists.

The forest industry in Illinois brings the state $4.5 billion annually and employs more than 68,000 people. Almost all of the state's forests are hardwoods, with the remainder made up mainly of conifers. Hardwoods grown in the state include black walnut, red oak, white oak (the state tree), yellow poplar, ash, hickory, hard maple, and soft maple.

Illinois is home to 123 state protected areas that include state parks, wildlife areas, recreation areas, nature reserves, and state forests. The largest state park is the Pere Marquette State Park, located on 8,050 acres (5,258 ha) of land in Grafton. Pere Marquette State Park is known as a winter home for many of the state's bald eagles. The U.S. Fish and Wildlife Service lists 26 animal and 10 plant species in Illinois as either threatened or endangered. Endangered animals include the Iowa Pleistocene snail, Karner blue butterfly, and the gray bat. The leafy prairie-clover and running buffalo clover are the only federally endangered plant species found within the state, the rest are listed as threatened. At the state level, the Illinois Department of Natural Resources has listed 161 animal and 332 plant species as threatened or endangered. The white-tailed deer is the state animal and the cardinal is the state bird. State programs such as the Conservation Stewardship Program and the Illinois Wildlife Action Plan attempt to address issues of environmental degradation to strengthen and redeem the natural world in the state.

Water: Abundant Freshwater Resources

Illinois is a water-rich state. Residents draw their water from surface as well as ground sources, and many of the large municipalities in the state, such as Chicago, obtain their water from a mixture of these sources. Illinois has jurisdiction over 1,526 square miles (3,952 sq km) of Lake Michigan, the only North American Great Lake located entirely within the United States. Lake Carlyle, an artificial lake that spans forty-one square miles, is the largest inland body of water.

Roughly 2,000 rivers and streams crisscross the land, covering 9,000 miles (13,480 km) or about three-and-a-half times the distance between New York City and San Francisco. The state's important rivers define its shape and form in several places. Among them are the Wabash and the Ohio Rivers, which form the southeastern and southern border respectively; the Mississippi River, which forms the western border of the state; and the Illinois, which does not define a border, but flows northeast to southwest across the central region, eventually meeting and disappearing into the Mississippi River. Bogs and wetlands are found in the northeast, and the state's southern tip contains cypress swamps like those found in southern states.

Illinois was ranked twenty-third for total nonfuel mineral production in 2010 with a value of $910 million. The state was the nation's number-one producer of industrial sand and gravel and tripoli in 2007. Other principal materials produced in the state are crushed stone, and portland cement.

Agriculture: The Bounty of the Breadbasket

Illinois is located in the breadbasket of the United States and its diverse fertile soils and unique climate represent a tremendous resource. According to the U.S. Department of Agriculture, the state has roughly 76,000 farms, which collectively cover 28 million acres (11 million ha) of Illinois land—nearly 80 percent of the state's territory. The top agricultural commodities produced in Illinois are soybeans, corn, and pig products. Farmers grow and raise many other agricultural commodities as well, including wheat, cattle, oats, sorghum, hay, sheep, poultry, fruits, and vegetables. Together, raw agricultural commodities account for a $9 billion per year industry in the state. In addition, food processing, the state's primary manufacturing activity, adds more than $14 billion annually to the state's economy.

Illinois is a leading state in terms of agricultural export to other nations—agricultural products account for 7 percent of total U.S. agricultural exports. The Illinois Local and Organic Food and Farm Task Force was established by statewide legislation in 2007 to increase the amount of locally grown and organically produced food. The task force's goal is to make Illinois the country leader in organic food production.

❧ Energy

Illinois carries the burden of being one of the top energy-consuming states in the nation. Analysts attribute the high energy demand to Illinois's large population and sizable industrial sector, which sucks resources to the state's energy-intensive aluminum, chemicals, metal casting, petroleum, and steel industries. The state's per capita energy consumption, however, ranks 16th lowest of the 50 U.S. states.

Illinois is one of the top energy-producing states in the country and is a net exporter of energy. Nuclear energy and coal constitute more than 95 percent of Illinois's energy generation. With eleven nuclear reactors and six power plants, Illinois is also the first in the United States in terms of nuclear energy production, generating more than 10 percent of the nation's total nuclear energy.

While Illinois is a top producer of nuclear energy, the industry has not been without its problems. In March 2011, Honeywell International, Inc., pleaded guilty to one felony offense for knowingly storing hazardous waste without a permit in violation of the Resource Conservation and Recovery Act (RCRA). Honeywell owns a uranium hexafluoride (UF6) conversion facility in Massac County. At the facility, natural uranium is converted to UF6 to be used as nuclear fuel. The waste that accumulates from this conversion is stored in 55-gallon (208 l) drums, from which uranium would eventually be reclaimed. Honeywell shut down part of the reclamation process, causing drums of the waste and all additional waste generated to be stored on site. The company did not have a permit to store the waste, which is considered corrosive and hazardous. An investigation by the EPA in 2009 found almost 7,500 illegally stored barrels of

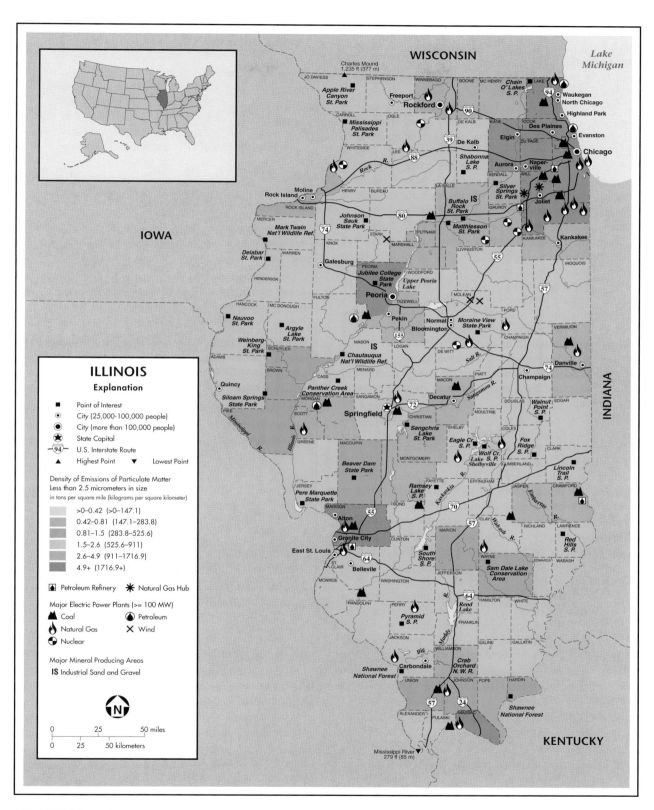

SOURCES: "County Emissions Map: Criteria Air Pollutants." *AirData*. U.S. Environmental Protection Agency. Available from http://www. epa.gov/air/data/geosel.html; *Energy Maps*. U.S. Energy Information Administration. Available from http://www.eia.gov/state; *Highest and Lowest Elevations*. U.S. Geological Survey. Available from http://egsc.usgs.gov/isb/pubs/booklets/elvadist/elvadist.html#Highest; *2007 Minerals Yearbook*. U.S. Geological Survey. Available from http://minerals.usgs.gov/minerals/pubs/state. © *2011 Cengage Learning.*

radioactive and hazardous waste. Honeywell was sentenced to a five-year term of probation, in which they must implement a community service project for the community surrounding the facility, and must also pay a criminal fine of $11.8 million.

The state contains about 10 percent of the country's recoverable coal reserves, the third most of any state in the nation. However, only a small fraction of these reserves are used to generate electricity in Illinois. Instead, Illinois receives much of its raw coal from other states, particularly Wyoming. The state then converts the imported coal into energy, and exports roughly half to other states, such as Indiana, Florida, Tennessee, and Missouri.

It is striking that Illinois contains such large coal reserves, but chooses to import other states' coal rather than develop its own capacity. Yet, there is logic to these trends. Illinois coal, like most of the Midwestern variety, contains very high amounts of sulfur, whereas western coal has relatively low levels of the chemical. Illinois ranks fourth among the 50 states in coal consumption for the generation of electricity, but electric utilities in the state tend to prefer low-sulfur coal to the high-sulfur type because low-sulfur coal produces considerably less pollution. In addition, Illinois has highly developed population centers that make the development of its coal reserves more difficult.

Despite the use of low-sulfur coal, the state's high consumption of coal has not been without its problems. A report released by the National Resources Defense Council in July 2011 included Illinois on its list of "Toxic 20" states for air pollution levels. The report points out that there are still some power plants in the state that lack pollution controls for toxic chemicals, which they claim as responsible for increased asthma rates in children. The report states that power plants released 5.6 million pounds (2.5 million kg) of chemicals in the state in 2009, equating to 23 percent of the state's pollution.

The Illinois Power Agency Act (Public Act 095-0481), adopted in 2007, require that Illinois obtain at least 25 percent of its energy from renewable resources by 2025. Solar, wind, biomass, and hydroelectric power are eligible sources. However, at least 75 percent of the energy used to meet the renewable standard must come from wind.

❧ Green Business, Green Building, Green Jobs

Green Business: Investing in Environmental Entrepreneurship

Diverse stakeholders in Illinois have recognized the value of green business to the state's future economy. Sustain Illinois is a collaborative business competition launched in 2009 by the Chicago Sustainable Business Alliance and the Chicago West Side Entrepreneurship Center. The

---

Illinois State Profile

Physical Characteristics

Land area	55,518 square miles (143,791 sq km)
Inland water area	836 square miles (2,165 sq km)
Coastal area	NA
Highest point	Charles Mound 1,235 feet (376 m)
National Forest System lands (2010)	298,000 acres (121,000 ha)
State parks (2011)	123

Energy Statistics

Total energy production (2009)	2,000 trillion Btu
State ranking in total energy production (2009)	11
Renewable energy net generation total (2009)	3.7 million megawatt hours
Hydroelectric energy generation (2009)	136,000 megawatt hours
Biomass energy generation (2009)	710,000 megawatt hours
Wind energy generation (2009)	2.8 million megawatt hours
Wood and derived fuel energy generation (2009)	NA
Crude oil reserves (2009)	66 million barrels (10.5 million cu m)
Natural gas reserves (2009)	NA
Natural gas liquids (2008)	NA

Pollution Statistics

Carbon output (2005)	230.0 million tons of CO_2 (208.7 million t)
Superfund sites (2008)	44
Particulate matter (less than 2.5 micrometers) emissions (2002)	29,988 tons per year (27,204 t/yr)
Toxic chemical releases (2009)	95.1 million pounds (43.1 million kg)
Generated hazardous waste (2009)	1 million tons (948,400 t)

SOURCES: AirData. U.S. Environmental Protection Agency. Available from http://www.epa.gov/air/data; *Energy Maps, Facts, and Data of the U.S. States.* U.S. Energy Information Administration. Available from http://www.eia.gov/state; *The 2012 Statistical Abstract.* U.S. Census Bureau. Available from http://www.census.gov/compendia/statab; *United States Energy Usage.* eRedux. Available from http://www.eredux.net/states.

© 2011 Cengage Learning.

---

competition sought to encourage green business development by offering financial rewards to entrepreneurs who developed sustainable companies. The Sustain Illinois competition awarded in 2009 a collective $22,500 in prizes to four Illinois businesses who best embodied sustainability, which is defined by the triple bottom line—"people, planet, profit."

Green Building: Government Agency Demands Green Office Space

The state of Illinois sought to lead by example in the green building movement, piloting in 2006 a program in which the Central Management Services (CMS) awarded its first-ever competitive bid for green building space. The Illinois CMS is charged with managing the state's 60 million square feet of leased and owned office space, and through the pilot program sought to lease green office space in Chicago for two of the state's agencies.

Landlords who took definitive steps to "green up" their properties were allowed to issue competitive bids to have the two state agencies as tenants. To qualify, landlords had to prove that they properly disposed of interior construction materials, used recycled materials for carpeting, and selected energy-efficient lighting fixtures. In piloting the program, the state of Illinois hoped to encourage other land owners to take similar measures, while also saving the state money by reducing the costs of operating their offices.

Green Jobs: Training Tomorrow's Workers

In January 2010, Illinois governor Pat Quinn announced a $1.7 million state grant to the Illinois Community College Sustainability Network (ICCSN), a consortium of community colleges geared toward advancing career development in energy efficiency and renewable energy. A large portion of the money went directly to three Illinois community college campuses for green jobs programs that allow Illinois workers to gain skills that will help them adapt to a green centric economy. The remainder of the grant funds went generally to the ICCSN itself.

❧ The Battle of the Asian Carp

Since the beginning of 2010, the state of Illinois has found itself at the center of legal disputes with its fellow Great Lakes states, most notably Michigan, over the issue of the invasive Asian carp. Four species of Asian carp—bighead, silver, grass, and black—were first imported into the United States in the 1960s and 1970s by Southern catfish farmers who used the fish to naturally remove algae and other matter from their farm ponds. Some carp were accidently released into local waterways of the Mississippi River Basin in the 1990s, as major flooding caused the catfish farm ponds to overflow into river areas. Since then, the carp have been steadily making their way upriver toward the Great Lakes. Asian carp can be quite large, weighing in at up to 100 pounds (45 kg). They are extremely prolific and eat large quantities of food. The greatest concern over the migration of the species into the Great Lakes is that, once there, they will disrupt the food chain by consuming large amounts of food that other native fish rely on, thereby becoming a dominating species in a relatively short amount of time.

Motions Filed and Denied

In the fall of 2009, reports indicated that genetic material from the Asian carp had been discovered in the Chicago-area waterway system that links the Mississippi river to the Great Lakes, approximately six miles from

Chicago, located on the banks of Lake Michigan, is one the country's major metropolises. © *Bryan Busovicki/ShutterStock.com*

Lake Michigan. No actual Asian carp were found in the waterway, but the announcement set of a flurry of legal actions to force immediate action toward preventing any further migration. In December 2009, the State of Michigan filed a motion with the Supreme Court which sought an injunction to force the state of Illinois to close the Chicago-area locks that link the waterways. The motion was denied in January 2010, in part because the U.S. Army Corp of Engineers argued that the presence of an electric barrier at the Chicago Sanitary and Ship Canal was a sufficient means of keeping the Asian carp contained. Several days after the Supreme Court decision, however, officials from the Corp acknowledged that genetic matter of the Asian carp had been discovered in the channel beyond the barrier. That month, U.S. Senator Debbie Stabenow (D-MI) and U.S. Representative Dave Camp (R-MI) introduced federal legislation titled "Close All Routes and Prevent Asian Carp Today," or the CARP Act (Senate 2946, House 4472). The proposed law, which is based on similar demands set by Michigan's motion for an injunction, could lead to a more permanent closure of the waterway.

The Response from Illinois

Officials from the state of Illinois are just as concerned about the potential threat to the Great Lakes environment as are officials from neighboring states. However, the state is opposed to even a temporary closure of the locks, since this could prove to be a major blow to the local economy, blocking trade along a much-used inland shipping route. Furthermore, the state has been working closely with the U.S. Army Corps of Engineers for some time on measures to control the migration and population of the Asian carp, including upgrades to the barrier system, the use of chemicals to kill the fish, and removal of the fish from local waterways. The state has also committed substantial resources for further Asian carp removal operations and intensive DNA monitoring and sampling programs along the waterways.

One potentially profitable approach to Asian carp control involves a public-private partnership between the Illinois Department of Commerce and Economic Opportunity, Big River Fisheries in Pearl, Illinois, and the Beijing Zhuochen Animal Husbandry Company, a meat processing company in China. There is a large market for wild Asian carp in China, and the Illinois carp are considered to be of high quality and taste. The agreement called for production of 30 million pounds (13.6 million kg) of fish by the end of 2011, thus providing a favorable boost to the local fishing industry and creating about 180 new jobs.

In a similar plan, two food processing plants are to open in the state dealing with Asian carp products. One plant in Havana would convert the by-products from processed Asian carp into pet food and fish oil. The other plant, in Grafton, will process the fish before sending the by-products to the Havana plant. Each plant should process from 50,000 to 100,000 pounds (22,680 to 45,360 kg) of fish per day. The idea behind this business venture is to create a new industry in the state and to provide more jobs for its residents. In recent years, Asian carp dishes have begun to pop up in restaurants and markets in other areas where the fish has been invading, and these plants hope to begin this same trend in Illinois. Whether or not this will help to stem the invasion of the Asian carp into the Great Lakes remains to be seen, but officials hope that it will at least help to control the fish's numbers.

In the long-term, the state plans to be an active participant in the Asian Carp Management and Control Implementation Task Force with the U.S. Fish and Wildlife Service, which has initiated a far-reaching plan encompassing 133 different actions that can be applied in all of the national watersheds where Asian carp are found.

The Battle Continues

In February 2010, Michigan issued another request to the Supreme Court for a preliminary injunction to close the Chicago locks. This renewed request was based on the DNA evidence found by the U.S. Army Corps of Engineers and on a study completed by researchers at Wayne State University entitled *Chicago Waterway System Ecological Separation: The Logistics and Transportation Related Cost Impact of Waterway Barriers*. This study concludes that closure of the waterways affected by such an injunction would amount to about $64 million to $69 million annually, which is considered to be far less than the state of Illinois initially suggested in its arguments against the action. The motion was again denied. This time then U.S. Solicitor General Elena Kagan issued an official memorandum on behalf of the Obama administration asserting that the federal government has already demonstrated its commitment to protecting the Great Lakes from the Asian carp through the ongoing work of the Army Corps of Engineers, and that this work should be allowed to continue, rather than be hindered by legal debates. The statement essentially placed the federal government strongly on the side of the state of Illinois.

In response to the Wayne State University study, the Illinois Chamber of Commerce released an economic analysis in April 2010 that was conducted by economist Dr. Joseph Schwierterman of DePaul University. This report suggests that the economic impact of closing the waterways would amount to $582 million the first year and $531 million each year for the subsequent seven years, resulting in a net loss of $4.7 billion over a twenty-year period.

In June 2010, a commercial fisherman hired by the state of Illinois to conduct routine sampling in the area found a nineteen pound (8.6 kg) Asian carp in Lake Calumet in Chicago, about six miles (9.6 km) downstream from Lake Michigan and above the electric barrier. The news sparked yet another flurry of debate and complaint. On July 20, Michigan, Wisconsin, Minnesota, Ohio, and Pennsylvania filed a joint suit in the U.S. District Court for the Northern District of Illinois against the U.S. Army Corps of Engineers and Metropolitan Water Reclamation District of Greater Chicago. This lawsuit claims that in failing to stop the progress of the carp toward the lakes, these agencies have created a public nuisance that threatens the public resources of the waters and fisheries of the Great Lakes. The suit also calls for an official review of the actions of the Corps under the Administrative Procedures Act, which allows legal challenges to federal agency actions to determine if they were arbitrary or unlawful.

In early August 2010, the Illinois Department of Natural Resources reported that testing conducted on the Asian carp discovered in June indicated that the fish may have been placed in Lake Calumet by humans, rather than it having migrated past the barrier on its own.

The case calling for the injunction to close the locks was heard in September and October 2010. In December, Judge Robert Dow, Jr., of the U.S. District Court issued an opinion that denied the request for an injunction, stating that the plaintiffs had not met the necessary burden of proof to obtain the injunction, in part by failing to show sufficient proof of irreparable harm if the situation remains the same. In the official opinion paper, the judge acknowledged the potential environmental and economic threats associated with the migration of the carp into the lakes, but noted that federal and state agencies are well aware of the situation and have been working on solutions to the problem.

At the national level, the Asian Carp Prevention and Control Act (S 1421—111th Congress) passed in Congress and was signed into law on December 14, 2010. The law adds the bighead carp species of Asian carp to the list of injurious species that are prohibited from being imported or shipped in the United States under the Lacey Act.

In March 2011, the U.S. Army Corps of Engineers released a research report on the operation of the electric dispersal barrier system in the Chicago Sanitary and Ship Canal (CSSC). The information that the Corps gathered indicated that the barrier was working as designed, successfully immobilizing fish as small as 5.4 inches (13.7 cm) in length. The report stated that carp smaller than 5.4 inches would not likely appear near the barrier, since the closest spawning population of Asian carp is located 25 miles (40 km)—and three locks—downstream. This distance is more than an Asian carp is able to travel during its first year of life, proving that by the time a juvenile made it to the barrier, it would exceed 5.4 inches. The U.S. Army Corps of Engineers report provides an answer to those that were unsure of the effectiveness of the barrier, and to those that may have thought the only solution was closing the locks. For now, it seems that the Asian carp have been prevented from entering the Great Lakes.

More Asian carp DNA was discovered in Lake Calumet in June and July of 2011, which lead to a four-day intensive fishing expedition by federal officials in early August. The purpose of the expedition was to determine whether or not the Asian carp has made its way into the locks that are designed to keep them from entering Lake Michigan. Biologists and commercial fisherman laid half-mile-wide nets to sweep large portions of Lake Calumet and also sample fish along the shoreline using electrofishing. The expedition produced no actual physical specimens of the invasive fish; however, environmentalists have challenged the fishing approach and continue to point to DNA evidence of invasion.

❧ High-speed Rail is on the Fast Track in Illinois

In January 2010, the U.S. federal government unveiled $8 billion in stimulus grants for the development of high-speed rail in the country. Illinois was one of the largest beneficiaries of the funds, pulling in $1.2 billion worth of grants for several projects across the state. The vast majority of the Illinois-designated funds ($1.1 billion) were earmarked for improvements to modernize the Chicago to Saint Louis, Missouri, rail line. Immediate track and infrastructure improvements will allow passenger trains to travel the route considerably faster, reducing travel time by 25 percent and paving the way for future modernizations.

Although Illinois obtained more than one-eighth of the federal dollars given in the January 2010 package, the awarded sum represented a fraction of the funds requested by the state, and some Illinois advocates wanted more. Many state lawmakers regarded the federal dollars as a down payment on a broader high-speed train network that reaches other important regional centers as well.

Illinois advocates and lawmakers envision Chicago as the major high-speed train hub in the country, connecting numerous dynamic Midwestern cities—from Cleveland to Minneapolis—with modern, comfortable, fast, and reliable service. But Illinois's high-speed rail advocates were thrilled to have received the billion dollar grant and view it as a complement to the Capital Construction Bill signed by Illinois governor Pat Quinn in July 2009, which allocated $850 million of state funds to rail infrastructure and $400 million for high speed rail.

Can Illinois Build on the Momentum?

The Midwest High-speed Rail Association (MHSRA) is a Chicago-based, member-supported, non-profit pressure group that works to advance all areas of high-speed rail in Illinois. MHSRA mobilizes support for high-speed rail projects and works to pressure state and federal lawmakers to support ambitious drives for high-speed rail in the state and region. The MHSRA's core plan for high-speed rail hedges on three principal steps: creating a web of core 220 miles per hour (354 km per hour) commuter trains to connect major routes, upgrading the entire Amtrak network to 90 miles per hour (145 km per hour) plus trains and tracks, and creating a reliable network of fast sleeper trains.

Like many lawmakers, the MHSRA looked at the federal grant dollars awarded to Illinois in January 2010 and said, essentially, "let's build on this." In March 2010, MHSRA worked with Illinois legislators to pass Senate Bill (SB 2571), which would create an Illinois and Midwest High-Speed Rail Commission. The bill would have tasked the commission with preparing a report recommending the best governmental structure for a public-private partnership to design, build, operate, and maintain the state's high-speed rail network; however, it did not pass the Illinois House before the end of the 2010 legislative session.

Illinois state officials announce the next phase of high speed rail construction at an Amtrak maintenance building Tuesday, March 22, 2011, in Chicago. © *AP Images/Charles Rex Arbogast*

Environmentally Friendly Travel

Roughly 27 percent of greenhouse gas emissions in the country come from the transportation sector, and as of 2010, 90 percent of Midwestern travel was by car. Compared to automobile travel, high-speed rail produces considerably less emissions of harmful pollutants, including key greenhouse gases, such as volatile organic compounds (VOC), carbon monoxide (CO), and nitrous oxides (NO_2). In addition, 110 miles per hour (177 km per hour) trains—the mainstay of the Midwest's high-speed rail plan—produce less VOC and CO emissions per million of passenger miles than air travel.

In September 2010, Governor Quinn announced the start of the project, which involved upgrading 90 miles (145 km) of railroad track between Alton and Lincoln along the Chicago to St. Louis route, to enable it to permit train operations at up to 110 miles per hour (177 km per hour). IDOT indicated the track should be ready for high-speed service by 2012.

In February 2011, additional studies, including an Environmental Impact Statement (EIS), were begun on the Chicago to St. Louis high-speed rail by the Illinois Department of Transportation (IDOT) and the Federal Railroad Administration (FRA). The purpose of the EIS will be to study the impacts of potential improvements to the rail system.

For Illinois, the Chicago to St. Louis corridor is the top priority for passenger rail development. Ultimately, the Illinois high-speed rail program focuses on a trio of objectives: creating more options for sensible, fast personal travel in the state; bringing jobs to the state's high-technology and green sectors; and building environmentally friendlier ways to get from one place to another. With billions of dollars of stimulus grants flooding into the state to support similar programs, energy-efficient, high-speed rail is positioned to become a reality in Illinois.

BIBLIOGRAPHY

Books

Chapman, Patrick, and Piotr Wiczkowski. *Wind-powered Electrical Systems: Highway Rest Areas, Weigh Stations, and Team Section Buildings.* Urbana: Illinois Center for Transportation, 2009.

Northeastern Illinois Regional Greenways and Trails Plan: 2009 Update. Chicago: Chicago Metropolitan Agency for Planning, 2010.

A Report on Wind Energy. Springfield: Illinois Commission on Government Forecasting and Accountability, 2008.

Winckler, Suzanne, and Michael Forsberg. *The Smithsonian Guides to Natural America: The Heartland–Nebraska, Iowa, Illinois, Missouri, Kansas.* Washington, DC: Smithsonian Books, 1996.

Web Sites

"Asian Carp and Chicago Canal Litigation" Great Lakes Environmental Law Center. Available from http://www.greatlakeslaw.org/blog/asian-carp

"Asian Carp may have been planted near lake." *Chicago Sun-Times.* August 5, 2010. Available from http://www.suntimes.com/news/metro/2569700,asian-carp-lake-michigan-planted-080510.article

Asian Carp Prevention and Control Act (S 1421—111th Congress). U.S. Congress. Available from http://www.govtrack.us/congress/billtext.xpd?bill=s111-1421

"Chicago Sustainable Business Alliance." Available from http://csba.foresightdesign.org

Davey, Monica. "Fight Against Asian Carp Threatens Fragile Great Lakes Unity." The New York Times. January 3, 2010. Available from http://www.nytimes.com/2010/01/03/science/earth/03states.html

Dries, Kate. "New air pollution report calls Illinois one of the 'Toxic 20.'" WBEZ. July 21, 2011. Available from http://www.wbez.org/story/new-air-pollution-report-calls-illinois-one-toxic-20-89426

"Economic Impacts of Climate Change on Illinois." University of Maryland, Center for Integrative Environmental Research. Available from http://www.cier.umd.edu/climateadaptation/Illinois%20Economic%20Impacts%20of%20Climate%20Change.pdf

"Gov. Blagojevich sets goal to dramatically reduce greenhouse gas emissions in Illinois." Office of the Governor. Available from http://illinois.gov/PressReleases/ShowPressRelease.cfm?SubjectID=2&RecNum=5715

"Governor Quinn Announces Illinois as First State to Begin High-Speed Rail Construction." Illinois Department of Transportation. September 17, 2010. Available from http://www.dot.il.gov/press/r091710.html

"Governor Quinn Announces New Initiative to Control Asian Carp Population." Illinois Department of Commerce and Economic Opportunity. July 13, 2010. Available from http://www.illinois.gov/PressReleases/ShowPressRelease.cfm?SubjectID=1&RecNum=8624

Guarino, Mark. "Asian carp: DNA evidence finds something fishy near Lake Michigan." *The Christian Science Monitor.* August 5, 2011. Available from http://www.csmonitor.com/Environment/2011/0805/Asian-carp-DNA-evidence-finds-something-fishy-near-Lake-Michigan

Guarino, Mark. "Will Asian carp turn up in fishing expedition near Lake Michigan?" *The Christian*

Science Monitor. August 1, 2011. Available from http://www.csmonitor.com/Environment/2011/0801/Will-Asian-carp-turn-up-in-fishing-expedition-near-Lake-Michigan

"Honeywell Pleads Guilty in Illinois to Illegal Storage of Hazardous Waste/Corporation sentenced to pay $11.8 million criminal fine." U.S. Environmental Protection Agency. March 11, 2011. Available from http://yosemite.epa.gov/opa/admpress.nsf/d0cf6618525a9efb85257359003fb69d/def2-f68123e736b38525785000721a93!OpenDocument

Hood, Joel. "Price tag of closing locks to Asian carp: $4.7 billion, new study says." *Chicago Tribune.* April 7, 2010. Available from http://articles.chicagotribune.com/2010-04-07/news/ct-met-0408-asian-carp-study-20100407_1_locks-study-chicago-river

"Illinois Climate Change Advisory Group: Final Recommendations to the Governor." Illinois Climate Change Advisory Group. Available from http://www.epa.state.il.us/air/climatechange/documents/final-recommendations.pdf

"Illinois Community College Sustainability Network." Available from http://ectolearning.com/partners/ilccsn/htmsite/pages/home.shtml

"Illinois Forest Facts." Illinois Forestry. University of Illinois Extension. Available from http://web.extension.illinois.edu/forestry/il_forest_facts.html

Illinois High-Speed Rail. Available from http://www.idothsr.org/

"Illinois Local and Organic Food and Farm Task Force." Illinois Department of Agriculture. Available from http://www.agr.state.il.us/marketing/Mkt_ILOFFTaskForce.html

"Listings and occurrences for Illinois." Species Reports. U.S. Fish and Wildlife Service. Available from http://ecos.fws.gov/tess_public/pub/stateListingAndOccurrenceIndividual.jsp?state=IL&S8fid=112761032792&S8fid=112762573902

"Midwest High-speed Rail Association." Available from http://www.midwesthsr.org

Miller, Marc "Illinois Asian Carp Control Efforts." Illinois Department of Natural Resources. February 9, 2010. Available from http://transportation.house.gov/Media/file/water/20100209/Miller%20Testimony.pdf[SJT1]

"New Environmental Study to Begin For Chicago to St. Louis High-Speed Rail." February 21, 2011. Illinois Department of Transportation. Available from http://www.idothsr.org/pdf/tier%201%20eis%20press%20release-%20february%202011.pdf

Official IDOT Illinois High Speed Rail–Chicago to St. Louis. Available from http://www.idothsr.org/

Pere Marquette State Park. Available from http://www.greatriverroad.com/pere/pereindex.htm

Smothers, Michael. "Asian carp: 'If you can't beat 'em, eat 'em.'" January 23, 2011. PJStar.com. Available from http://www.pjstar.com/business/x1390758830/Asian-carp-If-you-cant-beat-em-eat-em

State of Michigan, State of Wisconsin, State of Minnesota, State of Ohio, and Commonwealth of Pennsylvania v. United States Army Corps of Engineers and Metropolitan Water Reclamation District of Greater Chicago. Available http://www.greatlakeslaw.org/files/mi_carp_complaint_dist_ct.pdf

Taylor, John C., and James L. Roach. *Chicago Waterway System Ecological Separation: The Logistics and Transportation Related Cost Impact of Waterway Barriers.* State of Michigan, Department of Attorney General. Available from http://www.glu.org/sites/default/files/carp/TR_chicago_canal_report_feb10.pdf

Indiana

Indiana, situated in the north-central United States, ranks 38th in size among the 50 states. The Hoosier State shares borders with Michigan to the north, Ohio to the east, Kentucky to the south, and Illinois to the west. The state has a short northwestern shoreline along Lake Michigan. The northern terrain of slightly rolling hills becomes more rugged in the southeastern portion of the state. The southwest corner of the state is part of the Illinois Basin, an area rich in coal, petroleum, and other minerals.

Indiana's Department of Environmental Management celebrated its twenty-fifth anniversary in 2011. During the years of its existence, the department has succeeded in improving air, land, and water quality for all Hoosiers. By 2009, all counties had air quality that met national standards, which represented a great improvement—in 2005, many areas had unacceptable levels of ozone and fine particulate matter in the air.

Climate

Indiana's climate features four distinct seasons and marked seasonal changes in temperature and precipitation produce bitterly cold winters and hot, humid summers. Such changes also create an agriculture-friendly environment that has made the state a leading national producer of corn and soybeans, potentially important biofuels.

Climate Change Impacts and Response

According to a 2008 study from Indiana's Purdue University Climate Change Research Center, if greenhouse gas concentrations continue to increase in the region, the resulting rise in temperatures and fluctuation in precipitation levels could create a serious threat to the environment, and particularly to local farmlands. For example, the study projects that total annual precipitation could increase by more than 20 percent by 2100 in some regions, but the increase would occur during the early winter and early spring, thus leading to greater flood risks

at these times. At the same time, summertime precipitation could decline by up to 9 percent. Added to the potential for higher summer temperatures and prolonged occurrences of extreme heat, these impacts of climate change are likely to have an adverse affect on crop production.

Indiana is one of a handful of states that have not established a formal climate action change plan, and government officials have been reluctant to adopt the aggressive greenhouse gas reduction targets that others have imposed in recent years. The economy lies at the heart of the issue. Opponents of action to reduce greenhouse gas emissions cite to the *State Greenhouse Gas Programs: An Economic and Scientific Analysis*, a 2003 study from the Chicago-based Heartland Institute, for the argument that greenhouse gas emissions goals are costly. This study found that a modest target of reducing greenhouse gas emission by 7 percent below 1990 levels by 2010–2012 would cost Indiana $3.3 billion per year in direct expenses and lost revenues. Rather than pursuing greenhouse gas emissions goals, the state has chosen instead to focus on economic development projects that encourage the use of alternative transportation fuels and renewable energy sources and promote energy efficiency and energy independence, noting that such developments will in turn reduce the amount of greenhouse gas emissions.

⚜ Natural Resources, Water, and Agriculture

Natural Resources: Conserving and Preserving a Valuable Natural Heritage

Indiana has more than 4.6 million acres (1.9 million ha) of forests, covering 20 percent of its total land area. Nearly 96 percent of these forests contain high-quality commercial hardwoods, allowing Indiana to lead the nation in forest-based businesses and wood furniture manufacturing. With active management, however, forest areas continue to grow by about 100,000 acres (40,470 ha) every three years. Primary tree species include oak, hickory, beech, maple, and yellow poplar (the state tree). Soft maple, pin oak, and sycamore are also found.

More than two thousand plant species are found in the state, of which 25 percent are nonnative. The red fox is the only common carnivorous animal in Indiana. Other native mammals include white-tail deer, raccoons, opossum, skunks, muskrats, squirrels, and cottontail rabbits. There are a variety of bird and waterfowl species, including the barn owl, Canada goose, field sparrow, and the cardinal (the state bird). Various catfish, pike, bass, and sunfish are native to the state. The state has 25 state parks and 229 dedicated nature preserves.

According to the U.S. Fish and Wildlife Service, there are 26 animal species and 5 plant species listed as threatened or endangered. Endangered animals include the Indiana bat, the piping plover, and four varieties of pearlymussel. Endangered plants found within the state include the running buffalo clover and Short's goldenrod.

Coal is also an important natural resource. Indiana routinely ranks second (after Texas) among the U.S. states in coal consumption for electricity generation. Primary nonfuel minerals include cement (Portland and masonry), crushed stone, construction sand and gravel, dimension stone (for which the state ranked second in 2007), and lime. The state was ranked twenty-fifth overall in total nonfuel mineral production with a value of $837 million in 2010.

Water: Rivers and Lakes Worth Conserving

Though only a small portion of Lake Michigan lies on the northwest border of the state, Indiana officials consider the Great Lake to be an important state resource and participate in a variety of cooperative conservation efforts with other Great Lakes states. The state is also a party to the Great Lakes–St. Lawrence River Basin Water Resources Compact. Indiana is home to more than four hundred inland lakes, the largest of which are Wawasee, Maxinkuckee, Freeman, and Shafer. Indiana's Wabash River flows westward across the north central region and turns southward to empty into the Ohio River, which forms the southern border of the state. About four-fifths of the state's land is drained by the Wabash and its tributaries. The northern region is drained by the Maumee River, which flows into Lake Erie at Toledo, Ohio, and by the Kankakee River, which joins the Illinois River in Illinois.

In April 2011 it was announced that three officials of a wastewater treatment facility in Indianapolis had been sentenced for felony violations of the Clean Water Act (CWA). Ecological Systems, Inc. (ESI) had intentionally discharged untreated wastewater and stormwater from its facility directly into the city's sewer system. The company's vice president and two managers were

sentenced to varying terms of probation, fines, and community service after pleading guilty to a total of four counts of CWA violations. The Indiana Department of Environmental Management was alerted in 2009 after receiving complaints from Indianapolis residents that "thick, oily wastewater" had flowed into their yards from sewer manholes after a heavy rainfall. ESI did not have the required storage capacity to handle the wastewater, so the company discharged the water directly into the sewer system. Around 300,000 gallons (1.1 million l) of untreated water were pumped into the sewers over the course of 8 hours. The heavy rainfall occurred in the hours after the untreated water had been discharged, leading to the waste reemerging from sewer manholes downstream from the ESI facility. The investigation into the incident revealed that ESI had not been adequately treating waste for some time, that major pieces of equipment needed to be repaired or replaced, and the facility did not have enough storage space. The company had also provided the Environmental Protection Agency with misleading data in order to hide the fact that it was not in compliance with the CWA.

The Threat of Asian Carp

The invasive Asian carp has gained attention recently as more and more of the potentially dangerous fish have been found throughout the waterways leading to the Great Lakes. Two species of Asian carp, the bighead and silver carp, have been reported in Indiana waters since the mid-1990s. The state has been monitoring the populations of these fish ever since. In August 2010, the silver carp made headlines as a local fisherman videoed an encounter of hundreds of the fish jumping out of the Wabash River in an area north of Terre Haute. The primary concern for many is that these fish do not make their way into the Great Lakes, where the extremely prolific species would most likely edge out the native species in competitions for food. Within the state, there is concern that the carp could migrate from the Wabash River to the Maumee River, the latter of which connects to Lake Erie. While the rivers are not directly connected, the waters do comingle during certain flood conditions. In July 2010, the Indiana Department of Natural Resources (DNR) announced plans to install a barrier along part of Eagle Marsh, a wetland area near Fort Wayne, which could block the potential passage of the Asian carp from the Wabash River into the Maumee River during such flood conditions. The 1,200-foot (366-m) long and 8-foot (2.4-m) tall chain-link fence was completed in October 2010. The fencing is bolstered by 120 concrete barriers. Funding for this project was provided through the U.S. Environmental Protection Agency and the U.S. Fish and Wildlife Service through the Great Lakes Restoration Initiative.

So far, that state of Indiana has remained somewhat neutral amid the flurry of carp-related lawsuits that have

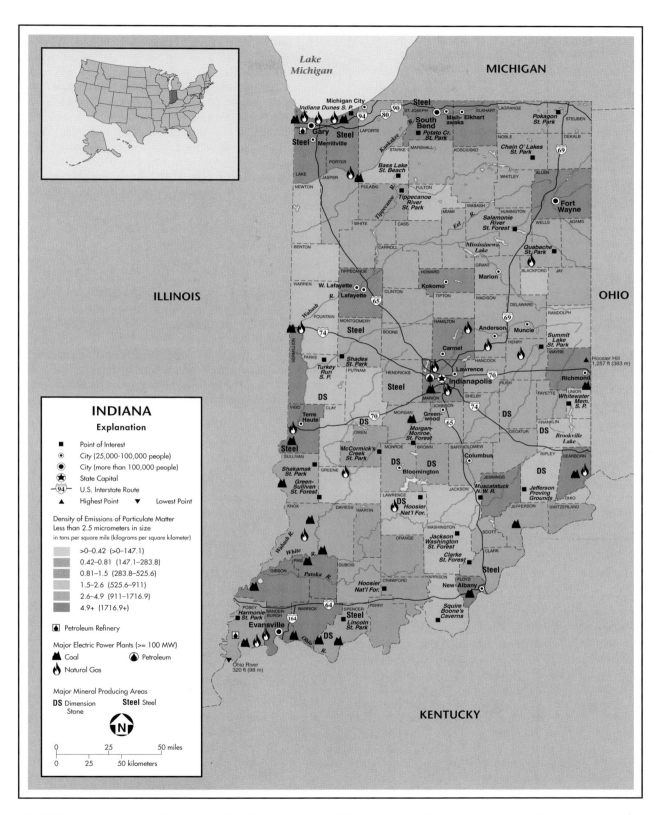

SOURCES: "County Emissions Map: Criteria Air Pollutants." *AirData*. U.S. Environmental Protection Agency. Available from http://www.epa.gov/air/data/geosel.html; *Energy Maps*. U.S. Energy Information Administration. Available from http://www.eia.gov/state; *Highest and Lowest Elevations*. U.S. Geological Survey. Available from http://egsc.usgs.gov/isb/pubs/booklets/elvadist/elvadist.html#Highest; *2007 Minerals Yearbook*. U.S. Geological Survey. Available from http://minerals.usgs.gov/minerals/pubs/state. © 2011 Cengage Learning.

Indiana State Profile

Physical Characteristics

Land area	35,823 square miles (92,781 sq km)
Inland water area	361 square miles (935 sq km)
Coastal area	NA
Highest point	Hoosier Hill 1,257 feet (383 m)
National Forest System lands (2010)	203,000 acres (82,000 ha)
State parks (2011)	25

Energy Statistics

Total energy production (2009)	950 trillion Btu
State ranking in total energy production (2009)	20
Renewable energy net generation total (2009)	2.2 million megawatt hours
Hydroelectric energy generation (2009)	503,000 megawatt hours
Biomass energy generation (2009)	303,000 megawatt hours
Wind energy generation (2009)	1.4 million megawatt hours
Wood and derived fuel energy generation (2009)	NA
Crude oil reserves (2009)	8 million barrels (1.3 million cu m)
Natural gas reserves (2009)	NA
Natural gas liquids (2008)	NA

Pollution Statistics

Carbon output (2005)	235.1 million tons of CO_2 (213.3 million t)
Superfund sites (2008)	32
Particulate matter (less than 2.5 micrometers) emissions (2002)	49,327 tons per year (44,748 t/yr)
Toxic chemical releases (2009)	132.5 million pounds (60.1 million kg)
Generated hazardous waste (2009)	778,500 tons (706,200 t)

SOURCES: AirData. U.S. Environmental Protection Agency. Available from http://www.epa.gov/air/data; *Energy Maps, Facts, and Data of the U.S. States.* U.S. Energy Information Administration. Available from http://www.eia.gov/state; *The 2012 Statistical Abstract.* U.S. Census Bureau. Available from http://www.census.gov/compendia/statab; *United States Energy Usage.* eRedux. Available from http://www.eredux.net/states.

been initiated by Michigan and the other Great Lakes states. In March 2010, Indiana filed an *amicus curiae* in support of Michigan's motion to reopen an earlier case for a preliminary injunction to close shipping locks near Chicago as an emergency measure to prevent the further migration of the carp. The amicus brief supported the motion to reopen the case, but did not represent a position on how the case should be decided. While the brief noted the concerns of the state toward protecting Lake Michigan and the lake ecosystems, it also noted the economic importance of the Chicago ship canal to Indiana industries. More than four hundred barges transit the route between the O'Brien Lock and the Port of Indiana-Burns Harbor each year. This activity brings in about $350 million in business revenues and supports

about 3,000 jobs with $84 million in personal income. The closing of the locks could also lead to additional environmental problems for Indiana's Calumet region, since the state does not have adequate levees to contain the back flow that could be caused by the closure.

In December 2010, researchers from the University of Notre Dame released results of a sampling study that showed there was no evidence of Asian carp within Eagle Marsh. This study represented the largest sampling of Indiana waterways for environmental DNA (eDNA) that would indicate the presence of Asian carp. Researchers collected 247 water samples from the ditches and stream associated with the 705-acre (285-ha) wetland area. All of the samples were tested for bighead and silver carp eDNA and all of them came back negative. The Notre Dame researchers expect to continue monitoring projects with funding assistance through the Great Lakes Restoration Initiative.

Michigan's February motion was soon denied, as was a second request for an injunction made in July 2010. The December 2010 opinion of the U.S. District Court stated that the plaintiffs had not met the necessary burden of proof to obtain the injunction, in part by failing to show sufficient proof of irreparable harm if the locks remained open. The judge acknowledged the potential environmental and economic threats associated with the migration of the carp into the lakes, but noted that federal and state agencies are well aware of the situation and have been working steadily on solutions to the problem. At the national level, the Asian Carp Prevention and Control Act (S 1421—111th Congress) passed in Congress and was signed into law on December 14, 2010. The law adds the bighead carp species of Asian carp to the list of injurious species that are prohibited from being imported or shipped in the United States under the Lacey Act.

In March 2011, Sweetwater Springs Fish Farm of Peru, Indiana, was found guilty of trying to transport over 6,000 pounds (2,720 kg) of live Asian carp into Canada. The fish were found during an inspection of one of the company's trucks at Blue Water Bridge in Point Edward, Ontario. The fish are prohibited in the province, and the company was fined $20,000.

Agriculture: Harvesting Food and Fuel

State officials hope to focus on agriculture as a primary sector for economic growth. The state is already a leading producer of corn and soybeans. These crops serve as staples for American tables, and can be used in the production of biofuels—a growing segment of the state economy. The state's agricultural strategic plan promotes the development of biofuel crops, while also expanding hardwood forestry sector and redeveloping what was once a thriving pork industry.

Organic farming has been encouraged throughout the state as the market for such produce increases. The

Indiana State Department of Agriculture sponsors a cost-share program to reimburse farmers for some of the costs of applying for organic certification under the Indiana Certified Organic (ICO) program.

❧ Energy

More than 90 percent of the state's electricity is produced at coal-fueled plants; about half of the state's coal supply is produced locally from small mines in the Illinois Basin. These Indiana mines account for about 3 percent of annual total nationwide production, but the state also relies on imports from Wyoming, West Virginia, and Illinois to fulfill local demand. Large amounts of coal are used by Indiana's industrial sector, particularly its steel industry. Other energy-intensive industries include aluminum and glass production.

Indiana is one of the nation's top consumers of distillate fuels. Indiana's industrial sector also relies on natural gas resources, using about half of the natural gas supplies in the state. Additionally, two-thirds of all households in the state use natural gas as a primary source of energy for home heating. While there are nearly five hundred oil and gas fields in the southwestern Illinois Basin region of the state, production at these sites is relatively low in light of high consumer and industrial demand. A majority of the state's crude oil and natural gas supplies are imported from the Gulf Coast region and Canada. Since 2009, additional supplies of natural gas have come from Colorado and Wyoming via the Rockies Express Pipeline system.

The state is a net exporter of electricity, producing much more than is needed for local demand. Given their reliance on natural gas for home heating, Indiana households use less electricity than the national average though per capita energy consumption is among the highest in the nation. There are no nuclear power plants in the state.

Alternative Energy: BioTown, USA

Indiana seeks to be a national leader in the development, production, and promotion of alternative energy sources. In 2005, the town of Reynolds, Indiana, made headlines as it launched an innovative and ambitious renewable energy project nicknamed BioTown, USA. The long-term goal of the program is to completely convert the town's reliance on fossil fuels to renewable energy resources. While some of the key initiatives of the program have been delayed by the national recession, some progress has been made. For instance, Habitat for Humanity has teamed up with BioTown partners in a project to design and build new homes using green building standards.

Wind power is emerging as a potential source of alternative energy for Indiana. In 2009, Indiana was ranked as the third fastest-growing state for wind energy

In 2005, the town of Reynolds, Indiana, made headlines as it launched an innovative and ambitious renewable energy project nicknamed BioTown, USA. © *AP Images/John Harrell*

by the American Wind Energy Association. In 2009 and 2010, the state increased its installed wind capacity tenfold. The Fowler Ridge Wind Farm in Benton County is the largest U.S. wind farm east of the Mississippi River.

In August 2011, municipal utility Richmond Power and Light of Indiana announced plans to switch its 100 MW Whitewater Valley coal-fired generating station to burn gas produced from solid waste. Estimated to cost $150 to $160 million, the utility hopes to make the conversion by the spring of 2013. The process involves refining municipal solid waste into resource derived fuel, and then having it go into a gasification process which produces the gas that is burned to generate electricity. Such technology has been used in Japan and Europe, but has not been used on a large-scale commercially in the United States until Richmond announced its plans. The municipal utility decided to make the conversion for both economic and environmental reasons, and they hope that these steps will help to phase-out the use of coal in southwestern Indiana.

Hoosier Homegrown Energy and Indiana's Clean Energy Portfolio Standard

Indiana's strategic energy plan sets a goal of producing 25 percent of all energy consumed by alternative sources by 2025. The plan is outlined in the 2006 publication Economic Growth from Hoosier Homegrown Energy, which details three primary goals: to trade current energy imports for future Indiana economic growth (energy independence); to produce electricity, natural gas, and transportation fuels from clean coal and bioenergy; and to improve energy efficiency and infrastructure.

Indiana's Clean Energy Portfolio Standard (CPS) was created in May 2011 by the passage of Senate Bill

The Fowler Ridge Wind Farm, with more than 200 wind energy turbines, will eventually generate enough carbon-free electricity to power more than 200,000 average American homes.
© *ZUMA Press/newscom*

0251. Only public utilities can participate in the program, which sets a voluntary goal of 10 percent clean energy by 2025. Fifty percent of qualifying energy obtained by utilities participating in the program must come from within the state. Utilities that participate in the program become eligible for incentives which will help them pay for compliance projects.

⚜ Green Business, Green Building, Green Jobs

Green Jobs: Indiana Gets It

In January 2010, the Indiana Department of Workforce Development (DWD) was awarded a $6 million grant from the U.S. Department of Labor for green jobs training. The money will be used toward establishing the Indiana Green Energy Technology Instruction and Training (I Get It) initiative, which is expected to offer training opportunities, along with tuition assistance, for nearly 2,200 unemployed Hoosiers, including autoworkers. The DWD will establish the Indiana Advanced Energy Training Center to facilitate the program. The center's focus will be on developing a curriculum for education in the green energy sector.

Green Building: Seeking Common Ground

In 2008, Governor Mitch Daniels issued an executive order (EO8-14) that placed Indiana among the ranks of thirty-three other states that require all newly constructed state-owned buildings to meet national green building standards under the Leadership in Energy and Environmental Design (LEED) rating system of the U.S. Green Building Council (USGBC). Controversy over green building requirements took root in February 2010, when the Indiana House of Representatives passed a bill that would require all municipal governments to meet certain LEED standards in the new construction of their own buildings, including schools. Opponents of the bill claim that cities should be allowed to consider the costs and benefits of green building projects on a case-by-case basis, rather than being required to adopt a level of standards that they may not be prepared to meet. Those in favor of the bill argue that the construction of more energy-efficient buildings benefit both the taxpayers and the environment in the long run. The bill was referred to the Senate Committee on Energy and Environmental Affairs for further review and amended to increase discretion but was not presented for a full senate vote. In the meantime, a variety of companies and organizations have taken the steps toward LEED certification through the Indiana Branch of the USGBC. At the end of 2009, there were 35 certified building projects in the state, including two sites that have received the highest LEED rating, platinum status.

Green Business: Building on the Indy Tradition

In 2008, the Central Indiana Corporate Partnership launched the statewide Energy Systems Network (ESN), a major economic initiative that focuses on the development of the "cleantech" sector by actively recruiting businesses involved in research, development, and production of alternative energy sources. The Greater Indianapolis Chamber of Commerce (Indy Chamber) launched its Indy Green Business Initiative in 2008 to promote green practices in both new and existing businesses throughout the area. The Indy Chamber offers a wide variety of resources or business owners and entrepreneurs interested in going green.

THINK City hits the Road

Building on its history in auto parts manufacturing, Indiana has taken a leading role in development of next-generation batteries and electric drive vehicles. In December 2010, the THINK manufacturing facility in Elkhart presented the first American made all-electric passenger vehicles to the State of Indiana for use in the government fleet. With headquarters in Oslo, Norway, THINK is a leading international vehicle manufacturing company that is dedicated to production of electric vehicles. The THINK City model cars that were presented to the state feature advanced lithium-ion batteries that were manufactured in Indiana by Ener1, Inc.

While only fifteen cars were presented in the December ceremony, the state expected to roll out a fleet of one hundred or more by the end of 2011, with assistance from the Project Plug-IN initiative of the Energy Systems Network. Project Plug-IN is an industry-led, commercial-scale pilot program based in the Indianapolis area that is designed to promote the production and use of plug-in electric vehicles and related smart-grid technology. Officials from the Indiana-based Energy Systems Network will work to support the production and delivery of the additional THINK City vehicles for the state fleet and the necessary charging infrastructure to maintain the vehicles.

The THINK City is a zero emissions car that can travel for about 100 miles on a single charge. The model was first developed for urban commuters and fleet operations in Scandinavia and has been safety certified in Europe since 1999. THINK planned to make the City model available in other select U.S. cities by the end of 2011 as well. The facility's plans hit a snag in 2011, however, when THINK's parent company declared bankruptcy. Production had slowed down in the spring due to parts shortages that were the result of the issues that lead to the company declaring bankruptcy. In July 2011, the parent company was sold in a Norwegian bankruptcy court to Mr. Borris G. Zingarevich, who has investment operations in St. Petersburg, Russia. Zingarevich has indicated that he wants to maintain the plant's presence in the United States and continue production. This came as a relief to workers and residents in Elkhart, who were unsure if production in the plant would continue. Mayor Dick Moore stated that the facility's goal of employing 415 workers by 2013 is still attainable, despite the short disruption in production.

❧ Biofuels: The Highway to the Future

Drawing on its strength as a leading producer of corn and soybeans, and with a little help from the federal government, Indiana has proven itself as a leader in the development and production of transportation biofuels. Biofuels generally produce fewer emissions of air toxics than gasoline. Made from renewable sources, biofuels offer a greater degree of energy security for the state and the nation as well. Local production of biofuels also creates jobs and boosts local economies.

Ethanol, an alcohol-based alternative fuel made from corn, is primarily produced and distributed in the form of E85, a fuel containing 85 percent ethanol and 15 percent unleaded gasoline. E85 is used in flex-fuel vehicles that can run on gasoline or the ethanol based substitute. However, even most ordinary vehicles can use a fuel blend that contains up to 10 percent ethanol (E10), and much of the unleaded gasoline sold in Indiana contains some ethanol. Another alternative fuel produced in Indiana is biodiesel, which can generally be used in any diesel vehicles. Biodiesel can be made from animal fats, discarded restaurant grease, and vegetable oils, such as soy. B20, a blend of 20 percent biodiesel and 80 percent regular diesel, is one of the most common fuel blends produced in Indiana.

Known as the Crossroads of America, the state of Indiana was an obvious choice as one of the partners in the I-65 Clean Biofuels Corridor project sponsored, in part, by the U.S. Department of Energy (USDOE). An initial USDOE grant allowed for the construction of nineteen public biofuels filling stations in Indiana. But that was only a jumpstart for the growing industry. As of 2010, there were 130 biofuels filling stations in the state, supplied by twelve ethanol plants (with one under construction) and five biodiesel plants. The total production capacity of the plants is more than 850 million gallons (3.2 billion liters). The 2009 estimate for the total value of Indiana ethanol and its byproducts was $1.3 billion. More than $29 million ends up in the pockets of Indiana corn and soybean farmers. Continued research and development in biofuels technologies is expected to have a major impact on the economy as it involves a wide variety of sectors, including agriculture, research and development, manufacturing, and transportation/distribution.

In March 2011, POET—an ethanol producer with 27 plants in the United States—opened its fourth plant in Cloverdale, Indiana. POET purchased the plant from Altra Biofuels in 2010. The company has invested $30 million in upgrades to the 90 million-gallon-per-year facility, which includes POET's Total Water Recovery System that cuts wastewater discharge. The facility provides up to 45 jobs, the majority of which will be filled from the local community. POET's other Indiana ethanol plants are located in Alexandria, North Manchester, and Portland.

A number of organizations work together to further Indiana's biofuels industry. The Indiana Economic Development Corporation actively recruits new businesses that focus on energy technology solutions. The Indiana Corn and Indiana Soybean Alliance offer resources and assistance for farmers in the production and marketing of crops within the biofuels industry and Purdue University has formed active partnerships with government and business entities to promote the growth and development of better, more cost-effective biofuel production technologies. All things considered, Indiana is clearly on the fast track to success in the biofuels industry.

BIBLIOGRAPHY

Books

Sanders, Scott R. *A Conservationist Manifesto*. Bloomington: Indiana University Press, 2009.

Strutin, Michal, and Gary Irving. *The Smithsonian Guides to Natural America: The Great Lakes–Ohio, Indiana,*

Michigan, Wisconsin. Washington, DC: Smithsonian Books, 1996.

Web Sites

Amicus Curiae the State of Indiana in Support of Motion to Reopen State of Michigan v. State of Illinois et. al. (February 19, 2010). Great Lakes Environmental Law Center. Available from http://www.greatlakeslaw.org/files/indiana_carp_amicus_supporting_motion_to_reopen.pdf

Asian Carp Prevention and Control Act (S 1421—111th Congress). U.S. Congress. Available from http://www.govtrack.us/congress/billtext.xpd?bill=s111-1421

Associated Press. "Indiana company fined for Asian carp possession." *The Wall Street Journal*. March 8, 2011. Available from http://online.wsj.com/article/AP0ddaa2ab8473441e8d2e67a182ab9fa4.html

Associated Press. "Indiana crews complete Asian carp fencing barrier." *Bloomberg Businessweek*. October 21, 2010. Available from http://www.businessweek.com/ap/financialnews/D9J05F701.htm

Central Indiana Corporate Partnership. Available from http://www.cincorp.com/

"DNR to put up carp barrier in Allen Co." Wane.com. July 14, 2010. Available from http://www.wane.com/dpp/news/dnr-to-erect-carp-barrier-in-allen-county

Foulkes, Arthur. "There's something fishy going on Wabash River: Asian carp causing problems." The Tribune-Star. August 10, 2010. Available from http://tribstar.com/news/x1491234966/Theres-something-fishy-going-on-Asian-carp-causing-problems

Green.indy. "Indiana Lands $6 million Green Jobs Grant," January 21, 2010. Available from http://green.indy.com/posts/indiana-lands-6m-green-jobs-grant

Impacts of Climate Change for the State of Indiana. The Purdue Climate Change Research Center. Available from http://www.purdue.edu/climate/pdf/ClimateImpactsIndiana.pdf

IN.gov. E85/B20 for I-65 and Beyond: Indiana. Available from http://www.in.gov/oed/2401.htm

Indiana Corn and Indiana Soybean Alliance. Available from http://www.indianasoybean.com/

Indiana State Department of Agriculture & Reynolds, Indiana. The BioTown, USA. Sourcebook of Biomass Energy. Available from http://www.in.gov/oed/files/Biotown_Sourcebook_040306.pdf

Indy Partnership: Indy Green Business Initiative. "Indianapolis Region: Renewable Energy,

Components Manufacturing." Available from http://www.indypartnership.com/media/docs/clean%20tech%20docs/Clean-Tech_Presentation.pdf

Lane, Jim. "POET opens 90 million gallon ethanol plant in Indiana with advanced yields, water recovery." March 16, 2011. *Biofuels Digest*. Available from http://biofuelsdigest.com/bdigest/2011/03/16/poet-opens-90-million-gallon-ethanol-plant-in-indiana-with-advanced-yields-water-recovery/

Matyi, Bob. "Indiana muni to switch 100-MW coal plant to solid waste gasification." Platts. August 2, 2011. Available from http://www.platts.com/RSSFeed-DetailedNews/RSSFeed/Coal/6339911

Memorandum Opinion and Order: Case No. 10-CV-4457. December 2, 2010. U.S. District Court for the Northern District of Illinois. Available from http://www.greatlakeslaw.org/files/dist_ct_pi_opinion_order.pdf

"New Supreme Court filings in Asian carp dispute." Great Lakes Environmental Law Center. Available from http://www.greatlakeslaw.org/blog/2010/03/new-supreme-court-filings-in-asian-carp-dispute.html

Peterson, Mark. "THINK electric car production to resume in Elkhart." WNDU. July 25, 2011. Available from http://www.wndu.com/hometop/headlines/THINK_electric_car_production_to_resume_in_Elkhart_126141658.html

POET. Available from http://www.poet.com/index.asp

Senate Bill 251: An Act to amend the Indiana Code concerning utilities. Indiana Legislature. Available from http://www.in.gov/legislative/bills/2011/SE/SE0251.1.html

Spalding, Tom. "State leads charge on electric cars." *Indianapolis Star*. December 17, 2010. Available from http://green.indy.com/posts/state-leads-charge-on-electric-cars

State Greenhouse Gas Programs: An Economic and Scientific Analysis—Impact on Indiana. The Heartland Institute. Available from http://www.heartland.org/bin/media/publicPDF/CO2-Indiana.pdf

"THINK delivers its first U.S.-built electric cars." THINK. Available from http://www.thinkev.com/Press/Press-releases/THINK-delivers-its-first-U.S.-built-electric-cars

25th Anniversary State of the Environment 2011. Indiana Department of Environmental Management. Available from http://www.in.gov/idem/files/state_of_environment_2011.pdf

U.S. Energy Information Administration: Independent Statistics and Analysis. "Table 26: U.S. Coal Consumption by End User Sector, by Census Division and State, 2008, 2007." Report released September 18, 2009. Available from http://www. eia.doe.gov/cneaf/coal/page/acr/table26.html

"Vice president, two managers of waste treatment facility sentenced for Clean Water Act felonies." United States Environmental Protection Agency. April 4, 2011. Available from http://yosemite.epa.gov/ opa/admpress.nsf/0/FA3D07020EE935AF85257 86800799BB2

Wind Energy Facts: Indiana. American Wind Energy Association. Available from http://www.awea. org/learnabout/publications/upload/ Indiana.pdf

Iowa

Conservation of natural resources is important to Iowans. A majority of citizens surveyed in 2010 considered preservation of resources to be critical to the state's economic health. Though Iowa is the smallest of the Midwest states, it is one of the most valuable in terms of natural resources. About 90 percent of the state's land is used for agriculture, which forms the foundation of the economy. The state ranks as second in the nation for the value of agricultural products, ranking first in the production of corn and soybeans. Building on the strength of agriculture, the state has also become first in the nation in the production of ethanol. Iowa's rich soils are generally cited as the source of such success, but that resource is in danger, as erosion from wind and water wipes away tons of topsoil each year. The state also faces some challenges in protecting waterways and natural habitats, particularly dwindling prairielands. In an effort to meet those challenges, Iowa voters passed a constitutional amendment to establish a Natural Resources and Outdoor Recreation Trust Fund, which will serve as a permanent, protected funding source for environmental conservation, improvement, and protection efforts. In terms of energy, the state is still largely dependent on imported coal, petroleum and natural gas, but the government has already taken a number of steps toward a goal of energy independence, primarily in the form of legislation that promotes the use of biofuels and other clean energy technologies.

Climate

Iowa lies in the humid continental zone and generally features four distinct seasons, with hot summers, cold winters, and wet springs. Temperatures vary widely during the year, with an annual average of 49°F (9°C). The state averages 166 days of full sunshine and 199 cloudy or partly cloudy days.

Climate Change

According to the National Wildlife Federation, if greenhouse gas emissions are not cut back in Iowa, temperatures in the state could increase between 9 and 22°F (−13 to −6°C). Such a dramatic increase would create dire consequences for the state's ecosystems. Higher temperatures and drier conditions could destroy up to 91 percent of the state's critical wetland habitats, which would result in a severe decline in waterfowl. Warming temperatures will also cause changes to prairie grassland habitats, which would shift many of the state's grassland bird species north and possibly out of the state. Along with these habitat changes, climate change is projected to cause increased flooding and extreme droughts, which would adversely affect the state's important crop yields.

To address the issue of climate change, the Iowa Climate Change Advisory Council (ICCAC) was established by the legislature in 2007 (Senate File 485) with a mandate to complete a report that would include the necessary policies and strategies to reduce statewide greenhouse gas emissions. The ICCAC was charged to consider a scenario that would reduce greenhouse gas emissions by 50 percent by 2050 and allowed to consider additional scenarios. It also examined a scenario to a reduce emissions 90 percent by the same date. The December 2008 final report included fifty-six policy options, of which 38 were quantified for greenhouse gas emissions reductions and cost-effectiveness. According to the ICCAC, implementing all 38 quantified policy options would lead to a 90 percent reduction from 2005 levels. These options primarily focus on the development of energy efficiency and clean energy technologies. In addition to creating the ICCAC, the 2007 legislation also required the Iowa Department of Natural Resources to complete an annual inventory of greenhouse gas emissions in Iowa. Having fulfilled its mandate, the ICCAC was officially disbanded on July 1, 2011, as part of the 2010 State Government Reorganization.

🍁 Natural Resources, Water, and Agriculture

Natural Resources

With forest covering only about 7 percent of the state, the forest and wood products industry is fairly small. In 2005 there were about twenty-nine sawmills producing saw logs, pulpwood, veneer logs, poles, and similar products. Some of the common tree species include oak, hickory, black walnut, and sugar maple. Silver maple and cottonwoods can be found along the flood plains.

There are ten state forests, including the Shimek State Forest, which is one of the largest remaining single pieces of contiguous forest in Iowa. Stephens State Forest is the largest in geographical area and is one of the most popular sites for wild turkey hunts. There are fifty-two state parks, several of which are managed by county conservation boards. The Lewis & Clark and Mormon Pioneer national trails pass through parts of Iowa.

Some of the most common wildlife species found throughout the state include red and gray foxes, raccoon, woodchuck, muskrat, common cottontail, white-tailed deer, and opossum. The state sponsors three active birding trails. The Makoke Trail in central Iowa is home to more than 300 bird species, including the bobolink, yellow-headed blackbird, cardinal, and eastern goldfinch (the state bird). Peregrine falcons and bald eagles are on the state's threatened and endangered list, but can still be found in some areas.

The U.S. Fish and Wildlife Service listed 13 animal and five plant species in Iowa as threatened or endangered in 2011. Animal species included the Iowa Pleistocene snail, the Indiana bat, and the piping plover. Threatened plant species included the prairie bush-clover and both the eastern and western prairie fringed orchid.

Bringing Back the Prairies

While tallgrass prairies once covered more than 80 percent of the state, less than one-tenth of one percent remains today. Settlement and agriculture are the main reasons for the decline. A number of environmental groups are involved in activities to revive the prairies. At the state level, the Iowa Department of Natural Resources sponsors the Prairie Resource Center, through which it has organized a number of replanting projects on public lands, relying heavily on the support of volunteers. Butterfly milkweed, prairie cord grass, big bluestem, prairie smoke, and purple prairie clover are only a few of the numerous native wildflowers and grasses.

In 2007, Iowa was ranked second in the nation for crude gypsum production. Other important nonfuel minerals produced in the state include limestone, cement, and construction sand and gravel. The state was ranked thirty-second overall for total nonfuel mineral production in 2010, with a value of $542 million.

Water: Mississippi, Missouri, and the Iowa Great Lakes

The history of settlement, agriculture, and trade in Iowa is inextricably linked to the great resources of the Mississippi and the Missouri rivers. Many early settlers came to the state by way of the rivers, which then became major routes for trade and further exploration. The rivers are just as important today, serving as a gateway to one of the nation's most extensive inland waterway systems. In Iowa, the terminal ports of Dubuque and Davenport on the Mississippi and Sioux City and Council Bluffs on the Missouri are the most active, handling shipments of coal, grain, petroleum, and other commodities bound for ports in Chicago, Houston, St. Paul, and New Orleans. The Des Moines and the Iowa Rivers are major tributaries of the Mississippi. The Grand and Big Sioux are tributaries of the Missouri.

There are numerous lakes and ponds across the state, though many of them are very small. The largest is Lake Red Rock, a reservoir created as a flood control project by the U.S. Army Corps of Engineers through the construction of the Red Rock Dam on the Des Moines River. The Iowa Great Lakes region in the northwest contains a group of natural glacial lakes that are the largest natural lakes in the state. They include Spirit Lake, West Okoboji, and East Okoboji.

Many rivers, streams, and lakes are popular sites for sports fishing, with rainbow trout, catfish, walleye, and yellow fish among the most popular catches.

In 2011, a concentrated animal feeding operation (CAFO) in Council Bluffs was issued an administrative compliance order for violations of the federal Clean Water Act. The S&S Cattle Company was found to discharge manure, litter, and processed wastewater into a series of drainage ditches that flow into a tributary of Mosquito Creek in Pottawattamie County. Such waste often violates water quality standards and can cause problems with human health, can threaten aquatic life in the state's rivers, and impair the use of waterways. The Iowa feedlot that received the order has a capacity of 999 cattle and was confining 730 head at the time of their inspection. The lot was ordered by the U.S. EPA to apply for a National Pollutant Discharge Elimination System (NPDES) permit and to construct feedlot waste controls or reduce the number of cattle it confines to meet regulatory requirements. Five other feedlots in Kansas and Nebraska were also issued orders.

The majority of feedlot operators in this region are in compliance with the Clean Water Act, as water is a vital resource for the agriculture-rich area. Because the water supply is critical, the EPA was scrutinizing all operations in the Midwest, to ensure that the water supply is not compromised in the future.

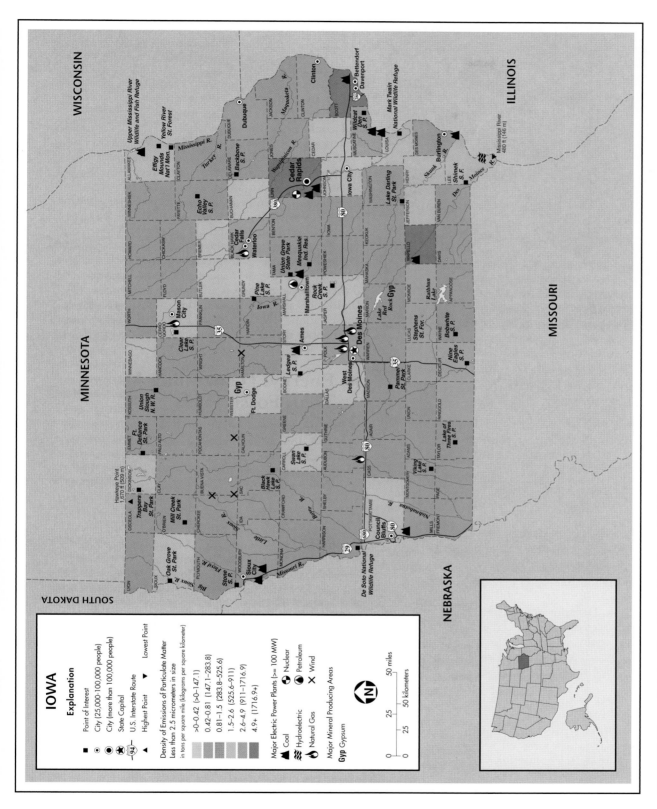

SOURCES: "County Emissions Map: Criteria Air Pollutants." *AirData.* U.S. Environmental Protection Agency. Available from http://www.epa.gov/air/data/geosel.html; *Energy Maps.* U.S. Energy Information Administration. Available from http://www.cia.gov/state; *Highest and Lowest Elevations.* U.S. Geological Survey. Available from http://egsc.usgs.gov/isb/pubs/booklets/elvadist/elvadist.html#Highest; *2007 Minerals Yearbook.* U.S. Geological Survey. Available from http://minerals.usgs.gov/minerals/pubs/state. © 2011 Cengage Learning.

Peregrine falcon. © mlorenz/ShutterStock.com

Agriculture: The Legacy of the Glaciers

With more than 90 percent of the state's landscape used for agriculture, it is no surprise that Iowa consistently ranks among the top agricultural states in the nation. In 2010, Iowa ranked as second in the nation for overall crop values. The state ranks first in the production of corn for grain, soybeans, eggs, and hogs and pigs, while coming in second for the production of beef. According to the Iowa Corn Promotion Board, ethanol production accounted for 39 percent of the Iowa corn market in 2009. Iowa is third in the nation for the number of individual farms and ninth for the number of organic farms. In 2009, there were more than 200 farmers' markets throughout the state, generating an estimated $38 million in sales.

The Iowa Department of Agriculture and Land Stewardship is accredited by the USDA National Organic Program to certify all aspects of the organic farm production, including crops, food products, feed, livestock, and the handling and processing of organic products.

The success of Iowa's farms is directly attributed to the state's rich soils. The root systems and organisms of Iowa's past tallgrass prairies transformed the raw deposits, which were left behind thousands of years ago by the glaciers that once covered the state, into its rich topsoil. In fact, Iowa's topsoils (about 450 types) are among the richest and deepest in the country.

However, the valuable resource of rich topsoil is dwindling through soil erosion, caused primarily by wind and water. Vulnerability to erosion is ironically a direct result of agriculture practices, which leave the soil vulnerable to forces of nature. In 2008, an estimated 50 tons of soil per acre was lost due to increased and more intense rainfall. According to a report from the Iowa Climate Change Impacts Committee, waterlogged soil is an issue that needs to be addressed as well. Changes in climate will lead to increased precipitation and could make the region more prone to flooding. Waterlogged soil can cause crops to have shallower root systems making them more vulnerable to diseases, nutrient deficiencies, and drought stress. Waterlogged soil is responsible for up to 32 percent of crop yield loss. As a result, soil conservation is a primary concern for the state's government and landowners. The Iowa Department of Agriculture and Land Stewardship's Soil Conservation Division is the primary agency responsible for leadership in soil protection and management efforts. Since a vast majority of farms are privately owned, the agency serves as an important link between landowners and officials from the various soil and water conservation districts that have been established throughout the state.

❦ Energy: Demanding More Than Fossil Fuels

With no proven reserves of oil or natural gas, and very little coal, Iowans have relied almost entirely on imports to fill local energy demands. The transportation sector is the largest consumer of basic petroleum products, but the agricultural sector also demands a large quantity of liquefied petroleum gas. About 70 percent of the electrical supply is generated from coal-fired plants, which are primarily supplied with low-sulfur coal imported from Wyoming. Wind power accounts for the next largest source of electricity, and is the fastest-growing source of power in Iowa. Wind power contributes approximately 20 percent of Iowa's electricity generation. The Duane Arnold nuclear plant generates about 10 percent of the state's electricity. Small amounts of power are generated by natural gas, hydropower, and petroleum. More than 60 percent of residents use natural gas for home heating.

Considering the Alternatives

Since the 1990s, the state has made significant strides in the use of alternative and renewable energy sources. Wind power is catching on in Iowa, with nearly 20 percent of the total electricity supply produced through wind turbines, primarily located in the west, northwest, and northcentral regions of the state. That percentage is likely to increase as public utilities and independent power producers begin to fulfill regional and national renewable energy goals and requirements by building more wind farms in Iowa. In early 2011, Iowa boasted the second-

Iowa State Profile

Physical Characteristics

Land area	55,858 square miles (144,672 sq km)
Inland water area	415 square miles (1,075 sq km)
Coastal area	NA
Highest point	Hawkeye Point 1,670 feet (509 m)
National Forest System lands (2010)	NA
State parks (2011)	86

Energy Statistics

Total energy production (2009)	470 trillion Btu
State ranking in total energy production (2009)	25
Renewable energy net generation total (2009)	8.6 million megawatt hours
Hydroelectric energy generation (2009)	971,000 megawatt hours
Biomass energy generation (2009)	168,000 megawatt hours
Wind energy generation (2009)	7.4 million megawatt hours
Wood and derived fuel energy generation (2009)	NA
Crude oil reserves (2009)	NA
Natural gas reserves (2009)	NA
Natural gas liquids (2008)	NA

Pollution Statistics

Carbon output (2005)	78.9 million tons of CO_2 (71.5 million t)
Superfund sites (2008)	11
Particulate matter (less than 2.5 micrometers) emissions (2002)	16,561 tons per year (15,023 t/yr)
Toxic chemical releases (2009)	43.3 million pounds (19.6 million kg)
Generated hazardous waste (2009)	40,300 tons (36,600 t)

SOURCES: AirData. U.S. Environmental Protection Agency. Available from http://www.epa.gov/air/data; *Energy Maps, Facts, and Data of the U.S. States.* U.S. Energy Information Administration. Available from http://www.eia.gov/state; *The 2012 Statistical Abstract.* U.S. Census Bureau. Available from http://www.census.gov/compendia/statab; *United States Energy Usage.* eRedux. Available from http://www.eredux.net/states.

© 2011 Cengage Learning.

highest amount of installed capacity of wind power, behind Texas.

The 1983 Iowa Alternative Energy Law (Iowa Code 476.41 et seq.) was the first such requirement for utilities to purchase or own renewable energy resources. The law requires the state's two investor-owned utilities, MidAmerican Energy and Alliant Energy Interstate Power and Light, to contract for a combined total of 105 megawatts of their generation from renewable energy resources. The utilities met this requirement in the 1990s primarily through the use of wind power and biomass. Since that time, Iowa governors Tom Vilsack and Chet Culver have set additional wind power goals, including reaching 25 percent wind power by 2025.

Corn-Fed Alternatives

As the leading state in corn production, Iowa has also become the leading producer of ethanol, with over three dozen operating ethanol plants. However, while production is high, local consumption has been relatively low, as the vast majority of the ethanol produced in Iowa is exported to other states. Iowa's low level of ethanol consumption is attributed in part to the fact that Iowa is among the states that still allow the use of conventional gasoline. The states that receive Iowa's ethanol generally require a blend of motor fuel and ethanol in some areas, since such a blend tends to produce a lower level of toxic emissions. The production–consumption imbalance in Iowa is changing rapidly, however, as the legislature passed a renewable fuel standard with a goal to replace 15 percent of the state's total gasoline sales with biofuels by 2015 and 25 percent by 2020 (House File 2754; Iowa Code 422.11N). By executive order (3-2007), at least 60 percent of the fuel purchased for state-owned flexible fuel vehicles must be E85 (a fuel that contains approximately 85 percent ethanol).

Another boost for the use of biofuels came in 2011 with the governor's signature on Senate File 531. This new renewable fuels law establishes the nation's first specific E15 incentive for local retailers and provides additional incentives for biodiesel producers. The law offers retailers a 3 cent per gallon state income tax credit on sales of E15, a mid-level 15 percent ethanol blend that is currently available for flexible fuel vehicles. The U.S. EPA is expected to approve the use of E15 in all 2001 and newer model cars and light trucks by the end of 2011.

The law also provides variable state income tax credits for the production and sale of biodiesel blends. In 2012, retailers can receive a credit of 2 cents per gallon for B2. A retail credit of 4.5 cents per gallon will be offered for B5 sales in 2012 and 2013. Biodiesel producers will earn a production sales tax credit of 3 cents per gallon in 2012. This incentive will drop to 2.5 cents per gallon in 2013 and to 2 cents per gallon in 2014. The credits are limited to the first 25 million gallons per producer. Additional provisions in the new law include an appropriation of $3 million per year in funding for Iowa's Renewable Fuels Infrastructure Program, designed to provide grants for the installation of blenders and dispensers of ethanol fuels and biodiesel.

Proposed Ethanol Pipeline: Dream or Reality? An ethanol pipeline was proposed in early 2010, which would connect Iowa and other ethanol-producing states to northeastern markets. The 1,700-mile (2,740-km) pipeline, if approved, would carry ten million gallons (38 million l) of ethanol per day. However, the pipeline is controversial and its development remains far from assured. Skeptics predict that the pipeline would be subject to malfunction and failure over time because of the corrosiveness of ethanol. Additionally, corn-based ethanol critics argue that the fuel represents a less-than-efficient power source, requiring unjustifiably high energy inputs—from those associated with agricultural cultivation to the energy inputs linked to running of the production facilities—to produce the finished product. Moreover, the notion of diverting potential food supplies and arable land to meet energy demands troubles some critics as being unethical. In July of 2010, a study from the U.S. Department of Energy determined that the project was "economically unfeasible." This is because the pipeline would need to carry 50 percent more ethanol annually than the originally proposed pipeline for the project to be possible without financial incentives. However, some executives and legislators remain positive, as the study indicated that despite costs, the project would be possible under certain conditions.

The Iowa Office of Energy Independence

One of the most significant changes in state energy policy procedures came in 2007 with the passage of energy independence legislation (House File 918). This legislation created the Iowa Office of Energy Independence (OEI) and the Iowa Power Fund. The OEI is charged with developing strategic plans that will advance state efforts for achieving energy independence through partnerships with business and industry, community leaders, government and public agencies, and other stakeholders. The Iowa Power Fund was created to support and promote these plans by providing financial assistance for the research and development of clean energy technologies and projects that increase the awareness of and demand for such technologies. Each year, the OEI publishes an Energy Independence Plan that reviews the past year's progress toward meeting set goals and sets forth new or adjusted recommendations for reducing the state's consumption of energy, dependence on foreign sources of energy, and use of fossil fuels. The OEI also continues to support the long-term goals of the 2010 plan, which include reducing energy use in facilities by 30 percent by 2025, increasing Iowa's wind energy consumption to 30 percent by 2020 and installing a total of 20 gigawatts of wind turbine capacity, and increasing the use of Iowa-produced biofuels by 50 percent by 2025. The 2011 plan established key new recommendations, which include identifying ways to make energy project implementation less time-intensive and more financially viable; conducting consumer education about how to purchase flex fuel vehicles and encourage owners of flex fuel vehicles to use higher blends of ethanol; and to support the research and development and

commercialization of Iowa's biochemical industry to displace petrochemicals

🌿 Green Business, Green Building, Green Jobs

Green Business: Iowa City Welcomes Moss Green Urban Village

Iowa City may soon be welcoming a number of eco-friendly businesses as it becomes home to what is being billed as the nation's first "macro green" business park. In June 2010, Eco-4 Partners and the Moss Green Development Corp. got the green light for a proposed 170-acre (69-ha) Moss Green Urban Village at the site of what was once the Moss Dairy Farm. The concept for the village is to create a district of office buildings, retail shops, restaurants, housing, and recreation areas, all built with sustainable design and construction practices, using the latest in energy efficiency technologies. Moss Green Development Corporation broke ground for the project in June 2011.

Another new organization committed to the development of green businesses is the Iowa Green Team, with a mission to provide a platform of services, programs, events, and partnership opportunities for the growth of the green economy. The team offers green coaching and consulting services in support of businesses and organizations that want to "grow green." They have also launched a Turn Iowa Green initiative to provide a more general forum for networking and the promotion and support of green businesses.

Iowa Power Fund

The state provides financial and technical assistance for companies involved in the development of clean energy technologies or production of related technologies through the Iowa Office of Energy Independence (OEI) and the Iowa Power Fund. From its inception in 2007, through December 2010, the legislature appropriated a total of $95 million for the fund. In 2011 the OEI completed a study that summarized the economic impact of funded projects through 2010 and offered estimates on the potential impact of ongoing and similar new projects through 2033. The results indicate that annual economic activity associated with ongoing project operations from 2007 through 2014 could reach $22.7 million. These projects are expected to provide at least two hundred jobs each year and state tax revenues of more than $859,000 annually.

From 2014 through 2033, funded projects could result in an economic output of more than $40.3 billion, with more than 8,400 jobs and state tax revenues of $475 million. In May 2011, the OEI listed forty-five Iowa Power Fund approved projects. Recipients include Hybrid Power Centers, LLC in Des Moines, which is at work on a project to develop a hybrid power plant that will combust both coal and biomass in a single integrated system, and the TPI Iowa in Newton, which is working on ways to foster the mass production of wind turbines through its Advanced Manufacturing Innovation Initiative. Fifteen approved projects involved the development of biofuels.

Green Building: Going for Gold-Level Certification

The state building code (IAC 661) that took effect on January 1, 2010, includes updated sections for energy efficiency and conservation. The International Energy Conservation Code (IECC) of 2009 was adopted by reference to provide the basic guidelines for residential and commercial building energy conservation. However, these standards may change within the next few years, depending on a review by the Commission on Energy Efficiency Standards and Practices. This commission was established by the legislature in 2008 (Iowa Code 103A.27) with the charge to evaluate and report on the current building energy efficiency standards and to recommend new and improved standards that would be applicable to all new residential, commercial, or industrial construction. The commission's final report in January 2011 encouraged the adoption of succeeding editions of the IECC, while also urging state officials to consider additional improvements in energy efficiency standards that go beyond the standard international code.

The Iowa Department of Public Safety has also developed a set of sustainable design standards that projects must meet to qualify for additional tax incentives. For example, commercial building construction projects can be certified as sustainably designed if they meet the criteria for gold-level certification under the U.S. Green Building Council Leadership in Energy and Environmental Design (LEED) rating system or its equivalent. The Iowa City Fire Station No. 2, completed in 2008, is an example of a LEED Gold demolition and reconstruction project.

The energy efficiency standards for state-owned and managed buildings have evolved over the years as early goals were met and new ones established. Under Executive Order 41 (2005), state agencies were required to reduce energy consumption by an average of 15 percent by 2010, relative to 2000 levels. In 2008, Executive Order 6, known as the Green Government Initiative, rescinded that measure and replaced it with a directive to reduce energy consumption by at least another 15 percent by 2015. The expected reduction applies to the use of electricity, natural gas, fuel oil, and water. The Green Government Initiative also created three supporting green building and energy efficiency task forces: the Energy Excellent Buildings Task Force, Sustainable Materials Task Force, and Biofuels Task Force.

In addition to efficient buildings, Iowa is a leader in energy efficiency programs sponsored by gas and electric utilities. These programs help customers adopt and use a wide range of energy-efficient technologies, from appliances and lighting to insulation, and save millions of kilowatt-hours of electricity or therms of gas every year.

Green Jobs: Introducing the Iowa Green Jobs Task Force

From about 1995 to 2007, Iowa's green economy focused primarily on recycling and waste management. The number of green jobs in clean energy and construction has increased, however, most likely as a result of statewide alternative energy and energy efficiency initiatives, along with several financial incentives for green business. Recognizing that a commitment to a clean energy future comes with the need for a skilled green industry workforce, the governor established the Iowa Green Jobs Task Force in 2009 (Executive Order 16). The task force is charged with finding ways to create new jobs and provide training for workers in the renewable energy industry. In January 2010, the state received a three-year, $5.9 million grant from the U.S. Department of Labor in support of these efforts.

Iowa Workforce Development (IWD) has followed suit by launching the Iowa's New Energy Economy website, designed to provide information on the local green economy for job seekers and employers alike. In Spring 2010, IWD published *Green Registered Apprenticeships* in Iowa, a brief report that introduces job seekers to the types of green trade jobs available throughout the state, along with projected wages and demand. The state's efforts have paid off, as shown by the Des Moines-West Des Moines area being named as one of the American cities with the fastest green jobs growth by Fox Business in 2011. The rate of green job growth was 11.4 percent per year, largely due to the efforts of Des Moines mayor T. M. Franklin Cownie.

Young adults can gain experience through two green job training programs associated with AmeriCorps. Green Iowa AmeriCorps provides opportunities within the field of energy efficiency and conservation, while Conservation Corps Iowa provides work and educational experiences through natural resource-based projects on public lands.

❧ Iowa's Water and Land Legacy

When Iowa voters went to the polls in November 2010, Question #1 was whether or not to approve a major constitutional amendment to protect the environment for generations to come.

Question #1 proposed an amendment to the state constitution to establish the Natural Resources and Outdoor Recreation Trust Fund within the state treasury as a permanent and protected funding source for the improvement and protection of the state's water and land resources. In the state legislature, the proposed amendment was formally known as the Natural Resources and Outdoor Recreation Act. The Conservation Campaign, which was leading the call for approval of the amendment, referred to it as Iowa's Water & Land Legacy Amendment.

The final voter-approval stage of the amendment came after about three years of research and campaigning among some of the state's most prominent conservation and environmental groups, with overwhelming support from state and local agencies and the state legislature. The proposed amendment was agreed on by both branches of the Iowa General Assembly in 2008. The accompanying joint resolutions placing the amendment in the hands of the voters were passed by both branches in 2009. The amendment passed in November 2010, after which the Natural Resources and Outdoor Recreation Trust Act was enrolled pursuant to Senate File 2310, which had been approved by the governor in April 2010. Under the new law, the Natural Resources and Outdoor Recreation Trust Fund is established as a permanent source for conservation funding, administered under guidelines that will be set by the legislature and subject to annual audits through a public oversight committee. Money for the fund will be obtained by the allocation of three-eighths of one cent from the sales tax revenues generated the next time that the state legislature raises the sales tax. In other words, the next time the state raises the sales tax by one cent, three-eighths of the revenues from the increase will be earmarked for the trust fund. The law itself will not result in a tax increase. It simply establishes a preexisting condition for future sales tax increases.

According to information provided by Iowa's Water & Land Legacy campaign, the law may eventually lead to an additional $150 million per year for much needed environmental protection and conservation efforts. Over 90 percent of the state's land is used for agriculture, which provides a solid foundation for Iowa's economy. The success of Iowa's farms is directly attributed to the state's rich soils. However, nearly five tons of soil per acre is lost each year due to erosion from wind and water. More than four hundred of the state's waterways are believed to be impaired, with about 53 percent of Iowa's waters rated as poor. Despite the importance of Iowa's natural resources, the state ranks at forty-seventh in the nation for per capita conservation spending. The Sustainable Natural Resources Recovery Committee from the Iowa Department of Agriculture has identified several categories for future funding, including natural resources management, agriculture and land stewardship, watershed protection, lake restoration, resource enhancement and protection (REAP), local conservation partnership programs, and trails.

While some voters may have been concerned about the potential increase in sales taxes and the reliability of

Waubonsie State Park, Iowa.　© *Charles L Bolin/ShutterStock.com*

administering bodies, support for the amendment came from all walks in Iowa, as the benefits of cleaner water, improved parks and wildlife areas, and a generally more stable and sustainable environment were available to all residents. In a poll taken about the time of the vote, Iowa's Water & Land Legacy campaign reported that 90 percent of Iowans considered protection of the state's land, water, and recreational opportunities as critical for the state's economy and 75 percent supported an increase in funding for conservation and protection.

BIBLIOGRAPHY

Books

Anderson, J.L. *Industrializing the Corn Belt*. DeKalb, IL: Northern Illinois University Press, 2009.

Faldet, David S. *The Upper Iowa River and Its People*. Iowa City: University of Iowa Press, 2009.

Winckler, Suzanne, and Michael Forsberg. *The Smithsonian Guides to Natural America: The Heartland—Nebraska, Iowa, Illinois, Missouri, Kansas*. Washington, DC: Smithsonian Books, 1996.

Web Sites

"American Cities with the Fastest Green Jobs Growth." Fox Business. July 15, 2011. Available from http://www.foxbusiness.com/markets/2011/07/15/american-cities-with-fastest-green-jobs-growth/

American Council for an Energy Efficient Economy. *The 2009 State Energy Efficiency Scorecard.* Available from http://www.aceee.org/pubs/e097.htm

Birding Iowa. *The Makoke Trail: A Guide to Birding in Central Iowa.* Available from http://www.iowa-birds.org/places/documents/Makoke_Trail.pdf

"Branstad Signs Bill to Boost E15 Sales and Biodiesel Production." Iowa Renewable Fuels Association. May 26, 2011. Available from http://www.iowarfa.org/pr052611.php

Climate Change Impacts on Iowa. Iowa Climate Change Impacts Committee. January 1, 2011. Available from http://www.water.iastate.edu/Documents/CompleteReport,%20final.pdf

Commission on Energy Efficiency Standards and Practices: Final Report. Iowa Commission on Energy Efficiency Standards and Practices. Available from http://www.dps.state.ia.us/fm/building/energy/PDF/commission_on_energy_efficiency_standards_and_practices_final_report.pdf

"Energy Conservation in Construction." Iowa Department of Public Safety. Available from http://www.dps.state.ia.us/fm/building/energy/index.shtml

"Ethanol Facts." Iowa Corn Promotion Board. Available from http://www.iowacorn.org/User/Docs/Iowa%20Ethanol%20talking%20points%20FINA_9-21-09_L.pdf

"Fishes of Iowa." Iowa Department of Natural Resources, Fish and Fishing. Available from http://www.iowadnr.gov/fish/iafish/iafish.html

Garden-Monheit, Hannah. "Iowa Receives $5.9 Million Grant for Green Jobs Training." *Iowa Senate Democrats.* January 20, 2010. Available from http://www.senate.iowa.gov/democrats/iowa-receives-5-9-million-grant-for-green-jobs-training

General Assembly of the State of Iowa. *Code of Iowa, Chapter 476. Public utility regulation alternate energy production facilities.* Available from http://www.newamerica.net/files/IA_RPS_Iowa_-Code_476.41.pdf

General Assembly of the State of Iowa. *House File 918 (2007): An Act Establishing the Office of Energy Independence and the Iowa Power Fund and Related Provisions.* Available from http://www.energy.iowa.gov/Legislation/docs/HouseFile918.pdf

General Assembly of the State of Iowa. *House File 2754: Establishment of Renewable Fuel Standards.* Available from http://search.legis.state.ia.us/NXT/gateway.dll?qt=&f=templates&xhitlist_q=ethnaol+promotion&fn=default.htm&xhitlist_d=current-legislation

General Assembly of the State of Iowa. *Senate File 485: An Act relating to Greenhouse Gas Emissions.* Available from http://www.iowadnr.gov/air/prof/ghg/files/SF485.pdf

General Assembly of the State of Iowa. *Senate File 2310: The Natural Resources and Outdoor Recreation Act.* Available from http://coolice.legis.state.ia.us/Cool-ICE/default.asp?Category=billinfo&Service=Billbook&menu=false&ga=83&hbill=SF2310

General Assembly of the State of Iowa. *Senate Joint Resolution 1: The Natural Resources and Outdoor Recreation Trust Fund.* Available from http://coolice.legis.state.ia.us/Cool-ICE/default.asp?Category=billinfo&Service=Billbook&menu=false&ga=83&hbill=SJR1

"Global Warming and Iowa." The National Wildlife Federation. Available from http://www.nwf.org/Global-Warming/~/media/PDFs/Global%20Warming/Global%20Warming%20State%20Fact%20Sheets/Iowa.ashx

Green Iowa Americorps. Available from http://green-iowaamericorps.com

IAC 103A.27: Commission on Energy Efficiency Standards and Practices. Iowa Administrative Code. Available from http://coolice.legis.state.ia.us/Cool-ICE/default.asp?category=billinfo&service=IowaCode&input=103A.27

"Information about Iowa's Wildlife." Iowa Department of Natural Resources, Wildlife. Available from http://www.iowadnr.gov/wildlife/files/wildinfo.html

"Iowa." U.S. Department of Agriculture, National Agricultural Statistics Service. Available from http://www.nass.usda.gov/Statistics_by_State/Iowa/index.asp

Iowa Climate Change Advisory Council. *Iowa Climate Change Advisory Council Final Report.* Available from http://www.iaclimatechange.us/capag.cfm

"Iowa Condition of the State Address 2003." The Pew Center on the States. Available from http://www.stateline.org/live/details/speech?contentId=16147

"Iowa Condition of the State Address 2008." The Pew Center on the States. Available from http://www.stateline.org/live/details/speech?contentId=272866

Iowa Department of Agriculture and Land Stewardship. Available from http://www.agriculture.state.ia.us

Iowa Department of Natural Resources. *Iowa's Forestry Resource Base.* Available from http://www.iowadnr.gov/education/backinfo/foresorc.pdf

Iowa Department of Public Safety. *Sustainable Design Standards*. Available from http://www.dps.state.ia.us/fm/building/sustainable/index.shtml

Iowa Office of Energy Independence. *2010 Energy Independence Plan*. Available from http://www.energy.iowa.gov/OEI/docs/2010WebEnergyIndependencePlan.pdf

"Iowa Pathways: Iowa Soils." Iowa Public Television. Available from http://www.iptv.org/iowapathways/mypath.cfm?ounid=ob_000144&h=no

"Iowa Power Fund Approved Projects." Iowa Office of Energy Independence. Available from http://www.energy.iowa.gov/files/RevisedPFApproved%20Projects071410.pdf

Iowa Power Fund Economic Impact Study. Iowa Office of Energy Independence. Available from http://www.state.ia.us/government/governor/energy/files/PowerFundFullEconomicImpactAnalysis121610.pdf

Iowa Utilities Board. *Wind-powered Electricity Generation in Iowa*. Available from http://www.state.ia.us/government/com/util/energy/wind_generation.html

Iowa Workforce Development. *Green Registered Apprenticeships in Iowa, Spring 2010*. Available from http://www.iowaworkforce.org/apprenticeship/GreenRegisteredApprenticeships.pdf

Iowa's New Energy Economy. Available from http://www.iowaworkforce.org/newenergy

"Iowa's State Forests." Iowa Department of Natural Resources. Available from http://www.iowadnr.gov/forestry/forests.html

Iowa's Water & Land Legacy. Available from http://www.iowaswaterandlandlegacy.org/ourland.aspx

Lake Red Rock. Available from http://www2.mvr.usace.army.mil/RedRock/default.cfm

"Listings and Occurrences for Iowa." Species Reports. U.S. Fish and Wildlife Service. Available from http://ecos.fws.gov/tess_public/pub/stateListingAndOccurrenceIndividual.jsp?state=IA&s8fid=112761032792&s8fid=112762573902&s8fid=24012960761772

"Minerals of Iowa." Iowa Geological & Water Survey. Available from http://www.igsb.uiowa.edu/browse/minerals/minerals.htm

Moss Green Urban Village. Available from http://www.eco-4.net/moss-green-urban-village

National Waterways Conference. *Iowa Waterway Facts*. Available from http://lsgreview.com/documents/nationalwate/StateFactSheet-iowa2.pdf

Prairie Resource Center. Iowa Department of Natural Resources. Available from http://www.iowadnr.gov/wildlife/files/seedharvest.html

Senate File 531: An Act Relating to Motor Fuels. Iowa General Assembly. Available from http://coolice.legis.state.ia.us/Cool-ICE/default.asp?Category=billinfo&Service=Billbook&menu=false&hbill=SF531

Soil Conservation Division, Iowa Department of Agriculture and Land Stewardship. Available from http://www.agriculture.state.ia.us/soilConservation.asp

"State Energy Profiles: Iowa." United States Energy Information Administration. Available from http://tonto.eia.doe.gov/state/state_energy_profiles.cfm?sid=IA

State of Iowa Building Code: Chapter 16. Iowa Administrative Code. Available from http://www.legis.state.ia.us/Rules/Current/iac/661iac/66116/66116.pdf

State of Iowa, Executive Department. *Executive Order Number Three (2007)*. Available from http://publications.iowa.gov/5190/1/03-070621.pdf

State of Iowa, Executive Department. *Executive Order Number Six (2008): Green Government*. Available from http://www.energy.iowa.gov/green_govt/docs/ExecutiveOrder6-GreenGov'tInitiative.pdf

State of Iowa, Executive Department. *Executive Order Number Sixteen (2009): Green Jobs Task Force*. Available from http://www.governor.iowa.gov/files/Executive_Order_No16.pdf

State of Iowa, Executive Department. *Executive Order Number Forty-One (2005)*. Available from http://publications.iowa.gov/2619/1/EO_41.pdf

Turn Iowa Green. Available from http://turniowagreen.com

2011 Energy Independence Plan. Iowa Office of Energy Independence. Available from http://www.state.ia.us/government/governor/energy/files/2011EnergyIndpPlanLowResFINAL121410.pdf

Waddington, Lynda. "Iowa CAFO cited in EPA compliance orders." **Iowa Independent**. August 22, 2011. Available from http://iowaindependent.com/60435/iowa-cafo-cited-in-epa-compliance-orders

Waterways Council, Inc. *Iowa State Profile*. Available from http://www.waterwayscouncil.org/WWSystem/State%20Profiles/Iowa.pdf

Kansas

Known as both the "Sunflower State" and the "Wheat State," Kansas is one of the most productive agricultural states in the United States. It leads the nation in wheat and sorghum production, and ranks behind the Dakotas in the production of sunflowers and sunflower seed and oil products. Located in the western northcentral United States, Kansas is the second-largest Midwestern state (after Minnesota) and ranks thirteenth in size among the fifty states.

Climate

Kansas's continental climate is highly changeable. The average mean temperature is 55°F (13°C). Normal annual precipitation ranges from slightly more than 40 in (102 cm) in the southeast to as little as 16 in (41 cm) in the west. Overall annual precipitation for the state averages 27 in (69 cm), although years of drought have not been uncommon. About 70 to 77 percent of the precipitation falls between April and September. The annual mean snowfall ranges from about 36 in (91 cm) in the extreme northwest to less than 11 in (28 cm) in the far southeast. Tornadoes are common Kansas. Dodge City is said to be the windiest city in the United States, with an average wind speed of 14 mph (23 km/h).

According to the National Wildlife Federation, warming temperatures in Kansas due to climate change could have detrimental effects on the state's winter wheat crops. If global warming continues unabated, farmers in the state may have to shift to different crops, which would impact the state's most vital industry. Climate change could also result in the drying of Kansas's wetlands, which would prove detrimental to the many migratory bird species and waterfowl that depend upon them. The breeding range of the state's songbird species could also shift out of the state due to the effects that climate change would have on habitats and food sources.

In response to concerns about global climate change then-Governor Kathleen Sebelius issued Executive Order No. 08-03 on March 21, 2008, which established the Kansas Energy and Environmental Planning Advisory Group (KEEP). From 2008 to 2009, this group worked to identify how Kansas should respond to the challenge of global climate change. They developed and recommended short-, medium-, and long-term goals for statewide reductions of greenhouse gas emissions. At the state's request, the Center for Climate Strategies prepared a report, "DRAFT Kansas Greenhouse Gas Inventory and Reference Case Projections 1990–2025," which was designed to provide information that KEEP and others could use in developing policy. Along with these goals, KEEP analyzed climate mitigation policies in all economic sectors in Kansas through 2025 in order to meet greenhouse gas reduction goals.

In 2010, Republican Sam Brownback was elected governor. In his first "State of the State" address in January 2011, Governor Brownback pledged his support for renewable energy development, but did not mention his goals for the state in reducing greenhouse gases.

❧ Natural Resources, Water, and Agriculture

Natural Resources

Native grasses cover one-third of Kansas. Bluestem—both big and little—has the greatest forage value. Other native grasses include buffalo grass, blue and hairy gramas, and alkali sacaton. The state flower is the wild sunflower, which is found throughout the state. Other wildflowers include wild daisy, ivy-leaved morning glory, and smallflower verbena. The western prairie fringed orchid and Mead's milkweed were listed as threatened, and the running buffalo clover was listed as endangered by the U.S. Fish and Wildlife Service in 2011.

While trees were rare in Kansas at the time of European settlement, today the state has more than 2.2 million acres (890,000 ha) of natural and planted forestland, most of which is found in the eastern part of the state. The cottonwood is the most common tree, and is also the state tree. One native conifer, eastern red cedar, is found generally throughout the state. Although this species is native, it is very invasive and is considered to be a problem species in many areas. Other common trees include hackberry, green ash, black walnut, and bur oak. Black walnut is the most commercially valuable tree in the state. There are no native pines. Private individuals own 95 percent of the state's forestland, while 5 percent is publicly owned. One million additional acres (400,000 ha) of forestland are planted and maintained by Kansas's communities.

Kansas has over 50 sawmills and timber buyers that harvest over 3.3 million cubic feet from Kansas forests annually. The forest industry employs more than 6,700 people, and forest products contribute $1.3 billion annually to the state economy.

Kansas's only big game animal is the white-tailed deer. Other popular game animals include Mule deer and Pronghorn Antelope. In addition, the Kansas Department of Wildlife, Parks, and Tourism lists limited elk hunting in Kansas. Other native mammals include the common cottontail, black-tailed jackrabbit, black-tailed prairie dog, muskrat, opossum, and raccoon. The state bird is the western meadowlark, and Kansas has the largest flock of prairie chickens remaining in North America. The U.S. Fish and Wildlife Service named 12 animal species as threatened or endangered in 2011. Among these are the gray bat, American burying beetle, Topeka shiner, and black-footed ferret. Efforts in the 1990s and early 2000s brought back the black-footed ferret population from about 50 individuals to 650 individuals in 2007. Programs to reintroduce black-footed ferrets to the wild aim to have a base of 240 individuals for captive breeding while reintroducing their offspring. There were an estimated 1,500 individuals in the wild in 2011, and while the population will likely never be as prevalent as it has been in the past, reintroduction programs should keep the population from continuing to decline.

Minerals

According to the U.S. Geological Survey, Kansas's raw nonfuel mineral production was valued at $1.1 billion in 2010. Kansas is the nation's leading producer of Grade-A helium and crude helium (both extracted from natural gas). It is one of only two states that produce crude helium. Other minerals produced in the state include salt, portland cement, crushed stone, crude gypsum, and common clays.

Water

More than 10,000 miles (16,100 km) of streams and rivers run through Kansas, and there are hundreds of artificial lakes and reservoirs. One of the state's naturally occurring lakes, of which there are few, is Lake Inman. Most of Kansas's large reservoirs were built in the 1960s for flood control, water supply, and recreation. The reservoirs provide sport fishermen with crappie, white bass, varieties of catfish, largemouth bass, walleye, striped bass, and wipers. Major rivers include the Missouri, which defines the state's northeastern boundary; the Arkansas, which runs through Wichita; and the Kansas (Kaw), which runs through Topeka and joins the Missouri at Kansas City.

One of the state's two natural bodies of water, Cheyenne Bottoms, is a Ramsar Wetland of International Importance. This wetland is not only a habitat for the endangered whooping crane, but is also an important site for over 800,000 migratory birds each year. Located in the southcentral portion of the state, the salt marshes of the Quivira National Wildlife Refuge (also a Ramsar site) serve as a nesting, migration, and winter habitat for over 320 bird species.

Agriculture

Kansas is home to some 65,500 farms on 46.2 million acres (18.7 million ha) of land. The state's top crops were wheat, corn, forage, sorghum, and soybeans. Kansas was ranked first in the nation for wheat and sorghum acreage, with 8.5 million acres (3.4 million ha) and 2.6 million acres (1.1 million ha), respectively. The state also ranked second in the nation for cattle and calves (6.7 million) and ninth in the nation for hogs and pigs (1.9 million). Kansas is also one of the top producers of sunflowers and sunflower products in the nation, behind only the Dakotas.

The United States Department of Agriculture (USDA) has launched the Ogallala Aquifer Initiative, which provides research funding for projects that aim to improve agricultural sustainability. Research could focus on irrigation systems and technologies, irrigation management, and economic assessments and impacts. The federal agency supports research projects in any of the eight aquifer states, and Kansas has secured several of these projects. For example, irrigation research in southwest Kansas indicated that cotton crops were more productive using drip irrigation; the top soil tended to be warmer with drip irrigation compared to traditional seasonal irrigation techniques. Another study from Tribune, Kansas found that improved management of irrigation practices increases crop yield. In particular, pre-season irrigation, used to make up for decreased availability of water during the regular planting season, helped to increase grain yields of 20–30 bushels per acre (8–12 bushels per ha) which increased profitability by $50–100 per acre ($200–400 per ha). Researchers concluded that with declining well capacities,

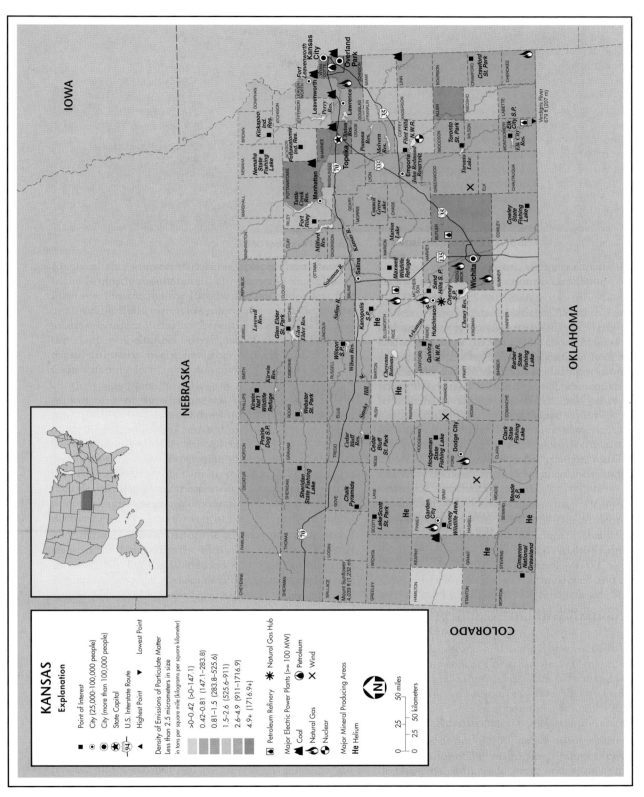

pre-season irrigation may be necessary for optimum crop production.

According to the U.S. Department of Agriculture, Kansas had 83 USDA-certified organic operations in 2008. These operations covered more than 51,000 acres (20,600 ha) of land. The state had over 1,700 organic heads of cows and pigs, and small numbers of organic poultry. By far, the organic crop that had the most acreage in the state was for organic grains, which covered more than 26,000 acres (10,500 ha). These crops include corn, wheat, oats, barley, and sorghum. Kansas also had more than 9,000 acres (3,600 ha) of organic fallow, 7,000 acres (2,800 ha) of organic hay and silage, and more than 2,600 acres (1,050 ha) of organic beans. The state also produced organic fruits, vegetables, and potatoes. There were also 771 acres (312 ha) of certified organic sunflower crops.

❧ Energy

Kansas has considerable fossil fuel reserves, mostly in the southern part of the state. The Hugoton Gas Area is the fifth-largest natural gas field in the United States. Kansas consumes the majority of its natural gas output and transports most of the remainder to neighboring states. There are also has untapped reserves of coalbed methane in the southeast. Natural gas production from this unconventional resource is rapidly expanding. About three-fourths of Kansas households use natural gas as their primary energy source for home heating.

The state's southeastern corner is home to minor reserves of bituminous coal, however the majority of the coal used in Kansas's power plants is shipped by railcar from other states. Coal-fired power plants supply about 75 percent of the state's electricity, and the Wolf Creek nuclear plant in Burlington supplies the remainder.

Concerns were raised about the Wolf Creek nuclear power plant in May 2011. With the Fukushima disaster in Japan in March, followed by the tornado in nearby Joplin, Missouri, in May, inspections to the Wolf Creek plant found that some emergency equipment and storage sites may not survive a tornado. Vehicles and equipment needed to fight fires, retrieve fuel for emergency generators, and resupply water to keep nuclear fuel cool were found not to be secure. Tornadoes in Alabama and Virginia had already knocked out power and exposed vulnerabilities to nuclear plants in those states. What these instances have revealed is that while safety systems at the plants are designed to withstand tornadoes and other natural disasters, the related plant emergency equipment is not necessarily secure. Wolf Creek Nuclear Operating Corporation immediately began to take the necessary steps to correct these issues.

Kansas State Profile

Physical Characteristics

Land area	81,762 square miles (211,763 sq km)
Inland water area	516 square miles (1,336 sq km)
Coastal area	NA
Highest point	Mount Sunflower 4,039 feet (1,231 m)
National Forest System lands (2010)	108,000 acres (44,000 ha)
State parks (2011)	24

Energy Statistics

Total energy production (2009)	840 trillion Btu
State ranking in total energy production (2009)	23
Renewable energy net generation total (2009)	2.9 million megawatt hours
Hydroelectric energy generation (2009)	13,000 megawatt hours
Biomass energy generation (2009)	NA
Wind energy generation (2009)	2.9 million megawatt hours
Wood and derived fuel energy generation (2009)	NA
Crude oil reserves (2009)	259 million barrels (41.2 million cu m)
Natural gas reserves (2009)	3,279 billion cubic feet (92.9 billion cu m)
Natural gas liquids (2008)	162 million barrels (25.8 million cu m)

Pollution Statistics

Carbon output (2005)	79.9 million tons of CO_2 (72.5 million t)
Superfund sites (2008)	11
Particulate matter (less than 2.5 micrometers) emissions (2002)	11,000 tons per year (9,979 t/yr)
Toxic chemical releases (2009)	21.1 million pounds (9.6 million kg)
Generated hazardous waste (2009)	222,800 tons (202,200 t)

SOURCES: AirData. U.S. Environmental Protection Agency. Available from http://www.epa.gov/air/data; *Energy Maps, Facts, and Data of the U.S. States.* U.S. Energy Information Administration. Available from http://www.eia.gov/state; *The 2012 Statistical Abstract.* U.S. Census Bureau. Available from http://www.census.gov/compendia/statab; *United States Energy Usage.* eRedux. Available from http://www.eredux.net/states.

© 2011 Cengage Learning.

In addition to fossil fuel resources, the state's flat plains offer some of the highest wind power potential in the country, ranking it one of the top ten wind-producing states in the nation. As of 2007, the state had 364 megawatts of installed wind capacity. The state's cornfields also offer a major feedstock for ethanol production. The state's 13 ethanol-producing plants supply the United States with more than 130 million gallons (492 million l) of ethanol annually. However, total renewable energy production contributes only minimally to Kansas's electricity supply, providing less than 3 percent of the state's total electricity production.

Renewable Portfolio Standard

In May 2009, Kansas adopted a renewable portfolio standard that requires utilities to acquire one-tenth of their energy from renewable sources by 2011 and one-fifth by 2020. The required generation capacity can be produced by wind, solar thermal, photovoltaics, dedicated crops grown for energy production, methane from landfills or wastewater treatment, clean and untreated wood products such as pallets, hydropower, or fuel cells using hydrogen produced by an eligible renewable resource.

❧ Green Business, Green Building, Green Jobs

Green Business and Green Jobs

In 2009, then-Governor Kathleen Sebelius signed legislation to modify the Kansas Economic Revitalization and Reinvestment Act in order to draw new renewable energy jobs and businesses to the state. Senate Bill 108 revises the act to provide economic incentives to eligible wind or solar energy projects. Eligible projects relate to the research, development, engineering, or manufacturing of a product for either of those industries. Projects must employ a minimum of 200 full-time employees within five years, which should significantly improve the green economy within the state.

According to the Kansas Department of Labor's *2009 Kansas Green Jobs Report*, Kansas had over 46,000 green jobs that year. Over half of these jobs were in energy efficiency. The rest were concentrated in agriculture and natural resource conservation, pollution prevention and environmental cleanup, and producing renewable energy. The industries with the largest numbers of green jobs were specialty trade contractors, building construction, administrative and support services, and professional, scientific, and technical services. Together, these industries accounted for more than half of Kansas's green jobs. According to the Pew Charitable Trusts, Kansas was home to 591 clean energy businesses in 2007. They also predict that the clean energy economy will grow 51 percent from 2007 to 2017, one of the fastest rates in the country.

Cloud County Community College in Concordia is the only college in Kansas that is approved to offer an Associate of Applied Science degree in Wind Energy Technology. The college also offers a basic certificate in Wind Energy Technology, as well. Graduates of the program will be qualified to work for a modern commercial wind farm operation or pursue a career related to the production and utilization of wind energy. Wichita State University's College of Engineering is also performing wind energy research projects, and Kansas State University's Wind Application Center works to educate engineers and hosts a number of wind energy-related projects.

Green Building

In 2007, the Kansas State Legislature established the 2006 International Energy Conservation Code (IECC) as the state's commercial building code. The Kansas Corporation Commission (KCC) is responsible for providing commercial and residential energy code training and educational seminars. An energy efficiency disclosure by the builder or seller of new residential buildings to the buyer is required according to these standards.

The state also offers a number of incentives and rebates for commercial and residential buildings that make the effort to become more energy efficient. The Kansas City Board of Public Utilities offers Commercial, Residential, and Homebuilder Energy Efficiency Rebate Programs. Rebates for the commercial program are available for qualifying air-source, water-source, and ground-source heat pumps; package terminal heat pumps; resistance heating systems; electric boilers; and electric water heaters.

Perhaps one of Kansas's best examples of green building is the city of Greensburg. In 2007, the city was leveled by a 2 mile-wide (3.2 km) EF5 tornado. Shortly after, the town began making plans to rebuild as a green town. The town's municipal building boasts the latest in window, HVAC, and other energy-saving technologies and is the first municipal LEED Platinum building in the United States. The town is also home to a wind farm that opened in 2009, and the county seat now has the world's highest per capita concentration of geothermal wells. The wind farm generates enough power for 4,000 homes, and since the town has a population of only 1,400, it sells the excess power. The town has also become a center for environmental awareness and green energy education. Over 1,000 ecotourists have visited the town since it began its green initiatives. The town's "Chain of Eco-Homes" project will consist of 12 model homes that will serve as living laboratories to teach visitors about sustainable building techniques, energy-efficient features, and green products. Other green programs in the town include the high school's Green Club, a farmer's market, and the Reclaimed Lumber Project that re-uses wood salvaged from trees felled by tornadoes.

❧ Irrigating Kansas's Farms: The Depleting Ogalla Aquifer

Western Kansas sits on part of an underground water stock that is almost equal to two of the Great Lakes. The Ogallala aquifer, also called the High Plains aquifer, underlies 174,000 square miles (451,000 sq km) of eight

According to the National Wildlife Federation, warming temperatures in Kansas due to climate change could have detrimental effects on the state's winter wheat crops.
© iStockPhoto.com/TriggerPhoto

states: Kansas, South Dakota, Wyoming, Nebraska, Colorado, Oklahoma, New Mexico, and Texas. As the most abundant water source in this region, the agricultural industry relies on it as a source for irrigating crops. However, the aquifer is not an infinite water source, and people are using more of its supply of groundwater than it can replenish. Aquifers renew very slowly, and can take anywhere from decades to millennia to restock themselves. Not only are irrigation and consumption depleting the aquifer, but overuse has depressed water tables, degraded ecosystems, deteriorated the quality of the groundwater, and caused conflicts among those that use the aquifer.

Researchers and government officials are searching for ways to improve the management of the aquifer. For example, researchers from the Kansas Geological Survey and Michigan State University are working together to examine the interactions between the aquifer and the region's landscape, atmosphere, and socioeconomic conditions. Using this information, they will be able to predict the potential effects of adjustments in land management policies and the establishment more sustainable water-use practices.

In addition to research efforts, there are also important changes in the way the aquifer is managed. The Kansas Department of Agriculture is actively promoting efforts to manage groundwater more sustainably. Part of this effort involves collecting more information on water levels in the aquifer. In 2004, the Department of Agriculture's Basin Management Team added nearly 100 wells to the monitoring network in northwest Kansas. This investment provides a clearer picture of the state of the aquifer and allows for more informed aquifer management. Currently, there are 156 wells that are measured annually, with additional measurements collected tri-annually. The Department of Agriculture also offers voluntary incentive programs to help sustain groundwater. For example, the Water Transition Assistance Program, is designed to help restore aquifers and streams in critical areas. Three areas that have been approved for the program include Rattlesnake Creek Subbasin, Prairie Dog Creek Basin, and Groundwater Management District #4 High Priority Areas. This five year pilot program requires the participant to permanently dismiss or significantly reduce their irrigation rights to decrease consumptive groundwater use. Landowners that give up their irrigation rights are compensated based on a number of factors outlined in the program's rules and regulations. The land that will no longer be irrigated must be transitioned to dry land, which will be planted with permanent vegetation. Limited irrigation is permitted for up to three years after rights are given up, in order for vegetation to be established.

In July 2011, an economic summit on the future of the aquifer was held in Colby. The summit, hosted by Governor Sam Brownback, focused on how to extend the life of the aquifer. The state's water requirements were targeted, as they are now considered outdated and can prompt farmers to irrigate unnecessarily. Ideas developed at the meeting could be presented at the state's 2012 Legislature. As both the state and federal government work on programs and strategies to maintain the Ogallala aquifer, all parties agree that more research is necessary to inform decision making. More information is needed to better understand the aquifer, its recharge rate, and the long term impacts of current and alternative water use patterns.

BIBLIOGRAPHY

Books

Blakeslee, Donald J. *Holy Ground, Healing Water: Cultural Landscapes at Waconda Lake, Kansas.* College Station, TX: TAMU Press, 2010.

Buchanan, Rex. *Kansas Geology: An Introduction to Landscapes, Rocks, Minerals, and Fossils.* 2nd ed. Lawrence: University Press of Kansas. 2010.

Gress, Bob. *Faces of the Great Plains: Prairie Wildlife.* Lawrence, KS: University Press of Kansas, 2003.

Miner, Craig. *Kansas: The History of the Sunflower States, 1854–2000.* Lawrence, KS: University Press of Kansas, 2002.

Miner, Craig. *Next Year Country: Dust to Dust in Western Kansas. 1890–1940.* Lawrence, KS: University Press of Kansas, 2006.

Montrie, Chad. *Making a Living: Work and Environment in the United States.* Chapel Hill, NC: University of North Carolina Press, 2008.

Shortridge, James R. *Cities on the Plains: The Evolution of Urban Kansas.* Lawrence, KS: University Press of Kansas, 2004.

Winckler, Suzanne, and Michael Forsberg. *The Smithsonian Guides to Natural America: The Heartland–Nebraska, Iowa, Illinois, Missouri, Kansas.* Washington, DC: Smithsonian Books, 1996.

Web Sites

"About Kansas Fishing." Kansas Department of Wildlife and Parks. Available from http://www.kdwp.state.ks.us/news/Fishing/About-Kansas-Fishing

Brownback, Governor Sam. "2011 State of the State Address." Available from https://governor.ks.gov/media-room/speeches/2011/01/12/2011-State-of-the-State-Message

Cappiello, Dina and Matthew Daly. "Wolf Creek Nuclear Plant in 'Tornado Alley' Not Fully Twister-Proof." The Huffington Post. May 26, 2011. Available from http://www.huffingtonpost.com/2011/05/27/wolf-creek-nuclear-plant-tornado-twister_n_867987.html

Center for Climate Strategies. "Draft Kansas Greenhouse Gas Inventory and Reference Case Projections 1990–2025." May 2008. Available from http://www.ksclimatechange.us/ewebeditpro/items/O1F17410.pdf

"Cheyenne Bottoms Wildlife Area." Great Bend Convention and Visitors Bureau. Available from http://visitgreatbend.com/Cheyenne_Bottoms.asp

"The Clean Energy Economy: Kansas." The Pew Charitable Trusts. Available from http://www.pewcenteronthestates.org/uploadedFiles/wwwpewcenteronthestatesorg/Fact_Sheets/Clean_Economy_Factsheet_Kansas.pdf

"Data Sets: Organic Production." Economic Research Service. U.S. Department of Agriculture. Available from http://www.ers.usda.gov/Data/Organic/

"Energy Efficiency Programs." Kansas City Board of Public Utilities. Available from http://www.bpu.com/customer_service/commercialOverview.jsp

Gleeson, Tom, et al. "Groundwater sustainability strategies." *Nature Geoscience*, no. 3(2010):378–379. Available from http://www.kgs.ku.edu/General/Personnel/rs/mas/2010/Gleeson_Nature_Geoscience_Groundwater_sustainability.pdf

"Global Warming and Kansas." National Wildlife Federation. Available from http://www.nwf.org/~/media/PDFs/Global%20Warming/Global%20Warming%20State%20Fact%20Sheets/Kansas.ashx

Greensburg GreenTown. Available from http://www.greensburggreentown.org/

"Kansas." *2007 Minerals Yearbook.* U.S. Geological Survey. Available from http://minerals.usgs.gov/minerals/pubs/state/2007/myb2-2007-ks.pdf

"Kansas." U.S. Energy Information Administration. Accessed from http://www.eia.doe.gov/state/state_energy_profiles.cfm?sid=KS

Kansas Association of Ethanol Processors. Available from http://www.ethanolkansas.com/

"Kansas Energy and Environmental Policy Advisory Group (KEEP)." Kansas Climate Change Advisory Group. Available from http://www.ksclimate-change.us/index.cfm

Kansas Energy Plan 2008. Kansas Energy Council. Available from http://kec.kansas.gov/energy_plan/energy_plan_08.pdf

Kansas Forest Resource Assessment and Strategy. Kansas Forest Service. June 2010. Available from http://www.kansasforests.org/Kansas_FRAS.pdf

Kansas Forest Service. Available from http://www.kansasforests.org/

"Kansas Governor Signs Bill to Attract Renewable Energy Jobs." Kansas News. U.S. Department of Energy. April 7, 2009. Available from http://apps1.eere.energy.gov/states/state_news_detail.cfm/news_id=12445/state=KS

"Kansas studies dwindling Ogallala Aquifer." *The Kansas City Star.* July 24, 2011. Available from http://www.kansascity.com/2011/07/24/3034387/kansas-studies-dwindling-ogallala.html

Kansas Sunflower Commission. Available from http://www.kssunflower.com/

"Kansas: 2009 State Agricultural Overview." U.S. Department of Agriculture. Available from http://www.nass.usda.gov/Statistics_by_State/Ag_Overview/AgOverview_KS.pdf

Kansas Wind Applications Center. Available from http://www.ece.ksu.edu/psg/wac/

"Listings and occurrences for Kansas." Species Reports. U.S. Fish and Wildlife Service. Available from http://ecos.fws.gov/tess_public/pub/

stateListingAndOccurrenceIndividual.jsp?state=KS&
s8fid=112761032792&s8fid=112762573902&s
8fid=24012936441342

Lyons, Larry. "The amazing return of the black footed
ferret." *Niles Daily Star.* February 15, 2011.
Available from http://www.nilesstar.com/2011/
02/15/larry-lyons-the-amazing-return-of-the-
black-footed-ferret/

National Sunflower Association. Available from http://
www.sunflowernsa.com/default.asp

Ogallala Aquifer. Agricultural Research Service. U.S.
Department of Agriculture. Available from http://
www.ogallala.ars.usda.gov/

"The Ogallala Aquifer." High Plains Underground Water
Conservation District No. 1. Available from http://
www.hpwd.com/the_ogallala.asp

"Ogallala-High Plains Aquifer." Basin Management
Team. Kansas Department of Agriculture. Available
from http://www.ksda.gov/subbasin/content/204

"Ogallala-High Plains Aquifer Information." Kansas
Geological Survey. The University of Kansas. Avail-
able from http://www.kgs.ku.edu/HighPlains/
OHP/index.shtml

*Ogallala-High Plains Fringe Area 2009 Field Analysis
Summary.* Basin Management Team. Kansas
Department of Agriculture. Available from http://

www.ksda.gov/includes/document_center/
subbasin/Ogallala/Ogallala_2009_Field_
Summary.pdf

"Research keys on Ogallala Aquifer." *Omaha World-
Herald.* October 25, 2010. Available from http://
www.omaha.com/article/20101025/NEWS01/
710259931

"Rules and Regulations of the Water Right Transition
Assistance Pilot Project Program." State Conservation Commission of Kansas. Available from http://
scc.ks.gov/sccdocs/waterConservation/wtap/
WTAPRegs.pdf

State Conservation Commission of Kansas. Available
from http://scc.ks.gov/

"Sustainable Energy Solutions." Wichita State University.
Available from http://webs.wichita.edu/?u=sus-
tainability&p=

2009 Kansas Green Jobs Report. Kansas Department
of Labor. Available from http://www.dol.ks.gov/
LMIS/GoingGreen/KansasGreenJobs
Report.pdf

"Voluntary Incentive Programs." Basin Management
Team. Kansas Department of Agriculture. Available
from http://www.ksda.gov/subbasin/content/316

"Wind Energy Technology." Cloud County Community
College. Available from http://www.cloud.edu/
academics/wind/

Kentucky

Kentucky faces a quandary. As the federal government debates the merits of energy bills designed to reduce greenhouse gas emissions and wean the nation from its dependency on fossil fuels, the state of Kentucky faces a particular challenge. Kentucky's coal industry is the foundation of the state's economy. The state ranks third in the nation for the production of coal and relies on coal heavily for instate production of electricity. Yet, the state government recognizes the increasing need to develop cleaner, efficient, and more sustainable sources of energy. The Kentucky legislature and various state agencies are currently considering new strategies and incentives for the development of a climate action plan and renewable energy and energy efficiency standards that will reach statewide energy and environmental goals, while maintaining the integrity of the coal industry.

Climate: The Kentucky Climate Action Plan Council

Kentucky has a temperate climate with cold winters and warm, humid summers. Rainfall is heaviest in the month of July, but generally adequate throughout the spring and summer months. Winter snow can vary considerably, but is generally moderate.

With a strong reliance on fossil fuels for electricity, the state has one of the largest carbon footprints of any state in the nation. According to a survey from the U.S. Energy Information Administration, in 2009 Kentucky ranked seventh in the nation for carbon dioxide emissions from the electric power industry. According to the *Final Kentucky Greenhouse Gas Inventory and Reference Case Projections 1990–2030*, published by the Center for Climate Strategies (CCS) in June 2010, greenhouse gas (GHG) emissions in Kentucky increased by 33 percent from 1990 to 2005. If no actions are taken, emissions could rise to 62 percent above 1990 levels by 2030.

While some debate the extent to which GHG emissions affect global warming, reports indicate that climate change could pose a serious threat for the state and the region. According to the National Wildlife Federation, average temperatures within the state could rise as much as 6.75°F (3.75°C) by 2100. Such an increase in temperatures, along with a potential increase in the severity of both floods and droughts, could lead to a decline in the state's timber industry and a loss of wildlife, the latter of which could lead further to a loss of hunting, fishing, and tourist dollars.

The state is already committed to taking action toward the reduction of GHG emissions, primarily through the development of energy efficiency and alternative energy industries. In support of such development, the governor published the state's first comprehensive energy plan, *Intelligent Energy Choices for Kentucky's Future*, in 2008. The plan calls for a reduction of GHG emissions by 20 percent of 1990 levels by 2025.

In recognition of the relationship between environmental protection, energy, and economic development, Governor Steven Beshear created the Kentucky Energy and Environment Cabinet (EEC) in June 2009. Three departments within the EEC—the Department for Environmental Protection, the Department for Natural Resources, and the Department for Energy Development and Independence—have banded together to form the Kentucky Climate Action Plan Council. As of 2011, the council was still in the process of creating a statewide action plan to address the challenges of global climate change and recommend short- and long-term strategies to achieve the statewide GHG reduction goals. The Center for Climate Strategies (CCS), a nonprofit research organization, was called in to assist the council in these efforts.

However, at the same time, the state legislature has been considering a joint resolution that would declare Kentucky a "sanctuary state" for the coal industry, thereby exempting the coal industry from adherence to federal regulations under the Clean Air Act and the

Clean Water Act. Senate Joint Resolution 99 (11RS) states that the regulatory actions of the U.S. EPA are in violation of the Kentucky constitution, which protects the pursuit of safety and happiness and the protection of property. It also claims that the EPA is in violation of the Ninth Amendment of the U.S. Constitution, since federal regulation of the Kentucky coal industry could lead to economic devastation for many citizens and "the right to be free from imperial power by the federal government over the states that deprives the citizens of economic security and wellbeing is fundamental and understood by all citizens of the United States." The resolution would specifically exempt coal mining and processing activities from all federal regulations. This resolution was sent to the Committee for Natural Resources and Environment in March 2011.

🍁 Natural Resources, Water, and Agriculture

Natural Resources: Hardwoods and Bluegrass

About 47 percent of the state is forested, with the most heavily forested areas found in the Cumberland Plateau and the Appalachian mountains. Hardwood forests of oak (red and white) and hickory predominate, accounting for about 72 percent of the forestland. Walnut, maple, cherry, and yellow poplar (tulip poplar) are also found in the hardwood forests. There are significant areas of pine forest, with common species including Virginia, pitch, loblolly, and eastern white pine.

About 97 percent of the state's forestland is considered available for timber production. Kentucky ranks second in the nation for the production of hardwood and the state's wood industries generate more than $4.5 billion in revenue each year.

Pastures of the famous Kentucky bluegrass are found throughout the state, but are most notable in the north-central area known as the Bluegrass Region. In this region, known for its horses and cattle, fields of Kentucky bluegrass are generally used as forage. Several turf-type varieties of Kentucky bluegrass are widely used for lawns and sports fields, particularly in the northeastern and north-central states.

There are fifty-two state parks, two national parks, and one national recreation area in the state. Hunting is fairly popular throughout the state, with a number of common wildlife species considered to be game animals. Deer, elk, wild turkey, bobcat, beaver, wood duck, Canada goose, and squirrel are hunted in season. There are also occasional black bear hunting seasons. Coyote, groundhog, and wild hog can be trapped year-round. The venomous copperhead, western cottonmouth, timber rattlesnake, and western pigmy rattlesnake are all found in Kentucky. Among the state's protected species

are the gray bat, Virginia big-eared bat, bald eagle, and the red-cockaded woodpecker. The U.S. Fish and Wildlife Service lists thirty-six animal and eight plant species in the state as federally threatened or endangered, including the Cumberlanddarter, Kentucky cave shrimp, and four types of pearlymussel.

Kentucky is a leading state in the production of lime and primary aluminum, ranking third in the nation for total production of both in 2007. Kentucky produces significant amounts of crushed stone, which accounts for nearly 53 percent of the state's nonfuel raw mineral production value. Other mineral resources produced in the state include portland cement, common clays, and construction sand and gravel. The state was ranked twenty-seventh overall for nonfuel mineral production in 2010 witha value of $742 million.

Water: Ports and Caves

The Ohio and Mississippi rivers that border the state have always served as important transportation routes. Other important rivers, including the Kentucky, Cumberland, Tennessee, Big Sandy, Green, Licking, and Tradewater, are all tributaries of the Ohio. Kentucky's inland waterways provide links to the Great Lakes and the Gulf of Mexico, with goods transported to markets in Canada, Mexico, and South America. The state is home to seven active operating public river ports, with five more under development. The Port of Louisville along the Ohio River is one of the largest inland ports in the nation. The largest lakes in Kentucky are artificial. Lake Cumberland is the largest of these entirely within the state. Kentucky Lake (shared with the state of Tennessee) was created by the 8,422-foot (2,567-m) long TVA Kentucky Dam and is the largest reservoir in the eastern United States. Others include Lake Barkley and Dale Hollow Lake. All of these are popular recreational areas. The largest natural lake is Swan Lake.

Water drainage through porous limestone rock has created a number of underground caves and passages throughout the central portion of the state, the best known of which is Mammoth Cave. With more than 365 miles (587 km) of passageways, the Mammoth Cave system is the longest surveyed cave in the world.

Pollution of surface waters caused by runoff from mining, agriculture, residential and commercial wastes, and other activities is a significant concern for the state. In 2009, results of a study by the federal government, published in *Journal of the American Water Resources Association*, indicated that the region around Louisville was among the likely sources of phosphorus pollution runoff that was contributing to the Gulf of Mexico's oxygen-depleted "dead zone."

While fishing is not a major commercial industry within Kentucky, there are a number of small catfish farms throughout the state. The Wolf Creek National Fish Hatchery by Lake Cumberland in Jamestown

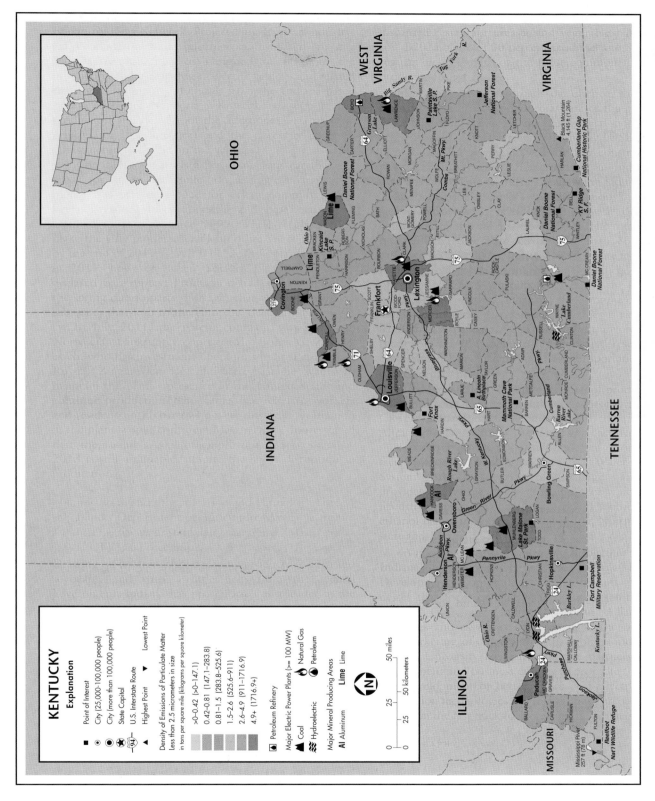

SOURCES: "County Emissions Map: Criteria Air Pollutants." *AirData*. U.S. Environmental Protection Agency. Available from http://www.epa.gov/air/data/geosel.html; *Energy Maps*. U.S. Energy Information Administration. Available from http://www.eia.gov/state; *Highest and Lowest Elevations*. U.S. Geological Survey. Available from http://egsc.usgs. gov/isb/pubs/booklets/elvadist/elvadist.html#Highest; *2007 Minerals Yearbook*. U.S. Geological Survey. Available from http://minerals.usgs.gov/minerals/pubs/state. © 2011 Cengage Learning.

Water drainage through porous limestone rock has created a number of underground caves and passages throughout the central portion of the state, the best known of which is Mammoth Cave. © *Caitlin Mirra/ShutterStock.com*

produces about one million rainbow and brown trout each year to stock nearly one hundred public fishing waters throughout the state.

Agriculture: Tobacco, Bourbon, and Ginseng

Tobacco is the most important agricultural crop for the state. While Kentucky ranks second in the nation in the overall production of tobacco (after North Carolina), the state ranks first in the production of burley tobacco, which is primarily used in cigarettes. It also comes in first for the production of dark fire-cured and dark air-cured tobacco, which are used in smokeless tobacco products such as snuff, pipe tobacco, and chewing tobacco. Hay is another major agricultural product, along with corn and soybeans.

Kentucky was once one of the largest grape and wine producers in the nation, but the industry declined rapidly during Prohibition. In recent years, however, viniculture has been making a comeback. In 2010, there were more than 113 grape producers in the state and sixty small farm wineries. Bourbon, named after one of the original counties of Kentucky, is one of the state's most famous products. In 1964, the U.S. Congress officially recognized bourbon as a distinctive product of the

United States, prompting Kentucky bourbon distillers to call it "America's Official Native Spirit." The bourbon industry generates more than $125 million in tax revenues each year and supports 10,000 jobs.

The state is one of nineteen in the country that sponsors a wild ginseng program. Wild ginseng, a perennial herb that can be used for medicinal purposes, is considered to be at risk and is a protected plant under federal and Kentucky state laws. Marketing and export of wild ginseng grown in Kentucky is strictly regulated by the Kentucky Department of Agriculture (KYDOA), which has established that only licensed dealers can buy or sell the product. Ginseng for export must be certified by the U.S. Fish and Wildlife Service in order to be in compliance with the Convention on International Trade and Endangered Species (CITES) treaty.

Kentucky has ranked first in the nation for equine breeding and sales, which includes horses, ponies, mules, burros, and donkeys. However, the state is best known for its thoroughbred horse industry, which includes the breeding and sale of horses, the racing industry, and support activities. In 2008, there were 540 thoroughbred farms in the state. In 2009, some 14,257 thoroughbred foals were recorded in Kentucky, which is nearly 45

Kentucky State Profile

Physical Characteristics

Land area	39,492 square miles (102,284 sq km)
Inland water area	919 square miles (2,380 sq km)
Coastal area	NA
Highest point	Black Mountain 4,145 feet (1,263 m)
National Forest System lands (2010)	814,000 acres (329,000 ha)
State parks (2011)	52

Energy Statistics

Total energy production (2009)	3,100 trillion Btu
State ranking in total energy production (2009)	5
Renewable energy net generation total (2009)	3.7 million megawatt hours
Hydroelectric energy generation (2009)	3.3 million megawatt hours
Biomass energy generation (2009)	101,000 megawatt hours
Wind energy generation (2009)	NA
Wood and derived fuel energy generation (2009)	263,000 megawatt hours
Crude oil reserves (2009)	20.0 million barrels (3.2 million cu m)
Natural gas reserves (2009)	2,782 billion cubic feet (78.8 billion cu m)
Natural gas liquids (2008)	101 million barrels (16.1 million cu m)

Pollution Statistics

Carbon output (2005)	143.0 million tons of CO_2 (129.7 million t)
Superfund sites (2008)	14
Particulate matter (less than 2.5 micrometers) emissions (2002)	30,372 tons per year (27,553 t/yr)
Toxic chemical releases (2009)	142.6 million pounds (64.7 million kg)
Generated hazardous waste (2009)	132,700 tons (120,400 t)

SOURCES: AirData. U.S. Environmental Protection Agency. Available from http://www.epa.gov/air/data; *Energy Maps, Facts, and Data of the U.S. States.* U.S. Energy Information Administration. Available from http://www.eia.gov/state; *The 2012 Statistical Abstract.* U.S. Census Bureau. Available from http://www.census.gov/compendia/statab; *United States Energy Usage.* eRedux. Available from http://www.eredux.net/states.

© 2011 Cengage Learning.

percent of all foals recorded in North America. Thoroughbred sales at public auction amounted to about $1.1 billion in 2007. About 76 percent of all Kentucky Derby winners were Kentucky-bred horses. However, only about 20 percent of the horses in the state are involved in racing. The majority are involved in non-racing competitions, recreational opportunities, and other activities (i.e., breeding, farming, and equine therapy).

The Kentucky Organic Program, overseen by the KYDOA, is based on the requirements for the U.S. National Organic Program. Organic farming in Kentucky is slowly taking root. According to the USDA, there were 11 certified organic operations in Kentucky in 2006, and

57 by 2008. The KYDOA promotes the sale of local produce and agricultural products through Kentucky Proud, a program that helps producers establish local markets and draws consumers to those markets.

Energy

Oil and Natural Gas

While Kentucky produces only a small amount of crude oil, it has two refineries (Catlettsburg and Somerset) for local processing, with additional crude oil supplies shipped in from Tennessee and West Virginia. Petroleum products are also shipped into the state by pipelines and river barge. A reformulated ethanol blend of gasoline is required for use in the Louisville metropolitan area and in the Kentucky suburbs that are part of the greater Cincinnati, Ohio–Northern Kentucky metropolitan area. As of 2010, the state had two ethanol production facilities and three biodiesel facilities.

While there are some reserves of natural gas in eastern Kentucky, most of the state's supply comes from the Gulf Coast by pipeline. The state's industrial sector is a major consumer of natural gas, using about 50 percent of the state's supply. More than 40 percent of all households use natural gas for home heating.

Coal and Electricity

Kentucky has ranked as one of the three largest coal-producing states in the country for more than fifty years, currently standing at third after Wyoming and West Virginia. Production takes place in both underground and surface mines. The of mountain top mining, which involves the removal of surface soils along a mountain ridge in order to reach the underlying coal seam, is a highly controversial activity, as many environmentalists are concerned that such practices cause permanent damage to the landscape and mountain ecosystems. Kentucky coal accounts for 10 percent of total U.S. coal production and 25 percent of production east of the Mississippi river. It is no surprise then that more than 90 percent of the electricity produced in the state comes from coal-fired plants. Most of the remainder is produced by petroleum-fired plants, though there are a few hydroelectric power plants as well. More than 40 percent of all households use electricity for home heating.

Setting New Standards in Renewable Energy and Efficiency

Such a strong dependency on coal and other fossil fuels is a cause for concern, both economically and environmentally. While the state recognizes the benefits of developing more energy efficient and renewable sources of energy, the importance of the coal industry to the state is such that the use of coal as an energy source cannot be seriously discredited. With this in mind, the state

Mining practices which involve the removal of surface soils from farmland or along a mountain ridge in order to reach the underlying coal seam, are controversial, as many environmentalists are concerned that such practices cause permanent damage to the wildlife habitats ecosystems. © *Emory Kristof/National Geographic/Getty Images*

legislature is currently considering two different bills, one of which is likely to end up as the new renewable energy and efficiency portfolio standard.

House Bill 408 would require utilities to reduce electricity use by at least 10.25 percent of retail sales by 2020. It would further require that 12.5 percent of electricity must come from renewable sources by 2020, including 2 percent through solar power. Other eligible sources would include wind, hydropower, geothermal energy, biomass, landfill gas, and anaerobic digestion. HB 408 includes a mandate for utilities to develop comprehensive weatherization programs that would lead to cost-savings for low-income residents. The bill places a major focus on the establishment of residential energy efficiency programs sponsored by utility companies. House Bill 408 does not address nuclear power or carbon capture and storage technology.

By comparison, House Bill 3 would require utilities to reduce electricity use by 6 percent of retail sales by 2018. At least 10 percent of all electricity would come from renewable sources by 2022. This bill would create a new low-carbon energy standard to encourage the development of nuclear power, carbon capture and storage, and coal gasification facilities as acceptable alternative sources of energy. HB 3 would require utilities to generate up to 4 percent of retail sales by low carbon sources by 2012 and 20 percent by 2022. HB 3 could also add natural-gas derived liquid fuels as an alternative transportation fuel. As of 2011, both HB 3 and HB 408 were stalled in the Natural Resources and Environment Committee.

However, the Clean Energy Opportunity Act (HB 239) was introduced to the state house in February 2011. The new bill calls for a renewable portfolio standard of 12.5 percent of utility retail sales by 2021, along with a mandate for utilities to increase energy efficiency measures to achieve annual retail savings of up to 10.25 percent by 2021.

Intelligent Energy Choices for Kentucky's Future

Both bills support some of the strategies for energy independence that were outlined by Governor Steven Beshear in the 2008 publication of *Intelligent Energy Choices for Kentucky's Future*, which is meant to serve as an action plan for the development of more efficient and sustainable energy solutions. The report presents seven primary strategies, which include the development of renewable and efficiency portfolio standards, an alternate transportation fuel standard, and aggressive carbon capture and storage projects to improve the marketability of Kentucky coal while allowing for a decrease in greenhouse gas emissions. The report sets a goal of ensuring that 50 percent of all state coal-based energy facilities will be equipped with carbon management technologies by 2025. The report also calls for research and development into the potential for nuclear energy.

To address the goal for developing alternative transportation fuels, the governor established an Executive Task Force on Biomass and Biofuels in 2009. In December of that year, the task force presented a report entitled *Biomass and Biofuels Development in Kentucky*, which detailed the potential for a sustainable biomass and biofuels industry in the state. The report places existing biomass production capabilities between 12 and 15 million tons per year. Under the mandates of the Federal Renewable Fuels Standard, the state can expect a demand for 10 million tons of biomass for 2022 for the production of 700 million gallons (2.6 billion l) of liquid transportation fuels. If the state adopts a renewable portfolio standard, demand for biomass for electricity generation could jump as well. An additional 15 million tons of biomass could be used to produce enough renewable electricity to account for 18 percent of total generation by 2025. Therefore, the total demand for biomass for transportation fuel and electricity generation could reach 25 million tons of biomass per year by 2025. The task force concludes that a 25 million ton per year biomass industry could be feasible for the state, with minimal land use changes and the adoption of renewable portfolio standards, and with capital investments in excess of $10 billion. Once established, the industry could have a net annual output of more than $3.4 billion.

⚘ Green Business, Green Building, Green Jobs

Green Business

The growth of a green economy has been relatively slow in Kentucky, but shows potential for improvement as the state begins to promote research and development in renewable and alternative energy technologies. According to a report published in 2009 by Pew Charitable Trusts, there were 778 clean energy businesses in the state in 2007, supporting about 9,300 jobs. From 2006–2008, there was no report of venture capital funds. A similar report from the National Governor's Association Center for Best Practices showed that venture capital investment in clean technology had decreased from more than $4 million in 2001 to less than $2 million in 2003. Since these figures were published, however, the state has implemented a number of incentives to promote energy efficiency standards in commercial, residential, and state properties and has begun to work on the development of renewable energy and energy efficiency portfolio standards. These actions are likely to lead to an increase in businesses and jobs related to the development of alternative and renewable energy sources.

Green Building for KEEPS

The Kentucky legislature adopted a high-performance building standard for state-owned buildings in April 2008 through the passage of House Bill 2. Under this law all construction or renovation of public buildings that are funded by the state at 50 percent or more must meet requirements for certification under the U.S. Green Building Council's Leadership in Energy and Environmental Design (LEED) program. The level of certification for each building will depend on the budget and size of the project. In general, higher budget projects will require higher levels of certification. All building leases for state agencies will be expected to meet the same standard by July 1, 2018. HB 2 further requires public schools to be enrolled in the Kentucky Energy Efficiency Program for Schools (KEEPS). Administered through the Kentucky Resource Center for Environmental Sustainability at the University of Louisville J.B. Speed School of Engineering, the program aims to reduce energy consumption and lower operating costs at all public school facilities.

Greening the People's Home

Taking the theme of going green to heart, the state's first family has taken steps to reduce energy consumption and improve energy efficiency at the governor's mansion. Kentucky First Lady Jane Beshear has been proactive in working toward the goal to reduce energy consumption at the mansion by 15 percent by the end of 2010 and by 30 percent by 2014. Some of the changes made in this effort include the use of energy efficient appliances and fixtures, fuel-efficient vehicles and groundskeeping equipment, and recycling projects. The first lady has also planted three 16 by 24 foot (4.9 by 7.3 m) garden plots on the grounds of the mansion to provide food for family and guests and to serve as a model for what can be done in backyards throughout the state. The program of greening the mansion is part of a larger initiative known as the Kentucky Green Team, which is designed to promote and inspire sustainable environmental practices within communities.

Setting an example for the greening of the commercial sector, the award winning Green Building opened in Louisville in the fall of 2008, becoming the first commercial building in the city to gain LEED Platinum certification. The privately owned building is a mixed-use facility housing a café, offices, and event spaces.

General Electric (GE) unveiled a LEED Platinum data center at its Louisville headquarters in 2011. The company wanted to reduce data center energy consumption and lower their environmental impact. GE's achievement is significant considering data center emissions are growing faster worldwide than any other kind of emissions. The center is 34 percent better in terms of energy savings than a typical code-compliant building, and water consumption is 42 percent lower than the industry baseline. GE also installed high-density servers to reduce the size of the data center floor by half, which means that less energy is needed to cool the space. The site also utilizes off-site renewable energy sources.

Green Jobs

According to a report published in 2009 by the Pew Charitable Trusts, more than 67 percent of the green jobs in Kentucky are in conservation and pollution mitigation. A growing number of jobs are developing in energy efficiency businesses, as the state has supported legislation and initiatives aimed toward reducing energy consumption and costs in state, commercial, and residential buildings. In January 2010, the state was awarded a grant of more than $4.7 million as part of the State Energy Partnership and Training grant program of the U. S. Department of Labor for the development of training opportunities in energy efficiency and renewable energy jobs. The funds will provide educational opportunities for more than 600 workers in the Cumberland and West Kentucky Workforce Investment Areas who are dislocated workers, unemployed individuals, out-of-school youth, and veterans. Participants will earn degrees and/or industry-recognized certification in green job industries including energy assessment, Smart Grid technology, chemical engineering, plumbing, and pipefitting.

The Future of Kentucky Coal

As the quest for energy independence through renewable energy sources sweeps the nation, the state of Kentucky is faced with a significant environmental and economic challenge. How can the state preserve its thriving coal industry while meeting demands to provide cleaner, more efficient energy sources?

Kentucky, one of the country's top coal producing states, accounts for 10 percent of total U.S. coal production and 25 percent of production east of the Mississippi River. The state exports coal to thirty states and eleven foreign countries. These exports bring in more than $4.3 billion each year. In 2006, revenues from the sale of Kentucky coal reached $5.4 billion. Most of the state's own electricity needs are supplied by coal-fired power plants.

Balancing the Environment with Economy

Some leaders believe that Kentucky must work aggressively to transition the state's economy away from its heavy reliance on coal. The state recognizes the benefits of developing more energy efficient and renewable sources of energy, but the coal industry is far too important to the economy of the state to be disregarded. In response to the challenge to balance environmental concerns with economic progress, the state government has initiated a variety of strategies and legislation that look toward the development of advanced carbon technologies and the diversification of coal products as the key to future success.

The first step is research. In 2007, the state legislature passed House Bill 1, which authorized funding for research by the Kentucky Geological Survey in the areas of carbon dioxide-enhanced oil and gas recovery and the geological storage of carbon dioxide, more commonly known as carbon capture and sequestration (CCS). This research project began in 2008 through the work of the Kentucky Consortium for Carbon Storage and is expected to continue until 2012. Another group currently working on the research and development of CCS technologies is the Carbon Management Research Group, a consortium of the University of Kentucky's Center for Applied Energy Research, the Kentucky Energy and Environment Cabinet, and the state's major power companies. The group will lead a $24 million, ten-year program of research to develop and demonstrate cost-effective and practical technologies for managing carbon dioxide emissions in coal-fired electric plants.

The next step is development. These research projects will serve as a major key for achieving the goals set in the 2008 publication of *Intelligent Energy Choices for Kentucky's Future*. The report presented seven primary goals and strategies for providing a sustainable and independent energy future for the state. Strategy 6 calls for the initiation of aggressive CCS projects to retrofit existing coal-fired power plants with advanced carbon management technologies, which would improve the efficiency of the plants while also reducing greenhouse gas emissions. Strategy 5 focuses on the diversification of the coal industry through the development of coal-to-gas technology, a process which creates synthetic natural gas from coal. The state has set a goal to produce the equivalent of 100 percent of the annual natural gas requirement by augmenting instate natural gas production with coal-to-gas processing by 2025.

The Challenge of Refining Coal's Role in Kentucky

To be implemented, the governor's plan needs support from the legislature. Legislation to support renewable energy and to improve the environmental performance of coal mining and coal-fired power generation plants was introduced in both 2010 and 2011. However, as of late 2011, none of the bills had been passed. During the summer of 2011, water contamination from the coal mining industry came under scrutiny. An alliance of environmental groups in the state discovered that two mining companies, International Coal Group and Frasure Creek Mining, had exceeded their pollution permit limits more than 4,000 times in the first quarter of the year alone. The two companies are the largest producers of mountaintop-removal-mined coal in Kentucky. The environmental groups had notified the companies of their intent to sue the previous year over more than 20,000 violations of the Clean Water Act, but the companies only ended up being fined a fraction of what would be imposed under the Clean Water Act. A flaming drinking water well in Pike County brought the public's attention to the alleged abuses of big coal companies. The well began burning and water in the area began running gray, orange, and black after explosions beneath homes were heard in January 2011. Excel Mining runs a nearby coal mine and has been fingered as the culprit. Excel offered to install a water filtration system, but only if residents signed a liability waiver. They refused. Only some families have received assistance, such as bottled water, and some have been instructed to evacuate but most cannot afford to do so. If big coal companies are working towards cleaner solutions for their industry, they may also want to keep the trust of local residents by dealing with current pollution issues as well.

The Legislative Research Commission in Kentucky projected that the legislation to regulate the storage and disposal of coal ash was likely to come before the legislature in the 2012 session.

While environmental groups might favor more drastic steps away from fossil fuels, the coal industry is too important to the state, and the nation, to be abandoned, which means that innovative approaches to the diversification of the coal industry and the development of advanced coal technologies will provide the key to Kentucky's economic future.

BIBLIOGRAPHY

Books

Hopkins, Bruce. *The Smithsonian Guides to Natural America: Central Appalachia–West Virginia, Kentucky, Tennessee.* Washington, DC: Smithsonian Books, 1996.

Web Sites

Beshear, Steven L. *Intelligent Energy Choices for Kentucky's Future: Kentucky's 7-Point Strategy for Energy Independence.* Available from http://www.energy.ky.gov/NR/rdonlyres/C3E2E625-AF3C-483D-955F-99FF57D74C64/0/FinalEnergyStrategy.pdf

Biomass and Biofuels Development in Kentucky. Executive Task Force on Biomass and Biofuels, Commonwealth of Kentucky. Available from http://agpolicy.ky.gov/Documents/091210_BiomassTaskForce_FinalReport.pdf

Bruggers, James. "Kentucky, Indiana key contributors to 'dead zone'." Hypoxia: the Northern Gulf of Mexico. Available from http://www.gulfhypoxia.net/news/default.asp?XMLFilename=200904122133.xml

Caves of the Central Kentucky Karstlands. Available from http://www.kentuckycaves.org

The Clean Energy Economy: Kentucky. The Pew Charitable Trusts. Available from http://www.pewcenteronthestates.org/uploadedFiles/wwwpewcenteronthestatesorg/Fact_Sheets/Clean_Economy_Factsheet_Kentucky.pdf

Clean Energy Opportunity Act (HB 239). Kentucky Legislature. Available from http://www.lrc.ky.gov/record/11RS/HB239.htm

"Conditions amp; Closures: Climate in Kentucky." Daniel Boone National Forest, USDA Forest Service. Available from http://www.fs.fed.us/r8/boone/conditions/clim.shtml

Division of Biofuels, Kentucky Department for Energy Development & Independence. http://energy.ky.gov/biofuels/Pages/default.aspx

Draft Kentucky Greenhouse Gas Inventory and Reference Case Projections 1990–2030. Center for Climate Strategies. Available from http://www.kyclimatechange.us/ewebeditpro/items/O122F22500.pdf

"GE Unveils Platinum LEED-Certified Data Center." Sustainable Plant. August 24, 2011. Available from http://www.sustainableplant.com/2011/08/ge-unveils-platinum-leed-certified-data-center/

Ginseng. University of Kentucky Cooperative Extension Service. Available from http://www.uky.edu/Ag/NewCrops/introsheets/ginseng.pdf

Global Warming and Kentucky. National Wildlife Federation. Available from http://www.nwf.org/Global-Warming/~/media/PDFs/Global%20Warming/Global%20Warming%20State%20Fact%20Sheets/Kentucky.ashx

The Green Building. Available from http://www.thegreenbuilding.net

Hall, Marvin. *Kentucky Bluegrass.* Pennsylvania State University. Available from http://cropsoil.psu.edu/extension/facts/agfact50.pdf

House Bill 1: An act relating to the advancement of energy policy, science, technology, and innovation in the Commonwealth, making an appropriation therefore, and declaring an emergency. Kentucky Legislature. Available from http://www.lrc.ky.gov/record/07S2/HB1.htm

House Bill 2 08RS: An act relating to the promotion of the efficient use of energy. Kentucky Legislature. Available from http://www.lrc.ky.gov/record/08rs/hb2.htm

House Bill 3 10RS: An act relating to the advancement of clean energy use and production. Kentucky Legislature. Available from http://www.lrc.ky.gov/record/10rs/hb3.htm

House Bill 408 10RS: An act relating to energy. Kentucky Legislature. Available from http://www.lrc.ky.gov/record/10RS/HB408.htm

"Hunting/Trapping and Wildlife." Kentucky Department of Fish and Wildlife Resources. Available from http://fw.ky.gov/navigationdual.aspx?cid=741

Issues Confronting the 2012 Kentucky General Assembly. Informational Bulletin No. 236, Legislative Research Commission. Available from http://www.lrc.ky.gov/lrcpubs/IB236.pdf

Kentucky Agricultural Statistics 2008–2009 Bulletin. United States Department of Agriculture, National Agricultural Statistics Service, Kentucky Field Office. Available from http://www.nass.usda.gov/Statistics_by_State/Kentucky/Publications/Annual_Statistical_Bulletin/B2009/b2009.html

Kentucky Association of Riverports. Available from http://kentuckyriverports.com

Kentucky Bourbon Trail. Available from http://www. kybourbontrail.com

Kentucky Climate Action Plan Council. Available from http://www.kyclimatechange.us/home.cfm

Kentucky Climate Center. Available from http://kyclim. wku.edu

Kentucky Coal Facts: 2007–2008 Pocket Guide. Kentucky Coal Association. Available from http://www. kentuckycoal.org/documents/CoalFacts08.pdf

Kentucky Consortium for Carbon Storage. Available from http://www.uky.edu/KGS/kyccs

Kentucky Department of Agriculture. Available from http://www.kyagr.com

Kentucky Department of Fish and Wildlife Resources. Available from http://fw.ky.gov

Kentucky Energy Efficiency Program for Schools (KEEPS). Available from https://louisville.edu/ kppc/keeps.

Kentucky Green Team. Available from http://green-team.ky.gov

"Kentucky Lakes and Rivers." Kentucky Tourism. Available from http://www.kentuckytourism.com/ explore/lakes_rivers.aspx

Kentucky: Profile of the Green Economy. National Governors Association Center for Best Practices. Available from http://www.nga.org/Files/pdf/09 GREENPROFILEKY.PDF

Kentucky Proud. Available from http://www.kyproud. com

"Kentucky receives $4.74 million green jobs grant." Kentucky at Work: Governor Steve Beshear's Communications Office. Available from http:// migration.kentucky.gov/Newsroom/governor/ 20100122greenJobs.htm

Kentucky Resource Center for Environmental Sustainability. Available from https://louisville.edu/kppc/ home.html.

Kentucky: 2007 Minerals Yearbook. United States Geological Survey. Available from http://minerals. usgs.gov/minerals/pubs/state/2007/myb2-2007-ky.pdf

"Kentucky's Forest Facts." Kentucky Department of Natural Resources, Division of Forestry. Available from http://forestry.ky.gov/Pages/Kentuckys' ForestFacts.aspx

"Kentucky's Threatened and Endangered Species." Kentucky Department of Fish and Wildlife Resources. Available from http://fw.ky.gov/ telst.asp

Kentucky Thoroughbred Association and Kentucky Thoroughbred Owners and Breeders. Available from https://www.kta-ktob.com/AboutUs/WhoWeAre. aspx

Senate Joint Resolution 99 (11RS). Kentucky Legislature. Available from http://www.lrc.ky.gov/ record/11RS/SJ99.htm

"State Energy Profiles: Kentucky" U.S. Energy Information Administration. Available from http:// tonto.eia.doe.gov/state/state_energy_profiles.cfm? sid=KY

"The State of Freight in Kentucky." Kentucky Transportation Cabinet. April 2011. Available from http://transportation.ky.gov/Planning/

Sturgis, Sue. "Flaming drinking-water well in Kentucky illuminates Big Coal's abuses." Facing South. August 19, 2011. Available from http://www. southern studies.org/2011/08/flaming-drinking-water-well-in-kentucky-illuminates-big-coals-abuses.html

The 2009 Guide to the Kentucky Horse Industry. The Kentucky Horse Council. Available from http:// www.kentuckyhorse.org/industry-table-of-con tents

Wolf Creek National Fish Hatchery. Available from http://www.fws.gov/wolfcreek/index.htm

Louisiana

Time and time again, Louisiana has found itself recovering from an environmental setback. From devastating hurricanes in 2005 to a major offshore oil spill in 2010, the state generally known for its sultry bayous and the city of New Orleans has faced great challenges in rebuilding, preserving, and managing sustainable habitats for wildlife and human populations. A year after the devastating April 2010 Deepwater Horizon oil spill in the Gulf of Mexico, Louisiana's natural and business environments were beginning to return to normal. While biologists from the Louisiana Department of Wildlife and Fisheries (LDWF) had continued to recover oil-covered birds in the region into January 2011, on April 19, 2011, the National Oceanic and Atmospheric Administration (NOAA) reopened to commercial and recreational fishing the last of the federal waters that had been closed after the oil spill. Still, the extent of the damage to the environment from the spill remains undetermined. In February 2011, researchers from Georgia had reported that thick patches of crude oil remained on the Gulf floor and were thicker than expected.

In some ways, these challenges have inspired state officials and residents alike to embrace a more sustainable lifestyle. The city of New Orleans, for instance, now participates in the U.S. Department of Energy's Solar American Cities Project, rebuilding homes and businesses with solar technology. Taking stock of the state's existing resources, there appears to be some promise for the development of the biofuels industry, with wood and wood wastes as fuel for electric energy and sugarcane converted to ethanol for transportation. However, the 2010 oil spill in the Gulf of Mexico will have long-lasting effects on the environment and the economy.

Climate

The climate of Louisiana is semitropical, with warm, humid summers and mild winters. Its location on the Gulf Coast places the state in line for sometimes deadly tropical storms and hurricanes, particularly in the late summer and fall. In August 2005, the southeastern region of the state was devastated by the arrival of one such storm, Hurricane Katrina. High winds and flooding brought on by the category four storm led to a failure in the levee system around New Orleans, unleashing floodwaters that covered more than 80 percent of the city, with depths as high as 20 feet (6.3 m). One month later, Hurricane Rita arrived, making landfall near Johnson's Bayou on September 23. More than 1,800 people died as a result of the storms, which caused physical damages in excess of $81 billion.

The environmental effects of the storms were severe. Chemicals and toxins were released into the air and floodwaters as homes, businesses, and vehicles were destroyed and submerged. Public health was jeopardized for many months following the storms, as sewage and water systems were slowly rebuilt and as the sometimes toxic debris was collected for disposal. The coastal wildlife habitats in the region were left just as devastated. Even as the floodwaters receded, contamination by chemical pollutants and saltwater left many wildlife habitats, and their returning native inhabitants, at risk for disease. Cleanup efforts were slow, but relatively steady. However, six parishes—Jefferson, Orleans, Plaquemines, St. Bernard, St. Tammany, and Terrebonne—were still considered to be under a declared state of emergency, which was extended through September 30, 2011. (The declaration of a state of emergency authorizes and regulates a number of cleanup efforts, particularly those related to solid waste and hazardous waste management.)

As of 2011, Louisiana did not have a Climate Action Plan in place.

⚘ Natural Resources, Water, and Agriculture

Fast-Growing Trees Inspire an Industry

Nearly 50 percent of the state is covered in forests, with tree species ranging from loblolly and shortleaf pines in the uplands, to cypress and tupelo in the swamps, and hardwoods, including tupelo, along the Mississippi River. Slash pine is grown for timber production in wetter areas. With a mild climate and abundant rainfall, Louisiana has the fastest tree-growing cycle in North America. This creates the perfect environment for a thriving forest industry, which includes production of pulp and paper as well as lumber and pine plywood. Much of the state was once covered in longleaf pine savannah.

Diversity of Animals and Plants

Some of the most common mammals found in the Louisiana forests are squirrels, rabbits, armadillos, opossums, raccoons, deer, and bobcats.. Louisiana black bears, a threatened species, are limited to populations in the Atchafalaya and Tensas River Basins. The U.S. Fish and Wildlife Service lists 26 threatened or endangered animal species and four threatened or endangered plant species found in the state. Endangered animals include several species of sea turtle, the red-cockaded woodpecker, and the Florida panther. Endangered plant species include the American chaffseed and the Louisiana quillwort. The state has one national park, Kistachie, and 34 state parks and recreation sites, and 24 National Wildlife Refuges. Located within the city limits of New Orleans, Bayou Sauvage National Wildlife Refuge is the largest urban wildlife refuge in the country.

In February 2011, ten whooping cranes were reintroduced to a Louisiana conservation area. The whooping crane is the most endangered species of crane in the world and is found only in North America. The entire Louisiana population had been wiped out by the 1950s. As of 2011, there were only 560 birds in the wild and captivity combined. The birds started out in an enclosed pen in Louisiana's White Lake Wetlands Conservation Area, from which they werereleased into a 1.5-acre (0.6-ha) open pen. The birds will be closely monitored and encouraged to roost and breed. Another set of cranes were introduced in October 2011, with the entire project scheduled to last until 2021.

Louisiana was ranked as the top salt-producing state in the nation in 2007, and is home to the oldest working salt mine in the United States, which is located on Avery Island off the Louisiana Gulf Coast. In recent years, however, construction sand and gravel have become more profitable commodities for the state. The state was ranked thirty-third for overall nonfuel mineral production in 2010 with a value of $492 million.

Water: Bountiful Bayous

The legendary Louisiana bayous are part of a vast network of wetlands that characterizes the southern portion of the state. Louisiana has the largest area of wetlands in the United States. Catahoula Lake, in LaSalle and Rapides parishes, was designated as a Ramsar Wetland of International Importance in 1991 and serves as a major habitat for several species of migratory birds, along with resident duck species, such as mottled ducks and wood ducks. Catahoula is also the largest freshwater lake in the state. Lake Pontchartrain, while larger, is actually a brackish coastal estuary.

The Mississippi River has always been a major asset for the state, serving as a major transportation route for domestic and foreign products passing through Louisiana ports. The Port of South Louisiana, which includes the ports of New Orleans, Fouchon, and Baton Rouge, is the largest tonnage port in the Western Hemisphere. The ports of New Orleans, Baton Rouge, and Plaquemines are among the busiest ports in the nation. Other important rivers include the Red, Pearl, Atchafalaya, and Sabine.

The coastal waters of Louisiana support a major fishing industry that ranks second in the nation (after Alaska). Shrimp, oysters, blue crab, menhaden, and drum (including redfish and speckled trout) are all caught along the coastal regions. Following the April 2010 Deepwater Horizon explosion and oil spill, however, fishing in the Gulf of Mexico was suspended for a four-month period. Prior to the 2010 oil spill, Louisiana ranked first in the nation for the production of seafood, providing one-third of the total U.S. supply. Fisheries statistics for 2010 would not be available until late in 2011, but experts predicted that none of the Gulf Coast ports that ranked in the top ten in 2009 (and in most previous years) would appear on 2010's list.

The typical freshwater catch includes red and white crawfish, though a large amount of crawfish—and catfish—are produced through farms.

Sport fishing is also popular, with bass and crappie among the more popular catches. The state of Louisiana's sport fishing was in serious peril as a result of the Deepwater Horizon oil spill. In December 2010, BP agreed to pay the Louisiana Department of Wildlife and Fisheries (LDWF) $2.56 million to compensate the department for lost revenue associated with the decline in recreational fishing license sales.

The Rising Mississippi 2011

The state faced a number of environmental and economic challenges as a result of heavy flooding along the Mississippi River and its tributaries beginning in March 2011. State officials and residents alike were particularly concerned when the rising river prompted the U.S. Army Corps of Engineers to take the drastic measure of opening the Morganza spillway for the first time in nearly forty years. The Morganza spillway is part of the flood control system of locks and levees built after the

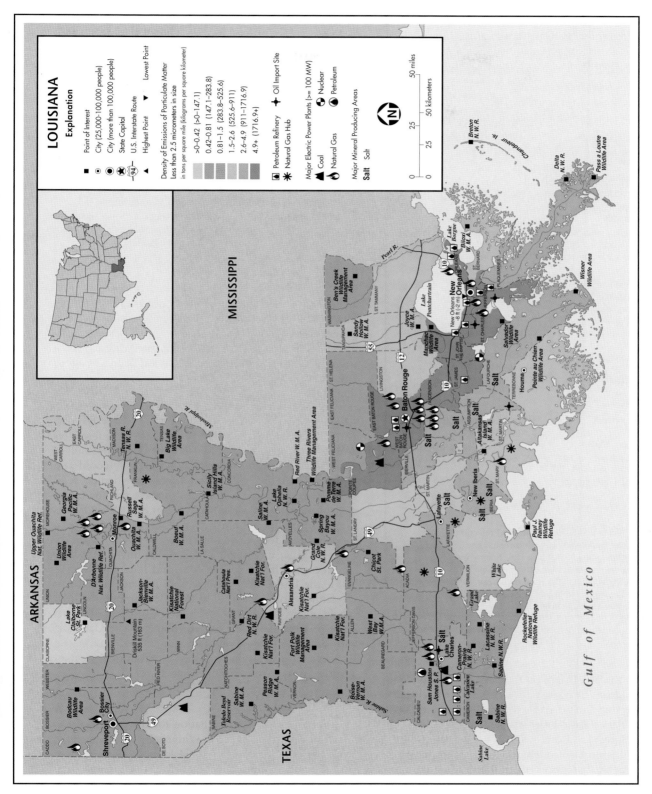

SOURCES: "County Emissions Map: Criteria Air Pollutants." *AirData.* U.S. Environmental Protection Agency. Available from http://www.epa.gov/air/data/geosel.html; *Energy Maps.* U.S. Energy Information Administration. Available from http://www.eia.gov/state; *Highest and Lowest Elevations.* U.S. Geological Survey. Available from http://egsc.usgs.gov/isb/pubs/booklets/elvadist/elvadist.html#Highest; *2007 Minerals Yearbook.* U.S. Geological Survey. Available from http://minerals.usgs.gov/minerals/pubs/state. © 2011 Cengage Learning.

Louisiana State Profile

Physical Characteristics

Land area	43,199 square miles (111,885 sq km)
Inland water area	4,433 square miles (11,481 sq km)
Coastal area	1,951 square miles (3,140 sq km)
Highest point	Driskill Mountain 535 feet (163 m)
National Forest System lands (2010)	604,000 acres (244,000 ha)
State parks (2011)	22

Energy Statistics

Total energy production (2009)	6,200 trillion Btu
State ranking in total energy production (2009)	3
Renewable energy net generation total (2009)	3.6 million megawatt hours
Hydroelectric energy generation (2009)	1.2 million megawatt hours
Biomass energy generation (2009)	67,000 megawatt hours
Wind energy generation (2009)	NA
Wood and derived fuel energy generation (2009)	2.3 million megawatt hours
Crude oil reserves (2009)	370.0 million barrels (58.8 million cu m)
Natural gas reserves (2009)	20,688 billion cubic feet (585.8 billion cu m)
Natural gas liquids (2008)	231.0 million barrels (36.7 million cu m)

Pollution Statistics

Carbon output (2005)	179.1 million tons of CO_2 (162.5 million t)
Superfund sites (2008)	8
Particulate matter (less than 2.5 micrometers) emissions (2002)	26,950 tons per year (24,448 t/yr)
Toxic chemical releases (2009)	119.5 million pounds (54.2 million kg)
Generated hazardous waste (2009)	3.9 million tons (3.5 million t)

SOURCES: AirData. U.S. Environmental Protection Agency. Available from http://www.epa.gov/air/data; *Energy Maps, Facts, and Data of the U.S. States.* U.S. Energy Information Administration. Available from http://www.eia.gov/state; *The 2012 Statistical Abstract.* U.S. Census Bureau. Available from http://www.census.gov/compendia/statab; *United States Energy Usage.* eRedux. Available from http://www.eredux.net/states.

© 2011 Cengage Learning.

Water is released by the U.S. Army Corps of Engineers at the Morganza Spillway May 14, 2011. The opening of the floodgates for the first time in nearly forty years was intended to lower the crest of the flooding Mississippi River at Baton Rouge and downriver to New Orleans. © *Mario Tama/Getty Images*

great flood of 1927. It was designed to relieve the pressure of the Mississippi on the levees of Baton Rouge and New Orleans by diverting waters into the Atchafalaya Basin. The decision to open the spillway put residents along the Atchafalaya River at risk, particularly in the town of Butte La Rose, which was placed under a mandatory evacuation order as the floodwaters were predicted to reach higher than fifteen feet (4.6 m). However, after the spillway was opened on May 14, 2011, the waters moved in an unexpected trajectory that ultimately caused less severe flooding than expected. By early June, mandatory evacuation orders had been lifted and many residents were able to return to their homes.

Even so, the total impact of the floods on the economy included losses sustained by agriculture, fishing, and other businesses.

The flood called the actions of the Army Corps of Engineers into question. Congress, flood-plain managers, and other major interests have criticized the Corps' continued investment in the old system of flood management, stressing the need for a new system. Some would like to go back to allowing the river to flow naturally, which may help filter out some of the fertilizers and pesticides that have caused a dead zone in the Gulf of Mexico. Allowing the river to flow naturally could also replenish local marshes which have been denied sediments that the river would normally have provided. The disappearing marshes also make cities like New Orleans more vulnerable to hurricanes. The Corps has been dredging the delta and controlling the river's course to keep the navigation channel open, but this just adds to the negative effects on the delta and local marshes. In 2011, the Environmental Defense Fund announced that it planned to sponsor a worldwide competition that would invite experts to redesign the delta so that it reconciles the needs of the environment, flood control, and navigation. Ideas from such a competition could help to find common ground between environmental groups and the Army Corps of Engineers.

Agriculture

Louisiana ranks first in the nation for the production of sugarcane and third for rice. With such an abundance of sugarcane, researchers from the Audubon Sugar Institute of Louisiana State University have been conducting research and feasibility studies that could lead to the development of a prominent biofuels industry, with sugarcane converted into ethanol. Cotton is also a major crop, which may become even more significant as the state welcomes the construction of two major yarn-producing textile mills by Zagis USA. Sweet potatoes and pecans are also important local crops. One of the state's most famous products, Tabasco Sauce, is produced by the McIlhenny family from peppers grown on Avery Island.

The Louisiana Organic Certification Program matches the standards outlined by the U.S. Department of Agriculture. As of 2011, there were 13 certified organic operations in the state.

⚜ Energy

Oil and Gas Resources Support the Louisiana LOOP

Louisiana has rich supplies of oil and natural gas from both onshore and offshore sources. The state ranks fourth in the nation for the production of crude oil from state-operated facilities and fifth in the nation for natural gas. However, large quantities of these resources are found in the federally administered Outer Continental Shelf (OCS) in the Gulf of Mexico. When the amount of crude oil and natural gas from the Louisiana section of the OCS is added with the state total, Louisiana ranks first in the nation for oil production and second for natural gas. Several state ports also serve as points of entry for large amounts of imported crude oil. The Louisiana Offshore Oil Port (LOOP) is the only U.S. port that can accommodate deep-draft tankers.

With 17 operating oil refineries, the state ranks second in the nation (after Texas) for production of petroleum products. About 75 percent of all refined petroleum products are exported to other states. However, statewide consumption of both oil and natural gas is very high, primarily to meet the high demand of the industrial sector. About 50 percent of residents use natural gas as a primary energy source for home heating.

Electricity

Nearly 50 percent of the state's electricity is produced by natural gas–fired plants. Another 25 percent comes from coal-fired plants, with an additional 20 percent produced at the state's two nuclear power plants. Two coal mines in the northwestern region of the state supply lignite coal to nearby power plants. Additional supplies of sub-bituminous coal are imported, primarily from Wyoming. The per capita consumption of electricity in the residential sector is relatively high, due to the widespread use of electricity as a source for home cooling and heating.

Renewable Energy Sources

The state has demonstrated some potential for the use of alternative energy sources. Wood and wood waste are used to produce about 3 percent of the state's electricity supply. There is also a small amount of energy produced through hydroelectric power. There are a growing number of biofuel facilities within the state, encouraged by state tax incentives for businesses using alternative fuel vehicles and by the adoption of the Louisiana Biofuel Standard (2006), which mandates that all gasoline sold within the state will eventually contain 2 percent ethanol. However, the Biofuel Standard will not go into effect until six months after the time when the state has reached a goal of producing fifty million gallons (189 million l) of ethanol per year (RS 3:4674).

New Orleans is one of 25 cities selected by the U.S. Department of Energy for participation in its Solar America Cities project, a program that encourages the use of solar technology in the construction of homes and businesses.

While the state has not yet adopted a Renewable Portfolio Standard, a public hearing on the topic was hosted by the Louisiana Public Service Commission in April 2010. In January 2011, the Louisiana Public Service Commission sponsored a staff conference to study the possible development of financial incentives for utilities to improve their energy efficiency.

⚜ Green Business, Green Building, Green Jobs

Louisiana's green economy is small, but has shown signs of growth through the collective efforts of state and local officials, business organizations, and educational institutions, all of which are working to promote a greener business climate. Growing Green represents one such cooperative effort. Officially known as the Louisiana and Mississippi Green Jobs Consortium, Growing Green is a partnership between the Louisiana Workforce Commission, Louisiana State University, the Mississippi Department of Employment Security, and Mississippi State University. With a $2.3 million grant from the U.S. Department of Labor (awarded in November 2009), Growing Green has begun to compile research on the regional green economy, with the intent of forming solid economic development strategies and workforce training programs that will support the growth of green collar jobs.

The Louisiana Blue Ocean Initiative

More firmly on the state level, in 2010 Louisiana Economic Development (LED) finalized and began implementation of its Blue Ocean Initiative, a development strategy designed to identify specific growth industries and create the necessary action plans to push those target industries forward. While this might be considered more of a high-tech industry initiative than one for a green economy, the six target industries include next generation automotive manufacturing (including electric vehicles), renewable and energy efficiency, and water management.

Green Building

In 2007, the Louisiana legislature passed a bill that requires the use of energy efficiency measures for construction and renovations of state-owned facilities (Senate Bill 240/Act 270). The law states that major facilities must be designed, constructed, and certified to exceed the requirements of the state energy code by at least 30 percent. The Louisiana Division of Administration was empowered to set energy efficiency goals for state facilities for 2009, 2010, and 2011. While certification under the Leadership in Energy and Environmental Design (LEED) program of the U.S. Green Building Council is not required within the state, there are several new construction projects underway that have been designed to meet some level of LEED certification, particularly in the Greater New Orleans area. The first LEED gold-certified building in Louisiana is Northpark, which opened in 2008 and serves as the headquarters for Chevron's Gulf of Mexico Business Unit. Green building initiatives in the rebuilding of the Ninth Ward of New Orleans following Hurricane Katrina have been supported by such celebrities as actor Brad Pitt, whose Make It Right Foundation provides financial support for the construction of affordable and sustainable homes for working families.

Green Jobs

Most of the existing green jobs in the state are in the fields of conservation and pollution mitigation; however, the energy efficiency and renewable energy subsector is beginning to grow, in part due to financial incentives offered to businesses through Louisiana Economic Development. As the green economy begins to take shape, several organizations have been established to provide educational and training opportunities in green collar jobs. The Louisiana Green Corps was established as a United Way Agency program in 2008 through a grant from the U.S. Department of Labor National Emergency Grant program to provide green job training opportunities for unemployed, underemployed, and at-risk young adults (ages 17–24) in the Greater New Orleans area. Louisiana CleanTech is a statewide, nonprofit organization supporting the development of green industries, in part, by providing training programs in solar electric systems and installation.

❧ Gulf of Mexico Oil Spill 2010

The Effect of the Oil Spill on Louisiana's Shoreline and Economy

On September 19, 2010, the U.S. government officially declared the BP Macondo oil well to be dead. The site of a catastrophic blowout and subsequent spill in April 2010, the well was permanently sealed in a process that began on July 15, when a cap was put in

Crude oil (due to the continued leaking of the BP Deepwater Horizon oil rig) is shown in a marsh area May 26, 2010, in Blind Bay, Louisiana. © Win McNamee/Getty Images

place. Scientists immediately sought funding to begin gathering data, sampling, and research to evaluate the effects of the spill on the water and wildlife of the Gulf of Mexico. The final report from the U.S. federal panel investigating the incident was released on January 11, 2011. The panel found that BP, along with Halliburton and Transocean, made decisions in order to work faster and more cheaply, overlooking safety needs and therefore helping to trigger the explosion and resulting massive oil spill.

Louisiana governor Bobby Jindal declared a state of emergency for the coastal regions on April 29, 2010, as state and parish officials began to implement environmental protection action plans, in cooperation with BP and the Coast Guard. The first traces of the oil slick resulting from the spill were seen along the Louisiana coast by April 28. By mid-May, as the spill reached further into the barrier islands system of Louisiana, state government officials began to call on the federal government and BP to create nearly 80 miles (129 km) of sand berms to provide further protection for the delicate nesting grounds located on coastal habitats. The plan was not immediately approved, however, as some officials believed such an effort would not be sufficient and could not be completed quickly enough to provide greater protection than the booms and patrols already in place. Some also noted that dredging and pumping operations necessary for such an operation would cause further damage to marshlands and wildlife. However, on June 2, 2010, BP announced that it would provide $360 million to fund the U.S. government's construction of six sections of sand berms to protect the barrier islands.

In December 2010, five months after the well was capped, Louisiana was in the final stages of constructing sand berms to block and capture residual oil. This activity stirred debate, since scientists argued that the oil was too dispersed to be blocked by the berms, which had only captured 1,000 barrels of oil out of the estimated 1.85 million barrels that were spilled. Political analysts questioned whether the state was continuing the project because it would mar Governor Jindal's image if left unfinished. Federal and state agencies voiced their opposition to the construction of sand berms as well, suggesting that the project could be harmful to wildlife and that funds earmarked for sand berms—amounting to $220 million—could have been spent on other restoration projects. Yet state officials kept at it, arguing that they needed to do everything they could to keep the oil at bay. In the end, the sand berms appear not to have done much good. The report of the National Commission on the BP Deepwater Horizon Oil Spill and Offshore Drilling, issued in January 2011, concluded that the berms "were not a success."

A fishing ban, in effect from May 2 (before the well was capped) until July 23, placed hundreds of Louisiana fishermen out of work. The National Oceanic and Atmospheric Administration (NOAA) was prompted to begin lifting the fishing ban when no fish caught in these areas tested positive for contamination. In April 2011, the NOAA lifted the ban on the last areas of the ocean to have been closed following the April 2010 Deepwater Horizon oil spill.

The shrimp catch, which typically peaks from May through December, was adversely affected, but not entirely lost, for 2010. BP eventually initiated a program to train and employ local residents, including many of the unemployed fishermen, to assist in cleanup operations.

A January 2011 report, commissioned by claims administrator Kenneth Feinberg, suggested that shrimp, crabs, oysters, and finfish would likely recover 30 percent of their populations by the end of 2011 and would fully recover by 2012. The report was prepared by the Harte Research Institute for Gulf of Mexico Studies at Texas A&M University–Corpus Christi.

In July 2011, Louisiana State University released a report that detailed the health impacts of the spill on coastal residents. The study found that depression, physiological symptoms, disruption to daily routines, and widespread psychosocial stress were substantial among residents. This was particularly evident among residents who either worked or had immediate family who worked for an industry directly affected by the disaster. Physiological impacts from the stress caused by the spill included headaches or migraines, joint and muscle aches, and stomachaches. When it came to illness caused by physical contact with oil, the Louisiana state health department reported that residents and cleanup workers alike experienced nausea, dizziness, headaches, and throat and eye irritations.

In February 2011, the National Oceanic and Atmospheric Administration (NOAA) and the Department of Interior (DOI) announced that they were developing a Programmatic Environmental Impact Statement (PEIS) in order to advance the restoration of the Gulf of Mexico environment. These efforts are part of an ongoing Natural Resource Damage Assessment (NRDA) in the states affected by the spill. Louisiana, along with Florida, Mississippi, Alabama, Texas, NOAA, and DOI, are working on a comprehensive assessment of the damage that the spill incurred to the Gulf Coast region's fish and wildlife habitats. Each of the Gulf Coast states held public scoping meetings as the first step in the PEIS process. These meetings discussed actions that could be taken to restore or rehabilitate injured resources. The comments provided during these meetings will be used to create an outline of the PEIS, which will be reviewed by the public again later in the year.

The oil spill has been both an environmental and economic disaster for Louisiana well beyond the Gulf fishing industry. On May 27, 2010, President Barack Obama declared a six-month suspension of exploratory drilling activity in the Gulf of Mexico. While this suspension was meant to be a cautionary measure while the Deepwater Horizon explosion was under investigation and drilling safety measures are reevaluated, the administration received complaints from groups and citizens representing the estimated 103,000 maritime services workers whose livelihoods depend on Gulf oil drilling activity. Due to the six-month suspension, thirty-three active deepwater drilling operations along the gulf's Outer Continental Shelf were required to shut down. On July 30, BP announced that it would establish a $100 million fund to support rig workers unemployed and facing hardship as a result of the moratorium.

On August 23, 2010, the responsibility for receiving and processing claims for losses related to the oil spill transferred from BP to the Gulf Coast Claims Facility (GCCF). Under independent administrator Kenneth R. Feinberg, the GCCF began processing claims for emergency payments to individuals and businesses. According to a report released by BP in August 2011, payments made to all claimants from both BP and the GCCF totaled more than $7 billion. Out of that amount, Louisiana received a total of more than $400 million.

New drilling rules were issued on September 30, 2010, to ensure the safety of offshore drilling. The regulations also set the terms under which drilling resumed on November 30, 2010.

BIBLIOGRAPHY

Books

Canney, Donald L. *In Katrina's Wake: The U.S. Coast Guard and the Gulf Coast Hurricanes of 2005.* Gainesville, FL: University Press of Florida, 2010.

Melosi, Artin, ed. *Environment, vol. 8 of The New Encyclopedia of Southern Culture.* Chapel Hill, NC: University of North Carolina Press, 2007.

White, Mel, TriaGiovan, and Jim Bones. *The Smithsonian Guides to Natural America: The South Central*

States—Texas, Oklahoma, Arkansas, Louisiana, Mississippi. Washington, DC: Smithsonian Books, 1996.

Web Sites

"Agriculture, Food & Wood Products." Louisiana Economic Development. Available from http://www.louisianaeconomicdevelopment.com/opportunities/key-industries/agriculture,-food–wood-products.aspx

Audubon Sugar Institute. Louisiana State University AgCenter. Available from http://www.lsuagcenter.com/en/our_offices/departments/Audubon_Sugar_Institute

Broder, John M., and Tom Zeller Jr. "Gulf Oil Spill Is Bad, but How Bad." *The New York Times*, May 3, 2010. Available from http://www.nytimes.com/2010/05/04/us/04enviro.html

"Claims and Government Payments, Gulf of Mexico Oil Spill." BP. August 23, 2011. Available from http://responsedata.bp.com/files/PublicClaimsStatusTracking08_23_2011.pdf

The Clean Energy Economy: Louisiana. The Pew Charitable Trusts. Available from http://www.pewcenteronthestates.org/uploadedFiles/wwwpewcenteronthestatesorg/Fact_Sheets/Clean_Economy_Factsheet_Louisiana.pdf

Dykes, Brett Michael. "Researchers find thick patches of crude still on Gulf floor." February 22, 2011. Yahoo News. Available from http://news.yahoo.com/s/yblog_thelookout/20110222/ts_yblog_thelookout/researchers-find-thick-patches-of-crude-still-on-gulf-floor

"Federal Natural Resource Trustees Announce Next Step in BP Deepwater Horizon Spill Gulf Restoration Process." February 19, 2011. National Oceanic and Atmospheric Administration. Available from http://www.noaanews.noaa.gov/stories2011/20110219_gulfspillrestoration.html

"Fifth Extension of Sixteenth Amended Declaration of Emergency and Administrative Order." State of Louisiana Department of Environmental Quality. Available from http://www.deq.louisiana.gov/portal/portals/0/news/pdf/Fifthextensionofsixteenthdeclarationofemergency.pdf

"Global Warming and Louisiana." The National Wildlife Federation. Available from http://www.nwf.org/~/media/PDFs/Global%20Warming/Global%20Warming%20State%20Fact%20Sheets/Louisiana.ashx

Growing Green. Available from http://www.laworks.net/Green/GG_Main.asp

Guillot, Craig. "Oil Spill Hits Gulf Coast Habitats." *National Geographic Daily News*. April 30, 2010. Available from http://news.nationalgeographic.com/news/2010/04/100430-energy-oil-spill-hits-gulf-coast

Gulf Coast Claims Facility. "Louisiana Program Statistics." Available from http://www.gulfcoastclaimsfacility.com/GCCF_Louisiana_Status_Report.pdf

Hammer, David. "Maritime Industry Workers Question Whether Drilling Moratorium Is Worth the Economic Pain." *The Times-Picayune*, June 4, 2010. Available from http://www.nola.com/news/gulf-oil-spill/index.ssf/2010/06/maritime_industry_workers_ques.html

"Louisiana Incentives and Laws for Ethanol." U.S. Department of Energy. Available from http://www.afdc.energy.gov/afdc/laws/laws/LA/tech/3252

Louisiana Public Service Commission, Staff Technical Conference, Docket Number R-31106. "Rulemaking to Study the Possible Development of Financial Incentives for the Promotion of Energy Efficiency by Jurisdictional Electric and Natural Gas Utilities." January 25, 2011. Available from http://www.lpsc.org/_docs/_General/R-31106%20Jan%2025%20Tech%20Conf.pdf

Louisiana State Legislature. *SB 240/Act 270: Louisiana major facility project; energy efficiency and conservation requirements*. Available from http://ssl.csg.org/dockets/2010cycle/30B/30Bbills/0330b06laenergypublicfacilities.pdf

Make It Right Foundation: Helping to Rebuild New Orleans' Lower 9th Ward. Available from http://www.makeitrightnola.org/

McIlhenny Company. "Welcome to Avery Island: Home of Tabasco." Available from http://www.tabasco.com/tabasco_history/avery_island.cfm#targ

Morganza Floodway. Available from http://www.mvn.usace.army.mil/bcarre/morganza.asp

National Commission on the BP Deepwater Horizon Oil Spill and Offshore Drilling. *Report to the President: Deepwater: The Gulf Oil Disaster and the Future of Offshore Drilling,*. January 2011. Available from http://www.oilspillcommission.gov/final-report

"President Barack Obama Suspends Drilling at 33 Wells in the Gulf of Mexico." *The Times-Picayune*, May 27, 2010. Available from http://www.nola.com/news/gulf-oil-spill/index.ssf/2010/05/president_barack_obama_suspend.html

Rioux, Paul. "Mississippi River flooding forecasts now seem like cries of 'Wolf!' to some in Butte La Rose." *The Times–Picayune*. June 1, 2011. Available from http://www.nola.com/environment/index.ssf/2011/06/although_relieved_that_forecas.html

Robertson, Campell. "Hopes Rise in South as Waters Do Not." *The New York Times.* May 24, 2011. Available from http://www.nytimes.com/2011/05/25/us/25flood.html?_r=1&pagewanted=print

Russell, James S. "U.S. Army Corps Flood Failures on Mississippi Demand New Vision." Bloomberg. August 23, 2011. Available from http://www.bloomberg.com/news/2011-08-23/u-s-army-corps-flood-failures-on-mississippi-demand-new-vision.html

Scott, Robert Travis. "Gulf oil spill will not cause cash flow problems for state, Gov. Bobby Jindal says." *The Times-Picayune*, May 4, 2010. Available from http://www.nola.com/news/gulf-oil-spill/index.ssf/2010/05/gulf_oil_spill_will_not_cause.html

"State Energy Profiles: Louisiana." United States Energy Information Administration. Available from http://tonto.eia.doe.gov/state/state_energy_profiles.cfm?sid=LA

State of Louisiana, Department of Environmental Quality. Sixteenth Amended Declaration of Emergency and Administrative Order: Hurricane Katrina and its Aftermath. Available from http://www.deq.state.la.us/portal/portals/0/news/pdf/Katrina16th Amended.pdf

Stephenson, Emily. "Endangered cranes to be reintroduced in Louisiana." February 8, 2011. Reuters. Available from http://www.reuters.com/article/2011/02/08/us-cranes-idUSTRE7176K 820110208

Stokstad, Erik. "Politics Buried Science in Louisiana Sand Berms, Oil Commission Finds." Science Insider, December 17, 2010. Available from http://news.sciencemag.org/scienceinsider/2010/12/politics-buried-science-in-louisana.html

Tunnell, John W. Jr. "An expert opinion of when the Gulf of Mexico will return to pre-spill harvest status following the BP Deepwater Horizon MC 252 oil spill." January 31, 2011. Available from http://gulfcoastmaritime.com/wp-content/uploads/2011/02/20110131-GCCF-Final-Report.pdf

Maine

With a land territory of just under 31,000 square miles (80,290 sq km), Maine is the largest state in New England and the 11th smallest state in the United States. Maine can be divided into three climatic regions: the southern interior zone, the coastal zone, and the northern half of the state, located in between the Canadian provinces of Quebec and New Brunswick. The northern zone is defined by its dry and cool climate relative to the other zones, while the coastal zone is the most moderate of the three regions year-round.

A coastal state with a huge forestry sector, climate change is a major concern for Maine. Rising sea levels and ocean temperatures, and increased hurricane intensities, also associated with climate change, could severely impact Maine, fundamentally changing the complexion and ecology of Maine's coastline and its interior, which could have substantial impacts on agricultural and silvicultural resources critical to the state's economy. According to the Center for Integrative Environmental Research (CIER) at the University of Maryland, the forest industry in the northeast United States will likely face production declines of as much as 17 percent as a result of global climate change. Since Maine's forestry sector is robust and economically vital to the state, declining production could have a severe impact. Due to the possibility of a decline in the forestry sector and a recognition of the connection to releases of greenhouse gases from conventional energy sources, Maine has been making efforts to boost wind energy and even tidal energy production.

Responding to these challenges, Maine's state legislature enacted a law in 2003 that charged the state's Department of Environmental Protection (DEP) with producing a climate change action plan, the first such legal requirement of its kind in the nation. In December 2004, the Maine DEP unveiled its action plan for the state, which set a goal of reducing greenhouse gas emissions to 1990 levels by 2010, and 10 percent below those levels by 2020. In its third biennial progress report on reducing the emissions, released in January 2010, Maine's DEP reported that the state was on track to achieving the action plan's 2010 objective.

Maine is a member of the Regional Greenhouse Gas Initiative, a cooperative cap-and-trade program involving ten Northeastern and Mid-Atlantic states. The program is designed with the goal to reduce power sector carbon dioxide emissions by 10 percent by 2018. To that end, the regional cap established by the group was set at 188 million short tons of carbon dioxide per year from 2009 to 2014. Starting in 2015 the cap will decrease by 2.5 percent each year. Carbon dioxide allowances for power plants can be obtained or traded in quarterly auctions. Each state may then reinvest its auction proceeds in programs that support the growth of a clean energy economy. In Maine, the state's auction proceeds are earmarked for electric and fossil fuel energy efficiency programs under the direction of the Efficiency Maine Trust. The first three-year control (or compliance) period began on January 1, 2009 and was set to end on December 31, 2011. At that time, each regulated power plant must submit one allowance for each ton of carbon dioxide emitted during the control period. The RGGI represents the first mandatory, market-based carbon dioxide emissions program in the United States.

❧ Natural Resources, Water, and Agriculture

Heavy Forests Adjoin Rich Ocean Waters

Maine's forests serve as one of the state's greatest natural resources, and operate as a boon for Maine's economy. Maine is home to the largest contiguous block of undeveloped forestland east of Mississippi. The state's forests, which in recent years have covered as much as 90 percent of the state (more than any other U.S. state) are largely comprised of softwoods, chiefly red and white spruces, balsam fir, eastern hemlock, and white and red

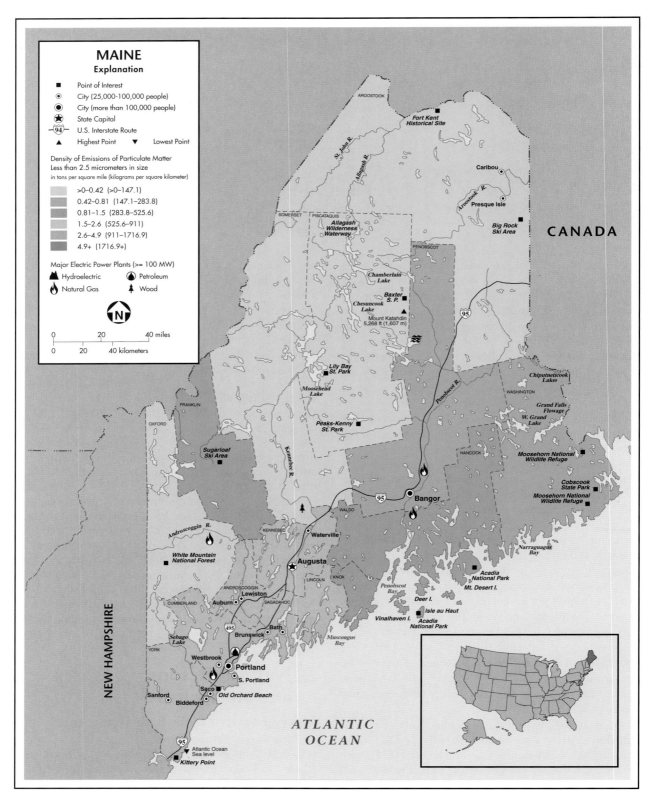

MAINE
Explanation

- ■ Point of Interest
- ◉ City (25,000–100,000 people)
- ⦿ City (more than 100,000 people)
- ★ State Capital
- —94— U.S. Interstate Route
- ▲ Highest Point   ▼ Lowest Point

Density of Emissions of Particulate Matter
Less than 2.5 micrometers in size
in tons per square mile (kilograms per square kilometer)

- >0–0.42 (>0–147.1)
- 0.42–0.81 (147.1–283.8)
- 0.81–1.5 (283.8–525.6)
- 1.5–2.6 (525.6–911)
- 2.6–4.9 (911–1716.9)
- 4.9+ (1716.9+)

Major Electric Power Plants (>= 100 MW)

- ▲ Hydroelectric   ⬤ Petroleum
- ⬤ Natural Gas   🌲 Wood

0   20   40 miles
0   20   40 kilometers

SOURCES: "County Emissions Map: Criteria Air Pollutants." *AirData*. U.S. Environmental Protection Agency. Available from http://www.epa.gov/air/data/geosel.html; *Energy Maps*. U.S. Energy Information Administration. Available from http://www.eia.gov/state; *Highest and Lowest Elevations*. U.S. Geological Survey. Available from http://egsc.usgs.gov/isb/pubs/booklets/elvadist/elvadist.html#Highest; *2007 Minerals Yearbook*. U.S. Geological Survey. Available from http://minerals.usgs.gov/minerals/pubs/state.   © 2011 Cengage Learning.

Leatherback sea turtle hatchling leaves a nest marked for evaluation. © *Chris Johnson/Alamy*

pine. Important hardwoods include beech, yellow and white birches, sugar and red maples, white oak, black willow, black and white ashes, and American elm. These trees represent the backbone of Maine's vibrant wood products industry, which contributes more than $4 billion to the state's economy each year and provides more than 50,000 jobs.

There are forty-eight state parks and historic sites in Maine, bringing in more than 2 million visitors each year. In addition, the state is home to Acadia National Park, notable as the first national park east of the Mississippi and home to Cadillac Mountain, the tallest mountain on the eastern coast and, during a portion of the year, the first place in the U.S. to see the sunrise. It is one of the most visited within the national park system.

The U.S. Fish and Wildlife Service lists 15 animal and 3 plant species in Maine as either federally threatened or endangered, including three species of whale, the leatherback sea turtle, and the eastern prairie fringed orchid. The state maintains special management plans for fifteen mammal species, including the raccoon, beaver, Eastern coyote, American black bear, river otter,

snowshoe hare, and moose. There are also twenty-two management plans involving birds, including general strategies for island nesting seabirds and waterfowl and specific plans for some species such as wild turkey, harlequin duck, grasshopper sparrow, and the golden and bald eagles. Blanding's turtle, eastern box turtle, spotted turtles, northern black racer, Clayton's copper butterfly, and Tomah mayfly each have their own plans as well.

Maine was ranked forty-fifth for overall nonfuel mineral production in 2010 with a value of $114 million. The state produces construction sand and gravel, crushed stone, portland cement, dimension stone, and peat.

Water: Not Just a Rocky Coast

A water-rich state, Maine boasts more than 2,200 lakes and ponds. The two largest lakes in the state are Moosehead Lake and Sebago Lake; the former is the largest lake located entirely within one state east of the Mississippi River. Of the more than 5,000 rivers in the state, the most important include the Penobscot River, the largest river totally within Maine's borders, the Androscoggin, the Kennebec, and the Saco rivers. The St. John River, which extends into Canada and defines part of Maine's northern border, also represents a historically vital river.

The importance of Maine's portion of the Atlantic Ocean to the state and region also cannot be overstated. In terms of recreation, housing, and commercial fishing, the Atlantic Ocean waters are invaluable to the state. According to the Nature Conservancy, the Gulf of Maine functions as one of the world's ten most productive marine systems. More than 20 species of whale troll the waters off the state's coast.

The most important Maine fishery product today is the lobster. According to the Gulf of Maine Research Institute, Maine is the largest lobster-producing state in the nation, with lobster landings increasing considerably over the past two decades. The rich fisheries in Maine's portion of the Atlantic Ocean are also used to harvest an array of other popular fish and sea animals, including flounder, halibut, scallops, and shrimp.

Agriculture: World Leader in Blueberries

According to 2009 USDA figures, Maine boasted roughly 8,100 farms, which took up more than 2,100 square miles (5,440 sq km) of land. Although Maine's cold climate and short growing season have impeded growth in Maine's overall agricultural economy, the state does lead the region, the country, and even the world in certain areas of agriculture.

Maine ranks first in the world in the production of blueberries, producing over 25 percent of the total blueberry crop and over 50 percent of the world's wild blueberries. Maine is also the regional leader in potato production, and ranks sixth nationally in terms of total acres devoted to potato cultivation. Nationally, Maine also ranks second in maple syrup production.

Organic farming is a growing sector of agriculture in the state. In 2009, there were a total of 380 certified organic farms in Maine, which as a proportion of total farms in the state, was the second most in the United States, behind Vermont.

❧ Energy

Oil and Natural Gas

Because Maine has no fossil fuel reserves of its own, all of its oil and gas must be imported via barge and pipeline to the state, a majority of which originates in Canada. The ports of Portland, Searsport, and Calais receive petroleum products from other countries as well.

Maine residents consume a significant amount of fuel oil—which is used by about 80 percent of all households for home heating—but also exports nearly 50 percent of its supply to other New England markets. Like several of the Northeast states, consumption of fuel oil is particularly high during the cold winter months, making the state vulnerable to distillate fuel oil shortages and dramatic price spikes. Maine benefits from the

Northeast Home Heating Oil Reserve, which was established by the U.S. Department of Energy in July 2000. In the event of a shortage, the reserve provides Northeast consumers adequate supplies of oil for about ten days, the time required for ships to carry heating oil from the Gulf of Mexico to New York Harbor. The storage terminals for the reserve are located in New Jersey and Connecticut.

Electricity

About 44 percent of the electricity generated in the state is produced at natural gas–fired plants. A large portion of the remaining supply is generated from renewable energy sources. About 27 percent of the electricity supply is generated from hydroelectric power. Nearly 20 percent comes from wood and woodwaste facilities, which places Maine as one of the nation's top producers of electricity from woodwaste. About 1.5 percent of the electricity supply comes from wind power.

Recognizing Maine's Renewable Energy Potential in Wind and Waves

The development of wind energy is a major goal for the state government. Pursuant to the Maine Wind Energy

Cadillac Mountain, Acadia National Park, Maine. © *Doug Lemke/ShutterStock.com*

Act (Maine Revised Statute Title 35-A, Chapter 34), the state has set a series of goals to develop at least 2,000 megawatts of installed wind energy capacity by 2015 and at least 8,000 megawatts of installed capacity by 2030. To tap into this potential, the U.S. Department of Energy announced in October 2009 a leveraged $8 million grant to the Maine Offshore Wind Initiative at University of Maine (UMAINE) for deepwater offshore wind research. In June 2010, following a visit to the center by U.S. energy secretary Steven Chu, an additional $20 million was dedicated to the project, which has set a goal of building the world's first floating wind turbine by 2012. These Department of Energy grants are part of the American Recovery and Reinvestment Act. In August 2011 Interior Secretary Ken Salazar toured the center and was impressed, vowing to move quickly to identify offshore energy zones. The Offshore Wind Initiative is a project of the UMAINE Advanced Structures and Composites Center. A supporting grant of $12.4 million was offered to the university by the U.S. Commerce Department's National Institute of Standards and Technology to build the Advanced Nanocomposites in Renewable Energy Laboratory, which will also provide significant research facilities for offshore wind technology. UMAINE is also a leader of the DeepCWind Consortium, which is a group of nonprofits, utilities, and businesses involved in offshore wind, and firms with expertise in wind project siting.

Also in June 2010, state voters approved a $26 million bond issue for energy projects, with $11 million earmarked for research on the floating turbines.

The potential for tidal power is once again being explored in Maine, with several projects under development. Tidal power involves the use of hydrokinetic devices that generate electricity from the force of the tides. This concept is not new for Maine, dating back to the 1930s. The Tidal Energy Device Evaluation Center (TEDEC) of the Maine Maritime Academy (MMA) and three industry partners are developing a tidal energy project in Castine harbor and the Bagaduce River. In addition, Tidewalker Associates of Trescott, Maine, has revived a project in Half Moon Cove in Washington County, where a major project demonstrated technical feasibility in the 1970s, although economic restraints prohibited completion at the time. Tidewalker received a preliminary permit from the Federal Energy Regulatory Commission in December 2010 to study the feasibility of the Half Moon Cove Project, and was considering undertaking a project that would involve the construction of a 1,200-foot-long (366-m) rock-filled barrage and a four-turbine generating station with a total capacity of 9.0 megawatts at Half Moon Cove. In addition, a 7.1-mile-long (11.4-km) transmission line would be constructed to distribute the estimated 45,000 megawatt-hours of electricity per year that the project would provide.

Maine State Profile

Physical Characteristics

Land area	30,841 square miles (79,878 sq km)
Inland water area	2,282 square miles (5,910 sq km)
Coastal area	613 square miles (987 sq km)
Highest point	Mount Katahdin 5,268 feet (1,606 m)
National Forest System lands (2010)	54,000 acres (22,000 ha)
State parks (2011)	32

Energy Statistics

Total energy production (2009)	180 trillion Btu
State ranking in total energy production (2009)	42
Renewable energy net generation total (2009)	8.2 million megawatt hours
Hydroelectric energy generation (2009)	4.2 million megawatt hours
Biomass energy generation (2009)	273,000 megawatt hours
Wind energy generation (2009)	299,000 megawatt hours
Wood and derived fuel energy generation (2009)	3.4 million megawatt hours
Crude oil reserves (2009)	NA
Natural gas reserves (2009)	NA
Natural gas liquids (2008)	NA

Pollution Statistics

Carbon output (2005)	23.3 million tons of CO_2 (21.1 million t)
Superfund sites (2008)	12
Particulate matter (less than 2.5 micrometers) emissions (2002)	4,332 tons per year (3,930 t/yr)
Toxic chemical releases (2009)	8.5 million pounds (3.9 million kg)
Generated hazardous waste (2009)	3,700 tons (3,300 t)

SOURCES: AirData. U.S. Environmental Protection Agency. Available from http://www.epa.gov/air/data; *Energy Maps, Facts, and Data of the U.S. States.* U.S. Energy Information Administration. Available from http://www.eia.gov/state; *The 2012 Statistical Abstract.* U.S. Census Bureau. Available from http://www.census.gov/compendia/statab; *United States Energy Usage.* eRedux. Available from http://www.eredux.net/states.

© 2011 Cengage Learning.

Renewable Portfolio Standard

In September 1999, Maine adopted its first renewable portfolio standard, which required that the state's electricity providers use renewable resources to fuel at least 30 percent of their power generation. Under the standard, eligible renewable resources included wind, biomass, solar, fuel cells, geothermal, tidal, solid waste in conjunction with recycling, and hydroelectric. In 2006, Maine adopted a new renewable portfolio goal to increase the capacity for new (placed into service after September 1, 2001) renewable energy by 10 percent by 2017. The goal became a mandatory standard under Public Law 403 of 2007. In 2007, Public Law 403 made the goal a mandatory standard and set dates for implementation.

❦ Green Business, Green Building, Green Jobs

Maine Helps Green Businesses Grow

The Office of Innovation and Assistance, a function of Maine's Department of Environmental Protection, offers an impressive menu of resources for local businesses that are interested in saving money through green practices. In addition to offering technical support for the state's green businesses, the Office of Innovation promotes these businesses on their Web site and offers a certification and branding program that allows local, participating businesses to market themselves as Maine Environmental Leaders.

Additionally, the Office of Innovation and Assistance offers the Small Business Technical Assistance Program (SBTAP) to help businesses in Maine with less than 100 employees comply with federal and statewide environmental regulations and reduce pollution and waste. The SBTAP's services are free of charge and small business owners receive assistance not just in environmental compliance but in pollution prevention and cost-effective methods and technology for improving operations.

Many companies are attracted to Maine because of its abundance of natural resources. The Environmental and Energy Technology Council of Maine (E2 Tech) is working on repurposing the decommissioned Brunswick Naval Air Station into a renewable energy park. The park will serve as a place for renewable energy businesses to relocate to Maine and to conduct research and development, along with light manufacturing. Still in the conceptual phase, the aim is to pattern the park after the University of California at Irvine's Research Power Park.

Green Building

Under the terms of ME Executive Order 8 (FY 04/05), new construction, expansions, or renovations of buildings that are owned or operated by a state agency are expected to incorporate the standards of the U.S. Green Building Council Leadership in Energy and Environmental Design program as they pertain to design, construction, operation, and maintenance of the building. However, these standards will only be enforced when deemed to be cost-effective over the life cycle of the building. The order applies to state-sponsored institutes of higher learning, but school administrative districts and municipalities are not subject to the order. In addition, the state joined the federal Energy Star Challenge in 2005. Under this program, the state government has vowed to encourage energy-efficiency strategies in buildings throughout the state and has pledged to set an example by tracking energy use and greenhouse gas emissions from its own government buildings in order to find ways to improve the energy efficiency of those buildings. Pursuant to the 2009 passage of Act 372, the state has also created the Task Force to Advance Energy Efficiency Conservation and Independence at State Facilities, which has provided recommendations to the government concerning initiatives, actions, and investments that are most likely to lead to greater energy independence for the state.

Efficiency Maine

Several organizations exist in Maine to facilitate and support both the green building movement and the cause of greater energy-efficiency. Most prominent among these organizations is Efficiency Maine, a state-run organization that seeks to "save energy, reduce energy costs, help the environment, and promote sustainable economic development." Created by the Act to Strengthen Energy Conservation in 2002, the initial mandate for Efficiency Maine was to promote a more efficient use of electricity and, as a result, lower electricity costs for consumers. In 2010, the mission was expanded pursuant to the Act Regarding Maine's Energy Future (2009). This act created the Efficiency Maine Trust, which became responsible for producing a plan that would achieve a series of energy reduction goals, including: 30 percent reduction in electricity and natural gas consumption by 2020, a 20 percent reduction in heating fuel consumption by 2020, the weatherization of 100 percent of homes and 50 percent of businesses by 2030, reducing consumption of liquid fossil fuels by at least 30 percent by 2030, and reducing peak-load electric energy consumption by 100 megawatts by 2020. The program differs from similar energy-efficiency mandates in other states in scope by covering more than just electricity and by focusing on consumer support and action rather than focusing primarily on utilities.

Efficiency Maine provides an array of services that aim to help residents and businesses owners use less energy more wisely. For the small business owner in the state, Efficiency Maine offers free energy audits, in which an energy auditor will spend a portion of a day touring a business facility and providing suggestions for easy and cost sensible energy savings. For a homeowner looking to reduce their electric bills, Efficiency Maine provides cash rebates for new, energy efficient appliances they have purchased. Programs are funded in part by a small percentage of all of Maine's electricity bills. For 2010, Efficiency Maine received funding for some projects under the American Recovery and Reinvestment Act and from the regional Greenhouse Gas Initiative.

Green Jobs

According to a 2009 study by the Pew Charitable Trusts, jobs in Maine's clean energy economy grew at a rate of 22.7 percent between 1998 and 2007, while traditional jobs grew by only 3.3 percent over that period. In 2007, 725 clean energy businesses were located in Maine, providing 6,000 green jobs. Future green sector job growth looked less promising, however, as Maine did not attract any venture capital to its clean energy economy from 2006 to 2008.

❧ Sustainable Fishing: Countering Depletion

As with many natural resources, human beings have historically perceived the bounty of the ocean—fish and ocean wildlife—to be inexhaustible resources and endless sources of food. As human populations have expanded across the globe, however, and demand for fish and seafood has steadily increased, many people have begun to recognize that the human appetite for some fish is quickly outpacing their availability. In places like the Gulf of Maine, where fishing has not only served as a source of food but represents an economic lifeblood and cultural bedrock, this reality has hit locally with force. Analysts have noted that fishers in Maine, who for decades were accustomed to bringing home thousands of pounds of fish per day, often travel farther today than ever before, while returning with far smaller and less lucrative catches. The problem has grown to the point that, in the 1990s, for the first time in history, official organizations declared that the Atlantic cod stock in the Gulf of Maine had collapsed.

With fish supplies in the Gulf of Maine dwindling well below their historic levels, many Maine fishermen moved to different regions, closed down their operations entirely, or transferred their energies towards lobsters—the sea creature that serves today as the most important and abundant fishery product in Maine. However, the turmoil in the Gulf of Maine underscored to many statewide, regional, and national policy makers the need for proactive policy prescriptions for the situation.

The increase in lobster landings in the state has also raised concerns. A report released in 2011 pointed out that Maine's dependence on this abundance could have them locked in a so-called "gilded trap." Researchers are calling for a restoration of the diversity of the Gulf. A few decades ago, Maine fisheries also included cod, hake, haddock, halibut, and swordfish, which were just about eliminated by intense fishing. Many of these were lobster predators, whose elimination—along with food from baited traps—allowed lobsters to flourish. Researchers say the overcrowding of lobsters would be disastrous if outbreaks of parasite infestations and shell disease were to occur, as they have done in southern New England waters. Researchers are unsure of how an increase in biodiversity would affect lobster yields, stating that the whole ecology of the Gulf has changed, and they aren't even sure yet if it is a good or bad thing. Still, many lobstermen remain concerned about the rapid expansion of lobster catches and what that means for the future of the Gulf.

Leaders Stand Together

In 1989 the governors and premiers of all the U.S. states and Canadian provinces that border the Gulf of Maine joined together to form the Gulf of Maine Council on the Environment. The mission of the organization is to "maintain and enhance environmental quality in the Gulf of Maine and to allow for sustainable resource use by existing and future generations." Every five years, the Gulf of Maine Council on the Environment puts together an action plan that outlines a strategy for the next five years on how to work towards the Council's mission. The five-year plans regularly emphasize the importance of sustainable fishing.

The state of Maine has also taken independent steps to address, develop, and support sustainable fisheries in the state. In 2000, the Maine Department of Marine Resources unveiled a strategic plan, which listed the development of sustainable fisheries high among its priorities. The strategic plan envisioned and supported the goal of having Maine's coastal communities reformulate their economic base toward sustainable fisheries and aquaculture.

Sustainable Fishing: Facing the Challenge

The Food and Agricultural Organization of the United Nations defines sustainable fishing as the conscious effort to ensure that "fisheries resources [are] not depleted beyond their natural capacity of renewal and passed as such to future generations." Sustainable fishing can include traditional commercial fishing as well as aquaculture, or fish farming (although these practices raise issues of waste, and the impact of releases of genetically modified organisms on wild populations). The key objective is to ensure that the way the fish are harvested is in accord with the natural balance of the local ecosystem.

While such foresight is commendable, it is difficult to actualize. Fishery experts, such as Ellen Marsden of the University of Vermont, have identified many impediments to the successful implementation of sustainable fisheries. Prominent among these are the challenges of data uncertainty—the inability to know exactly how many fish there are in a given ecosystem, the complexity of ecosystem dynamics, the political unwillingness to make decisions that hurt fishermen or the fishing industry, and consumer awareness.

Community-Based Fisheries

Several Maine organizations see community-based fisheries as a path towards sustainability in the sector. The Penobscot East Resource Center, a partner with the Nature Conservancy, is one Maine organization that seeks to promote local, community-centric fisheries. Port

Clyde Fresh Catch embodies the type of economically and environmentally sustainable fishing enterprise that is changing the way Mainers consume and think about fish. Port Clyde Fresh Catch is a direct distribution network that pairs sustainably minded fishermen with local consumers interested in receiving fresh, sustainably caught seafood. Port Clyde uses environmentally friendly gear that reduces "bycatch"—fish caught unintentionally—and engages in seasonal fishing, which ensures that one species is not harvested all year round. Together, organizations and businesses like Port Clyde Fresh Catch and the Penobscot East Resource Center have helped Mainers conceive of themselves as active stakeholders in the sustainable fishing future of Maine.

BIBLIOGRAPHY

Books

Cenkl, Pavel. *Nature and Culture in the Northern Forest*. Iowa City: University of Iowa Press, 2010.

Collette, Bruce B. and Grace Klein-McPhee. *Bigelow and Schroeder's Fishes of the Gulf of Maine*, 3rd ed. Washington, DC: Smithsonian Books, 2002.

Tree, Christina, and Nancy English. *Explorer's Guide Maine Coast & Islands*. New York: W. W. Norton & Co., 2010.

Wetherell, W. D. *The Smithsonian Guides to Natural America: Northern New England–Vermont, New Hampshire, Maine*. Washington, DC: Smithsonian Books, 1995.

Web Sites

Adams, Glenn. "Interior secretary sees Maine wind energy center." Chem.Info. August 18, 2011. Available from http://www.chem.info/News/FeedsAP/2011/08/topics-alternative-energy-interior-secretary-sees-maine-wind-energy-center/

"An Act Regarding Maine's Energy Future (Public Law, Chapter 372 LD 1485, item 1)." Maine State Legislature. Available from http://www.efficiencymaine.com/docs/AgencyRules/LD-1485.pdf.

"An Act to Strengthen Energy Conservation Public Law, Chapter 624 HP 330-LD 420)." Maine State Legislature. Available from http://www.mainelegislature.org/ros/LOM/lom120th/4Pub601-650/Pub601-650-23.htm.

Dean, Cornelia. "Lobsters Find Utopia Where Biologists See Trouble." *The New York Times*. August 22, 2011. Available from http://www.nytimes.com/2011/08/23/science/23lobster.html

"Efficiency Maine." Available from http://www.efficiencymaine.com/

"Indicators for Sustainable Development of Fisheries." Food and Agricultural Organization of the United Nations. Available from http://www.fao.org/docrep/W4745E/w4745e0f.htm

"Magnuson-Stevens Fishery Conservation and Management Act: As Amended through January 12, 2007." National Oceanic and Atmospheric Administration. Available from http://www.nmfs.noaa.gov/msa2005/docs/MSA_amended_msa%20_20070112_FINAL.pdf

Maine Deepwater Offshore Wind Report. The University of Maine. Available from http://www.deepcwind.org/docs/OfficialOffshoreWindReport-22311.pdf.

Maine: Incentives/Policies for Renewables & Efficiency. U.S. Department of Energy, Database of State Incentives for Renewables & Efficiency. Available from http://www.dsireusa.org/incentives/incentive.cfm?Incentive_Code=ME01R

"Maine Renewable Portfolio Standard." Maine Public Utilities Commission. Available from http://www.mainelegislature.org/legis/statutes/35-A/title35-Asec3210.html

Maine State Forest Assessment and Strategies. Maine Forest Service, Department of Conservation. Available from http://www.maine.gov/doc/mfs/mfs/state_assessment/downloads/maine_assessment_and_strategy_final.pdf

Maine Tidal Power. Available from http://www.maine-tidalpower.com/index.html.

The Maine Wind Energy Act (Maine Revised Statute Title 35-A,Chapter 34) . State of Maine. Available from http://www.mainelegislature.org/legis/statutes/35-a/title35-Ach34.pdf

Morgan, William. "Maine Voters Approve Offshore Wind Funding." Offshore Wind Wire. June 9, 2010. Available from http://offshorewindwire.com/2010/06/09/roundup-maine-approves-funding

Regional Greenhouse Gas Initiative: Maine State Investment Program. Available from http://www.rggi.org/rggi_benefits/program_investments/Maine.

Report of the Task Force to Advance Energy Efficiency, Conservation and Independence at State Facilities. State of Maine. Available from http://www.maine.gov/bgs/energy/documents/FinalReportJanuary2010.pdf

"Rule Chapters for the Public Utilities Commission." State of Maine. Available from http://www.maine.gov/sos/cec/rules/65/chaps65.htm.

"Seafood Watch: All Regions." Monterey Bay Aquarium. Available from http://www.montereybayaquarium.org/cr/SeafoodWatch/web/sfw_regional.aspx

"State Energy Profiles: Maine." U.S. Energy Information Administration. Available from http://tonto.eia.doe.gov/state/state_energy_profiles.cfm?sid=ME

"State of Organic Agriculture in Maine 2009." Colby College. Available from http://wiki.colby.edu/display/stateofmaine2009/State+of+Organic+Agriculture+in+Maine

"Strategic Plan." Maine Department of Marine Resources. Available from http://www.maine.gov/dmr/Strategic%20Plan%202000.htm

Turkel, Tux. "Feds earmark $20M for deepwater wind power research." *Morning Sentinel.* June 25, 2010. Available from http://www.onlinesentinel.com/news/Feds-earmark-20-million-for-deepwater-wind-power-reserach.html#

"Understanding the Dichotomy Between Industrial Agriculture and Sustainable Agriculture: Types and Characteristics of Maine Farms." Sustainable Agriculture Program. University of Maine. Stewart Smith, Pamela Bell, and Andrew Files. Available from http://www.sag.umaine.edu/more/types-and-characteristics-o.pdf

University of Maine Advanced Structures & Composites Center, Available from http://www.aewc.umaine.edu

Valigra, Lori. "Cleantech industry finds a natural home in Maine." Mass High Tech. August 3, 2011. Available from http://www.masshightech.com/stories/2011/08/01/weekly10-Cleantech-industry-finds-a-natural-home-in-Maine.html

Maryland

The Chesapeake Bay—the largest and most biologically productive estuary in the United States and Maryland's main waterway—is the heart of the state. Maryland is one of the ten smallest states in the nation, composed of a total land area of just 12,407 square miles (27,092 sq km). Geographically, however, the state is full of diversity and beauty.

The Chesapeake Bay plays a significant role in defining Maryland's topography, which can be divided into three distinct regions. In the far west, along Maryland's border with West Virginia, is the Appalachian Mountain region of the state. This geographically slight area boasts the highest elevations in Maryland and is home to Backbone Mountain, at 3,360 feet (1,025 m) the state's highest peak. The Appalachian Mountains descend east into the Piedmont Plateau, Maryland's second physiographic area, which is an uplands region with gorges and fast flowing rivers. Finally, the Pediment Plateau graduates east into Maryland's Atlantic Coastal Plain, a low-lying region bisected by the massive Chesapeake Bay.

Small State Belies Great Climate Diversity

Despite Maryland's small size, the state displays tremendous climatic diversity. The western reaches of the state—in the mountains —are naturally cooler than in the east, along the Chesapeake Bay, and average annual temperatures in the two areas diverge by more than ten degrees (48°F [8.9°C] in the western highlands; 59°F [15°C] in the southeast). Global climate change represents a significant challenge for the state, as a large portion of Maryland sits on the low-lying coastal plain, along the Atlantic Coast or the Chesapeake Bay. This region is highly developed, with major cities, such as Baltimore and Annapolis, sitting right along the water. As sea levels rise, these population centers are at risk.

According to the National Wildlife Federation, global warming is already taking its toll on the state, with water levels in the Chesapeake Bay already rising twice as fast as the global average rate of sea level rise. This rise threatens the many small islands in the bay, threatening coastal habitats for shorebirds that pass through the region each spring. Sea level rise has also destroyed nearly one-third of the marshes at the Blackwater Wildlife Refuge since 1938. This area is home to one of the largest concentrations of nesting bald eagles on the east coast. If nothing is done to slow global warming, the marshes could disappear entirely in the next thirty years.

In April 2007, Maryland's governor signed Executive Order 01.01.2007.07, which created the Maryland Climate Change Commission and charged it with developing a climate change action plan. In August 2008, the Maryland Climate Change Commission unveiled this plan. The core premise of the action plan was that global warming is "unequivocally" occurring and is likely caused by an increase in greenhouse gas emissions. Thus, the plan advocated for dramatically and progressively reducing Maryland's greenhouse gas (GHG) emissions, aiming for a 10 percent reduction from 2006 levels by 2012; a 15 percent reduction by 2015; a 25 to 50 percent reduction by 2020; and a 90 percent reduction by 2050. In May 2009, Maryland governor Martin O'Malley signed into law the Greenhouse Gas Emissions Reduction Act of 2009, which embraced the core findings of the state's climate change action plan, and established a greenhouse gas reduction target of 25 percent below 2006 levels by 2020.

Maryland is a member of the Regional Greenhouse Gas Initiative (RGGI), a cooperative cap-and-trade program involving ten Northeastern and Mid-Atlantic states. The program is designed with the goal to reduce power sector carbon dioxide emissions by 10 percent by 2018. To that end, the regional cap established by the group was set at 188 million short tons of carbon dioxide per year from 2009 to 2014. Starting in 2015 the cap will decrease by 2.5 percent each year. Carbon dioxide allowances for power plants can be obtained or traded in quarterly auctions. Each state may then reinvest its auction proceeds in programs that support the growth of a clean energy economy. In Maryland, the state's auction proceeds have been used to establish the Strategic Energy Investment Fund, which supports energy efficiency, conservation, renewable energy, and residential energy bill assistance programs. The first three-year control (or compliance) period began on January 1, 2009, and was set to end on December 31, 2011. At that time, each regulated power plant must submit one allowance for each ton of carbon dioxide emitted during the control period. The RGGI represents the first mandatory, market-based carbon dioxide emissions program in the United States.

❧ Natural Resources, Water, and Agriculture

Forests

Maryland's forests cover 41 percent of the state, or about 2.6 million acres (1.1 million ha). While there are more than 160 native or naturalized tree species in the state, yellow poplar, red maple, loblolly pine, and red and white oaks are among the most common. Hickory, beech, blackgum, and white ash are also found throughout the state. About 76 percent of the forests are privately owned. The forest industries are important to the state, with 92 percent of the forested lands classified as timberland. The total annual payroll for the forest product industry has been estimated at $420 million.

Parks and Wildlife

Maryland is home to 66 state parks and 16 national parks, including the Assateague Island National Seashore, which is shared with Virginia. Maryland boasts a tremendous diversity of plants and animals, with more than 80 species of mammals, 85 species of reptiles and amphibians, more than 233 species of birds, and more than 3,000 types of plants. Some of the most common animals include the cottontail rabbit, gray and southern flying squirrel, woodchuck, raccoon, red fox, and the white-tailed deer. Coyote and black bear can also be found in the state. The common raven, common crow, mocking bird, mourning dove, Carolina chickadee, and piping plover are among the many birds sighted.

The U.S. Fish and Wildlife Service lists 21 animal and 10 plant species in Maryland as federally threatened or endangered. Among the species listed are several ocean-dwelling species, such as the leatherback sea turtle and three species of whale. Also listed are some species unique to Maryland, such as the Maryland darter—one of the rarest fish species in the world. The Maryland Wildlife and Heritage Service lists at least one hundred species as threatened or endangered under its own State Nongame and Endangered Species Conservation Act.

One of the great challenges for Maryland is the preservation of its natural resources. Maryland's booming population directly threatens its forests and other natural resources and urban sprawl strains the limits of the natural world.

Minerals

In terms of mineral resources, crushed stone, construction sand and gravel, and masonry cement are the most important nonfuel minerals produced in the state, accounting for roughly 99 percent of total production. According to the U.S. Geological Survey, the total value of Maryland's nonfuel mineral production was $438 million in 2010, less than 1 percent of total U.S. production. Although this figure seems small, Maryland was ranked thirty-fifth among U.S. states in total nonfuel mineral production, considerably higher than its ranking in size.

The Chesapeake Bay Watershed

Nearly all of Maryland is situated within the Chesapeake Bay's massive watershed. Principal rivers in the state include the Potomac, which forms much of the southern and western border of the state; the Patapsco, which runs through central Maryland and empties into the Chesapeake Bay at Baltimore; the Patuxent, draining the Western Shore; and the Susquehanna, crossing the Pennsylvania border and emptying into the Chesapeake Bay in northeastern Maryland. Many lakes and creeks, none of any great size, as well as thirty-eight other rivers are also found in Maryland. Deep Creek Lake, a popular seasonal resort destination in far western Maryland, at 3,900 acres (1,578 ha), is the largest freshwater lake in the state.

Coastal Habitats

Chesapeake Bay is the largest estuary is the United States and the third largest in the world. The bay is home to more than 350 fish species, including pumpkinseed, summer flounder, and American shad, and numerous birds and waterfowl, such as osprey, sanderling, and piping plover. The Atlantic waters of the state are home to several species of marine mammals, including the common and bottlenose dolphin, harbor porpoise, minke and humpback whales, harbor and gray seals, and leatherback and green sea turtles.

Fishing and Commerce

Sport fishing enthusiasts enjoy a variety of catches from the state's rivers and lakes, with popular species that include largemouth and small mouth bass, striped bass, yellow and white perch, herring, northern pike, walleye, and several species of trout. The seafood industry of

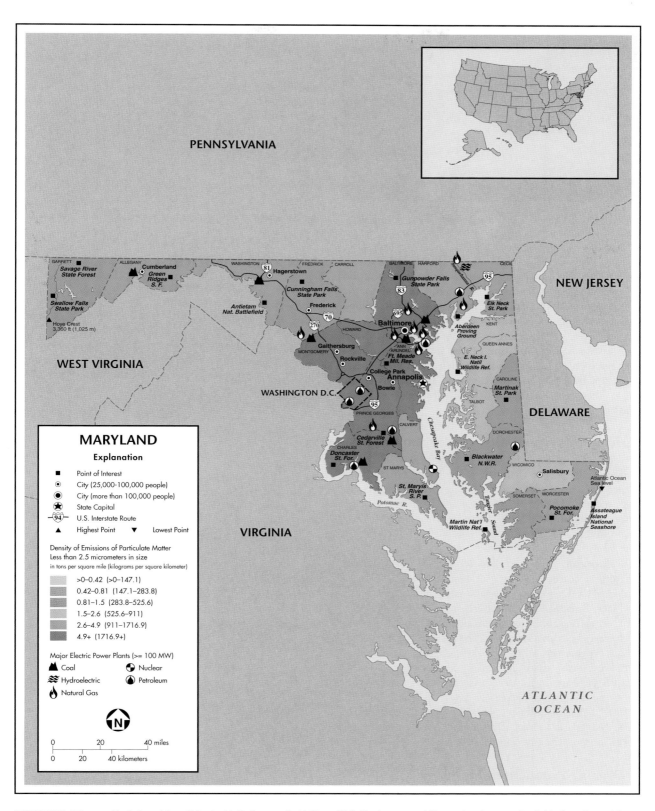

PENNSYLVANIA

NEW JERSEY

WEST VIRGINIA

WASHINGTON D.C.

VIRGINIA

DELAWARE

ATLANTIC
OCEAN

MARYLAND

Explanation

■ Point of Interest
◉ City (25,000-100,000 people)
◉ City (more than 100,000 people)
★ State Capital
〜94〜 U.S. Interstate Route
▲ Highest Point ▼ Lowest Point

Density of Emissions of Particulate Matter
Less than 2.5 micrometers in size
in tons per square mile (kilograms per square kilometer)

>0–0.42 (>0–147.1)
0.42–0.81 (147.1–283.8)
0.81–1.5 (283.8–525.6)
1.5–2.6 (525.6–911)
2.6–4.9 (911–1716.9)
4.9+ (1716.9+)

Major Electric Power Plants (>= 100 MW)

▲ Coal   ◉ Nuclear
〜 Hydroelectric ◐ Petroleum
◖ Natural Gas

N

0   20   40 miles
0   20   40 kilometers

Savage River State Forest, Cumberland, Green Ridges S.F., Swallow Falls State Park, Hoye Crest 3,360 ft (1,025 m), Antietam Nat. Battlefield, Hagerstown, Cunningham Falls State Park, Frederick, Gaithersburg, Rockville, College Park, Annapolis, Bowie, Prince Georges, Gunpowder Falls State Park, Baltimore, Aberdeen Proving Ground, Elk Neck St. Park, Ft. Meade Mil. Res., E. Neck I. Natl Wildlife Ref., Martinak St. Park, Cedarville St. Forest, Calvert, Doncaster St. For., Blackwater N.W.R., Salisbury, St Marys, St. Marys River S.P., Pocomoke St. For., Assateague Island National Seashore, Atlantic Ocean Sea level, Martin Nat'l Wildlife Ref., Tangier Sound, Potomac R., Chesapeake Bay

GARRETT, ALLEGANY, WASHINGTON, FREDRICK, CARROLL, BALTIMORE, HARFORD, CECIL, KENT, QUEEN ANNES, CAROLINE, TALBOT, DORCHESTER, WICOMICO, WORCESTER, SOMERSET, CHARLES, ST MARYS, CALVERT, PRINCE GEORGES, ANN ARUNDEL, HOWARD, MONTGOMERY

A Maryland Blue Crab resting on the beach in on the Chesapeake Bay. © Lone Wolf Photos/ShutterStock.com

Chesapeake Bay, including fish landings and seafood processing, contributes more than $400 million to the state economy each year. Blue crabs, soft clams, striped bass, and oysters are important catches.

The Port of Baltimore is one of the busiest cargo ports in the nation, and one of the top ports handling products such as coal, oil, motor vehicles, and metal waste and scrap. In 2009, Baltimore ranked as fifteenth in the nation for total tonnage and twelfth for value of cargo handled.

Agricultural Sector Mirrors Maryland's Size

In terms of sales, Maryland's agricultural sector is proportionally larger than the state itself, but remains smaller than average for a U.S. state. According to the most recent U.S Department of Agriculture (USDA) figures, Maryland's 12,000 farms extended over 9,767 square miles (25,296 sq km) of land and produced more than $2.4 billion in annual sales.

Historically, tobacco has served as the principle agricultural commodity in Maryland, and as a share of total U.S. tobacco sales, Maryland is still an above average producer. But the agricultural sector has clearly shifted to favor other commodities, such as chickens and chicken products—the top agricultural products in terms of sales today. To put this shift into perspective, consider that there were more than fifty times more acres devoted to tobacco production in 1978 than in 2007, significantly outpacing the decline of total land devoted to agriculture. In 2007, farmland still occupied 78 percent of the total in 1978. Maryland ranks thirteenth among states for producing poultry and poultry products.

In Organic Production, Maryland is Growing

Due to increased consumer demand, organic farming is a growing agricultural sector in Maryland. In 2004, the Maryland Organic Certification Program had certified seventy-eight organic farms. By the 2008 USDA

Organic Production Survey, 129 farms in Maryland were listed as organic certified or exempt. At the time of the Organic Production Survey, Maryland's organic farms were generating, at $10 million in annual sales, more revenue than those in sixteen states in the nation. Maryland's organic production was roughly on par with its overall agricultural production, falling below average for a U.S. state in total sales, but high for its size. As a share of total organic sales, livestock and poultry products were the largest commodity group in Maryland.

⚘ Energy: Low-Input Economy Keeps Energy Consumption Low

Maryland consumes considerably less energy per capita than most U.S. states, with only eight states consuming less energy per person than Maryland. The transportation sector leads all others in total energy consumption, but not by much. Maryland industry is the only sector in the state that demands considerably less energy than the others, requiring less than half of the energy resources demanded by the commercial, the residential, and the transportation sectors.

In terms of energy production, Maryland's coal fired plants supply a majority of the electricity produced in the state. Maryland has some coal reserves in the western region of the state, but is not rich in energy resources. Thus, much of the coal burned at Maryland power stations arrives from neighboring states with large coal reserves, such as West Virginia and Pennsylvania. Maryland's lone nuclear power plant, a dual unit plant located in Calvert Cliffs along the Chesapeake Bay, produces approximately one-fifth of the electricity generated in the state. Petroleum and natural gas fired plants supply much of the remainder of the electricity produced in the state.

Renewable Potential

At present, Maryland's renewable energy portfolio is limited. However, the state holds considerable potential for developing renewable energy, particularly wind resources off the state's Atlantic coast and in the Appalachian Mountains. Recognizing the imperative to move in the renewable energy direction, Maryland enacted its first renewable portfolio standard (RPS) in 2004, with revisions implemented in 2006, 2007, and 2010. Under the revised standard, Maryland's electricity suppliers must obtain a set rate of their electricity from specifically designated renewable resources, with the peak objective of the RPS coming in 2022, when a full 20 percent of electricity must be supplied by pre-approved renewable resources (including a 2 percent minimum for solar energy). Maryland's RPS

Maryland State Profile

Physical Characteristics

Land area	9,705 square miles (25,136 sq km)
Inland water area	736 square miles (1,906 sq km)
Coastal area	1,854 square miles (2,984 sq km)
Highest point	Hoye Crest 3,360 feet (1,024 m)
National Forest System lands (2010)	NA
State parks (2011)	45

Energy Statistics

Total energy production (2009)	270 trillion Btu
State ranking in total energy production (2009)	38
Renewable energy net generation total (2009)	2.4 million megawatt hours
Hydroelectric energy generation (2009)	1.9 million megawatt hours
Biomass energy generation (2009)	376,000 megawatt hours
Wind energy generation (2009)	NA
Wood and derived fuel energy generation (2009)	175,000 megawatt hours
Crude oil reserves (2009)	NA
Natural gas reserves (2009)	NA
Natural gas liquids (2008)	NA

Pollution Statistics

Carbon output (2005)	78.8 million tons of CO_2 (71.5 million t)
Superfund sites (2008)	19
Particulate matter (less than 2.5 micrometers) emissions (2002)	19,473 tons per year (17,665 t/yr)
Toxic chemical releases (2009)	35.9 million pounds (16.3 million kg)
Generated hazardous waste (2009)	33,700 tons (30,600 t)

SOURCES: AirData. U.S. Environmental Protection Agency. Available from http://www.epa.gov/air/data; *Energy Maps, Facts, and Data of the U.S. States.* U.S. Energy Information Administration. Available from http://www.eia.gov/state; *The 2012 Statistical Abstract.* U.S. Census Bureau. Available from http://www.census.gov/compendia/statab; *United States Energy Usage.* eRedux. Available from http://www.eredux.net/states.

© 2011 Cengage Learning.

provides graduated renewable energy targets for electricity providers, which ease them into full 2022 compliance.

In September 2011, Constellation Energy began construction on a 16.1 megawatt photovoltaic solar power plant in Emmitsburg. It was the largest project of its kind in the state as of that date. Maryland's Department of General Services and the University System of Maryland Power have entered into 20-year agreements with Constellation Energy to purchase power from the plant beginning in 2012. The project was part of the Maryland's Generating Clean Horizons initiative, initiated in December 2009. The initiative, a partnership with the University System of Maryland, has the goal of supporting the development of large-scale, commercial renewable energy projects that can supply power to the grid before 2014.

Green Business, Green Building, Green Jobs

Green Business

Maryland has a number of programs that help or encourage businesses in the state "green" their operations. One of Maryland's preferred methods of encouragement is the tax incentive, which applies to companies that engage in green practices. The Brownfields Revitalization Incentive Program (BRIP), run through the Maryland Department of Business and Economic Development, represents one outstanding incentive-based environmental business program in the state. BRIP encourages businesses in Maryland to cleanup brownfield sites by offering substantial tax credits for the increased value of the remediated property. Here's how it works.

A business decides to purchase an old building with deeply contaminated soil for $100. The company decides to remediate the soil, and consequently, the property doubles in value, as more and more people become interested in moving there. Under most tax systems, the company would have to pay tax on the true value of the property—$200. But because the company helped improve Maryland's environment and helped recycle a property that would otherwise go to waste, Maryland rewards that company by giving it, for up to five years, a real property tax credit between 50 and 70 percent of the increased value of the site.

The Brownfields Revitalization Incentive Program is just one example of incentive-based environmental programs for businesses in the state. BRIP is compelling because it addresses one of the chief environmental concerns in Maryland—population sprawl. In this way, Maryland's land reuse programs help to slow human encroachment on the natural world.

Maryland Becomes a Force for Green Building

In 2006, Maryland's General Assembly passed House Bill 1211, which created the Green Building Task Force. Maryland's Green Building Task Force was charged with reviewing regional and national green building initiatives to determine the most cost effective ways to encourage green building in Maryland. In December 2007, the Green Building Task Force completed its review and produced a final report, which strongly advocated for the authorization of green building tax incentives in Maryland.

One program on which the Green Building Task Force focused was the Maryland Green Building Tax Credit, a $25 million fund created in 2001 to encourage green building in the state. The program was scheduled to last until 2011, but was exhausted in 2005 due to its extreme popularity. The Green Building Task Force therefore called for reauthorized funding for a modified green building tax credit. Because demand outpaced supply of the initial tax credits, the task force advanced the idea of raising qualifying standards for green built buildings from traditional LEED Certification to LEED Gold Certification (the second highest certification offered through the U.S. Green Building Council). Although the proposal to raise qualifying standards to LEED Gold Certification was not implemented, funding for the green building tax credit has been reauthorized in Maryland.

Today, a tax credit of up to 8 percent of the total building cost is offered to individuals who construct a LEED Silver certified building of 20,000 square feet (1,858 sq m) or more on an approved site. Approved sites include qualified brownfields locations or priority funding areas that are not wetlands.

Leading by example, the state legislature enacted the Maryland High Performance Buildings Act (SB 208) in 2008. This law requires that all new construction or major renovations of state buildings must meet the criteria for LEED Silver certification or higher, or obtain a comparable numeric rating on a similar nationally recognized system. New schools built with state assistance are also required to meet this standard. To assist in these efforts, for fiscal years 2010 through 2014 the state has pledged to pay 50 percent of the local share of the extra costs that will be incurred by school districts as a result of these requirements.

In 2011, Montgomery County launched the Residential Energy Efficiency Rebate Program. The program provides incentives of up to $3,000 to owners of single-family homes and condominiums who make energy efficiency improvements, such as geothermal heat pumps and solar water heating and appliances. The program works with other incentives from companies such as Pepco, BG&E, Potomac Edison, and Maryland Energy Administration Programs. The rebate is part of the county's American Recovery and Reinvestment Act grant. Montgomery County also offers property tax credits for renewable energy and energy efficiency measures.

Maryland Emphasizes Green Jobs Despite Losses

Although Maryland runs many incentive-based environmental programs and has attracted in recent years more venture capital to the clean energy economy than forty-four of the fifty U.S. states, the number of clean energy jobs in Maryland broke with overall U.S. trends and decreased from 1998 to 2007. According to the Pew Charitable Trusts, Maryland had, with 12,908, more clean energy jobs than thirty states in the nation in 2007. However, the downward pressure on clean energy jobs

was certainly distressing for public policy makers in Maryland.

In September 2009, the Governor's Workforce Investment Board published a twenty-eight page energy industry workforce report, entitled, "Preparing Today's Workers for Tomorrow's Opportunities." The report focused almost exclusively on green jobs and the importance of growing that sector in the state. The report advanced a commonsense approach for how to develop a green economy workforce. Three key objectives were highlighted: attracting workers to the green economy by cultivating a buzz around green jobs; making information about the green economy readily accessible to workers in the state; and identifying and developing short-term courses that train workers for specific duties in the green economy.

❧ Chesapeake Bay Cleanup

The Chesapeake Bay is the largest, most biologically productive estuary in the United States, and the third largest in the world. Formed about 12,000 years ago from glacier melt, the bay is a shallow but highly productive resource with average depths (including its tributaries) of only 21 feet (6 m). Roughly 3,600 species of plant and animal life are found in the bay, which harbors a robust fishing industry that brings in some 500 million pounds of seafood every year.

The Chesapeake Bay is also a deeply threatened resource. Each year, about 300 million pounds (136 million kg) of nutrient pollution and 4.8 million tons (4.4 metric tons) of sediment enter into the bay from farm fields, sewage plants, septic tanks, suburban lawns, airborne pollutants, roads and parking lots. This astonishing figure, which carries dramatic environmental consequences for the bay, is easier to understand when one considers the massive size of the Chesapeake Bay watershed. The watershed—the area that drains into the Chesapeake Bay through rivers, streams and groundwater—extends 64,000 square miles (165,760 sq km) and reaches into six states: parts of New York, Delaware, and West Virginia; a large section of Pennsylvania; most of Virginia; almost all of Maryland; and all of the District of Columbia.

As populations expand across this area, more and more toxic runoff enters the Chesapeake Bay. According to the Chesapeake Bay Foundation's (CBF) 2008 State of the Bay Report, the bay's health rated 28 out of 100 that year. A score of 70 would constitute a "saved" bay. Since the early 1980s, when the bay's health was the worst (CBF estimates that the bay's health would have rated a 23 out of 100 at that time), several governing bodies across the Chesapeake Bay Watershed have joined together to begin the process of improving the health of the bay. But several challenges remain.

Historical Efforts

Competing interests have bottlenecked the pollution management of the watershed for years. Efforts to restore the Chesapeake Bay began as early as the mid-1970s, when U.S. Senator Charles Mathias, of Maryland, sponsored a congressionally funded, $27 million, five-year study by the U.S. Environmental Protection Agency (EPA) analyzing the rapid loss of wildlife in the bay. The study, which concluded in the early 1980s, found that excess nutrient pollution—high amounts of nitrogen and phosphorous from fertilizers, septic systems, wastewater treatment plants, etc.—was responsible for the Chesapeake Bay's degradation. In 1983, soon after Mathias's study was published, the original Chesapeake Bay Agreement was signed by a group that later became known as the Chesapeake Executive Council: the governors of Maryland, Virginia, and Pennsylvania; the mayor of Washington, DC; the administrator of the EPA; and the chair of the Chesapeake Bay Commission, a tri-state legislative body.

The council agreed to meet regularly to discuss and agree on environmental management practices for the Chesapeake Bay. In 1987, and again in 2000, the council wrote new Chesapeake Bay Agreements that adjusted for new on-the-ground realities in the bay. In 2000, the governors of New York and Delaware agreed to comply with the water quality section of the Chesapeake 2000 agreement, and in 2002, West Virginia joined New York and Delaware as additional signatories. However, while critics commended these agreements as good first steps, they hungered for more measurable action and results.

Federal Government Gets Involved

One of the key objectives of the Chesapeake 2000 agreement was to resolve the bay's water quality problems by 2010. Through a number of strategies, including increasing riparian buffers—areas of trees, shrubs, and other vegetation adjacent to streams—by at least 10,000 miles (16,000 km) in the bay area, the agreement aimed to "correct [by 2010] the nutrient- and sediment-related problems in the Chesapeake Bay and its tidal tributaries sufficiently to remove the Bay and the tidal portions of its tributaries from the list of impaired waters under the Clean Water Act." According to the agreement, if the water quality goals of the agreement were not met, a court ordered Chesapeake Bay Total Maximum Daily Load (TMDL) would be imposed by May 12, 2011.

On May 12, 2009, in an acknowledgement that this objective would not be met, U.S. President Barack Obama issued the Chesapeake Bay Protection and Restoration executive order, conceding that, despite significant efforts by everyone involved, water quality remained poor and progress toward meeting the goals of the Clean Water Act was moving too slow. The executive order created the Federal Leadership Committee, charged with overseeing the management and development of Chesapeake Bay cleanup strategies, and required the administrator of the EPA to publish a proposal for federal land management in the Chesapeake Bay.

Exactly one year after issuing the May 2009 executive order, the Obama administration rolled out an ambitious plan to remove all of the tidal waters of the Bay from the EPA's List of Impaired Waters within fifteen years. Known as the "Strategy for Protecting and Restoring the Chesapeake Bay Watershed," the plan includes regulations to restore clean water, implement new conservation practices on several million acres of farms, and conserve two million acres of undeveloped land. Additionally, the plan establishes two-year milestones, to help bolster the accountability of the plan.

The Obama administration's restoration plan corresponded with the settlement of a joint lawsuit brought against the EPA by the Chesapeake Bay Foundation, four former elected officials from Maryland, Virginia and Washington, D.C., and organizations representing watermen and sport fishermen, which claimed that the EPA had not done enough to protect the Chesapeake Bay watershed from pollution. Under the settlement, the EPA agreed to establish a Chesapeake Bay TMDL.

A TMDL represents the maximum amount of pollution a body of water can receive while still meeting set water quality standards. Covering an area of 64,000 square miles (165,760 sq km), the Chesapeake Bay TMDL established in December 2010 is the largest and most complex TMDL ever developed in the nation. It is designed to place the bay on a strict "pollution diet" by limiting the amount of acceptable pollution from major sources. Specifically, the Bay TMDL places annual limits at 185.9 million pounds (84.3 million kg) of nitrogen, 12.5 million pounds (5.7 million kg) of phosphorus, and 6.45 billion pounds (2.9 billion kg) of sediment. These figures represent a 25 percent reduction in nitrogen, a 24 percent reduction in phosphorus, and a 20 percent reduction in sediment. The stated goal of the TDML is to ensure that all control measures needed to fully restore the bay are in place by 2025, with at least 60 percent of those measures established by 2017.

Although environmentalists welcomed the news of the Obama administration's plan, many remained cautious, since so many plans in the past have failed. Environmental watchdog groups submitted still-dismal reports for the health of the bay for the year 2010. EcoCheck, representing a partnership of the NOAA and the University of Maryland Center for Environmental Science, gave the bay an overall grade of C- in its 2010 Chesapeake Bay Report Card, with failing marks given for the ecosystems of the Lower Western Shore of Maryland and the Patapsco and Back Rivers. The group noted an overall health decline from 46 percent throughout 2009 to 42 percent in 2010. The Potomac River saw a grade decline from 49 percent in 2009 to 34 percent for 2010, with higher levels of phosphorus and sediment noted as a result of two major storm events that contributed to higher streamflow. However, the Chesapeake Bay Foundation raised its assessment of the bay from a health index of 28 in 2008 to 31 (out of 100) in 2010. Failing marks were noted for pollution levels, which is consistent with the EcoCheck reports, but the foundation also gives marks for habitat and fishery renewal actions, which showed some increase throughout the year.

In the wake of August 2011's Hurricane Irene, scientists were interested in how the storm's heavy rainfall would affect the estuary. Large infusions of rainwater can cause crabs to concentrate further south because they will not have to move north to access the fresh water they prefer. Oysters, another important Chesapeake Bay catch, don't fare as well in fresh water. Also, the runoff from such heavy rainfall can smother oyster beds with sediment and increase the amount of nitrogen and phosphorous in the water—substances the TMDL has been working to lessen. The U.S. Geological Survey started sampling waters along the East Coast to test for increased pesticides, *E. coli*, nutrients, and sediment. While the long-term effects of the hurricane on water quality are not yet known, scientists said Hurricane Irene could be a "defining event for 2011."

BIBLIOGRAPHY

Books

Forbes Travel Guide: Mid-Atlantic. Chicago: Forbes Travel Guide, 2010.

Ross, John, and Bates Littlehales. *The Smithsonian Guides to Natural America: The Atlantic Coast and Blue Ridge–Maryland, District of Columbia, Delaware, Virginia, North Carolina.* Washington, DC: Smithsonian Books, 1995.

Titus, James G., and K. Eric Anderson. *Coastal Sensitivity to Sea-level Rise: A Focus on the Mid-Atlantic Region.* Washington, DC: U.S. Climate Change Science Program, 2009.

Web Sites

"Brownfield Revitalization Program." Maryland Department of Business and Economic Development. Available from http://www.choosemaryland.org/businessresources/Pages/Brownfields.aspx

"Certified Maryland Organic Farms." Maryland Department of Agriculture. Available from http://www.mda.state.md.us/md_products/certified_md_organic_farms/index.php

Chesapeake Bay Foundation. Available from http://www.cbf.org

"Chesapeake Bay." National Wildlife Federation. Available from http://www.nwf.org/Wildlife/Wild-Places/Chesapeake-Bay.aspx

"Chesapeake Bay Preservation and Restoration Executive Order." Office of the Press Secretary. The White House. Available from http://www.whitehouse.gov/the_press_office/Executive-Order-Chesapeake-Bay-Protection-and-Restoration/

"Chesapeake Bay Report Card 2010." EcoCheck. Available from http://ian.umces.edu/pdfs/ecocheck_report_card_311.pdf

"Chesapeake Bay TMDL." U.S. Environmental Protection Agency. Available from http://www.epa.gov/chesapeakebaytmdl/

"Chesapeake 2000." Chesapeake Bay Program. Available from http://www.chesapeakebay.net/content/publications/cbp_12081.pdf

"The Clean Energy Economy." Pew Charitable Trusts. Available fromhttp://www.pewcenteronthestates.org/uploadedFiles/Clean_Economy_Report_Web.pdf

"Climate Change Impacts on Maryland and the Cost of Inaction." Center for Integrative Environmental Research. The University of Maryland. Available from http://www.cier.umd.edu/climateadaptation/Chapter3.pdf

"Creature Feature: Maryland Darter." Maryland Department of Natural Resources. Available from http://www.dnr.state.md.us/mydnr/CreatureFeature/md_darter.asp

Dishneau, David. "Irene leaves outages, worries in Mid-Atlantic wake." HometownAnnapolis.com. August 28, 2011. Available from http://www.hometownannapolis.com/news/reg/2011/08/28-58/Irene-leaves-outages-worries-in-Mid-Atlantic-wake.html

"Executive Order 01.01.2007.07." Office of the Governor. Available from http://www.gov.state.md.us/executiveorders/01.07.07ClimateChange.pdf

"Greenhouse Gas Emissions Reduction Act of 2009." Maryland General Assembly. Available from http://mlis.state.md.us/2009rs/bills/sb/sb0278e.pdf

Halsey, Ashley III. "Chesapeake Bay Settlement has EPA Agreeing to Enforce Pollution Reduction Goals." *The Washington Post.* Available from http://www.washingtonpost.com/wp-dyn/content/article/2010/05/11/AR2010051105212.html

"Governor Martin O'Malley Announces Clean Energy Projects to Spur Economic Growth, Promote Sustainability." December 8, 2009. Office of Governor Martin O'Malley. Available from http://www.gov.state.md.us/pressreleases/091208.asp

High Performance Buildings Act (Chapter 124, Senate Bill 208). State of Maryland. Available from http://mlis.state.md.us/2008rs/chapters_noln/Ch_124_sb0208T.pdf

The Importance of Maryland's Forest: Yesterday, Today and Tomorrow. Maryland Department of Natural Resources. Available from http://www.dnr.state.md.us/forests/download/forests_ytt.pdf

"Maryland at a Glance." Maryland State Archives. Available from http://www.msa.md.gov/msa/mdmanual/01glance/html/mdglance.html

"Maryland's Green Building Tax Credit: Qualifications for the Tax Credit." Maryland Energy Administration. Available from http://www.energy.state.md.us/incentives/business/greenbuilding/greenbuilding_qualifications.pdf

Maryland Wildlife and Heritage Service. Available from http://www.dnr.state.md.us/wildlife

"Montgomery County Launches Program to Help Residents Improve Energy Efficiency of their Homes." Maryland Real Estate Rama. August 26, 2011. Available from http://maryland.realestaterama.com/2011/08/26/montgomery-county-launches-program-to-help-residents-improve-the-energy-efficiency-of-their-homes-ID0271.html

"1983 Chesapeake Bay Agreement." The Chesapeake Bay Program. Available from http://www.chesapeakebay.net/content/publications/cbp_12512.pdf

"Organic Production Survey 2008." U.S. Department of Agriculture. Available from http://www.agcensus.usda.gov/Publications/2007/Online_Highlights/Organics/ORGANICS.pdf

Port of Baltimore (Maryland Port Administration). Available from http://mpa.maryland.gov/index.php

Regional Greenhouse Gas Initiative: Maryland State Investment Plan. Available from http://www.rggi.org/rggi_benefits/program_investments/Maryland

"Renewable Energy Portfolio Standard of 2010." Public Service Commission of Maryland. Available from http://webapp.psc.state.md.us/Intranet/Reports/MD%20RPS%202010%20Annual%20Report.pdf

"Rivers in Maryland." Maryland Geological Survey. Available from http://www.mgs.md.gov/esic/fs/fs3.html

State of the Bay 2010. Chesapeake Bay Foundation. Available from http://www.cbf.org/Document.Doc?id=596

"State Fact Sheets: Maryland." U.S. Department of Agriculture. Available from http://www.ers.usda.gov/StateFacts/MD.htm

"Strategy for Protecting and Restoring the Chesapeake Bay Watershed." U.S. Environmental Protection Agency. Available from http://yosemite.epa.gov/opa/admpress.nsf/d0cf6618525a9efb85257359003fb69d/efd-fab237bdc4c9a8525772100465d3d!OpenDocument

"2007 Census of Agriculture: Maryland." U.S. Department of Agriculture. Available from http://www.agcensus.usda.gov/Publications/2007/Full_Report/Volume_1,_Chapter_1_State_Level/Maryland/mdv1.pdf

"2007 Final Report of the Green Building Task Force." Maryland Department of Planning. Maryland Department of Housing and Community Development. Available from http://www.dnr.state.md.us/ed/2007FinalReportGBTF.pdf

Massachusetts

The expansive shoreline of Cape Cod Bay and the outer Atlantic Coast represent both the beauty and challenge of the environment of Massachusetts. The Cape Cod National Seashore serves as a habitat for more than 450 species of amphibians, reptiles, fish, birds, and mammals, but there are potential threats to that habitat. Global climate change could bring a rise in sea levels that would affect these precious resources, impacting both marine and land species. More immediately, some residents are focused on an offshore wind farm in Nantucket Sound, which could be operational by 2013, and which poses aesthetic and other concerns. Others consider it represents progress in combating carbon emissions. Inland, the state government is attempting to balance the potential for the development of biomass energy with concerns about exploitation of forest resources, as it also promotes the use of solar energy and other energy efficiency projects through many new initiatives, such as its Green Communities Program. While the large-scale Cape Wind proposal has drawn considerable press and controversy, other smaller, behind-the-scenes programs, such as the Pathways Out of Poverty initiative or the promotion of the Cranberry Harvest Trail Guide, have quietly advanced. This range of large-scale alternative energy plans and small-scale initiatives demonstrates the commitment of state officials and residents alike to developing sustainable, environmentally friendly communities and a stronger, greener economy.

Climate

In general, the state experiences a humid continental climate with four distinct seasons. The potential effects of global climate change pose a great concern for the state, particularly for the coastal regions, where fish and wildlife habitats would suffer from the erosion and saltwater infiltration that accompany a rise in sea levels. According to the National Wildlife Federation, already rising sea levels have contributed to the spread of West Nile virus and Lyme disease. Barrier island refuges such as Monomoy National Wildlife Refuge and the Parker River National Wildlife Refuge could be lost to sea level rise, eliminating vital habitats for threatened and endangered bird species such as the piping plover and roseate tern.

In one step toward addressing the potential challenge, the Massachusetts legislature passed the Global Warming Solutions Act of 2008 (Chapter 298), which called on the state Secretary of Energy and Environmental Affairs to set a legally enforceable greenhouse gas (GHG) emissions limit that would fall between 10 percent and 25 percent below 1990 levels by 2020 and 80 percent below by 2050. The act also established two new advisory bodies—the Climate Protection and Green Economy Advisory Committee and the Climate Change Adaptation Advisory Committee—to assist the Massachusetts Executive Office of Energy and Environmental Affairs in making the final limit decision and developing a reasonable plan of action to reach that goal. In December 2010, the Secretary placed the statewide GHG emissions reduction goal at the maximum 25 percent below 1990 levels by 2020, and 80 percent below by 2050. At the same time, he released the final *Clean Energy and Climate Plan for 2020*. The plan presents a portfolio of expanded and new policy recommendations that are expected to support the success of established policies, while providing additional outlets for clean energy use and development, which ultimately will lead to not only lower emission levels, but also a stronger green economy.

Massachusetts is a member of the Regional Greenhouse Gas Initiative (RGGI), a cooperative cap-and-trade program involving ten Northeastern and Mid-Atlantic states. The program is designed with the goal of reducing power sector carbon dioxide emissions by 10 percent by 2018. To that end, the regional cap established by the group was set at 188 million short tons of carbon dioxide per year from 2009 to 2014. Starting in 2015 the cap will decrease by 2.5 percent each year. Carbon dioxide allowances for power plants can be obtained or traded in quarterly auctions. Each state may then reinvest its auction proceeds in programs that support the growth of a clean energy economy. In Massachusetts, the state's auction proceeds have been used to support a variety of consumer benefit programs, particularly utility-administered energy efficiency programs. The first three-year control (or compliance) period began on January 1, 2009 and was set to end on December 31, 2011. At that time, each regulated power plant must submit one allowance for each ton of carbon dioxide emitted during the control period. The RGGI represents the first mandatory, market-based carbon dioxide emissions program in the United States.

❧ Natural Resources, Water, and Agriculture

Natural Resources: Wood Imports Needed Despite Abundant Woodlands

About 62 percent of the state is covered in forest and woodland, with over 75 percent under private ownership. The state has established strong environmental laws concerning timber harvesting operations and sustainable forestry, and according to the MassWoods Forest Conservation Program, about 98 percent of the wood needed to support the state's paper, pulp, and wood product manufacturing is imported. Some of the most common tree species found within the state include the eastern white pine, red maple, eastern hemlock, northern red oak, and sugar maple. Production and sale of Christmas trees is a primary forest industry.

Massachusetts has one of the largest state park systems in the nation with more than one hundred protected parks, forests, and historic sites. Common animal species across the state include white-tailed deer, skunk, raccoon, grey fox, red and gray squirrels, cottontail rabbits, and woodchucks. Bobcats are the only wild cat species found in the state and black bears can also be found in some areas. ("Fisher cats" are found throughout the state except in Cape Cod and the islands, but they are actually members of the weasel family). Common birds include the blue jay, cardinal, song sparrow, bobwhite quail, great horned and screech owls, and mockingbird. The U.S. Fish & Wildlife Service lists 22 animal and 5 plant species in the state as either threatened or endangered, including five species of sea turtles and five species of whales.

The mining industry within the state produces common clays, lime, marble, sand and gravel, silica, quartz, granite, limestone, sandstone, slate, and traprock. The state was ranked at fortieth in the nation in overall nonfuel mineral production in 2010 with a value of $194 million.

Water: The Quabbin and Wachusett Reservoirs

The longest river in the state is the Connecticut River, with major tributaries that include Deerfield, Westfield, Chicopee, and Millers. The Charles and the Mystic flow into Boston Harbor. Other notable rivers include the Taunton, Blackstone, Housatonic, and Merrimack. Native inland fish include brook trout, chain pickerel, brown bullhead, and yellow perch. Mallard ducks and Canadian geese are common waterfowl species.

There are more than 1,100 lakes and ponds within the state. The largest lake is the artificial Quabbin Reservoir, which at a capacity of about 412 billion gallons (1,560 billion l) is one of the largest manmade public water supplies in the United States. The second-largest body of water in the state, the Wachusett Reservoir, lies east of the Quabbin. Together, these two reservoirs provide water for most of the greater Boston area. The largest natural lake is Assawompsett Pond in southern Massachusetts. Another large lake—Lake Chargoggagogmanchaugagochaubunagungamaug (also known as Lake Webster—is notable for having the longest name.

Trade and Tourism Thrive from Boston Harbor to Cape Cod Bay

At Boston Harbor, the Port of Boston is the oldest continuously active major port in the Western Hemisphere. More than 15 million tons (13.6 million metric tons) of cargo pass through Boston each year. The Port at Gloucester, one of America's oldest fishing ports, also supports a major fishing industry. The most valuable products of the Massachusetts commercial catch include quahog, lobster, and sea scallops.

The deepwater Port of New Bedford consistently ranks as first in the nation for value of fish landings, at over $280 million per year. With nearby seafood processing plants and wholesale companies, fishing is a billion dollar industry for the city. The port will soon be a major center of support for the wind energy industry as well. In October 2010, the governor announced plans to build a new 21-acre (8.5-hectare), multipurpose marine commerce terminal at New Bedford, with the primary purpose of serving as a support facility for Cape Wind, the private developer that is expected to build a large-scale, controversial offshore wind farm in Nantucket Sound. The new terminal will be designed to accommodate the vessels that deliver wind turbine parts, along with barges that can transport these and other components to the offshore installation site. Officials expect that the new terminal will give Massachusetts a competitive edge as the "first mover" in offshore wind for projects along the Atlantic coast. The terminal will also be used for traditional maritime commerce as well. This new $35 million port project will be financed by state, federal, and municipal governments and operated by a consortium of state and local agencies.

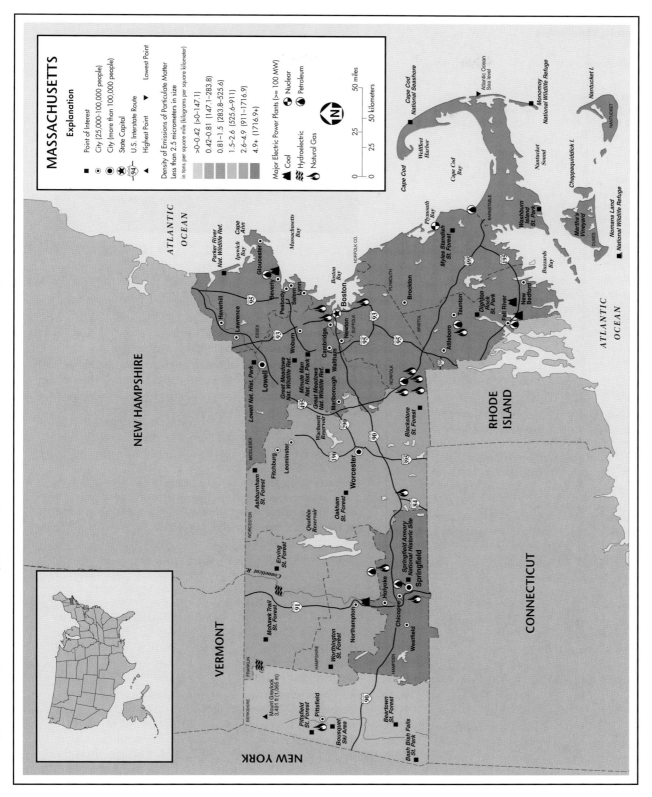

SOURCES: "County Emissions Map: Criteria Air Pollutants." *AirData*. U.S. Environmental Protection Agency. Available from http://www.epa.gov/air/data/geosel.html; *Energy Maps*. U.S. Energy Information Administration. Available from http://www.eia.gov/state; *Highest and Lowest Elevations*. U.S. Geological Survey. Available from http://egsc.usgs.gov/isb/pubs/booklets/elvadist/elvadist.html#Highest; *2007 Minerals Yearbook*. U.S. Geological Survey. Available from http://minerals.usgs.gov/minerals/pubs/state. © 2011 Cengage Learning.

Massachusetts State Profile

Physical Characteristics

Land area	7,801 square miles (20,204 sq km)
Inland water area	461 square miles (1,194 sq km)
Coastal area	977 square miles (1,572 sq km)
Highest point	Mount Greylock 3,491 feet (1,064 m)
National Forest System lands (2010)	NA
State parks (2011)	143

Energy Statistics

Total energy production (2009)	110 trillion Btu
State ranking in total energy production (2009)	44
Renewable energy net generation total (2009)	2.4 million megawatt hours
Hydroelectric energy generation (2009)	1.2 million megawatt hours
Biomass energy generation (2009)	1.1 million megawatt hours
Wind energy generation (2009)	6,000 megawatt hours
Wood and derived fuel energy generation (2009)	115,000 megawatt hours
Crude oil reserves (2009)	NA
Natural gas reserves (2009)	NA
Natural gas liquids (2008)	NA

Pollution Statistics

Carbon output (2005)	87.0 million tons of CO_2 (78.9 million t)
Superfund sites (2008)	30
Particulate matter (less than 2.5 micrometers) emissions (2002)	5,067 tons per year (4,596 t/yr)
Toxic chemical releases (2009)	5.4 million pounds (2.4 million kg)
Generated hazardous waste (2009)	32,500 tons (29,500 t)

SOURCES: AirData. U.S. Environmental Protection Agency. Available from http://www.epa.gov/air/data; *Energy Maps, Facts, and Data of the U.S. States.* U.S. Energy Information Administration. Available from http://www.eia.gov/state; *The 2012 Statistical Abstract.* U.S. Census Bureau. Available from http://www.census.gov/compendia/statab; *United States Energy Usage.* eRedux. Available from http://www.eredux.net/states.

© 2011 Cengage Learning.

The coasts of Cape Cod Bay and the Atlantic provide a variety of shellfish, including mussels and oysters, while also serving as habitats for a wide variety of common and rare animal species. The Cape Cod National Seashore, established in 1961, covers 44,600 acres (18,050 ha) of shoreline and upland landscapes and serves as a habitat for more than 450 species of amphibians, reptiles, fish, birds, and mammals. About twenty-five federally protected species can be found in this national park, including the piping plover.

Nantucket was once the home base for a major whaling industry. Now, visitors can take whale watch or seal scouting cruises out of the Nantucket Sound and Cape Cod Bay, with guarantees of glimpsing a few of these marine mammals.

At Boston Harbor, the Port of Boston is the oldest continuously active major port in the Western Hemisphere. More than 15 million tons (13.6 million metric tons) of cargo pass through Boston each year. © *Juan Vte. Muñoz/Shuttrstock.com*

Agriculture: Tourists Welcome on the Cranberry Harvest Trail

While the state is generally not considered to be a major farming area, agritourism is on the rise, especially through the promotion of the state's most famous crop: cranberries. The southeastern Cape Cod region of the state is home to more than 14,000 acres (5,666 ha) of cranberry bogs, most of which are included on the Cranberry Harvest Trail Guide published for tourists by the Cape Cod Cranberry Growers' Association. Massachusetts ranks second in the nation for the production of both cranberries and wild blueberries and is within the top ten for maple syrup and raspberries. Over 95 percent of the state's farms are categorized as small farms, with sales below $250,000 per year. More than 80 percent of all farms are family owned.

Baystate Organic Certifiers is the USDA National Organic Program accredited certifying agency responsible for maintaining national organic standards for growers and food processors throughout Massachusetts and seven other New England States. Throughout the year, more than 600 farmers' markets and roadside stands can be found in the state by those looking for locally grown produce and products.

Wine production is a growing activity in the state, increasing by 21 percent between 2007 and 2010. There are a total of 36 wineries across the state, of which more than seven have opened since 2007. Wineries range from vineyards to small urban operations. Officials from the Department of Agriculture believe that this increase is in part due to increased interest in buying local products. Many local vintners take advantage of the state's cranberry production and specialize in making cranberry wine and other fruit wines. Wineries also received permission from the state Department of Agriculture to sell their wines at local farmers' markets, which for the smaller wineries, provides a great venue through which they can market their products while cutting the costs of using a wholesaler.

⚜ Energy: Dependent on Imported Fossil Fuels

With no fossil fuel resources of its own, no refineries, and no natural gas storage facilities, Massachusetts relies on imports to supply its petroleum and natural gas needs. Natural gas is received through pipelines from the U.S. Gulf Coast and Canada, with additional wintertime supplies from storage sites in New York, Pennsylvania, and Ohio. The state is home to three liquefied natural gas (LNG) import terminals, two of which are located offshore near Boston and one onshore at Everett. These terminals supply markets throughout the Northeast.

In 1995, Massachusetts became one of only a few states to require the statewide sale and use of ethanol-blended reformulated gasoline (RFG). The RFG formulas in use are consistent with the guidelines established by the federal RFG program under the U.S. Clean Air Act.

Electricity: Leading the Nation in Landfill Gas-to-Energy Systems

About 30 percent of the state's supply of electricity is produced through natural-gas fired plants. Plants that burn coal and petroleum each produce about a quarter of the state's supply, with the rest coming from nuclear, hydroelectric, and renewable energy sources.

In recent years, Massachusetts has become one of the nation's top producers of electricity from landfill gas (methane) and municipal solid waste. As of 2010, the state had at least fifteen active landfill gas-to-energy (LGTE) sites producing a total of about 50.6 megawatts of power. Several other LGTE systems are under construction or in the planning stages. Biomass energy from cordwood, wood chips, and wood pellets has been proven to be a viable alternative for businesses, though some organizations have voiced concerns that the rapid development of wood-fueled energy systems could pose a serious threat to the state's woodlands. There is considerable potential for the development of wind power operations, particularly in the Berkshire Mountains and offshore along the Atlantic Coast, but many residents are divided about wind turbines on top of the Berkshire hills.

In one of several efforts to place Massachusetts as a national leader in research and development of wind energy, the Massachusetts Clean Energy Center has partnered with the U.S. Department of Energy's National Renewable Energy Laboratory to build a world-class Wind Technology Testing Center in Charleston.

Construction of the facility began in 2009, with $24.7 million in funding from the American Recovery and Reinvestment Act and $13.2 million in grants and loans from the Massachusetts Clean Energy Center. Opened in May 2011, the facility is the first large blade testing station in the nation, testing and certifying turbine blades up to 295 feet (90 m) in length.

Opportunities for wind power were expanded even further in August 2011, when eight Massachusetts communities received $16 million in low-interest federally subsidized financing for renewable energy projects. Belchertown, Cohassett, Deerfield, Fairhaven, Gill, Haverhill, Kingston, and Marshfield will each receive a share of the funds. Three companies will each receive $1.3 million to install wind turbines in the area. One company—Conservation Wind Partners LP—will install a 900 kW turbine on the Trustees of Reservations Whitney Thayer Woods Reservation in Cohasset. Two more turbines will be installed by Fairhaven Wind LLC in Fairhaven, and another two in Kingston by No Fossil Fuel LLC.

Massachusetts 2008 Energy Bill: The Green Communities Act

In 2008, the state government approved a substantial energy bill known as the Green Communities Act (SB 2768). The act includes an expansion of the previously adopted renewable portfolio standard, and takes several leaps further by mandating greater investments in electric and natural gas energy efficiency programs and the use of renewable energy sources.

The renewable portfolio standard (RPS) approved by the act requires utilities to use renewable energy sources for 15 percent of generated supply by 2020 and 25 percent by 2030. The act includes an additional alternative energy portfolio standard that promotes the development and use of specific alternative generation technologies through a mandate that requires utilities to produce a minimum of 5 percent of annual electric sales through one or more of these sources. Qualifying alternative generation systems include combined heat and power, paper-derived fuel, energy efficient steam technologies, and gasified coal with carbon capture and permanent sequestration.

Beginning in 2010, retail suppliers were expected to provide a portion of their renewable energy through qualified in-state interconnected solar facilities, as established through the RPS Solar Carve-Out Program. This program offers incentives to residential, commercial, public, and non-profit entities to install onsite photovoltaic systems with a capacity of 2 megawatts or less and connect them to the utility grid.

The Green Communities Act is so called because it also establishes a statewide Green Communities Program, designed to provide financial assistance for energy efficiency and conservation programs at the municipal level.

❧ Green Business, Green Building, Green Jobs

Green Business

In an April 2010 report from Clean Edge, Inc. Massachusetts was ranked as second in the nation (after California) in a survey focused on clean energy leadership and innovation. *A Future of Innovation and Growth: Advancing Massachusetts's Clean-Energy Leadership* outlines the success that the state has had in developing and promoting the growth of a clean energy economy, and considers the potential for green business growth in the future. The report noted the state's world-class academic and research centers as a primary factor in the current and anticipated success of the clean energy economy.

The University of Massachusetts, for instance, supports a number of major centers that add support to the development of green business, including the Advanced Technology and Manufacturing Center at UMass-Dartmouth and the Center for Energy Efficiency and Renewable Energy and the National Environmental Technology Institute, both at UMass-Amherst. The spirit of innovation promoted by these centers has attracted a number of clean tech and clean energy companies, including A123 Systems (advanced electric batteries), Konarka (organic photovoltaics), and Evergreen Solar. However, green business is a global business, with global competition. In 2011, Evergreen Solar closed its doors, unable to compete with cheaper solar panels produced in China).

Strong government leadership and policy support were also noted as important factors in the state's success in green business, now and for the future. That state government commitment to a new green economy is evident in the *Massachusetts Clean Energy and Climate Plan for 2020*. The plan was released in December 2010 as a result of the Global Warming Solutions Act of 2008. While the primary focus of the plan was to address the issue of setting and achieving statewide greenhouse gas emission goals, the portfolio of new policies recommended by the plan are designed to support the already growing number of green businesses associated with energy efficiency, advanced building, and renewable energy generation. Officials are hopeful that full implementation of the plan could lead to the creation of between 42,000 and 48,000 new jobs by 2020.

Green Building: Massachusetts LEED Plus

In 2007, the governor of Massachusetts initiated a green building and energy efficiency standard for state-owned buildings through Executive Order 484, "Leading by Example—Clean Energy and Efficient Buildings." The order calls for an overall energy consumption reduction in state-owned and state-leased buildings equal to at least 20 percent by 2012 and 35 percent by 2020. Energy consumption from the year 2004 was established as the baseline. Additionally, state government facilities are expected to procure 15 percent of their annual energy consumption from renewable sources by 2012 and 30 percent by 2020. The order further mandates that all new construction and significant renovations of state facilities over 20,000 square feet (1,858 sq m) in size must meet the Massachusetts LEED (Leadership in Energy and Environmental Design) Plus green building standard that has been established by the Commonwealth of Massachusetts Sustainable Design Roundtable as of 2006. This LEED Plus standard adds to the national standards by incorporating requirements for an overall energy performance of 20 percent better than the Massachusetts Energy Code, reducing outdoor water consumption by 50 percent, and reducing indoor water consumption by 20 percent.

In related measures, the governor's Zero Net Energy Buildings Task Force published its final report, *Getting to Zero*, in 2009. It contains recommendations for policies to promote the construction of commercial and residential facilities that consume less energy.

The Lyndon P. Lorusso Applied Technology Center at Cape Cod Community College, commonly referred to as the Green Technology Center, was the first LEED-certified building in the state, gaining Gold-level certification under the U.S. Green Building Council LEED program.

Green Jobs: Pathways Out of Poverty through the Massachusetts Green Jobs Act

The Massachusetts Green Jobs Act of 2008 (HB 5018, Chapter 307) established the Massachusetts Clean Energy Center as the state's lead agency for the development of a green economy. The center promotes job creation by encouraging the development of new clean energy companies through seed grants and related market research projects and by funding training programs for the necessary green workforce. The act was promoted in part by the Massachusetts Green Jobs Coalition (MAGJC), a statewide alliance that supports the creation of a green economy as a pathway out of poverty for underdeveloped communities. The official Pathways Out of Poverty initiative was incorporated into the Green Jobs Act in the form of a competitive grant program for companies and organizations that provide training for low-income workers. The first round of grantees included the Jobs for Youth (JYF) Networks' Weatherization Technician Training Program in Lowell; Quinsigamond Community College in Worcester; the Regional Employment Board of Hampden County, Inc. in Springfield; Massasoit Community College in Brockton; and Berkshire Community College in Pittsfield.

❧ Nantucket Sound Wind Farm

For a number of years, the private developer Cape Wind has been working on plans to build a 420-megawatt wind farm on Horseshoe Shoal in Nantucket Sound. As the nation's first proposed offshore wind farm, it has gained much attention through a complex and unprecedented permitting process and has caused a great deal of controversy among homeowners, environmental organizations, and local officials, as some extol the benefits of developing this renewable energy resource, while others are concerned about impacts on their local environment.

Ten Years in the Making

The idea for an offshore wind farm in Nantucket Sound was first introduced by a representative from Cape Wind in 2000, with an initial proposal for fifty wind turbines. Since then, the proposal has grown to include 130 wind turbines. Cape Wind has not released any official data on the expected final cost to build and has admitted that the project will not necessarily result in immediate savings on electricity for consumers. Residential cost savings are expected in the long-term, however, as Cape Wind expects to develop a number of fixed-priced contracts with suppliers, thereby stabilizing the cost of electricity.

Supporters of the project cite a much greater range of benefits beyond the cost of electricity for the average consumer. Clean Power Now, one of the local organizations standing in support of the project, has reported that the Cape Wind farm could displace up to 733,000 tons of carbon dioxide, the equivalent of taking 175,000 cars off the road each year. The state governor, Deval Patrick, has declared his support for the project, claiming that the development of a stable, renewable energy source could lead to a stronger, stable economy in the future. Cape Wind reports that the project will create thousands of short-term jobs in construction and assembly and at least 150 permanent jobs as the project goes online. Most supporters cite greater energy independence and cleaner air for the region as strong points for the project.

Opponents of the project paint a different picture. The Alliance to Protect Nantucket Sound, the initiator of the Save Our Sound campaign, reports that the cost of the electricity produced by Cape Wind would be two or three times greater than the current wholesale prices in the area, producing an unreasonable increase in costs for consumers. The Alliance and many other opponents claim that the project will lead to economic declines, particularly through a drop in tourism as the wind turbines would dramatically alter the natural landscape of the sound. The Massachusetts Fisherman's Partnership has further argued that the wind farm will displace the commercial fishing industry of the sound.

A number of environmental groups have noted concerns that the project could threaten the habitat of native marine and avian species, in part by simply displacing them from their habitats, but also through the potential threat of an oil spill or other forms of chemical contamination in the sound. The Alliance to Protect Nantucket Sound notes that the proposed wind turbines and the electrical service platform would contain more than 64,700 gallons (244,900 l) of oil necessary for operations. If any of the oil storage tanks ruptured, the resulting oil spill could cause severe damage to the coastal environments of Cape Cod and the island of Nantucket.

In the Home Stretch?

As the debate continued, spring 2010 brought a series of victories for Cape Wind. In April 2010, the U.S. Interior Secretary Ken Salazar released an official Record of Decision for Cape Wind, announcing Federal approval for the wind farm. Almost immediately, a number of lawsuits were threatened, by opponents claiming the decision violates the Endangered Species Act, the Outer Continental Shelf Lands Act, and other laws. In May, the Federal Aviation Administration released a report concluding that the farm would not be a hazard for air navigation. In the same month, the utility company National Grid announced a tentative agreement to buy some of the electricity that would be produced by the farm, representing a major move forward for Cape Wind and its plans to secure long-term, fixed-rate contracts.

That agreement became official in November 2010 as the Massachusetts Department of Public Utilities (DPU) approved a fifteen-year contract between National Grid and Cape Wind. According to the terms of the contract, National Grid will purchase 50 percent of the output of the Cape Wind offshore facility at an initial price of 18.7 cents per kilowatt-hour in 2013. The price will rise annually by 3.5 percent for fifteen years, after which time National Grid has the right to a one-time extension of the contract for ten years. These costs are expected to translate into an increase in consumer costs by 1.3 percent to 1.7 percent, while commercial and industrial customers could see an increase of 1.7 percent to 2.2 percent. In the written order of approval (DPU 10-54), the DPU states that the contract is cost-effective, with benefits that support the public interest by creating protections for tax payers in light of rising fuel costs. The DPU further stated that the contracts fulfill a mandate under the Green Communities Act that calls on the government to facilitate the development of renewable energy generation. Opponents claim the cost is still too high, perhaps double that of other renewable energy sources, such as hydroelectric power or onshore wind. Notably, the DPU did not approve a second contract submitted by

Environmental groups have noted concerns that the Nantucket Wind Sound project could threaten the habitat of native marine and avian species. © *Todd Warshaw/ZUMA Press/newscom*

Cape Wind for the remaining 50 percent of output. This proposal did not specify a contracting party.

In January 2011, Cape Wind completed the permitting process with the receipt of permits from the U.S. Environmental Protection Agency (air quality) and the U.S. Army Corps of Engineers. In response, the Alliance to Protect Nantucket Sound and the Wampanoag Tribe of Gay Head/Aquinnah filed a petition requesting a new review of the EPA air quality permit, but that request was denied in May 2011 as the EPA determined that the petitioners did not meet the necessary burden of proof to warrant the action.

In April 2011, Cape Wind cleared another hurdle as the Bureau of Ocean Energy Management, Regulation, and Enforcement (BOEMRE) approved the construction and operations plan for the project. But the legal wrangling continued in May as the Alliance to Protect Nantucket Sound and the Associated Industries of Massachusetts filed appeals with the Massachusetts Supreme Judicial Court to overrule the November decision of the DPU. Oral arguments on this case were expected to be heard in September or October 2011, which is when Cape Wind hoped to break ground. Also in May, Cape Wind received notice from the U.S. Department of Energy (DOE) that their application for a federal loan guarantee has been placed on hold until more funding for the loan program becomes available. The application had an original process deadline of September 30, 2011. In the meantime, Siemens AG, Europe's largest engineering company, stated they were

willing to provide financing for Cape Wind. While officials from Cape Wind stated their intention to continue to pursue the loan, the DOE could not give any assurances as to when sufficient budget resources would be available from Congress, thus placing the future of the Cape Wind project in a financial quandary.

BIBLIOGRAPHY

Books

Finch, Robert, and Jonathan Wallen. *The Smithsonian Guides to Natural America: Southern New England— Connecticut, Rhode Island, Massachusetts.* Washington, DC: Smithsonian Books, 1996.

Kershner, Bruce, and Robert T. Leverett. *The Sierra Club Guide to the Ancient Forests of the Northeast.* San Francisco, CA: Sierra Club Books, 2004.

Murdy, Edward. *Fishes of Chesapeake Bay.* Washington, DC. Smithsonian Books, 2002.

Web Sites

"About Reformulated Gasoline (RFG)." Massachusetts Department of Environmental Protection. Available from http://www.mass.gov/dep/air/community/rfg.htm

Adams, Steve. "Number of Mass. wineries is growing like a vine." *Patriot Ledger.* August 29, 2011. Available from http://www.patriotledger.com/business/x865771063/Number-of-Mass-wineries-is-growing-like-a-vine

The Alliance to Protect Nantucket Sound. Available from http://www.saveoursound.org/site/PageServer

Cape Cod Cranberry Association. Available from http://www.cranberries.org/about/overview.html

Cape Wind. Available from http://www.capewind.org/index.php

Cape Wind Energy Project: Horseshoe Shoal, Nantucket Sound—Record of Decision. U.S. Department of the Interior, Minerals Management Service. Available from http://www.doi.gov/news/doinews/upload/Cape-Wind-ROD.pdf

Cassidy, Patrick "Gulf Oil Spill Soils Federal Agency's Reputation." *Cape Cod Times.* May 29, 2010. Available from http://www.capecodonline.com/apps/pbcs.dll/article?AID=/20100529/NEWS/5290318/-1/SPECIAL01

The Commonwealth of Massachusetts, Executive Department. *Executive Order No. 484: Leading by Example—Clean Energy and Efficient Buildings.* Available from http://www.mass.gov/Agov3/docs/Executive%20Orders/Leading%20by%20Example%20EO.pdf

"Department of Public Utilities Approves Contract for Offshore Wind Power." Massachusetts Executive Office of Energy and Environmental Affairs. November 22, 2010. Available from http://www.mass.gov/?pageID=eoeeapressrelease&L=5&L0=-Home&L1=Grants+%26+Technical+Assistance&L2=Guidance+%26+Technical+Assistance&-L3=Agencies+and+Divisions&L4=Department+of+Public+Utilities+(DPU)&sid=Eoeea&b=pressrelease&f=101122_pr_cape_wind&csid=Eoeea

Environment Northeast. *Massachusetts 2008 Energy Bill: An Act Relative to Green Communities, Senate Bill No. 2768.* Available from http://www.env-ne.org/public/resources/pdf/MA_Energy_Bill_Summary.pdf

A Future of Innovation and Growth: Advancing Massachusetts' Clean-Energy Leadership. Clean Edge, Inc. Available from http://www.masscec.com/masscec/file/A%20Future%20of%20Innovation%20and%20Growth%20Advancing%20Massachusetts'%20Clean-Energy%20Leadership.pdf

General Court of the Commonwealth of Massachusetts. *Chapter 307 of the Acts of 2008: An Act Relative to Green Jobs in the Commonwealth.* Available from http://www.mass.gov/legis/laws/seslaw08/sl080307.htm

"Global Warming and Massachusetts." National Wildlife Federation. Available from http://www.nwf.org/~/media/PDFs/Global%20Warming/Global%20Warming%20State%20Fact%20Sheets/Massachusetts.ashx

"Massachusetts Ag Facts & Statistics." Massachusetts Department of Agricultural Resources. Available from http://www.mass.gov/agr/facts/index.htm

Massachusetts Clean Energy Center. Available from http://www.masscec.com

Massachusetts Clean Energy and Climate Plan for 2020.. Massachusetts Executive Office of Energy and Environmental Affairs. Available from http://www.mass.gov/Eoeea/docs/eea/energy/2020-clean-energy-plan.pdf

"Massachusetts Communities Receive Funds To Install Wind Turbines." North American Windpower. August 26, 2011. Available from http://www.nawindpower.com/e107_plugins/content/content.php?content.8475

"Massachusetts Leading the Way in Landfill Gas-To-Energy Generation." Massachusetts Department of Environmental Protection. Available from http://www.mass.gov/dep/public/publications/0707land.htm

Massachusetts List of Endangered Species. Massachusetts Department of Fish and Game (DFG). Available from http://www.mass.gov/dfwele/dfw/nhesp/species_info/mesa_list/mesa_list.htm

MassWoods: Forest Conservation Program. University of Massachusetts Amherst. Available from http://www.masswoods.net/index.php/forests

"Multiple Groups Appeal Cape Wind National Grid Contract." The Alliance to Protect Nantucket Sound. December 13, 2010. Available from http://saveoursound.org/p/salsa/web/press_release/public/?press_release_KEY=110

"New Beford Port terminal to host offshore wind assembly and construction." Office of the Governor of Massachusetts. October 20, 2010. Available from http://www.mass.gov/?pageID=gov3pressrelease&L=1&L0=Home&sid=Agov3&b=pressrelease&f=101020_new_bedford_wind&csid=Agov3

Norton, Michael, and Matt Murphy. "Department of Public Utilities OKs Cape Wind contract; appeals expected." Masslive.com. November 23, 2010. Available from http://www.masslive.com/news/index.ssf/2010/11/department_of_public_utilities.html

"Our Green Campus Commitment." Cape Cod Community College. Available from http://www.capecod.edu/web/occ/green#lorusso

"Overview of the Global Warming Solutions Act 2008." Massachusetts Department of Environmental Protection, Air & Climate. Available from http://www.mass.gov/dep/air/climate/gwsa.htm

Petition of Massachusetts Electric Company and Nantucket Electric Company (DPU 10-54). Massachusetts

Department of Public Utilities. Available from http://www.env.state.ma.us/dpu/docs/electric/10-54/112210dpufnord.pdf

Regional Greenhouse Gas Initiative: Massachusetts State Investment Plan. Available from http://www.rggi.org/rggi_benefits/program_investments/Massachusetts

"State Energy Profiles: Massachusetts." U.S. Energy Information Administration. Available from http://tonto.eia.doe.gov/state/state_energy_profiles.cfm?sid=MA

"Timber." MassWoods Forest Conservation Program, University of Massachusetts Amherst. Available from http://www.masswoods.net/index.php/timber

"Wind Farms." *Cape Cod Times.* Available from http://www.capecodonline.com/apps/pbcs.dll/section?category=special01

"Wind Technology Testing Center." Massachusetts Clean Energy Center. Available from http://www.masscec.com/index.cfm/page/Wind-Technology-Testing-Center-/pid/10463

Wingfield, Brian. "Siemens Willing to Finance Cape Wind as U.S. Postpones Backing, CFO Says." Bloomberg. June 21, 2011. Available from http://www.bloomberg.com/news/2011-06-21/siemens-willing-to-finance-cape-wind-as-u-s-postpones-backing-cfo-says.html

Michigan

Sharing a border with four of the five Great Lakes, water is by far Michigan's most significant natural resource. The Great Lakes support commercial shipping for the state's industries (notably the automobile industry), providing transportation of raw materials and finished products. Protecting the Great Lakes from pollutants and invasive species, while developing responsible management plans in cooperation with the governments of Canada and the other Great Lakes states, is a high priority for Michigan. The state has turned its sights toward other environmental concerns as well, particularly those relating to the development of alternative and renewable energy sources, particularly wind and solar energy. As the home of automotive giants, the state has taken steps to encourage the development of biofuels and hybrid or alternative fueled vehicles.

Climate

Michigan enjoys a temperate, agriculture-friendly climate that features four distinct seasons. Addressing the effects of climate change is a leading environmental concern. According to data published by the National Wildlife Federation, temperatures in Michigan are already rising. If no actions are taken to reduce greenhouse gas emissions average summer temperatures could increase by 13°F (7.2°C) by 2100. Cold-water fish species will be adversely affected as the waters in their habitat warm and water levels decrease. The shoreline wetlands of the Great Lakes will also be affected, causing changes in breeding and migratory habitat for waterfowl in the region. In March 2009, the Michigan Climate Action Council published an action plan calling for a reduction of greenhouse gas emissions of 20 percent below 2005 levels by 2020 and 80 percent below 2005 levels by 2050.

Natural Resources, Water, and Agriculture

Natural Resources: Forests

Forest—most classified as timberland—covers more than half of the state's total land area, some 19.3 million acres (7.8 million ha). Maple, birch, aspen, and pine are the most tree common species. The state flower, the apple blossom, was chosen to signify the importance of trees and shrubs throughout the state that produce fruit such as cherries, strawberries, raspberries, blueberries, and cranberries. The state's forest products industry produces pulp, paper, lumber and solid wood products, and wood furniture. Furniture manufacturing accounts for the greatest number of employees and annual wages for the forest products industry, followed by paper manufacturing. Overall, the industry is the fourth—largest manufacturing industry in the state, directly employing over 59,000 residents and providing direct and indirect economic benefits of more than $14 billion to the state.

Natural Resources: Parks and Wildlife

Protected lands cover about 20 percent of Michigan's land area. Hunting, fishing, and other outdoor activities are enjoyed at many sites throughout the state, including ninety-eight state parks and several state forest areas. Due to the economic downturn of 2008–10 the state has experienced budget cuts of nearly 63 percent for its Forest Recreation Program. As a result, the Michigan Department of Natural Resources proposed the closure of at least twenty-three state forest campgrounds by the end of 2011. These state forest campgrounds are separate from the state park system and generally consist of rustic sites offering few amenities. Alternative sources of funding, including an optional license plate fee, are being proposed. The state is also home to five national parks.

Michigan's most common animals are deer, raccoons, cottontail and snowshoe rabbits, and squirrels. Moose and nearly all of the state's remaining wolves are found in Isle Royale in Lake Superior. Despite the University of Michigan's athletic mascot, there are no wild wolverines in Michigan. There are more than 300 bird species, including the common robin (the state bird) and the endangered Kirtland's warbler. Ruffed grouse, bobwhite quail, and ducks and geese are hunted throughout the state. The U.S. Fish and Wildlife Service lists twenty-four animal and plant species that are federally threatened or endangered. Along with Kirtland's warbler, endangered animal species include the Indiana bat and Hungerford's crawling water beetle. The Michigan monkey-flower and American chaffseed are the state's endangered plant species, with seven more plants listed as threatened.

Natural Resources: Minerals

The state has significant quantities of iron ore and has ranked as second in the nation for production of this commodity. The state has also ranked within the top five for the production of potash, construction sand and gravel, and portland cement, and among the top ten for salt, crude gypsum, and masonry cement. In 2007 the state ranked first for production of magnesium compounds. A small amount of copper is mined for sale. There has also been some exploration for gold, nickel, palladium, silver, uranium, and zinc. In 2010 the state was ranked as tenth overall for total nonfuel mineral production with a value of $1.96 billion.

Water: A Land of Great Lakes

Water is by far Michigan's most significant natural resource. In addition to borders on four of the five Great Lakes, the state has about 35,000 inland lakes and ponds. The largest lake completely within the state is the Lower Peninsula's Houghton Lake (31 sq mi or 80 sq km). The state's leading river is the Grand, flowing through the Lower Peninsula into Lake Michigan. Other major rivers that flow into Lake Michigan include the St. Joseph, Kalamazoo, Muskegon, Pere Marquette, and Manistee. On the eastern side of the peninsula, the Saginaw River and its tributaries form the state's largest watershed. Wetlands account for about 15 percent of the total land area of the state. Despite vast freshwater resources, Michigan has the most state households served by private wells (about 1.12 million), with approximately 25,000 domestic wells drilled per year.

Whitefish, perch, and lake trout (the state fish) are native to the Great Lakes, while perch, bass, and pike are indigenous to inland waters. The commercial fishing industry involves two fairly equal components: state-licensed operations and Native American tribe-licensed operations. Great Lakes whitefish is the primary commercial species. The state supports six fish hatcheries and five permanent salmonid egg take stations.

Agriculture: Milk, Corn, and Soybeans

There are about 55,000 farms in the state, covering approximately 10 million acres (4 million ha) of land. The southern half of the Lower Peninsula is the principal agricultural region; however, potatoes are profitable in northern Michigan and the fruit-belt areas along the lakeshores are favorable for fruit production. The south-central and southeastern counties are major centers of soybean production. Milk, corn, and soybeans are the top three agricultural commodities; the state ranks third (behind California and Florida) in floriculture products, such as bedding plants, perennials, and potted plants.

Organic farming is an important, and growing, segment of agriculture. In 1998, the Michigan Department of Agriculture created the Michigan Organic Advisory Committee (MOAC) to develop a strategic plan for the production, processing, and marketing of the state's organically grown products. In 2009, the MOAC registry included 275 registered organic farm parcels, covering more than 17,650 acres (7,143 ha).

In early 2011, the state House of Representatives passed two bills (HB 4212 and HB 4213) that promote the expansion of the Michigan Agricultural Environmental Assurance Program (MAEAP) and place that program within the state's legal statutes. The MAEAP was established in 1998 as a voluntary environmental assessment and compliance program representing the interests of farmers, the Michigan Department of Agriculture (MDA), and the Michigan Farm Bureau. The MAEAP is designed to engage farmers in a process that will prevent or minimize agricultural pollution risks and reduce legal and environmental risks related to farm activities. In order to gain and retain MAEAP verification, farmers must complete a comprehensive three-step process that involves education, on-farm technical assessment, and the verification of development and implementation of an appropriate action plan for each farm. The MDA provides the necessary educational and technical support, and completes the final inspection that verifies compliance. Farmers are expected to repeat the entire process every three years in order to maintain verified status.

HB 4212 was passed by both houses and signed into law in March 2011. HB 4213 passed in the house and went to Senate committee in February 2011. The new legislation establishes state approval and ongoing support for the program, bringing assurance to farmers that the program is both legitimate and long lasting. Under the new statutes, the program will continue to be voluntary, but this state-level recognition could inspire more farmers to participate. As of 2011, more than 1,000 Michigan farmers were MAEAP-verified and an additional 10,000 had started the verification process.

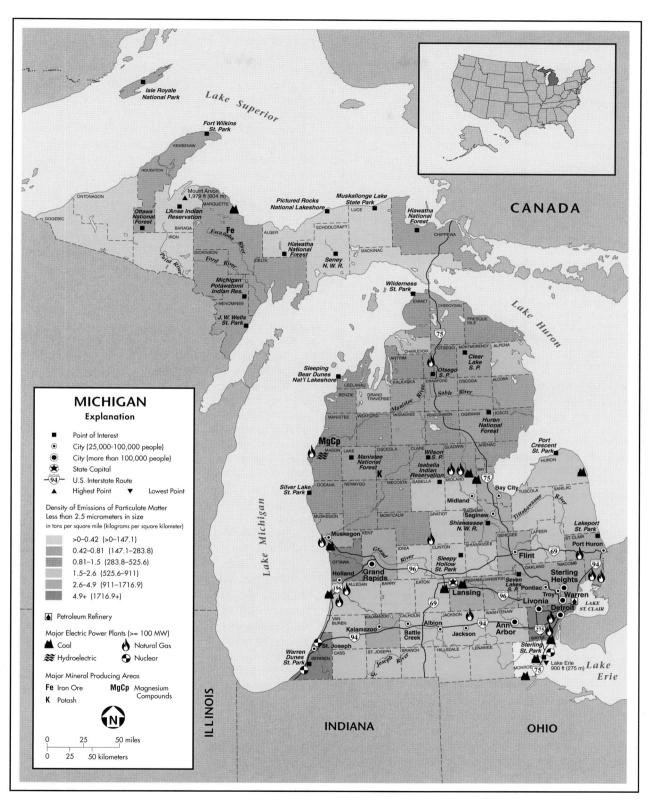

MICHIGAN

Explanation

■ Point of Interest

◉ City (25,000–100,000 people)

◉ City (more than 100,000 people)

★ State Capital

〔94〕 U.S. Interstate Route

▲ Highest Point ▼ Lowest Point

Density of Emissions of Particulate Matter
Less than 2.5 micrometers in size
in tons per square mile (kilograms per square kilometer)

	>0–0.42 (>0–147.1)
	0.42–0.81 (147.1–283.8)
	0.81–1.5 (283.8–525.6)
	1.5–2.6 (525.6–911)
	2.6–4.9 (911–1716.9)
	4.9+ (1716.9+)

🅿 Petroleum Refinery

Major Electric Power Plants (>= 100 MW)

▲ Coal 🔥 Natural Gas

〰 Hydroelectric ◓ Nuclear

Major Mineral Producing Areas

Fe Iron Ore MgCp Magnesium Compounds

K Potash

0   25   50 miles
0   25   50 kilometers

SOURCES: "County Emissions Map: Criteria Air Pollutants." *AirData*. U.S. Environmental Protection Agency. Available from http://www. epa.gov/air/data/geosel.html; *Energy Maps*. U.S. Energy Information Administration. Available from http://www.eia.gov/state; *Highest and Lowest Elevations*. U.S. Geological Survey. Available from http://egsc.usgs.gov/isb/pubs/booklets/elvadist/elvadist.html#Highest; *2007 Minerals Yearbook*. U.S. Geological Survey. Available from http://minerals.usgs.gov/minerals/pubs/state. © 2011 Cengage Learning.

Michigan State Profile

Physical Characteristics

Land area	56,528 square miles (146,407 sq km)
Inland water area	2,164 square miles (5,605 sq km)
Coastal area	NA
Highest point	Mount Arvon 1,979 feet (603 m)
National Forest System lands (2010)	2.9 million acres (1.2 million ha)
State parks (2011)	98

Energy Statistics

Total energy production (2009)	790 trillion Btu
State ranking in total energy production (2009)	28
Renewable energy net generation total (2009)	4.0 million megawatt hours
Hydroelectric energy generation (2009)	1.4 million megawatt hours
Biomass energy generation (2009)	834,000 megawatt hours
Wind energy generation (2009)	300,000 megawatt hours
Wood and derived fuel energy generation (2009)	1.5 million megawatt hours
Crude oil reserves (2009)	33.0 million barrels (5.2 million cu m)
Natural gas reserves (2009)	2,763 billion cubic feet (78.2 billion cu m)
Natural gas liquids (2008)	43 million barrels (6.8 million cu m)

Pollution Statistics

Carbon output (2005)	184.9 million tons of CO_2 (167.7 million t)
Superfund sites (2008)	66
Particulate matter (less than 2.5 micrometers) emissions (2002)	21,247 tons per year (19,275 t/yr)
Toxic chemical releases (2009)	71.4 million pounds (32.4 million kg)
Generated hazardous waste (2009)	284,300 tons (257,900 t)

SOURCES: AirData. U.S. Environmental Protection Agency. Available from http://www.epa.gov/air/data; *Energy Maps, Facts, and Data of the U.S. States.* U.S. Energy Information Administration. Available from http://www.eia.gov/state; *The 2012 Statistical Abstract.* U.S. Census Bureau. Available from http://www.census.gov/compendia/statab; *United States Energy Usage.* eRedux. Available from http://www.eredux.net/states.

© 2011 Cengage Learning.

❧ Energy

Fighting the Michigan Coal Rush

About 60 percent of the state's electricity is produced by coal-fired plants, with coal imported primarily from Wyoming and Montana, but also from West Virginia, Kentucky, and Pennsylvania. Such a heavy reliance on this high-emissions fossil fuel has sparked controversy, as proponents of green energy speak out against the future of coal-fired plants within the state. In February 2009, amid what has been called the Michigan Coal Rush, the governor delayed approval for the construction of eight new coal-fired plants, stating that the delay would allow time for government agencies to consider alternative

energy resources. Later that year, Consumers Energy received approval for the construction of a new 800-megawatt advanced supercritical pulverized clean coal plant (SCPC) on the site of its Karn/Weadock Generating Complex near Bay City. The SCPC process operates at higher temperatures and steam pressures, which allows for the creation of more energy with less coal. Consumers Energy argues that the new plant will translate into higher efficiency and fewer emissions. The plant is expected to be operational in 2017. On the other hand, the conversion to biomass fuels seems to be a more popular energy alternative. In 2007, the L'Anse Warden Electric Company converted an existing coal-, oil- and natural gas-fired generating station to biomass.

Nuclear Power and Natural Gas

The state has three nuclear power plants, which generate about 25 percent of its electricity supply. In the search for renewable power generation, some plants have experimented with wood and wood waste fuel, as well as methane recovered from landfills; however, only a very small percentage of electricity is generated through these types of renewable sources. Most of the remaining supply is generated using natural gas.

Michigan has the most substantial natural gas reserves among all of the Great Lakes states. Primary gas wells are located in the Antrim fields in the northern Lower Peninsula, which are among the largest United States gas fields. About 30 percent of the statewide demand for natural gas is met with local resources. The state imports additional reserves from Illinois, Louisiana, Texas, and Oklahoma, placing much of it in storage. Michigan boasts of having the largest underground natural gas storage capacity in the United States, which it uses to supply natural gas to neighboring states, particularly in the winter months.

Renewable Energy: Wind and Biofuels

Michigan has adopted an Integrated Renewable Portfolio Standard (RPS), through which the government has pledged to use renewable energy sources to generate at least of 10 percent of the state's energy supply by 2015. To that end, energy technology manufacturers have stepped forward to create the largest renewable energy park in the country. The project involves the conversion of an abandoned automobile factory in Wixom into a facility that will produce solar panels and large-scale batteries.

In January 2011, officials from Muskegon County began their search for a private firm to build a large-scale wind farm at the county's 11,000-acre (4,452-ha) wastewater treatment site (in Egelston and Moorland townships). Howard & Howard, the county's energy consultant firm, hopes to find a developer to build a project that will produce between 100 and 150 megawatts of electricity. The site is considered to be a viable location in part because it already has two sets of power lines that span the large property. The area has also shown adequate wind speeds to support a wind energy project. Negotiations with development teams began in July 2011, with officials hoping to sign a contract with a developer by the end of that year.

Michigan's major automobile manufacturers have all demonstrated a commitment to research and development in the development of energy efficient vehicles that use alternative fuels. The first of several biodiesel production plants in the state was opened in 2006 in Bangor and Michigan manufacturers are also gearing up to make electric vehicles.

Green Business, Green Building, Green Jobs

Green Business: Growing a Green Economy

Michigan is home to six regional sustainable-business forums, which serve as a major statewide network for businesses that are actively pursuing strategies to promote long-term growth, responsible environmental management, and social equity—a combination of goals known as the triple bottom line. Such groups are expected to serve as a valuable resource for the growing number of entrepreneurs in Michigan's growing green economy. In the *Michigan Green Jobs Report 2009*, a survey of green businesses in operation from 2005 to 2008 found that nearly 20 percent were start-ups.

Green Building: Taking the LEED

The green building movement gained momentum in Michigan throughout the early 2000s, producing both environmental and financial benefits. According to the 2005 report, Building Green for the Future, Michigan ranked eighth nationally for quantity of green development projects in progress and sixth nationally for projects certified by the national Leadership in Energy and Environmental Design (LEED) rating system. The Grand Rapids Art Museum was recognized as the world's first Gold LEED certified art museum in 2008. In 2006, the General Motors Lansing Delta Township Assembly Plant became the first automotive manufacturing plant in the world to receive LEED certification.

In August 2010, Ford announced plans to partner with Detroit Edison to build a 500-kilowatt solar energy production system at its Michigan Assembly Plant in Wayne. The primary purpose is to provide power for production of the electric and non-electric versions of the Ford Focus, with two new hybrid models expected to be in production at the plant in 2012. The project also includes a secondary solar energy system to provide lighting for the facility. The system is the largest solar power array in the state and saves the company $160,000

Michigan has three nuclear power plants, which generate about 25 percent of its electricity supply. © Vitaly Korovin/ShutterStock.com

per year in energy costs. Major funding for the project came from the Michigan Public Service Commission and the SmartCurrents Program operated by the local electric utility, DTE Energy.

The state government has sponsored several initiatives to encourage green building practices. Under Executive Directives 2005–4 and 2007–22, all new state buildings or renovations in excess of $1 million must be energy efficient and environmentally sustainable, and government agencies are expected to reduce grid-based energy purchases in public facilities by 20 percent by the end of 2015. In 2010, the state legislature considered amendments to the Michigan Business Tax law to allow taxpayers to claim a tax credit for a percentage of the total cost of new green construction or existing building renovations attempting LEED certification (HB 4927). The bill died in committee at the close of the 2009–10 session, with no immediate plans to reintroduce.

Green Jobs: Driving the New Economy

As part of its Green Jobs Initiative, Michigan has defined a green economy as comprising industries that offer products and services in five categories: agriculture and natural resource conservation, clean transportation and fuels, increased energy efficiency, pollution prevention or environmental cleanup, and renewable energy product. In 2009, green jobs accounted for about 3 percent of Michigan's overall private sector employment. To help prepare a new generation of workers for green economy growth, the Michigan Department of Energy, Labor & Economic Growth has launched a $6 million Green Jobs

Initiative to help businesses develop green training and education programs.

Reflecting Michigan's history as a leader in the automotive industry, clean transportation and fuels are the driving forces in Michigan's green economy, accounting for 41 percent of all green jobs in 2009. This industry is expected to be a major source of new green collar jobs as automotive companies continue their research and development projects in renewable and alternative fuel sources. Companies involved in increasing energy efficiency account for about 23 percent of all green jobs.

❧ The Great Lakes: Shared Management For Shared Water Supplies

Protecting and managing the vast resources of the Great Lakes is a major priority for Michigan. As the largest surface freshwater system in the world, the Great Lakes are an important source of drinking and agricultural irrigation water and are also commercially important for fishing and transportation. The Great Lakes' moderating effect on the climate of the region, the *lake effect,* provides for the fruit-belt environments that are so important to the state's orchards and farms.

Michigan shares jurisdiction over four of the five Great Lakes—Michigan, Superior, Huron, and Erie—with the governments of bordering states and Canadian provinces, and with the federal governments of the United States and Canada. As a result, there are state, federal, and international laws and agreements regarding the protection, management, and restoration of the variety of bountiful Great Lakes resources. Michigan is also part of the Council of Great Lakes Governors, a major organization for collaboration on Great Lakes issues.

Responsible Great Lakes management poses a formidable challenge. While the water supply of the Great Lakes is great, it is not inexhaustible. The question of whether or not to allow the diversion of lake waters to other areas of the country is a hot topic among bordering

Michigan is home to five national parks, including Pictured Rocks National Lakeshore. © *Jason Patrick Ross/ShutterStock.com*

states. The government of Michigan has consistently voted against diversion proposals.

Changing patterns of water levels in the lakes from climatic fluctuations also contribute to water supply concerns. While some seasonal fluctuations are common for the region, significant climate changes—such as recent spells of warm, dry weather—can dramatically alter temperature and precipitation patterns and affect the well-being of lakeshore plant and animal life. Changes in lake effect weather patterns pose problems for agriculture as well. Finally, there are ongoing concerns over pollution in both the water and air of the Great Lakes system.

Can Asian Carp and Other Invasive Species Be Stopped?

The introduction of approximately 185 non-native aquatic species into the Great Lakes is a major regional issue. About 10 percent of these species are considered invasive, meaning they pose a threat to the natural ecosystem. The sea lamprey *(Petromyzon marinus)*, a primitive jawless fish native to the Atlantic Ocean, is one of the most notable invaders. Sea lampreys entered Lake Erie through manmade locks in the 1920s and migrated to Lake Superior by 1983. The state governments have sponsored numerous programs to control the population of this parasite, but the challenge is constant.

Michigan officials believe that shipping locks near Chicago connecting Lake Michigan to the Mississippi River Basin will allow the invasive Asian carp to move into the Great Lakes. Michigan, Minnesota, New York, Ohio, Wisconsin, and the Canadian province of Ontario have asked the U.S. Supreme Court to order Illinois to close these locks. On January 19, 2010, the U.S. Supreme Court denied the request; on the same day, the U.S. Army Corps of Engineers reported that they might have detected DNA evidence of Asian carp in Lake Michigan.

The Battle Continues

In February 2010, Michigan Attorney General Mike Cox issued another request to the Supreme Court for a preliminary injunction to close the Chicago locks. This renewed request was based on the DNA evidence found by the U.S. Army Corps of Engineers and on a study completed by researchers at Wayne State University entitled *Chicago Waterway System Ecological Separation: The Logistics and Transportation Related Cost Impact of Waterway Barriers.* This study concludes that a temporary closure of the waterways affected by such an injunction would not have the dramatic effect on the economy that the state of Illinois has suggested in its arguments against the action. Opposing Michigan, U.S. Solicitor General Elena Kagan issued an official memorandum on behalf of the Obama administration asserting that the federal government has already demonstrated its commitment to protecting the Great Lakes from the Asian carp through the ongoing work of the Army Corps

of Engineers, and that this work should be allowed to continue, rather than hindered by legal debates. The Supreme Court again denied Michigan's motion.

In June 2010, a commercial fisherman hired by the state of Illinois to conduct routine sampling in the area found a 19-pound (8.6-kg) Asian carp in Lake Calumet, about 6 miles (9.6 km) downstream from Lake Michigan and above the electric barrier at the Chicago Sanitary and Ship Canal that has been considered the last major line of defense against the carp. The news sparked yet another flurry of debate and complaint. On July 20, 2010, Cox announced that his office had filed a new suit in the U.S. District Court for the Northern District of Illinois against the U.S. Army Corps of Engineers and Metropolitan Water Reclamation District of Greater Chicago. This lawsuit claimed that in failing to stop the progress of the carp toward the lakes, these agencies created a public nuisance that threatens the public resources of the waters and fisheries of the Great Lakes. The suit also called for an official review of the actions of the Corps under the Administrative Procedures Act, which allows legal challenges to federal agency actions to determine if they were arbitrary or unlawful.

The case was heard in September and October 2010. In December, Judge Robert Dow Jr. of the U.S. District Court issued an opinion that denied the request for an injunction, stating that the plaintiffs had not met the necessary burden of proof to obtain the injunction, in part by failing to show sufficient proof of irreparable harm if the situation remains the same. In the official opinion paper, the judge acknowledged the potential environmental and economic threats associated with the migration of the carp into the lakes, but noted that federal and state agencies are well aware of the situation and have been working on solutions to the problem.

More Asian carp DNA was discovered in Lake Calumet in June and July of 2011, which led to a four-day intensive fishing expedition by federal officials in early August. The purpose of the expedition was to determine whether or not the Asian carp has made its way into the locks that are designed to keep them from entering Lake Michigan. Biologists and commercial fisherman laid half-mile-wide nets to sweep large portions of Lake Calumet and also sample fish along the shoreline using electrofishing. The expedition produced no actual physical specimens of the invasive fish; however, environmentalists have challenged the fishing approach and continue to point to DNA evidence of invasion[SJT3].

At the national level, the Asian Carp Prevention and Control Act (S 1421—111th Congress), sponsored by Michigan's senator Carl Levin, passed in Congress and was signed into law on December 14, 2010. The law adds the bighead carp species of Asian carp to the list of injurious species that are prohibited from being imported or shipped in the United States under the Lacey Act.

🍁 Kalamazoo River Oil Spill

On July 26, 2010, a section of pipeline leaked oil into a stream that adjoins the Kalamazoo River, causing the largest oil spill to date in Midwest history. The U.S. Environmental Protection Agency (EPA) has estimated that the pipeline released over 1 million gallons (3.8 million liters) of oil approximately 60 miles (97 km) east of Lake Michigan. However, Enbridge Energy Partners, the Houston-based company that operates the pipeline, estimates the spill volume at 843,444 gallons (3.2 million liters). The 1,900-mile (3,058-km) Lakehead pipeline system, where the spill occurred, was built in 1969 to move oil from Indiana to Ontario. Correspondence with the Pipeline and Hazardous Materials Safety Administration (PHMSA) has revealed that in the past decade, Enbridge has received multiple warnings, citations, and fines for violation of safety and performance standards. Though post-rupture evaluations revealed corrosion on sections of the pipeline, the cause of the leak is still undetermined. A 140-foot (43-m) section of the pipe was shipped to Washington, D.C., for analysis by the U.S. National Transportation Safety Board (NTSB), and Michigan's attorney general's office announced an investigation regarding the causes of the spill. The analysis, along with interviews of various Enbridge employees, was expected to be completed by the end of 2011. The National Oceanic and Atmospheric Administration (NOAA) has also embarked on a long-term assessment to evaluate the extent of damage to the Talmadge Creek and Kalamazoo River systems.

Enbridge claims to have detected the leak on July 26, 2010. Upon discovery of the rupture, the flow of oil was stopped by closing isolation valves on the pipeline. Though spillage was contained in a 25-mile (40-km) section of the river between Marshall and Battle Creek, Michigan, officials estimated that cleanup and recovery could take months or even years. Enbridge completed an eleven-part work plan that was approved by the EPA in August 2010, which contained measures for dealing with all aspects of cleanup and recovery. Since the leak was discovered, the EPA oversaw up to 2,000 workers, who snaked more than 110,000 feet (33,530 m) of absorbent booms over contaminated areas. As cleanup continued into the winter months, some of these boom lines were removed to prevent problems with ice flow, but officials noted that freezing weather actually helped, as frozen oil solids became easier to remove. The booms were scheduled for replacement beginning in March 2011, as the spring thaw got underway. According to reports posted from both Enbridge and the U.S. EPA, more than 13.7 million gallons (51.9 million l) of oily water had been collected by mid-December. Enbridge estimated that nearly 700,000 gallons (2.6 million l) of oil would be salvaged for future commercial use.

Workers place containment boom on the Kalamazoo River to contain an oil spill (July 28, 2008). © *Jim West/Alamy*

The U.S. Fish and Wildlife service oversaw the aid effort for affected animals. Focus Wildlife International, a West Coast company specializing in rehabilitating oil-contaminated animals, also provided assistance, particularly through management of the temporary housing complex in Marshall known as Turtle City, which served as home to 470 turtles and one toad that were affected by oil contamination. Caretakers at the facility expected to release their charges back into their original habitats at some time in the spring of 2011. As of February 2011, a total of more than 2,200 animals had been rehabilitated and released through the combined efforts of participating groups.

The Calhoun County Health Department administered ongoing air, water, and soil tests to determine what additional actions need to be taken. In February 2011, a representative from the Michigan Department of Natural Resources and the Environment noted that there had been no signs of groundwater contamination in the affected areas; however, monitoring was expected to continue for several years as officials hope for complete recovery of the ecosystem before 2015. The affected sections of Talmadge Creek and the Kalamazoo River have been closed to the public since the spill occurred. Officials hoped to have oil-affected parts of the Kalamazoo River open for public use by late December 2011, clean-up is ongoing.

As of May 2011, the U.S. EPA had spent more than $20 million on clean-up efforts, which will be billed to Enbridge. Enbridge reported expenses of at least $550 million at the same time. Enbridge initially pledged to reimburse all citizens and businesses affected by the spill; the Enbridge website provides information on filing and claim and says that the claims process will be kept open until at least July 25, 2011. However, not all citizens of the area affected were satisfied by the company's response. An attorney representing ten households in Marshall and Battle Creek filed a suit in Calhoun Circuit County court on behalf of residents who had not been able to obtain satisfactory settlements from Enbridge for damages to property and health. The clients accused Enbridge of nuisance and neglect in failing to adequately maintain the pipeline. However, Enbridge has argued that it should not be held liable for the spill, since the company had followed all relevant laws and regulations and, therefore, the damage was unforeseeable.

Other lawsuits were been filed as well. A six-plaintiff class-action suit was filed in August 2010 with similar complaints. That month, the Great Lakes Environmental Law Center also gave notice of its intention to file a suit seeking up to $100 million in civil financial penalties against Enbridge for violations of the Clean Water Act. Center officials have stated that they would delay or dismiss the case if the federal or state governments file suit against the company instead. In March 2011, David Uhlmann, the former chief of the U.S. Department of Justice's environmental crisis section, predicted that Enbridge would most likely face federal criminal charges under the Clean Water Act, similar to the charges that BP could face for the 2010 Gulf Oil Spill.

On August 31, 2010, a pressure test of Line 6B, the affected part of the pipeline, was deemed successful and no leaks were detected. By September 22, Enbridge had received approval to restart Line 6B, and the line was successfully returned to service on September 28, 2010.

In January 2011, a number of state and local environmental advocates marked the six-month anniversary of the spill with a call to U.S. Representative Fred Upton (R–St. Joseph) to use his influence in Washington to support legislation that would prevent such environmental disasters in the future. The newly founded Coalition for New Priorities (est. November 2010) sponsored the Rally to Remember the Kalamazoo River Oil Spill on January 26, 2011, at Western Michigan University as part of this effort. Upton was chosen as the chairman of the House Energy and Commerce Committee for the 2011 session of Congress. Michigan environmentalists are particularly concerned that

proposed funding cuts to government agencies charged with regulating oil and pipeline industries could set the stage for future disasters. However, Upton may not be easily convinced, as he is a strong supporter of the Keystone XL pipeline, a large-scale Canadian-sponsored project to build a line that will transport Canadian crude oil from Alberta to the gulf coast of Texas.

A study released in August 2011 from the Michigan Department of Community Health received criticism when it stated that there are no long-term health effects related to human contact with submerged oil. Scientists with the National Wildlife Federation stated that more research is needed and that the study is therefore incomplete, particularly because eight chemicals found in submerged oil were not included in the study. The EPA has continued to monitor the air, sediment, and ground water for chemicals released from the oil. According to news reports, officials have said that no chemicals have been found in drinking water. Nonetheless, a study by the Calhoun County Health Department showed that about 60 percent of residents who lived near the river reported acute health effects, such as headaches and bloody noses. Enbridge was ordered to have 200 acres (81 ha) of submerged oil cleaned up by the end of December 2011; clean-up is ongoing.

BIBLIOGRAPHY

Books

Leonetti, Ron. *Of Woods and Water: A Photographic Journey across Michigan* Bloomington: Quarry Books/Indiana University Press, 2008.

Montrie, Chad. *Making a Living: Work and Environment in the United States.* Chapel Hill, NC: University of North Carolina Press, 2008.

Strutin, Michal, and Gary Irving. *The Smithsonian Guides to Natural America: The Great Lakes–Ohio, Indiana, Michigan, Wisconsin.* Washington, DC: Smithsonian Books, 1996.

Web Sites

"Asian Carp and Chicago Canal Litigation" Great Lakes Environmental Law Center. Available from http://www.greatlakeslaw.org/blog/asian-carp.Associated Press

"Asian Carp may have been planted near lake." *Chicago Sun-Times.* August 5, 2010. Available from http://www.suntimes.com/news/metro/2569700,asian-carp-lake-michigan-planted-080510.article

Asian Carp Prevention and Control Act (S 1421–111th Congress). U.S. Congress. Available from http://www.govtrack.us/congress/billtext.xpd?bill=s111-1421

A Bill to Amend the Michigan Business Tax Code (HB 4927-2009). Michigan Legislature. Available from http://www.legislature.mi.gov/documents/

2009-2010/billintroduced/House/pdf/2009-HIB-4927.pdf

Building Green for the Future: Case Studies of Sustainable Development in Michigan. Available from http://www.michigan.gov/documents/deq/deq-ess-p2-green-handbook_282422_7.pdf

"Cleaning up wildlife after the oil spill," WWMT, July 27, 2010. Available from http://www.wwmt.com/articles/west-1379517-cleaning-wildlife.html

Dolan, Matthew. "Michigan Oil Spill Prompts Evacuations, Finger-Pointing," Matthew Dolan, *Wall Street Journal*, July 29, 2010. Available from http://online.wsj.com/article/SB1000142405274870357810457539761381889174-0.html?mod=googlenews_wsj

Egan, Dan "Asian carp discovered near Lake Michigan." Milwaukee-Wisconsin *Journal Sentinel*. June 23, 2010. Available from http://www.jsonline.com/news/wisconsin/97003199.html

Enrolled House Bill No 4212. Michigan Legislature. Available from http://www.legislature.mi.gov/documents/2011-2012/billenrolled/House/pdf/2011-HNB-4212.pdf

"EPA gets $13M for Michigan spill; will seek reimbursement from Enbridge," The Associated Press, August 2, 2010. Available from http://www.woodtv.com/dpp/news/local/kalamazoo_and_battle_creek/EPA-gets-up-to-13M-for-Mich-oil-spill

"EPA notes improvements at Michigan oil spill site," The Associated Press, August 1, 2010. Available from http://www.google.com/hostednews/ap/article/ALeqM5hbazNv8HPBELUpCXxcRQmC-xaO3DgD9HB1D9G0

Gaertner, Eric. "Muskegon County requests proposals from wind developers interested in wastewater site." *Muskegon Chronicle*. January 26, 2011. Available from http://www.mlive.com/news/muskegon/index.ssf/2011/01/muskegon_county_requests_propo.html

Gaertner, Eric. "Wind-farm negotiations for Muskegon County wastewater site to begin." Mlive.com. July 14, 2011. Available from http://www.mlive.com/news/muskegon/index.ssf/2011/07/wind-farm_negotiations_for_mus.html

"Global Warming and Michigan." National Wildlife Federation. Available http://www.nwf.org/Global-Warming/~/media/PDFs/Global%20Warming/Global%20Warming%20State%20Fact%20Sheets/Michigan.ashx

Guarino, Mark. "Asian carp: DNA evidence finds something fishy near Lake Michigan." *The Christian Science Monitor*. August 5, 2011. Available from http://www.csmonitor.com/Environment/2011/0805/Asian-carp-DNA-evidence-finds-something-fishy-near-Lake-Michigan

Guarino, Mark. "Will Asian carp turn up in fishing expedition near Lake Michigan?" *The Christian Science Monitor*. August 1, 2011. Available from http://www.csmonitor.com/Environment/2011/0801/Will-Asian-carp-turn-up-in-fishing-expedition-near-Lake-Michigan

Hornbeck, Mark; Charlie Cain; and Gary Heinlein. "Governor pushes green power." *The Detroit News*, February 4, 2009. Available from http://detnews.com/article/20090204/POLITICS/902040388/Governor-pushes-green-power

Killian, Chris. "Six months after Kalamazoo River oil spill, environmental groups urge U.S. Rep. Fred Upton to provide greater oil-pipeline oversight." *Kalamazoo Gazette*. January 26, 2011. Available from http://www.mlive.com/news/kalamazoo/index.ssf/2011/01/environmental_groups_urge_us_r.html

Kleseno, David D. "Michigan 2008–2009 Highlights." Michigan Field Office, National Agricultural Statistics Service. Available from http://www.nass.usda.gov/Statistics_by_State/Michigan/Publications/MichiganFactSheets/STHILGTS.pdf

Klug, Fritz. "About 75 Kalamazoo River residents attend Battle Creek meeting on oil spill, get information on lawsuit." MILive.com. August 21, 2011. Available from http://www.mlive.com/news/kalamazoo/index.ssf/2011/08/75_kalamazoo_river_residents_a.html

Klug, Fritz. "National Wildlife Federation says health study of Kalamazoo River oil spill is incomplete." MILive.com. August 19, 2011. Available from http://www.mlive.com/news/kalamazoo/index.ssf/2011/08/national_wildlife_federation_s.html

Lambert, Sara. "Oil spill victims file class-action lawsuit," *Battle Creek Enquirer*, August 1, 2010. Available from http://www.battlecreekenquirer.com/article/20100801/OILSPILL/8010330/Oil-spill-victims-file-class-action-lawsuit

Lawrence, Eric D. "Workers try to grasp Michigan oil spill toll on wildlife," *Detroit Free Press*, July 30, 2010. Available from http://www.freep.com/article/20100730/NEWS06/7300362/1322/Workers-try-to-grasp-Michigan-oil-spill-toll-on-wildlife

"List of Biodiesel and Ethanol Stations in Michigan." Michigan Department of Agriculture. Available at http://www.michigan.gov/mda/0,1607,7-125–187045–,00.html

Melzer, Eartha Jane. "Enbridge denies responsibility for oil spill." *The Michigan Messenger.* January 31, 2011. Available from http://michiganmessenger.com/46106/enbridge-denies-responsibility-for-oil-spill

Melzer, Eartha Jane. "Enbridge increases estimate of oil spilled in Kalamazoo River." *The Michigan Messenger.* December 23, 2010. Available from http://michiganmessenger.com/45137/enbridge-increases-estimate-of-oil-spilled-in-kalamazoo-river

Melzer, Eartha Jane. "Enbridge expected to face criminal charges on Michigan oil Spill." *The Michigan Messenger.* March 7, 2011. Available from http://michiganmessenger.com/47099/enbridge-expected-to-face-criminal-charges-over-michigan-spill#

Memorandum Opinion and Order: Case No. 10-CV-4457. December 2, 2010. U.S. District Court for the Northern District of Illinois. Available from http://www.greatlakeslaw.org/files/dist_ct_pi_opinion_order.pdf

Michigan Agricultural Environmental Assurance Program. Available from http://www.maeap.org/maeap

Michigan Green Jobs Report 2009. Michigan Department of Energy, Labor & Economic Growth. Available from http://www.michigan.gov/documents/nwlb/GJC_GreenReport_Print_277833_7.pdf

"Michigan." National Park Service. Available from http://www.nps.gov/state/mi/index.htm?program=parks

Michigan's Natural Resources and Environment: A Citizen's Guide. Michigan Legislature, Legislative Service Bureau, Science and Technology Division. Available from http://www.legislature.mi.gov/documents/Publications/NaturalResources.pdf

Michigan 2007 Minerals Yearbook. U.S. Geological Survey. Available from http://minerals.usgs.gov/minerals/pubs/state/2007/myb2-2007-mi.pdf

Mikalonis, Saulius. "LEEDing Legislation in Michigan. " Greening of the Great Lakes. Available from http://www.greeningofthegreatlakes.com/public_policy/leed_legislation.php

Neavling, Steve, and Christina Hall. "EPA: A lot of work ahead in Michigan oil cleanup," *Detroit Free Press,* August 2, 2010. Available from http://www.freep.com/article/20100802/NEWS05/8020357/1322/EPA-A-lot-of-work-ahead-in-Michigan-oil-cleanup

Neavling, Steve, and Christina Hall. "Oil pipeline section to be analyzed in Washington, D.C.," *Detroit Free Press,* August 2, 2010. Available from http://www.freep.com/article/20100802/NEWS05/8020358

Office of the Governor, State of Michigan. *Executive Directive No. 2005–4: Energy Efficiency in State Facilities and Operations.* Available from http://www.michigan.gov/gov/0,1607,7-168-21975_22515-116177–,00.html

Office of the Governor, State of Michigan. *Executive Directive No. 2007–22: Enhanced Energy Efficiency and Conservation by State Departments and Agencies.* Available from http://www.michigan.gov/gov/0,1607,7-168-36898_45122-180298–,00.html

Oosting, Johnathan. "Using solar to build electric: Ford to revamp Wayne plant with focus on sustainability " Mlive.com. August 16, 2010. Available from http://www.mlive.com/auto/index.ssf/2010/08/using_-solar_to_build_electric.html

"Organic Registration Page." Michigan Department of Agriculture. Available from http://www.michigan.gov/mda/0,1607,7-125-1569_25516—,00.html

Rogers, Christina. "Wixom plant will get new life." *The Detroit News.* September 11, 2009. Available from http://detnews.com/article/20090911/AUTO01/909110345/Wixom-plant-will-get-new-life

Sea Grant Michigan. Available from http://www.miseagrant.umich.edu

"State and Local Climate and Energy Program: Michigan." United States Environmental Protection Agency. Available from http://www.epa.gov/statelocalclimate/state/tracking/individual/mi.html#a05-e

"State Energy Profiles: Michigan." U.S. Energy Information Administration. Available at http://tonto.eia.doe.gov/state/state_energy_profiles.cfm?sid=MI

Substitute House Bill No. 4213. Michigan Legislature. Available from http://www.legislature.mi.gov/documents/2011-2012/billengrossed/House/pdf/2011-HEBH-4213.pdf

Taylor, John C. and James L. Roach. *Chicago Waterway System Ecological Separation: The Logistics and Transportation Related Cost Impact of Waterway Barriers.* State of Michigan, Department of Attorney General. Available from http://www.glu.org/sites/default/files/carp/TR_chicago_canal_report_-feb10.pdf

Thompson, Carol. "Clean-up continues through winter as oil spill damage lingers." Capital News Service. February 4, 2011. Available from http://capitalnewsservice.wordpress.com/2011/02/04/clean-up-continues-through-winter-as-oil-spill-damage-lingers

"Trends in Michigan's Forest Products Industry." Michigan forest Products Council. Available from http://www.michiganforest.com/documents/treds2010.pdf

"Turtle City Prepares Oil-Contaminated Reptiles for Return to the Wild." State of Michigan. February 24, 2011. Available from http://www.michigan.gov/som/0,1607,7-192-53480_56420-251802-,00.html

"Value and Rank of Nonfuel Mineral Production in the U.S., 2010 p/1/ (Rank Based on Value of Raw Material Produced)." National Mining Association. Available from http://www.nma.org/pdf/m_value_rank.pdf

Wood, Michael. "Enbridge spill clean-up will take months," QMI Agency, August 1, 2010. Available from http://www.torontosun.comnews/world/2010/08/01/14896256.html

Minnesota

Known as the Land of 10,000 Lakes, Minnesota is at the crossroads of three types of terrain, with grassland plains and prairies to the west and south, coniferous (cone-bearing) forest to the north, and hardwood forest, once known as the "Big Woods" to the east. The state's famous waters, together with forests, parks, and wilderness areas, offer residents and tourists a variety of outdoor recreational opportunities. They also sustain the state's forestry, farming, and mining industries.

A Varied Climate

Minnesota has a continental climate, with cold, often frigid winters and warm summers. The growing season is 160 days or more in the south central and southeastern regions, but 100 days or less in the northern counties. Average temperatures range from 8°F (-13°C) in January to 66°F (18°C) in July for Duluth, and from 12°F (-11°C) in January to 74°F (23°C) in July for the Twin Cities, Minneapolis and St. Paul.

Precipitation is lightest in the northwest, where it averaged 19 inches (48 cm) per year. Heavy snowfalls occur from November to April, averaging about 70 inches (178 cm) annually in the northeast and 30 inches (76 cm) in the southeast. Tornadoes occur mostly in the southern part of the state; on average there are eighteen tornadoes in the state each year.

In 2003, the Minnesota Pollution Control Agency's Climate Change Action Plan determined that effects of climate change for Minnesota will involve substantial warming, particularly in winter, and likely increased precipitation. Increased heavy rainfall will result in more incidents of flooding, resulting in more soil runoff and drought in the summer as more moisture runs off and less is stored in soils. Climate change could also shorten the winter season by at least a month due to warming during early and late winter months. Since the state is at a crossroads of a variety of landscapes, scientists believe this could cause extreme changes along these boundaries, such as the retreat of the boreal forest of the north into Canada, habitat shifts for cold water fish species into extreme northern Minnesota, and the northern establishment of animal and plant species normally found far south of the state

The Minnesota Climate Change Advisory Group released a report to the state legislature in 2008 that included a greenhouse gas (GHG) inventory and 46 recommended policy actions to reduce GHG emissions. Some of these actions include minimizing savings from utility conservation improvement programs, improving statewide building codes, and a program to reduce emissions of nonfuel high-global-warming-potential GHGs.

Natural Resources, Water, and Agriculture

Natural Resources

One-third of Minnesota's nearly 80,000 square miles (207,200 sq km) of land area is made up of fifty-eight state forests and two national forests, the Chippewa National Forest and the Superior National Forest, which includes the Boundary Waters Canoe Area Wilderness. The state is home to the nation's largest jack pine and largest white spruce, according to the Minnesota Department of Natural Resources. Forest products have an annual economic impact of $6–7 billion, with 40,000 acres (16,187 ha) of timber harvested in 2002. In 2007, more than 4 million trees were planted on state land and more than 3 million on private land in a reforestation effort.

The state also boasts 66 state parks and one national park—Voyageurs National Park, which is the only national park without a road. The state's natural lands are home to more than 550 pairs of bald eagles, 1,600 timber wolves, 12,000 common loons (the state bird), moose, black bear, and white-tailed deer. According to

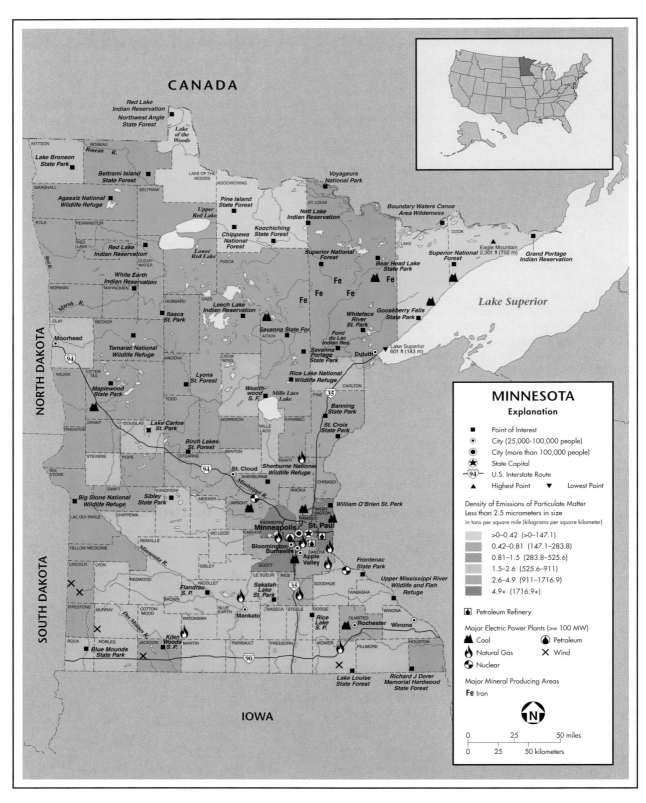

SOURCES: "County Emissions Map: Criteria Air Pollutants." *AirData*. U.S. Environmental Protection Agency. Available from http://www.epa.gov/air/data/geosel.html; *Energy Maps*. U.S. Energy Information Administration. Available from http://www.eia.gov/state; *Highest and Lowest Elevations*. U.S. Geological Survey. Available from http://egsc.usgs.gov/isb/pubs/booklets/elvadist/elvadist.html#Highest; *2007 Minerals Yearbook*. U.S. Geological Survey. Available from http://minerals.usgs.gov/minerals/pubs/state. © 2011 Cengage Learning.

the U.S. Fish and Wildlife Service, there are fifteen federally endangered or threatened plant and animal species in the state, which include the dwarf trout lily, gray wolf, Topeka shiner, and the piping plover.

In 2011, federal officials began efforts to attempt to delist gray wolves of the Great Lakes region from the federal Endangered Species List. The protections for the wolves remained in place until December 2011 when the Obama administration declared that the gray wolf populations in Michigan, Minnesota, Wisconsin, and parts of adjoining states had recovered sufficiently enough to be removed from the endangered species list. Only recently had the wolves in the Great Lakes region been classified as two species—the gray wolf and the eastern wolf—including hybrids of the two species. Some biologists cite that recent discovery as another reason why protections should have been left in place, to give scientists a better opportunity to understand the population.

Minnesota has commercial mines for iron ore (for which the state ranked first in the nation in 2007), quartzite, granite and gabbro, limestone/dolomite, peat, silica sand, and kaolin clay. There are six mines in the state that produce low-grade iron ore (or active taconite), of which 40 million long tons of pellets were produced in 2006. In 2010 Minnesota was ranked fourth for overall total nonfuel mineral production with a value of $3.9 billion.

Pollution from mining operations is a concern in the state, as illustrated through the proposed Polymet NorthMet copper-nickel and precious metals mining project. The state has sought to enact some environmental protections while allowing mining companies to continue or expand extraction of the state's mineral resources.

In August 2011, Minnesota and U.S. Steel came to an agreement, called a schedule of compliance, that permitted the company to expand production at one plant while capturing polluted wastewater at another. The schedule of compliance deal is similar to a contract and specifies actions the company will need to take at its two Minnesota plants, located in Iron Range and Mountain Iron. While the Minnesota Pollution Control Agency claims that the deal will protect the environment without interfering with the Iron Range's economic development, environmentalists and some state Indian tribes have expressed concerns. They do not believe that the pollution-reducing technology adopted for the plant will be effective. Additionally, the expansion of the one plant will cause more air pollution. U.S. Steel aims to solve this issue by installing dry scrubbers and other technology in its smoke stacks to capture air pollutants. Indian tribes and environmentalists are skeptical of this technology as well. While officials are convinced that the schedule of compliance will improve environmental performance, the effectiveness of pollution-reducing technologies remains to be seen.

Minnesota State Profile

Physical Characteristics

Land area	79,607 square miles (206,181 sq km)
Inland water area	4,782 square miles (12,385 sq km)
Coastal area	NA
Highest point	Eagle Mountain 2,301 feet (701 m)
National Forest System lands (2010)	2.8 million acres (1.2 million ha)
State parks (2011)	75

Energy Statistics

Total energy production (2009)	350 trillion Btu
State ranking in total energy production (2009)	34
Renewable energy net generation total (2009)	7.5 million megawatt hours
Hydroelectric energy generation (2009)	809,000 megawatt hours
Biomass energy generation (2009)	887,000 megawatt hours
Wind energy generation (2009)	5.0 million megawatt hours
Wood and derived fuel energy generation (2009)	796,000 megawatt hours
Crude oil reserves (2009)	NA
Natural gas reserves (2009)	NA
Natural gas liquids (2008)	NA

Pollution Statistics

Carbon output (2005)	102.4 million tons of CO_2 (92.9 million t)
Superfund sites (2008)	25
Particulate matter (less than 2.5 micrometers) emissions (2002)	4,348 tons per year (3,944 t/yr)
Toxic chemical releases (2009)	22.2 million pounds (10.1 million kg)
Generated hazardous waste (2009)	106,800 tons (96,900 t)

SOURCES: AirData. U.S. Environmental Protection Agency. Available from http://www.epa.gov/air/data; *Energy Maps, Facts, and Data of the U.S. States.* U.S. Energy Information Administration. Available from http://www.eia.gov/state; *The 2012 Statistical Abstract.* U.S. Census Bureau. Available from http://www.census.gov/compendia/statab; *United States Energy Usage.* eRedux. Available from http://www.eredux.net/states.

© 2011 Cengage Learning.

Water in the Land of 10,000 Lakes

Ten thousand years ago, most of Minnesota was covered in glaciers more than a mile thick. These would eventually melt to form the more than 15,000 lakes, rivers, streams, and extensive wetlands that give the state more inland water than any other, except Alaska. Large inland lakes include Lower and Upper Red Lake, Mille Lacs, and Leech Lake. A total of 2,212 square miles (5,729 sq km) of Lake Superior lies within Minnesota's jurisdiction. Lake Itasca, in the northwest, is the source of the Mississippi River, which drains about three-fifths of the state and, after meeting with the St. Croix River below Minneapolis-St. Paul, forms part of the state's eastern boundary with Wisconsin. Other major rivers include the

According to the Minnesota Department of Agriculture, there were more than 650 organic farms and more than 200 certified organic processing facilities across the state. © *ZUMA Press/newscom*

Minnesota River, the Red River of the North, and the North River.

In April 2011, the Minnesota Pollution Control Agency (MPCA) announced that it was seeking grant proposals from local governments to reduce nonpoint source water pollution. Nonpoint source pollution is pollution that comes from many sources, such as farm fields or urban areas, and not a single point, such as from an industrial facility. The MPCA has made $2.5 million available for development, education, applied research, or restoration projects.

Ranked first in the nation in the per capita sales of fishing licenses, Minnesota boasts 3.8 million acres (1.5 million ha) of fishing waters and 15,000 miles (24,140 km) of fishable streams. In 2010, 3.5 million pounds (1.6 million kg) of fish were commercially harvested, which included herring and smelts from Lake Superior, whitefish and yellow pike from inland lakes, and carp and catfish from the Mississippi and Minnesota rivers. Sport fishing attracts some 1.5 million anglers annually to the state's fishing lakes and streams, which are stocked with trout, bass, pike, muskellunge ("muskie"), and other fish by the Division of Fish and Wildlife of the Department of Natural Resources.

Agriculture: Talking Turkey

About half of Minnesota's land area, 42,031 square miles (108,860 sq km), is used for agriculture. As of 2009, Minnesota had 81,000 farms. The state ranks first in the nation for sugar beet production. Other top crops include corn for grain, for which the state ranks fourth in the United States, and soybeans for beans, for which the state

ranks third. When it comes to livestock, Minnesota is ranked first in the nation for turkey, its top livestock item, and third for hogs and pigs.

According to the Minnesota Department of Agriculture, there were more than 650 organic farms and more than 200 certified organic processing facilities across the state in 2010. There are also 16,530 head of organic cattle, hogs, pigs, sheep and lamb, and 155,833 organic poultry.

Energy

Ethanol, Petroleum, and Natural Gas

Minnesota is among the nation's top producers of ethanol, with over a dozen corn-based production plants located primarily in the southern part of the state. There is a statewide requirement for the use of oxygenated motor gasoline blended with 10 percent ethanol, due to a program started in 1992 put in place to support ethanol production and consumption. Minnesota also offers incentives to encourage the adoption of E85—a mixture of 85 percent ethanol with 15 percent motor gasoline— and now has more E85 refueling stations than any other state.

Several pipeline systems bring crude oil to Minnesota from Canada for refining at two plants in the Minnesota-St. Paul area. The MinnCan Project, completed in 2009, involved the construction of a 304-mile (489-km) pipeline from Clearbrook in Clearwater County to the Flint Hills Resources refinery in Rosemont in Dakota County to carry Canadian crude oil.

Natural gas is supplied mostly by pipelines from Canada and from North and South Dakota, with over

Minnesota is among the nation's top producers of ethanol, with over a dozen corn-based production plants located primarily in the southern part of the state (such as this one that opened in 2009). The vertical structures are evaporation towers; the large horizontal structures are drying mills for drying corn. © *ZUMA Press/newscom*

two-thirds of Minnesota households using it as their primary heating fuel during the winter. Over four-fifths of the natural gas that the state receives is shipped to Iowa and Wisconsin on its way to other Midwestern U.S. markets.

Electricity and Renewable Resources

Coal, brought into Minnesota by rail from Montana and Wyoming, powers three-fifths of Minnesota's electricity generation. Two nuclear plants near the Twin Cities produce one-fourth of the state's electricity, with the Prairie Island Plant licensed to operate through 2014, and the smaller Monticello plant licensed through September 2030.

Minnesota installed its first wind farm in 1987 at Crookston. More than 60 wind farms have followed since then, with a total wind energy capacity of 2196 MW as of January 1, 2011. Wind farms in the southwest area of the state produce nearly 5 percent of Minnesota's electricity. In 2011, Minnesota was ranked fourth in the nation for wind energy output, behind Texas, California, and Iowa. Legislation passed in 2005 has made it a state goal to have 25 percent of energy come from wind resources by 2025.

Creating Standards for Renewable Energy

In 2007, Minnesota enacted legislation that created a renewable portfolio standard (RPS) for the state's major utility, Xcel Energy and another RPS for other electric utilities. The Xcel Energy RPS aims to have 25 percent of the utility's energy come from renewable sources by 2016, while the RPS for other utility companies aims to have 25 percent of their energy from renewable sources by 2025. Also in 2007, the state modified its existing non-mandatory renewable energy objective to require

that 7 percent of electricity sold to retail customers come from eligible renewable energy sources by 2010. Eligible renewables are generated by solar, wind, hydroelectric facilities less than 100 megawatts (MW), hydrogen and biomass.

In January 2011, the Minnesota Department of Commerce and the Minnesota Pollution Control Agency released the *Annual Legislative Proposal Report on Greenhouse Gas Emission Reductions and Biennial Greenhouse Gas Emissions Reduction Report*. According to the report, the state met its energy requirements for 2009, and was on track to meet its 2010 renewable energy requirements of at least 7 percent of statewide retail electricity sales from renewable resources. The report also made a number of suggestions of actions that could be taken to help the state reach its ultimate goal of receiving 25 percent of its energy from renewable sources by 2025. These suggestions included an expanded power grid to better accommodate wind and solar power and improving and streamlining the process of applying for energy efficiency incentives.

⚘ Green Business, Green Building, Green Jobs

Green Business: A Variety of Opportunities

Minnesota boasts a variety of organizations poised to expand the growing green economy. The organization Windustry, located in Minneapolis, serves as a statewide resource for high quality wind energy information. The organization has a special focus on helping rural and local communities reap the economic development benefits of new wind energy projects. Another organization promoting the growth of Minnesota's green economy is Sundays Energy. Sundays Energy provides a variety of services to aspiring environmentally friendly entrepreneurs, including help with everything from business proposals to branding, and taking care of the many logistics necessary for a successful business to operate.

Green Building: "Greening" the Community

In 2001, the Minnesota Legislature required the Department of Administration and Commerce to develop mandatory sustainable building design guidelines for all new state bonded buildings. In 2008, this legislation was expanded to include all major renovations. New state-bonded buildings and major renovations must exceed the state energy code by at least 30 percent and focus on achieving the lowest possible lifetime costs. Building projects must also encourage continual energy conservation improvements, exceed air quality and lighting standards, create and maintain a healthy environment, and specify ways to reduce material costs.

The statewide initiative Minnesota Green Communities—a collaboration of the Greater Minnesota Housing Fund, the Family Housing Fund, and Enterprise's national Green Communities initiative—seeks to ensure that all new affordable housing in Minnesota is green, and aims to "green rehab" or retrofit 10,000 units of existing affordable housing by 2015. The program uses environmentally beneficial materials and conservation-minded land use planning to reduce energy costs and provide healthier environments for families and communities. Nearly 380 green homes have been built or are underway in cities from Minneapolis and Duluth to Bloomington.

The city of Minneapolis also adopted a policy in 2006 requiring all new and significantly renovated buildings financed by the city of Minneapolis to be built to a LEED Silver level of quality with an emphasis on energy efficiency.

Controversy in Minnesota's green building arena erupted in December of 2010, when the Builders' Association of the Twin Cities (BATC) sued Minnesota Green Star (GreenStar). Unlike most states that have incorporated LEED standards into their green regulations, Minnesota created GreenStar, its own green building certification standard. Originally partnered with BATC, the Minnesota chapter of the National Association of the Remodeling Industry, and the Minneapolis-based Green Institute, BATC withdrew from the organization with the downturn of the economy. BATC sued GreenStar because it claimed that it developed and owns the intellectual property to the organization's "Green Homebuilding Guidelines," and also claimed that it is owed over $300,000 dollars from GreenStar. BATC also filed a temporary restraining order to keep GreenStar from altering or selling the manual, though they may continue to use it in ongoing projects. The withdrawal of BATC's funding and participation in GreenStar threatens the existence of the state's green building guidelines. Since the state also partially funded the GreenStar program, they also may have a stake in ownership and may be brought into the legal fray or be forced to develop or integrate new state guidelines. A temporary injunction hearing was held on January 24, 2011. GreenStar and BATC were still seeking an amicable solution as of fall 2011.

Green Jobs: Re-Training the Workforce

According to the Minnesota Department of Employment and Economic Development, the top three green growth careers in Minnesota are environmental engineering, hazardous waste management, and engineering geology. In 2009, some 9,477 Minnesotans were employed in the renewable energy sector, and 22,441 were employed in green services, with both of those numbers expected to increase.

The Minnesota chapter of the Blue-Green Alliance received a $5 million Energy Training Partnership Grant in January 2010 to fund its GreenPOWER (Green Partnership of Workforce and Employer Resources) job training program. The program partners cities, labor unions, manufacturers, and technical colleges to train workers in green manufacturing and energy jobs. One specific group targeted by the program will be displaced autoworkers, such as those affected by the closing of the Ford Motor Company's Twin Cities Assembly Plant, though the program will also reach outside that area into southwest Minnesota and the Iron Range.

In August 2011, the state received a boost in green jobs training when the Saint Paul Port Authority (SPPA) received a $300,000 Brownfields Job Training Grant from the EPA. The Port Authority received the grant because the EPA recognized them as a leader in redeveloping underutilized contaminated or "brownfield" sites, such as the location of the former 3M Company's international headquarters, which has been redeveloped as the Beacon Bluff Business Center. The grant, managed by Employer Solutions Inc., will train students in environmental jobs. The training will consist of six three-week sessions with courses on hazardous materials management, energy management, and reducing environmental releases and emissions.

🌱 PolyMet Mining, Inc./ NorthMet Project: Back to the Drawing Board

Once the world's iron ore capital, Minnesota's mining industry experienced a dramatic decline in the late nineteenth century, causing many jobs to disappear. In the early twenty-first century, increased demand for metals by developing countries revitalized Minnesota's mining culture and prompted new exploration, a new steel mill, and plans for mine development. PolyMet Mining, Inc. recently proposed the NorthMet Project, which would develop an open pit mine on public land managed by the Superior National Forest and refurbish and modify a former taconite ore processing facility previously owned by LTV Steel Mining. The facility would extract copper and precipitates of nickel, cobalt, and precious metals.

The environmental question related to this mine relates to the techniques that must be used to extract these minerals, which are part of sulfide rock. When that rock is brought to the surface and exposed to air and water, the sulfur in the rock links with hydrogen and oxygen in the atmosphere to form sulfuric acid. Rainwater and snow melt that runs over these rocks becomes acidic. When it flows into streams and wetlands, it then creates conditions where plants and wildlife cannot live. Residents have been concerned about the mine's effect on the local landscape, near Babbitt and Hoyt Lakes in northwestern Minnesota. Of the steps that would be taken to mitigate the mine's effect on the environment. To offset damage to the 848 acres (343 ha) of wetlands of affected by the project, PolyMet initially proposed construction of about 1,100 acres (445 ha) of wetlands off-site and, at closure, reconstruction of 175 acres (71 ha) of wetlands on-site. To reduce contamination of local waterways by AMD, PolyMet planned to mine ore with a minimal amount of sulfide at 0.7 percent—far less than other mines where sulfide concentrations can reach as much as 30 percent. Finally, PolyMet proposed to engineer foundations, drains, liners, and covers as a collection system for all water that contacts exposed mining rock in the stockpiles and mine pit. Perimeter dykes would seek to prevent water from entering or leaving the mine site and contaminating area water supplies. Upon closure of the mine, PolyMet would cap any remaining waste rock stockpiles with the potential to create acid with a geomembrane and cover this with soil and vegetation.

In February 2010, the U.S. Environmental Protection Agency (EPA) rejected the draft EIS and PolyMet's mitigation plans as environmentally inadequate. The EPA found that the actions included in the draft proposal would result in water pollution exceeding water quality standards; in addition, the agency stated that the EIS failed to provide mitigation for all impacts to wetlands. In October 2010, the Minnesota DNR, the U.S. Army Corps of Engineers, the U.S. Forest Service, and St. Paul District, published a Notice of Intent to begin preparations for the supplemental draft statement. As of April 30, 2011, PolyMet reported that it had spent $33.648 million on environmental review and permitting.

Once the modeling confirms that the project meets state and federal standards, a third party contractor will put together the preliminary supplemental draft Environmental Impact Statement (SDEIS), expected in the fall of 2011. In June 2011 it was reported that the air, wetlands, and geotechnical modeling and evaluations required for the SDEIS were well defined and modeling had started. The SDEIS was still on track to be published in the fall of 2011. Residents of Minnesota, where the legacy of mining is strong, will have to wait and see whether PolyMet can successfully develop a new mine, while addressing environmentalists' and the EPA's concerns.

Increased heavy rainfall will result in more incidents of flooding, resulting in more soil runoff and drought in the summer as more moisture runs off and less is stored in soils (such as this 1997 flooding). © *AP Images/David J. Phillip, File*

particular concern are the local wetlands and ground and surface water quality, since approximately 2.5 square miles (5 of the 13 sq km) the proposed mine would cover are covered by wetlands, which would be destroyed. Another concern is for the disposal of the millions of tons of waste rock, some containing sulfide mineralization that has the potential to cause acid mine drainage (AMD). AMD can hinder streambed ecosystems, smothering animal and plant life on the streambed. AMD discharge can also potentially contain elevated levels of toxic metals, especially nickel and copper, with lower levels of such trace and semimetal ions as lead, arsenic, aluminum, and manganese.

In November 2009, the Minnesota Department of Natural Resources (DNR) published a draft of an environmental impact statement (EIS), documenting

BIBLIOGRAPHY

Books

McCarron, Robert. *Technical Assistance Project for the Minnesota Pollution Control Agency.* Golden, CO: National Renewable Energy Laboratory, 2006.

Shepard, Lansing, and Tom Bean. *The Smithsonian Guides to Natural America: The Northern Plains– Minnesota, North Dakota, South Dakota.* Washington, DC: Smithsonian Books, 1996.

Tober, Dwight A. *Big Bluestem Biomass Trials in North Dakota, South Dakota, and Minnesota.* Bismarck,

ND: U.S. Department of Agriculture, Natural Resources, Conservation Service, 2008.

Web Sites

Annual Legislative Proposal Report on Greenhouse Gas Emission Reductions and Biennial Greenhouse Gas Emissions Reduction Report. Minnesota Department of Commerce and the Minnesota Pollution Control Agency. Available from http://www.state.mn.us/mn/externalDocs/Commerce/Greenhouse_Gas_Emissions_Reduction_Report_2011_122910041040_GreenhouseGasEmissions2010.pdf

"B3 State of Minnesota Sustainable Building Guidelines." The State of Minnesota Sustainable Building Guidelines (MSBG). Available from http://www.msbg.umn.edu/index.html

"Building the Framework for a Clean Energy Future in Minnesota." Blue-Green Alliance. Available from http://www.bluegreenalliance.org/states/minnesota

Demos, Telis. "Minnesota's Mining Boom." *Fortune.* November 21, 2007. Available from http://money.cnn.com/2007/11/21/news/minnesota_mining.fortune/index.htm

"Discover Green Jobs." Minnesota Department of Employment and Economic Development. Available from http://www.positivelyminnesota.com/JobSeekers/Discover_Green_Jobs/index.aspx

"Draft Environmental Impact Statement (EIS) PolyMet Mining, Inc./NorthMet Project." Minnesota Department of Natural Resources. Available from http://www.dnr.state.mn.us/input/environmentalreview/polymet/eis_toc.html

"EPA Awards Job Training Grant to Saint Paul Port Authority." U.S. Environmental Protection Agency. August 24, 2011. Available from http://yosemite.epa.gov/opa/admpress.nsf/0/a3bd4d1ad1ad8561852578f60055bc20?OpenDocument

"Federal Agencies Publish Notice of Intent for PolyMet EIS." PolyMet Mining. Available from http://www.polymetmining.com/uploads/PolyMet_NR_2010_6.pdf

Flesher, John. "Great Lakes wolves could come off endangered list." April 15, 2011. *Houston Chronicle.* Available from http://www.chron.com/disp/story.mpl/ap/top/all/7523963.html

Hemphill, Stephanie. "Mining pollution may be hurting Minn's wild rice." November 29, 2010. Minnesota Public Radio News. Available from http://minnesota.publicradio.org/display/web/2010/11/28/wild-rice-standards/

Hemphill, Stephanie. "State, U.S. Steel strike deal to expand production, clean up pollution at Iron Range plants." August 19, 2011. Minnesota Public Radio News. Available from http://minnesota.publicradio.org/display/web/2011/08/19/us-steel-iron-range-plants-pollution-clean-up-expansion/

"Leading by Example: Government Policies." Minneapolis: City of Lakes. Available from http://www.ci.minneapolis.mn.us/sustainability/policies.asp

"Minneapolis Living Well 2010 Sustainability Report." The City of Minneapolis. Available from http://www.ci.minneapolis.mn.us/sustainability/docs/2010MinneapolisLivingWellReport.pdf

"Minneapolis St. Paul: Green Cities Green Jobs." Mayor's Initiative on Green Manufacturing. Available from http://www.ci.stpaul.mn.us/DocumentView.aspx?DID=5757

"Minnesota Climate Change Action Plan: A Framework for Climate Change Action." Minnesota Pollution Control Agency. Available from http://aeromt.org/PDFs/mnclimate-action-plan.pdf

Minnesota Department of Agriculture. Available from http://www.mda.state.mn.us/

Minnesota Department of Natural Resources. Available from http://www.dnr.state.mn.us/index.html

Minnesota Green Communities. Available from http://www.mngreencommunities.org/

"Minnesota State Minerals Information." U.S. Geological Survey, Minerals Information. Available from http://minerals.usgs.gov/minerals/pubs/state/mn.html

"Minnesota, US Steel reach pollution deal." *The Washington Examiner.* August 19, 2011. Available from http://washingtonexaminer.com/news/2011/08/minnesota-us-steel-reach-pollution-deal

"Minnesota Wind Facts." National Wind. Available from http://www.nationalwind.com/minnesota_wind_facts

"MPCA offering $2.5 million in grants for water quality projects." April 19, 2011. *Hometown Source.* Available from http://hometownsource.com/2011/04/11/mpca-offering-2-5-million-in-grants-for-water-quality-projects/

"Notification of SB 2030." Minnesota Sustainable Building 2030. Available from http://www.mn2030.umn.edu/notice.html

Polymet Mining. Available from http://www.polymet-mining.com/index.php

"PolyMet Mining Inc./NorthMet Project." Minnesota Department of Natural Resources. Available from http://www.dnr.state.mn.us/input/environmental-review/polymet/index.html

"PolyMet's NorthMet Proposal." Save Our Sky Blue Waters. Available from http://www.sosbluewaters.org/projects.htm

"PolyMet Updates Status of Environmental Review." April 15, 2011. Mining Minnesota. Available from http://www.miningminnesota.com/news_view.php?id=336

"PolyMet Updates Status of Environmental Review." MineWeb. June 1, 2011. Available from http://www.mineweb.com/mineweb/view/mineweb/en/page674?oid=128420&sn=Detail&pid=102055

"Renewables Portfolio Standard." Minnesota Incentives/Policies for Renewables & Efficiency. Available from http://www.dsireusa.org/incentives/incentive.cfm?Incentive_Code=MN14R&re=1&ee=1

Shapiro, Shari. "A Star is Falling—Builders' Association of the Twin Cities Sues Minnesota Green Star." December 19, 2010. *CleanTechies*. Available from http://blog.cleantechies.com/2010/12/19/a-star-is-falling-builders-association-of-the-twin-cities-sues-minnesota-green-star/

Status of Organic Agriculture in Minnesota. Minnesota Department of Agriculture. Available from http://www.mda.state.mn.us/~/media/Files/news/govrelations/organicstatusreport.ashx

Windustry. Available from http://www.windustry.org/

Mississippi

Mississippi is a relative powerhouse in terms of energy. The three refineries located within the state account for about 2 percent of the total U.S. refining capacity. One of the nation's largest natural gas processing plants is located in Pascagoula and Richton is home to one of the storage sites for the U.S. Strategic Petroleum Reserve. The state, however, has taken steps to encourage the development of green industries as well. The Mississippi Clean Energy Initiative, passed in April 2010, provided significant tax incentives for companies that manufacture systems or components to generate renewable energy. Several such companies have already moved into the state, including those that focus strongly on solar energy and biofuels production. As the state's rebuilding efforts continue following the devastating effects of Hurricane Katrina in 2005, many organizations have chosen to embrace green building practices, constructing both homes and businesses with greater energy efficiency. And while there has been progress on that front, the state faced even more economic and environmental concerns after the 2010 Deepwater Horizon Oil Spill in the Gulf of Mexico and the damage caused by a series of deadly tornadoes and Mississippi River floods in the spring of 2011.

Climate

Mississippi has a humid subtropical climate, characterized by mild winters and long, hot summers. Rainfall averages about 50 to 65 inches (127–165 cm) annually, with a generally even distribution throughout the year. However, the state does experience extreme conditions of drought and severe storms, including tornadoes and hurricanes. In the 2005 hurricane season, Katrina and Rita caused the death of more than one hundred people, along with millions of dollars of damage to homes, businesses, and the coastal environment.

Spring snowmelt and severe storms contributed to major flooding in several states along the Mississippi River and its tributaries beginning in March 2011. The floodwaters destroyed or severely damaged at least eight hundred homes, including nearly all of the three hundred homes of the small riverside town of Tunica Cutoff. Then, in April 2011, a series of at least thirty-four tornadoes swept through the state, with storms that caused additional floods and destruction in thirty-three of the state's eighty-two counties. At least six of the tornadoes were rated at an intensity of EF-3, with winds up to 150 miles per hour. One catastrophic EF-5 storm with winds up to 205 miles per hour passed through the city of Smithville, killing at least fifteen people and injuring forty more. In total, at least 35 deaths and 160 injuries were reported. At least twenty-nine of the affected counties were declared disaster areas by the federal government, with more than $8 million in federal assistance approved for the state in May 2011. At that time, the impact of the floods and storms on the economy, including losses sustained by agriculture, fishing, and other businesses, was still being assessed. Damage to the environment was also being surveyed.

Climate Change

According to a 2009 report from the National Wildlife Federation (NWF), average summer temperatures in Mississippi could increase by 5.8°F (3.2°C) by 2100 if no mitigating measures are taken to curb the production of greenhouse gas emissions. Projections also indicate that the sea level along the Mississippi Gulf Coast could rise by 15 inches (38 cm) by 2100, leading to significant coastal erosion and the loss of important wildlife habitats. The state has not taken any formal legislative actions concerning climate change, but has created financial incentives for companies that reduce their use of fossil fuels through renewable energy sources. The NWF also cites MIT research showing hurricanes and other storms have increased in duration and intensity since the 1970s, and are linked to increases in sea surface temperatures. In 2004 and 2005, hurricanes caused million of dollars in damage to the coastline and turned several counties into disaster areas.

🌼 Natural Resources, Water, and Agriculture

Forests and Parks

About 65 percent of Mississippi is covered in forests, with about 70 percent owned by private non-industrial landowners. More than 53 percent of the forests are hardwood and oak-pine types, while 33 percent are pine. About 13 percent of the land is considered to be regenerating as forest. Nearly all of the forest land is classified as timberland. Some common tree species include white, cherrybark, and live oaks; red, Florida, and swamp red maples; spruce and longleaf pines; magnolia; hickory; and pond and bald cypress. Timber has generally been noted as one of the three most valuable agricultural crops in more than sixty-five of the state's eighty counties. As such, the statewide annual timber production has been valued at more than $1 billion annually. Forestry and related industries together contribute between $11 billion and $14 billion to the state economy each year and account for 8.5 percent of all jobs in the state.

The Mississippi Forestry Association sponsors a popular tree farm program that is affiliated with the American Tree Farm System. To be listed as a certified tree farm, private landowners must develop a management plan based on strict environmental standards and pass annual inspections. Mississippi has more than 3,000 tree farms, more than any other state in the nation.

Throughout the state there are a number of invasive plant species that threaten the habitats of native wildlife and other native plants. Congograss, an invasive grass that is considered to be one of the worst weeds in the world, is found in 62 of the 82 counties in the state. Other threatening plant species include kudzu, Chinese tallow, and alligatorweed.

The state hosts nine national wildlife refuges, six national forests, seven national parks, 24 state parks, and forty-two state wildlife management areas. These areas serve as home to a variety of wildlife species, including swamp rabbit, cottontail, wild turkey, eastern gray squirrel and the eastern fox squirrel, bobcat, mink, muskrat, white-tailed deer, alligator, American black bear and Louisiana black bear, otter, coyote, nutria, and wild hogs. In August 2011, the U.S. Fish and Wildlife Service listed 37 animal and four plant species that occur in the state as threatened or endangered. Endangered animal species include the Mississippi sandhill crane, red-cockaded woodpecker, and five varieties of sea turtle. American chaffseed, Price's potato-bean, Pondberry, and Louisiana quillwort are the state's endangered plant species.

Minerals

The value of nonfuel minerals has fluctuated significantly in the first decade of the twenty-first century, primarily due to fluctuating demands for the state's primary products, construction sand, gravel, and crushed stone. In 2000, the estimated value of nonfuel mineral production was at $157 million. By 2006, that value increased to $270 million, only to decrease in 2007 to $238 million. The state also produces fuller's earth, portland cement, ball clay, and bentonite. Mineral operations provide more than 7,000 direct and indirect jobs.

Water

The largest lakes in the state, all manmade, include the Grenada, Sardis, Enid, and Arkabutla. The Ross Barnett Reservoir, commonly referred to as The Rez, was created along the Pearl River to serve as a major source of drinking water for the state. It is under the management of the Pearl River Valley Water Supply District.

Ports and Commerce

The Mississippi River flows along the western border of the state, providing a vital link between the Gulf of Mexico to inland river states as far away as Minnesota. The Mississippi is the largest commercial river in the country and the third-largest river system in the world. Within the state, there are five river ports along the Mississippi River—Natchez, Vicksburg, Yazoo County, Greenville, and Rosedale. Mississippi's longest inland river is the Pearl. Other major rivers include the Big Black and Yazoo Rivers.

The Tennessee-Tombigbee Waterway (Tenn-Tom), located in the northeast portion of the state, links the Tennessee and Ohio Rivers with the Gulf of Mexico. There are six ports located along the Tenn-Tom.

Mississippi has two deepwater seaports, Gulfport and Pascagoula, both located on the Gulf of Mexico. The Port of Pascagoula is the largest, handling 35 million tons (32 million t) of cargo each year. The Port of Gulfport handles more than 2 million tons (1.8 million t) of cargo per year. The smaller Port Bienville is a shallow draft barge port that primarily serves the Port Bienville Industrial Park, which is part of a designated foreign trade zone.

Fishing

Commercial and farm fishing are major contributors to the local economy. In 2007, marine shrimping provided a total economic impact of more than $114 million. Blue crab and oysters are also important to the annual commercial catch.

Mississippi is the national leader in catfish farming, which had a value of $218 million in 2010. There are smaller operations for the production of hybrid striped bass and alligator produced for meat and leather. The state operates 19 freshwater fishing lakes.

In recent years, there has been an increasing concern over the presence of various invasive fish species that threaten both the environment and the economy of the state. Species that find their way into the Mississippi River

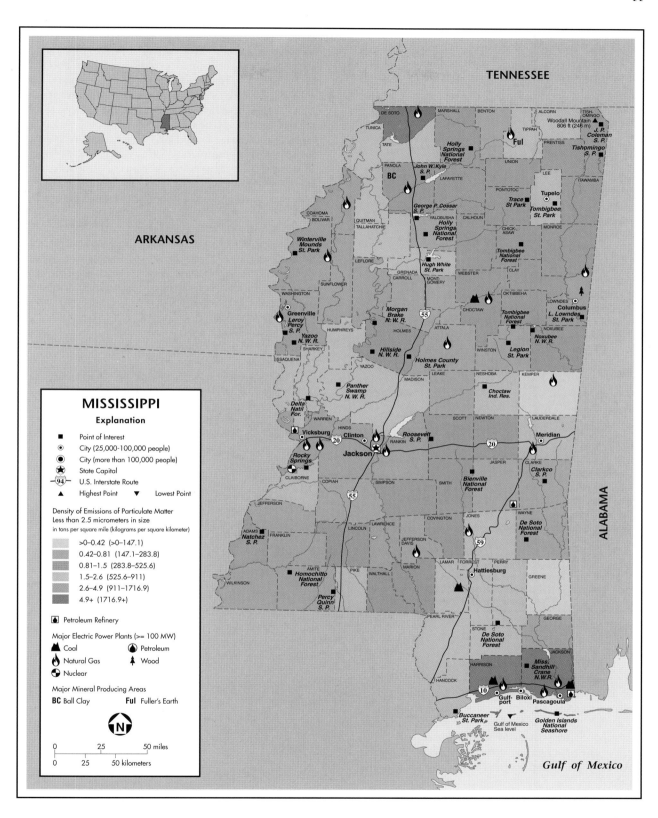

SOURCES: "County Emissions Map: Criteria Air Pollutants." *AirData*. U.S. Environmental Protection Agency. Available from http://www. epa.gov/air/data/geosel.html; *Energy Maps*. U.S. Energy Information Administration. Available from http://www.eia.gov/state; *Highest and Lowest Elevations*. U.S. Geological Survey. Available from http://egsc.usgs.gov/isb/pubs/booklets/elvadist/elvadist.html#Highest; *2007 Minerals Yearbook*. U.S. Geological Survey. Available from http://minerals.usgs.gov/minerals/pubs/state.   © 2011 Cengage Learning.

Mississippi State Profile

Physical Characteristics

Land area	46,920 square miles (121,522 sq km)
Inland water area	772 square miles (1,999 sq km)
Coastal area	591 square miles (951 sq km)
Highest point	Woodall Mountain 806 feet (246 m)
National Forest System lands (2010)	1.2 million acres (475,000 ha)
State parks (2011)	24

Energy Statistics

Total energy production (2009)	420 trillion Btu
State ranking in total energy production (2009)	32
Renewable energy net generation total (2009)	1.4 million megawatt hours
Hydroelectric energy generation (2009)	NA
Biomass energy generation (2009)	7,000 megawatt hours
Wind energy generation (2009)	NA
Wood and derived fuel energy generation (2009)	1.4 million megawatt hours
Crude oil reserves (2009)	244 million barrels (38.8 million cu m)
Natural gas reserves (2009)	917 billion cubic feet (26.0 billion cu m)
Natural gas liquids (2008)	4 million barrels (0.6 million cu m)

Pollution Statistics

Carbon output (2005)	62.1 million tons of CO_2 (56.4 million t)
Superfund sites (2008)	4
Particulate matter (less than 2.5 micrometers) emissions (2002)	12,683 tons per year (11,505 t/yr)
Toxic chemical releases (2009)	54.3 million pounds (24.6 million kg)
Generated hazardous waste (2009)	1.7 million tons (1.5 million t)

SOURCES: AirData. U.S. Environmental Protection Agency. Available from http://www.epa.gov/air/data; *Energy Maps, Facts, and Data of the U.S. States.* U.S. Energy Information Administration. Available from http://www.eia.gov/state; *The 2012 Statistical Abstract.* U.S. Census Bureau. Available from http://www.census.gov/compendia/statab; *United States Energy Usage.* eRedux. Available from http://www.eredux.net/states.

© 2011 Cengage Learning.

pose a threat to the environments of many Midwestern water sources as well, and some, such as the Asian carp, have made their way north to the Great Lakes region. In November 2009, the Mississippi Department of Environmental Quality presented the final draft of the Mississippi State Management Plan for Aquatic Invasive Species. The plan lists the invasive species of concern and provides specific actions and regulations as potential solutions to the spread or increase of these species. Species of concern include tilapia, zebra mussel, Asian carp (including silver, bighead, and common species), and the Australian red claw crawfish. Invasive aquatic plants include alligatorweed, Brazilian waterweed, and water hyacinth.

Agriculture

Agriculture accounts for much of the employment opportunity in Mississippi, providing jobs for about 29 percent of the workforce on more than 11.5 million acres (4.7 million ha) of farmland. However, manufacturing has taken over as the state's largest industry, a spot previously held by agriculture. The total market value of all agriculture products in the state totaled $4.9 billion. Poultry and eggs are the primary commodities, with a value of $2.4 billion in 2009. Soybeans, corn, cotton and rice are the next most important commodities. The state ranks among the top five in the nation for production of cotton and cottonseed. Wheat, sweet potatoes, and peanuts are also produced.

The state has been fairly successful in attracting companies focused on biofuel production. With soybeans and corn as major commodities for the state, there is a hope that the development of biofuels markets and production facilities will bring an even greater boost for the agricultural section suppliers. In August 2010, KiOR, a biofuels company based in Texas, committed to locating five biofuel production facilities in Mississippi, investing more than $500 million into the operations and creating at least 1,000 new jobs.

The Mississippi Department of Agriculture and Commerce (MDAC) Organic Certification Program began in 2005. In 2008, there were only 23 certified organic operators in the state.

Energy

Oil

Oil wells in the southern portion of the state produce a minimal amount of crude oil. However, Mississippi is a relative powerhouse in oil refining. The three refineries located within the state account for about 2 percent of the total U.S. refining capacity. The Pascagoula refinery along the Gulf Coast is the largest of the three. It processes oil imported from Central and South America to supply markets throughout the South and Southeast United States. New oil and gas field deposits have been discovered in the Black Warrior Basin in the north part of the state, as well as offshore along the Gulf Coast. According to the U.S. Energy Information Administration, geologists believe further exploration of these areas could result in new oil and gas reserves.

Mississippi is one of a small number of states that allow the statewide use of conventional motor gasoline, rather than a reformulated blend. About 21 percent of all Mississippi households use liquefied petroleum gasses for home heating. There is a major propane hub located in Hattiesburg.

Strategic Petroleum Reserve

Richton is home to one of the storage sites for the U.S. Strategic Petroleum Reserve. The Strategic Petroleum

Reserve was developed as a result of the 1975 Energy Policy and Conservation Act, which, among other things, sought to create a safe reserve of oil for use in an energy emergency. The total reserve, with a capacity of 727 million barrels, is stored in more than 500 salt domes along the Gulf of Mexico. It represents the largest emergency oil reserve in the world, and the site was chosen in part because its inland location shelters it from the threat of hurricanes. The Richton salt domes have a capacity of 160 million barrels.

Natural Gas from the U.S. and Africa

As with oil, Mississippi produces very little natural gas of its own, but has developed a strong processing sector. Pascagoula is home to one of the largest natural gas processing plants in the nation, with supplies provided from the federally administered Outer Continental Shelf of the Gulf of Mexico. The state also purchases natural gas from neighboring states to supply local demand. About 37 percent of households use natural gas as a primary source for home heating. A liquefied natural gas import terminal at the Port of Pascagoula will serve as a receiving station for international imports. The $1.1 billion project is one of two liquefied natural gas terminals proposed in Pascagoula. It was being developed by Gulf LNG Energy and was expected to be operational by the end of 2011. Gulf LNG Energy represents the partnership of the Crest Group, El Paso Corp., and Sonangol (the state-owned energy company in Angola).

Electricity

Nearly 48 percent of the state's electric supply is generated from natural-gas fired plants. Another 26.6 percent comes from coal-fired plants, with coal imported from Colorado, Kentucky, and Illinois. There is one coal mine in Choctaw County that produces lignite coal for the onsite 440-megawatt power plant that uses clean coal technology. About 22 percent of the electric supply is generated from the Grand Gulf Nuclear Power Station. To meet total demand, Mississippi imports electricity from neighboring states. About 40 percent of households use electricity as a source for home heating. The larger household demand for electricity stems from the extensive use of air conditioning systems during the hot summer months.

Renewables

Approximately 2.9 percent of the state's electricity supply is generated from wood and wood derived fuels. While the use of renewable energy sources is currently quite low, a 2010 report from the nonprofit, statewide coalition Advance Mississippi indicates that there is strong potential for the development of biomass energy sources and some potential for the development of hydropower and geothermal energy. In the same assessment, the potential for solar and wind energy was considered to be very low.

The state does not have an official renewable portfolio standard. The state energy program administered through the Mississippi Development Authority (MDA) focuses primarily on encouragement for energy efficiency programs. The MDA has also supported programs that promote the use of alternative fuels throughout the state.

❧ Green Business, Green Building, Green Jobs

Green Business: Announcing the Mississippi Clean Energy Initiative

While the green economy of Mississippi is relatively small, there is a solid potential for growth that is just being explored and promoted by state officials. The primary growth area is expected to be in biofuels and renewable energy technologies.

In support of the renewable energy technology sector, the state legislature passed the Mississippi Clean Energy Initiative (HB 1701) in April 2010. This initiative provides significant tax incentives for companies that manufacture systems or components that can be used to generate renewable energy, such as solar, wind, biomass, and hydropower. To qualify, a business must make a minimum investment of $50 million and create 250 full-time jobs. Those who do are given a ten-year exemption on state income and franchise taxes and a sales and use tax exemption. One company that may qualify for this new incentive is Twin Creek Technologies, which announced in April 2010 that it would build a state-of-the-art solar panel manufacturing plant in northwest Mississippi.

A Boom in Biofuels

The state has been fairly successful in attracting companies focused on biofuel production. As of 2011, the Canada-based Enerkem Corporation was building a waste-to-biofuels plant in Pontotoc at the Three Rivers Landfill Site. The plant was expected to be operational by the end of 2012 with a capacity to produce 10 million gallons (38 million l) of ethanol per year. As of July 2010, BlueFire Ethanol Fuels Inc. was in the second phase of financing for the construction of a cellulosic biofuels plant in Fulton. In August 2010, the state provided a $75 million loan package for KiOR, Inc., which was expected to build five renewable crude oil production facilities throughout the state. The first three were expected to be completed by 2015.

Green Jobs

These efforts in boosting the clean energy industry were expected to result in a good number of new jobs. The opening of the Twin Creek Technologies solar panel manufacturing plant was expected to create 500 new jobs. Likewise, the first three KiOR renewable crude oil production facility projects were expected to create more than 1,000 direct and indirect jobs from 2010 through 2015. In support of these job creating industries, the Mississippi Development Authority developed the Mississippi Job Protection through Energy Economic Development Program. Through this program, eligible businesses may receive funding for energy efficient retrofits and upgrades to help them cut costs, reduce energy consumption, and create or retain jobs. In 2009, the authority allocated $10 million of funding from the American Recovery and Reinvestment Act (ARRA) toward this job protection program.

Green Building

While Mississippi has not imposed legislation that requires green building practices, the state encourages and promotes energy efficiency standards and building practices as part of the state energy program. Under the Mississippi Energy Management Law (SB 3113), all state-owned or state-leased buildings and facilities must implement a state energy management program, which is monitored through the Energy Division of the Mississippi Development Authority. The program calls for the use of energy efficient practices, noted through monitoring of energy consumption. Recent support for these efficiency efforts has come in the form of significant funding from U.S. Department of Energy as part of the American Recovery and Reinvestment Act (ARRA) program. In 2009, the Mississippi Development Authority was allocated $40.4 million in support of the state energy program. Approximately $14.6 million has been allocated for programs that will reduce energy consumption in public buildings. An additional $9.6 million will be awarded to public and private entities that are investing in renewable energy systems.

Mississippi's power companies offer a number of rebates and incentives for homes that wish to become more energy efficient. An incentive program from the Tennessee Valley Authority, the Generation Partners Program, offers a production-based incentive to Valley homeowners and businesses for the installation of renewable generation systems from solar, wind, low-impact hydropower, and biomass. Mississippi Power offers rebates to its customers to help offset the cost of converting from gas equipment to energy efficient electric equipment. Rebates are available for heat pumps, HVAC systems, geothermal heat pumps, and water heaters.

Green Re-Building After the Storm

Green building practices have taken root in Mississippi, in part as a result of the 2005 tragedy of Hurricane Katrina. Thousands of homes and buildings were destroyed by the devastating storm, and in the aftermath, many chose to rebuild with green practices in mind. In August 2010, the Grand Bay Coastal Resource Center of the National Estuarine Research Reserve became the first state-owned project in Mississippi to gain certification under the U.S. Green Building Council Leadership and Energy and Environmental Design (LEED) program. The $7 million facility, built to gold-level certification standards, includes offices, laboratories, classrooms, an interpretative center, and living quarters for visiting scientists.

The state's first LEED Platinum home was also completed in 2010 through the efforts of Habitat for Humanity Bay-Waveland Area. This Bay St. Louis-based local chapter was organized a few months after the storm, with the intention to serve those left homeless in an area where 53 percent of the housing stock had been severely damaged or destroyed. Since 2008, all of the group's construction staff have been trained as certified green professionals by the National Association of Home Builders (NAHB). As of 2009, the chapter has made a commitment that all new homes will meet or exceed the silver standards for green building as set by the NAHB.

⚘ The Impact of the Oil Spill

From April 20 through July 15, 2010, nearly 4.9 million barrels of oil—205 million gallons—were released into the Gulf of Mexico as a result of the explosion on the Deepwater Horizon oil-drilling rig, located about 50 miles (80 km) from the coast of Louisiana. While the full impact of the disaster might not be assessed for many years, preliminary reports show that the economy of South Mississippi took a significant hit as a result of what has already been noted as the worst oil spill in U.S. history.

Initial Findings

In June and July 2010, David L. Butler and Edward Sayre, researchers at the University of Southern Mississippi, published a series of three white papers noting their initial findings concerning the economic impact of the Deepwater Horizon oil spill on South Mississippi. Their research was conducted primarily through interviews with business owners and employees as they determined the estimated impact on revenue, employment, and tax revenues. The primary losses were noted in the tourism and related service sectors. During the time of the spill, many Gulf Coast beaches were affected by temporary closures and/or swimming advisories as oil and tar balls eventually washed onto the shores. This led to a decline in tourism at what is generally considered to be a peak season for the Mississippi coast.

According to the Butler-Sayre reports, the coastal counties of Hancock, Harrison, and Jackson experienced an estimated loss in revenues of $119.4 million from May–August 2010, representing a decline of 5 percent from the same period in 2009. Non-casino hotels showed a particularly high percentage of loss for May

Workers clean up tar balls and residue left on an oil-stained Mississippi beach by the ongoing Deepwater Horizon oil blowout, July 14, 2010. © *A.J. SISCO/UPI/newscom*

2010, with revenues down by about 50 percent from that of May 2009. The loss in tax revenues for the same sectors was estimated at $11 million for the same three coastal counties, representing a decline of 6.6 percent from 2009 figures. While there was an increase in unemployment claims in these counties, it was not clear how many job losses were directly related to the events of the spill. Reports indicated that some of those who lost jobs during the spill found new temporary employment with BP or other clean-up contractors, while others filed loss claims with BP directly rather than file for unemployment.

The Butler-Sayre findings did not include potential losses in the commercial fishing industry, noting that such figures might be more difficult to ascertain. There seems to be some hope, however, that the industry outlook will not be quite as bleak as expected. Federal waters adjacent to Mississippi waters were closed to commercial and recreational fishing due the presence of oil and concerns over how the mixture of oil and chemical dispersants used to reduce the effects of the spill would affect the seafood catch. These waters were reopened on September 2, 2010, in light of the fact that no oil had been documented in the area since July 12. Most areas of the Mississippi territorial waters were temporarily closed to commercial and recreational fishing by July 1; however,

they were all reopened by August 25. According to a September 2010 report from the Mississippi Department of Marine Resources, biweekly sampling of fish, shrimp, crabs, and oysters conducted from May 23 through September 12 showed that the levels of possible contaminants were well below the levels of concern, indicating that the seafood is safe for consumption. Biweekly sampling ended in October 2010, in favor of monthly sampling. For April 2011, the levels of possible contaminants were again well below the levels of concern. While the overall catch for the 2010 season may have declined, some seafood prices increased, thus providing a bit of an offset for fishermen.

As of April 2011, the Mississippi Department of Environmental Quality reported that there were still approximately 280 people working on efforts involved in clean up and monitoring of the shorelines following the Deepwater Horizon oil spill. About 152 vessels were continuing to conduct sampling operations and more than 4,057 tons of recyclable waste, including oily liquids and solid waste, had been processed.

Controversy for the Governor

In the early stages of the disaster, Governor Haley Barbour was criticized by the media and some local officials for his lack of significant response to the disaster.

An oil boom as it protects an inlet in Pass Christian, Mississippi from the BP Deepwater Horizon platform disaster. The economy of south Mississippi took a significant hit as a result of the disaster. © STAN HONDA/AFP/Getty Images/newscom

The governor's early comments to the media indicated his belief that the oil spill was not nearly as severe as initial reports indicated and that overreaction and exaggeration from the media were causing the most harm to the state, by making would-be tourists nervous about their plans for a Mississippi Gulf Coast holiday. Barbour's public comments softened a bit as the first signs of oil were reported on Mississippi shores in mid-June 2010. But criticism continued, with new complaints that Barbour's lack of concern was evident as he seemed to maintain his business-as-usual travel schedule, which took him out of state for all or part of 28 days during the 85-day spill.

Governor Barbour declared a state of emergency on April 30, 2010, in which he noted the potential threat that the spill posed to the state's land, water, and wildlife. At the same time, he issued an executive order giving authority to the adjutant general of the Mississippi National Guard to take whatever actions were deemed necessary and requisite for the assistance of state and local authorities. On May 13, 2010, the governor announced his request to the U.S. Small Business Administration for funds to assist those businesses affected by the spill.

In May 2010, President Barack Obama established the National Commission on the BP Deepwater Horizon Oil Spill and Offshore Drilling. The commission was tasked with examining the cause of the spill and developing options to guard against and mitigate the impact of oil spills associated with offshore drilling in the future. The commission presented its findings to the president in January 2011. The report included recommendations, such as establishing an independent agency for regulating offshore drilling, new safety regulations to update and enhance current drilling operations, greater cooperation among federal agencies with a stake in offshore drilling and greater scientific and technical research in all areas related to offshore drilling.

BIBLIOGRAPHY

Books

Canney, Donald L. *In Katrina's Wake: The U.S. Coast Guard and the Gulf Coast Hurricanes of 2005.* Gainesville: University Press of Florida, 2010.

Emison, Gerald, and John C. Morris, eds. *Speaking Green with A Southern Accent: Environmental Management and Innovation in the South.* Lanham, MD: Lexington Books, 2010.

Melosi, Artin, ed. *Environment*, vol. 8 of *The New Encyclopedia of Southern Culture.* Chapel Hill: University of North Carolina Press, 2007.

White, Mel, Tria Giovan, and Jim Bones. *The Smithsonian Guides to Natural America: The South Central States– Texas, Oklahoma, Arkansas, Louisiana, Mississippi.* Washington, DC: Smithsonian Books, 1996.

Web Sites

"Aquaculture in Mississippi." Mississippi State University Extension Service. Available from http://msucares.com/aquaculture/index.html

Associated Press. "Mississippi governor's frequent travels produce friction back home." Nola.com. October 9, 2010. Available from http://www.nola.com/politics/index.ssf/2010/10/mississippi_governors_frequent.html

Butler, David L., and Edward Sayre. *Economic Impact of the Deepwater Horizon Oil Spill on South Mississippi: Initial Findings on Employment.* The University of Southern Mississippi. Available from http://www.usm.edu/oilspill/files/white-papers/White_Paper_Employment_FINAL.pdf

Butler, David L., and Edward Sayre. *Economic Impact of the Deepwater Horizon Oil Spill on South Mississippi: Initial Findings on Revenue.* The University of Southern Mississippi. Available from http://www.usm.edu/oilspill/files/white-papers/Oil-Spill-Economic-Impact-Butler-Sayre.pdf

Butler, David L., and Edward Sayre. *Economic Impact of the Deepwater Horizon Oil Spill on South Mississippi: Initial Findings on Tax Revenue.* The University of Southern Mississippi. Available from http://www.usm.edu/oilspill/files/white-papers/WhitePaper-ButerSayreTax.pdf

Enerkem: Pontotoc, Mississippi. Available from http://www.enerkem.com/en/our-locations/plants/pontotoc-mississippi.html

Executive Order 1308 (State of Emergency and National Guard Authority in response to the Gulf Oil Spill). Mississippi Office of the Governor. Available from http://www.governorbarbour.com/news/2010/apr/Orders%20for%20Coast.pdf

"Fulton Project Advances to Phase 2 of Loan Guarantee Process." BlueFire Ethanol Fuels, Inc. Available from http://bluefireethanol.com/pr/78

"Global Warming and Mississippi." National Wildlife Federation. Available from http://www.nwf.org/Global-Warming/~/media/PDFs/Global%20Warming/Global%20Warming%20State%20Fact%20Sheets/Mississippi.ashx

"Governor Barbour Welcomes Biofuel Producer To Mississippi. " Mississippi Development Authority. August 26, 2010. Available from http://www.mississippi.org/index.php?id=866

"Grand Bay Dedicates New 'Green' Building." National Estuarine Research Reserve System. Available from http://www.nerrs.noaa.gov/News.aspx?id=328

"Gulf Islands National Seashore." National Parks Service. Available from http://www.nps.gov/guis

Gulf LNG. Available from http://www.elpaso.com/gulflng/default.shtm

Habitat for Humanity Bay-Waveland Area. Available from http://www.habitatbaywaveland.org/index.html

"Invasive Species." Mississippi State Conservation Center. Available from http://www.stateconservation.org/miss/?q=4

"Invasive Species: State Resources—Mississippi." National Agricultural Library. U.S. Department of Agriculture. Available from http://www.invasivespeciesinfo.gov/unitedstates/ms.shtml#thr

Kelly, Johnny. "Over 30 tornadoes tore across Mississippi during historic tornado outbreak." *The Examiner.* May 1, 2011. Available from http://www.examiner.com/weather-in-jackson/over-30-tornadoes-tore-across-mississippi-during-historic-tornado-outbreak

Lach, Eric. "How Long Can Mississippi's Governor Keep Downplaying the Oil Spill?" TPM LiveWire. June 4, 2010. Available from http://tpmlivewire.talkingpointsmemo.com/2010/06/mississippi-gov-keeps-downplaying-oil-spill.php

"Listings and occurrences for Mississippi." Species Reports. U.S. Fish and Wildlife Service. Available from http://ecos.fws.gov/tess_public/pub/stateListingAndOccurrenceIndividual.jsp?state=MS&s8-fid=112761032792&s8fid=112762573902&s8-fid=24012986458132

Making the Grade: An Assessment of Renewable Energy Sources for Mississippi. Advance Mississippi. Available from http://www.advancemississippi.com/documents/msrenewablesib.pdf

Mississippi Clean Energy Initiative (HB 1701). Mississippi Legislature. Available from http://billstatus.ls.state.ms.us/documents/2010/pdf/HB/1700-1799/HB1701SG.pdf

Mississippi Department of Agriculture and Commerce. Available from http://www.mdac.state.ms.us/index.asp

Mississippi Department of Wildlife, Fisheries, & Parks. Available from http://home.mdwfp.com

Mississippi Emergency Management Agency. Available from http://www.msema.org/gulfrecovery

"Mississippi Energy Facts." Institute of Energy Research. Available from http://www.instituteforenergyresearch.org/state-regs/pdf/Mississippi.pdf

Mississippi Energy Management Law (SB 3113). Mississippi Legislature. Available from http://www.mississippi.org/assets/docs/energy/sbill3113.pdf

"Mississippi Establishes Model for Other States in Pursuit of Clean Energy Future." 15 by 25 Resource. Available from http://blog.25x25.org/?p=1841

Mississippi Forestry Association. Available from http://msforestry.net

Mississippi Seafood Safety—September 2010. Mississippi Department of Marine Resources. Available from http://www.dmr.state.ms.us/Publications/201009-ms-seafood-safety-newsletter.pdf

Mississippi's Assessment of Forest Assessment and Forest Resource Strategy. Mississippi Forestry Association. Available from http://www.mfc.ms.gov/pdf/Forest_Assessment/MS_Assessment_Resource_Strategy_2010.pdf

"Mississippi State Energy Management Program." Mississippi Development Authority. Available from http://www.mississippi.org/index.php?id=17

"Mississippi State Energy Program." Mississippi Development Authority. Available from http://www.mississippi.org/index.php?id=659

Mississippi State Management Plan for Aquatic Invasive Species. Mississippi Department of Environmental Quality. Available from http://www.deq.state.ms.us/MDEQ.nsf/pdf/Main_MSMPAIS/$File/MAISManPlanNov2009.pdf?OpenElement

Mississippi State Port Authority at Gulfport. Available from http://www.shipmspa.com

Mississippi: 2007 Minerals Yearbook. United States Geological Survey. Available from http://minerals.usgs.gov/minerals/pubs/state/2007/myb2-2007-ms.pdf

Office of the Mississippi State Climatologist. Available from http://geosciences.msstate.edu/stateclimatologist.htm

"Oil Spill Commission Landmark Report On Gulf Disaster Proposes Urgent Reform Of Industry And Government Practices To Overhaul U.S. Offshore Drilling Safety. " National Commission On The BP Deepwater Horizon Oil Spill and Offshore Drilling. January 11, 2011. Available at http://www.oilspill-commission.gov/final-report

Port of Pascagoula. Available from http://www.portof-pascagoula.com/port-facts.html

"Residential Rebates." Mississippi Power. Available from http://www.mississippipower.com/earthcents/ec_rebate.asp

Ross Barnett Reservoir. Available from http://www.therez.ms/about.html

"State Energy Profiles: Mississippi." U.S. Energy Information Administration. Available from http://tonto.eia.doe.gov/state/state_energy_profiles.cfm?sid=MS

"State of Mississippi Pledges Financial Support for Five KiOR Biofuel Facilities." Business Wire. August 30, 2010. Available from http://www.businesswire.com/news/home/20100830005782/en

"Strategic Petroleum Reserve." U.S. Department of Energy. Available from http://fossil.energy.gov/programs/reserves/spr

The Tennessee-Tombigbee Waterway. Available from http://www.tenntom.org/about/ttwkeycomponents.htm

"Transocean Drilling Incident Response 2010." Mississippi Department of Environmental Quality. Available from http://www.deq.state.ms.us/MDEQ.nsf/page/Main_OilSpillLinksandPublicInformation2010?OpenDocument

"TVA: Green Power Switch Generation Partners." Tennessee Valley Authority. Available from http://www.tva.com/greenpowerswitch/partners/

U.S. Energy Information Administration. U.S. States Analysis: Mississippi. Available at http://www.eia.gov/state/state-energy-profiles-analysis.cfm?sid=MS

Missouri

The state of Missouri's size, topography, and geographic location make it a rich source of farmlands and natural resources. With a total land area of 68,886 square miles (178,568 sq km), Missouri ranks eighteenth in size among the fifty U.S. states. Researchers, environmentalists and corporations are continuously exploring the vast possibilities the state holds, including options like wind power in the northwest quadrant, ethanol and other biomass plants in the north, and hydroelectric power. The state's jewel of a park system, combined with a multitude of lakes and rivers, provide tourism and recreation opportunities as well. The two largest rivers in North America, the Missouri and the Mississippi, converge in the state. More than 6,300 caves have been discovered in Missouri, many with navigable water running through them. However, wildlife that thrives in the forests, rivers, and caverns are threatened by climate change, invasive species, and other factors. There are multiple agencies within the state that are tracking greenhouse gas emissions and recommending changes to stem future detrimental consequences.

Topographically, Missouri can be divided into four regions. The Dissected Till Plains, which lie north of the Missouri River and form part of the U.S. Central Plains, are comprised of fertile flatlands, prairies, and rolling hills. This region is the breadbasket of the state and boasts extraordinarily rich soils. The western region of the state, known as the Osage Plains, represents an unglaciated prairie ecoregion, occasionally interrupted by gentle, rounded hills. The Ozark Highlands, the largest region of the state, is an ancient, uplifted plateau filled with caves, which spans across the southern portion of Missouri. This region contains the highest point in the state, Taum Sauk Mountain, which rises 1,772 feet (540 m). Finally, the southeast corner of the state, known as the Mississippi Alluvial Plain, is a region of swamps and bottomland forest.

Climate: Strong Seasonality, Rising Temperatures

Missouri has a continental climate defined by strong seasonality. Regional climate variation does exist, but not along any concrete geographic boundaries. From summer to winter, strong variations occur in both temperature and precipitation, with winters generally maintaining a cold and dry character, and summers a hot and moist one. Spring and fall in Missouri are the most volatile seasons, and significant climatic variations can occur abruptly within these seasons, due to successive, fast moving fronts.

Scientists estimate that temperatures in Missouri will rise up to nearly 7°F (3.9°) over the next 100 years due to climate change. Most scientists believe that this temperature rise will be accompanied by greater precipitation—as much as a 20 percent increase. According to the United States Global Change Research Program, the precipitation increase in Missouri and across the Midwest will likely cause a rise in extreme flood and drought conditions. In periods of flooding, the risk of waterborne diseases will increase. Missouri could see increases in its growing season and greater crop yields due to rising temperatures. However, environmentalists temper these predictions by warning that greater flooding, drought, and invasive species could challenge the gains farmers attain from the expanded growing season.

According to the National Wildlife Federation, climate change could also lead to warmer water temperatures, which would reduce fish habitat in the state. This would harm populations of recreational fish such as smallmouth bass and wild Ozark rainbow trout. Climate change will likely impact the state's overall tourism revenue as well. Nearly 4 million people spent upwards of $3 billion on hunting, fishing, and wildlife viewing in Missouri each year. The state could also see an increase in the lifespan of mosquitoes carrying diseases, such as St. Louis encephalitis. Another detrimental effect of climate change could be the reduction of up to 91 percent of the wetlands in the Prairie Pothole Region. This area is one of the most important waterfowl breeding grounds in North America. The reduction of these wetlands could lead to a significant decline in the number of waterfowl, such as ducks, breeding in the region, reducing the population of important species such as mallards, gadwall, blue-winged teal, and northern pintails.

Climate Action Options

To address the issue of climate change, the Missouri Energy Center, a part of the Missouri Department of Natural Resources, first completed a baseline greenhouse gas (GHG) emissions inventory for 1990, then followed up with *Greenhouse Gas Emission Trends and Projections for Missouri, 1990–2015*. This latter report indicates that GHG emissions increased by 13 percent from 1990 to 1996, with carbon dioxide emissions from fossil fuel combustion for energy use providing the greatest portion of the increase. Though carbon dioxide emissions from fossil fuel combustion are projected to increase even more by 2015, the report projects a decrease in perflourinated carbon (PFC) emissions associated with aluminum manufacturing. The report suggests that as increases from some sources are offset by decreases in others, the total GHG emissions for 2015 will be only slightly higher than they were in 1990.

After analysis and discussion of this data, the Missouri Energy Center published *Missouri Actions Options to Reduce Greenhouse Gas Emissions* in July 2002. This report provides a number of action options to reduce statewide GHG emissions from electricity generation, residential and commercial buildings, transportation, agriculture, forestry, and solid waste management operations. Many of these options involve the development of programs, policies, and incentives that focus on energy efficiency and energy-use reduction across all sectors of the statewide community. Since the report was published, the state has implemented several programs related to the recommended options.

❦ Natural Resources, Water, and Agriculture

With rich soils across the state, a network of stunning caves in the south, and portions of the two largest rivers in North America, Missouri boasts a collection of unique and precious natural resources.

Reintroducing Fire to Help Forests Flourish

Forests cover about 35 percent of Missouri—about half of their historic range. The oak-hickory forest type is the most common in the state, with white, black, scarlet, and northern red oak the most common of the oaks. Oak-pine forest is found primarily in the southern and southeastern Ozarks, with shortleaf pine accounting for between 25 and 50 percent of the stands. However, changing climates could alter the look of the state's forests, as an increasing number of southern pines replace the oak and hickory present in southern Missouri and the Ozarks. Mixed hardwoods can be found in the southeast. Missouri forests produce wood for a number of commercial products, including pallets, flooring lumber, oak and walnut veneer fence posts and furniture. Missouri is a leading producer of wooden barrels, charcoal, and red cedar gift items. Christmas trees are also produced. Wood industries contribute about $3 billion to the state's economy each year.

Missouri's forestlands represent one of the most vulnerable natural resources in the state. Despite adding roughly one million new trees each decade, the health of Missouri forests is in jeopardy. The threats Missouri woodlands face are varied but one of the most pronounced stems from a lack of ground fires, the natural cycle of destruction and regeneration. According to the United States Department of Agriculture and other organizations, fire suppression represents one of the great ecological challenges for the state. Without ground fires, the composition of the state's woodlands become fundamentally skewed because the forests become overstocked. Closed canopies stifle the growth of the ground flora essential to a healthy forest, and biodiversity declines. For more than 8,000 years, Native Americans living in the Missouri region recognized the importance of ground fires for forest regeneration and would engage in prescribed burns. However, as European settlers developed the region, wildfire became a tremendous fear—as it would occasionally destroy settlements—and the new settlers worked to suppress all forms of fire. As education expanded in more recent times, the Missouri Department of Conservation began reintroducing prescribed fire as a way to increase the health of the state's woodlands.

Remediation efforts have also helped the Department of Conservation address other issues that threaten Missouri's forests, such as invasive species, feral hogs, unauthorized logging, and soil erosion. Important future issues for Missouri's forestry include climate change, ecosystem management and forest stress from timber production.

Wondrous Wildlife

Missouri state park system includes eighty-five parks and historic sites with more than 200,000 acres (80,937 ha) available to the public. The state is also home to six national historic trails, including the popular Lewis & Clark Trail and the Pony Express Trail. The system also has the longest developed Rails To Trails project in the United States at 225 miles (362 km) long. In terms of wildlife, Missouri boasts more than 3,000 types of plants and more than 20,000 species of mammals, fish, insects, and other creatures, including the common cottontail, the muskrat, the gray and red foxes, and the bluebird, the state bird. As of August 2011, the U.S. Fish and Wildlife Service noted thirty-one plant and animal species found in

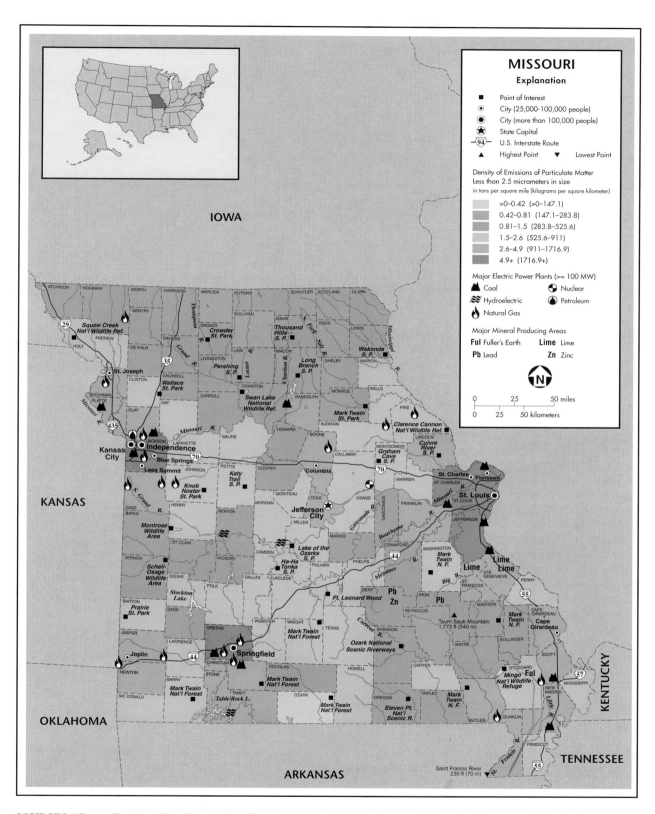

MISSOURI
Explanation

■ Point of Interest
⊙ City (25,000–100,000 people)
◉ City (more than 100,000 people)
★ State Capital
94 U.S. Interstate Route
▲ Highest Point ▼ Lowest Point

Density of Emissions of Particulate Matter
Less than 2.5 micrometers in size
in tons per square mile (kilograms per square kilometer)

>0–0.42 (>0–147.1)
0.42–0.81 (147.1–283.8)
0.81–1.5 (283.8–525.6)
1.5–2.6 (525.6–911)
2.6–4.9 (911–1716.9)
4.9+ (1716.9+)

Major Electric Power Plants (>= 100 MW)
▲ Coal ☢ Nuclear
≋ Hydroelectric ◗ Petroleum
🔥 Natural Gas

Major Mineral Producing Areas
Ful Fuller's Earth **Lime** Lime
Pb Lead **Zn** Zinc

Ⓝ

0   25   50 miles
0   25   50 kilometers

IOWA
KANSAS
OKLAHOMA
ARKANSAS
TENNESSEE
KENTUCKY

SOURCES: "County Emissions Map: Criteria Air Pollutants." *AirData*. U.S. Environmental Protection Agency. Available from http://www. epa.gov/air/data/geosel.html; *Energy Maps*. U.S. Energy Information Administration. Available from http://www.eia.gov/state; *Highest and Lowest Elevations*. U.S. Geological Survey. Available from http://egsc.usgs.gov/isb/pubs/booklets/elvadist/elvadist.html#Highest; *2007 Minerals Yearbook*. U.S. Geological Survey. Available from http://minerals.usgs.gov/minerals/pubs/state. © 2011 Cengage Learning.

Missouri that are listed as federally threatened or endangered. These include the American burying beetle, the running buffalo clover, the Ozark cavefish, the Ozark big-eared bat, and the pallid sturgeon.

Minerals: A Leader in Lead

According to the United States Geological Survey, Missouri ranked in the top ten states in terms of the total value of nonfuel mineral production in 2008. That year, the state ranked as first in the nation for the production of lead, lime, and fireclay. Missouri regularly produces more than one-half the nation's lead output, the most of any U.S. state.

Missouri's success as a leading producer of lead has not come without its drawbacks. In October of 2010, it was announced that Doe Run Resources Corp. of St. Louis agreed to spend $65 million to correct violations of environmental laws at ten of its lead mining, milling, and smelting facilities. For years the residents of Herculaneum and other southeastern Missouri communities have been exposed to high levels of lead, putting children at great risk. The company ultimately decided to shut down its lead smelter in the town of Herculaneum by December 31, 2013, and will provide an initial $8.14 million to guarantee cleanup work at the facility. The closing of the smelter will lead to significant improvements in the environment by reducing greenhouse gas emissions and pollutants in an area that is currently violating federal air standards for lead, ozone, and particulate matter. The settlement also requires Doe Run to set up trust funds for the cleanup of other active or former mining facilities, and to take steps to come into compliance with more strict Clean Water Act permits at ten of its facilities. In addition, the EPA is issuing a new administrative order requiring Doe Run to sample residential properties near the Herculaneum smelter for high lead soil concentrations, and to clean up properties with concentrations of 400 parts per million or higher. Doe Run will also improve its transportation methods for lead-bearing materials, and take part in community mitigation projects over the next four years.

In 2008, Missouri also ranked within the top ten states for production of fuller's earth, portland cement, crushed stone, copper, zinc, cadmium, silver, and aluminum.

Caverns and Convergences: Water in Missouri

Missouri's water resources are tremendous, and rivers alone snake across more than 56,000 miles (90,123 km) of the state. To put this into perspective, consider that if the state's rivers were stacked end to end, they could circumnavigate the globe more than two times. Missouri bears witness to the convergence of the two largest rivers in North America and two of the greatest in the world—the Mississippi and the Missouri Rivers. The largest lake in the state is the artificial Lake of the Ozarks, which covers 93 square miles (241 sq km).

Missouri State Profile	
Physical Characteristics	
Land area	68,716 square miles (177,974 sq km)
Inland water area	987 square miles (2,556 sq km)
Coastal area	NA
Highest point	Taum Sauk Mountain 1,772 feet (540 m)
National Forest System lands (2010)	14.9 million acres (6.0 million ha)
State parks (2011)	83
Energy Statistics	
Total energy production (2009)	180 trillion Btu
State ranking in total energy production (2009)	39
Renewable energy net generation total (2009)	2.4 million megawatt hours
Hydroelectric energy generation (2009)	1.8 million megawatt hours
Biomass energy generation (2009)	73,000 megawatt hours
Wind energy generation (2009)	499,000 megawatt hours
Wood and derived fuel energy generation (2009)	2,000 megawatt hours
Crude oil reserves (2009)	NA
Natural gas reserves (2009)	NA
Natural gas liquids (2008)	NA
Pollution Statistics	
Carbon output (2005)	137.2 million tons of CO_2 (124.5 million t)
Superfund sites (2008)	32
Particulate matter (less than 2.5 micrometers) emissions (2002)	13,544 tons per year (12,287 t/yr)
Toxic chemical releases (2009)	76.1 million pounds (34.5 million kg)
Generated hazardous waste (2009)	238,200 tons (216,100 t)

SOURCES: AirData. U.S. Environmental Protection Agency. Available from http://www.epa.gov/air/data; *Energy Maps, Facts, and Data of the U.S. States.* U.S. Energy Information Administration. Available from http://www.eia.gov/state; *The 2012 Statistical Abstract.* U.S. Census Bureau. Available from http://www.census.gov/compendia/statab; *United States Energy Usage.* eRedux. Available from http://www.eredux.net/states.

© 2011 Cengage Learning.

In addition to large surface water resources, the state also contains substantial groundwater resources—some of which are accessible to humans through Missouri's breathtaking network of underground caves, more than 6,300 strong.

Ports and Fishing

The Port of St. Louis on the Mississippi represents the northernmost point on the river that remains accessible throughout the year (since the river does not freeze there). The port handles more than 32 million tons of freight each year and is noted as the third largest inland port in the Midwest, serving as a storage, transfer and distribution point for goods heading all over the world. The Kansas City Port at the confluence of the Missouri and Kansas rivers is one of the largest storage and distribution centers on the Missouri. There are nine other ports throughout the state; the Missouri port system combined handles about $4.1 billion in cargo annually. Some commercial fishing takes place along the Mississippi, Missouri, and St. Francis rivers. There are also several fish farms throughout the state, with catfish, baitfish, and ornamental fish being the primary commercial aquaculture species. Popular game fish for sports anglers include crappie, bluegill, muskie, paddlefish, trout, and walleye.

The Threat of Asian Carp

The rapidly growing population of Asian carp along the Missouri River has raised serious concerns for environmentalists and fishermen in the state. The three species of Asian carp found most often in the Missouri—bighead, silver, and black—were first imported into the United States in the 1960s and 1970s by Southern catfish farmers who used the fish to naturally remove algae and other matter from their farm ponds. Some carp were accidently released into local waterways of the Mississippi River Basin in the 1990s, as major flooding caused the catfish farm ponds to overflow into river areas. Since then, the carp have been steadily making their way upriver and have been reproducing at alarming rates. They are extremely prolific and eat large quantities of food, thereby depleting the supply for native species. The Asian carp can be quite large, with some weighing in at up to one hundred pounds. Boaters along the Missouri have reported numerous incidents in which presumably panicked fish have jumped out of the water at and into their boats, causing injuries to those hit by the flying fish and damage to the boats. While live Asian carp minnows were once used as live bait by local fishermen, this practice is now illegal, as state and federal agents continue to consider ways to contain the growing population. Toward that end, a major study on the life cycle of the species is being conducted by the U.S. Geological Survey through the Columbia Environmental Research Center in Columbia, Missouri. Officials hope that the results of the Invasive Carp Research Program will provide important information for developing effective and sustainable management plans for the invasive species. In the meantime, Asian carp continue to threaten native aquatic life in the Mississippi River, as well as in other nearby waterways. Federal scientists fear that extensive flooding of the Mississippi River in 2011 may have resulted in Asian carp being introduced to smaller lakes, ponds, and rivers.

Steady Farming Prevails in Missouri

According to the United States Department of Agriculture's (USDA) 2010 statistics, Missouri's 108,000 farms spanned about 29 million acres, covering about 66 percent of the state's total land area. Unlike many other states, where the agricultural sector fluctuates significantly over time, one finds in Missouri little variation in the amount of land and the number of farms devoted to agriculture over the past three decades. Missouri is a top producing state in poultry, cattle, and hogs. In 2009, the state ranked as fifth in the nation for the production of rice, sixth for soybeans and cotton, eighth for grain sorghum, and ninth in corn. Forage items, such as hay and grass silage, are also important crops. According to the 2007 USDA agricultural census, the total value of agricultural products sold in Missouri was more than $7.5 billion—the twelfth most in the United States. However, soil erosion continues to be a challenge for Missouri farmers. In a 2005 report, the Missouri Department of Natural Resources stated that as recently as 1995 Missouri ranked second in the nation for its rate of soil erosion. However, Missouri voters have passed a Parks and Soils Sales Tax, the proceeds of which are dedicated to fighting soil erosion, several times in the state's history. Missouri was the first—and remains the only—state in the nation to approve a sales tax for soil conservation. The tax was renewed for ten years by 76 percent of the voters in 2006.

According to a USDA survey, Missouri had 140 certified organic farming operations in 2008.

❧ Energy: Robust Coal Consumer

On both a per capita and an absolute basis, Missouri consumes an average amount of energy for a U.S. state. Yet when it comes to coal consumption, Missouri ranks among the top twelve states in total use. Coal remains the dominant source of electricity in Missouri and constitutes more than 80 percent of total production. The vast majority of coal burned in Missouri—more than 90 percent—arrives on railcars from Wyoming, which is famous for its desirable low sulfur, cleaner burning coal. It is ironic that Missouri, the first state west of the Mississippi to harvest coal commercially, today relegates that duty to other western states and harvests little itself. However, this is attributable to the character of Missouri coal, which has a higher sulfur content than western coals. Nuclear energy produced at the lone reactor in the state—the Callaway nuclear plant in Fulton—supplies much of the state's non-coal electricity.

Roughly 60 percent of homes in the state use natural gas as their dominant heating source, and Missouri attains this fuel via pipeline from Kansas, Arkansas, Oklahoma, and Nebraska. Of the substantial quantities of natural gas imported into the state, more than 80 percent is rerouted and exported to Illinois and Iowa for reshipment. Major petroleum pipelines also pass through the state as well, but much of the petroleum that enters Missouri is also exported to other Midwestern states, where the petroleum is refined.

As of 2011, only about 3 percent of Missouri's electricity is produced with renewable resources—principally hydroelectric. However, standards adopted in November 2008 require that 5 percent of total electricity be produced with renewable sources by 2014, 10 percent by 2018, and 15 percent by 2021. According to the National Wildlife Federation, Missouri was ranked eighteenth in the United States for wind power in 2008. The American Wind Energy Association ranked the state twentieth in terms of its future wind potential. Estimates are that the state has 5,960 MW of potential capacity.

Another option in Missouri is biomass renewable energy. As of 2011, there were six ethanol plants in northern Missouri. Those plants produced some 200 million gallons (757 million l) of corn ethanol annually. There were also three biodiesel plants producing 50 million gallons (189 million l) of biodiesel a year from soy and animal fats. There are several examples of industrial corporations using wood waste for direct heating, and more proposals for additional biomass-fed power plants.

Good Faith Energy Efficiency Effort Gets Teeth

In June 2007, Missouri created its first renewable energy and efficiency objective for the state's investor-owned utilities, requiring each utility to make a "good faith effort" to generate or procure electricity from eligible renewable energy resources. The objective set a series of goals for the utilities: that they generate at least 4 percent of sales from eligible renewable resources by 2012, 8 percent by 2015, and 11 percent by 2020. In November 2008, Missouri voters expanded this objective, approving a ballot initiative that eliminated the "good faith" clause in the state's energy and efficiency objective, and established mandates for similar goals. Under the revised standard, 15 percent of electric sales from investor-owned utilities must come from eligible renewable resources by 2021. Of the 15 percent renewable mandate, 2 percent must come from solar energy (0.3% of total energy sales). It is important to note that both the 2007 and 2008 standards only applied to investor-owned utilities, however, and no requirements were placed on municipal utilities or electric cooperatives.

❧ Green Business, Green Building, Green Jobs

Growing Green Businesses: Mizzou Jumps on Board

The green business sector is growing in Missouri. From 1998 to 2007, the number of clean energy businesses in Missouri expanded from 1,026 to 1,062, and twenty-five new patents in the clean energy sector were registered to Missouri residents and businesses over that period. (In terms of clean energy patents, however, this was below average for a U.S. state.) State-funded organizations, such as the University of Missouri, have developed strategies that make it easier for businesses in the state to improve efficiency and reduce their carbon footprint.

The University of Missouri boasts two centers devoted to improving efficiency among Missouri's businesses and industries: The Missouri Industrial Assessment Center and the Missouri Environmental Assistance Center (MEAC). The industrial assessment center, which is funded primarily by the U.S. Department of Energy, offers free energy audits for small to medium-sized manufacturers in the state. Eligible companies can apply for an energy audit through the assessment center and a team from the university will arrive to conduct an energy assessment. In addition to "greening" the texture of manufacturing in the state, the Missouri Industrial Assessment Center also offers hands-on training for its students in the energy engineering sector, ultimately making the Missouri workforce more competitive in the field.

The Missouri Environmental Assistance Center (MEAC), on the other hand, offers great general information to all Missouri businesses on how to save money by improving efficiency. The "energy efficiency" tab of the MEAC Web site offers links to tax incentive programs in Missouri and also lists simple modifications that small business owners can make to improve efficiency.

Evergreen Institute Invests Big in Missouri Green Building

Green Building in Missouri is bolstered by an array of local organizations that help homeowners and educators in the state familiarize themselves with the details of the movement. The Evergreen Institute, whose main campus is located in Gerald, Missouri, just outside of St. Louis, represents one organization that is committed to growing the sector in the state. The Evergreen Institute offers a host of classes and workshops for educators, homeowners, business men and women, and building professionals to help them grapple with green building issues and gain continuing education credit through the U.S. Green Building Council (USGBC). In addition to running more conventional green building workshops, the Evergreen Institute offers "deep green" natural building workshops, which allow individuals to work with natural plasters, earthen floors, and other natural materials that expand green building beyond more conventional materials.

The state has also implemented measures to improve its green building portfolio. Senate Bill 649, which took effect in 2007, requires that all large (more than 5,000 sq ft/465 sq m) state buildings constructed or substantially renovated after July 1, 2009, achieve the U. S. Green Building Council's Silver certification or higher. Additionally, SB 649 offers a number of tax incentives for taxpayers who construct a green building or renovate an existing structure into a green building.

Federal Funding Grows Green Jobs

From 1998 to 2007, green jobs grew at 5.4 percent in the state, significantly outpacing Missouri's 2.1 percent conventional job growth over that period. According to the Pew Charitable Trusts, more than $24 million in venture capital funds poured into the clean energy sector of the state from 2004–2006, contributing to a swelling in the number of green businesses in the state. The 2009 American Recovery and Reinvestment Act (ARRA) added significantly to the development of the green jobs sector in Missouri. ARRA earmarked at least $500 million to Missouri to prepare state workers for careers in the energy efficiency and renewable energy fields.

❧ Hidden Wonders: Missouri's Caves and Karst Landscape

Missouri's unique geology maintains conditions ripe for caves. More than 6,300 caves have been discovered in Missouri, and each year that number increases as new discoveries are made (roughly 100 per year). With the exception of the northwest region of the state, caves can be found throughout Missouri. However, the southern half of the state—particularly the Ozarks, which is defined by a karst topography—holds the highest number of caves.

A karst topography, out of which most caves are formed, is marked by soluble rock formations (in the case of Missouri, limestone and dolomite geologic formations). As time passes, surface streams and water pick up carbon dioxide from air and dead plant debris and erode through these soluble rock layers to form the three features that define a karst terrain:

1. Sinkholes—rounded depressions in the landscape formed by water slowly dissolving the rock below

2. Losing streams—surface streams that sacrifice substantial flow to the subsurface through bedrock openings; the cavernous spaces underground known as

3. Caves, and springs (where water exits from the underground flow, often from caves, and reappears on the land surface).

Technically, a cave is simply a natural opening that is large enough for human entry. In Missouri, caves serve as homes to many unique forms of life—from bats to blind cavefish to other sun-sheltered organisms—and operate as critical transitways for the state's groundwater. Many of Missouri's caves carry tremendous volumes of water, which flow hidden underground before emerging at the surface as springs, visibly feeding the state's rivers and streams. Many people think of caves and springs as fundamentally different. In reality, a spring is nothing more than the outlet of a cave that contains water.

Missouri's caves are also ancient formations, and historic evidence shows that Native Americans used caves as shelter, sources of water, and depositories of minerals, such as clay, for some 10,000 years. In more recent times, humans have used Missouri's extensive network of caves for recreation, ecotourism, beer brewing (as caves provide ideal, constant temperatures for the "laagering" of beer), and adventure. In fact, Missouri's network of caves has hosted a number of speakeasies, taverns, and ballrooms over time.

But these activities, and others, have come with costs.

Underground Cathedrals of Karst: A Threatened Ecosystem

The splendor of Missouri's caves—particularly those in the karst terrains of the Ozarks—is threatened. The Missouri Caves and Karst Conservancy notes that urban development has nearly eliminated the once robust network of caves in certain sections of the state, including the St. Louis region. Some sewer districts in Missouri use caves as part of their sewer system, and many small towns exploit sinkholes as local garbage dumps. When it rains, when toilets flush, when showers run, heavy amounts of pollution can travel down into the groundwater below, severely disrupting the water quality and the life that depends upon it.

In the karst terrains, water flows easily. Unlike with traditional groundwater systems, where a natural filtration process takes effect as water passes through incredibly small openings in rock, there is virtually no natural filtration in the karst terrains. This means the entire network is extremely vulnerable to surface as well as direct pollution. According to the Missouri Speleological Survey, Missouri's caves shelter roughly 900 different species of wildlife, including several endangered species, such as the gray bat. These animals remain tremendously vulnerable to the effects of pollution.

Cavesnail Comes Close to Extinction The Tumbling Creek cavesnail is one cave animal in Missouri that was driven nearly to extinction because of water pollution. This unique snail species is found in only one cave in the entire world—the Tumbling Creek Cave in southern Missouri. When a farm above that cave was converted to a feedlot, sediments from the lot began to enter the groundwater. These sediments choked the

Falling Water Falls in the middle of the Ozark National Forest.   © *Ross Ellet/ShutterStock.com*

Tumbling Creek Cave stream, and consequently, the Tumbling Creek cavesnail, which nearly went extinct. Neighbors and environmentalists noticed the problem, and were able to improve the water quality by restoring the farm land to more natural conditions, but the event underscored the deep vulnerability of the karst terrains and the animals that depend on them. Tumbling Creek Cave has also been designated as a Priority 1 gray bat cave, deeming it essential in preventing that species' extinction. The Tumbling Creek cavesnail and numerous other Missouri cave species remain on the Endangered Species list.

Preserving Missouri Caves and Karst

Karst and cave preservation depends on public education. One of the most important elements of maintaining Missouri's cave treasures involves informing the public about their vulnerabilities. In addition to the tremendous threat of water pollution—from sewers, septic tanks, farms, and fertilizers—Missouri's caves and karst are also threatened by direct human activity and vandalism. Newly discovered caves are significant targets for vandals who will often enter the structures to "tag" the walls with noxious chemical sprays or remove ancient formations as artifacts to display.

Thus, one element of cave preservation is secrecy. Missouri residents who discover a new cave are urged to keep it secret from the public and the news media. Installed gates can also be effective deterrents to vandals and unauthorized visitors, and the Missouri Department of Conservation can help residents design ecologically friendly gates for caves and springs on their properties.

The challenges of cave and karst conservation are significant, but like the great, man-made cathedrals that certain communities have maintained around the world for centuries, it is up to Missouri's residents to protect the natural cathedrals that dot and deeply enrich their landscape today.

BIBLIOGRAPHY

Books

Chapman, Shannon S. *Ecoregions of Iowa and Missouri.* Reston, VA: USGS Information Services, 2002.

Iffrig, Greg F., et al. *Pioneer Forest: A Half Century of Sustainable Uneven-aged Forest Management in the Missouri Ozarks.* Asheville, NC: U.S. Department of Agriculture, Forest Service, 2008.

Winckler, Suzanne and Michael Forsberg. *The Smithsonian Guides to Natural America: The Heartland—*

Nebraska, Iowa, Illinois, Missouri, Kansas. Washington, DC: Smithsonian Books, 1996.

Web Sites

"2006 Minerals Yearbook: Missouri." U.S. Geological Survey. Available from http://minerals.usgs.gov/minerals/pubs/state/2006/myb2-2006-mo.pdf

"2007 Census of Agriculture: Organic Production Survey (2008)." United States Department of Agriculture. Available from http://www.agcensus.usda.gov/Publications/2007/Online_Highlights/Organics/ORGANICS.pdf

"2009 State Agricultural Overview: Missouri." United States Department of Agriculture. Available from http://www.nass.usda.gov/Statistics_by_State/Ag_Overview/AgOverview_MO.pdf

"Caring for Your Karst." Missouri Speleological Survey. Available from http://mospeleo.org/docs/Caring%20for%20your%20karst.pdf

"Charting a New Path for Missouri's Electricity Generation and Use." National Wildlife Federation. Available from http://www.nwf.org/Global-Warming/~/media/PDFs/Global%20Warming/Clean%20Energy%20State%20Fact%20Sheets/MISSOURI_10-22-6.ashx

"Clean Energy Economy: Missouri." Pew Charitable Trusts. Available from http://www.pewcenteronthestates.org/uploadedFiles/wwwpewcenteronthestatesorg/Fact_Sheets/Clean_Economy_Factsheet_Missouri.pdf

The Evergreen Institute. Available from http://67.199.86.177//index.cfm?action=DisplayMain

Foster, Mary. "Mississippi Flooding May Have Spread Asian Carp." Associated Press. June 10, 2011. Available from http://www.columbiamissourian.com/stories/2011/06/10/mississippi-flooding-may-have-spread-invasive-fish/

"Global Climate Change Impacts in the United States: Midwest." United States Global Change Research Program. Available from http://www.globalchange.gov/images/cir/region-pdf/MidwestFactSheet.pdf

"Global Warming and Missouri." National Wildlife Federation. Available from http://www.nwf.org/Global-Warming/~/media/PDFs/Global%20Warming/Global%20Warming%20State%20Fact%20Sheets/Missouri.ashx

Greenhouse Gas Emission Trends and Projections for Missouri, 1990-2015. Missouri Energy Center. Available from http://www.dnr.mo.gov/energy/cc/ghg.htm.

"Invasive Carp Research Program." Columbia Environmental Research Center. Available from http://www.cerc.usgs.gov/Branches.aspx?BranchId=40.

Kavanaugh, Lee Hill. "Asian carp, the new bullies of America's inland waters, are crazy, high-flying fish." McClatchy-Tribune News Service. September 1, 2010. Available from http://www.cleveland.com/nation/index.ssf/2010/09/asian_carp_the_new_bullies_of.html.

MASWCD: 65 Years of Progress. Missouri Association of Soil and Water Conservation Districts. Available from http://www.maswcd.net/historydoc.htm

"MDC Discover Nature: Missouri Forests Today." Missouri Department of Conservation. Available from http://mdc.mo.gov/discover-nature/habitats/forests/missouri-forests-today.

Missouri Action Options for Reducing Greenhouse Gas Emissions. Missouri Energy Center. Available from http://www.pewclimate.org/docUploads/MO%20ActionOptions%202002.pdf.

Missouri Aquaculture Association. Available from http://moaquaculture.org.

Missouri Caves and Karst Conservancy. Available from http://www.mocavesandkarst.org/

"Missouri: Incentives /Policies for Renewables and Efficiency." Database of State Incentives for Renewables and Efficiency. Available from http://www.dsireusa.org/incentives/incentive.cfm?Incentive_Code=MO08R&state=MO&CurrentPageID=1&RE=1&EE=1

Missouri Port Authorities. Available from http://www.missouriports.org/ports.html.

Missouri 2008 Minerals Yearbook. United States Geological Survey. Available from http://minerals.usgs.gov/minerals/pubs/state/2008/myb2-2008-mo.pdf.

Moving Energy Forward. Missouri Department of Natural Resources. Available from: http://blogs.mo.gov/energy/2011/07/29/what-is-res/

"North America's Largest Lead Producer to Spend $65 Million for Environmental Violations at Missouri Facilities." United States Environmental Protection Agency. Available from http://yosemite.epa.gov/opa/admpress.nsf/6427a6b7538955c585257359003f0230/1510175059ac92c3852577b6005e1e47!OpenDocument

"Ozark: Cave/Karst Systems." National Park Service. Available from http://www.nps.gov/ozar/naturescience/cave.htm

"A Renewable Portfolio Standard for Missouri's Electric Utilities." Missouri Public Service Commission. Available from http://www.psc.mo.gov/electric/missouri-energy-task-force/renewable_portfolio_standard.pdf

"Senate Bill Number 649." Missouri State Legislature. Available from http://www.senate.mo.gov/07info/pdf-bill/intro/SB649.pdf

"Species Report: Listings and Occurrences for Missouri." U.S. Fish and Wildlife Service. Available from http://ecos.fws.gov/tess_public/pub/stateListingAndOccurrenceIndividual.jsp?state=MO&s8fid=112761032792&s8fid=112762573902&s8fid=2401279126 1753

"State Energy Profile: Missouri." U.S. Energy Information Administration. Available from http://tonto.eia.doe.gov/state/state_energy_profiles.cfm?sid=MO

Strategic Plan 2005–2009. Missouri Department of Natural Resources. Available from http://www.dnr.mo.gov/s_plan/s-plan2005.pdf

"2008 Organic Survey." United States Department of Agriculture. Available from http://www.agcensus.usda.gov/Publications/2007/Online-Highlights/Organics/index.asp

"Use of Prescribed Fire." Missouri Department of Conservation. Available from http://mdc4.mdc.mo.gov/Documents/9173.pdf

Montana

The state of Montana has a diverse economy, including contributions from aerospace, agriculture, biotechnology, healthcare, manufacturing, natural resources, technology, and tourism. Agriculture and tourism are the state's biggest sectors, as the state is home to both Yellowstone and Glacier National Parks. The Williston Basin that covers eastern Montana and western North Dakota contains three of the largest one hundred oil fields in the nation, with two of these located within Montana. Montana is known as "The Treasure State" for its wealth of nonfuel minerals, including copper, platinum, gold, and palladium. The state has also shown potential in the development of wind and hydroelectric energy sources. Montana is facing a few challenges in the development of a green economy, but the legislature is working to develop consensus on issues concerning climate change and the development of clean energy resources. The state is currently facing a challenge in wildlife management as well, as Montana Fish, Wildlife & Parks address legal issues concerning the recent relisting and subsequent delisting of the gray wolf to the federal Endangered Species List for the region.

Climate

The Continental Divide that crosses through the northwest portion of the state creates two distinct climatic regions. The eastern region has cold winters, warm summers, and heavy precipitation in late spring and early summer. The western region generally has milder winters and cooler summers.

Climate Change

By most accounts, the effects of climate change have already had a significant impact on the landscape of Montana. According to information available from the Montana Department of Environmental Quality, one of the most dramatic effects is seen in the diminishing glaciers of Glacier National Park. When the park was first established in 1910, there were 150 glaciers along the mountains. As of 2010, there are twenty-seven glaciers

remaining, and these could disappear by 2022 under current weather pattern predictions. If the general increase in temperatures continues, winter precipitation will more often come in the form of rain instead of snow, meaning earlier runoff causing the land to become drier as a result. This drier land could also cause an increase in forest fires during the summer. Changes in habitat could also affect the state's fish and wildlife populations, which in turn could affect the state's tourism and recreation sectors.

According to the *Montana Greenhouse Gas Inventory and Reference Case Projections 1990–2020*, published by the Center for Climate Strategies, greenhouse gas emissions in Montana increased by 14 percent from 1990 to 2005. During the same time period, national emissions increased by 19 percent. The principle sources for these emissions are from electricity use and agriculture, which each account for 27 percent of the state's gross GHG emissions. Under certain reference case projections, it is estimated that greenhouse gas emissions could increase by 30 percent above 1990 levels by 2020, without appropriate mitigating actions.

In response to these reports, the Montana Climate Change Advisory Committee issued the *Montana Climate Change Action Plan* (2007), which includes fifty-four policy recommendations concerning measures the state could take to reduce greenhouse gas emissions to 1990 levels by 2020. A majority of the reductions would come from incentives for building; energy supply; agriculture, forestry, and waste management; and light duty vehicle clean car standards.

Montana and the Western Climate Initiative (WCI)

Montana is a member of the Western Climate Initiative (WCI), a regional action group committed to developing a joint strategy for the reduction of greenhouse gas emissions. In 2008, the WCI announced the development of a greenhouse gas emissions cap-and-trade program that is expected to take effect in participating states and

Canadian provinces beginning January 2012. Since its inception, most states have backed out of the WCI's reduction strategies and have not passed reduction cap and trade legislation. Montana is one of the states that has not passed cap and trade legislation.

🍃 Natural Resources, Water, and Agriculture

Natural Resources

Forests cover about 25 percent of the land area of Montana. About 85 percent of forests is available for harvest. West of the Continental Divide, the most common forest tree species are firs, lodgepole, Douglas fir, grand fir, spruce, larch, and western hemlock. To the east of the divide, ponderosa pine is the most prevalent. About 96.5 percent of the land forested in the early 1600s is still forested today. Since 2007, the presence of mountain pine beetles has been an ongoing concern in several of Montana's forest and urban areas.

Parks and Wildlife

Montana has fifty-three state parks, three national parks, 15 wilderness areas, and part of the Bighorn Canyon National Recreation Area. The Lewis & Clark National Historic Trail also crosses through the state. Yellowstone National Park, the northern edge of which is in Montana, was established in 1872 as the first national park. It serves as home to the largest concentration of mammals in the lower 48 states, including bison, bobcats, mountain lions, grizzly bears, elk, bighorn sheep, moose, coyote, and white-tailed deer. At least 318 species of bird have been documented in the park. Rubber boas and prairie rattlesnakes can also be found.

The state's wildlife habitats are home to black and grizzly bears, pronghorn (antelope), and mountain goat, along with numerous small common mammals, such as beavers, rabbits, squirrels, and skunks. Some common birds include the eastern and western meadowlarks, mountain chickadee, American kestrel, prairie falcon, and various types of hummingbirds, sparrows, swallows, ducks, and geese.

Montana Fish, Wildlife & Parks lists thirty-seven mammals as species of concern or of potential concern, including the black-tailed and white-tailed prairie dogs, wolverine, black-tailed jackrabbit, and free-ranging herds of American bison. The burrowing owl, great gray owl, great blue heron, and golden eagle are among more than eighty species of bird listed as species of concern by the state.

The U.S. Fish and Wildlife Service lists eleven animal and three plant species as either threatened or endangered in Montana. Endangered animal species include the whooping crane, pallid sturgeon, and black-footed ferret.

The three threatened plant species are Spalding's catchfly, water howellia, and Ute ladies'-tresses.

The gray wolf has been at the center of controversy for the state and the region as legal battles ensue concerning the federal protection status assigned to the wolf. Successful recovery and management programs have resulted in significant growth in the gray wolf population of Montana over the years. The federal government removed the species from the region's list of endangered species in 2009, but legal challenges from environmental groups led to the relisting of the gray wolf in 2010. Ultimately, the wolf was once again delisted in 2011, with full management of the species returned to the state.

Minerals: The Treasure State

With a wealth of nonfuel minerals, Montana is known as "The Treasure State." Nonfuel mineral production is valued at more than $1 billion annually ($1.1 billion in 2010), with copper, molybdenum, platinum, gold, and palladium accounting for about 79 percent of production. Montana is the only state that produces palladium and platinum. The state also ranks as a leading producer of talc, silver, bentonite clay, and industrial garnets. A significant quantity of construction sand and gravel is also produced.

Water: The Triple Divide

The Continental Divide that separates the watersheds draining into the Pacific Ocean from those that drain into the Atlantic (at the Gulf of Mexico) crosses through the northwest portion of Montana. Triple Divide Peak in Glacier National Park additionally marks a dividing point between waters that flow into the Pacific, the Atlantic, and the Arctic Ocean (through Hudson Bay).

Rivers and Lakes

Ft. Peck Reservoir, created by a dam on the Missouri River, is the largest manmade lake in the state and the fifth largest in the nation. The largest natural lake in the state is Flathead Lake. The state has more than 170,000 miles (273,600 km) of streams and rivers, with the Missouri River being one of the most important. Red Rock Creek and the Yellowstone River, both tributaries of the Missouri, are also important.

There are several hydroelectric plants along Montana's rivers, producing a little more than 35 percent of the total supply of electricity.

Fishing

Most fishing in the state is for sport, with the exception of some waters that are open for commercial catches of whitefish. Some favorite catches include cutthroat trout, shovelnose sturgeon, sauger, channel catfish, paddlefish, and lake trout. Montana is home to eleven state fish

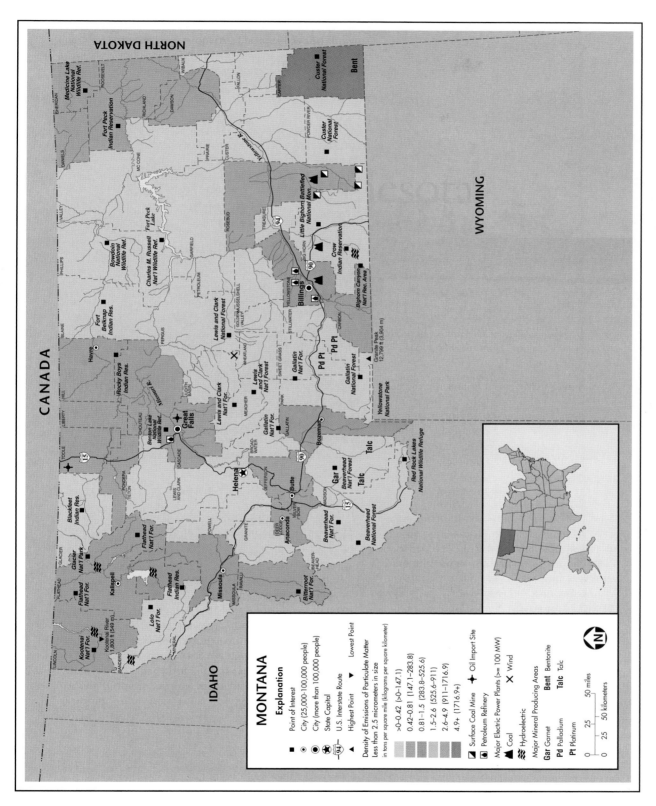

SOURCES: "County Emissions Map: Criteria Air Pollutants." *AirData*. U.S. Environmental Protection Agency. Available from http://www.epa.gov/air/data/geosel.html; *Energy Maps*. U.S. Energy Information Administration. Available from http://www.eia.gov/state; *Highest and Lowest Elevations*. U.S. Geological Survey. Available from http://egsc.usgs.gov/isb/pubs/booklets/elvadist/elvadist.html#Highest; *2007 Minerals Yearbook*. U.S. Geological Survey. Available from http://minerals.usgs.gov/minerals/pubs/state. © 2011 Cengage Learning.

St. Mary Lake, Glacier National Park. *© Charles L Bolin/ShutterStock.com*

hatcheries and two national hatcheries. Creston National Fish Hatchery specializes in rainbow trout and westslope cutthroat trout. Ennis National Fish Hatchery works as part of the National Broodstock Program, producing about twenty million rainbow trout eggs annually for research facilities, universities and federal, state, and tribal hatcheries in twenty-three states.

The Land of Wheat and Honey

Montana ranks as second in the nation for total acres of land in farms and ranches. The state is typically ranked among the top five for production of wheat, barley, honey, lentils, dry edible peas, Austrian winter peas, flaxseed, and safflower. Additionally, the state ranks among the top ten in production of cows (particularly for beef), sheep and lambs, wool, alfalfa hay, pinto beans, garbanzo beans, sugar beets, and canola.

The Montana Department of Agriculture is accredited to certify organic produce and handlers under the USDA National Organic Program and under the International Standards Organization. In 2010, there were at least eighty certified producers and handlers listed in the program database. Montana ranks first among states in the production of certified organic wheat and second in organic production of all grains, peas, lentils, and flax.

✿ Energy

Fossil Fuels: Coal

Montana is home to large reserves of coal and oil. With nearly 25 percent of the nation's total estimated recoverable coal reserves, Montana produces about 4 percent of the total U.S. production of coal each year. Most of the coal comes from surface mines in the Powder River Basin that lies along the border with Wyoming. About 25 percent of the coal produced is used for electricity generation within the state. The remainder is exported to at least fifteen other states, with Minnesota and Michigan as the largest buyers.

Fossil Fuels: Oil & Natural Gas

The Williston Basin that covers eastern Montana and western North Dakota contains three of the largest one hundred oil fields in the nation. Two of these are located

Montana State Profile

Physical Characteristics

Land area	145,541 square miles (376,949 sq km)
Inland water area	1,498 square miles (3,880 sq km)
Coastal area	NA
Highest point	Granite Peak 12,799 feet (3,901 m)
National Forest System lands (2010)	17.0 million acres (6.9 million ha)
State parks (2011)	53

Energy Statistics

Total energy production (2009)	1,200 trillion Btu
State ranking in total energy production (2009)	16
Renewable energy net generation total (2009)	10.4 million megawatt hours
Hydroelectric energy generation (2009)	9.5 million megawatt hours
Biomass energy generation (2009)	NA
Wind energy generation (2009)	821,000 megawatt hours
Wood and derived fuel energy generation (2009)	95,000 megawatt hours
Crude oil reserves (2009)	343 million barrels (54.5 million cu m)
Natural gas reserves (2009)	976 billion cubic feet (27.6 billion cu m)
Natural gas liquids (2008)	12 million barrels (1.9 million cu m)

Pollution Statistics

Carbon output (2005)	32.7 million tons of CO_2 (29.7 million t)
Superfund sites (2008)	16
Particulate matter (less than 2.5 micrometers) emissions (2002)	4,881 tons per year (4,428 t/yr)
Toxic chemical releases (2009)	41.2 million pounds (18.7 million kg)
Generated hazardous waste (2009)	37,800 tons (34,300 t)

SOURCES: AirData. U.S. Environmental Protection Agency. Available from http://www.epa.gov/air/data; *Energy Maps, Facts, and Data of the U.S. States.* U.S. Energy Information Administration. Available from http://www.eia.gov/state; *The 2012 Statistical Abstract.* U.S. Census Bureau. Available from http://www.census.gov/compendia/statab; *United States Energy Usage.* eRedux. Available from http://www.eredux.net/states.

© 2011 Cengage Learning.

within Montana. Crude oil production within the state accounts for nearly 2 percent of the national total. Refineries in the Billings area produce petroleum products for regional markets. Montana requires the use of oxygenated gasoline in the Missoula area during the winter months. In 2005, the legislature passed a bill (SB 293) that requires a 10 percent ethanol blend in all non-premium gasoline.

There are small quantities of natural gas produced in the state, about 40 percent of which is shipped to out-of-state markets. About 60 percent of Montana households use natural gas as a primary source for home heating.

Yellowstone Oil Spill

On July 1, 2011, an ExxonMobil pipeline ruptured about 10 miles (16 km) west of Billings. The Silvertip pipeline released oil into the Yellowstone River for about 30 minutes until the pipeline was shut down. An estimated 42,000–54,000 gallons (159,000–204,000 l) of oil were released into the river, with 60 percent of the downstream shoreline found to be contaminated. Initially, officials evacuated the nearby town of Laurel in case of a possible explosion. The residents were allowed to return about four hours later, once fumes from the oil had dissipated. Clean-up crews immediately began to lay down absorbent sheets along the banks of the river in an effort to mop up some of the oil. Over 1,000 people worked to clean up the spill. Later that same month, it was revealed that federal inspectors had discovered a problem in the pipeline a month before it ruptured, yet decided it was not significant enough to force a shutdown. A review of pipeline records also showed that the pipeline had about 20 percent external corrosion, reported in inspections from 2004 and 2009. The rupture occurred as the river flooded due to heavy rains, and some reports indicate that the entire pipeline was severed, rather than springing a leak. The cause of the spill was still under investigation as of November 2011. The spill raised concerns about drinking water safety, fish consumption advisories, and led to a bill in the House of Representatives calling for more stringent pipeline rules.

Williston Basin and the Bakken Formation

The Williston Basin contains part of the Bakken shale formation, which is one of the largest shale plays in the nation. The formation covers parts of eastern Montana and western North Dakota and stretches northward into Canada. The marine shales found in this formation are petroleum source rocks that produce hydrocarbons. In the oil and gas industry, the term "play" refers to a geographic region where an economic quantity of oil or gas is likely to be found. According to the U.S. Geological Survey, the Bakken Formation contains an estimated mean of 3.65 billion barrels of undiscovered oil, 1.85 trillion cubic feet of associated and dissolved natural gas, and 148 million barrels of natural gas liquids.

A number of drilling and pipeline companies have begun development around the Bakken Formation. Baker, Montana, is being touted as a hub for Bakken oil, lying at the heart of planned pipeline intersections and serving as a headquarters for investing companies. Bridger and Belle Fourche Pipeline intends to build a series of three collector pipelines that will transport Bakken oil through Baker and TransCanada Pipelines has proposed a similar project that will transport oil from the Canadian portion of the formation to U.S. refineries along the Gulf Coast.

Electricity and Renewables

A little more than 58 percent of the electricity supply is generated from coal-fired plants, but the state has shown a great potential for and commitment to incorporating renewable and clean technology energy sources in its energy mix. Six of the ten largest electricity generating plants within the state are operating on hydropower. In total, hydropower generates a little more than 35 percent of the total supply of electricity. About 3 percent of electricity comes from wind farms in central Montana.

Since 2007 and the passage of House Bill 25, the state has had a de facto ban on the approval of new coal-fired plants. Under HB 25, new coal plants cannot be pre-approved unless they present plans to sequester 50 percent of the carbon dioxide produced, or until the federal or state government passes a requirement for carbon sequestration. Since the technology to meet the 50 percent requirement is not commercially available, the bill essentially places a temporary ban on new coal-fired plants.

Renewable Portfolio Standard

The Montana renewable portfolio standard (RPS) was enacted in 2005 by the passage of the Montana Renewable Power Production and Rural Economic Development Act (MCA 69-3-2001). Under the act, public utilities are required to obtain 15 percent of their retail electricity sales from eligible renewable resources by 2015. Eligible renewable resources include wind, solar, geothermal, hydroelectric, landfill or farm-based methane gas, wastewater treatment gas, biomass, and fuel cells where hydrogen is produced from renewable fuels. In 2010, the legislature's Energy and Telecommunications Interim Committee voted to draft and support a bill to amend the RPS by increasing the required minimum of renewable source electricity to 20 percent by 2020 and 25 percent by 2025.

Energy Policy

In October 2005, Governor Brian Schweitzer launched a series of meetings and discussions that led to the development of what is now referred to as the Schweitzer Energy Policy. The policy is primarily an outline for economic development through the promotion of renewable and clean-technology energy sources and energy efficiency and conservation projects, all of which will lead to a more sustainable and independent energy future for the state.

In 2009, the Energy and Telecommunications Interim Committee of the Montana Legislature was charged with the task of reviewing current energy policy legislation and proposing policy changes that would promote new energy developments. The committee was able to reach a consensus on a number of topics, including transmission line development and energy efficiency, but could not reach a consensus on the language used for projects including fossil fuel resources for electricity. For instance one major policy issue focused on the concept of increasing the supply of

On July 1, 2011, an ExxonMobil pipeline ruptured about 10 miles (16 km) west of Billings. It was quickly contained but the spill stretched over dozens of miles. © *AP Images/Matthew Brown*

low-cost electricity through coal-fired generation. Some committee members hoped to redefine the issue to move in a direction away from fossil-fuels, but other committee members (and lobbyists) preferred the inclusion of statements that support fossil fuels over other resources. Some committee members also asked for wording that would make reference to and concessions for climate change, while others countered with claims that there was no evidence to support the reality of climate change. As a result, the committee did not reach a consensus on findings and recommendations to support a change in energy policy, and therefore, chose not to pursue any legislative changes.

✿ Green Business, Green Building, Green Jobs

Green Jobs Montana: Examination and Estimation

There are conflicting reports concerning the number of green businesses and green jobs available in the state of

Montana. In 2009, the Montana Department of Labor and Industry published a report that highlighted the challenges faced by many in defining and assessing the extent of the green economy as noted by the number of green jobs. *Green Jobs Montana: Examination and Estimation*, particularly notes the lack of a single standard definition for "green jobs" and the fact that in certain industries that are not immediately considered as "green," employees may be conducting green activities part of the time. With these challenges in mind, the report presents seven different estimates of the number of green jobs available in the state, based on seven different methodologies. Using employment figures from 2008, these estimates range from 4,079 green jobs to as many as 22,060.

As in most states, the greatest potential for the growth of a green economy seems to be in the development of renewable and clean energy resources. In 2010, Headwaters Economics, an independent nonprofit research group based in Bozeman, released a report entitled *Clean Energy Leadership in the Rockies: Competitive Positing in the Emerging Green Economy*, which examines and compares the use and development of clean energy resources in five Rocky Mountain states—Colorado, New Mexico, Montana, Utah, and Wyoming. According to this report, there were 408 green establishments in Montana in 2007, supporting 2,155 jobs. In this comparison study, Montana came in fourth of five in the number of green jobs created from 1995 to 2007, falling well behind Utah, Colorado, and New Mexico. The study suggests that the Montana government will need to make a stronger legislative commitment to the development and use of renewable energy, coupled with an investment in education and research, in order to attract investors.

Green Jobs Training

Outside of the political arena, there are groups surging forward in the promotion of green jobs through designated job training programs. In 2009, the Montana Electrical Joint Apprenticeship and Training Committee, which is part of the International Brotherhood of Electrical Workers (IBEW), received a grant of about $5 million through the American Recovery and Reinvestment Act for training programs related to wind, solar, and hydropower energy sources. More than one thousand IBEW members are expected to benefit from the grant. In 2010, the Pure Energy Center opened in Lavina, Montana, to provide job training for those seeking careers in conservation, energy efficiency, and the use of natural and renewable energy sources. Classes are available, for building science, weatherization, energy auditing, energy use analysis, and the Building Performance Institute Building Analyst Certification Program. The center also sponsors a special Green Jobs Training for Women program, with classes taught by women for women. The University of Montana College of

Technology has an energy technician training program as well, with many courses offered online.

Green Building

In 2009, the state legislature passed a bill (SB 49) setting energy efficiency standards for state-owned and state-leased buildings. Pursuant to the act, all new construction and major renovation projects for state-owned and leased buildings must exceed the effective International Energy Conservation Code by 20 percent, to the extent that it is cost effective. The Montana Department of Labor was also called on to work in collaboration with the state university system and other state agencies to develop and adopt high performance building standards for use in state agencies.

For residents and business owners, the state Department of Environmental Quality provides a variety of programs and incentives focused on creating energy efficient spaces and lifestyles. Organizations such as the Montana Building Industry Association and Montana chapter of the U.S. Green Building Council promote programs to encourage residents and private business owners to go green. The Missoula Federal Credit Union is an example of a platinum-level construction project, certified under the U.S. Green Building Council Leadership in Energy and Environmental Design (LEED) program. The building was constructed in such a way that 80 percent of the regularly occupied spaces receive natural daylight and more than 40 percent of the building materials content, by value, was manufactured using recycled materials.

❧ Legal Wrangling Over the Gray Wolf

The gray wolves that were once abundant in the western region of the United States were nearly extinct in Montana by the 1930s, primarily due to loss of habitat and conflict with the ever-growing human population. In 1980, the U.S. Fish and Wildlife Service (USFWS) approved the Northern Rocky Mountain Wolf Recovery Plan, designed to restore the species to the three targeted recovery areas of northwest Montana, central Idaho, and the Greater Yellowstone Area.

The plan seems to have worked very well, as the recovery of the wolf population in the Northern Rockies is considered to be one of the fastest comebacks of an endangered species on record. In the mid-1990s, more than sixty wolves were released into Yellowstone National Park and central Idaho to boost the local population. The minimum recovery goal was to develop a population of at least 300 individual wolves and thirty breeding pairs throughout the region for three consecutive years. The goal was met in 2002, with an increasing population noted every year since. According to information posted by Montana Fish, Wildlife & Parks (FWP), the wolf population in the Northern Rocky Mountain region was estimated at a total of 1,706 individual wolves with 115 breeding pairs at the end of 2009. The state of Montana was home to 524 of those wolves, with 37 breeding pairs.

The success of the recovery program might also be attributed to effective wolf management plans. Montana completed its own federally approved plan in 2004 and secured a cooperative agreement with the USFWS to implement as much of the state plan that is allowed under federal regulations, with federal funding for support.

In April 2009, the U.S. Fish & Wildlife Service delisted (removed) the gray wolf from the endangered species list for Montana and Idaho, thus relinquishing wildlife management responsibilities to state agencies. Montana Fish, Wildlife & Parks is the agency responsible for implementing the state's federally approved Gray Wolf Program. The program is designed to maintain a stable wolf population, while providing legal measures to protect livestock from becoming prey. From 1995 to 2007, wolves were responsible for 803 confirmed livestock deaths in Montana, including cattle, sheep, llamas, goats, and horses. In 2009, there were 309 confirmed deaths, with other injury or death losses that were not confirmed, but considered probable. Under state management regulations, livestock owners were permitted to kill wolves that were found in the act of chasing or harassing livestock. The state also sponsored a hunting season as a measure to keep the wolf population in check.

However, the 2009 delisting was challenged in a U.S. District Court by a coalition of thirteen environmental groups, including Defenders of Wildlife, the Sierra Club, and the Humane Society of the United States. The suit was focused on the federal decision to delist the gray wolf in Montana and Idaho, but not in Wyoming. All three states are part of the larger Northern Rocky Mountain region, which has been noted as having the largest wolf population in the American West. The plaintiffs argued that the federal Endangered Species Act does not allow the federal government to subdivide a distinct population segment, providing legal protection for the wolves in one region, while delisting them in another. Furthermore, it was noted that the state of Wyoming did not have a federally approved management plan and therefore would not be prepared to adequately protect the wolf population to federal standards. The case was heard by U.S. District Judge Donald Molloy in Missoula, who agreed that the delisting had been inappropriate and reinstated federal protection for the entire region. His ruling to relist the gray wolf was issued on August 5, 2010.

In Montana, this meant that the wolves in the northwest region of the status were reclassified as endangered, while the wolves of the southern region were reclassified as experimental. Endangered wolves cannot be harassed, hazed, or killed by hunters, livestock owners, or other private citizens. Endangered species can only be killed in self-defense or in defense of the life of another person. Experimental wolves can be hazed and harassed by livestock owners, but cannot be killed simply for being found in proximity to livestock. They may be killed if they are found actively chasing or attacking livestock, but the incident must be reported to the FWP within twenty-four hours. Experimental species can be killed in self-defense or the in defense of another, but cannot be hunted or trapped.

The Montana FWP Commission immediately passed a resolution urging the U.S. Department of Interior and the U.S. Fish and Wildlife Service to appeal the ruling. The Montana Environmental Quality Council (a legislative committee) and Montana governor Brian Schweitzer sent similar letters to the Department of Interior and the U.S. Department of Justice. The FWP also submitted a permit application to the USFWS for permission to go forward with a previously scheduled statewide conservation hunt for the fall of 2010. The application was denied and the FWP cancelled the hunt. The state filed an appeal with the district court on October 1, 2010.

While FWP officials have noted that the current wolf population is secure, they are concerned that the numbers could increase quickly and significantly without the balance provided by conservation hunts and other local actions. State officials also point out that the local wolf population is not significantly endangered, but rather well managed.

Defenders of Wildlife, one of the groups fighting for increased federal protection of the wolves, states that the total number of wolves for the region dropped from 2,000 at the beginning of 2009 to 1,650 at the end of that year, primarily as a result of managed hunts in Montana and Idaho. They argue that additional hunts in these states could quickly lead to significant losses in the overall wolf population.

Montana found itself back in control of its wolf populations once again in April 2011. Congress attached a rider to a federal appropriations bill that delisted wolves in Montana and Idaho. The rider also states that the rule will not be subject to judicial review. Environmental groups argued in court in July 2011 that Congress overstepped its authority with the rider. They claim the rider is unconstitutional because the wolf case was being appealed with a decision pending, and it therefore interfered with the judicial branch. Legal experts disagree, stating that the environmental groups face difficult odds, since Congress is in full rights to order a rule exempt from judicial review if it has authored all rules involved. Montana again holds authority over its wolf populations and plans on holding a wolf hunting season in the fall of 2011. The state has set a quota of 220 wolves for its hunt.

BIBLIOGRAPHY

Books

Baron, Jill. *Rocky Mountain Futures: An Ecological Perspective.* Washington, DC: Island Press, 2002.

Corum, Nathaniel. *Building a Straw Bale House: The Red Feather Construction Handbook.* New York, NY: Princeton Architectural Press, 2005.

Eagan, Timothy. *The Big Burn: Teddy Roosevelt and the Fire that Saved America.* Boston, MA: Houghton Mifflin Harcourt, 2009.

Johnson, Jerry. *Knowing Yellowstone: Science in America's First National Park.* Lanham, MD: Taylor Trade Publishing, 2010.

Manning, Richard. *Rewildling the West: Restoration in a Prairie Landscape.* Berkeley, CA: University of California Press, 2009.

Schmidt, Jeremy and Thomas Schmidt. *The Smithsonian Guides to Natural America: The Northern Rockies–Idaho, Montana, Wyoming.* Washington, DC: Smithsonian Books, 1995.

Stiller, David. *Wounding the West: Montana, Mining, and the Environment.* Lincoln, NE: University of Nebraska Press, 2000.

Sullivan, Gordon. *Saving Homewaters: The Story of Montana's Streams and Rivers.* Woodstock, VT: The Countryman Press, 2008.

Swanson, Frederick H. *The Bitterroot and Mr. Brand borg: Clearcutting and the Struggle for Sustainable Forestry in the Northern Rockies.* Salt Lake City, UT: University of Utah Press, 2011.

Wyckoff, William. *On the Road Again: Montana's Changing Landscape.* Seattle, WA: University of Washington Press, 2006.

Web Sites

An Act Generally Revising the Electric Utility Industry Restructuring and Customer Choice Laws (HB 25). Montana Legislature. Available from http://data. opi.mt.gov/bills/2007/billhtml/HB0025.htm

An Act Requiring the Department of Administration to Establish High-Performance Building Standards for State-Owned Buildings (SB 49). Montana Legislature. Available from http://data.opi.mt.gov/bills/ 2009/billhtml/SB0049.htm

An Act Revising Laws Related to Alternative Fuels and Petroleum Products (SB 293). Montana Legislature. Available from http://data.opi.mt.gov/bills/2005/ billhtml/SB0293.htm

Assessment of Undiscovered Oil Resources in the Devonian-Mississippian Bakken Formation, Williston Basin Province, Montana, and North Dakota, 2008. United States Geological Survey. Available from http:// pubs.usgs.gov/fs/2008/3021/pdf/FS08-3021_508.pdf

"Beetles." Montana Department of Natural Resources and Conservation. Available from http://www. beetles.mt.gov

Clean Energy Leadership in the Rockies: Competitive Positing in the Emerging Green Economy. Headwaters Economic. Available from http://www. headwaterseconomics.org/greeneconomy/ CleanEnergyLeadership.pdf

"Climate Change in Montana." Montana Department of Environmental Quality. Available from http://deq. mt.gov/ClimateChange/default.mcpx

Daly, Matthew. "Ruptured Montana oil pipeline had earlier problem." Associated Press. July 20, 2011. Available from http://www.google.com/ hostednews/ap/article/ALeqM5gJCBl2PKLYLb 77_ZBPs2qynPn0-w?docId=dbf7a3482e504041b 50b6bf6c0a2f6a2

Dennison, Mike. "Panel OKs increasing renewable energy mandates." *Independent Record.* July 31, 2010. Available from http://helenair.com/news/arti-cle_69a5d4d6-9c68-11df-8386-001cc4c002e0.html

"Energy Conservation." Montana Department of Environmental Quality. Available from http:// deq.mt.gov/Energy/conservation/default.mcpx

"Facts about Montana Agriculture." Montana Depart ment of Agriculture. Available from http://agr.mt. gov/dept/info.asp

"Fort Peck Dam/Lake." U.S. Army Corps of Engineers. Available from http://www.nwo.usace.army.mil/ html/Lake_Proj/fortpeck/welcome.html

Glacier National Park. National Parks Service. Available from http://www.nps.gov/glac/index.htm

Green Jobs in Montana: Examination and Estimation. Montana Department of Labor and Industry. Available from http://researchingthegreenecon-omy.com/docfolder/stateresearch/3602_green_ jobs%5B1%5D.pdf

"IBEW Wins More That $20 Million in Green Jobs Training Grants." International Brotherhood of Electrical Workers. January 8, 2009. Available from http://www.ibew.org/articles/10daily/1001/ 100108_GreenTraining.htm

"Idaho-Montana wolf issues head back to court on Tuesday." The Spokesman-Review. July 25, 2011. Available from http://www.spokesman.com/ blogs/outdoors/2011/jul/25/idaho-montana-wolf-issues-head-back-court-tuesday/

"Listings and occurrences for Montana." Species Reports. U.S. Fish and Wildlife Service. Available from http://ecos.fws.gov/tess_public/pub/state-ListingAndOccurrenceIndividual.jsp?state=MT&S8-fid=112761032792&S8fid=112762573902

"A Look at Montana Agriculture." Agriculture in the Classroom. Available from http://www.agclass-room.org/kids/stats/montana.pdf

"Missoula Federal Credit Union." U.S. Green Building Council, Missoula Chapter. Available from http://chapters.usgbc.org/montana/documents/MissoulaFCULEEDSheet-small_000.pdf

"Montana Animal Species of Concern." Montana Fish, Wildlife & Parks. Available from http://mtnhp.org/reports/MASOC_2009.pdf

Montana Climate Change Action Plan. Montana Climate Change Advisory Committee. Available from http://deq.mt.gov/ClimateChange/plan.mcpx

Montana Climate Office. Available from http://www.cfc.umt.edu/mco

Montana Field Guides. Available from http://fieldguide.mt.gov

"Montana Fishing Guide." Montana Fish, Wildlife and Parks. Available from http://fwp.mt.gov/fishing/guide

"Montana Forests." Montana Wood Products Association. Available from http://www.montanaforests.com/forests

"Montana Green Building Program." Montana Building Industry Association. Available from http://www.montanabia.com/green.html

Montana Greenhouse Gas Inventory and Reference Case Projections 1990–2020. Center for Climate Strategies. Available from http://www.mtclimatechange.us/ewebeditpro/items/O127F13145.pdf

"Montana Lakes and Reservoirs." U.S. Bureau of Reclamation, Great Plains Region. Available from http://www.usbr.gov/gp/lakes_reservoirs/montana_lakes.htm

"Montana Organic Program." Montana Department of Agriculture. Available from http://agr.mt.gov/organic/Program.asp

"Montana Renewable Power Production and Rural Economic Development Act (MCA 69-3-2001)." *Montana Annotated Code 2009.* Available from http://data.opi.mt.gov/bills/mca_toc/69_3_20.htm

Montana State Parks. Available from http://fwp.mt.gov/parks

Montana Watercourse. Available from http://www.mtwatercourse.org/index.php

"Montana Wolf Program." Montana Fish, Wildlife and Parks. Available from http://fwp.mt.gov/wild-things/management/wolf/default.html

Montana's Energy Policy Review. Montana Legislature, Energy, and Telecommunications Interim Committee. Available from http://www.leg.mt.gov/content/Publications/committees/interim/2009_2010/2010-energy-policy.pdf

"Northern Rockies and Yellowstone Area Wolves." Defenders of Wildlife. Available from http://www.defenders.org/programs_and_policy/wildlife_conservation/imperiled_species/wolves/wolf_recovery_efforts/northern_rockies_wolves/index.php

O'Connor, Anahad. "Ruptured Pipeline Spills Oil Into Yellowstone River." *The New York Times.* July 2, 2011. Available from http://www.nytimes.com/2011/07/03/us/03oilspill.html?scp=1&sq=Ruptured%20Pipeline%20Spills%20Oil%20Into%20Yellowstone%20River&st=cse

PPL Montana—Hydroelectric Plants. Available from http://www.pplmontana.com/producing+power/power+plants/PPL+Montana+Hydro.htm

Pyburn, Evelyn. "Montana Gets Second Chance at Bakken Oil." *Big Sky Business Journal.* September 22, 2010. Available from http://www.bigskybusiness.com/index.php?option=com_content&view=article&id=1501:montana-gets-second-chance-at-bakken-oil&catid=7:features&Itemid=112

"The Schweitzer Energy Policy." Montana Department of Commerce. Available from http://commerce.mt.gov/Energy/energypolicy.mcpx

"State Energy Policy: Interim Legislative Energy Committee Update." August 2010. Montana Environmental Information Center. http://meic.org/energy/energy_policy/2009-state-energy-policy

"State Energy Profiles: Montana." U.S. Energy Information Administration. Available from http://tonto.eia.doe.gov/state/state_energy_profiles.cfm?sid=MT

2007 Minerals Yearbook: Montana. United State Geological Survey. Available from http://minerals.usgs.gov/minerals/pubs/state/2007/myb2-2007-mt.pdf

"U.S. House wants better pipeline rules." UPI. July 28, 2011. Available from http://www.upi.com/Business_News/Energy-Resources/2011/07/28/US-House-wants-better-pipeline-rules/UPI-63151311857655/?spt=hs&or=er

"Yellowstone National Park." National Park Service. Available from http://www.nps.gov/yell/index.htm

Nebraska

Located in the Great Plains of the midwestern United States, Nebraska is a leading farming and ranching state. Ranking as the third highest producer of corn in the nation, Nebraska has been able to utilize this resource and become a leading producer of the alternative fuel ethanol, much of which is shipped for use in other states. In 2011, Nebraskans fought to keep up the growth of renewable energy sources in their state, as they have been fighting the construction of the Keystone XL crude oil sands pipeline. The pipeline would pass under over the Ogallala Aquifer and the Nebraska Sandhills, possibly putting the local ecosystem in danger.

Climate

Nebraska has a continental climate, with highly variable temperatures from season to season and year to year. Average yearly precipitation in Omaha is about 30 inches (76 cm); 17 inches (43 cm) in the semiarid panhandle in the west; and in the southeast, 30 inches (76 cm). Snowfall in the state varies, with the northwest corner of the state receiving the most. Blizzards, droughts, and windstorms have plagued Nebraska throughout its history.

Climate Change Initiatives

Nebraska does not have a climate change action plan. The state is, however, part of the Western Governors' Association (WGA), which in 2006 signed resolutions with a goal to meet 30,000 megawatts of clean energy by 2015 and a 20 percent increase in energy efficiency by 2020. The WGA also encourages states to get adequate funding for state energy efficiency and renewable generation programs.

In 2007, Nebraska—as well as Iowa, Indiana, Illinois, Minnesota, Michigan, Kansas, Ohio, South Dakota, North Dakota, and Wisconsin—signed the Midwestern Energy Security and Climate Stewardship Platform. The platform follows goals that include supporting the state's bioeconomy, and supporting the management and creation of a carbon dioxide storage infrastructure, renewable fuel usage, and new megawatts of wind energy.

✿ Natural Resources, Water, and Agriculture

Forests and Plants

Nebraska is home to 1.3 million acres (530,000 ha) of forestland. The state has an array of forest types, and common species include the cottonwood, American elm, green ash, ponderosa pine, oak, walnut, aspen, eastern redcedar, and birch. The live gross volume of Nebraska's forest resources is 2.9 billion cubic feet (80 million cu m), making woody biomass a readily available energy source for Nebraska. The state produces a variety of products from wood, including lumber, furniture, gunstocks, pallets, wood pallets and chips for fuel, and decorative mulch. Nebraska's wood products manufacturing industry had an output of $286 million in 2002, and employed more than 2,200 workers.

The cottonwood is the primary commercial tree species in Nebraska. However, cottonwood regenerates slowly and continues to do so because of drought conditions, current land uses, and dams. The eastern redcedar regenerates rapidly and has been replacing the cottonwood. If measures aren't taken to regenerate cottonwood trees and conditions continue to remain the same, Nebraska may lose its most economically important hardwood species. Nebraska also has 38 million ash trees, which means that the emerald ash borer (EAB)—a nonnative insect that kills ash trees—will have a significant economic and environmental impact if it arrives in the state. In Lincoln alone, costs to remove, dispose of, and replant trees lost to EAB will most likely exceed $137 million.

Nebraska's tallgrass prairie includes various slough grasses and needlegrasses, along with big bluestem and prairie dropseed. Western wheatgrass and buffalo grass are found in mixed prairie regions. Nebraska's wild-flowers consist of wild rose, phlox, petunia, columbine, goldenrod, and sunflower. Four plant species were federally threatened as of 2011: Ute lady's tresses, Colorado butterfly plant, and both the eastern and western prairie fringed orchids. The blowout penstemon was listed as endangered that year.

Nebraska's Animals

Some of Nebraska's native mammal species include the pronghorn, white-tailed and mule deer, badger, kit fox, prairie vole, and two skunk species. Some of the state's 400 bird species are the mourning dove, barn swallow, and western meadowlark (the state bird). Popular game animals include deer, turkey, antelope, elk, and bighorn sheep. The Nebraska Game and Parks Commission reported that the state earned more than $13 million issuing hunting permits in 2009. The U.S. Fish and Wildlife Service listed thirteen animal species (vertebrates and invertebrates) as threatened or endangered in 2011, which were the American burying beetle, whooping crane, piping plover, black-footed ferret, Topeka shiner, pallid sturgeon, interior least tern, Salt Creek tiger beetle, gray wolf, Higgins eye mussel, winged mapleleaf, scale-shell mussel, and Eskimo curlew.

Mining

According to the U.S. Geological Survey, in 2010 Nebraska's top nonfuel mineral commodities were cement, crushed stone, and construction sand and gravel. Total nonfuel raw mineral production was valued at $181 million that same year. The state also produces some clay, shale, steel, and uranium. Fly ash is used in the production of portland cement, concrete, and as a soil stabilization material.

Rivers, Lakes, and Wetlands

The majority of Nebraska is prairie, however the state does have some water resources. The Sand Hills region is dotted with small natural lakes; in the rest of the state, the main lakes are manmade. The Missouri River forms the northeast and eastern eastern part of the northern boundaryies of Nebraska. Three rivers cross the state from west to east: the Platte River flows through the heart of the state for 310 mi (499 km), the Niobrara River traverses the state's northern region, and the Republican River flows through southern Nebraska.

Three of Nebraska's has three wetland areas include: the Rainwater Basin wetlands, the Big Bend reach of the Platte River, and the Sand Hills wetlands. These areas serve as important migrating and breeding grounds for waterfowl and nongame birds. Carp, catfish, bass, walleye, bluegill, trout, and perch are fished for sport. Commercial fish in Nebraska include black bullhead, yellow bullhead, freshwater drum, and yellow perch.

Agriculture

In 2010, Nebraska was home to more than 47,000 farms covering 45.6 million acres (18.5 million ha). The state ranked first in the nation for commercial red meat production that same year. It ranked second for pinto beans; third for cattle and calves and corn; fourth in soybean production; and fifth for hay production. The state also ranks sixth for hogs and pigs with over 3 million head. Because the state is one of the top producers of corn, it has become a leader in corn-based ethanol production.

According to the U.S. Department of Agriculture, Nebraska had 211 certified organic operations in 2008, covering more than 183,000 acres (74,000 ha). The state has more than 6.5 million heads of organic poultry, and over 12,000 heads of organic livestock. The state produces organic grains such as corn, wheat, oats, sorghum, millet, and rye. Nebraska also has crops of organic beans, sunflowers, hay, and small amounts of vegetables, fruit, and herbs.

❧ Energy

Most of Nebraska's small oil reserves are located in the western half of the state. A network of petroleum product pipelines connects Nebraska markets to refining centers in nearby states. The 2,148-mi (3,460-km) Keystone Pipeline, which became operational in the summer of 2010, transports crude oil from Alberta, Canada through eastern Nebraska to other Midwest markets. Over two-thirds of Nebraska households use natural gas as their primary fuel for home heating. The state relies on interstate transfers to meet virtually all of that demand. Nebraska ships over three-fifths of the natural gas it receives to Iowa, Missouri, and South Dakota.

According to the U.S. Energy Information Administration, coal-fired power plants supply two-thirds of the state's electricity. A small amount is also generated by the state's two nuclear power plants and by hydroelectric dams along the Platte River. Nebraska ranks sixth in the United States in wind potential, but twenty-fourth in wind production. The entire state is classified as fair or good according to the U.S. Department of Energy National Renewable Energy Laboratory.

Flooding along the Missouri River in June 2011 threatened Nebraska's two nuclear plants, calling into question their reliability and safety as a power source, particularly in the wake of the March 2011 meltdown at the Fukushima plant in Japan. One of the plants, Fort Calhoun Station, had been shut down since April for refueling, so officials opted to keep it shut down due to the impending floods. The other, Cooper Nuclear Station, is on higher ground and kept operating. Concern about the Fort Calhoun plant also came about in part due to the Nuclear Regulatory Commission citing it for not being adequately prepared for floods in 2010. Flood

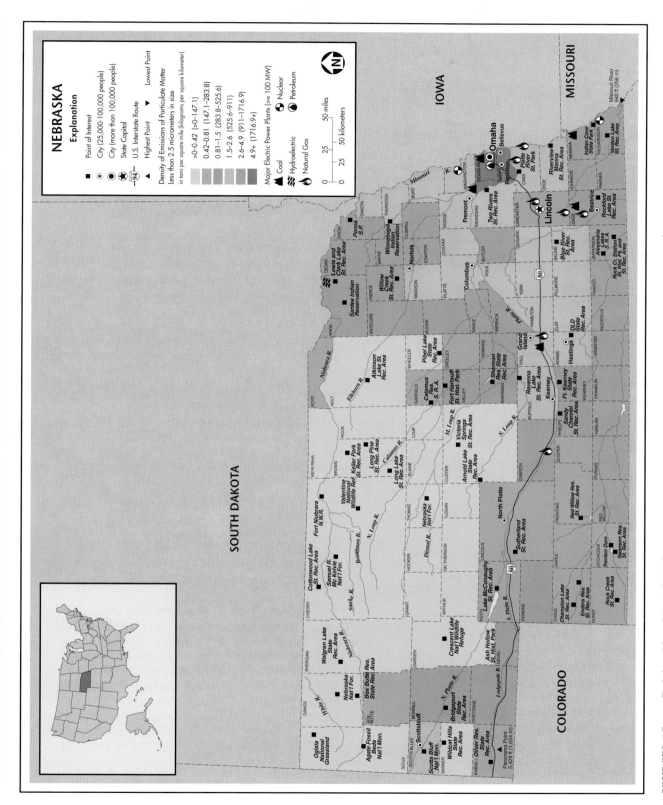

SOURCES: "County Emissions Map: Criteria Air Pollutants." *AirData.* U.S. Environmental Protection Agency. Available from http://www.epa.gov/air/data/geosel.html; *Energy Maps.* U.S. Energy Information Administration. Available from http://www.eia.gov/state; *Highest and Lowest Elevations.* U.S. Geological Survey. Available from http://egsc.usgs.gov/isb/pubs/booklets/elvadist/elvadist.html#Highest; *2007 Minerals Yearbook.* U.S. Geological Survey. Available from http://minerals.usgs.gov/minerals/pubs/state. © 2011 Cengage Learning.

Nebraska State Profile

Physical Characteristics

Land area	76,825 square miles (198,976 sq km)
Inland water area	524 square miles (1,357 sq km)
Coastal area	NA
Highest point	Panorama Point 5,424 feet (1,653 m)
National Forest System lands (2010)	352,000 acres (142,000 ha)
State parks (2011)	87

Energy Statistics

Total energy production (2009)	300 trillion Btu
State ranking in total energy production (2009)	37
Renewable energy net generation total (2009)	900,000 megawatt hours
Hydroelectric energy generation (2009)	434,000 megawatt hours
Biomass energy generation (2009)	66,000 megawatt hours
Wind energy generation (2009)	383,000 megawatt hours
Wood and derived fuel energy generation (2009)	NA
Crude oil reserves (2009)	9 million barrels (1.4 million cu m)
Natural gas reserves (2009)	NA
Natural gas liquids (2008)	NA

Pollution Statistics

Carbon output (2005)	43.2 million tons of CO_2 (39.2 million t)
Superfund sites (2008)	13
Particulate matter (less than 2.5 micrometers) emissions (2002)	2,001 tons per year (1,815 t/yr)
Toxic chemical releases (2009)	29.6 million pounds (13.4 million kg)
Generated hazardous waste (2009)	28,200 tons (25,600 t)

SOURCES: AirData. U.S. Environmental Protection Agency. Available from http://www.epa.gov/air/data; *Energy Maps, Facts, and Data of the U.S. States.* U.S. Energy Information Administration. Available from http://www.eia.gov/state; *The 2012 Statistical Abstract.* U.S. Census Bureau. Available from http://www.census.gov/compendia/statab; *United States Energy Usage.* eRedux. Available from http://www.eredux.net/states.

waters eventually caused a berm to collapse around the plant, allowing flood waters to reach containment buildings and forcing electrical power to be shut down. Backup generators proceeded to cool nuclear material, which along with the fact that the plant had not been operational, protected the public from any dangers that may have come from the flooding.

Alternative Fuels: A Leading Producer of Ethanol

As one of the nation's top producers of corn, Nebraska is also among the nation's top producers of corn-based ethanol. There are currently 24 operating ethanol plants concentrated in the central and eastern parts of the state. The state's ethanol production is mostly sent for use in

A petroleum storage and distribution terminal on a pipeline in Nebraska. © *Jim Parkin/Alamy*

other states. Most states require the use of specific gasoline blends due to air-quality considerations, and Nebraska is one of the few states in the nation that does not require this and allows the statewide use of conventional motor gasoline.

Nebraska opened its first commercial biodiesel facility in 2006. Horizon Biofuels, Inc. has the capacity to produce 5 million gallons (19 million l) of biodiesel per year by refining crude soybean oil. Construction is expected to begin in 2011 on a new biodiesel plant in South Sioux City. Nature's BioReserves will use tallow leftover from beef processing done at nearby Beef Products, Inc. The plant will produce 60 million gallons (227 million l) of fuel a year.

As of 2011, Nebraska did not have a Renewable Portfolio Standard.

⚘ Green Business, Green Building, Green Jobs

Green Business and Green Jobs

According to the Pew Charitable Trusts, in 2007 Nebraska had more than 5,200 jobs in the clean energy sector in 368 businesses. Another report, from the National Governor's Association, indicated that in 2009 Nebraska was a national leader in the green transportation sector. Green transportation also had the highest number of workers out of all the green sectors, with about 2,100. The state also had a high employment concentration in the sectors of recycling and waste, water and wastewater, and air and environment.

The Nebraska Business Development Center at University of Nebraska at Omaha provides Nebraska businesses with information about waste reduction, grant programs for small businesses, and energy efficiency assistance. One of the programs they offer is an

The Fort Calhoun nuclear power station, which was shut down for refueling, surrounded by flood waters from the Missouri River, June 14, 2011. © *AP Images/Nati Harnik*

Environmental Kaizen, which brings together a team of 10–15 employees who go through a week-long waste reduction effort for the business. The kaizen, a Japanese word meaning "improvement" or "change for the better," helps the business develop a plan for solutions and aids them in implementing that plan.

Nebraska colleges and universities offer a variety of green training programs, some of which apply directly to the strengths of the state's green economy. Northeast Community College in Norfolk offers a certificate or Associate of Applied Science degree in Renewable Fuels Technology. The program focuses on the state's thriving ethanol industry. Students have hands-on experience with process control trainers and an ethanol plant simulator. In addition, they gain knowledge in electricity, environmental compliance, microbial ecology, process dynamics, and distillation and evaporation. The college also offers a diploma in Wind Energy, which trains students in wind energy fundamentals and the mechanics of wind turbine systems.

The University of Nebraska at Lincoln houses the Nebraska Center for Energy Sciences Research. The center was established in 2006 to conduct research on renewable energy sources, energy efficiency, and energy conservation; and to expand economic opportunities and improve quality of life in Nebraska. Along with research opportunities, the Center offers a minor in Energy Sciences. Designed for students in any major, courses focus on how energy production and use affect the economy and environment. Along with its core courses, the minor offers upper-level elective courses in four thematic areas that the students can choose from: energy and natural resources, plant and animal bioenergy, energy engineering and energy economics, and policy and human dimensions.

Green Building

In July 2005, the Nebraska Energy Code, which is based on the 2003 International Energy Conservation Code (IECC) replaced the 1983 Model Energy Code. The Code applies to all new state-owned and state-funded buildings, or renovations of or additions to any existing state buildings. However, only those renovations that will cost more than 50 percent of the replacement cost of the building must comply with the Code. Cities and counties are able to adopt codes that differ from the Nebraska Energy Code, however, state law requires the adopted code to be equivalent to the Nebraska Energy Code.

The state also offers a number of rebates and grants for businesses that want to become more energy efficient. Lincoln Electric System offers a Commercial and Industrial Energy-Efficiency Innovation Grant of up to $50,000. The grant is available to businesses for project design assistance and developing measures to improve energy-demanding processes. Nebraska Public Power District offers a Commercial Energy Efficiency Rebate Program. This program offers multiple rebates for their commercial and industrial customers for energy efficient lighting, HVAC measures, high efficiency motors, and variable speed drives.

On the county and municipal level, Douglas County Environmental Services formed a Green Roof Committee in 2007. This Committee aims to incorporate more green roofs in the metropolitan Omaha area to minimize the negative impacts of stormwater runoff. In the summer of 2010, the Committee hosted a Green Roof tour, which included the roof of the Douglas County Health Center. In January of 2010, Omaha mayor Jim Suttle announced that he had signed the United States Conference of Mayors' Climate Protection Agreement, in which supporting mayors pledge to reduce carbon dioxide emissions in their communities. As part of his goal to make Omaha more energy efficient, the city began the Program for City Building Energy Efficiency, a comprehensive plan focused on energy efficiency and conservation efforts within the operations and maintenance of existing buildings. One hundred city buildings were audited, and once those audits were complete, the city began plans to retrofit the buildings to improve their energy efficiency.

❦ Is It Safe? Moving Tar Sands Crude Oils Through Nebraska

The extraction of oil from tar sands has long been controversial. It takes a significant amount of energy to obtain the fuel, resulting in a high level of greenhouse gas emissions. Also, once the fuel is extracted, toxic ponds and lakes are left behind, putting water supply and the local environment at risk. A report released in February 2011 focused on the potential dangers of tar sands crude oil that are transported through buried pipelines. The proposed TransCanada Keystone XL pipeline would carry tar sands crude oil from Canada through the middle of the United States from Alberta to Houston, Texas. Because this raw oil is more corrosive and acidic, there are worries that spills and ruptures in the pipeline would cause significant damage to the wetlands and aquifers through which it will be traveling.

Normally, oil is processed and goes through an upgrade that makes it into synthetic crude oil before being shipped. This synthetic oil is less corrosive than tar sands crude oil. Groups such as the Natural Resources Defense Council (NRDC) and the Sierra Club are concerned that the tar sands crude oil—also called DilBit—will be shipped via a pipeline that is designed for synthetic crude oil, and therefore there will be a higher chance of ruptures and spills. The Keystone XL Pipeline would transport up to 900,000 barrels per day along 1,600 miles (2,575 km) of pipeline, putting the center of the United States at risk for oil spills. Part of the issue is that there have not been many studies done on how to monitor DilBit, which can be more difficult to work with. Recent analysis researchers for the U.S. Army Corps of Engineers suggests that the risks of catastrophic pipeline ruptures at Sand Hills river crossings have been underestimated by Trans-Canada. The Keystone XL pipeline would cross 92 miles (148 km) of the Sand Hills, 65 miles (105 km) of which are less than 10 feet (3 m) near groundwater sources, meaning the pipeline will be sitting in or very near groundwater. Where it crosses under Sand Hills rivers, it will certainly be in contact with the aquifer, putting local drinking water sources at risk. While TransCanada claims that its safety technology and procedures are top-notch, many are still concerned because of the recent disasters such as the Gulf of Mexico and Michigan's Kalamazoo River.

Environmental groups have been trying to discourage President Obama from approving the pipeline for these reasons. Along with the report about the dangers of the pipeline, an ad campaign has been launched against it as well. Groups have also been keeping track of spills associated with another of Keystone's DilBit pipelines, the Keystone I, which has had 11 spills reported through June 2011. Groups have also been focusing on the areas through which the pipeline will travel. It will cross the Ogallala aquifer, which covers most of Nebraska and provides one-third of the country's drinking water. The aquifer has already been facing threats of contamination and depletion due to irrigation. The pipeline will also pass below the reach of the Platte River, a crucial stopping point for both the sandhill crane and the endangered whooping crane. The Deep Fork Wildlife Area in Oklahoma is another fragile area through which the pipeline will travel, as it is home to a variety of animals that include bald eagles and bobcats.

DilBit is also more difficult than conventional oil to clean up when a spill does occur. Because it is composed of raw bitumen, it is heavier than water and more likely to sink into the water column and wetland sediments. This means that spills will require more dredging than a conventional oil spill and will need more personnel, equipment, and supplies. Another factor that should be taken into consideration is the higher number of spills that the Alberta hazardous liquid pipeline has experienced due to internal corrosion. Alberta has experienced 218 spills between 2002 and 2010, sixteen times higher than in the United States. These spills are greater than 26 gallons (98 l) per 10,000 miles (16,000 km) of pipeline.

In their report, the NRDC outlined steps that the United States should take to prevent future spills of DilBit. First, they call for new U.S. pipeline safety regulations that will address the transportation of DilBit. They also state that the oil pipeline industry should take special precautions for pipelines that transport DilBit, using available technologies to protect against corrosion and spills until new regulations are in place. Spill response planning for DilBit pipelines should also be outlined, due to the difficulty of cleaning up a DilBit spill. The report also suggests that the U.S. should reduce demand for oil by investing in alternatives to oil and enforcing existing reduction programs. The most important step that the NRDC suggests is for new DilBit pipeline construction to be halted until adequate safety regulations are in place. The risks of these pipelines should be thoroughly evaluated so that proper safety regulations can be written with the least amount of accidents occurring in the meantime.

In May 2011, Legislative Bill 629 was passed in an attempt at a compromise between parties that oppose the pipeline and those that believe it will help the state economically. The bill requires entities that harbor oil pipelines in the state to be responsible for reclamation costs due to construction, operation, and management of their infrastructure. State Senator Jim Smith believes that the bill is a proper compromise, yet those that are concerned for the environment believe the bill's monetary focus fails to adequately protect Nebraska's environment from risk of pollution.

On January 18, 2010, President Obama rejected the proposed Keystone XL pipeline—not on the basis of the project itself—but because he felt the Congress-imposed deadline did not allow time for sufficient and proper review of the project relative to the assessment of the pipeline's full impact on not only the U.S. environment, but the health and safety of its citizens. The State Department indicated that the decision did not preclude any subsequent applications for the pipeline.

BIBLIOGRAPHY

Books

Cragin, Susan. *Nuclear Nebraska: The Remarkable Story of the Little County that Couldn't be Bought.* New York, NY: AMACOM Books, 2007.

Farrar, Jon. *Field Guide to Wildflowers of Nebraska and the Great Plains.* 2nd ed. Iowa City, IA: University of Iowa Press, 2011.

Johnsen, Carolyn. *Raising a Stink: The Struggle over Factory Hog Farms in Nebraska.* Lincoln, NE: Bison Books, 2003.

Johnsgard, Paul A. *The Nature of Nebraska: Ecology and Biodiversity.* Lincoln, NE: University of Nebraska Press, 2001.

Johnsgard, Paul A. *The Niobara: A river Running through Time.* Lincoln, NE: University of Nebraska Press, 2007.

Laresn, Lawrence Harold. *Upstream Metropolis: An Urban Biography of Omaha and Council Bluffs.* Lincoln, NE: University of Nebraska Press, 2007.

Light, Daniel S. *Ecology and Economics of the Great Plains.* Lincoln, NE: University of Nebraska Press, 2010.

Montrie, Chad. *Making a Living: Work and Environment in the United States.* Chapel Hill, NC: University of North Carolina Press, 2008.

Powers, Tom. *Audobon Guide to the National Wildlife Refuges. Northern Midwest: Illinois, Indiana, Iowa, Michigan, Minnesota, Nebraska, North Dakota, Ohio, South Dakota, Wisconsin.* New York, NY: St. Martin's Press, 2000.

Winckler, Suzanne and Michael Forsberg. *The Smithsonian Guides to Natural America: The Heartland–Nebraska, Iowa, Illinois, Missouri, Kansas.* Washington, DC: Smithsonian Books, 1996.

Web Sites

Augustine, Jonathon. "Keystone XL pipeline debate rages on." NewsNetNebraska. July 8, 2011. Available from http://www.newsnetnebraska.org/nnn/keystone-xl-pipeline-debate-rages-on/

"The Clean Energy Economy: Nebraska." The Pew Charitable Trusts. Available from http://www.pewcenteronthestates.org/uploadedFiles/wwwpewcenteronthestatesorg/Fact_Sheets/Clean_Economy_Factsheet_Nebraska.pdf

Great Plains Tar Sands Pipelines. Plains Justice. Available from http://tarsandspipelines.wordpress.com/

"Green Roof Working Committee." Douglas County Environmental Services. Available from http://www.douglascounty-ne.gov/envservcms/green-roof-committee

Hack, Mace A. "Midlands Voices: Pipeline's safety far from guaranteed." *Omaha World-Herald.* July 20, 2011. Available from http://www.omaha.com/article/20110720/NEWS0802/707209965

Kerley, David, et al. "Nebraska Residents in No Danger After Floods Hit Nuke Plant: Waters Breach Berm at Fort Calhoun Nuclear Station." ABC News. June 27, 2011. Available from http://abcnews.go.com/US/nebraska-residents-danger-floods-hit-nuke-plant-waters/story?id=13932406

Legislative Bill 629. For an Act relating to pipelines; to adopt the Oil Pipeline Reclamation Act; to provide severability; and to declare an emergency. Nebraska Legislature. May 26, 2011. Available from http://nebraskalegislature.gov/FloorDocs/Current/PDF/Slip/LB629.pdf

Linck, Michelle. "South Sioux City to build new biodiesel plant; fuel to be made of beef tallow." *Sioux City Journal.* December 18, 2010. Available from http://siouxcityjournal.com/news/local/article_73fdb550-03eb-5efc-acfe-270c8d5de463.html

Lincoln Electric System (LES)—Commercial and Industrial Energy-Efficiency Innovation Grant. Available from http://www.les.com/

"Listings and occurrences for Nebraska." U.S. Fish and Wildlife Service. Available from http://ecos.fws.gov/tess_public/pub/stateListingAndOccurrenceIndividual.jsp?state=NE&s8fid=112761032792&s8fid=112762573902&s8fid=24012940878091

"Mayor Suttle: Energy Audits for Public Buildings." The Mayor's Official Website for the City of Omaha. Available from http://www.cityofomaha.org/mayor/mayors-office-home/archives/552

Meneguzzo, Dacia N., et al. *Nebraska's Forests: 2005.* United States Department of Agriculture Forest Service. Available from http://www.nfs.unl.edu/documents/impactreports/NFSFIAReport.pdf

"Nebraska." State Energy Profiles. U.S. Energy Information Administration. Available from http://www.eia.doe.gov/state/state_energy_profiles.cfm?sid=NE

"Nebraska–Canada Facts." Government of Canada. Available from http://www.canadainternational.gc.ca/san_diego/commerce_can/2010/ne.aspx?lang=eng

Nebraska Center for Energy Sciences Research. University of Nebraska at Lincoln. Available from http://ncesr.unl.edu/

"Nebraska Energy Codes." Nebraska Energy Office. Available from http://www.neo.ne.gov/home_const/iecc/iecc_codes.htm

Nebraska Game and Parks: Fishing. Available from http://outdoornebraska.ne.gov/fishing.asp

Nebraska Game and Parks: See You Out There. 2009 Annual Report. Nebraska Game and Parks Commission. Available from http://outdoornebraska.ne.gov/admin/annual_reports/2009_Annual_Report.pdf

"Nebraska: Profile of the Green Economy." NGA Center for Best Practices. Available from http://www.nga.org/Files/pdf/09GREENPROFILENE.pdf

Nebraska Public Power District—Commercial Energy Efficiency Rebate Programs. Available from http://www.nppd.com/EnergyWise/business.asp

"Nebraska's Biodiesel Production Capacity." Nebraska Energy Statistics. Official Nebraska Government Website. Available from http://www.neo.ne.gov/statshtml/138.htm

Oatman, Maddie. "A Sticky Situation for TransCanada's Keystone XL Pipeline." *MotherJones.* February 17, 2011. Available from http://motherjones.com/blue-marble/2011/02/transcanada-keystone-tar-sands-oil

Piva, Ronald J., and Dennis M. Adams. *Nebraska Timber Industry——An Assessment of Timber Output and Use, 2006.* United States Department of Agriculture Forest Service. Available from http://www.nfs.unl.edu/documents/ruralforestry/NE%20TPO%202006.pdf

Renewable Fuels Technology Program. Northeast Community College. Available from http://www.northeast.edu/Degrees-and-Programs/Renewable-Fuels-Technology/

"State Actions on Climate Change: A Focus on How Our Communities Grow." Environmental and Energy Study Institute. Available from http://www.eesi.org/100709_state_plans_factsheet

Sulzberger, A.G. and Matthew L. Wald. "Flooding Brings Worries Over Two Nuclear Plants." *The New York Times.* June 20, 2011. Available from http://www.nytimes.com/2011/06/21/us/21flood.html

Sustainability and Green Business Practice. Nebraska Business Development Center. Available from http://nbdc.unomaha.edu/about/greenbusiness.cfm

Swift, Anthony, et al. *Tar Sands Pipelines Safety Risks.* National Resources Defense Council. Available from http://www.sierraclub.org/dirtyfuels/downloads/2011-02-safety.pdf

Tar Sands Invasion: How Dirty and Expensive Oil from Canada Threatens America's New Energy Economy. National Resources Defense Council. Available from http://www.nrdc.org/energy/files/TarSandsInvasion.pdf

"2009 State Agricultural Overview: Nebraska." United States Department of Agriculture. Available from http://www.nass.usda.gov/Statistics_by_State/Ag_Overview/AgOverview_NE.pdf

Wind Energy Diploma. Northeast Community College. Available from http://www.northeast.edu/Degrees-and-Programs/Wind-Energy/

Nevada

While Nevada may be best known for the neon lights of Las Vegas, the state also features vast expanses of natural scenery. With a total land area of just under 110,000 square miles (286,000 sq km), Nevada ranks seventh in size among the fifty U.S. states. Sandwiched between the Rocky Mountains to the east and the Sierra Nevada to the west, Nevada is located almost entirely within the Great Basin—the largest contiguous closed drainage basin in North America. The state's topography and climate largely reflect this location. Nevada is one of the driest states in the nation. While the few rivers that lie outside the Great Basin drain into the Colorado or Snake Rivers (in the southeast and extreme north, respectively) most of the state's rivers run to marshes, wetlands, or playas that evaporate seasonally in alkali sinks and dry lake beds. During the winter, temperatures in the north and west in the mountains can get extremely cold. Meanwhile, summers in the south can be scorching and hot.

According to the U.S. Global Climate Change Research Program, from a baseline in 1960–79 to 2009, average temperatures in the southwestern United States have risen about 1.5°F (0.8°C). By 2080–2099, increases of 4 to 10°F (2.2 to 5.6°C) were predicted, depending on the extent to which we are able to control carbon emissions. This will produce reduced precipitation for Nevada ranging from about a 40 percent decline in the very southern tip of the state to no perceptible change in the extreme northeastern corner. Most of the Colorado River basin will experience a 20 to 40 percent decline in precipitation, which, along with reduced snowpack will produce not only reduced flow, but also increased seasonal variability of flow. Scientists at the University of Maryland's Center for Integrative Environmental Research (CIER) note that as temperatures rise in Nevada, the state's already diminishing water supplies could grow more strained, energy demand could increase (as residents use more electricity to cool their homes in the summer), and

Nevada's attractiveness as a tourist destination—a major economic boon for the state—could decrease. According to The National Wildlife Federation, the strain on Nevada's water resources that global warming would cause could put stress on the state's wetland regions, resulting in the decline of waterfowl species that use the wetlands as breeding grounds. This decline could also lead to outbreaks of rangeland grasshoppers and other pests that would normally be kept in check by breeds of songbirds whose breeding range would shift out of the state.

On April 10, 2007, Nevada governor Jim Gibbons created by executive order the Nevada Climate Change Advisory Committee (NCCAC), which he charged with providing recommendations for how Nevada can reduce greenhouse gas emissions. One year later, the NCCAC submitted its final report. High among the committee's recommendations was the development of a climate change action plan. Nevada had not published its action plan as of June 2010.

🍂 Natural Resources, Water, and Agriculture

Unique Climate, Unique Resources: Forests

Forests cover about 12 percent of the state, with more than 92 percent under the management of the U.S. Forest Service and the Bureau of Land Management. The forests are divided into two types: timberland and woodlands. The woodlands consist primarily of a pinyon-juniper type, including Nevada's state tree—the single-leaf pinyon. There is some mountain mahogany at higher elevations. Various species of conifers dominate Nevada's timberlands, featuring ponderosa, western white, lodgepole, and Jeffrey pines; white and red fir; and incense cedar. The primary timber harvest is related to fuel management, which is the thinning of trees of in dense areas that are susceptible to forest fires. The

Nevada Division of Forestry (NDF) has been considering the potential for woody biomass collected in the state's forestlands. With a grant from the U.S. Forest Service, the NDF has implemented successful biomass energy production projects at the Northern Nevada Correctional Center in Carson City and David E. Norman Elementary School in Ely.

Parks and Wildlife

Nevada hosts 24 state parks and recreation areas and two national parks. Death Valley National Park (shared with California) contains some of the harshest desert lands in the nation, but still supports a variety of native species, including 51 species of mammals, 307 species of birds, 39 reptiles and amphibians, and more than 1,000 kinds of plants. Annual precipitation in the park ranges from 1.9 inches (4.8 cm) in the valley to more than 15 inches (38 cm) in the mountain ranges. The new Van Sickle CA/NV Bi-State Park opened in July 2011. Located on the California-Nevada boundary in South Lake Tahoe, it is the only bi-state park in the United States with a single entrance that provides access to both sides of the state line. The park contains land donated to the Nevada Division of State Parks by Jack Van Sickle in 1989 and additional land purchased by the State of California.

About 81 percent of the state is classified as rangeland, or shrub lands, with a variety of vegetation zones that featuring sagebrush (particularly in the north), salt desert scrub and Mojave mixed scrub, creosote (in the southern valleys), bitterbrush and mountain shrub, dry meadows, and perennial and annual grasslands.

According to Landscope, a land conservancy organization affiliated with the National Geographic Society, Nevada ranks eleventh among the 50 states in overall biodiversity, sixth in number of endemic species, third in the number of species at risk, and eleventh in the number of species extinctions. Native mammals include the desert bighorn sheep, black bear, white-tailed and mule deer, antelope, Rocky Mountain elk, river otter, and numerous nocturnal species adapted to avoid the daytime heat. Wild horses are also common in the state. Native bird species include the mountain bluebird, bald eagle, goshawk, red-tailed hawk, and peregrine falcon. The U.S. Fish and Wildlife Service lists thirty-four plant and animals species as threatened or endangered, including the desert tortoise, the cui-ui, a sucker fish found only in the saline Pyramid Lake, and the Devils Hole pupfish, a small bright bluish-colored fish isolated in a single cavern in southwestern Nevada just across the state line from Death Valley, California. Landscope's analysis of Nevada's conservation challenges cites the state's designation as one of the fastest growing states in the nation as a major factor in maintaining wildlife habitats. As more people inhabit Nevada, space and water will become greater challenges for conservationists.

Gold, Silver, and Abandoned Mines

The discovery of the Comstock Lode in 1859 is considered by many to be the most important event in U.S mining history. It was the first major silver discovery in the nation, with that precious metal accounting for about 57 percent of ore extracted from the district. The presence of gold in the lode was quickly discovered as well, accounting for about 42 percent of the take. This event marked the end of the California gold rush, as many miners in the region flocked to what is now Nevada in search of new claims. Nevada has been ranked as first in the nation for gold production since 1981, producing more than 70 percent of the nation's total in 2010. Nevada's gold production makes it the fourth largest producer in the world. The state has consistently ranked in first or second place for silver for many years, accounting for about 19 percent of total U.S. production in 2007. The state has ranked within the top ten for production of copper, barite, diatomite, lime, pumice, kaolin, and crude gypsum. Some mines produce mercury as a byproduct of gold and silver processing. Nevada is the only state that produces magnesite and lithium carbonate minerals.

As the gold and silver rush of the late 1800s drew to an end, numerous mines were left abandoned. As of 2011, the U.S. Bureau of Land Management reported an estimated 300,000 abandoned mine lands in the state, with about 50,000 considered to pose a significant risk to human health and safety. Of those, 50,000, nearly 600 have been permanently closed through the combined efforts of federal, state, and private agencies. About 15,000 have been discovered, inventoried, and fenced. Efforts to contain the rest are ongoing.

With Water, the Devil Is in the Desert

Nevada is one of the driest states in the nation and faces several water-related challenges. In total, water covers 663 square miles (1,717 sq km) of Nevada land, although much of Nevada's surface water is highly saline, and most Nevada communities rely primarily on groundwater for their domestic supply.

There are a number of large lakes and several large saline marshes, known as sinks. The largest lake is Pyramid in the west. Nevada shares Lake Tahoe with California, and Lake Mead—created by the Hoover Dam on the Colorado River in the southwest—with Arizona. The Humboldt River is the longest in the state, flowing through the north into the Humboldt Sink. The Walker, Truckee, and Carson Rivers drain the western part of Nevada.

In the 2000s, Nevada's water problems have been exacerbated by ongoing drought in the Colorado River Basin, the primary source of domestic water for the Las Vegas Valley, where more than 50 percent of Nevada's population resides. According to the Southern Nevada Water Authority—the agency responsible for

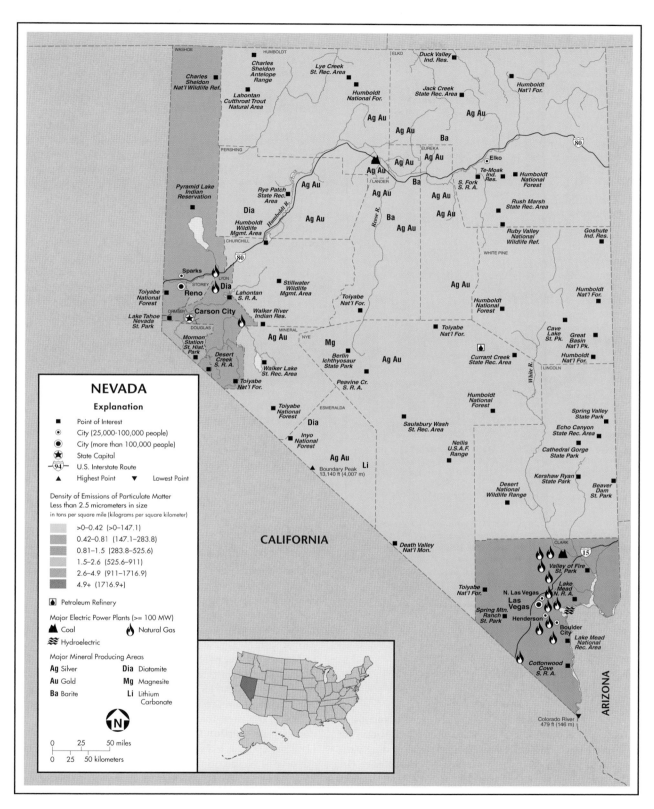

NEVADA

Explanation

■ Point of Interest
⊙ City (25,000-100,000 people)
◉ City (more than 100,000 people)
★ State Capital
—94— U.S. Interstate Route
▲ Highest Point   ▼ Lowest Point

Density of Emissions of Particulate Matter
Less than 2.5 micrometers in size
in tons per square mile (kilograms per square kilometer)

	>0–0.42 (>0–147.1)
	0.42–0.81 (147.1–283.8)
	0.81–1.5 (283.8–525.6)
	1.5–2.6 (525.6–911)
	2.6–4.9 (911–1716.9)
	4.9+ (1716.9+)

⬢ Petroleum Refinery

Major Electric Power Plants (>= 100 MW)
▲ Coal   ◗ Natural Gas
≋ Hydroelectric

Major Mineral Producing Areas

Ag Silver   Dia Diatomite
Au Gold   Mg Magnesite
Ba Barite   Li Lithium
                    Carbonate

Ⓝ

0   25   50 miles
0   25   50 kilometers

SOURCES: "County Emissions Map: Criteria Air Pollutants." *AirData*. U.S. Environmental Protection Agency. Available from http://www.
epa.gov/air/data/geosel.html; *Energy Maps*. U.S. Energy Information Administration. Available from http://www.eia.gov/state; *Highest
and Lowest Elevations*. U.S. Geological Survey. Available from http://egsc.usgs.gov/isb/pubs/booklets/elvadist/elvadist.html#Highest;
2007 Minerals Yearbook. U.S. Geological Survey. Available from http://minerals.usgs.gov/minerals/pubs/state. © *2011 Cengage Learning.*

Nevada State Profile

Physical Characteristics

Land area	109,780 square miles (284,329 sq km)
Inland water area	792 square miles (2,051 sq km)
Coastal area	NA
Highest point	Boundary Peak 13,140 feet (4,005 m)
National Forest System lands (2010)	5.7 million acres (2.3 million ha)
State parks (2011)	25

Energy Statistics

Total energy production (2009)	60 trillion Btu
State ranking in total energy production (2009)	46
Renewable energy net generation total (2009)	4.3 million megawatt hours
Hydroelectric energy generation (2009)	2.4 million megawatt hours
Biomass energy generation (2009)	NA
Wind energy generation (2009)	NA
Wood and derived fuel energy generation (2009)	1,000 megawatt hours
Crude oil reserves (2009)	NA
Natural gas reserves (2009)	NA
Natural gas liquids (2008)	NA

Pollution Statistics

Carbon output (2005)	43.3 million tons of CO_2 (39.3 million t)
Superfund sites (2008)	1
Particulate matter (less than 2.5 micrometers) emissions (2002)	4,731 tons per year (4,291 t/yr)
Toxic chemical releases (2009)	183.4 million pounds (83.2 million kg)
Generated hazardous waste (2009)	11,100 tons (10,100 t)

SOURCES: AirData. U.S. Environmental Protection Agency. Available from http://www.epa.gov/air/data; *Energy Maps, Facts, and Data of the U.S. States.* U.S. Energy Information Administration. Available from http://www.eia.gov/state; *The 2012 Statistical Abstract.* U.S. Census Bureau. Available from http://www.census.gov/compendia/statab; *United States Energy Usage.* eRedux. Available from http://www.eredux.net/states.

© 2011 Cengage Learning.

water supply to communities of Southern Nevada—water runoff into the Colorado River Basin was down 34 percent from 1999 to 2008, resulting in declining water levels in Lakes Mead and Powell.

As Nevada deals with a growing population, increased temperature and reduced precipitation due to climate change will exacerbate the problem of supplying water to people in the driest desert in North America. In 2008, the Southern Nevada Water Authority began construction of a third intake pipe, designed to take water from the deepest part of Lake Mead. The project was scheduled for completion in 2014, which officials hope will be before lake levels fall below one of the two existing intake structures. The $700-million project came at a time when water levels on Lake Mead had already dwindled well below historic levels, clearly evidenced by an ominous and growing "bathtub ring" around the reservoir.

Harsh Climate Limits Farming

Because Nevada's arid environment is not conducive to widespread farming, the state's agricultural sector remains relatively small. According to the U.S. Department of Agriculture (USDA), Nevada's 3,100 farms spanned roughly 5.9 million acres of land. The primary agricultural activity in the state is range livestock production, with cattle and calves predominating. Sheep and lambs are next in importance, with smaller operations of hogs, poultry, and horses. There are several dairy farms in the state as well. The primary agricultural crop is alfalfa hay, which is processed in cubes and compressed bales for export. Alfalfa seed is also produced for sale. Other main crops include potatoes, barley, winter and spring wheat, corn, and oats. Some types of apples are produced in the state, including gala, cameo, and red and golden delicious. Pistachios and pecans are important commodities in Nye County, in south-central Nevada.

The Nevada Department of Agriculture (NDOA) began its organic certification program in 1998. In August 2011, NDOA listed thirty-nine certified organic producers and handlers in the state. Nevada's organic farmers produce an assortment of food and farm products, from cut flowers to wheat to artichokes to livestock feeds. The USDA put the total value of Nevada's organic product sales at $2.8 million in 2008.

✿ Energy

Leader in Renewable Energy

Nevada's total energy consumption is low for a U.S. state, in part because Nevada's economy trends away from the energy intensive manufacturing sector in favor of tourism and recreation. The two largest sources of electricity for Nevada are natural gas and coal—imported fuels that supply roughly half and two-fifths of electricity generated in Nevada, respectively. Much of the natural gas used in Nevada is piped into the state from Utah and other Rocky Mountain states. Large, interstate pipelines crisscross Nevada, providing residents in Nevada—and California—access to this fuel. Interestingly, almost 70 percent of the natural gas piped into Nevada ends up supplying California. Coal, likewise, is also a largely imported fuel, arriving in Nevada on railcars and mixed with water via a 275-mile (550-km) pipeline from Arizona—the only such coal delivery pipeline in the world. The remainder of the electricity generated in Nevada (roughly 10 percent) is supplied by renewable energy supplies, such as geothermal, hydroelectric, and, increasingly, solar energy. In 2003, the Nevada legislature established a program to provide rebates and incentives to encourage development of solar energy systems for residential, business and public building use. The program was expanded in 2008 and renamed RenewableGenerations.

When the Hoover Dam (known as Boulder Dam until 1947) was completed in 1936, Nevada immediately became a leader in the renewable energy sector. Today, the state maintains that position. Although California is the largest beneficiary of energy produced at the Hoover Dam, Nevada continues to obtain tremendous amounts of electricity from the Hoover Dam as well—more than 23 percent of total production according to the U.S. Energy Information Administration. The state is also a leader in solar and geothermal energy production. In fact, California is the only state in the nation that provides more geothermal energy than Nevada.

Nevada was one of the first states in the nation to implement a renewable portfolio standard (RPS), putting forward its first RPS in 1997. In 2009, Nevada unveiled a new, more rigorous renewable portfolio standard, which mandated that at least 25 percent of its electricity come from renewable sources by 2025. Additionally, the standard required that 6 percent come from solar energy by 2016.

❧ Green Business, Green Building, Green Jobs

Rebates Reward Nevada's Renewable Businesses

Under Nevada's RenewableGenerations program, Nevada offers financial incentives to residents and small business owners, farmers, and school superintendents who install renewable energy systems on their properties and grounds. In doing so, the state effectively subsidizes certified Nevada businesses that operate in the green energy sector. Under the RenewableGenerations program, residents and business owners who hire a certified Nevada energy contractor to install green energy systems on their properties receive generous rebates for those systems. The RenewableGenerations Web site actively promotes Nevada-certified contractors, and offers a host of resources, training, and workshop opportunities to keep those businesses on the cutting edge of the field.

Sin City LEEDs with Silver Certifications

Because Nevada residents grapple with population growth, water shortages, and, in some cases, year-round air conditioning, analysts believe that green building will play an increasingly important role in Nevada. In addition to statewide and federally funded green building programs, large cities in the state have launched their own green building initiatives. In October 2006, the City of Las Vegas approved the Green Building Resolution, which jumpstarted the city's green building program.

Under the initial terms of the Las Vegas green building program, the city was required to make its "best effort" to ensure that city buildings and facilities were constructed to meet the U.S. Green Building Council's Silver LEED certification or higher. In August 2009, Las Vegas expanded this program, putting forth incentive packages for owners of residential and commercial buildings who make strides towards green design. The Green Building Special Revenue Fund increases the program's accessibility to funding by siphoning 25 percent of any incremental increase in utility franchise fees, up to $2.5 million per year.

Green Jobs

According to the Pew Charitable Trusts, Nevada experienced strong growth (nearly 29 percent) in the green jobs sector from 1998 to 2007. During those years, green job growth outpaced overall job growth in the state. In 2007, Nevada boasted more than 3,600 jobs in the clean energy economy, a sector that was attracting millions of dollars in venture capital each year. According to Nevada senator Harry Reid's web site, at least $3.15 billion of the 2009 American Recovery and Reinvestment Act poured into Nevada for environmental and clean energy projects, including a $97.5 million grant for clean energy job creation.

The University of Nevada at Reno is home to the Renewable Energy Center, where the university has centralized its research into renewable energy sources. In 2007, the university began offering a minor in Renewable Energy. The program has two tracks, one for engineering students who wish to add an additional specialization of alternative energy sources, and the second for students of other disciplines. The objective of the interdisciplinary minor is to provide students with technical skills, economic and political background, and analysis and design skills that will help them to apply the knowledge gained in their major to the important issues of alternative and renewable energy.

❧ Desert and Drought Strain Water Resources in Southern Nevada

Thirsty Las Vegas

As anyone who travels to Las Vegas knows, the city functions as a booming metropolis within the expansive Nevada desert, an artificial oasis within a sea of sand. From 1985 to the 2000 U.S. Census, the population of Las Vegas has more than doubled. Thus, city planners have been challenged to develop systems that allow ample freshwater resources to flow to this desert city and surrounding area. As of 2011, Las Vegas received roughly 90 percent of its water from Lake Mead, the famous reservoir created by impounded water from the Hoover Dam in 1936. However, there are serious questions about the sustainability of Lake Mead and the Colorado River, which feeds Lake Mead, as water sources.

Under the 1922 Colorado River Compact, sixteen million acre-feet of water are allocated per year from the Colorado River to the upper basin states (Colorado, New Mexico, Utah, and Wyoming), the lower basin states (Arizona, California, and Nevada), and Mexico—7.5 million acre-feet, 7.5 million acre-feet, and 1 million acre-feet, respectively. Yet these quotas overestimate how much water the Colorado River can actually supply. Flow on the Colorado River has only reached or exceeded sixteen million acre-feet per year in 28 of the past 80 years. Additionally, a sustained drought, which began in 1998, has further reduced water levels in Lake Mead. The drought caused water levels in Lake Mead to fall to their lowest level on record in 2010, requiring the Southern Nevada Water Authority (SNWA) to develop contingency options to supply the necessary water. However, the region received good news in the summer of 2011, when the lake's surface level rose 30 feet (9 m) due to a wet winter and a substantial snowpack in the Rocky Mountains. With the possibility of another rise of 40 feet (12 m) by the end of 2012, there seemed reason to hope that potential water shortages might be postponed.

A Race Against Time: Constructing the "Third Straw."

Supplying water to the growing Las Vegas population will be a major concern for generations of Nevada residents, but a more urgent, short-term concern has demanded immediate and expensive action from the state. The water level of Lake Mead had been falling dangerously below the two intake pipes that channel water from the lake to the city of Las Vegas and other localities. And while substantial snowpack in the Rocky Mountains during the previous winter resulted in elevated lake levels in 2011, there is still cause for concern. The prognosis for the possibility of water shortages was revised from 2011 to 2014. In 2008, the SNWA embarked on an ambitious project to construct a third intake pipe, commonly known as "the third straw." Positioned deeper than the other two intake pipes, the third straw will allow the SNWA to continue to draw water from the reservoir if water levels drop below the existing intake pipes. The $700-million project was expected to be completed by 2014. Given the difficult drought conditions gripping the area, project planners have expressed a deep sense of urgency about the project. "Failure is not an option," said Patricia Mulroy, the general manager of the SNWA in April 2010, of the third

intake project, tapping this sentiment. "[When water levels on Lake Mead fall to] 1,050 feet, we'll see the end of the Hoover Dam." As Mulroy made her ominous comments, water levels on Lake Mead stood precariously at a little over 1,080 feet (329 m), falling a dramatic 150 feet (46 m) from 2000 levels. If water levels declined to 1,050 feet (320 m), one of the two existing intake pipes would no longer be able to draw water, causing significant water challenges in Las Vegas. The second intake pipe fails to draw in water at 1,000 feet (305 m). In October 2010, the water level fell lower than it ever has since it was constructed 75 years ago, dropping to 1,083 feet (330 m) above sea level. However, the low level of Lake Mead illustrated the urgency for alternative water sources for the region and the continued construction of the intake pipe.

Construction of the intake pipe was proceeding according to plan until July 1, 2010, when an accident occurred as excavators hit a fault zone 600 feet (183 m) underground, causing a leak that slowly filled the excavated cavern. No workers were injured, but the accident temporarily ceased work. As of early 2011, the project's starter tunnel had filled up with mud and water three times. The contractor now plans on abandoning the tunnel and rerouting it in another direction in order to avoid the fault line that has been causing the issues so far. The original finish date for the project was 2013, but these construction changes delayed the projected completion until 2014. These setbacks bring attention to the possibility that engineering is not a fool-proof equalizer of demography combined with the effects of climate change on our resources.

Beyond the Hoover Dam

The SNWA also promotes other projects aimed at satisfying the water needs of Las Vegas and southern Nevada residents. One of these proposed projects would require construction of a 327-mile (526-km) underground pipeline, which would transport water from underground aquifers in central and eastern Nevada to the city. The pipeline would cost an eye-popping $3.5 billion, not including the cost of water transport. At a June 2011 University of Colorado conference focused on the Colorado River, SNWA head Pat Mulroy addressed the need for the pipeline and emphasized that cooperation among the states involved will be the key to resolving issues surrounding the sharing of water aquifers, such as the Snake Valley aquifer, which straddles the borders of Nevada and Utah.

Transporting the water would itself require feeding huge amounts of electricity to energy-hungry water pumps—an expensive task. Taking aim at the energy aspect of the project, the SNWA purchased in May 2010 a lease on several thousand acres of eastern Nevada land to explore the possibility of constructing a geothermal plant to power the pipeline. According to the *Las Vegas*

Nevada shares Lake Mead—created by the Hoover Dam on the Colorado River in the southwest—with Arizona. © Andy Z./ ShutterStock.com

Sun, the water authority was, at the time of the land lease, already the largest consumer of electricity in southern Nevada.

Clearly, the SNWA's efforts are driven by a constant demand for water. The need to address the underlying issue of consumption—and the question of how to reduce it—also remain critical aspects of the water authority's planning. SNWA officials set a goal in 2002 to reduce water use to 199 gallons per capita per day (GPCD) by 2035 in southern Nevada. Under the plan, southern Nevada reduced its water use by 25 percent from 2002 to 2009, from 314 GPCD to 240 GPCD. Conservation incentives play a critical role in reducing water consumption among Nevada residents. The Water Smart Landscapes Rebate program represents one incentive-based program run by SNWA to reduce water demand. Under the program, residents are given $1.50 per square foot per year (up to 5,000 square feet/465 sq m) to replace grass with water-saving desert landscaping. Since the program's inception, more than 150 million square feet (14,000,000 sq m) of lawn has been transformed into water-saving landscaping, which,

according to SNWA, has saved the community billions of gallons of water. While water conservation efforts by SNWA have been vigorous and commendable since implementation of their plan in 2002, comparisons with other cities in the southwestern United States demonstrate they still have ample opportunities for additional demand reduction. (See "Hidden Oasis: Water Conservation and Efficiency in Las Vegas" in the bibliography section below).

Looking to the Future, Looking to the East?

Even with successful per capita water reduction programs, as climate change continues and the Las Vegas population booms, Nevada will continue to experience challenges associated with water supply. These challenges will certainly generate innovative, if controversial, proposals—from the development of desalination plants, to wastewater regeneration, to proposals that advocate population stability rather than growth. The general manager of the SNWA advocated in February 2009 for the diversion of Midwestern water to the western United States to address water shortages. "We can't conserve our way out of a massive Colorado River drought," general manager Patricia Mulroy began. "We can't desalt our way out of a massive Colorado River drought. If the West is growing drier and the Midwest is growing wetter, I see that as an opportunity." Indeed, in Nevada, all options are on the table.

However, the Midwest states surrounding the Great Lakes are not so receptive to the idea. In 2008, Congress passed the Great Lakes-St. Lawrence River Basin Water Resources Compact, which gives the Midwest states affected greater control over the water in their region. Part of that compact is designed to prevent diverting water resources to Western and Southern states unless all eight Great Lakes states approve it. With non-neighboring states unwilling to share water resources, Nevada may have to continue its innovative ways to find new means of securing water for its growing population.

BIBLIOGRAPHY

Books

Donahue, Debra L. *The Western Range Revisited: Removing Livestock from Public Lands to Conserve Native Biodiversity.* Norman: University of Oklahoma Press, 2000.

Grayson, Donald K. *The Great Basin: A Natural Prehistory*, rev. ed., Berkeley, CA: University of California Press, 2011.

Holing, Dwight. *The Smithsonian Guides to Natural America: The Far West–California, Nevada.* Washington, DC: Smithsonian Books, 1996.

Web Sites

Barringer, Felicity. "Lake Mead Hits Record Low Level." October 18, 2010. *The New York Times.* Available from http://green.blogs.nytimes.com/2010/10/18/lake-mead-hits-record-low-level/?scp=2&sq=lake%20mead&st=Search

Brean, Henry. "Third Straw Excavation: Lake Mishap 'Not Devastating.'" *Las Vegas Review-Journal*. July 16, 2010. Available from http://www.lvrj.com/news/lake-mishap–not-devastating–98587584.html

"Biomass Program." Nevada Division of Forestry. Available from http://forestry.nv.gov/forestry-resources/biomass-program

"Certified Organic Producers and Handlers." Nevada Department of Agriculture. Available from http://agri.state.nv.us/Plant_PDF/MembersList.pdf

"Clean Energy Economy: Nevada." Pew Charitable Trusts. Available from http://www.pewcenter onthestates.org/uploadedFiles/wwwpewcenter onthestatesorg/Fact_Sheets/Clean_Economy_Factsheet_Nevada.pdf

Climate Change and the Economy. Nevada: Assessing the Costs of Climate Change. CIER Center. University of Maryland. Available from http://www.cier.umd.edu/climateadaptation/Climate%%20change–NEVADA.pdf

"Colorado River Compact." Available from http://www.usbr.gov/lc/region/pao/pdfiles/crcompct.pdf>

"Design Change to Delay Vegas Intake from Lake Mead." January 21, 2011. *Las Vegas Sun*. Available from http://www.lasvegassun.com/news/2011/jan/21/nv-vegas-water-lake-mead-1st-ld-write-thru/

"Economic Impacts of Climate Change on Nevada." CIER Center. University of Maryland. Available from http://www.cier.umd.edu/climateadapta tion/Nevada%%20Economic%%20Impacts%%20of%%20Climate%%20Change.pdf

"Economic Recovery Plan." Senator Harry Reid. Available from http://reid.senate.gov/issues/economy_arra.cfm#arraprojects

Edwards, Jerome. "Comstock Lode." ONE: Online Nevada Encyclopedia. Available from http://www.onlinenevada.org/comstock_lode

"Exporting Eastern Nevada Groundwater to Las Vegas." Sierra Club. Available from http://nevada.sierra club.org/conservation/pipelines/index.html

"First Detailed Map of Land-Cover Vegetation." U.S. Geological Survey. Available from http://www.usgs.gov/newsroom/article.asp?ID=2509

"Global Climate Change's Impacts on the U.S.: South west Region." United States Global Change Research Program. Available from http://www.globalchange.gov/publications/reports/scientific-assessments/us-impacts/full-report/regional-cli mate-change-impacts/southwest

"Global Warming and Nevada." The National Wildlife Federation. Available from http://www.nwf.org/Global-Warming/~/media/PDFs/Global%20Warming/Global%20Warming%20State%20Fact%20Sheets/Nevada.ashx

"Green Building Program." City of Las Vegas. Available from http://www.lasvegasnevada.gov/files/Green-BuildingProgramFINAL.pdf

"Hidden Oasis: Water Conservation and Efficiency in Las Vegas." The Pacific Institute. Available from http://www.westernresourceadvocates.org/media/pdf/hidden_oasis_low_res.pdf

"Hoover Dam Hydroelectric Plant." U.S. Energy Infor mation Administration. Available from http://www.eia.doe.gov/kids/energy.cfm?page=Hoover_Dam

"Low Water." National Park Service. United States Department of the Interior. Available from http://www.nps.gov/lake/naturescience/lowwater.htm

"Nevada Climate Change Advisory Committee Final Report." State of Nevada. Available from http://www.cier.umd.edu/climateadaptation/Nevada%20Economic%20Impacts%20of%20Climate%20Change.pdf

Nevada Department of Agriculture. Available from http://agri.nv.gov/AgInNevada.htm

"Nevada Minerals." U.S. Department of the Interior, Bureau of Land Management. Available from http://www.blm.gov/nv/st/en/prog/minerals.html

"Nevada Wildlife Action Plan." Landscope. Available from http://www.landscope.org/nevada/priorities/

"Nevada's Economic Recovery Projects." Senator Harry Reid. Available from http://reid.senate.gov/issues/economy_arra.cfm#arraprojects

Nevada 2007 Minerals Yearbook. United States Geolog ical Survey. Available from http://minerals.usgs.gov/minerals/pubs/state/2007/myb2-2007-nv.pdf

"Organic Production Survey (2008)." U.S. Department of Agriculture. http://www.agcensus.usda.gov/Publications/2007/Online_Highlights/Organics/ORGANICS.pdf

Renewable Energy Center. University of Nevada at Reno. Available from http://www.unr.edu/energy/index.html

"RenewableGenerations." Available from http://www.nvenergy.com/renewablesenvironment/renewable-generations/

Saulny, Susan. "Ban Near On Diverting Water To The Great Lakes." *The New York Times.* Available from http://www.nytimes.com/2008/09/23/us/23lakes.html

Shine, Conor. "Lake Mead's Water Level Rises 30 Feet After Wet Winter." *Las Vegas Sun* August 17, 2011. Available from http://www.lasvegassun.com/news/2011/aug/17/lake-meads-water-level-rises/

"Species Reports: Nevada. U.S. Fish and Wildlife Service." Available from http://ecos.fws.gov/tess_public/pub/stateListingAndOccurrenceIndividual.jsp?state=NV&s8fid=112761032792&s8fid=112762573902&s8fid=24012785214823

State Natural Resource Assessment. Department of Conservation and Natural Resources, Nevada Division of Forestry. Available from http://forestry.nv.gov/wp-content/uploads/2010/09/NV_state_assessment_web.pdf

"Van Sickle CA/NV Bi-State Park." Nevada Division of State Parks. Available from http://parks.nv.gov/masterplans/VanSickle/Van%20Sickle.htm

"Water Authority Eyes Power for Pipeline Plan." *Las Vegas Sun.* Available from http://www.lasvegassun.com/news/2010/may/31/water-authority-eyes-power-pipeline-plan/

"Water Smart Landscape Rebate." Southern Nevada Water Authority. Available from http://www.snwa.com/html/cons_wsl.html

New Hampshire

Nicknamed "the granite state" in reference to its geology and its tradition of self-sufficiency, New Hampshire is a small New England state, ranking forty-fourth in land area in the United States. New Hampshire's major recreational attractions include skiing, snowmobiling and other winter sports, hiking and mountaineering, observing the fall foliage, and summer cottages along many lakes and the seacoast. The White Mountain National Forest links the Vermont and Maine portions of the Appalachian Trail, and for those who do not hike, there is the Mount Washington Auto Road, where visitors may drive to the top of 6,288-foot (1,917-m) Mount Washington. Since the state relies heavily on recreation and the tourism industry, it has become vital to preserve and protect New Hampshire's environment, and in 2005 Governor John Lynch issued an executive order making the environment a priority for the state, establishing initiatives to steer the state towards a clean energy economy. These include requiring Energy Star equipment for all state agencies and departments, tracking and reducing energy and water use by state agencies, and other measures.

Climate

Like many New England states, New Hampshire has a varied climate. Each of the four seasons differ greatly in their daily temperatures and weather patterns. Climate variations can also result from distance from the ocean, mountains, lakes, or rivers. Spring arrives mid-March and with it the most unpredictable weather patterns of the year. Snow can be seen well into April. The varied weather patterns in the spring are replaced in mid-June by warm, sunny days and cool, clear nights during the summer months. Starting in late September to early October, the leaves begin to turn and the evening temperatures start dipping below freezing. The days, however, are usually fairly sunny and mild. Winter begins in late October when the first snow usually arrives and continues through March.

Taking Action against Climate Change. According to the National Wildlife Federation, climate change would have dire consequences for the state of New Hampshire. Forests are likely to shift from conifer and mixed forests to temperate deciduous forests, and species such as the sugar maple, of importance to hundreds of maple syrup producers, could disappear. Climate change has already had a significant impact on sugar maple trees, as ice storms and drought have caused widespread damage to groves in New Hampshire and other New England states. The value of the maple syrup crop remains significant, however, at about $5 million a year, constituting a small but vital part of the New Hampshire tourism experience. Animal species, such as the purple finch (the state bird), could also disappear as they shift out of state due to global warming, and higher water temperatures are likely to cause a decline in cold-water fish species in rivers. The sea level at Portsmouth Harbor is projected to rise 18 inches (46 cm) by 2100, which would cause the loss of sand beaches that could only be replenished at great cost.

In 2009, New Hampshire governor John Lynch's Climate Change Policy Task Force developed the New Hampshire Climate Change Action Plan. The purpose of the plan is to reduce greenhouse gas emissions while providing the greatest possible long-term economic benefits at the same time. The ultimate goal of the plan is to reduce emissions to 80 percent below 1990 levels by 2050, with a mid-term goal of 20 percent below 1990 levels by 2025. To do this, the Task Force made sixty-seven recommendations on ways to reduce emissions from buildings, electric generation, and transportation; protect natural resources; support regional and national initiatives to reduce greenhouse gases; develop an integrated education, outreach, and workforce training program; and adapt to the existing and potential climate change impacts. To accomplish this, the Task Force recommended the formation of the New Hampshire Energy and Climate Collaborative to oversee the implementation of the plan using a phased-in approach. The eighteen-member collaborative

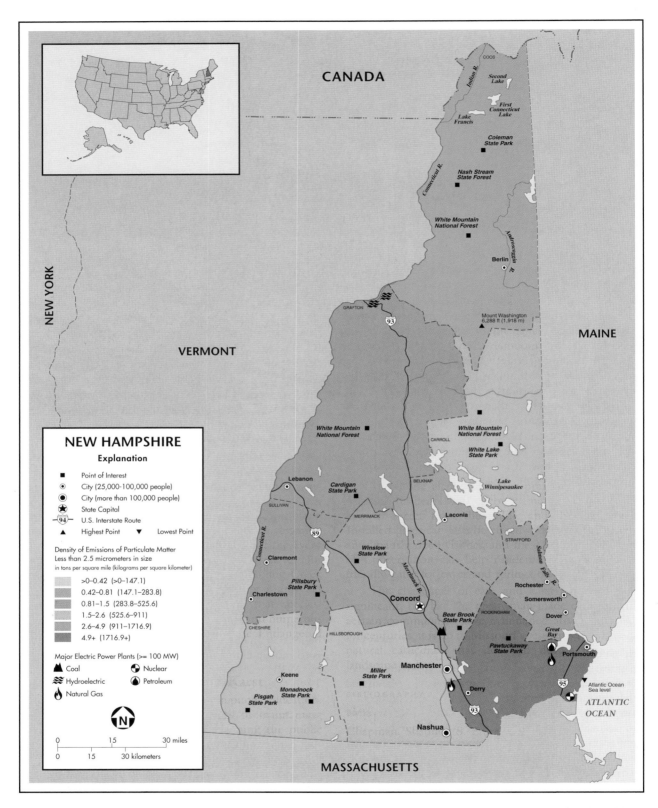

SOURCES: "County Emissions Map: Criteria Air Pollutants." *AirData.* U.S. Environmental Protection Agency. Available from http://www. epa.gov/air/data/geosel.html; *Energy Maps.* U.S. Energy Information Administration. Available from http://www.eia.gov/state; *Highest and Lowest Elevations.* U.S. Geological Survey. Available from http://egsc.usgs.gov/isb/pubs/booklets/elvadist/elvadist.html#Highest; *2007 Minerals Yearbook.* U.S. Geological Survey. Available from http://minerals.usgs.gov/minerals/pubs/state. © 2011 Cengage Learning.

consists of leaders from business, nonprofit, and public sectors. The group provides annual reports on its progress via a public website and provides resources for how New Hampshire residents can reduce their energy and water use.

New Hampshire is a member of the Regional Greenhouse Gas Initiative (RGGI), a cooperative cap-and-trade program involving ten Northeastern and Mid-Atlantic states. The program is designed with the goal to reduce power sector carbon dioxide emissions by 10 percent by 2018. To that end, the regional cap established by the group was set at 188 million short tons of carbon dioxide per year from 2009 to 2014. Starting in 2015 the cap will decrease by 2.5 percent each year. Carbon dioxide allowances for power plants can be obtained or traded in quarterly auctions. Each state may then reinvest its auction proceeds in programs that support the growth of a clean energy economy. In New Hampshire, the state's auction proceeds have been used to establish the Greenhouse Gas Emissions Reduction Fund. At least 10 percent of this fund is allocated in support of energy efficiency programs for low income consumers. The rest supports a variety of electric and fossil fuel energy efficiency programs. The first three-year control (or compliance) period began on January 1, 2009 and was set to end on December 31, 2011. At that time, each regulated power plant must submit one allowance for each ton of carbon dioxide emitted during the control period. The RGGI represents the first mandatory, market-based carbon dioxide emissions program in the United States.

❧ Natural Resources, Water, and Agriculture

Natural Resources

New Hampshire has 75 state parks, 58 state forests, and 32 wildlife management areas. The state's forests support an abundance of elm, maple, beech, oak, pine, hemlock, and fir trees. Among wild flowers, several orchids are considered rare. Nearly 84 percent of the state is covered with trees, and according to the University of New Hampshire Cooperative Extension, forest-based manufacturing is the third largest manufacturing industry in the state. The contribution of the forest industry and forest-related tourism to the New Hampshire economy is more than $2 billion each year, or 4 percent of the Gross State Product. Direct payment of the timber tax to municipalities averages $4 million each year. In addition, the registration of logging trucks, trailers and other equipment contributes hundreds of thousands of dollars each year to the State of New Hampshire and its municipalities.

Among native New Hampshire mammals are the white-tailed deer, muskrat, beaver, porcupine, and snowshoe hare. Hunting in New Hampshire remains popular, despite decreases in registered hunters. Popular animals to hunt include the white-tailed deer, the black bear, moose, and wild turkey. Trapping for furs is also popular, with the 2008/2009 fur harvest valuing $102,767 based on average pelt value.

The U.S. Fish and Wildlife Service lists nine animal species occurring in the state as federally threatened or endangered, including the Karner blue butterfly, Canada lynx, and leatherback sea turtle. There are three listed endangered plant species, which are the northeastern bulrush, Jesup's milk-vetch, and small whorled pogonia.

Since 2000, the state legislature has funded a Land and Community Heritage Program (LCHIP). In 2002, several organizations—the Audubon Society of New Hampshire, the New Hampshire Division of Forests and Lands, the New Hampshire Fish and Gem Department, the Society for the Protection of New Hampshire Forests, the Nature Conservancy, and the University of New Hampshire Cooperative Extension—joined together to establish the Living Legacy Project, which built on the Ecological Reserve System Project established in 1995. The Living Legacy Project's objective is to coordinate efforts to protect the biodiversity of the state through voluntary preservation of public and private lands.

While New Hampshire does not have any fossil fuel reserves, non-fuel minerals are a vital part of the state's economy. According to a 2008 U.S. Geological Survey, the value of New Hampshire's non-fuel minerals was $101 million. And based on a 2007 report from the National Mining Association, the industry in New Hampshire employed 850 workers in 129 mines with an average annual income of $51,000. All told, New Hampshire's mining operations resulted in $120 million worth of mineral, metal and fuel products. Minerals mined in the state include gemstones, sand and gravel for construction, and crushed and dimension stone.

Water

There are nearly 1,000 lakes and ponds larger than 10 acres and more than 3,000 small ponds in New Hampshire, of which the largest is Lake Winnipesaukee, covering 70 square miles (181 sq km). According to the New Hampshire Department of Environmental Services, some lakes, such as Lake Massabesic in Manchester and Penacook Lake in Concord, are used as public water supplies and have partial or total restrictions on recreational uses, but the most popular uses for most lakes are swimming and boating, followed by fishing. In fact, New Hampshire has approximately 170 public beaches on lakes and ponds. Some of the most popular sports fishing catches include smallmouth and largemouth bass; brook, rainbow, lake, and brown trout; pickerel; white and yellow perch; landlocked salmon; and northern pike.

The principal rivers are the Connecticut (forming the border with Vermont), Merrimack, Salmon Falls,

The Mount Washington Hotel, a National Historic Landmark, opened in 1902. © *Chee-Onn Leong/ShutterStock.com*

Piscataqua, Saco, and Androscoggin. Near the state's 18 miles of seacoast are the nine rocky Isles of Shoals, three of which belong to New Hampshire. According to a report from the University of New Hampshire Cooperative Extension, commercial fish landings were valued at about $17.3 million in 2009. While the annual catch generally includes about thirty commercial species of fish, American lobster, Atlantic cod, and pollock account for nearly 90 percent of the overall catch by economic value. These three species along with Atlantic herring and spiny dogfish account for 90 percent of the overall catch by weight. Four species of sea turtles and the finback whale can be found in the coastal waters; all of these are included on the federal list for threatened or endangered species.

About 10 percent of the state land area is covered by wetlands, which include tidal marshes and mud flats, freshwater red maple swamps, bogs, vernal pools, Atlantic white cedar swamps, and wet meadows.

Agriculture

According to the U.S. Department of Agriculture, in 2009 New Hampshire was home to 4,150 farms covering 470,000 acres of land. Top crop items in the state are forage, corn for silage, vegetables, cut Christmas trees, and apples. Top livestock items were layers (hens that produce eggs), pullets (hens that lay eggs for flock replacement), cattle and calves, chickens for meat, and horses and ponies. When it comes to value of sales by commodity group, the nursery and floriculture industry ranks highly at $65 million annually in sales.

Relative to the size of the state, organic farming is a small enterprise in New Hampshire. According to the U.S. Department of Agriculture, there were 102 certified organic operations in the state in 2008 covering a total of 8,447 acres (3,418 ha) with total sales of $10.7 million. While most organic production is dedicated to livestock and poultry, the state's organic farms also produce hay, vegetables, a small amount of fruit, and maple syrup.

✤ ENERGY

New Hampshire does not have any fossil fuel reserves. The state receives petroleum products from the United States and abroad at Portsmouth, on the Atlantic coast. New Hampshire households are among the most petroleum-dependent in the United States, as more than one-half of New Hampshire homes use fuel oil as their

New Hampshire State Profile

Physical Characteristics

Land area	8,952 square miles (23,186 sq km)
Inland water area	328 square miles (850 sq km)
Coastal area	NA
Highest point	Mount Washington 6,288 feet (1,917 m)
National Forest System lands (2010)	736,000 acres (298,000 ha)
State parks (2011)	75

Energy Statistics

Total energy production (2009)	140 trillion Btu
State ranking in total energy production (2009)	43
Renewable energy net generation total (2009)	2.9 million megawatt hours
Hydroelectric energy generation (2009)	1.7 million megawatt hours
Biomass energy generation (2009)	151,000 megawatt hours
Wind energy generation (2009)	62,000 megawatt hours
Wood and derived fuel energy generation (2009)	984,000 megawatt hours
Crude oil reserves (2009)	NA
Natural gas reserves (2009)	NA
Natural gas liquids (2008)	NA

Pollution Statistics

Carbon output (2005)	20.5 million tons of CO_2 (18.6 million t)
Superfund sites (2008)	20
Particulate matter (less than 2.5 micrometers) emissions (2002)	2,696 tons per year (2,445 t/yr)
Toxic chemical releases (2009)	2.9 million pounds (1.3 million kg)
Generated hazardous waste (2009)	4,500 tons (4,100 t)

SOURCES: AirData. U.S. Environmental Protection Agency. Available from http://www.epa.gov/air/data; *Energy Maps, Facts, and Data of the U.S. States.* U.S. Energy Information Administration. Available from http://www.eia.gov/state; *The 2012 Statistical Abstract.* U.S. Census Bureau. Available from http://www.census.gov/compendia/statab; *United States Energy Usage.* eRedux. Available from http://www.eredux.net/states.

© 2011 Cengage Learning.

primary energy source for home heating during the state's long, cold winters. As a result of this, New Hampshire, along with much of the Northeast, is vulnerable to distillate fuel oil shortages and price spikes during the winter months. In July 2000, then President Bill Clinton directed the U.S. Department of Energy to establish the Northeast Heating Oil Reserve in order to avoid future shortages. The Reserve gives Northeast consumers adequate supplies of oil for about 10 days, the time required for ships to carry heating oil from the Gulf of Mexico to New York Harbor. Because four counties in densely populated areas of southeastern New Hampshire have had high levels of ground-level ozone, in order to comply with federal Clean Air Act requirements the state now requires gasoline stations in areas not attaining clean air standards to supply reformulated motor gasoline. Reformulated gasoline is a blended fuel that evaporates more slowly, and has lower benzene content, adequate oxygen content, and no heavy metals.

Natural gas is piped into the state from Maine and Canada, and about half of the supply that comes into the state is shipped on to Massachusetts. Consumption of natural gas in the state is relatively low, but demand is growing for electricity consumption.

From the early 1990s to 2002, the 1,245-megawatt Seabrook nuclear plant, the largest nuclear reactor in New England, supplied about half of the state's electrical power. It now supplies about 39 percent, while coal, natural gas, and petroleum together supply a little less than half of the state's electrical power. Renewables, which are growing rapidly, and hydropower make up about 10 percent.

Promoting Renewable Energy

Lacking fossil fuel reserves, New Hampshire has focused on its potential for renewable energy. In addition to tapping hydroelectric potential, the state has initiatives to develop energy from wind, solar, wood, landfill gas, and municipal solid waste. The Sustainable Energy Division of the Public Utility Commission administers the state's new Renewable Energy Fund and the Greenhouse Gas Emissions Reduction Fund. The two funds support energy efficiency and renewable energy projects and initiatives.

Working together, the Renewable Energy and Energy Efficiency Business Loan Program of the New Hampshire Business Resource Center (BRC) and People's United Bank provide low-interest loans to small businesses to purchase structural and equipment improvements that reduce energy consumption. A variety of energy efficiency measures and renewable energy systems are eligible for financing of $10,000 or more, with a maximum term of seven years. Participants use energy cost savings to repay the loan.

In 2009 the New Hampshire Public Utilities Commission selected the New Hampshire Business Finance Authority (BFA) to establish a revolving-loan program for businesses in the state to finance energy efficiency upgrades. All businesses, including nonprofits, are eligible to apply, and the minimum loan begins at $100,000. The BFA was provided $2 million to start the program, and it will work with interested applicants to customize a loan package that results in increased energy efficiency and financial savings for the company.

In 2007, New Hampshire enacted a renewable portfolio standard (RPS). The RPS requires that 25 percent of the state's electricity be generated from renewable sources by 2025. This is to be met by providers acquiring renewable energy certificates (RECs) equivalent to 23.8 percent of retail electricity sold to end-use customers by 2025.

❧ Green Business, Green Building, Green Jobs

Green Business

Following the implementation of the state's Climate Action Plan, the Green Launching Pad was founded at the University of New Hampshire (UNH), and is affiliated with Recovery.gov (the U.S. government's official website that provides easy access to data related to American Recovery and Reinvestment Act spending) and the New Hampshire Office of Energy and Planning. The Green Launching Pad supports and stimulates the emergence of new green businesses in the state, using a team made up of technical, scientific, and business faculty and students at UNH and statewide. The organization also plans to host seminars and information sessions to reach out to entrepreneurs, to existing green businesses that may have new product or process ideas, and to faculty at New Hampshire universities. Another role the Green Launching Pad aims to play is helping new companies form, create jobs, and contribute to the state's economy, while at the same time reducing the state's carbon emissions and energy use in sustainable ways. An example of a company taking part in the program is EnerTrac, a company that provides low-cost remote monitoring equipment for a variety of industries. This company participated in the inaugural year of The Green Launching Pad program, and developed smart meters designed to help fuel oil and propane companies monitor and reduce greenhouse gas emissions. "Creating and encouraging ventures like this is at the heart of our mission at UNH, and it is critical to helping our nation compete in an emerging green and global economy," said Mark Huddleston, President of the University of New Hampshire.

In 2008, the New Hampshire Department of Environmental Services (NHDES) published the *Making Your Business Greener Workbook.* The book provides basic guidance to small businesses to make their facilities and operations "greener." Checklists are provided to guide the reader through a series of decisions for implementing a number of initiatives. Some of these initiatives are more general and can apply to all businesses, while some are more business-specific. The workbook is intended as a starting point for businesses to begin making decisions on greening their operations, and experts and consultants may need to be utilized when it comes to more specific technologies and needs. The workbook supplements a series of factsheets and guidebooks issued by NHDES, including its *2007 Planning for Profits, a Guide to Pollution Prevention for NH Businesses,* and its Pollution Prevention technical assistance program, that provides non-regulatory, free and confidential assistance to New Hampshire businesses, municipalities, public agencies, organizations and residents. The Pollution Prevention assistance program helps businesses comply with environmental regulations and find improvements in process or changes in material use that avoid waste and pollutant releases, and provides information on vendors of greener products and equipment.

Green Building

In 2002, New Hampshire adopted a mandatory statewide building code based on the 2000 International Energy Conservation Code (IECC). Senate Bill 81 was enacted in July 2007, which upgraded the New Hampshire Energy Code to the 2006 IECC, and it was upgraded again in December 2009. The New Hampshire State Building Code Review Board adopted IECC 2009 as the new statewide code effective April 1, 2010. By implementing the 2009 IECC statewide, New Hampshire businesses and homeowners are projected to save an estimated $16 million annually by 2020 and $31 million annually by 2030 in energy costs due to more energy efficient buildings. Additionally, implementing the code will help avoid about 3 trillion Btu of primary annual energy use by 2030 and annual emissions of more than 0.2 million metric tons of CO_2 by 2030.

Also, in 2005, New Hampshire's governor John Lynch signed Executive Order 2005-04, committing the state to the Energy Star Challenge of improving energy efficiency in state-occupied buildings by 10 percent. The New Hampshire Department of Administrative Services (DAS) was required to implement an energy information system, including an energy efficiency rating, to measure agencies' progress towards achieving this goal. All agencies and departments were required to implement this system to track energy and water usage and to benchmark energy. Agencies and departments are also required to purchase Energy Star equipment unless exempt by a waiver from the DAS. The order specifies that new construction and renovation designs should exceed the state energy code by at least 20 percent, and energy modeling should be used during the design processes.

Along with these state programs, the Home Builders and Remodelers Association of New Hampshire's (HBRANH) Build Green NH program offers verification and certification services to home builders in the state, assuring buyers that their homes meet the strict benchmarks established by the National Association of Home Builders' Green Building Program, or NAHBGreen. To qualify for NAHBGreen certification, homes must meet energy-efficiency benchmarks at least 15 percent more stringent than most building codes or equivalent to the voluntary Energy Star program of the U.S. Department of Energy and Environmental Protection Agency. Homes must also meet criteria for water and other resource efficiency, indoor environmental quality, and lot and site development. They also come with operations and maintenance materials for homeowners to help them maximize the benefits of a green home.

Green Jobs

In 2011 The Brookings Institute released its report on the green economy called "Sizing The Clean Economy." This report addressed the state of the nation's energy situation and green economy in the wake of a recession that began in 2008. The number of New Hampshire's green jobs fell slightly from 2009 to 2011, but still held strong at nearly 13,000 jobs, with an average wage of $40,773. According to a 2009 report, "New Hampshire's Green Economy and Industries: Current Employment and Future Opportunities," from researchers at the Whittemore School of Business & Economics at the University of New Hampshire, nearly 50 percent of those jobs fell under the category of smart technology industries. Those are defined as jobs that provide research, production, or services that directly or indirectly relate to technological improvements in the four other categories noted in the survey: energy efficiency, renewable energy, green transportation, and environmental services. The largest smart technology industries in the state were noted as electronic instruments and computer and electronic manufacturing. About 25 percent of the total green jobs were in energy efficiency, followed by 20 percent in environmental services, 3 percent in green transportation, and 1 percent in renewable energy. From 2001 to 2007, the number of green jobs within the state increased overall by about 1.7 percent. Jobs in renewable energy increased by 15 percent during this time period. While this data indicates that the state shows a particular strength in the field of smart technology, state policies that support the use of renewable energy, such as the 2007 renewable Portfolio Standards and participation in the regional Greenhouse Gas Initiative, are intended to promote growth in all of the cited sectors.

❧ The University of New Hampshire's Stormwater Center: Working to Reduce Stormwater Runoff Pollution

Uncontrolled stormwater runoff is a big source of water pollution in many places across the United States, and there are national stormwater regulations that are requiring cities to act on this issue. Stormwater runoff occurs when rain and snowmelt runs over impervious surfaces and does not percolate into the ground. As it runs over the surface, the water accumulates debris, chemicals, sediment, or other pollutants that could adversely affect water quality if the runoff is discharged into rivers, streams, lakes, or coastal waters untreated.

In response to the need to educate communities about how to better handle this issue, the University of New Hampshire created their Stormwater Center. The mission of the Center is the protection of water resources through effective stormwater management, and the Center runs a facility that conducts controlled testing of stormwater management designs and devices. The Center's field research facility serves as a site for testing stormwater treatment processes and for technology demonstrations and workshops. The testing results and technology demonstrations are meant to assist in the planning, design, and implementation of effective stormwater management strategies for resource managers.

Along with the Primary Field Facility, the Center has a "pervious" concrete (allowing water to penetrate instead of running off) parking lot and an asphalt parking lot that is also porous. Future testing sites include a green roof and pervious pavement. Stormwater controls that have been or are currently being tested include:

- 6 Conventional Best Management Practices (BMPs), some of which include different types of swale—a drainage ditch that is lined with either stones or vegetation to filter out pollutants and direct stormwater—and a detention basin that is designed to protect against flooding and downstream erosion by storing water for a limited period of a time.

- 8 Low Impact Development Devices, some of which include bioretention systems which use vegetation, such as trees, shrubs, and grasses, to remove pollutants from stormwater runoff. Sources of runoff are diverted into bioretention systems directly as overland flow or through a stormwater drainage system. Alternatively, a bioretention system can be constructed directly in a drainage channel or swale. Another device is a subsurface gravel wetland—a system that approximates the look and function of a natural wetland, effectively removing sediments and other pollutants commonly found in runoff, while enhancing the visual appeal of the landscape. It relies on a dense root mat, crushed stone, and a microbe rich environment to treat water quality.

- 11 Manufactured Devices, some of which include 5 hydrodynamic separators (HDS)—and systems that use the physics of flowing water to remove a variety of pollutants and are characterized by an internal structure that creates a swirling vortex. By using the vortex flow of water, along with supplemental features to reduce velocity, the system separates floatables such as trash, debris, oil, and settleable particles, like sediment, from stormwater. However, HDS systems alone, without settling or retention systems, are not effective for the removal of very fine solids or dissolved pollutants.

Efforts to reach out to and educate the community about stormwater runoff include routine Stormwater Technology Demonstration Workshops and annual meetings for professional associations and government agencies. As of 2010, about 1,700 people had participated in the workshops. The Center also publishes a Biannual Data Report on stormwater system performance, has presentations at regional and national venues, website resources, an Innovative Stormwater Management Database for the region, and provides publications in refereed journals. The Center's Technical Advisory Board includes academics, state and federal regulators, local government officials, and industry representatives that provide advice and expertise on dealing with the issue of stormwater runoff.

BIBLIOGRAPHY

Books

Collette, Bruce B., and Grace Klein-McPhee. *Bigelow and Schroeder's Fishes of the Gulf of Maine*, 3rd ed. Washington, DC: Smithsonian Books, 2002.

Wetherell, W. D. *The Smithsonian Guides to Natural America: Northern New England–Vermont, New Hampshire, Maine*. Washington, DC: Smithsonian Books, 1995.

Web Sites

Carbee, Hunter, and Sarah Smith. "Forest Products Road Manual." University of New Hampshire Cooperative Extension. Available from http://extension.unh.edu/resources/files/Resource000252_Rep272.pdf

The Clean Energy Economy: New Hampshire. The Pew Charitable Trusts. Available from http://www.pewcenteronthestates.org/uploadedFiles/wwwpewcenteronthestatesorg/Fact_Sheets/Clean_Economy_Factsheet_NewHampshire.pdf

"The Economic Importance Of New Hampshire's Forest-Based Economy: 2011." New Hampshire Division of Forests & Lands. Available from http://www.nefainfo.org/NEFA%20NH%20Forest%20Econ%20Impor%202011.pdf

Gittell, Ross, et al. *New Hampshire's Green Economy and Industries: Current Employment and Future Opportunities*. University of New Hampshire. Available from http://carbonsolutionsne.org/resources/reports/pdf/green_jobs_report_final.pdf

Global Warming and New Hampshire. The National Wildlife Federation. Available from http://www.nwf.org/Global-Warming/~/media/PDFs/Global%20Warming/Global%20Warming%20State%20Fact%20Sheets/NewHampshire.ashx

"Gov. Lynch, U.S. Energy Secretary Chu, UNH President Huddleston Announce Companies Chosen For Green Launching Pad." University of New Hampshire. April 28, 2011. Available from http://www.unh.edu/news/cj_nr/2011/apr/lw28green.cfm

Green Economy: The Current Status of Green Jobs in New Hampshire. State of New Hampshire. Available from http://www.nh.gov/nhes/elmi/pdfzip/specialpub/infocus/GreenEconomy.pdf

Green Launching Pad. Available from http://www.greenlaunchingpad.org/home

Lynch, John. Executive Order 2005-4. Available from http://www.sos.nh.gov/EXECUTIVE%20ORDERS/Lynch2005-4.pdf

Magnusson, Matt. "The Economic Impact of New Hampshire's Seafood Industry:Opportunity for Sustainability." University of New Hampshire Cooperative Extension. Available from http://extension.unh.edu/CommDev/documents/Seafood_Economy.pdf

Making Your Business Greener Workbook. New Hampshire Department of Environmental Services. Available from http://des.nh.gov/organization/commissioner/pip/publications/general/green_business_wkbook.pdf

"Mining in New Hampshire." National Mining Association. Available from http://www.nma.org/pdf/states/econ/nh.pdf

New Hampshire. U.S. Energy and Information Administration. Available from http://www.eia.doe.gov/state/state_energy_profiles.cfm?sid=NH

The New Hampshire Climate Action Plan. New Hampshire Climate Change Policy Task Force. Available from http://des.nh.gov/organization/divisions/air/tsb/tps/climate/action_plan/documents/nhcap_final.pdf

New Hampshire Division of Forests and Lands. Available from http://www.nhdfl.org/

New Hampshire Energy & Climate Collaborative. Available from http://www.nhcollaborative.org/index.shtml

New Hampshire Renewable Portfolio Standard. Available from http://www.puc.state.nh.us/Sustainable%20Energy/Renewable_Portfolio_Standard_Program.htm

New Hampshire State Parks. Available from http://www.nhstateparks.org/explore/state-parks.aspx

New Hampshire Water Resources Primer. New Hampshire Department of Environmental Services. Available from http://des.nh.gov/organization/divisions/water/dwgb/wrpp/documents/water_resources_primer.pdf

"NH BFA—Business Energy Conservation Revolving Loan Fund." New Hampshire Incentives/Policies for Renewables & Efficiency. Available from http://www.dsireusa.org/incentives/incentive.cfm?Incentive_Code=NH35F&re=1&ee=1

NH Climate. NewHampshire.com. Available from http://www.newhampshire.com/about-nh/nh-climate-info.aspx

Organic Production Data Sets. U.S. Department of Agriculture. Available from http://www.ers.usda.gov/Data/Organic/

Regional Greenhouse Gas Initiative: New Hampshire State Investment Plan. Available from http://www.rggi.org/rggi_benefits/program_investments/New_Hampshire

"Renewable Energy and Energy Efficiency Business Loan." New Hampshire Incentives/Policies for Renewables & Efficiency. Available from http://www.dsireusa.org/incentives/incentive.cfm?Incentive_Code=NH16F&re=1&ee=1

2009 State Agricultural Overview: New Hampshire. U.S. Department of Agriculture. Available from http://www.nass.usda.gov/Statistics_by_State/Ag_Overview/AgOverview_NH.pdf

University of New Hampshire Stormwater Center. Available from http://www.unh.edu/erg/cstev/

U.S. Fish and Wildlife Service Species Reports: Listings and occurrences for New Hampshire. Available from http://ecos.fws.gov/tess_public/pub/stateListingAndOccurrenceIndividual.jsp?state=NH&s8fid=112761032792&s8fid=112762573902&s8fid=24012845832973

Value of Maple Syrup Crop. Available from http://www.nass.usda.gov/Statistics_by_State/New_England_includes/Publications/0605mpl.pdf

New Jersey

Though it ranks as one of the smallest states in the union, New Jersey is a powerhouse when it comes to existing and potential energy resources. The state is positioned as a major Northeastern distribution center for natural gas and petroleum products and is home to the largest of three storage terminals that make up the Northeast Home Heating Oil Reserve. At home, New Jersey's three nuclear power plants provide more than 50 percent of the electric supply for the state. Despite this abundance of more traditional energy sources, the state is actively exploring the potential of cleaner, renewable energy sources through the 2008 adoption of an Energy Master Plan, designed to support development of new green energy infrastructure. This greening of the Garden State is expected to change the face of the local economy, creating new jobs for the state and positioning the state as a national leader in renewable energy resources. Chief among these is offshore wind power, which is emerging as the leading option for renewable energy. As of 2011, there were multiple wind farm projects in the works.

Climate

Most of New Jersey has a moderate climate with cold winters and warm, humid summers. The average annual rate of precipitation throughout the state is about 45 inches (114 cm). The climate is strongly affected by the westerlies, the prevailing winds that generally flow west to east. These winds generally have a moderating effect on the climate, but sometimes bring violent thunderstorms and an occasional hurricane.

The Global Warming Response Act Rising temperatures and rising sea levels as a result of global climate change could have a serious impact on the state's natural resources. According to a report from the National Wildlife Federation, sea levels along the Atlantic Coast of the state could rise by as much as 27 inches (68.5 cm) by 2100, inundating existing coastal ecosystems. Rising temperatures, particularly in the summer months, could create an unhealthy breeding environment for the state's songbirds, which are important to the state because of their appetite for certain invasive pests.

In response to the potential threats of climate change, the state initiated the New Jersey Global Warming Response Act in 2007. This law mandates a statewide reduction of greenhouse gas emissions to 1990 levels by 2020, followed by a further reduction to 80 percent below 2006 levels by 2050. Strategies for achieving these goals are outlined in *Meeting New Jersey's 2020 Greenhouse Gas Limit: New Jersey's Global Warming Response Act Recommendations Report*, published in 2009. A dominant strategy focuses on energy efficiency and energy conservation, the development of alternative energy sources is important as well.

The Global Warming Response Act is supplemented by the New Jersey 2008 Energy Master Plan (EMP), which sets statewide energy reduction and energy efficiency goals. The six action items proposed in the EMP were projected to reduce statewide energy consumption by 20 percent by 2020 and also bring about a significant decrease in the amount of greenhouse gas emissions from the electricity and heating sector through the development of clean energy technologies, particularly wind and solar energy sources. According to the 2008 EMP, implementation of the EMP scenario could achieve greenhouse gas emissions in 2020 that are 23 percent below the target set by the Global Warming Act of reaching 1990 levels by that time.

New Jersey was a founding member of the Regional Greenhouse Gas Initiative (RGGI), a cooperative cap-and-trade program involving ten Northeastern and Mid-Atlantic states that started controlling carbon dioxide emissions from the power sector in 2009. The program is designed with the goal to reduce these emissions by 10 percent by 2018. To that end, a regional cap on carbon dioxide emissions was established by the group and set at 188 million short tons of CO_2 emissions per year from 2009 to 2014. Starting in 2015 the cap will decrease by 2.5 percent each year. Carbon dioxide allowances for power plants can be obtained or traded in quarterly auctions. Each state may then reinvest its auction proceeds in programs that support the growth of a clean energy economy. The first three-year control (or compliance) period began on January 1, 2009, and was set to end on December 31, 2011. At that time, each regulated power plant must submit one allowance for each ton of carbon dioxide emitted during the control period. The RGGI represents the first mandatory, market-based carbon dioxide emissions program in the United States. However, in May 2011, Governor Chris Christie announced New Jersey would withdraw from the program, saying it was an ""ineffective"" way to reduce emissions. Christie said the state instead would focus on bolstering other energy sources like solar, wind, and natural gas. Remaining members of the cooperative cited the more than $700 million in clean energy investments resulting from RGGI as proof of its success. Critics called it a blow to the state"s efforts to reduce its reliance on conventional and typically higher-emitting power sources.

⚘ Natural Resources, Water, and Agriculture

The Pine Barrens

About 42 percent of New Jersey is forested. The state's most notable forest region is the Pinelands National Reserve, also known as the Pine Barrens. Established by an act of Congress in 1978, the Pinelands National Reserve was the first national reserve in the country. Located in the Atlantic Outer Coastal Plain of the southern part of the state, the reserve occupies about 22 percent of the state's land area. Low, dense forests of pine and oak are predominant in the region, with cedar and hardwood swamps in some areas as well. There are about 12,000 acres of pygmy forest here, consisting of mature pine and oak trees that are less than 11 feet (3.3 m) tall. The region also supports more than 850 plant species, including the rare curly grass fern and broom cowberry. Urban development and invasive plant and insect species are the primary challenges to forest health.

The Delaware Water Gap and Gateway national recreation areas cover parts of New Jersey. New Jersey has 54 state parks, forests, and recreation areas covering more than 422,000 acres (170,778 ha). According to the New Jersey Division of Fish and Wildlife, the state is home to more than 400 vertebrate wildlife species. Some common species of mammal include opossum, raccoon, cottontail rabbits, a variety of squirrels, muskrats, voles, and red and grey fox. Black bears and eastern coyote can be found in some parts of the state. The U.S. Fish and Wildlife Service lists 21 species of plants and animals currently found in the state as threatened or endangered. The animals include the Indiana bat, dwarf wedgemussel, shortnose sturgeon, and bog turtle, while the plants include the seabeach amaranth and small whorled pogonia.

The primary minerals produced in the state include crushed stone and construction sand and gravel. New Jersey is the only state that produces greensand marl, which is used as an organic soil conditioner and fertilizer and as a water filtration medium to remove soluble iron and manganese from well water.

Water: Ports for Shipping and Fishing

New Jersey's major rivers include the Delaware, Passaic, Hackensack, and Raritan. The largest natural lake in the state is Lake Hopatcong. The Delaware River Basin, which covers more than 13,500 square miles in New Jersey, Pennsylvania, New York, and Delaware, serves as a major resource for more than 15 million people, providing water for drinking, agricultural, and industrial use. This important resource is managed primarily through the work of the Delaware River Basin Commission (DRBC). The commission was established in 1961 through the passage of concurrent legislation in the four basin states and with the accompanying signature of President John F. Kennedy. The compact that formed the commission created the first regional body to share equal authority with the federal government in the management of a river system. Since then, the commission has been instrumental in providing programs for water quality protection, supply allocation, conservation efforts, drought and flood management, watershed planning, and recreation. The commissioners include the governors of New Jersey, New York, Pennsylvania, and Delaware and a federal representative, with each commissioner having one vote of equal power.

According to the New Jersey Division of Fish & Wildlife, there are about 134 freshwater fish species throughout the state, with native species that include several types of shad, the American eel, brook trout, white catfish, and rainbow smelt. The state sponsors two fish hatcheries. The Pequest Trout Hatchery produces more than 600,000 rainbow, brook, and brown trout for stocking the public waters of New Jersey each year. The Hackettstown State Fish Hatchery (also known as the Charles O. Hayford State Fish Hatchery) produces fifteen different species of cool and warm water fish, including channel catfish, bluegill, largemouth and smallmouth bass, walleye and northern pike.

New Jersey is bordered by the Atlantic on the east coast and its ports have a major impact on the economy of the state. The Port of New York and New Jersey is the largest port on the East Coast and the third largest, by tonnage, in the nation, generating more than $2 billion in annual tax revenues for state and local governments. In 2010, the port handled 5.3 million containers, an increase over the previous year. The Port Authority of New York

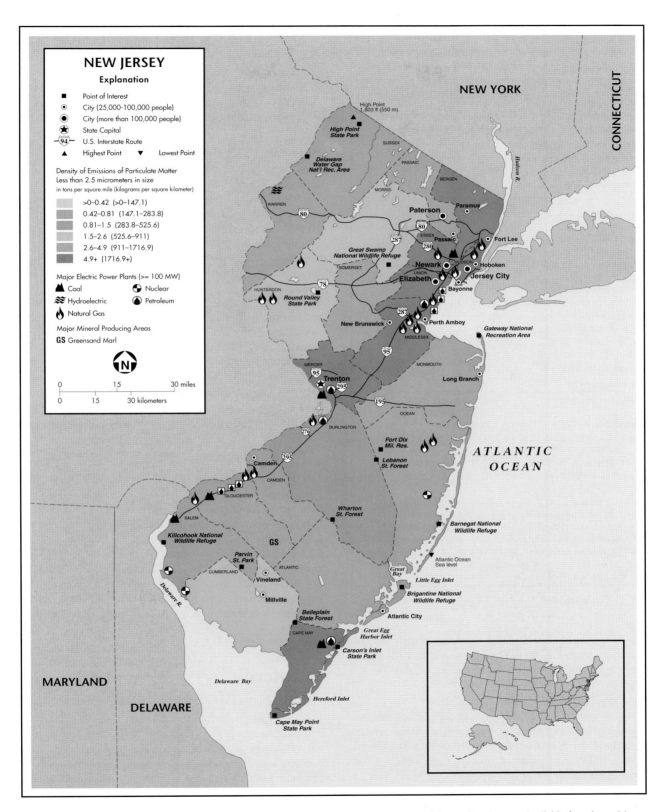

NEW JERSEY

Explanation

■ Point of Interest
⊙ City (25,000-100,000 people)
◉ City (more than 100,000 people)
★ State Capital
—94— U.S. Interstate Route
▲ Highest Point   ▼ Lowest Point

Density of Emissions of Particulate Matter
Less than 2.5 micrometers in size
in tons per square mile (kilograms per square kilometer)

>0–0.42 (>0–147.1)
0.42–0.81 (147.1–283.8)
0.81–1.5 (283.8–525.6)
1.5–2.6 (525.6–911)
2.6–4.9 (911–1716.9)
4.9+ (1716.9+)

Major Electric Power Plants (>= 100 MW)
▲ Coal   ⊛ Nuclear
≋ Hydroelectric   ◗ Petroleum
🔥 Natural Gas

Major Mineral Producing Areas
GS Greensand Marl

Ⓝ

0   15   30 miles
0   15   30 kilometers

NEW YORK
CONNECTICUT

High Point
1,803 ft (550 m)
High Point
State Park
SUSSEX
Delaware
Water Gap
Nat'l Rec. Area
PASSAIC
MORRIS
BERGEN
Hudson R.
WARREN
Paterson   Paramus
80
287   80
ESSEX   Passaic   Fort Lee
280
Great Swamp
National Wildlife Refuge
HUDSON
SOMERSET   Newark   Hoboken
78   Elizabeth   Jersey City
UNION   Bayonne
HUNTERDON
Round Valley
State Park
287   Perth Amboy
New Brunswick
95   MIDDLESEX   Gateway National
Recreation Area
MERCER
95   MONMOUTH
Trenton
295   Long Branch
195
OCEAN
276
BURLINGTON
Fort Dix
Mil. Res.
Camden   Lebanon
295   St. Forest
CAMDEN
GLOUCESTER   Wharton
St. Forest
SALEM
Killcohook National
Wildlife Refuge
GS
Parvin
St. Park
Delaware R.   CUMBERLAND   ATLANTIC
Vineland
Millville
Belleplain
State Forest
CAPE MAY
Carson's Inlet
State Park

ATLANTIC
OCEAN

Barnegat National
Wildlife Refuge
Atlantic Ocean
Sea level
Great
Bay   Little Egg Inlet
Brigantine National
Wildlife Refuge
Atlantic City
Great Egg
Harbor Inlet

MARYLAND   Delaware Bay
DELAWARE   Hereford Inlet
Cape May Point
State Park

SOURCES: "County Emissions Map: Criteria Air Pollutants." *AirData*. U.S. Environmental Protection Agency. Available from http://www.epa.gov/air/data/geosel.html; *Energy Maps*. U.S. Energy Information Administration. Available from http://www.eia.gov/state; *Highest and Lowest Elevations*. U.S. Geological Survey. Available from http://egsc.usgs.gov/isb/pubs/booklets/elvadist/elvadist.html#Highest; *2007 Minerals Yearbook*. U.S. Geological Survey. Available from http://minerals.usgs.gov/minerals/pubs/state. © 2011 Cengage Learning.

New Jersey State Profile

Physical Characteristics

Land area	7,354 square miles (19,047 sq km)
Inland water area	458 square miles (1,186 sq km)
Coastal area	402 square miles (647 sq km)
Highest point	High Point 1,803 feet (550 m)
National Forest System lands (2010)	NA
State parks (2011)	50

Energy Statistics

Total energy production (2009)	360 trillion Btu
State ranking in total energy production (2009)	35
Renewable energy net generation total (2009)	1.0 million megawatt hours
Hydroelectric energy generation (2009)	32,000 megawatt hours
Biomass energy generation (2009)	928,000 megawatt hours
Wind energy generation (2009)	21,000 megawatt hours
Wood and derived fuel energy generation (2009)	NA
Crude oil reserves (2009)	NA
Natural gas reserves (2009)	NA
Natural gas liquids (2008)	NA

Pollution Statistics

Carbon output (2005)	123.7 million tons of CO_2 (112.2 million t)
Superfund sites (2008)	112
Particulate matter (less than 2.5 micrometers) emissions (2002)	6,474 tons per year (5,873 t/yr)
Toxic chemical releases (2009)	13.1 million pounds (5.9 million kg)
Generated hazardous waste (2009)	555,800 tons (504,200 t)

SOURCES: AirData. U.S. Environmental Protection Agency. Available from http://www.epa.gov/air/data; *Energy Maps, Facts, and Data of the U.S. States.* U.S. Energy Information Administration. Available from http://www.eia.gov/state; *The 2012 Statistical Abstract.* U.S. Census Bureau. Available from http://www.census.gov/compendia/statab; *United States Energy Usage.* eRedux. Available from http://www.eredux.net/states.

© 2011 Cengage Learning.

and New Jersey is currently working on projects to expand its cargo handling capabilities in anticipation of an increase in trade from the completion of the Panama Canal expansion in 2014.

There are six major commercial fishing ports in New Jersey, with clams, scallops, tuna, swordfish, lobster, and flounder providing some of the most valuable catches. According the New Jersey Division of Fish & Wildlife, there are about 336 marine finfish in the state's waters throughout the year.

The Atlantic Coastal Plain, a flat area with swamps and sandy beaches, provides habitat for numerous birds and marine life. The Edwin B. Forsyth National Wildlife Refuge in southern New Jersey was designated as a Ramsar Wetland of International Importance in 1986, in recognition of its importance as a breeding and wintering ground for more than 70,000 birds. More than 80 percent of the refuge consists of tidal salt meadow and marsh. Peregrine falcons, ospreys, and bald eagles are all found in the refuge. Several species of whale and dolphin have been noted off the coast on New Jersey, along with harbor, gray, and harp seals.

Agriculture: Jersey Fresh, Jersey Grown

New Jersey, also known as the Garden State, ranks second in the nation for the production of blueberries and third for the production of cranberries, freestone peaches, and bell peppers. New Jersey has more than 10,000 farms across the state, covering more than 730,000 acres (292,000 ha). To support local farmers, the New Jersey Department of Agriculture sponsors Jersey Fresh, a program that promotes community and roadside farmers markets and agritourism events. Jersey Grown is a similar program started in 2004 for the promotion of the state's nurseries and garden centers. According to the 2007 census by the U.S. Department of Agriculture (USDA), New Jersey's floriculture, nursery, and greenhouse industry ranked among the top states nationwide when it came to market value of products, with a value of $440 million. All Jersey Grown participants are certified by the state department of agriculture and must maintain disease- and pest-free plant material and nursery stock that meets or exceeds standards set by the American Nursery and Landscape Association.

The New Jersey Organic Certification Program was established in 2006 and has earned National Organic Program Accreditation to certify crops, livestock, and handling operations. As of the 2008 Organic Survey taken by the USDA census, there have been more than 122 farms certified as organic, and the state is home tomore than 3,330acres (1.332 ha) of organic land. As of 2010, there were also 22 state-certified organic handling facilities, producing a variety of products that include pasta, hummus, and non-dairy organic frozen desserts.

❧ Energy

Oil and Natural Gas: Storage and Distribution

Though New Jersey has no fossil fuel reserves of its own, it is part of a major northeastern distribution center for natural gas and petroleum products. Crude oil from overseas comes in through New York Harbor en route to the state's six oil refineries. The state is linked to the Buckeye Pipeline, which supplies petroleum products to Northeast and Midwest markets, and the Colonial Pipeline, which carries supplies from the Gulf Coast to New York Harbor. New York Harbor houses the largest petroleum hub in the United States, with a petroleum bulk terminal storage capacity of more than 75 million barrels.

New Jersey law requires the statewide use of a reformulated blend of motor gasoline that includes ethanol. Supplies of ethanol from the Midwestern United States, Brazil, and the Caribbean are received at a large ethanol storage facility in Sewaren, New Jersey, from which it is then redistributed to northeast markets. Demand for transportation fuel is high in New Jersey, primarily due to the large number of residents who work out-of-state in places such as New York City and Philadelphia.

Natural gas is piped into the state through systems that emerge from Pennsylvania. A new liquefied natural gas (LNG) pipeline, the Crown Landing LNG project, has been in the planning stages for several years, but has stalled a number of times, most recently as a result of a dispute between New Jersey and neighboring Delaware concerning the location of the pier that would receive overseas imports. If completed, the project will supply LNG for the Philadelphia area. However, in 2009 Hess LNG bought the project from BP America and in May 2010 requested more time from the Federal Energy Regulatory Commission (FERC) to consider the project's size, scope and location. The company was considering downsizing the project, which was estimated to cost $600 million when first proposed in 2003. In May 2011, the company again asked for an extension from the FERC, this time because of a dispute over the accuracy of a computer program designed to assess spill and fire risks.

Fracking in New Jersey?

While there are currently no natural gas drilling operations in the state of New Jersey, residents and lawmakers alike are concerned about the potential dangers of the drilling process known as hydraulic fracturing, or fracking, which is already being used in operations in Pennsylvania to access resources from the Marcellus Shale. Pennsylvania is believed to hold the thickest deposits of Marcellus Shale in the country and has been attracting investments in this area at a breakneck pace. The fracking technique that allows access to the deep deposits involves a high-pressure injection of water, sand, and various chemicals to fracture the underlying rock and release the natural gas. Many believe that the wastewater produced from this process poses a serious threat to public health, especially if it mingles with large residential drinking supplies, such as that of the Delaware River Basin.

In the spring of 2011, the Delaware River Basin Commission (of which New Jersey governor Chris Christie is a member) was still working on a set of regulations to address the environmental concerns that could arise from fracking operations in Pennsylvania along the Delaware River. A lawsuit over the issue was filed in August 2011 by such entities as the National Parks Conservation System Association, Riverkeeper, and the Delaware River Keepers Networks against the U.S. Army Corps of Engineers and the Delaware River Basin Commission. The lawsuit asks federal regulators to suspend plans to develop natural gas resources in the river basin until there is a greater understanding of the environmental impact of the plan. However, concern over the dangers of fracking has compelled legislators from New Jersey to ban the practice within their own state. In March 2011, the state senate unanimously passed Senate Bill 2576, which very simply prohibits the use of the drilling technique within the state. The Assembly passed the bill in June 2011. The bill was hailed as an important preventive measure by some officials who are concerned that the rush to tap the Marcellus Shale could lead companies to shift their focus toward the potential of the Utica Shale, which lies a few thousand feet below the Marcellus and extends slightly into northern New Jersey. There are currently no other New Jersey state regulations concerning natural gas exploration. However, New Jersey Governor Chris Christie conditionally vetoed the bill in August 2011, and it was returned to the Senate for reconsideration. Governor Christie sought to convert the proposed ban into a one year moratorium, and also requested that the NJ Department of Environmental Protection be required to conduct an independent study of fracking.

The Northeast Home Heating Oil Reserve

Perth Amboy is the site of the largest of three storage terminals that make up the Northeast Home Heating Oil Reserve. The reserve was created to alleviate the strain of frequent shortages of fuel oil in the northeastern states, particularly during the winter months when demand is at its peak. The Perth Amboy storage facility has a capacity of about one million barrels.

About 20 percent of New Jersey residents use fuel oil as their primary source for home heating, while about 66 percent use natural gas.

Electricity: Nuclear, Wind and Solar

New Jersey's three nuclear power plants provide more than 50 percent of the electricity supply for the state. The Oyster Creek Nuclear Generating Station, established in 1969, is the oldest operating nuclear plant in the country. Natural gas and coal-fired plants are responsible for most of the remaining supply of electricity, with coal imported from West Virginia, Virginia, and Pennsylvania. A small portion of electricity is generated from landfill gas and municipal solid waste. The state has strong potential for offshore wind energy. In 2010, there were at least three proposed wind farm projects in the works, including a major 350-megawatt wind farm to be located about twenty miles off the coast of South Jersey.

Though solar is still a small part of the energy portfolio in New Jersey, the state reached a milestone in

New Jersey's three nuclear power plants provide more than 50 percent of the electric supply for the state. © *Aerial Archives/Alamy*

July 2011 with more than 380 megawatts (MW) generated by 10,000 solar arrays statewide. New Jersey is second only to California in both installed solar capacity and number of installations. In a draft of his 2011 Energy Master Plan, Gov. Christie called for more solar projects to occur on brownfields and landfills. In 2011, the New Jersey Meadowlands Commission began a project designed to transform a closed landfill into a 12,000 panel solar farm that will generate up to 3 MW of electricity.

Renewable Portfolio Standard (RPS)

The New Jersey Board of Public Utilities approved the state's most recent renewable portfolio standard in 2006 (New Jersey Administrative Code, Title 14, Chapter 8). The RPS requires that utilities generate 22.5 percent of their retail electrical supply from renewable sources by 2021. In 2010, a New Solar Advancement and Fair Competition Act (A3520) went into effect, which requires utilities to produce at least 2,158 gigawatt-hours of electricity from solar electric generators during energy

year 2021 (June 2020–May 2021), with 5,316 gigawatt hours produced in energy year 2026 and each year after that.

The 2008 Energy Master Plan

The state's renewable portfolio standard is supported and supplemented by the state's Energy Master Plan (EMP) process. The last EMP was issued in 2008, and a 2011 update was pending. Created under the direction of Governor Corzine, the EMP is designed to support the development of a new green energy infrastructure for the state, in part by setting a series statewide of energy reduction and energy efficiency goals. The 2008 EMP sets a target to reduce statewide energy consumption by 20 percent by 2020. The 2008 EMP also proposes the more ambitious renewable energy goal of generating 30 percent of all power from renewable energy sources by 2020.

❧ Green Business, Green Building, Green Jobs

New Jersey Going Green: Business

The development of green business and green jobs in New Jersey is intrinsically linked to the development of the New Jersey 2008 Energy Master Plan (EMP), which sets forth a number of energy efficiency and energy reduction goals for not only the government, but for the commercial and residential sectors of the state as well. To support the goals set forth by the EMP, the New Jersey Economic Development Authority initiated Clean Energy Solutions (CES), a series of financing programs for commercial, industrial, and institutional entities that are going green. Funding options under CES include grants and interest-free loans available through programs such as Clean Energy Solutions Capital Investments and the Clean Energy Manufacturing Fund.

New Jersey Going Green: Jobs

According to *New Jersey Going Green*, a report published by the New Jersey Department of Labor and Workforce Development (LWD), there were 20,764 companies in New Jersey in 2009 that were either already serving green functions or that could "turn green" through the implementation of clean energy technologies or by producing such technologies. Those companies employed nearly 192,000 workers, accounting for about 5 percent of the state's total employment. Full implementation of the 2008 Energy Master Plan was projected to create an additional 20,000 jobs.

The largest increase in both green businesses and jobs is expected to be in the energy efficiency sector, particularly in construction and weatherization.

The Jersey-Atlantic wind farm was the first wind farm in New Jersey. © *MShieldsPhotos/Alamy*

Additional jobs in clean energy production through wind and solar installations, operation, and maintenance are also expected.

To prepare the workforce for the new green economy, the LWD has developed a number of training initiatives, of which the most prominent is the Green Job Training Partnership Program (GJTP), supported in part by a $300,000 grant from the Conserve to Preserve Foundation of the New Jersey Resources Corporation. The program provides entry-level training opportunities for underserved urban men, women, and youth and additional training for incumbent workers who simply hope to enhance their skills.

Isles, Inc., a nonprofit community development and environmental organization, has also made great strides in promoting green job training and green business growth through its Isles E4 (Energy, Environment, Equity, Employment) program, which focuses on the home energy efficiency market. In promoting these efforts, Isles E4 has created the Center for Energy and Environmental Training (CEET), which provides energy efficiency job training programs at community-based organizations across the state. Graduates from the CEET have found entry-level jobs earning up to $17 per hour.

Green Building

In January 2008, the state adopted a high performance green building standard that requires all new state-owned buildings larger than 15,000 square feet be designed to achieve silver certification under the U.S. Green Building Council's Leadership in Energy and Environmental Design (LEED) program (New Jersey Statute 52:32). An additional provision was added in 2007 that requires all state agencies to purchase Energy Star products when available (New Jersey Statute 52:34). Under Executive Order 24 (2002), all new schools must be designed to incorporate LEED Version 2.0 guidelines.

The New Jersey Clean Energy Program, administered by the Office of Clean Energy of the New Jersey Board of Public Utilities, provides financial incentives, educational programs, and technical services for residents and business owners who want to go green in new building or retrofitting projects.

In June 2010, the state was home to eighty-seven LEED certified projects. The New Jersey Meadowlands Commission Center for Environmental & Scientific Education in Lyndhurst and the Willow School Art Barn in Gladstone are the state's only platinum certified facilities at that time. PNC Bank has fifteen branch facilities within the state that were certified at either silver or gold level.

❧ A Turn in the Right Direction for Offshore Wind Development

In June 2010, New Jersey marked a major milestone toward the development of wind energy with the passage of the Offshore Wind Economic Development Act (S 2036). The act is seen as an important step in reaching the New Jersey 2008 Energy Master Plan (EMP) goal of 3,000 megawatts of offshore wind energy generation, or 13 percent of the state's total electric supply. The act also positions the state as a strong contender in the race to develop the first offshore wind farm on the East Coast.

Offshore Wind Renewable Energy Certificate

At the heart of the act is a major incentive package that creates an Offshore Wind Renewable Energy Certificate (OREC) program. The ORECs will work exactly like standard Renewable Energy Certificates, which serve as proof that a utility has complied with local standards for the production of electricity by renewable sources. Generally, a utility will receive one certificate for one megawatt hour of electricity generated. The utility will be required to hold a certain number of certificates by a given deadline. These certificates can be earned, traded, bought, and sold. The New Jersey ORECs will be distributed by the New Jersey Board of Public Utilities (BPU), which will determine the amount of ORECs that each supplier must hold as a percentage of the total kilowatt hours sold. The Offshore Wind Economic Development Act mandates that the OREC program must support a total of 1,100 megawatts of energy.

As an additional incentive, the act also established a 100 percent tax credit for capital investments of $50 million or more for new offshore wind facilities. As of 2010, the credit was capped at $100 million, but the New Jersey Economic Development Authority has the ability to increase the amount, as long as the total amount of credits issued under the program does not exceed $1.5 billion.

The Race to Be First Offshore

Passage of the act was good news for Garden State Offshore Energy, which in 2008 proposed developing a 350-megawatt wind farm to be located about twenty miles off the coast of South Jersey. The project has already been approved by the New Jersey Board of Public Utilities. If all goes well, the farm will be up and operating in 2013. It is expected to produce more than 1.2 billion kilowatt-hours of electricity each year, or enough to supply more than 110,000 households.

NRG Bluewater Wind may also benefit from the act, as this developer plans to build a 350-megawatt farm about sixteen miles off the coast of Atlantic City. In 2008, the company received a $4 million grant from the state government for work on the project, which will consist of between eighty to one hundred turbines. Fishermen's Energy of Cape May received approval in May 2011 to build a demonstration-scale six turbine wind farm. This project was planned for the waters off the coast of Atlantic City. Fishermen's Energy, founded by New Jersey commercial fishermen, planned to eventually install a 20-megawatt, nine-turbine project about three miles (5 km) offshore and has made additional plans for a 350-megawatt farm about ten miles (16 km) out. While approval for the demonstration project placed them ahead in the race to build wind farms off the New Jersey coast, they still needed to complete the permitting process with the state Board of Public Utilities and obtain the necessary federal permits before the project moved forward.

Wind energy development is happening elsewhere in the state as well. In May 2010, the Port Authority of New York and New Jersey announced plans to build a five-turbine wind farm on the Port Jersey Peninsula that will support the port's cargo operations and help the Port Authority reach its own environmental and sustainability goals, including the reduction of greenhouse gas emissions by 80 percent of 2005 levels by 2050. The New Jersey Office of Clean Energy has awarded a $3.6 million grant for development of the Port Authority project.

BIBLIOGRAPHY

Books

Belton, Thomas J. *Protecting New Jersey's Environment.* New Brunswick, NJ: Rivergate Books, 2011.

Kershner, Bruce, and Robert T. Leverett. *The Sierra Club Guide to the Ancient Forests of the Northeast.* San Francisco, CA: Sierra Club Books, 2004.

Walter, Eugene and Jonathan Wallen. *The Smithsonian Guides to Natural America: The Mid-Atlantic States–New York, Pennsylvania, New Jersey.* Washington, DC: Smithsonian Books, 1996.

Web Sites

"Clean Energy Solutions." New Jersey Economic Development Authority. Available from http://www.njeda.com/web/Aspx_pg/Templates/Pic_Text.aspx?Doc_Id=1080&topid=722&midid=1357

"Christie Administration Advances Commitment To Renewable Energy Development." New Jersey Board of Public Utilities. July 25, 2011. Available from http://www.njcleanenergy.com/files/file/Renewable_Programs/10000%20Solar%20Milestone%20Press%20Release.pdf

Delaware River Basin Commission. Available from http://www.state.nj.us/drbc/whoweare.htm

Edwin B. Forsyth National Wildlife Refuge. Available from http://www.fws.gov/northeast/forsythe/wildlife.html

Executive Order 24#x2013;2002. State of New Jersey, Office of the Governor. Available from http://www.state.nj.us/infobank/circular/eom24.htm

Fishermen's Energy. Available from http://www.fishermensenergy.com/index.html

Garden State Offshore Energy. Available from http://www.gardenstatewind.com

"Global Warming." State of New Jersey. Available from http://www.state.nj.us/globalwarming/home/news/approved/070706.html

Global Warming and New Jersey. National Wildlife Federation. Available from http://cf.nwf.org/globalwarming/pdfs/newjersey.pdf

Global Warming Response Act. State of New Jersey Legislature. Available from http://www.nj.gov/globalwarming/home/documents/pdf/nj_global_warming_response_act.pdf

"Green Job Training Partnership." New Jersey Department of Labor and Workforce Development. Available from http://www.njcleanenergy.com/files/file/Green_Job_Training/Green%20Job%20Training%20Partnership%20Program.pdf

"Groups Challenge Delaware River Basin Fracking Plan." Thomson Reuters. August 4, 2011. Available from http://newsandinsight.thomsonreuters.com/Legal/News/2011/08_-_August/Groups_challenge_Delaware_River_Basin_fracking_plan/

Gruen, Abby. "Preparation for groundbreaking offshore wind farm project begins in Atlantic City." May 1, 2010. NJ.com. Available from http://www.nj.com/news/index.ssf/2010/05/preparation_for_first_us_wind.html

Isles E4 (Energy, Environment, Equity, Employment). Available from http://isles.org/main/services/financial-self-reliance/isles-e4-energy-environment-equity-employment

Jersey Fresh. Available from http://www.state.nj.us/jerseyfresh

Jersey Grown. Available from http://www.jerseygrown.nj.gov

Johnson, Tom. "Lawmakers Declare New Jersey a No-Fracking Zone." NJ Spotlight. March 11, 2011. Available from http://www.njspotlight.com/stories/11/0310/2151

Johnson, Tom. "State Issues First Permits for Offshore Wind Farm." NJ Spotlight. April 7, 2011. Available from http://www.njspotlight.com/stories/11/0407/0049

Lawrence, Gregory. "The Race is On: N.J. Legislature Passes Offshore Wind Incentive Package." *Green Energy News.* July 9, 2010. Available from http://www.green-energy-news.com/contribute/articles2010/2010sub003.html

"LEED Certified & Registered Projects in New Jersey." U.S. Green Building Council New Jersey. Available from http://www.usgbcnj.org/page2.php?id=8

Meeting New Jersey's 2020 Greenhouse Gas Limit: New Jersey's Global Warming Response Act Recommendations Report. New Jersey Department of Environmental Protection. Available from http://www.nj.gov/globalwarming/home/documents/pdf/njgwra_final_report_and_appendices_dec2009.pdf

National Agricultural Statistics Services: New Jersey. Available from http://www.nass.usda.gov/Statistics_by_State/New_Jersey/index.asp

Navarro, Mireya. "Christie Pulls N.J. From 10-State Climate Initiative." *New York Times*. May 26, 2011. Available from http://www.nytimes.com/2011/05/27/nyregion/christie-pulls-nj-from-greenhouse-gas-coalition.html

New Jersey Administrative Code, Title 14, Chapter 8: Renewable Energy and Energy Efficiency. Available from http://www.dsireusa.org/documents/Incentives/NJ05Rb.htm

New Jersey Clean Energy Program. Available from http://njcleanenergy.com/residential/technologies/renewable/renewable

New Jersey Division of Fish & Wildlife. Available from http://www.state.nj.us/dep/fgw

New Jersey Energy Master Plan. Available from http://www.state.nj.us/emp

Senate Bill 2576 (2010–2011): An act concerning certain drilling techniques. State of New Jersey Legislature.

Available from http://www.njleg.state.nj.us/2010/Bills/S3000/2576_I1.HTM

New Jersey Fishing and Aquaculture: Harvesting the Garden State's Waters. Available from http://www.state.nj.us/seafood/seafoodreport.pdf

New Jersey Forest Service: Forest Health. Available from http://www.state.nj.us/dep/parksandforests/forest/njfs_forest_health.html

New Jersey Going Green: A Demand-Supply Analysis Of Current And Potential Green Jobs And Green Skills. New Jersey Department of Labor and Workforce Development. Available from http://lwd.dol.state.nj.us/labor/lpa/pub/studyseries/njgreen.pdf

New Jersey Meadowlands Commission Center for Environmental & Scientific Education. Available from http://www.njmeadowlands.gov/environment/cese.html

New Jersey Pinelands Commission. Available from http://www.state.nj.us/pinelands/reserve

New Jersey Resources. Available from http://www.njresources.com/index.asp

New Jersey Statute 52:32—Definitions relative to energy savings for construction of certain State buildings. State of New Jersey. Available from http://www.dsireusa.org/documents/Incentives/NJ16Ra.htm

New Jersey Statute 52:34—State required to purchase "Energy Star" products. State of New Jersey. Available from http://www.dsireusa.org/documents/Incentives/NJ16Rb.htm

New Jersey 2007 Minerals Yearbook. United States Geological Survey. Available from http://minerals.usgs.gov/minerals/pubs/state/2007/myb2-2007-nj.pdf

New Jersey Weather & Climate Network. Available from http://climate.rutgers.edu/njwxnet

"Northeast Home Heating Oil Reserve." U.S. Department of Energy. Available from http://www.fossil.energy.gov/programs/reserves/heatingoil

NRG Bluewater Wind. Available from http://www.bluewaterwind.com/current.htm

Offshore Wind Economic Development Act (S 2036). State of New Jersey Legislature. Available from http://www.njleg.state.nj.us/2010/Bills/S2500/2036_R2.PDF

Port of New York and New Jersey. Available from http://www.panynj.gov/port/about-port.html

Regional Greenhouse Gas Initiative: New Jersey State Investment Plan. Available from http://www.rggi.org/rggi_benefits/program_investments/New_Jersey

The Solar Energy Advancement and Fair Competition Act (A3520). New Jersey State Legislature. Available from http://www.njleg.state.nj.us/2008/Bills/A4000/3520_R3.PDF

"State Energy Profiles: New Jersey." U.S. Energy Information Administration. Available from http://tonto.eia.doe.gov/state/state_energy_profiles.cfm?sid=NJ#

"Statements Regarding New Jersey." Regional Greenhouse Gas Initiative. Available from http://www.rggi.org/news/njstatements

"2009 Economic Development Strategies–Organic Industry." State of New Jersey Department of Agriculture. Available from http://www.state.nj.us/agriculture/conventions/2009/organic.html

"USA: Hess Considers Changes in Crown Landing LNG Project." *LNG World News.* May 13, 2010. Available from http://www.lngworldnews.com/usa-hess-considers-changes-in-crown-landing-lng-project/

"USA: Hess Delays Crown Landing LNG Project." *LNG World News.* May 6, 2011. Available from http://www.lngworldnews.com/usa-hess-delays-crown-landing-lng-project/

"Willow School, Gladstone, New Jersey." Somerset County Business Partnerships. Available from http://www.scbp.org/member/documents/willow.pdf

New Mexico

New Mexico is one of the largest and most ecologically diverse states in the nation. The state boasts a diverse landscape, featuring the southernmost part of the Rocky Mountains and the Chihuahuan Desert. Roughly 21 percent of New Mexico is forestland, most of which (62 percent) is administered by government agencies. New Mexico relies on a combination of surface water and groundwater for human consumption and agriculture. While there is abundant groundwater, much of it is too salty to drink, leading the state to forge ahead with multiple projects looking into desalination plants to supply New Mexico with a supplementary water source.

Climate

The state has a mild, continental climate characterized by light precipitation totals, abundant sunshine, low relative humidity, and a relatively large annual and diurnal temperature range. The highest mountains, being part of the Rocky Mountains, have climate characteristics common to that range.

Established in 2005, the New Mexico Climate Change Advisory Group (CCAG) completed a study in December 2006, which indicated that by the mid- to late-twenty-first century, climate change could cause air temperatures to increase by 6 to 12 °F (3.3–6.7°C) on average, but more in winter, at night, and at high elevations. It could also cause more episodes of extreme heat, fewer episodes of extreme cold, and a longer frost-free season; more intense storm events and flash floods; and winter precipitation falling more often as rain, less often as snow. Some climate models project that average precipitation will increase, while others predict a decrease. A plan put together in December 2006 proposes to lower New Mexico's total greenhouse gas emissions (GHG) to 2000 levels by 2012, 10 percent below 2000 levels by 2020, and 75 percent by 2050.

Controversy Brews over Greenhouse Gas Emissions

Since January 1, 2011, the day that Republican governor Susana Martinez took office, there has been a great deal of controversy concerning new regulations passed by the state's Environmental Improvement Board (EIB) in November and December of 2010. The first was a provision that will allow the state to move forward in participation with a regional cap-and-trade market alliance. The second calls for an annual reduction in greenhouse gas emissions by 3 percent from 2010 levels, with an ultimate goal of reducing emissions by 25 percent below 1990 levels by 2020. When the regulations were passed in 2010, then–Governor-elect Martinez vowed to repeal the measures on taking office. She argued that the regulation of heat-trapping emissions was burdensome for industry and harmful to the state's economy, and that the EIB acted out of political rather than common sense economic motives in approving the cap-and-trade provision after such a proposal was rejected by state lawmakers. In her first week in office, Martinez issued an order to suspend "all proposed and pending regulations" from publication as codified state law for at least ninety days while under review by a newly created Small-Business-Friendly Task Force. She then fired all of the members of the EIB to replace them with her own appointees.

Lawyers for the New Mexico Environmental Law Center, however, argued that her actions in issuing the executive order were "underhanded" and "illegal." On January 26, 2011, the New Mexico Supreme Court agreed in a unanimous ruling that Martinez had violated the state constitution by preventing the rules from publication. As it stands, the new EIB can only rescind the regulations after the required period of public hearings and public comment. However, the matter made its way into the new session of the state legislature in the form of Senate Bill 489. The bill did not reverse either regulation, but proposed a new law prohibiting the EIB or any other local board from adopting "a rule more stringent than federal law or regulation for reporting, verifying, limiting, trading, or capping emission of greenhouse gases." That bill, however, died in the state's Senate Judiciary Committee in 2011. In September

A variety of flora and rock formations in the extreme desert conditions of New Mexico.
© *John S. Sfondilias/ShutterStock.com*

2011, an environmental group, New Energy Economy filed a motion with the board, requesting that three of its members recuse themselves from discussion regarding rescinding the regulations, citing testimony the three made prior to being appointed to the board.

❧ Natural Resources, Minerals, Water, and Agriculture

From Forests to Deserts

Just over 20 percent of New Mexico is forestland, with major species including ponderosa pine, spruce, pinon, and juniper forests and mixed conifer woodlands. The majority of forests are on federal land, where the New Mexico Forestry Division requires a permit for timber harvest on any area greater than 25 acres (10 ha), as well as a plan for forest regeneration. In 2001, the federal government initiated a Collaborative Forest Restoration Program (CFRP), which has awarded more than 100 grants to organizations (one-third of which are Native American tribes) working throughout New Mexico, CFRP projects have created over 300 forest related jobs in the state, while vigorously working to preserve and restore New Mexico's woodlands.

New Mexico has 61 wildlife management areas across the state, many of which are GAIN properties. GAIN—Gaining Access Into Nature—is a state program that offers wildlife viewing and other activities on State Game Commission owned wildlife management areas. GAIN activities include camping, photography, hiking, and horseback riding, during which visitors may see a number of indigenous animals, such as pronghorn antelope, deer, elk, wild turkey, and black bears.

Desert areas of the state include the shrub-dominant Chihuahuan Desert in the southeastern part of the state, which includes White Sands National Monument and Carlsbad Caverns National Park. White Sands, the location of the world's largest gypsum dune field, is the home of well-known desert dwellers such as the tarantula, the giant desert centipede, and a variety of snakes and other reptiles. Plants found in the area include a variety of cacti and the flowering centaury and wooly paperflower.

Carlsbad Caverns National Park is a prime example of the diversity of New Mexico's plant and wildlife. The park is an important year-round habitat for top predators such as the cougar, and nesting habitat for migratory species, such as the large colonies of cave swallows and Brazilian (Mexican) free-tailed bats that raise their young in Carlsbad Cavern. It also contains Rattlesnake Springs, which, along with the Carlsbad Cavern Natural Entrance, has been designated as an Important Bird Area (IBA) by the National Audubon Society. Vegetation in the park varies from desert shrublands and semigrasslands to montane grasslands and woodlands.

Thirty-three New Mexican animal species and 13 plant species were listed as threatened or endangered

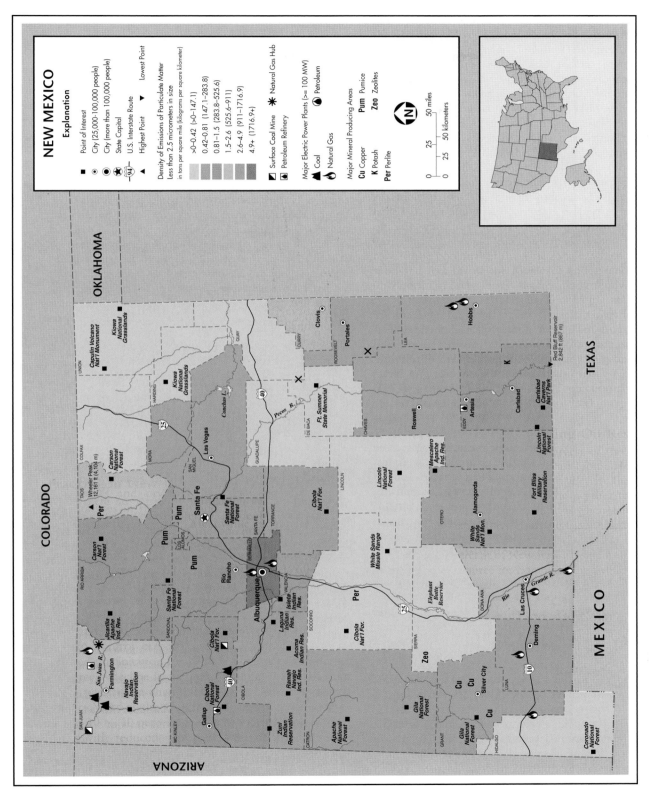

SOURCES: "County Emissions Map: Criteria Air Pollutants." *AirData*. U.S. Environmental Protection Agency. Available from http://www.epa.gov/air/data/geosel.html; *Energy Maps*. U.S. Energy Information Administration. Available from http://www.eia.gov/state; *Highest and Lowest Elevations*. U.S. Geological Survey. Available from http://egsc.usgs.gov/isb/pubs/booklets/elvadist/elvadist.html#Highest; *2007 Minerals Yearbook*. U.S. Geological Survey. Available from http://minerals.usgs.gov/minerals/pubs/state. © 2011 Cengage Learning.

Exceptionally dry weather conditions and high winds led to an outbreak of wildfires in the state in April 2011. © *Brad Wilson/Getty Images*

by the U.S. Fish and Wildlife Service in 2010. Endangered animal species included the Mexican long-nosed bat, jaguar, and the New Mexican ridge-nosed rattlesnake. Threatened and endangered plant species included five varieties of cacti, the Sacramento prickly poppy, and the Pecos sunflower. On May 18, 2010, the New Mexico Department of Game and Fish released a statement acknowledging that the desert bighorn sheep had met the requirements to be removed from the state endangered species list and proposed that the State Game Commission take the appropriate action.

Exceptionally dry weather conditions and high winds led to an outbreak of wildfires in the state in April 2011. The Rabbit Ear Fire outside of Clayton (northeast) affected 23,000 acres of grassland and pinyon-juniper forest. The Tire Fire, named for the vehicle tire blowout that caused it, affected 17,000 acres in an area south and west of Clovis, destroying three homes. Several smaller fires occurred throughout the month, but no casualties were reported. As a precaution, the U.S Bureau of Land Management implemented fire restrictions for more than a dozen counties in southern New Mexico, including a ban on smoking, except in enclosed vehicles or buildings, and on the use of charcoal and wood burning, except in developed recreation sites.

Minerals

Nonfuel minerals production totaled $1.6 billion in 2008, according to U.S. Geological Survey data. New Mexico ranks fifteenth in the United States in nonfuel mineral production value, with copper and potash leading the way. Along with construction sand and gravel, Portland cement, and molybdenum concentrates, these minerals make up about 94 percent of the state's total nonfuel raw mineral production value. Copper alone accounts for about 45 percent of the total value. Many other valuable minerals, such as gold, silver, crude gypsum, gemstones, perlite, pumice, and salt, can be found in New Mexico.

Rivers and Reservoirs

The major rivers of New Mexico include the Rio Grande, Pecos, San Juan, Canadian, and Gila. The largest bodies of inland water are the Elephant Butte Reservoir and Conchas Reservoir, both created by dams. There is no commercial fishing in New Mexico, however sport fishing is popular, with numerous fish species introduced into state lakes and reservoirs for this purpose. New Mexico also has two government-sponsored fish hatcheries and technology centers in Dexter and Mora. The Dexter National Fish Hatchery and Technology Center is the only facility in the nation dedicated to studying and distributing endangered fish for restocking in waters where they naturally occur. Some of the species that the Center breeds include the Rio Grande silvery minnow, the Colorado pikeminnow, and the razorback sucker, all river fish.

Agriculture

In 2010, New Mexico had 21,000 farms totaling 43 million acres. Leading crops included hay and corn for grain, with values of over $200 million and $58.8 million, respectively. The state also produces significant amounts of wheat, potatoes, and chiles, which are grown primarily in the southwest part of the state centered around Hatch, which calls itself the "Chile Capital of the World." New Mexico ranks fourth in the United States in cheese production and ninth for milk production. Milk is the number-one cash commodity in New Mexico, producing more than $1 billion in revenue. Pecan exports reached more than 25 million pounds (11.3 million kg) in 2007 and 2008, earning approximately $40 million in net sales for growers. Looking ahead at the issues facing agriculture in the state, the New Mexico Department of Agriculture created a Strategic Plan 2009–2013 that addressed areas for concern and set strategic goals to overcome those challenges. The report cited eight areas that were priorities for the state, including food safety and security, natural resources and environmental quality, regulatory compliance, food health, and consumer awareness and alternative energy, among others.

According to the USDA's 2008 Census, New Mexico had nearly 200 organic farms with a total of 117,676 acres and more than 15,000 certified heads of organic livestock. Organic product sales totaled $33.4 million. The New Mexico Organic Farming Conference is held yearly and hosts speakers and has workshops that address topics such as soil, livestock, weed and pest management, and farm support. The New Mexico Farmer's Marketing Association reports over fifty farmer's markets across the state that provide fresh and organic produce to communities. The Association also helps communities start their own markets and assists with organizational development, grower recruitment, finding volunteers and developing revenue streams to help markets become self-sustaining.

⚘ Energy

Oil and Natural Gas

As a leading U.S. producer of crude oil and natural gas, New Mexico's natural gas production accounts for almost one-tenth of the U.S. total. Approximately one-third of all natural gas produced in New Mexico is coalbed methane. The San Juan Basin, the leading coalbed methane-producing region in the United States, also holds the Blanco Hub, which is a major transportation point for Rocky Mountain natural gas supplies heading to West Coast markets. While state natural gas consumption is low, primarily due to New Mexico's small population, more than two-thirds of its households use natural gas as their primary energy source.

New Mexico's crude oil wells produce an output that is 3.1 percent of the U.S. total, with production in the Permian and San Juan Basins. In fact, the Permian Basin is home to three of the 100 largest oil fields in the United States. The state has three oil refineries with several pipelines connecting these refineries to state and area markets. New Mexico has one ethanol plant in Portales with a capacity of 30 million gallons per year. Ethanol is mixed with gasoline in order to increase its oxygen content, and New Mexicans consumed 804,000 barrels in 2008.

Coal and Electricity

The majority of New Mexico's coal comes from two major mines in the San Juan Basin, with about three-fifths of it used within the state. Coal-fired power plants dominate the New Mexico electricity market and supply over four-fifths of the state's electricity generation. Just over one-tenth of New Mexico households use electricity as their main energy source for home heating.

An Emerging Leader in Renewable Energy

New Mexico has some of the best potential for solar, wind, and geothermal energy of any state in the country. The state ranks second behind Arizona when it comes to solar energy output. The Cimarron I Solar Project, built by First Solar and operated by Southern Company and Turner Renewables, became fully operational in December 2010. A 30-megawatt (AC) photovoltaic solar power project covering more than 250 acres (101 ha), it can provide power to approximately 9,000 homes serving an estimated 18,000 residents, and will displace over 45,000 tons of carbon dioxide per year. In April 2011, the Public

---

New Mexico State Profile

Physical Characteristics

Land area	121,297 square miles (314,158 sq km)
Inland water area	293 square miles (759 sq km)
Coastal area	NA
Highest point	Wheeler Peak 13,161 feet (4,011 m)
National Forest System lands (2010)	9.4 million acres (3.8 million ha)
State parks (2011)	35

Energy Statistics

Total energy production (2009)	2,500 trillion Btu
State ranking in total energy production (2009)	10
Renewable energy net generation total (2009)	1.9 million megawatt hours
Hydroelectric energy generation (2009)	271,000 megawatt hours
Biomass energy generation (2009)	34,000 megawatt hours
Wind energy generation (2009)	1.5 million megawatt hours
Wood and derived fuel energy generation (2009)	NA
Crude oil reserves (2009)	700 million barrels (111.3 million cu m)
Natural gas reserves (2009)	15,598 billion cubic feet (441.7 billion cu m)
Natural gas liquids (2008)	715 million barrels (113.7 million cu m)

Pollution Statistics

Carbon output (2005)	57.62 million tons of CO_2 (52.3 million t)
Superfund sites (2008)	13
Particulate matter (less than 2.5 micrometers) emissions (2002)	8,854 tons per year (8,032 t/yr)
Toxic chemical releases (2009)	15.3 million pounds (6.9 million kg)
Generated hazardous waste (2009)	1 million tons (978,600 t)

SOURCES: AirData. U.S. Environmental Protection Agency. Available from http://www.epa.gov/air/data; *Energy Maps, Facts, and Data of the U.S. States*. U.S. Energy Information Administration. Available from http://www.eia.gov/state; *The 2012 Statistical Abstract*. U.S. Census Bureau. Available from http://www.census.gov/compendia/statab; *United States Energy Usage*. eRedux. Available from http://www.eredux.net/states.

© 2011 Cengage Learning.

Service Company of New Mexico (PNM), the largest electricity producer in New Mexico, dedicated its Albuquerque Solar Energy Center, the first of five large-scale solar power plants that the company planned for operation in 2011. The Albuquerque facility consists of 30,000 solar photovoltaic panels covering 20 acres (8 ha) and can produce up to 2 megawatts of power, or enough to serve about 630 average households. Four additional facilities, located in Los Lunas, Deming, Alamogordo, and Las Vegas, will be larger, each with an expected capacity of 5 megawatts. Together, the five plants will offset 44 million pounds of carbon, which is equivalent to taking 4,500 cars off the road.

New Mexico also produces a large amount of energy from wind resources. The city of Albuquerque is part of the Sky Blue Program, a renewable wind energy program offered by the PNM, under which the city government has achieved the goal of purchasing 20 percent of the city's total kilowatt-hour usage in the form of wind-generated electricity in order to reduce the city's carbon footprint, greenhouse gas emissions, and fossil fuel usage. The wind energy used in Albuquerque is created by 136 turbines on a field covering 9,600 acres (3,885 ha) at the New Mexico Wind Energy Center near Clovis, New Mexico. In March 2007, New Mexico adopted a renewable portfolio standard that requires 20 percent of an electric utility's power to come from renewable energy sources by 2020.

❧ Green Business, Green Building, Green Jobs

Setting High Standards for Green Building

In 2006, the governor signed an executive order that called for all executive branch state agencies, including the higher education department, to adopt the U.S. Green Buildings Council's Leadership in Energy and Environmental Design (LEED) rating system. Newly constructed public buildings over 15,000 square feet and/or using over 50 kilowatts peak electrical demand (and similarly sized renovations involving the replacement of two of the three major systems—HVAC, lighting, and plumbing) must achieve a minimum rating of LEED Silver and significant energy savings. Smaller building projects must achieve a minimum delivered energy performance standard of one-half of the U.S. energy consumption for that building type as defined by the U.S. Department of Energy. All other new construction, renovations, repairs, and replacements of state buildings must employ cost-effective, energy efficient, green building practices to the maximum extent possible.

In April 2007, New Mexico's Senate Bill 463 established a personal and corporate tax credit for sustainable buildings. Commercial buildings that meet the requirements for the LEED Silver or higher certification for new construction, existing buildings, core and shell, or commercial interiors are eligible. Eligible residential buildings include single-family homes and multi-family homes, which are certified as either Build Green NM Silver or higher or LEED-H Silver or higher, and Energy Star certified manufactured homes. The amount of the credit varies according to square footage for both commercial and residential buildings. The Navajo Nation's Baca/Dlo'ay azhi Community School in Prewitt was the first LEED-certified building in New Mexico (and the first U.S. Department of the Interior building) to receive the

designation. Certified in 2004, the community school, which is operated by the Bureau of Indian Affairs, boasts an optimized heating and air conditioning system and the use of recycled steel.

On the municipal level, the city of Albuquerque established the Green Path Program in 2005, in order to encourage and facilitate voluntary design and construction of energy efficient buildings. The program issues certificates with the building permit at the completion of high-performance green building projects. The certificates are official recognition by the Green Path administrator of the level of achievement that each building project represents. The city is also part of the 2030 Challenge, which is a global initiative that encourages cities to design all new buildings, developments, and major renovations to meet a fossil fuel, GHG-emitting, energy consumption performance standard of 50 percent of the regional or country average for that building type. The energy consumption performance standard will be increased every five years in order for the city to eventually become carbon-neutral by 2030.

For homebuilders in New Mexico, the Home Builders Association of Central New Mexico (HBA CNM), with the Green Building Initiative, started the Build Green NM (BGNM) program in 2006. A voluntary program, BGNM encourages builders to use technologies, products, and practices that will provide greater energy efficiency and reduce pollution, reduce water usage, and preserve natural resources. Each home that meets the criteria can attain one of four possible levels: bronze, silver, gold, and the highest, emerald.

Encouraging Green Business

There are many rebate and incentive programs which encourage green business in New Mexico. Two programs that emerged in 2009 were the Solar Energy Improvement Special Assessment Act and the Renewable Energy Financing District Act. The Renewable Energy Financing District Act provides financing for property owners to install renewable energy technologies that include photovoltaics, solar thermal, geothermal and wind technologies. The Solar Energy Improvement Special Assessment Act authorizes each county to create a solar energy improvement special assessment provision, which allows the county to create rules for certifying certain private banks and financing institutions as "solar energy improvement financing institutions." Certified institutions can loan property owners up to 40 percent of the assessed value of the property for purposes of solar energy (photovoltaic or solar thermal) improvements.

Working for a "Greener" New Mexico

According to a Pew Charitable Trusts report released in 2009, New Mexico's green jobs economy grew more than twenty-five times faster than overall jobs between

1998 and 2007. While the size of the green jobs economy is small, its growth is fast, increasing by 50.1 percent over ten years. By 2007, the state had 4,815 clean energy jobs and 577 green businesses. Of these green jobs, the majority are in conservation and pollution mitigation, with others in energy efficiency, clean energy and training and support. Of these sectors, jobs in energy efficiency grew the most over the past ten years, by 184 percent.

In an effort to enhance clean energy and clean technology economic development and job creation in the state, Governor Bill Richardson created a Green Jobs Cabinet in 2009. A *New Mexico Green Jobs Guidebook* is available through the New Mexico Economic Development Web site. Developed by the Green Jobs Cabinet, the guidebook provides an accessible overview to green jobs in New Mexico for students and job seekers.

When it comes to green jobs training and education, New Mexico's universities have an abundance of programs available. On April 17, 2007, New Mexico State University president Michael Martin signed an agreement making New Mexico State University (NMSU) a member of the American College and University Presidents Climate Commitment. The purpose of the commitment is to make the university a positive example within the community by enacting policies that encourage climate neutrality, sustainability, and energy conservation on campus. Second, the university is charged with the task of educating the next generation of citizens, scientists, and community leaders to be sensitive to the issues of climate change and sustainability and to provide them the knowledge and skills necessary to achieve climate neutrality. NMSU faculty incorporates sustainability related issues into their courses, and the Sustainability at NMSU website keeps an inventory of courses across a myriad of disciplines with sustainability, climate, and environmental themes.

The state's community colleges are also involved in developing training programs for emerging fields. Both Santa Fe and San Juan Community Colleges have renewable energy training programs, Mesalands Community College has a wind power training program, and Central New Mexico Community College has a selection of "green" training programs.

Encouraging Citizens To Become "Greener"

New Mexico has programs in place to encourage not only businesses but homeowners to be greener in their daily life. The New Mexico Solar Market Development Tax Credit provides financing up to 10 percent of the cost of a solar photovoltaic (PV) or solar thermal system. To qualify, the system had to have been installed after 2009 and only provides up to $9,000, but the effort can be combined with a federal tax credit for up to 30 percent of the cost of the project. Up to $5 million in state tax support is available through 2016 for the program.

Plenty of Water, Too Salty to Drink: Groundwater Desalination

Despite dealing with periodic drought, New Mexico does not have a water shortage. However, at least 75 percent of its groundwater is too salty to drink. With the cost of desalination—the treatment of salty water into potable water—now comparable to the cost of treating of river water, New Mexico has been able to tap into a plentiful resource: its brackish groundwater. To supply drinking water to a growing population, some communities are turning to the option of desalination of these brackish groundwater reserves to supplement the surface and groundwater they already use.

The Brackish Groundwater National Desalination Research Facility was opened in Alamogordo, New Mexico in 2007. The center focuses on developing technologies for the desalination of brackish groundwater found in the inland states with the expertise of researchers from federal government agencies, universities, the private sector, research organizations, and state and local agencies.

In 2004, the Alamogordo Regional Water Supply Project—also known as the Snake Tank wells project— received a permit to build 10 wells on the Bureau of Land Management's (BLM) land north of Tularosa, New Mexico. The plan was to deliver water collected from these wells to a desalination plant near the Brackish Groundwater National Desalination Research Facility. The 2004 permit was met with protests and was appealed, but officials received a new permit—issued in 2008—that allowed them to go ahead with the project. The initiative will permit the facility to draw and divert up to 4,000 acre-feet (an acre-foot can supply two average households a year) of water per year, which equates to 1,303.6 million gallons per year. This will allow the production of up to five million gallons a day of water on peak days as needed. In May 2010, the city received funding for the first 15 miles of water transmission pipeline from the Snake Tank field to the city. Officials are also in discussions with nearby Holloman Air Force Base for co-use of the Bonito Lake pipeline, which would alleviate the need for approximately 13 miles of new pipeline.

In August 2010, the Draft Environmental Impact Statement (EIS) for the project was released. The draft EIS evaluates potential biological, economic, and social consequences that could result from the project and its alternatives. The draft and eventually the final EIS will help the Bureau of Land Management determine whether or not they should authorize a right-of-way to the city of Alamogordo to develop the well sites and pipeline infrastructure. The draft statement did not have an alternative plan, other than that of no action. After the public comments on the draft are gathered, an alternative plan will be constructed from these comments and incorporated into the final EIS. As the final EIS has yet to be released, the Snake Tank Wells project has yet to become a reality.

Another project, started in January 2010, involved plans for a desalination plant in Sandoval County, which would be capable of processing five million gallons of brackish water daily from an aquifer in the Rio Puerco basin, near Rio Rancho. Engineers estimate that the aquifer contains between a half million acre-feet to 2.5 million acre-feet of water. The project does not come without obstacles, however. Planners are striving to make sure they can cover the costs of technology, find energy sources for the plant, and identify cost-efficient methods of handling the waste byproducts of the desalinization process.

In April 2010, the project hit a legal snag as there were disputes over the ownership of the land on which two wells were drilled. At that time, the county was considering looking into other potential well sites. In December 2010, Sandoval County agreed to let Arizona-based developer Recorp/Aperion assume responsibility for developing the desalination plant. This agreement settles a lawsuit the developer filed against the county over access to the site. Recorp has eight years to transform the exploration wells the county drilled into a water utility project for Sandoval County customers. The developer must also reimburse the county the $6 million it has invested in the project either in cash, land, or a combination of both. If Recorp does not develop a water utility within eight years, the county will have the option to take over the project again.

New Mexico's supply of surface and ground water has been coming up short for citizens as the population grows, so if these and other desalination projects are successful, then the state will find itself with a plentiful new resource.

BIBLIOGRAPHY

Books

Benedict, Audrey Delella. *The Naturalist's Guide to the Southern Rockies: Colorado, Southern Wyoming, and Northern New Mexico*. Golden, CO: Fulcrum Publishing, 2008.

Donahue, Debra L. *The Western Range Revisited: Removing Livestock from Public Lands to Conserve Native Biodiversity*. Norman, OK: University of Oklahoma Press, 2000.

Hamilton, Lisa. *Deeply Rooted: Unconventional Farmers in the Age of Agribusiness*. Berkeley, CA: Counterpoint Press, 2010.

Nagle, John Copeland. *Law's Environment: How the Law Shapes the Places We Live*. New Haven, CT: Yale University Press, 2010.

Page, Jake, and George H. H. Huey. *The Smithsonian Guides to Natural America: The Southwest–New Mexico, Arizona*. Washington, DC: Smithsonian Books, 1995.

Web Sites

"The 2030 Challenge." Architecture 2030. Available from http://www.architecture2030.org/2030_challenge/index.html

"Alamogordo Regional Water Supply Project Environmental Impact Statement." U.S. Department of the Interior. Available from http://www.blm.gov/nm/st/en/fo/Las_Cruces_District_Office/alamogordo_regional.html

Associated Press. "Wildfire scorches 23,000 acres in eastern NM." KBO Eyewitness News 4. April 11, 2011. Available from http://www.kob.com/article/stories/S2061054.shtml?cat=525.

"Baca/Dlo'ay azhi Consolidated School." The U.S. Department of the Interior. Available from http://www.doi.gov/greening/awards/2004/baca.html

Barringer, Felicity. "2 Environmental Rules Halted in New Mexico." January 6, 2011. *The New York Times*. Available from http://www.nytimes.com/2011/01/07/us/07emit.html?pagewanted=print

"Brackish Groundwater National Desalination Research Facility." U.S. Department of the Interior. Available from. http://www.usbr.gov/pmts/water/research/tularosa.html

Bryan, Susan Montoya. "Recusal of NM Regulators Sought in Emissions Case." Business Week/Associated Press. September 1, 2011. Available from http://www.businessweek.com/ap/financialnews/D9PFUVN81.htm

"Build Green NM." Available from http://www.buildgreennm.com/

"Carlsbad Caverns National Park." Available from http://www.nps.gov/cave/index.htm

"Cimarron Solar energizes first 10 megawatts." Tri-State Generation and Transmission Association, Inc. Available from http://www.tristategt.org/NewsCenter/NewsItems/Renewable-Project-Update.cfm

"Clean Energy Tax Incentives: Solar Market Development Tax Credit." New Mexico Energy, Minerals & Natural Resources Department. Available from http://www.emnrd.state.nm.us/ECMD/CleanEnergyTaxIncentives/solartaxcredit.htm

"Climate Change Action Plan." Climate Change Advisory Group. Available from http://www.nmclimatechange.us/ewebeditpro/items/O117F10150.pdf

"Desalination of saline and brackish water becoming more affordable." Sandia National Laboratories.

Available from https://share.sandia.gov/news/resources/news_releases/desalination-of-saline-and-brackish-water/

"Desert Bighorns may be removed from state endangered species list." New Mexico Department of Game and Fish. Available from http://www.wildlife.state.nm.us/publications/press_releases/documents/2010/051810bighorns.html

"The Dexter National Fish Hatchery and Technology Center." Available from http://www.fws.gov/southwest/fisheries/dexter/index.html

"A dozen counties face fire restrictions." KRQE News 13. April 11, 2011. Available from http://www.krqe.com/dpp/weather/wildfires/a-dozen-counties-face-fire-restrictions.

"Energy Efficiency Standards for State Buildings (New Mexico)." Available from http://en.openei.org/wiki/Energy_Efficiency_Standards_for_State_Buildings_%28New_Mexico%29

"Greenhouse Cap-and-Trade Provisions (Title 20, Chapter 2, part 350)." New Mexico Environmental Improvement Board. Available from http://www.nmenv.state.nm.us/cc/documents/20_2_350_NMAC_final.pdf.

"The Green Path Program." Albuquerque Official City Website. Available from http://www.cabq.gov/albuquerquegreen/green-goals/green-building

"Local Option—Renewable Energy Financing District/Solar Energy Improvement Special Assessments." New Mexico Incentives/Policies for Renewables and Efficiency. Available from http://www.dsireusa.org/incentives/incentive.cfm?Incentive_Code=NM28F&re=1&ee=1

Martinez, Susana. *Executive Order 2011-001: Formation Of A Small Business-Friendly Task Force.* Office of the Governor, State of New Mexico. Available from http://www.governor.state.nm.us/uploads/FileLinks/1e77a5621a1544e28318ba93fcd47d49/EO-2011-001.pdf.

New Mexico Fire Information. Available from http://nmfireinfo.wordpress.com.

"New Mexico Governor Loses Bid to Overturn Greenhouse Gas Cap." Environment News Service. January 26, 2011. Available from http://www.ens-newswire.com/ens/jan2011/2011-01-26-091.html.

"New Mexico Wildlife, Waterfowl, and Fisheries Management Areas." Available from http://www.wildlife.state.nm.us/conservation/wildlife_management_areas/index.htm

"New Mexico's Green Economy: Capitalizing on Assets and Opportunities." New Mexico Green Jobs Cabinet. Available from http://www.edd.state.nm.us/greenEconomy/governorsGreenJobsCabinetReport.pdf

"NMDA Strategic Plan 2009–2013." New Mexico Department of Agriculture. Available from http://nmocc.state.nm.us/events-and-publications-folder/Strategic%20Plan_2009-2013.pdf

O'Brien, Renee A. "New Mexico's Forest Resources, 2000." U.S. Forest Service Treesearch. Available from http://www.treesearch.fs.fed.us/pubs/6272

"Organic Production." United States Department of Agriculture's Economic Research Service. Available from http://www.ers.usda.gov/Data/Organic/

"Pew Report: New Mexico Clean Energy Economy Jobs Grew 25 Times Faster than Overall Jobs." Available from http://www.pewglobalwarming.org/cleanenergyeconomy/pdf/NM_Release_09-0610.pdf

"PNM's First Large-Scale Solar Plant Up and Running." PNM. April 20, 2011. Available from http://www.pnm.com/news/2011/0420_abq_solar_dedication.htm.

"PNM Sky Blue Program." Public Service Company of New Mexico (PNM). Available from http://www.pnm.com/customers/sky_blue.htm?source=enviro_home

"Potential effects of climate change on New Mexico." New Mexico Environment Department. Available from http://www.nmenv.state.nm.us/aqb/cc/Potential_Effects_Climate_Change_NM.pdf

Rayburn, Rosalie. "Desalination Plant a Go." *Albuquerque Journal.* Available from http://www.allbusiness.com/government/government-bodies-offices-regional/13834644-1.html

Rayburn, Rosalie. "Sandoval County, Developer Settle Dispute Over Desalination Plant Site." December 30, 2010. *Albuquerque Journal.* Available from http://www.abqjournal.com/abqnews/abqnewseeker-mainmenu-39/26129-sandoval-county-developer-settle-dispute-over-desalination-plant-site.html

Reichbach, Matthew. "Bill to restrict board's greenhouse gas regs clears committee." *The New Mexico Independent.* March 1, 2011. Available from http://newmexicoindependent.com/69068/bill-to-restrict-enviro-boards-greenhouse-gas-regs-clears-committee.

"Renewables Portfolio Standard." New Mexico Incentives/Policies for Renewables and Efficiency. Available from http://www.dsireusa.org/incentives/incentive.cfm?Incentive_Code=NM05R&state=NM&CurrentPageID=1

"Schools blaze path to LEED-certified construction status." New Mexico Business Weekly.

Available from http://albuquerque.bizjournals.com/albuquerque/stories/2006/03/13/story7.html

"Sustainability at NMSU." New Mexico State University. Available from http://sustainability.nmsu.edu/

"Sustainable Building Tax Credit (Personal) SB 463." New Mexico Incentives/Policies for Renewables and Efficiency. Available from http://www.dsireusa.org/incentives/incentive.cfm?Incentive_Code=NM15F&re=1&ee=1

"2008 Minerals Yearbook: New Mexico." U.S. Geological Survey. March 2011. Available from http://minerals.usgs.gov/minerals/pubs/state/2008/myb2-2008-nm.pdf

"Wind Energy." Albuquerque Official City Website. Available from http://www.cabq.gov/albuquerquegreen/green-goals/energy-and-emissions/wind-energy

New York

Driving across the Empire State, as New York is known, one cannot help but notice its topographic diversity. The western part of the state—the Great Lakes Plain—is relatively low and flat, whereas large parts of the remainder of the state progress into more mountainous terrain. The Adirondack Mountains in the northeast and the Taconic Mountains in the relative southeast, serve as the state's highlands. Roughly 40 percent of New York is situated at an elevation of one thousand feet or more.

Located in the northeastern United States, New York ranks thirtieth in size among the 50 states. The total land area of New York is 47,214 square miles (127,190 sq km). The state lies entirely within North America's humid continental zone, but there is climatic variation from region to region. The state's three main climatic regions are the southeastern lowlands, with the warmest temperatures and longest season between frosts; the uplands of the Catskills and Adirondacks, where winters are cold and summers cool; and the snow belt along the Great Lakes, one of the snowiest areas of the United States.

New York Acts on Climate Change

Multiple state agencies have been involved in identifying the impacts of climate change and finding ways to reduce greenhouse gas emissions, as well as create new sources of renewable energy. New York's Department of Environmental Conservation cites effects such as warmer temperatures, higher sea levels, increases in high-precipitation weather events and stressors on native species like the sugar maple that may threaten their survival as a direct result from climate change. Successive New York gubernatorial administrations have taken steps to address climate change in the state. Three-term governor George Pataki (in office 1995–2006) began this process in June 2001, when he formed the New York State Greenhouse Gas Task Force. The task force was charged with developing policy recommendations for reducing the

state's greenhouse gas emissions; in 2003, it recommended a greenhouse gas reduction target of 5 percent below 1990 levels by 2010, and 10 percent by 2020. Governor David Paterson, who assumed the office in 2008, outlined even more ambitious greenhouse gas reduction targets upon taking office. In August 2009, Paterson signed Executive Order 24, which established a greenhouse gas reductions target of 80 percent from the levels released in 1990 by 2050. Additionally, EO 24 created the Climate Action Council (CAC), which was charged with preparing an official Climate Action Plan (CAP) for New York. The New York State Climate Action Plan Interim Report was released in November of 2010. The report puts forth a number of strategies and policy suggestions to help the state reach its goal of reducing greenhouse gas emissions 80 percent below 1990 levels by 2050. Input on suggested policy options is still being collected, and work on the final Climate Action Plan will continue during 2011.

New York is a member of the Regional Greenhouse Gas Initiative (RGGI), a cooperative cap-and-trade program involving nine Northeastern and Mid-Atlantic states. The program is designed with the goal to reduce power sector carbon dioxide emissions by 10 percent by 2018. To that end, the regional cap established by the group was set at 188 million short tons of carbon dioxide emissions per year from 2009 to 2014. Starting in 2015 the cap will decrease by 2.5 percent each year. Carbon dioxide allowances for power plants can be obtained or traded in quarterly auctions. Each state may then reinvest its auction proceeds in programs that support the growth of a clean energy economy. In New York, the state's auction proceeds are jointly administered by the New York State Energy Research Development Authority, the Department of Environmental Conservation, and the Public Service Commission. Proceeds are invested in projects related to improvements in energy efficiency, the development of clean and renewable energy technologies, and the expansion of a green workforce, among others.

The first three-year control (or compliance) period began on January 1, 2009, and was set to end on December 31, 2011. At that time, each regulated power plant must submit one allowance for each ton of carbon dioxide emitted during the control period. The RGGI represents the first mandatory, market-based carbon dioxide emissions program in the United States, and originally boasted ten member states. However, in May 2011, the governor of New Jersey withdrew his state from the cooperative, calling it "ineffective." New York Department of Environmental Conservation Commissioner Joseph Martens reaffirmed New York's commitment to the effort through a statement released May 26, 2011. In it, he says "In New York, investment of RGGI auction proceeds in energy efficiency improvements is leading to savings for thousands of New York residents and businesses, and to the creation of thousands of high quality jobs. Regionwide, emissions from the power plants covered by RGGI have gone down much faster than expected, providing New York and its partners in RGGI with the opportunity to further strengthen the RGGI program."

❧ Natural Resources, Water, and Agriculture

Natural Resources: Forests

New York boasts roughly 150 species of trees, with forests covering more land today (18.6 million acres or 62 percent of the state) than at any time since the mid-1800s. Observers attribute New York's great forest reclamation to the rise of eco-consciousness at the end of the 19th century and the realization that forests were not an inexhaustible resource. Nearly three million acres of these forests are found in the Adirondack and Catskills Forest Preserves, which hold tremendous biodiversity. The forest industries, including recreation, employ more than 70,000 people and contribute about $8.8 billion annually to the economy. The most common forest type is northern hardwood, followed by elm-ash-red maple and oak-hickory types. White and red pine, spruce, and fir are commonly found among the forests as well. Christmas trees and maple syrup are notable forest products for the state, with sales totaling about $25 million in 2005. New York ranks seventh in the United States in sales of Christmas trees. About 90 percent of New York's timberlands are owned by family forest owners or business concerns.

Natural Resources: Parks and Wildlife

There are 178 state parks and 22 national parks within the state. In total, over 600 species of mammals, birds, and reptiles live in New York. White-tailed deer, snowshoe hare, common and New England cottontails, woodchuck, squirrel, muskrat, and raccoon are among

As of 2011, the statewide black bear population was estimated at 6,000–7,000, with the largest concentration (4,000–5,000) found in the Adirondack region. *jadimages/ShutterStock.com*

the most common mammals. Bobcat, red and gray fox, and Eastern coyote can also be found in some park and forest areas. Several types of warblers, sparrows, and woodpeckers are among the common birds. The bluebird was designated the state bird in 1970; the beaver was adopted as the state animal in 1975. The U.S Fish and Wildlife Service lists 27 New York plant and animal species that are federally threatened or endangered. Endangered animals include the shortnose sturgeon and the Indiana bat, while endangered plant species include the northeastern bulrush and the sandplain gerardia.

The black bears that were once found primarily in large forested areas of the state have expanded their range throughout the state since the 1990s, occasionally being sighted in nearly every upstate county. As of 2011, the statewide black bear population was estimated at 6,000–7,000, with the largest concentration (4,000–5,000) found in the Adirondack region. Due to the growing number of conflicts between bears and people, in January 2011, the state Department of Environmental Conservation (DEC) announced a change to the state regulation that prohibits the feeding of black bears. While the intentional feeding of bears has always been discouraged, the new ban also applies to indirect feeding through food attractants, such as improperly packaged garbage and refuse or bird feeders that are easily accessible to bears. The new regulation gives the DEC the authority to remove such attractants if they are determined to be nuisances.

Historically, New York has been at the forefront of the conservation movement. In 1908, New York became the first state to require a hunting license for the taking of wildlife and soon after, in 1925, New York established The Conservation Fund to help manage and protect fish and wildlife in the state. These efforts have continued into the new millennium. The New York Division of Fish, Wildlife and Marine Resources completed in 2005 a

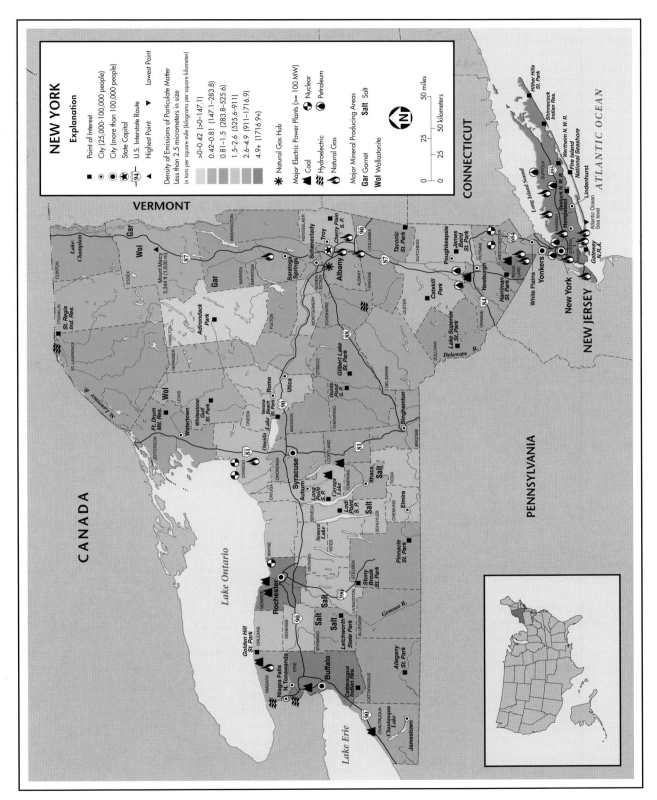

SOURCES: "County Emissions Map: Criteria Air Pollutants." *AirData*. U.S. Environmental Protection Agency. Available from http://www.epa.gov/air/data/geosel.html; *Energy Maps*. U.S. Energy Information Administration. Available from http://www.eia.gov/state; *Highest and Lowest Elevations*. U.S. Geological Survey. Available from http://egsc.usgs.gov/isb/pubs/booklets/elvadist/elvadist.html#Highest; *2007 Minerals Yearbook*. U.S. Geological Survey. Available from http://minerals.usgs.gov/minerals/pubs/state. © 2011 Cengage Learning.

Comprehensive Wildlife Conservation Strategy (CWCS), which established a strategy for state wildlife conservation and funding. In addition to requiring detailed monitoring of species, habitats, and statewide threats to wildlife, the CWCS also ensured that New York would be eligible to receive State Wildlife Grant (SWG) funds through the U. S. Fish and Wildlife Service. The grants can ease the financial burden of wildlife conservation.

Natural Resources: Minerals

Reserves of mineral and metal ores are found throughout New York State, supporting a $1.5 billion-a-year mining industry. Approximately 90 percent of state mining revenue is earned through the extraction of sand, gravel, and limestone. Mining occurs in every county in New York State except some surrounding New York City (Bronx, Kings, New York, Queens, and Richmond counties). New York is the only state that produces wollastonite, a mineral used to improve the performance of plastics, paints and coatings, ceramics, and metals. Nationally, New York ranks second in output of industrial garnet, and third in salt production. It dropped in 2008 from the fifth spot to sixth for production of zinc and cadmium in zinc concentrates. It also dropped to third from second in peat production, but New York remains a significant producer of peat in the United States.

Water

New York State is endowed with more than 7,600 freshwater lakes, ponds and reservoirs, as well as portions of two of the five Great Lakes. The most notable of these bodies of water include the Finger Lakes—five large, finger-like bodies of water in central New York; Lake Ontario and Erie—the two Great Lakes that border the state to the north; and Lake Champlain. New York also has thousands of rivers and streams that traverse the state and flow into larger bodies of water. Overall, more than seventy thousand miles of rivers and streams crisscross the state. Notable rivers include the Hudson, Susquehanna, Delaware, and Saint Lawrence. The Niagara River forms part of New York's border with the Canadian province of Ontario, and connects Lake Erie and Lake Ontario. Niagara Falls on the Niagara River cascades about 175 feet (53 m) and provides an important source of hydroelectric power.

The Delaware River Basin, which covers more than 13,500 square miles in New York, Pennsylvania, New Jersey, and Delaware, serves as a major resource for more than 15 million people, providing water for drinking and agricultural and industrial uses. This important resource is managed primarily through the work of the Delaware River Basin Commission (DRBC). The commission was established in 1961 through the passage of concurrent legislation in the four basin states and with the accompanying signature of President John F. Kennedy. The compact that formed the commission created the

New York State Profile	
Physical Characteristics	
Land area	47,126 square miles (122,056 sq km)
Inland water area	1,979 square miles (5,126 sq km)
Coastal area	977 square miles (1,572 sq km)
Highest point	Mount Marcy 5,344 feet (1,629 m)
National Forest System lands (2010)	16,000 acres (6,000 ha)
State parks (2011)	178
Energy Statistics	
Total energy production (2009)	900 trillion Btu
State ranking in total energy production (2009)	21
Renewable energy net generation total (2009)	32.1 million megawatt hours
Hydroelectric energy generation (2009)	27.6 million megawatt hours
Biomass energy generation (2009)	1.7 million megawatt hours
Wind energy generation (2009)	2.3 million megawatt hours
Wood and derived fuel energy generation (2009)	536,000 megawatt hours
Crude oil reserves (2009)	NA
Natural gas reserves (2009)	196 billion cubic feet (5.6 billion cu m)
Natural gas liquids (2008)	NA
Pollution Statistics	
Carbon output (2005)	214.3 million tons of CO_2 (194.4 million t)
Superfund sites (2008)	87
Particulate matter (less than 2.5 micrometers) emissions (2002)	16,483 tons per year (14,953 t/yr)
Toxic chemical releases (2009)	23.3 million pounds (10.6 million kg)
Generated hazardous waste (2009)	1 million tons (936,800 t)

SOURCES: AirData. U.S. Environmental Protection Agency. Available from http://www.epa.gov/air/data; *Energy Maps, Facts, and Data of the U.S. States.* U.S. Energy Information Administration. Available from http://www.eia.gov/state; *The 2012 Statistical Abstract.* U.S. Census Bureau. Available from http://www.census.gov/compendia/statab; *United States Energy Usage.* eRedux. Available from http://www.eredux.net/states.

© 2011 Cengage Learning.

first regional body to share equal authority with the federal government in the management of a river system. Since then, the commission has been instrumental in providing programs for water quality protection, supply allocation, conservation efforts, drought and flood management, watershed planning, and recreation. The commissioners include the governors of New York, New Jersey, Pennsylvania, and Delaware and a federal representative, with each commissioner having one vote and all votes having equal power.

The state's inland waters are home to more than 165 fish species, including several types of catfish, perch, and pike. The waters of the Atlantic Coast, including the Long Island Sound and New York Bay, are home to

Niagara Falls on the Niagara River are an important source of hydroelectric power.   © *Byron Jorjorian/Alamy*

numerous species of marine fish, crabs, mussels, clams, and more. Marine mammals include the six types of whale and the harbor seal. About five species of sea turtle travel through New York waters from June through November. Commercial fishing is important to the local economy. Some of the top marine species include Atlantic surfclam, silver hake, longfin squid, scup, golden tilefish, hard clam (quahog), and sea scallops. The New York Department of Environmental Conservation operates twelve fish hatcheries throughout the state, producing a variety of fish including brown, rainbow, and brook trout; steelhead, coho, and chinook salmon; muskellunge, walleye, and lake sturgeon.

Ports at Buffalo (on Lake Erie), Albany (on the Hudson River), and Jefferson (on Long Island Sound) are important points for commercial trade. The extensive, 524-mile (201-km) New York State Canal System connects the Hudson River with the Great Lakes, Finger Lakes, and Lake Champlain. The Port of New York and New Jersey is the largest port on the East Coast and the third largest in the nation by tonnage, generating more than $ billion in annual tax revenues for state and local governments. The Port Authority of New York and New Jersey is currently working on projects to expand its cargo handling capabilities in anticipation of an increase in trade from the completion of the Panama Canal expansion in 2014.

Massive Hudson River Cleanup. The Hudson River Cleanup, a project that aims to reclaim a huge section of the Hudson River severely damaged by industrial dumping, represents one of the most costly and complicated environmental cleanups in U.S. history. The stretch of river on which the project focuses extends about two hundred miles, from Hudson Falls in eastern, upstate New York to the Battery in New York City. For three decades (1947–1977), General Electric (GE), a major American corporation, dumped more than one million pounds of polychlorinated biphenyls (PCBs) from two capacitor manufacturing plants into the Hudson River. PCBs, when ingested in sufficient quantities by humans through contaminated fish, can cause a host of health problems including low birth weight, thyroid disease, and learning, memory, and immune system disorders.

From May 15 through November 2009, GE, under Environmental Protection Agency (EPA) oversight, began dredging the PCB-laden sediment out of the river as phase one of a multi-part cleanup. The toxic sediment was then transported by rail to Texas, where it was placed in a landfill approved to accept PCB-contaminated material.

Reviews of phase one by both GE and the EPA took place throughout 2010 in order to consider the successes and challenges presented by the process. Phase one suffered several delays and setbacks when the PCB-infused river muck was discovered to be far thicker than original probing projected. Additionally, GE claimed that the sediment removal process had released PCBs into the river and that fish from the affected areas tested with higher levels of PCBs after the dredging than before the cleanup work began. The EPA report disputed GE's data, suggesting that the rising PCB levels in the fish stock were unlikely to be permanent. Most notably, the final evaluation reports from both GE and the EPA each indicated that, despite the use of the best available dredging technology and controls and strict adherence to EPA guidelines, phase one still fell short of achieving the Engineering Performance Standards (EPS) set by the EPA. However, the EPA also noted that phase one proved to be successful in that both the sediment volume and the PCB mass removed met or exceeded the amounts initially estimated for this part of the process.

As a result of these evaluations, in March 2011 the EPA announced a new set of standards for phase two of the cleanup and extended the time frame for removal of all affected sediment, from five years to seven. Dredging during phase two will involve deeper digging than that employed in the first phase, and new procedures should ensure that fewer dredging passes will be necessary. GE launched phase two in June 2011; during this phase, GE aims to remove 350,000 cubic yards, or 400,000 tons, of PCB containing sediment from the river by October via barges with multiple dredges mounted on them. The project will employ about 500 workers. Over the life of the Phase 2 project, about 2.4 million cubic yards of sediment will be removed and disposed of at federally approved facilties.

Agriculture: From Milk to McIntoshes

New York is home to over 36,000 farms, which collectively account for 23 percent of the state's total land area. Agriculture is a multibillion dollar-a-year industry and produces a vast array of consumables—from meat and dairy products to the state's renowned McIntosh apples and tart cherries. Milk is the most economically important agricultural product in the state, accounting for more than $2 billion in revenues a year—half of total agricultural receipts in New York. New York is also known for its grapes, grape juices, and award-winning wines, with major grape-growing areas surrounding the Finger Lakes, the Hudson River Valley, Lake Erie, and the eastern end of Long Island.

Organic Farming Grows in Popularity in New York. The Northeast Organic Farming Association of New York (NOFA-NY) has certified organic farms since 1984, and operates in a growing industry. As of 2011, the Northeast Organic Farming Association had certified more than 600 farms, dairies, or processors certified organic in New York. Several other organizations, both inside and outside of New York, can also certify state farms as organic. Figures updated in 2009 from the Economic Research Service of the U.S. Department of Agriculture showed 803 farms in New York as certified organic in 2008.

✿ Energy: Exploring New Pipelines

New York consumes more energy than most U.S. states, yet on a per capita basis, consumes among the least energy in the nation. The average New York household consumes half the energy of the average U.S. household—an accomplishment attributed to widely used urban public transportation systems.

The two largest power sources in New York—nuclear energy and natural gas—each account for about 30 percent of New York's electric power consumption. Four locally operated nuclear reactors generate all of the nuclear energy for the state. Hydroelectric power also functions as a major power source for New York, with the strong currents of the Hudson and Niagara rivers being harvested for electricity. The Robert Moses hydroelectric plant—on the Niagara River—is one of the largest hydroelectric facilities in the world, capable of producing 2,353 megawatts of clean, renewable power.

As of 2010, New York led the rest of the United States in converting landfill gas to energy. In that year, there were 21 landfill gas recovery facilities in the state, which generate energy via the natural breakdown of solid waste through anaerobic micro-organisms. According to New York's Department of Environmental Conservation, landfill gas-to-energy projects "control the migration of explosive gases, treat emissions and can offset tons of sulfer dioxide emissions which could be produced by fossil-fuel power generation."

Much of the state's natural gas is imported from Canada and other U.S. states. The state has begun to consider the exploitation of the natural gas reserves of the black shale Marcellus formation, which extends deep underground from Ohio and West Virginia northeast into Pennsylvania and southern New York. Drilling activity in New York is expected to focus on areas where the Marcellus shale is deeper than 2,000 feet, using the controversial hydraulic fracturing mining method, commonly known as fracking.

However, state officials determined that this new process of mining would require a new set of rules and regulations, particularly in regards to environmental

Oil shipping pipelines in New York City. © 2011 Kim Steele/Jupiterimages Corporation

protection. As a result, in September 2009, the New York Department of Environmental Conservation (DEC) released its Draft Supplemental Generic Environmental Impact Statement (Draft SGEIS) concerning issues related to fracking. The public review period that ended in December 2009 resulted in more than 10,000 comments, but the DEC did not move forward to formalize any proposals regarding fracking permits at that time. Instead, a revised draft was requested to take a closer look at the potential impact of the process. The revised draft report was released in July 2011, and residents were given until December 12, 2011, to comment.

As citizens' concerns mounted, in November 2010 the New York State Assembly passed legislation that could have placed a six-month moratorium on the use of fracking for oil and gas exploration throughout the state. That bill was vetoed by Governor David A. Peterson in December 2010, as he determined that the terms of the moratorium were too broad and that the Draft SGEIS should be revised in order to reflect a greater review of

public comments. As an alternative measure, Peterson issued Executive Order 41, which called for the completion of the new draft from the DEC by June 1, 2011, and placed a moratorium on "high-volume, horizontal hydraulic fracturing," while allowing a continuation of the permitting process for vertical wells, which rarely use fracking techniques.

In the wake of this decision, in February 2011, the City Council of Buffalo unanimously passed an ordinance to prohibit fracking within the city and to ban the storage, transport, treatment, or disposal of fracking waste within the city. While no such drilling operations have yet been proposed for Buffalo, city officials fear that fracking wastewater from neighboring areas could end up in the city sewer system. A number of other towns and cities have begun to consider similar bans as well. One of the most prevalent concerns is the potential for contamination of rivers, streams, and drinking water systems.

In the spring of 2011, the Delaware River Basin Commission (of which New York governor Andrew Cuomo is a member) was also at work on a set of regulations to address the environmental concerns that could arise from fracking operations, specifically those in Pennsylvania along the Delaware River.

The 182-mile (293-km) Millennium Pipeline, operational since 2008, could potentially be used to transport natural gas mined from the Marcellus shale to the high-demand markets of northern New Jersey and New York City. This 30-inch diameter natural gas pipeline runs from Corning in Steuben County across New York's Southern Tier and down the western side of Sullivan and Orange counties, ending at Ramapo in Rockland County.

A proposed ethanol pipeline connecting Iowa to New York City could provide New York with access to more renewable energy resources. The proposed 1,700-mile (2,736-km), $3 billion pipeline, if approved, would carry ten million gallons (37,854 l) of ethanol per day. However, the pipeline is controversial and, as of early 2010, its development remained far from assured. Skeptics predict that the pipeline would be subject to malfunction and failure over time because of the corrosiveness of ethanol. Additionally, corn-based ethanol critics argue that the fuel represents a less-than-efficient power source, requiring unjustifiably high energy inputs—from those associated with agricultural cultivation to the energy inputs linked to running of the production facilities—to produce the finished product. Moreover, the notion of diverting potential food supplies and arable land to meet energy demands troubles some critics and smacks others as unethical. In July 2010, a study from the U.S. Department of Energy determined that the project was feasible under certain circumstances, but would require financial incentives, because the pipeline would need to carry 50 percent more ethanol annually than the originally proposed pipeline. Though physically possible within the parameters of the project, there would need to be a significantly increased need for E85 ethanol fuel. [SJT3]However, some executives and legislators remain positive, as the study indicated that despite costs, the project was possible under certain conditions.

In September 2004, the New York Public Service Commission (PSC) adopted a Renewable Portfolio Standard (RPS) for the state. The RPS originally had a target for 25 percent of state electricity consumption to come from renewable sources by 2013. The plan was expanded in January 2010 to have a goal of 30 percent of electricity to come from renewable sources by 2015.

❧ Green Business, Green Building, Green Jobs

Green Business: Accredited Sustainability

The New York State Department of Environmental Conservation (DEC) helps New York businesses transform themselves into sustainable and green enterprises. One DEC initiative is the Green Hotel Certification Pilot Program that invites hotels and lodges across the state to "green up" for official recognition. Companies receive green accreditation based on evaluations measuring their carbon footprint, waste generation, and their conservation and/or appropriate use of natural resources. Once accredited, those companies are officially recognized as "green" and can display their accreditation to consumers as a marketing tool.

Green Building: LEEDing by Example

State legislation passed in 2000 established a Green Building Tax Credit for businesses and individuals in the state who own or live in buildings that pass certain "green" standards. The measure aimed to increase energy efficiency, improve indoor air quality, and reduce the environmental impact of large commercial and residential buildings. To accomplish these objectives, the Green Building Tax Credit encouraged owners and tenants to press for sustainability in their buildings or living spaces by providing tax relief for those who own or lease establishments that meet the green criteria.

In 2005, New York City adopted Local Law 86, which requires that all new city buildings or substantial renovations in excess of $2 million must seek Leadership in Energy and Environmental Design (LEED) Silver certification or its equivalent. The law came into effect in 2007. In 2008, New York State adopted a similar measure, the State Green Building Construction Act. This state law came into effect in 2010 and requires the development of green building standards for newly constructed or substantially renovated New York State government buildings.

Green Jobs: Jump-starting Weatherization and Energy Efficiency Employment

Despite seeing declining jobs—both in the traditional and clean energy jobs sectors—in recent years, New York has remained a leader in green jobs. According to the Pew Charitable Trusts, New York had more clean energy jobs in 2007 than 90 percent of U.S. states and was attracting hundreds of millions of dollars in venture capital funds to that sector. Efforts to expand green jobs in New York have also received boosts from state and federal programs.

In October 2009, New York governor David Paterson signed the Green Jobs/Green New York Act, which aimed to create 14,000 green jobs and stimulate investment in weatherization and energy efficiency improvements for residential and commercial building. By eliminating one of the major barriers to renovation aimed at improving energy efficiency—the high upfront costs of retrofitting a home—the bill hoped to jump-start the creation of highly skilled jobs in the green industry. To accomplish this objective, the bill set up a $70 million revolving door for "green" residential home retrofitting, among other programs.

The 2009 American Recovery and Reinvestment Act (ARRA) also gave New York a large financial toolbox to build the state's green jobs sector. In total, $1.6 billion was awarded to the state for Department of Energy (DOE) projects. The vast majority of those funds dealt specifically with the clean energy sector. Of particular consequence for green job creation in the state was the nearly $400 million of ARRA funds awarded to New York for weatherization assistance. The Department of Energy expects the funding to help weatherize 45,400 homes and to fund job programs that train New York workers for these green jobs.

❧ Catskill Mountains Watershed: New York City's Clean Drinking Water Supply

The Catskill Mountains Watershed, which provides drinking water to New York City, its surrounding areas, and the roughly nine million people who live there, is the largest unfiltered drinking water system in the United States. Essentially this means that the natural water purification process in the Catskills Watershed works well enough that large-scale artificial purification measures such as filtration are not needed. However, several issues—from fertilizer runoff to an aging network of pipes—threaten the integrity of the system, which, if you ask any New York City resident, provides some of the best drinking water in the country.

The Catskill Mountains Watershed is located in rural upstate New York, just southwest of Albany. Farms are plentiful in the area, and a major water supply concern is fertilizer runoff into the watershed. In 1990, when this issue began gaining momentum in the New York City area, the interests of New York City residents and local Catskills farmers began to clash. Farmers in the area of the watershed, who don't drink the water themselves, complained that they would shoulder the costs of runoff reduction. Those farmers argued that New York City should invest a projected $6–8 billion in a filtration system, such as those operated by the majority of other municipalities across the country.

However, a dose of marketing creativity eased this issue in 1993, when concerned partners created the nonprofit Watershed Agricultural Council (WAC). The WAC encouraged farmers in the Catskills region to engage in environmentally friendly practices by offering tangible economic incentives for their cooperation. One of the incentives developed was the "Pure Catskills" label, which can be attached to food products produced by cooperating farmers in the watershed region. In this way, New York City residents can make a decision to support the upstate farmers, whose stewardship makes clean, New York City drinking water possible.

In January 2010, another issue threatening New York City's drinking water was resolved when New York's attorney general reached a settlement with five hospitals and nursing homes in the watershed area that were caught flushing pharmaceutical waste down toilets and sinks. Because sewage plants were not designed to filter the medications—ranging from hormones to antidepressants—those chemicals were likely to end up running off into and contaminating the watershed. In the settlement, the hospitals and nursing homes agreed to stop flushing the medicine and to pay fines for past violations. In September 2010, after months of negotiation between state and city officials and health care institutions, efforts were taken in order to assist facilities caught flushing prescriptions to dispose of them properly. For example, Catskill Watershed Corporation executives helped to transport 79 pounds (36 kg) of pharmaceuticals from nursing homes in Delaware County to the Dutchess County Resource Recovery Facility where they were incinerated.

Because the interests of upstate residents and New York City water consumers may conflict, New York City's Department of Environmental Protection works to develop varied and visionary approaches to ensure the long-term viability of the watershed. Since 2007, New York City has committed $541 million to land purchases around the watershed—part of the $1.5 billion total the city has invested in watershed protection programs. The land-grab program continued in 2010 and 2011, with New York City approving purchases of several thousand acres of land around the reservoirs during those years. Analysts have noted that the stagnating U.S. real estate market improved the city's land acquisition program, as it drove down outside purchasing competition. According to the City of New York in February 2011, since the program's inception more than 116,000 acres of watershed land have been protected via the purchasing program. Officially, New York City's watershed purchasing program will end in January 2012. However, by all accounts the city is looking to extend the program by at least a decade. Ultimately, New York City's purchasing efforts indicate a belief that the best way to ensure the watershed's longevity is to gain control over the treasured resource.

BIBLIOGRAPHY

Books

Kershner, Bruce, and Robert T. Leverett. *The Sierra Club Guide to the Ancient Forests of the Northeast*. San Francisco, CA: Sierra Club Books, 2004.

McGreevy, Patrick Vincent. *Stairway to Empire: Lockport, the Erie Canal, and the Shaping of America*. Albany, New York: SUNY Press, 2009.

Stradling, David. *Making Mountains: New York City and the Catskills*. Seattle, WA: University of Washington Press, 2007.

Walter, Eugene, and Jonathan Wallen. *The Smithsonian Guides to Natural America: The Mid-Atlantic States–New York, Pennsylvania, New Jersey*. Washington, DC: Smithsonian Books, 1996.

Web Sites

Assemblywoman Donna A. Lupardo, Assembly District 126. "Assemblywoman Lupardo's State Green Building Construction Act Signed by Governor Paterson." November 5, 2008. Available from http://assembly.state.ny.us/mem/? ad=126&sh=story&story=29301

Associated Press. "NYC Buys More Upstate Watershed Land." *Crain's New York Business*. Available from http://www.crainsnewyork.com/article/ 20100719/REAL_ESTATE/100719865

Bridges, Todd et al. "Hudson River EPS Peer Review Report (Draft)." U.S. Environmental Protection Agency. Available from http://www.hudsondredgingdata.com/

"Buffalo N.Y. bans hydraulic fracturing." Reuters. February 8, 2011. Available from http://www.reuters.com/article/2011/02/08/us-energy-natgas-usa-buffalo-idUSN0810753020110208

Case 03-E-0188: Renewable Portfolio Standard. New York State Public Service Commission. Available from http://www3.dps.state.ny.us/W/PSCWeb.

nsf/All/1008ED2F934294AE85257687006F38
BD?OpenDocument

"Certified Organic Producers 2000–2007, by State."
United States Department of Agriculture, Economic
Research Service. Available from http://www.ers.
usda.gov/Data/Organic/

City of New York, Mayor's Office of Operations, Office of
Environmental Coordination. 2008. *Local Law 86 of
2005 Annual Report.* Available from http://www.nyc.
gov/html/oec/downloads/pdf/LL86/LL86AP.pdf

"The Clean Energy Economy." The Pew Charitable
Trusts. Available from http://www.pewcenter
onthestates.org/uploadedFiles/Clean_Economy_
Report_Web.pdf

"Comprehensive Wildlife Conservation Strategy Plan."
New York Department of Environmental Conserv
ation. Available from http://www.dec.ny.gov/
animals/30483.html

"CWC Collects Pharmaceuticals from Nursing Homes."
Sierra Activist. October 6, 2010. Available from
http://sierraactivist.org/2010/10/06/cwc-colle
cts-pharmaceuticals-from-nursing-homes/#hide

"Department of Energy Recovery Act State Memos: New
York." U.S. Department of Energy. Available from
http://www.energy.gov/recovery/documents/
Recovery_Act_Memo_New_York.pdf

"Draft Supplemental Generic Environmental Impact
Statement on the Oil, Gas and Solution Mining
Regulatory Program." New York State Department
of Environmental Conservation Division of Mineral
Resources; Bureau of Oil & Gas Regulation.
Available from ftp://ftp.dec.state.ny.us/dmn/
download/OGdSGEISFull.pdf

*The Economic Importance and Wood Flows from New
York's Forests, 2007.* The North East State Foresters
Association. Available from http://www.dec.
ny.gov/docs/lands_forests_pdf/economic.pdf

"Executive Order 24: Establishing a goal to reduce
greenhouse gas emissions eighty percent by the year
2050 and preparing a climate action plan." New
York State Governor's Office. Available from
http://www.state.ny.us/governor/executive_
orders/exeorders/eo_24.html

"Executive Order No. 41: Requiring Further Environ
mental Review." Marcellus Shale. New York State
Department of Environmental Conservation. Avail
able from http://www.dec.ny.gov/energy/46288.
html#41

"GE to Perform Second Phase of Hudson River
Dredging Project." December 23, 2010. The
Hudson River Dredging Project. GE Corporate
Environmental Programs. Available from http://

www.hudsondredging.com/news/press_release/
20101223_19/

Geiger, Bob. "Study casts doubt on ethanol pipeline."
Dolan Newswires. July 21, 2010. Available from
http://dailyreporter.com/blog/2010/07/21/
study-casts-doubt-on-ethanol-pipeline/

Hager, Emily B. "City Buys Buffer Land Around
Reservoirs." *The New York Times.* Available from
http://cityroom.blogs.nytimes.com/2010/06/
15/city-buys-buffer-land-around-reservoirs/

The Hudson River Dredging Project. Available from
http://www.hudsondredging.com

Hudson River PCB Superfund Site. Available from:
http://www.hudsondredgingdata.com

Landfill Gas Recovery Facilities – NYS Dept. of
Environmental Conservatism. Available from:
http://www.dec.ny.gov/chemical/23679.html.

"Listings and Occurrences for New York." *Species
Reports.* The U.S. Fish and Wildlife Service. Available
from http://ecos.fws.gov/tess_public/pub/state
ListingAndOccurrenceIndividual.jsp?state=NY&s8
fid=112761032792&s8fid=112762573902&s8fid=
24012961469042

New York State Climate Action Plan Interim Report.
New York State Climate Action Council. Available
from http://www.nyclimatechange.us/Interim
Report.cfm

New York State Office of Parks, Recreation & Historic
Preservation. Available from http://www.nysparks.
com/parks

"Organic Production Data Sets." U.S. Department of
Agriculture. Available from http://www.ers.usda.
gov/Data/Organic/

"Phase 1 Evaluation Report Hudson River PCBs Superfund Site." General Electric Company. Available
from http://www.hudsondredging.com/about_
the_project/key_technical_reports/
20100308P1ER_text.pdf

"Recommendations to Governor Pataki For Reducing
New York State Greenhouse Gas Emissions." The
Center for Clean Air Policy. Available from http://
www.ccap.org/docs/resources/534/NYGHG_
Report.pdf

Regional Greenhouse Gas Initiative: New York State
Investment Plan. Available from http://www.rggi.
org/rggi_benefits/program_investments/
New_York

"Species Report, New York." United States Fish and
Wildlife Service. Available from http://ecos.fws.
gov/tess_public/pub/stateListingAndOccurren-
ceIndividual.jsp?state=NY

"State, City Announce Landmark Agreement To Safe guard New York City Drinking Water." New York City Environmental Projection. Feb. 16, 2011. Available from http://www.nyc.gov/html/dep/html/press_releases/11-11pr.shtml

"Statement From New York DEC Commissioner Joseph Martens." Regional Greenhouse Gas Initiative. May 26, 2011. Available from http://www.rggi.org/docs/Martens_Statement.pdf

"Statewide Ban on Feeding Black Bears Now in Effect." New York State Department of Environmental Conservation. January 21, 2011. Available from http://www.dec.ny.gov/press/71953.html?showprintstyles

"2008 Minerals Yearbook New York." U.S. Geological Survey. Available from http://minerals.usgs.gov/minerals/pubs/state/2008/myb2-2008-ny.pdf

Watershed Agricultural Council. Available from http://www.nycwatershed.org

Zeller, Tom, Jr. "New York Governor Vetoes Fracking Bill." *The New York Times.* December 11, 2010. Available from http://green.blogs.nytimes.com/2010/12/11/new-york-governor-vetoes-fracking-bill

North Carolina

From the Blue Ridge Mountains to the Atlantic Coast, the natural wonders of North Carolina provide a wealth of resources for the enjoyment and sustainment of all the state's inhabitants and visitors. The western Appalachian Mountains feature the Blue Ridge and Great Smoky Mountains, home to some of the highest peaks east of the Mississippi River. Several state forests and parks are found in the mountains and in the rolling hills and red clay plateau of the central Piedmont Region, while the coastal plain of the Atlantic features several protected habitats rich in their diversity of plant and wildlife. A long chain of barrier islands, called the Outer Banks, lies off the state's Atlantic Coast and encloses one of the largest estuary systems in the nation. These islands attract about 5 million visitors each year. Management of the state's seventeen river basins, more than 18 million acres of forest, and the delicate coastal habitats on the Atlantic is a priority for the state. The state has the potential to become a national leader in the production of wind energy, even though the construction of large wind facilities, particularly in the western mountain regions has become a point of controversy. Home to Research Triangle Park, one of the oldest and largest research parks in the country, the state is already a leader in the research and development of clean energy and sustainable practices that promote green lifestyles for residents as well as industries.

Climate

The climate of North Carolina is subtropical with short, mild winters and often humid summers. During late summer and early autumn, the coastal region is vulnerable to high winds and flooding from hurricanes, the effects of a pressure system known as the Azores High (or Bermuda High).

The effects of global climate change, particularly as they may relate to the coastal ecosystems, are a concern for state officials. According to a report from the National Wildlife Federation, average temperatures in the state could rise by 5.4°F (3°C) by 2100 if global warming continues unabated. Some areas of North Carolina's coastline have already experienced a sea level rise of about 2 inches (5 cm) during the last century. Such increases have led to a more rapid erosion of beaches and coastal developments. In 1999, the Cape Hatteras Lighthouse was moved 2,900 feet (884 m) inland in order to keep this 132-year-old landmark from collapsing under the rising waters of the Atlantic Ocean. Researchers project that sea levels could rise by an additional 12 inches (30 cm) by 2100. Such a rise could have a dramatic affect on the state's more delicate coastal habitats, which serve as home to species such as the brown pelican and the loggerhead sea turtle.

To address these issues, the state established the Climate Action Plan Advisory Group, which presented a series of detailed recommendations concerning climate change policies in its 2008 report. A number of those policies have already been implemented by the government. To further the cause, the NC Legislative Commission on Global Climate Change was established to conduct a more in depth examination of the expected effects of climate change on North Carolina and the effectiveness of programs that have already been established to adapt to the anticipated challenges of climate change. The commission was also called on to provide recommendations to the legislature for further actions. The final report of the commission was presented to the General Assembly in May 2010. It included seven legislative proposals including one to create a permanent legislative commission on climate change, one to develop a climate change adaptation strategy, and one that calls for an evaluation of the carbon sequestration potential of the state's agriculture and forestlands. All seven bills were filed in the 2009–10 session, with most referred to committees as the session ended in July 2010. None of the bills were reintroduced for the 2011–2012 session.

❧ Natural Resources, Water, and Agriculture

Natural Resources: From the Great Smoky Mountains to the Sea

More than 59 percent of the state's land area is covered with forests, with nearly 97 percent classified as commercial timberland. Hardwoods are found in most forest areas, with stands of oak, pine, and other conifers also common. Cypress and gum trees can be found in the swamp areas closer to the coast. While saw logs, pulpwood, veneer logs, and Christmas trees are primary products, North Carolina is also a leading manufacturer of wood furniture. The state consistently ranks among the top three in the nation for the sale of Christmas trees.

The Great Smoky Mountains National Park, shared with Tennessee, is the state's only national park. With acres of relatively untouched land, the park features more than 3,500 plant species and the largest block of virgin red spruce forest on earth. The park was inscribed as a UNESCO World Heritage Site in 1983. The state is also home to two national seashores (Cape Lookout and Cape Hatteras), along with other national historic sites and trails.

The state park system includes 35 parks, 20 natural areas, 7 lakes, 4 rivers, and 4 recreation areas. Mount Mitchell State Park, the first established in the state, features the highest peak east of the Mississippi River. The newest park, Grand Mountain State Park, was established in 2009 and covers 2,456 acres (994 ha) along the crest of the mountain, an area known as the backcountry of this popular site. A 2008 economic study by North Carolina State University's Department of Parks, Recreation, and Tourism Management estimated the state park system's total economic impact at $412 million. All told, in 2010 the state parks system saw more than 14 million visits, which nearly broke the state record set in 2009 of 14.2 million visits.

North Carolina has nearly 3,000 varieties of flowering plants, including several native species of orchids. White-tailed deer and coyotes can be found throughout the state, while black bears are part of the attraction of the Great Smoky Mountains National Park. Wild boars can be found in the southwestern areas of the state. Small common mammal species include raccoons, muskrats, and several types of squirrel. Common game birds include the bobwhite quail, mourning dove, wild turkey, and several types of duck and geese. In 2011, the U.S. Fish & Wildlife Service listed 62 animal and plant species in the state as threatened or endangered, including the West Indian manatee, Indiana bat, Carolina northern flying squirrel, 5 species of sea turtles, and 4 species of whale. Threatened and endangered plant species include 2 species of pitcher plant, Schweinitz's sunflower, Cooley's meadowrue, and the white irisette.

Minerals

Crushed stone was North Carolina's leading nonfuel mineral resource, according to a 2010 update of the U.S. Geological Survey. Phosphate rock, sand and gravel, clay, feldspar, and crude mica round out other minerals found in the state. North Carolina leads the nation in production of feldspar and crude mica, and is the only state that produces pyrophyllite. It is one of four states in the United States producing phosphate rock, and one of two states producing olivine (a magnesium iron silicate).

Water

There are seventeen distinct river basins across the state. The largest, and one of four that are completely contained within the state, is the Cape Fear River Basin at the center of the state, which contains 6,386 miles (10,277 km) of streams and rivers, 31,135 acres (12,600 ha) of lakes, and 31,753 acres (15,278 ha) of estuary. The Hiwassee, Little Tennessee, French Broad, Watauga, and New River Basins are part of the larger Mississippi River Basin that drains into the Gulf of Mexico. All of the others eventually flow into the Atlantic. Since the late 1980s, the North Carolina Department of Environment and Natural Resources (DENR) has maintained a separate water quality management program for each of the seventeen basins, with updates made every five years.

More than half of the state's residents get their drinking water from groundwater, via private and municipal wells. Consequently, contamination of the state's groundwater from historic pesticide use on agricultural lands and from leaking underground petroleum storage tanks continues to be a significant concern to state policy-makers.

There are several dams and hydroelectric plants located along the central and western rivers. Lake Norman, the largest artificial lake in the state, was formed by the Cowans Ford Dam on the Catawba River and hosts four hydroelectric generators. Nearly all of the state's natural lakes are found in the outer coastal plain. The largest of these is Lake Mattamuskeet (67 sq mi/ 174 sq km), followed by lakes Phelps and Waccamaw. Freshwater lakes are home to a variety of fish species, including catfish, pickerel, and perch. Trout and small-mouth bass are found in mountain streams.

The waters of the Atlantic Coast and around the islands of the Outer Banks offer habitats for numerous marine species. Channel bass, striped bass, and flounder are common fish. Shrimp, crabs, and clams are the most sought-after shellfish. The state's total catch for hard blue crab accounted is often one of the highest in the nation.

The Pamlico and Albemarle Sounds form the second-largest estuarine system of the contiguous states. Several types of pelicans, terns, herons, and egrets are

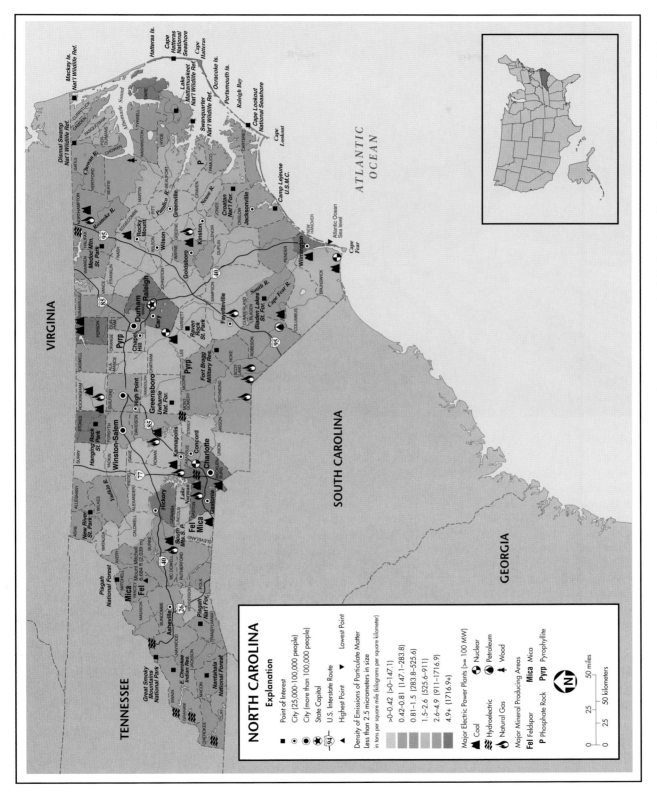

NORTH CAROLINA

Explanation

■ Point of Interest

⊙ City (25,000–100,000 people)

◉ City (more than 100,000 people)

✪ State Capital

〔94〕 U.S. Interstate Route

▲ Highest Point ▼ Lowest Point

Density of Emissions of Particulate Matter
Less than 2.5 micrometers in size
in tons per square mile (kilograms per square kilometer)

>0–0.42 (>0–147.1)	
0.42–0.81 (147.1–283.8)	
0.81–1.5 (283.8–525.6)	
1.5–2.6 (525.6–911)	
2.6–4.9 (911–1716.9)	
4.9+ (1716.9+)	

Major Electric Power Plants (>= 100 MW)

▲ Coal ☢ Nuclear

✹ Hydroelectric ♦ Petroleum

♦ Natural Gas ♠ Wood

Major Mineral Producing Areas

Fel Feldspar **Mica** Mica

P Phosphate Rock **Pyrp** Pyrophyllite

0 ___ 25 ___ 50 miles

0 ___ 25 ___ 50 kilometers

SOURCES: "County Emissions Map: Criteria Air Pollutants." *AirData.* U.S. Environmental Protection Agency. Available from http://www.epa.gov/air/data/geosel.html; *Energy Maps.* U.S. Energy Information Administration. Available from http://www.cia.gov/state; *Highest and Lowest Elevations.* U.S. Geological Survey. Available from http://egsc.usgs. gov/isb/pubs/booklets/elvadist/elvadist.html#Highest; *2007 Minerals Yearbook.* U.S. Geological Survey. Available from http://minerals.usgs.gov/minerals/pubs/state. © 2011 Cengage Learning.

The Blue Ridge Parkway in North Carolina. © *Tim Mainiero/ShutterStock.com*

among the water birds found in the coastal areas. Four species of whale and five species of sea turtle are listed as endangered species. Wetlands cover about 5.7 million acres (2.3 million ha) of the state, and about 70 percent of the species on the threatened and endangered list depend on wetlands for survival. The state's landmark Coastal Habitat Protection Plan offers a long-term comprehensive blueprint for restoring and enhancing the state's valuable coastal resources.

The Atlantic Intracoastal Waterway, an interconnected system of rivers, bays, and canals along the Atlantic coast, passes along the entire length of eastern North Carolina and serves as a protected thoroughfare for ships. One popular spot along the waterway is the Dismal Swamp Canal, located along the Great Dismal Swamp of Virginia and North Carolina. It is the oldest operating artificial waterway in the nation. The entire Atlantic Intracoastal Waterway is maintained by the U.S. Army Corp of Engineers. The ports of Wilmington and Morehead City serve as important trade stops.

Agriculture: Tobacco and Cotton Still Abound

Quotas on tobacco were eliminated in 2004 with the passage of the Fair and Equitable Tobacco Reform Act.

This act changed U.S. tobacco farm policy and provided buyout payments to growers. Producers were then free to grow any type of tobacco in any amounts. Those who continued to grow tobacco after quotas were lifted planted more acres of tobacco on average; this trend was predicted to continue, with tobacco acreage per farm continuing to grow, through 2013. As of 2010, North Carolina ranked first in the nation in the production of tobacco, a crop with a value of around $500 million. The state ranks among the top three in the nation in sweet potatoes, hogs, pigs, turkeys, and poultry and eggs. Cucumbers, strawberries, peanuts, blueberries, and tomatoes are also significant crops. Cotton is still a major crop in some counties close to the South Carolina border. In recognition of the growing market for organic foods, the North Carolina Department of Agriculture and Consumer Services (DACS) sponsors the Organic Farmers Assistance Program to offer support for growers seeking national organic certification. For consumers, the DACS maintains a directory of farms and markets that produce organic products and sponsors a Certified Roadside Farm Markets program designed to encourage the marketing of locally grown produce. In 2008 there were 246 certified organic farms in North Carolina; these farms produced crops with an estimated value of value of $52 million.

❧ Energy

Oil, Natural Gas, and Coal: Dependent on Fossil Fuels

North Carolina depends heavily on imported oil, natural gas, and coal to satisfy its energy needs. Oil and natural gas comes into the state via pipelines from the Gulf Coast. While the industrial sector is the largest consumer of natural gas, 24 percent of all households use natural gas for home heating. Nearly 60 percent of the state's electricity is produced by coal-fired plants, which are primarily supplied by mines in West Virginia and Kentucky. North Carolina's three nuclear power plants provide about 33 percent of the state's electricity and just over 6 percent of the nation's total, placing the state as one of the top nuclear power producers in the nation. Hydroelectric and gas-powered plants supply most of the remaining demand; however, wind and wood energy are gaining much attention as the state considers cleaner sources of energy. Forty-nine percent of all households rely on electricity for home heating and cooling.

Alternative Energy: The Winds of Change

The development of renewable energy resources is a major focus for the state, which became the only southeastern state to adopt a Renewable Energy and Energy Efficiency Portfolio Standard (REPS) in 2007. The REPS requires all investor-owned utilities to produce 12.5 percent of their supply through renewable sources by 2021 (Session Law 2007-397). Along with that, municipalities that sell electric power and electric member corporations must meet 10 percent of demand via renewable sources by 2018. The challenge to meet such a goal has inspired a number of businesses, organizations, and residents to seek out new ways to create and conserve energy.

Wind power is a likely starting point for meeting the statewide goal. North Carolina ranks among the top ten states in the nation in capacity for wind power; however, the development of utility-scale wind farms, particularly in the western mountain areas, has led to a great deal of controversy within the state legislature, as some believe that the construction of such facilities could have an adverse effect on the view and the environment of the pristine mountain areas.

A 2010 report from the National Wildlife Federation (NWF), *Offshore Wind in the Atlantic*, indicated a significant potential for offshore wind energy developments for North Carolina. The report echoed findings from a University of North Carolina study that estimated a potential for the development of more than 55 gigawatts of wind beyond the Pamlico Sound. According to the NWF report, this represents more than 20 percent of the total offshore wind potential of the Atlantic coast. The report also suggests that development in this area could

As of 2010, North Carolina ranked first in the nation in the production of tobacco. © *Robert Donovan/ShutterStock.com*

lead to an increase of between 10,000 and 20,000 new manufacturing jobs.

There are several groups within the state working toward the development of wind power, including the North Carolina Wind Working Group at Appalachian State University and the regional Southern Alliance for Clean Energy.

The state's first proposed offshore wind project is the Outer Banks Ocean Energy Project, which was launched in 2008 by Outer Banks Ocean Energy (OBCE). OBCE was acquired by Apex Wind Energy in July 2010. Apex Wind has since applied for a federal exploratory lease for an area of about 213 square miles (552 sq km) located 20 miles (32 km) off the North Carolina coast in Onslow Bay. If the application is approved, the company will support a five-year site assessment study to consider the feasibility of a project that would involve the construction of between 380 and 525 wind turbines (depending on size) and produce up to 1,900 megawatts of power,

North Carolina State Profile

Physical Characteristics

Land area	48,619 square miles (125,923 sq km)
Inland water area	4,044 square miles (10,474 sq km)
Coastal area	NA
Highest point	Mount Mitchell 6,684 feet (2,037 m)
National Forest System lands (2010)	1.3 million acres (508,000 ha)
State parks (2011)	34

Energy Statistics

Total energy production (2009)	560 trillion Btu
State ranking in total energy production (2009)	26
Renewable energy net generation total (2009)	7.1 million megawatt hours
Hydroelectric energy generation (2009)	5.2 million megawatt hours
Biomass energy generation (2009)	131,000 megawatt hours
Wind energy generation (2009)	NA
Wood and derived fuel energy generation (2009)	1.8 million megawatt hours
Crude oil reserves (2009)	NA
Natural gas reserves (2009)	NA
Natural gas liquids (2008)	NA

Pollution Statistics

Carbon output (2005)	146.2 million tons of CO_2 (132.6 million t)
Superfund sites (2008)	36
Particulate matter (less than 2.5 micrometers) emissions (2002)	25,834 tons per year (23,436 t/yr)
Toxic chemical releases (2009)	62.7 million pounds (28.4 million kg)
Generated hazardous waste (2009)	71,800 tons (65,100 t)

SOURCES: AirData. U.S. Environmental Protection Agency. Available from http://www.epa.gov/air/data; *Energy Maps, Facts, and Data of the U.S. States.* U.S. Energy Information Administration. Available from http://www.eia.gov/state; *The 2012 Statistical Abstract.* U.S. Census Bureau. Available from http://www.census.gov/compendia/statab; *United States Energy Usage.* eRedux. Available from http://www.eredux.net/states.

© 2011 Cengage Learning.

enough to power about 550,000 homes. However, the project hit a stumbling block in 2011, when a federal task force ruled that two-thirds of North Carolina's ocean waters, including Apex's potential area in Onslow Bay, were off limits to wind farms. The task force deemed only about 3,600 square miles (9,324 sq km) of ocean suitable for wind farm exploration, down from more than 10,000 square miles (25,900 sq km) of available area. The task force cited military operations and habitat issues. An Apex Wind Energy representative told the Raleigh News & Observer that the ruling won't deter the company, and that there is still potential area for development within the 3,600 square miles (9.3 sq km).

Meanwhile, in May 2011 the North Carolina Utilities Commission approved an application from Oregon-based Iberdrola Renewables Inc. to build a 150-turbine, 300-megawatt wind farm in the northeastern counties of Pasquotank and Perquimans. This Desert Wind Power Project, so named for the flat land on which it would be built, could generate enough electricity to power 55,000 to 70,000 homes. If the rest of the regulatory process goes smoothly, the company could begin construction by the end of 2011. The project cost is estimated at about $600 million. Iberdrola Renewables is a U.S. subsidiary of the Spanish company Iberdrola.

Yet another wind farm was proposed in September 2011 by Invenergy, a Chicago-based company that was operating 26 wind farms across the country at that time. The proposed North Carolina project, called Pantego, consists of 49 wind turbines on 11,000 acres (28,490 ha) in the eastern part of the state. It was estimated that Pantego had the potential to generate 80 megawatts of power and, if approved, could begin generating electricity in December 2012.

Other Alternative Energy

Meanwhile, groups such as Environment North Carolina and the North Carolina Solar Center of NC State University are among several groups promoting solar energy. In 2010, the Environment North Carolina Research and Policy Center released a study that quantified environmental and economic benefits if the state could reach a goal of generating 14 percent of its electricity supply from solar sources by 2030. In *Working with the Sun: How Solar Power Can Protect North Carolina's Environment and Create New Jobs*, the group asserts that reaching this goal would prevent ten million metric tons of carbon dioxide and seventeen million pound of nitrogen oxide emission into the air. Such a program could also save five billion gallons water per year that is usually used in steam and cooling operations for fossil-fueled and nuclear power plants.

NC GreenPower, an independent, nonprofit organization, provides a unique approach for businesses and residents willing to support the alternative power supply goals of the state. NC GreenPower supports the production of renewable energy through voluntary contributions and carbon offset products from businesses, organizations, and individual citizens. The first of its kind in the nation, NC GreenPower was established through an initiative of the North Carolina Utilities Commission and is administered through Advanced Energy, an independent, nonprofit corporation in Raleigh. For as little as $4 per month, individuals can add one block of 100 kilowatt-hours of green energy to the state supply. A $4 per month contribution can also mitigate 500 pounds of carbon dioxide. Businesses, corporations, or larger groups may contribute towards 100 or more blocks of energy for as low as $2.50 per block.

🍃 Green Business, Green Building, Green Jobs

North Carolina Green Business Fund

In 2007, the North Carolina Green Business Fund was established by the state legislature to oversee a major grant program for new businesses investigating the development, production, and use of alternative energy sources and technologies. The fund is administered under the North Carolina Board of Science and Technology. In 2008 and 2009, twenty-seven businesses received grants ranging from $18,000 to $100,000. In each of those years, the general assembly allocated $1 million to the fund. For 2010, however, the governor approved a state budget that allocated $10 million in federal American Recovery and Reinvestment Act (ARRA) funds for the enlargement of the Green Business Fund.

For 2011, no state funds were appropriated, as the program was still funded through ARRA resources. In all, sixteen awards were granted for a total of more than $4.5 million. Top recipients included Storms Farms, a swine farm, which received $500,000 for a biogas-to-energy system; and Biowheels, Inc., which will use its $375,000-plus award to install solar-supported electric vehicle charging stations in partner communities. In its 2010 report, the North Carolina Innovation Council recommended that the Green Business Fund should continue with state appropriations of at least $3 million annually on a recurring basis.

New and existing green businesses may be eligible for one or more of the many financial assistance and tax credit programs sponsored in part by the Department of Environment and Natural Resources. These include a renewable energy property tax credit for the construction or installation of a solar energy system to heat, cool, or provide hot water to a building, and a conservation tax credit for private landowners who voluntarily conserve their land.

Green Buildings: HealthyBuilt Homes and Sustainable Schools

One of the first significant pieces of legislation in support of green building practices within the state is the Conservation of Energy and Water Act (SB 668), which passed in 2007. The act called for the creation of sustainable, energy efficient building standards to be applied to all state-owned buildings and all buildings associated with the University of North Carolina and the North Carolina Community College System. The act mandates that all of these buildings establish energy efficiency requirements of 30 percent by 2015. The Independent Energy Efficiency Administrator Act was first introduced to the legislature in April 2009 (HB 1050) and was refiled in 2011 (HB 874). The bill calls for

the creation of a new organization, NC Save$ Energy, which will set and support energy efficiency and conservation programs for residential, commercial, and local government buildings as well. As of May 2011, the bill had passed the first reading of the house and was referred to the Committee on Public Utilities.

In December 2010, the North Carolina Building Code Council voted on new standards that could provide an even more significant boost for the green building industry. The council approved a much debated plan to increase energy efficiency standards in new commercial construction by 30 percent beyond the existing code (based on the 2009 IECC and 2009 IRC). Energy efficiency standards for new residential buildings were set to increase by 15 percent above existing codes. In addition, the council voted to establish a voluntary compliance program for residential builders that choose a 30 percent efficiency standard for new homes. These new standards are expected to lead to consumer savings of between $30 and $100 per month on average. A number of new jobs in the energy efficiency technology and building sectors are also expected.

The new building code is expected to take effect in January 2012. However, the December decision was strongly opposed by members of the North Carolina Home Builders Association (NCHBA), who argue that the new standards will be too costly. Several other groups involved in building design and construction echoed this claim, and voiced concern that the expected costs in savings versus implementation were highly exaggerated. The NCHBA announced that it would send letters of opposition to the state general assembly for the 2011 legislative session, in hope that legislators will delay or abolish the new code.

Green building practices in commercial and residential sectors have begun to grow through the help of voluntary certification programs offered by such groups as NC HealthyBuilt Homes and the Western North Carolina Green Building Council. The world's largest model of green building practices is the U.S. Environmental Protection Agency's North Carolina campus at Research Triangle Park, which is home to the National Health and Environmental Effects Research Laboratory and the National Exposure Research Laboratory.

Green Jobs

According to the *Green Jobs in North Carolina 2008 Assessment,* there were an estimated 63,000 green jobs in the state, with about 25,000 in the environmental technology field. About 14,000 of the total jobs came from the recycling sector. The passage of legislation concerning the adoption of energy efficiency standards has helped create a market for a new green economy, as meeting these standards often requires the creation of new jobs. The 2010 North Carolina Renewable Energy and Energy Efficiency Industries Census, published by the North Carolina Sustainable Energy Association, placed the number of jobs in this sector at 12,500 full-time equivalent employees. This represented a 22 percent increase from 2009. The highest percentage of energy-efficiency sector jobs was found in manufacturing, representing 32 percent of the estimated total jobs. Research and development followed with 24 percent. This census also indicated that about 11 percent of the renewable energy jobs were offered by firms involved in solar energy, while another 10 percent came from firms involved in wind energy development. Together, the companies that participated in the census anticipate a 20 percent increase in employment throughout 2011.

To meet the needs of a green economy, several new green job training programs have been developed by various organizations within the state. The Asheville Green Opportunity Corps (Asheville GO) offers a paid training and placement program for unemployed young adults just getting started in green careers in and around the Asheville area. The Career Center at the University of North Carolina Wilmington offers special educational and placement resources for students in the field of environmental science. The North Carolina Community College System offers industry training and degree programs in the life sciences through their BioNetwork program.

Green Jobs: Working with the Sun

A 2010 study from the Environment North Carolina Research & Policy Center has placed a spotlight on the potential benefits of solar energy both on the economy and the environment. *Working with the Sun: How Solar Power Can Protect North Carolina's Environment and Create New Jobs* examines the benefits that would arise if the state could develop enough solar power facilities to supply 14 percent of statewide electrical consumption by 2030. According to the report, Achieving this goal could lead to the creation of more than 28,000 jobs. Considering the number of businesses already involved in solar power development, this goal may not be too far-fetched. The report noted that there are already more than one hundred businesses within the state that manufacture, install, or market solar energy systems. Durham-based Carolina Solar Energy is responsible for the installation of the 4-acre (1.6-ha), 650-kilowatt solar park at Person County Business and Industrial Center. Completed in 2009, it is one of the largest solar installations in the state; it generated 837,000 kilowatt hours the first year. The report also suggests that there are nearly three hundred companies within the state that have the technical potential to manufacture solar energy system components. In 2008, these businesses employed more than 16,000 people. According to the study, all green electric power businesses in the state, including solar, wind, biomass and energy efficiency, employed more than 10,000 people in 2009.

In September 2011, the proposed merger by Duke Energy and Progress Energy was given conditional authorization by the Federal Energy regulatory Commission. The resulting company will be the largest energy company in the nation. It was considered a threat to solar power progress by critics, including a coalition of environmental groups, which includes the Sierra Club and Environmental Defense Fund. These groups believe that the merger will restrict competition among smaller solar-focused companies and other renewable energy producers. The state Utilities Commission completed public hearings on the merger on September 22, but had not issued an order as of November 2011. One state-based environmental group asked that if the merger were approved by the Utilities Commission, it should be required to pay $75 million a year into a public fund to help pay for weatherization and other programs.

❧ Chasing the Wind: The Controversy of Mountain Wind Turbines

The U.S. Department of Energy (DOE) ranks North Carolina as one of the top ten states in the nation in capacity for wind power; however, the development of utility-scale wind farms, particularly in the western mountain areas, has become a controversial issue for legislators, environmental groups, and residents alike. The controversy is rooted in the interpretation of the Mountain Ridge Protection Act of 1983, commonly referred to as the Ridge Law (GS 113A-205). The Ridge Law prohibits the construction of "tall buildings or structures" of more than 40 feet (12 m) high on ridges that are 3,000 feet (914 m) or more above sea level. Buildings of more than 500 feet (15 m) high on the adjacent valley floor are also prohibited by this law. However, the law offered exemptions for "any equipment for the transmission of electricity" and "windmills."

Opponents of wind facilities in the mountains have argued that the "windmill" exemption of the Ridge Law relates to small windmills that are associated with a particular residence and operated solely to power that residence, not the construction of commercial, utility-scale wind farms. However, the issue has not been decided in the courts and is still an open legal question subject to varying interpretations. Nevertheless, the uncertainty around this issue has created a barrier to development of wind facilities in the mountains by discouraging investors and wind developers.

In spring 2009, a bill (SB 1068) was introduced to establish a formal regulatory process for the permitting and siting of wind energy facilities. The legislation would also amend the Ridge Law by expanding the "windmill" exemption to specifically include "wind turbines for the development of electricity" to the extent authorized by local governments. According to an impact survey conducted by the U.S. DOE, the economic benefits in North Carolina for the development of 1,000 megawatts of wind energy could reach $1.1 billion within the first twenty years, with about $20.4 million per year funneled into local economies and over 3,000 temporary and long-term jobs. The environmental benefits would include the reduction in carbon dioxide emissions by about 2.9 million tons per year and a water savings of more than 1.5 million gallons per year. As the state struggles with the cost of imported fossil fuels and the challenge to meet the goals set in the 2007 Renewable Energy and Energy Efficiency Portfolio Standard, many are looking to wind power as one sector that will assist in reaching the state's long-term economic and environmental goals. However, the Ridge Law presents a major barrier toward wind farm development.

Concerns about wind farms range from noise and bird impacts to the possibility of creating a hazard for air navigation. The most prominent outcry, however, has been about aesthetics, as local politicians claim that the unsightly structures would ruin the pristine views of the regions mountain recreational areas. However, in a survey conducted by North Carolina Wind Energy of Appalachian State University, most residents were in favor of the development of wind power and were not opposed to the construction of wind turbines in mountain areas. More than 65 percent believed that wind turbines should not be prohibited. Current laws already prohibit the development of wind power in national and state parks and other protected conservation areas, leaving only about 5 percent of the state's ridgelines available as potential wind facility sites. That 5 percent represents two-thirds of the state's onshore wind potential.

The controversy in the legislature was so great that the Senate Finance Committee eventually agreed to remove the "wind turbine" amendment and simply redefine the "windmill" exemption to fit the personal residence definition, providing that the structure is no taller than 100 feet and only serves a particular residence. The regulatory process section of the bill was kept intact. In August 2009, this new edition of the bill passed its third reading in the state senate by a vote of 43 to 1, which could have placed a ban on wind turbines within the mountain areas. However, the bill was later referred to the House Committee on Energy and Energy Efficiency, where it died at the end of the 2009–2010 session. It was not reintroduced for 2011–2012

BIBLIOGRAPHY

Books

Barnes, Jay. *North Carolina's Hurricane History.* Chapel Hill: University of North Carolina Press, 2001.

Blevins, David. *Wild North Carolina: Discovering the Wonders of Our State's Natural Communities.* Chapel Hill: University of North Carolina Press, 2011.

Emison, Gerald, and John C. Morris, eds. *Speaking Green with a Southern Accent: Environmental Management and Innovation in the South.* Lanham, MD: Lexington Books, 2010.

Melosi, Artin, ed. *Environment,* vol. 8 of *The New Encyclopedia of Southern Culture.* Chapel Hill: University of North Carolina Press, 2007.

Nash, Steve. *Blue Ridge 2020: An Owner's Manual.* Chapel Hill: University of North Carolina Press, 1999.

Robinson, Peter J. *North Carolina Weather and Climate.* Chapel Hill: University of North Carolina Press, 2005.

Ross, John and Bates Littlehales. *The Smithsonian Guides to Natural America: The Atlantic Coast and Blue Ridge–Maryland, District of Columbia, Delaware, Virginia, North Carolina.* Washington, DC: Smithsonian Books, 1995.

Silver, Timothy. *Mount Mitchell and the Black Mountains: An Environmental History of the Highest Peaks in Eastern America.* Chapel Hill: University of North Carolina Press, 2003.

Web Sites

"Apex Wind Energy Acquires Outer Banks Ocean Energy, LLC." Apex Wind Energy, Inc. July 14, 2010. Available from http://www.apexwind.com/news/docs/Apex_OBOE_Release_FINAL.pdf

Asheville Green Opportunity Corp. Available from http://www.greenopportunities.org/asheville-go

Atlantic Intracoastal Waterway. Available from http://www.nao.usace.army.mil/Technical%20Services/Operations%20Branch/atlantic%20intracoastal%20waterway/homepage.asp

Broadwell, Fred. *Green Jobs in North Carolina 2008 Assessment.* Sustainable Economics Consulting. Available from http://www.sustainable-economies.com/nc_green_jobs_2008.pdf

"Climate Change in North Carolina." *Our North Carolina, Naturally.* Available from http://www.climatechange.nc.gov

Final Report to the General Assembly and the Environmental Review Commission. Legislative Commission on Global Climate Change, North Carolina General Assembly. Available from http://www.ncleg.net/documentsites/committees/LCGCC/Commission%20Report%202010/LCGCC%20Final%20Report%205-20-10.pdf

"Financial Assistance and Tax Credits." North Carolina Department of Environment and Natural Resources. Available from http://www.enr.state.nc.us/html/tax_credits.html

General Assembly of North Carolina. *General Statute 113A-205: Mountain Ridge Protection Act of 1983.* Available from http://www.ncga.state.nc.us/

EnactedLegislation/Statutes/pdf/ByArticle/ Chapter_113A/Article_14.pdf

General Assembly of North Carolina. *House Bill 1050: Independent Energy Efficiency Administrator.* Available from http://www.ncleg.net/Sessions/ 2009/Bills/House/PDF/H1050v1.pdf

General Assembly of North Carolina. *Senate Bill 1068: Permitting of Wind Energy Facilities.* Available from http://www.ncga.state.nc.us/sessions/2009/bills/ senate/pdf/s1068v3.pdf

General Assembly of North Carolina. *Session Law 2001-546, SB 668: An Act to Promote the Conservation of Energy and Water Use in State, University, and Community College Buildings.* Available from http://www.ncga.state.nc.us/Sessions/2007/ Bills/Senate/PDF/S668v6.pdf

"Global Warming and North Carolina." National Wildlife Federation. Available from http://www.nwf.org/ Global-Warming/~/media/PDFs/Global% 20Warming/Global%20Warming%20State%20Fact% 20Sheets/NorthCarolina.ashx

Madsen, Travis, and Elizabeth Ouzts. *Working with the Sun: How Solar Power Can Protect North Carolina's Environment and Create New Jobs.* Environment North Carolina Research & Policy Center. Available from http://www.environmentnorthcarolina.org/ uploads/ca/80/ca809d139d551c92990e082edc6e 4b15/Working-with-the-Sun.pdf

McGrath, Gareth. "Onslow Bay looked at for first N.C. wind farm." *Star News.* August 19, 2010. Available from http://www.starnewsonline.com/article/ 20100819/ARTICLES/100819557/1004?

Murawski, John. "Critics of Duke-Progress Deal Beat Deadline." *Charlotte Observer.* September 8, 2011. Available from http://www.charlotteobserver.com/ 2011/09/08/2590290/critics-of-duke-progress-merger.html

Murawski, John. "Panel Limits Ocean Waters For Offshore Wind Farms." *Raleigh News & Observer.* May 17, 2011. Available from http://blogs.news-observer.com/business/ncs-ocean-waters-off-limits-to-offshore-wind-farms#storylink=misearch

Murawski, John. "Plan For Wind Farm Floated." *Charlotte Observer.* September 6, 2011. Available from http:// www.charlotteobserver.com/2011/09/08/ 2590290/critics-of-duke-progress-merger.html

North Carolina Department of Agriculture and Consumer Services. Available from http://www.ncagr. gov/index.htm

North Carolina Department of Agriculture and Consumer Services: Marketing Division, Field Crops,

Tobacco. Available from http://www.ncagr.gov/ markets/commodit/horticul/tobacco/

North Carolina Green Business Fund homepage. Available from http://www.ncscitech.com/gbf/index.htm

"North Carolina OKs $600 million Iberdrola wind farm." Reuters. May 3, 2011. Available from http:// af.reuters.com/article/energyOilNews/ idAFN0316807320110503

North Carolina Renewable Energy and Energy Efficiency Portfolio Standards: A Citizen's Guide. North Carolina Sustainable Energy Association. Available from http://www.ncsustainableenergy.org/media/ NCSEA%20-%202007%20A%20Citizens%20Guide% 20-%20The%20NC%20REPS%20-%20Nov% 202007.pdf

North Carolina Wind Energy at Appalachian State University. Available from http://www.wind.app-state.edu/index.php

Robinson, Julie. "NC Building Code Council Approves Compromise on Energy Conservation Code." NCSEA News. December 14, 2010. Available from http://energync.org/blog/ncsea-news/2010/12/ 14/nc-building-code-council-approves-compro-mise-on-energy-conservation-code

"State Energy Profiles: North Carolina." United States Energy Information Administration. Available from http://tonto.eia.doe.gov/state/state_energy_ profiles.cfm?sid=NC

2008 Annual Report. North Carolina Division of Forest Resources. Available from http://www.dfr.state.nc. us/NCDFRAnnualReport.pdf

Making North Carolina the State Where Innovation Thrives: Initial Recommendations. North Carolina Innovation Council. Available from http://www. ncscitech.com/PDF/reports/Innovation_Council_ Initial_Recommendations.pdf

"2007 Mineral Yearbook: North Carolina." U.S. Geological Survey. Available from http://minerals. usgs.gov/minerals/pubs/state/2007/myb2-2007-nc.pdf

2010 North Carolina Renewable Energy & Energy Efficiency Industries Census. North Carolina Sustainable Energy Association. Available from http://energync.org/assets/files/2010%20Ind ustry%20Census.pdf

"2011 Annual Report." North Carolina Division of Parks and Recreation. Available from http://www. ncparks.gov/News/media_room/docs/ 2011_annual_rpt.pdf

United States Environmental Protection Agency, Research Triangle Park homepage. Available from http://www.epa.gov/rtp/aboutrtp.htm

North Dakota

North Dakota was a great place to be in 2011 for those responsible for balancing the state budget. An oil boom in the Bakken Formation of North Dakota has had a dramatic affect on the state's economy, creating a state budget surplus as most of the country struggles under the weight of the recession. But the state, which has significant resources in oil, coal, and natural gas, is not resting on the laurels of its recent wealth in fossil fuels. The *EmPower ND Comprehensive State Energy Policy Report 2010–2025* was released in the summer of 2010, with a primary goal to double North Dakota's energy production from all sources by 2025. However, since there has been little alternative energy developed thus far in the state, even doubling alternative energy production will still represent a relatively small percentage of the state's total. The plan provides action items for development of a full range of energy resources, including wind, biomass, natural gas, oil, solar, geothermal, and coal gasification.

Climate

North Dakota lies in the northwestern continental interior of the United States. Characteristically, summers are quite hot and winters very cold. Annual precipitation is varied, with semiarid conditions in the west and higher precipitation in the east. The state is subject to cyclical droughts and other extreme weather conditions, such as blizzards, tornadoes, hailstorms, thunderstorms, floods, and high winds.

In June 2011, residents of Minot, North Dakota, witnessed the worst flooding event in the city's history. Bigger than Minot's 1881 and 1969 floods, 12,000 residents were forced to evacuate their homes. Unusually heavy rains coupled with the melting of thick mountain snowpack caused the flash flooding beginning at the Souris River source and the Assiniboine River in Saskatchewan. The flood waters finally stopped rising on June 26, 2011, but most of the Minot and Burlington Souris river valley area was already flooded. The river

reached 1,562 feet (473 m) above sea level, 4 feett (1.2 m) higher than the 130-year-old record. It is estimated that over 4,000 homes were damaged, many with damage too great to repair. Homes even a fair distance away from the river flooded up to ceiling rafters. As the flood waters slowly began to recede in July 2011, officials and scientists acknowledged that the United States was on track to set a record for the cost of weather-related disasters that year, and that these disasters were evidence of changes in the earth's background climate system. The Souris River flood was just one of eight weather disasters experienced from January to June 2011 that exceeded $1 billion in damage. The previous record was nine disasters in 2008. Bismarck also suffered from major flooding from the Missouri River, which over-flowed its banks at the same time as the Souris River.

Climate Change

According to a report on climate change in North Dakota published by the Center for Integrative Environmental Research (CIER), temperatures in the northern and central Great Plains have risen by about 2°F (1.1°C) in the past one hundred years. The Intergovernmental Panel on Climate Change predicts that North Dakota could see a rise in average temperatures by 6.75°F (3.75°C) by 2100, if global warming continues unabated. Such a change could result in even greater weather extremes and an increase in the number and intensity of storm events. In the 2008 publication, *Economic Impacts of Climate Change on North Dakota*, the CIER considers the direct economic impacts that could be experienced in the state as a result of climate change. The report suggests that the greatest negative impacts could be seen in agriculture and water supply, both of which can be seriously altered by extreme drought and rainfall events. Changes to natural habitats as a result of climate change could lead to loss of wildlife, which could in turn have a serious impact on the hunting, fishing, and tourism industries.

As of 2011, North Dakota was one of several states that does not have a climate change action plan.

❧ Natural Resources, Water, and Agriculture

Natural Resources: Forests

Less than 5 percent of the total land area of North Dakota is forested, with the most abundant native forestland consisting of elm-ash forest types located along the rivers of the state. The largest concentration of forest can be found in the Turtle Mountains, where aspen-birch type forests predominate. Bur oak and aspen-ash forest types are located in Devils Lake Hills and Pembina Gorge. Some of the southwest counties support isolated stands of western conifer forests, including ponderosa pine and Rocky Mountain juniper.

Rural tree planting programs have played an important role in environmental conservation since the late 1800s, with a particular focus on such efforts during the Dust Bowl years of the 1930s. One of the most notable programs was the Prairie States Forestry Project, launched by President Franklin D. Roosevelt in 1935 in a multistate effort to minimize soil erosion on farmlands throughout the Great Plains. Tree lines planted as shelterbelts can now be found around many of the state's farms.

While the state does not have a significant forest product industry, the Towner State Nursery produces 1.2 million confiner seedlings each year for use as shelterbelts and other conservation planting efforts.

About 58 percent of all forests are owned by families or individuals. About 22 percent are federally owned, while 6 percent are state owned. The North Dakota Parks and Recreation Department manages fifteen state parks and four day use recreation areas.

Parks and Prairies

Theodore Roosevelt National Park is home to the colorful and dramatic rock formations that mark the Badlands. The park provides protective habitats for a number of large grazing animals, including bison, feral horses, elk, white-tail and mule deer, and longhorn steers. More than 185 species of bird inhabit that park, with some of the most notable including golden eagles, wild turkey, black-capped chickadees, and great-horned owls.

The Drift Prairie that covers most of the eastern portion of the state supports many native species of grasses and forbs, with predominant vegetation that includes prairie junegrass, green needle grass, Western wheat grass, pasque flower, Western wallflower, and prairie rose. This region features a number of animal species that are among those considered to be species of

conservation priority by the state, including the arctic and pygmy shrews, bobolink, American bittern, and Canadian toad. Black-tailed prairie dogs are among the more common smaller mammals throughout the state. Overall, the North Dakota Comprehensive Wildlife Conservation Strategy, more commonly referred to as the Wildlife Action Plan, identifies one hundred species of conservation priority overall.

The U.S. Fish and Wildlife Service lists seven animal and one plant species as threatened or endangered in North Dakota. Endangered animal species include the least interior tern and the pallid sturgeon. The state's single threatened plant species is the western prairie fringed orchid.

Minerals

While the state produces significant amounts of crude oil and natural gas, construction sand and gravel are the most valuable nonfuel minerals produced by the state. The state also produces lime and leonardite, an oxidized lignite that is used for viscosity control in oil well drilling muds, as a dispersant, a soil conditioner, and as a stabilizer for ion-exchange resins. The state's nonfuel mineral production was valued at $88 million in 2010.

In the mid-1950s, lignite containing uranium was discovered and mined in North Dakota, but extracting the uranium from the lignite proved difficult. By 1962, a procedure was developed where the lignite was burned in pits at the mine site, in a process that took from 30 to 60 days. The resulting ash could then be further processed. Mining was discontinued in 1967 after total production of approximately 85,000 tons (77,100 t) of ore resulting in 270 tons (245 t) of "yellow cake" (U_3O_8). Nuclear power fell out of favor in the United States in the 1980s, and all the mines closed. There is concern about the ongoing health risks posed by radioactive dust that spread from the lignite burn sites. However, in 2011, there was renewed interest in North Dakota's uranium resources, despite the fact that state's uranium reserves represent a fraction of 1 percent of the total U.S. reserves.

Water: Rivers and Lakes

Major rivers of North Dakota are the Red River and the Missouri River. The Sheyenne is a major tributary of the Red River. The largest natural lake (and second-largest body of water) in the state is Devils Lake, which flows into the Sheyenne River. The largest body of water is Lake Sakakawea, which was created along the Missouri River by construction of Garrison Dam, which is the fifth largest earthen dam in the nation. Sakakawea is the third-largest manmade lake in the United States (after Lake Mead and Lake Powell). The Oahe Dam on the Missouri River created Lake Oahe which is the fourth-largest humanmade reservoir in the nation. This lake extends

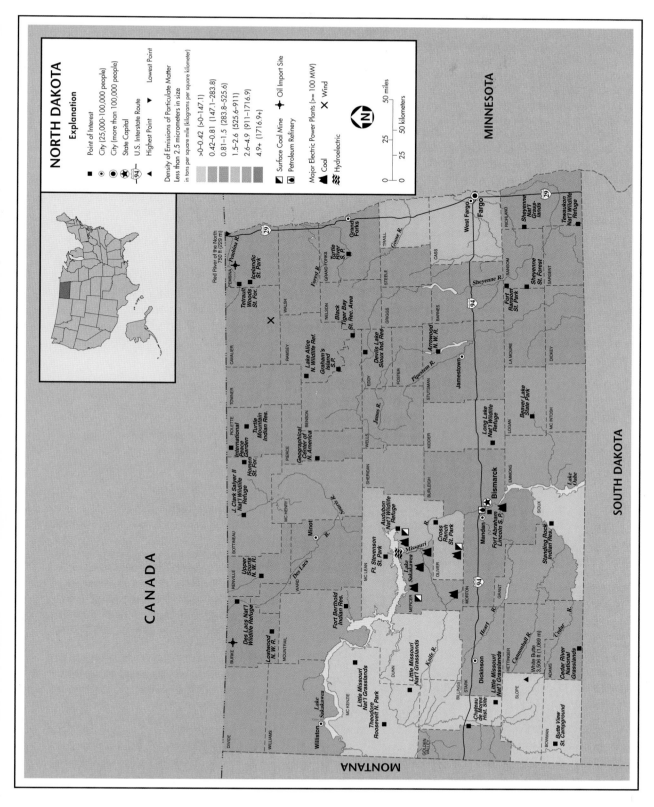

NORTH DAKOTA

Explanation

- Point of Interest
- ⊙ City (25,000–100,000 people)
- ◉ City (more than 100,000 people)
- ★ State Capitol
- 〈94〉 U.S. Interstate Route
- ▲ Highest Point
- ▼ Lowest Point

Density of Emissions of Particulate Matter
Less than 2.5 micrometers in size
in tons per square mile (kilograms per square kilometer)

- >0–0.42 (>0–147.1)
- 0.42–0.81 (147.1–283.8)
- 0.81–1.5 (283.8–525.6)
- 1.5–2.6 (525.6–911)
- 2.6–4.9 (911–1716.9)
- 4.9+ (1716.9+)

- ◪ Surface Coal Mine
- ◪ Petroleum Refinery
- ✦ Oil Import Site
- ✕ Wind

Major Electric Power Plants (>= 100 MW)
- ▲ Coal
- 〰 Hydroelectric

SOURCES: "County Emissions Map: Criteria Air Pollutants." *AirData*. U.S. Environmental Protection Agency. Available from http://www.epa.gov/air/data/geosel.html; *Energy Maps*. U.S. Energy Information Administration. Available from http://www.cia.gov/state; *Highest and Lowest Elevations*. U.S. Geological Survey. Available from http://egsc.usgs.gov/isb/pubs/booklets/elvadist/elvadist.html#Highest; *2007 Minerals Yearbook*. U.S. Geological Survey. Available from http://minerals.usgs.gov/minerals/pubs/state. © 2011 Cengage Learning.

North Dakota State Profile

Physical Characteristics

Land area	69,001 square miles (178,712 sq km)
Inland water area	1,697 square miles (4,395 sq km)
Coastal area	NA
Highest point	White Butte 3,506 feet (1,069 m)
National Forest System lands (2010)	1.1 million acres (448,000 ha)
State parks (2011)	19

Energy Statistics

Total energy production (2009)	880 trillion Btu
State ranking in total energy production (2009)	18
Renewable energy net generation total (2009)	4.5 million megawatt hours
Hydroelectric energy generation (2009)	1.5 million megawatt hours
Biomass energy generation (2009)	12,000 megawatt hours
Wind energy generation (2009)	3.0 million megawatt hours
Wood and derived fuel energy generation (2009)	NA
Crude oil reserves (2009)	1.1 billion barrels (166.3 million cu m)
Natural gas reserves (2009)	1.1 trillion cubic feet (30.6 billion cu m)
Natural gas liquids (2008)	104.0 million barrels (16.5 million cu m)

Pollution Statistics

Carbon output (2005)	50.7 million tons of CO_2 (46.0 million t)
Superfund sites (2008)	0
Particulate matter (less than 2.5 micrometers) emissions (2002)	7,583 tons per year (6,879 t/yr)
Toxic chemical releases (2009)	21.2 million pounds (9.6 million kg)
Generated hazardous waste (2009)	530,500 tons (481,300 t)

SOURCES: AirData. U.S. Environmental Protection Agency. Available from http://www.epa.gov/air/data; *Energy Maps, Facts, and Data of the U.S. States.* U.S. Energy Information Administration. Available from http://www.eia.gov/state; *The 2012 Statistical Abstract.* U.S. Census Bureau. Available from http://www.census.gov/compendia/statab; *United States Energy Usage.* eRedux. Available from http://www.eredux.net/states.

© 2011 Cengage Learning.

through part of South Dakota as well. About 4 percent of the state supply of electricity comes from hydroelectric power, with the largest facility located at the Garrison Dam. Hundreds of other dams have been built to conserve water and provide irrigation.

Prairie Potholes

About 2.5 million acres (1 million ha) of land are classified as wetlands. These are primarily found in the prairie lands and consist of prairie potholes (glacial depressions) that provide water for wildlife and livestock. The prairie potholes are important habitats for migrating birds. Nearly half of the duck population of the state originates from the Prairie Pothole Region of North America (extending from north-central Iowa to central Alberta).

In 1958 the U.S. Congress amended the Duck Stamp Act to authorize the U.S. Fish and Wildlife Service (USFWS) to use money from the sale of federal duck stamps to purchase wetland areas to be designated as waterfowl production area (WPA). Nearly 95 percent of all WPAs are located in four states: North and South Dakota, Minnesota, and Montana. North Dakota's WPAs represent 39 percent of the country's 36,000 total WPAs as of 2011. The smallest WPA, at just 0.1 acres (0.04 ha), is the Ward County WPA in North Dakota.

Fish and Fishing

While there is little commercial fishing in North Dakota, the Garrison Dam National Fish Hatchery produces several species of stock fish, including walleye, yellow perch, northern pike, and brown, cutthroat, and rainbow trout. The Valley City National Fish Hatchery produces some of these same species, along with tiger muskies, bluegill, and pallid sturgeon.

Agriculture: First in Sunflowers, Flaxseed, and Honey

Agriculture is a leading industry for the state, with nearly 24 percent of population employed in production agriculture or agriculture-related industries. Additionally, North Dakota's farms and ranches provide food and habitat for 75 percent of the state's wildlife. In 2009, the state ranked first in the nation for production of spring and durum wheat, sunflowers, barley, dry edible beans, canola, flaxseed, lentils, and honey. Ninety percent of the nation's produced supply of canola and 95 percent of flaxseed production comes from North Dakota. Cattle outnumber people in the state by about three to one. Besides cows (for meat and dairy), hogs, sheep, and lambs, ranches throughout the state also raise horses, bison, elk, and nontraditional livestock, such as white-tailed deer. The state produces about two million wild turkeys each year.

Organic Agriculture

North Dakota is a leading state in the production of organic oats, buckwheat, and rye. In 2008, the state ranked as third in the nation in the number of certified organic cropland acres, at more than 216,000 acres (87,400 ha). As of 2009, more than forty companies were certified to handle or process organic products. The North Dakota Organic Advisory Board has been established to provide help and information for producers, consumers, industry, and others interested in organic agriculture. National organic certification rules apply.

⚜ Energy

Oil and Natural Gas

North Dakota provides about 3 percent of the total U.S. production of crude oil and about 1 percent of the U.S. total for natural gas production. In 2010, there were 4,905 producing oil wells in North Dakota, marking an all-time record for the state. One petroleum refinery, located near Bismarck, primarily processes oil extracted from the Williston Basin, which covers eastern Montana and western North Dakota and contains three of the largest one hundred oil fields in the nation.

North Dakota is the nation's largest producer of synthetic natural gas, with the Great Plains Synfuels plant in Beulah being the primary source. Each year, the plant produces more than 54 billion cubic feet of gas from coals. As of 2010, there were thirteen natural gas processing plants operating in western North Dakota. Most of the state's supply of natural gas is transported to Midwestern and Canadian markets.

About 43 percent of households use natural gas as a primary source for home heating, while 16 percent rely on liquefied petroleum gases and 9 percent use fuel oil. Due to severe winters, North Dakota has one of the highest per capita energy consumption rates in the nation.

Coal and Electricity

There are several large surface coalmines in the central portion of the state that supply most of the local demand. Over 85 percent of the electricity supply is generated from coal-fired plants and 29 percent of all households rely on electricity for home heating.

Renewables: Increasing Potential for Wind and Ethanol

North Dakota is commonly known as being a windy state, and is considered to have great potential for further developments in wind energy. In 2010, the total wind production capacity was greater than 1,200 megawatts, with projects in the works to add another 6,000 megawatts. A little more than 8 percent of the electricity supply is produced by wind power. Another 4 percent is produced through hydroelectric power, with the largest facility located at the Garrison Dam.

In 2010, there were five ethanol plants operating in the state, with a total capacity of about 350 million gallons (3,185,645 l) per year. While the use of conventional gasoline is allowed statewide, recent incentives and campaigns to promote the use of ethanol have proven to be quite successful. In 2009, the state legislature passed a bill that created the Biofuel Blender Pump Incentive Fund (2009 SB 2228), a $2 million program that provides up to $5,000 in tax incentives to retailers for each ethanol blender pump that they install. Blender pumps allow consumers to choose from several blends of ethanol ranging from E10 (a 10% ethanol blend) to E85 (an 85% blend). By mid-2010, more than 150 blender pumps had been installed throughout the state with another 172 applications pending. With the help of local marketing campaigns, local consumption of ethanol has increased substantially as a result of the program. The North Dakota Corn Council reported that more than 167,000 gallons (632,000 l) of renewable fuels had been used in the first eight months of 2009. In the first eight months of 2010, local consumption rose to more than 351,000 gallons (1.33 million l).

Energy Plans and Goals: EmPower ND

In 2007, the state legislature enacted a State Renewable and Recycled Energy Objective (2007 HB 1506) with a voluntary goal of generating 10 percent of all retail electricity sold in the state from renewable energy and recycled energy sources by 2015. Also in 2007, the legislature passed the Energy Independence Initiative (2007 HB 1462) adopting the nationwide 25 by '25 initiative with a goal to derive at least 25 percent of all energy produced in America from renewable sources by 2025. This initiative created EmPower ND, a committee of the state department of commerce that was given a mandate to develop a comprehensive energy policy to stimulate the development of renewable and traditional fossil-based energy within the state. EmPower ND Comprehensive State Energy Policy Report 2010–2025 was released in the summer of 2010. The plan introduces twenty goals with fifty-one policy statements and ninety-eight action items noted as means to reach those goals. One of the primary goals includes a drive to double North Dakota's energy production from all sources by 2025 in an environmentally friendly way (using 2007 figures as a baseline). The plan provides action items for development of a full range of energy resources, including wind, biomass, natural gas, oil, solar, geothermal, and lignite and coal conversion. Action plans are also added to expand energy transmission capabilities and utility infrastructures.

⚜ Green Business, Green Building, Green Jobs

Green Business

As in most states, the development of a green economy in North Dakota will be largely dependent on improvements and developments in clean and renewable energy. In 2007, the state legislature passed a bill that led to the formation of the Renewable Energy Council with a mission to promote the growth of renewable energy industries through research, development, marketing, and education. Under its Renewable Energy Program, the council provides financial and technical assistance for companies and organizations working to develop renewable energy sources and related industrial use technologies. In 2009, the legislature made a continuing appropriation of $3 million for the program. Some of the projects funded by the program have included the Biomass Testing Laboratory at North Dakota University, an ethanol fuels promotion campaign sponsored by the ND Ethanol Producers Association, and the purchase of equipment to extract corn oil at Blue Flint Ethanol.

Green Jobs Development

Developments in wind energy could bring the greatest boom in new green jobs. According to research from the Environmental Law & Policy Center, each new 250-megawatt wind project for the state could create and support hundreds of direct and indirect jobs during each year of the construction phase and as many as one hundred permanent jobs during the operational phase. However, in 2009 the state's largest wind tower manufacturer, DMI Industries, laid off 160 workers by eliminating its weekend shifts. Company officials cited a lack of product demand as the cause, noting that a number of anticipated wind projects were delayed as would-be operators struggled to secure financing during the recession. As more stimulus funds become available for wind energy projects, the market is expected to grow, as will the number of jobs added to the sector. The involvement of high-profile investors may provide a boost for the industry as well. In 2010, Google bought a $38.8 million stake in two North Dakota wind farms operated by NextEra Energy Resources.

Job Training at Centers of Excellence

The state government has placed the development of jobs in energy research and related industries as one of the top twenty goals of the EmPower ND Energy Policy, which was released in 2010. Two schools that have already gained national acclaim for programs in energy education are Bismarck State College and the University of North Dakota. Bismarck State College is home to the National Energy Center of Excellence, which offers programs in power plant, process plant, electric power, electrical transmissions, and nuclear power technologies. Students can also pursue a degree in energy management and benefit from programs at the center's Electric Power Research Institute. The University of North Dakota is home to the National Center for Hydrogen Technology, which provides a number of educational and outreach workshops, courses (including online), and resources for students and professionals of all ages.

Green Building: Energy Codes under Review

Effective on January 1, 2011, the North Dakota Building Code went into effect. The state's code consists of the 2009 International Building Code, International Residential Code, International Mechanical Code, and International Fuel Gas Code published by the International Code council. Parts of the building code include a number of measures designed to reach the statewide energy-efficiency and infrastructure goals introduced in the EmPower ND Energy Policy of 2010, which hope to move the state toward greater energy independence.

Green Building Sites

In the meantime, a number of organizations are at work to promote green building practices for commercial, industrial, and residential buildings. As of 2010, the Green Building Committee of the North Dakota Department of Health had developed a plan to implement best management practices that lead to decrease in energy use and an increase in energy efficiency in three of its main office complexes. The Great River Energy facility in Bismarck became the state's first gold-certified building under the U.S. Green Building Council Leadership in Energy and Environmental Design program in 2009. As of 2010, there were only three other LEED-certified buildings in the state: Turtle Mountain Replacement High School in Belcourt, the Gagnon Office Building in Bismarck, and North Dakota State University (NDSU) Downtown in Fargo. A North Dakota Chapter of the U.S. Green Building Council has been in place since December 2009.

❧ The Bakken Oil Boom

Since 2008, the state of North Dakota has experienced a major boom in oil production, primarily thanks to recent technological developments that have opened the vast resources of the Bakken Formation. The Bakken shale formation of the Williston Basin is a one of the largest shale plays in the nation. In the oil and gas industry, the term "play" refers to a geographic region where an economic quantity of oil or gas is likely to be found. Shale is a type of sedimentary rock containing organic compounds that produce liquid hydrocarbons. The Bakken Formation covers parts of eastern Montana and western North Dakota and stretches northward into Canada. According to a 2008 report from the U.S. Geological Survey (USGS), working in conjunction with the North Dakota Geological Survey, the Bakken Formation contains an estimated mean of 3.65 billion barrels of technically recoverable oil, meaning that the oil can be accessed using technologies that are currently available. More recent figures from the USGS indicate that the field could contain up to 4.3 billion barrels of recoverable oil.

The Bakken Formation is not a new discovery. Oil companies have been interested in the potential of the formation since the 1950s, but lacked the technology to easily and economically extract the crude oil, which lies nearly 10,000 feet (3,050 m) below ground. In the early 2000s, the process of horizontal drilling and hydraulic

The Painted Canyon in Theodore Roosevelt National Park. © *Pierdelune/ShutterStock.com*

fracturing (commonly known as fracking) made shale oil recovery a more economically viable operation. In this process, a well is first drilled downward to the same level as the formation, then drilling continues horizontally into the play. A large volume of water, mixed with chemicals, is then blasted into the formation to "fracture" the rocks, thus releasing the oil inside.

Using this process, oil production at the Bakken Formation has increased dramatically since about 2007. North Dakota has doubled its production of oil in that timeframe, moving up the ranks to become the fourth largest oil producer in the nation after Texas, Alaska, and California. The resulting economic boom has allowed the state to fare better than most during the recession, keeping unemployment below 5 percent and creating a state budget surplus.

The rapid growth of the industry has not come without challenges and concerns. The increase in job opportunities with oil companies has brought workers from across the country to the area surrounding the Bakken Formation. The relatively small town of Williston, North Dakota, which lies at the heart of local operations, has experienced a population increase from about 15,000 to 18,000 in just a few years. Unfortunately, the town does not have enough affordable housing or temporary residential options (such as hotels) to accommodate the new residents, most of whom are men who lost their jobs in their own hometowns and come with very little money to start out with. At least three "man camps" have opened in the area to provide temporary shelters, some of the most basic of which consist of large storage containers outfitted with bunk beds. Some new workers simply live out of their cars and trucks.

Hotels and apartment buildings have been or are in the process of being constructed in Williston, but with the local economic boom the cost of housing has increased dramatically, posing concerns that even those with some of the higher paying jobs will have trouble meeting expenses. Safety and security has become another issue of concern. Since the arrival of so many new residents, the Williams County Sheriff's Department has noted an increase in the number of incidents involving bar fights, domestic disturbances, and the use and possession of illegal drugs. Housing shortages and infrastructure needs extend beyond Williston as well, causing shortages and similar issues in other areas, such as Minot.

Naturally, there are environmental concerns regarding the increase in oil operations as well. The fracking process is controversial in several areas of the country, as environmentalists raise concerns that it could lead to the contamination of groundwater sources. However, oil companies claim that the level of chemicals in the fracking fluid does not pose a toxic threat. Oil leaks are another concern. In 2010, there were at least two leaks in North Dakota that were associated with fracking operations. In September 2010, a well operated by Denbury Resources spilled about 222 barrels of crude and 1,534 barrels of hydraulic fracturing fluid as a result of a failed pipe casing. Officials claimed that the oil and fluid did not pose a risk to the drinking water supply in the area. Valve failure was noted as the cause of a Whiting Petroleum Corp. spill in November 2010. A leak from the Keystone pipeline was reported in May 2011, caused by a bad valve. About 500 barrels of oil were released, most of which was contained by a berm around the pumping station.

Yet another concern involves recent debates over the area of the Bakken Formation that lies under Theodore Roosevelt National Park. As part of his 2010 campaign for the U.S. House of Representatives, Republican candidate Rick Berg suggested that income earned from horizontal drilling into the national park could provide funding to stabilize the national Social Security system. Using horizontal drilling, wells could be constructed outside of the boundaries of the park, thus protecting the natural landscape at the surface while gaining access to what lies below. The Democratic incumbent Earl Pomeroy spoke out against such a practice. The Republican North Dakota governor John Hoeven issued a statement against drilling in the national parks through his spokesman.

The flooding of the Souris River around Minot in 2011 caused concerns about the effects that the disaster would have on the state's economy, particularly in light of its oil boom. Officials have acknowledged that the flooding will set the state back as far as development goes, but considering the upward trend the state has seen while the rest of the country has struggled, officials and residents are confident that the state will continue to prosper.

BIBLIOGRAPHY

Books

Disilvestro, Roger L. *Theodore Roosevelt in the Badlands: A Young Politician's Quest for Recovery in the American West.* New York, NY: Walker & Company, 2011.

Hamilton, Lisa. *Deeply Rooted: Unconventional Farmers in the Age of Agribusiness.* Berkeley, CA: Counterpoint Press, 2010.

Hoganson, John W. *Geology of the Lewis & Clark trail in North Dakota.* Missoula, MT: Mountain Press Publishing, 2003.

Lewis, Meriwether. *A Vast and Open Plain: The Writings of the Lewis and Clark Expedition in North Dakota, 1804-1806.* Bismarck, ND: State Historical Society of North Dakota, 2003.

Marshall, Joseph M, III. *To You We Shall Return: Lessons about Our Planet from the Lakota.* New York, NY: Sterling Ethos, 2010.

Nagle, John Copeland. *Law's Environment: How the Law Shapes the Places We Live.* New Haven, CT: Yale University Press, 2010.

Powers, Tom. *Audobon Guide to the National Wildlife Refuges. Northern Midwest: Illinois, Indiana, Iowa, Michigan, Minnesota, Nebraska, North Dakota, Ohio, South Dakota, Wisconsin.* New York, NY: St. Martin's Press, 2000.

Schermeister, Phil. *Dakotas: Where the West Begins.* Washington, DC: National Geographic Society, 2008.

Shelby, Ashley. *Red River Rising: The Anatomy of a Flood and the Survival of an American City.* St, Paul, MN: Borealis Books, 2003.

Shepard, Lansing and Tom Bean. *The Smithsonian Guides to Natural America: The Northern Plains–Minnesota, North Dakota, South Dakota.* Washington, DC: Smithsonian Books, 1996.

Web Sites

Assessment of Undiscovered Oil Resources in the Devonian-Mississippian Bakken Formation, Williston Basin Province, Montana, and North Dakota, 2008. United States Geological Survey. Available from http://pubs.usgs.gov/fs/2008/3021/pdf/FS08-3021_508.pdf

Bevill, Kris. "Blender Pump Boom: North Dakota's Tremendous Growth Sets an Example." Ethanol Producer Magazine. December 2010. Available from http://www.ethanolproducer.com/article.jsp?article_id=7132

Biofuel Blender Pump Incentive Fund (2009 SB 2228). Legislative Assembly of North Dakota. Available from http://www.legis.nd.gov/assembly/61-2009/bill-text/JBOR0300.pdf

"Biofuels Blender Pump Program." North Dakota Department of Commerce. Available from http://www.communityservices.nd.gov/energy/biofuels-blender-pump-program

Caselman, Ben. "Oil Industry Booms—in North Dakota." *The Wall Street Journal.* February 6, 2010. Available from http://online.wsj.com/article/SB10001424052748703795004575087623756596514.html

"Dams and Reservoirs of the Upper Missouri River." North Dakota Water Science Center. Available from http://nd.water.usgs.gov/lewisandclark/dams.html

Economic Impacts of Climate Change on North Dakota. The Center for Integrative Environmental Research,

University of Maryland. Available from http://www.cier.umd.edu/climateadaptation/North%20Dakota%20Economic%20Impacts%20of%20Climate%20Change%20Full%20Report.pdf

EmPower North Dakota. Available from http://www.communityservices.nd.gov/energy/empower-north-dakota-commission-information

Empower North Dakota: Comprehensive State Energy Plan 2010—2025. Available from http://www.communityservices.nd.gov/energy/empower-north-dakota-commission-information

Energy Independence Initiative (2007 HB 1462). Legislative Assembly of North Dakota. Available from http://www.legis.nd.gov/assembly/60-2007/bill-text/HBBM0400.pdf

Falstad, Jan. " Bakken Play: Boom of Burden? Paying the Price." *Billings Gazette.* August 16, 2010. Available from http://billingsgazette.com/news/state-and-regional/montana/article_36b89f80-a8da-11df-bc67-001cc4c002e0.html

Garrison Dam National Fish Hatchery. Available from http://www.fws.gov/garrisondam

Goode, Darren. "GOP candidate suggests drilling for oil in Teddy Roosevelt National Park." *The Hill.* September 10, 2010. Available from http://thehill.com/blogs/e2-wire/677-e2-wire/118055-gop-candidate-suggests-drilling-in-teddy-roosevelt-park-to-pay-for-social-security

"Green Building Committee Action Plan." North Dakota Department of Health. Available from http://www.ndhealth.gov/wm/Publications/GreenBuilding-CommitteeActionPlan.pdf

The Greening of NDSU Downtown. Michael J. Burns Architects, Ltd. Available from http://ala.ndsu.edu/fileadmin/ala.ndsu.edu/Web_Site_Resource_-Files/ndsu_downtown_green_tour.pdf

"Growing North and South Dakotas' Green Economy." Environmental Law & Policy Center. Available from http://www.repoweringthemidwest.org/wp-content/uploads/2009/06/dakotas-wind-industry-supply-chainapril2009.pdf

"Hydraulic Fracking 101." Earthworks. Available from http://www.earthworksaction.org/FracingDetails.cfm

Kolpack, Dave. "Company shuts down oil well after spill near New Town." *Bismarck Tribune.* November 22, 2010. Available from http://www.bismarcktribune.com/news/state-and-regional/article_7701d4e0-f64f-11df-8906-001cc4c002e0.html

"LEED Projects: North Dakota." U.S. Green Building Council. Available from http://www.usgbc.org/LEED/Project/CertifiedProjectList.aspx?CMSPageID=244

Legendary Forests: State Forests Guide. North Dakota Forest Service. Available from http://www.ndsu.edu/fileadmin/ndfs/docs/st_forest/07_state_forest.pdf

"Listings and occurrences for North Dakota." Species Reports. U.S. Fish and Wildlife Service. Available from http://ecos.fws.gov/tess_public/pub/stateListingAndOccurrenceIndividual.jsp?state=ND&S8fid=112761032792&S8fid=112762573902

MacPherson, Jams. "Google invests in North Dakota wind farms." Mother Nature Network. May 7, 2010. Available from http://www.mnn.com/earth-matters/energy/stories/google-invests-in-north-dakota-wind-farms

"Major Crops and Livestock of North Dakota." Available from http://www.agdepartment.com/PDFFiles/agbrochure2010.pdf

McEwan, Craig. "West Fargo wind tower manufacturer DMI slashes 100 jobs." *AGWeek.* April 8, 2009. Available from http://www.agweek.com/event/article/id/43189/publisher_ID/5

"Mineral Resources of North Dakota." North Dakota Geological Survey. Available from https://www.dmr.nd.gov/ndgs/Mineral/mineralnew.asp.

National Center for Hydrogen Technology: Outreach. Available from http://www.undeerc.org/NCHT/midOutreach/default.aspx

National Energy Center of Excellence, Bismarck State College. Available from http://info.bismarckstate.edu/energy/energyed/NECE.asp

"ND Chapter of the US Green Building Council Organizing." *County News.* May/June 2010. Available from http://www.ndaco.org/?id=138

North Dakota Advisory Board. Available from http://www.ndorganics.nd.gov/information.html

"North Dakota Lakes and Reservoirs." U.S. Department of the Interior, Bureau of Reclamation, Great Plains Region. Available from http://www.usbr.gov/gp/lakes_reservoirs/north_dakota_lakes.htm

North Dakota State Building Code. Department of Commerce, Division of Community Services. January 1, 2011. Available from http://www.communityservices.nd.gov/uploads%5Cresources%5C601%5C2010-north-dakota-state-building-code-book-final-1.26.pdf

North Dakota Statewide Assessment of Forest Resources and Forest Resource Strategy. North Dakota Forest Service. Available from http://www.ndsu.edu/fileadmin/ndfs/docs/home_ndfs/ndstate_assess_strat_final_approv9_15_10.pdf

North Dakota 2007 Minerals Yearbook. U.S. Geological Survey. Available from http://minerals.usgs.gov/minerals/pubs/state/2007/myb2-2007-nd.pdf

North Dakota Water Science Center. Available from http://nd.water.usgs.gov

O'Toole, Molly. "Weather disasters seen costly sign of things to come." Reuters. July 29, 2011. Available from http://www.reuters.com/article/2011/07/29/us-climate-disasters-hearing-idUSTRE76-S0UC20110729

"Our LEED Buildings." Great River Energy. Available from http://www.greatriverenergy.com/aboutus/ourleedbuildings

"Renewable Energy Program." North Dakota Industrial Commission. Available from http://www.nd.gov/ndic/renew-infopage.htm

"State Energy Profiles: North Dakota." U.S. Energy Information Administration. Available from http://tonto.eia.doe.gov/state/state_energy_profiles.cfm?sid=ND

"State Parks in North Dakota." North Dakota Parks and Recreation Department. Available from http://www.parkrec.nd.gov/parks/index.html

State Renewable and Recycled Energy Objective (2007 HB 1506). Legislative Assembly of North Dakota. Available from http://www.legis.nd.gov/assembly/60-2007/bill-text/HBIO0300.pdf

Sulzberger, A.G. "Even Boom States Get the Blues." *The New York Times.* June 26, 2011. Available from http://www.nytimes.com/2011/06/27/us/27flood.html?ref=northdakota

"Theodore Roosevelt National Park." National Park Service. Available from http://www.nps.gov/thro/index.htm

Valley City National Fish Hatchery. Available from http://www.fws.gov/valleycity/major spp.htm

"Wetlands of North Dakota." North Dakota Water Science Center, U.S. Geological Survey. Available from http://nd.water.usgs.gov/wetlands/index.html

"Wetlands of the Prairie Pothole Region: Invertebrate Species Composition, Ecology, and Management." Northern Prairie Wildlife Research Center, U.S. Geological Survey. Available from http://www.npwrc.usgs.gov/resource/wetlands/pothole/prairie.htm

Wildlife Action Plan. North Dakota Game and Fish Department. Available from http://gf.nd.gov/conservation/cwcs.html

Ohio

With more than 41,000 square miles (106,190 sq km) of land, Ohio takes its place as thirty-fifth in size among the 50 U.S. states. Ohio can be divided into three distinct topographical areas: the rolling Allegheny Mountain foothills of the east; the Lake Erie shore to the north; and the generally flat central plains of the west. However, Ohio's environmental landscape is far less clear cut, with battles ensuing over issues such as natural gas drilling, clean energy mandates and invasive species in Lake Erie on Ohio's northern border.

Ohio lies in the humid continental zone and epitomizes a temperate, four-season state. Winters are generally quite cold, with the frequent occurrence of lake effect storms. While temperatures can vary dramatically by season and location, Ohio's southern region boasts the warmest temperatures and a growing season that averages 198 days, longer than that of the rest of the state, which averages between 150 to 178 days.

Climate change has and will continue to have profound impacts on Ohio—particularly in the area of water supply. According to the National Wildlife Federation (NWF), studies have shown that Ohio cities are at an especially high risk of heat waves due to global warming, with the number of days over 99°F (32°C) each year potentially tripling if global warming pollution continues to increase. NWF also estimates that by 2100, average summer temperatures in the state could increase between 7 and 9°F (3.9 and 5°C) if greenhouse gas emissions are not reduced; this could produce increases in extreme weather conditions such as flooding and drought. Along with the lowering water level of Lake Erie, warmer waters due to global warming would also cause habitat decline for fish that live in cooler waters, and could increase populations of non-native species. Changes in dominant tree species in Ohio's forests would also lead to drastic changes in the current ecosystem. The state has developed several programs in order to combat climate change in Ohio. Some of these programs include the Ohio Fuel Cell Initiative and the Ohio Wind Production and Manufacturing Incentive Program, which research development potential in the areas of solar/hydrogen and wind energy, respectively.

Natural Resources, Water, and Agriculture

Forests

Forests cover about 30 percent of the state, with about 97 percent of all forest land classified as productive timberland. While more than 100 tree species have been identified in the state, about half of the forests are of the oak/hickory type, which includes yellow-poplar, red maple, white oak, northern red oak, white ash, hickory, and walnut. Sugar maples are also prevalent. A relative of the horse chestnut, the Ohio buckeye (the official state tree) can been identified by a cluster of cream-colored flowers that bloom in spring and later form large, brown, nuts that are inedible for humans. Ohio's forest industries, including lumber harvesting and the manufacturing of products such as paper, furniture, and home products, generate more than $15 billion annually. Furniture alone accounted for more than $1.6 billion of that, which earned Ohio the rank of sixth in the nation for wood-manufactured furniture. Ohio's primary and secondary forest industry sectors employ more than 35,000 people each year. More than 70 percent of state forests are family-owned.

Parks and Wildlife

In total, there are 74 state parks on 174,000 acres (70,416 ha) of land that attract more than 55 million visitors each year. Ohio also has 20 state forests, and 132 nature preserves under the authority of the Ohio Department of Natural Resources. Ohio's Cuyahoga Valley National Park is one of the most-visited in the national park system. It preserves 33,000 acres of land and wildlife habitat, along the Cuyahoga River and the Ohio & Erie Canal between Cleveland and Akron, Ohio. The Cleveland Metroparks, which form an "Emerald Necklace" of parks around the greater Cleveland area, is one of the notable municipal park systems.

Ohio's native wildlife includes 56 species of mammals, 200 species of breeding birds, and 84 species of amphibians and reptiles. Some of the most common mammals include the white-tailed deer, red and gray fox, coyote, badger, raccoon, beaver, and woodchuck. Bobcats, once believed to be extirpated from the state, seem to be returning, with more than 350 verified reports from 1970 through 2009. Common birds include the eastern great blue heron, mourning dove, eastern belted kingfisher, and a variety of ducks, woodpeckers, and warblers. The cardinal is the state bird. Ruffed grouse and wild turkey are favorite game species. Amphibian and reptile species include Fowler's toad, bullfrog, and marbled and red-backed salamanders, and three poisonous snakes—northern copperhead, eastern massasauga (swamp rattler), and timber rattlesnake. The state has more than 2,500 plant species. The United States Fish and Wildlife Service lists 19 Ohio plant and animal species as either threatened or endangered, including the Karner blue butterfly, Scioto madtom, copper belly watersnake, lakeside daisy, eastern prairie fringed orchid and northern wild monkshood.

In an effort to restore some of Ohio's natural flora and fauna, central Ohio's Metro Parks system is constructing a nature center to oversee a bison habitat designed for public viewing and education. The project has been undertaken in preparation for the 2012 International Ecosummit—the first to be held in the United States. Darby Creek Metro Park will become a permanent home for a starting number of six bison, and in order to accommodate the animals the land will be restored to the way it was nearly two centuries ago. Volunteer groups helped to prepare for the arrival of the bison with prairie plantings, seed harvesting, and by constructing fences, decking, walkways and an observation tower. The hope is that with the reintroduction of the bison in the area, other native species may be encouraged to return, such as the sandhill crane. As the herd of bison grows, they will be able to move to other parks within the system. The fences were in place by September 2010, and the bison moved in February 2011. The nature center and observation tower were expected to open in 2012.

Water

The majority of Ohio's 2,500 lakes are situated in the eastern region of the state. The single most important water resource in the state is Lake Erie, one of the five North American Great Lakes. Ohio shares Lake Erie with neighboring states and Ontario, Canada. Lake Erie is the shallowest and smallest (by volume) of the North American Great Lakes and is also the most biologically productive, often producing more pounds of fish than all of the other North American Great Lakes combined.

Higher temperatures have decreased snowmelt runoff and have caused higher rates of evaporation on Lake Erie. As a result, analysts predict that Ohioans will increasingly rely on ground water sources to satisfy demand. The state's manufacturing and shipping industries, which rely heavily on Lake Erie and other waterways to ship goods, will also be affected by lower water levels. Lake Erie also experienced a toxic algae bloom in 2011 that was estimated at two-and-a-half times greater than the last algae bloom in the early 2000s. Algae blooms occurring in lakes result from increased levels of phosphorus in the water from fertilizer runoff, and is toxic to mammals. The water from Lake Erie during the blooms can be treated by water treatment facilities for use as clean tap water, but requires extra treatment measures that sap already tight county and municipal budgets.

The Lake Erie–Ohio River Drainage Divide zigzags from the northeast corner of Ohio to the middle of the western border of the state, separating Ohio topographically between the northern Lake Erie basin region, which constitutes about one-third of the state, and the southern Ohio River basin region, which takes up roughly two-thirds. North of the divide, water flows into the Maumee, Portage, Sandusky, Cuyahoga, and Grand rivers, which flow north and empty into Lake Erie. South of the ridge, the water flows to the Ohio River, through the Muskingum, Hocking, Raccoon, Scioto, Little Miami and Miami rivers.

Sport fishing is popular at many lakes and rivers, with channel catfish and largemouth, smallmouth, and white bass among the popular catches. Walleye, yellow perch, steelhead, white bass, and smallmouth bass are popular Lake Erie fish. The state maintains six fish hatcheries producing rainbow and brown trout, walleye, yellow perch, muskellunge, and largemouth bass, among others. There is some commercial fishing along Lake Erie, and in 2006, 14 commercial operations were handed up indictments for racketeering and theft for falsifying yellow perch catch documents and illegally selling more perch than the catch quota. The investigation was considered to be the largest ever involving the state wildlife division. The case involved ""illegal netting and selling of 40 tons of yellow perch,"" according to the *Toledo Blade*.

Can Asian Carp and Other Invasive Species Be Stopped?

The introduction of approximately 185 non-native aquatic species into the Great Lakes is a major regional issue. About 10 percent of these species are considered invasive, meaning they pose a threat to the natural

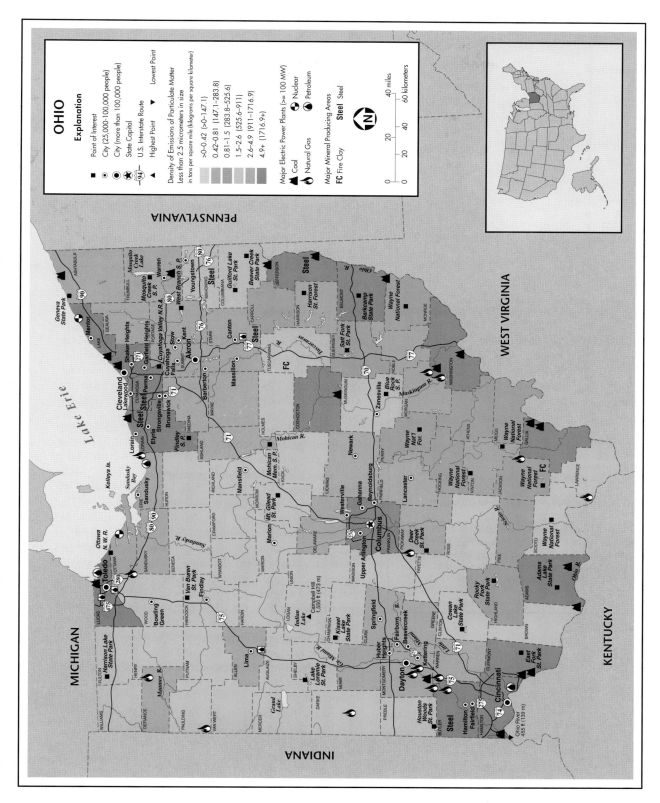

SOURCES: "County Emissions Map: Criteria Air Pollutants." *AirData.* U.S. Environmental Protection Agency. Available from http://www.epa.gov/air/data/geosel.html; *Energy Maps.* U.S. Energy Information Administration. Available from http://www.eia.gov/state; *Highest and Lowest Elevations.* U.S. Geological Survey. Available from http://egsc.usgs.gov/isb/pubs/booklets/elvadist/elvadist.html#Highest; *2007 Minerals Yearbook.* U.S. Geological Survey. Available from http://minerals.usgs.gov/minerals/pubs/state. © 2011 Cengage Learning.

Ohio State Profile

Physical Characteristics

Land area	40,858 square miles (105,822 sq km)
Inland water area	467 square miles (1,210 sq km)
Coastal area	NA
Highest point	Campbell Hill 1,550 feet (472 m)
National Forest System lands (2010)	241,000 acres (98,000 ha)
State parks (2011)	74

Energy Statistics

Total energy production (2009)	1,100 trillion Btu
State ranking in total energy production (2009)	17
Renewable energy net generation total (2009)	1.2 million megawatt hours
Hydroelectric energy generation (2009)	528,000 megawatt hours
Biomass energy generation (2009)	210,000 megawatt hours
Wind energy generation (2009)	14,000 megawatt hours
Wood and derived fuel energy generation (2009)	410,000 megawatt hours
Crude oil reserves (2009)	38.0 million barrels (6.0 million cu m)
Natural gas reserves (2009)	896.0 billion cubic feet (25.4 billion cu m)
Natural gas liquids (2008)	NA

Pollution Statistics

Carbon output (2005)	265.5 million tons of CO_2 (240.9 million t)
Superfund sites (2008)	35
Particulate matter (less than 2.5 micrometers) emissions (2002)	65,948 tons per year (59,827 t/yr)
Toxic chemical releases (2009)	158.7 million pounds (72.0 million kg)
Generated hazardous waste (2009)	1.3 million tons (1.2 million t)

SOURCES: AirData. U.S. Environmental Protection Agency. Available from http://www.epa.gov/air/data; *Energy Maps, Facts, and Data of the U.S. States.* U.S. Energy Information Administration. Available from http://www.eia.gov/state; *The 2012 Statistical Abstract.* U.S. Census Bureau. Available from http://www.census.gov/compendia/statab; *United States Energy Usage.* eRedux. Available from http://www.eredux.net/states.

ecosystem. The sea lamprey (*Petromyzon marinus*), a primitive jawless fish native to the Atlantic Ocean, is one of the most notable invaders. Sea lampreys entered Lake Erie through manmade locks in the 1920s and migrated to Lake Superior by 1983. The state governments have sponsored numerous programs to control the population of this parasite, but the challenge is constant.

Officials believe that shipping locks near Chicago connecting Lake Michigan to the Mississippi River Basin will allow the invasive Asian carp to move into the Great Lakes. Michigan, Minnesota, New York, Ohio, Wisconsin, and the Canadian province of Ontario have

asked the U.S. Supreme Court to order Illinois to close these locks. On January 19, 2010, the U.S. Supreme Court denied the request; on the same day, the U.S. Army Corps of Engineers reported that they might have detected DNA evidence of Asian carp in Lake Michigan.

The Battle Continues

In February 2010, Michigan Attorney General Mike Cox issued another request to the Supreme Court for a preliminary injunction to close the Chicago locks. This renewed request was based on the DNA evidence found by the U.S. Army Corps of Engineers and on a study completed by researchers at Wayne State University entitled *Chicago Waterway System Ecological Separation: The Logistics and Transportation Related Cost Impact of Waterway Barriers.* This study concludes that a temporary closure of the waterways affected by such an injunction would not have the dramatic effect on the economy that the state of Illinois has suggested in its arguments against the action. Opposing Michigan, U.S. Solicitor General Elena Kagan issued an official memorandum on behalf of the Obama administration asserting that the federal government has already demonstrated its commitment to protecting the Great Lakes from the Asian carp through the ongoing work of the Army Corps of Engineers, and that this work should be allowed to continue, rather than hindered by legal debates. The Supreme Court again denied the motion.

The case was heard in September and October 2010. In December, Judge Robert Dow Jr. of the U.S. District Court issued an opinion that denied the request for an injunction, stating that the plaintiffs had not met the necessary burden of proof to obtain the injunction, in part by failing to show sufficient proof of irreparable harm if the situation remains the same. In the official opinion paper, the judge acknowledged the potential environmental and economic threats associated with the migration of the carp into the lakes, but noted that federal and state agencies are well aware of the situation and have been working on solutions to the problem. In August 2011, the ruling was upheld by the Seventh Circuit Court of Appeals. However, the court ruled that if the urgency of the matter increased, it may revisit the request for an injunction.

At the national level, the Asian Carp Prevention and Control Act (S 1421—111th Congress) passed in Congress and was signed into law on December 14, 2010. The law adds the bighead carp species of Asian carp to the list of injurious species that are prohibited from being imported or shipped in the United States under the Lacey Act.

In the meantime, scientists have found Lake Erie to be able to sustain the Asian carp, despite previous assertions that the water is too cold and the tributaries too short for spawning. Scientists at the U.S. Geological Survey compared Lake Erie's shallow waters with those in China and Russia, and found Lake Erie to be a suitable habitat for the invasive fish.

Minerals

Ohio has ranked within the top five states in the nation for production of fire clays, lime, and salt. Rock salt is produced from two large mines located beneath Lake Erie, with Morton Salt and Cargill Inc. being the major salt producers. The Belden Brick Company, Ohio's largest building brick producer, uses a variety of clay from the state resources. Ohio clay and shale is also used to produce cement and lightweight aggregate applications. The state produces significant quantities of high silica sandstone (used in glass manufacturing), gravel, and crushed stone. While the state is a major producer of metals such as aluminum, beryllium, and raw steel, these are processed from imported materials.

Agriculture

Agriculture represents a major industry in Ohio, with more than 75,000 farms covering more than 26.7 million acres. These farms grow a diversity of crops, thanks, in part, to the state's fertile and diverse soils. Corn and soybeans are among the top commodities. The state has ranked within the top ten nationally for production of both crops, along with tomatoes, pumpkins, bell peppers, and oats. Ohio is also a leading producer of animal products. According to U.S. Department of Agriculture 2008 statistics, Ohio ranked second (behind Iowa) in egg production and chicken livestock, and the state also holds the title for number one Swiss cheese-producing state in the nation. Maple syrup, apples, grapes, and greenhouse and nursery material are also significant Ohio products. As a whole, agriculture contributes about $93 billion annually to the state economy. About 93 percent of the state's corporate farms are owned by family corporations, with 84 percent of all farms run by the families residing on the farms.

Statistics from the U.S. Department of Agriculture (USDA) in 2009 listed 629 Ohio farms as certified organic, with a value of $25 million. While year-to-year data indicates a growing number of organic farms in Ohio, negative attitudes among conventional farmers towards organic farming inhibit organic market entry in Ohio. Changing those attitudes represents a major challenge for policymakers and organizations in the state. The Ohio Ecological Food and Farm Association is one grassroots membership-based organization that works to promote and support sustainable, ecological, and healthful food systems, including organic, in Ohio.

In an effort to reinvent their economy, residents and officials in Williams County, Ohio are beginning to revitalize their agricultural sector into a green economy. In addition to producing food, green farmers would also use their crops to produce electricity and crop-based fuels to replace engine oil. Research institutions such as Battelle Memorial Institute and the Ohio State University are working on ways to offset the high cost of such endeavors. Possible new technologies that may pop up around the state are anaerobic digesters, which convert manure and crop waste into methane-generated electricity, and small bio-refineries that turn stalks, cobs, wood chips, and yard wastes into fuels. Pond-grown algae may also be used to make bio-diesel for trucks.

A unique new crop that will be grown in Ohio is the Russian dandelion. The weeds of this plant, which Americans normally spend money to eradicate, are ideal for making tires. This new resource will be needed because rubber-tree forests in southeastern Asia can no longer keep up with rubber demand from numerous growing economies. Variations of the Russian dandelion are being tested at research centers in the state, and it has been found to thrive more successfully in Ohio's climate than in its native one. Another aspect that makes the dandelion such an ideal crop is that once the roots are harvested, the remainder of the plant may be used for fuel. It has been estimated that the dandelion could begin to be grown commercially within five years.

If initiatives such as these come to fruition, it would mean more jobs and new business development for a state that has been struggling with job creation, particularly in rural areas.

🌿 Energy

Ohio's sizeable industrial sector and large population make it one of the major energy consuming states in the nation. Ohio industry is famous for energy-intensive products, such as steel, glass, and chemicals, and more than 33 percent of total electricity demand in Ohio can be attributed to the manufacturing sector. Coal serves as the most significant source of domestic energy production in the state, accounting for 90 percent of Ohio's total energy generation. Ohio ranks third (behind Texas and Indiana) in the consumption of coal for electricity generation. Two nuclear power facilities along Lake Erie—Perry and Davis-Besse—generate most of Ohio's remaining energy. Both are operated by FirstEnergy Corp.

In 2002, a hole was found in the lid of the Davis-Besse nuclear reactor, and the Nuclear Regulatory Commission counted it as the fifth most dangerous U.S. nuclear situation since 1979. Had the hole not been found when it was, the NRC estimated a meltdown would have occurred sometime in the next 60 days to 22 months. The reactor was taken offline for nearly two years and a new reactor lid was installed. In February 2010, extensive cracking was found in components on the lid, leading once again to a shutdown. The plant was allowed to restart in June 2010, under the agreement that it would operate for 14 months and then would undergo another lid replacement.

Ohio is situated in the northern portion of the Appalachian Coal Basin, which is one of the largest coal fields in the United States. Geologists estimate that Ohio contains 11.5 billion tons of economically recoverable coal reserves. However, less than one third of Ohio's coal-fired energy production is fueled by domestic supplies. Instead, the majority of the coal that feeds Ohio's power plants is imported by other states in the region, such as Pennsylvania and West Virginia.

Renewable Energy in Ohio

Multiple projects are studying the offshore wind potential of Lake Erie's waters, both shallow and deep. Solar, too, emerged as a shining star for the Buckeye state. An 80-acre (32-ha) solar project in Wyandot County was completed in 2010 and generates 12 megawatts of electricity, supplying more than 1,400 homes annually. A significantly larger project that could provide up to 300 megawatts of electricity was announced in 2010 by American Municipal Power, which supplies electricity to 128 municipalities in six states including Ohio. Construction on the project will span five years and consist of facilities in multiple states, including Ohio.

The Future of Fracking in the Utica Shale

Relatively small amounts of oil and natural gas have been produced from the eastern portion of the state associated with the Appalachian Basin and the Marcellus Shale. But some analysts are predicting a drilling boon will sweep the state as geologists produce estimates of the potential oil and gas deposits of the Utica Shale. The Utica Shale lies between 3,000 and 7,000 feet (914 and 2,135 m) below the mile-deep (1.6-km) Marcellus Shale and extends further into Ohio than the Marcellus. In March 2011, Lawrence Wickstrom of the Ohio Geological Society offered an "educated guess" that the Ohio shale deposits could contain about 3.75 trillion cubic feet of gas and 1.31 billion barrels of oil.

The possibility of striking it rich in Ohio has already drawn some investors. Since 2005, the state has issued 67 drilling permits for the Marcellus Shale, resulting in the 44 operating wells. Then in 2010, a number of large drilling companies, including Chesapeake Energy, became more active in leasing mineral rights throughout many of Ohio's eastern counties. In early 2011, prospects for shale gas drilling brightened considerably as the Ohio governor announced his own support for opening state parks for drilling as part of his overall budget proposal. In March 2011, House Bill 133 was introduced in the state assembly, calling for the creation of a five-member, governor-appointed Oil and Gas Leasing Board that would have exclusive authority to lease any portion of land that is owned or controlled by a state agency. A similar bill was introduced in the state senate.

Environmental groups are understandably opposed to the idea, not only for the commercial use of protected lands, but because of the drilling methods that would be employed. Shale gas and oil is extracted through a process known as horizontal hydraulic fracturing, or fracking. In this process, a well is first drilled downward to the same level as the formation, then drilling continues horizontally into the formation. A large volume of water, mixed with chemicals, is then blasted into the formation to "fracture" the rocks, thus releasing the oil inside. The fracking process is controversial in several areas of the country, as environmentalists raise concerns that it could lead to the contamination of groundwater sources. However, oil companies claim that the level of chemicals in the fracking fluid does not pose a toxic threat, a sentiment that was mirrored by Wickstrom in his March interview. Oil leaks are another concern. Controversy over this new moneymaking plan has also grown as the governor's budget proposes $73.2 million in funding cuts for the Ohio Department of Natural Resources and the Ohio Environmental Protection Agency. County soil and water conservation districts could also see a cut in state aid of about $6.4 million, or 44 percent.

In September 2011, Cleveland-area state Senator Michael Skindell introduced a bill (S.B. 213) proposing a two-year moratorium on fracking in Ohio until the results of an U.S. Environmental Protection Agency study are released. The study will address potential environmental impacts raised by critics of the fracking process. The Ohio Chamber of Commerce also has commissioned a study on the potential economic benefits of gas drilling, according to a Businessweek article.

Advanced Energy Portfolio Standard

In May 2008, Ohio governor Ted Strickland signed the Senate Bill 221 into law, establishing the Advanced Energy Portfolio Standard. The Advanced Energy Portfolio Standard requires that by 2025 Ohio generate at least 25 percent of its electricity from advanced energy sources, including wind, solar, advanced nuclear, and "clean coal." At least half of the required energy, 12.5 percent of electricity sold, must be generated by renewable sources such as wind, solar, hydropower, geothermal or biomass. Additionally, at least half of this renewable energy must be generated in-state. However, a bill (S.B. 216) introduced in September 2011 had the potential to strip the law signed by Strickland of its alternative energy mandates. The bill's sponsor, State Senator Kris Jordan, cited the recession and the potential for higher energy bills as the reason for the proposed rollback.

❧ Green Business, Green Building, Green Jobs

Green Business

Growing the "green" and advanced energy sectors of the economy is a major priority for the state's policy makers. In addition to making Ohio "greener," the state's Advanced Energy Portfolio Standard also represents a mandate for job and business growth in the Ohio's green sector by requiring substantial local production of renewable energy. The state's Energy Gateway Fund, which was established in 2010, represents another policy initiative that is designed to stimulate investment in the green business sector of Ohio's economy. The fund will leverage $40 million of federal and state stimulus dollars to encourage additional private investment in advanced energy technologies. Returns on investment will be reinvested in the fund to allow for sustained support of transformational green energy projects, as well as continued job creation.

Ohio's private sector are also leading the charge to revitalize the state's green business environment. The Cleveland-based Entrepreneurs for Sustainability (E4S) represents one such group, and carries a mission to educate entrepreneurs on how to develop sustainable businesses. Several Cleveland-area startups, such as A Piece of Cleveland, have credited E4S with providing them the resources to develop and grow. A Piece of Cleveland carves out its niche in the "waste-stream," by reclaiming material that would otherwise be thrown out. The company, which has garnered considerable national attention, deconstructs abandoned houses in Cleveland and uses the reclaimed material to make new furniture.

The first business in Ohio to have its company Certified Green Plus by the Institute of Sustainable Development was Cleveland-based Taylor Furniture. The company redirects over 90 percent of its waste from landfills by recycling and composting. Taylor's facility is also constructed on a revitalized brownfield property, and the facility was made to be energy efficient, reducing the company's energy consumption by over 58 percent.

Green Building

While a host of local green building organizations exist in the state, Ohio state government has also entered into the green building dialogue and bolstered the movement by mandating green building certifications on some of the state's projects. The Green Schools Initiative, which aims to make public schools run smarter and greener, represents one of these programs. Launched by the Ohio School Facilities Commission (OSFC) in 2007, the initiative mandates that all schools awarded OSFC funding after 2007 meet at least the Leadership in Energy and Environmental Design (LEED) silver certification, with the goal of having schools meet the more ambitious LEED gold certification. Operating on a point-based system, LEED buildings are graded in eight categories, such as water efficiency, materials and resources, and awareness and education. The points are aggregated to place the building within one of the four LEED certifications: Certified, Silver, Gold, and Platinum.

Green Jobs

According to the Pew Charitable Trusts 2009 Clean Energy Economy report, Ohio was one of the few states that lost jobs from 1998–2007 in its overall economy, but gained jobs in the clean energy sector. The report showed that Ohio attracted nearly $75 million in venture capital to firms in green sector of the economy from 2006 to 2008. Ohio ranked fourth nationally in terms of total jobs in the clean energy economy—behind only California, Texas, and Pennsylvania—with more than thirty-five thousand jobs. Additionally, the state ranked first in the nation in green jobs created by the 2009 American Recovery and Reinvestment Act.

❧ The Clean Ohio Fund

The Clean Ohio Fund consists of four competitive statewide programs to improve and revitalize the natural environment of the state. Approved by voters in 2000, the program allocated $400 million to fund its initiatives. In 2008, Ohio voters overwhelmingly approved Issue 2, allowing the state to issue another $400 million in bonds to support the Fund's four major program areas:

- The Clean Ohio Brownfield Revitalization Fund, supporting cleanup to encourage redevelopment activities at brownfield sites.

- The Clean Ohio Agricultural Easement Purchase Program, assisting landowners and communities with the goal of preserving farmland.

- The Clean Ohio Green Space Conservation Program, funding the preservation of open spaces, sensitive ecological areas, and stream corridors.

- The Clean Ohio Trails Fund, working to improve outdoor recreational opportunities for Ohioans by funding trails for outdoor pursuits of all kinds.

When voters approved the Clean Ohio Fund in 2000, half of the total money—$200 million—was set aside for the Brownfield Revitalization Fund. The Brownfield Revitalization Fund offers a particularly compelling example of economic renewal through environmental cleanup.

Brownfield sites are defined as vacant or underused properties that were originally built for, and then polluted

Brownfield site in Dayton, Ohio (the former Dayton Electroplate plant). © *AP Images/Tom Uhlman*

by, industrial or commercial purposes. Brownfield buildings and the soils on which they sit are frequently filled with dangerous and environmentally damaging chemicals, such as asbestos or polychlorinated biphenyls (PCBs). Many times, these buildings are not just community eye sores—they are health risks and environmental nightmares consigned to decay. Brownfields are common in Ohio and around the country because the costs of their cleanup are simply too high to justify the investment. New companies would rather build on untainted ground.

Some 174 applicants have been awarded funding through Ohio's brownfield program, which delivered $1.4 million as an average grant. In many cases, Clean Ohio Brownfield Revitalization Fund grants were leveraged by matching funds from companies that benefited from the remediation efforts and revitalized buildings or spaces.

Funding Revitalizes a Landmark

The historic landmark known as The Airdock in Akron, Ohio, is held up as a model for the Brownfield Revitalization Fund's success. The Airdock was built by the Goodyear-Zeppelin Corporation in 1929 as a facility to construct enormous, lighter-than-air ships, including the famous Goodyear Blimp. The building itself is an imposing presence, twenty-two stories high and the length of two Washington Monuments stacked end-to-end.

Lockheed Martin acquired The Airdock in 1996 but soon discovered that the fireproofed layer within the structure's protective steel covering was beginning to flake. Hazardous, tar-based material containing PCBs was beginning to rain down and contaminate the site's soil. In 2006, the Clean Ohio Fund offered a $3-million grant for remediation, which Lockheed Martin immediately matched. According to Clean Ohio Fund statistics, ninety-three jobs were created through this remediation

effort and hundreds of jobs were saved. Following the cleanup, Lockheed Martin used the facility to develop a prototype high-altitude airship for the U.S. Missile Defense Agency.

BIBLIOGRAPHY

Books

Callender, Heidi L., ed. *Wind Energy in Ohio*. Concord Twp, OH: Lake Publishing, 2010.

McCormac, James S. *Wild Ohio: The Best of Our Natural Heritage*. Kent, OH: Kent State University Press, 2008.

Strutin, Michal, and Gary Irving. *The Smithsonian Guides to Natural America: The Great Lakes—Ohio, Indiana, Michigan, Wisconsin*. Washington, DC: Smithsonian Books, 1996.

Sustainable Cleveland 2019: Action and Resource Guide. Cleveland: Sustainable Cleveland, 2011.

Web Sites

"American Municipal Power and Standard Energy Announce 300 Megawatt Solar Energy Development." AMP's Newsroom. June 8, 2010. Available from http://amppartners.org/newsroom/american-municipal-power-and-standard-energy-announce-300-megawatt-solar-energy-development/

"Asian Carp and Chicago Canal Litigation" Great Lakes Environmental Law Center. Available from http://www.greatlakeslaw.org/blog/asian-carp

Asian Carp Prevention and Control Act (S 1421—111th Congress). U.S. Congress. Available from http://www.govtrack.us/congress/billtext.xpd?bill=s111-1421

Bell, Kelley. "No Bull! We've Got Bison!" *(614) Magazine*. Available from http://614columbus.com/magazine/08-01-2010/no-bull-weve-got-bison

Bennish, Steve. "Global warming already hitting Ohio, study says." *Dayton Daily News*. Available from http://www.daytondailynews.com/news/dayton-news/global-warming-already-hitting-ohio-study-says-859552.html

Carr Smythe, Julie. "Ohio Opponents To Seek Moratorium On Gas Drilling." *Businessweek* September 7, 2011. Available from http://www.businessweek.com/ap/financialnews/D9PJMDM81.htm

"Cuyahoga Valley National Park." U.S. National Park System. Available from http://www.nps.gov/cuva/index.htm.

"Entrepreneurs for Sustainability." Available from http://www.e4s.org/content/index.asp

"Fishing." Ohio Department of Natural Resources Division of Wildlife. Available from http://www.dnr.state.oh.us/Home/FishingSubhomePage/tabid/6518/Default.aspx.

Funk, John. "FirstEnergy Restarts Davis-Besse Nuclear Reactor." *Cleveland Plain Dealer*. June 29, 2010. Available from http://www.cleveland.com/business/index.ssf/2010/06/firstenergy_restarts_davis-bes.html

Funk, John. "Frack drilling for natural gas could be boon for Ohio, but environmentalists alarmed." *The Plain Dealer*. March 11, 2011. Available from http://www.cleveland.com/business/index.ssf/2011/03/frack_drilling_for_natural_gas.html.

Funk, John, and Mangels, John. "Ohio's Nuclear Near Miss." *Cleveland Plain Dealer*. September 21, 2004. Available from http://www.cleveland.com/powerplants/plaindealer/index.ssf?/powerplants/more/1095759100318143.html

"Global Warming and Ohio." The National Wildlife Federation. Available from http://www.nwf.org/Global-Warming/~/media/PDFs/Global%20Warming/Global%20Warming%20State%20Fact%20Sheets/Ohio.ashx

"Green Jobs Created or Saved by the Recovery Act. " The Council on State Governments. Available from http://www.csg.org/about/pressreleases/documents/CSGGreenJobsReport.pdf

"Green Schools Initiative." Ohio School Facilities Commission. Available from http://www.osfc.state.oh.us/Library/GreenSchools/tabid/137/Default.aspx

House Bill 133: Oil and Gas Leasing Board. General Assembly of the State of Ohio. Available from http://www.legislature.state.oh.us/BillText129/129_HB_133_I_Y.pdf.

Hunt, Spencer. "Oil, natural-gas drilling proposed for park land." *The Columbus Dispatch*. March 16, 2011. Available from http://www.dispatchpolitics.com/live/content/local_news/stories/2011/03/16/copy/oil-natural-gas-drilling-proposed-for-park-land.html?sid=101.

"Lake Erie Strategic Plan." Ohio Department of Natural Resources. Available from http://www.dnr.state.oh.us/Home/FishingSubhomePage/fisheriesmanagementplaceholder/fishingfairportstratplan/tabid/6167/Default.aspx

McPeek, Marshall. "Bison Moving Into The Metro Parks." NBC4i. Available from http://www2.nbc4i.com/news/2010/aug/11/bison-moving-metro-parks-ar-188539/

Memorandum Opinion and Order: Case No. 10-CV-4457. December 2, 2010. U.S. District Court for the Northern District of Illinois. Available from http://www.greatlakeslaw.org/files/dist_ct_pi_opinion_order.pdf

"Ohio Agriculture: A Profile." U.S. Department of Agriculture. Ohio Department of Agriculture. Available from http://www.nass.usda.gov/Statistics_by_State/Ohio/Publications/PRO07.pdf

"Ohio: Assessing the Costs of Climate Change." National Council of State Legislatures in collaboration with the University of Maryland's Center for Integrative Environmental Research. Available from http://www.cier.umd.edu/climateadaptation/Climate%20change–OHIO.pdf

Ohio Ecological Food and Farm Association. Available from http://www.oeffa.org/

"Ohio Energy Gateway Fund." Ohio Department of Development: Ohio Energy Resources Division. Available from http://uceao.org/pdf/Ohio_Energy_Gateway_Fund_RFP.pdf

"Ohio Forest Industry Fact Sheet." Ohio Forest Association, Inc. Available from http://www.ohioforest.org/pdf/factsheet.pdf

Ohio Forests 2006. U.S. Forest Service. Available from http://www.nrs.fs.fed.us/pubs/rb/rb_nrs36.pdf.

Ohio Forestry Association. Available from http://www.ohioforest.org.

"Ohio Senate Bill 221." Available from http://www.legislature.state.oh.us/BillText127/127_SB_221_EN_N.pdf

Ohio State Park and Recreational Area Study Committee Report (2009). Available from http://www.dnr.state.oh.us/Portals/2/PDFs/StParksStudyRpt_27Feb09.pdf.

Ohio 2008 Minerals Yearbook. U.S. Geological Society. Available from http://minerals.usgs.gov/minerals/pubs/state/2008/myb2-2008-oh.pdf.

"A Piece of Cleveland." Available from http://www.apieceofcleveland.com/

Pollick, Steve. "Commercial Perch Netters Could Face Tougher Rules." *Toledo Blade*. February 12, 2006. Available from http://www.toledoblade.com/StevePollick/2006/02/12/Commercial-perch-netters-could-face-tougher-rules

Provance, Jim. "Ohio Renewable Energy Law In Danger." *Toledo Blade*. September 9, 2011. Available from http://www.toledoblade.com/State/2011/09/09/Ohio-renewable-energy-law-in-danger.html

Scott, Michael. "Ohio poised to take center stage in natural gas drilling debate as it considers tapping park lands." *The Plain Dealer*. March 27, 2011. Available from http://blog.cleveland.com/metro/2011/03/ohio_poised_to_take_center_sta.html.

"State Park Lands and Shale Gas Exploration." Ohio Department of Natural Resources, Ohio State Parks. Available from http://www.dnr.state.oh.us/tabid/23360/Default.aspx.

Strooh, Desmond. "Algae Bloom In Lake Erie Causing Increased Toxicity." WTOL 11. August 29, 2011. Available from http://www.wtol.com/story/15355174/algae-bloom-in-lake-erie-causing-increased-toxicity

The Taylor Companies. Available from http://www.thetaylorcompanies.com/taylorCompanies.php?targetScript=home.taylor.php

2010–11 Wildlife Population Status Report. Ohio Department of Natural Resources, Division of Wildlife. Available from http://www.dnr.state.oh.us/Home/wild_resourcessubhomepage/ResearchandSurveys/WildlifePopulationStatusLandingPage/tabid/19230/Default.aspx.

Oklahoma

Located in the south central region of the United States, Oklahoma is the twentieth-largest state. A major producer of natural gas, oil, and agriculture, Oklahoma relies on an economic base of aviation, energy, telecommunications, and biotechnology. An up and coming industry in the state is weather, with the National Weather Center located in Norman. The northeastern corner of the state was once home to a thriving zinc-lead mining industry. Since the mines closed, the area around Tar Creek has suffered from contaminated water and soils, and cave-ins. Efforts have been underway in recent years to clean the contaminated water using passive treatment systems.

Climate

Oklahoma has a continental climate with cold winters and hot summers. Normal daily average temperatures in Oklahoma City range from 37°F (2°C) in January to 82°F (27°C) in July. Dry, sunny weather generally prevails throughout the state. Precipitation varies from an average of 15 inches (38 cm) annually in the northwestern panhandle to over 50 inches (127 cm) in the southeast. Oklahoma City is one of the windiest cities in the United States, with an average annual wind speed of 13 mph (20 km/h).

Oklahoma is also tornado-prone. One of the most destructive windstorms was the tornado that tore through Ellis, Woods, and Woodward counties on April 9, 1947, killing 101 people and injuring 782 others. More recently, the May 3, 1999, outbreak spawned at least 66 tornadoes, including an F5 tornado that killed 48 people and caused more than $1 billion in damage.

As of 2011, Oklahoma did not have a climate change action plan. The Oklahoma Climatological Survey did, however, release a statement on climate change in 2007. This document outlines the impacts that climate change could have on the state, such as an increase in heat waves, a higher likelihood of droughts, and an increased risk of forest fires. While rain-free periods will increase, individual rainfall events will be more intense, leading to flash flooding. The climate change statement offers four recommendations of actions the state can take to prepare for, and mitigate the future effects of, climate change. First, the state should take a comprehensive assessment of its vulnerability to climate change; second, the state should fund the Oklahoma Water Resources Board's Comprehensive Water Plan study to identify existing as well as projected needs for water (ongoing in 2011); third, the state should develop efficiency programs to reduce its growing demand for energy; and fourth, the state should invest in renewable energy technology and production.

❧ Natural Resources, Water, and Agriculture

Forests and Wildlife

Grasses grow in abundance in Oklahoma. Bluestem, buffalo, sand lovegrass, and grama grasses are native, with the bluestem found mostly in the eastern and central regions, and buffalo grass most common in the western counties, known as "short grass country." There are more than 10 million acres (4 million ha) of forest in Oklahoma. Deciduous hardwoods are found in the eastern part of the state, and red and yellow cactus blossoms brighten the Black Mesa area in the northwest. The forest industry contributes more than $2 billion to the state's economy annually. The vast majority of Oklahoma's forests (95 percent or more) are not owned by the federal government or large forest products companies, but by thousands of private individuals. There are 47 state parks in Oklahoma.

The white-tailed deer is found in all counties, and Rio Grande wild turkeys are hunted across much of the state. Pronghorn (antelope) inhabit the panhandle area, and elk survive in the Wichita Mountains National

Weather plays a key role in the state of Oklahoma—the National Weather Center is located in Norman. © *Ryan McGinnis/Alamy*

Wildlife Refuge. A few herds of American bison (buffalo) are also preserved in the Wichita Mountains refuge, and in the Nature Conservancy's J.T. Nickel Family Nature and Wildlife Preserve and Tallgrass Prairie Preserve which is the world's largest preserved tract of native tallgrass prairie. Hunting is a popular pastime in Oklahoma, and is also an important economic activity. The total economic effect of deer hunting in 2006 was estimated at nearly $500 million. The total economic effect from all hunting activity that same year was estimated to be $843 million. Game animals include pronghorn, deer, elk, bear, and feral hogs. The bobwhite quail, ring-necked pheasant, dove, and prairie chicken are common game birds; waterfowl hunting is also common.

As of 2011, the U.S. Fish and Wildlife Service listed 18 animal and two plant species as threatened or endangered in Oklahoma. Endangered species include the Indiana bat, the American burying beetle and the red-cockaded woodpecker. The Ozark cavefish, leopard darter, Neosho madtom, piping plover, and Arkansas River basin shiner were listed as threatened. Both the eastern and western prairie fringed orchids were threatened plant species. The state's Department of Wildlife Conservation lists four species as threatened or endangered. The longnosed darter, Neosho mucket, and Oklahoma cave crayfish are listed as endangered, and the black-sided darter is listed as threatened.

Mineral Resources

Minerals mined in Oklahoma include limestone, building stone, sand and gravel, gypsum, clay and shale, granite, volcanic ash, Tripoli, salt, bentonite, iron ore, and chat. The state also produces the liquid and gaseous minerals iodine and helium. The state ranked thirtieth nationally in nonfuel mineral production in 2010. The value of nonfuel mineral production in 2010 was estimatedat $646 million from 766 mines that employed more than 5,000 workers. Also, the Oklahoma Department of Mines recorded approximately 1.4 million tons of bituminous coal was produced from nine mines in seven counties in 2010.

Water

Not quite two-thirds of Oklahoma is drained by the Arkansas River, and the remainder by the Red River. Within the state, the Arkansas is joined by the Verdigris, Grand (Neosho), and Illinois Rivers from the north and northeast, and by the Cimarron and Canadian Rivers from the northwest and west. The Red River, which marks most of the state's southern boundary, is joined by the Washita, Salt Fork, Blue, Kiamichi, and many smaller rivers. The only natural lakes in the state are oxbow lakes, a U-shaped body of water formed when a wide meander from the main stem of a river is cut off to create a lake. However, there are many humanmade lakes, of which the largest is Lake Eufaula, covering 102,500 acres (41,500 ha).

Native sport fish include largemouth, smallmouth, white, and spotted bass; catfish; crappie; sunfish and paddlefish. Sport fishermen bring in 3.8 million pounds of fish from state reservoirs every year. Along with surface water reservoirs, groundwater aquifers are important drinking water sources in the state.

Agriculture

According to the U.S. Department of Agriculture, in 2010 Oklahoma had 86,500 farms on more than 35 million acres (14 million ha) of land. The highest valued crops were hay, wheat, corn, soybeans, and cotton. In terms of acreage, Oklahoma ranked fourth in the nation for forage, and fifth for both wheat for grain and sorghum for grain. For livestock, the state ranked fifth in the nation in terms of inventory for cattle and calves, and eighth for hogs and pigs.

Fifty-eight percent of the state experienced extreme drought conditions during the first half of 2011. The dry conditions have caused many wheat farmers to consider changing to different crops, since many are experiencing major losses of wheat crops, or they are simply not growing. Hundreds of grassfires have been sparked by the drought, causing dozens to lose their homes. The state eased commercial vehicle restrictions in July 2011 in order to speed the delivery of hay to cattle whose grazing areas have been decimated by the drought. Bigger trucks were allowed to operate and to haul heavier loads.

As of 2010, there were 105 certified organic operations in the state. In 2007, the U.S. Department of Agriculture estimated that Oklahoma was home to more than 22,000 acres (8,900 ha) used for organic farming. Some organic crops produced in the state include vegetables, fruit, berries, field crops, and live-stock.

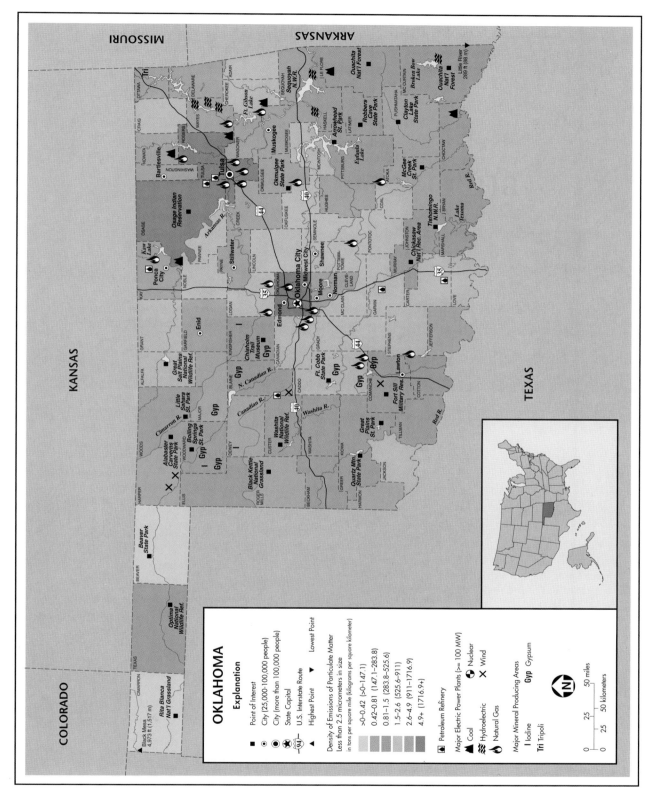

OKLAHOMA

Explanation

■ Point of Interest

⊙ City (25,000–100,000 people)

◉ City (more than 100,000 people)

✪ State Capital

▬94▬ U.S. Interstate Route

▲ Highest Point ▼ Lowest Point

Density of Emissions of Particulate Matter
Less than 2.5 micrometers in size
in tons per square mile (kilograms per square kilometer)

>0–0.42 (>0–147.1)

0.42–0.81 (147.1–283.8)

0.81–1.5 (283.8–525.6)

1.5–2.6 (525.6–911)

2.6–4.9 (911–1716.9)

4.9+ (1716.9+)

⬡ Petroleum Refinery

Major Electric Power Plants (>= 100 MW)

▲ Coal ☢ Nuclear

⚒ Hydroelectric ✕ Wind

⚘ Natural Gas

Major Mineral Producing Areas

I Iodine **Gyp** Gypsum

Tri Tripoli

0 — 25 — 50 miles

0 — 25 — 50 kilometers

SOURCES: "County Emissions Map: Criteria Air Pollutants." *AirData.* U.S. Environmental Protection Agency. Available from http://www.epa.gov/air/data/geosel.html; *Energy Maps.* U.S. Energy Information Administration. Available from http://www.eia.gov/state; *Highest and Lowest Elevations.* U.S. Geological Survey. Available from http://egsc.usgs.gov/isb/pubs/booklets/elvadist/elvadist.html#Highest; *2007 Minerals Yearbook.* U.S. Geological Survey. Available from http://minerals.usgs.gov/minerals/pubs/state. © 2011 Cengage Learning.

Approximately 58 percent of Oklahoma experienced extreme drought conditions during the first half of 2011. Hundreds of grassfires were attributed to the dry drought conditions, which caused dozens to lose their homes. © *Jeff R Clow/Getty Images*

⚜ Energy

Oklahoma is known for its abundant oil and natural gas resources. The state ranks third in the nation in natural gas production, and fifth in the nation in crude oil production. There are more than 125,000 producing oil and natural gas wells. These wells produce more than 61 million barrels of oil. With five petroleum refineries that have a combined capacity of more than 500,000 barrels per day, the state produces 3 percent of the total U.S. capacity.

Eight percent of the nation's natural gas reserves are in Oklahoma, and three-fifths of the state's residents use natural gas as their primary energy source for home heating. There are also large reserves of coalbed methane in the Arkoma Basin and the Cherokee Platform in the eastern part of the state. Extraction of those resources has grown in recent years. Oklahoma sends natural gas via pipeline to neighboring states, the majority to Kansas, including the natural gas trading hubs in Texas and Kansas. Almost 90 percent of the natural gas that enters the state arrives via pipelines from Texas and Colorado.

Oklahoma produces most of its electricity from coal and natural gas. The state also contains the most significant deposits of bituminous coal west of the Mississippi River and east of the Rocky Mountains, but it imports the majority of the coal it uses from Wyoming. Remaining energy production comes from renewable sources, primarily wind and hydroelectric power. As of 2009, the state had 11 wind farms. The Blue Canyon II wind farm had the highest capacity at 151.5 megawatts (MW).

Oklahoma's Renewable Energy Goal

In May of 2010, Oklahoma passed House Bill 3028. This bill created the Oklahoma Energy Security Act, which provides a renewable energy goal for the state. The act calls for 15 percent of the total installed generation capacity in Oklahoma to be derived from renewable sources by 2015. Eligible renewable energy resources include wind, solar, hydropower, hydrogen, geothermal, biomass, and other renewable energy resources approved by the Oklahoma Corporation Commission (OCC). Energy efficiency may be used to meet up to 25 percent of the goal.

⚜ Green Business, Green Building, Green Jobs

Green Business and Green Jobs

According to the National Governors Association Center for Best Practices, Oklahoma has a strong

Oklahoma State Profile

Physical Characteristics

Land area	68,603 square miles (177,681 sq km)
Inland water area	1,296 square miles (3,357 sq km)
Coastal area	NA
Highest point	Black Mesa 4,973 feet (1,516 m)
National Forest System lands (2010)	461,000 acres (187,000 ha)
State parks (2011)	50

Energy Statistics

Total energy production (2009)	2,600 trillion Btu
State ranking in total energy production (2009)	8
Renewable energy net generation total (2009)	6.5 million megawatt hours
Hydroelectric energy generation (2009)	3.6 million megawatt hours
Biomass energy generation (2009)	163,000 megawatt hours
Wind energy generation (2009)	2.7 million megawatt hours
Wood and derived fuel energy generation (2009)	68,000 megawatt hours
Crude oil reserves (2009)	622 million barrels (98.9 million cu m)
Natural gas reserves (2009)	22,769 billion cubic feet (644.7 billion cu m)
Natural gas liquids (2008)	985 million barrels (156.6 million cu m)

Pollution Statistics

Carbon output (2005)	103.3 million tons of CO_2 (93.7 million t)
Superfund sites (2008)	8
Particulate matter (less than 2.5 micrometers) emissions (2002)	6,976 tons per year (6,328 t/yr)
Toxic chemical releases (2009)	29.6 million pounds (13.4 million kg)
Generated hazardous waste (2009)	41,900 tons (38,000 t)

SOURCES: AirData. U.S. Environmental Protection Agency. Available from http://www.epa.gov/air/data; *Energy Maps, Facts, and Data of the U.S. States.* U.S. Energy Information Administration. Available from http://www.eia.gov/state; *The 2012 Statistical Abstract.* U.S. Census Bureau. Available from http://www.census.gov/compendia/statab; *United States Energy Usage.* eRedux. Available from http://www.eredux.net/states.

© 2011 Cengage Learning.

concentration of green business activity in energy infrastructure, and is growing in the areas of business services and air and environment. The state also attracted cleantech venture capital in both 2004 and 2007. According to this study, employment concentration in businesses services increased the most out of all green segments.

According to another state profile put together by the Pew Charitable Trusts, Oklahoma's clean energy economy grew three times as fast as total jobs between 1998 and 2007. Their profile states that as of 2007, Oklahoma had more than 5,400 green jobs in 693 businesses. More than 77 percent of these jobs are in conservation and pollution mitigation.

Wind power in Oklahoma seems to have the most potential for building green businesses and jobs. In 2007, the state was ranked eighth in the U.S. for wind mill utility operation. The state's potential wind power capacity is nearly 82,000 megawatts more than its actual projects currently use. Oklahoma State University has a wind turbine technology degree program in place to train workers in the state to harness this potential. Oklahoma City Community College offers a Wind Turbine Technician Certificate program, where students study basic electricity, industrial electronics, electromechanical devices, programmable controller systems, and instrumentation and control operations along with wind energy industry fundamentals. On September 10, 2008, the University of Oklahoma signed an historic agreement with Oklahoma Gas & Electric Company (OG&E) to purchase 100% percent of its OG&E-supplied electricity from renewable energy sources by 2013. This commitment is instrumental in enabling OG&E to build the OU Spirit Wind Farm—along with the required distribution lines to the grid—in northwestern Oklahoma. A number of other technology centers and community colleges offer training for wind energy technology in Oklahoma.

Tulsa Community College offers both an Associate's of Applied Science and a Certificate in Alternative Energy, which includes the study of wind energy, solar energy, biofuels, and hydrogen power conversion systems.

Green Building

House Bill 3394, signed in 2008, requires the state to meet the certification guidelines of either the U.S. Green Building Council's (USGBC) LEED system or the Green Building Initiative's Green Globes rating system. State construction or renovations of buildings larger than 10,000 square feet (929 sq m) must meet the standards of either rating system. In August 2010, the Environmental Protection Agency (EPA) named four Oklahoma state buildings as Energy Star buildings, including the state Capitol, the attorney general's building, the Jim Thorpe Building, and the Kerr-Edmondson building. The National Weather Center also has an experimental green roof.

On the municipal level, the city of Tulsa has been making efforts to make the city more sustainable, which include green building. The city released energy plans in 2007, 2009, and 2010. These plans outline goals in various categories with an aim to make the city more energy efficient. Some of the goals from the 2010 plan include: Reducing the amount of energy used by Tulsa facilities by 15 percent below 2008 levels by December 31, 2011; obtaining 30 percent of all energy in Tulsa facilities from renewable sources by June 30, 2013; and performing all new city of Tulsa construction, major renovations, and retrofits to a high performance certification program standard by June 30, 2011.

The city of Norman also has a "Green Team," which is working to replace traditional gasoline with compressed natural gas for city vehicles, replacing old traffic signals with LED lights, and adopting a city-wide fuel conservation policy. The city also adopted the Norman 2025 Land Use and Transportation Plan, which aims to achieve a desired land use pattern in response to growth rates, public utility constraints, and environmental conditions.

🌿 Passive Water Treatment at Tar Creek

Tar Creek was one of the first sites designated for the federal Superfund program, a government plan for identifying and cleaning up toxic waste sites. The site is centered near the former communities of Picher and Cardin, Oklahoma, and covers roughly 40 square miles (104 sq km). The waste was a result of over 70 years of lead and zinc mining that left behind miles of tunnels, waste piles, bore holes, and mine shafts. When mining ceased, water filled the void spaces and reacted with the remaining minerals, becoming acid mine water. The mining also left behind massive piles of chat, which is a term for fragments of siliceous rock, limestone, and dolomite waste rejected in the lead-zinc milling operations that accompanied mining. These chat piles also contain significant amounts of lead, zinc, cadmium and other metals.

In 1996, 31.2 percent of Picher's children between the ages of 1 and 5 had elevated blood lead levels and many of the town's children were also found to have learning disorders. The state began offering buyouts to the residents in 2004, with a federal buyout following in 2006, and today the town is nearly empty. However, environmental contamination sources remain.

University of Oklahoma researchers from the College of Engineering's Center for Restoration of Ecosystems and Watersheds, with the help of the design/build firm CH2M Hill, completed the nine-acre (3.6-ha) Mayer Ranch Passive Treatment System, located near Commerce in 2008. This system uses natural processes to clean the contaminated water that flows from the mine pool to Tar Creek. The system is made up of ten manmade ponds, each of which has a different role in cleaning the water. Gravity causes the water to flow between the ponds. Using oxidation ponds, surface flow wetlands, vertical flow bioreactors, re-aeration ponds (using solar and wind power) and horizontal flow limestone beds, it takes about three weeks for the water to flow through the entire system, after which it is released into a tributary of Tar Creek. The first step in the process puts air into the water which helps to remove iron. In later units water flows vertically through organic material that helps sequester contaminants. Another infusion of air by wind- and solar-

powered aeration pumps follows, with the final steps serving to remove any remaining contaminants. The system cleans about 20 percent of the contaminated water in the watershed.

In 2009, only a year into the project, the system was already dubbed a success. The team of scientists and students were able to reduce the level of metals that were polluting Tar Creek to below target levels, and water that was once orange now runs clear. As of October 2010, the system had removed over 100 tons (91 t) of iron, 6 tons (5 t) of zinc, 80 pounds (36 kg) of lead, 20 pounds (9 kg) of cadmium, and 20 pounds (9 kg) of arsenic. The system is expected to last for twenty to thirty years without extensive repair.

In early 2011, Robert Nairn, director of OU's Center for Restoration of Ecosystems and Watersheds, announced that initial grant funding for the project had ended, and the team is looking for new funding opportunities to continue their work. Securing funds for the project is critical, since Nairn estimates that water quality issues will continue at the site for centuries and the current project only focuses on a small part of an area that includes a network of affected streams. In the meantime, the research team has been sampling the water on a quarterly basis, and looking into ways to recycle contaminants that are taken from the water. The team has also been working on another passive water treatment system in the high desert Andes of Bolivia.

BIBLIOGRAPHY

Books

Baird, W. David, and Danny Goble. *Oklahoma, a History.* Norman, OK: University of Oklahoma Press, 2008.

Chang, David A. *The Color of the Land: Race, Nation, and the Politics of Landownership in Oklahoma, 1832-1929.* Chapel Hill, NC: University of North Carolina Press, 2010.

Franks, Kenny, and Paul F. Lambert. *Oklahoma: The Land and Its People.* Norman, OK: University of Oklahoma Press, 1997.

Henderson, Caroline A., and Alvin O. Turner. *Letters from the Dust Bowl.* Norman, OK: University of Oklahoma Press, 2001.

Lowitt, Richard. *American Outback: The Oklahoma Panhandle in the Twentieth Century.* Lubbock, TX: Texas Tech University Press, 2006.

Mathis, Nancy. *Storm Warning: The Story of a Killer Tornado.* New York, NY: Simon & Schuster, 2007.

Miller, Rudolph J. *Fishes of Oklahoma.* University of Oklahoma Press, 2004.

White, Mel, Tria Giovan, and Jim Bones. *The Smithsonian Guides to Natural America: The South Central States—Texas, Oklahoma, Arkansas, Louisi ana, Mississippi.* Washington, DC: Smithsonian Books, 1996.

Woodhouse, S. W. *A Naturalist in Indian Territory: The Journals of S. W. Woodhouse, 1849-1850.* Norman, OK: University of Oklahoma Press, 1996.

Web Sites

Alternative Energy. Tulsa Community College. Available from http://www.tulsacc.edu/60070/

Bogart, Rachel. "USDA Offers Aid to Severe Weather-Impacted States." Yahoo! News. July 17, 2011. Available from http://news.yahoo.com/usda-offers-aid-severe-weather-impacted-states-183600947.html

Branson, Hailey. "Only a Few Hearty Souls Left in Picher." March 11, 2010. *Routes.* Available from http://routes.ou.edu/story.php?storyID=180

Branson, Hailey. "OU students, researchers help clean up Tar Creek." April 16, 2010. *Routes.* Available from http://routes.ou.edu/story.php?storyID=246

Center for Restoration of Ecosystems and Watersheds. University of Oklahoma. Available from http://crew.ou.edu/

"The Clean Energy Economy: Oklahoma." The Pew Charitable Trusts. Available from http://www.pewcenteronthestates.org/uploadedFiles/wwwpewcenteronthestatesorg/Fact_Sheets/Clean_Economy_Factsheet_Oklahoma.pdf

House Bill 3028: An Act relating to energy; creating the Oklahoma Energy Security Act. Oklahoma State Legislature. Available from http://dsireusa.org/incentives/incentive.cfm?Incentive_Code=OK05R&re=1&ee=1

House Bill 3394: An Act relating to public buildings and public works. Oklahoma State Legislature. Available from http://dsireusa.org/incentives/incentive.cfm?Incentive_Code=OK04R&re=1&ee=1

Juozapavicius, Justin. "2011 Drought: Oklahoma Sees Driest 4 Months Since 1921." The Huffington Post. April 6, 2011. Available from http://www.huffingtonpost.com/2011/04/06/2011-drought-oklahoma_n_845419.html

Kelleher, James B. "Drought-stricken Oklahoma to ease truck rules to save cattle." Reuters. July 21, 2011. Available from http://www.reuters.com/article/2011/07/21/us-oklahoma-drought-idUS-TRE76K7HL20110721

"Listings and occurrences for Oklahoma." U.S. Fish and Wildlife Service Species Reports. Available from http://ecos.fws.gov/tess_public/pub/stateListingAndOccurrenceIndividual.jsp?state=OK&s8fid=112761032792&s8fid=112762573902&s8fid=24012920127552

Matthews, Elizabeth. "Ecological engineering cleans contaminated water at Tar Creek area." October 7, 2009. KOAM News. Available from http://www.koamtv.com/global/story.asp?s=11276954

Oklahoma Forestry Services. Available from http://www.forestry.ok.gov/

"Oklahoma Map—State Parks." Oklahoma's Official Travel and Tourism Site. Available from http://www.travelok.com/maps/view.parks

"Oklahoma Organic Producers & Processors." Oklahoma Department of Agriculture, Food and Forestry. Available from http://www.oda.state.ok.us/forms/food/ogl.pdf

"Oklahoma: Profile of the Green Economy." NGA Center for Best Practices. Available from http://www.nga.org/Files/pdf/09GREENPROFILEOK.pdf

Oklahoma Is Wind Energy. Oklahoma Department of Commerce. Available from http://www.okcommerce.gov/Site-Selection/Industry-Profiles/Wind

Oklahoma Wind Power Initiative. Available from http://www.seic.okstate.edu/owpi/default.asp

Snead, Mark C., and Suzette Bartha. "The Economic Impact of Oklahoma's Oil & Natural Gas Industry." Center for Applied Economic Research. Oklahoma State University. Available from http://www.oerb.com/Portals/0/docs/State%20Oil%20Gas%20Impact%20Draft%2020080916.pdf

Snead, Mark C., and Suzette Bartha. "The Local Impact of Oil and Gas Production and Drilling in Oklahoma." Center for Applied Economic Research. Oklahoma State University. Available from http://www.oerb.com/Portals/0/docs/Local%20Oil%20Gas%20Impact%20Draft%2020080916.pdf

"Statement on Climate Change and its Implications for Oklahoma." Oklahoma Climatological Survey. Available from http://climate.ok.gov/newsmedia/climate_statement.pdf

Tar Creek Information Site. Local Environmental Action Demanded, Inc. Available from http://www.tarcreek.org/

2006–2007 Annual Report. Oklahoma Mining Commission Department of Mines. Available from http://www.ok.gov/mines/documents/ANNUALREPORT2006-2007Oct%2014%202008.pdf

"2009 State Agriculture Overview: Oklahoma." United States Department of Agriculture. Available from http://www.nass.usda.gov/Statistics_by_State/Ag_Overview/AgOverview_OK.pdf

"2010 Energy Plan." The City of Tulsa. Available from http://www.cityoftulsa.org/environmental-programs/office-of-sustainability/2010-energy-plan.aspx

Wilkerson, April. "OU Team Targeting Tar Creek." OU Engineering Blog. February 28, 2011. Available from http://ouccoe100.blogspot.com/2011/02/ou-team-targeting-tar-creek.html

Wind Energy Training Program. Oklahoma City Community College. Available from http://www.occc.edu/corporatelearning/WindEnergy.html

Wind Turbine Technology. Oklahoma State University. Available from http://www.osuokc.edu/wind/

Oregon

Oregon's environment is diverse—ranging from the Pacific Coast, to the Willamette Valley, to the high desert of the central part of the state, to the spectacular scenery of Mount Hood and the Columbia River Gorge. With a total land area of almost 96,000 square miles (248,640 sq km), Oregon ranks tenth in size among the 50 U.S. states. The Cascade Mountains, which run from north to south through west-central Oregon, divide the state into two easily conceptualized regions, each with considerable variation. Immediately west of the Cascades Mountains lies Oregon's heartland. Here, the slopes of the Cascade Mountains descend into the state's fertile valleys and farmlands, the largest being the Willamette Valley. Further west, adjacent to the Pacific Ocean, is Oregon's Coast Range, a low lying mountain system that rises from the beaches, bays, and headlands of the Pacific coast. On the eastern side of the Cascade Mountains lie the other two-thirds of Oregon, where expansive arid plateaus extend for miles, with the occasional interruption of a river canyon. The Cascade Mountains themselves contain nine volcanic peaks that rise more than 9,000 feet (2,743 m) above sea level.

Just as the Cascade Mountains divide the state topographically, they also split Oregon climatically. Heavy precipitation and moderate temperatures define the western third of the state, whereas the region east of the Cascade Mountains has an arid climate with more extreme temperatures.

State government reports estimate that climate change could have large, perverse impact on Oregon. Scientists worry that rising temperatures could increase precipitation and snow in some regions of the state, contributing to increased flooding. Additionally, rising sea levels threaten Oregon's beaches, sandy bluffs, and coastal wetlands. According to the National Wildlife Federation, average temperatures in Oregon could rise about 5.4°F (3°C) by 2100 if measures are not taken to abate global warming. The effects of warming temperatures in the state have already been noted. In 2005, the temperature of the water along the Pacific coast was 2 to 5°F (1.1 to 2.8°C) higher than normal. This resulted in huge declines of phytoplankton and krill. That year, gray whales that feed on krill and other small crustaceans were so malnourished that their bodies were deformed by the time they reached the coast. Also, warmer river temperatures have resulted in a decline in salmon, steelhead, and trout species. Scientists trawling for young salmon in 2005 noted extremely low counts in the spring and fall seasons.

To address these challenges, the Oregon governor signed House Bill 3543 in August 2007. HB 3543 set the goals of reducing greenhouse gas emissions to 10 percent below 1990 levels by 2020 and to 75 percent below those levels by 2050. Additionally, HB 3543 directed the state to arrest growth in greenhouse gas emissions by 2010. HB 3543 also created the Oregon Global Warming Commission, a 25-member advisory group that works to develop and implement long-term policy recommendations to prepare for and adapt to climate change. In March 2011, the Commission delivered its biennial report to the legislature, which detailed the state's progress toward its climate goals and 40 actions to help Oregon reach these goals. The report states that Oregon's greenhouse gas emissions through 2010 are expected to be flat, with emissions going on a downward trend in the next few years. At this point, the state looks to be on track when it comes to halting the growth of greenhouse gas emissions. However, progress toward reducing those emissions in order to meet the 2020 and 2050 goals remains uncertain at this point.

Good news returned for anglers in 2011, with the announcement from the Oregon Department of Fish & Wildlife that the fall chinook salmon numbers were expected to be the highest since 2004 for the Columbia River. Officials there expected more than 750,000 prized mid- and upriver bright salmon to return. These fish are desirable for their size and food quality. The large return came just three years after what some officials considered

Chinook salmon migrate upstream to their spawning beds in the Columbia River, Oregon. © *Buddy Mays/Alamy*

a total collapse of the fall chinook in the Sacramento River, which runs from the Pacific Ocean through California and Oregon. In April 2008, the Pacific Fishery Management Council issued the largest salmon fishing closure ever for the California and Oregon coastlines. Numbers rebounded in 2010 and were expected to continue to rebound in 2011.

Natural Resources, Water, and Agriculture

Oregon Proactively Protects Its Forests

Oregon's greatest natural resources are its forests and its fish, which together offer huge economic opportunities for the state. Almost 50 percent of Oregon is covered in forest—92 percent of the forest cover present in 1850. These forests support Oregon's famous, and highly regulated, wood products industry. The combined value of forestry services and wood products manufactured from the forests totals about $13 billion annually in sales. That equates to 11 percent of the state's economic output. Each year, more than 100 million new trees are planted in a proactive reforestation effort, mandated under the Oregon Forest Practices Act. When trees are harvested, new seedlings must be planted to replace the trees that are harvested. Every harvested acre must be replanted within two years—and be "free-to-grow" and well established within six years. The Oregon Forest Practices Act requires land owners not only to replant but also to comply with a variety of other forest management rules that protect fish and water resources and provide for wildlife.

In the eastern portion of Oregon, the ponderosa pine is the dominant species. In the west, the Douglas fir,

western hemlock, and Sitka spruce are prominent conifers. Together, these forests harbor a tremendous diversity of wildlife. Oregon's more than 190 state parks, recreation areas, and natural sites are home to some 130 species of mammal, including the cougar and black bear, native to Oregon. Other important animals in the state include the black-tailed and mule deer, the elk, and, of course, the salmon, which is a staple of Oregon's commercial and recreational fishing industries.

The U.S. Fish and Wildlife Service lists 56 plant and animal species native to Oregon as either threatened or endangered. This list includes the leatherback sea turtle, the gray wolf (which was reintroduced after many years of absence) and the humpback whale, as well as plant species such as the western lily (*Lilium occidentale*), Willamette daisy (*Erigeron decumbens var. decumbens*) and Cook's Lomatium (*Lomatium cookii*).

In April 2011, the National Marine Fisheries Service initiated a status review to determine whether the upper Klamath River spring wild chinook salmon should be protected under the Endangered Species Act. The Klamath River chinook population, found in southern Oregon, has suffered from major declines due to dam building, logging and irrigation. Once the third-largest producer of salmon and steelhead on the West Coast, the river in 2011 only had an estimated 300 to 3,000 wild-spawning spring Chinook, compared to tens of thousands in the early 2000s.

Invasive species represent an ominous threat to Oregon's natural resources. As global trade increases, and more ships from abroad dock at Oregon's coastal ports, the number of invasive species in Oregon tends to grow. Oregon has taken several steps to address this issue, including the creation of the Oregon Invasive Species Council, and the development of an Invasive Species Action Plan. The goal behind both is to address new invasive species immediately, before they have a chance to proliferate and when it is least costly for the state. Invasive species found in Oregon include the feral swine, mute swan and the emerald ash borer.

Oregon's nonfuel mineral production was valued at $493 million in 2007. Industrial minerals accounted for all of the state's nonfuel mineral production, such as crushed stone, construction sand and gravel, and portland cement. Also in 2007, Oregon ranked second in the nation in production of gemstones and crude perlite and third in the production diatomite. Diatomite, which is porous and light, can be used as a filtration aid, or to absorb liquid, among other uses.

Water

Although Oregon is a coastal state with many lakes and rivers, including the deepest lake in the United States (Crater Lake) and the third largest river in the nation by volume (the Columbia River), water is unevenly distributed across the state. The southeastern portion of the

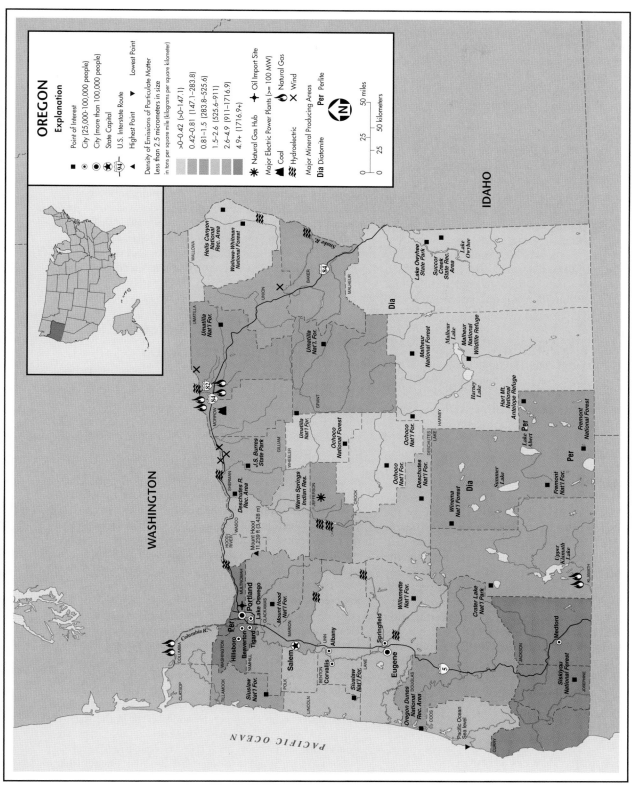

SOURCES: "County Emissions Map: Criteria Air Pollutants." *AirData.* U.S. Environmental Protection Agency. Available from http://www.epa.gov/air/data/geosel.html; *Energy Maps.* U.S. Energy Information Administration. Available from http://www.eia.gov/state; *Highest and Lowest Elevations.* U.S. Geological Survey. Available from http:// egsc.usgs.gov/isb/pubs/booklets/elvadist/elvadist.html#Highest; *2007 Minerals Yearbook.* U.S. Geological Survey. Available from http://minerals.usgs.gov/minerals/pubs/ state. © 2011 Cengage Learning.

state extends into the Great Basin—a large interior drainage basin known for its aridity. Meanwhile, the western third of Oregon is far wetter than other regions of the state. Of the many natural lakes in Oregon, nineteen have surface areas greater than 4.5 square miles (11.6 sq km). The Upper Klamath Lake, the largest lake in the state, has more than 92 square miles (238 sq km) of surface area.

The network of rivers that run through Oregon has proved invaluable to the state's energy infrastructure. The Columbia River hosts Oregon's four largest electricity generation facilities, all of which are hydroelectric plants.

The commercial fishing industry is one of the most important in the state. In 2009, the state landed 211.5 million pounds of fish. Onshore landings alone had a value of $104.4 million. During 2008, there were 886 vessels that had an Oregon-based home port, and they made more than 18,000 deliveries to Oregon ports. In total, both onshore and offshore commercial fishing brought workers $398 million in personal income.

Agriculture

According to the United States Department of Agriculture (USDA), Oregon had 38,600 farms in 2009, which took up 25,625 square miles of the state's land. The average size of an Oregon farm—425 acres (172 ha) —was commensurate with the average American farm. In 2008, Oregon was a top producer of cut Christmas trees. Oregon also took the top spot for field and grass seed crops, and the third spot for greenhouse, nursery and floriculture products with more than 1,800 greenhouses and nurseries located in the state.

The USDA's 2008 Organic Production Survey ranked Oregon, with 657 organic farms, as one of the top five states in terms of certified or exempt organic farms. Oregon's organic farmers brought in more than $155 million in sales in 2008, the fourth most in the United States. Oregon's organic roots are deep as the state is the home of Oregon Tilth, a nonprofit organization that offers education about organic products to residents statewide, as well as offers product certification internationally. Organizers at Oregon Tilth, which began in 1982 to certify local growers, collaborated with officials in Washington and California to write standards and procedures for production that later became the blueprint for the National Organic Program.

⚜ Energy

Renewable Energy Powers Oregon

Oregon consumes less energy—and produces more through renewable means—than most of the other 50 states. Oregon is situated in the twenty-fifth percentile in per capita energy consumption (39 states consume more energy per capita than Oregon). Likewise, of the energy produced in Oregon, a tremendous amount comes from renewable sources, particularly hydroelectric. A leading state in the production of hydroelectric power, Oregon obtains roughly two-thirds of its domestic electricity generation from that clean, renewable power source. The forceful Columbia River, which wends through Oregon and empties into the Pacific Ocean, fuels Oregon's four largest power generation stations. Wind, geothermal, and wood waste (sawdust, shavings, and wood chips) are other significant renewable resources used to produce energy in Oregon.

Although Oregon boasts a robust menu of renewable resources, the state also imports energy. Coal-fired plants in Utah, Montana, and Wyoming shoot energy into Oregon's electric grid, and natural gas is piped into Oregon from Canada and Rocky Mountain states.

In 2007, Oregon adopted its first renewable portfolio standard, which required the state's largest utilities to obtain at least 25 percent of their electricity from renewable sources by 2025.

⚜ Green Business, Green Building, Green Jobs

Green Business

Green business is a booming sector of Oregon's economy. In 2009, the American Council for an Energy-Efficient Economy listed Oregon as one of the top five states in energy efficiency—for the second year in a row. One of the reasons that Oregon has been so successful in adopting green practices is that both the public and private sectors have been supportive of green businesses in the state. Two examples of public and private sector support are the Green Business Tax Credit program, which is run through the Oregon Department of Energy, and Sustainable Business Oregon, a private publication devoted to the research and support of green businesses in the state.

The Green Business Tax Program offers substantial tax credits to businesses that make investments in energy conservation, recycling, renewable energy resources, and clean-burning fuels. Under the program, the standard tax credit covers 35 percent of eligible project costs, paid out at 10 percent per year. However, certain projects, such as renewable energy resource generation, can receive a tax credit as high as 50 percent of eligible project costs. Meanwhile, Sustainable Business Oregon provides detailed information about the green business sector in the state— where Oregon ranks, what businesses in the state are doing, and who they are. The "Green Pages" is one publication launched by Sustainable Business Oregon that enables people to see, and patronize, sustainable businesses in Oregon.

The Green Spot, a directory of environmentally friendly businesses in central Oregon, released an updated edition in April 2011. The publication boasts a variety of

Mt. Hood. © *iStockPhoto.com/Danny Warren*

businesses, which include carpet cleaning services to earth-friendly gifts. Each business is labeled with symbols based on which sustainable criteria they meet. The directory also contains a resource guide, featuring government organizations and nonprofit groups that relate to sustainability. The Green Spot is put together by the Central Oregon Environmental Center and is distributed free in central Oregon.

Green Building

In the 1990s, as awareness spread about the impacts of housing on the environment, public policy makers in Oregon began to consider ways to expand green building in the state. In 1998, the Oregon Housing and Community Services Department (OHCS) initiated a special project on green building, eventually producing a Green Building Task Force—a group of experts in the building and housing fields charged with developing the framework for an "environmentally sensitive building initiative" for Oregon.

Two years after its creation, the Green Building Task Force produced a report of recommendations, which focused on four objectives:

1. Departmental Action (what OHCS is doing internally to embody the principles of green building);

2. Subsidies and Incentives (tax credits and weatherization assistance to individuals and businesses);

3. Education (creating public awareness about sustainable design and building);

4. Interface with Regulatory Process (making sure that building codes and regulations are conducive to green design).

As of 2011, OHCS played a critical role in helping to achieve those objectives, hosting a website that offers residents and businesses great information about green building and available incentives. Oregon also introduced a green building policy that requires all new state government buildings to be constructed to meet U.S. Green Building Council Silver LEED certification or higher. On the municipal level, in 2001 the city of Portland adopted a Green Building Policy that requires all new city buildings and major renovations to achieve LEED certification. The policy was updated in 2005 to require that new buildings meet the LEED Gold standard and renovated buildings meet the Silver standard.

In April 2011, a new 6.5 megawatt cogeneration power plant at Oregon State University (OSU) was awarded LEED Platinum certification. The OSU Energy Center, a natural gas-run plant that combines heating and

Oregon State Profile

Physical Characteristics

Land area	95,985 square miles (248,600 sq km)
Inland water area	1,063 square miles (2,753 sq km)
Coastal area	74 square miles (119 sq km)
Highest point	Mount Hood 11,239 feet (3,426 m)
National Forest System lands (2010)	15.7 million acres (6.3 million ha)
State parks (2011)	192

Energy Statistics

Total energy production (2009)	410 trillion Btu
State ranking in total energy production (2009)	33
Renewable energy net generation total (2009)	37.3 million megawatt hours
Hydroelectric energy generation (2009)	33.0 million megawatt hours
Biomass energy generation (2009)	128,000 megawatt hours
Wind energy generation (2009)	3.5 million megawatt hours
Wood and derived fuel energy generation (2009)	674,000 megawatt hours
Crude oil reserves (2009)	NA
Natural gas reserves (2009)	NA
Natural gas liquids (2008)	NA

Pollution Statistics

Carbon output (2005)	40.4 million tons of CO_2 (36.7 million t)
Superfund sites (2008)	13
Particulate matter (less than 2.5 micrometers) emissions (2002)	6,559 tons per year (5,950 t/yr)
Toxic chemical releases (2009)	17.3 million pounds (7.8 million kg)
Generated hazardous waste (2009)	61,900 tons (56,100 t)

SOURCES: AirData. U.S. Environmental Protection Agency. Available from http://www.epa.gov/air/data; *Energy Maps, Facts, and Data of the U.S. States.* U.S. Energy Information Administration. Available from http://www.eia.gov/state; *The 2012 Statistical Abstract.* U.S. Census Bureau. Available from http://www.census.gov/compendia/statab; *United States Energy Usage.* eRedux. Available from http://www.eredux.net/states.

© 2011 Cengage Learning.

electricity generation, is the nation's first LEED Platinum power plant. The plant allows OSU to generate almost half of its electrical needs on site, dramatically lowering its energy costs and reducing carbon dioxide emissions by 38 percent. The plant also utilizes rainwater harvesting, hot water generated by heat recovery from the steam system, a white reflective roof, water-efficient landscaping, recycled building materials, and natural lighting. The Energy Center will also serve as a learning lab for OSU students.

Green Jobs

Because Oregon is heavily invested in the renewable energy sector, the state has been a leader in attracting and supporting green jobs. According to the Pew Charitable Trusts, more than 1 percent of total jobs in Oregon were related to the clean energy economy in 2007—a greater share than any state in the nation. Additionally, from 1998 to 2007, clean energy jobs have grown in Oregon at more than 50 percent, significantly outpacing job growth in the traditional economy, which grew at 7.5 percent. From 2006 to 2008, Oregon attracted more than $70 million in venture capital to the clean energy economy.

One example of statewide job growth originated from the city of Portland's Bureau of Planning and Sustainability. Clean Energy Works Oregon started in Portland and has been lauded for its early job creation successes. In April 2011, officials announced the program would expand to other parts of the state. Clean Energy Works Oregon is a nonprofit that focuses on home energy efficiency upgrades. Though in its beginning stages in 2011, the program was expected to create 1,300 jobs through 6,000 residential projects, with a result of significant energy savings over the course of three years.

Oregon's institutions of higher education offer residents plenty of opportunities to receive training for green careers. Located in Eugene, the Northwest Energy Education Institute (NEEI) offers four two-year degrees, four certifications, and custom training to prepare students to enter the green workforce. Students can earn degrees in energy management, renewable energy, water conservation, and resource conservation. There are also certificates available for energy management, a sustainable building advisor, building operator, and a residential energy auditor and inspector. NEEI is located in the Science Department at Lane Community College, and its programs are geared toward practicing professionals in the energy industry.

In June 2010, Oregon governor Ted Kulongoski announced that the state had received $1 million under the American Recovery and Reinvestment Act to develop a new green job training center, to help workers develop skills in energy efficient retrofitting and weatherization.

Shepherds Flat Wind Farm

The use of wind energy isn't entirely new for the state of Oregon, which as of December 2009 ranked as fourth in the nation for existing capacity. The Stateline Wind Energy Center that straddles the Oregon–Washington border at Pendleton, Oregon, is the largest commercial wind electricity–generating facility in the Northwest, with 454 wind turbines (operating in both states) producing a maximum of 300 megawatts, enough to power about 72,000 homes. While most other wind facilities in Oregon are of much smaller capacity, several have plans to expand within the next few years, building upon the state's potential. In September 2009, three Oregon wind farms that came online during 2009 received federal stimulus grants for their expansion projects. These were the Horizon Wind Energy Wheat Field wind farm in Arlington and the Iberdrola Renewable Pebble Springs and Hay Canyon wind farms in Arlington and Moro respectively.

In April 2010, the U.S. Department of Defense nearly derailed a major wind farm construction project that promises to be the largest land-based wind energy project in the world. Construction of the Shepherds Flat wind farm, under development by Caithness Energy, began in March 2010, but came to a sudden halt in mid-April when the Pentagon moved to block the final U.S. Federal Aviation Administration (FAA) permit, citing that the wind farm would disrupt the nearby U.S. Air Force radar system in Fossil, Oregon. The Pentagon's permit refusal set in motion a major lobbying campaign led by Oregon's Democratic senators Ron Wyden and Jeff Merkley and Republican U.S. representative Greg Walden. While the Pentagon argued on issues of national security, the Oregon team countered with arguments that national security and energy security are one and the same, and pushed for officials to reconsider any options that would let the project go forward. In late April 2010, the Pentagon dropped its opposition to the wind farm, and groundbreaking proceeded in early May.

A much-needed boost to the local economy was also put in jeopardy by the government standoff. The Shepherds Flat project is set to be built across 30 miles of land within the rural, economically depressed counties of Gilliam and Morrow. With 338 wind turbines, the facility is expected to have a generating capacity of 845 megawatts, surpassing the 781-megawatt farm near Roscoe, Texas, that now holds the distinction of being the largest in the world. Shepherds Flat will generate enough energy to power 235,000 homes. The populations of Gilliam and Morrow counties are estimated at 1,645 and 11,533 respectively. Hundreds of construction jobs will be created as the facility is built, while 35 permanent jobs are expected to be created within the first year of operation. The project is expected to collect $4–5 million per year in property taxes for the host counties and $2.7 million a year in royalties over the next ten years for about two dozen farmers and ranchers who are allowing turbines to be placed on their land. Local officials hope the project will attract new residents and businesses to the areas as local revenues from the facility will be invested in schools, libraries, and infrastructure improvements.

After a few weeks of intense debate, the Pentagon officially dropped its objections to the project with a decision to provide improvements to the local radar system that would address the concerns of the FAA. The Department of Defense has indicated that this latest approval does not set a precedent for future wind farms in the area, which will be assessed on a case-by-case basis.

The project cleared another hurdle in October of 2010, when it received a $1.3 billion stimulus loan from the U.S. Department of Energy. Secretary of Energy Steven Chu pointed out that providing funds for this project is an example of the Obama administration's commitment to increase renewable energy generation and to create jobs. The Shepherds Flat project has a projected completion date for 2012. The facility has already signed a supply and service contract with GE, which will supply the wind turbines and provide operational and maintenance services for ten years. The facility will supply electricity for Southern California Edison, which is expected to secure 33 percent of its power from renewable sources by 2020. It is expected to reduce carbon emissions by more than a million tons each year, which is the equivalent of taking 212,141 cars off of the road.

While the Shepherds Flat Wind Farm has been moving along, questions have arisen in the first few months of 2011 about how much the project will end up costing taxpayers. The project has been able to take advantage of multiple state and federal tax subsidies, with the money to cover the subsidies—adding up to over $1 billion—coming from the taxpayers. This has some residents of the area up in arms, stating that it is a waste of money for a project that would have gone ahead anyway, with or without subsidies.

BIBLIOGRAPHY

Books

Chasan, Daniel Jack, and Tim Thompson. *The Smithsonian Guides to Natural America: The Pacific Northwest–Washington, Oregon*. Washington, DC: Smithsonian Books, 1995.

Donahue, Debra L. *The Western Range Revisited: Removing Livestock from Public Lands to Conserve Native Biodiversity*. Norman: University of Oklahoma Press, 2000.

Grayson, Donald K. *The Great Basin: A Natural Prehistory*, rev. ed., Berkeley: University of California Press, 2011.

Walker, Peter A., and Patrick T. Hurley. *Planning Paradise: Politics and Visioning of Land Use in Oregon*. Tucson: The University of Arizona Press, 2011.

Web Sites

2007 Minerals Yearbook: Oregon. U.S. Geological Survey. Available from http://minerals.usgs.gov/minerals/pubs/state/2007/myb2-2007-or.pdf

"ACEEE: Recession Not Dimming States' Growing Focus on Energy Efficiency as 'First Fuel,' with CA, MA and CT Rated Best on Implementing Energy Efficiency." American Council for an Energy-

Efficient Economy. Available from http://www.aceee.org/press/e097pr.htm

"Briefing Report: Oregon Commercial Fishing Industry Preliminary Economic Contributions In 2009." Oregon Department of Fish & Wildlife. January 2011. Available from http://www.dfw.state.or.us/fish/commercial/docs/OR_Comm_Fish_Ec_Impacts_Prelim_2009.pdf

"Business Energy Tax Credits." Oregon Department of Energy. Available from http://www.oregon.gov/ENERGY/CONS/BUS/BETC.shtml

City of Portland Green Building Policy. Office of the City Auditor. City of Portland, Oregon. Available from http://www.portlandonline.com/auditor/index.cfm?&a=250416&c=34835

"The CleanEnergy Economy: Repowering Jobs, Businesses and Investments Across America." The Pew Charitable Trusts. Available from http://www.pewcenteronthestates.org/uploadedFiles/Clean_Economy_Report_Web.pdf

Eilperin, Juliet. "Pentagon Objections Hold Up Oregon Wind Farm." *The Washington Post.* April 15, 2010. Available from http://www.washingtonpost.com/wp-dyn/content/article/2010/04/15/AR2010041503120.html

"First LEED Platinum Power Plant: Oregon State University." April 13, 2011. *Sustainable Business.* Available from http://www.sustainablebusiness.com/index.cfm/go/news.display/id/22238

"Forest Practices Administrative Rules and Forest Practices Act." Oregon Department of Forestry. Available from http://www.oregon.gov/ODF/privateforests/docs/guidance/FPArulebk.pdf

"Global Warming and Oregon." National Wildlife Federation. Available from http://www.nwf.org/Global-Warming/~/media/PDFs/Global%20Warming/Global%20Warming%20State%20Fact%20Sheets/Oregon.ashx

"Green Building in Oregon." Oregon Housing and Community Services Department. Available from http://www.oregon.gov/OHCS/DO_Green-Building.shtml#Green_Building_Activities_

"Green Building Task Force: Recommendations Report." Oregon Housing and Community Services. Available from http://www.oregon.gov/OHCS/DO/docs/RecommendationsReport.pdf?ga=t

"Green Business Initiative." University of Oregon. Available from http://www.law.uoregon.edu/greenbizlaw/

Hagemeier, Heidi. "The Green Spot directory now out." April 13, 2011. *The Bulletin.* Available from http://www.bendbulletin.com/article/20110413/NEWS0107/104130304/

"Improved Sacramento River Chinook Allow First Major California, Oregon Ocean Fishery Since 2007." The Columbia Basin Fish & Wildlife News. April 15, 2011. Available from http://www.cbbulletin.com/407671.aspx

Learn, Scott. "Pentagon Drops Opposition to Bug Oregon Wind Farm." *The Oregonian.* April 30, 2010. Available from http://www.oregonlive.com/environment/index.ssf/2010/04/air_forces_drops_opposition_to.html

Mortenson, Eric. "Three Oregon Wind Farms Win $140 Million in Federal Stimulus." *The Oregonian.* September 1, 2009. Available from http://www.oregonlive.com/environment/index.ssf/2009/09/three_oregon_wind_farms_win_14.html

Northwest Energy Education Institute. Available from http://www.nweei.org/

"Oregon Global Warming Commission recommends 40 key actions." March 17, 2011. Oregon Department of Energy. Available from http://www.oregon.gov/ENERGY/news/1125OGWC.shtml

"Oregon Invasive Species Action Plan." Oregon Department of Fish and Wildlife. Available from http://www.oregon.gov/OISC/docs/pdf/oisc_plan6_05.pdf?ga=t

"Organic Production Survey 2008." U.S. Department of Agriculture. Available from http://www.agcensus.usda.gov/Publications/2007/Online_Highlights/Organics/ORGANICS.pdf

"Oregon Tilth: History." Oregon Tilth. Available from http://tilth.org/about/history

"Portland's Energy Efficiency Remodel Program A Win For Homeowners And Community." Portland Bureau of Planning & Sustainability. April 27, 2011. Available from http://www.portlandonline.com/bps/index.cfm?c=44851&a=346818

"Shepherd's Flat Wind Farm: Large-Scale Sustainable Business Comes to Oregon." October 19, 2010. CleanTechies.com. Available from http://blog.cleantechies.com/2010/10/19/shepherds-flat-wind-farm-large-scale-oregon/

Sickinger, Ted. "The cost of green: Huge eastern Oregon wind farm raises big question about state, federal subsidies" March 12, 2011. OregonLive.com. Available from http://www.oregonlive.com/politics/index.ssf/2011/03/post_20.html

Sickinger, Ted. "Shepherds Flat wind farm: What's the cost to taxpayers?" March 12, 2011. OregonLive.com. Available from http://www.oregonlive.com/politics/index.ssf/2011/03/post_19.html

"Species Reports: Listings and occurrences for Oregon." U.S. Fish and Wildlife Service. Available from http://ecos.fws.gov/tess_public/pub/

stateListingAndOccurrenceIndividual.jsp?state=OR&s8fid=112761032792&s8-fid=112762573902&s8fid=24012792965633

Stateline Wind Energy Center. Available from http://www.rnp.org/projects/stateline.html

"Strong Fall Chinook Returns Expected For Columbia River." Oregon Department of Fish & Wildlife. July 27, 2011. Available from http://www.dfw.state.or.us/news/2011/july/072711.asp

"Sustainable Business Oregon." Available from http://www.sustainablebusinessoregon.com/index.html

"Upper Klamath River Chinook Salmon One Step Closer to Endangered Species Act Protection." April 11, 2011. Center for Biological Diversity. Available from http://www.biologicaldiversity.org/news/press_releases/2011/chinook-salmon-04-11-2011.html

"U.S. Economic Impacts of Climate Change and the Costs of Inaction. Regional Highlight: Pacific Northwest." Center for Integrative Environmental Research. University of Maryland. Available from http://www.cier.umd.edu/documents/Pacific%20Northwest-Economic%20Impacts%20of%20Climate%20Change.pdf

Pennsylvania

Pennsylvania is a state with rich resources and a strong history of industrial innovation. Keeping the two thriving while protecting and preserving the environment has challenged the state's leaders. Pennsylvanian Rachel Carson helped launch the environmental movement with her 1962 work, *Silent Spring.* Pennsylvania was also the site of the most serious nuclear power plant accident in U.S. history, at the Three Mile Island nuclear power plant near Middletown on March 28, 1979.

The second largest of the Mid-Atlantic states, Pennsylvania covers nearly 45,000 square miles (116,550 sq km) of land and ranks 32nd in size among the 50 U.S. states. A topographically diverse state, Pennsylvania can be divided into more than a dozen distinct physiographic regions. However, it is perhaps easiest to conceive of the state in six, broad geographic regions.

In the northwest along Lake Erie sits the Central Lowlands Province, a flat, low-lying region that is the smallest of the state's provinces. To the southeast of the Central Lowlands is the Appalachian Plateau Province, an expansive province, which covers roughly the western and northern thirds of the state. The Ridge and Valley Province is situated to the east and south of the Appalachian Plateau Province, and represents the Appalachian Mountains section of the state. Below the Ridge and Valley Province are the Piedmont and New England Provinces, with the latter maintaining slightly higher elevations. And, finally, at the southeast corner of the state is the Atlantic Coastal Plain, a small, very low-lying section of Pennsylvania.

Climate

Pennsylvania lies entirely within the humid continental zone, but corresponding to the diversity of elevations, its climate varies from region to region. In the west, along Lake Erie and the Ohio Valley, Pennsylvania has the warmest climate with the longest growing season. There, summers tend to be hot. The rest of the state, with its higher elevations, has cold winters and cool summers.

According to the University of Maryland's Center for Integrative Environmental Research (CIER), climate change will likely have a significant impact on Pennsylvania's environment and economy. Depending on the scenario, CIER scientists believe that annual temperatures could rise in Pennsylvania during the twenty-first century between 3.6 and 12.6°F (2 and 7°C). The most obvious manifestation of this temperature rise will be warmer winters. However, scientists believe it could also increase the levels of precipitation in the state, thus contributing to larger floods and more pollution runoff into Pennsylvania's water supplies.

Higher temperatures are also associated with decreasing water levels on major rivers and lakes, such as Lake Erie. Because Pennsylvania relies heavily on ports to ship goods, lower water levels could require expensive dredging projects or the construction of overland shipping routes. Climate change will also negatively affect populations of cold-water fish species, such as brook and rainbow trout. According to the National Wildlife Federation, climate change could also adversely affect the health of Pennsylvanians. Currently, "red alert" air-quality days happen an average two days per summer in Pittsburgh. Estimates are that by the mid-twenty-first century, this number could climb to five days per summer. Ozone levels already exceed the EPA's healthy standard ten days out of the year, and have the potential to climb to 22 days if steps aren't taken to decrease ozone levels.

Sensing the challenges associated with climate change, and Pennsylvania's contribution to the problem (at the end of 2009, the state was responsible for a full 1 percent of world greenhouse gas emissions), the state compiled and published the Pennsylvania Climate Change Action Plan in October 2009. The action plan called for Pennsylvania to reduce greenhouse gas emissions by at least 30 percent from 2000 levels by 2020.

❧ Natural Resources, Water, and Agriculture

Vast Woodlands

Forests cover more than 60 percent of Pennsylvania's land, and represent a growing resource in the state. Maple, walnut, poplar, oak, pine, ash, beech, linden, and Hemlock, the state tree, are found throughout the state's expansive forests. According to a 2004 report from the Pennsylvania Forest Products Association, the state's forest industry generates $5.5 billion in sales every year, and employs over 90,000 people at 3,000 facilities across the state.

Pennsylvania's dense woodlands provide an ideal habitat for numerous animal species, including the iconic American black bear, the grey and red foxes, and Pennsylvania's state animal, the white-tailed deer. The U.S. Fish and Wildlife Service lists 15 plant and animal species native to Pennsylvania as federally threatened or endangered. Endangered animals include the shortnose sturgeon and Indiana bat, while endangered plant species include the northeastern bulrush. Pennsylvania is home to 117 state parks and 24 national parks and historic sites. The state parks system was awarded the 2009 National Gold Medal for Excellence in Parks and Recreation Administration by the National Recreation and Park Association. Each year more than 34 million people enjoy the state parks system. The newest of Pennsylvania's national parks is the Flight 93 National Memorial Site, which commemorates the events of September 11, 2001, when the actions of the passengers and crew aboard Flight 93 resulted in an attack on the U.S. Capitol being averted. Phase 1 of the memorial was dedicated on September 10, 2011, with a ceremony that followed the next day remembering the tenth anniversary of the event.

Pennsylvania has a tremendous endowment of mineral wealth as well—from its Marcellus Shale, considered to be the densest and most economically valuable in the country, to its Anthracite coal reserves, which are the largest in the nation. The state also has significant amounts of sand and soft coal reserves. And despite declining values, Pennsylvania ranked second in the nation in crushed stone produced in 2008, and third in production of Portland cement. Pennsylvania produced significant amounts of cadmium metal acquired from out-of-state sources, ranking it first of three cadmium-producing states.

Water Abounds in Pennsylvania

Pennsylvania's location in the humid continental zone naturally provides the state with tremendous amounts of surface water—rivers, streams, and lakes—including a portion of Lake Erie, one of the five North American Great Lakes. However, Pennsylvania's largest fresh water resources are locked under the ground—more than 30 times the aggregate of Pennsylvania's surface water. This groundwater is stored in slowly moving underground aquifers, which eventually discharge into the state's rivers and streams, providing, on average, more than 60 percent of the water flow in these resources. The largest, most important rivers in the state are the Delaware, Monongahela, Allegheny, and Ohio rivers, all of which played significant roles in Pennsylvania's early commercial development. The Delaware River provides Pennsylvania direct access to the Atlantic Ocean.

The Delaware River Basin, which covers more than 13,500 square miles in New Jersey, Pennsylvania, New York, and Delaware, serves as a major resource for more than 15 million people, providing water for drinking, agricultural, and industrial use. This important resource is managed primarily through the work of the Delaware River Basin Commission (DRBC). The commission was established in 1961 through the passage of concurrent legislation in the four basin states and with the accompanying signature of President John F. Kennedy. The compact that formed the commission created the first regional body to share equal authority with the federal government in the management of a river system. Since then, the commission has been instrumental in providing programs for water quality protection, supply allocation, conservation efforts, drought and flood management, watershed planning, and recreation. The commissioners include the governors of New Jersey, New York, Pennsylvania, and Delaware and a federal representative, with each commissioner having one vote of equal power.

Pennsylvania is home to 15 fish hatcheries, producing species such as striped bass, walleye, catfish, muskellunge, largemouth bass, smallmouth bass, pike, and pickerel. These fish hatcheries help support Pennsylvania's fishing industry, which along with other fishing related activities generates more than $1.6 billion for the state each year. However, that industry may be threatened with the potential introduction of the invasive species Asian carp into the waters of Lake Erie. Pennsylvania is one of five states (along with Michigan, Ohio, Minnesota, and Wisconsin) that sued the U.S. Army Corps of Engineers and an Illinois waterway management agency to close links from the Mississippi River to the Great Lakes. The Asian carp is prevalent in the Mississippi River, and with 2011 flooding, may have invaded smaller rivers and lakes in Missouri. A U.S. District judge denied the states' request, and an appeals court upheld the ruling in August 2011. The states maintain the Asian carp, which reproduces quickly and competes for food with native species, is a serious threat to a $7 billion sportfishing and tourism industry in the Great Lakes.

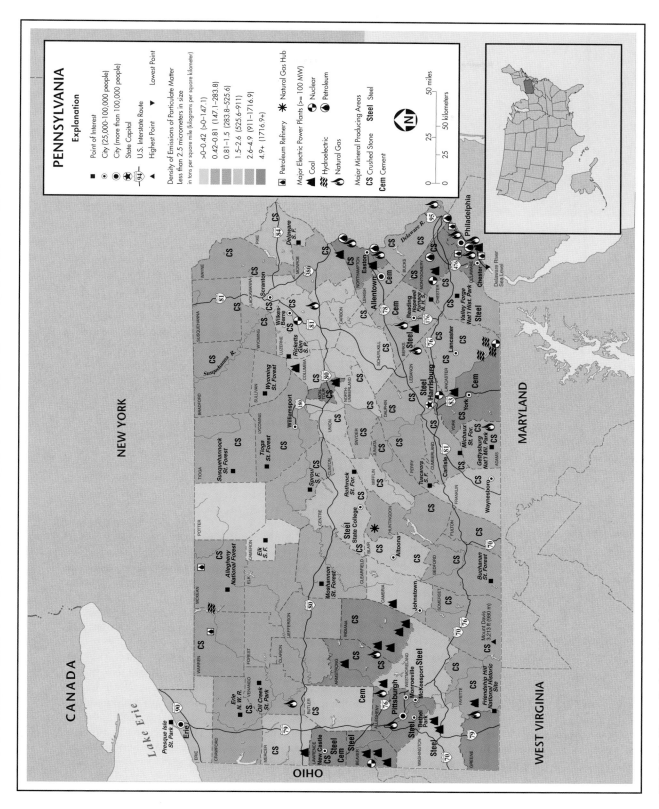

PENNSYLVANIA

Explanation

■ Point of Interest

⊙ City (25,000–100,000 people)

◉ City (more than 100,000 people)

★ State Capital

🛣94 U.S. Interstate Route

▲ Highest Point   ▼ Lowest Point

Density of Emissions of Particulate Matter
Less than 2.5 micrometers in size
in tons per square mile (kilograms per square kilometer)

>0–0.42 (>0–147.1)
0.42–0.81 (147.1–283.8)
0.81–1.5 (283.8–525.6)
1.5–2.6 (525.6–911)
2.6–4.9 (911–1716.9)
4.9+ (1716.9+)

◉ Petroleum Refinery   ✳ Natural Gas Hub

Major Electric Power Plants (>= 100 MW)

⬥ Coal   ◐ Nuclear

⬥ Hydroelectric   ◑ Petroleum

⬥ Natural Gas

Major Mineral Producing Areas

CS Crushed Stone   **Steel** Steel

Cem Cement

N

0   25   50 miles
0   25   50 kilometers

CANADA

NEW YORK

Lake Erie

Presque Isle St. Park ■

Erie ⊙ 🛣90

Erie N.W.R. ◐

Oil Creek St. Park ■

Venango

CRAWFORD

MERCER

CS

LAWRENCE

New Castle ■ **Steel**

Cem **Steel**

BEAVER 🛣79

WASHINGTON

Steel 🛣70

GREENE

WEST VIRGINIA

WARREN

CS

FOREST

Allegheny National Forest

McKEAN ◈

ELK

Elk S.F.

CAMERON

CS

JEFFERSON

CLARION

🛣80

ARMSTRONG

CS

BUTLER

CS

INDIANA

CS

Pittsburgh ◉

Monroeville ◐

Bethel Park

ALLEGHENY

McKeesport **Steel**

🛣76

WESTMORELAND **Steel**

Johnstown ⊙

CAMBRIA

CS

Friendship Hill National Historic Site

FAYETTE 🛣70

Mount Davis 3,213 ft (980 m) ▲

CS

SOMERSET 🛣70 🛣76

POTTER

TIOGA

Tioga St. Forest ■

CS

Sproul S.F.

CLINTON

CENTRE

Moshannon St. Forest

CS

CLEARFIELD

Altoona ⊙

BLAIR

Steel

State College ⊙ ✳

CS

Rothrock St. For.

MIFFLIN

HUNTINGDON

BEDFORD

CS

Buchanan St. Forest

FULTON 🛣70

SUSQUEHANNA

CS

Scranton ⊙ 🛣81

Wilkes-Barre ⊙ 🛣81

LUZERNE

Ricketts Glen S.P.

Williamsport ⊙ 🛣180

LYCOMING

Sussquehannock St. Forest ■

SULLIVAN

Wyoming St. Forest ■

CS

COLUMBIA

UNION

CS

SNYDER

JUNIATA

PERRY

Carlisle ⊙

CUMBERLAND 🛣81

Michaux St. For.

CS

Gettysburg Nat'l Mil. Park ■

ADAMS

Waynesboro ⊙

FRANKLIN

MARYLAND

WAYNE

PIKE 🛣84

MONROE 🛣380

CARBON

LACKAWANNA

WYOMING

NORTH-UMBERLAND

MONT-OUR

DAUPHIN

Harrisburg ★ **Steel**

LEBANON 🛣83

York ⊙ **Cem**

YORK

Susquehanna R.

Delaware S.F.

NORTHAMPTON

Easton ⊙

LEHIGH

Allentown ◉ 🛣78

BERKS

Reading ⊙ **Cem**

Hopewell Furnace N.H.S.

Valley Forge Nat'l Hist. Park

Lancaster ⊙ **Steel**

SCHUYLKILL

🛣76

MONTGOMERY

CHESTER

BUCKS

Cem

🛣95

Philadelphia ◉

DELAWARE

Chester ⊙ **Steel**

Delaware River Sea Level ▼

🛣476

Delaware R.

OIHO

WORLDMARK ENCYCLOPEDIA OF U.S. AND CANADIAN ENVIRONMENTAL ISSUES

SOURCES: "County Emissions Map: Criteria Air Pollutants." *AirData.* U.S. Environmental Protection Agency. Available from http://www.epa.gov/air/data/geosel.html; *Energy Maps.* U.S. Energy Information Administration. Available from http://www.eia.gov/state; *Highest and Lowest Elevations.* U.S. Geological Survey. Available from http://egsc.usgs.gov/isb/pubs/booklets/elvadist/elvadist.html#Highest; *2007 Minerals Yearbook.* U.S. Geological Survey. Available from http://minerals.usgs.gov/minerals/pubs/state. © 2011 Cengage Learning.

Evidence of drought along Lake Erie. © *AP Images/Emilio DiValerio*

Small and Nimble Organic Farms Bring in the Bucks

Organic farming serves as a major industry in Pennsylvania, and the state ranked third in the nation in total organic product sales in 2008, only behind California and Washington. That year, more than 583 farms were listed as certified organic in the state. According to the Center for Rural Pennsylvania, the average organic farm in Pennsylvania generated in 2008 more than quadruple the sale receipts of the average conventional farm in the state. Looked at in the context of organic farming nationally, Pennsylvania's organic farming sector was even more impressive. Whereas the average organic farm in the United States spanned 285 acres, Pennsylvania organic farms averaged just a fraction of that—96 acres. Yet Pennsylvania's small organic farms still generated considerably more revenue than their larger organic peers across the country. The sales receipts for the average organic farm in the country were just $217,700, compared to $386,000 in Pennsylvania. No wonder that when surveyed, more than 70 percent of the state's organic farmers said that they would maintain or increase their organic production over the next few years. Local farmers have an invaluable resource right in their own state, too. Pennsylvania Certified Organic is a USDA-accredited organization that works to certify area farms, and has expanded its reach to include farms in neighboring states like Ohio, West Virginia, and New York, among others.

The reason that Pennsylvania's organic farms appeared so much more productive than other regions' could have to do with the history of agriculture in Pennsylvania. During the colonial period, German immigrants farmed the fertile land in southeastern Pennsylvania, making the state a leader in agricultural production. Unlike farmers in other states, who worked the soil until it was depleted and then moved on, these farmers carefully cultivated the same plots year after year,

using crop rotation techniques that kept the land productive.

A March 2010 report from the U.S. Department of Agriculture (USDA) showed that more than 13,000 square miles (33,670 sq km) of Pennsylvania land are used to harvest agricultural products on more than 63,000 farms. The state's food-processing industry is also one of the largest in the United States, with 2,300 companies located in the state. The state's top crops include corn, soybeans, oats, wheat, and apples.

Nonrenewable Energy Continues to Attract Investment

Pennsylvania ranks sixth in energy production among the fifty states, despite having below average per capita energy consumption. The state is rich with energy resources and serves as an important hub for traditional nineteenth- and twentieth-century nonrenewable energy supplies, such as coal. At the same time, Pennsylvania's wealth of natural, renewable energy resources, such as wind and water, could help it emerge as a leader in twenty-first century renewables.

The Appalachian basin, which covers most of the state, famously holds huge reserves of coal, and the state contains the largest remaining reserves of anthracite coal in the nation. Anthracite coal is a rare, high-value, and high-carbon coal that burns cleanly with little soot. Minor fields of oil and natural gas are also found in this region and the first oil well in the world, the Drake Well, was drilled in the state. In March and April 2010, the Pennsylvania Public Utility Commission was meeting to discuss the future development of Marcellus Shale. Pennsylvania is believed to hold the thickest deposits of Marcellus Shale in the country and has been attracting investments in this area at a breakneck pace. Nuclear energy provides roughly one-third of the state's energy, and with five operating reactors, Pennsylvania has the second-highest nuclear energy generating capacity, behind Illinois.

Renewable energy is not being ignored in the Keystone State. Possible areas for development include hydropower via the state's Susquehanna River and its multiple smaller river basins. There is also the potential of wind energy development in the Appalachian and Allegheny mountain ranges. The Lake Erie coastline to the north also offers wind potential. Another bright spot for the state is solar energy. During the summer of 2011, solar energy generation in the state eclipsed the 100-megawatt mark, which is enough to power more than 12,000 homes. However, that bright spot may not shine much past its 2011 success unless the alternative energy portfolio standard goals for solar are increased. The solar advances had already met the goals for 2013 by the fall of

Pennsylvania State Profile

Physical Characteristics

Land area	44,739 square miles (115,873 sq km)
Inland water area	567 square miles (1,469 sq km)
Coastal area	NA
Highest point	Mount Davis 3,213 feet (979 m)
National Forest System lands (2010)	513,000 acres (208,000 ha)
State parks (2011)	120

Energy Statistics

Total energy production (2009)	2,800 trillion Btu
State ranking in total energy production (2009)	6
Renewable energy net generation total (2009)	6.0 million megawatt hours
Hydroelectric energy generation (2009)	2.7 million megawatt hours
Biomass energy generation (2009)	1.6 million megawatt hours
Wind energy generation (2009)	1.1 million megawatt hours
Wood and derived fuel energy generation (2009)	694,000 megawatt hours
Crude oil reserves (2009)	10.0 million barrels (1.6 million cu m)
Natural gas reserves (2009)	6,985 billion cubic feet (197.8 billion cu m)
Natural gas liquids (2008)	NA

Pollution Statistics

Carbon output (2005)	271.4 million tons of CO_2 (246.2 million t)
Superfund sites (2008)	95
Particulate matter (less than 2.5 micrometers) emissions (2002)	64,795 tons per year (58,781 t/yr)
Toxic chemical releases (2009)	123.3 million pounds (55.9 million kg)
Generated hazardous waste (2009)	290,800 tons (263,800 t)

SOURCES: AirData. U.S. Environmental Protection Agency. Available from http://www.epa.gov/air/data; *Energy Maps, Facts, and Data of the U.S. States.* U.S. Energy Information Administration. Available from http://www.eia.gov/state; *The 2012 Statistical Abstract.* U.S. Census Bureau. Available from http://www.census.gov/compendia/statab; *United States Energy Usage.* eRedux. Available from http://www.eredux.net/states.

2011, and without any incentives to buy additional, more expensive, solar power, the traditional energy companies will stop producing it. That, in turn, will reduce the amount of funding for future renewable energy projects.

In 2004, Pennsylvania adopted an alternative energy portfolio standard, which mandated that electric distribution companies generate 18.5 percent of the state's energy from renewable sources by 2020. In 2008, Pennsylvania governor signed H.B. 2200, which required that utilities work with customers to cut energy use by 1 percent by 2011, and 3 percent by 2013. The bill also required utilities to install "smart meters" on all homes and businesses in Pennsylvania within 15 years.

Three Mile Island was the site of the most serious nuclear power plant accident in U.S. history, on March 28, 1979. © *iStockPhoto.com/Dobresum*

❧ Green Business, Green Building, Green Jobs

Create Synergy, Spread Ideas, Produce Green

Pennsylvania's green business movement is driven primarily by major state universities, such as the Center for Sustainability at Penn State University, and institutions within Pennsylvania's large cities. The Pittsburgh-based Champions for Sustainability (C4S), an outgrowth of Sustainable Pittsburgh, represents one organization that is actively building a green business climate in Pittsburgh and its surrounding areas. C4S, which is funded and supported by several large Pennsylvania-based philanthropic organizations, aims to create synergy between business and academic leaders, entrepreneurs and community advocates to create a foundation ripe for sustainable businesses in and around Pittsburgh. By encouraging information exchanges and networking between businesses that are invested in sustainable practices or are interested in moving in that direction, C4S seeks create dynamism in the sustainability sector. C4S also promotes innovative, green businesses in their "spotlight" section, which highlights local companies that are doing exciting things with sustainability. The Sustainable Business Network of Philadelphia seeks to promote similar objectives in and around Philadelphia.

A LEEDer in the Green Building Movement

If the number of LEED certified buildings indicates a state's commitment to green building, then Pennsylvania has in recent years been a leader in the green building movement, boasting the third most LEED-certified properties of any state. This effort has been bolstered and supported by the state's political organs. The Pennsylvania Department of Environmental Protection was one of the first organizations in the country to pilot the U.S. Green Building Council's LEED standards when constructing one of its regional offices in 1997. Likewise, the Pennsylvania Department of Conservation and Natural Resources aims to achieve LEED certifications on all of its buildings and facilities. The Governor's Green Government Council (GGGC) also plays a huge role in the state's green building movement. The GGGC was created in 1998 with the explicit purpose of facilitating "the incorporation of environmentally sustainable practices into the government's planning, operations, and policymaking and regulatory functions." Emphasized within the GGGC is green building.

Shedding Jobs, but Growing Capital

According to the Pew Charitable Trusts, Pennsylvania shed jobs from 1998–2007, including in the clean energy sector, but still boasted the third most green jobs of the U.S. states, with nearly 39,000. According to the Pennsylvania Department of Labor and Industry, these jobs fell into five industry sectors: energy efficiency, renewable energy, clean transportation, pollution prevention and cleanup, and agriculture and resource conservation. It is estimated in the Pennsylvania Green Jobs Report from January 2010 that between 2010 and 2012, $10 billion in public and private sector funds for green projects would combine to create 115,000 jobs for the state. Pennsylvania was also a leader in attracting venture capital to state's advanced and clean energy sector, drawing more than $230 million in venture capital funds to the state's clean energy economy from 2006–2008.

🍃 Marcellus Shale: Old Resource, New Debate

Marcellus Shale is a hydrocarbon-rich, black shale formation found throughout Pennsylvania. Geologists estimate that the entire Marcellus Shale formation, which extends deep underground from West Virginia and Ohio, through Pennsylvania, and into southern New York, holds between 128 and 516 trillion cubic feet of natural gas. However, extracting this gas from Marcellus Shale, a tight geologic formation, was long considered prohibitively expensive.

Soaring natural gas prices in recent years coupled with new extraction methods have since removed many of those barriers. But environmental concerns weigh heavy on the debate. The Marcellus Shale is considered to be at its thickest in Pennsylvania, underlying roughly two thirds of the state, so it is here that the debate is perhaps the most pronounced. In the beginning months of 2010, natural gas companies in Pennsylvania were breaking ground on three new Marcellus Shale wells per day, triple the rate of 2009. Environmental groups, however, were fighting back, pressuring authorities to curb the practice,

A natural gas triple play

Some drilling companies are exploring other shale formations in Pennsylvania in addition to the Marcellus Shale. The Utica Shale lies several thousand feet (600 m) deeper than the Marcellus. The Upper Devonian Shales are shallower than the Marcellus. Shale is formed from marine life deposited on ancient sea beds. The formations vary in thickness, natural gas content, and depth. Appalachian shales are deeper to the East — the Marcellus is about 9,000 ft. (2,743 m) deep in northeastern Pennsylvania — and grow shallower and thinner in Ohio to the West.

Source: The Penn State Marcellus Center for Outreach and Research, Geology.com, American Association of Petroleum Geologists
Graphic: Mike Placentra, The Philadelphia Inquirer © 2011 MCT

Map of the Northeast U.S. locating the Marcellus, Upper Devonian and Utica shale formations. © Placentra/MCT/newscom

particularly in ecologically sensitive areas, such as the Delaware River Watershed.

Discovery

Beginning in the mid-nineteenth century, many Pennsylvania residents along Lake Erie installed natural gas wells in the shallow Devonian shales to heat and light their homes and businesses. By the 1930s, some individuals, hungry for more gas, were pushing these wells deeper into the earth. Occasionally, as the drills penetrated deeper, they worked into the bands of the Marcellus Shale. Huge bursts of fast-flowing gas would often emerge, then quickly die. Geologists concluded that Marcellus Shale contained pockets of natural gas that could not be easily or economically harvested by the vertical wells of the time. For decades the Marcellus Shale was ignored. By the late 1980s, however, a new technology known as horizontal drilling emerged, making the Marcellus Shale gas far more accessible.

Horizontal drilling enables gas companies to bore down thousands of feet vertically, as they had done for decades, and then bend the drill-head at a 90 degree angle to start drilling horizontally. Horizontal drilling allows companies to greatly increase their exposure to the Marcellus Shale, because it enables them to tunnel directly through it.

Environmental Concerns

Environmentalists in Pennsylvania criticize the Marcellus Shale natural gas development primarily because of its potential to pollute and overuse local water supplies. In order to harvest the gas from the geologically tight Marcellus Shale formation, gas companies must employ a process known as hydraulic fracturing ("fracking"). To "frack" a well, gas companies must pump enormous amounts of water, sand, and chemicals through the drill hole at extremely high pressure. Once the water, sand, and chemical solution reaches the Marcellus Shale portion of the drill hole, it is forced through small, localized, and deliberately made perforations in the cement casing, which encloses the entire drill hole to protect the surrounding formations from its contents.

The fracking process of a single well demands incredible amounts of water—sometimes more than one million gallons of water per day. When one considers that an Olympic-sized swimming pool filled to capacity would often be unable to provide enough water to operate a single well a single day, one can appreciate the concerns over water usage. Additionally, the fracking process requires substantial amounts of "lubricants," which are special chemical solutions drilling companies use to help break up the shale and release its gas. Before the lubricants reach the shale, however, they must travel through Pennsylvania's groundwater (in sealed cement casing).

Environmentalists worry that some of these chemicals might leak out into the groundwater aquifers. Gas companies exacerbate these concerns by refusing to disclose the contents of these lubricants, claiming they are proprietary information.

The U.S. Environmental Protection Agency (EPA) ruled in 2004 that no evidence indicated that fracking threatened drinking water quality. However, prominent environmentalists, including EPA officials, have disputed this finding. In March 2010, the EPA announced that it would launch a study examining the effects of fracking on the environment and human health. The draft study was submitted for peer review in February 2011, after which the agency revised the draft plan. Initial results from the study will be available in late 2012 with an additional report on further research in 2014. The purpose of this study is to research the lifespan of water that is put through the fracking process, including the water's treatment and disposal. In March 2011, the EPA sent a letter to the state, asking it to test water from waste treatment plants and drinking water facilities for radioactivity and to review the permits of state treatment plants handling wastewater from natural gas drilling. EPA officials are concerned that biosolids, or sludge created from heavier contaminants during the treatment process, may be improperly applied as fertilizers and thereby contaminate water sources. Testing will be performed at 14 public water authorities and 25 wastewater plants.

The Chesapeake Bay Foundation, along with other environmental groups, has called for the federal government to conduct a more comprehensive analysis of hydraulic fracturing in the six states under which the Marcellus Shale lies. The foundation wants this review to not only cover drilling's affect on drinking water, but also its impact on air pollution, groundwater, and other areas. The foundation filed a petition for an environmental impact statement in April 2011 under the National Environmental Policy Act.

In part to appease the environmental concerns over Marcellus Shale drilling, the Pennsylvania House of Representatives passed in May 2010 House Bill 2235, which would put a three-year freeze on new leases for gas drilling in state forests. The bill eventually moved to the Pennsylvania Senate where it died. However, in March 2011 Representative Greg Vitali, a Democrat from Delaware County, reintroduced the legislation as House Bill 150. Vitali also introduced House Bill 33, which would impose a tax on Marcellus Shale gas production. Both bills were stalled in committee as of late 2011. Pennsylvania is the only major gas-producing state that does not have a drilling tax or fee.

The Delaware River Watershed

In 2010, perhaps no area of Pennsylvania was so mired in the Marcellus Shale debate as the northeast Delaware River Watershed region. The Delaware River Watershed region boasts tremendous reserves of carbon-rich Marcellus Shale, with some experts contending that the region can become the most productive gas field in the nation. But the Delaware River Watershed also provides drinking water to fifteen million people, and it offered marvelous, unspoiled grounds for trout fishermen and outdoorsmen. As such, a frenzied lobbying effort ensued in 2010 over whether to open the region to Marcellus Shale development.

Advocates for drilling included landowners and farmers, some struggling to make ends meet, who felt that it was their right to use their land to create wealth. Outdoorsmen, environmental groups, and anti-drilling neighbors opposed the development, contending that the benefits of drilling would affect only a small slice of the population, whereas the costs and potential consequences would be felt by everyone in the region—possibly, even, by generations to come.

One Pennsylvania town has suffered the negative effects of fracking on their drinking water supply. In late 2009, residents from Dimock in Susquehanna County sued Cabot Oil and Gas Company for contaminating their wells with methane—the main component of natural gas—and other toxic industrial solvents. Residents also claimed they had health problems, such as neurological and gastrointestinal illnesses, and at least one person's blood tests showed toxic levels of the same metals found in the contaminated water. The company supplied some residents with drinking water after the wells were found to be contaminated, but claimed that their operations were not the cause of the contamination. However, in both 2009 and 2010, Cabot sent more than 44,000 barrels of well wastewater to a treatment facility, and this water was subsequently discharged into a creek that provides drinking water to more than 300,000 residents. So far, Pennsylvania has been the only state that allows waterways to be used as the primary disposal place for wastewater from hydraulic fracturing. But in light of recent controversy, all ten of the biggest drillers in the state claim that they have now eliminated river discharges or significantly reduced them. In December of 2010, Cabot and nineteen Dimock residents came to a settlement that established escrow accounts for the households that total $1.4 million. Cabot will also offer house water treatment systems for each home.

Another accident—called the most serious in the history of fracking—occurred in April 2011. It underscored the potential for fracking to go wrong. Chesapeake Energy suspended the practice in northeast Pennsylvania when a gas well sustained a blowout during a late-night operation resulting in thousands of gallons of water—and the toxic chemicals used in the process—spilling into a nearby waterway. The company used a combination of plastic, ground up tires, and mud to block the well from leaking further. The environmental ramifications were still being evaluated months later.

Eager drilling companies have already leased thousands of acres of watershed land. If the Delaware River Basin Commission—the federal-interstate compact agency that monitors the water supplies in the region—gives the go ahead, gas, along with royalty checks, would start flowing soon after. In the spring of 2011, the Delaware River Basin Commission (of which Pennsylvania governor Tom Corbett is a member) was still working on a set of regulations to address the environmental concerns that could arise from fracking operations in Pennsylvania along the Delaware River.

BIBLIOGRAPHY

Books

Kershner, Bruce and Robert T. Leverett. *The Sierra Club Guide to the Ancient Forests of the Northeast.* San Francisco, CA: Sierra Club Books, 2004.

Nash, Steve. *Blue Ridge 2020: An Owner's Manual.* Chapel Hill: University of North Carolina Press, 1999.

Walter, Eugene and Jonathan Wallen. *The Smithsonian Guides to Natural America: The Mid-Atlantic States–New York, Pennsylvania, New Jersey.* Washington, DC: Smithsonian Books, 1996.

Web Sites

"Cabot Oil and Gas Corporation Announces Global Settlement with the Pennsylvania Department of Environmental Protection." December 15, 2010. Cabot Oil & Gas Corporation. Available from http://phx.corporate-ir.net/staging/phoenix.zhtml?c=116492&p=irol-newsArticleright&ID=1508409&highlight=

"Center for Sustainability at Penn State." Pennsylvania State University. Available from http://www.cfs.psu.edu/index.aspx?p=1

"Champions for Sustainability." Sustainable Pittsburgh. Available from http://www.c4spgh.org/

"Economic Impacts of Climate Change on Pennsylvania." University of Maryland: Center for Integrative Environmental Research (CIER). Available from http://www.cier.umd.edu/climateadaptation/Pennsylvania%20Economic%20Impacts%20of%20Climate%20Change%20Full%20Report.pdf

"EPA Submits Draft Hydraulic Fracturing Study Plan to Independent Scientists for Review/The draft plan is open for comment." February 8, 2011. U.S. Environmental Protection Agency. Available from http://yosemite.epa.gov/opa/admpress.nsf/d0cf6618525a9efb85257359003fb69d/26195e235a35cb3885257831005fd9cd!OpenDocument

"Global Warming and Pennsylvania." The National Wildlife Federation. Available from http://www.nwf.org/Global-Warming/~/media/PDFs/Global%20Warming/Global%20Warming%20State%20Fact%20Sheets/Pennsylvania.ashx

Hopey, Dan. "Dark Times Ahead For Solar Power." *Pittsburgh Post-Gazette.* Sept. 5, 2011. Available from http://www.post-gazette.com/pg/11248/1172283-454.stm

"House Bill 2200: Smart Meters Installation." Available from http://www.puc.state.pa.us/electric/pdf/Act129/HB2200-Act129_Bill.pdf

"House Bill Would Impose Temporary Moratorium on State Forest Land Gas Leasing." March 14, 2011. PA Environment Digest. Available from http://www.paenvironmentdigest.com/newsletter/default.asp?NewsletterArticleID=18381&SubjectID=

"Hydraulic Fracturing." U.S. Environmental Protection Agency. Available from http://water.epa.gov/type/groundwater/uic/class2/hydraulicfracturing/index.cfm

Lustgarten, Abraham. "Pa. Residents Sue Gas Driller for Contamination, Health Concerns." November 20, 2009. *ProPublica.* Available from http://www.propublica.org/article/pa-residents-sue-gas-driller-for-contamination-health-concerns-1120

"Marcellus Shale." Pennsylvania Public Utility Commission. Available from http://www.puc.state.pa.us/naturalgas/naturalgas_marcellus_Shale.aspx

McAllister, Edward. "Driller Halts Pennsylvania Fracking After Blowout." Reuters. April 21, 2011. Available from http://www.reuters.com/article/2011/04/21/us-chesapeake-blowout-idUSTRE73-K5OH20110421

"Newsletter March/ April 2010." Center for Rural Pennsylvania. Available from http://www.rural.palegislature.us/newsletter.html#6

"PA State Fish Hatcheries: Engines for Rural Economic Development." Pennsylvania Fish and Boat Commission. Available from http://www.fish.state.pa.us/hatchinfsm.pdf

"Pennsylvania Allows Gas-Well Wastewater to Flow Into Rivers." January 3, 2011. *PennLive*. Available from http://www.pennlive.com/midstate/index.ssf/2011/01/pennsylvania_allows_gas-well_w.html

"Pennsylvania Alternative Energy Portfolio Standard." Available from http://paaeps.com/credit/

"Pennsylvania Climate Change Action Plan." Pennsylvania Department of Environmental Protection. Available from http://www.elibrary.dep.state.pa.us/dsweb/Get/Document-77736/ALL%20OF%20VOLUME%201%20AND%202.pdf

"Pennsylvania Climate Change Roadmap." Pennsylvania Environmental Council. Available from http://www.pecpa.org/files/downloads/PEC_Climate_-Change_Roadmap_Executive_Summary.pdf

"Pennsylvania Executive Orders." Pennsylvania Office of Administration. Available from http://www.portal.state.pa.us/portal/server.pt/community/executive_orders/708/1990_-_1999/208254

"The Pennsylvania Green Jobs Report." The Pennsylvania Department of Labor and Industry. Available from http://www.paworkforce.state.pa.us/portal/server.pt/community/pa_workforce_development/12865

"Physiographic Provinces of Pennsylvania." Pennsylvania Department of Conservation and Natural Resources. Available from http://www.dcnr.state.pa.us/topogeo/maps/map13.pdf

Urbina, Ian. "Pennsylvania Calls for More Water Tests." April 7, 2011. *The New York Times*. Available from http://www.nytimes.com/2011/04/08/science/earth/08water.html?_r=1&hpw

Wang, Marian. "Pa. Environmental Agency Butts Heads with Gas Drilling Company Over Town's Water Woes." October 1, 2010. *ProPublica*. Available from http://www.propublica.org/blog/item/pa.-environmental-agency-and-gas-drilling-company-butt-heads-over-dimocks-

Rhode Island

Once known for its prosperous Providence Plantations, Rhode Island, the smallest state in the United States, has developed an economy based on services and manufacturing rather than agriculture. Moving into the twenty-first century, the state hopes to transform its economy yet again to include more green industries, particularly through the development of alternative energy sources such as wind power. The state is also at work to revitalize its precious commercial fishing industry, which has been challenged in years past by high levels of pollutants in its coastal waters.

Climate

Rhode Island's climate is humid, with cold winters and short, mild summers. Average annual temperatures are about 50°F (10°C), with average January temperatures in the high 20s (just below 0°C), and July temperatures in the low 70s (low 20°C). The state sees a fair amount of rain and snow

The Effects of Climate Change

Although the state's summers are mild, it has been predicted that Rhode Island's summers will begin to see more days above 90°F (32°C). Rising temperatures in the state have the potential to cause a host of future problems for residents of the state, and some are already seeing the damaging effects. Rising sea levels will impact the wildlife and natural habitats of the coastal regions, as well as the thirty-eight islands in the bay and sound areas of the state.

In an effort to reduce the impact climate change has had and will continue to have on the state's environment and natural resources, Rhode Island became part of the New England Governors and Eastern Canadian Premiers (NEG/ECP) regional Climate Change Action Plan 2001. In July of 2002, Rhode Island's Department of Environmental Management and the State Energy Office completed the *Rhode Island Greenhouse Gas Process* (RI GHG), an action plan that outlines fifty-two options the state could implement to reduce greenhouse gas emissions. On January 1, 2006, the rules and regulations governing the state's renewable energy standard went into effect. In 2004 the state instituted a program of consumer rebates for the purchase of energy efficient vehicles. The program was expanded in 2009, when the state received approximately $882,000 from the federal government for rebates to consumers who purchased qualifying energy-efficient appliances.

Rhode Island is also a member of the Regional Greenhouse Gas Initiative (RGGI), a cooperative cap-and-trade program that at its inception involved ten Northeastern and Mid-Atlantic states. The program was designed with the goal of reducing power sector carbon dioxide emissions by 10 percent by 2018. To that end, the regional cap established by the group was set at 188 million short tons of carbon dioxide per year from 2009 to 2014. Starting in 2015 the cap will decrease by 2.5 percent each year. Carbon dioxide allowances for power plants can be obtained or traded in quarterly auctions. Each state may then reinvest its auction proceeds in programs that support the growth of a clean energy economy. In Rhode Island, the state's auction proceeds are distributed through the Office of Energy Resources, in consultation with the Department of Environmental Management and the Energy Efficiency and Resources Management Council. Sixty percent of the proceeds are used to support energy efficiency projects of National Grid, the state's major utility. The remaining 40 percent is earmarked to support new partnerships, research, and financing projects designed to promote energy efficiency and energy savings for consumers. The first three-year control (or compliance) period began on January 1, 2009 and was set to end on December 31, 2011. By that date, each regulated power plant must submit one allowance for each ton of carbon dioxide emitted during the control period. The RGGI represents the first mandatory, market-based carbon dioxide emissions program in the United States. In May 2011, New Jersey Governor Chris Christie announced his state was withdrawing from the

Beavertail Lighthouse on the coast of Rhode Island. © *iStockPhoto. com/christopher martin*

RGGI by the end of the year, calling it a "failure." As of late 2011, no other state has followed suit.

Energy Independence and Climate Solutions Act

The Rhode Island Energy Independence and Climate Solutions Act was first introduced to the state senate in 2009 (S0488/H5706) as an effort to further address global warming concerns by instituting mandatory greenhouse gas emissions reporting measures and imposing statewide limitations on emissions. It also called for the creation of a Global Warming Solutions Working Group, to advise and assist in the development of measures that would realize statewide reduction goals, and a special Global Warming Pollution Control Fund that would collect fees from those in violation of new emissions standards. The bill was delayed in committees, however, as legislators considered the economic and environmental factors involved in developing appropriate climate change solutions. To keep the discussion going, in 2010 the assembly established the Rhode Island Climate Change Commission with a charge to study the impacts of climate change on the state and to consider which adaption and mitigation efforts could reduce the effects and promote environmental sustainability, while still supporting economic growth and sustainability. The Energy Independence and Climate Solutions Act was reintroduced in 2010 (S2039) and in 2011 (S0724) to maintain an active status while the commission completes its study. The final report from the commission was expected in early 2012.

❧ Natural Resources, Water, and Agriculture

Distinct Geographies

Two geographic regions are distinguished in the state: the New England Upland and the Coastal Lowlands. The Coastal Lowlands include the Narragansett Bay islands, the land east of the bay, and more than half of the state's mainland. Cattails and asters populate marshlands off coastal areas, and meadows and white daisies and wild carrots can be found in meadowlands. The New England Upland, sometimes referred to as the Western Rocky Upland, comprises the northern and western regions of Rhode Island.

Flora and Fauna

Forests cover more than half of the state, and Rhode Island is home to a variety of flora. The red maple is the state's tree, but other common trees are the ash, birch, black walnut, cedar, elm, hickory, maple, oak, pine, poplar, red cedar, tulip tree, and willow. Flowering plants include the azalea, dogwood, blue gentian, iris, lily, orchid, and violet (the state's flower). The sandplain gerardia is a known endangered plant species.

Coyotes, beavers, foxes, minks, otters, rabbits, white-tailed deer and woodchuck are among the wild mammals in the state. Common woodland birds are the barred owl, blue jay, catbird, robin, ruffed grouse and screech-owl. Along the coast loons, ospreys and terns can be found, among other species of shore birds. Birds hunted for game throughout the state include partridges, pheasants, quail, wild ducks, and woodcocks.

According to the U.S. Fish and Wildlife Service (FWS), the American burying beetle; shortnose sturgeon; hawksbill, Kemp's ridley and leatherback sea turtles; and finback, humpback, and right whales are endangered species in Rhode Island and its surrounding waters. All told, Rhode Island has 14 animal and plant species listed as endangered or threatened. With assistance from the FWS, the Rhode Island National Wildlife Refuge Complex was created along Atlantic coastal regions of the state, comprising five centers for protecting and conserving natural habitats for migratory shorebirds and other wildlife species.

Mineral Production Increases

Rhode Island produces valuable minerals for construction and building materials. Granite, sand and gravel are most commonly mined, although other mined products include limestone and traprock. The state has seen an overall increase in production in recent years. Production from 2005 to 2006 increased by more than one-third, and from 2006 to 2007 by more than ten percent. In 2007 there was a slight drop in production, but the production value still increased by more than 20 percent because of an increase in the marketable value of sand and gravel.

Cumberlandite, a stone considered to be very rare and unique, is the official Rhode Island state rock. This stone has only been found along the sides of the Narragansett Bay and has not been discovered outside the state. Rhode Island is known by geologists and rock enthusiasts worldwide for this large and very pure rare ore deposit.

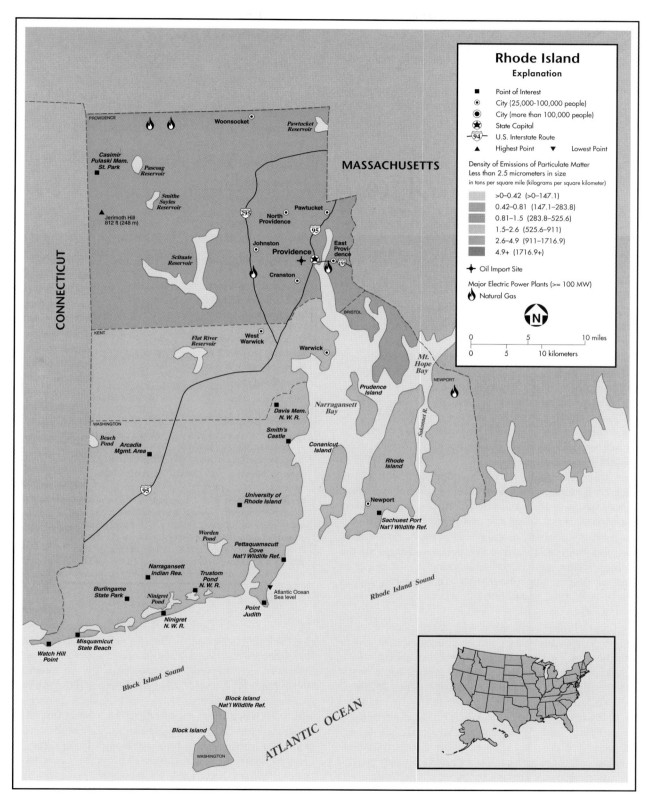

Rhode Island
Explanation

- ■ Point of Interest
- ⊙ City (25,000-100,000 people)
- ◉ City (more than 100,000 people)
- ★ State Capital
- 〔94〕 U.S. Interstate Route
- ▲ Highest Point   ▼ Lowest Point

Density of Emissions of Particulate Matter
Less than 2.5 micrometers in size
in tons per square mile (kilograms per square kilometer)

- >0–0.42 (>0–147.1)
- 0.42–0.81 (147.1–283.8)
- 0.81–1.5 (283.8–525.6)
- 1.5–2.6 (525.6–911)
- 2.6–4.9 (911–1716.9)
- 4.9+ (1716.9+)

✛ Oil Import Site

Major Electric Power Plants (>= 100 MW)
🔥 Natural Gas

0   5   10 miles
0   5   10 kilometers

MASSACHUSETTS
CONNECTICUT

PROVIDENCE
Woonsocket
Pawtucket Reservoir
Casimir Pulaski Mem. St. Park
Pascoag Reservoir
Smithe Sayles Reservoir
Jerimoth Hill 812 ft (248 m)
Scituate Reservoir
Pawtucket
North Providence
Johnston
Providence
East Providence
Cranston
BRISTOL
KENT
Flat River Reservoir
West Warwick
Warwick
Mt. Hope Bay
NEWPORT
Prudence Island
Sakonnet R.
Davis Mem. N.W.R.
Narragansett Bay
Smith's Castle
Conanicut Island
Rhode Island
WASHINGTON
Beach Pond
Arcadia Mgmt. Area
University of Rhode Island
Newport
Sachuest Port Nat'l Wildlife Ref.
Worden Pond
Pettaquamscutt Cove Nat'l Wildlife Ref.
Narragansett Indian Res.
Trustom Pond N.W.R.
Burlingame State Park
Ninigret Pond
Ninigret N.W.R.
Atlantic Ocean Sea level
Point Judith
Misquamicut State Beach
Watch Hill Point
Rhode Island Sound
Block Island Sound
Block Island Nat'l Wildlife Ref.
Block Island
WASHINGTON
ATLANTIC OCEAN

SOURCES: "County Emissions Map: Criteria Air Pollutants." *AirData*. U.S. Environmental Protection Agency. Available from http://www. epa.gov/air/data/geosel.html; *Energy Maps*. U.S. Energy Information Administration. Available from http://www.eia.gov/state; *Highest and Lowest Elevations*. U.S. Geological Survey. Available from http://egsc.usgs.gov/isb/pubs/booklets/elvadist/elvadist.html#Highest; *2007 Minerals Yearbook*. U.S. Geological Survey. Available from http://minerals.usgs.gov/minerals/pubs/state. © 2011 Cengage Learning.

Bays, Estuaries, Rivers

Water is an abundant and key resource for the state of Rhode Island, once used to power the state's mills and factories. The Narragansett Bay is the largest estuary in New England, and provides a rich and diverse array of support to the state's economy, from fisheries to tourism and recreational opportunities. A 2003 study estimated that the Bay brings in more than $2 billion in revenue from tourism-related activities. Revenues from commercial fishing activities were estimated at around $77 million in the mid-1990s.

Rhode Island's best known island is Block Island, which lies south of the state in the Atlantic Ocean. Rhode Island has thirty-eight other islands, all located in Narragansett Bay, the best known being Prudence, Conanicut, and Aquidneck Islands. The northern end of Mt. Hope Bay reaches into Massachusetts, and the lower part of the bay (bordered by Rhode Island on the east and west sides) empties into Narragansett Bay to the west and connects with the Sakonnet River, an inlet of the Atlantic Ocean separating Aquidneck and the eastern mainland to the south.

Major rivers in Rhode Island are the Pawtuxet, Blackstone/Seekonk, Woonasquatucket, Moshassuck, and Pawcatuck. The Blackstone is the main river flowing into the Providence River, an estuary of Narragansett Bay. Lakes, ponds, and reservoirs are plentiful and can be found throughout the state. The largest body of water is the Scituate Reservoir. The state has about 65,000 acres (26,305 ha) of wetlands.

Coastal and bay waters are populated with clams, bluefish, flounder, jellyfish, lobster, mackerel, sea bass, striped bass, swordfish, and tuna. Common freshwater fish include bass, brook trout, eel, perch, pickerel, and trout.

A variety of edible fish and shellfish provide a diverse catch for commercial fishers. Lobster and scallops are the leading catches, and the state is a leading producer of flounder and squid. Other fish commercially caught include cod, fluke, hake, herring, mackerel, scrod, scup, whiting, and yellowtail.

Point Judith was once the largest commercial fishing port in the state, but has downsized in recent years because of the protection and restoration efforts of government and environmental groups such as the New England Fisheries Management Council (NEFMC). The NEFMC, one of eight regional councils set up by the 1976 federal Magnuson Fishery Conservation and Management Act, manages fishery resources within the 200-mile limit off the New England coastline, and has placed limits on commercial harvesting of many species to prevent overfishing and rebuild fish stocks. The NEFMC in 2009 enacted a catch "shares" program, which is in line with a national policy by the National Oceanic and Atmospheric Association (NOAA) that designates quotas and catch limits for individual operations in order to reduce

Rhode Island State Profile

Physical Characteristics

Land area	1,034 square miles (2,678 sq km)
Inland water area	187 square miles (484 sq km)
Coastal area	9 square miles (14 sq km)
Highest point	Jerimoth Hill 812 feet (247 m)
National Forest System lands (2010)	NA
State parks (2011)	22

Energy Statistics

Total energy production (2009)	4 trillion Btu
State ranking in total energy production (2009)	48
Renewable energy net generation total (2009)	100,000 megawatt hours
Hydroelectric energy generation (2009)	5,000 megawatt hours
Biomass energy generation (2009)	145,000 megawatt hours
Wind energy generation (2009)	NA
Wood and derived fuel energy generation (2009)	NA
Crude oil reserves (2009)	NA
Natural gas reserves (2009)	NA
Natural gas liquids (2008)	NA

Pollution Statistics

Carbon output (2005)	11.4 million tons of CO_2 (10.3 million t)
Superfund sites (2008)	12
Particulate matter (less than 2.5 micrometers) emissions (2002)	181 tons per year (164 t/yr)
Toxic chemical releases (2009)	400,000 pounds (200,000 kg)
Generated hazardous waste (2009)	4,500 tons (4,100 t)

SOURCES: AirData. U.S. Environmental Protection Agency. Available from http://www.epa.gov/air/data; *Energy Maps, Facts, and Data of the U.S. States.* U.S. Energy Information Administration. Available from http://www.eia.gov/state; *The 2012 Statistical Abstract.* U.S. Census Bureau. Available from http://www.census.gov/compendia/statab; *United States Energy Usage.* eRedux. Available from http://www.eredux.net/states.

© 2011 Cengage Learning.

overfishing. The program also allows greater traceability for catches with the goal of ensuring a safe food supply. However, not everyone is happy with the new regulations, and a lawsuit was filed in 2010 by two Massachusetts mayors, along with several fishermen who were negatively impacted by the restrictions. The lawsuit alleges the new program ignores a requirement in the Magnuson Act to hold a referendum on what the filers considered a "limited access" program. Creators of the catch shares program say it is an open system, which does not require a referendum. In June 2011, a federal judge rejected the referendum claim, and a notice of appeal was filed in August 2011.

Freshwater fishing is a popular recreational activity in Rhode Island, and the state's water diversity provides plenty of opportunities. Additionally, the state raises around 200,000 fish per year in hatcheries. Hatcheries in Rhode Island contain brown, brook and rainbow trout, largemouth and smallmouth bass, Atlantic salmon, and golden shiners.

The Greenwich Bay Fish Kill

In August 2003, more than one million fish died in what became known as the Greenwich Bay Fish Kill. The RI Department of Environmental Management (RI DEM) determined that the event was caused by oxygen depletion (anoxia)—that is, the fish essentially suffocated. Menhaden, other finfish, eels, crabs and softshell clams were affected. The fish kill coincided with a very large number of beach closings due to poor water quality and rainstorms, also contributing to the runoff of polluted waters into Narragansett Bay. RI DEM published a report that recommended upgrading sewage treatment plants, improving the management of septic systems, and better management of stormwater. The fish kill came just months after a barge spilled tens of thousands of barrels of oil in Buzzards Bay, Massachusetts, bordering Rhode Island's Narragansett Bay area.

Agriculture

The Rhode Island Red chicken, developed on a small farm in Little Compton in the mid-1800s, was designated as the state bird because of its national success as a dual-purpose chicken breed. Rhode Island's farmland occupies less than 10 percent of the state, with about 1,220 farms total, according to a 2008 USDA Census. The top crops are now greenhouse and nursery products used in commercial and residential landscaping, which amounts to a $40 million a year industry. Milk also provides a substantial source of farming income. Other dairy products, chicken, eggs, hay, potatoes, and corn are also produced, but are not the most significant source of income.

Rhode Island developed its own organic certification program in 1990. When the USDA National Organic Program went into effect in 2002, the state Department of Environmental Management (RI DEM) became a nationally accredited state certification agency. The Rhode Island Organic Certification Program is administered by the RI DEM Plant Industry Section of the Division of Agriculture and Resource Marketing. In 2010, there were twenty-six certified organic producers listed by the RI DEM.

❧ Energy

Electricity

Rhode Island is one of only two states with no coal-generated electric power. Electricity is mostly generated from natural gas, accounting for almost 98 percent of the state's electricity (more than any other state). The

remaining 2 percent comes from renewable sources such as hydroelectric power, municipal solid waste, and landfill gas. Petroleum and conventional hydroelectric are also sources, but very minimal power is produced from them. Rhode Island has the lowest per capita energy consumption in the nation. In 2007 the state conducted a series of meetings on offshore wind energy to discuss the findings of a study commissioned by the state that determined that 15 percent of Rhode Island's electricity needs could be met by offshore wind energy. In July 2010, governors Donald Carcieri of Rhode Island and Deval Patrick of Massachusetts signed an agreement to jointly explore the potential for offshore wind energy in federal waters adjacent to both states.

In August 2011, U.S. Department of the Interior Secretary Ken Salazar announced the federal government would begin accepting proposals for wind farms in the "area of mutual interest" adjacent to both Rhode Island and Massachusetts. He estimated a lease could be agreed upon as early as 2012, and cited a National Renewable Energy Lab (a division of the U.S. Department of Energy) report that shows tremendous potential through wind farms in the area.

Renewable Energy Standards

As part of the Regional Greenhouse Gas Initiative, greenhouse gas emission caps have been imposed on power plants. In 2005, the state adopted Air Pollution Control Regulation 37, the Rhode Island Low Emissions Vehicle Program, which is a regulation similar to standards established in California.

The state's Renewable Energy Standard was enacted in 2004, requiring 16 percent of electricity providers' supply to come from renewable resources by the end of 2019. Renewable energy sources have been identified as: direct solar radiation, wind, ocean power, geothermal, hydroelectric (facilities cannot be greater than 30 megawatts in capacity), biomass (using eligible biomass fuels), and fuel cells that use renewable resources. In June 2009 a new standard was introduced as part of the Renewable Energy Standard, called the Long Term Contracting Standard for Renewable Energy. Under this standard, electricity suppliers must enter long-term contracts for energy from new renewable energy facilities. The deadline for submission of these contracts is the end of 2013, and they are subject to review by the Public Utilities Commission before they will be approved.

One effort to promote the development and use of renewable energy within the state was introduced through the Rhode Island Renewable Energy Coordinating Board Act (2011 S0722), which called for the creation of a new five-member board with a mandate to develop and recommend a strategic renewable energy implementation plan for the state. The bill passed and was signed by the governor in July 2011.

Energy Efficiency

Rhode Island has also attempted to green the state through the Rhode Island Energy Efficiency and Resource Management Council (EERMC), established in 2007 under the state's Comprehensive Energy Conservation, Efficiency, and Affordability Act of 2006. The purpose of the EERMC is to advocate for energy consumers, and recommend and oversee programs that promote energy efficiency and the diversification of energy resources.

According to a report issued by the EERMC in 2010, Rhode Island ranked ninth in the nation in 2009 in the State Energy Efficiency Scorecard by the American Council for an Energy Efficiency Economy (ACEEE). The state has worked to put more than $50 million in federal funds obtained through the American Recovery and Reinvestment Act (ARRA) to use through the implementation of the State Energy Plan, Weatherization Assistance Program, and Energy Efficiency and Conservation Block Grants.

❧ Green Business, Green Building, Green Jobs

Green Business: Stimulating the Local Green Economy

Rhode Island is seeking to build a greener economy by promoting clean energy resources and green jobs. The Rhode Island Economic Development Corporation (RIEDC) manages the state's Renewable Energy Fund and is committed to stimulating the growth of a green collar economy by providing grants and loans for renewable projects. The fund provides incentives for: business, commercial, and institutional projects; affordable housing developments; municipal energy renewable projects; and research studies. In February 2010 the RIEDC put out a working draft report, *A Roadmap for Advancing the Green Economy in Rhode Island*. The report outlined initiatives to include building green manufacturing industries, revising efficiency standards, supporting small business and scientific and technological research, and developing the state's offshore wind power potential.

Deepwater Wind on Thin Ice

In September 2010, the offshore wind development company Deepwater Wind announced it would be relocating its headquarters to a newly expanded facility in Providence, Rhode Island, and that it would establish a regional manufacturing facility in Quonset. The announcement was hailed by many as a great opportunity for the state as it embraces a new green industry and joins the race to develop the first offshore wind farm in the United States.

To establish the new manufacturing facility, the state of Rhode Island and Deepwater Wind negotiated a joint development agreement under which Deepwater is expected to invest $1.5 billion in the state. The operation of this facility, which will produce support structures for wind turbines and towers, is expected to create close to eight hundred jobs, bringing in about $60 million in annual wages. Both this facility and the new headquarters will strengthen Deepwater Wind's presence in the state, and provide additional support for plans to build the Block Island Wind Farm about three miles off the southeastern coast of Block Island.

Deepwater Wind was chosen by the state as the developer for the Block Island Wind Farm in 2008. The proposed 28.8 megawatt facility would consist of five to eight turbines and could generate enough power to supply Block Island entirely, with an additional supply to cover about 15 percent of Rhode Island's remaining demand. The project would also bring in much needed jobs and stimulate economic growth in local green industries. Moving forward in 2009, Deepwater Wind signed a twenty-year power purchase agreement with National Grid, the state's largest utility, through which Deepwater agreed to sell electricity at 24.4 cents per kilowatt-hour in the first full year of operation with a price increase of 3.5 percent for each following year. The anticipated first year of operation was set for 2013. But when the Rhode Island Public Utilities Commission (RI PUC) approved the power purchase agreement in August 2010, a swell of legal appeals stalled construction plans.

Two companies, Toray Plastics Inc. and Polytop Corp., filed suits with the Rhode Island Supreme Court calling for an appeal of the RI PUC decision on the grounds that the accepted price for electricity was not "commercially reasonable," a primary requirement for consideration in such contracts. Company managers argue that the higher costs for electricity associated with the contract would pose an unfair burden for them, putting their future at risk during a difficult economic time. Then-state attorney general Patrick C. Lynch and the Conservation Law Foundation also filed suits based on what they called an unfair review process that resulted in a "sweetheart deal" for Deepwater Wind and National Grid.

The basis for this argument stemmed from the fact that the RI PUC initially denied a similar contract in early 2010 on the grounds that the cost was not commercially reasonable. At that time the state general assembly passed an amendment to the existing Long-Term Contracting Standard for Renewable Energy in order to provide for an expanded review process (2010 S2819). The assembly and the governor then compelled the RI PUC to take a second look at the contract, which led to its approval. In this second round, all three commissioners agreed that the project promised significant environmental benefits, including a push toward greater energy independence and the reduction of greenhouse gas emissions as the wind project replaces the diesel generators currently used on Block Island. However, only two of the three believed the contract was commercially reasonable.

In February 2011, the state's new attorney general Peter Kilmartin dropped the suit filed by his predecessor, stating his support for wind energy as a cornerstone for the state's energy future. In April 2011, the Rhode Island Supreme Court ruled that the Conservation Law Foundation did not have a legal right to appeal the decision, but did recognize the rights of Toray Plastics Inc. and Polytop Corp. to challenge the contract. However, the state's Supreme Court upheld the contract, and the project was allowed to proceed. Deepwater Wind plans to prepare the site in 2012 and to go online by sometime in 2013.

Green Building

In March 2009, Rhode Island updated its state building codes (H 5986) in compliance with the International Energy Conservation Code (IECC). Additionally, legislation enacted in November 2009 (SB 232) required new public building construction (5,000 square feet or greater) and public building renovations (10,000 square feet or greater) to be certified under the U.S. Green Building Council Leadership in Energy and Environmental Design (LEED) program.

Green building standards implemented by the state are supported by the Rhode Island chapter of the United States Green Building Council, which provides educational and informational resources on LEED certification, and works to develop partnerships that facilitate the realization of green building projects.

Save the Bay Center

In 2005, prior to the revision of energy codes, a new Save the Bay Center was created on an old dump site in Providence, on Narragansett Bay. Save the Bay, an independent nonprofit organization devoted to "protecting, restoring and encouraging stewardship of Rhode Island's most precious resource" received the land through donation and worked under a tight budget to redevelop the land and construct a building that could accommodate the needs of the organization without further damaging the surrounding environment. The completed project exceeded the expectations of Save the Bay staff. The rooftop is covered with local vegetation, giving the impression that the building is part of, or slips into, the land. Construction and design elements provide protection from sun and, in turn, keep the building cool. Water is conserved through waterless urinals and dual-flush toilets, and recycled content was used in much of the construction. Despite a decision not to include the extra cost of LEED certification, the project is notably one of the state's largest green building accomplishments.

Green Jobs

Unemployment in Rhode Island has had a lasting impact on the state's economy since the beginning of the 2008–09 economic downturn. The state government has taken action to rebuild the local economy, utilizing federal ARRA funds to implement new programs that promote a cleaner environment, green jobs, and reduced energy costs. According to a study conducted by the Pew Charitable Trusts, renewable energy jobs in Rhode Island are growing. In 2007 there were more than 2,300 green-energy jobs.

The Green Jobs-Green Rhode Island Act (S0451) introduced in the state assembly in 2011 is intended to provide a much-needed boost for both the local green economy and efforts toward greater energy efficiency. The act calls for the creation of a program that would provide energy-efficient retrofits for residential properties at no initial costs to the owner, with a goal of improving at least 300,000 homes in a five-year period. Since such a program would create thousands of new jobs, the act also calls for the launch of new job training programs to prepare new workers in the field of energy efficiency services. The bill was heard by the Senate Committee on Environment and Agriculture in April 2011.

❧ Improved Narragansett Bay Water Quality Signals Relief for Commercial Shellfish Harvesting Industry

The Narragansett Bay was once home to a thriving commercial shellfish harvesting industry, providing economic stability and livelihood to coastal towns. By the middle of the twentieth century, pollutants and disease had already taken their toll and commercial fisheries were nearly wiped out. In the 1990s oysters in the bay became inflicted with dermo disease, caused by a single-celled protozoan parasite. The oyster population was almost completely eradicated at that time, with only 10 percent of the original population surviving.

Water pollution, contaminants, and disease have continued to be a problem for the bay. Swimming is often prohibited in parts of the Bay, and bans have been placed on shellfish harvesting because of safety issues. Unanticipated closures create disruptive economic losses for many businesses in management areas, the commercial harvesting industry, and surrounding communities. The state's Department of Environmental Management has had to closely monitor the water, particularly testing conditions after heavy rain or storms.

Shellfish harvesting is prohibited in smaller bodies of water near the bay, such as Little Narragansett Bay, Pawcatuck River, Watch Hill Cove, and Mastuxet Brook. Pollution fosters dangerous levels of bacteria in the water, which then does not meet water quality and safety standards. Tests performed on the waters between 2005 and 2010 have found increasing levels of fecal coliform and enterococci bacterias. Swimming remains prohibited in these areas.

In May 2010 the state announced that it would be reopening an additional several hundred acres of water to shellfish harvesting in the Greenwich and Upper Narragansett Bays. This signals that the water quality in and around Narragansett Bay is improving. The annual rise in water bacteria levels occurs in the dry season, though experts have not yet been able to determine the cause. The areas were opened in May on a conditional basis and contamination levels will continue to be closely monitored.

Aquaculture in Rhode Island has seen increased support from the state and outside agencies. In 2009 a project aimed at restoring the oyster population and funded through the Natural Resources Conservation Service's (NRCS) Environmental Quality Incentives Program (EQIP) was launched. Save the Bay works on an annual bay scallop restoration project, the North Cape Shellfish Restoration Program. Save the Bay's web site is regularly updated with status reports on the project. With improving water quality and shellfish restoration activism, Rhode Island is steadily working to recover their waters and repopulate them with local fish.

BIBLIOGRAPHY

Books

Finch, Robert, and Jonathan Wallen. *The Smithsonian Guides to Natural America: Southern New England–Connecticut, Rhode Island, Massachusetts.* Washington, DC: Smithsonian Books, 1996.

Kershner, Bruce, and Robert T. Leverett. *The Sierra Club Guide to the Ancient Forests of the Northeast.* San Francisco, CA: Sierra Club Books, 2004.

Small Wind Electric Systems: A Rhode Island Consumer's Guide. Washington, DC: U.S, Department of Energy, Energy Efficiency. and Renewable Energy, Wind and Hydropower Technologies Program, 2003.

Web Sites

"About Us." Rhode Island National Wildlife Refuge Complex, U.S. Fish & Wildlife Service. Available from http://www.fws.gov/ninigret/complex/aboutus.html

"About Us." State of Rhode Island Department of Environmental Management. Department of Agriculture. Available from http://www.dem.ri.gov/programs/bnatres/agricult/index.htm

Barrett, Chris. "Deepwater Wind lawsuit allowed to proceed in R.I. Supreme Court." *Providence Business News.* April 22, 2011. Available from http://www.pbn.com/Deepwater-Wind-lawsuit-allowed-to-proceed,57443

Barrett, Chris. "PUC approves Deepwater Wind-National Grid power deal, but appeals expected." *Providence Business News.* August 11, 2010. Available from http://www.pbn.com/PUC-approves-Deepwater-Wind-National-Grid-power-deal-but-appeals-expected,51687

Buford, Talia. "For Some R.I. Communities, Cleanup of Superfund Sites Means a Long Haul." June 16, 2010. *The Providence Journal.* Available from http://www.projo.com/news/content/SMITH FIELD_SUPERFUNDS_06-14-10_LLINVCN_v22.1ace7d4.html

Cartledge, James. "Offshore Wind Developer Moves HQ to Rhode Island." BrighterEnergy. September 2010. Available from http://www.brighterenergy.org/16327/news/wind/offshore-wind-developer-moves-hq-to-rhode-island/

The Clean-Energy Economy. Pew Center of the States, Pew Charitable Trusts. Available from http://www.pewcenteronthestates.org/uploadedFiles/Clean_Economy_Report_Web.pdf

"Climate Change Action Plan 2001." Committee on the Environment and the Northeast International Committee on Energy of the Conference of New England Governors and Eastern Canadian Premiers. Available from http://negc.org/documents/NEG-ECP%20CCAP.PDF

"Confronting Climate Change in the U.S. Northeast." Union of Concerned Scientists. Available from http://www.climatechoices.org/assets/documents/climatechoices/rhode-island_necia.pdf

Cuddy, Don. "Oyster 'Gardens' May Help Restore Narragansett Bay Fishery." *SouthCoast Today.* Available from http://www.southcoasttoday.com/apps/pbcs.dll/article?AID=/20100328/NEWS/3280327

"DEM Announces Reclassification of Shellfish Water and Seasonal Shellfish Closures that Take Effect on May 29." RI Dept. of Environmental Management. Available from http://www.dem.ri.gov/news/2010/pr/0526102.htm

Dohner, Janet Vorwald. "Rhode Island Red Chickens: Heritage Poultry Breeds." *Mother Earth News.* July 2010. Available from http://www.motherearthnews.com/sustainable-farming/Rhode-Island-Red-heritage-poultry-zeylaf.aspx

Dupuis, Emily. "DEM: Water Quality in Rivers Needs Improving." *The Westerly Sun.* August 21, 2010. Available from http://www.thewesterlysun.com/news/article_572c9af2-ace3-11df-9176-001cc4c03286.html

"Energy Efficiency and Management Programs." Office of Energy Resources, State of Rhode Island. Available from http://www.energy.ri.gov/programs/efficiency.php

Gaines, Richard. "New Suit Targets Need For Catch Share 'Referendum.'" *The Gloucester Times*. Dec. 14, 2010. Available from http://www.gloucestertimes.com/fishing/x1666503922/New-suit-targets-need-for-catch-share-referendum

Gonchar, Joann. "Save the Bay Center." *GreenSource Magazine*. Available from http://greensource.construction.com/projects/0710_BayCenter.asp

"Governor Carieri Commends Deepwater Wind's Relocation of Headquarters to Rhode Island." Office of the Governor, State of Rhode Island. Available from http://www.ri.gov/GOVERNOR/view.php?id=12204

"Greenhouse Gas Action Plan." Rhode Island Greenhouse Gas Stakeholder Process. Available from http://righg.raabassociates.org/Articles/GHGPlanBody7-19-02FINAL.pdf

"The Greenwich Bay Fish Kill—August 2003." Rhode Island Department of Environmental Management. Available from http://www.dem.ri.gov/pubs/fish-kill.pdf

"House Bill 5986." State of Rhode Island General Assembly. Available from http://www.rilin.state.ri.us/BillText/BillText09/HouseText09/H5986.pdf

Howard, Jordan. "Ken Salazar: Offshore Wind Farms Will Rise In Rhode Island." Huffington Post. Aug. 17, 2011. Available from http://www.huffingtonpost.com/2011/08/17/rhode-island-offshore-wind-farms-ken-salazar_n_929426.html?ncid=edlinkusaolp00000008

"Incentives/Policies for Renewables & Efficiency: Rhode Island." Database of State Incentives for Renewables & Efficiency. Available from http://www.dsireusa.org/incentives/incentive.cfm?Incentive_Code=RI08R&re=1&ee=1&printable=1

"Interior Launches Leasing Process For Commercial Wind Energy Offshore Rhode Island and Massachusetts." U.S. Department of the Interior. Aug. 17, 2011. Available from http://www.doi.gov/news/pressreleases/Interior-Launches-Leasing-Process-for-Commercial-Wind-Energy-Offshore-Rhode-Island-and-Massachusetts.cfm

Kuffner, Alex. "R.I. 'Green' Jobs Grow Faster Than Overall Rate." *The Providence Journal*. Available from http://www.projo.com/news/content/BZ_GREEN_JOBS_06-19-09_VLENS7O_v21.2ff7d8a.html

Maranhas, Nicole. "Breaking Point." *Rhode Island Monthly*. December 2009. Available from http://www.rimonthly.com/Rhode-Island-Monthly/December-2009/Breaking-Point/index.php?cparticle=2&siarticle=1#artanc

"Mayors, Cities File To Appeal Fisheries Ruling." *The Gloucester Times*. Aug. 18, 2011. Available from http://www.gloucestertimes.com/local/x175567237/Mayors-cities-filed-to-appael-fisheries-ruling

Morgan, Thomas. "Update: DEM Declares Most RI Shellfish Areas Safe." *Providence Journal*. April 16, 2010. Available from http://newsblog.projo.com/2010/04/dem-oks-extra-shellfishing.html

"Organic Certification Program." Rhode Island Department of Environmental Management, Division of Agriculture. Available from http://www.dem.ri.gov/programs/bnatres/agricult/orgcert.htm

Pacheco, Andrada, and Tyrrell, Timothy. "The Economic Value of Narragansett Bay." Department of Environmental and Natural Resources Economics, University of Rhode Island. February 2003. Available from http://www.ci.uri.edu/Projects/PNB/Documents/3.%20Tim%202-24-03pres.pdf

Regional Greenhouse Gas Initiative: Rhode Island State Investment Plan. Available from http://www.rggi.org/rggi_benefits/program_investments/Rhode_Island

"Rhode Island." EPA State and Local Climate and Energy Program. Available from http://www.epa.gov/statelocalclimate/state/tracking/individual/ri.html

"Rhode Island." U.S. Energy Information Administration. Available from http://www.eia.doe.gov/state/state_energy_profiles.cfm?sid=RI#

"Rhode Island and Massachusetts Sign Agreement to Collaborate on the Development of Offshore Wind in Federal Waters." July 26, 2010, Rhode Island Government press release. Available from http://www.ri.gov/press/view.php?id=11879

"Rhode Island Aquaculture Producers Complete First Set in 2009 Oyster Restoration Project." USDA Natural Resources Conservation Service. Available from http://www.ri.nrcs.usda.gov/news/PDF/Oyster-RestorationProject6_09.pdf

"Rhode Island Climate and Energy." Environment Northeast. Available from http://www.env-ne.org/projects/open/p/id/339/state/Rhode%20Island

"Rhode Island Energy Facts." Institute for Energy Research. Available from http://www.instituteforenergyresearch.org/state-regs/pdf/Rhode%20Island.pdf

Rhode Island Energy Independence and Climate Solutions Act (2011 S0724). State of Rhode Island

General Assembly. Available from http://www.rilin. state.ri.us/billtext11/senatetext11/s0724.pdf

"Rhode Island Fish Hatcheries." EarthWatch Rhode Island. NBC News Report. September 17, 2006. Available from http://www.dem.ri.gov/earthwatch/pdf/16.pdf

"Rhode Island Offshore Wind Energy and Fishing." Warwick Online. May 23, 2010. Available from http://www.offshorewind.biz/2010/05/23/rhode-island-offshore-wind-energy-and-fishing-usa/

Rhode Island Renewable Energy Coordinating Board Act (2011 S0722). State of Rhode Island General Assembly. Available from http://www.rilin.state.ri.us//BillText11/SenateText11/S0722.pdf

"Rhode Island Symbols, Rock: Cumberlandite." SHG Resources: State Handbook & Guide. Available from http://www.shgresources.com/ri/symbols/rock/

"RI GHG Stakeholders Strategies Status 4/26/04." State of Rhode Island Department of Environmental Management. Available from http://www.dem.ri.gov/programs/bpoladm/stratpp/pdfs/status.pdf

"A Roadmap for Advancing the Green Economy in Rhode Island." Rhode Island Economic Development Corporation. Available from http://publications.riedc.com/qgcju.pdf

Rules and Regulations Governing the Implementation of a Renewable Energy Standard. State of Rhode Island and Providence Plantations Public Utilities Commission. Available from http://www.ripuc.org/eventsactions/docket/3659-RES-FinalRules%2812-7-05%29.pdf

"Scallop Restoration." Save the Bay. Available from http://www.savebay.org/Page.aspx?pid=611

"Senate Bill 232 Substitute B." State of Rhode Island General Assembly. Available from http://www.rilin.state.ri.us/PublicLaws/law09/law09212.htm

"Species Reports." U.S. Fish and Wildlife Service. Available from http://ecos.fws.gov/tess_public/pub/stateListingAndOccurrenceIndividual.jsp?state=RI&s8fid=112761032792&s8fid=112762573902&s8fid=24012838826983

2007 Minerals Yearbook: Rhode Island. U.S. Geological Survey. Available from http://minerals.usgs.gov/minerals/pubs/state/2007/myb2-2007-ri.pdf

2009 State Agriculture Overview: Rhode Island. National Agricultural Statistics Service. Available from http://www.nass.usda.gov/Statistics_by_State/Ag_Overview/AgOverview_RI.pdf

"Water Resources of Rhode Island." U.S. Geological Survey. Available from http://ri.water.usgs.gov/

"Water Withdrawals." Office of Water Resources, State of Rhode Island Dept. of Environmental Management. Available from http://www.dem.ri.gov/programs/benviron/water/withdraw/index.htm

"Wildlife Conservation Strategy." State of Rhode Island Department of Environmental Management Division of Fish and Wildlife. Available from http://www.dem.ri.gov/programs/bnatres/fishwild/swgindex.htm

South Carolina

Tourists flock each year to the coastal communities of South Carolina. Atlantic beaches and coastal wildlife reserves, combined with the state's rich history, provide much for visitors to enjoy. The state's forests also provide a substantial amount of tourist income, as well as significant revenues from forest-based industries. The value of construction minerals mined from the state has been increasing steadily since 2004, and commercial fishing, particularly shrimping, has remained strong. However, apart from environmental protection efforts, the growth of a green economy within the state has been relatively slow. Some business and government leaders hope that proposed legislation encouraging the development of renewable energy sources and energy efficiency programs will lead to a brighter future for the state. Yet, while such renewable energy legislation is being deliberated, the nuclear power cluster is set to grow through the construction of two new nuclear reactors by 2016.

Climate

South Carolina has a humid, subtropical climate with average temperatures that range from 68°F (20°C) on the coast to 58°F (14°C) in the northwest. Cooler temperatures prevail in the mountains. Summers are hot, particularly in the central part of the state where temperatures often exceed 90°F (32°C). Rainfall is ample throughout the state, but snowfall is minimal. The state is vulnerable to weather extremes that include both drought and hurricanes.

Climate Change Impacts. According to a report from the National Wildlife Federation, the average sea level of the coastal waters of South Carolina has risen by about 9 inches (22 cm) throughout the last century. The report suggests that an additional rise of about 19 inches (48 cm) could occur by 2100, if climate change continues at current rates. The beach erosion and saltwater incursion that such a change could bring would have a major impact on the environment, destroying several wildlife habitats and affecting the estimated $14 billion coastal tourist industry. Additionally, an increase in average sea surface temperatures could lead to an increase in the intensity of storms and hurricanes throughout the state.

In efforts to address the issues of climate change, the state commissioned the Center for Climate Strategies to produce the *South Carolina Greenhouse Gas Inventory and Reference Case Projects, 1990–2020.* According to this report, greenhouse gas emissions within the state increased by 39 percent from 1990 to 2005. In the same time period, national emissions rose by only 16 percent. Under reference case projections, greenhouse gas emissions could continue to increase by 87 percent of 1990 levels by 2020, if no mitigating actions are taken. To facilitate the development of such mitigation, on February 16, 2007, Governor Mark Sanford appointed a Climate, Energy, and Commerce Advisory Committee. In July 2008, the committee presented their final report and action plan, which included recommendations for fifty-one specific policies to reduce greenhouse gas emissions, while also addressing the issues of climate, energy, and commerce. The plan calls for a voluntary statewide goal to reduce greenhouse gas emissions by 5 percent below 1990 levels by 2020.

🍃 Natural Resources, Water, and Agriculture

Natural Resources

Forests cover about 67 percent of the state's landscape, with most of the forest area designated as timberland. Softwoods account for about 46 percent of all timberland, with common species that include balsam fir and yellow pine. Oak, hickory, ash, and maple are also prominent. South Carolina's forest product industries, including logging, primary wood products, and

The beach has eroded from around the homes and they are in danger of collapsing. Beach erosion along with saltwater incursion continue to have a major impact on homes in the area as well as the environment. © artcphotos/ShutterStock.com

furniture manufacturing, have an economic impact of more than $17 billion annually, employing more than 36,000 people. Timber is the state's number one cash crop at $679 million annually, according to the South Carolina Forestry Commission, which manages four state forests, including Sand Hills, Manchester, Harbison, and Wee Tee. Exports of forest products doubled from 2001 to 2010, with a slight dip attributed to the recession in 2009.

There are 47 state parks and one national park in South Carolina. Congaree National Park, awarded park status in 2003, was previously Congaree National Monument. It contains the largest contiguous tract of old-growth bottomland hardwood forest in the United States and one of the tallest deciduous forests in the world. The state also contains eight additional national park service sites, including historic sites and monuments.

South Carolina is home to a wide variety of wildlife. Common woodland mammals include opossum, gray and red foxes, beavers, and raccoons. White-tailed deer, black bears, coyote, muskrat, turkey, and feral hogs are among the popular game mammals. Alligators are hunted in season as well. The U.S. Fish and Wildlife Service's list of threatened or endangered species includes forty-one animal and plant species that occur within the state. Listed animals include the West Indian manatee, five types of sea turtle, and three types of whale; listed plants include two types of trillium and Schweinitz's sunflower.

Mining

The mining industry has been very productive in the twenty-first century, with the value of nonfuel minerals steadily increasing. In 2004, the value of South Carolina's nonfuel minerals was at $532 million. In 2007, nonfuel mineral production was up to a value of $789 million. Cement, crushed stone, and construction sand and gravel accounted for 95 percent of production. South Carolina ranked first of two states producing vermiculite, and second in production of kaolin. It ranked third in the nation in masonry cement production, which, combined with portland cement, led the state's increase in value in 2006.

Water

There are three primary river systems that drain most of the state—the Pee Dee, Santee, and Savannah. Most of the state's lakes are manmade reservoirs that support hydroelectric power facilities. Lake Marion, the largest lake in the state, was formed by a dam along the Santee River. Sport fishing is popular among many of the state's rivers and streams, with trout, striped and largemouth bass, and blue catfish among the popular freshwater catches. The state operates five fish hatcheries.

The beaches along the Atlantic Coast attract numerous visitors each year, making coastal tourism a significant part of the local economy. Four of South Carolina's state parks are located along the coast, providing habitats for numerous marine birds. Manatees and at least four species of sea turtles can be found along the coastal areas. Seven species of jellyfish and nearly 2,000 acres (809 ha) of intertidal oysters can be found within the coastal waters. Shrimp is by far the most valuable commercial fish commodity for the state, but crabs, clams, and oysters contribute to the mix. In 2008, commercial fishing accounted for about $16.7 million in state revenues, and employed more than 600 people.

The Atlantic Intracoastal Waterway, an interconnected system of inland rivers, bays, and canals along the Atlantic, crosses slightly inward along the South Carolina coast and serves as a protected thoroughfare for ships. It has also become a favorite trail for kayakers. The waterway is maintained by the U.S. Army Corp of Engineers.

The Port of Charleston is one of the busiest container ports in the United States. It was ranked as ninth in the nation for dollar value of international shipments in 2009. Primary commodities handled by the port include agricultural products, consumer goods, machinery, metals, chemicals, and vehicles. The Charleston port is set to get even larger, too. Plans for a 10-year, $1.3 billion expansion includes plans for a new terminal set to open in 2018. The new terminal will boost container capacity by 50 percent. Trade through the Port of Georgetown includes steel, petroleum, coke, and wood briquettes. The economic impact of both ports combined is about $45 billion per year.

Agriculture: Certified South Carolina

Broilers, turkeys, and eggs are among the top commodities from the state's agricultural sector, with broilers alone accounting for more than 30 percent of total agricultural sales. South Carolina has also ranked as one of the top five

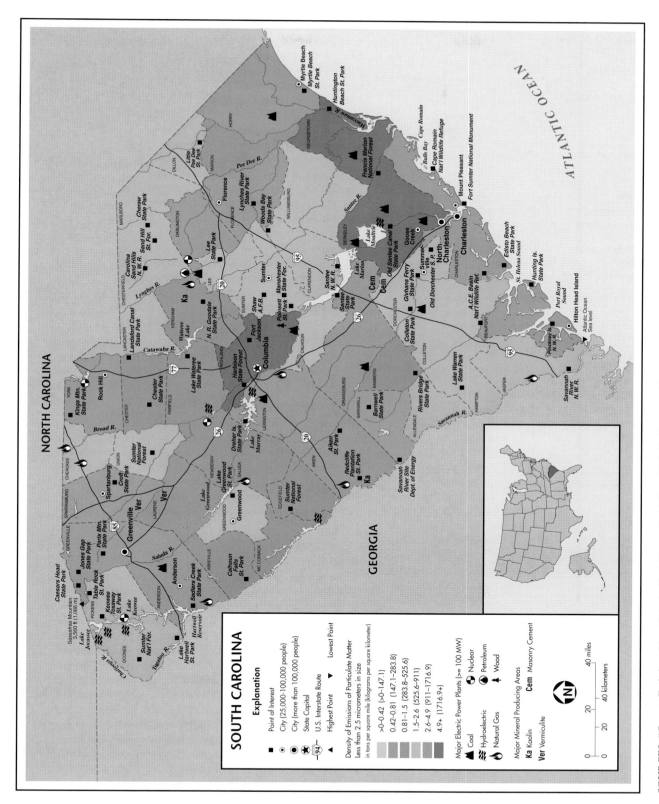

SOURCES: "County Emissions Map: Criteria Air Pollutants." *AirData*. U.S. Environmental Protection Agency. Available from http://www.epa.gov/air/data/geosel.html; *Energy Maps*. U.S. Energy Information Administration. Available from http://www.eia.gov/state; *Highest and Lowest Elevations*. U.S. Geological Survey. Available from http://egsc.usgs.gov/isb/pubs/booklets/elvadist/elvadist.html#Highest; *2007 Minerals Yearbook*. U.S. Geological Survey. Available from http://minerals.usgs.gov/minerals/pubs/state. © 2011 Cengage Learning.

South Carolina State Profile

Physical Characteristics

Land area	30,070 square miles (77,881 sq km)
Inland water area	1,044 square miles (2,704 sq km)
Coastal area	74 square miles (119 sq km)
Highest point	Sassafras Mountain 3,560 feet (1,085 m)
National Forest System lands (2010)	631,000 acres (255,000 ha)
State parks (2011)	47

Energy Statistics

Total energy production (2009)	630 trillion Btu
State ranking in total energy production (2009)	24
Renewable energy net generation total (2009)	4.1 million megawatt hours
Hydroelectric energy generation (2009)	2.3 million megawatt hours
Biomass energy generation (2009)	137,000 megawatt hours
Wind energy generation (2009)	NA
Wood and derived fuel energy generation (2009)	1.6 million megawatt hours
Crude oil reserves (2009)	NA
Natural gas reserves (2009)	NA
Natural gas liquids (2008)	NA

Pollution Statistics

Carbon output (2005)	79.2 million tons of CO_2 (71.8 million t)
Superfund sites (2008)	26
Particulate matter (less than 2.5 micrometers) emissions (2002)	21,850 tons per year (19,822 t/yr)
Toxic chemical releases (2009)	49.4 million pounds (22.4 million kg)
Generated hazardous waste (2009)	102,000 tons (92,600 t)

SOURCES: AirData. U.S. Environmental Protection Agency. Available from http://www.epa.gov/air/data; *Energy Maps, Facts, and Data of the U.S. States.* U.S. Energy Information Administration. Available from http://www.eia.gov/state; *The 2012 Statistical Abstract.* U.S. Census Bureau. Available from http://www.census.gov/compendia/statab; *United States Energy Usage.* eRedux. Available from http://www.eredux.net/states.

© 2011 Cengage Learning.

states for the production of quail. According to the 2007 USDA agricultural census, the state ranked third in the nation for the production of tobacco. The Charleston Tea Plantation on Wadmalaw Island is owned by Bigelow and produces the blend sold as American Classic Tea. It is the larger of only two commercial tea producers in the continental United States. Soybeans, corn, peaches, and cotton are also significant commodities.

The South Carolina Department of Agriculture sponsors the Certified South Carolina program as a marketing program designed to promote the sale of local produce and food products. Certified products are marked with the program's logo, and the initiative is supported by its own website featuring lists of certified farmers markets, restaurants, and other locations where South Carolina-certified products can be found. Grocery stores and farmer's markets that sell local products may also display the logo to attract customers. Restaurants that serve locally grown produce are certified under the program's Fresh on the Menu label. The state of South Carolina owns and manages three regional state farmers markets in Columbia, Florence, and Greenville. A new state-of-the-art market facility opened in Lexington County in 2010. Along with vendor booths, the new facility features an exhibition kitchen, a specialty foods shop, and an on-site restaurant. The state's farmers markets also host plant and flower festivals in the spring and fall to promote South Carolina-grown floriculture and horticulture products. The state's nursery, greenhouse, and floriculture industry had a value of $220 million in 2007.

The Clemson University Department of Plant Industry serves as the local U.S. Department of Agriculture (USDA) accredited certifying agency for organic certification. According to a survey from the USDA, South Carolina was home to eighteen 34 certified organic farming operations in 2008.

Energy

Petroleum and Natural Gas

With no reserves or refineries of its own, South Carolina imports its petroleum and natural gas via pipelines from the Gulf of Mexico. About 26 percent of all households in the state use natural gas for home heating, but since winters are generally mild, overall demand is fairly low. South Carolina is one of the few states that allow the use of conventional motor gasoline, rather than a reformulated blend.

Electricity

South Carolina is one of the top nuclear power producers in the nation, with four active nuclear plants in 2010 and two new nuclear reactors scheduled to go online in 2016. About 52 percent of the state's electric supply comes from these nuclear plants. A little over 35 percent comes from coal-fired generating plants, with coal supplies imported from Kentucky, Pennsylvania, West Virginia, and Tennessee. Natural gas-fired plants account for just under 10 percent of the electric supply. Per capita electricity consumption within the state is one of the highest in the nation. Electricity is the primary energy source for heating and air conditioning systems, the latter of which are used extensively during the hot summer months. Industrial use is also high.

Renewables: Water, Wind, and Landfills

The state's only local energy resource is water, but hydroelectric generating plants located along the rivers and lakes supply only about 2 percent of the state's electricity. A small amount of electricity is derived from wood and wood fuels.

Since 2001, a small amount of electricity has come from the Santee Cooper Green Power Program, which uses landfill gas (methane) as its primary energy source. Santee Cooper is a state-owned electric and water utility that serves as the largest power producer in South Carolina. All of South Carolina's twenty electric cooperatives and eight cities and towns purchase green power through this program. Santee Cooper also operates solar energy projects at eighteen schools in the state.

As of the beginning of 2011, South Carolina did not have a renewable portfolio standard. However, the Energy Conservation Plans Act (A318, R389, H4766) that was enacted in 2008 sets a statewide goal for state agencies to reduce energy use by 20 percent of 2000 standards by 2020. That act also established the Wind Energy Production Farms Feasibility Study Committee, which was given a mandate to review, study, and make recommendations regarding the feasibility of wind farms in the state. The committee presented its first report in January 2010. Having concluded that the state could benefit from wind energy projects both on and offshore, *South Carolina's Role in Offshore Wind Energy Development* presents eighteen recommendations for the state government concerning ways to promote and support such development.

In March 2011, a state senate bill called for the creation of a renewable energy portfolio standard for the state, requiring at least 4 percent of electricity to come from renewable sources by 2015. The requirement increases to 16 percent by 2020 and 20 percent by 2022 and beyond. The legislation also called for the creation of standards relating to biomass combustion processes that would deliver electric power to suppliers. The legislation calls on the Public Service Commission to monitor compliance and enforce the regulations, as well as report on progress related to renewable energy sources annually. The legislation, South Carolina Senate Bill 719, was referred to the Senate Judiciary Committee in May 2011.

✿ Green Business, Green Building, Green Jobs

Green Businesses and Green Jobs

South Carolina's green economy is relatively small, but there are several business leaders and state officials at work to promote the growth of green business and green industry, particularly in the fields of renewable energy and energy efficiency. According to a report from The Pew Charitable Trusts, South Carolina had 884 clean energy businesses in 2007, supporting 11,255 jobs. Some officials believe that number could grow substantially if

An ancient live oak tree in South Carolina. © *John Wollwerth/ ShutterStock.com*

the state supports legislation focused on the development of renewable energy sources. Between 1998 and 2007, green sector jobs grew 36 percent. However, venture capital investments had yet to take hold as of 2007, with none on file.

Organizations such as S.C. Businesses for Clean Energy are calling for the creation of new energy efficiency policies as well. In an August 2010 roundtable discussion hosted by the group, presenters noted that new energy efficiency standards could create 22,000 new jobs in South Carolina over a fifteen-year span.

Testing Facility a Windfall for the Local Economy

The Clemson University Restoration Institute is a driving force in the race to develop sustainable technologies that support a green economy. Established in 2004, the Restoration Institute is involved in research and development programs in six focus areas, including community revitalization, historic preservation and materials conservation, renewable energy, resilient infrastructure, restoration ecology, and advanced materials, process and systems. In 2009, Clemson University received a $45 million grant from the U.S. Department of Energy to build and operate a large-scale wind turbine drive train testing facility at the Restoration Institute campus. The university has also acquired $53 million in matching funds from the state and private sectors. The windfall is being hailed as a major economic opportunity for the region, with some officials hopeful that the testing facility will provide an anchor for a local wind energy manufacturing cluster. The facility is expected to be operational by the fall of 2012, and will be constructed in an 82,000-square foot (7,618-sq m) building at the former Charleston Naval Station. The U.S. Department of Energy estimates that the wind power industry could bring 10,000 to 20,000 new jobs to South Carolina within the next twenty years. Construction of the facility should open up at least 113 temporary jobs. In June 2011 the institute awarded the main contracts for design and construction of the facility.

Green Building

Under the Energy Independence and Sustainable Construction Act of 2007, all major facility projects in the state must be designed and built in such a manner as to qualify for silver-level certification under the U.S. Green Building Council Leadership in Energy and Environmental Design (LEED) program or two globes under the Green Globes Rating System. Schools, correctional intuitions, and some other types of buildings are exempt from this requirement. In 2008, this act was amended by the Energy Conservation Plans Act (A318, R389, H4766), which requires all state agencies and public schools to adopt energy conservation plans with a target goal to reduce energy use by 1 percent of 2000 of levels each year from 2008 through 2013 and by 20 percent by 2020.

The first publically funded LEED-certified project in the state was the Clemson University Advanced Materials Research Laboratory. The $22 million project earned Silver-LEED certification in 2005 and boasts of energy savings at $241,800 per year. In the same year, the University of South Carolina was awarded Silver-LEED certification for its Green Quad residence hall; the first LEED certified residence hall in the nation. The Franciscan Monastery of St. Clare in Travelers Rest is the first monastery in the nation to receive LEED (Silver) certification.

🌱 Going Nuclear

At a time when many states are forging ahead to develop and support renewable and sustainable energy, South Carolina is also forging ahead to promote its own nuclear energy cluster. South Carolina is one of the top nuclear power producers in the nation, with four active nuclear plants generating 52 percent of the state's electric supply and more than 11 percent of the national supply of nuclear power. Those percentages could increase within the next decade, as the state prepares to add two new nuclear reactors to the Virgil C. Summer Nuclear Station in Fairfield County by 2016. While some key state utilities and business groups are pleased at the prospect, environmental organizations are not.

The most notable objections have come from the Sierra Club and Friends of the Earth. The South Carolina Public Service Commission approved the new reactor project in 2009. However, representatives from the Sierra Club and Friends of the Earth have argued that the projects sponsors, South Carolina Electric and Gas Co. (SCE&G) and the state-owned Santee Cooper Electric Co-operative, violated the National Environmental Policy Act by neglecting to seriously consider renewable

alternatives, such as offshore wind, and the suitability of alternative programs to meet anticipated demands. The groups took their concerns to the Atomic Safety and Licensing Board of the Nuclear Regulatory Commission (NRC). The board initially dismissed the objections as vague and presented a recommendation for approval in January 2010. However, the five NRC commissioners sent the matter back to the board for a second look, claiming that the board had not provided a sufficient rationale for dismissing the questions concerning the suitability of demand programs.

In March 2010, the board provided a more detailed brief, with the conclusion that the NRC is not required or expected to second-guess the findings of the utility companies concerning their future power demands and their own conclusion concerning how those demands will be best supported. The SCE&G has projected that its baseload capacity will increase by 24 percent by 2021, and since alternative forms of energy are not sufficiently developed as of yet, the addition of the two nuclear reactors is the best option for increased baseload generation. The NRC board also indicated that the burden of proof concerning the merits of alternative options does not fall with the commission, but with the environmental organizations raising the objections.

In August 2010, the NRC commissioners officially affirmed the board's decisions and terminated the contested portion of the proceedings. A final environmental impact statement (EIS) was released by the NRC and the U.S. Army Corps of Engineers in April 2011, with a recommendation to approve the issuance of the combined construction permits and operating licenses for Units 2 and 3 at the V.C. Summer Nuclear Station. Construction on the $9.8 billion project is already underway, with Unit 2 expected to become operational in 2016, followed by Unit 3 in 2019. The new units will each consist of a 1,100-megawatt Westinghouse AP 1000 Pressurized Water Reactor. When added to the existing reactor (which has been approved for operation until 2042), the facility will be capable of generating 3,200 megawatts of electricity, enough to power more than 2.2 million homes in South Carolina. The existing Summer Station employs about 800 people. Up to 3,000 jobs could be created during the construction phase of the station expansion, with between 800 and 1,000 permanent jobs added once the new units are fully operational.

Nuclear is not entirely without its troubles in the state, though. The H.B. Robinson plant, owned by Progress Energy and located near Hartsville, South Carolina, supplies energy to both North and South Carolina. It experienced four unplanned shutdowns, two electrical fires and a power failure in one 12-month period in 2009-2010. The NRC put it on a watch list and cited Progress Energy with more than a dozen violations, but allowed it to continue operating, saying the violations were not serious safety concerns. In July 2011, the nuclear plant was removed from the watch list.

Meanwhile, state businesses are poised to benefit from the expansion of the nuclear power industry. New Carolina (formally known as South Carolina's Council on Competitiveness) has received a promise of $600,000 in funding from the U.S. Small Business Administration as part of the latter's Innovative Economies initiative. New Carolina will use the funds to develop the state's nuclear cluster by identifying gaps in the nuclear supply chain, determining which small businesses are needed or suited to fill those gaps, and providing opportunities for those suppliers to connect with customers locally, nationally, and worldwide.

BIBLIOGRAPHY

Books

Melosi, Artin, ed. *Environment*, vol. 8 of *The New Encyclopedia of Southern Culture*. Chapel Hill: University of North Carolina Press, 2007.

Nash, Steve. *Blue Ridge 2020: An Owner's Manual*. Chapel Hill: University of North Carolina Press, 1999.

Strutin, Michal, and Tony Arruza. *The Smithsonian Guides to Natural America: The Southeast–South Carolina, Georgia, Alabama, Florida*. Washington, DC: Smithsonian Books, 1996.

Web Sites

"Atlantic Intracoastal Waterway." U.S. Army Corps of Engineers. Available from http://www.nao.usace.army.mil/Technical%20Services/Operations%20Branch/atlantic%20intracoastal%20waterway/homepage.asp

Behr, Peter. "Environmental Groups' Challenge to Reactor Project Faces Uphill Path at NRC." *The New York Times*. August 27, 2010. Available from http://www.nytimes.com/cwire/2010/08/27/27climatewire-environmental-groups-challenge-to-reactor-pro-5382.html

Certified South Carolina. Available from http://www.certifiedscgrown.com

"The Clean Energy Economy: South Carolina." The Pew Charitable Trusts. Available from http://www.pewcenteronthestates.org/uploadedFiles/wwwpewcenteronthestatesorg/Fact_Sheets/Clean_Economy_Factsheet_SouthCarolina.pdf

Clemson University Restoration Institute. Available from http://www.clemson.edu/restoration

"Clemson University Restoration Institute Lands $98 Million Funding to Develop Next-generation Wind Turbines." Clemson University Newsroom. November 23, 2009. Available from http://www.clemson.edu/media-relations/article.php?article_id=2432

Congaree National Park. Available from http://www.nps.gov/cong

Energy Conservation Plans Act (A318, R389, H4766). South Carolina General Assembly. Available from http://www.scstatehouse.gov/sess117_2007-2008/bills/4766.htm

Energy Independence and Sustainable Construction Act of 2007. South Carolina General Assembly. Available from http://www.scstatehouse.gov/sess117_2007-2008/bills/376.htm

Final Draft South Carolina Greenhouse Gas Inventory and Reference Case Projection, 1990–2020. Center for Climate Strategies. Available from http://www.scclimatechange.us/ewebeditpro/items/O60F19091.pdf

Final Environmental Impact Statement for Combined Licenses for Virgil C. Summer Nuclear Station, Units 2 and 3 (NUREG-1939). United States Nuclear Regulatory Commission. Available from http://www.nrc.gov/reading-rm/doc-collections/nuregs/staff/sr1939

Gamble, Jack. "New Nuclear Construction: V.C. Summer 2 and 3." Nuclear Fissionary. January 31, 2011. Available from http://nuclearfissionary.com/2011/01/31/new-nuclear-construction-v-c-summer-2-3

"Increasing Vulnerability to Hurricanes: Global Warming's Wake-up Call for U.S. Gulf and Atlantic Coasts." National Wildlife Federation. Available from http://www.nwf.org/~/media/PDFs/Global-Warming/Hurricanes_FNL_LoRes.ashx

"Green Economic Recovery Program Impact on South Carolina." Political Economy Research Institute. Available from http://www.peri.umass.edu/fileadmin/pdf/other_publication_types/green_economics/south_carolina.pdf

Green Means Green: The Economic Impact of South Carolina's Natural Resources. Division of Research, Moore School of Business, University of South Carolina. Available from http://www.dnr.sc.gov/green/greenreport.pdf

"Metals and Minerals." Mining Association of South Carolina. Available from http://www.scmines.com

Murawski, John. "Progress On Hook For $24M." *Raleigh News & Observer*. September 17, 2011. Available from http://www.newsobserver.com/2011/09/17/1494494/progress-on-hook-for-24m.html

New Carolina. Available from http://www.newcarolina.org/clusters/tourism.aspx

"Organic Certification." Clemson University Public Service Activities. Available from http://www.clemson.edu/public/regulatory/plant_industry/organic_certification/index.html

Renewable Energy Plan (H3628). South Carolina General Assembly. Available from http://www.scstatehouse.gov/sess118_2009-2010/bills/3628.htm

Santee Cooper Green. Available from http://www.santeecoopergreen.com/portal/page/portal/SanteeCooper_Green

"Saving South Carolina's Coast." The Nature Conservancy. Available from http://www.nature.org/wherewework/northamerica/states/southcarolina/marine

Senate Bill 719. South Carolina Legislature. March 2011. Available from http://www.scstatehouse.gov/cgi-bin/query.exe?first=DOC&querytext=renewable%20energy&category=Legislation&session=119&conid=6691745&result_pos=0&keyval=1190719

SC Businesses for Clean Energy. Available from http://southcarolinacleanenergy.biz/about.html

"SC Green Projects." U.S. Green Building Council–South Carolina Chapter. Available from http://www.usgbcsc.org/site/?page_id=12

South Carolina Climate, Energy, and Commerce Advisory Committee, Final Report. Available from http://www.scclimatechange.us/ewebeditpro/items/O60F19029.PDF

South Carolina Department of Agriculture. Available from http://agriculture.sc.gov

South Carolina Department of Natural Resources. Available from http://www.dnr.sc.gov

"South Carolina Energy Facts." Institute for Energy Research. Available from http://www.instituteforenergyresearch.org/state-regs/pdf/South%20Carolina.pdf

South Carolina Forestry Commission. Available from http://www.state.sc.us/forest/index.htm

"South Carolina Nuclear Profile." U.S. Energy Information Administration. Available from http://www.eia.doe.gov/cneaf/nuclear/state_profiles/south_carolina/sc.html

South Carolina Ports. Available from http://www.scspa.com/search_results.asp?cx=011144877965471174217%3Acas37w_vop8&cof=FORID%3A11&q=statistics#990

"South Carolina Potential Green Jobs." South Carolina Department of Commerce. Available from https://www.sconestop.org/admin/gsipub/htmlarea/uploads/SCgreenJobs.pdf

South Carolina State Parks. Available from http://www.southcarolinaparks.com

South Carolina 2007 Minerals Yearbook. United States Geological Survey. Available from http://minerals.usgs.gov/minerals/pubs/state/2007/myb2-2007-sc.pdf

"State Energy Profiles: South Carolina." U.S. Energy Information Administration. Available from http://tonto.eia.doe.gov/state/state_energy_profiles.cfm?sid=SC#

South Carolina's Role in Offshore Wind Energy Development. Wind Energy Production Farms Feasibility Study Committee. Available from http://www.energy.sc.gov/publications/Wind%20Energy%20Production%20Farms%20Feasibility%20Study%20Committee%20Final%20Report%2012-09%20(2).pdf

Wenger, Yvonne. "Experts call for energy efficiency." *The Post and Courier.* August 25, 2010. Available from http://www.postandcourier.com/news/2010/aug/25/experts-call-for-energy-efficiency

South Dakota

Home to Mount Rushmore and the Crazy Horse Memorial, South Dakota is the seventeenth largest state in the union. The Missouri River flows through the state. Most of the population in concentrated east of the Missouri River, where agriculture reigns supreme. West of the river the economy focuses on ranching, tourism, and the defense industry, centered around Rapid City and Ellsworth Air Force Base. Tourists flock to the western part of the state to visit Mount Rushmore, the Black Hills, and motorcycle enthusiasts ride into Sturgis for the annual Sturgis Motorcycle Rally.

Agriculture is one of the state's most important industries, and along with its unique soil is one of its most important natural resources. Houdek soil, a type of well-drained, loamy soil formed under the influence of prairie grasses, is found only in South Dakota and covers at least 600,000 acres (242,800 ha) of land. Clearing and draining land for agriculture has contributed to the state's economic growth but has also created controversy. Eastern South Dakota, an area known as the Prairie Pothole Region, features a high density of wetlands. Whether to drain or preserve the wetlands has been the subject of debate and disagreement among citizens for decades.

As a leading producer of corn and soybeans, the state has also become a leading producer of ethanol, with total production estimated at 1 billion gallons (3.8 billion l) per year. As for other energy resources, more than 53 percent of the electric supply is generated by hydroelectric power, with the Missouri River being a primary source. The state has great potential for developments in wind energy, with nearly 5 percent of the electricity supply already generated from wind power. Developments in wind and other renewable energy resources will most likely serve as the foundation for the state's green economy.

Climate

South Dakota has an interior continental climate with hot summers and extremely cold winters. Average annual precipitation ranges from 17 to 20 inches (43 to 51 cm) in the central regions to 20 to 27 inches (51 to 69 cm) in the east. The state is sometimes affected by La Niña, which brings below average temperatures in the winter and below average levels of precipitation in the eastern portion of the state. The state is also susceptible to weather extremes including severe thunderstorms and drought.

Climate Change

According to a report from the Intergovernmental Panel on Climate Change, the average temperatures in South Dakota could rise by about 6.75°F (3.75°C) by 2100 if global warming continues unabated. Such a change could have a significant effect on some of the state's most important habitat areas. For instance, warmer temperatures and drier conditions in the Prairie Pothole Region could diminish wetlands found there, which in turn would affect the numerous nesting and migrating birds and waterfowl that depend upon the region.

The Climate Change Lesson in Public Schools

The state is one of several that has not adopted a climate change action plan. Debate over the potential causes and effects of global warming may be a factor in the state's hesitancy to develop such a plan. A 2010 concurrent resolution of the state legislature indicates that there are a number of politicians who are concerned as to the validity of climate change science. (Concurrent resolutions do not have the force of law, however, and they are not signed by the governor.) In February 2010, the state house of representatives passed House Resolution 1009, which urges public school teachers throughout the state to balance their approach to lessons on global warming by presenting it as a scientific theory, rather than a proven fact. The original text of the resolution also asked educators to inform students that there are a number of factors affecting world weather conditions, including "astrological" and "cosmological." Educators were also

Needles Highway is located in the scenic Black Hills of South Dakota. © *Jay Stuhlmiller/ShutterStock.com*

asked to note that "political and philosophical viewpoints have complicated and prejudiced the scientific investigation of global warming phenomena." The original language used to justify the resolution indentified carbon dioxide as a "highly beneficial ingredient for all plant life on earth" rather than a pollutant and noted that more than 31,000 American scientists have stated (by petition to the president) that there is no convincing scientific evidence that greenhouse gases cause catastrophic heating of the atmosphere or disruption of the Earth's climate. The state senate amended the resolution by deleting much of this language, including references to astrology and the benefits of carbon dioxide. This amended version was then passed by both houses.

⚜ Natural Resources, Water, and Agriculture

Forests

Though less than 4 percent of the state is covered with forest, these areas are important to the state as recreational areas and as habitat for a variety of wildlife. Most of the forested area (about 77 percent) is in the Black Hills, with ponderosa pine as the primary species. This coniferous forest area also includes white spruce (also known as the Black Hills spruce), rocky mountain juniper, and eastern red cedar. The Black Hills National Forest contains a large portion of this region, which serves as home to more than two hundred species of wildlife, including mountain lion, ruffed grouse, and mountain goat. A portion of the national forest is open to cattle grazing. The Black Hills National Forest was the site of the first federal government-regulated timber sale in 1899. A moderate timber industry continues to operate from the national forest, supporting about 2,000 jobs.

The upland forests of the southeastern portion of the state account for about 20 percent of the total forest. Common species there include elm, ash, bur oak, and aspen. About two-thirds of these upland hardwood forests are privately owned. Bottomland forest is found along the flood plains and tributaries of the Missouri River. Common tree species there include cottonwood, willow, green ash, and elm. Numerous shelterbelts have been planted in the open areas of the state to protect farms and homes against storm damage and soil erosion.

Parks and Monuments, Prairies, and Wildlife

Mixed grass and tall grass prairies cover large portions of the state. The state's two national parks each contain areas of mixed grass prairie serving as protected habitats for bison, elk, pronghorn, mule deer, coyote, and prairie dogs. Wind Cave National Park contains one of the longest and most complex cave systems in the world. Wind Cave is the fourth longest cave in the world. It consists of more than 132 miles (212 km) of explored passages, with more explored each year. Jewel Cave National Monument, located in the Black Hills, is the second-longest cave in the world with over 151 miles (243 km) of mapped passages. South Dakota is also home to Mount Rushmore, located near Keystone. Sculpted by Gutzon Borglum and later by his son Lincoln Borglum, Mount Rushmore features 60-foot (18-m) sculptures of the heads of former United States presidents George Washington, Thomas Jefferson, Theodore Roosevelt, and Abraham Lincoln. Badlands National Park protects a barren region of land that has one of the most extensive mammal fossil beds in the world. The Badlands also contain the largest expanse of protected prairie ecosystem within the national park system. Several successful reintroduction programs for native wildlife species, including the black-footed ferret, swift fox, bison, and bighorn sheep, have been carried out there. The park also supports populations of bobcat, black-tailed prairie dog, prairie rattlesnake, and black-billed magpie.

The eastern two-fifths of South Dakota is prairie, including mixed grass and tall grass ecosystems. Wildlife species that rely on these habitats include the northern bobwhite quail, gray partridge, greater prairie chicken, sage and sharp-tailed grouse, and wild turkey. Common species of small mammals include pocket gophers, ground squirrels, tree squirrels, porcupine, and opossum.

The U.S. Fish and Wildlife Service listed 11 animal and 1 plant species as threatened or endangered in 2011. Endangered animals include the black-footed ferret, whooping crane, and the American burying beetle. A single plant species, the western prairie fringed orchid, is listed as threatened.

South Dakota maintains 12 state parks, along with several other natural areas that provide homes for the state's abundant wildlife and preserve its natural resources.

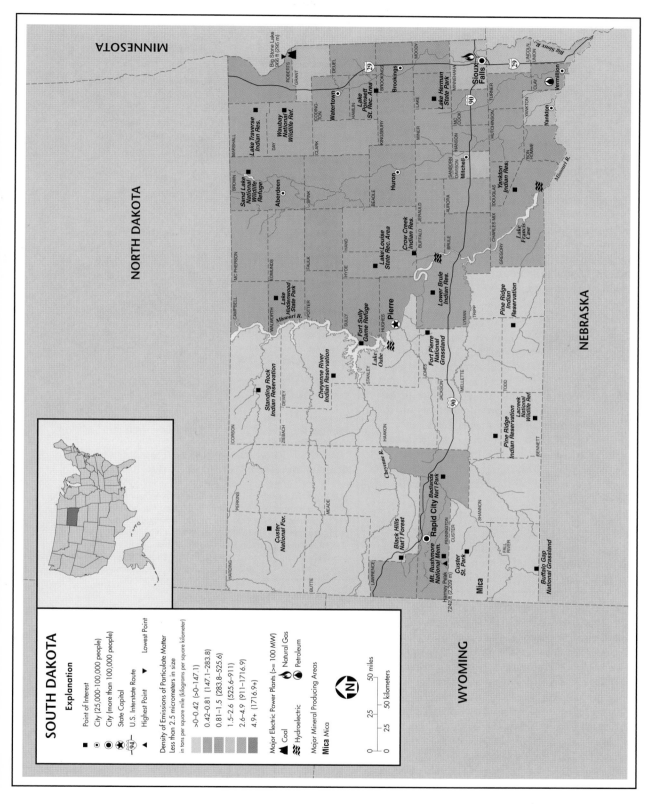

SOURCES: "County Emissions Map: Criteria Air Pollutants." *AirData*. U.S. Environmental Protection Agency. Available from http://www.epa.gov/air/data/geosel.html; *Energy Maps*. U.S. Energy Information Administration. Available from http://www.eia.gov/state; *Highest and Lowest Elevations*. U.S. Geological Survey. Available from http://egsc.usgs.gov/isb/pubs/booklets/elvadist/elvadist.html#Highest; *2007 Minerals Yearbook*. U.S. Geological Survey. Available from http://minerals.usgs.gov/minerals/pubs/state. © 2011 Cengage Learning.

Hunting is a popular and economically significant sport in South Dakota, with pheasant being the chief game. Deer and elk hunting are also popular and important for controlling the populations of these animals. The South Dakota Game, Fish, and Parks department reported that more than 167,000 licensed pheasant hunters (69,949 state residents and 97,350 nonresidents) spent an estimated $219.8 million in the state during the 2009 season.

In 2005 the state began offering a license, for state residents only, to hunt mountain lions. In addition, Custer State Park offers ten mountain lion hunting licenses, which are awarded by lottery. Hunters may apply for both licenses, but they must adhere to the limit of one mountain lion per season. The mountain lion season typically runs from January 1 through March 31, or until the season's quota has been reached. In 2011, the season's quota of 45 was reached on February 21, which marked the end of the season.

Minerals

Gold is a leading mineral commodity in terms of value, accounting for a gross value of more than $52 million in 2008. Gold production has increased since 2007 as gold prices have also risen. In 2007 Wharf Resources (the only South Dakota company producing gold) produced 57,628 ounces of gold. In 2009 production was up to 67,738 ounces. More than $3 million worth of silver was produced in 2007. Other geological resources produced throughout the state include sand and gravel, quartzite, limestone, portland cement, and dimension stone. Total nonfuel mineral production in the state was valued at $298 million in 2010.

Water

Most of South Dakota falls within the Missouri River watershed, draining into the Gulf of Mexico. The Missouri River and its tributaries, including the Grand, Cheyenne, Bad, Moreau, White, James, Vermillion, and Big Sioux, are the most important rivers in the state. Four of the Missouri's six main stem dams are in South Dakota. The dams—Gavins Point, Ft. Randall, Big Bend, and Oahe—provide water for irrigation, flood control, and hydroelectric power. The Oahe Dam on the Missouri River created Lake Oahe which is the fourth-largest manmade reservoir in the nation. This reservoir extends through part of North Dakota as well. The stretch of the Missouri River below Gavins Point Dam (from Pickstown, South Dakota, to Ponca, Nebraska) is a National Recreational River, administered by the National Park Service.

The northeast corner of the state is drained by the Red River and is separated from the Missouri River basin by a continental divide, draining ultimately into Hudson Bay, Canada.

The spring of 2011 saw record flooding of the Missouri River, affecting areas around Pierre and

South Dakota State Profile

Physical Characteristics

Land area	75,811 square miles (196,350 sq km)
Inland water area	1,305 square miles (3,380 sq km)
Coastal area	NA
Highest point	Harney Peak 7,242 feet (2,207 m)
National Forest System lands (2010)	2.0 million acres (816,000 ha)
State parks (2011)	58

Energy Statistics

Total energy production (2009)	160 trillion Btu
State ranking in total energy production (2009)	41
Renewable energy net generation total (2009)	4.9 million megawatt hours
Hydroelectric energy generation (2009)	4.4 million megawatt hours
Biomass energy generation (2009)	6,000 megawatt hours
Wind energy generation (2009)	421,000 megawatt hours
Wood and derived fuel energy generation (2009)	NA
Crude oil reserves (2009)	NA
Natural gas reserves (2009)	NA
Natural gas liquids (2008)	NA

Pollution Statistics

Carbon output (2005)	13.7 million tons of CO_2 (12.4 million t)
Superfund sites (2008)	2
Particulate matter (less than 2.5 micrometers) emissions (2002)	711 tons per year (645 t/yr)
Toxic chemical releases (2009)	4.6 million pounds (2.1 million kg)
Generated hazardous waste (2009)	1,200 tons (1,100 t)

SOURCES: AirData. U.S. Environmental Protection Agency. Available from http://www.epa.gov/air/data; *Energy Maps, Facts, and Data of the U.S. States.* U.S. Energy Information Administration. Available from http://www.eia.gov/state; *The 2012 Statistical Abstract.* U.S. Census Bureau. Available from http://www.census.gov/compendia/statab; *United States Energy Usage.* eRedux. Available from http://www.eredux.net/states.

© 2011 Cengage Learning.

Dakota Dunes and leading South Dakota to receive a Presidential Disaster Declaration. The flooding was caused by unusually heavy rains, especially on May 19 and 20, when 2–4 inches (5–10 cm) of heavy rain fell in the Black Hills and in western South Dakota. May that produced over a year's worth of rain in the upper Missouri River basin. This was coupled with melting snowpack from the Rocky Mountains that added to the floodwaters. By June 1, almost 3,000 people were evacuated from Pierre and Fort Pierre. Two days later, Governor Dennis Daugaard encouraged residents of Dakota Dunes to evacuate as well, stating that residents may not be able to return to their homes for up to two months. At least two people lost their lives, and the cost of the flooding was estimated at $13.2 million for Pierre alone. In July 2011, the state Department of Health began holding free cleanup training sessions for homeowners and businesses impacted by the flooding. These sessions were designed to help educate home and business owners about mold and other contaminants that may be present from the flooding. The flood has initiated debate in multiple states about flood control procedures. It has also lead to questions about whether the river is still viable as a commerce route, or if more of the river water should be kept in reservoirs in North and South Dakota for recreation in order to boost the region's economy.

Fish and Fishing

Approximately 100 species of freshwater fish inhabit the lakes and waterways of South Dakota. Some of the most common species include largemouth and smallmouth bass, walleye, common carp, and brown, rainbow, and brook trout. Eastern South Dakota is home to some rare species of fish, including the black buffalo, blue sucker, silver chub, and troutperch. The Missouri River contains several primitive fishes such as sturgeon, paddlefish, gar, and bowfin. Virtually all fishing is recreational. The D. C. Booth Historic National Fish Hatchery is one of the oldest operating hatcheries in the country. The facility primarily produces trout to stock the Black Hills region of the state. The Gavins Point National Fish Hatchery, one of four state hatcheries, raises endangered pallid sturgeon and paddlefish.

Agriculture

One of state's most important natural resources is its soil. Houdek soil, a type of well-drained, loamy soil formed under the influence of prairie grasses, is found only in South Dakota and covers at least 600,000 acres (242,800 ha) of land. Over 650 different soil types have also been found in the state. Agriculture is a leading industry that provides more than 40 percent of all jobs in the state and shows an economic impact of about $21 billion per year.

Sunflower seeds and sunflower oil are important products, with the state ranked second in the nation for production of both. The state has also ranked within the top ten for production of corn, wheat, and soybeans. The beef and pork industries are also significant, with rankings in the top five nationwide. The state regularly ranks first in the nation for production of pheasants.

Organic farms and products are certified under national guidelines. In 2008, there were 103 organic certified operations in the state.

❧ Energy

Oil and Natural Gas

The state of South Dakota has very few fossil fuel resources and must rely on imports from neighboring states to meet local demand for petroleum products and natural gas for fuel. Fortunately, demand for energy is relatively low, due to the fact that South Dakota is one of the least-populated states in the union. About 48 percent of all households rely on natural gas for home heating, while 22 percent rely on liquefied petroleum gases and 7 percent use fuel oil.

In addition to a reformulated ethanol blend, South Dakota also allows the use of conventional gasoline. The state is one of the leading producers of ethanol. In 2010, there were at least fifteen ethanol plants operating in the state with total production estimated at 1 billion gallons (3.8 billion l) per year.

Coal and Electricity

A little more than 39 percent of the state's supply of electricity is generated from coal-fired plants, with most of the coal imported from Wyoming. More than 53 percent of the electric supply is generated by hydroelectric power, with the Missouri River being a primary source. About 20 percent of households rely on electricity as their source for home heating.

Renewables

The state has great potential for developments in wind energy, with nearly 5 percent of the electricity supply already generated from wind power. There are also several locations in the south-central region of the state that show potential for developments in geothermal energy.

Energy Plans and Goals

In 2008 the state legislature enacted legislation (HB 1123) that established a voluntary objective that 10 percent of all retail sales of electricity in the state should be obtained from renewable source and recycled energy by 2015. The South Dakota Public Utilities Commission is responsible for establishing the standards for eligible sources, which include solar, hydroelectric, wind, geothermal, and biomass. In 2009 additional legislation was passed (SB 57) to include "conserved energy," which involves the effective use of energy efficiency and conservation measures.

The South Dakota State Energy Plan, funded by the U.S. Department of Energy and implemented by the South Dakota Energy Management Office, is designed to promote energy efficiency and energy cost savings by providing incentives and resources that help state institutions implement cost-effective energy efficiency improvement measures.

In 2009 the legislature mandated that the Bureau of Administration conduct a study of energy use and efficiency measures at state agencies in order to determine what new measures might be enacted as part of an overall Energy Master Plan to lower energy usage and costs (SB 202). The *State of South Dakota Statewide Energy*

Auditing for Energy Master Plan was completed by Minnesota-based SebestaBlomberg in December 2009. The final report indentifies 1,168 energy conservation measures that could lead to a 22 percent reduction in energy consumption and potential energy savings of $1.1 million per year if all of the measures are adopted.

⚘ Green Business, Green Building, Green Jobs

Green Business

As in many states, the development of a green economy in South Dakota will be largely dependent on improvements and developments in clean and renewable energy sources, particularly wind energy. A 2009 report from the Center for Rural Affairs notes that South Dakota has the wind potential to power about 50 percent of the nation's electrical demands. Yet, while the state is ranked as fourth in the nation for wind energy potential, it ranked as twentieth for installed capacity in 2009. To move the industry along, the state introduced two new financial incentive plans in March 2010. The Wind Transmission Construction Tax Refund (HB 1060) offers a refund of 45 percent for projects costing $10 million or more, with a refund of 55 percent available for project costs of $40 million or more. The program applies to new and expanded wind energy facilities and will run until January 1, 2013. The Renewable Energy System Exemption (SB 58) provides a property tax exemption for facilities that generate electricity using wind, solar, hydro, and biomass resources. The exemption applies to facilities with a capacity of 5 megawatts or less and offers an exemption on the first $50,000 or 70 percent of the assessed value of eligible property (whichever figure is greater).

Green Jobs

In January 2010 the South Dakota Department of Labor was awarded a $2.5 million grant from the American Recovery and Reinvestment Act for green jobs training programs. In May 2010, $100,000 was granted to Western Dakota Technical Institute in Rapid City to support a revised curriculum that provides training in green building construction, energy generation, and transportation. Another $100,000 was awarded to POET of Sioux Falls, a company that operates ethanol production plants in Big Stone, Chancellor, Hudson, and Mitchell, as well as several out-of-state. The company intended to use the money to provide training for up to 600 ethanol plant workers. The State Department of Labor has also awarded $150,000 to South Dakota State University to support courses and workshops for students pursuing careers in the ethanol and biofuels industry or relating to sustainable energy systems.

Green Building

A mandate for high performance standards in state buildings was enacted in 2008 (SB 91). The act requires all new state agency construction projects and renovations that cost more than $500,000 or include more than 5,000 square feet of space to meet the requirements of silver certification under the U.S. Green Building Council Leadership in Energy and Environmental Design (LEED) or a two-globe rating under the Green Building Initiative Green Globe rating system. Alternatively, projects can meet the requirements of a comparable rating under an accredited sustainable building certification program. The South Dakota Office of the State Engineer may issue a waiver of this requirement for special circumstances, such as projects for which meeting these standards would conflict with historic property laws or if the buildings in question will have minimal human occupancy.

The headquarters of Heartland Consumer Power District was the first newly constructed building in the state to earn LEED Platinum certification, which is the highest level of green certification under the program. The building was designed to be 44 percent more energy efficient with at least 70 percent of the building's energy coming from renewable sources, including wind energy and roof-mounted solar panels. The Museum of Visual Materials, one of the oldest buildings in downtown Sioux Falls, was the first LEED-Platinum certified renovated building in South Dakota.

⚘ Prairie Pothole Wetlands

South Dakota and states to the northeast are peppered with shallow depressions, mostly round in shape, that were left as the glaciers retreated about 12,000 years ago. These depressions, known as prairie potholes, range in size from a fraction of an acre to hundreds of acres. Most are found east and north of the Missouri River. Also called ponds, marshes, sloughs, swamps, or simply low spots, prairie potholes are often filled with water, creating marshy wetlands that provide habitat and breeding grounds for waterfowl and other species. An estimated 50–80 percent of the U.S. waterfowl population is bred in this region. In years of drought, the number of these wetlands decreases. In addition to providing habitat, the potholes also help to replenish the groundwater supply and provide water for foraging livestock.

Management of the state's prairie potholes (wetlands) have triggered heated controversy. The question of whether to preserve them or drain them has generated many legislative hearings and community debates over property rights, economics, and the value of wetlands. South Dakotans have struggled for decades to chart a course that will preserve this

Prairie potholes are shallow, mostly round depressions that were left as the glaciers retreated about 12,000 years ago. *© john t. fowler/Alamy*

important environment while allowing for economic development.

The prairie pothole controversy dates back to the late 1800s (and perhaps earlier) when South Dakota farmers began to seek ways to drain marshes to allow the land to be cultivated. In the period after World War II (1939–1945), when crop prices were rising, the U.S. Department of Agriculture provided technical and financial assistance to farmers seeking to drain wetlands. Over the decades, some 50–60 percent of wetlands in the region (North Dakota, Iowa, Minnesota, Montana, and neighboring Canadian provinces, in addition to South Dakota) were drained to make way for agriculture and commercial development.

As more wetlands disappeared, it became obvious that wildlife was being affected. The U.S. Fish and Wildlife Service (USFWS) began to provide technical and financial support to landowners to encourage them to preserve wetlands. Those in favor of preserving wetlands cited their benefits, including flood control. Wetlands absorb and store snowmelt and rain water, releasing it slowly back into the groundwater supply or the atmosphere. By replenish the groundwater supply, wetlands provide water for agriculture and consumer use and protect agricultural lands from the effects of drought.

In 1958 the U.S. Congress amended the Duck Stamp Act to authorize the USFWS to use money from the sale of federal duck stamps to purchase wetland areas outright. The first waterfowl production area (WPA) purchased under this program was in South Dakota. Nearly 95 percent of all WPAs were located in four states as of 2011: North and South Dakota, Minnesota, and Montana.

Managing wetlands effectively is a complex issue. Over the years, governmental departments took different sides on the issue of whether to drain wetlands or preserve them. Citizens were similarly divided, with their positions often based on their economic priorities. Farmers sought to maximize land available for crop cultivation, so they generally favored draining the wetlands to make way for crops. Others sought to preserve the wetlands, but their position had a less-quantifiable economic value; they cited the benefits to wildlife and people from preservation of wetlands and the important role wetlands play in hydrology (the movement of water through the landscape).

In 1998 South Dakota received a grant from the U. S. Environmental Protection Agency (EPA) to develop a state wetland policy. Representatives from the Department of Agriculture, the Department of Environment and Natural Resources, the Department of Game, Fish and Parks, and the Department of Transportation formed the South Dakota Interagency Wetlands Working Group (IWWG). A resulting policy, published in 2001, provides guidelines for how various state agencies should work together to protect the state's wetlands and its economic interests.

Also in 1998 the Sand Lake National Wildlife Refuge, a freshwater cattail marsh, was designated as a Ramsar Wetland of International Importance. This refuge is home to more than 230 species of birds, 55 mammals, 35 reptiles, 17 amphibians, and a variety of fish. Lying within the Prairie Pothole Region, this area is particularly important as a habitat for migrating waterfowl, with about 25 species visiting the refuge. These include the American black duck, mallard, northern pintail, wood duck, green-winged teal, and hooded and common merganser. The wetlands also provide breeding and nesting habitat for marsh and water birds, such as American bitterns and black-crowned night herons.

Mitigation

One way to address the competing priorities is through a mitigation program. A wetland mitigation bank is a permanently protected tract of land that has been preserved or restored and managed for wildlife habitat, water quality, and flood control. Wetland mitigation banks are established to counter threatened wetlands elsewhere. Those who own wetland mitigation banks may sell wetland credits to developers and others who need to compensate for adverse affects on wetlands caused by their projects. In 2008 the Army Corps of Engineers and the EPA published new guidelines for all forms of mitigation, including wetland banks. These rules promote national consistency for all mitigation programs, which are used to help restore many kinds of natural resources.

In 2008 the Food, Conservation, and Energy Act of 2008 (commonly referred to as the 2008 Farm Bill) established guidelines for the Wetlands Reserve Program (WRP), including how to set the value of land being purchased for wetlands easement or restoration; increasing the number of acres that can be enrolled in the program; and other parameters for the enrollment of wetlands in the program.

Recognizing the need for a wetland mitigation bank in South Dakota, government agencies and farmers worked together to establish one in the Big Sioux Watershed. The wetland mitigation bank will help to preserve wetlands, improve water quality, and allow farmers increased flexibility. Farmers (or other developers) who want to convert farmed wetlands on their property to non-wetlands are required to purchase wetland credits. These producers do not mitigate on their own farms for the wetland conversion, but on land that is part of the mitigation bank. The overall approach to developing a mitigation bank is to allow for the establishment of a larger contiguous wetland area able to replace the functions and values of the lost wetlands.

In May 2011 the Plains and Prairie Potholes Landscape Conservation Cooperative's (PPP LCC) steering committee approved nine projects for the 2011 fiscal year. One such project, done in conjunction with the Prairie Pothole Joint Venture, has developed high-resolution climate model projections to aid avian management and conservation of the wetlands. These models illustrate what the climate of the area may be like in the future based on a number of factors. The results of the climate model projections will be combined with hydrologic and vegetation models to give biologists a detailed picture of the possible effects of climate change on the wetlands. This will allow them to better manage the area in order to preserve it for the future. Data from the project will be available for distribution through the U.S. Geological Survey Climate Data Portal, along with fact sheets and scientific manuscripts on wetland, plant, and migrant bird responses to climate change.

Wetlands are still being drained to supply resources to meet growing demands from the expanding population, and the reserve program contracts expire in 2012, but South Dakotans are working together to reverse the trend. Agencies supporting this effort include the Nature Conservancy, Ducks Unlimited, and Pheasants Forever (the latter two are nonprofit organization made up of hunting enthusiasts dedicated to preserving waterfowl and wildlife habitats).

BIBLIOGRAPHY

Books

Carrels, Peter. *Uphill against Water: The Great Dakota Water War.* Lincoln, NE: University of Nebraska Press, 1999.

Marshall, Joseph M, III. *To You We Shall Return: Lessons about Our Planet from the Lakota.* New York, NY: Sterling Ethos, 2010.

Powers, Tom. *Audobon Guide to the National Wildlife Refuges. Northern Midwest: Illinois, Indiana, Iowa, Michigan, Minnesota, Nebraska, North Dakota, Ohio, South Dakota, Wisconsin.* New York, NY: St. Martin's Press, 2000.

Raventon, Edward. *Island in the Plains: A Black Hills Natural History.* Boulder, CO: Johnson Books, 1994.

Schermeister, Phil. *Dakotas: Where the West Begins.* Washington, DC: National Geographic Society, 2008.

Schnell, Herbert Samuel and John E. Miller. *History of South Dakota.* Pierre, SD: South Dakota State Historical Society Press, 2004.

Shepard, Lansing and Tom Bean. *The Smithsonian Guides to Natural America: The Northern Plains–Minnesota, North Dakota, South Dakota.* Washington, DC: Smithsonian Books, 1996.

Tekiela, Stan. *Birds of the Dakotas Field Gide.* Cambridge, MN: Adventure Publications, 2003.

Web Sites

An act to allow the use of energy efficiency and conservation to count toward the state's renewable and recycled energy objective (2009 SB 57). South Dakota Legislature. Available from http://legis.state.sd.us/sessions/2009/Bill.aspx?File=SB57ENR.htm

An act to establish design and construction standards for newly constructed or renovated state buildings (2008 SB 91). South Dakota Legislature. Available from http://legis.state.sd.us/sessions/2008/Bills/SB91P.pdf

An act to establish a state renewable and recycled energy objective (2008 HB 1123). South Dakota Legislature. Available from http://legis.state.sd.us/sessions/2008/Bills/HB1123ENR.pdf

An act to require the Bureau of Administration to prepare a report regarding the energy efficiency of state agencies (2009 SB 202). South Dakota Legislature. Available from http://legis.state.sd.us/sessions/2009/Bills/SB202ENR.pdf

"Black Hills National Forest." U.S. Forest Service. Available from http://www.fs.fed.us/r2/publications/briefing/BB-BlkHills.pdf

A concurrent resolution, calling for balanced teaching of global warming in the public schools of South Dakota (2010 HR 1009); enrolled version. South Dakota Legislature. Available from http://legis.state.sd.us/sessions/2010/Bills/HCR1009ENR.pdf

A concurrent resolution, calling for balanced teaching of global warming in the public schools of South Dakota (2010 HR 1009); printed version. South Dakota Legislature. Available from http://legis.state.sd.us/sessions/2010/Bills/HCR1009P.pdf

"Dams and Reservoirs of the Upper Missouri River." North Dakota Water Science Center. Available from http://nd.water.usgs.gov/lewisandclark/dams.html

D.C. Booth Historic National Fish Hatchery. Available from http://www.fws.gov/dcbooth/

"Eastern South Dakota Wetlands." Northern Prairie Wildlife Research Center, U.S. Geological Survey. Available from http://www.npwrc.usgs.gov/resource/wetlands/eastwet/overview.htm

"Ethanol Facilities Capacity by State and Plant." Government of Nebraska. Available at http://www.neo.ne.gov/statshtml/122.htm

"Flood cleanup training this week." KSFY News. July 18, 2011. Available from http://www.ksfy.com/story/15097294/flood-cleanup-training-this-week

Gavins Point National Fish Hatchery. Available from http://www.fws.gov/gavinspoint

"Global Warming and South Dakota." National Wildlife Federation. Available from http://www.nwf.org/Global-Warming/~/media/PDFs/Global%20Warming/Global%20Warming%20State%20Fact%20Sheets/SouthDakota.ashx

"Heartland Headquarters Earns LEED Platinum Certification." Koch Hazard Architects. Available from http://www.kochhazard.com/News/Press Releases/HeartlandLEEDPlat.pdf

"Labor Department awards POET $100,000 for green jobs training." South Dakota Department of Labor. May 12, 2010. Available from http://dol.sd.gov/news/releases10/nr051210_poet_energy_grant.pdf

"Labor Department awards WDT $100,000 for green jobs training." South Dakota Department of Labor. May 12, 2010. Available from http://dol.sd.gov/news/releases10/nr051210_wdt_energy_grant.pdf

"Listings and occurrences for South Dakota." Species Reports. U.S. Fish and Wildlife Service. Available from http://ecos.fws.gov/tess_public/pub/stateListingAndOccurrenceIndividual.jsp?state=SD&S8fid=112761032792&S8fid=112762573902

Museum of Visual Materials. Available from http://www.sfmvm.com

Ode, Dave. "LandScope America: South Dakota Conservation Summary." Available from http://www.landscope.org/south-dakota/overview/

Renewable Energy and Economic Potential in Iowa, Kansas, Nebraska, South Dakota. The Center for Rural Affairs. Available from http://files.cfra.org/pdf/Renewable-Energy-and-Economic-Potential.pdf

Renewable Energy System Exemption (2010 SB 58). South Dakota Legislature. Available from http://legis.state.sd.us/sessions/2010/Bills/SB58ENR.pdf

Sand Lake National Wildlife Refuge. Available from http://www.fws.gov/sandlake

Sand Lake Wetland Management District: Annual Narrative Report, 2003. Sand Lake National Wildlife Refuge. Available from http://www.fws.gov/sandlake/2003_wmd.pdf

SebestaBlomberg. *State of South Dakota Statewide Energy Auditing for Energy Master Plan.* Available from http://www.state.sd.us/boa/ose/Final%20Report/SD%20Energy%20Dft%20Rpt%20Rev%202009Dec01%20FINAL.pdf

"South Dakota Agriculture's Economic Impact Increases to $21.3 Billion." South Dakota Department of Agriculture. April 28, 2009. Available from http://www.state.sd.us/news/showDoc.aspx?i=10630

South Dakota Department of Agriculture. Available from http://sdda.sd.gov

South Dakota Department of Environment and Natural Resources. *The 2010 South Dakota Integrated Report for Surface Water Quality Assessment.* March 29, 2010. Available from http://denr.sd.gov/documents/10irfinal.pdf

South Dakota Game, Fish and Parks. Available from http://gfp.sd.gov

South Dakota Game, Fish, and Parks. Hunting Big Game. Available from http://gfp.sd.gov/hunting/big-game/

South Dakota Game, Fish and Parks. Pheasant Economics. http://gfp.sd.gov/hunting/small-game/pheasant-economics.aspx

South Dakota Game, Fish and Parks. Pheasant Statistics for South Dakota. Available from http://gfp.sd.gov/hunting/small-game/pheasant-stats.aspx

"South Dakota Lakes and Reservoirs." U.S. Department of the Interior, Bureau of Reclamation, Great Plains Region. Available from http://www.usbr.gov/gp/lakes_reservoirs/south_dakota_lakes.htm

South Dakota: National Park Service. Available from http://www.nps.gov/applications/parksearch/state.cfm?st=sd

South Dakota Office of Climatology. Available from http://climate.sdstate.edu/climate_site/climate.htm

"South Dakota State Receives $150,000 for green education." South Dakota State University. Available from http://www3.sdstate.edu/news/articles/green-education.cfm

"South Dakota State Soil (Houdek)." U.S. Department of Agriculture, Natural Resources Conservation Service. Available from http://www.sd.nrcs.usda.gov/technical/houdeksoil.html

South Dakota—2008 Mineral Summary. South Dakota Department of Environment & Natural Resources, Minerals and Mining Program. Available from http://denr.sd.gov/des/mm/documents/2008stat.pdf

"State Energy Profiles: South Dakota." U.S. Energy Information Administration. Available from http://tonto.eia.doe.gov/state/state_energy_profiles.cfm?sid=SD

Strickland, Jennifer. "South Dakota: No Ducking Climate Change Impacts to Prairie Pothole Wetlands." U.S. Fish and Wildlife Service. June 2, 2011. Available from http://www.fws.gov/news/blog/index.cfm/2011/6/2/South-Dakota-No-Ducking-Climate-Change-Impacts-to-Prairie-Pothole-Wetlands

Sulzberger, A.G. "After Floods, Debate Over Missouri River Rolls On." *The New York Times.* July 23, 2011. Available from http://www.nytimes.com/2011/07/24/us/24missouri.html

U.S. Department of Agriculture, Natural Resources Conservation Service. "Farm Bill 2008 At a Glance: Wetlands Reserve Program." May 2008. Available from http://www.nrcs.usda.gov/programs/farmbill/2008/pdfs/WRP_At_A_Glance_062608final.pdf

"Water Resources of South Dakota." South Dakota Water Science Center. Available from http://sd.water.usgs.gov

Wind Transmission Construction Tax Refund (2010 HB 1060). South Dakota State Legislature. Available from http://legis.state.sd.us/sessions/2010/Bills/HB1060ENR.pdf

Tennessee

The state of Tennessee features beautiful landscapes, from its mountain regions to its rivers and valleys. However, the state, like many others, struggles with balancing the natural beauty of its lands with its energy policies and efforts to keep it pristine. Governor Bill Haslam proclaimed the week of April 10–16, 2011 as Natural Areas Week to celebrate the fortieth anniversary of the Tennessee Natural Areas Preservation Act. Tennessee protects eighty-one natural areas, comprising 120,000 acres (48,562 ha), across the state. Tennessee is located in the southeastern United States. It is the thirty-sixth largest state in terms of land area, but the seventeenth largest in population. The Appalachian Mountains are found in the eastern part of the state where a section of the famous Appalachian Trail winds through the Great Smoky Mountains National Park. Tennessee is bordered on the west by the Mississippi River. Tennessee's major industries include agriculture, manufacturing, and tourism.

Climate

Tennessee's varied topography leads to a wide variety of climatic conditions, though generally the state has a temperate climate. The warmest parts of the state are the Gulf Coastal Plain—which extends from the Tennessee River to the Mississippi River in the western portion of the state, the Central Basin—also known as the Nashville Basin, located in the center of the state, and the Sequatchie Valley in the eastern portion of the state. Growing seasons are the longest in these three areas at up to 235 days, while in the mountainous areas in the east the growing season can be as short as 130 days. Severe storms occur infrequently, the greatest rainfall occurs in the winter and early spring, and snowfall is more prevalent in the east. The early fall months, particularly September and October, are the driest.

As noted in the recent report "Climate Change Impacts in the Southeastern United States," the southeast region, of which Tennessee is a part, may be one of the most vulnerable regions to climate change. The changes could include increasing heat waves leading to deleterious impacts on human health and to more wildfires; damage to native trees; loss of agricultural crops, such as soybeans; and, a loss of wildlife. According to the Tennessee Wildlife Resources Agency, climate change could cause a decline in bird and mammal populations as well as aquatic species. In 1999, the Center for Electric Power at Tennessee Technological University published "Tennessee Greenhouse Gas Emissions Mitigation Strategies" which provided a number of policy options designed to limit the impact of climate change. However, the report has not been updated, nor does Tennessee have a statewide climate action plan in place. Mayors from seven cities in Tennessee have signed onto the U.S. Conference of Mayors Climate Protection agreement that commits the cities to meet or beat the targets set forth in the Kyoto Protocol for greenhouse gas emission reduction.

✿ Natural Resources, Water, and Agriculture

Natural Resources

The state of Tennessee's natural lands are rich in aesthetic beauty and biological diversity. Tennessee has fifteen state forests, covering half of the state. The largest of these forests is the Natchez Trace at over 36,000 acres (14,569 ha), or over 56 square miles (145 sq km). Hardwood forest types occupy the vast majority of the state's forest land, with oak-hickory as the dominant group. Of the 150 native tree species, the tulip poplar (the state tree), shortleaf pine, and black, and red oaks are commonly found in the eastern part of the state, while the gum maple, black walnut, sycamore, and cottonwood grow in the west. The majority of forest land in Tennessee is owned by nonindustrial private forest landowners, with the rest publicly administered by local, state, or federal agencies. In 2006, forest exports totaled about $881 million, including products like paper, wood and furniture, among

Barge on the Kentucky Dam canal lock on the Tenessee River.
© Visions of America, LLC/Alamy

others. The state combines agriculture and forestry into one industry, and in 2006 that industry pumped $79 billion into the Tennessee economy.

Tennessee boasts 53 state parks, where native mammals such as the raccoon (the state animal), white-tailed deer, black bear, bobcat, woodchuck, and red and gray foxes reside. There are over 250 bird species in the state, over fifty amphibian species, and over fifty reptile species as well. Hunting and fishing are big business in Tennessee, with over 490,000 hunting licenses sold in 2009. Popular big game animals include elk, turkey, and wild hog, and popular small game mammals include beaver, muskrat, and mink. Bobwhite quail, ruffed grouse, mourning dove, and mallard duck are the most common game birds. Of the 186 fish species in Tennessee's lakes and streams, catfish, bass, pike, and trout are among the leading game fish.

According to the U.S. Fish and Wildlife Service, there are eighty-six plant and animal species that are either threatened or endangered in Tennessee. Some of these animals include the gray bat, the Nashville Crayfish, and the Carolina northern flying squirrel. Some of the plant species include the Tennessee purple coneflower, the green pitcher-plant, and Price's Potato-bean.

Mining: A Top Producer of Zinc and Ball Clay

According to the Tennessee Department of Environment and Conservation, mining in Tennessee contributes $800 million annually in product value, and $8.8 billion total in direct and indirect economic impact. Energy minerals found in the state include coal, oil, natural gas, oil shales, and radioactive materials, of which only coal, oil, and natural gas are being recovered. Construction materials mined in the state include sandstone, marble, crushed stone, limestone, clay for making cement, sand, and gravel.

Two of the most economically important minerals in the state are zinc and ball clay. The second largest producer of zinc in the nation, mines and mills are found in the middle and eastern portions of the state. The mines in Smith County produce the highest-grade zinc concentrate in the world and are also one of the world's largest sources of germanium, a critical material that is used in fiber optics, infrared systems, and semiconductors. A plant in Clarksville accounts for 28 percent of total U.S. production, producing 105,000 tons of zinc per year. Tennessee is also the top producer of ball clay in the United States, which is used primarily for products such as dinnerware, floor and wall tile, and pottery. Ball clay accounts for about four percent ($29 million) of Tennessee's annual mineral production value.

Water

Tennessee possesses a total of 1,062 miles (1,709 km) of waterways—its three major rivers are the Tennessee, the Mississippi, and the Cumberland. The Tennessee River trisects the state, and the Mississippi River provides the state's western border with Missouri and Arkansas. Memphis is the fourth-largest inland port in the United States, situated on the Mississippi River. Most of the state is drained by the Mississippi River system. Waters from the Tennessee and the Cumberland flow into the Ohio River in Kentucky and join the Mississippi at Cairo, Illinois. Formed in Kentucky, the Tennessee flows southwestward through the Great Valley into northern Alabama, then curves back into the state and flows northward, back into Kentucky. Tributaries of the Tennessee include the Clinch, Duck, Elk, Hiwassee, and Sequatchie rivers. The Cumberland River rises in southeastern Kentucky, flows across central Tennessee, and then turns northward back into Kentucky. In the western part of the state, the Forked Deer and Wolf rivers are among those flowing into the Mississippi.

The Tennessee Valley Authority (TVA), a federally operated energy corporation, operates nineteen hydroelectric dams in the state of Tennessee and provides management services, including flood controls, for thirty-two reservoirs and large portions of the Tennessee River system. The Kentucky Reservoir (shared with the state of Kentucky) was created by the 8,422-foot-long TVA Kentucky Dam and is the largest reservoir in the eastern United States. Since its opening in 1945, the filling of the reservoir opened the Tennessee River for year-round navigation and provided a link between the Tennessee Valley and the U.S. Inland Waterway System.

More than 72 percent of the state's major rivers and reservoirs are open to commercial fishing, but the industry is small and declining. According to the 2006–2012 strategic plan from the Tennessee Wildlife Resources Agency, sales of commercial fishing license declined by about 5 percent annually from 1994 to 2004 and were projected to decline by 12 percent annually from 2005 through 2012, as aging fishermen retire and

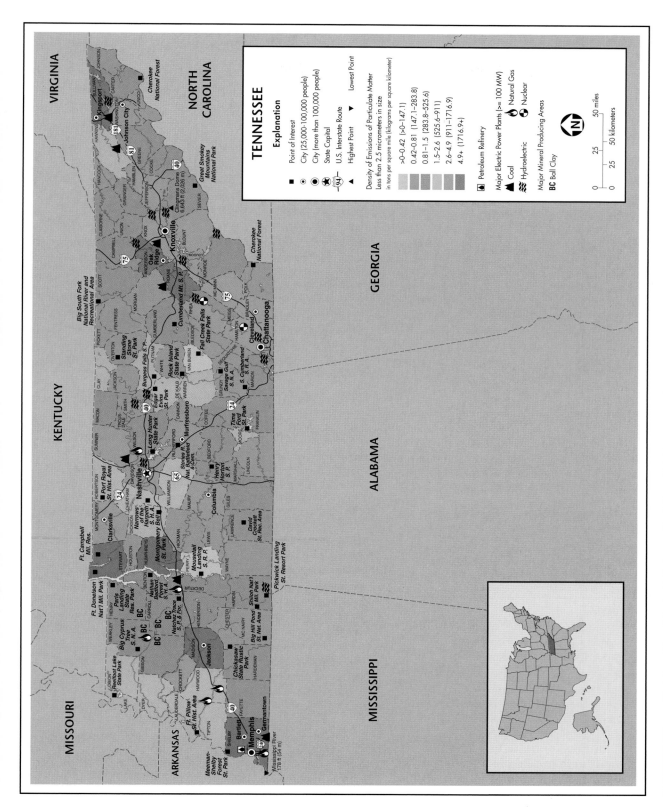

SOURCES: "County Emissions Map: Criteria Air Pollutants." *AirData*. U.S. Environmental Protection Agency. Available from http://www.epa.gov/air/data/geosel.html; *Energy Maps*. U.S. Energy Information Administration. Available from http://www.eia.gov/state; *Highest and Lowest Elevations*. U.S. Geological Survey. Available from http:// egsc.usgs.gov/isb/pubs/booklets/elvadist/elvadist.html#Highest; *2007 Minerals Yearbook*. U.S. Geological Survey. Available from http://minerals.usgs.gov/minerals/pubs/ state. © 2011 Cengage Learning.

Tennessee State Profile

Physical Characteristics

Land area	41,235 square miles (106,798 sq km)
Inland water area	910 square miles (2,357 sq km)
Coastal area	NA
Highest point	Clingmans Dome 6,643 feet (2,025 m)
National Forest System lands (2010)	718,000 acres (291,000 ha)
State parks (2011)	53

Energy Statistics

Total energy production (2009)	480 trillion Btu
State ranking in total energy production (2009)	29
Renewable energy net generation total (2009)	11.2 million megawatt hours
Hydroelectric energy generation (2009)	10.2 million megawatt hours
Biomass energy generation (2009)	36,000 megawatt hours
Wind energy generation (2009)	52,000 megawatt hours
Wood and derived fuel energy generation (2009)	862,000 megawatt hours
Crude oil reserves (2009)	NA
Natural gas reserves (2009)	NA
Natural gas liquids (2008)	NA

Pollution Statistics

Carbon output (2005)	120.1 million tons of CO_2 (108.9 million t)
Superfund sites (2008)	14
Particulate matter (less than 2.5 micrometers) emissions (2002)	36,022 tons per year (32,678 t/yr)
Toxic chemical releases (2009)	89.2 million pounds (40.5 million kg)
Generated hazardous waste (2009)	78,600 tons (71,300 t)

SOURCES: AirData. U.S. Environmental Protection Agency. Available from http://www.epa.gov/air/data; *Energy Maps, Facts, and Data of the U.S. States.* U.S. Energy Information Administration. Available from http://www.eia.gov/state; *The 2012 Statistical Abstract.* U.S. Census Bureau. Available from http://www.census.gov/compendia/statab; *United States Energy Usage.* eRedux. Available from http://www.eredux.net/states.

© 2011 Cengage Learning.

the number of new recruits each year has diminished. Nearly 46 percent of the annual commercial harvest comes from the Kentucky Reservoir. For 2005, the wholesale value of the commercial harvest was estimated at $2.7 million, with catfish and buffalo fish the most valuable catches. However, another lucrative catch—paddlefish, which is harvested for its eggs to be sold as caviar— ran into federal roadblocks in 2009. The U.S. Fish & Wildlife Service denied commercial anglers there the ability to export paddlefish and its products (the caviar) that came from Kentucky Lake outside the United States. The federal agency said commercial harvests there were not adhering to international export laws regarding sustainable harvests. About 63 percent of all caviar is

harvested in Tennessee, according to the U.S. Fish & Wildlife Service. The state sponsors ten fish hatcheries to stock the state's waterways. Five of these are dedicated to coldwater trout production. The five warmwater/coolwater facilities produce species that include crappie, striped bass, walleye, sauger, catfish, and sunfish.

Agriculture

Tennessee has a total of 78,300 farms across 10.9 million acres. As of 2010, the state ranked fourth in the United States in tobacco production, tenth in cotton, and twelfth in forage—land used for all hay, haylage, and grass silage. When it comes to livestock, Tennessee ranked sixth in the nation for horses and ponies.

According to the Southern Organic Resource Guide, there are a total of 14 certified organic farming operations in Tennessee, totaling over 600 acres of crops that include wheat, hay and silage, vegetables, fruit, and herbs. As of 2008, Tennessee had 125 heads of certified organic livestock. Farmer's markets in Memphis, Jackson, Nashville, Chattanooga and Knoxville are open year-round, and the Tennessee Department of Agriculture provides listings of even more markets that provide residents with organic products.

Energy

Tennessee leads the nation in per capita residential electricity consumption, with more than 60 percent of households using electricity as their primary source of energy for home heating. The Tennessee Valley Authority (TVA) is responsible for more than 90 percent of the state's electricity-generating capacity and serves nearly the entire state. Within the state of Tennessee, the TVA operates seven coal-fired power plants, two nuclear plants, six combustion turbine sites, and nineteen hydroelectric dams, with a total generating capacity of more than 19,655 megawatts. Approximately 50 percent of the electricity produced in the TVA region comes from coal-fired power plants. These coal plants rely mainly on coal shipped from other states, which include Wyoming, Illinois, Colorado, Kentucky, West Virginia, and Virginia.

Crude oil is also shipped in from out of state via the Capline pipeline, which ships the oil to the state's only refinery (Premcor Refining Group, Inc.) in Memphis. Tennessee also receives petroleum products from the Colonial and Plantation pipelines.

There are two nuclear plants in the southeastern part of the state—the Sequoyah and the Watts Bar Nuclear Plant—both near Chattanooga. The Watts Bar Nuclear Unit 1 came online in 1996, and was the last new reactor to do so in the United States. Construction on the Watts Bar Nuclear Unit 2 was temporarily suspended in 1985 as TVA was required to submit a more detailed Nuclear Performance Plan (NPP) to address corporate and

Approximately 50 percent of the electricity produced in the TVA region comes from coal-fired power plants such as this one located on the Clinch River in Tennessee. © *David R. Frazier Photolibrary, Inc./Alamy*

near Obion, online since 2008, produces 110 million gallons (416,395,320 l) per year, bringing the state's total production capacity to 177 million gallons (670,017,924 l) of ethanol per year. There are 34 public-access ethanol fueling stations in the state, which make up 1.5 percent of the U.S. total.

The Tennessee and Cumberland River systems make the state of Tennessee a major hub of hydroelectric power and one of the top hydroelectric power producers east of the Rocky Mountains, providing 12 percent of total electricity production. TVA operates nineteen hydroelectric dams within the state and one pumped-storage hydroelectric plant at Raccoon Mountain. The Kentucky Dam, at 8,422 feet (2,567 m) long and 206 feet (63 m) high, is the longest dam on the Tennessee River. The accompanying hydroelectric facility consists of five units with a capacity of 199 megawatts of electricity. The Raccoon Mountain Pumped Storage Plant consists of four generating units with a capacity of 1,532 megawatts.

Other renewable sources including wood, wood waste, solar, and wind, contribute minimally to the state's electricity production. TVA operates fourteen solar facilities in the state, with the largest being the 85-kilowatt facility at Finley Stadium in Chattanooga. TVA also operates an 18-turbine wind farm on Buffalo Mountain with a 24-megawatt capacity and an 8-megawatt methane gas generator at the Memphis wastewater treatment plant.

As of 2011, the state of Tennessee does not have a Renewable Portfolio Standard. However, in March 2011, TVA presented a new integrated resource plan that calls for an increase in the capacity for renewable and clean energy resources throughout the TVA system into 2029.

site-specific issues. Construction on Unit 2 resumed in 2007, with a construction permit completion date of March 31, 2013. The unit will add more than 1,100 megawatts of nuclear generating capacity to the grid. A little more than 34 percent of the electricity generated in the state is from nuclear power.

Considerable potential for greater and cost-effective energy efficiency exists in the state, according to *Energy Efficiency in the South*, a report prepared by the Georgia Institute of Technology and Duke University. The report lists high potential in Tennessee when it comes to reducing energy consumption and costs by using heat pump water heaters, geothermal heat pumps, and super boilers. Costs could be reduced from 44 to 72 percent by the implementation of these technologies.

Renewable Energy Sources: A Leader in Ethanol and Hydroelectric Production

Tennessee has two operating ethanol plants, making it the second-highest state in ethanol production in the southern United States after Texas. The ethanol plant

Energy Research

Once dedicated primarily to the pilot-scale production and separation of plutonium for the World War II-era Manhattan Project, the Oak Ridge National Laboratory (ORNL) is now a major center for research and development in a wide variety of fields. The energy science division of ORNL includes programs on bioenergy, energy efficiency and electricity technologies, renewable energy, and electricity delivery technologies, among others. A recent project involved the creation of a 3-D nanocone-based solar cell platform that can boost the light-to-power conversion efficiency of photovoltaics by nearly 80 percent. This technology can eventually be used to create solar cells at lower costs. Researchers at ORNL are also working on projects to develop low-cost, net-zero energy housing by 2020 and zero-energy commercial buildings by 2025. ORNL is managed by UT-Battelle, a partnership between the University of Tennessee and Battelle (a non-profit charitable trust).

❧ Green Business, Green Building, Green Jobs

Green Business: A Growing Hub for Solar Power

The state of Tennessee offers a number of grants, loans, and tax credits for businesses that take steps to go green. The Small Business Energy Loan provides low-interest loans to companies with fewer than 300 employees to help upgrade the level of energy efficiency in their buildings, plants, and manufacturing processes. The Tennessee Clean Energy Technology Grant Program offers grants to businesses of any size installing solar electric generating equipment, wind energy systems, or hydrogen fuel cells. The state also has a number of tax credits for green energy supply chain manufacturers in the areas of carbon charges, pollution control equipment.

State incentives have played a large role in bringing green business to Tennessee. The Hemlock Semiconductor plant in Clarksville broke ground in 2009, with a completion date set for 2012. The plant will create approximately 500 full-time jobs producing polysilicon, the base material for solar panels. The Germany-based Wacker Chemical plant near Chattanooga has yet to break ground, but acquired the land necessary for the project in 2009, and will also create another 500 jobs for the state producing hyperpure polycrystalline silicon. Both of these facilities will cost approximately $1 billion dollars each to complete. Tennessee (Memphis) is already host to Sharp Electronics, a major producer of solar modules. Since 2003 the manufacturing facility has turned out more than 2 million modules capable of powering more than 65,000 average-sized homes.

To push the solar industry forward, the state received and invested $62.4 million in funds from the State Energy Program of the American Recovery and Reinvestment Act to launch its Volunteer State Solar Initiative. This initiative represents a comprehensive solar energy and economic development program focused on job creation, education, research, and renewable energy production within the state.

The program consists of two branches, the Tennessee Solar Institute (TSI) and the West Tennessee Solar Farm. TSI involves programs offered through the University of Tennessee and the Oak Ridge National Laboratory that are designed to bring together scientists, educators, students, policy makers, and industry partners for collaborative efforts toward advancing solar energy production. The West Tennessee Solar Farm in Haywood County is a five-megawatt demonstration facility designed to serve as an educational site, a research facility, and a showcase for Tennessee-made solar products and components. The electricity generated at the facility will be distributed under purchase agreements with Tennessee Valley Authority and Chickasaw Electric Cooperative.

Green Building

In 2008, Senate Bill 116 was enacted, which made the use of the 2003 International Energy Conservation Code (IECC) mandatory for any new residential building construction as of January 1, 2009. The legislation also encourages builders of new residential and commercial construction to voluntarily use the 2006 IECC energy conservation standards for new construction. However, in 2009, Senate Bill 2300 granted the State Fire Marshal authority to select the specific ICC code edition to be implemented.

On the municipal level, Memphis Light, Gas, and Water Division (MLGW), a three-service public utility company in the area, offers the EcoBUILD Program. This voluntary program creates energy and environmental awareness through the promotion and use of energy-efficient and environmentally-friendly technology, materials, and techniques in new home construction. Homes built using EcoBUILD save on average 34 percent in electricity and 54 percent in natural gas. EcoBUILD standards include the use of recycled materials, low e-windows to minimize heat gain and reduce UV damage, radiant barrier to reduce heat gain through the roof, hard sheet metal ductwork to reduce duct leakage, and the use of native or adapted plants to reduce landscape watering.

Green Jobs: Increasing Educational Opportunities

According to the 2008 report from the Tennessee Department of Labor and Workforce Development (TDLWD), *Growing Green: The Potential for Green Job Growth in Tennessee*, the most promising areas for green job growth in the state were biomass, geothermal heat pumps, hydropower, solar photovoltaic, wind, and energy efficiency. Estimates at the time of the report were that with accelerated investment efforts, the state could gain 4,233 jobs in wind and 400 in solar by 2015. Additionally, an estimated 4,000 jobs in biofuels could be created in rural counties. The report also suggested that an investment of $1.9 billion in the development of green technologies could add more than 40,000 jobs.

The TDLWD followed up this report by conducting a green jobs survey throughout 2010. The results published in *Tennessee's Green Jobs Report* (May 2011) indicate that there were 43,804 green jobs throughout the state in 2010. A green job was defined as one in which an individual spent 50 percent or more of his or her time in one or more of the green economic activities also defined by the report. For 2010, there were also an estimated 3,645 vacancies in green jobs across the state. Construction and manufacturing showed the highest percentages of jobs, at 22 percent each. Most of these jobs involved energy efficiency activities.

The green economy is expected to grow even more through the development of a number of investment partnerships. In 2010, the state partnered with Nissan to develop a charging network for its plug-in electric vehicles. Nissan North America is headquartered in Tennessee and will be manufacturing the Nissan LEAF zero-emission vehicle beginning in 2012. In May 2010, construction began on Nissan's manufacturing facility in Smyrna, which will produce the lithium-ion batteries needed for the Nissan LEAF. In Chattanooga on May 24, 2011, Volkswagen inaugurated a new $1 billion assembly plant, where high fuel-efficiency cars designed specifically for the North American market will be manufactured.

Two professors from the Business & Economic Research Center at Middle Tennessee State University released a report in 2011 to measure the impact of six green projects in the works in Tennessee. Those projects were the Hemlock Conductor, Wacker Chemie AG, Volkswagen, Nissan LEAF and storage battery manufacturing, Tennessee Solar Institute and West Tennessee Solar Farm, and eTec Battery Charging Stations. The report showed in the construction phase of the projects, the green investment will total more than $5.5 billion by 2014, with a resulting 5,674 green jobs in 2011. Projecting to the operations phase of the projects, the professors predict more than 16,000 permanent jobs, more than 10,000 of which will be green jobs. The report estimates green manufacturing jobs as a part of these projects will account for 1.5 percent of the state's total manufacturing jobs.

In July 2010, Southwest Tennessee Community College (STCC) announced it was partnering with Memphis Bioworks Foundation to create a green training program. The Memphis Bioworks Foundation received a $2.9 million Energy Training Partnership from the Department of Labor for the program, of which STCC will receive $1.4 million. Some of the funds will be used to purchase energy-related equipment that will be used to enhance green strategies in the classroom. STCC is the principal training partner in a group that also includes Dyersburg State Community College, Jackson State Community College, the University of Memphis BEST Program, and Mid-South Community College. The training program is aimed toward dislocated and unemployed workers in West Tennessee, initially targeting current workers who need upgraded training. The project will have an extensive network of employers, labor representatives, educators, and community based organizations available for students. Training should be available in energy-efficiency building, construction and retrofit, renewable electric power, and manufacturers producing sustainable products. In the eastern part of the state, Pellissippi State Community College was awarded the 2010 Governor's Environmental Stewardship Award for Higher Education in part because of its extensive number of green jobs curriculum offerings.

The Tennessee Valley Authority Coal Ash Spill

On December 22, 2008, an earthen containment wall burst at the Tennessee Valley Authority (TVA) Kingston Fossil Fuel Plant in Roane County, releasing more than 1.1 billion gallons of toxic coal ash slurry into the nearby Emory and Clinch Rivers and covering over 300 acres (121 ha) of land. Three homes were destroyed and 42 were damaged, roads were washed out, electrical power was disrupted, a natural gas line was ruptured, and the sludge was up to 6-feet (2 m) deep in some areas. An entire neighborhood near the plant had to be evacuated.

Coal ash slurry is a mixture of water and fly ash, which is one of the residues generated when coal is burned and is captured in the chimneys of coal-fired power plants. The toxic chemicals that are found in fly ash can vary based upon the makeup of the coal bed it comes from. The chemicals found in the fly ash involved in the spill were arsenic, thallium, antimony, lead, cadmium, mercury, and boron. Arsenic has been known to cause increased lung cancer mortality in those exposed. Hundreds of fish were found dead downstream from the plant after the spill, though there was some debate at the time if their deaths were caused by the spill or the cold temperatures.

In early January 2009, an environmental advocacy group's independent tests revealed levels of arsenic, lead, chromium and other metals 2 to 300 times higher than drinking water standards in the Emory River near the site of the spill. The results were much higher than TVA's initial tests, which made citizens concerned that TVA was initially not being transparent with their test results.

Also in January 2009, TVA acknowledged that the plant's containment ponds had leaked twice before in the previous five years, and that repairs had been made with inexpensive patches rather than a more extensive and adequate repair. The seepages had occurred in 2003 and 2005, and could have possibly contributed to the disaster in 2008, though they occurred in different areas from where the containment wall burst. TVA has continued to claim that a combination of 12°F-temperatures (−11°C) combined with 6 inches (15 cm) of rain in ten days were factors that caused the containment wall to breach, though environmentalist groups have argued that the spill was still preventable. As a result, the Senate Environment and Public Works Committee started calling for better oversight of TVA's plants and to declare coal ash a hazardous waste. They promised to press for new regulations because of the disaster and apologized for not overseeing TVA's operations more thoroughly in the past.

As a result of the Senate's call to action, the Obama administration promised to propose new regulations governing coal combustion waste. In June 2010, the EPA presented a proposal with two options. The first was a recommendation to designate coal-ash as hazardous waste under the federal Resource Conservation and Recovery Act, a move that would require federal regulation and oversight of companies handling the material. A second option would keep the substance listed as nonhazardous, but provide stricter storage guidelines under local oversight. These proposals have inspired quite a bit of controversy in Congress. In an April 2011 hearing before the U.S. House, the primary speakers argued strongly against the idea of placing coal combustion waste under EPA regulations for hazardous substances, claiming that such a designation would ultimately result in a loss of jobs and increased utility costs. They also argued that the designation could have an adverse affect on companies that produce safe products made from coal ash, including wallboard and concrete.

By April of 2009, TVA had spent more than $20 million buying up properties tainted by the coal ash. This amount was not included in the original estimate that it would take $825 million to completely clean up the spill. Such property purchases represented settlements, and residents accepting the offer agreed not to sue the agency later. At that time, six property owners had turned down the offer, and may have joined one of several federal lawsuits against it. TVA ended up buying out more than 170 property owners, spending over $40.2 million. TVA then announced in September of that year that it would spend $43 million in economic development projects in Roane County, in order to make up for the lack of tourism and devaluation of property that the coal ash spill had caused. The amount allows for $10 million a year over the course of four years—the current estimated amount of time it will take to completely clean up the coal ash. Current estimates are that the spill will take $1.2 billion to clean up, including the $43 million set aside for economic development. In June of 2010, TVA was hit with penalties totaling $11.5 million for the spill, adding to those costs.

Long-term health effects to residents in the area of the coal ash spill have yet to be determined. Immediately after the spill, some residents reported nosebleeds and burning throat sensations. The Tennessee Department of Health released a Public Health Assessment in 2009, reporting that while it is unlikely that someone would be harmed by touching the coal ash, it may cause skin irritation. The report also stated that while drinking water and groundwater resources were not affected, it was unsafe to use the Emory River at the site of the spill. Health effects from breathing the ash and dust from the spill were inconclusive in the report, though it was mentioned that it could have aggravated symptoms in those with respiratory conditions or pre-existing heart conditions. Complaints of respiratory symptoms were widespread in the area, despite the report's inconclusive results. The one effect that the report could confirm, however, was that the spill caused elevated levels of stress and anxiety in residents living near the site—a result that could only be expected.

According to TVA, the first phase of cleanup concluded with the reopening of the Emory River May 29, 2010. The company, under the oversight of the U.S. Environmental Protection Agency and the Tennessee Department of Environment and Conservation, removed more than 3.5 million cubic yards (2.6 cubic m) of ash and sediment from the river. TVA officials say they are continuing to monitor air and water quality, and have "strengthened internal accountabilities and organizational effectiveness to reduce the likelihood of such events in the future."

Within the first year after the spill, there were numerous lawsuits filed against TVA for damages. Many of these suits have been consolidated, with a bench trial occurring in September 2011, before U.S. District Judge Thomas Varlan in Knoxville. Varlan has already dismissed those cases that specifically seek punitive damages. During the trial, the inspector general for the TVA said the company had ignored internal reports about the danger of a potential spill as early as 1985, as well as the guidance of several consultants. TVA's lawyers said the spill caused no lasting damage to residents or the environment. The trial concluded in October and Judge Varlan is expected to make a ruling in early 2012. Meanwhile, numerous other property owners are looking to file lawsuits before the end of the year.

Meanwhile, cleanup efforts are ongoing, with TVA's own cleanup plan expected to continue through 2014. It looks as if it will be some time before the long-term effects of the spill on human health and the environment will ultimately be known, though residents and experts will agree that the area will likely never be the same again.

BIBLIOGRAPHY

Books

Hopkins, Bruce. *The Smithsonian Guides to Natural America: Central Appalachia–West Virginia, Kentucky, Tennessee.* Washington, DC: Smithsonian Books, 1996.

Huso, Deborah. *Great Smoky Mountains National Park.* Berkeley, CA: Avalon Travel Publications, 2011.

Nash, Steve. *Blue Ridge 2020: An Owner's Manual.* Chapel Hill: University of North Carolina Press, 1999.

Web Sites

Annual Workforce Report 2010. Tennessee Department of Labor and Workforce Development. Available from http://www.tn.gov/labor-wfd/Publications/EmploymentSecurity/AnnualWorkforceReport2010.pdf

Arik, Murat, and Penn, David. "Green Jobs In Tennessee: Economic Impact of Selected Green Investments." Business of Economic Research Center, Middle Tennessee State University. June 2011. Available from http://www.sourcetn.org/admin/gsipub/htmlarea/uploads/TNGreenInvestmentStudy.pdf

Broder, John M. "Plant That Spilled Coal Ash Had Earlier Leak Problems." *The New York Times.* Available from http://www.nytimes.com/2009/01/09/us/09coal.html?fta=y

Brown, Marilyn, et.al. "State Profiles of Energy Efficiency Opportunities in the South: Tennessee." *Energy Efficiency in the South.* Georgia Institute of Technology and Duke University. Available from http://www.seealliance.org/se_efficiency_study/tennessee_efficiency_in_the_south.pdf

"The Clean Energy Economy: Tennessee." The Pew Charitable Trusts. Available from http://www.pewcenteronthestates.org/uploadedFiles/wwwpewcenteronthestatesorg/Fact_Sheets/Clean_Economy_Factsheet_Tennessee.pdf

"Climate Change and Potential Impacts to Wildlife in Tennessee: An Update to Tennessee's State Wildlife Action Plan." Tennessee Wildlife Resources Agency. Available from http://www.state.tn.us/twra/pdfs/tnclimatechange.pdf

"Climate Change Impacts in the Southeastern United States." Stratus Consulting. Available from http://www.tennessean.com/assets/pdf/DN161153721.PDF

"Climate Data for Tennessee." Office of the State Climatologist. University of Tennessee Knoxville. Available from http://climate.tennessee.edu/climate_data.html

Dewan, Shaila. "Administration Plans New Regulations on Coal-Ash Ponds." *The New York Times.* Available from http://www.nytimes.com/2009/03/08/us/politics/08ash.html?fta=y

Dewan, Shaila. "Metal Levels Found High in Tributary After Spill." *The New York Times.* Available from http://www.nytimes.com/2009/01/02/us/02sludge.html?fta=y

Dewan, Shaila. "T.V.A. to Pay $43 Million on Projects in Spill Area." *The New York Times.* Available from http://www.nytimes.com/2009/09/15/us/15ash.html?fta=y

"EcoBUILD." Memphis Light, Gas, and Water Division (MLGW). Available from http://www.mlgw.com/SubView.php?key=about_ecobuild

"Economic Impacts of Tennessee Agriculture & Forestry." Tennessee Department of Agriculture.

Available from http://www.tn.gov/agriculture/general/impact.shtml

"Energy Grants, Loans and Tax Incentives." Tennessee Department of Economic and Community Development. Available from http://www.tennessee.gov/ecd/CD_energy_grantloans.html

"EPA Approves TVA's $268M Cleanup Plan for Coal-Ash Spill." Sustainable Business.com. Available from http://www.sustainablebusiness.com/index.cfm/go/news.display/id/20345

"Export Permits to be Denied For Wild Paddlefish Products From Tennessee's Kentucky Lake." U.S. Fish & Wildlife Service. June 18, 2009. Available from http://www.fws.gov/news/NewsReleases/showNews.cfm?newsId=F69496C5-AA58-9830-0F1283385C9565A4

"Fact Sheet: Kingston Ash Recovery Project." Tennessee Valley Authority. June 6, 2011. Available from http://www.tva.gov/kingston/pdf/Kingston%20Ash%20Recovery%20Project%20Fact%20Sheet%20Final%2006-06-2011.pdf

"Forestry Division." Tennessee Department of Agriculture. Available from http://www.state.tn.us/agriculture/forestry/

"Growing Green: The Potential for Green Job Growth in Tennessee." Tennessee Department of Labor and Workforce Development. Available from http://www.state.tn.us/labor-wfd/Publications/EmploymentSecurity/GrowingGreenInTN2008.pdf

Hemlock Semiconductor. Available from http://www.hscpoly.com/default.aspx?bhcp=1

Integrated Resource Plan: TVA's Environmental & Energy Future. Tennessee Valley Authority. Available from http://www.tva.gov/environment/reports/irp/pdf/Final_IRP_complete.pdf

"Kingston Recovery." Tennessee Valley Authority. Available from http://www.tva.com/kingston/index.htm

Oak Ridge National Laboratory. Available from http://www.ornl.gov

Poovey, Bill. "TVA Inspector General Testifies At Coal Ash Trial." *Forbes.* September 23, 2011. Available from http://www.forbes.com/feeds/ap/2011/09/23/business-us-tva-coal-ash-tennessee_8696931.html

"Public Comment Draft TVA Coal Ash Release Public Health Assessment." Tennessee Department of Health. Available from http://health.state.tn.us/Environmental/PDFs/pha-fs-TVA-coalash-120809.pdf

"Region 4: TVA Kingston Fossil Plant Fly Ash Release." U.S. Environmental Protection Agency. Available from http://epa.gov/region4/kingston/index.html

Simms, Richard. "Hunting License Sales Increase in 2009." *The Chattanoogan.* Available from http://www.chattanoogan.com/articles/article_168226.asp

"Southwest Tennessee Community College to train students for green jobs." *Memphis Business Journal.* Available from http://memphis.bizjournals.com/memphis/stories/2010/07/12/daily1.html

"Species Reports: Listings and occurrences for Tennessee." U.S. Fish and Wildlife Service. Available from http://ecos.fws.gov/tess_public/pub/stateListingAndOccurrenceIndividual.jsp?state=TN&s8fid=112761032792&s8fid=112762573902&s8fid=24012798954163

"Sustainable mobility comes to United States with dedication of Nissan LEAF production site." Nissan News: Technology. Available from http://www.nissanusa.com/leaf-electric-car/news/technology/sustainable_mobility_comes_to_united_states#/leaf-electric-car/news/technology/sustainable_mobility_comes_to_united_states

"Tennessee: Fine Levied for Coal Ash Spill." *The New York Times.* Available from http://www.nytimes.com/2010/06/15/us/15brfs-tennessee.html?ref=coal

"Tennessee Greenhouse Gas Emissions Mitigations Strategies." Center for Electric Power, Tennessee Technological University. Available from http://www.tennessee.gov/ecd/pdf/greenhouse/entiredocument.pdf

"Tennessee Organic Statistics." Southern Organic Resource Guide. Available from http://www.attra.ncat.org/sorg/tn/#stats

Tennessee Solar Institute. Available from http://solar.tennessee.edu

"Tennessee State Energy Code for Buildings." Tennessee Incentives/Policies for Renewables and Efficiency. Available from http://www.dsireusa.org/incentives/incentive.cfm?Incentive_Code=TN03R&re=1&ee=1

"Tennessee State Parks." Tennessee Department of Environment and Conservation. Available from http://tn.gov/environment/parks/

Tennessee Natural Areas Week. Available from http://tn.gov/environment/na/events/seasonal.shtml

Tennessee Valley Authority. Available from http://www.tva.com

Tennessee Wildlife Resources Agency 2006–2012 Strategic Plan. Available from http://www.state.tn.us/twra/pdfs/StratPlan06-12.pdf

Tennessee's Green Jobs Report. Tennessee Department of Labor and Workforce Development. Available from http://www.sourcetn.org/admin/gsipub/htmlarea/uploads/GreenJobsReport2011.pdf

"Tennessee's Mineral Industry." Tennessee Department of Environment and Conservation. Available from http://tn.gov/environment/tdg/mineralind.shtml

Theobald, Bill. "House GOP pushes different coal ash debate." *The Tennessean.* May 1, 2011. Available from http://www.tennessean.com/article/20110501/COLUMNIST0106/305010110/Bill-Theobald-House-GOP-pushes-different-coal-ash-debate

"2009 State Agricultural Overview: Tennessee." United States Department of Agriculture. Available from http://www.nass.usda.gov/Statistics_by_State/Ag_Overview/AgOverview_TN.pdf

"Utility Rejects Many Requests as It Buys Land Tainted by Tennessee Coal-Ash Spill." *The New York Times.* Available from http://www.nytimes.com/2009/04/12/us/12spill.html?fta=y

"Wacker Tennessee." Wacker Chemie AG. Available from http://www.wacker.com/cms/en/regions/usa/tennessee/tennessee.jsp

West Tennessee Solar Farm. Available from http://solarfarm.tennessee.edu

Woods, Jeff. "Tennessee captures more green business." *Nashville City Paper.* Available from http://nashvillecitypaper.com/print/495994

Texas

While the Lone Star state has a reputation for its oil fields and cattle ranches, there are a surprising number of alternative resources that offer great potential in the growth of green industries. Texas is ranked first in the nation for the production of wind energy and is home to the largest wind power facility in the world. Furthermore, several state and private organizations are at work to encourage research and development in other alternative energy sources, including solar power and biomass, with the state's largest solar farm opening in late 2010, and two new bills introduced in the state legislature to boost the cause of solar energy in 2011. Texas was one of the first states to sponsor an organic certification program and is the second-largest agricultural producer in the nation.

Forging ahead, however, the state needs to address the serious challenge of providing enough water resources to supply the increasing demands of a growing population. The state may also face some difficulties associated with its status as one the largest producers and consumers of fossil fuels, which leaves the state with the highest carbon dioxide and sulfur dioxide emission rates in the country.

Average temperatures and precipitation vary widely from city to city across the state; but in general, the eastern coastal regions enjoy a maritime climate, while a more continental climate is found on the plains in the west. Annual rainfall varies widely—from 10 to 70 inches (25–178 cm)—across the state. Summer and winter are the two basic seasons, with hot summers stretching from April through October and winters stretching from November through March.

Extreme Weather Events Are Common

Dramatic weather disasters are not uncommon in Texas. Northcentral Texas experiences severe thunderstorms, which can be accompanied by an atmospheric condition known as convective turbulence. Microbursts, powerful convective turbulence, can cause catastrophic results for airplane flight. One example is the incident on August 2, 1985, when a Delta Air Lines flight landing a Dallas/Fort Worth International Airport was struck by a microburst, which slammed the airplane into the ground short of the runway. Of the 166 people on board, only 30 survived.

September and October mark the major hurricane season for the Gulf Coast region. In August 2005, Hurricane Katrina devastated the coastal regions of Louisiana and damaged Texas-operated oil production sites in the Gulf of Mexico. The state also lies in the area known as Tornado Alley, which stretches across the U.S. central plains. One of the worst tornado events occurred September 19–23, 1967, when 115 tornadoes were reported in the wake of Hurricane Beulah.

Periodic flooding and periods of drought are also common, particularly in the south and central regions of the state. During the 1950s, all but 10 of the state's 254 counties were declared disaster areas by the federal government due to a seven-year drought. The drought of 2007–09 cost the state more than $3.6 billion in loss of crops and livestock. The water situation continued to be a concern, as Texas experienced its hottest summer in the country's history in 2011, resulting in the driest 11-month span since records started being kept.

Texas Challenges the EPA

As the federal government has debated the actions and initiatives necessary to mitigate the effects of climate change, officials from the state of Texas have initiated a number of legal suits against the U.S. EPA to protest what they deem to be inappropriate federal control over state affairs. In February 2010, Governor Rick Perry and State Attorney General Greg Abbott issued a joint statement on their intent to challenge the U.S. Environmental Protection Agency's December 2009 report that found carbon dioxide emissions and other pollutants to be a cause of global warming. The report laid the groundwork for the development of new federal laws aimed at reducing and regulating greenhouse gas emissions throughout the country. In their joint statement, Perry and Abbott have argued that the EPA findings are based on incomplete and biased research data. While pointing out the significant steps that the state has already taken voluntarily toward the reduction of greenhouse gas emissions and the search for alternative energy sources, the governor argued that federal mandates concerning greenhouse gas emissions would have a serious negative impact on the state's economy.

As the year progressed and it became clear that the U.S government expected to move forward with the nationwide implementation of new regulations concerning greenhouse gas emissions, Texas responded with an additional suit. In an August 2010 petition filed with the U.S. District Circuit Court of Appeals for the District of Columbia, Governor Perry specifically attacked the proposed "tailoring rule," which is designed to limit greenhouse gas permits for some of the largest emitters. Perry stated that the rule is "arbitrary and capricious and is contrary to the Clean Air Act." At the same time, officials from the Texas Commission on Environmental Quality (TCEQ) issued a letter to the EPA, claiming that the state would not comply with any federal mandates concerning changes in the permitting process for greenhouse gas emissions.

This letter served to address a second battle with the EPA over its concerns for the state's flexible permitting program, which was implemented in Texas in 1994 and has been challenged by the EPA since about that time. The flex permit, which applies to some of the largest industrial plants in the state, regulates the overall emissions from a facility, rather than the pollution that comes from each individual unit within the facility. The EPA claims that the flex program does not fulfill the requirements of the Clean Air Act and threatened to override Texas policy by issuing greenhouse gas permits directly to Texas industries if the state would not comply.

Portions of the federal law went into effect as scheduled on January 2, 2011. The state of Texas refused to comply and filed for an immediate stay of action to keep the EPA from issuing permits without regard for Texas law, claiming that by doing so, the EPA would overstep its authority. The stay was denied. In response to the state's refusal to comply, the EPA imposed a federal implementation plan enforcing the authority of the agency over the permitting process in Texas. In February 2011 the state of Wyoming and the National Mining Association, as well as a handful of power companies, joined the suit, saying the EPA did not give them enough time to meet new requirements before taking over the permitting process.

A test of Texan resolve came on January 26, 2011, as the TCEQ met to approve an air-quality permit for the proposed Las Brisas coal-fired power plant in Corpus Christi. Earlier in the month, the EPA sent a letter to the TCEQ requesting that they deny the permit application

until the agency and the state had resolved their various issues and concerns. The Texas administrative law panel also recommended that the permit be denied. While the approval of the air-quality permit is significant, under federal law the plant is required to obtain a greenhouse gas emissions permit from the EPA.

The EPA then took the unusual step of working directly with flexible permit companies in Texas to come to a mutual agreement on permitting. In July 2011, the EPA announced that all flexible permit companies had agreed to apply for approved air permits at the federal level. In a statement released in July 2011, the EPA recognized several large businesses for being far ahead in the permitting process, including BP Products North America, Conoco Phillips Company, Exxon Mobil Corporation, and Marathon Petroleum Company LP. Despite the resolution at the federal level between regulators and the companies, Texas leaders remain critical of the EPA and continued to pursue the lawsuit challenging the federal agency's take on the flexible permitting process.

Texas still had a lawsuit pending against the EPA in regards to the imposition of the federal implementation plan, which the state claims is a violation of federal authority. That case was transferred from the Fifth Circuit Court of Appeals in New Orleans to the U.S. Court of Appeals for the District of Columbia in February 2011, as the former court determined the case was "national in scope." Still, the debate has continued at both the state and federal levels. On March 24, 2011, the U.S. House Energy and Commerce Subcommittee on Energy and Power held a field hearing in Houston to discuss several issues concerning the federal air quality and greenhouse gas regulations. The hearing was attended by Texas attorney general Greg Abbott, along with members from several Texas industry and environmental groups. Kathleen Hartnett White from the Texas Public Policy Foundation presented a paper outlining the high costs that the EPA regulations will have on both the state of Texas and the country, particularly given Texas's position as the "energy bread-basket of the U.S." The paper calls on U.S. legislators to consider amendments to the Clean Air Act and other federal environmental statutes that could have a serious impact on an already weakened economy.

Texas filed another lawsuit against the EPA in September 2011 in an effort to block pending pollution regulations that directly impact the state''s energy companies. State officials say the regulations curbing sulfurdioxide and nitrogen-oxide emissions would result in lost jobs and potentially cause blackouts. Luminent Generation Company, a Dallas power plant, also filed suit against the EPA, saying the proposed regulations would force it to close two power-generation units and multiple coal mines, resulting in the loss of 500 jobs. The suit was filed in the U.S. Court of Appeals for the District of

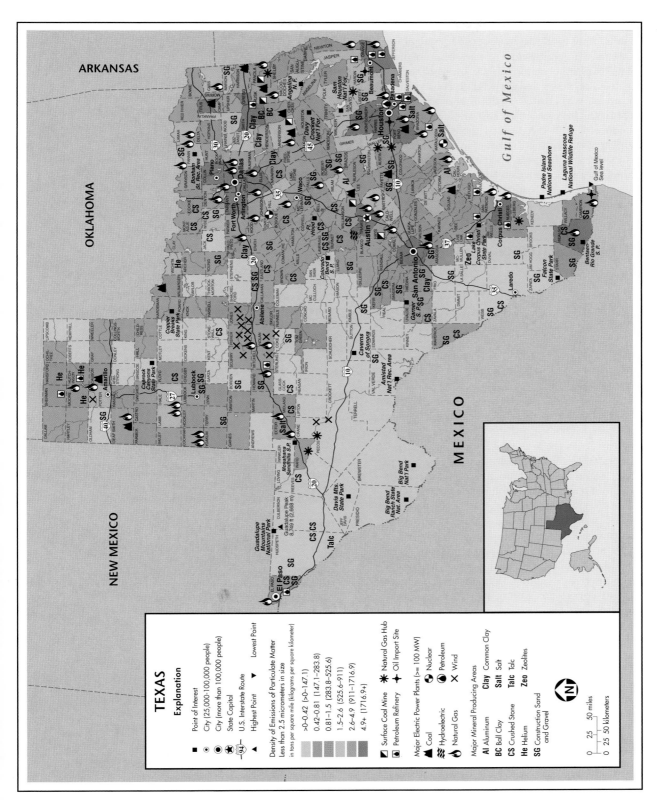

SOURCES: "County Emissions Map: Criteria Air Pollutants." *AirData.* U.S. Environmental Protection Agency. Available from http://www.epa.gov/air/data/geosel.html; *Energy Maps.* U.S. Energy Information Administration. Available from http://www.eia.gov/state; *Highest and Lowest Elevations.* U.S. Geological Survey. Available from http://egsc.usgs.gov/isb/pubs/booklets/elvadist/elvadist.html#Highest; *2007 Minerals Yearbook.* U.S. Geological Survey. Available from http://minerals.usgs.gov/minerals/pubs/state. © 2011 Cengage Learning.

Columbia Circuit. The state of Kansas also filed suit around the same time to block the proposed regulations.

Texas is one of a about a dozen states in the nation with no climate change action policy in place or in progress. It does, however, have a wildlife conservation action plan, which was created in 2005 and was being revised in 2011. The plan identified 880 wildlife species as "species of concern" and categorized them in order of threat. The plan also identified recommended conservation actions in eleven categories, such as direct management of natural resources, species restoration/recovery, land use planning, and creation of new habitat or ecological processes, among others.

❧ Natural Resources, Water, and Agriculture

Forests, Parks, and Wildlife

Most forested land, including most of the commercial timberland, is located in the Pineywoods region of east Texas. The loblolly-shortleaf pine is a predominant species in this region, though oak and hickory are also prevalent. Other native trees across Texas include magnolia, American elm, flowering mimosa, black persimmon, weeping juniper, cedar, mesquite, and pecan (the state tree). The state is home to four national forests and five state forests. Unlike most states, the vast majority of open lands in Texas are in private hands.

Orchids and other subtropical plant species can be found in southcentral Texas and more than 500 species of grasses can be found in the plains and prairies of the Lone Star State. The prickly pear cactus can survive the drought seasons in some of the driest regions of the state, but also inhibits the growth of other grasses and small plants.

There are more than 825 bird species in Texas, with the most abundant communities found along the coastal plains and the lower Rio Grande Valley. Bobcats, white-tailed deer, and coyote are among the more common mammal species, as are smaller mammals such as squirrels, prairie dogs, and raccoons. Twenty-six species of whales and dolphins have been noted in the coastal waters of Texas, with the bottlenose dolphin being most common. The nine-banded armadillo is one of the state's most unusual inhabitants. There are more than one hundred species of snakes across the snake, including the Texas coral snake and fifteen others that are poisonous. According to the U.S. Fish & Wildlife Service, there are 58 animal and plant species threatened or endangered in the state of Texas. The animal species on the list include 5 types of sea turtles, 3 salamanders, 7 types of beetles, and the whooping crane. Plant species on the list include 7 types of cacti, the Texas trailing phlox, and Texas prairie dawn flower.

Recurring drought conditions, combined with high winds, create the threat of frequent wildfires. In April

Texas State Profile

Physical Characteristics

Land area	261,226 square miles (676,572 sq km)
Inland water area	5,607 square miles (14,522 sq km)
Coastal area	406 square miles (653 sq km)
Highest point	Guadalupe Peak 8,749 feet (2,667 m)
National Forest System lands (2010)	755,000 acres (306,000 ha)
State parks (2011)	133

Energy Statistics

Total energy production (2009)	12,024 trillion Btu
State ranking in total energy production (2009)	1
Renewable energy net generation total (2009)	22.1 million megawatt hours
Hydroelectric energy generation (2009)	1.0 million megawatt hours
Biomass energy generation (2009)	429,000 megawatt hours
Wind energy generation (2009)	20.0 million megawatt hours
Wood and derived fuel energy generation (2009)	649,000 megawatt hours
Crude oil reserves (2009)	5.0 billion barrels (795.9 million cu m)
Natural gas reserves (2009)	80.4 trillion cubic feet (2.3 trillion cu m)
Natural gas liquids (2008)	3.4 billion barrels (545.6 million cu m)

Pollution Statistics

Carbon output (2005)	670.2 million tons of CO_2 (608.0 million t)
Superfund sites (2008)	49
Particulate matter (less than 2.5 micrometers) emissions (2002)	52,181 tons per year (47,337 t/yr)
Toxic chemical releases (2009)	196.4 million pounds (89.1 million kg)
Generated hazardous waste (2009)	13.5 million tons (12.2 million t)

SOURCES: AirData. U.S. Environmental Protection Agency. Available from http://www.epa.gov/air/data; *Energy Maps, Facts, and Data of the U.S. States.* U.S. Energy Information Administration. Available from http://www.eia.gov/state; *The 2012 Statistical Abstract.* U.S. Census Bureau. Available from http://www.census.gov/compendia/statab; *United States Energy Usage.* eRedux. Available from http://www.eredux.net/states.

© 2011 Cengage Learning.

2011, such conditions led to the outbreak of more than eighty fires affecting all but two of the state's 254 counties. The Possum Kingdom Complex fires, caused by the convergence of four separate blazes in parts of Stephens and Palo Pinto counties, affected more than 147,000 acres (59,489 ha) of land, destroying more than 30 homes. In total, the statewide wildfires destroyed more than 100 homes and led to the death of at least two volunteer firefighters. Officials reported that more that 90 percent of the fires were caused by humans. In September 2011, more fires raged through parts of southeastern Texas, scorching more than 55 square miles (142 sq km). The fire burned through a thick loblolly pine area, which was the largest remaining habitat for the Houston toad. Much of the toad's habitat was in the Bastrop State Park, a popular 6,000-acre (2,428-ha) state park. All but about 100 acres (40 ha) were consumed by the wildfires, which left scientists concerned about the future, not only of the park, but of the Houston toad.

Minerals

Oil, natural gas, and coal are the most valuable mineral resources in the state, making Texas a leading national producer of all three resources. However, the state is also a top producer of several nonfuel minerals, including crushed stone, construction sand and gravel, portland cement, gypsum, talc, and common clays.

Agriculture

The Texas Department of Agriculture (TDA) is headed by a commissioner, who is chosen in a statewide election to a four-year term. In 2007, Texas ranked first in the nation in market value of livestock and poultry and second in the total value of agricultural products. Texas is the nation's leading producer of cotton and cottonseed, producing both American upland and pima cotton. Other major crops include sorghum, wheat, corn, and hay, all of which are planted primarily in the northcentral and western plains region. Grapefruit is an important crop in the Rio Grande Valley region. The greenhouse and nursery sector is among the top five in the nation. This thriving agricultural sector, however, is vulnerable to periods of drought, which can lead to billions of dollars lost in failed crops and compromised livestock.

Texas became one of the first ten states in the nation to develop an Organic Certification Program in agriculture, which was first implemented in 1988. The Texas Department of Agriculture (TDA) has since adopted the national organic standards of the U.S. Department of Agriculture, and a certification program for livestock production and processing was adopted in 2003. Local produce for local consumption is promoted through the GO TEXAN program of the TDA. Under the GO TEXAN Restaurant Program, restaurants may obtain special certification for partnering with local producers for meat, fresh produce, and processed foods.

Water

Caddo Lake, which is connected to the Red River and shared between Texas and Louisiana, is considered to be the largest natural lake in the state, even though the total area of the lake has been increased by the construction of a river dam. Caddo Lake was designated as a Ramsar Wetland of International Importance in 1993. This wetland system supports one of the best examples of a mature flooded bald cypress forest, with trees up to four hundred years old. The area is also home to diverse, native freshwater fish communities, which include the American paddlefish and the American eel. The state has over two hundred major artificial reservoirs, including Amistad (shared with Mexico) and Toledo Bend (shared with Louisiana) on the Sabine River.

The Rio Grande serves as the international boundary with Mexico. Its total length of 1,896 miles (3,051 km) includes segments in Colorado and New Mexico, making it the nation's second-longest river (after the Missouri-Mississippi river system). The Colorado River, extending about 600 miles (970 km) across central and southeastern Texas to the Gulf of Mexico, is the longest river wholly within the state. Other important rivers include the Nueces, San Antonio, Brazos, Trinity, Sabine, Red, and Canadian. The San Jacinto overlaps the Houston Ship Channel that connects the Port of Houston with the Gulf of Mexico. As such, the San Jacinto is one of the most heavily trafficked rivers in North America.

The Gulf of Mexico serves as a major channel for commerce and industry for the nation as well as the state. Texas is home to 13 major deepwater ports along the Gulf, including the ports of Beaumont, Corpus Christi, Freeport, Houston, and Texas City, which are consistently ranked among the top 25 U.S. ports in tonnage handled. The ports are connected to one another and to the national inland waterway system through the Gulf Intercoastal Waterway, which runs from Carrabelle, Florida, to Brownsville, Texas. Port facilities along the Gulf of Mexico handle over 50 percent of all U.S. foreign imports and exports. Shrimping is a major commercial fishing industry in the state. Other commercial shellfish include blue crabs and oysters. The saltwater commercial fish catch also includes yellowfin tuna, red snapper, swordfish, and flounder.

⚜ Energy

Oil

Texas is the national leader when it comes to oil. The state's production of crude oil accounts for nearly 20 percent of the national total, and nearly 24 percent of the nation's proven oil reserves are located within the state. The type of crude oil found in the state, known as West Texas Intermediate, is of such high quality that it serves as the benchmark for oil found throughout the Americas. The Houston area hosts the largest refining center in the United States, including the Baytown refinery, which is the largest in the nation. A total of 23 Texas petroleum refineries process more than 4.7 million barrels per day, accounting for about 27 percent of the nation's annual oil refining capacity.

Texas is just as important to the nation in the production of natural gas, with production of marketed natural gas accounting for over 32 percent of the national total. Natural gas reserves in Texas account for 38 percent of total U.S. reserves for natural gas liquids and nearly 32 percent of the U.S. total for dry natural gas. With seven natural gas market hubs and the largest natural gas storage capacity in the nation, Texan natural gas is easily distributed from coast to coast.

Texas is also the nation's largest consumer of petroleum and natural gas. The state's petrochemical industry requires massive amounts of liquefied petroleum gases (LPG), pushing the state's LPG consumption to over 53 percent of the national total.

Electricity

According to reports from the U.S. Energy Information Administration, about half of the state's entire supply of electricity is produced by natural-gas fired plants, with coal-fired plants accounting for most of the rest. However, the Electric Reliability Council of Texas (ERCOT), which manages the power flow for about 85 percent of the state's electric grid, has reported that the use of coal is becoming more prominent, at least within their own management area. In 2010, coal accounted for about 39 percent of ERCOT managed electricity, while natural gas accounted for about 38 percent and nuclear for 13 percent.

Texas has eleven major surface coal mines, five of which are ranked among the 50 largest in the nation. However, most of the coal produced within the state is lignite (or brown coal), which is the lowest grade of coal. Lignite is lower in energy content than other types of coal and produces higher carbon dioxide and sulfur dioxide emission levels. As a result, Texas has the highest carbon dioxide and sulfur dioxide emission rates in the nation. All of the coal produced within the state is consumed locally, with additional supplies imported from Wyoming. There are two nuclear power plants in the state: the South Texas Project and Comanche Peak. Together, these plants produce only one-tenth of the state's supply of electricity. Since Texans rely heavily on electricity for home cooling (and heating), they use significantly more electricity per capita than the national average.

Alternative Energy

The state's first Renewable Portfolio Standard was adopted in 1999 (Senate Bill 7) with a mandate that electricity providers collectively generate 2,000 megawatts of additional renewable energy by 2009. In 2005, the legislature expanded the mandate to require the generation of 5,880 megawatts of renewable energy by 2015 and 10,000 megawatts by 2025 (Senate Bill 20). In looking for alternative energy sources, Texas has become the largest wind energy producer in the nation. While only about 3 percent of the state's electricity is produced by wind (enough to power about one million homes), the wind power capacity of Texas accounts for nearly 27 percent of the national total. The Horse Hollow Wind

Texas has become the largest wind energy producer in the nation. © *Ellisphotos/Alamy*

Energy Center in central Texas is the largest wind power facility in the world. Texas has also become a leading producer of biodiesel transportation fuel, with potential for producing more than 100 million gallons (378,541,200 l) per year.

Solar energy could also play a major role in the state's energy future. In November 2010, the state's largest solar farm opened and became operational in the San Antonio area. This Blue Wing Solar Project consists of 214,500 solar photovoltaic modules that are expected to produce more than 26,570 megawatt-hours of electricity per year, which is enough to power about 1,800 households. With the opening of this facility, Texas was ranked as the tenth-largest photovoltaic market in the nation for 2010 by the Solar Energies Industries Association in their annual *U.S. Solar Market Insights* report. While this shows promise for solar energy, the state legislature has been slow to lend support, as some solar energy incentive bills failed to pass in 2010. For the new 2011 session, at least two bills have been introduced to boost the cause of solar energy. Senate Bill 492 could provide a rebate for businesses and homeowners who install solar panels. House Bill 2961 could create a special fund for solar development projects by adding a $1 per month charge to home electric bills, $5 per month for each commercial meter, and $50 per month for each industrial meter. Individuals and small companies would be allowed to opt out of the program. Both bills remained in committee as of late 2011.

❧ Green Business, Green Building, Green Jobs

Green Building

The first green building standards were adopted by the state legislature in 1989. Commonly referred to as the Texas Standard, the Energy Conservation Design

Standard for New State Buildings is based on the American Society of Heating, Refrigerating and Air Conditioning Engineers Standard 90.1 and applies to all new construction and major renovations of state buildings. This code was updated by the adoption of the 2000 International Energy Conservation Code (IECC) and the 2000 International Residential Code (IRC). A mandatory statewide energy code, based on the 2000 IRC and the 2000 IECC, was established for residential and commercial buildings in 2001. In 2009, the legislature began consideration of a bill to update these standards to the 2009 IECC and 2009 IRC (House Bill 2783). As of late 2011, the bill had not yet been brought to a final vote.

Some cities, such as Austin, Houston, and Dallas, have adopted their own green building certification and incentive programs. The Far Southeast Austin EMS Station, completed in 2004, was the first building in Texas to achieve a gold rating from the Leadership in Energy and Environmental Design (LEED) rating standards of the U.S. Green Building Council. The Shangri La Botanical Gardens & Nature Center in Orange, completed in 2008, is a recent example of a platinum-rated building project, which is the highest standard in the LEED system.

Green Business

The renewable energy industry in Texas is regarded as a major growth industry for the economy. According to *The Texas Renewable Energy Industry and Workforce Development Assessment in 2008*, there were more than 470 companies involved in wind energy generation that year, including those involved in component manufacturing, repairs, and maintenance; sales and marketing, and research and development. There were about 270 companies in the energy conservation services sector. More than 150 companies represented the solar power sector, while nearly 140 companies were noted in the geothermal sector.

In support of the renewable energy industry, the state legislature created the Emerging Technology Fund in 2005 (House Bill 1188). The fund distributes awards to educational institutions, research organizations, and existing and new businesses that are committed to excellence in promoting research and commercialization of clean technologies. In 2007, the legislature revised the tax code to create property and franchise tax deductions for companies involved in the manufacture, sale, or installation of solar and wind devices (Tax Code Chap. 171). Additionally, a number of city and regional organizations have developed to provide networking, educational, and other resources that attract and grow green businesses. The non-profit Texas Foundation for Innovative Communities and the Texas Workforce Commission have initiated the first Texas Clean Energy Park in Austin. The park, which is in its first phase of development, will serve as a collaborative community for renewable energy companies, educational institutions, and research and development organizations working together to develop innovative solutions for the new green economy.

Green Jobs

According to a survey published by The Pew Charitable Trusts, Texas ranked second in the nation for the number of clean energy economy jobs in 2007, with over 55,600 jobs in 4,800 clean energy businesses. Conservation and pollution mitigation, clean (renewable) energy, and environmentally friendly production were the three largest sectors in the survey.

Recognizing the need to place workforce development as a key factor in promoting the green economy, the state legislature passed House Bill 1935 (2009), which called for the creation of the Jobs and Education for Texans (JET) Fund under the administration of the state comptroller. The JET Grant program is designed to support qualifying educational programs at public junior colleges, public technical institutes, and other eligible nonprofit organizations that focus on high-demand occupations and green jobs. A JET scholarship program is also available for eligible students at participating schools. In 2009, the state designated $90 million of Recovery Act funds for the Skills Development Fund, which can also be used to offer training in green jobs.

The non-profit Texas Foundation for Innovative Communities (TFIC) and Good Company Associates, an Austin-based business development consulting firm specializing in energy efficiency, renewable, and smart grid applications, are working toward the development of a more comprehensive Green Jobs Initiative for the state. The two companies co-hosted a one-day Green Jobs Initiative Conference at the Texas State Capitol in March 2010 as a way to gather and share ideas on making the initiative a reality.

❧ Water Scarcity

In fall 2007, the south and central regions of Texas entered into a two-year season of drought that was regarded as one of the worst in fifty years. During that time, eighty counties within the state were marked as being in extreme or exceptional drought conditions, which are the two most severe levels of drought noted by the U.S. Department of Agriculture (USDA). In April 2009, the USDA listed seventy counties as primary natural disaster areas. With record high temperatures and record low rainfall, the agricultural losses in both crops and livestock topped $3.6 billion. Though the rains returned to normal in the fall of 2009, there has been some concern that the water levels of area lakes, reservoirs, and aquifers have not returned to pre-drought

Texas experienced its hottest summer in the country's history in 2011, resulting in the driest 11-month span since records started being kept. © *Texas/Alamy*

levels. That issue continued in 2011, which saw an 11-month-span that was the driest on record, coupled with the hottest summer in history.

Water is a finite resource, and for a state that ranks second in the nation in terms of population and agricultural production, the need for water is great. Most of the state's water demand is supplied by surface water and groundwater. Approximately 51 percent of the state's surface water and 80 percent of groundwater is used for agriculture, while municipal demands account for 26 percent of surface water and 15 percent of groundwater. The population of Texas was estimated at more than 2.4 million in 2009. According to the Texas Water Development Board, that figure is expected to increase to nearly 46 million in 2060, accompanied by a 27 percent increase in demand for water. Over the same period, the state's existing water supply is expected to decrease by 18 percent.

In order to adapt for these changes, a major reduction in water use and demand will be necessary. Stepping up to the challenge, several cities across the state have already made some progress in creating and implementing rules and policies that promote water conservation among residents. In *Drop by Drop: Seven Ways Texas Cities Can Conserve Water*, officials from the National Wildlife Federation and the Lone Star Chapter of the Sierra Club have summarized the conservation efforts of nineteen Texas cities, and have considered seven major actions that have proven to be effective in local water conservation plans. For instance, some cities, such as San Antonio and Austin, have had great success in promoting toilet replacement programs that offer rebates to residents who purchase newer low-flush models. Similar programs to encourage the switch to water-conserving showerheads and washing machines are in place in some cities as well. Likewise, some cities have implemented outdoor watering ordinances that restrict lawn watering to once a week

or no more than twice a week. However, the report also highlights some of the areas that may need greater attention at the municipal level, such as consumer education and conservation funding. The Low Colorado River Association (LCRA) also addressed drought concerns in fall 2011. Its director asked the state in September 2011 to "significantly curtail" water for downstream agriculture use if water levels did not rise by spring 2012.

At the statewide legislative level, public officials have begun to take a serious look at existing policies for water management, in consideration of the changes that may be necessary in order to protect the state's most valuable natural resource. A 2009 report from the Environmental Defense Fund, *Down to the Last Drop*, highlights two major statewide issues of concern. First is the failure of current laws to address the interconnectivity of surface and groundwater systems, since current water laws consider the management of surface and groundwater as two separate categories of concern, with separate plans for administration. The second issue involves concerns that the current Groundwater Management Area (GMA) process may not be suitable for protecting the state's water resources in the long run.

The Texas Water Development Board has delineated sixteen GMAs, all but one of which is divided into a number of groundwater conservation districts. The formation of these districts was considered a necessary step toward amending the existing rule of capture that has been in place since 1904. According to the rule of capture, groundwater is the private property of the owner of the overlying land. Therefore, landowners have the right to pump, or capture, their own water from their own land. Since such unregulated access to groundwater is contrary to the need for tighter policies for conservation, the GMAs were designed to bring private owners and public officials together in efforts to promote local groundwater management policies. While some districts have issued modifications on the rule of capture, there have been lingering concerns that the districts might come into major conflict with landowners if they attempt to adopt and enforce new, more aggressive conservation measures to ensure a more sustainable future.

A partial response to this concern came in March 2011 as the state legislature passed a new groundwater bill that reaffirmed the interests of landowners under the rule of capture (by establishing it as a legislative act), but clarified the right of conservation districts to limit the amount of water that landowners can pump from the ground. While some believe this measure simply clarifies an already accepted standard, others believe that it could lead to more lawsuits, since some landowners may claim rights over larger volumes of groundwater.

BIBLIOGRAPHY

Books

Carlson, Paul Howard. *Deep Time and the Texas High Plains: History and Geology.* Lubbock: Texas Tech University Press, 2005.

Hamilton, Lisa. *Deeply Rooted: Unconventional Farmers in the Age of Agribusiness.* Berkeley, CA: Counter point Press, 2010.

Shallat, Todd. *Structures in the Stream: Water, Science, and the Rise of the U. S. Army Corps of Engineers.* Austin: University of Texas Press, 1994.

Todd, David, and David Weisman, eds. *The Texas Legacy Project: Stories of Courage and Conservation.* College Station: Texas A&M University Press, 2010.

White, Mel, Tria Giovan, and Jim Bones. *The Smithsonian Guides to Natural America: The South Central States—Texas, Oklahoma, Arkansas, Louisiana, Mississippi.* Washington, DC: Smithsonian Books, 1996.

Web Sites

Associated Press. "Texas defies EPA, approves coal-fired plant permit." Chron.com. January 26, 2011. Available from http://www.chron.com/disp/story. mpl/ap/tx/7399150.html

Associated Press. "Texas vs. EPA: Fight over pollution regulations growing fierce." *San Marcos Daily Record.* January 2, 2011. Available from http:// www.sanmarcosrecord.com/local/x2131360344/ Texas-vs-EPA-Fight-over-pollution-regulations-growing-fierce

Caddo Lake Institute. Available from http://caddolakeinstitute.us/index.html

"Clean Air and Air Permitting Milestones." U.S. Environmental Protection Agency. July 12, 2011. Available from http://yosemite.epa.gov/opa/adm press.nsf/8b770facf5edf6f185257359003fb69e/ 01990cda867a6107852578cb00588e80!Open Document

Drew, James. "Texas challenges EPA ruling on green house gas threat." *The Dallas Morning News,* February 17, 2010. Available from http://www. dallasnews.com/sharedcontent/dws/news/ washington/stories/DN-epasuit_17tex.ART.State. Edition2.4bb1e87.html

Drop by Drop: Seven Ways Texas Cities Can Conserve Water. National Wildlife Federation and the Lone Star Chapter of the Sierra Club. Available from http://www.texaswatermatters.org/pdfs/Drop ByDrop.pdf

"EPA Air Rules Slammed in Houston hearing." Argus Media. March 24, 2011. Available from http:// www.argusmedia.com/pages/NewsBody.aspx? id=745338&menu=yes

"ERCOT Region Electricity Use Up 3.5% in 2010." Electric reliability Council of Texas. January 10, 2011. Available from http://www.ercot.com/ news/press_releases/2011/nr01-10-11

Galbraith, Kate. "Court Denies Texas Request to Halt Greenhouse Gas Permitting." *The Texas Tribune.* January 12, 2011. Available from http://www. texastribune.org/texas-environmental-news/envir onmental-problems-and-policies/court-denies-tex as-request-halt-greenhouse-gas-per/

Galbraith, Kate. "Texas Leads Resistance to EPA Climate Action." *The The Texas Tribune.* September 23, 2010. Available http://www.texastribune.org/ texas-state-agencies/attorney-generals-office/texas-leads-resistance-to-epa-climate-action/

Galbraith, Kate. "Texas Solar Advocates Hope for Legislative Boost." *The Texas Tribune.* April 7, 2011. Available from http://www.texastribune.org/texas-energy/energy/texas-solar-advocates-hope-for-legislative-boost.

Galbraith, Kate. "Texas vs. EPA Permitting Battle Intensifies." *The Texas Tribune.* December 7, 2010. Available from http://www.texastribune.org/texas-environmental-news/environmental-problems-and-policies/texas-v-epa-permitting-battle-intensifies/

Hanna, Bill. "Texas Senate passes groundwater legislation." *Star-Telegram.* March 30, 2011. Available from http://www.star-telegram.com/2011/03/ 30/2962706/texas-senate-passes-groundwater. html.

"History of the General Land Office." Texas General Land Office. Available from http://www.glo.state. tx.us/archives/history/glo_today.html

Kollipara, Puneet, and Fowler, Tom. "Texas Joins Effort To Delay Pending EPA Pollution Law." *San Antonio Express-News.* September 22, 2011. Avail able from http://www.mysanantonio.com/default/ article/Texas-joins-effort-to-delay-pending-EPA-pol lution-2182948.php

Marbury, Laura Brock, and Mary E. Kelly. *Down to the Last Drop—2009 Update: Spotlight on Groundwater Management in Texas.* Environmental Defense Fund. Available from http://www.texaswatermat ters.org/pdfs/lastdrop.pdf

Nelson, Gabriel. "Texas Joins Challengers to EPA's Greenhouse Gas 'Tailoring' Rule." *The New York Times.* August 5, 2010. Available from http://www. nytimes.com/gwire/2010/08/05/05greenwire-texas-joins-challengers-to-epas-greenhouse-gas-25612.html

Nelson, Gabriel. "Wyo. Joins Texas In Suing EPA Over Rollout of Greenhouse Gas Regulations." *The New York Times.* February 16, 2011. Available from http://www.nytimes.com/gwire/2011/02/16/16greenwire-wyo-joins-texas-in-suing-epa-over-roll-out-of-g-86597.html?scp=2&sq=texas%20epa%20lawsuit&st=Search

The Pew Charitable Trusts. *The Clean Energy Economy: Texas Factsheet.* Available from http://www.pewcenteronthestates.org/uploadedFiles/wwwpewcenteronthestatesorg/Fact_Sheets/Clean_Economy_Factsheet_Texas.pdf

Plushnick-Masti, Ramit. "EPA Says All Texas Plants Will Get New Permits." *San Antonio Express-News.* July 12, 2011. Available from http://www.mysanantonio.com/default/article/EPA-says-all-Texas-plants-will-get-new-air-permits-1462638.php

Ramos, Mary G. "Oil and Texas: A Cultural History." *Texas Almanac.* Available http://www.texasalmanac.com/history/highlights/oil.

"State Energy Profiles: Texas." United States Energy Information Administration. Available from http://tonto.eia.doe.gov/state/state_energy_profiles.cfm?sid=TX.

"Texas Conservation Action Plan." Texas Parks & Wildlife. September 2005. Available from http://www.tpwd.state.tx.us/landwater/land/tcap/

"Texas Drought: Drought Approaches Worst In History." Low Colorado River Association. September 22, 2011. Available from http://www.lcra.org/water/drought/index.html

Texas Legislature. *Senate Bill 7 (1999).* Available from http://www.capitol.state.tx.us/tlodocs/76R/billtext/html/SB00007F.htm

Texas Legislature. *Senate Bill 20 (2005).* Available from http://www.capitol.state.tx.us/tlodocs/79I/billtext/pdf/SB00020F.pdf

Texas Legislature. *House Bill 1188 (2005).* Available from http://members.texasone.us/site/DocServer/HB01765F.pdf?docID=581

Texas Legislature. *House Bill 1935 (2009).* Available from http://www.legis.state.tx.us/tlodocs/81R/billtext/pdf/HB01935F.pdf

Texas Legislature. *House Bill 2783 (2009).* Available from http://www.capitol.state.tx.us/tlodocs/81R/billtext/pdf/HB02783S.pdf

Texas Legislature. House Bill 2961 (2011): Relating to the creation of a program for the development of solar energy industry in this state. Available from http://www.legis.state.tx.us/tlodocs/82R/billtext/pdf/HB02961I.pdf#navpanes=0.

Texas Legislature. Senate Bill 492 (2011): Relating to the creation of a distributed solar generation incentive program. Available from http://www.legis.state.tx.us/tlodocs/82R/billtext/pdf/SB00492I.pdf#navpanes=0.

Texas Legislature. *Tax Code Chapter 171: Franchise Tax.* http://www.statutes.legis.state.tx.us/Docs/TX/htm/TX.171.htm#171.056

Texas Ports Association. Available at http://www.texasports.org

"Texas Tax Codes Related to Renewable Energy Systems." State Energy Conservation Office. Available from http://www.seco.cpa.state.tx.us/re_incentives-taxcode-statutes.htm#171107

Tompkins, Shannon. "Flames From Bastrop Fire Will Be Felt For a Long Time." *San Antonio News-Express>.* September 21, 2011. Available from http://www.mysanantonio.com/news/local_news/article/Flames-from-Bastrop-fire-will-be-felt-for-a-long-2180436.php#photo-1613873

2009 State Agriculture Overview: Texas. National Agriculture Statistics Service, U.S. Department of Agriculture. Available from http://www.nass.usda.gov/Statistics_by_State/Ag_Overview/AgOverview_TX.pdf

U.S. Solar Market Insight: 2010 Year in Review. Solar Energy Industries Association. Available from http://www.seia.org/galleries/pdf/SMI-YIR-2010-ES.pdf.

White, Kathleen Hartnett. *EPA's GHG and Clean Air Act Regulations: A Focus on Texas' Economy, Energy Prices, and Jobs.* Texas Public Policy Foundation. Available from http://republicans.energycommerce.house.gov/Media/file/Hearings/Energy/032411/White.pdf.

Utah

Utah has abundant natural resources and spectacular natural scenery. National parks, ski resorts, Great Salt Lake, and Lake Powell combine to make the state an interesting place to live and attractive to tourists. Nearly 76 percent of the population lives in one of four counties along the northern Wasatch Front. Population and industrial growth in this region have posed a significant challenge for local officials in managing the region's air quality to comply with Environmental Protection Agency (EPA) standards. But the state is already at work implementing several programs and policies designed to provide cleaner air and a better environment for all.

Climate

The climate of Utah is generally semiarid to arid. With average annual precipitation at 10–15 in (25–38 cm), Utah is one of the driest states in the nation. However, annual precipitation differs dramatically from one region of the state to another depending on elevation and prevailing weather patterns. High-elevation mountains in the northeast may receive 50 inches (127 cm) annually whereas low-elevation deserts in the southwest may receive less than 5 inches (12.7 cm). Weather also varies dramatically from year to year with periods of drought alternating with periods of high moisture.

The Great Salt Lake influences precipitation along the Wasatch Front by a "lake effect." Most prominently noted in fall and spring, the lake effect is most substantial when cold winds from the northwest flow over the warmer water of Great Salt Lake, which enhances evaporation, increasing moisture in the air. When the moisture-laden air contacts the southeastern shore and is compressed as it pushes against the Wasatch Mountains, it produces precipitation that is a major source of rain and snow for the area, including the production of abundant, light and fluffy snow that is esteemed by skiers from around the world.

Winter surface inversions occurring along the Wasatch Front affect the weather and air quality. Usually, the temperature of air in the atmosphere becomes cooler with altitude. This is because most of the suns energy is converted to sensible heat at the ground, which in turn warms the air at the surface. The warm air rises in the atmosphere, where it expands and cools. An inversion occurs when the temperature of air actually increases with height. Having warm air on top of cooler air is referred to as a temperature inversion, because the temperature profile of the atmosphere is "inverted" from its usual state. The cooler air that is trapped under warmer air also traps pollutants closer to the surface. The state has initiated a number of policies and programs to address this issue.

Climate Change

State officials have already recognized the effects of global warming on the climate of Utah. In 2006, the governor established the Blue Ribbon Advisory Council (BRAC) on Climate Change to consider the current and potential impacts of climate change on the state. The council's 2007 report, *Climate Change and Utah: The Scientific Consensus*, notes that the average temperature in Utah during the period 1997–2007 was higher than that observed during any other comparable period of the past century. Average precipitation was also unusually high during the twentieth century, though there was also an increase in the severity and length of drought seasons in the past one hundred years. Continued warming trends are expected to result in fewer frost days, a decrease in mountain snowpack, and earlier snow melt patterns, all of which can reduce the year-round supply of drinking water. Such changes can also have a negative effect on wildlife and forest health, as some wildlife and tree species cannot thrive under these changing weather conditions.

Climate Change Action

The 2007 report *Utah Greenhouse Gas Inventory and Reference Case Projections, 1990–2020* from the Center for Climate Strategies has noted that greenhouse gas emissions in Utah increased by 40 percent from 1990 to 2005, a rate well above the national average of 16 percent for the same time period. In response to these reports and the recommendations for action provided by the BRAC, the state has set a goal to reduce greenhouse gas emissions to 2005 levels by 2020.

Utah and the Western Climate Initiative

In 2007, under former governor Jon Hunstman, Utah became a member of the Western Climate Initiative (WCI), a regional action group committed to developing a joint strategy for reduction of greenhouse gas emissions. In 2008, the WCI announced the development of a greenhouse gas emissions cap-and-trade program that is expected to take effect in participating states and Canadian provinces beginning January 2012. The cap-and-trade program is the primary action in the group's plan to reduce greenhouse gas emissions by 15 percent by 2020. However, in February 2009, the Utah House of Representatives passed a resolution (HR 3) urging the governor to withdraw from the WCI. Some state officials believe that the cap-and-trade program would lead to job losses and a decrease in business investment at a time when the economy is already struggling, since it could be expensive for some company owners to make the operational changes necessary to limit emissions. State Representative Mike Noel (Republican), the sponsor of the bill, told the press that he does not believe global warming is caused by human activity. In February 2010, the Utah legislature passed an additional joint resolution (HJR 12) urging the federal government to stop negotiations toward national cap-and-trade legislation and to refrain from further nationwide regulation of carbon dioxide emissions.

Distrust of environmental scientists and advocates may contribute to the anti-emissions reduction stance of some legislators and their supporters. The original text of the resolution, sponsored by Representative Kerry Gibson (Republican), called for the immediate halt of carbon dioxide reduction policies "until a full and independent investigation of the climate data conspiracy and global warming science can be substantiated." The original also stated that the Clean Air Act is based on "flawed" climate data. For the final version of the resolution, Gibson agreed to remove the word "conspiracy" from the text and changed the word "flawed" to "questionable." Several other controversial phrases were also amended. Encouraged by the state legislature, in 2010 the governor's office announced that Utah would not participate in the WCI cap-and-trade program, but hoped to remain a member of the group in order to work on complementary policies.

❧ Natural Resources, Water, and Agriculture

Woods and Wildlife

Forests cover about one-third of the state of Utah. According to the *Utah Statewide Forest Resource Assessment & Strategy Guide 2010*, about 17 percent of all forested lands are under private ownership. The rest is found on public lands Woodlands generally occur at elevations of 4,500 feet (1,370 m) and above, with piñon-juniper and oak-maple forests at lower elevations and aspen, fir (Douglas and white), Engelmann spruce, and pine (ponderosa, lodgepole, limber, bristlecone) at higher elevations. About 21 percent of forested lands are classified as timberlands, with aspen being the most prevalent commercial species. The state is home to forty-three state parks and five national parks. Part of the Glen Canyon National Recreation Area lies in Utah, as do four national historic trails.

There are more than 600 vertebrate species found in Utah, including American bison, bobcat, coyote, brown bear, Canada lynx, white-tailed deer, gray wolf, and Utah prairie dog. Black bear, bighorn sheep, elk, Rocky Mountain goat, and moose are popular for big game hunters. Turkey, sage grouse, pheasant, and swan, are also hunted. Among the many bird species are the bald eagle, grasshopper sparrow, burrowing owl, black swift, and the mountain plover, all of which are noted as wildlife species of concern by the Utah Department of Natural Resources. Popular sport fish include brook trout, black crappie, cutthroat trout, and northern pike. The desert tortoise, Gila monster, Mojave rattlesnake, and western banded gecko are among the reptiles listed as species of concern, while the Columbia spotted frog and the boreal toad (western toad) are noted amphibians on the list.

According to the U.S. Fish and Wildlife Service, there were 18 animal and 25 plant species listed as threatened or endangered in 2011. Endangered animals include the kanab ambersnail, the black-footed ferret, and the southwestern willow flycatcher. Threatened species include the Mexican spotted owl and the desert tortoise. The autumn buttercup, San Rafael cactus, Holmgren milk-vetch, and Barneby ridge-cress are some of the state's endangered plant species. Endangered fish include three varieties of chub and the razorback sucker.

Minerals

The production of clay and lime products and salt from Great Salt Lake were some of the first successful commercial ventures in the state. By the early 1900s, Utah was one of the largest mining and smelting centers in the western United States. Estimates from the U.S.

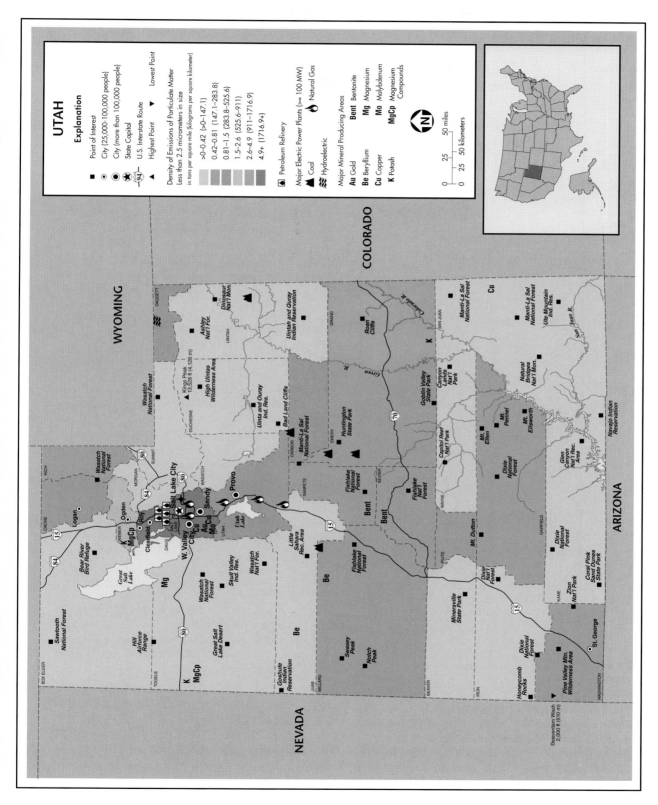

SOURCES: "County Emissions Map: Criteria Air Pollutants." *AirData.* U.S. Environmental Protection Agency. Available from http://www.epa.gov/air/data/geosel.html; *Energy Maps.* U.S. Energy Information Administration. Available from http://www.eia.gov/state; *Highest and Lowest Elevations.* U.S. Geological Survey. Available from http://egsc.usgs.gov/isb/pubs/booklets/elvadist/elvadist.html#Highest; *2007 Minerals Yearbook.* U.S. Geological Survey. Available from http://minerals.usgs.gov/minerals/pubs/state. © 2011 Cengage Learning.

Utah State Profile

Physical Characteristics

Land area	82,191 square miles (212,874 sq km)
Inland water area	2,706 square miles (7,009 sq km)
Coastal area	NA
Highest point	Kings Peak 13,528 feet (4,123 m)
National Forest System lands (2010)	8.2 million acres (3.3 million ha)
State parks (2011)	43

Energy Statistics

Total energy production (2009)	1,200 trillion Btu
State ranking in total energy production (2009)	14
Renewable energy net generation total (2009)	1.3 million megawatt hours
Hydroelectric energy generation (2009)	835,000 megawatt hours
Biomass energy generation (2009)	48,000 megawatt hours
Wind energy generation (2009)	160,000 megawatt hours
Wood and derived fuel energy generation (2009)	NA
Crude oil reserves (2009)	398 million barrels (63.3 million cu m)
Natural gas reserves (2009)	7,257 billion cubic feet (205.5 billion cu m)
Natural gas liquids (2008)	116 million barrels (18.4 million cu m)

Pollution Statistics

Carbon output (2005)	62.4 million tons of CO_2 (56.6 million t)
Superfund sites (2008)	16
Particulate matter (less than 2.5 micrometers) emissions (2002)	8,058 tons per year (7,310 t/yr)
Toxic chemical releases (2009)	147.4 million pounds (66.9 million kg)
Generated hazardous waste (2009)	59,400 tons (53,900 t)

SOURCES: AirData. U.S. Environmental Protection Agency. Available from http://www.epa.gov/air/data; *Energy Maps, Facts, and Data of the U.S. States.* U.S. Energy Information Administration. Available from http://www.eia.gov/state; *The 2012 Statistical Abstract.* U.S. Census Bureau. Available from http://www.census.gov/compendia/statab; *United States Energy Usage.* eRedux. Available from http://www.eredux.net/states.

© 2011 Cengage Learning.

Geological Survey placed the value of nonfuel minerals at about $4.4 billion for 2010. As such, Utah ranks third in the nation in the value of nonfuel minerals, producing nearly 7 percent of the total U.S. value. In 2010, Utah ranked second for production of copper, potash, and magnesium compounds and third for molybdenum concentrates, gold, and bentonite clay. Utah is the only state that produces beryllium concentrates and magnesium metals.

Great Salt Lake

Great Salt Lake is the largest lake in Utah and the fourth largest salt lake in the world. Salt production from the lake was a major industry for the Church of the Latter-day Saints from 1891 until 1918, when the Morton Salt Company purchased the business. Salt drawn from the lake is used for numerous products and applications, including salt cake, detergent filters, chemical processing, plastics, and road salt, as well as standard table salt. Magnesium chloride and sulfate of potassium (potash) are also drawn from the lake.

More than 250 species of birds can be found in habitats around Great Salt Lake. Due to high salinity, there are no fish, leaving brine shrimp and brine flies as the largest aquatic animals in the lake. The North Arm of the lake has an average salinity concentration of 26 to 28 percent, while the South Arm, which receives freshwater from the Bear and Weber rivers, has a salinity of about 13 percent. Higher salinity in the North Arm makes an ideal habitat for two types of bacteria, halobacterium and halococcus, which give the water a purple or reddish color.

Freshwater Lakes and Rivers

Major freshwater lakes include Utah Lake and Bear Lake (shared with Idaho). Many reservoirs created by dams on streams and rivers form manmade lakes throughout the state. Lake Powell, formed by the Glen Canyon Dam on the Colorado River just south of the Arizona border, is the largest of these.

Major rivers include (from north to south) the Bear, Weber, Jordan, and Sevier of the Great Basin (these rivers drain to terminal lakes, such as Great Salt Lake, instead of flowing to the ocean) and the Green, Duchesne, White, San Rafael, Dirty Devil, and San Juan, all of which flow into the Colorado River upstream of or within Lake Powell. Snowmelt supplies more than one hundred lakes and rivers, which are the primary source of fresh water for the state.

Fish and Fishing

The state maintains ten fish hatcheries that supply rivers, lakes, and reservoirs for sport fishing. There are also two national fish hatcheries in the state—Jones Hole and Ouray. Brook, brown, and rainbow trout are popular catches for anglers. The June sucker, an endemic species from Utah Lake, is on the federally endangered species list, while the Utah Lake sculpin, once endemic, has become extinct. Bear Lake is home to five endemic species—Bonneville cisco, Bonneville whitefish, Bear Lake whitefish, Bear Lake sculpin, and the Bea Lake cutthroat. The razorback sucker Colorado pikeminnow, roundtail chubs, humpback chub, and southwestern willow flycatcher are among the native species of the Green River that are now endangered. The Bonneville cutthroat trout, the state fish, is also noted as wildlife species of concern by the Utah Department of Natural Resources.

The Great Salt Lake. © *Marco Regalia/ShutterStock.com*

Agriculture

Agricultural production generates total cash receipts (direct output) of more than $1 billion annually. Agricultural processing and manufacturing are even more significant. Dairy products and cattle are among the top commodities. The state ranks among the top ten in the nation for production of tart and sweet cherries, sheep and goats, onions, apricots, and pears. Sweet corn, tomatoes, barley, wheat, and dry edible beans are also important crops. Certification for organic produce, products, and producers is available through the Utah Department of Agriculture and Food, which certifies to the standards of the USDA National Organic Program.

🍃 Energy

Oil and Natural Gas

Crude oil production in Utah accounts for about 1 percent of total U.S. production, while natural gas production in the state accounts for 2 percent of the U. S. total. Drilling operations for both oil and natural gas are concentrated in the Unita basin of eastern Utah. This basin is part of the greater Green River Formation that extends through portions of Colorado, Utah, and Wyoming. The Green River Formation contains the largest known oil shale deposits in the world. Oil shale is a type of sedimentary rock containing bituminous materials that can be mined and processed to generate oil. The federally owned Green River Formation contains an estimated 800 billion barrels of recoverable oil, an amount that is three times greater than the proven oil reserves of Saudi Arabia. However, the recovery process has thus far proven to be too complex and too expensive to be an economically feasible option for oil production.

About 20 percent of the natural gas produced in the state is from coal-bed methane (a type of natural gas produced from coal seams). About 50 percent of the natural gas produced within the state is consumed locally, while the other half is exported to neighboring states. Nearly 80 percent of all Utah households rely on natural gas as a primary source for home heating. The state has five oil refineries, all located in the Salt Lake City area. Petroleum consumption in the state is relatively low. The state requires the use of a low volatility blend of fuel for Salt Lake City and Provo/Orem areas, but conventional gasoline can be used in all other areas.

Coal and Electricity

A little more than 82 percent of the state's supply of electricity is generated from coal-fired plants, with most of the required coal mined from reserves within the state. Coal production in Utah accounts for more than 2 percent of the total U.S. production. About 15 percent of electricity comes from natural gas-fired plants.

Renewable Portfolio

Less than 2 percent of the state's supply of electricity is generated from hydropower and even less is generated from the state's two geothermal generating facilities. However, some efforts are being made to promote development of renewable and clean-tech energy resources. In 2008, the state legislature enacted the Energy Resource and Carbon Emission Reduction Initiative (SB 202), which established a renewable portfolio goal for the state. The act encourages utilities to use eligible renewable energy sources to produce 20 percent of their adjusted retail electric sales by 2025. The law only requires a utility to meet this goal if it is deemed cost-effective. Initially, eligible renewable energy sources included solar, wind, biomass, hydroelectric, geothermal, waste gas and waste heat, and wave, tidal, or ocean thermal energy. Amendments passed in 2010 added municipal solid waste, compressed air energy storage, and methane gas from abandoned coal mines or coal degassing operations as eligible sources (HB 192, HB 228, SB 104).

❧ Green Business, Green Building, Green Jobs

Green Business and Green Jobs

While the number of green businesses (and green jobs) is on the rise in the state, the rate of increase is relatively slow, and some reports indicate that the state could be doing more to create the necessary environment to build a green economy. In January 2010, Clean Energy Utah, a non-profit, non-partisan public interest organization, published *Building the Clean Energy Economy: A Study on Jobs and Economic Development of Clean Energy in Utah*, a study that considered the economic benefits associated with the full implementation of what is referred to as the "20 Percent Clean Energy Scenario." This scenario assumes the full implementation of the state's energy efficiency policy (established in 2006), which calls for a 20 percent increase in energy efficiency in all sectors by 2015, and the implementation of the renewable portfolio goal introduced in 2008 (SB 202), which encourages utilities to use eligible renewable energy sources to produce 20 percent of their adjusted retail electric sales by 2025. The study projects the addition of 7,000 new ongoing jobs by 2020 under the 20% Clean Energy Scenario, resulting in $310 million in new annual earnings and $300 million net annual increase in gross domestic product by state (GDPS).

However, as of 2011, the state had not adopted a required renewable portfolio standard, choosing instead to promote a renewable energy goal for utilities to use eligible renewable energy sources to produce 20 percent of their adjusted retail electric sales by 2025, if such a target is deemed cost-effective. In June 2010, Headwaters Economics published a study entitled *Clean Energy Leadership in the Rockies: Competitive Positioning in the Emerging Green Economy*, which compared the economies and policies of five states—Colorado, New Mexico, Montana, Utah, and Wyoming—to consider how well they were adapting their vast energy resources to create a greener economy. The study indicated that the state of Utah was lagging behind other states in the region in attracting clean energy businesses, in part due to the lack of a mandated renewable portfolio standard and few clean technology incentives.

Throughout 2010, the state has taken steps to establish a better green business climate. In June 2010, the governor announced the beginning of the formal planning process for a major ten-year strategic energy plan. As outlined in *Energy Initiatives and Imperatives: Utah's 10-Year Strategic Energy Plan*, the plan consists of a nine-objective approach that includes a directive to create new energy-related manufacturing opportunities and jobs. The Governor's Office of Economic Development held its first Renewable Energy Business Summit on November 15, 2010, as a means to encourage government, business, and academic leaders to work together for the development of new green economy. The governor issued a report in March 2011, summarizing the goals of the plan and providing information on its implementation.

Green Building

The State Building Energy Efficiency Program was launched through the passage of the Energy Savings in State Buildings act (HB 80) in 2006 and is implemented through the state Division of Facilities Construction and Management (DFCM). Under the program, the DFCM is responsible for setting guidelines, procedures, and incentives for energy efficiency in state facilities. Pursuant to the act, each state agency or assisting agency must develop an energy efficiency and cost conservation plan for associated facilities and appoint a staff member to oversee the plan. Also, all state building projects started after June 1, 2009 must be certified with a silver rating under the U.S. Green Building Leadership in Energy and Environmental Design (LEED) program. In 2005, the Daybreak Elementary and Community Center became the first public school in Utah to be LEED certified (Silver). That same year, the OSHA Salt Lake Technical Center was also certified as LEED Silver. The Daybreak Corporate Center became the first LEED Platinum certified building in Utah in 2008.

❦ Something in the Air on the Wasatch Front

The four northern counties of Davis, Salt Lake, Utah, and Weber lie along the western edge of the Wasatch Mountain Range, which is generally referred to as the Wasatch Front. This area is home to nearly 76 percent of the state's total population, with most living in Salt Lake City, Ogden, Provo, Layton, and adjacent suburban communities. With such a high population density, air pollution is a significant problem. Automobiles and industry are primary contributors to high levels of ozone and carbon monoxide. While pollutant levels are generally within an acceptable range much of the year, winter weather can cause higher concentrations of particulate matter (PM) to build up, which can lead to serious health problems for some individuals.

Particulate matter is a mixture of very fine dust, soot, and chemical particles that form in the atmosphere as secondary pollutants. During the winter, atmospheric conditions can create a condition known as surface inversion, which occurs when a front of warm air passes over a mass of cold air, trapping the cold air closer to the ground. When this happens, pollutants are trapped near the ground as well. People with existing lung or heart conditions such as asthma, emphysema, chronic obstructive pulmonary disease (COPD), and congestive heart failure may experience shortness of breath or the development of serious respiratory infections as a result of higher pollutant levels. Children and the elderly are also at risk for symptoms that can lead to hospitalization and premature death.

Local government officials along the Wasatch Front, and in the Cache Valley near Logan where inversions also occur, are well aware of the problem and have established a number of strategies to monitor and control the effects of winter inversions and secondary pollutants. There are 24 air monitoring stations located across the Wasatch Front. The four Wasatch Front counties have vehicle inspection programs in place to reduce automobile emissions. Carpooling and mass transit park and ride programs are also strongly encouraged. There are also a variety of regulatory controls placed on industrial facilities in an attempt to reduce PM emissions.

During winter, automobile traffic and use of wood burning stoves and fireplaces are regulated through the Red Light, Green Light program. When an inversion occurs and PM levels are elevated, the Air Monitoring Center of the Utah Division of Air Quality calls a "red light day," which means that wood burning is prohibited. Residents are asked to drive as little as possible and industries are expected to minimize their release of emissions. Residents with health issues are warned to refrain from strenuous outdoor activities, such as snow shoveling. On "yellow light days," residents and industries alike are asked to do what they can to minimize pollutants in order to avoid a more serious red light day. On "green light days," wood burning is permitted for all residents. The program season generally runs from November through March.

Since 2006, state officials have been struggling to face the challenge posed by a change in air quality standards imposed by the U.S. Environmental Protection Agency (EPA). The standards in question relate to the concentration of PM2.5 found in the air. PM2.5 is particulate matter that has an aerodynamic diameter of 2.5 microns or smaller. Such fine particles can be inhaled deeply into the lungs and are difficult to dispel. The EPA sets annual and twenty-four hour average standards for the presence of PM2.5 in the air. In 1997, the EPA set the twenty-four hour standard at 65 micrograms per cubic meter or lower and the state of Utah had no trouble meeting this requirement. However, in 2006, the EPA lowered this standard to 35 micrograms per cubic meter or lower, immediately placing the Wasatch Front out of compliance with federal health standards.

During the first half of 2011, Salt Lake County residents have been fighting local Kennecott Utah Copper's attempts to expand its Bingham Canyon Mine. The mine, which produces gold, copper, silver, and molybdenum, hopes to extend its operations for an extra nine years with the expansion. For an area that is already out of compliance with federal health standards, residents are angry that Kennecott would consider expanding their mine and possibly cause even more air pollution. In May 2011, the Utah Air Quality Board gave the mine permission to expand and mine deeper into the Oquirrh Mountains, increasing the amount of materials removed from 197 million tons to 260 million tons annually. Despite this increase, the company is claiming that the expansion, also called the Cornerstone project, will not lead to more air pollution but will instead see a decrease in emissions. The company states that better dust-suppression techniques, more fuel-efficient vehicles, and the conversion of a coal-fired power plant to natural gas are some of the techniques they will be employing to lessen harmful emissions. However, organizations such as Utah Physicians for a Healthy Environment, the Utah Clean Air Alliance, and Utah Moms for Clean Air are not at all receptive. EPA officials have also criticized the company's expansion, stating that their preliminary determination is that the project will not be approvable. In May, the Utah Air Quality Board approved a plan to lift the state's cap on PM10 emissions to accommodate the expansion, despite the EPA's misgivings. Another environmental permit for the project was approved in June 2011, bringing the project closer to reality, and making Utah residents feel that their concerns are being ignored.

Utah air quality officials are working to develop an EPA-approved implementation plan that will place the state back in compliance again. In the meantime, the

An aerial view of Kennecott's Bingham Canyon Mine—an open-pit copper mine—largest human-made excavation on earth. *© Lee Prince/ ShutterStock.com*

governor announced a statewide Clean Air Challenge, designed to encourage all residents to do their part to minimize air pollutants by driving less, carpooling more, and minimizing wood burning activities. In February 2010, researchers from the University of Utah received $1.2 million in funds from the National Science Foundation for a three-year study of winter inversion conditions, in efforts to learn more on how this meteorological effect contributes to the development of pollutants and overall air quality.

BIBLIOGRAPHY

Books

Alton, James M. *The River Knows Everything: Desolation Canyon and the Green.* Logan, UT: Utah State University Press, 2009.

Donahue, Debra L. *The Western Range Revisited: Removing Livestock from Public Lands to Conserve Native Biodiversity.* Norman, OK: University of Oklahoma Press, 2000.

Gordon, Greg. *Landscape of Desire: Identity and Nature in Utah's Canyon Country.* Logan, UT: Utah State University Press, 2003.

Grayson, Donald K. *The Great Basin: A Natural Prehistory,* rev. ed. Berkeley, CA: University of California Press, 2011.

Hengesbaugh, Mark. *Creatures of Habitat: The Changing Nature of Wildlife and Wild Places in Utah and the Intermountain West.* Logan, UT: Utah State University Press, 2001.

Lamb, Susan and Tom Bean. *The Smithsonian Guides to Natural America: The Southern Rockies–Colorado, Utah.* Washington, DC: Smithsonian Books, 1996.

Powell, James Lawrence. *Dead Pool: Lake Powell, Global Warming, and the Future of Water in the West.* Berkeley, CA: University of California Press, 2008.

Sullivan, Tim. *No Communication with the Sea: Searching for an Urban Future in the Great Basin.* Tucson, AZ: University of Arizona Press, 2010.

Webb, Robert H. *Cataract Canyon: A Human and Environmental History of the Rivers in Canyonlands.* Salt Lake City, UT: University of Utah Press, 2004.

Whitley, Colleen K., ed. *From the Ground Up: The History of Mining in Utah.* Logan, UT: Utah State University Press, 2006.

Web Sites

Agriculture in the Classroom: Utah State University Cooperative Extension. Available from http://extension.usu.edu/AITC

"As Interest in Renewable Energy Job Grows State Takes Action." Utah Governor's Office of Economic Development. October 19, 2010. Available from http://business.utah.gov/news/articles/vocus/116431

Associated Press. "Bill urging exit from climate initiative passes." Ksl.com. February 24, 2009. Available from http://www.ksl.com/?nid=148&sid=5688083

"The Basics of Winter Air Pollution in Utah." Utah Department of Environmental Quality. Available from http://www.cleanair.utah.gov/docs/BasicsofWinterAirPollutioninUtah.pdf

"Bear Lake, an Endemical Wonder." Angler Guide. Available from http://www.anglerguide.com/articles/710.html

Bernick, Bob, Jr. "Utah Legislature: House formally questions global warming." *Deseret News.* February 10, 2010. Available from http://www.deseretnews.com/article/700008370/Utah-Legislature-House-formally-questions-global-warming.html

Bon, Roger L., and Ken Krahulec. *2009 Summary of Mineral Activity in Utah.* Utah Geological Survey. Available from http://geology.utah.gov/online/c/c-111.pdf

Building the Clean Energy Economy: A Study on Jobs and Economic Development of Clean Energy in Utah. Utah Clean Energy. Available from http://utahcleanenergy.org/files/u1/Economic_Development_Study_Full_Report_FINAL.pdf

Clean Energy Leadership in the Rockies: Competitive Positioning in the Emerging Green Economy. Headwaters Economics. Available from http://www.headwaterseconomics.org/greeneconomy/CleanEnergyLeadership.pdf

Climate Change and Utah: The Scientific Consensus. Utah Governor's Blue Ribbon Advisory Council on Climate Change. Available from http://www.deq.utah.gov/BRAC_Climate/docs/Final_Report/Sec-A-1_SCIENCE_REPORT.pdf

Climate Change Joint Resolution (HJR 12 enrolled). Utah State Legislature. Available from http://le.utah.gov/~2010/bills/hbillenr/hjr012.htm

Climate Change Joint Resolution (HJR 12 introduced). Utah State Legislature. Available from http://le.utah.gov/~2010/bills/hbillint/hjr012.htm

Endangered and Threatened Animals of Utah. Utah Department of Natural Resources, Division of Wildlife Resources. Available from http://wildlife.utah.gov/habitat/pdf/endgspec.pdf

Energy Resource and Carbon Emission Reduction Initiative (SB 202). Utah State Legislature. Available from http://le.utah.gov/~2008/bills/sbillenr/sb0202.pdf

Energy Savings in State Buildings (HB 80). Utah State Legislature. Available from http://www.le.state.ut.us/~2006/bills/hbillenr/hb0080.pdf

Fahys, Judy. "Kennecott expansion clears another Utah hurdle." *The Salt Lake Tribune*. June 28, 2011. Available from http://www.sltrib.com/sltrib/news/52083340-78/kennecott-pollution-permit-quality.html.csp

"Farm Facts." Utah Department of Agriculture and Food. Available from http://ag.utah.gov/news/publications/documents/FarmFacts.pdf

"Fishing in Utah." Utah Department of Natural Resources, Division of Wildlife Resources. Available from http://wildlife.utah.gov/dwr/fishing

Great Salt Lake Ecosystem Program. Available from http://wildlife.utah.gov/gsl/index.php

Herbert, Gary R. *Energy Initiatives and Imperatives: Utah's 10-Year Strategic Energy Plan*. State of Utah, Office of the Governor. Available from http://www.utah.gov/governor/docs/Energy-Initiatives-Imperatives.pdf

"Kennecott Land's Daybreak Corporate Center Achieves LEED Platinum Certification." Kennecott Land. December 3, 2008. Available from http://www.kenecottland.com/library/media/Kennecott%20Lands%20Daybreak%20Corporate%20Center%20Achieves%20LEED%20Platinum%20Certification.pdf

"Listings and occurrences for Utah." Species Reports. U.S. Fish and Wildlife Service. Available from http://ecos.fws.gov/tess_public/pub/stateListingAndOccurrenceIndividual.jsp?state=UT&S8-fid=112761032792&S8fid=112762573902

Lomax, Simon. "Utah won't join regional cap-and-trade program in 2012." *Deseret News*. April 24, 2010. Available from http://www.deseretnews.com/article/700027066/Utah-wont-join-regional-cap-and-trade-program-in-2012.html

"Management of Air Quality in Utah." Utah Department of Environmental Quality. Available from http://www.deq.utah.gov/references/FactSheets/Air_Quality.htm

National Park Service: Utah. Available from http://www.nps.gov/applications/parksearch/state.cfm?st=ut

O'Donoghue, Amy Joi. "New study aims to capture information on Utah's inversion." *Deseret News*. February 2, 2010. Available from http://www.deseretnews.com/article/700006699/New-study-aims-to-capture-information-on-Utahs-inversion.html

O'Donoghue, Amy Joi. "Ozone levels see decrease along Wasatch Front." *Deseret News*. September 27, 2010. Available from http://www.deseretnews.com/article/700069074/Ozone-levels-see-decrease-along-Wasatch-Front.html

Oil Shale Resources of the Uinta Basin, Utah and Colorado. United States Geological Survey. Available from http://pubs.usgs.gov/dds/dds-069/dds-069-bb

"Organic Program." Utah Department of Agriculture and Food. Available from http://ag.utah.gov/divisions/plant/organic/index.html

"PM 2.5 Nonattainment Designations." Utah Department of Environmental Quality. Available from http://www.deq.utah.gov/Issues/hottopics/pm25.htm

Renewable Energy–Methane Gas (HB 192). Utah State Legislature. Available from http://le.utah.gov/~2010/bills/hbillenr/hb0192.pdf

Renewable Energy Modifications (SB 104). Utah State Legislature. Available from http://le.utah.gov/~2010/bills/sbillenr/sb0104.pdf

Renewable Energy Source Amendments (HB 228). Utah State Legislature. Available from http://le.utah.gov/~2010/bills/hbillenr/hb0228.pdf

Resolution on Energy Policy (HR 3). Utah State Legislature. Available from http://le.utah.gov/~2009/bills/hbillenr/hr0003.htm

"State Building Energy efficiency Program." Utah Division of Facilities Construction and Management. Available from http://dfcm.utah.gov/energyEff/index.html

"State Energy Profiles: Utah." U.S. Energy Information Administration. Available from http://tonto.eia.doe.gov/state/state_energy_profiles.cfm?sid=UT

Stettler, Jeremiah. "Pollution fears cloud approval of Kennecott expansion." *The Salt Lake Tribune*. May 27, 2011. Available from http://www.sltrib.com/

sltrib/politics/51752890-90/kennecott-expansion-mine-board.html.csp

Utah Conservation Data Center. Utah Natural Resources Division of Wildlife Resources. Available from http://dwrcdc.nr.utah.gov/ucdc

Utah Department of Agriculture and Food. Available from http://ag.utah.gov/index.html

Utah Forest Facts. Utah State University Forestry Extension. Available from http://extension.usu.edu/forestry/Reading/Assets/PDFDocs/NR_FF/NRFF011.pdf

"Utah Greenhouse Gas Goal." Utah Department of Environmental Quality http://www.deq.utah.gov/Climate_Change/GHG_goal.htm

Utah Greenhouse Gas Inventory and Reference Case Projections, 1990–2020. Center for Climate Strategies. Available from http://utahcleanenergy.org/files/u1/tah_Greenhouse_Gas_Inventory_Report_2007_CCS.pdf

"Utah Hunting." Utah Division of Wildlife Resources. http://dwrcdc.nr.utah.gov/ucdc

"Utah Lakes and Reservoirs." Utah Department of Environmental Quality, Division of Water Quality. Available from http://www.waterquality.utah.gov/watersheds/lakes.htm

"Utah LEED Buildings." U.S. Green Building Council: Utah Chapter. Available from http://www.usgbcutah.org/leedbuildings/default.aspx

"Utah Legislature: Climate change resolution advances in Senate." *Deseret News.* February 25, 2010. Available from http://www.deseretnews.com/article/700012160/Utah-Legislature-Climate-change-resolution-advances-in-Senate.html

Utah Sensitive Species List. State of Utah Department of Natural Resources, Division of Wildlife Resources. May 11, 2010. Available from http://dwrcdc.nr.utah.gov/ucdc/ViewReports/SSL_20100511.pdf

Utah Statewide Forest Resource Assessment & Strategy Guide 2010. Utah Department of Natural Resources, Division of Forestry, Fire and State Lands. Available from

Utah State Parks. Available from http://stateparks.utah.gov

"Utah's Winter Air Quality Program: Red Light, Green Light." Utah Department of Environmental Quality. Available from http://www.deq.utah.gov/references/FactSheets/Red-Green_light_program.htm

Ward, Ruby A., Paul M. Jakus, and Dillon Feuz. *The Economic Impact of Agriculture on the State of Utah.* Available from http://ag.utah.gov/news/documents/USUageconstudy2010-02.pdf

Water in Utah. Utah Department of Natural Resources, Division of Water Resources. Available from http://www.water.utah.gov/Brochures/WIU_BROC.HTM

Vermont

In recent years, the Green Mountain state has established the objective of creating a new clean, green economy. The state has joined the national 25 by '25 Initiative, which sets goals for the development of renewable energy sources found in forests, farms, and fields in the form of woody biomass, energy crops, wind, solar, and geothermal power. Vermont has also established the Sustainably Priced Energy Enterprise Development (SPEED) Program, which provides incentives for utilities to include increasing amounts of renewable resources in their power generation mix. These and other initiatives are complemented by a number of green economic development strategies, such as *Engineering beyond Green*, with the aim of promoting environmental engineering as a key economic sector, and the Vermont Sustainable Jobs Fund, with a primary mission to accelerate development of the green economy. The greatest incentive for change, however, comes in the potential 2012 closing of the state's nuclear power plant, which currently supplies about one-third of the state's energy requirements, and nearly three-fourths of its electricity. If the Vermont Yankee nuclear plant goes offline as scheduled, utility companies and state officials will need to fill the energy gap as efficiently and economically as possible.

Climate

Vermont experiences a moist continental climate with average temperatures that vary depending on elevation. Temperatures can also vary quite a bit throughout a single day, with an average daily temperature range of 20 or 30°F (−6.6 or −1°C). In summer, for instance, temperatures typically range from a daytime high of 80° F (27°C) or above to an overnight low in the 60s (15°C) or lower. Winter is generally quite cold, with some areas of the state experiencing several sequential days of below zero temperatures.

Climate Change

The effects of global warming have already been noted within the state. According to a report from the National Wildlife Federation, average temperatures across the New England region have risen by 2.2°F (1.2°C) within the last century. Some estimates indicate that Vermont could experience an average rise of up to 5°F (2.8°C) by 2100. Warmer winter temperatures in Vermont could lead to the loss of several prominent tree species in the state's forests, including the sugar maples that have made Vermont the national leader in maple syrup production. Along with damage done to the environment and ecosystems, loss of wildlife and habitats could translate into a major loss in tourism dollars as well.

The state report, *Vermont Greenhouse Gas Emissions Inventory Update, 1990–2008*, released in September 2010, shows that Vermont's greenhouse gas emissions declined 10 percent from 2005 levels. They are, however, 3 percent higher than in 1990. Emissions are largely attributed to the transportation, residential, commercial, and industrial heating sectors. Transportation alone was responsible for nearly 47 percent of emissions. Residential and commercial use came second, accounting for 26 percent of emissions. The contribution to the total reported from the residential and commercial sectors was significantly higher than the national average for 2008, which was estimated as 8 percent, because of the relatively lower amounts of commercial activity and heavy industry in the state.

The last report, which updated the Final Vermont Greenhouse Gas Inventory and Reference Case Projections 1990–2030, was issued in 2007. This report considered two projection scenarios, a low-emissions model and a high-emissions model. The low-emissions scenario was based on the expected implementation of already approved reduction programs and a cleaner energy approach to filling the anticipated energy gap if the Vermont Yankee nuclear plant license expires in 2012. (The Nuclear Regulatory Commission renewed Vermont Yankee's license for an additional 20 years in March 2011, but state approval has been denied.) Under the low-emissions scenario, GHG emissions are expected to increase by about 7 percent from 2005 through 2030. Under the high-emissions scenario, the increase would be about 32 percent because it is expected that fossil fuel sources will be used to replace the electricity provided by the plant.

The state has already taken a number of actions designed to reduce greenhouse gas emissions, primarily through programs that promote the development and use of clean energy technology and renewable energy sources. A 2006 law created a legislative commission on global climate change that established goals to reduce greenhouse gas emissions: by 25 percent below 1990 levels by 2012, followed by a reduction of 50 percent by 2028, and 75 percent by 2050. To that end, the Vermont Agency of Transportation prepared its own Climate Change Action Plan in 2008, which features a three-pronged approach to GHG emissions reduction: developing and promoting the use of biofuels, increasing vehicle efficiency, and increasing efficiency in the transportation system. The state has already adopted the standards set by the California Low Emission Vehicle Program, so that most vehicles model year 2000 and up that are sold in Vermont must meet the same low-emission certification standards as those sold in California.

Vermont is also a member of the Regional Greenhouse Gas Initiative (RGGI), a cooperative cap-and-trade program involving ten Northeastern and Mid-Atlantic states. The program is designed with the goal of reducing power sector carbon dioxide emissions by 10 percent by 2018. To that end, the regional cap established by the group was set at 188 million short tons of carbon dioxide per year from 2009 to 2014. Starting in 2015 the cap will decrease by 2.5 percent each year. Carbon dioxide allowances for power plants can be obtained or traded in quarterly auctions. Each state may then reinvest its auction proceeds in programs that support the growth of a clean energy economy. In Vermont, the state's auction proceeds are used to support whole building heating and energy efficiency projects and to facilitate appropriate fuel switching plans. At least half of the projects are designed to benefit low income consumers. The first three-year control (or compliance) period began on January 1, 2009 and was set to end on December 31, 2011. At that time, each regulated power plant must submit one allowance for each ton of carbon dioxide emitted during the control period. The RGGI represents the first mandatory, market-based carbon dioxide emissions program in the United States. In May 2011, New Jersey Governor Chris Christie announced that his state would withdraw from the RGGI by the end of the year, calling it a "failure." The rest of the states continued to be committed to the program, and Vermont governor Peter Shumlin released a statement at the time expressing his disappointment in Christie's decision. "RGGI is something to be proud of

and to embrace, not something to raid for short-term budget gains—as has occurred in some states recently—or to reject for political gain," Shumlin said in his statement. "We cannot deny the impact of greenhouse gas emissions on our planet; we should not abandon our responsibility to future generations who count on us to do the right thing. I believe we must redouble our efforts to reduce our impact on the climate."

🍁 Natural Resources, Water, and Agriculture

Natural Resources: Christmas Trees and Maple Syrup

The Green Mountain state has more than 4.46 million acres (1,861,562 ha) of forest, covering more than 75 percent of the state. Sugar maples are the most common tree species in the state, and Vermont is the largest producer of pure maple syrup in the United States. Two thousand maple producers in the state made 1.14 million gallons (4,315,370 l) of maple syrup in 2011, an increase of 28 percent over 2010. The state's maple syrup industry had a production value of $30 million in 2010. Fir trees are plentiful throughout the state as well; fir, spruce, and white pine all contribute to the healthy Vermont Christmas tree industry. Overall, the forest-based sector accounts for about $1 billion in value of shipments annually, or 9.3 percent of total manufacturing sales for the state. Forest-related recreation and tourism is estimated by the state to be worth an additional $485 million per year.

In 2010, wood was used a source for nearly 5 percent of the state's energy needs, with a growing number of households and institutions using wood for heating systems and two wood-burning electrical power generators. Under the Vermont 25 x '25 Initiative, designed to produce 25 percent of the energy consumed within the state through the use of renewable sources by 2025, the state hopes to boost the use of wood biomass to generate 9 percent of the state's energy needs by 2025.

Parks and Quarries

The state maintains fifty-two state parks, serving as home to some of the state's most popular wildlife species, including white-tailed deer, coyote, red fox, beavers, wild turkey, and, in some areas, moose. The Green Mountain National Forest serves as a habitat for several endangered or threatened species, including the gray wolf, eastern cougar, and the Canada lynx. The bald eagle, peregrine falcon, and common loon are on the regional forester's list of sensitive species. The U.S. Fish & Wildlife Service lists five animal and plant species occurring in the state as federally threatened or endangered, including the Indiana bat and the northeastern bulrush.

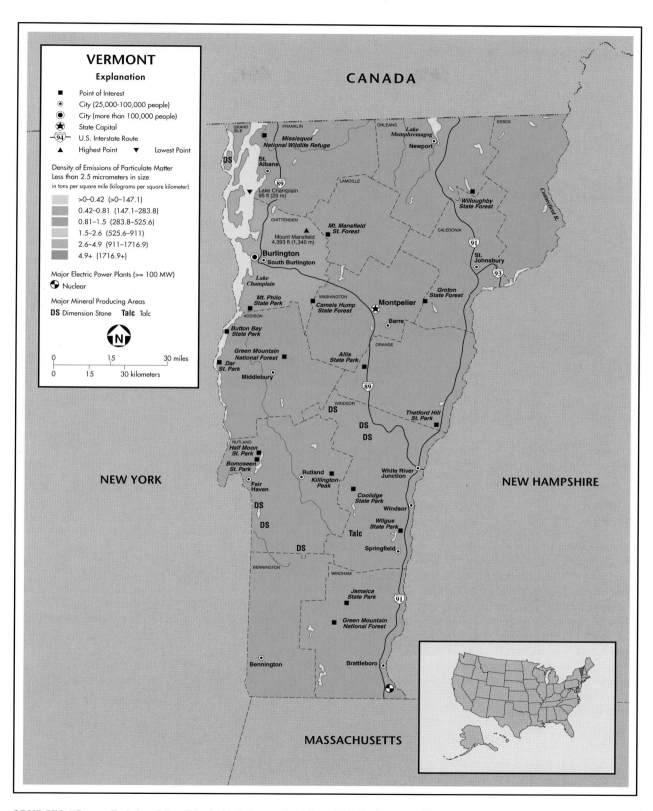

VERMONT

Explanation

- ■ Point of Interest
- ◉ City (25,000-100,000 people)
- ◎ City (more than 100,000 people)
- ★ State Capital
- 94 U.S. Interstate Route
- ▲ Highest Point   ▼ Lowest Point

Density of Emissions of Particulate Matter
Less than 2.5 micrometers in size
in tons per square mile (kilograms per square kilometer)

- >0–0.42 (>0–147.1)
- 0.42–0.81 (147.1–283.8)
- 0.81–1.5 (283.8–525.6)
- 1.5–2.6 (525.6–911)
- 2.6–4.9 (911–1716.9)
- 4.9+ (1716.9+)

Major Electric Power Plants (>= 100 MW)
- ⬤ Nuclear

Major Mineral Producing Areas
DS Dimension Stone   **Talc** Talc

Ⓝ

0   15   30 miles
0   15   30 kilometers

CANADA

NEW YORK

NEW HAMPSHIRE

MASSACHUSETTS

GRAND ISLE · FRANKLIN · ORLEANS · ESSEX · LAMOILLE · CHITTENDEN · CALEDONIA · WASHINGTON · ADDISON · ORANGE · WINDSOR · RUTLAND · BENNINGTON · WINDHAM

Missisquoi National Wildlife Refuge
St. Albans
Lake Memphremagog
Newport
Willoughby State Forest
Lake Champlain 95 ft (29 m)
Mt. Mansfield St. Forest
Mount Mansfield 4,393 ft (1,340 m)
Burlington
South Burlington
St. Johnsbury
Lake Champlain
Groton State Forest
Mt. Philo State Park
Camels Hump State Forest
Montpelier
Barre
Button Bay State Park
Green Mountain National Forest
Allis State Park
Dar St. Park
Middlebury
Thetford Hill St. Park
Half Moon St. Park
Bomoseen St. Park
Rutland
Killington Peak
White River Junction
Fair Haven
Coolidge State Park
Windsor
Wilgus State Park
Talc
Springfield
Jamaica State Park
Green Mountain National Forest
Bennington
Brattleboro
Connecticut R.

SOURCES: "County Emissions Map: Criteria Air Pollutants." *AirData.* U.S. Environmental Protection Agency. Available from http://www. epa.gov/air/data/geosel.html; *Energy Maps.* U.S. Energy Information Administration. Available from http://www.eia.gov/state; *Highest and Lowest Elevations.* U.S. Geological Survey. Available from http://egsc.usgs.gov/isb/pubs/booklets/elvadist/elvadist.html#Highest; *2007 Minerals Yearbook.* U.S. Geological Survey. Available from http://minerals.usgs.gov/minerals/pubs/state.   © 2011 Cengage Learning.

Tourst dollars spent in places such as Stowe contribute to the state's forest-related recreation and tourism industries. © *iStockPhoto.com/ Amy Riley*

Granite, marble, and slate are important mineral resources for the state. The Danby Quarry is the largest underground marble quarry in the world and the first marble production center to have its entire product line certified under the GREENGUARD Program, which requires a manufacturer to meet certain requirements for environmental responsibility, including use of safer chemicals and limiting particle emissions. In 2008, the state's nonfuel raw mineral production was valued at $111 million, with crushed stone, dimension stone, and construction sand and gravel accounting for most of the production. Vermont ranked third in the nation for production of crude talc, and dropped from being ranked third to a ranking of sixth in the nation for production of dimension stone.

Water

The major river in the state is the Connecticut River, forming the border with New Hampshire, and fed by important tributaries the White, Passumpsic, and Ottauqueechee and West Rivers. The Missisquoi, Lamoille, and Winooski rivers flow into Lake Champlain on the state's western border, and the Black and Clyde rivers flow into Lake Memphremagog on the northern border. The largest lake completely within the state is the manmade Harriman Reservoir, also referred to as Lake Whitingham. Sport fishing is popular at many sites, with brook trout, lake trout, landlocked salmon, largemouth bass, and yellow perch among the most popular catches. The state supports five fish hatcheries to stock lakes and streams and reestablish native fish populations. Hydroelectric power plants along the Connecticut River and Lake Champlain generate about 20 percent of the electrical supply in the state.

Wetlands cover about 4 percent of the land area of the state. These areas include wet meadows of wool grass, sedges, and sensitive fern; bogs of small cranberry, high brush blueberry, and sphagnum mosses; and marshes with wild rice, rushes, and cattails.

Agriculture

Vermont's agricultural sector is dominated by dairy, with sales of milk and other dairy products at nearly $500 million per year and more than 100 million pounds of cheese produced annually. Vermont is also a leading New England producer of beef. Apples are a top crop as well. A wide variety of vegetables and berries are grown

Vermont State Profile

Physical Characteristics

Land area	9,217 square miles (23,872 sq km)
Inland water area	400 square miles (1,036 sq km)
Coastal area	NA
Highest point	Mount Mansfield 4,393 feet (1,339 m)
National Forest System lands (2010)	400,000 acres (162,000 ha)
State parks (2011)	55

Energy Statistics

Total energy production (2009)	70 trillion Btu
State ranking in total energy production (2009)	45
Renewable energy net generation total (2009)	1.9 million megawatt hours
Hydroelectric energy generation (2009)	1.5 million megawatt hours
Biomass energy generation (2009)	24,000 megawatt hours
Wind energy generation (2009)	12,000 megawatt hours
Wood and derived fuel energy generation (2009)	393,000 megawatt hours
Crude oil reserves (2009)	NA
Natural gas reserves (2009)	NA
Natural gas liquids (2008)	NA

Pollution Statistics

Carbon output (2005)	6.5 million tons of CO_2 (5.9 million t)
Superfund sites (2008)	11
Particulate matter (less than 2.5 micrometers) emissions (2002)	237 tons per year (215 t/yr)
Toxic chemical releases (2009)	300,000 pounds (136,000 kg)
Generated hazardous waste (2009)	1,500 tons (1,400 t)

SOURCES: AirData. U.S. Environmental Protection Agency. Available from http://www.epa.gov/air/data; *Energy Maps, Facts, and Data of the U.S. States.* U.S. Energy Information Administration. Available from http://www.eia.gov/state; *The 2012 Statistical Abstract.* U.S. Census Bureau. Available from http://www.census.gov/compendia/statab; *United States Energy Usage.* eRedux. Available from http://www.eredux.net/states.

© 2011 Cengage Learning.

throughout the state, with much sold locally to stores, restaurants, or through farmers markets.

Certification for organic farming and products is carried out through Vermont Organic Farmers, a branch of the Northeast Organic Farming Association of Vermont. In 2010, there were at least 580 certified producers with 102,637 acres of certified organic farmland. Total gross sales for organic products was estimated at more than $125 million for that year.

Energy Crops

The Vermont Agency of Agriculture, Food and Markets (VAAFM), has been playing a major role in the design and implementation of the Vermont 25 x '25 Initiative.

Through this program, officials hope to produce more than 11 percent of the state's total energy needs through bioenergy crops and related technologies by 2025. In 2009, about 665 acres of oilseed crops were dedicated for biodiesel production. The first on-farm facility to make biodiesel was State Line Farm in North Bennington. State Line Farm has worked with the University of Vermont's Center For Sustainable Agriculture on the process of harvesting oilseed and converting it in a biodiesdel processing facility. The Vermont Grass Energy Partnership, funded in part by the Vermont Sustainable Jobs Fund, has taken the lead in conducting applied research on the use of perennial grasses for biomass energy production. In January 2011, the partnership released a report on the pros and cons of grass pellets for fuel, and came up with two recommendations for expanding the use of grass fiber as a heating fuel: to blend grass with wood pellets to meet existing industry norms and to build a new market for 100 percent grass pellets by developing appliances able to burn grass fuels. (Grass fuels are n'ot as feasible with current burning equipment because of high ash content and corrosive flue gas.) The report recommended more studies to determine production costs of a grass/wood blended pellet and to gauge commercial interest.

Also in 2009, the VAAFM was awarded $300,000 from the state's Clean Energy Development Fund in support of the Renewable Energy for Agriculture Grant Program (VT REAP) to promote the use of on-farm biomass energy programs, such as anaerobic digesters to produce electricity or heat from agricultural waste and animal manure. In 2009, there were eight operational farm digester systems in the state with two more operating as experimental facilities. Fourteen new digester projects were approved in late 2009.

Energy

Oil and Natural Gas

Vermont ranks last in the nation for both total energy consumption and demand for petroleum products and natural gas. With no fossil fuel resources of its own, Vermont imports petroleum products, used primarily for transportation fuel, from neighboring states and Canada. Vermont is one of the few states in the country that allows the statewide use of conventional motor oil, as opposed to a special reformulated blend.

About 60 percent of residents use fuel oil as a primary source for home heating. With often severe weather, increased demand for heating fuel during the harsh winter months can lead to distillate fuel shortages and dramatic increases in fuel costs. However, Vermont, along with its New England neighbors, benefits from inclusion in the Northeast Heating Oil Reserve. The reserve was created by a directive from President Bill Clinton in 2000 in an effort to alleviate the strain of winter shortages of fuel oil in the Northeastern states. The two million barrel reserve is meant to supply enough fuel oil for ten days, which is the estimated amount of time it takes for oil supplies to travel from the Gulf of Mexico to New York Harbor. Storage terminals for the reserve are located in Perth Amboy, New Jersey, and Groton and New Haven, Connecticut.

The relatively small amount of natural gas needed for residential use is supplied by Canada.

Electricity

Vermont and Rhode Island are the only two states in the union that do not have coal-fired power plants. Vermont generates a higher percentage of electricity from nuclear power than any other state in the union, according to the U.S. Energy Information Administration. About 35 percent of the statewide electrical supply comes from the Vermont Yankee nuclear power plant. Most of the remainder comes from renewable sources, with hydropower generating more than 30 percent of the electrical supply and wood and wood waste accounting for about 5 percent. The state is in the process of reorganizing its electrical supply, however, if the license for Vermont Yankee expires in 2012. (As of late 2011, the plant's owner, Entergy Corporation, was suing to overturn the state's refusal to permit the plant; the Massachusetts' Attorney General has filed a brief in support of Vermont's action. If the permit is ultimately denied, it would be the first nuclear power plant to close against the power plant owner's wishes.)

The SPEED Program for Renewable Energy

The state has considerable potential for further development of biomass, wind, solar, and hydropower sources of energy and the government has promoted a number of initiatives to encourage such development. Legislation enacted in 2005 established the Sustainably Priced Energy Enterprise Development (SPEED) Program (30 VSA §8001 et seq.). The SPEED Program provides incentives for utilities to include increasing amounts of renewable resources in their power generation mix. A primary focus is on encouraging utilities to establish long-term power purchase agreements with renewable energy source generators that are certified by the Vermont Public Service Board (PSB) as SPEED projects. Utilities may develop their own SPEED projects as well. An amendment enacted in 2008 as part of the Vermont Energy Efficiency and Affordability Act (SB 209) established a statewide goal to generate 20 percent of all electric retail sales by SPEED projects before July 1, 2017. The SPEED program serves as a non-binding renewable portfolio goal subject to review by the PSB. According to the initial act, the PSB is required to evaluate the program by the end of 2011 in order to determine the amount of SPEED project electricity that

has been supplied to Vermont consumers. If the goals have not been met voluntarily, they will become mandatory, and all utilities will be required to meet any new increase in electric retail sales through renewable sources or the purchase of renewable energy credits.

In June 2010, the state legislature passed a renewable energy bill (Act 159; H 781) that calls for the PSB to consider whether or not a more permanent renewable portfolio standard should be enacted to replace the SPEED program. The PSB is expected to provide a report on their findings by October 1, 2011.

Energy Plans and the Vermont 25 x '25 Initiative

The state's first comprehensive energy plan was published in 1998 as *Fueling Vermont's Future: Comprehensive Energy Plan and Greenhouse Gas Action Plan*. An additional twenty-year *Vermont Electric Plan* was published in 2005. Then in 2009, the energy plan and the electric plan were combined into one more fully updated *Vermont Comprehensive Energy Plan 2009*, which addresses issues of energy supply and demand, not only from a local perspective, but in regional, national, and global contexts as well.

In 2008, the state legislature set a new statewide target for producing 25 percent of all energy consumed within the state through renewable energy sources by 2025 (10 VSA §580). This legislation led to the establishment of the Vermont 25 x '25 Initiative, a local chapter of the national 25 x '25 Alliance that serves as a forum for members from several government agencies as they work toward reaching this set goal. Under the Vermont 25 x '25 Initiative, the overall 25 x '25 goal is broken down into smaller energy production goals that will be met through the development of energy crops, agricultural waste, woody biomass, wind, solar, hydroelectric, and geothermal sources.

❧ Green Business, Green Building, Green Jobs

Green Business

Green business is not a particularly new concept for Vermont, as there are a number of statewide and regional groups that have been promoting sustainable and environmentally responsible business practices for more than two decades, and a state pollution prevention program devoted to helping them improve their environmental performance. Recently the state has seen an increase in the number of clean tech businesses, and the state has also begun to more actively encourage developments in energy efficiency and renewable energy resources. According to a survey from the Pew Charitable Trust, there were 311 clean tech companies in the state in 2007. A report from Collaborative Economics, a group that advises "civic entrepreneurs," indicates that energy generation has been a leading segment of the clean tech industry, with energy efficiency seen as a major growth sector.

Going Green and Beyond

The growth of the green economy has been sparked by several state government initiatives and incentives and public-private partnerships, all focused on encouraging and supporting green business. In 2007, the governor established the Vermont Environmental Engineering Advisory Council as part of a major initiative to promote environmental engineering as a key economic sector in the state. The council's 2008 report, *Engineering Beyond Green: Capturing the Emerging Market for Holistic Innovation and Expertise*, provided a series of recommendations for the legislature on necessary steps for growing the green economy. These had a particular focus on investments in education, training, and recruitment of qualified professionals in the industry.

Also in 2008, the Vermont Agency of Commerce and Community Development published *Promoting and Fostering the Green Economy in Vermont: A Strategic Plan for a Green Future*. This document summarizes some of the key goals set by the Department of Economic Development for growing the green economy, which include providing continued support for existing green businesses while actively recruiting new businesses to the state. The report also lists some of the organizations assisting in the growth of the green economy, including the Vermont Center for Emerging Technologies and the Vermont Environmental Consortium.

Vermont Sustainable Jobs Fund

One major, statewide green business and green job initiative is the Vermont Sustainable Jobs Fund (VSJF), which was created by an act of legislation in 1995 with a primary mission to accelerate the development of the state's green economy (10 VSA 15A). The VSJF provides grant funding and technical assistance to a wide variety of business owners and entrepreneurs who are developing businesses and markets that lead to new jobs. Many of the VSJF-sponsored projects focus on sustainable energy products, such as the Vermont Biofuels Initiative. But the group is also involved in projects such as the Farm to Plate Initiative, which is focused on creating jobs in the agriculture and food service and production sectors by expanding markets for Vermont grown and made foods.

Green Jobs: Vermont Green

To help recruit and train those looking for careers in the growing fields of energy efficiency and renewable energy, the Central Vermont Community Action Council (CVCAC) has created the Vermont Growing Renewable Energy/Efficiency Employment Network, more commonly called Vermont Green. The program involves a statewide public-private partnership designed to provide training in weatherization and other energy efficiency trades, green building practices, renewable energy sources, recycling and waste reduction, and environmental protection. The program particularly targets those who are unemployed or underemployed. In January 2010, the CVCAC was awarded a grant of $4.86 million through the American Recovery and Reinvestment Act for the Vermont Green program.

Green Building

The basic energy efficiency building standards for both commercial and residential buildings are linked to those set by the most recent International Energy Conservation Code. However, in 2008, Vermont enacted legislation that set a number of building efficiency goals (10 VSA §581). The state hopes to improve the energy efficiency of at least 20 percent of the entire housing stock (which would amount to more than 60,000 housing units) by 2017 and 25 percent by 2025 (80,000 units). Another goal involves the reduction of total fossil fuel consumption in all buildings by 6 percent annually by 2017 and 10 percent annually by 2025.

There are several organizations throughout the state that are encouraging the use of green building practices in all residential, commercial, and industrial projects. The Vermont Green Building Network (VGBN) was founded in 2002 as the local chapter of the United States Green Building Council. The VGBN works to establish a market for green building in the state as well as providing support for businesses involved in green building. Building for Social Responsibility, the Vermont chapter of the Northeast Sustainable Energy Association, sponsors the Vermont Building Greener Program, a voluntary certification program for residential buildings. This was the first program of its kind in the Northeast.

🍁 Vermont Yankee Nuclear

The heated debate over the future of the Vermont Yankee Nuclear plant has erupted into a legal war as the local subsidiaries of Entergy, the company that operates the plant, have filed a lawsuit to prevent the state from shutting the plant down in March 2012. A trial resulting from the lawsuit began in September 2011. The core of the matter lies in conflicting opinions over the validity of a 2006 state law requiring the approval of the state legislature for the plant's license renewal. The plant began operating in March 1972 under a 40-year license set to expire in 2012. Under the terms of a 2002 Memorandum of Understanding signed by two of Entergy's subsidiaries, Entergy Nuclear Vermont

The Vermont Yankee nuclear power plant provides 35 percent of the state's electrical supply. © AP Images/Toby Talbot

Yankee, LLC (ENVY) and Entergy Nuclear Operations Inc. (ENOI), the companies agreed to apply for a certificate of public good from the Vermont Public Service Board if they wanted to extend the plant's operating license beyond 2012. However, in 2006, the state legislature passed Act 160, which gave the general assembly the power to vote on the matter and made legislative approval a primary factor in license renewal. As of 2011, Vermont was the only state with such a law on its books.

In February 2010, the Vermont senate voted 26 to 4 against a license extension for the Vermont Yankee nuclear plant. The senate vote is historically significant in that it marks the first time that a state legislature has voted to close a nuclear plant. While several states have held popular referendums on the closure of nuclear reactors, the only one to succeed was in California, when voters called for the closing of the Rancho Seco reactor in 1989.

The outcome was not entirely unexpected. Several state officials have been working on alternative energy source options for a number of years, with a goal to lessen the state's dependency on nuclear energy as its primary source of electricity. But the issue took on a greater urgency in January 2010 when Vermont Yankee notified the Vermont Department of Health that groundwater samples taken in November 2009 contained traces of the radioactive material tritium. The company began an immediate investigation with oversight by the Nuclear Regulatory Commission and discovered the source to be an aging and badly corroded underground pipe that was leaking nuclear steam. The threat of radioactive contamination may have been enough of an incentive for legislators to question the renewal of the plant's license, but an additional issue of trust was involved: In 2007, following a collapse of one of the plant's cooling towers, plant officials had claimed

that there were no underground pipes that could leak tritium.

Additional support for the state government's stand against nuclear power came in the wake of the reactor leaks at the Fukushima Daiichi Nuclear Power Plant in Japan as a result of the March 11, 2011 earthquake and tsunami. Vermont Yankee uses the same type of General Electric Mark 1 boiling water reactor as the now crippled Fukushima plant did. Many Vermont politicians immediately pointed to Fukushima as further justification for the legislative and executive decision to close Vermont Yankee. However, supporters of the plant pointed out that the Vermont location is unlikely to experience the same devastating natural disaster that was the immediate cause of the reactor failures at Fukushima. Furthermore, just one day before the earthquake, the U.S. Nuclear Regulatory Commission voted to approve a twenty-year license renewal for Vermont Yankee, a decision based on an extensive five-year safety and environmental review.

As the state stands firm on its resolve to see Vermont Yankee closed in 2012, Entergy filed its lawsuit against the state in federal district court on April 18, 2011. According to a statement from Entergy, the complaint is based on the belief that the passage of Act 160 in 2006 represented a breach of the 2002 Memorandum of Understanding between the state and the company's subsidiaries. Company officials state that they did not agree with the 2006 law, but at the time, were willing to try to work with the state government, rather than resort to litigation. This explains the actions taken by the company in applying for the certificate of public good in 2008. According to the Entergy statement, the complaint is based in part on the legal principles of the Atomic Energy Act and a precedent set by the U.S. Supreme Court in 1983 in a similar case involving Pacific Gas & Electric, which affirmed that a state has no authority over the environmental and safety aspects of nuclear power licensing or operations. According to this argument, the state of Vermont does not have the right to shut down the operations of a federally licensed nuclear power plant. A few days after filing the lawsuit, Entergy also filed a request for a preliminary injunction to keep the state from closing the plant until the courts have ruled on the suit.

Vermont's governor Peter Shumlin issued a statement claiming that Entergy did, in fact, support the 2006 law allowing for state jurisdiction in the matter and that the company is violating its own agreement to abide by the state relicensing process.

In response to the suit, the state legislature inserted into the Vermont Energy Act 2011 a "bill-back" provision, which could require Entergy to pay all of the state's legal fees in the federal suit. The Vermont Energy Act 2011 was passed in May 2011 and covers energy development measures involving net metering, the promotion of biomass and hydropower, and the creation of a Clean Energy Development Fund. The "bill-back" provision was added near the end of deliberations and caused controversy among legislators, as some believed that this rule, which is commonly used to cover the cost of expert testimony in trials involving utility companies, should not apply to other fees, such as legal counsel. Others believe the state simply does not have the authority to support such a measure and that it will inevitably be challenged in court.

Meanwhile, the state's largest utilities have been taking matters into their own hands by negotiating new deals with a variety of energy companies as they seek alternative sources to nuclear energy. In May 2010, Green Mountain Power and Central Vermont Power signed agreements with Granite Reliable Wind, which is currently developing a 99-megawatt wind farm in Coos County, New Hampshire. In August 2010, the same two entities signed a twenty-six-year deal with the Canadian company Hydro-Quebec. The state has received power from Hydro-Quebec since the 1980s. The new deal is designed to ensure competitive prices over the next twenty-six years and to provide nearly 25 percent of the state's electricity during that time. The starting price for the electricity is set at $58.07 per megawatt-hour and will be adjusted in future years based on regional and national electricity prices. The contract was approved by the Vermont Public Service Board in April 2011 and is expected to go into effect in November 2012. Vermont Yankee had offered a similar contract that involved a first-year price of $49 per megawatt-hour followed by market-adjusted pricing. A few days after the Hydro-Quebec deal was approved, the board of the Vermont Electric Cooperative, the state's third-largest utility, also rejected a 20-year contract with Vermont Yankee.

BIBLIOGRAPHY

Books

Dunbar, Bethany. *Kingdom's Bounty: A Sustainable, Eclectic Edible Guide to Vermont's Northeast Kingdom.* New York: Umbrage, 2011.

New England 2011: Connecticut, Maine, Massachusetts, New Hampshire, Rhode Island, and Vermont. Chicago, IL: Five Star Travel Corp., 2011.

Wetherell, W. D. *The Smithsonian Guides to Natural America: Northern New England–Vermont, New Hampshire, Maine.* Washington, DC: Smithsonian Books, 1995.

Web Sites

Act 159 (H 781): An Act Relating to Renewable Energy. Vermont State Legislature. Available from http://www.leg.state.vt.us/docs/2010/Acts/ACT159.pdf

Act 160: An Act Relating to a Certificate of Public Good for Extending the Operating License of a Nuclear Power Plant. Vermont State Legislature. http://www.leg.state.vt.us/docs/legdoc.cfm?URL=/docs/2006/acts/ACT160.htm

Barlow, Daniel. "26-year power deal inked between Hydro-Quebec and Vermont." Times Argus. August 13, 2010. Available from http://www.timesargus.com/article/20100813/NEWS02/708139955/1003/NEWS02

Building for Social Responsibility. Available http://www.bsr-vt.org/index.html

"The Clean Energy Economy: Vermont." The Pew Charitable Trust. Available from http://www.pewcenteronthestates.org/uploadedFiles/wwwpewcenteronthestatesorg/Fact_Sheets/Clean_Economy_Factsheet_Vermont.pdf

Climate Change and Vermont. Available from http://www.anr.state.vt.us/air/planning/htm/Climate Change.htm

"CVPS to purchase Deerfield Wind power." Central Vermont Public Service. September 9, 2010. Available from http://www.cvps.com/AboutUs/news/viewStory.aspx?story_id=295

Engineering Beyond Green: Capturing the Emerging Market for Holistic Innovation and Expertise. Vermont Engineering and Environment Advisory Council. Available from http://www.dca.state.vt.us/documents/VtEEACPrelimReport-Feb08.pdf

Final Vermont Greenhouse Gas Inventory and Reference Case Projections, 1990–2030. Center for Climate Strategies. Available from http://www.anr.state.vt.us/air/Planning/docs/Final%20VT%20GHG%20Inventory%20&%20Projection.pdf

Fueling Vermont's Future: Comprehensive Energy Plan and Greenhouse Gas Action Plan. Vermont Department of Public Service. Available from http://publicservice.vermont.gov/pub/state-plans-comp energy.html

"Global Warming and Vermont." National Wildlife Federation. Available from http://www.nwf.org/Global-Warming/~/media/PDFs/Global%20Warming/Global%20Warming%20State%20Fact%20Sheets/Vermont.ashx

"Grantee: State Line Biofuels." Vermont Sustainable Jobs Fund. Available from http://www.vsjf.org/case-studies/8/grantee-state-line-biofuels

Green Mountain National Forest. Available from http://www.fs.fed.us/r9/forests/greenmountain/htm/greenmountain/g_home.htm

GREENGUARD Certification Programs. Available from http://www.greenguard.org/en/CertificationPrograms.aspx

"Industrial Minerals of Vermont: 200 Years and Going Strong." Vermont Geological Survey. Available from http://www.anr.state.vt.us/dec/geo/industrial mins.htm

"Investigation into Tritium Contamination at Vermont Yankee Nuclear Power Station." Vermont Depart ment of Health. Available from http://healthver mont.gov/enviro/rad/yankee/tritium.aspx

"Low-Emission Vehicle Regulations and Test Procedures." California Air Resources Board. Avail able from http://www.arb.ca.gov/msprog/ levprog/test_proc.htm

"Maple Syrup 2011." U.S. Department of Agriculture. June 13, 2011. Available from http://www.nass. usda.gov/Statistics_by_State/New_England_ includes/Publications/0605mpl.pdf

Promoting and Fostering the Green Economy in Vermont: A strategic Plan for a Green Future. Vermont Agency of Commerce and Community Develop ment. Available from http://www.thinkvermont. com/Portals/0/Green_Strategy.pdf

Regional Greenhouse Gas Initiative: Vermont State Investment Plan. Available from http://www.rggi. org/rggi_benefits/program_investments/Vermont

Renewable Energy for Agriculture Grant Program. Available from http://www.vermontagriculture. com/energy/documents/REAPGrantSummary.pdf

Senate Bill 209: The Vermont Energy Efficiency and Affordability Act. The State of Vermont Legislature. Available from http://www.leg.state.vt.us/docs/ legdoc.cfm?URL=/docs/2008/bills/passed/ S-209.HTM

"State Energy Profiles: Vermont." U.S. Energy Inform ation Administration. Available from http:// tonto.eia.doe.gov/state/state_energy_profiles.cfm? sid=VT

"Technical Assessment of Grass Pellets As Boiler Fuel In Vermont." Vermont Grass Energy Partnership. January 2011. Available from http://www.vsjf.org/ assets/files/RFPs/VT%20Grass%20Pellet%20Feasi bility%20Study%202010.pdf

Trans Climate Change Action Plan. Vermont Agency of Transportation. Available from http://www.aot. state.vt.us/planning/Documents/Planning/ VTransClimateActionPlanfinal1.pdf

Vermont Agency of Agriculture. Available from http:// www.vermontagriculture.com/index.htm

Vermont Center for Emerging Technologies. Available from http://www.vermonttechnologies.com

Vermont Comprehensive Energy Plan 2009. Vermont Department of Public Services. Available from http://publicservice.vermont.gov/planning/

CEP%20%20WEB%20DRAFT%20FINAL% 206-4-08.pdf

Vermont Danbury Marble. Available from http://www. vermontquarries.com/marble/index.html

Vermont Division of Forestry. Available from http:// www.vtfpr.org/htm/forestry.cfm

"Vermont Energy Facts." Institute for Energy Research. Available from http://www.instituteforenergyre search.org/state-regs/pdf/Vermont.pdf

Vermont Environmental Consortium. Available from http://www.vecgreenvalley.org

Vermont Fish and Wildlife Department. Available from http://www.vtfishandwildlife.com/index.cfm

Vermont Grass Energy Partnership. Available from http://www.vsjf.org/project-details/11/vermont-grass-energy-partnership

Vermont Green. Available from http://www.vtgreen.org

"Vermont Greenhouse Gas Emissions Inventory Update: 1990-2008." Vermont Agency of Natural Resources. September 2010. Available from http:// www.anr.state.vt.us/anr/climatechange/Pubs/ Vermont%20GHG%20Emissions%20Inventory% 20Update%201990-2008%20FINAL_0927 2010.pdf

Vermont Maple Syrup. Available from http://vermon tmaple.org/index.php

Vermont Organic Farmers. Available from http://nofavt. org/programs/organic-certification

"Vermont: Profile of the Green Economy." Collaborative Economics. Available from http://www.nga.org/ Files/pdf/09GREENPROFILEVT.PDF

Vermont SPEED. Available from http://vermontspeed. com

Vermont State Climate Office. Available from http:// www.uvm.edu/~ldupigny/sc

Vermont Statutes Annotated: Greenhouse Gas Redu ction Goals (10 VSA §578). Available from http:// www.leg.state.vt.us/statutes/fullsection.cfm? Title=10&Chapter=023&Section=00578

Vermont Statutes Annotated: Renewable Energy Programs (30 VSA §8001 et seq.). Available from http://www.leg.state.vt.us/statutes/fullchapter. cfm?Title=30&Chapter=089

Vermont Statutes Annotated: The Sustainable Jobs Fund Program (10 VSA 15A). Available from http:// www.leg.state.vt.us/statutes/sections.cfm? Title=10&Chapter=015A

Vermont Statutes Annotated: 25 by 25 State Goal (10 VSA §580). Available from http://www.leg.

state.vt.us/statutes/fullsection.cfm?Title=10&-Chapter=023&Section=00580

Vermont Sustainable Jobs Fund. Available from http://www.vsjf.org

"Vermont Utils to Buy Wind Power from New Hampshire." Reuters. May 20, 2010. Available from http://www.reuters.com/article/idUSN2019488420100520

"Vermont Yankee Nuclear Plant." Burlington Free Press. Available from http://www.burlingtonfreepress.

com/section/TOPICS0202/Vermont-Yankee-Nuclear-Plant

"Wetlands Factsheet 2: What Is a Wetland." Vermont Department of Environmental Conservation, Wetland Office. Available from http://www.anr.state.vt.us/dec//waterq/wetlands/docs/wl_factsheet2.pdf

"Wildlife Viewing in Vermont State Parks." Vermont State Parks. Available from http://www.vtstate-parks.com/htm/nature_wildlife.htm

Virginia

With the Blue Ridge and Allegheny Mountains region in the west and northwest, the piedmont plateau in the central section of the state, and the Atlantic coastal plain, or tidewater, in the east, Virginia has something for everyone. Virginia is the thirty-seventh largest state (land area of 39,594 square miles or 102,548 sq km) and is known for its great biologic and mineral diversity.

Starting in the west, Virginia's Blue Ridge and Allegheny Mountains section functions as a geologically diverse region with high elevations. Highly wooded mountains with rounded peaks dot this beautiful region of the state, which is home to Virginia's tallest peak, Mt. Rogers, which stands 5,729 feet (1,746 m) above sea level. Moving east, the Blue Ridge Mountains descend into Virginia's piedmont plateau, which functions as a foothills region and a buffer between Virginia's mountain region and its coastal plain. In this triangularly shaped region, elevations range from 1,000 feet (305 m) in the west to 300 feet (91 m) in the east, where the Atlantic Coastal Plain, an ecologically hyper productive region sitting adjacent to the Atlantic Ocean, begins.

Virginians are justifiably proud of their natural heritage, even enshrining it in the state's constitution. Entitled "Conservation," Article XI provides, among other things, that "it shall be the Commonwealth's policy to protect its atmosphere, lands, and waters from pollution, impairment, or destruction, for the benefit, enjoyment and general welfare of the people of the Commonwealth."

Climate and Climate Change: Responses

Although Virginia has considerable climatic diversity, a mild but humid climate defines most of Virginia. The western region of the state, as altitudes rise, tends to have cooler temperatures. But milder weather reigns dominant across the state, with average annual temperatures floating close to 56°F (13.2°C).

The Appalachian (Allegheny) and Blue Ridge Mountains have a significant climatic impact in Virginia, particularly on the valleys that are sandwiched between

them—the New River and Shenandoah River valleys. These valleys receive a double rain shadow effect from the mountain ranges that rise on each side. When moist air flows from west to east, it loads the western side of the Appalachian Mountains with precipitation, while leaving the valleys on the east almost totally dry. Likewise, when moist air flows from east to west, from the Atlantic Ocean, the Blue Ridge Mountains cast a westward rain shadow on those same valleys. As a result, the New River and the Shenandoah River valleys are the driest places in the state, and unusually arid zones for the eastern U.S.

Global climate change could have profound and devastating impacts on Virginia. Scientists from the Center for Ocean-Land-Atmosphere Studies (COLA) in Maryland predict average temperatures across Virginia to rise by 5.6°F (3.1°C) from 2000 to 2099, and believe that the temperature rise could be accompanied by a precipitation increase of 11 percent across the state. Particularly worrying for Virginia, however, is the potential sea level rise. Many Virginian communities occupy low lying areas along the Atlantic Ocean, and these communities could be devastated by rising ocean levels. According to the Virginia Institute of Marine Science, the Virginia coastal zone is the second most vulnerable region in the United States to the predicted impacts of climate change, behind New Orleans.

In 2007, Virginian governor Timothy Kaine issued Executive Order 59, which created the Governor's Commission on Climate Change. The commission was charged with compiling a climate change action plan for the state to help Virginia cope with the disruptive impacts of climate change and to develop a climate change policy. In December 2008, the Governor's Commission on Climate Change delivered on that task. Virginia's climate change action plan advocates for statewide climate policies that correspond with federal efforts. Thus, Virginia's climate change action plan offers a list of recommendations structured around federal action, even advancing the idea of Virginia lobbying the U.S.

Congress to implement policies deemed advantageous to the state such as passing climate change legislation that funds, for example, key industries in the state as well as colleges and universities that advance green technologies. Furthermore, the action plan called on the governor to press Congress to adopt a tough cap and trade program that surpasses in rigor the greenhouse gas reduction goals advanced in the Virginia Energy Plan (The Virginia Energy Plan, released in 2007, called for a 30 percent reduction in greenhouse gas emission by 2025).

⚘ Natural Resources, Water, and Agriculture

Diverse Topography and Climate Supports Great Resources

Virginia's unique environment and topography support tremendous geologic and biologic diversity. From the lowlands near the Atlantic Ocean to the stunning peaks in the west, the dramatic change in Virginia's landscape is a visible reflection of the more subtle forms of diversity, both mineral and biological.

Minerals

According to the U.S. Geological Survey, the value of Virginia's nonfuel raw mineral production has steadily increased since 1990, and generates more than $1 billion a year in revenue. In 2007, Virginia ranked twenty-second in the nation for total nonfuel mineral production, accounting for roughly 2 percent of total U.S. nonfuel mineral production. The most prominent nonfuel mineral produced in Virginia is crushed stone. Construction sand, gravel, lime, and zirconium represent other economically important nonfuel minerals in the state. Virginia is the only state that mines kyanite, an aluminum silicate that is sometimes used as a gemstone, but often used in the manufacture of refractory products such as bricks, mortar, and foundry molds. In 2007, the state ranked second in the nation for production of zircon and vermiculite, third in iron oxide pigments, and fourth in fuller's earth clay. Virginia also is the leading state in the nation for the production of ilmenite, out of two states that produce the mineral. It can be converted into titanium dioxide, which is useful as a pigment in paint.

Forests, Parks, and Wildlife

Forests cover more than 62 percent of the state, provide more than $27.5 billion annually for the state economy, and result in more than 248,000 jobs. The most common tree species are yellow poplar; loblolly and Virginia pine; chestnut, white, northern red, scarlet, and black oak; red maple; American holly; sweet gum; and flowering dogwood. About 80 percent of the forestland is under private ownership, by families or individuals. Less than 4 percent of the forestland is owned by forest product firms. Eleven percent is owned by the federal government, while about 5 percent is owned by state and local government entities. Besides timber and wood products, forest industries produce a number of specialty products, including naval stores (turpentine, pin resin), pine cones and pine straw, maple syrup, fruits and nuts, and a variety of medicinal plants.

Virginia is home to 35 state parks, 20 state forests, and 21 national parks, along with numerous national historical sites, landmarks, and battlefields. The state is rich with America's history, including key Civil War sites and architecture dating back to the eighteenth century.

Virginia boasts tremendous plant and animal diversity. Some of the most common mammal species include white-tailed (Virginia) deer, woodchuck, raccoon, beaver, opossum, nutria, red and gray foxes, and spotted and striped skunks. Elk, black bear, coyote, and bobcat can also be found in the state. Bird watchers can find more than four hundred species represented throughout the state. Ruffed grouse (commonly called pheasant in Virginia), wild turkey, bobwhite quail, mourning dove, and woodcock are popular game birds. More than 200 species of dragonflies and damselflies are found in Virginia, possibly more than any other state.

Several biological "hotspots"—areas with unusual amounts of biodiversity and rare species—are dotted across the state. The most prominent biological hotspot is the far southwestern corner of the state. This region is defined by a limestone subsurface, which like most of western Virginia supports a karst topography—da cavernous geologic landscape known to produce caves and springs. Virginia's karst region, and the caves and springs that accompany it, are known to support a host of unusual and rare species, such as eyeless fish, cave bats, salamanders, and cave beetles.

The U.S. Fish and Wildlife Service lists sixty-eight plant and animal species found in Virginia as federally threatened or endangered. Among the animals listed are several cave dwellers, such as the gray, Indiana, and Virginia big-eared bats; and the Lee County and Madison cave isopods. The Virginia Department of Game and Inland Fisheries identified 925 species of greatest conservation need in its 2005 Wildlife Action Plan, 60 percent of which are aquatic. More than fifty species of mussels are listed by the state as threatened or endangered in the 10-year action plan. The state has special wildlife management plans for the Dutch Gap black vulture, piping plovers, raptors, peregrine falcon, and golden eagles, among other animals. Those on the list have received rankings of critical, very high, high and moderate in terms of their conservation need. The partners involved in creating the Action Plan have formed working groups in order to accomplish the goals set out by the plan, and will have a formal revision by 2015 based on the activities accomplished by the working groups.

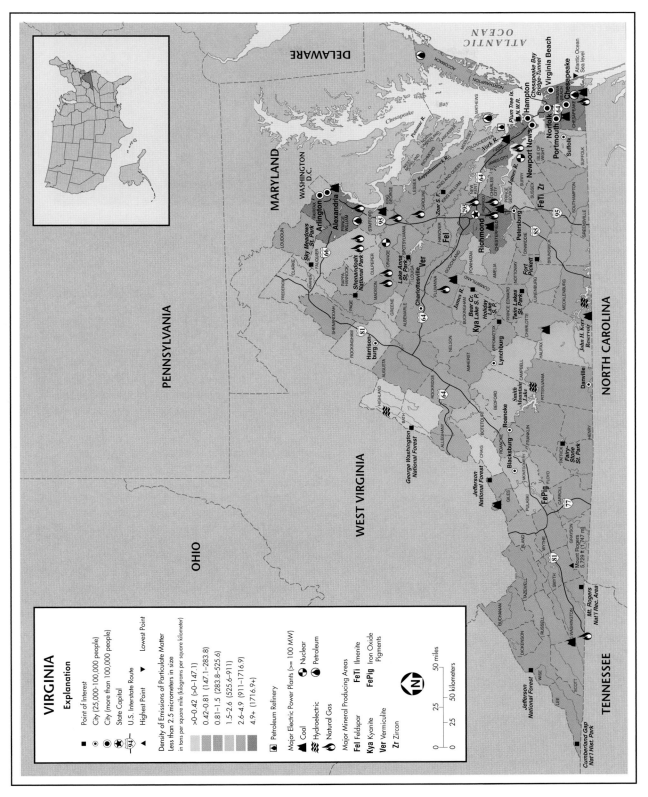

SOURCES: "County Emissions Map: Criteria Air Pollutants." *AirData*. U.S. Environmental Protection Agency. Available from http://www.epa.gov/air/data/geosel.html; *Energy Maps*. U.S. Energy Information Administration. Available from http://www.cia.gov/state; *Highest and Lowest Elevations*. U.S. Geological Survey. Available from http://egsc.usgs.gov/isb/pubs/booklets/elvadist/elvadist.html#Highest; *2007 Minerals Yearbook*. U.S. Geological Survey. Available from http://minerals.usgs.gov/minerals/pubs/state. © 2011 Cengage Learning.

Virginia State Profile

Physical Characteristics

Land area	39,493 square miles (102,286 sq km)
Inland water area	1,106 square miles (2,865 sq km)
Coastal area	1,729 square miles (2,783 sq km)
Highest point	Mount Rogers 5,729 feet (1,746 m)
National Forest System lands (2010)	1.7 million acres (673,000 ha)
State parks (2011)	35

Energy Statistics

Total energy production (2009)	1,200 trillion Btu
State ranking in total energy production (2009)	15
Renewable energy net generation total (2009)	3.9 million megawatt hours
Hydroelectric energy generation (2009)	1.5 million megawatt hours
Biomass energy generation (2009)	709,000 megawatt hours
Wind energy generation (2009)	NA
Wood and derived fuel energy generation (2009)	1.7 million megawatt hours
Crude oil reserves (2009)	NA
Natural gas reserves (2009)	3.1 trillion cubic feet (87.5 billion cu m)
Natural gas liquids (2008)	NA

Pollution Statistics

Carbon output (2005)	122.6 million tons of CO_2 (111.2 million t)
Superfund sites (2008)	31
Particulate matter (less than 2.5 micrometers) emissions (2002)	24,230 tons per year (21,981 t/yr)
Toxic chemical releases (2009)	56 million pounds (25.4 million kg)
Generated hazardous waste (2009)	51,000 tons (46,300 t)

SOURCES: AirData. U.S. Environmental Protection Agency. Available from http://www.epa.gov/air/data; *Energy Maps, Facts, and Data of the U.S. States.* U.S. Energy Information Administration. Available from http://www.eia.gov/state; *The 2012 Statistical Abstract.* U.S. Census Bureau. Available from http://www.census.gov/compendia/statab; *United States Energy Usage.* eRedux. Available from http://www.eredux.net/states.

© 2011 Cengage Learning.

Virginia has 1,262 square miles (3,269 sq km) of freshwater wetland and more than 370 square miles (958 sq km) of tidal or coastal wetlands. © *Aurora Photos/Alamy*

Chesapeake Bay Watershed Defines Much of Virginia

Virginia is fortunate to have an abundance of natural water resources. More than 51,000 miles (82,077 km) of streams and rivers crisscross Virginia and some 203 square miles (525 sq km) of publically owned lakes are found in the state. Virginia's wetlands are also robust, and the state has 1,262 square miles (3,269 sq km) of freshwater wetland and more than 370 square miles (958 sq km) of tidal or coastal wetlands. Virginia's wetland resources, while substantial, represent just a fraction of their historic range. According to the Environmental Protection Agency (EPA), Virginia lost from 1780 to 1980 more than 40 percent of its wetlands, much of which could be attributed to development and agriculture. The Virginia Department of Environmental Quality attempts to mitigate the impacts of development on Virginia's wetlands by offering a regulatory framework that protects wetlands under conservation easement, restrictive covenant, or those considered a national heritage resource. However, not all of Virginia's wetlands receive these designations, and developers are allowed to build on most private lands, even wetland ecosystems, if no conservation protection is in place.

According to the Virginia Department of Conservation and Recreation, roughly 60 percent of Virginia is located within the Chesapeake Bay Watershed, a drainage zone that covers some 64,000 square miles (165,759 sq km) in the mid-Atlantic region of the United States. Four of the most important rivers in the state, the Rappahannock, York, James, and the Potomac, are all located within the Chesapeake Bay Watershed. These rivers offer plentiful fishing and recreation opportunities, and boast an array of aquatic species. Several species of bass, trout, and catfish are popular fishermen catches, along with walleye, yellow perch, northern pike, and muskellunge.

In 1988, the Virginia General Assembly enacted the Chesapeake Bay Preservation Act stating that "healthy state and local economies and a healthy Chesapeake Bay are integrally related." Virginia is also a party to the multistate Chesapeake 2000 Agreement, a compact whereby Maryland, Pennsylvania, Virginia, and the District of Columbia committed to multiple goals—including preserving 20 percent of the land in each party's portion of the watershed by 2010—in order to protect the water quality of Chesapeake Bay. Virginia has encouraged conservation easements that remove development rights on private lands as a key tool in protecting the Chesapeake Bay and its tributaries. As a result of a partnership between regional, state and federal leaders, many of the goals set out by the agreement and the resulting Chesapeake Bay Action Plan have been accomplished or are ongoing efforts. However, significantly more needs to be done. For example, a hurricane and tropical storm in 2011 caused the Susquehanna River to flood, creating what scientists called a "sediment plume" to drain into the Chesapeake Bay. The plume, according to a report in the Virginian-Pilot newspaper, was loaded with runoff from area farms, as well as tree limbs and potentially polluted wastes. In the fall of 2011, scientists were watching the impact of the plume on the recovering ecosystem of the Bay.

Other ecologically vital rivers are found elsewhere in the state. According to NatureServe, a national conservation organization based in Virginia, the upper Clinch River, located in southwest Virginia, has the highest number of globally imperiled and vulnerable freshwater species in the United States, including twenty-nine rare mussel species. The water resources in this largely unexplored area, rich with caves and springs, are threatened by environmentally unsound forestry and farming practices, as well as coal mining.

Virginia's portions of the Chesapeake Bay and the Atlantic Ocean are also very important to the state, providing important recreation and fishing opportunities for Virginia's residents and offering potentially massive energy resources, both renewable and conventional. Virginia has 120 miles (193 km) of Atlantic Ocean coastline. The Atlantic waters are home to a variety of marine species, including the Atlantic bottlenose dolphin, striped dolphin, harbor porpoise, harbor seal, humpback whale, and five species of sea turtles.

Commercial fishing still plays an important role in the local economy. In 2009, Virginia ranked third in the nation for total poundage of fish landings (after Alaska and Louisiana), with the port of Reedville ranking third in the nation for fish landings based on poundage at individual ports (after Dutch Harbor-Unalaska and Empire-Venice). Sea scallop landings were valued at more than $63 million in 2009, with blue crab the next single most valuable catch, at more than $25 million. The most valuable commercial catches of finfish include Atlantic croaker, striped bass, and summer flounder.

Deep Agricultural Roots Continue to Grow

Virginia's agricultural sector is immense. According to the National Agricultural Statistical Service (NASS) 2009 State Agricultural Overview, Virginia's 47,000 farms spanned 12,500 square miles (32,365 sq km), a little under one-third of the total land area in the state. Although agricultural commodity sales are roughly $2.9 billion per year, the overall economic impact of the agricultural sector is far bigger. Agriculture and its related industries bring in roughly $55 billion ($79 billion when forestry is included) in revenue annually. According to the Virginia Department of Agriculture and Consumer Services (VDACS), Virginia's agricultural sector directly

and indirectly employs more than 350,000 people, including some 60,000 farmers and workers. Numerous state programs exist to support agriculture, including purchasing development rights and the Land Preservation Tax Credit. It serves, by far, as the largest sector in the state.

Broilers—chickens raised specifically for their meat—are Virginia's top agricultural product in terms of sales. That commodity alone generates more than half a billion dollars in sales per year. However, the largest agricultural commodity by share of total U.S. production is tobacco. Virginia remains one of the top five tobacco producing states in the nation. And though small in comparison to the tobacco harvest, Virginia's wine grape production has flourished from the early 1980s to present day. In 2007, the state saw 5,600 tons (2,540 kg) of wine grapes produced to make 350,000 cases of wine, according to VDACS. Those numbers ranked Virginia eighth in the United States in grape production, and resulted in cash receipts of more than $7.5 million.

Certified Organic: Growing in Popularity

Consistent with national trends, the organic farming industry in Virginia is rapidly expanding. According to the U.S. Department of Agriculture's (USDA) 2008 Organic Production Survey, Virginia had more certified or exempt farms (180) than twenty-nine states in the nation. The Virginia Department of Agriculture and Consumer Services actively supports organic farmers in the state. In 2006, the department hired its first organic specialist, whose job involves helping farmers in Virginia obtain organic certification and helping organic farmers market their crops. Organic growers and producers are eligible to apply for funds to offset the cost of organic certification, under the provisions of the Federal Farm Bill. The reimbursement amounted to up to 75 percent of the cost of certification, providing an incentive to become certified organic.

❧ Energy: Traditional Fuels Dominate Energy Grid

On a per capita basis, Virginia consumes an average amount of energy for a U.S. state. The transportation sector, which leads all others in demand, consumes roughly 40 percent of the total energy in the state, and relies predominantly on liquid fuels derived from petroleum, such as gasoline and diesel. However, the residential and commercial sectors, which together consume more than 50 percent of the state's total energy, rely on electricity.

Virginia's coal-fired power plants dominate the electric market in the state, producing nearly 50 percent of the electricity generated in Virginia. Much of the raw coal used to power these facilities comes from Virginia coal mines, which are located almost exclusively in the

Virginia coal production peaked in 1990, when the state produced 46.5 million tons of the raw fuel. Since then, it has been steadily declining. © *iStockPhoto.com/AdShooter*

southwestern portion of the state. However, these mines, bucking the overall coal trends in the United States, are experiencing declining production. Virginia coal production peaked in 1990, when the state produced 46.5 million tons of the raw fuel. Since then, it has been steadily declining.

Nuclear power, which is produced at two nuclear power stations in the state, serves as the second largest source of electricity in Virginia, generating roughly one-third of Virginia's electricity. Natural gas and petroleum fired power plants account for a majority of the rest. Bringing that electricity to market has raised its own environmental concerns. In recent years, the location of new electrical transmission towers has generated much debate across the Commonwealth.

Renewable Potential

Virginia has considerable potential for renewable energy generation, particularly wind potential off Virginia's Atlantic coast. As in other states, planning for offshore windmills have raised questions about the impacts on scenic views. But a report from the Virginia Coast Energy

Research Consortium shows offshore wind could produce enough power to meet at least 10 percent of the state's electricity needs and create thousands of career-length green-sector jobs in the process. The group identified 25 lease blocks that are beyond the visual horizon offshore "that could support approximately 3,200 MW of offshore wind farm capacity," according to the consortium's 2010 report. However, the state's renewable portfolio remains limited. According to the U. S. Energy Information Administration, wood and wood products provide roughly 2.5 percent of total electricity generated in Virginia, and other renewable sources, such as hydroelectric, wind, solar, municipal solid waste, and other renewable sources, contribute minimally.

In April 2007, Virginia established a voluntary renewable portfolio standard, which challenged utilities to produce 12 percent of base-year 2007 electric sales from renewable sources by 2022 and 15 percent by 2025.

⚜ Green Business, Green Building, Green Jobs

Attracting Green Businesses with Multi-Year Incentives

Over the years, Virginia has taken several steps to develop the green business sector in the state. In 1995, Virginia led a charge for developing the domestic solar manufacturing industry in the state by implementing the Solar Manufacturing Incentive Grant (SMIG) program, which still exists. SMIG provides annual grants—up to $4.5 million per year—to encourage the production of photovoltaic panels in Virginia. Virginia companies that manufacture and sell photovoltaic panels can apply for a six-year grant program that offers graduated rebates depending on the rated capacity of the panel and the year sold.

Under the plan, if you manufacture in Virginia and sell a 100 watt solar panel, you will receive a $75 rebate each year for the first 2 years ($0.75/ watt), $50 for years 3 and 4 ($0.5/watt), and $25 for years 5 and 6 ($0.25/ watt). Other similarly oriented programs, such as the Biofuels Productions Incentive Grants (BPIG) program, have also been launched in the state in successive years.

The American Recovery and Reinvestment Act (ARRA) also promises to significantly bolster the green business investment in the state as well. In total, ARRA earmarked more than $422 million to clean energy projects across Virginia.

Carrot-and-Stick Approach Grows Green Building

Arlington County, located in northeast Virginia, provides a case study for how local and county governments in Virginia are bolstering the green building movement in the state. Arlington County offers a host of incentives (and disincentives) that encourage energy efficient design and construction across the county. One example of this carrot-and-stick approach to green building is Arlington's Green Building Fund. Under the fund's provisions, site developers who do not build green are charged a onetime fee of $.045 per square foot of building space. A newly built, 100,000 square foot building that did not aim for LEED certification would thus contribute $4,500 to the fund. This graduated fee is roughly equal to what the U.S. Green Building Council would charge for registration and evaluation of a formal LEED application. The money contributed to Arlington's Green Building Fund is then used to promote green building education and outreach across the country. A similar effort is underway in Fairfax County known as the "Greening of Tysons Corner" that seeks to transform one of the largest shopping and employment centers in the country by mandating green construction standards for all new buildings.

At the state level, according to Executive Order 82 (2009): Greening of State Government, all new buildings of greater than 5,000 gross feet in size for use by state executive branch agencies and institutions must conform to LEED Silver or Green Globes two-globe standards, unless an exemption is granted by the Department of General Services. Renovation projects where the cost of the renovation exceeds 50 percent of the value of the building are also expected to meet these standards. The order also requires all state agencies to encourage the private sector to adopt green building standards by giving preference to facilities that meet LEED or Green Globe standards when leasing office space.

Green Jobs Wait for Capital Kick
According to the Pew Charitable Trusts, Virginia had more clean energy jobs (nearly 17,000) in 2007 than most states in the nation (seventeenth), but fell below average among U.S. states in the share of total jobs produced by that sector. That year, less than one half of one percent of total jobs in Virginia were clean energy jobs and thirty-seven of the fifty U.S. states had a greater share of jobs generated by the clean energy economy than Virginia. From 1998 to 2007, the clean energy sector grew at a slower rate than in most U.S. states, and conventional job growth outpaced clean energy job growth.

Still, Virginia continued to attract substantial amounts of clean energy-designated venture capital, more than all but seventeen states in the nation from 2006 to 2008. During that period, Virginia attracted more than $70 million in venture capital to the clean energy economy—outpacing several clean energy heavyweights, such as Oregon, and undoubtedly laying a foundation for future green sector job growth.

In April 2010, Virginian governor Bob McDonnell signed into law a tax credit program that gives companies a $500 tax credit for each green job created. The tax credit was applicable for taxable years beginning on or after January 1, 2010, and required that eligible jobs have a baseline salary of $50,000 of higher.

National Drilling Debate Knocks Near Virginia's Shores

Fifty miles off of Virginia's coast is the source of one of the most contentious political and environmental battles in the United States. Beneath the sea floor sits a lake of oil, estimated by the federal government to hold 130 million barrels worth, as well as 1.14 trillion cubic feet of natural gas. Energy companies hunger for access to these resources; politicians long for the jobs they could help create; and environmentalists worry about the impact these resources—specifically their harvesting—could have on species such as the leatherback sea turtle, the finback whale, and the brown pelican.

The official name of this lake of oil beneath the sea floor is Lease Sale 220, a 2.9 million acre plot, which begins about fifty miles off Virginia's Atlantic coast and extends east. U.S. president Barack Obama fueled the drilling debate when he announced in March 2010 a controversial plan to open this entire area, along with other, large sections of the country, to offshore drilling. Companies could have started bidding on contracts and conducting exploratory drilling here as early as 2011 or 2012 had Obama's plan moved forward. Instead, an oil-related environmental disaster in the Gulf of Mexico caused President Obama to cancel this lease sale and Virginia's lawmakers to reassess their positions on offshore drilling.

Distant Disaster Reverberates in Virginia
On 20 April 2010, a deep-sea oil rig operated by British Petroleum (BP)—similar to what might be used in Lease Sale 220 one day—exploded and created what many consider to be one of the worst environmental disasters in U.S. history. For nearly three months, huge volumes of oil gushed from the BP well into the Gulf of Mexico and onto area beaches. Fishing communities were devastated, huge numbers of wildlife were killed, and an entire ecosystem was disrupted. By the time BP contained the leak, in mid-July, the Gulf of Mexico oil spill was already, by far, the largest oil spill in U.S. history, with unknown and potentially severe long-term environmental consequences for the region. The 2010 Gulf of Mexico oil spill was also a case study in the dangers of deep-sea offshore drilling, as the depth at which the rig operated was largely understood as a principle barrier to expeditious containment.

Environmental Groups Praise Obama's Decision
When President Obama announced on May 27, 2010, that he was cancelling Lease Sale 220, environmental

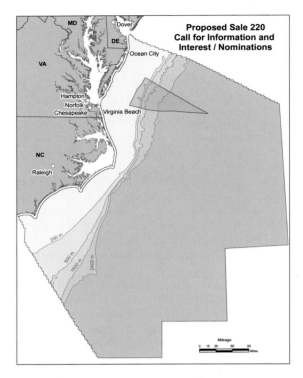

Lease Sale 220. *Courtesy of The Bureau of Ocean Energy Management, Regulation and Enforcement*

groups across Virginia welcomed the move. "The economic and environmental disaster that is currently unfolding on the Gulf Coast underscores the inherent and unavoidable risks that would come with drilling off Virginia's coast," said Glen Besa of the Virginia chapter of the Sierra Club. "It's unfortunate that it took a disaster such as this to finally bring to light just how mistaken it would be to drill off Virginia's coast." Besa and other environmentalists found in the U.S. Department of Defense (DoD) an unusual ally in the campaign against offshore drilling in Virginia. The DoD protested plans to open Lease Sale 220 to drilling because rig operations in that region would disrupt regional naval exercises, which are launched regularly from sizable naval bases along Virginia's shore. According to James P. Moran, a U.S. Congressman from Virginia who is opposed to drilling, "When you come down to it, the Navy's operations are much more important to the Virginia economy, let alone national security, than these drilling operations."

But even after the Gulf of Mexico oil disaster and protests by DoD officials, many Virginian lawmakers, including Republican governor Bob McDonnell and Eric Cantor, the minority whip in the U.S. House of Representatives, continued to support offshore drilling in Virginia. "Just as Americans did not quit or retreat from innovation after tragedies in space exploration, so must we learn, change, and persevere in advancing energy

independence by using all our natural resources," Governor McDonnell said immediately after President Obama canceled Lease Sale 220. "It is my hope that the President's action does not signal the end of offshore energy exploration and production off Virginia in the years ahead."

McDonnell made the campaign for offshore drilling a focal point of his administration, campaigning on the idea of using oil and gas proceeds to make road improvements across the state. However, even if drilling moved forward under the original timeline laid out by President Obama in March 2010, Virginia would not be entitled to any royalties from drilling unless Congress passed legislation explicitly allowing it. Congress passed a similar measure in 2006 that allowed Gulf Coast states to take home 37.5 percent of offshore oil revenue. Still, McDonnell was encouraged by the job creation prospects of drilling, and cited "conservative" estimates that offshore oil and natural gas drilling could create thousands of jobs for Virginians.

Politicians Weigh Costs and Benefits

Looked at in context of the overall U.S. energy needs, the oil and gas locked in Lease Sale 220 is but a drop in a pool of water. According to the *Washington Post*, the entire estimated supply of oil in Lease Sale 220 could meet about six days worth of U.S. demand. Likewise, the 1.14 trillion cubic feet of natural gas could not supply U.S. needs for a single month. But the job prospects of drilling and the potential windfall for state revenue—if Congress passed a revenue sharing bill—could cause the political calculus to shift.

In August 2010, Governor Bob McDonnell remained confident that Virginians would eventually move to support drilling again. "I really believe that people will strengthen again their support for offshore resources," McDonnell said in a radio interview, "because they understand that we cannot continue to rely on foreign countries and get into global economic conflicts over energy." Meanwhile, other state political and environmental leaders took more cautious positions on drilling in the wake of the Gulf disaster. Mark Warner, a U.S. Senator from Virginia and a Democrat, strongly supported offshore drilling before the Gulf disaster but moderated his stand as the biggest oil spill in U.S. history rattled the Gulf Coast. "We don't want to see any new areas drilled until after we've had a full investigation and know exactly what happened in the Gulf of Mexico," Warner said on May 27, 2010, shortly after President Obama cancelled Lease Sale 220. "This disaster has revealed problems at the Minerals Management Service that we need to sort through and correct. It also raises questions about what we should expect from the oil and gas industry, and the relationships between local, state, and federal government agencies in terms of both prevention and response."

Warner's response seemed to typify Virginia's moderation with regard to drilling. While never ruling out future support for offshore drilling in Virginia, Warner recognized the fact that the 2010 Gulf of Mexico oil spill should raise questions among even the staunchest supporters of offshore drilling. Ultimately, it is too early to tell which way the Lease Sale 220 debate will tip, since federal legislators are still divided over the issue. In April 2011, the U.S. House Committee on Natural Resources recommended HR 1230: Restarting American Offshore Leasing Now Act for consideration during the U.S. House's 2011–2012 session. This bill, passed by the House in May 2011, was designed to reverse Obama's decision and to force the scheduled lease sales to proceed in a prompt and safe manner. The House also passed HR 1231, reversing President Obama's Offshore Moratorium Act, which called for the release of at least half the available land within each Outer Continental Shelf planning area. As of late 2011, the Senate had not yet acted on either bill.

BIBLIOGRAPHY

Books

Melosi, Artin, ed. *Environment*, vol. 8 of *The New Encyclopedia of Southern Culture*. Chapel Hill: University of North Carolina Press, 2007.

Nash, Steve. *Blue Ridge 2020: An Owner's Manual.* Chapel Hill: University of North Carolina Press, 1999.

Ross, John, and Bates Littlehales. *The Smithsonian Guides to Natural America: The Atlantic Coast and Blue Ridge–Maryland, District of Columbia, Delaware, Virginia, North Carolina.* Washington, DC: Smithsonian Books, 1995.

Web Sites

Chesapeake Bay Preservation Act. Code of Virginia. Available from http://leg1.state.va.us/cgi-bin/legp504.exe?000+cod+TOC10010000021000000000000

"The Clean Energy Economy." Pew Charitable Trusts. Available from http://www.pewcenteronthestates.org/uploadedFiles/Clean_Economy_Report_Web.pdf

"Climatology Office." University of Virginia. Available from http://climate.virginia.edu/home.htm

"Constitution of Virginia." Available from http://legis.state.va.us/laws/search/constitution.htm

"Final Report: A Climate Change Action Plan." Governor's Commission on Climate Change. Available from http://www.deq.virginia.gov/export/sites/default/info/documents/climate/CCC_Final_Report-Final_12152008.pdf

Fisheries of the United States—2009. NOAA Fisheries. Available from http://www.st.nmfs.noaa.gov/st1/fus/fus09/index.html

"Green Building." Arlington County Virginia. Available from http://www.co.arlington.va.us/departments/environmentalservices/epo/EnvironmentalServicesEpoGreenBuildings.aspx

Greening of State Government (EO 82-2009). Commonwealth of Virginia, Office of the Governor. Available from http://www.dsireusa.org/documents/Incentives/VA12R.pdf

Harper, Scott. "Plume of Muck From Recent Storms Heading Our Way." The Virginian-Pilot. September 16, 2011. Available from http://www.hamptonroads.com/2011/09/plume-muck-recent-storms-heading-our-way

Helderman, Rosalind S. "Oil Drilling Off Va's Shore Would Interfere With Military, Defense Study Says." *The Washington Post.* Available from http://www.washingtonpost.com/wp-dyn/content/article/2010/05/18/AR2010051804656.html

"Initiative for Coastal Climate Change Research." Virginia Institute for Marine Science. Available from http://www.vims.edu/research/units/programs/icccr/index.php

Kaiser, Ann. "McDonnell Backs Offshore Drilling in Virginia Amidst Moratorium." *Virginia Statehouse News.* Available from http://virginia.statehousenewsonline.com/482/mcdonnell-backs-offshore-drilling-in-virgina-amidst-moratorium/

"Lease Sale Cancellation Makes Sense." Office of Senator Mark R. Warner. Available from http://warner.senate.gov/public/index.cfm?p=Blog&ContentRecord_id=230d77e2-7557-4251-a5dd-071ddb4edb58&ContentType_id=ec227f31-cc52-4e56-87db-385a02e2bceb

"Lee County Cave Isopod." Virginia Department of Conservation and Recreation. Available from http://www.dcr.virginia.gov/natural_heritage/documents/fscaveisopod.pdf

Michaels, Patrick J. and Paul C. Knappenberger. "Science and Economics of Climate Change." The Virginia Institute. Available from http://www.virginiainstitute.org/publications/climate_change.php#9

"Odonata of Virginia." Northern Prairie Wildlife Research Center. United States Geological Survey. Available from http://www.npwrc.usgs.gov/resource/distr/insects/dfly/va/toc.htm

"Office of Wetlands and Water Protection." Virginia Department of Environmental Quality. Available from http://www.deq.state.va.us/wetlands/#Is_it_legal

Pollard, Trip. "A Green Makeover for Tysons Corner." *The Washington Post*, September 7, 2008. Available from http://www.washingtonpost.com/wp-dyn/

content/article/2008/09/05/
AR2008090503137.html

"Restarting American Offshore Leasing Now Act (HR 1230)." U.S. House of Representatives Committee on Natural Resources. Available from http://naturalresources.house.gov/News/DocumentSingle.aspx?DocumentID=231014

"Report on Business Incentives 2008–09." Virginia Department of Commerce and Trade. Available from http://www.ltgov.virginia.gov/initiatives/JCC/EconomicallyDistressedAreas/EconDisArea_BusinessIncentivesReport_2008-2009.pdf

"Rivers of Life: Critical Watersheds For Protecting Freshwater Biodiversity." NatureServe. Available from http://www.natureserve.org/library/riversoflife.pdf

"Statement of Governor Bob McDonnell on President's Offshore Energy Decision." Virginia Secretary of Natural Resources. Available from http://www.naturalresources.virginia.gov/News/viewRelease.cfm?id=192

"Senate Bill 623." General Assembly of Virginia. Available from http://leg1.state.va.us/cgi-bin/legp504.exe?101+ful+CHAP0722+pdf

"Species Report: Virginia." U.S. Fish and Wildlife Service. Available from http://ecos.fws.gov/tess_public/pub/stateListingAndOccurrenceIndividual.jsp?state=VA&s8fid=112761032792&s8-fid=112762573902&s8fid=24012804170143

"2006 Minerals Yearbook: Virginia." United States Geological Survey. Available from http://minerals.usgs.gov/minerals/pubs/state/2006/myb2-2006-va.pdf

"Virginia Agriculture—Facts and Figures." Virginia Department of Agriculture and Consumer Services. Available from http://www.vdacs.virginia.gov/agfacts/index.shtml

Virginia Department of Game and Inland Fisheries. Available from http://www.dgif.virginia.gov

"Virginia Lease Sale 220." Bureau of Ocean Energy Management, Regulation, and Enforcement. Available from http://www.boemre.gov/offshore/220.htm

"Virginia Offshore Wind Studies." Virginia Coastal Energy Research Consortium. April 2010. Available from http://www.vcerc.org/VCERC_Final_Report_Offshore_Wind_Studies_Full_Report_newest.pdf

"Virginia Recovery Act Snapshot." U.S. Department of Energy. Available from http://www.energy.gov/recovery/va.htm

"Virginia: State Energy Profile." U.S. Energy Information Administration. Available from http://tonto.eia.doe.gov/state/state_energy_profiles.cfm?sid=VA

Virginia Statewide Assessment of Forest Resources. Virginia Department of Forestry. Available from http://www.dof.virginia.gov/info/resources/2010-State-Assessment_06-15_reduced.pdf/

"Virginia Sustainable Business Network." Available from http://www.vsbn.org/

"Virginia Wildlife Action Plan: Executive Summary." Virginia Department of Game and Inland Fisheries. August 2005. Available from http://www.bewildvirginia.org/wildlifeplan/summary.pdf

"Wetlands: Status and Trends." U.S. Environmental Protection Agency. Available from http://www.epa.gov/OWOW/wetlands/vital/status.html

Washington

While the Evergreen State may be well known for its pine forests (which cover over half of the state), much of the state is mountainous, and the coastal marine resources of the Pacific Ocean are just as important as the timberlands when it comes to providing healthy habitats for both humans and wildlife. The Olympic Mountains to the west are home to temperate rainforests that receive some 150 inches (381 cm) of rain annually. More centrally located, the Cascade Range of mountains is home to several volcanic cones, including Mount Rainier, which at 14,410 feet (4,395 m) is the highest peak in the state, and Mount St. Helens, whose 1980 eruption flattened forests and forever changed the surrounding landscape. Dams on the Columbia and Snake Rivers serve as major sources of hydropower for the region, making Washington one of the largest producers of hydroelectric power in the nation. The waters of the Outer Coast and the Puget Sound offer significant resources that support a diverse marine life, as well as the human population.

Climate

The Cascade Mountains divide Washington both topographically and climatically. Due in part to its location in the rain shadow of the Olympic Mountains, western Washington experiences a mild, though often rainy climate. Areas east of the Cascades have a climate characterized by cold winters, hot summers and sparse rainfall.

Impacts of Climate Change

In February 2009, the Climate Impacts Group of the University of Washington, issued the results of a study on the environmental consequences of climate change. According to *The Washington Climate Change Impacts Assessment*, without concerted effort to curb the current rate of greenhouse gas emissions, the state could see a major change in precipitation and temperature patterns, with wetter autumns and drier, hotter summers.

Warmer winter temperatures could lead to a decrease in snowpack by nearly 30 percent by 2020 and 40 percent by 2040. A shift in the timing of spring snow melt could have a significant effect on the municipal and agricultural water supplies: an earlier spring melt decreases the amount of water available for use in summer. A decreased summer water level in major rivers also could lead to a decrease in hydroelectric power production during those months and could affect salmon migration to and from spawning grounds. Furthermore, sea levels along the coast are projected to rise by between 2 inches and 13 inches by 2100, depending on location, increasing erosion and negatively affecting the state's shellfish industry.

However, Washingtonians have not have not been complacent about climate change. In 2005, Seattle Mayor Greg Nickels initiated the U.S. Mayor's Climate Protection Agreement, challenging major U.S. cities to reduce their emissions to below 1990 levels, in line with the Kyoto Protocol.

Washington and the Western Climate Initiative

As early as 2003, the governors of Washington, Oregon and California joined to form the West Coast Global Warming Initiative. That group grew to include seven states and four Canadian provinces and took on the name the Western Climate Initiative (WCI). In 2008, the WCI proposed a regional emissions reduction target of 15 percent below 2005 levels by 2020 to be met through a market-based approach that would also spur investment in and development of clean-energy technologies, create green jobs, and protect public health. A regional cap-and-trade program, set to go into effect on January 1, 2012, is a major part of the initiative. It is one officials say will reduce emissions without negatively impacting the local economy and local businesses. The cap-and-trade program covers the following emissions: carbon dioxide, methane, nitrogen trifluoride, sulfur hexafluoride, perfluorocarbons, hydroflurocarbons, and nitrous oxide. The emission sources include transportation fuel use, industrial processes and fuel combustion, electricity generation, and residential and commercial fuel use. Phase One, which is designed to reduce emissions from industrial processes and fuel combustion and electricity generation, goes into effect in 2012. The second phase, focusing on residential and commercial fuel use and transportation, is scheduled to take effect in 2015.

The Washington State Department of Ecology contracted with ECONorthwest in Oregon to assess the potential economic impacts to Washington of the proposed initiative. The results of the *Washington Western Climate Initiative Economic Impact Analysis* were published in February 2010, with a general conclusion that the implementation of the WCI plan as designed could result in an increased economic output of $3.3 billion in Washington State by 2020, and the creation of 19,300 jobs.

The state government also has implemented policies, laws, and initiatives designed to reduce greenhouse gas emissions while focusing on the development of a clean energy economy for the state. In 2008, the state legislature set its own greenhouse gas emissions reduction targets, calling for a reduction to 1990 levels by 2020, followed by a reduction to 25 percent below 1990 levels by 2035, and by 50 percent by 2050 (RCW 70.235.020). In 2009, the governor issued an executive order (EO 09-05) that charged the state Department of Ecology with the task of working with major industries to help them achieve these reduction benchmarks. Pursuant to Senate Bill 5560, passed in April 2009, the state departments of Ecology, Agriculture, Commerce, Fish and Wildlife, Natural Resources, and Transportation are charged with developing a comprehensive, integrated climate change response strategy that will bring all these efforts together. The initial state strategy is due out in December 2011.

❧ Natural Resources: The Evergreen State

Forests

The forests of the Evergreen State are key ecological and economic resources. With about 16.2 million acres classified as timberland, production of wood and wood products is a major industry. Common species include Sitka spruce, Douglas fir, western hemlock, western red cedar, big leaf maple, black cottonwood, and western yew. The state manages only about 2.1 million acres of forested trust lands; the federal government oversees eight national forest areas covering 9.2 million acres. Each year, the forestry industry contributes more than $15 billion to the state's economy through the wood, construction, and paper sectors, as well as recreational and biomass industries. However, the timber harvest was in decline in the mid-2000s due in part to fluctuations in regional and international markets.

Parks and Wildlife

There are 119 state parks and thirteen national parks within the state. Olympic National Park, noted for its glacier-clad mountains and the longest undeveloped coast in the contiguous United States, is also a World Heritage Site.

Washington is home to more than 1,300 plant species, including the western rhododendron, the state flower. The forest and mountain regions serve as habitats for species such as the Columbia black-tailed deer and black bear. The most common smaller mammals include western fisher, raccoon, muskrat, porcupine, marten, and mink. The Roosevelt elk, named after President Theodore Roosevelt, is indigenous to the Olympic Mountains. Washington boasts more bald eagles than any other state except Alaska. Game birds include the ruffed grouse, bobwhite quail, and ring-necked pheasant. The U.S. Fish and Wildlife Service lists 28 animal species and 9 plant species occurring within the state as federally threatened or endangered.

Minerals

Washington is one of only two states (with North Carolina) that produces olivine, a silicate mineral used in the aluminum foundry process. The state has ranked within the top ten nationally for the production of zinc, cadmium, lead, and construction sand and gravel. Washington also produces generous quantities of crush stone, portland cement, and industrial sand and gravel.

A State with Two Coasts: The Pacific Coast and Puget Sound

Washington has two distinct coastal regions: the Pacific Coast and the Puget Sound. The Pacific Coast provides seasonal homes for many protected species, including the migrating gray and humpback whales, and a year-round residence for the threatened western snowy plover. The Puget Sound is the second-largest estuary in the nation (after Chesapeake Bay). It serves as a home for over two hundred fish species, one hundred seabird species, and at least thirteen types of marine mammals, including the orca (killer whale). The protection of both the Pacific Coast and Puget Sound is extremely important to the state, which has several active programs to address and resolve the issues of water pollution, erosion, and climate change that affect these areas.

2011 Clean Water Jobs Act

One effort to providing funding for water conservation and cleanup projects has become quite controversial. The 2011 Clean Water Jobs Act was introduced in the state

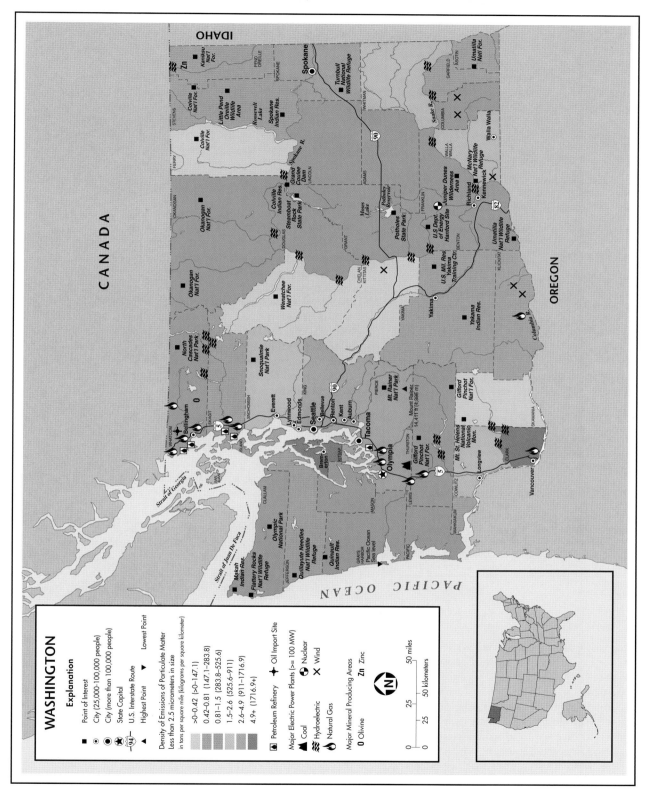

WASHINGTON

Explanation

- Point of Interest
- ⊙ City (25,000–100,000 people)
- ◉ City (more than 100,000 people)
- ★ State Capital
- 〔94〕 U.S. Interstate Route
- ▲ Highest Point   ▼ Lowest Point

Density of Emissions of Particulate Matter
less than 2.5 micrometers in size
in tons per square mile (kilograms per square kilometer)

- >0–0.42 (>0–147.1)
- 0.42–0.81 (147.1–283.8)
- 0.81–1.5 (283.8–525.6)
- 1.5–2.6 (525.6–911)
- 2.6–4.9 (911–1716.9)
- 4.9+ (1716.9+)

- ✦ Petroleum Refinery   ⊕ Oil Import Site

Major Electric Power Plants (>= 100 MW)
- ▲ Coal   ⊕ Nuclear
- 〰 Hydroelectric   ✕ Wind
- ⬦ Natural Gas

Major Mineral Producing Areas
- 0 Olivine   Zn Zinc

0   25   50 miles
0   25   50 kilometers

CANADA
IDAHO
OREGON
PACIFIC OCEAN

SOURCES: "County Emissions Map: Criteria Air Pollutants." *AirData.* U.S. Environmental Protection Agency. Available from http://www.epa.gov/air/data/geosel.html; *Energy Maps.* U.S. Energy Information Administration. Available from http://www.eia.gov/state; *Highest and Lowest Elevations.* U.S. Geological Survey. Available from http://egsc.usgs.gov/isb/pubs/booklets/elvadist/elvadist.html#Highest; *2007 Minerals Yearbook.* U.S. Geological Survey. Available from http://minerals.usgs.gov/minerals/pubs/state. © 2011 Cengage Learning.

Washington State Profile

Physical Characteristics

Land area	66,449 square miles (172,102 sq km)
Inland water area	1,646 square miles (4,263 sq km)
Coastal area	2,537 square miles (4,083 sq km)
Highest point	Mount Rainier 14,411 feet (4,392 m)
National Forest System lands (2010)	9.3 million acres (3.8 million ha)
State parks (2011)	141

Energy Statistics

Total energy production (2009)	980 trillion Btu
State ranking in total energy production (2009)	22
Renewable energy net generation total (2009)	78.0 million megawatt hours
Hydroelectric energy generation (2009)	72.9 million megawatt hours
Biomass energy generation (2009)	167,000 megawatt hours
Wind energy generation (2009)	3.6 million megawatt hours
Wood and derived fuel energy generation (2009)	1.3 million megawatt hours
Crude oil reserves (2009)	NA
Natural gas reserves (2009)	NA
Natural gas liquids (2008)	NA

Pollution Statistics

Carbon output (2005)	78.7 million tons of CO_2 (71.4 million t)
Superfund sites (2008)	48
Particulate matter (less than 2.5 micrometers) emissions (2002)	5,355 tons per year (4,858 t/yr)
Toxic chemical releases (2009)	15.7 million pounds (7.1 million kg)
Generated hazardous waste (2009)	317,200 tons (287,800 t)

SOURCES: AirData. U.S. Environmental Protection Agency. Available from http://www.epa.gov/air/data; *Energy Maps, Facts, and Data of the U.S. States.* U.S. Energy Information Administration. Available from http://www.eia.gov/state; *The 2012 Statistical Abstract.* U.S. Census Bureau. Available from http://www.census.gov/compendia/statab; *United States Energy Usage.* eRedux. Available from http://www.eredux.net/states.

© 2011 Cengage Learning.

legislature in early 2010 (SB 6851/HB 3181), and called for an increase in the state hazardous substance tax as applied to the wholesale value of refined petroleum products, pesticides, and other chemicals that pollute waterways, primarily through runoff. Opponents of the bill claim that the proposed tax increase from 0.7 percent to 2 percent is too excessive, and would likely lead to the loss of jobs in the petroleum industry, which stands to be the hardest hit by such taxation. Those opponents won out in 2010, with the bills becoming stalled. However, there was enough support to reintroduce new bills in 2011 that proposed a 1 percent tax on the chemicals (SB 5604/HB 1735). The money gained from the taxes would go to local municipalities for storm water pollution

mitigation efforts. Supporters claim that the significant increase in revenue for the state can be used to fund local infrastructure projects and conservation efforts that would create thousands of new jobs across the state. Touted as a polluter-pays bill, supporters also believe that the tax increase is not likely to have a serious impact on oil company profits. Opponents argue that only a third of the amount collected would be distributed to environmental projects, while the rest would end up in the state general fund. Opponents also see the imposition of such a long-term tax increase as detrimental to the growth of business during a rough economy. The 2011 bills were still being considered as of late 2011.

Global Warming and Marine Life

The Washington salmon catch is one of the largest in the nation by value, providing a great economic resource, as well as filling nationwide consumption demands. Salmon stocks have declined over the years, however, leading officials to place some species on the list for endangered or threatened species. According to a report from the National Wildlife Federation (NWF), the 2004 yearly run of sockeye salmon was down about 50% percent as a result of warmer waters. Additionally, in the summer of 2005, coastal ocean temperatures were reported at 2 to 5 degrees above normal, resulting in a decline in plankton and krill, the main source of food for many seabirds. According the NWF report, tens of thousands of Brandt's cormorants and common murres died from starvation that year. The presence of numerous Humbolt squid along the coastal waters also signals warmer water temperatures. These squid are usually found along the coast of Mexico and southern California.

Columbia and Snake: The Electric Rivers

The Columbia River is the longest (1,200 mi/1,900 km) and most powerful river in the state, running from British Columbia to the Pacific, and serving as a source of hydroelectric energy for the entire Pacific region. In volume, the Columbia ranks second only to the Mississippi, with an average discharge of 262,000 cubic feet (7,400 cu m) per second. It provides irrigation to over 600,000 acres (242,812 ha) as part of the Columbia Basin Project. Better known, however, is its Grand Coulee hydroelectric facility, the largest generating plant in the United States. The Snake River, the longest tributary of the Columbia, also is a major source of hydroelectric power. Overall, there are over 1,000 dams in Washington, owned and operated by the utilities or the federal government. The Yakima River, another major tributary of the Columbia, serves as a significant irrigation source for the agricultural lands in the Yakima River Basin, located in the south-central portion of the state.

Washington has numerous lakes, of which the largest is the artificial Roosevelt Lake, covering 123 square miles (319 sq km), created by the Grand Coulee Dam.

Grand Coulee Dam. © *aricvyhmeister/ShutterStock.com*

The 55-mile (89-km) long Lake Chelan and Lake Washington, near Seattle, are the largest natural lakes.

Major commercial ports for the state are found at Seattle, Tacoma, and Anacortes, all of which are located in the Puget Sound. Fishing has a significant impact on the local economy, with sport fishing generating about $1.1 billion annually and commercial fisheries generating an average of $1.6 billion annually. Dungeness crab and salmon are among the most valuable catches.

Agriculture: Apples, Cherries, and Potatoes

Washington is well known as the nation's leading producer of apples, accounting for 59 percent of total U.S. production. However, the state also ranks first in production of red raspberries, hops, and sweet cherries, and second in potatoes. To ensure the continued development of such a strong agricultural sector, the Washington State Department of Agriculture (WSDA) has developed the *Future of Farming: Strategic Plan for Washington Agriculture 2020 and Beyond*. The WSDA also has developed strategies to protect the environment and to anticipate the important challenges of climate change. The promotion of organic and sustainable farming practices is also a major focus within the state, using standards established through the WSDA Organic Food Program. According to the USDA's 2008 Organic Survey, Washington State has nearly 900 organic farms on more than 82,000 acres (33,184 ha) of land for a total value of $281 million.

❧ ENERGY

Energy: Oil and Natural Gas

While Washington does not have its own oil fields, the state serves as a principal refining center for Pacific Northwest markets. The five major refineries within the state receive crude oil primarily from Alaska and Canada. Washington also imports natural gas from Canada. About one-third of all households use natural gas a primary source for home heating.

Electricity

Washington leads the nation in the production of hydroelectric power, with nearly three-fourths of the state's electricity produced at hydroelectric power plants. The Grand Coulee facility has a capacity of 7,079 megawatts. The Columbia Generating Station, the only nuclear power plant in the state, generates 1,150 megawatts, about one-tenth of the state's supply of electricity. Washington is a major exporter of electricity. Through the Western Interconnection grid system, Washington sends large amounts of hydroelectric and wind power north to British Columbia and Alberta, Canada, and south through Oregon to California.

Moving Toward a Coal-Free Future

The TransAlta facility in the Centralia area is the state's only coal-fired power plant, and also the single largest source of air pollution in the state. Under Executive Order 09-05 (2009), the Department of Ecology was charged with the task of working specifically with TransAlta to ensure that the plant would meet the state's greenhouse gas emissions performance standards by no later than December 31, 2025. In early March 2011, the state and TransAlta forged an agreement that moved a major step further by deciding to phase out coal-fired operations completely by 2025. Under this agreement, the first of TransAlta's two boilers will be retired by December 31, 2020, with the second retired by December 31, 2025. In the interim, TransAlta will continue to sell coal power through its long-term contracts within the state, thereby providing financial stability for the company as it develops and implements technologies for the use of cleaner energy sources. The company will also install additional air pollution control technology by 2013 to reduce emissions of nitrogen oxide. On April 29, 2011, the governor signed Senate Bill 5769, the TransAlta Energy Transition Bill, which will provide state funding of about $10 million on projects that promote energy efficiency and conservation and to stabilize utility costs for local communities while the transition to clean energy is made. TransAlta will pay $30 million for local energy efficiency projects and $25 million for energy economic development in the Centralia, a move that is expected to help create a booming clean energy job market for the region. With this agreement, Washington will become a coal-free energy state by 2025.

Renewable Energy

Wind power is becoming an important source of renewable energy, producing nearly three percent of the state's electricity. In 2008, Washington ranked fifth in the

Discovery Point Lighthouse on Washington's West Point, jutting into Puget Sound.   © Thye Gn/Alamy

nation for wind energy capacity. Given the state's volcanic activity, geothermal energy offers great future potential. Biomass is also emerging as an important renewable opportunity, tapping into the vast forestry resources within the state. The state"s Department of Natural Resources (DNR) has initiated several pilot projects to partner with companies using biomass from state forests in renewable energy projects. The state legislature also passed a bill in 2010 allowing the DNR to enter into contracts to supply forest biomass, as well as lease state lands for the conversion of biomass. Washington's biomass production accounts for 3 percent of total U.S. generation. Drawing on these and other resources, the state has adopted a renewable energy standard that will require all utility companies serving 25,000 people or more to produce 15 percent of their energy from renewable sources by 2020.

🍃 Green Business, Green Building, Green Jobs

Climate Change and Green Collar Jobs Act

Moving into the twenty-first century, Washington state officials have made many bold and decisive choices in promoting the growth of a green economy. Recent legislation includes:

1. The Washington Climate Change Challenge (EO 07-02), prescribing the creation of 25,000 jobs in the clean energy sector by 2020.

2. The Climate Change and Green Collar Jobs Act (HB 2815), which marked workforce training and development as a key feature in the plan for statewide reduction in greenhouse gas emissions. In doing so, Washington became the first state in the nation to link workforce training with climate policy actions.

3. The Evergreen Jobs Act (HB 2227), calling for the creation of an additional 15,000 new green economy jobs by 2020, with a secondary goal that at least 30 percent of those jobs will go to veterans, National Guard members, and those from low-income or disadvantaged populations. The act also created the Evergreen Jobs Account, to serve as a grant program for curriculum development, workforce training, and retraining programs that prepare employees for green collar jobs.

According to the *2008 Washington State Green Economy Jobs.* report, there were about 47,190 existing green jobs throughout the state, accounting for about 1.6 percent of total employment. Most of those jobs were found in the category of businesses involved in energy efficiency.

To encourage further development in green energy, the Washington Clean Energy Leadership Council was formed in 2009 (SB 5921). The council was charged with the task of evaluating the strengths of the state's existing clean energy industries and developing a plan for the growth of clean energy businesses and jobs. The council's final report, *Accelerating Washington Clean Energy Job Growth*, was completed in October 2010. The plan identified three areas where Washington has an advantage: energy efficiency, renewable energy integration, and bioenergy. The plan also proposed ways to promote growth in these areas: by aligning clean energy policy and regulation, accelerating high profile clean energy development, and creating a focal point for clean energy economic development, primarily through the establishment of a Clean Energy Growth Partnership. A major theme of the plan is to ensure sustainable growth in targeted areas by supplementing public funds with non-state investment in clean energy. The formal recommendations of the council were presented to the legislature in January 2011. The council predicts that implementation of these recommendations could result in the creation of more than 50,000 direct and indirect clean energy jobs and approximately $2.3 billion in annual employment income by 2020.

For 2011, the state legislature passed and the governor signed (on April 11, 2011), a bill to create a new Puget Sound Corps (SB 5230/HB 1294), discussed below. The bill will create about 150 new jobs by 2013, and will help restore the Puget Sound. The legislature was also considering the above-mentioned 2011 Clean Water Jobs Act (SB 5604/HB 1735), a polluter-pays tax bill that would provide new revenue through increased taxes on the wholesale value of hazardous substances, would provide new funding to create jobs through local infrastructure projects and waterway cleanup efforts, particularly along the Puget Sound and Spokane River.

Green Buildings

In 2005, Washington became the first state to pass a law requiring all new construction and renovation of state-operated buildings to meet green building standards, as defined under the Leadership in Energy and Environmental Design (LEED) rating system of the U.S. Green Building Council. The High-Performance Public Buildings Act (39.35D RCW) mandates green building standards for public schools (including colleges and universities), as well as for government offices. The Washington Green Building Initiative is one part of the larger, 30-year *Beyond Waste Plan* that was initiated by the government in November 2004. The long-term goal

of the Initiative is to bring green building practices into the mainstream throughout the entire state, with a vision for 2035 in which 100 percent of all new construction and renovations adhere to the highest levels of green building standards.

Green Business

Green businesses continue to grow in Washington, partly in response to the enactment of laws and policies that have been designed to promote a green economy. In 2009, the Washington Department of Commerce published *Washington State's Green Economy: A Strategic Framework*. According to this report, many business leaders in the state favor government initiated policies and regulations for the environment, because such legislation creates and sustains a green market for products and services. In addition, to assist and encourage the growth and development of green businesses, the state Department of Ecology offers the Ecology for Business Web site, which provides basic information on starting and operating a business in Washington, plus important information on environmental regulations and how they affect the major economic sectors.

❧ The Puget Sound

The Puget Sound, on Washington's northwest coast, is the second-largest estuary in the United States, after Chesapeake Bay. Extending about 50 miles (80 km) inland from the Pacific, the Sound drains nineteen river basins. The sills and basins of its floor create areas of varying depth, from deep, open waters to shallow inlets, where tidal flows create a mixture of freshwater and saltwater. Such variance creates a habitat for diverse marine life, including more than two hundred species of fish, six hundred species of sea grasses, one hundred types of sea birds, and at least thirteen species of marine mammals. More than three thousand species of invertebrates are also found within the Sound.

The greater Puget Sound region covers twelve counties and includes waters from the Olympic and Cascade Mountains, as well as 2,800 miles (4,506 km) of inland marine waterways. The region is covered in forests, wetlands, lakes, and rivers, all of which serve as major resources for those living, working, and vacationing in the region. Ocean-related industries offer an estimated $3.8 billion in wages for the residents. Sport and commercial fishing are major activities in the Sound region, with salmon and geoducks (a very large species of saltwater clam) being among the most valuable catches. In all, the economic and recreational activities of the Puget Sound generate an estimated $20 billion per year.

Unfortunately, the same people who rely so heavily on the resources of the Sound also cause the greatest damage. Population growth and urbanization have led to a serious increase in the amount of pollutants dispersed into both the water and the air. An estimated 140,000 pounds of toxic chemicals are washed into the Puget Sound each day, with about 75 percent of all toxins carried by storm water runoff from roads, driveways, roofs, and other developed surfaces. Some of the most common contaminants include oil, grease, polychlorinated biphenyls (PCBs), copper, lead, and zinc. Reports indicate that the resident orcas of the Puget Sound are among the most PCB-contaminated mammals on earth. In addition, discharges from farms, sewage treatment plants, and failing septic systems have led to low levels of dissolved oxygen in some waters, resulting in the death of bottom-dwelling marine creatures. More than five hundred rivers, streams, and lakes in the Puget Sound basin have shown some level of contamination, affecting waters already strained by the population, which is expected to reach 5.1 million by 2020.

Puget Sound Partnership

While there are many organizations involved in work to restore, protect, and responsibly manage the resources of the Puget Sound, one of the most important initiatives is the *2020 Action Agenda* of the Puget Sound Partnership. The partnership was created by the state legislature in 2007 with a mandate to develop and coordinate efforts to restore and protect the Puget Sound. The comprehensive plan includes recommendations on actions that address a myriad of challenges, from continued population growth to the effects of climate change. The plan issues a call to local governments, private businesses, native tribes, and residents alike to form partnerships that address issues of waste management, pollution reduction, and responsible management of resources at local levels. The plan also includes specific actions that expand on existing salmon and orca recovery plans designed to improve the populations of these marine residents.

To further support these efforts of the Puget Sound Partnership, the state legislature enacted a bill to create a new Puget Sound Corps (SB 5230/HB1294). The bill, introduced in the state senate in January 2011 and signed into law in April 2011, consolidates some of the administrative duties of several agencies that are related to the Washington Conservation Corps (WCC) within the state Ecology Department. The WCC is a state-run program that provides paid internships for young adults (ages eighteen to twenty-five) to work in environmental conservation and monitoring projects. Currently, most of the WCC efforts have been focused on projects in the mountain regions and eastern Washington. The cost savings that result from the administrative consolidation could allow for the creation of a similar Puget Sound Corps, with a specific mandate to carry out the agenda of the Puget Sound Partnership. The cost of maintaining the proposed corps is estimated at about $5 million per year, with funding expected by shifting appropriations to the Ecology Department from the Natural Resources Department. Supporters also believe that the establishment of the Puget Sound Corps will attract federal funding for conservation efforts, as well as special grants from other conservation organizations. The bill, introduced by state senator Kevin Ranker (D) and in the house by Steve Tharinger (D) had bipartisan support.

The clean-up efforts hit a stumbling block in early 2011, however, when the health of a vital section of the sound—Samish Bay—was downgraded by the state Department of Health. The bay is home to more than 4,000 acres of commercial shellfish beds, which must be closed when pollution levels reach higher limits. In 2010 and 2011, the beds were closed for more than 100 days. Governor Chris Gregoire demanded the area be restored and the polluters identified by September 2012. In May 2011, the Partnership made public a 10-point plan that would help clean up and restore Samish Bay. Through these actions and more, the partnership endeavors to create a healthier Puget Sound that supports and preserves both the human and wildlife populations—all by the year 2020.

BIBLIOGRAPHY

Books

Chasan, Daniel Jack, and Tim Thompson. *The Smithsonian Guides to Natural America: The Pacific Northwest–Washington, Oregon.* Washington, DC: Smithsonian Books, 1995.

Donahue, Debra L. *The Western Range Revisited: Removing Livestock from Public Lands to Conserve Native Biodiversity.* Norman: University of Oklahoma Press, 2000.

Duffin, Andrew P. *Plowed Under: Agriculture & Environment in the Palouse.* Seattle: University of Washington Press, 2007.

Eagan, Timothy. *The Big Burn: Teddy Roosevelt and the Fire that Saved America.* Boston, MA: Houghton Mifflin Harcourt, 2009.

Books

Accelerating Washington Clean Energy Job Growth: Washington State Clean Energy Leadership Plan Report Executive Summary and Overview. Navigant Consulting, Inc. Available from http://www.washingtoncelc.org/filestore/CELC_Navigant%20Executive%20Summary_Final.pdf

An act relating to establishing the Puget Sound corps (SB 5230/HB 1294). Washington State Legislature. Available from http://apps.leg.wa.gov/documents/billdocs/2011-12/Pdf/Bills/Senate%20Bills/5230.pdf

"Coal Free Future for Washington." Environmental Priorities Coalition. Available from http://environmentalpriorities.org/coal-free

"Commissioner Goldmark Announces Pilot Projects In Biomass Initiative." Washington State Department of Natural Resources. Jan. 13, 2010. Available from http://www.dnr.wa.gov/BusinessPermits/News/Pages/nr10_003.aspx

Clean Water Act (SB 6851/HB 3181). Washington State Legislature. Available from http://apps.leg.wa.gov/documents/billdocs/2009-10/Pdf/Bills/Senate%20Bills/6851-S.pdf

Department of Ecology, State of Washington. *Beyond Waste Plan: 2009 Update*. Available from http://www.ecy.wa.gov/pubs/0907026.pdf

"Ecology for Business." Department of Ecology, State of Washington. Available from http://www.ecy.wa.gov/business/index.html

"Fish, Wildlife, and Washington's Economy." Washington Department of Fish and Wildlife. Available from http://wdfw.wa.gov/publications/01145/wdfw_01145.pdf

"Global Warming and Washington." National Wildlife Federation. Available from http://www.nwf.org/Global-Warming/~/media/PDFs/Global%20Warming/Global%20Warming%20State%20Fact%20Sheets/Washington.ashx

"Governor Gregoire Signs landmark legislation to transition state off of coal power." Office of the Governor, State of Washington. Available from http://www.governor.wa.gov/news/news-view.asp?pressRelease=1699&newsType=1

Hotakainen, Rob. "As Patience Runs Short, Puget Sound Cleanup Accelerates." *The Seattle Times*. Aug. 28, 2011. Available from http://seattletimes.nwsource.com/html/localnews/2016035078_puget-sound28.html

Office of the Governor, State of Washington. *Executive Order 07-02: Washington Climate Change Challenge*. Available from http://www.governor.wa.gov/execorders/eo_07-02.pdf

Office of the Governor, State of Washington. *Executive Order 09-05: Washington's Leadership on Climate Change*. Available from http://www.ecy.wa.gov/climatechange/2009EO/2009EO_signed.pdf

"Olympic National Park." World Heritage Convention. Available from http://whc.unesco.org/en/list/151.

Puget Sound Partnership. Available from http://www.psp.wa.gov

Radtke, Hands D. *Washington State Commercial Fishing Industry Total Economic Contribution*. Seattle Marine Business Coaltion. Available from http://www.fishermensnews.com/attachmentsPDF/RadtkeReport.pdf

Revised Code of Washington: Greenhouse gas emissions reductions (RCW 70.235.020). Available from http://apps.leg.wa.gov/rcw/default.aspx?cite=70.235.020

Schmidt, Katie. "Bill wants 'boots on the ground' to clean Puget Sound." *The News Tribune*. January 25, 2011. Available from http://www.thenewstribune.com/2011/01/25/v-printerfriendly/1515799/bill-wants-boots-on-the-ground.html

"State Energy Profiles: Washington." U.S. Energy Information Administration. Available at http://tonto.eia.doe.gov/state/state_energy_profiles.cfm?sid=WA

"2011 Clean Water Jobs Act." Environmental Priorities Coalition. Available from http://environmental-priorities.org/clean-water

The United States Conference of Mayors Climate Protection Center. Available from http://www.usmayors.org/climateprotection/revised

Washington Clean Energy Leadership Council homepage. Available at http://www.washingtoncelc.org

Washington Clean Energy Leadership Council: Recommendations for Implementing Navigant/CELC Strategy. Available from http://www.washingtoncelc.org/filestore/CELC%20Recommendations%20_%20Transmittal%20Letter_Final.pdf

The Washington Climate Change Impacts Assessment: Evaluating Washington's Future in a Changing Climate. The Climate Impacts Group, University of Washington. Available from http://cses.washington.edu/cig/files/waccia/wacciafullreport.pdf

"Washington Reaches Agreement with TransAlta to Reduce Emissions." GovMonitor. March 7, 2011. Available from http://www.thegovmonitor.com/world_news/united_states/washington-reaches-agreement-with-transalta-to-reduce-emissions-47290.html

Washington State Department of Agriculture homepage. Available from http://agr.wa.gov

Washington State Department of Natural Resources homepage. Available from http://www.dnr.wa.gov/Pages/default.aspx

Washington State Employment Security Department: Labor Market and Economic Analysis. *2008 Washington State Green Economy Jobs*. Available from http://www.workforceexplorer.com/admin/uploadedPublications/9463_Green_Jobs_Report_2008_WEXVersion.pdf

Washington State Greenhouse Gas Inventory and Reference Case Projections, 1990–2020. Center for Climate Strategies. Available from http://www.ecy.wa.gov/climatechange/docs/WA_GHGInventoryReferenceCaseProjections_1990-2020.pdf

Washington State Legislature. "High-Performance Buildings: Chapter 39.35D." *Revised Code of Washington.* Available from http://apps.leg.wa.gov/RCW/default.aspx?cite=39.35D&full=true#39.35D.010

Washington State Legislature. *House Bill 2227: Evergreen Jobs Act.* Available from http://apps.leg.wa.gov/billinfo/summary.aspx?bill=2227&year=2009

Washington State Legislature. *House Bill 2815: Climate Change Framework/Green-Collar Jobs Act.* Available from http://apps.leg.wa.gov/documents/billdocs/2007-08/Pdf/Bills/Session%20Law%202008/2815-S2.SL.pdf

Washington State Legislature. Senate Bill 5560: An act relating to state agency climate leadership. Available from http://apps.leg.wa.gov/documents/billdocs/2009-10/Pdf/Bills/Senate%20Passed%20Legislature/5560-S2.PL.pdf

Washington State Legislature. Senate Bill 5769 (2011): Regarding coal-fired electric generation facilities.

Available from http://apps.leg.wa.gov/billinfo/summary.aspx?bill=5769

Washington 2007 Minerals Yearbook. United States Geological Survey. Available from http://minerals.usgs.gov/minerals/pubs/state/2007/myb2-2007-wa.pdf

Washington Western Climate Initiative Economic Impact Analysis. ECONorthwest. Available from http://www.ecy.wa.gov/climatechange/docs/20100707_wci_econanalysis.pdf

"Washington's Forests, Timber Supply and Forest-Related Industries." Washington State Department of Natural Resources. Jan. 24, 2008. Available from http://www.dnr.wa.gov/Publications/em_fwfeconomiclow1.pdf

"The WCI Cap & Trade Program." Western Climate Initiative. Available from http://www.westernclimateinitiative.org/the-wci-cap-and-trade-program

West Virginia

Nestled within the Appalachian Highlands, the rugged beauty of the Mountain State attracts thousands of outdoor tourists each year to natural habitats rich in biodiversity. Most recently, however, it is the state's most famous underground resource that has drawn the most critical attention. Coal has been a major industry in West Virginia for a great portion of the state's history, yet, the coal industry is set for major changes. As national concerns increase over greenhouse gas emissions, adverse impacts of mining, and coal combustion waste disposal, many have embraced policies promoting the development of cleaner, more sustainable energy sources. State officials and industry leaders have begun to meet the challenge of change by investing in the development of "clean coal" technologies, designed to produce fewer emissions with higher energy efficiency. But these new developments may not come fast enough if the U.S. Congress moves as quickly as needed in passing legislation designed to limit greenhouse gas emissions, and substantially reduce the demand for coal.

Climate

West Virginia has a continental climate, with four distinct seasons ranging from hot, humid summers, to briskly cold winters. Considering that major industries are the production of coal, natural gas, and other fossil fuels the topics of greenhouse gas emissions and global warming are highly charged, for residents, industry leaders, and politicians alike.

West Virginia does not yet have a Climate Action Plan in place. While the U.S. Congress considers the merits of the proposed American Clean Energy and Security (ACES) Act of 2009, state officials believe that federal attempts to regulate emissions through such a program could create unnecessary volatility in the energy market, leading to a drop in the state's gross domestic product of $750 million by 2020 and a loss of 10,000 jobs during the same period. State legislators instead

advocate greater investment in "clean coal" technologies. However, the true costs of coal include documented dramatic health impacts from fossil fuels and significant savings from Cap-and-Trade programs such as those proposed by ACES. Recent published studies (Hill, et al) show that health benefits from reduced air pollution far outweigh economic costs of Cap-And-Trade and document (Hendryx and Ahearn) that there are $5 in health costs associated with every dollar of coal revenue generated.

❧ Natural Resources, Water, and Agriculture

Natural Resources

West Virginia is the third most heavily forested state in the nation (after Maine and New Hampshire), with forests covering about 78 percent of the total land area. Hardwoods such as oak, ash, walnut, hickory, and chestnut are among the most common forest trees. Maple, hemlock, pine, and spruces are also prevalent. The wood products industry generates about $3.2 billion per year and results in about 30,000 jobs.

The beauty of the Appalachian Mountains draws numerous visitors to more than thirty state parks and forests, which provide safe habitats for such wildlife as the white-tailed (Virginia) deer, black bear, and wildcat, along with some more common animals as raccoons, opossums, gray and red foxes, and cottontail rabbits. Some of the most common birds are sparrows, woodpeckers, swallows, warblers, cardinals, hawks, and owls. Wild Turkey and bobwhite quail are common game animals. Poisonous copperheads and rattlesnakes are also abundant.

According to the U.S. Fish and Wildlife Service, West Virginia is home to thirteen threatened endangered animal species and six threatened or endangered plant species. Endangered animals in the state include three varieties of bat and five varieties of freshwater mussels. Endangered plants include the northeastern bulrush and the running buffalo clover.

In March 2011, a federal judge reinstated endangered status for the West Virginia northern flying squirrel. The squirrel had been removed from the endangered list in 2008. However, a lawsuit was filed by a number of environmental groups in 2009 that alleged that the U.S. Fish and Wildlife Service did not follow its own recovery plan concerning the species and therefore violated the Endangered Species Act. Recovery plans contain science-based criteria, which are developed by teams of scientists who are experts on the species of concern. These criteria measure whether the species' endangered status should be changed. The ruling acknowledged that not all of the criteria were met in the West Virginia flying squirrel's recovery plan.

While coal, oil, and natural gas reserves are by far the state's most important mineral resources, nonfuel minerals such as cement, lime, sand, and gravel have significant economic value for the state.

Water

The two major rivers are the Potomac and the Ohio. The Ohio River has a long history as a major inland transportation route. The Port of Huntington Tri-state is the largest inland river port in the nation and the sixth largest of all U.S. ports. The Monongahela and Kanawha, tributaries of the Ohio, are also navigable. The Shenandoah is the principal tributary of the Potomac. There are several subterranean streams throughout the state, producing caverns such as Seneca Caverns, Smoke Hole Caverns, and Organ Cave. West Virginia has no natural lakes, but numerous reservoirs provide recreation, fishing, water supply, and flood protection. Ground water is used extensively, both for domestic water supplies and an emerging bottled water industry.

More than 100 species of fish are found in West Virginia's rivers, including smallmouth bass, rainbow trout, and brook trout (the state fish). While there is little commercial fishing, there are some trout farms, two state hatcheries, and one national fish hatchery in the state.

Agriculture

Most of West Virginia's 23,200 farms are small and privately owned, with 80 percent of all farms bringing in less than $10,000 per year and 95.2 percent operated by a family or individual. Livestock and livestock products are the primary agricultural commodities, with poultry, eggs, cattle, and dairy products as the top commodities. Tree fruit (apples and peaches) are the most economically important crops, although acreage of corn and hay crops is also significant. A number of native medicinal plants,

including ginseng, goldenseal, bloodroot, and sassafras are harvested as cash crops.

In the interest of marketing and development, the West Virginia Department of Agriculture sponsors a number of promotional programs for locally grown produce and food products. The Farmer to Chef initiative forges partnerships between farmers and restaurants and resorts that agree to use local products. The Department is also working on the development of a halal and kosher certification program to increase the marketability of West Virginia products in East Coast cities. Organic farmers may be certified through the National Association of State Organic Programs, which maintains an official contact at the WV Department of Agriculture. According to the U.S. Department of Agriculture's 2008 Organic Survey, West Virginia had more than 50 certified organic operations in the state.

Energy

Oil and Gas

The state produces very small amounts of crude oil but about 2 percent of the nation's natural gas. The only oil refinery, located in Newell, primarily produces lubricants and process oils, with small amounts of conventional gasoline and diesel fuel. West Virginia is one of a few states that do not require the use of specific gasoline blends, which are generally adopted to reduce vehicle emissions. The industrial sector consumes about 30 percent of the state's supply of natural gas. About 50 percent of all households use natural gas as their primary source for home heating.

Though production of natural gas is low, the state has a relatively large underground storage capacity, enough to supply several Northeastern states during the winter months. In the hopes of increasing natural gas production, the West Virginia Geological and Economic Survey has been compiling data on the potential for unconventional natural gas resources, including reserves found in Marcellus Shale and tight gas deposits, which are found deeply imbedded in hard rock. However, the technique primarily used for recovering natural gas from such hard rock deposits, known as hydraulic fracturing or "fracking," is highly controversial.

On March, 18, 2010, the U.S. Environmental Protection Agency (EPA) announced that it would conduct a comprehensive study of the impact of hydraulic fracturing on water quality and public health. The draft study was submitted for peer review in February 2011, after which the agency revised the draft plan. Initial results from the study will be available in late 2012 with an additional report on further research in 2014. The purpose of this study is to research the lifespan of water that is put through the fracking process, including the water's treatment and disposal.

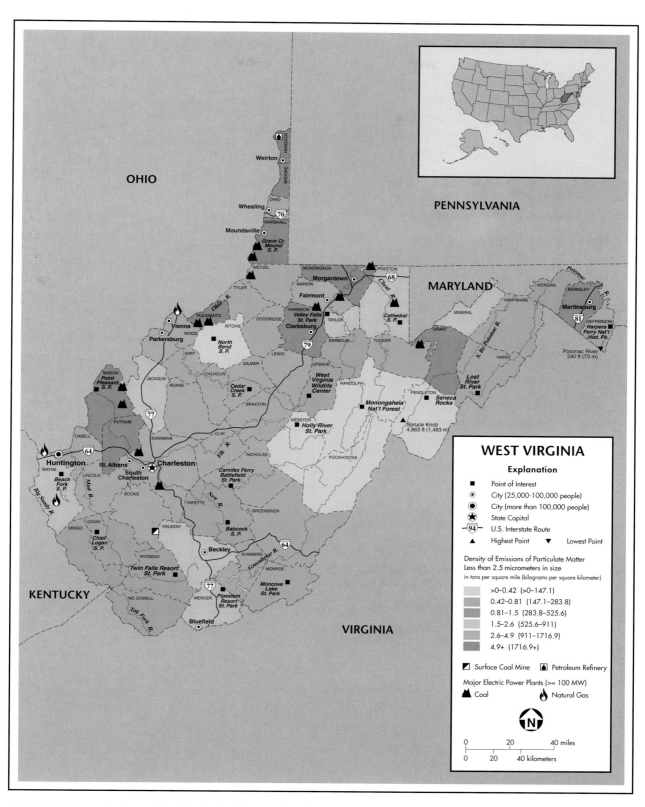

WEST VIRGINIA

Explanation

- ■ Point of Interest
- ◉ City (25,000-100,000 people)
- ◉ City (more than 100,000 people)
- ★ State Capital
- ⬡94 U.S. Interstate Route
- ▲ Highest Point   ▼ Lowest Point

Density of Emissions of Particulate Matter
Less than 2.5 micrometers in size
in tons per square mile (kilograms per square kilometer)

- >0–0.42 (>0–147.1)
- 0.42–0.81 (147.1–283.8)
- 0.81–1.5 (283.8–525.6)
- 1.5–2.6 (525.6–911)
- 2.6–4.9 (911–1716.9)
- 4.9+ (1716.9+)

▨ Surface Coal Mine   ◉ Petroleum Refinery

Major Electric Power Plants (>= 100 MW)

▲ Coal   ♦ Natural Gas

0   20   40 miles
0   20   40 kilometers

SOURCES: "County Emissions Map: Criteria Air Pollutants." *AirData*. U.S. Environmental Protection Agency. Available from http://www.epa.gov/air/data/geosel.html; *Energy Maps*. U.S. Energy Information Administration. Available from http://www.eia.gov/state; *Highest and Lowest Elevations*. U.S. Geological Survey. Available from http://egsc.usgs.gov/isb/pubs/booklets/elvadist/elvadist.html#Highest; *2007 Minerals Yearbook*. U.S. Geological Survey. Available from http://minerals.usgs.gov/minerals/pubs/state. © 2011 Cengage Learning.

Appalachian Mountains of West Virginia. © *Aurora Photos/Alamy*

In addition to environmental concerns of the effects of drilling in the Marcellus Shale, recent accidents occurring at drilling sites are likely to increase pressure on state and federal agencies for greater regulation of inland drilling practices. On June 7, 2010, a fireball and explosion at a Marcellus Shale natural gas drilling site outside Moundsville, West Virginia, burned seven workers. Less than a week earlier, a blowout had occurred at a Pennsylvania Marcellus Shale natural gas drilling site.

In March 2011, the Morgantown City Council proposed two resolutions concerning Marcellus Shale drilling. The first resolution called for a special session to pass drilling regulations, while the second resolution called for a moratorium on drilling permits while these regulations are being developed. Members of the oil and gas industry, along with city residents, students, engineers, and members of environmental organizations spoke during the council meeting about the advantages and disadvantages of a moratorium and the need for drilling regulations. A resolution was finally adopted that, while silent on the issue of a moratorium, calls for a special session to pass drilling legislation. In June 2011 the council voted to ban the practice of "fracking" within the city limits, as well as within one mile of the city's borders. However, a county court removed the ban in August, after Northeast Natural Energy sued for the right to drill its wells situated across the Monongahela River from Morgantown.

In September 2011, West Virginia state legislators contemplated permit fees of $10,000 for drilling the first Marcellus Shale gas welland $5,000 for each well thereafter. Drilling industry groups expressed concern about the fees, calling them "excessive." According to media reports, drilling organizations say the fees would eclipse any of those in neighboring states, thereby making it difficult for West Virginia to compete for new projects. Prior permit fees were in the hundreds of dollars, and in Pennsylvania, operators pay between $3,000 and $4,000 for a permit. Legislators hoped to have the bill passed by the end of 2011.

West Virginia State Profile

Physical Characteristics

Land area	24,038 square miles (62,258 sq km)
Inland water area	192 square miles (497 sq km)
Coastal area	NA
Highest point	Spruce Knob 4,863 feet (1,482 m)
National Forest System lands (2010)	1 million acres (422,000 ha)
State parks (2011)	36

Energy Statistics

Total energy production (2009)	4,200 trillion Btu
State ranking in total energy production (2009)	4
Renewable energy net generation total (2009)	2.4 million megawatt hours
Hydroelectric energy generation (2009)	1.6 million megawatt hours
Biomass energy generation (2009)	NA
Wind energy generation (2009)	742,000 megawatt hours
Wood and derived fuel energy generation (2009)	NA
Crude oil reserves (2009)	19.0 million barrels (3.0 million cu m)
Natural gas reserves (2009)	5,946 billion cubic feet (168.4 billion cu m)
Natural gas liquids (2008)	108.0 million barrels (17.2 million cu m)

Pollution Statistics

Carbon output (2005)	114.4 million tons of CO_2 (103.8 million t)
Superfund sites (2008)	9
Particulate matter (less than 2.5 micrometers) emissions (2002)	36,922 tons per year (33,495 t/yr)
Toxic chemical releases (2009)	43 million pounds (19.5 million kg)
Generated hazardous waste (2009)	92,400 tons (83,900 t)

SOURCES: AirData. U.S. Environmental Protection Agency. Available from http://www.epa.gov/air/data; *Energy Maps, Facts, and Data of the U.S. States.* U.S. Energy Information Administration. Available from http://www.eia.gov/state; *The 2012 Statistical Abstract.* U.S. Census Bureau. Available from http://www.census.gov/compendia/statab; *United States Energy Usage.* eRedux. Available from http://www.eredux.net/states.

© *2011 Cengage Learning.*

Coal

West Virginia produces more than 10 percent of the nation's coal supply and ranks second in the nation (after Wyoming) in the production of coal. Coal-fired plants produce nearly all of the state's electricity. The remainder is produced through several small hydroelectric facilities. Only about 30 percent of all households rely on electricity for home heating, which translates into a relatively low residential consumption rate. The production rate for electricity remains high, however, as West Virginia ranks second in the nation (after Pennsylvania) in net interstate electricity exports.

About 55 percent of the state's coal is produced from underground mines, with the remainder from surface mining methods that include contour mining, area mining, and mountaintop mining.

Mountaintop mining has been a topic of controversy for several years as citizens protest against a method that destroys the natural environment and leaves behind a variety of pollutants. By law, coal companies engaging in surface mining are expected to restore mined lands to their original contour and to reforest or replant the area as necessary in order to return the land it to its natural state. Opponents argue that complete restoration is rarely possible in the case of mountaintop mining. Furthermore, blasting on mountain peaks causes rocks and other debris to be deposited into nearby rivers and streams, producing what is commonly referred to as valley fill. This fill can contain pollutants that affect the water supply. The federal government has become a part of the debate, as tighter water quality regulations have been imposed at mountaintop mining sites.

Alternative and Renewable Energy Sources

As the federal government continues to implement energy policies that promote alternative and sustainable energy sources, with fewer greenhouse gas emissions, the future of the coal industry is a major concern for the state, which earns more than 12 percent of the gross state product from coal. Facing the challenge head on, a number of companies have begun to consider the development of advanced coal technologies, such as carbon capture and storage and coal gasification.

There is a growing interest in other alternative energy sources, such as solar and wind production. The Mountaineer Wind Energy Center in Tucker County is West Virginia's first commercial wind farm and has a capacity to produce 66 MW of electricity from 44 turbines. The Beech Ridge Wind Farm in Greenbriar County was given a green light for construction in January 2010, after working out an agreement with environmental groups to take measures that will protect the nearby Indiana bat population. The initial operation will include sixty-seven turbines, with an option to expand by adding thirty-three turbines in the future. Another existing wind farm is the NedPower Mount Storm in Grant County near Washington, D. C., which became fully operational in 2008 and has the ability to generate up to 264 MW of electricity, or enough to power 66,000 homes. Additional wind farms are proposed or under construction around the state.

West Virginia enacted its alternative and renewable energy portfolio standard in June 2009, mandating that investor-owned utilities supply at least 10 percent of electricity through alternative and renewable means by 2015. By 2025, the utilities are required to supply

Aerial view of mountaintop coal mining near Kayford Mountain, West Virginia. © *Aurora Photos/Alamy*

25 percent of electricity through alternative and renewable resources. The state made the stipulation, too, that 90 percent has to come from energy other than natural gas. Utilities had to submit their plans for resources by the beginning of 2011. According to the U.S. Department of Energy, in West Virginia alternative energy sources may include "coal technology, coal bed methane, natural gas, fuel produced by a coal gasification or liquification facility, synthetic gas, integrated gasification combined cycle technologies, waste coal, tire-derived fuel, pumped storage hydroelectric projects and recycled energy."

❦ Green Business, Green Building, Green Jobs

In 2007, West Virginia was ranked last among the fifty states in a *Forbes* magazine survey of America's greenest states, claiming the state was one of several suffering from, "a mix of toxic waste, lots of pollution and consumption and no clear plans to do anything about it." While the development of a green economy has been slow, state officials have made some progress in attracting green businesses to the state, but are focused primarily on existing industries. Appalachian Power, a subsidiary of American Electric Power (AEP), has invested more than $70 million in its Mountaineer Power Plant, which it claims will use an advanced coal technology known as carbon capture and sequestration to create electricity. Carbon capture and sequestration is an expensive and highly controversial technique, whereby the carbon dioxide produced as a result of burning coal is chilled with ammonium and then compressed and pumped far beneath the earth into rock formations. In a related industry, CertainTeed Gypsum has invested more than $100 million in its manufacturing facility located near the AEP Kammer-Mitchell power plant, from which it receives waste fly ash that is converted into high-quality synthetic gypsum wallboards.

Green Building

While there is no specific statewide high-efficiency, green building code, there are some groups throughout the state that are proving the potential for green building practices. The School Building Authority of West Virginia has broken ground on what may become the state's first school listed under the U.S. Green Building Council Leadership in Energy and Environmental Design (LEED) certification program. Spring Mills Primary School in Berkeley County was built from the ground up using green practices, including the use of a geothermal heat pump and a three-inch insulated white roof, both of which help keep heating and cooling costs under control. A storm water collection system was added to recycle rainwater for landscaping. The school opened in fall 2011 and has created a new addition in the curriculum for teachers to talk to students about recycling and conservation efforts.

The Woodlands Development Group in Elkins is working in cooperation with the West Virginia Housing Development Fund and the Davis Elkin College Sustainability Center with plans to build three green townhouses in Elkin for low-income residents. A solar hot water system will be a primary feature of the homes, which may become some of the first LEED certified residential buildings in the state.

West Virginia GREEN-UP Council

State officials have recognized the need for an educated workforce to serve as a cornerstone for a green economy. In January 2010, WorkForce West Virginia received a $6 million grant from the U.S. Department of Labor to support a new green jobs training program. The program is being developed largely through the efforts of the West Virginia GREEN-UP Council (West Virginia Growing Renewable and Efficient Energy Utilizing Partnerships). The GREEN-UP Council consists of representatives

from a variety of businesses, research firms, educational institutions, nonprofit organizations, and economic development officials. The purpose of the council is to develop educational and training programs that are specifically targeted on meeting the goals of the state's energy plan. In part, this will include the development of a GREEN-UP certificate program for community colleges, along with new wind energy technology and water and wastewater treatment programs. A number of training programs and informational seminars on green jobs are now being offered through WV GreenWorks, a nonprofit statewide organization that held its first class (Certified Home Energy Raters) in April 2010.

🍃 Mountaintop Mining: The Line Between Profit and Plunder

Mountaintop mining has been a topic of controversy for many years, as environmentalists argue that the method destroys the natural environment, while mining supporters claim the highly regulated process is the most efficient and environmentally responsible method of surface mining. In recent years, the debate has gone all the way to Washington, D.C., as the U.S. Environmental Protection Agency (EPA) has taken a more critical look at permitting standards, particularly those relating to valley fills and compliance with the federal Clean Water Act.

Mountaintop mining involves the stripping and removal of land through the use of explosives in order to expose coal seams, sometimes hundreds of feet below the surface. Heavy machinery is then used to remove the coal. The rock, dirt, and other debris set loose by the process are disposed of in adjacent lowlands, creating what are known as valley fills. Once the mining operation is complete, by law, coal companies are expected to restore the mined lands to their original contour and to reforest or revegetate the area as necessary in order to return the land it to its natural state.

Supporters of the method claim that the required restoration process makes mountaintop mining the most environmentally responsible method over time, and that most areas are successfully reforested or replanted. They further argue that mountaintop mining requires compliance with more stringent environmental regulations than would be imposed on public construction projects, such as highways, airports, shopping malls, and large manufacturing sites. These projects may also involve the stripping and removal of surface lands, with debris relocated in lower fill areas, and all such projects must adhere to the federal environmental guidelines concerning the acceptable and unacceptable levels of contaminants in fill placed near water sources.

Mining operators in West Virginia claim that they have been diligent in meeting the requirements imposed by federal regulations thus far and believe that they are being unfairly villianized by environmental organizations that are quick to post pictures and videos of mining operations, but rarely go back to document the effects of restoration.

Opponents argue that complete restoration is rarely possible in the case of mountaintop mining, since explosion and removal methods are so destructive. For instance, forests are stripped and frequently replaced by introduced grasses rather than native forests. Thus, habitats for migrating and nesting bird populations are destroyed, and some of those birds may not return to the area for many years, if at all. Furthermore, reports indicate that nearly 2,000 miles (3,219 km) of smaller mountain rivers and streams have been filled in completely by valley fills, thus affecting the natural environment, and that state regulators and inspectors have been lax in testing for contaminants in debris placed in valley fills near flowing rivers and streams, thus leaving the state's water supply at risk. A recent study has linked stream impacts to increased cancer rates among residents. Most importantly, homes and whole communities near or on mine sites may become unlivable, due to blasting, dust, and heavy equipment traffic.

For their part, the U.S. government has begun to impose tighter permitting regulations that may reduce mountaintop mining in the entire Appalachian region. In a 2008 report concerning the downstream effects of mountaintop mining, the EPA discovered that an unacceptable level of salts and other toxins have been released into streams draining from the mining debris in some valley fill areas as rainwater filters through it. In April 2010, the EPA announced stricter guidelines for valley fill permits, setting new, more stringent standards on acceptable levels of contaminants in debris. Analysts say that very few of the state's existing valley fills would meet the new standard, and anticipate that fewer valley fill permits will be approved in the future, as mining companies must now reevaluate their process to impose greater pollution control measures. Since mountaintop operations cannot take place without a valley fill permit, some believe the end is near for the practice.

The adoption of new regulations has put a number of permit applications on hold. Other permits that have passed the first stage of approval through the U.S. Army Corps of Engineers are being held for further review by the EPA, which holds power to veto such permits if it believes the environmental impact will be too great. One such permit belongs to Spruce Mine No. 1 of Arch Coal, Inc. In May 2010, the national coal industry group Federation for American Coal, Energy and Security (FACES of Coal) hosted a rally in Charleston to protest the threat of EPA interference, which it views as a political, rather than scientific move. Several hundred coal industry supporters attended the rally. In January 2011, the EPA exercised its veto of the mine's permit. West Virginia officials warn that the new standards will cause a serious blow to the state's economy and to the nation's coal supply chain. About 10 percent of the U.S. coal supply is produced through mountaintop mining. Officials further argue that, in focusing on a very specific water issue, the U.S. government is disregarding the wider social and economic issues at stake. Meanwhile, opponents claim that their concerns are ignored by state and federal officials and have protested mountaintop removal mines through sit-ins, demonstrations, and an on-going civil disobedience campaign, resulting in at least 150 arrests since 2009.

The National Mining Association filed a lawsuit that alleges the U.S. government has unlawfully blocked surface coal mining efforts by imposing additional requirements for obtaining permits. The EPA and the U.S. Army Corps of Engineers filed a motion to dismiss the lawsuit; however, a federal judge denied the motion in January 2011. The motion was denied because, under the Clean Water Act, the EPA is only to have a limited role in the issuing of permits. The National Mining Association claims that when the EPA tightened their guidelines for mining permits, they were implementing unlawful substantial changes to the process. The case was unresolved as of late 2011.

Residents opposed to mountaintop mining on Coal River Mountain in Raleigh County have suggested an alternative use for the land: installing a wind farm. Coal River Mountain is one of the last intact mountaintops in the region, and its forests are known for their biodiversity. Residents and experts hope that continuing to mine for coal underground and preserving the forests and landscape will bring more tourist dollars to the area. Installing a wind farm could also preserve jobs in an area that has been totally dependent on the coal industry. Coal executives have argued that flattened mountaintops are easier to develop for wind farms, but this has been refuted, since the higher the elevation of a wind farm, the more utility-scale wind there will be.

Coal executives and families that rely on the industry for their livelihoods, however, worry that replacing mining with wind turbines is simply unrealistic. Wind power cannot compete with coal production financially without substantial subsidies. While mountaintop mining would therefore keep the industry stable, it would only be in the short-term. The mountain's coal resources and the royalties that come from it easily surpass what a wind farm would produce. However, coal will run out, and once it does the coal companies will leave land that has been irreversibly changed. Residents that want to preserve Coal River Mountain's pristine landscape are hoping for a compromise that would involve the continuation of underground mining while bringing in a turbine production plant, which would begin a transition from coal-dependency to renewable energy. For now, coal remains the focal point in the area, and blasting has already begun on one corner of the mountain. However, that one area was the subject of a protest by four members of a group called Radical Action For Mountain People's Survival. The protest led to a lawsuit filed by Marfork Coal Company in September 2011. The coal company asked for a restraining order against the four members and their associates. The protestors staged a 30-day tree sit-in summer 2011, which caused a one-day delay in blasting at the site.

West Virginians on both sides of the mining question continue to fight in the hope of finding a balance that is both environmentally and economically friendly.

BIBLIOGRAPHY

Books

Hopkins, Bruce. *The Smithsonian Guides to Natural America: Central Appalachia–West Virginia, Kentucky, Tennessee.* Washington, DC: Smithsonian Books, 1996.

Riddel, Frank S. *The Historical Atlas of West Virginia.* Morgantown: West Virginia University Press, 2008.

West Virginia: Official State Travel Guide. South Charleston, WV: Miles Media Group, Inc., 2006.

Web Sites

Childs, Randall A. *West Virginia's Forests: Growing West Virginia's Future.* College of Business and Economic, West Virginia University, June 2005. Available from http://www.wvforestry.com/Economic%20Impact%20Study.pdf

"Court Gives Endangered Status Back to West Virginia Northern Flying Squirrel, Rules that Recovery Plans Must Be Followed." March 30, 2011. Center for Biological Diversity. Available from http://www.biologicaldiversity.org/news/press_releases/2011/west-virginia-northern-flying-squirrel-03-28-2011.html

Hendryx, M., and M. M. Ahearn. "Mortality in Appalachian Coal Mining Regions: The Value of Statistical Life Lost." *Public Health Reports* (124: 541–550). 2009.

Hill, J. S., et al. "Climate Change and Health Costs of Air Emissions from Biofuels and Gasoline." *Proceedings of the National Academy of Science* (106: 2077–2082), 2009.

Hitt, N. P., and M. Hendryx. "Ecological Integrity of Streams Related to Human Cancer Mortality Rates." *EcoHealth.* Published online April 2, 2010. Available from http://springerlink.com/content/lu7wgk595v1hhm64/fulltext.pdf

"Invenergy to Complete Construction of West Virginia Wind Farm Following Agreement to Protect Indiana Bat." Invenergy. Available from http://www. invenergyllc.com/news/Greenbrier_County_Agreement_F2doc.pdf

"Judge Overturns Drilling Ban." *The Gazette Mail.* August 14, 2011. Available from http://www.wvgazette.com/ap/ApTopStories/201108141206

Krafcik, Mike. "City of Morgantown Asks State to Stop Issuing Marcellus Shale Permits." March 28, 2011. *The State Journal.* Available from http://www.statejournal.com/story.cfm?func=viewstory&storyid=96755

"Listings and Occurrences for West Virginia." Species Reports. U.S. Fish and Wildlife Service. Available from http://ecos.fws.gov/tess_public/pub/stateListingAndOccurrenceIndividual.jsp?state=WV&s8-fid=112761032792&s8fid=112762573902&s8-fid=24012973648292

Moore, C.V. "Markfork Suing Activists Over Tree Sit At Mine Site." *The Register-Herald.* September 15, 2011. Available from http://www.register-herald.com/local/x1642552059/Marfork-suing-activists-over-tree-sit-at-mine-site

Mountaintop Mining: Viewpoint. Walker Machinery Company. Available from http://www.wvcoal.com/attachments/909_WALKER%20MMV%20LOW%20RES.pdf

"NedPower Mount Storm Wind Project Completed." Shell U.S. Media Center. December 8, 2008. Available from http://www.shell.us/home/content/usa/aboutshell/media_center/news_and_press_releases/2008/wind_energy_120808.html

Palmer, M. A., et al. "Mountaintop Mining Consequences." *Science* 327:148–149, 2010.

Pond, Gregory, et al. *Downstream Effects of Mountaintop Coal Mining: Comparing Biological Conditions using Family-and Genus-Level Macroinvertebrate Bioassessment Tools>.* The North American Benthological Society, 2008. Available from http://www.epa.gov/Region3/mtntop/pdf/downstreameffects.pdf

Plundering Appalachia: The Tragedy of Mountaintop-Removal Coal Mining. Available from http://www.plunderingappalachia.org

Smith, Vicki. "W.Va. Producers Oppose $10K Marcellus Permit Fee." Bloomberg BusinessWeek. September 20, 2011. Available from http://www.businessweek.com/ap/financialnews/D9PSE4E00.htm

"State Energy Profiles: West Virginia." United States Energy Information Administration. Available from West Virginia's Coal Mining Methods. West Virginia Coal Association. Available from http://www.wvcoal.com/mountain-top-mining/wv-coal-mining-methods.html?start=1

Umstead, Matthew. "Spring Mills Primary School about 85 percent complete." *Herald-Mail.* January 11,

2011. Available from http://articles.herald-mail.com/2011-01-11/news/27023681_1_don-zepp-spring-mills-primary-school-first-green-school

Ward, Ken Jr. "Hundreds Turn Out for EPA Mountaintop Removal Hearing." *Charleston Gazette*. May 18, 2010. Available from http://wvgazette.com/News/MiningtheMountains/201005180947

Ward, Ken Jr. "Latest, Longest Massey Tree-sit Protest Ends." *Charleston Gazette*. January 29, 2010. Available from http://www.wvgazette.com/News/MiningtheMountains/201001290665

West Virginia Department of Agriculture 2009 Annual Report. Available from http://www.wvagriculture.org/images/Executive/Annual/Contents.html

West Virginia Energy. West Virginia Department of Commerce. Available from http://wvcommerce.org/energy/default.aspx

West Virginia Geological and Economic Survey. Available from http://www.wvgs.wvnet.edu

"West Virginia Incentives/Policies For Renewables & Efficiency." Database of State Incentives For Renewables & Efficiencies. U.S. Department of Energy. Updated January 1, 2011. Available from http://www.dsireusa.org/incentives/incentive.cfm?Incentive_Code=WV05R&re=1&ee=1

"West Virginia Receives $6 million Green Grant for Work Force Training. WorkForce West Virginia." Available from http://www.workforcewv.org/logos/Green%20Job%20Grant%20Award%20Release.pdf

Wingfield, Brian, and Miriam Marcus. "America's Greenest States." *Forbes*, October 7, 2007. Available from http://www.forbes.com/2007/10/16/environment-energy-vermont-biz-beltway-cx_bw_mm_1017greenstates.html

WV GreenWorks. Available from http://wvgreenworks.org

Zeller Jr., Tom. " A Battle in Mining Country Pits Coal Against Wind." *The New York Times*. August 15, 2010. Available from http://www.nytimes.com/2010/08/15/business/energy-environment/15coal.html

Wisconsin

Often referred to as America's Dairyland, Wisconsin has a long farming tradition. It ranks second (after California) in the number of organic farms. Located in the eastern, north-central United States, Wisconsin ranks twenty-fifth in size among the 50 U.S. states. The state's land area can be divided into four approximately equal sized geographic regions. The Superior Upland, situated below Lake Superior and the border with the Michigan Upper Peninsula, is the defined by heavily forested rolling hills. A second upland region, the Driftless Area of southwest Wisconsin (and parts of surrounding states), features rugged terrain and elevations that reach more than twelve hundred feet. A comparatively flat, crescent-shaped lowland occupies the space immediately south of the highlands. Finally, a large, glaciated lowland plain is situated in the east and southeast along Lake Michigan.

Wisconsin has a continental climate. Summers are warm and winters notoriously cold, especially in the upper northeast and north-central lowlands. The average annual temperature ranges from 39°F (3.8°C) in the north to about 50°F (10°C) in the south. Because of its unique and cool climate, Wisconsin could be profoundly, and negatively, impacted by climate change. According to research conducted by the Nelson Institute for Environmental Studies at the University of Wisconsin-Madison, global climate change will significantly raise temperatures throughout Wisconsin by the end of the 21st century. According to the National Wildlife Federation, temperatures in the state could rise as much as 8 to 17°F (4.4 to 9.4°C) by the year 2100. Higher temperatures could increase the severity of droughts, further reduce water levels in Lake Michigan by as much as 1.5 to 8 feet (0.5 to 2.4 m) by the end of the century, impair the state's wetland habitats, and harm croplands and forests adapted to Wisconsin's cooler climate. Cool-water fish species could face serious declines in population as water temperatures rise, and the extent of forested areas could decline by as much as 55 to 70

percent due to drier conditions as a result of global warming.

🌳 Natural Resources, Water, and Agriculture

Forests, Parks, and Wildlife

Forestland covers about 46 percent of the state, with the most dominant forest type being maple/beech/birch (28 percent of forests). Oak/hickory and aspen/birch are other common types. About 68 percent of the forests are privately owned, while 7 percent are maintained by the state. The forest product industry, provides employment for more than 66,000 residents, primarily through the paper industry, which is a leading manufacturing industry for the state. Wood furniture and other wood products manufacturing are also important sectors. As of 2009, forest product jobs accounted for about 14 percent of all the manufacturing jobs in the state, and the industry contributes $18 billion to the state's economy annually. Forestry and forestry support services account for 13.5 percent of all businesses in Wisconsin.

Wisconsin has 53 state parks and recreation areas, 42 state trails, and 13 state forests, all home to a wide variety of plants and animals. The state is also home to Apostle Island National Lakeshore and the Ice Age National Scenic Trail. Common animals throughout the state include the white-tailed deer, red and grey foxes, and many of the 336 bird species found in the state. The Horicon National Wildlife Refuge, managed jointly by the U.S. Fish and Wildlife Service and the Wisconsin Department of Natural Resources, is the largest cattail marsh in the United States. It has been designated as a Ramsar Wetland of International Importance for its significance as a resting ground for thousands of migrating ducks and Canada geese. According to the

U.S. Fish and Wildlife Service, there are fifteen plant and animal species found in Wisconsin that are federally endangered or threatened, including the Canada lynx, and the eastern prairie fringed orchid.

The protections for the gray wolves remained in place until December 2011 when the Obama administration declared that the gray wolf populations in Michigan, Minnesota, Wisconsin, and parts of adjoining states had recovered sufficiently enough to be removed from the endangered species list. Only recently had the wolves in the Great Lakes region been classified as two species—the gray wolf and the eastern wolf—including hybrids of the two species. Some biologists cite that recent discovery as another reason why protections should have been left in place, to give scientists a better opportunity to understand the populations.

In 2001, the U.S. Congress launched the State Wildlife Grants Program to provide conservation funding to states that prepare a Wildlife Action Plan. In response, Wisconsin put forward an action plan that identified native wildlife species with low or declining populations and offered a menu of conservation actions to get threatened or endangered species permanently off those lists. Some of these plans will build on efforts that have already proven successful in the past decades. Since 1985, the Wisconsin Department of Natural Resources has noted an increase in the number of timber wolves from a little more than a dozen animals to nearly 700 in 2010. An elk reintroduction program has resulted in population growth from 25 in 1995 to 164 in 2010.

Minerals

Geologic diversity also makes Wisconsin an important hub for mineral mining. Both metallic and nonmetallic minerals are harvested in the state. The state established its first comprehensive mineral mining law in 1974, enabling the Wisconsin Department of Natural Resources to regulate the metallic mining industry. However, the state has taken measures to limit metallic mining because of negative environmental impacts. As of 2007, there were no active metal mines in the state. Non-metallic mining remains a common activity in Wisconsin, where roughly two thousand registered mines harvest an array of non-metallic minerals, such as sand, gravel, limestone, and dolomite. The state has ranked as a leading national producer of dimension stone, and ranks third in production of industrial sand and gravel.

Water: A Collectivist Approach

Wisconsin is a water-rich state. The Mississippi River borders its southwestern edge, and portions of the two Great Lakes (Superior and Michigan), more than 15,000 inland lakes, and 39,000 miles (62,764 km) of rivers and streams are found in the state. The state boasts more than 8,200 square miles (21,238 sq km) of ecologically diverse and environmentally important wetlands, and enough groundwater to cover the entire state in 100 feet of water.

Under the state's Public Trust Doctrine, all of Wisconsin's waters, lakes, and streams belong collectively to Wisconsin's citizens and are declared "common highways and forever free." An owner of a lakefront home or a piece of land with a stream running across it is permitted reasonable use of the water that borders or runs through the property, but if the owner's activity impedes public rights to the waters, the Wisconsin Supreme Court has ruled that public rights are primary to individual rights.

Ports and Fishing

Wisconsin's major ports—including Milwaukee and Manitowoc on Lake Michigan, Sturgeon Bay and Green Bay on an arm of Lake Michigan, and Superior on Lake Superior—handle more than 40 million tons of cargo valued at more than $8 billion each year. The commercial fishing industry of the Wisconsin Great Lakes has an economic impact of more than $31 million per year. Meanwhile, sport fishing in Wisconsin's lakes and streams is a popular pasttime and generates more than $2.75 billion in economic benefits each year. Lake rainbow, and brown trout; Chinook and coho salmon; largemouth bass; channel catfish; yellow and white perch; and walleye are popular catches.

The Threat of Asian Carp

In July 2010, Wisconsin and four other states in the Great Lakes region filed a lawsuit against the U.S. Army Corps of Engineers and the Metropolitan Reclamation District of Greater Chicago to force them to close the Chicago locks to try to prevent the invasive Asian carp from advancing into Lake Michigan. The suit requested that the locks be shut at all times, except in emergency situations. The states also requested more poisoning and netting programs for areas north of an electric barrier on the Chicago Sanitary and Ship Canal. This electric barrier was the first line of defense against the advancement of the Asian carp, but evidence has been found that the carp may have breached this barrier, including a fisherman's catch of a 20-pound (9-kg) specimen only six miles (9.6 km) from Lake Michigan. However, the Illinois Department of Natural Resources reported in early August that testing conducted on the Asian carp discovered in June indicated that the fish may have been placed in Lake Calumet by humans, rather than it having migrated past the barrier on its own.

Varieties of the Asian carp have been found in Wisconsin waters since as early as 1987, when the grass carp appeared. Bighead carp began appearing in 1998, and the first confirmed silver carp was found in 2008. No black carp have yet been sighted. Asian carp has proven to be highly detrimental to native aquatic plants that support native fish species.

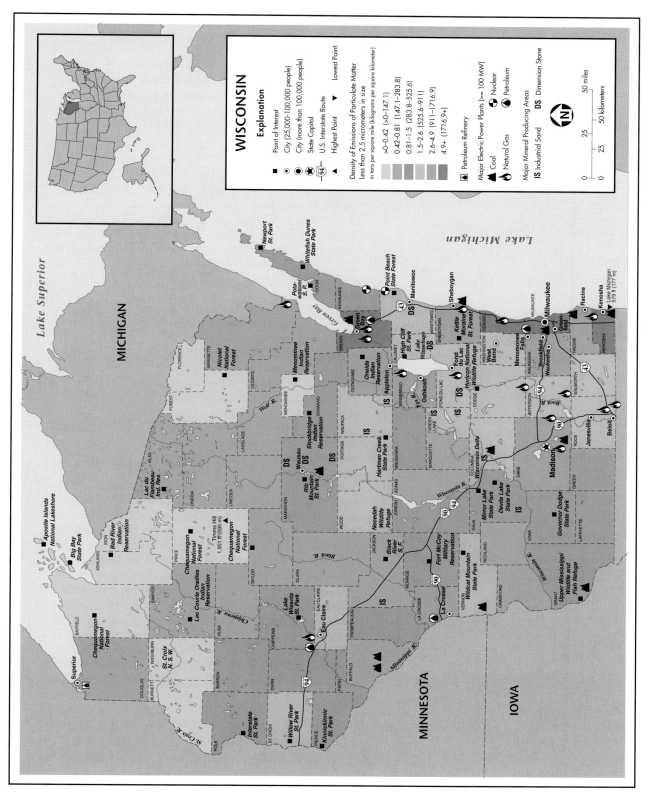

SOURCES: "County Emissions Map: Criteria Air Pollutants." *AirData.* U.S. Environmental Protection Agency. Available from http://www.epa.gov/air/data/geosel.html; *Energy Maps.* U.S. Energy Information Administration. Available from http://www.cia.gov/state; *Highest and Lowest Elevations.* U.S. Geological Survey. Available from http://egsc.usgs.gov/isb/pubs/booklets/elvadist/elvadist.html#Highest; *2007 Minerals Yearbook.* U.S. Geological Survey. Available from http://minerals.usgs.gov/minerals/pubs/state. © 2011 Cengage Learning.

Wisconsin State Profile

Physical Characteristics

Land area	54,154 square miles (140,258 sq km)
Inland water area	1,984 square miles (5,139 sq km)
Coastal area	NA
Highest point	Timms Hill 1,951 feet (595 m)
National Forest System lands (2010)	1.5 million acres (621,000 ha)
State parks (2011)	66

Energy Statistics

Total energy production (2009)	290 trillion Btu
State ranking in total energy production (2009)	36
Renewable energy net generation total (2009)	3.7 million megawatt hours
Hydroelectric energy generation (2009)	1.4 million megawatt hours
Biomass energy generation (2009)	519,000 megawatt hours
Wind energy generation (2009)	1.0 million megawatt hours
Wood and derived fuel energy generation (2009)	769 million megawatt hours
Crude oil reserves (2009)	NA
Natural gas reserves (2009)	NA
Natural gas liquids (2008)	NA

Pollution Statistics

Carbon output (2005)	104.8 million tons of CO_2 (95.1 million t)
Superfund sites (2008)	38
Particulate matter (less than 2.5 micrometers) emissions (2002)	10,897 tons per year (9,885 t/yr)
Toxic chemical releases (2009)	32.9 million pounds (14.9 million kg)
Generated hazardous waste (2009)	223,400 tons (202,700 t)

SOURCES: AirData. U.S. Environmental Protection Agency. Available from http://www.epa.gov/air/data; *Energy Maps, Facts, and Data of the U.S. States.* U.S. Energy Information Administration. Available from http://www.eia.gov/state; *The 2012 Statistical Abstract.* U.S. Census Bureau. Available from http://www.census.gov/compendia/statab; *United States Energy Usage.* eRedux. Available from http://www.eredux.net/states.

The case calling for the injunction to close the locks was heard in September and October 2010. In December, Judge Robert Dow Jr. of the U.S. District Court issued an opinion that denied the request for an injunction, stating that the plaintiffs had not met the necessary burden of proof to obtain the injunction, in part by failing to show sufficient proof of irreparable harm if the situation remains the same. In the official opinion paper, the judge acknowledged the potential environmental and economic threats associated with the migration of the carp into the lakes, but noted that federal and state agencies are well aware of the situation and have been working on solutions to the problem. The states appealed the ruling, but in August 2011, it was upheld by the Seventh Circuit Court of Appeals. However, the court ruled that if the urgency of the matter increased, it may revisit the request for an injunction.

At the national level, the Asian Carp Prevention and Control Act (S 1421—111th Congress) passed in Congress and was signed into law on December 14, 2010. The law adds the bighead carp species of Asian carp to the list of injurious species that are prohibited from being imported or shipped in the United States under the Lacey Act.

Problems with Phosphorus

In June 2010, the Wisconsin Natural Resources Board (WNRB) approved a series of controversial regulations designed to limit the amount of phosphorus that ends up in the state's lakes, rivers, and streams. Phosphorus pollution from agricultural, residential, and industrial runoff is a major concern in some areas, as this chemical commonly found in fertilizers lowers oxygen levels in the water, thereby contributing to the growth of deadly green-blue algae in some waterways and a decline in the fish population in others. As of June 2010, about 172 lakes and streams in Wisconsin were considered to be "impaired waters" due to high levels of phosphorus. The new regulations set a strict standard for the acceptable amount of phosphorus in local waterways and even tighter new limits on acceptable levels from public and industrial wastewater treatment facilities.

The controversy surrounding the new regulations was primarily one of finances. The WNRB has estimated that implementation of the regulations could cost more than $1 billion. At least one business-sponsored analysis put the estimated cost at more than $4 billion. Some community wastewater treatment facilities have estimated that residential sewage treatment rates could jump by as much as $900 per year. In addition, the new regulations promote a cost-sharing program with farmers, by which the state would pay up to 70 percent of the cost for non-point pollution controls. However, it was not clear how the state would fund such a program in the long-term.

In March 2011, in the midst of this controversy, Governor Scott Walker introduced a proposal to rewrite the rule. The proposal included a switch from a numeric standard for phosphorus levels to a "narrative" standard, which would provide a description of water quality expectations rather than a set limit. Walker also suggested that any phosphorus limits should not be stricter than the standards set by neighboring states. This proposal was immediately criticized by the WNRB and other environmental groups, all of which urged the governor to reconsider. In April 2011, Walker agreed to an alternative measure by suggesting a two-year delay on the implementation of the regulations. His primary motivation appeared to be a concern for the economic impact the new plans could have on an already weakened economy. However, supporters of the new regulations continue to voice concerns over the potential environmental impact associated with a delay in implementing adequate regulation.

Leader in Agriculture: Adapting to Changing Needs and Demands

Wisconsin's early agricultural economy was based on wheat. Farmers also grew barley and hops to feed the famous, early Milwaukee beer brewers—the Pabst and Miller Brewing Companies. After the Civil War, soil exhaustion and crop destruction caused by the chinch bug forced farmers to turn to other crops, including corn, oats, and hay, which could be used to feed hogs, sheep, cows, and other livestock.

Known as America's Dairyland, Wisconsin was ranked as first in the nation for dairy products in 2009, accounting for 46 percent of all statewide agricultural sales. In the same year, 127 of the 211 dairy manufacturing plants were producing some type of cheese. While cow's milk is the primary supply, the state also ranks as a national leader for the number of dairy goats. In efforts to more fully support and promote the dairy industry, the state has instituted a number of tax credits for cheesemakers working to modernize their dairy and livestock operations. The nonprofit Dairy Business Innovation Center launched in 2004 provides technical and development assistance to dairy farmers and boasts of having assisted in the opening of forty-three new dairy processing plants and the expansion of seventy plants from 2004 through 2010.

Besides dairy, Wisconsin also ranks as a leading state in the production of cranberries, oats, snap peas, maple syrup, sweet corn, green peas, and cucumbers for pickles.

As of 2010, there are approximately 78,000 farms in Wisconsin on 15.2 million acres (6,151,247 ha) of land. The U.S. Department of Agriculture (USDA) valued Wisconsin's agriculture products at nearly $9 billion in 2007, ninth among the 50 U.S. states.

Since 2002, Wisconsin has ranked behind only California in the number of organic farms. In 2009, the USDA National Organic Program listed more than one thousand farms as certified organic in Wisconsin; other organizations have identified hundreds more as organic, but uncertified. Wisconsin boasts more organic livestock, poultry, and dairy farms than any other state; in 2007, Wisconsin's organic dairy sales alone reached $57.6 million. To foster organic programs and involvement, the state created the Wisconsin Organic Advisory Council. With members appointed by the secretary of agriculture, the private sector body pulls together public and private resources and consults the state's agencies on critical organic farming matters, like production, processing, regulations, certification, and marketing. The council is one of many efforts the state makes to live up to former Governor Jim Doyle's 2004 goal of making Wisconsin the national leader in organic agriculture.

Modern Wisconsin dairy farm. © *Nancy Gill/ShutterStock.com*

The Wisconsin government has long supported preservation of its agricultural lands. The Wisconsin Working Lands Initiative, introduced to the state's biennial budget in 2009, provides options, funding, and incentives for state and local governments and private interests to work together to save Wisconsin farmland, promote agricultural enterprises, and to eliminate (or minimize) conflicts over land use and development.

🌳 Energy

Wisconsin's total energy usage—including personal, commercial, and industrial consumption—is average for a U.S. state.

Coal constitutes about two-thirds of Wisconsin's total energy generation, although little of that coal is mined domestically in the state. Instead, about four-fifths of the coal used in Wisconsin arrives on railcars from Wyoming, a state rich with desirable, low-sulfur coal. Natural gas plants and two nuclear reactors along Lake Michigan supply most of the remainder of the state's electricity. Small energy imports from other states, such as Illinois, also supplement Wisconsin's domestic energy generation.

Wisconsin's dependence on coal as a power source has led to concerns about mercury releases into the atmosphere. The state's coal-fired power stations produce a substantial amount of the mercury releases in the state—86 percent as of 2010. As a result, the state adopted (and revised in 2008) mercury laws that require large coal-fired power plants to reduce their mercury emissions by 90 percent by either January 1, 2015, or January 1, 2021, depending on the approach taken by each coal facility.

Reliance on high-carbon power sources such as coal and natural gas has prompted Wisconsin's leaders to take action on Global Warming. Governor Jim Doyle signed

Executive Order No. 191 in April 2007 to create a Task Force on Global Warming. Fifteen months later, the governor's task force released a 239-page final report on global warming, complete with policy recommendations for the state. The task force recommended several short-term and long-term goals for greenhouse gas emission reductions, including a 75 percent reduction from 2005 levels by 2050.

Many of the task force's recommendations, including the greenhouse gas emissions reductions, were drafted into statewide legislation known as the Clean Energy Jobs Act, which was introduced in January 2010. The bill called for a reduction of greenhouse gas emissions to 2005 levels by 2014, and to 75 percent of 2005 levels by 2050. The bill also called for a number of polices that would lower energy consumption and increase the amount of energy that public utilities would need to produce from renewable sources. The bill was controversial, with debate centering around the expected cost of setting such standards. The governor's Public Service Commission reported that the measures of the bill would save consumers $1.2 billion in energy costs over fifteen years. However, one senator issued a statement suggesting that Wisconsin electric utilities would need to spend $15 billion to build or buy renewable energy and utility customers would need to pay $10.5 billion in new energy efficiency taxes. Because of opposition, the bill was not scheduled for a senate vote before the assembly adjourned and expired with the legislative session.

Reducing state greenhouse gas emissions will require development of renewable energy resources. Fortunately, the network of rivers that crisscross the state offer ample opportunity for hydroelectric dams and the state's robust corn industry allows Wisconsin to produce substantial quantities of ethanol. In 2006, Governor Jim Doyle signed the Energy Efficiency and Renewables Act, which established a renewable portfolio standard for the state. The act mandated that domestic utilities produce 10 percent of their energy by 2015 using renewable sources, including solar, wind, hydroelectric power, biomass, geothermal technology, tidal or wave action.

In 2011 the Wisconsin legislature passed a bill expanding the type of hydroelectric plant from which energy could be derived. Prior to the bill, only small hydroelectric plants were counted toward the state's renewable portfolio standard. SB 81, however, expanded the criteria to include plants that generate more than 60 MW of electricity, opening the door for Wisconsin's utilities to import renewable energy from Canada. Critics of the bill say the move discourages the creation of local jobs and infrastructure for renewable energy. The final action, Wisconsin Act 34 of 2011, was scheduled to take effect on December 31, 2015.

Ready to Shine

A March 2010 report from Wisconsin Environment, *Ready to Shine: The Potential of Wisconsin's Solar Industry*, presents the case for building a solar energy sector in the new green economy as a means to decrease the state's dependency on fossil fuels, while also creating new jobs. The report notes that Wisconsin's solar resources are comparable to those of New Jersey, the latter of which has become a national leader in solar development. The report projects that the development of rooftop solar panel projects on suitable homes and businesses throughout the state could generate a total of 11.9 million megawatt-hours of electricity each year, enough to power two-thirds of the homes within the state. Additionally, solar hot water collectors in suitable homes could provide about 3.5 percent of the total energy used in Wisconsin households.

Other renewable energy sources explored by state leaders include biomass, biofuels, and waste-to-energy projects. On the biofuels front, the state mandates use of alternative fuels by the state fleet of vehicles, calling for a 50 percent reduction of unleaded fuels by 2015. With a mix of private funding and American Recovery and Reinvestment Act money, Wisconsin was able to install 18 alternative refueling stations and deploy more than 300 vehicles that use alternative fuels on the road, according to the 2011 Wisconsin Biofuels and Alternative Fuels Use Report. The state has four operating and two proposed biodiesel facilities. Meanwhile, Wisconsin ranks ninth for ethanol production in the United States, with 545 million gallons in annual capacity. There are twelve operating ethanol facilities and one proposed plant in the state.

⚘ Green Business, Green Building, Green Jobs

Green Business Support Networks Emerge

Wisconsin is encouraging green business development and private enterprises and state universities are also working to grow the green business field in the state. For example, the University of Wisconsin's School of Business is leading the charge with its Wisconsin Sustainable Business Council. The Sustainable Business Council focuses on supporting and mentoring businesses that have transitioned to or are interested in moving towards more green-centric business models. The philosophy behind the council is that business-to-business interchange and collaboration is vital to developing a healthy green business climate in Wisconsin. The Sustainable Business Council offers a host of information and networking opportunities for businesses with interests in or commitments to sustainability.

The Charge for Green Building and Design

The state of Wisconsin has made efforts to lead by example in the green building movement. In 2006, Wisconsin governor Jim Doyle signed Executive Order 145, mandating that all state buildings meet the U.S. Green Building Council's green building standards. All new and existing buildings in the state's portfolio must achieve at least the basic Leader in Environmental and Energy Design (LEED) certification. Additionally, EO 145 set the goal of reducing overall actual energy usage per square foot by 20 percent from 2005 baseline levels by 2010.

The Rise of Solar Power

The state showcased the possibilities of green building in December 2009, when it installed 48 photovoltaic, solar electric panels on the roof of the state capital. The solar panels were expected to cut the capital's carbon emissions by twelve metric tons annually, about the average energy usage of a typical household.

A few businesses throughout the state have installed similar rooftop projects that represent the potential for solar energy. At the Amherst headquarters of Gimme Shelter Construction, a company that specializes in green homes, solar panels provide 100 percent of the office's electricity. Most of the heating system is operated by solar energy as well. Solar panels installed on the rooftops of two Kohl's department stores in Waukesha provide 20 percent of the electricity needed at each store. At the Central Waters Brewing Company in Amherst, a 1,000-square-foot array of solar heat collectors has resulted in energy savings of 18 percent by decreasing the amount of natural gas needed to heat the water used in the brewing process.

Some of the state's energy projects are facing challenging times. One example is a program that encouraged energy efficiency among residents and businesses; this program experienced budget cuts and changes in 2011. The statewide Focus On Energy program, created in 2011, was handed over to an out-of-state corporation for management, which decided to roll back a popular rebate program that helped Wisconsin residents and businesses make energy-efficient modifications. The state cut the proposed budget for the program, though funding is not through state dollars but via a fund paid into by the state's utilities. The rollback of the rebate program and the budget cuts could negatively impact local solar, wind and biomass businesses, as well as those who engaged in weatherization.

Monastery LEEDs the Nation

In March 2010 the Benedictine Women of Madison's Holy Wisdom Monastery received the U.S. Green Building Council's Platinum distinction, earning the highest score (63 of a possible 69 points) of any building in the United States as of that date. Some of the features of the monastery project include photovoltaic energy generation, solar lights in the parking lot, pervious concrete in certain areas of the parking lot to allow storm water infiltration, geothermal wells under the parking lot, bamboo floors, green roofs, and rain barrels. Those at the monastery provide tours through the LEED-certified facility and consider it an opportunity to educate Madison-area residents about reducing the environmental impact of buildings.

Wisconsin Loses Green Jobs, but Ventures Forth

According to the Pew Charitable Trusts Clean Energy Economy 2009 report, Wisconsin was one of only eight states in the nation that shed jobs in the clean energy sector from 1998 to 2007. Moreover, Wisconsin represented only one of four states in the United States that, over that same period, was growing jobs in its overall economy while losing jobs in the clean energy sector. Still, the state took measures to grow clean energy sector jobs, and several key indicators offered encouraging signals about the future of green jobs in the state.

From 2006 to 2008, Wisconsin attracted nearly $50 million of venture capital funds to the clean energy sector. Additionally, the state launched a $150 million grant program, known as the Wisconsin Energy Independence Fund, to offer leveraged grants to clean energy businesses and projects in Wisconsin, creating jobs in the field. Members of Wisconsin's state legislator also attempted to create synergy in the green jobs sector, proposing the Clean Energy Jobs Act in January 2010. Although this bill failed to pass out of the legislature in its final session on Earth Day 2010, activists remain hopeful about green jobs growth potential in the state.

⚜ Groundwater: Wisconsin's Threatened and Invisible Wonder

So abundant and important is Wisconsin's groundwater that it is often referred to as the state's buried treasure. More than 800,000 private wells provide more than two-thirds of the state's residents with fresh groundwater each day. But while groundwater is inseparable from the daily lives of most Wisconsin residents, it is a greatly misunderstood, and threatened, resource.

Groundwater, like surface water, is intricately linked to the larger water cycle. Rainwater and snowmelt percolate down through soil and rock to fill underground aquifers. Yet, groundwater natural currents can pull it towards the major surface water resources. Wisconsin's rivers and lakes are partially fed by groundwater, thus allowing their levels to remain fairly constant, even in times of low precipitation or draught. It is no wonder that this resource is so vital to the state!

As of 2010, about 172 lakes and streams in Wisconsin were considered to be "impaired waters" due to high levels of phosphorus. © *Terry Donnelly/Alamy*

Wisconsin's groundwater faces several threats, some of which—like the groundwater itself—remain invisible, hidden beneath our feet. The two greatest threats to Wisconsin's groundwater are excessive withdrawal and toxic contamination. Toxic contamination represents a more visceral concern for Wisconsin residents and policy makers, as it relates to the fundamental question, is the water I am drinking safe? While the sources of toxic groundwater contamination are too varied to list, air pollution, farm fertilizers, and animal and human waste can all make their way into Wisconsin groundwater.

Excessive withdrawal occurs when groundwater resources are consumed at a rate that exceeds their natural replenishment. This issue arises most prominently in the state's urban areas, where heavy population concentrations demand substantial water resources. Urban areas also tend to be highly developed, with less green space and more pavement, asphalt, and concrete covering the ground. These artificial ground coverings prevent rain water and

snowmelt from being absorbed into the ground, denying thirsty, local aquifers a "recharge."

Wisconsin Responds with Groundwater Law

Wisconsin introduced comprehensive groundwater legislation in 1984 to address ground water toxicity. Chapter 160 of the Wisconsin Statutes, known as the groundwater law, outlined groundwater protection standards that have been hailed as the most comprehensive in the nation. The groundwater law affirmed Wisconsin's belief that all groundwater and all aquifers ought to be fit for human consumption by intentionally omitting the aquifer classification system—which allows certain groundwater aquifers to be written off as too polluted or too industrial for human consumption, and thus clean up.

Water advocates have, until recently, criticized Wisconsin for having weak regulatory powers over groundwater withdrawal. This issue received considerable attention when the bottled water company Perrier proposed to install a high-capacity well and bottle the state's water in 2000. Public outcry was so great that the company independently made the decision to open the plant in another state. The ordeal highlighted Wisconsin's impotence, at that time, in regulating companies or individuals who wished to consume large quantities of the state's groundwater. If Perrier had gone ahead with the plant, the state could have done little to stop it. Following the Perrier case, the state began to consider ways to put teeth into its regulation of high-capacity wells. On Earth Day 2004, these efforts materialized in a new groundwater protection law, the 2003 Wisconsin Act 310, which expanded Wisconsin's regulation of groundwater withdrawals.

In 2009, legislators considered a bill that would add another layer of groundwater management to already existing regulations and provide greater protection of the state's drinking water. The bill would have created standards for when groundwater has been degraded due to excessive withdrawals, as well as create groundwater attention areas to avoid excessive withdrawal of groundwater. The measure, SB 620, failed to pass out of senate committee in April 2010.

BIBLIOGRAPHY

Books

Huhti, Thomas. *Wisconsin.* Berkeley, CA: Avalon Travel, 2010.

Lewis, Ronald. *Transforming the Appalachian Countryside: Railroads, Deforestation, and Social Change in West Virginia, 1880–1920.* Chapel Hill: University of North Carolina Press, 1998.

Rygle, Kathy J. *The Treasure Hunter's Gem & Mineral Guides to the U.S.A., Volume 4: Northeast States.* Woodstock, VT: GemStone Press, 2011.

Strutin, Michal, and Gary Irving. *The Smithsonian Guides to Natural America: The Great Lakes—Ohio, Indiana, Michigan, Wisconsin.* Washington, DC: Smithsonian Books, 1996.

Web Sites

"Asian Carp and Chicago Canal Litigation" Great Lakes Environmental Law Center. Available from http://www.greatlakeslaw.org/blog/asian-carp

"Asian carp found in Wisconsin." Prairie State Outdoors. Available from http://www.prairiestateoutdoors.com/index.php?/pso/article/asian_carp_found_in_wisconsin/

"Asian Carp in Lake Calumet May Have Been Placed by Humans: Study." FOX Chicago News. Available from http://www.myfoxchicago.com/dpp/news/metro/asian-carp-lake-calumet-human-placed-study-20100805

Asian Carp Prevention and Control Act (S 1421–111th Congress). U.S. Congress. Available from http://www.govtrack.us/congress/billtext.xpd?bill=s111-1421

Berquist, Lee. "Board approves phosphorus limits in state waterways." *Journal Sentinel.* June 23, 2010. Available from http://www.jsonline.com/news/wisconsin/96995454.html

"Clean Energy Jobs Act." 2010. Available from http://www.legis.state.wi.us/2009/data/AB-649.pdf

Dairy Business Innovation Center. Available from http://www.dbicusa.org

Economic Impact of Wisconsin's Commercial Ports. Wisconsin Department of Transportation, Bureau of Planning and Economic Development. Available from http://www.dot.wisconsin.gov/travel/water/docs/ports-econ-report.pdf

Egan, Dan. "Asian carp discovered near Lake Michigan." Milwaukee-Wisconsin *Journal Sentinel.* June 23, 2010. Available from http://www.jsonline.com/news/wisconsin/97003199.html

"Executive Order No. 145: Creation of High Performance Green Building Standards for State Facilities." Available from http://www.wisgov.state.wi.us/journal_media_detail.asp?prid=1907&locid=19

"Executive Order No. 191: Creation of the Governor's Task Force on Global Warming." Available from http://www.wisgov.state.wi.us/docview.asp?docid=10963

"Global Warming and Wisconsin." National Wildlife Federation. Available from http://www.nwf.org/Global-Warming/~/media/PDFs/Global%20Warming/Global%20Warming%20State%20Fact%20Sheets/Wisconsin.ashx

"Highlights of Wisconsin's 2004 Forest Inventory and Analysis." Wisconsin Department of Natural Resources. Available from http://dnr.wi.gov/forestry/fia/highlights2004.htm

"Horicon National Wildlife Refuge." U.S. Fish and Wildlife Service. Available from http://www.fws.gov/midwest/horicon/docs/brochure.pdf

Kohler, Dan, and Rob Kerth. *Ready to Shine: The Potential of Wisconsin's Solar Industry.* Wisconsin Environment Research and Policy Center. Available from http://www.wisconsinenvironment.org/uploads/87/dd/87dd8f0bb1e1bc821e75-c704aa5a6c8a/Ready-to-Shine.pdf

Memorandum Opinion and Order: Case No. 10-CV-4457. December 2, 2010. U.S. District Court for the Northern District of Illinois. Available from http://www.greatlakeslaw.org/files/dist_ct_pi_opinion_order.pdf

Newman, Judy. "Major Changes For Focus On Energy Program." *Wisconsin State Journal.* June 26, 2011. Available from http://host.madison.com/wsj/business/article_e31b7a48-064c-5d15-b6ca-09abaee68fbf.html

"Organic Agricultural in Wisconsin: 2009 Report." University of Wisconsin–Madison; Center for Integrated Agricultural Systems. Available from http://www.cias.wisc.edu/wp-content/uploads/2010/02/org09final022310.pdf

"Organic Farming: Wisconsin Organic Advisory Council." Wisconsin Department of Agriculture, Trade & Consumer Protection. Available from http://datcp.wi.gov/Farms/Organic_Farming/Advisory_Council/index.aspx

Program Summary: Wisconsin Working Lands Initiative. Wisconsin Department of Agriculture, Trade and Consumer Protection. Available from http://datcp.wi.gov/uploads/Environment/pdf/ProgramSummaryNov2010.pdf

"The Public Trust Doctrine." Wisconsin Constitution; Article IX, Section I. Available from http://www.legis.state.wi.us/lrb/pubs/consthi/04consthiIV4.htm

"SB 620." 2009–2010 Wisconsin State Legislature. Available from https://docs.legis.wisconsin.gov/2009/proposals/sb620

"SB 81." 2011-2012 Wisconsin State Legislature. Available from https://docs.legis.wisconsin.gov/2011/proposals/sb81

Seely, Ron. "Walker withdraws effort to repeal phosphorus rule, now backs delay." *Wisconsin State Journal.* April 4, 2011. Available from http://host.madison.com/wsj/news/local/environment/article_4075da9a-5f07-11e0-bf8d-001cc4c002e0.html

Smith Laura, "Native animals making a comeback." WLUK-TV. November 10, 2010. Available from http://www.fox11online.com/dpp/news/local/north_counties/native-animals-making-a-come-back-wisconsins-wild-side-november-2010-series

Smith, Laura. "Wolf thrives after facing extinction." WLUK-TV. November 9, 2010. Available from http://www.fox11online.com/dpp/news/local/north_counties/wolf-thrives-after-facing-extinction-wisconsins-wild-side-november-2010-series

Smith, Neal. "Holy Wisdom Monastery—LEED Education Plan." Benedictine Women of Madison. September 3, 2009. Available from http://bene-dictinewomen.org/2009/holy-wisdom-mona stery-leed-education-plan/

State of Michigan, State of Wisconsin, State of Minnesota, State of Ohio, and Commonwealth of Pennsylvania v. United States Army Corps of Engineers and Metropolitan Water Reclamation District of Greater Chicago. Available http://www.greatlakeslaw.org/files/mi_carp_complaint_dist_ct.pdf

Vorpahl, Amelia. "Controversial Clean Energy Jobs Act pioneered by Gov. Jim Doyle was also delayed." The Badger Herald. April 21, 2010. Available from http://badgerherald.com/news/2010/04/21/controversial_clean.php

"The Waters of Wisconsin Annual Report." 2008. Wisconsin Department of Natural Resources. Avail able from http://dnr.wi.gov/org/water/success/annual_report_2008.pdf

"Wisconsin Biofuels and Alternative Fuels Use Report." Wisconsin State Energy Office. 2011. Available from http://energyindependence.wi.gov/docview.asp?docid=21585&locid=160

"Wisconsin Climate Change." Wisconsin Department of Natural Resources. Available from http://dnr.wi.gov/climatechange/

Wisconsin Department of Agriculture, Trade and Consumer Protection. Available from http://datcp.wi.gov

"Wisconsin Energy Independence Fund." Wisconsin Department of Commerce. Available from http://www.commerce.state.wi.us/BD/BD-WEIF.html

"Wisconsin's Forest Products Industry." Wisconsin Department of Natural Resources. Available from http://dnr.wi.gov/forestry/um/pdf/report/WisconsinForestProductsIndustry.pdf

"Wisconsin's Strategy for Reducing Global Warming." Governor's Task Force on Global Warming. Avail able from http://dnr.wi.gov/environmentprotect/gtfgw/documents/Final_Report.pdf

Wisconsin 2007 Minerals Yearbook. U.S. Geological Survey. Available from http://minerals.usgs.gov/minerals/pubs/state/2007/myb2-2007-wi.pdf

Wyoming

The state of Wyoming has some of the most significant fossil fuel resources in the nation, most of which are produced for export. Nearly 40 percent of the total U.S. mined supply of coal comes from the Powder River Basin of northwestern Wyoming. The Powder River Basin also serves as a major source of coalbed methane (a type of natural gas produced from coal seams), placing Wyoming as second in the nation for the production of coalbed methane. Overall production of natural gas generally adds up to about 10 percent of the U.S. production total with the majority coming from the Green River Basin. State production of crude oil accounts for about 3 percent of the national total, but there is great potential for oil recovery from the oil shale deposits of the Green River Formation. The state produces fossil fuels, but most are exported, resulting in greenhouse gas emissions occurring elsewhere. The challenges Wyoming must address are the environmental, economic, and social impacts from the mining, drilling, and transport of the materials. The state also must consider the challenge of protecting key wildlife and their habitats, such as the Pronghorn Migration Corridor and greater sage-grouse, while managing future development projects.

Climate

The climate in Wyoming varies by altitude. With a mean elevation of 6,700 feet (2,040 m), some of the coldest winter temperatures are experienced in the mountains and the warmest summer temperatures felt in the lower basins. A semiarid climate is experienced east of the mountains. Heavy snowfall occurs within the mountains, creating snowpack that in turn provides a large portion of the state's water supply. Wyoming also provides the headwaters in the Missouri-Mississippi, Green-Colorado, Snake-Columbia, and Great Salt Lake river basins. Most rainfall occurs in the spring and early summer. Hailstorms are the most destructive weather features affecting the state, having a tendency to lead to serious damage of crops and property.

Climate Change

According to a 2009 report from the National Wildlife Federation, the effects of global warming could have a fairly significant impact on the state of Wyoming. The report indicates that average temperatures in Wyoming could increase by an estimated 6.75°F (3.75°C) by 2100 if global warming continues unabated, though different climate change models have different predictions. Warmer winters could mean a decrease in mountain snowpack that would have a serious impact on the year-round water supply. Hotter summers could lead to increased periods of drought and a greater risk of forest and rangeland wildfires, which in turn may affect many wildlife habitats in the state. More severe rainstorms could also occur, leading to increased incidents of flash flooding.

Unraveling the Tailoring Rule

The state is one of several that does not have an official climate change action plan. State officials have generally been hesitant to commit to federal government proposals and actions that affect state control over environmental issues such as greenhouse gas emissions. In September 2010, Governor Dave Freudenthal sent a letter to the U.S. Environmental Protection Agency indicating that the state would not be able to comply with the federal greenhouse gas emissions regulation known as the Tailoring Rule. The rule requires existing large industrial facilities to obtain a permit for greenhouse gas emissions. The rule also calls for all new industrial facilities and renovation projects to employ the best available control technology for monitoring and reducing emissions. The rule was scheduled to take effect as of January 2, 2011. However, Governor Freudenthal noted that current Wyoming law prohibits the state from regulating greenhouse gas emissions, and any legislative changes to that rule would not occur until after the next session convened on January 11, 2011. Thus far, it looks like the state has been forced to go along with the rule. It has submitted a modified State Implementation Plan (SIP), which has been partially approved and partially disapproved by the EPA. The EPA is also proposing to approve Wyoming's May 2011 revision of the state's Prevention of Significant Deterioration (PSD) program.

The law referred to relates to HB 171, which was enacted in 1999 and prohibits state government agencies and officials from proposing or enacting any rules or regulations that call for the reduction of greenhouse gas emissions prior to the ratification of the Kyoto Protocol. The Kyoto Protocol was introduced in 1997 as part of the United Nations Framework Convention on Climate Change. The treaty encourages industrialized nations to fight global warming through the reduction of greenhouse gas emissions. The United States is a signatory of the treaty, but has shown no intention to ratify the document.

At least thirteen other states have questioned the Tailoring Rule, showing particular concern for the timeline, as most states believe the January launch is too soon to be practical.

❧ Natural Resources, Water, and Agriculture

Forests and the Mountain Pine Beetle

Wyoming has approximately 9.8 million acres (4 million ha) of forested land, accounting for about 16 percent of the total land area. About 8.2 million acres (3.3 million ha) are federally owned. Lodgepole pine is the most common forest type in the state, but these forests have been under attack since the 1990s from the regional mountain pine beetle epidemic.

The mountain pine beetle, also known as the Rocky Mountain pine beetle or Black Hills beetle, is native to pine forests in western North America. In the fall, the insects tunnel into the trunks of lodgepole and ponderosa pines to lay their eggs, which hatch in early spring. When weather conditions are just right, with warmer winter and spring temperatures and periods of drought, the beetles may begin to reproduce in higher numbers, setting in motion a process that kills an increasing number of trees year after year. Loss of wildlife habitats and an increased risk of wildfires are serious concerns for the state as a result. However, some see the problem as a possible boon for the dwindling timber industry of the state. Clearing of dead and infested trees is a primary course of action to minimize the ongoing threat of the epidemic, and some of that harvested wood can be sold locally for use as firewood or chips, which are used as biofuel for energy production. Demand for the wood as sawlogs is not very high, however, particularly due to the characteristic blue-tinged stain that results from a fungus left on the wood by the burrowing beetles. This lack of demand has led some conservationists to argue against the logging projects, claiming that the removal of the trees has little effect on

the spread of the beetles and, depending upon the removal method used, could pose a threat to the long-term health of the forest.

While the mountain pine beetles are targeting the lodgepole and ponderosa pines, the limber pine, whitebark pine, cottonwood, and aspen forests of the state also seem to be dwindling from a combination of diseases, fires, invasive plants, changes in water flow, and possibly changes in climate.

Parks and Wildlife

Wyoming is home to two national parks and nine national forests. Shoshone National Forest was the first national forest in the nation, just as Yellowstone National Park was the nation's first national park and Devils Tower National Monument was the nation's first national monument. Grand Teton National Park features 61 species of mammals, including bison, moose, and coyote. This park is also home to several trumpeter swans, the largest waterfowl in North America. The National Elk Refuge is located next to the Grand Teton National Park and serves as a feeding range for the continent's largest known herd of elk. Wyoming is also home to 11 state parks and 17 other historic sites, recreation areas, and tourist locations.

Mule deer and white-tailed deer are among the most abundant game mammals, with antelope and elk also hunted in season. Wild turkey, bobwhite quail, and several grouse species are leading game birds. There are several types of common sparrows, wrens, warblers, hawks, and owls. The state has special conservation programs in place for grizzly bear, bighorn sheep, and greater sage-grouse.

The U.S. Fish and Wildlife Service lists eleven animal and four plant species as threatened or endangered in Wyoming. Endangered animals include the Wyoming toad, black-footed ferret, and the Kendall Warm Springs dace. The blowout penstemon is the only endangered plant species in the state, with the Colorado butterfly plant, Ute ladies'-tresses, and desert yellowhead listed as threatened.

Legal Wrangling over the Gray Wolf

Wyoming is one of the three states involved in recent federal district court actions concerning the management of the gray wolf population of the Northern Rockies. The recovery of the wolf population in the Northern Rockies, which covers Wyoming, Montana, and Idaho, is considered to be one of the fastest comebacks of an endangered species on record. In the mid-1990s, more than sixty wolves were released into Yellowstone National Park and central Idaho to boost the local population. The minimum recovery goal was to develop a population of at least three hundred individual wolves and thirty breeding pairs throughout the region for three consecutive years. The goal was met in 2002, with an increasing

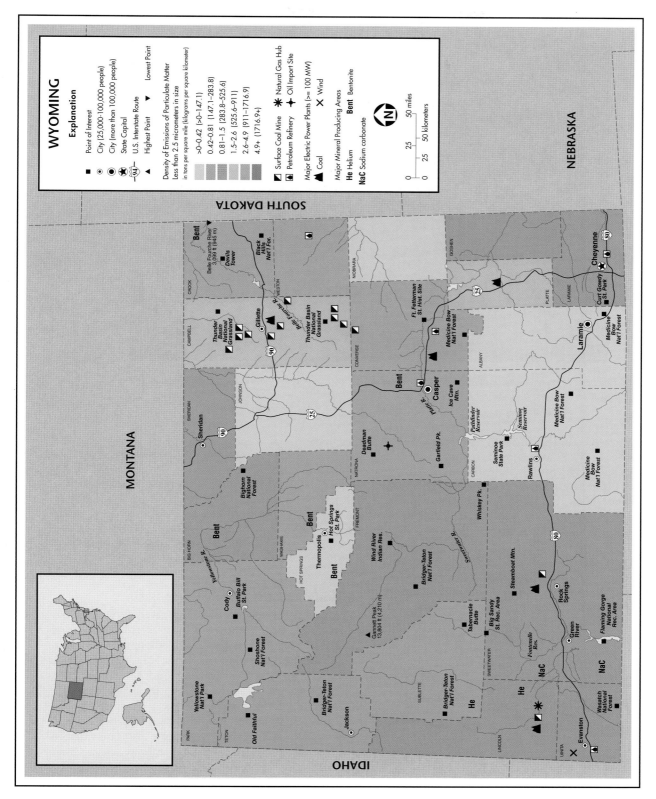

WYOMING

Explanation

■ Point of Interest
⊙ City (25,000–100,000 people)
◉ City (more than 100,000 people)
☆ State Capital
〔94〕 U.S. Interstate Route
▲ Highest Point   ▼ Lowest Point

Density of Emissions of Particulate Matter
Less than 2.5 micrometers in size
in tons per square mile (kilograms per square kilometer)

>0–0.42 (>0–147.1)
0.42–0.81 (147.1–283.8)
0.81–1.5 (283.8–525.6)
1.5–2.6 (525.6–911)
2.6–4.9 (911–1716.9)
4.9+ (1716.9+)

▣ Surface Coal Mine   ✳ Natural Gas Hub
◐ Petroleum Refinery   ✦ Oil Import Site

Major Electric Power Plants (>= 100 MW)
▲ Coal   ✕ Wind

Major Mineral Producing Areas
He Helium   **Bent** Bentonite
NaC Sodium carbonate

Ⓝ

0   25   50 miles
0   25   50 kilometers

MONTANA

SOUTH DAKOTA

IDAHO

NEBRASKA

SOURCES: "County Emissions Map: Criteria Air Pollutants." *AirData*. U.S. Environmental Protection Agency. Available from http://www.epa.gov/air/data/geosel.html; *Energy Maps*. U.S. Energy Information Administration. Available from http://www.cia.gov/state; *Highest and Lowest Elevations*. U.S. Geological Survey. Available from http://egsc.usgs.gov/isb/pubs/booklets/elvadist/elvadist.html#Highest; *2007 Minerals Yearbook*. U.S. Geological Survey. Available from http://minerals.usgs.gov/minerals/pubs/state. © 2011 Cengage Learning.

Forests of Wyoming have been under attack since the 1990s from the regional mountain pine beetle epidemic. © *Kinetic Imagery/Alamy*

population noted every year since. In 2009, the U.S. Fish & Wildlife Service delisted (removed) the gray wolf from the endangered species list for Montana and Idaho, thus relinquishing wildlife management responsibilities to state agencies once they produced a federally approved conservation plan. Wyoming was not included in the delisting because it does not have a federally approved protection plan.

The 2009 delisting was immediately challenged in a U.S. District Court by a coalition of environmental groups using the argument that the federal Endangered Species Act does not allow the federal government to subdivide a distinct population segment to provide legal protection for the wolves in one region, while delisting them in another. U.S. District Judge Donald Molloy agreed that the delisting had been inappropriate and reinstated federal protection for the entire region. His ruling to relist the gray wolf in all three states was issued on August 5, 2010. More recently, U.S. District Judge Alan Johnson ruled that the U.S. Fish and Wildlife Service was not justified in rejecting Wyoming's wolf management plan and sent the plan back for reconsideration. In April 2011, wolves were delisted in Montana and Idaho through legislative action when Congress attached a rider to a budget bill removing federal protection from the animals. Wyoming is negotiating with the federal government over future management of wolves outside of Yellowstone National Park using a

combination of trophy animal hunts during specified seasons and a year round hunt away from a buffer area around the park. Conservationists are concerned as this would allow more than half of the population outside the park to be removed. Scientists worry that such a large cut in the wolf population outside of national parks would isolate Yellowstone wolves, leading to inbreeding and possibly extinction. The deal was subject to negotiation in the fall of 2011.

Mining and the Green River Basin

The Green River Basin of southwestern Wyoming has the world's largest known deposit of trona, a natural hydrated sodium carbonate and sodium bicarbonate used to produce industrial soda ash. As a result, Wyoming ranks as first in the nation for the production of soda ash, which is used in the manufacturing of a number of products including glass, soap, detergents, and textiles, as well as in food products such as sodium bicarbonate (baking soda). The state also ranks first in the nation for production of bentonite clay. Other minerals produced by the state include crude gypsum, construction sand and gravel, crushed stone, and portland cement. Uranium, diamonds, placer gold, and copper have also been mined in the state. The total value of nonfuel minerals in Wyoming amounted to $1.9 billion in 2010.

Wyoming State Profile

Physical Characteristics

Land area	97,088 square miles (251,457 sq km)
Inland water area	724 square miles (1,875 sq km)
Coastal area	NA
Highest point	Gannett Peak 13,804 feet (4,207 m)
National Forest System lands (2010)	9.2 million acres (3.7 million ha)
State parks (2011)	25

Energy Statistics

Total energy production (2009)	10,900 trillion Btu
State ranking in total energy production (2009)	2
Renewable energy net generation total (2009)	3.2 million megawatt hours
Hydroelectric energy generation (2009)	967,000 megawatt hours
Biomass energy generation (2009)	NA
Wind energy generation (2009)	2.2 million megawatt hours
Wood and derived fuel energy generation (2009)	NA
Crude oil reserves (2009)	583.0 million barrels (92.7 million cu m)
Natural gas reserves (2009)	35.3 trillion cubic feet (999.1 billion cu m)
Natural gas liquids (2008)	1.0 billion barrels (160.6 million cu m)

Pollution Statistics

Carbon output (2005)	62.88 million tons of CO_2 (57.0 million t)
Superfund sites (2008)	2
Particulate matter (less than 2.5 micrometers) emissions (2002)	22,082 tons per year (20,032 t/yr)
Toxic chemical releases (2009)	25 million pounds (11.3 million kg)
Generated hazardous waste (2009)	3,500 tons (3,200 t)

SOURCES: AirData. U.S. Environmental Protection Agency. Available from http://www.epa.gov/air/data; *Energy Maps, Facts, and Data of the U.S. States.* U.S. Energy Information Administration. Available from http://www.eia.gov/state; *The 2012 Statistical Abstract.* U.S. Census Bureau. Available from http://www.census.gov/compendia/statab; *United States Energy Usage.* eRedux. Available from http://www.eredux.net/states.

© 2011 Cengage Learning.

Water

The Continental Divide that separates the watersheds draining into the Pacific Ocean from those that drain into the Atlantic (at the Gulf of Mexico) crosses diagonally through the state from the northwest to the south central border. Most of the major rivers in the state originate within state boundaries and flow into neighboring states. The Snake River, which flows into Idaho, is the largest river in the state in terms of annual water flow, followed by the Bighorn (including the Wind and Shoshone Rivers), and the Yellowstone, Green, and North Platte Rivers. Other notable rivers include the Belle Fourche, Cheyenne, Powder, Niobrara, and Bear Rivers.

Nearly 2 percent of the electricity supply for the state is from hydroelectric power. Seminoe and Buffalo Bill dams are two of the largest impoundment based hydroelectric facilities in the state. The Seminoe Reservoir is one of the largest in the state and serves as a major recreation area. The largest natural lake is Yellowstone, which lies at the heart of Yellowstone National Park.

The overall Wyoming State Water Plan coordinates seven individual river basins (and plans), with the Wind/Bighorn, Platte, and Green River basins being the largest by area.

Fish and Fishing

There is no significant commercial fishing in Wyoming, but anglers enjoy popular fishing spots along many of the well-stocked rivers and streams. Some of the native fish species include the burbot, channel catfish, cutthroat trout, mountain whitefish, Arctic grayling, and black bullhead. The Saratoga National Fish Hatchery provides lake trout eggs for the Great Lakes recovery program. This fishery also breeds the endangered Wyoming toad as part of a habitat reintroduction program. The Jackson National Fish Hatchery, located on the National Elk Refuge, is part of the U.S. Fish and Wildlife Service's National Broodstock Program.

Agriculture

Wyoming ranks first in the average size of farms and ranches in the nation. It is among the top ten states in the nation for the production of wool, sheep and lambs, pinto beans, other dry beans, barley, and sugar beets, but the most important crop in value is hay. Wheat, barley, corn for grain, and sugar beets are also important crops. The cattle industry is the most important agricultural sector, with annual production valued at more than $600 million. Sheep, lambs, and wool are important products, as are hogs and horses.

The state's primary organic and natural foods program is facilitated by the Wyoming Business Council. Programs and support of organic agriculture is also offered by the University of Wyoming Cooperative Extension Service (CES) and the Wyoming Department of Agriculture.

❧ Energy

Coal and the Powder River Basin

Wyoming has some of the largest fossil fuel deposits in the United States. The Powder River Basin occupies the northwestern region of Wyoming and the southeastern portion of Montana. It is the largest coal-producing region in the country, accounting for nearly 40 percent of the total U.S. mined supply, and it ranks Wyoming as second in the nation (after Montana) for estimated recoverable coal reserves. Since the coal seams of the

Powder River Basin are relatively close to the surface, extraction is less expensive than in other coal-producing regions of the country. The coal found there also has lower sulfur content then other types of coal, making it an even better choice for electricity generating companies hoping to lower greenhouse gas emissions. Wyoming coal is exported to more than thirty states.

Natural Gas and the Rockies Express Pipeline

The Powder River Basin is also a major source of coalbed methane, a type of natural gas produced from coal seams. Wyoming ranks second in the nation for production of coalbed methane (after Colorado) and is one of the leading states for overall production of natural gas, which generally adds up to about 10 percent of the U.S. production total. Conventional natural gas comes primarily from the greater Green River Basin. Only about 10 percent of the natural gas produced in the state is used locally, allowing the state to export large amounts of the supply to markets in California and the Midwest. The Midwestern supply is facilitated by the relatively new Rockies Express Pipeline, which became fully operational in November 2009 and is one of the largest pipelines in the country. Extending into eastern Ohio, the line has a capacity of 1.8 billion cubic feet of natural gas per day.

Oil and the Green River Formation

Oil production in Wyoming accounts for about 3 percent of the U.S. total, but there is even greater potential for oil recovery from the oil shale deposits of the Green River Formation. The Green River Formation extends through portions of Colorado, Utah, and Wyoming and contains what are believed to be the largest known oil shale deposits in the world. Oil shale is a type of sedimentary rock containing bituminous materials that can be mined and processed to generate oil. The federally owned Green River Formation contains an estimated total of 1 trillion barrels of oil. Conservative estimates indicate that about 800 billion barrels are recoverable, an amount that is three times greater than the proven oil reserves of Saudi Arabia. However, the recovery process has thus far proven to be too complex and too expensive to be an economically feasible option for oil production.

The state has five oil refineries. Since petroleum consumption in the state is low, much of the product is exported to neighboring states. Wyoming allows the statewide use of conventional gasoline, rather than the reformulated blends that are required in some states and certain metropolitan areas.

Electricity and Clean Coal Technology

A little more than 91 percent of the state's electricity supply is generated by coal-fired plants. In 2007, the state legislature created the Clean Coal Technologies Research Program (HB 301) as a means to promote research and development in marketable low-emissions coal technology. The Clean Coal Task Force that oversees an accompanying fund consists of members of the Wyoming Energy Resources Council at the University of Wyoming School of Energy Resources. Qualified research projects may receive a dollar-for-dollar match as a supplement to verifiable non-state funds. For 2010, the legislature appropriated a budget of $14 million for the Clean Coal Technology Fund.

Statewide consumption of electricity is relatively low, allowing the state to export much of its produced supply. To facilitate this exchange, the governors of California, Nevada, Utah, and Wyoming are working together on the development of a new high-capacity electric transmission line that could stretch for 1,300 miles (2,090 km) from Wyoming to the other three states and Colorado. Known as the Frontier Line, the proposed project stems from the 2003 Rocky Mountain Area Transmission Study launched by the governors of Wyoming and Utah to evaluate the transmission alternatives for the Rocky Mountain region. The Frontier Line is just one of the expansion projects recommended by the study.

Wind and Gateway West

The state shows much potential for wind energy, particularly along the gap in the Rocky Mountains known as the Southern Wyoming Corridor. As of 2010, about 4.8 percent of the electricity in the state is produced through wind power, but several officials hope to boost that percentage in the not too distant future. The state is trying to balance wind energy production with environmental (primarily sage-grouse and other wildlife habitat) and citizen concerns. Some plans for future wind development hinge on the success of various electric transmission line projects, since generating facilities must be linked to a larger transmission network in order to be most commercially successful. At least one such project, the Gateway West transmission line sponsored by Rocky Mountain Power, has been stalled as private landowners in the Commissary Ridge area are fighting against the addition of new power lines near their homes. An alternate route has been delineated through federal lands, and a draft Environmental Impact Statement (EIS) for the project is scheduled to be released in Fall 2011. Rocky Mountain Power (RMP), the largest wind developer in the state, owns and operates its own transmission network and has nine wind farms in Wyoming with a total capacity of 626.6 megawatts. Despite efforts to support the new transmission line, the company does not have plans to add any new wind generating projects through 2017.

Nearly 2 percent of the electricity supply for the state is from hydroelectric power.

Wyoming is one of several states that does not have a renewable portfolio standard. As part of the Western Governors' Association, the state participates in discussions for the Clean and Diversified Energy Initiative, which is detailed in the 2006 report *Clean Energy, a Strong Economy and a Healthy Environment*. The initiative sets a goal to develop 30,000 megawatts of clean energy for the region by 2015, from both traditional and renewable sources, and to achieve a 20 percent increase in energy efficiency by 2020.

❦ Green Business, Green Building, Green Jobs

Green Business

With a strong reliance on fossil fuels, the state of Wyoming lags behind other states in the region in the development of a clean energy or "green" economy. In 2010, Headwaters Economics, an independent non-profit research group, released a report entitled *Clean Energy Leadership in the Rockies: Competitive Positing in the Emerging Green Economy*, which examines and compares the use and development of clean energy resources in five Rocky Mountain states—Colorado, New Mexico, Montana, Utah, and Wyoming. According to the study, Wyoming had the lowest percentage of green jobs in the five-state region with only 5 percent. While Wyoming is believed to have great potential in the development of wind energy, the state has not passed or implemented significant clean energy and energy efficiency policies and, therefore, has been unable to attract major investments for green businesses. According to the Headwaters Economics report, Wyoming attracted only $38 million of venture capital for the clean technology sector in 2008. By comparison, Colorado collected nearly $800 million. Wyoming also ranked as forty-ninth in the nation for money received from federal stimulus grants from the U.S. Department of Energy, gaining only about $9.4 million. Colorado received more than $296 million, ranking fifteenth in the nation. While all these numbers are accurate, other reasons, such as a total population less than a Denver suburb and a tradition of not relying on the federal government for aid, are as likely to explain them as the state's lack of green policies.

Green Building

Wyoming has not yet set a statewide energy efficiency building standard for public buildings. However, the Wyoming Business Council oversees a number of incentive and grant programs for businesses and residents interested in creating more energy efficient workplaces and homes. There are also a number of organizations that are working to promote and support efforts in green building and energy efficiency practices in all sectors. These include the nonprofit Wyoming Energy Council, Wyoming's Energy Conservation Network (WyoEnergy), the Cooperative Extension Service and the School of Energy Resources at the University of Wyoming, and

the Wyoming Chapter of the U.S. Green Building Council.

With assistance from the Wyoming Business Council, the Laramie County Library in Cheyenne became the first public building in the state to achieve certification under the U.S. Green Building Council Leadership in Energy and Environmental Design (LEED) program. Completed in 2007, the building received LEED Silver certification. The library was designed to achieve a 40 percent reduction in energy costs and a 30 percent reduction in water use.

Green Jobs

The Wyoming Department of Employment launched its first survey of green jobs in August 2010 by selecting a number of businesses at random to receive questionnaires on the green economy. For the purpose of this survey, a green job was defined as one in which an employee produces a product or service that improves energy efficiency, expands the use of renewable energy, and supports environmental sustainability. The results indicated that 3.3 to 3.8 percent of those surveyed had at least a portion of their work time devoted to energy efficient activities. Twenty-eight percent of the construction firms surveyed indicated that they participated in energy efficiency activities, followed closely by manufacturing firms at 25 percent. In terms of employment, the manufacturing sector (14.9 percent) and the professional and business services sector (6.6 percent) indicated the highest levels of energy efficiency employment.

While the number of green jobs seems to be relatively small, there are a few schools with dedicated training programs for green occupations. The Wind Energy Technology program at Laramie County Community College has received national recognition for programs that include two associate degrees in wind energy. The Energy Resource Science program at the University of Wyoming offers a unique curriculum that combines studies in study geology and geophysics, engineering, economics and policy, environment and natural resources, and computational modeling to prepare professionals for careers involving energy asset management.

❦ The Path of the Pronghorn

The state that is home to the first national park, the first national monument, and the first national forest has also welcomed the nation's first designated wildlife migration corridor—the Path of the Pronghorn. The spring and winter migration of the western pronghorn between the Upper Green River Basin and Grand Teton National park represents the longest migration of an ungulate in the lower forty-eight states. Each year, herds consisting of as many as 800 (with some estimates counting as many as 1,500-2,000) pronghorn will travel south for the winter and return in the spring, taking a roundtrip journey somewhere between 175 to 330 miles (280 to 530 km). Researchers believe that the native pronghorn have followed the same migration route for thousands of years, though their population has dropped significantly.

Habitats and Obstacles

In the early 1800s, there were an estimated 35 million pronghorn living in the open spaces of the West. As of 2010, there are only about 700,000, with most living in Wyoming and part of Idaho. Pronghorn herds generally seek out areas of large open grasslands, where they can graze on a large variety of plants, including flowers, shrubs, and cacti, along with several types of plants that are toxic or simply unappealing to other herbivores. Being the fastest animal in North America, able to reach speeds of up to 65 miles per hour (100 km/h), larger fields provide safer homes for the pronghorn, who can usually outrun predators when there are no other obstacles in the way. Coyote targeting fawns are the primary such predators in the west. Human development has presented a number of obstacles, while also diminishing the size of and number of available grasslands for the animals.

While a number of pronghorn reside in the relative safety of the national parks, their migratory nature means that most herds will live or travel outside of protected areas at some time during each year. Over time, obstacles placed in and around the migration route have posed a great challenge. Roads and fences are the biggest threats for migrating herds. Each year, a number of pronghorn are killed by vehicles, but the fences built around roads and property, sometimes built to protect the animals from harm, usually block their travels. Unlike deer, pronghorn are unable to jump and will usually attempt to dig under the fence in order to get through. Besides simply slowing the herd down, attempts to dig and crawl under wire woven fences can lead to injury for the animals. In recent years there have been concerted efforts to make fences antelope-friendly by raising the lowest wire of barb wire fencing or replacing woven wire fencing.

Protection Efforts

The Wildlife Conservation Society (WCS) has been studying the habitat and migration patterns of the pronghorn for several years. The New York-based WCS represents a coalition of local, state, and federal agencies, along with conservation groups from across the country. This organization campaigned strongly for the protection of the western migration corridor as a means to protect the pronghorn from endangerment and extinction. Their efforts were rewarded in 2008 when the USDA Forest Service added the Pronghorn Migration

Corridor Forest Plan Amendment to the Bridger-Teton National Forest Land and Resources Management Plan. The amendment first designated the boundaries for the corridor within the national forest. It also set a mandate that all projects, activities, and infrastructures authorized in the corridor region must be designed and located to allow the successful migration of the pronghorn that summer in Jackson Hole and winter in the Green River Basin.

While the official designation of the Path of the Pronghorn (as it is commonly known) is a major step toward protecting the herds, it only applies to lands located within the national forest and national park systems. The corridor crosses a number of other public and private lands, and conservationists fear that continued development will jeopardize the safety of migrating herds. Groups such as the Green River Valley Land Trust are working with private landowners to improve management for pronghorn migration as well as developing conservation easements. Members of the WCS are particularly concerned about the possible effects of recent natural gas development projects in Wyoming. In September 2010, the WCS announced the beginning of a joint study with the Wyoming Game and Fish Department and Grand Teton National Park to monitor the migration of a number of animals in efforts to evaluate the potential threats and impediments to that migration. The study will take a close look at conditions on the southern winter range portion of the corridor, which lies on private and federal lands (under the Bureau of Land Management) and contains the largest oil and natural gas reserves in the United States that are currently under development. At least thirty pronghorn in Grand Teton have been already been outfitted with GPS collars to be monitored during the 2010–11 migration. So far the research team has made some interesting observations. In June 2011, they announced that the pronghorn's annual migration was delayed that year, likely due to the above-average snowpack in the region. The numbers of pronghorn arriving at Grand Teton National Park for the summer have been lower than usual, and researchers have speculated that pregnant does attempting the migration may have stayed behind if they gave birth to their fawns along the way. If this is the case, researchers are trying to determine if the does simply stay behind with their fawns, and if that causes the fawns to never learn to migrate. When it comes to long-term population management, researchers state that it is too early to say what effect the delayed migrations will have on the pronghorn.

Researchers at the University of Wyoming and elsewhere are involved in many studies to estimate the effects of various energy development projects (e.g., natural gas, coal, wind) on antelope and antelope migration.

BIBLIOGRAPHY

Books

Benedict, Audrey Delella. *The Naturalist's Guide to the Southern Rockies: Colorado, Southern Wyoming, and Northern New Mexico.* Golden, CO: Fulcrum Publishing, 2008.

Donahue, Debra L. *The Western Range Revisited: Removing Livestock from Public Lands to Conserve Native Biodiversity.* Norman, OK: University of Oklahoma Press, 2000.

Huser, Verne. *Wyoming's Snake River.* Salt Lake City, UT: University of Utah Press, 2001.

Johnson, Jerry. *Knowing Yellowstone: Science in America's First National Park.* Lanham, MD: Taylor Trade Publishing, 2010.

Schmidt, Jeremy, and Thomas Schmidt. *The Smithsonian Guides to Natural America: The Northern Rockies– Idaho, Montana, Wyoming.* Washington, DC: Smithsonian Books, 1995.

Smith, Robert Baer. *Windows into the Earth: The Geologic Story of Yellowstone and Grand Teton National Parks.* New York, NY: Oxford University Press, 2000.

Wolf, David A. *Industrializing the Rockies: Growth, Competition, and Turmoil in the Coalfields of Colorado and Wyoming, 1868-1914.* Boulder, CO: University Press of Colorado, 2003.

Web Sites

"About Oil Shale." Oil Shale & Tar Sands Programmatic EIS, U.S. Department of the Interior, Bureau of Land Management. Available from http://ostseis. anl.gov/guide/oilshale/index.cfm

An act relating to clean coal technology (HB 301). Wyoming Legislature. Available from http:// www.uwyo.edu/ser/_files/DOCS/cleancoal/ HB0301.pdf

An act relating to public health; prohibiting the proposal or promulgation of state regulations intended to reduce emissions of greenhouse gases (HB 171). Wyoming Legislature. Available from http://legisweb.state. wy.us/99sessin/engross/house/hb0171.htm

Bleizeffer, Dustin. "EPA's impending greenhouse gas regulations may decrease coal market." *Casper Star Tribune.* October 11, 2010. Available from http://trib.com/news/state-and-regional/ article_1b173580-b0b7-5a8b-ab0d-98f3c9196297. html

Bleizeffer, Dustin. "Rocky Mountain Power has no plans to build more turbines in Wyoming." *Casper Star Tribune.* October 18, 2010. Available from http:// trib.com/news/state-and-regional/article_33cd 05f0-25d9-5fa3-9bd0-6024bd6ff4f8.html

"Clean Coal Technology Fund." University of Wyoming, School of Energy Resources. Available from http:// www.uwyo.edu/ser/research/clean-coal/index. html

Clean Energy, a Strong Economy and a Healthy Environment. Western Governors' Association. Available from http://www.westgov.org/index.php?option= com_joomdoc&task=doc_details&gid=90&Itemid=85

Clean Energy Leadership in the Rockies: Competitive Positing in the Emerging Green Economy. Headwaters Economics. Available from http://www. headwaterseconomics.org/greeneconomy/ CleanEnergyLeadership.pdf

"Energy Resource Science Program." School of Energy Resources, University of Wyoming. Available from http://www.uwyo.edu/ser/energy-resource-science/index.html

Freudenthal, David. "Letter to U.S. Environmental Protection Agency." September 9, 2010. Available from http://governor.wy.gov/Media.aspx?Med iaId=1300

"The Frontier Line: A Transmission Project for the American West." Wyoming Public Service Comm ission. Available from http://psc.state.wy.us/ htdocs/subregional/Frontierline040105.pdf

Gateway West Transmission Line Project. Wyoming Bureau of Land Management. U.S. Department of the Interior. Available fromhttp://www.wy.blm. gov/nepa/cfodocs/gateway_west/index.html

Gearino, Jeff. "Residents speak out against power line route." *Casper Star Tribune.* June 19, 2010. http:// trib.com/news/state-and-regional/arti-cle_1180dfbd-3641-58a9-9909-c3b3e4fcbbb5.html

"Global Warming and Wyoming." National Wildlife Federation. Available from http://www.nwf.org/ Global-Warming/~/media/PDFs/Global% 20Warming/Global%20Warming%20State%20Fact% 20Sheets/Wyoming.ashx

"Grand Teton National Park." National Park Service. Available from http://www.nps.gov/grte/index. htm

Gruver, Mead. "Governor to EPA: Wyoming can't regulate greenhouse gas." *The Seattle Times.* Sep tember 10, 2010. Available from http://seattle times.nwsource.com/html/businesstechnology/ 2012865191_apusgreenhousegaswyoming.html

Kaufman, Leslie. "Wolves Could Lose Federal Protection in Wyoming." Green: A Blog about Energy and the Environment. *The New York Times.* July 7, 2011. Available from http://green.blogs.nytimes.com/ 2011/07/07/wolves-lose-federal-protection-in-wyoming/?partner=rss&emc=rss

"Laramie County Library." Southwest Energy Efficiency Project. Available from http://www.swenergy.org/publications/casestudies/wyoming/laramie/index.html

"A Look at Wyoming Agriculture." Agriculture in the Classroom. Available from http://www.agclass-room.org/kids/stats/wyoming.pdf

Manning, Patrick. "Results of the Baseline Survey." *Wyoming Labor Force Trends.* February 2011. Wyoming Department of Employment. Available from http://doe.state.wy.us/lmi/0211/a5.htm

"New Study Looks to Give the Pronghorn Room to Roam." Wildlife Conservation Society. September 22, 2010. Available from http://www.wcs.org/press/press-releases/room-to-roam-for-pronghorn.aspx

"Organic and Natural Foods Program." Wyoming Business Council. Available from http://www.wyomingbusiness.org/ag/ag_organicnatural.aspx

Pearson, Travis. "Snowpack hinders pronghorn migration north." *Pinedale Roundup.* June 30, 2011. Available from http://www.pinedaleroundup.com/V2_news_articles.php?heading=0&page=72&story_id=2097

Pelzer, Jeremy. "Beetle-kill epidemic a boon for Wyoming's timber industry?" *Casper Star Tribune.* October 5, 2010. Available from http://trib.com/news/state-and-regional/article_0832ccc4-191c-550e-963a-1a6809ba12b4.html

Pelzer, Jeremy. "Pine beetle epidemic kills Wyoming forests, generates debate." *Caspar Star Tribune.* Available from http://trib.com/news/state-and-regional/article_f70fe563-0e1a-5eea-b5b7-2e041b99093b.html

Pronghorn Migration Corridor forest Plan Amendment: Decision Notice & Finding of No Significant Impact. USDA Forest Service. Available from http://www.wyomingoutdoorcouncil.org/html/what_we_do/wildlife/pdfs/PronghornMigrationCorr-ROD.pdf

"Renewable and Efficient Energy—Solutions for Wyoming." Cooperative Extension Service, School of Energy Resources, University of Wyoming. Available from http://www.uwyo.edu/renew-energy/default_text.asp

"Rockies Express Pipeline." Kinder Morgan. Available from http://www.kindermorgan.com/business/gas%5Fpipelines/rockies%5Fexpress

Rocky Mountain Area Transmission Study. Wyoming Public Service Commission. Available from http://psc.state.wy.us/rmats/rmats.htm

"State Energy Profiles: Wyoming." U.S. Energy Information Administration. Available from http://tonto.eia.doe.gov/state/state_energy_profiles.cfm?sid=WY

"Water Resources." Wyoming State Geological Service. Available from http://www.wsgs.uwyo.edu/Topics/WaterResources

"The Wild West: A Pronghorn's Incredible Journey." Wildlife Conservation Society. Available from http://www.wcs.org/new-and-noteworthy/travel-guide-for-the%20path-of-the-pronghorn.aspx

"Wind Energy Technology." Laramie County Community College. Available from http://www.lccc.wy.edu/programs/windEnergy

Wyoming Chapter: U.S. Green Building Council. Available from http://www.usgbcwyoming.org

Wyoming Energy Conservation Network. Available from http://65.125.143.14/about_wyoenergy.asp

Wyoming Energy Council. Available from http://www.wyoec.org

"Wyoming Forest Health Report." Wyoming State Forestry Division. Available from http://slf-web.state.wy.us/forestry/adobe/wyfhm.pdf

"Wyoming Game and Fish Species List." Wyoming Game and Fish Department. Available from http://gf.state.wy.us/wildlife/nongame/SpeciesList/index.asp

"Wyoming Lakes and Reservoirs." United States Department of the Interior, Bureau of reclamation, Great Plains Region. Available from http://www.usbr.gov/gp/lakes_reservoirs/wyoming_lakes.htm

Wyoming State Climate Office. Available from http://www.wrds.uwyo.edu/sco/climate_office.html

"Wyoming State Energy Program." Wyoming Business Council. Available from http://www.wyomingbusiness.org/business/energy.aspx

Wyoming State Geological Survey. Available from http://www.wsgs.uwyo.edu/Topics/WYGeology/WYGeology-Page5.aspx

Wyoming State Parks, Historic Sites, and Trails. Available from http://wyoparks.state.wy.us/index.asp

Wyoming State Water Plan. Available from http://waterplan.state.wy.us

Wyoming 2007 Minerals Yearbook. United States Geological Survey. Available from http://minerals.usgs.gov/minerals/pubs/state/2007/myb2-2007-wy.pdf

Overview of Current Environmental Issues, Canada

Canada is the second-largest country in the world (after Russia). Geographically, Canada makes up the larger portion of the North American continent and shares its southern border with the United States and its northwestern border with the U.S. state of Alaska.

The land mass of Canada, including bodies of freshwater, totals 3,855,174 square miles (9,984,670 sq km). In 2011, Canada's population was approximately 34.5 million, ranking it thirty-third among the world's nations in population. The most populated areas of the country are located within 100 miles (160 km) of the southern border shared with the United States. Southern Ontario and Quebec have the highest population densities, while the northern regions are very sparsely populated.

❧ Early History

The geographic area that is now Canada was inhabited by various indigenous and Asian migrating peoples for several centuries prior to the arrival of the Europeans. There is physical evidence of Norse structures in the Atlantic region dating from the eighth century or earlier. The Norsemen did not settle and were gone by 1497, when John Cabot (c. 1450–c. 1499) claimed the land for England. The French explorers Jacques Cartier (1491–1557) and Samuel de Champlain (c. 1567–1635) began to explore and settle New France in 1534 and 1603, respectively.

The French settlers were involved with the fur trade in the areas surrounding the St. Lawrence River. The Hudson's Bay Company received a Charter in May 1670 that provided them with control of a large portion of land surrounding Hudson's Bay, including any land fed by water running into Hudson's Bay. Ownership of the land included control over Indian trade in the area, including the fur trade and lumber. Waterways provided access to the natural resources. The Hudson's Bay Company controlled this land, known as Rupert's Land, from 1670 to 1870. In 1763, the Treaty of Paris saw the French lose control of territories in eastern Canada to the English.

Canada comprises ten provinces and three territories. In 1867, after several constitutional conferences, four provinces formed Canada, a parliamentary federation. From 1870 to 1999, the four original provinces—Quebec, Ontario, New Brunswick, and Nova Scotia—were joined by other provinces and territories. Manitoba and the Northwest Territories joined the Confederation in 1870, British Columbia in 1871, Prince Edward Island in 1873, Yukon Territory in 1898, Alberta and Saskatchewan in 1905, Newfoundland in 1949, and Nunavut in 1999.

Jurisdiction over natural resources is set out in sections 91 and 92 of the Constitution Act, 1982 (formerly the British North America Act, 1867), with agricultural powers set in section 95. Most provincial governments were given jurisdiction over the sale of public lands and the timber on public lands; property rights; exploration, development, production, and export of nonrenewable natural resources and electricity; and taxation of resources. The federal government has jurisdiction over territory natural resources, oceans, and fisheries. The Prairie Provinces and territories were not legislated power over their natural resources at the time of joining Confederation. In 1930, the Canadian government passed three acts for the transfer of jurisdiction over natural resources to Manitoba, Saskatchewan, and Alberta.

Canadian Pacific Railway built a national railway during the 1880s. The railway provided land transportation, which served to unify the country from the Atlantic Ocean in the east to the Pacific Ocean in the west. The railway encouraged tourism to the national parks, settlement across the prairies, and allowed access and development of natural resources.

Canada is seen as a leader in environmental concern and activities. The 1960s and 1970s brought a new awareness about the need for environmental preservation and sustainable development. Several Canadian organizations sprang up to voice concern regarding pollution, decline of natural resources, and to promote sustainable development. Groups created in 1969 include the Vancouver-based Society Promoting Environmental Conservation (SPEC) and the Toronto-based Pollution Probe. In 1971, an Atlantic Canada group, the Ecology Action Centre, was formed, and in British Columbia, Greenpeace was born. The activists who created Greenpeace started their activities as the Don't Make a Wave Committee. In 1970, the group sent the fishing ship, christened Greenpeace, to protest against an underground nuclear bomb detonation, carried out by the United States at Amchitka off the southwest coast of Alaska. In 2011, both Alberta Environment and Environment Canada marked fortieth anniversaries.

In June 1972, the United Nations Conference on the Human Environment met in Stockholm to consider a way "to inspire and guide the peoples of the world in the preservation and enhancement of the human environment." The conference issued a sweeping declaration, covering topics from population control to environmental preservation to nuclear proliferation. The purpose of the declaration was to give the nations of the world a framework for development and environmental protection.

In 1983, the United Nations (UN) convened the World Commission on Environment and Development (WCED), popularly known as the Brundtland Commission, to review why the 1972 Stockholm Declaration had not been effective. Canada strongly supported the WCED and was instrumental in the work of the commission. In 1987, the WCED published *Our Common Future* (also known as the Brundtland Report), which provided a definition and framework for "sustainable development":

"Sustainable development is development that meets the needs of the present without compromising the ability of future generations to meet their own needs. It contains within it two key concepts: the concept of 'needs', in particular the essential needs of the world's poor, to which overriding priority should be given; and the idea of limitations imposed by the state of technology and social organization on the environment's ability to meet present and future needs."

Along with the definition, *Our Common Future* included seven critical strategies requiring national policy changes to achieve sustainable development worldwide. Among other things, the report noted the lack of integration of the environment and economy in Canada, and recommended that the Canadian government implement policies to improve in these areas. Following the report's release, Canada initiated several activities, including a Task Force, a National Roundtable on the Environment and the Economy, and many other groups to engage in policy studies and recommendations. In 1988, the Canadian Environmental Protection Act came into force, consolidating five separate pieces of legislation.

Canada played a prominent role in the negotiation of the Montreal Protocol (1989) that sought to encourage the world's nations to eliminate ozone-depleting substances.

Evaluating Progress

The Institute of International Sustainable Development, together with other agencies, presented a conference in October 2007 to look at progress related to sustainable development. Twenty years after the Brundtland Commission's report, the impetus for sustainable development had wavered and several strategies, such as a national fisheries strategy and national water quality standards, had not come to fruition. However, significant improvement in forestry and agricultural practices had been achieved.

A country with many natural resources, most of Canada's exports go to its largest trading partner, the United States. In 1855, the Unites States and British colonies in North America signed a Reciprocity Treaty allowing free trade. The treaty was cancelled in 1866, one year prior to Canadian Confederation. Free trade between Canada and the United States did not resume until 1988, under the United States–Canada Free Trade Agreement. In 1994, the North America Free Trade Agreement (NAFTA) added Mexico as a free trade partner.

Statistics Canada estimates for 2010 shows the Canadian gross domestic product (GDP) has increased in the area of services to 78 percent, followed by declines in both industry and agriculture to 20 percent and 2 percent respectively. Canada ranks fourteenth among the nations of the world in terms of GDP. Canada's GDP reflects the successful exploitation of the country's abundant natural resources.

The 2010 human development index (HDI), a global comparative index tool developed by the United Nations Development Program, gave Canada a value of 0.908, up from 0.789 in 1980. This is a very high rating, placing Canada sixth among the 187 nations included in the ranking. The HDI measures indicators related to a long and healthy life, access to knowledge, and a decent standard of living. The improvement in HDI accomplished by Canada in the thirty-year period (1980–2010) demonstrates more relative progress than other countries in the group.

Environmental Report Card: "Needs Improvement"

A 2009 Conference Board of Canada report, *How Canada Performs: A Report Card on Canada*, evaluated Canada's environmental performance in several areas: air quality, waste, water quality and quantity, biodiversity

Canadian Pacific Railway built the national railway, which provided land transportation that unified the country from sea to sea, during the 1880s. © *Justin Prenton/Alamy*

and conservation, natural resource management, and energy efficiency and climate change. The report shows that Canada compares poorly to its peer countries, especially on measures to address climate change and in waste generation and water consumption. Two provincial capitals, Victoria and St. John's, continue to release raw sewage into the ocean. Ironically, the exploitation of Canada's rich resources contributes to its lower environmental rating. Resource extraction requires water, generates waste products, and may affect air quality.

Ontario and Alberta have the highest emissions among the province and territories in Canada. The vast size of Canada contributes to the nation's environmental challenges: the energy expended to transport products across long distances to markets increases greenhouse gas emissions (GHG). Other areas of concern included in the report were municipal wastewater discharges as a large source of water pollution and pressures on biodiversity.

Canada's lowest ratings were for volatile organic compounds (VOC) emissions, municipal waste generation, water consumption, organic farming, marine trophic index, and GHG emissions. The highest rating (A) was for use of forest resources. The ratings suggest that Canada is not initiating sufficient steps to towards sustainability.

Climate

Canada has four climate zones, including dry climates, humid mesothermal climates, humid microthermal climates, and polar climates. Each zone or division has several climate types. The largest division by area is the humid microthermal climate according to the *National Atlas of Canada*.

Extreme weather is a perennial concern in Canada. In 2011, there were several floods, notably in Manitoba and Quebec, where flooding was experienced during spring and summer. Southern Ontario suffered through a summer heat wave with temperatures approaching record levels. Several areas of Canada experienced drought; in Alberta, drought conditions persisted through most of the first decade of the twenty-first century. By 2011, the dry conditions supported several wildfires, including one that destroyed the town of Slave Lake. Alberta has recorded just two larger wildfires—the Chinchaga fire (1950) and the Keane fire (1981). Severe weather affects infrastructure, natural resources, wildlife, and water resources.

The federal government lists fifteen acts and seven regulations that relate to climate change. These acts of legislation and policy relate to the implementation of

The exploitation of Canada's rich resources contributes to its lower environmental rating. Resource extraction requires water, generates waste products, and may affect air quality. © *Gunter Marx/VII/Alamy*

Kyoto Protocol; the development of agencies for sustainable development technologies; aviation, occupational health and safety, and motor vehicle safety regulations; emission reduction incentives; UN Framework Convention on Climate Change Privileges and Immunities Orders; and notice of a decision not to add certain species to the endangered species list. They also related to the establishment of Clean Air Day Canada and Canadian Environment Week. Environment Week is the first week in June, which includes June 5, World Environment Day, which was established by the United Nations General Assembly in 1972. Canada established Environment Week the same year. Clean Air Day was declared as the Wednesday of Environment Week; the first official Clean Air Day was celebrated on June 2, 1999. The goal of Clean Air Day is to increase public awareness of the need to sustain clean air and to take action to minimize climate change.

Canada has made a commitment to the Kyoto Protocol, becoming one of the nations to ratify it in 2002; however, citing that the Protocol "does not represent a way forward for Canada," Canada formally withdrew from the Protocol in December 2011. The country was the first to pull out of the global treaty. The Copenhagen Accord, which committed the country to reducing its greenhouse gas emissions by 17 percent of its 2005 levels by 2020, was signed by Canada in December 2009. The biggest emitters, the transportation and electricity generation sectors, are being targeted for regulations to reduce emissions.

A May 2011 report from the Conference Board of Canada, *Greenhouse Gas Mitigation in Canada*, states that Canada has a patchwork of action plans related to greenhouse gas emissions. The federal and provincial governments have not coordinated their efforts to reduce emissions. The report determines that several provincial governments have climate change action plans in place, although it is difficult to ascertain the progress. The lack of coordination among various federal and provincial programs and legislation makes any targets difficult to achieve. It is suggested that efforts to integrate federal and provincial plans may result in greater efficiency (and less bureaucracy) in achieving results in the area of carbon pricing.

❦ Natural Resources, Water, and Agriculture

Natural Resources

Parks Parks Canada marked its one-hundredth anniversary in 2011. The agency is dedicated to protecting Canada's natural places. In 1911 Canada created the first national service, with a mission to focus on establishing national parks, preserving significant historical sites, and conserving and protecting marine habitats. The first national park, Cave and Basin National Historic Site—later, Banff National Park—was established at Banff in 1885. Prior to 1911, mining and logging were allowed in the national parks; however these activities ceased in 1930 with the passing of the *National Parks Act*.

Canada boasts many firsts related to its parks service:

1. Gwaii Haanas National Marine Conservation Area in British Columbia is the only protected area in the world that extends from the floor of the ocean to the tops of mountains.

2. Jasper National Park is the largest dark sky preserve (area kept free of artificial light).

3. The Fundy National Park, home to Bay of Fundy, has the highest tides of anywhere in on earth.

4. Wood Buffalo National Park features the largest known beaver dam.

Forestry Canada has approximately ten percent of the world's boreal forest. There are 981,004 acres (397.3 million ha) of forest, other wooded land, and lands with tree cover from sea to sea. Approximately eight percent of Canada's forests are protected by legislation and

Jasper National Park is the largest dark sky preserve, i.e., area kept free of artificial light. © *Peter Adams Photography Ltd./Alamy*

40 percent of the total forest land base is protected by varying levels of land-use planning or forest management agreements. Less than one percent of Canada's forests are harvested annually.

Canada is the largest exporter of forest products in the world, and the United States is the largest importer of Canadian forest products. The global economic downturn of 2008–09 reduced the market for forestry products, as construction of residential and commercial buildings slowed. The forest industry's contribution to the Canadian GDP is approximately 1.7 percent. Direct employment in the forest industry in 2009 fell by 13 percent compared to 2008. Forestry accounts for about 50 percent of the economic base in some 200 Canadian communities. Forests harvested on public land are required to be managed and regenerated, with an estimated 72 percent of harvested forest on crown land regenerated with tree planting, seeding, or natural growth.

Like forests elsewhere in the world, Canadian forests face adverse effects from several factors:

1. Wildfires destroy forest land annually.

2. The Mountain Pine Beetle infestation affects a significant portion of forests in British Columbia and Alberta. Advancement of the infestation depends on winter weather conditions.

3. Drought conditions stress forest trees, making them susceptible to disease and infestations.

According to projections made by Natural Resources Canada, loss of forest will contribute to the increase in prairie area, already likely to expand as a consequence of climate change.

Wildlife

Canada is home to more than 70,000 known species of plants and wildlife. Approximately 400 of these are at risk, including the wood bison, woodland caribou, beluga whale, grey whale, and grizzly bear. Canada ranks seventh out of the twenty-nine countries ranked by the Organisation for Economic Co-operation and Development (OECD) for species at risk.

Habitats are being affected by human activity, climate change, and industrial development. When provincial governments refuse to review and enforce protection for endangered species, such as the woodland caribou, it is not uncommon for nonprofit organizations to bring pressure on the federal government to intervene to protect the species at risk. Court actions have also dealt with the effects of oil sands tailings ponds on the habitat of waterfowl.

The decline of fishing off eastern Canada in the 1990s was the result of overfishing of smaller fish and large-bodied fish predators, such as cod. A study published in *Nature* in July 2011 reported that forage fish ballooned to 900 percent;, with the lack of predators, resulting in the loss of food sources. The study also found that decline brought about a restructuring of the marine habitat, which did not result in a return to the original state of the fisheries.

Water

Canada has the third largest supply of freshwater in the world. Canada has 8,500 rivers and two million lakes. Water covers 8.9 percent of the country's total area. The Great Lakes are the largest bodies of freshwater, containing 18 percent of the world's surface freshwater. Canadians use a lot of water. Canada ranks twenty-eighth of twenty-nine OECD countries in per capita water consumption. Per capita water use in Canada is more than eight times that of Denmark, which ranks number one among the countries ranked, according to the Conference Board of Canada. Reasons for high water consumption include the ample supply, lack of water conservation programs and incentives, and the low cost of water. The high consumption has the potential to stress on the country's water resources and requires infrastructure to deliver, treat, and dispose of water.

Water

The two main agricultural zones in Canada are the western prairies and the east. Statistics Canada's census of agriculture, conducted every five years, confirmed what many Canadians already suspected: farming is on the decline in Canada. The total number of farms declined in Canada, from 246,923 in 2001 to 229,373 in 2006. Farm products with the highest production include indigenous pig, chicken, and cattle meat; wheat; rapeseed; fresh whole cow milk; peas, soybeans, and potatoes; and eggs.

Crop production in Canada can be strongly affected by weather events. The Prairie Provinces of Manitoba, Saskatchewan, and Alberta are the largest producers of wheat. Canada is a major global wheat producer, ranking sixth in the world with an annual average production of 24.5 million tons. Canada is also the global leader in production of lentils, dry peas, linseed, canary seed, and mustard seed.

In the early 1920s, many Canadian prairie farmers banded together to form wheat cooperatives. The farmers wanted more control over the grain marketing system. In 1935, the Canadian Wheat Board (CWB) was formed to control the market for grain products and ensure that Canadian farmers were receiving a fair price for their grain. Western farmers' participation was compulsory by 1943 under federal legislation, although some farmers in British Columbia all farmers in eastern Canada do not participate. As of 2011, only wheat and barley grains were marketed through the CWB. After 75 years of operation, some questioned whether the CWB was still relevant in the marketing of Canadian products. In 2011, the government surveyed farmers to determine their interest in continuing to operate the CWB; more than 50 percent of those surveyed voted in favor of preserving the CWB.

❧ Energy

Oil Fever

The first oil well in Canada was dug in Oil Springs, Ontario, between 1856 and 1858. The discovery of oil there triggered a fevered search for oil across the country, with Ontario the center of petroleum exploration and technology. The first Canadian natural gas discovery was in 1883 near Medicine Hat, Alberta.

Canada ranks third in the world, behind Saudi Arabia and Venezuela, for reserves of oil. Canada is the only non-OPEC member listed among the top five oil reserve countries. Oil sands form 97 percent of Canada's proven reserves. Oil sands are deposits that contain a combination of water, clay, sand, and a thick, heavy oil, which is called bitumen. While oil sands are found throughout the world, Canada's deposits are among the largest. A mere 7 billion barrels of the oil sands resource has been produced of the estimated 170 billion barrels of recoverable reserves. Technological advances are assisting in the production of the shrinking conventional oil and gas reserves in the country. However, severe weather events in Canada may affect oil and gas recovery in Canada. In the first half of 2011, such events led to a 4.2 percent decrease in oil and gas extraction. In addition, wildfires and other adverse weather conditions may cause slowdowns in support activities for mining, oil and gas extraction, drilling, and rig activities.

There is offshore oil and gas production in Newfoundland and Nova Scotia. The Hibernia fields in Newfoundland produce oil and associated gas, while the Nova Scotia fields produce solely gas. Not every province embraces oil exploration. Since 1972, the British Columbia government has had a moratorium on offshore drilling in place.

Activism and Protests

During the first decade of the twenty-first century, citizens and organizations became more political, with demonstrations against industrial activity and nonrenewable resource extraction, production, and transportation by pipeline. In 2011, ongoing protests were staged over TransCanada's plans to build a huge pipeline to carry oil from Alberta to Texas. TransCanada, a company based in Calgary, Alberta, had put forth its plans to construct the

1,700-mile (2,720-km) pipeline, known as the Keystone XL, in 2008. A final decision on the pipelines had been expected in 2011; protests were staged in Canada and Washington, D.C. And then, on January 18, 2012, President Barack Obama rejected the proposed Keystone XL pipeline—not on the basis of the project itself—but because he felt the Congress-imposed deadline did not allow time for sufficient and proper review of the project relative to the assessment of the pipeline's full impact on not only the U.S. environment, but the health and safety of its citizens. The State Department indicated that the decision did not preclude any subsequent applications for the pipeline. If and when the pipeline wins approval, construction would take two to three years. If the pipeline does not win approval, TransCanada expected to build a pipeline from Alberta to British Columbia, where the oil could then be shipped to Asian markets. Life-cycle and environmental impact assessment of projects, consultation, land-use framework, and integrated resource plans are just a few of the tools and policies put in place to evaluate whether such resource development projects are sustainable.

Several provinces are evaluating the feasibility of producing shale gas and the environmental effects of that process on the land and population. Western provinces were moving forward with shale gas exploration, as were New Brunswick and Nova Scotia. However, as of 2011, Quebec had a moratorium on shale gas exploration in place.

Coal Resources

Canada has significant coal deposits, which include estimates of 9 billion tons (8.7 billion t) of coal-in-place with 7 billion tons (6.6 billion t) recoverable with current technologies as of 2011. The largest Canadian deposits are found in British Columbia, Alberta, and Saskatchewan, with smaller deposits mined in New Brunswick and Nova Scotia. Seventeen of the twenty-two coal mines operating in Canada in 2007 were located in Alberta. Reserves that are not currently mined have been found in Ontario, Yukon Territory, Newfoundland and Labrador, Northwest Territories, and Nunavut.

Coal from Alberta and Saskatchewan, representing more than 40 percent of Canada's total production, is exported to Asian markets. Eastern Canadian, with smaller coal deposits and less production, imports some coal. Most of the coal produced in Canada is used to produce electricity. Provinces with the highest proportion of electricity produced by coal are Alberta, Saskatchewan, Nova Scotia, and Ontario.

Hydropower

Hydropower is produced in several areas due to the multitude of water resources available. British Columbia, Manitoba, and Quebec are the biggest producers of hydropower in Canada. In 1881, the Ottawa Electric Light Company was the first to produce electricity using

water at Chaudières Falls. The DeCew Falls generating plant, in operation since 1898 near Hamilton, Ontario, is the country's oldest high-head plant.

In 1965, the world's first 765-kilovolt transmission line was built in Quebec, linking Quebec City to Montreal. A second line was built in Manitoba in 1971. The Commission for the Centennial of Engineering in Canada recognized this technology as a significant engineering feat of the twentieth century. The technology has been applied in various worldwide projects.

Canada has many world-class hydropower facilities including the Daniel-Johnson Dam, the world's largest arch-and-buttress dam; the Robert-Bourassa generating station, the largest underground power station. Bothe facilities are in Quebec.

Canada produces almost 12 percent of the world's hydropower. Until 2004, when it was surpassed by China, Canada was the largest producer in the world. Hydropower accounts for well over half of the electricity produced in Canada.

Nuclear Power

Approximately 15 percent of the electricity produced in Canada comes from nuclear power. As of 2011, three provinces hosted the 18 existing nuclear reactors, which produced more than 12,600 MW of energy combined. The country was considering expanding nuclear capacity by building as many as nine more reactors. In 2008, nuclear power provided 53 percent of Ontario's electricity.

In 1944, Canadian researchers worked to develop the country's own nuclear power reactors. The National Research Experimental Reactor (NRX), at Chalk River, Ontario, commenced operation in 1947. In 1952, Atomic Energy of Canada Ltd. (AECL) was created as a crown corporation. Forty percent of the world supply of molybdenum-99 is provided by the National Research Universal (NRU) reactor built at Chalk River in 1957. Canada developed the Candu reactors, with the first going into operating in Ontario in 1971. As of 2011, some 32 Candu reactors were operating in seven countries. (Candu reactors produce nearly all of the global supply of radioisotopes for medical and sterilization use.)

Renewable Energy Resources

Canada has 4,611 MW of installed wind power capacity. The provinces with the highest wind power capacities are Ontario (1656 MW), Alberta (807 MW), and Quebec (663 MW). The Canadian Wind Energy Association reported in 2011 that there were some 129 wind farms in the country, with more in the planning stages. Wind energy was the fastest growing energy sector in Canada as of 2011. Alberta and Saskatchewan were the only provinces that have no provincial targets associated with wind power.

Canada has significant solar energy resources. The highest areas of solar energy are located in the Prairie Provinces (Alberta, Manitoba, and Saskatchewan),

Ontario, and Quebec. In 2009, Canada's photovoltaic projects increased to 62 megawatts. Another renewable energy source is geothermal power. In 2011, the Geological Survey of Canada released a report outlining significant potential for geothermal energy development in the country. While there appeared to be potential for geothermal energy development in broad areas of the country, data had only been collected to assess about 40 percent of the country's landmass as of 2011.

❧ Green Business, Green Building, Green Jobs

Green Business

The Canadian government funds many programs to encourage green projects. EcoAction Community Funding Program, created in 1995, encourages community organizations to undertake projects that will have positive, measurable changes on the environment.

According to Environment Canada's publication, *Canada's Emissions Trends*, several federal and provincial projects and measures have been instituted to reduce greenhouse gas (GHG) emissions. Nationally, the government has implemented passenger automobile and light-duty truck emissions regulations, electricity performance standards, and strengthened energy efficiency standards. On December 15, 2010, new regulations requiring an average renewable fuel content of five percent ethanol in gasoline and two percent in diesel fuel and heating oil went into effect.

The government's ecoENERGY program has provided incentives for energy-efficient and sustainable construction and development. In September 2011, the government announced that it would invest $78 million in 2012 and 2013 in initiatives designed to improve energy efficiency in residential and commercial buildings, industries, vehicles, and consumer appliances. Programs operated under the ecoENERGY umbrella included ecoENERGY Retrofit Initiative, ecoENERGY for Buildings and Houses, ecoENERGY for Industry, ecoFreight Program, ecoTechnology for Vehicles Program, ecoENERGY for Fleets, Public Transit Tax Credit, ecoENERGY for Renewable Heat, ecoAUTO Rebate Program, ecoENERGY for Personal Vehicles Initiative, National Vehicle Scrappage Program, Marine Shore Power Program, Renewable Fuels Development, ecoENERGY for Biofuels, ecoAGRICULTURE Biofuels Capital Initiative, Technology Development and Deployment, and ecoMobility.

Several provinces have initiated climate change action plans. British Columbia's provincial government states that the province is the first carbon neutral public sector in North America. From 2008 to 2011, British Columbia provided $75 million to fund 247 energy projects in government buildings, post-secondary institutions, hospitals, and schools. Every government building is required to be carbon neutral and regulations enforce the requirement to measure, reduce, and offset greenhouse gas emissions from buildings. The projects have encouraged innovation and helped create green jobs in British Columbia.

Green Building

The U. S. Green Building Council (USGBC) has recognized a number of green building projects in Canada. In a 2011 report, USGBC noted 378 commercial projects in Canada that qualified for some level of Leadership in Energy and Environmental Design (LEED) certification. More than 2,600 other commercial projects had been registered for LEED status in Canada, giving a total LEED green building footprint of 480 million square feet (44,593,642 sq m). Toronto is a major venue for LEED buildings, with more than 40 certified and 300 registered projects as of 2011.

Examples of Canadian projects receiving the LEED Gold or Gold EB (Existing Building) certification are the Royal Bank Plaza, Sun Life Financial Tower, Hydro One Networks, Fidelity Investments Canada, and Upper Canada College's William P. Wilder Arena & Sports Complex—all in Toronto. In 2011, Toronto hosted Greenbuild, the world's largest green building conference; it was the first time the conference had been held outside the United States.

Green Jobs

The Environmental Careers Organization Canada estimated environmental sector employment at more than 682,000 in 2010. Ontario's Green Energy Act legislation provided an incentive to create an estimated 50,000 jobs. The federal government's *Economic Action Plan (EAP) Year 2* provided almost $16 billion over two years to encourage infrastructure projects and create jobs. Of the 84,000 projected jobs created under the EAP, some 19,821 would be green jobs.

BIBLIOGRAPHY

Books

Demerse, Clare. *Reducing Pollution, Creating Jobs: The Employment Effects of Climate Change and Environmental Policies.* Calgary: The Pembina Institute, 2011.

Environmental Trends in British Columbia: 2007. Victoria, BC: British Columbia Ministry of Environment, 2007.

Greenhouse Gas Mitigation in Canada Report May 2011. Ottawa: Conference Board of Canada, 2011.

How Canada Performs: A Report Card on Canada. Ottawa: Conference Board of Canada, 2009.

Our Story: Notre Histoire. Ottawa: Parks Canada, 2011.

Working for the Environment. Gatineau, Quebec: Environment Canada. 2011.

Periodicals

Frank, Kenneth T., et al. "Transient dynamics of an altered large marine ecosystem". *Nature.* DOI:10.1038. Online 27 July 2011.

"Natural Resource Wealth, 2010." *EnviroStats: Service Bulletin.* 2011 (Fall) 5:3 (14–17).

Web Sites

Antón, J., S. Kimura and R. Martini, "Risk Management in Agriculture in Canada", *OECD Food, Agriculture, and Fisheries Working Papers*, No. 40, 2011, OECD Publishing. Available from http://dx.doi.org/10.1787/5kgj0d6189wg-en

The Atlas of Canada. Available from http://atlas.nrcan.gc.ca/site/english/index.htm

The Atlas of Canada: Climatic Regions. Available from http://atlas.nrcan.gc.ca/site/english/maps/archives/3rdedition/environment/climate/030?maxwidth=1600&maxheight=1400&mode=navigator&upperleftx=0&upperlefty=0&lowerrightx=3984&lowerrighty=2960&mag=0.0625

British Columbia Climate Action for the 21st Century, 2010. Ministry of Environment, British Columbia. Available from http://www.env.gov.bc.ca/cas/pdfs/climate_action_21st_century.pdf

"Canada Recognized for LEEDing the way in Green Buildings." *Building Strategies and Sustainability.* June 16, 2011. Available from http://bssmagazine.ca/CanadaRecognizedforLEEDingtheWay.aspx

Canada's Forests: Statistical Data: Key Facts. Canadian Forest Service. Available from http://cfs.nrcan.gc.ca/pages/242?lang=en_CA

Canadian Agriculture in 2008: An Overview of Key Events. Statistics Canada. 21-004-X Available from http://www.statcan.gc.ca/pub/21-004-x/21-004-x2009002-eng.pdf>

Canadian Association of Petroleum Producers (CAPP). *CAPP Statistical Handbook.* Available from http://www.capp.ca/library/statistics/handbook/Pages/default.aspx#pOCI3J1WX6ft

Canadian Hydropower Association. *Hydropower in Canada: Past, Present, and Future, 2008.* Available from http://www.canhydropower.org/hydro_e/pdf/hydropower_past_present_future_en.pdf

Canadian Wind Energy Association. Available from http://www.canwea.ca

Centre for Energy. Available from http://www.centreforenergy.com/AboutEnergy/

CIA World Factbook: Canada,. 2011. U.S. Central Intelligence Agency. Available from https://www.cia.gov/library/publications/the-world-factbook/geos/ca.html

"Climate Zones." Natural Resources Canada. Available from http://oee.nrcan.gc.ca/residential/personal/windows-doors/climate-zones.cfm?attr=4

"Coal Facts." Coal Association of Canada. Available from http://coal.ca/content/index.php?option=com_content&view=article&id=47&Itemid=56

"Confederation." *The Canadian Encyclopedia.* Available from http://www.thecanadianencyclopedia.com/index.cfm?PgNm=TCE&Params=a1ARTA0001842

"Ecology Action Centre: About the EAC." Available from http://www.ecologyaction.ca/content/about-eac

"Electric Power Generation, Transmission and Distribution, 57-202-X, 2009." Statistics Canada. Available from http://www.statcan.gc.ca/pub/57-202-x/57-202-x2007000-eng.pdf

"Energy Sector: Energy Sources: Coal: About Coal." Natural Resources Canada. Available from http://www.nrcan.gc.ca/eneene/sources/coacha-eng.php#production

"Everyone's Talking About Water: It's Time For Action." Environment Canada, 2011. Available from http://www.ec.gc.ca/Publications/B0D70C82-3263-4C05-9A76-AC005C913750/Everyones-TalkingAboutWater2011

"FAOStat: Canada, 2009." Food and Agriculture Organization of the United Nations. Available from http://faostat.fao.org/DesktopDefault.aspx?PageID=339&lang=en&country=33

"First Oil Well in Western Canada National Historic Site of Canada." Parks Canada. Available from http://www.pc.gc.ca/docs/v-g/pm-mp/lhn-nhs/puits-well_e.asp

Geothermal Energy Resource Potential of Canada, 2011. Geological Survey of Canada. Available from http://geopub.nrcan.gc.ca/moreinfo_e.php?id=288745

Greenpeace Canada: History. Available from http://www.greenpeace.org/canada/en/About-us/History/

Parks Canada. "First Oil Well in Western Canada National Historic Site of Canada." Available from http://www.pc.gc.ca/docs/v-g/pm-mp/lhn-nhs/puits-well_e.asp

"Hot Topic: Environment." July 2011. Conference Board of Canada. Available from http://www.conferenceboard.ca/hcp/hot-topics/environment.aspx

"Keystone XL Pipeline Decision: Delay Hasn't Stalled Debate." November 28, 2011. Public News Service.

Available from http://www.publicnewsservice.org/index.php?/content/article/23482-1

"Reduction of Carbon Dioxide Emissions from Coal-Fired Generation of Electricity Regulations, Proposed Regulations." *Canada Gazette Part I.* August 27, 2011. 2779–2842. Available from http://www.gazette.gc.ca/rp-pr/p1/2011/2011-08-27/pdf/g1-14535.pdf

"Report on Energy Supply and Demand in Canada. 57-003-X." Statistics Canada. Available from http://www.statcan.gc.ca/pub/57-003-x/57-003-x2009000-eng.pdf

"Report of the World Commission on Environment and Development: Our Common Future." United Nations. Available from http://www.un-documents.net/wced-ocf.htm

Road to Improvement. Indian and Northern Affairs Canada. May 2008. Available from http://www.reviewboard.ca/upload/ref_library/1217612729_ri08-eng.pdf

"Six Historical Events in the 100 Years of Canada's Petroleum Industry." Petroleum History Society. Available from http://www.petroleumhistory.ca/history/wells.html.

"Solar Power in Canada." Centre for Energy. Available from http://www.centreforenergy.com/AboutEnergy/Solar/Overview.asp?page=5

Solar Vision 2025. CanSIA. Available from http://www.cansia.ca/node/6512

Sustainable Development: From Brundtland to Rio 2012. Available from http://www.un.org/wcm/webdav/site/climatechange/shared/gsp/docs/GSP1-6_Background%20on%20Sustainable%20Devt.pdf

Tarasofsky, Richard. *Canada's Progress in Addressing the Strategic Imperatives Set Out in "Our Common Future".* Available from http://www.iisd.org/pdf/2007/facing_canada_progress.pdf

U.S. EIA Country Analysis Briefs, Canada, April 2011. Available from http://www.eia.gov/countries/cab.cfm?fips=CA

World Bank. *Hydropower.* Available from http://water.worldbank.org/water/topics/hydropower

World Nuclear Association. *Nuclear Power in Canada.* Available from http://world-nuclear.org/info/inf49a_Nuclear_Power_in_Canada.html

Alberta

Alberta, the most populous of Canada's three Prairie Provinces, is characterized in the southwest by the spectacular scenery of the Rocky Mountains, where the picture-postcard resorts of Banff, Jasper, Lake Louise, and Waterton are found. Covering a vast area of 255,284 square miles (661,185 sq km), the province is roughly the size of the state of Texas. About 90 percent of Alberta is made up of the vast interior plain that stretches across North America.

With Saskatchewan, Alberta is one of two landlocked provinces in Canada. Alberta's desert topography is a magnet to dinosaur hunters, who flock to the area between Calgary and Edmonton. Also in Northern Alberta, near Wembley and near Grande Prairie, a new fossil bed was the subject of a great deal of interest in 2011. Enthusiasts and scientists seek fossils and other relics from prehistoric times. The capital city of Edmonton is the primary supply and service hub for Canada's oil sands and other northern resource industries.

Climate

Alberta has a continental climate, characterized by vivid seasonal contrasts in which long, cold winters are balanced by mild to hot summers. Known as the "Sunshine Province," the climate also features an unusually high number of sunny days, with an average of 320 days per year—more than any other province—in all seasons. Although the entire province is covered in cold air in winter, in the southwest a mild wind, the "Chinook," frequently funnels through the mountains from the Pacific Ocean.

Average temperatures for the province can range from 10°F (-12°C) in January to 64°F (18°C) in July. However, extreme temperatures are not uncommon. According to statistics from Environment Canada, temperatures can range from as low as -65°F (-54°C) in January to 104°F (40°C) in July.

Action for Climate Change. Climate change would result in warmer Alberta winters, which would lead to changes in precipitation patterns (such as rain instead of snow), impacting snowpack and spring runoff. Alberta's current cold winters also translate into fewer pests and diseases lasting into spring. However, warming temperatures could change that, resulting in greater risk to forests and human health. In 2002, the Alberta government released a Climate Change Strategy; in January 2008, it released an updated version of the strategy. Particularly important for Alberta as the largest emitter of greenhouse gasses in Canada, the strategy's actions are based on three themes: Implementing carbon capture and storage; greening energy production; and conserving and using energy efficiently. Action taken for the first of these themes was the creation of the Alberta Carbon Capture and Storage Development Council, which developed a work plan for implementing carbon capture and storage. For the second theme, companies reduced their greenhouse gas emissions by at least 12 percent. As of 2008, this action resulted in approximately 2.5 million tons of actual reduction. For the third theme, the province launched Alberta's Conservation Team (ACT) in order to encourage Albertans to take action, and the creation of an incentive program to promote the use of energy efficient appliances and home improvements.

❧ Natural Resources, Water, and Agriculture

Natural Resources

Alberta has 2,947 known species of plants. In 2006, there were 10 threatened or endangered plant species, including the slender mouse-ear-cress and the western blue flag.

Alberta's mammal species include nine species of bats, black and grizzly bears, elk, moose, woodland caribou, cougar, lynx, bighorn sheep, mountain goat, wood bison, coyote, red fox, and gray wolf. There are ten species of amphibians and nine species of reptiles in the

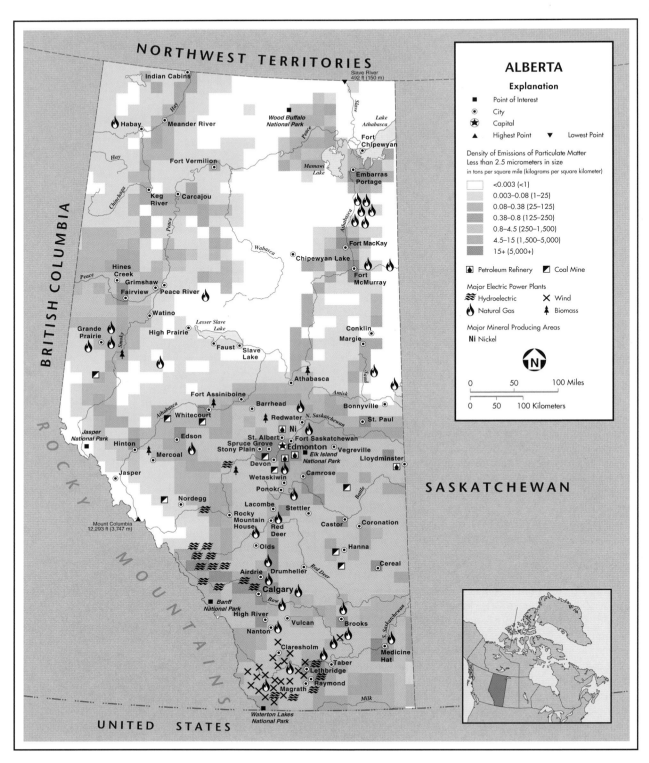

SOURCES: *Energy Facts and Statistics.* Centre for Energy. Available from http://www.centreforenergy.com/FactsStats/MapsCanada; "Geographical Highlights." *The Canadian Encyclopedia.* Available from http://www.encyclopediecanadienne.ca/geoHighlights/canmap_geog_v1_eng.swf; "Highest Points by Province and Territory." *The Atlas of Canada.* Natural Resources Canada. Available from http://atlas.nrcan.gc.ca/site/english/learningresources/facts/faq.html#points; "Mining in Canada: Map." *Mining in Canada.* The Mining Association of Canada. Available from http://www.mining.ca/site/images/MapofCanada.pdf; "Particulate Matter < 2.5 Micrometers (PM2.5) Emission in 2007." *CAC Density Maps.* Environment Canada. Available from http://www.ec.gc.ca/inrp-npri/default.asp?lang=en&n=BD725B2A-1. © *2011 Cengage Learning.*

Alberta Provincial Profile

Physical Characteristics

Land area	248,000 square miles (642,317 sq km)
Freshwater area	7,541 square miles (19,531 sq km)
Highest point	Mount Columbia 12,293 feet (3,747 m)
Forest lands (2011)	68.5 million acres (27.7 million ha)
Provincial parks (2011)	69

Energy Statistics

Total electricity generated (2009)	59.6 million megawatt hours
Hydroelectric energy generation (2009)	1.9 million megawatt hours
Wind energy generation (2009)	100,000 megawatt hours
Tidal energy generation (2009)	NA
Biomass energy capacity (2009)	193 megawatts
Crude oil reserves (2009)	1.5 billion barrels (237.7 million cu m)
Natural gas reserves (2009)	37.8 trillion cubic feet (1.1 billion cu m)
Natural gas liquids (2009)	661.4 million barrels (105.2 million cu m)

Pollution Statistics

Carbon output (2009)	124.3 million tons of CO_2 (112.7 million t)
Federal contaminated sites receiving funds (2008)	5
Particulate matter (less than 2.5 micrometers) emissions (2009)	438,363 tons per year (397,676 t/yr)

SOURCES: *Canada's Greenhouse Gas Emissions.* Environment Canada. Available from http://www.ec.gc.ca/ges-ghg/default. asp?lang=En&n=1357A041-1; *Canada Year Book, 2011.* Statistics Canada. Available from http://www.statcan.gc.ca/pub/11-402-x/11-402-x2011000-eng.htm; *Energy Facts and Statistics.* Centre for Energy. Available from http://www.centreforenergy.com/FactsStats/MapsCanada; *Federal Contaminated Sites.* Government of Canada. Available from http://www.federalcontaminatedsites.gc.ca/index-eng. aspx; "Forest Land by Province and Territory." Statistics Canada. Available from http://www40.statcan.gc.ca/l01/cst01/envi34a-eng.htm; "Geographical Highlights." *The Canadian Encyclopedia.* Available from http://www. encyclopediecanadienne.ca/geoHighlights/canmap_geog_v1_eng.swf; *National Pollutant Release Inventory.* Environment Canada. Available from http://ec.gc.ca/pdb/websol/emissions/ap/ap_query_e.cfm

© 2011 Cengage Learning.

province. Bird species include whooping crane, Cooper's hawk, blue grouse, bald eagle, great horned owl, American white pelican, long-billed curlew, bay-breasted warbler, and Canada goose. According to Alberta Sustainable Resource Development, there are 26 at-risk wildlife species in the province. Endangered mammals include the swift fox and Ord's kangaroo rat. Endangered birds include the burrowing owl, mountain plover, piping plover, and whooping crane.

Sustainable Forests. About 60 percent of the total land area of Alberta, or approximately 94.4 million acres (147,500 sq mi/38 million ha) is covered by forests. Alberta has four forest regions: boreal, aspen parkland, subalpine, and montane. The boreal is the largest region, taking up 35 percent of Canada's total land area and 77 percent of the country's total forest land. In Alberta, the boreal region covers the majority of the province, mainly in the northwest. The subalpine region runs along the bottom half of Alberta's western border, and covers much of the Rocky Mountains. The aspen parkland region lies in the southeastern part of the province, extending from the boreal region to the southern border. The montane region covers the east-west mountain valleys that extend from the foothills. These are the valleys that channel the "Chinook" winds, or warm Pacific air, into Alberta during the winter. Tree species found in the province include aspen poplar, balsam fir, black spruce, white birch, lodgepole pine (Alberta's provincial tree), alpine fir, Engelmann spruce, tamarack, and Douglas fir.

The provincial government owns 87 percent of Alberta's forestland, the federal government owns 9 percent, and private owners account for the remaining four percent. About 61 percent of the total forest area is classified as commercially productive forest land, and the forest industry provides approximately 44,000 jobs per year. The most important forestry products produced in terms of value of shipments are wood pulp, softwood lumber, and waferboard, with products such as newsprint, panelboard, particleboard, and cabinetry becoming more important. According to the Alberta Forest Products Association (AFPA), the forest products industry is Alberta's third largest economic sector, and contributes C$5.5 billion to the province annually. However, the decrease in North American housing production from 2004 to 2007 has caused the market value of Alberta's forest products to fall by 36 percent and 3,800 jobs have been lost. This downturn has led the Alberta government to begin working with the industry on a strategy for training and development in order to meet future workforce needs. In January 2011, the AFPA launched the Work Wild program, designed to attract younger generations to the forestry industry. The program includes presentations in Alberta schools and at community events, as well as marketing efforts such as a Web site and social media campaign.

Along with working to improve workforce training, Alberta also looks on the sustainability of its forests as a priority. The forest industry harvests at levels below natural growth rates, and plants two trees for each tree cut in order to maintain their forests.

Mining. Alberta mines oil sands, natural gas, coal, sand, dimension stone, ammonite shell, gravel, limestone, salt, shale, and gold. There are 15 major mines and quarries in Alberta. Of these, 11 are coal and oil sands mines, and four are quarries. The mining of oil

Moraine Lake in Banff National Park, Alberta. © *Caleb Foster/ShutterStock.com*

sands is big business in Alberta, with Syncrude Canada operating the largest mine in the world and using some of the largest mining trucks ever built. Coal and oil sands mining contribute C$3.3 billion dollars to the economy annually. Alberta is also a hub for cement manufacturing and has two major plants in Exshaw and Edmonton. Salt is recovered by solution mining, which involves pumping water down wells to dissolve the salt and pumping the resulting salt brine to the surface. Alberta's minerals industry directly employs an estimated 10,000 people.

Water

Approximately 2.2 percent of the Canada's water is found in Alberta. Northern Alberta has more high volume lakes and rivers with southern Alberta having lakes and rivers with lower volumes. Almost 87% of water in Alberta flows north to the Arctic Ocean. All water found in Alberta is owned and managed by the federal government even if found on privately owned land. It is thought that Alberta has more groundwater than surface water. Drought, climate change, and contaminants affect the quantity and quality of water. Irrigation requires the largest allocation of water usage for a specific activity.

Meanwhile, commercial fishing is regarded as a C$5 million-per-year industry, according to numbers from Alberta's Sustainable Resource Development. Prominent species sought include brown trout, eastern brook trout, northern pike, rainbow trout, walleye, and yellow perch.

As of 2010, Alberta had an estimated 300,000 anglers and 800 commercial fishing operations. Alberta is divided into three fish management zones; each is responsible for the maintenance of local stocks. The Fish Culture Branch of the Alberta Fish and Wildlife Service annually stocks lakes and streams with trout, walleye fry, and walleye fingerlings.

Agriculture

The *2006 Census of Agriculture*, a report of Alberta's Agriculture and Rural Development department, listed Alberta's total farm area as more than 52 million acres. Cattle farms, representing the largest category, numbered more than 20,000 in 2006, followed by grain and oilseed farms, and wheat farms.

In 2006, agricultural exports were valued at C$6 billion. About 40 percent of all exports are sent to the United States. Japan and Mexico are the next largest agricultural export markets. Alberta produces about 44 percent of the Canada's barley, 34 percent of the canola (oil seed), 28 percent of the wheat, and 23 percent of the oats.

Wheat is Alberta's primary crop, with 7.3 million tons produced in 2009. Barley production was at 3.8 million tons, oat production was at 303,527 tons, and canola production was at 3.11 million tons.

❦ Energy: A Hub of Coal and Oil Production

In 2010, the production of crude oil and its equivalents from other sources averaged 619,000 barrels per day, while natural gas production that same year averaged 10.9 billion cubic feet per day. The overwhelming bulk of Alberta's crude oil and natural gas production is exported, mainly to the United States. As of 2009, Alberta's proven reserves of conventional crude oil totaled 1.5 billion barrels, while another 169.3 billion barrels were in the province's oil sands, giving the province the third-largest oil reserve in the world behind Saudi Arabia and Venezuela. Alberta also accounts for 74.4 percent of the natural gas produced in the country.

The province's three refineries, the Imperial Oil Refinery, the Scotford Refinery, and Suncor Energy Refinery, are all located in Edmonton. The Interprovincial Pipe Line (IPL), which originates in Edmonton and passes through Saskatchewan, transports crude oil from both Alberta and Saskatchewan to markets in eastern Canada and the United States.

Alberta is by far Canada's largest producer of coal and holds 70 percent of Canada's coal reserves. Alberta coal reserves have a current estimate of 33.4 billion tons remaining to be mined according to the Energy Resources Conservation Board (ERCB). This massive

Alberta has three oil refineries, all located in Edmonton.
© iStockPhoto.com/Dan Barnes

energy resource supplies fuel for about 59 percent of the province's electricity generation in 2008. Alberta's total coal production in 2008 was approximately 32 million tons of marketable coal. The provincial government committed to investing C$2 billion to encourage carbon capture and storage projects for Alberta's coal-fired electric plants and facilities related to producing oil from the oil sands.

The majority of Alberta's electric power comes from thermal (steam, internal combustion, and combustion turbine) sources. In 2009, the province's installed power generating capacity stood at 13,734 megawatts (MW), of which hydroelectric was at 900 MW of generating capacity. Coal and gas held the highest capacities, at 5,692 MW and 5,189 MW respectively.

Renewable sources of energy remain viable in Alberta, as it is second behind Ontario in terms of wind power capacity. According to the Centre For Energy, Alberta has 26 wind farms as of June 2011 with installed capacity of 803 MW, or enough to power more than 640,000 homes a year. The largest facility, with a capacity of 81.6 MW, is near Trochu, north of Calgary.

❦ Green Business, Green Building, Green Jobs

Green Business

As of 2009, the city of Calgary has invested C$20 million in energy performance contracts with private sector firms to retrofit 226 municipal buildings. Under the contracts, energy service companies are paid to upgrade a building, applying technologies that will reduce electrical, heating, and other operating costs. The company, which typically assumes responsibility for financing the project, uses the savings in energy costs to pay off the retrofit loan over the contract's 10-year period. These contracts are expected to reduce the city's carbon dioxide emissions by 29,526 tons (30,000 t) per year. Plans to expand the program to C$50 million in contracts could increase emission reductions to up to 78,736 tons (80,000 t) per year. The energy performance contracts are part of a comprehensive strategy to reduce Calgary's carbon dioxide emissions by 157,472 tons (160,000 t) per year by 2012.

On the provincial level, in August 2010, the government of Alberta introduced a commercial lighting incentive program for business owners to increase their energy efficiency. Called Light it Right, the program offers business owners rebates between C$37,500 and C$375,000 for installing more energy-efficient lighting, depending on the building type and the type of retrofit. The program aims to reduce 188,000 tons of greenhouse gas emissions overall by 2020—the equivalent of taking 40,000 cars off the road. The program is run by the nonprofit Climate Change Central and was scheduled to continue until December 31, 2011, or until funding runs out.

Green Building

On the municipal level, cities in Alberta have been working towards providing incentives for green building projects. Environment Canada provides links to a number of such incentive programs on its web site. Examples include the city of Okotoks's LEED Incentive Program that provides rebates based on building permit values for different levels of LEED development and the city of Calgary's rebate program for green homes and incentives for residential toilet replacement. Depending on the level of certification, new or retrofitted buildings could receive a rebate of 20 to 60 percent of the project's building permit fee.

On the provincial level, the government of Alberta has dedicated over C$36 million to help citizens reduce greenhouse gas emissions through a number of rebates and incentives. Rebates are available for homeowners who choose to replace their clothes washers, domestic hot water heater, furnace or boiler, insulation, and toilets with more energy efficient appliances. There is also a rebate for those who participate in the pre-retrofit home energy evaluation, and for those purchasing a new EnerGuide labeled home.

Green Jobs

The 2009 report, "Green Jobs: It's Time to Build Alberta's Future," states that Alberta should turn its focus from creating jobs in the oil and gas sectors to green energy, as more jobs are likely to be created with such an investment. The report recommends strategies for the province to implement, such as creating policies for building Alberta's energy efficiency, expanding transit and high-speed rail, accelerating renewable energy development, and making sure to meet the skills demand with training and education programs.

Alberta's colleges and universities already have programs geared toward green careers. Three universities—the University of Alberta, the University of Calgary, and the University of Lethbridge—joined together to form the Canada School of Energy and Environment (CSEE), an innovative and integrated research and educational collaboration. In addition, the University of Calgary is home to the Institute for Sustainable Energy, Environment, and Economy (ISEEE), established in 2003 to ensure that the University is recognized internationally for its research, education, and innovation in energy and the environment. Using a multidisciplinary approach, ISEEE brings together the faculties of the Schulich School of Engineering, Haskayne School of Business, the School of Public Policy, and the faculties of science, law, and environmental design. Among the ISEEE programs is the Master of Science in Sustainable Energy Development.

Lethbridge College (formerly Lethbridge Community College) has an International Wind Energy Academy. This program provides education and teacher certification for the wind turbine industry. The college's location in southern Alberta, an area known for sustainable winds, makes the program ideally situated for preparing students for entry into clean energy jobs.

❧ Mining Oil Sands: A Precious and Controversial Resource

Oil sands are a naturally occurring mixture of sand or clay, water, and tar-like bitumen. Each grain of sand is covered by a thin layer of water and then by a layer of the highly viscous bitumen, which is a heavy form of crude oil. Bitumen is too thick to flow naturally or to be pumped out of the ground. To extract it, it must to be either heated or diluted with a solvent, before being upgraded into synthetic crude oil. The oil is extracted by surface mining when the deposits are less than 82 yards (75 m) underground. Deeper deposits are mined "in situ" (in place) using techniques that extract the bitumen underground, before pumping it to the surface.

In early 2009, oil sands operations produced 1.4 million barrels of bitumen per day, a figure which is projected to increase to 2.2 million barrels per day by 2015 and to 4.3 million barrels per day by 2030.

Environmental Damage

Mining of oil sands comes with dire environmental consequences. Alberta ranks number one among the provinces when it comes to industrial air pollutants. This dubious distinction comes mostly as a by-product of oil sands mining.

Alberta's oil sands cover an area about the size of the state of Florida in the United States, or approximately 54,363 square miles (140,800 sq km). The oil sands are found in three main deposits: Athabasca, Cold Lake, and Peace River. The surface mining area is found at Athabasca, which is an area that covers 1,834 square miles (4,750 sq km). Part of the surface mining process involves clearing the area of trees; as of 2008, more than 232 square miles (600 sq km) of boreal forest had been disturbed to allow oil sands mining. The government of Alberta has leased 30,502 square miles (79,000 sq km) of northeastern Alberta for oil sands development without prior environmental assessment.

Along with the destruction of forest habitat, oil sands mining produces three times more greenhouse gas emissions than conventional Canadian and U.S. oil production. Emissions from oil sands mining are expected to increase from 4 percent of Canada's emissions in 2006

Coal and oil sands mining contribute C$3.3 billion dollars to the economy annually. © Davewebbphoto/Dreamstime.com

to 12 percent by 2020—accounting for 44 percent of the total increase in emissions over that period. Overall, 5 percent of Alberta's greenhouse gases come from oil sands plants and upgraders.

The use of large amounts of water in oil sands extraction is also an environmental issue. For every single barrel of bitumen mined from oil sands, between two and four barrels of water are needed. Most of this water is taken from the Athabasca River. As of 2009, more than 550 million cubic meters of water from the Athabasca Basin had been licensed to be diverted for oil sands projects. This water, polluted with "tailings," cannot be returned to the natural water cycle. (Tailings are the toxic liquid waste products created by bitumen extraction in the mines.) Waste water that cannot be recycled remains in tailings lakes and ponds and toxic wastewater from in situ mining is reinjected underground. Tailings ponds have leached into the surrounding environment, spreading contamination. Tailings are toxic to mammals and aquatic organisms.

As of 2009, only 0.2 percent of the area disturbed by oil sands mining has been government-certified as reclaimed. The boreal forest disturbed by the mining will never return to its natural state, as much of it was wetlands, which cannot be recreated.

Thus important ecosystems have been permanently destroyed.

The Oil Sands Environmental Coalition (OSEC)—made up of the Pembina Institute, the Toxics Watch Society of Alberta, and the Fort McMurray Environmental Association, and represented by Ecojustice—has been working to raise awareness about the environmental effects of oil sands mining and have urged policymakers to take action. In August 2010, OSEC filed a submission calling on the Joint Review Panel to reject an application by Total E&P Canada for the company's Joslyn North Mine Project, citing significant environmental impacts, a deficient environmental assessment, and insufficient progress on government regulations to address oil sands environmental impacts. The Joslyn North Mine Project would result in 1.5 million tons more of greenhouse gas pollution each year and would destroy thousands of hectares of land. OSEC stated that the company's environmental assessment was not reliable and should be thrown out. However, in January 2011, the three-member Join Review Panel gave conditional approval for the project, provided Total E&P Canada follows through with 20 specified actions, including providing detailed plans prior to starting the project, adhering to strict discharge restrictions, providing detailed wildlife mitigation efforts, and working with local environmental groups to mitigate environmental effects from the project. The project is set to begin in 2017.

Three years after another panel—for the Imperial Kearl project—warned of the dangers of oil sands development, the government has made little progress in setting standards or finding solutions to reduce the environmental effects of oil sands mining. Despite a requirement for oil sands producers to implement reclamation plans for the lands they mine, few successful reclamations have been made.

Some progress is being made, however, On September 20, 2010, the Alberta government announced that mining company Suncor had transformed and reclaimed a 544-acre (220-ha) tailings pond. Alberta's premier noted that the reclamation demonstrated what is possible for the future of oils sands mining and environmental preservation.

The government itself is becoming even more organized and involved in monitoring the environmental impacts of oil sands mining. In July 2011, the government announced a new federal monitoring program proposal created with the input of nearly 100 Canadian scientists. The proposal called for increasing the number of monitoring sites and expanding the borders of monitored lands up to the Northwest Territories and south of the oil sands down to Fort McMurray. Costs for the proposed additional monitoring are expected to approach C$50 million, which is to be funded by the mining industry. The proposal addressed water quality, as well as habitat health for insects, fish, and other animals. The proposal is one step toward maintaining a healthy environment while tapping the reserves of the oil sands.

In November 2011, the Alberta government established an Oil Sand Information Portal accessible on the Internet. The portal is a one-window page with links to maps and searchable oil sands data sets related to greenhouse gas emissions, facilities water use, land disturbance, and reclamation and tailings pond size.

BIBLIOGRAPHY

Books

Banff National Park Management Plan. Gatineau, Quebec: Parks Canada, 2010.

Berkes, Fikret. *Breaking Ice: Renewable Resource and Ocean Management in the Canadian North*. Calgary: University of Calgary Press, 2005.

Hart, E. J. *J. B. Harkin: Father of Canada's National Parks*. Edmonton: University of Alberta Press, 2010.

Luxton, Eleanor G. *Banff: Canada's First National Park*. 2nd ed. Banff, AB: Summerthought Publications, 2008.

Richardson, Lee. *The Oil Sands: Toward Sustainable Development*. Ottawa: Standing Committee on Natural Resources, 2007.

Shiell, Leslie. *Greater Savings Required: How Alberta Can Achieve Fiscal Sustainability from Its Resource Revenues*. Ottawa: C.D. Howe Institute, 2008.

Waterton Lakes National Park Management Plan. Gatineau, Quebec: Parks Canada, 2010.

Wood Buffalo National Park Management Plan. Gatineau, Quebec: Parks Canada, 2010.

Web Sites

"Alberta's 2008 Climate Change Strategy." Government of Alberta Environment. Available from http://environment.gov.ab.ca/info/library/7894.pdf

"City of Calgary Uses Innovative Approach to Cut Energy Bills." Climate Change Central. Available from http://www.climatechangecentral.com/node/103

"Energy Facts & Statistics: Alberta." Centre For Energy. Available from http://www.centreforenergy.com/FactsStats/MapsCanada/AB-EnergyMap.asp

Energy Resources Conservation Board. Available from http://www.ercb.ca/portal/server.pt?

Facts about Water in Alberta. Alberta Environment. 2010. Available from http://environment.gov.ab.ca/info/library/6364.pdf

"Focus On Climate Change." Alberta Environment. January 2008. Available from http://environment.gov.ab.ca/info/library/7390.pdf

"Green Incentives Across Canada: Alberta." Environment Canada. Available from http://www.ec.gc.ca/financement-funding/default.asp?lang=En&n=E-F8AE9FC-1&offset=1&toc=show

Government of Alberta Agriculture and Rural Development. Available from http://www.agric.gov.ab.ca/app21/rtw/index.jsp

Government of Alberta Energy. Available from http://www.energy.alberta.ca/

Government of Alberta Environment. Available from http://environment.alberta.ca/

Government of Alberta Sustainable Resource Development. Available from http://www.srd.alberta.ca/

"An Integrated Oil Sands Environment Monitoring Plan." Environment Canada. July 2011. Available from http://www.ec.gc.ca/default.asp?lang=En&n=56D4043B-1&news=7AC1E7E2-81E0-43A7-BE2B-4D3833FD97CE

Institute for Sustainable Energy, Environment and Economy. University of Calgary. Available from http://www.iseee.ca/

Lethbridge College International Wind Energy Academy. Available from http://www.lethbridgecollege.ca/externalapps/oldsite/iwea//index.php?option=com_frontpage&Itemid=1

My Rebates. Climate Change Central. Available from http://www.climatechangecentral.com/my-rebates/air_sealing

Oil Sands Information Portal. Alberta Environment and Water. Available from http://environment.alberta.ca/apps/osip

Oil Sands Watch. Pembina Institute. Available from http://www.oilsandswatch.org/

"Premier Stelmach Calls Tailings Pond Reclamation a Historic Achievement." Government of Alberta press release. Available from http://www.alberta.ca/acn/201009/291914021A90B-DA12-B628-2C2768A2952D7F8E.html

Radler, Marilyn. "Total Reserves, Production climb on mixed results." *Oil and Gas Journal*, December 6, 2010. Available from http://www.ogj.com/articles/print/volume-108/issue-46/special-report/total-reserves-production-climb-on-mixed.html

"Report of the Joint Review Panel." Energy Resources Conservation Board. January 27, 2011. Available from http://www.ceaa.gc.ca/050/documents/47646/47646E.pdf

Simieritsch, Terra. "Oil Sands Environmental Coalition Calls on Panel to Reject Total Oil Sands Mine Application." The Pembina Institute, August 27, 2010. Available from http://www.pembina.org/media-release/2069

"Species Assessed by Alberta's Endangered Species Conservation Committee: Short List." Government of Alberta Sustainable Resource Development. Available from http://www.srd.alberta.ca/BioDiversityStewardship/SpeciesAtRisk/SpeciesSummaries/documents/SpeciesAssessed-EndangeredSpeciesConservationCommittee-ShortList-Jun03-2010.pdf

"Sport Fishing In Alberta In 2005: Performance, Value and Economic Impact Volume 1." Econometric Research Limited. November 2008. Available from http://www1.agric.gov.ab.ca/$Department/deptdocs.nsf/all/csi12823/$FILE/Volume-I-Fishing-Impacts-May-11.pdf

The Town of Okotoks LEED Green Building Incentive Program. Available from http://www.okotoks.ca/data/1/rec_docs/803_Town_of_Okotoks_LEED_Incentive_Program_Approved_December_12_2009.pdf

"Work Wild." Alberta Forest Products Association. Available from http://albertaforestproducts.ca/sites/default/files/downloads/AFPA%20Work%20Wild%20Fact%20Sheet.pdf

British Columbia

British Columbia has embarked on a number of ambitious strategies that aim toward a greener future for the economy and environment of the province. The primary 2009 British Columbia Energy Plan outlines the province's goals for achieving energy self-sufficiency through clean and renewable energy sources. This plan is supplemented by the *Energy Efficient Buildings Strategy: More Action, Less Energy*, which promotes green building end energy-efficiency strategies at residential, commercial, and industrial levels, and the *British Columbia Climate Action Plan*, which sets environmental conservation and preservation strategies for several sectors, including forestry and agriculture, along with energy, transportation, and industry. While many strategies focus on the development of a clean energy economy, the province has not ignored the importance of protecting its natural resources in agriculture and wildlife. Organic and sustainable farming practices are taking root in many areas and the province has established the Forest and Range Practices Act. Designed in part to conserve soils and reforest logged areas. One controversial policy is the *Grizzly Bear Conservation Strategy*, which is designed to protect the dwindling local population of grizzly, but still allows for annual trophy hunts for what is listed as a species of concern.

Climate

Climate varies by topography throughout the province. The coastal region has a fairly mild climate with abundant precipitation—from 51 to 150 inches (130 to 380 cm) of rain a year. The interior has a continental climate with long, cold winters and mild to hot summers.

Climate Change Provincial officials have already noted several changes in the climate over the last fifty to one hundred years. *Indicators of Climate Change for British Columbia 2002* detailed several of the past and anticipated impacts of global climate change on the environment. According to the report, average annual temperatures have risen by about 33.9°F (1.1°C) in the interior of the province and by 35°F (1.7°C) in the north. Rising temperatures have resulted in decreased snow depth and snow water content and earlier spring melts, all of which affect the summertime provincial water supply. Sea levels along the coast have already risen by between 2 and 5 inches (4 and 12 cm) and could rise by up to 88 centimeters over the next one hundred years.

The government has already initiated several climate action strategies to reduce greenhouse gas emissions and decrease reliance of fossil fuels. These include the goal of reducing greenhouse gas emissions by 33 percent of 2007 levels by 2020 and 88 percent by 2050. The Climate Action Plan published in 2008 details the government's strategies for reaching this and complementary goals in climate change mitigation and adaptation. The comprehensive plan includes actions and strategies for seven sectors, including agriculture, forestry, waste, buildings, transportation, energy, and industry. The 2010 publication of *British Columbia Climate Action for the 21st Century* provided an overview of the climate actions taken to date and the actions that the government expects to take in reaching target goals. Some of those goals included a carbon neutral core government by the end of 2010, as well as a revenue-neutral carbon tax and partnership within the Western Climate Initiative, a cap-and-trade system involving multiple West Coast states in the United States and British Columbia. The government announced in June 2011 that British Columbia's public sector was the first in North America to achieve carbon-neutral status.

❧ Natural Resources, Water, and Agriculture

Natural Resources

The Province is the most diverse of any province based on ecosystems, animal, plant and timber species. British

Columbia's forests support 1,345 animal and plant species and 49 native tree species.

British Columbia is covered by 149 million acres (596,000 sq km) of forest, which represents an area larger than France. (The province's total land area is 367,669 sq mi/952,263 sq km.) Different forest types that occur in the province are dry ponderosa pine forests in the south, boreal forest in the northeast, and the temperate rainforests along the Pacific coast. The principal species harvested are lodgepole pine, spruce, hemlock, balsam, Douglas fir, and cedar. Coastal forests consist primarily of hemlock, while lodgepole pine and spruce are the main interior species. The forest industry is a large part of the provincial economy, yet only a fraction of one percent of its immense forests is logged each year. Only two percent of its land has been permanently converted to other uses such as farming, ranching and urban development, and when public lands are logged, they are returned to forest.

In 2004, the government of British Columbia passed the Forest and Range Practices Act, which applies to any forest or range activities on public land, maintaining the province's high level of environmental protection. It specifies requirements to conserve soils, to reforest logged areas, and to protect riparian areas, fish and fish habitat, watersheds, biodiversity, and wildlife. It also specifies requirements for the construction, maintenance and deactivation of forest roads. Under the Act, forest companies are required to develop forest stewardship plans that outline how they will meet objectives set by government for soils, timber, wildlife, water, fish, biodiversity and cultural heritage resources. Public views and forest values must be considered before forest companies can harvest timber, build roads, or undertake other forest activities on public forest land.

Though in decline, the forestry industry still makes up about 13 percent of British Columbia's gross domestic product, and employs more than 200,000 people. According to the Council of Forest Industries, forestry accounts for more than C$3.5 billion in payments to the government. However, the industry is suffering because much of the wood s shipped to the United States, where there is declining demand due to a poor housing market. The industry has also been plagued by the mountain pine beetle infestation, which is was waning as of late 2011.

British Columbia is home to some 1,138 vertebrate species, including 142 mammal species, 488 bird species, 83 fresh water and 368 saltwater fish, 22 amphibians, and 18 reptile species. Invertebrate species are estimated at between 50,000 and 70,000, including 35,000 species of insects. There are an estimated 2,580 species of vascular plants (ferns and all plants that reproduce through seeds), 1,000 types of mosses and liverworts, 1,000 lichens, 522 species of attached algae, and more than 10,000 fungi species. Some of the more distinguishable mammal species are: shrew, mole, bat, rabbit, pika, beaver, porcupine,

gopher, squirrel, chipmunk, coyote, wolf, fox, cougar, lynx, bobcat, otter, sea lion, wolverine, marten, skunk, weasel, raccoon, black bear, grizzly bear, mountain goat, bighorn sheep, moose, deer, elk, and caribou.

In 2010, there were 58 plant species listed as threatened or endangered, including the golden paintbrush, water-plantain buttercup, yellow montane violet, and Lyall's mariposa lily. The same year, there were 93 vertebrate species listed as threatened or endangered. Endangered birds include the burrowing owl, the sage thrasher, and vesper sparrow. Endangered mammals include Pacific water shrew, Townsend's mole, and the Vancouver Island marmot. The Rocky Mountain tailed frog, the northern leopard frog, the western painted turtle, and white sturgeon are all endangered as well.

Mining Mining in British Columbia is a key component of the province's economy. According to the British Columbia Ministry of Energy, Mines, and Petroleum Products, as of 2009, there were more than 700 mineral exploration and mining companies with offices in Vancouver, many with worldwide projects. British Columbia is also ideally situated to serve Pacific Rim markets, as its ports are deep water, capable of servicing all vessel classes, and offer the shortest shipping times to Asia from the Americas. In 2008, there were five agreements signed between British Columbia-based companies and Asian companies and as of June, 2009, five more agreements had been signed. More than half (59 percent) of British Columbia's coal exports are destined for Asian markets.

Of all the provinces, British Columbia is ranked third in terms of the value of its mineral production. Minerals produced in the province include coal, copper, molybdenum, gold, silver, zinc, and lead; and industrial minerals, such as limestone, sulphur, aggregate, gypsum, quartzite, jade, barite, dimension stone, flagstone, dolomite, and magnesite. British Columbia's diverse geological environments also have the potential to produce many other mineral commodities, such as nickel and iron from metal deposits, and niobium, tantalum, and glacial clay from industrial mineral occurrences.

Water

The Pacific Ocean provides British Columbia's western border, and the province's longest river is the Fraser River at 850 miles (1,368 km), and its largest lake is Williston Lake, a reservoir, at 680 square miles (1,761 sq km). Other major rivers include the upper Columbia River and the Kootenay River. In northern British Columbia, the Stikine, Nass, and Skeena rivers flow toward the Pacific Ocean, and Peace River flows northeast toward the Arctic Ocean. Long, narrow lakes are found throughout the valleys of the southern and central interior. Among these are Atlin, Kootenay, Okanagan, Quesnel, and Shuswap lakes. Several high dams have impounded large reservoir lakes like Kinbasket Lake, particularly on the Columbia and Peace rivers.

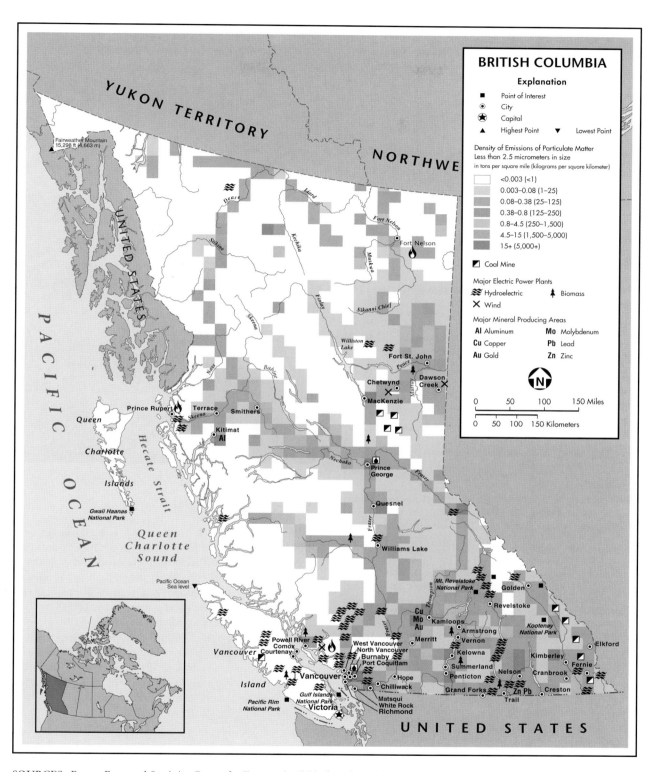

SOURCES: *Energy Facts and Statistics.* Centre for Energy. Available from http://www.centreforenergy.com/FactsStats/MapsCanada; "Geographical Highlights." *The Canadian Encyclopedia.* Available from http://www.encyclopediecanadienne.ca/geoHighlights/ canmap_geog_v1_eng.swf; "Highest Points by Province and Territory." *The Atlas of Canada.* Natural Resources Canada. Available from http://atlas.nrcan.gc.ca/site/english/learningresources/facts/faq.html#points; "Mining in Canada: Map." *Mining in Canada.* The Mining Association of Canada. Available from http://www.mining.ca/site/images/MapofCanada.pdf; "Particulate Matter < 2.5 Micrometers (PM2.5) Emission in 2007." *CAC Density Maps.* Environment Canada. Available from http://www.ec.gc.ca/inrp-npri/default.asp? lang=en&n=BD725B2A-1. © 2011 Cengage Learning.

British Columbia Provincial Profile

Physical Characteristics

Land area	357,216 square miles (925,185 sq km)
Freshwater area	7,548 square miles (19,549 sq km)
Highest point	Mount Fairweather 15,299 feet (4,663 m)
Forest lands (2011)	143.1 million acres (57.9 million ha)
Provincial parks (2011)	830

Energy Statistics

Total electricity generated (2009)	62.2 million megawatt hours
Hydroelectric energy generation (2009)	55.9 million megawatt hours
Wind energy generation (2009)	NA
Tidal energy generation (2009)	NA
Biomass energy capacity (2009)	190.1 megawatts
Crude oil reserves (2009)	113.2 million barrels (18.0 million cu m)
Natural gas reserves (2009)	18.9 trillion cubic feet (534.2 billion cu m)
Natural gas liquids (2009)	162.7 million barrels (25.9 million cu m)

Pollution Statistics

Carbon output (2009)	12.0 million tons of CO_2 (10.9 million t)
Federal contaminated sites receiving funds (2008)	77
Particulate matter (less than 2.5 micrometers) emissions (2009)	110,646 tons per year (100,376 t/yr)

SOURCES: *Canada's Greenhouse Gas Emissions.* Environment Canada. Available from http://www.ec.gc.ca/ges-ghg/default. asp?lang=En&n=1357A041-1; *Canada Year Book, 2011.* Statistics Canada. Available from http://www.statcan.gc.ca/ pub/11-402-x/11-402-x2011000-eng.htm; *Energy Facts and Statistics.* Centre for Energy. Available from http:// www.centreforenergy.com/FactsStats/MapsCanada; *Federal Contaminated Sites.* Government of Canada. Available from http://www.federalcontaminatedsites.gc.ca/index-eng. aspx; "Forest Land by Province and Territory." Statistics Canada. Available from http://www40.statcan.gc.ca/l01/ cst01/envi34a-eng.htm; "Geographical Highlights." *The Canadian Encyclopedia.* Available from http://www. encyclopediecanadienne.ca/geoHighlights/canmap_geog_v1_ eng.swf; *National Pollutant Release Inventory.* Environment Canada. Available from http://ec.gc.ca/pdb/websol/emissions/ap/ ap_query_e.cfm

Commercial fishing is big business in British Columbia, as it is the fourth largest industry in the province with more than 80 species of finfish, shellfish, and plants harvested. Dominant commodities include salmon, roe herring, groundfish, and shellfish species. In 2006, the wholesale value of the province's seafood products was more than C$1 billion. Seafood is British Columbia's number one food export with 85 percent of products shipped out of the country, and seafood processing occurs at 195 facilities in the province.

Organic kale growing in Pemberton, British Columbia. © *David Buzzard/Alamy*

With its scenic freshwater lakes, rivers and streams, British Columbia also has a vibrant sport fishing industry. According to a 2005 report on the economic impacts of sport fishing in the province, nearly half of all British Columbia adults have purchased anglers' licenses at one point in their lives. The sport pumps nearly C$500 million into the local economy and employs nearly 4,000 people.

Taking advantage of their water resources, British Columbia generates about 90 percent of its electricity from hydropower. There are 72 hydroelectric generating stations in the province, the majority of which are located in the Columbia and Kootenay Rivers area, in the lower mainland, and on Vancouver Island.

Agriculture and Aquaculture

Only about 5 percent of the total provincial land is considered arable. Of the 2.8 million hectares of farmland, nearly 1.7 million hectares are for pasture or grazing. Dairy farming is one of the largest components of the agricultural sector, with beef cattle and poultry production also significant. Floriculture is an important sector. Berries, grapes and tree fruits are also important in

Farmed salmon, from locations such as this salmon farm in the Broughton archipelago, is the single largest agricultural export of British Columbia. © *Chris Cheadle/Alamy*

terms of annual value. The Fraser River Delta and the Fraser Valley are the primary regions for vegetable, tree fruit, and floriculture, as the soil in these regions is considered to be among the richest in the nation. Food processing plays a significant role in the economy, contributing about C$2 billion to the provincial GDP.

Aquaculture is extremely important to the provincial economy, with farmed salmon being the single largest agricultural export. The province ranks among the top five largest producers of farmed salmon in the world, with Atlantic salmon as the primary farmed species. Pacific oyster and Manila clam are the primary farmed shellfish species. Seafood processing plays a role in the economy as well, with about C$974 million worth of fish and seafood products exported in 2006.

The Similikameen Valley claims the distinction of being "The Organic Capital of Canada," since nearly 60 percent of the farmers in the region have gone organic. There were nearly 500 certified organic farms in British Columbia, representing 2.8 percent of the total number of farmers in the province and 13 percent of the all organic farmers in Canada. That year, more than one hundred farms were in transition to become organic. Organic farming standards and certification is provided through the Ministry of Agriculture and Lands.

Energy

Non-Renewables: Oil, Natural Gas, and Coal

British Columbia is ranked second among the provinces in production of natural gas. The primary reserves are

found in the Ladyfern, Greater Sierra, Monkman, and Horn River fields in the northeast portion of the province. Most of this gas is exported through two major pipelines. Spectra Energy operates gathering and transmission systems that extend to Huntington/Sumas on the border with the United States and TransCanada operates a transmission system that extends from the western border of Alberta to Kingsgate.

In 2010, Canada's three western provinces formed the New West Partnership. This partnership creates barrier-free trade, labor mobility, competitiveness, regulatory streamlining, and investment between the three provinces. Late in 2010, an Energy Memorandum of Understanding was signed to improve access to Asian markets.

In September 2011, the provincial government announced plans to create a robust liquefied natural gas (LNG) industry in British Columbia as part of a wider proposal to create jobs. Part of that plan included bringing three new LNG terminals online by 2020. One project, the Kitimat terminal in the northwest quadrant of British Columbia, received the necessary environmental approvals to move forward. Proposed by Apache Canada Ltd., EOG Resources Inc., and Encana Corporation, the terminal and accompanying pipeline would provide LNG to markets in the Asia Pacific region.

In 2009, the province had 1,061 operating oil wells producing a total of about 23,070 barrels of oil per day and 10,881 barrels of condensate. These wells are concentrated mainly along the northeast border of the province. While there are two refineries in the province—Prince George and Burnaby—the province must import petroleum products in order to meet local demand.

In 2009, there were nine active coal mines in the province found in the three main coalfields of East Kootenay in the southwest corner of the province, Peace River in the central region, and Comox on Vancouver Island. Nearly all of the coal produced within the province is exported.

Electricity: Earth, Wind, and Water

About 90 percent of the electricity supply is produced from hydropower. The province has seventy-three hydroelectric generating plants, the largest of which is the 2,730-megawatt G. M. Shrum station on the Peace River. The province has four natural-gas fired thermal electric generation facilities, the largest of which is the 950-megawatt Burrard station near Vancouver. There are six thermal electric facilities that are operated with woodwaste. There is also one 102-megawatt wind farm located near Dawson Creek.

The BC Energy Plan

The 2009 British Columbia Energy Plan outlines the province's ambitious goals for achieving energy self-sufficiency through clean and renewable energy sources. The plan is broken down into four main categories: energy conservation and efficiency, electricity, alternative energy, and oil and gas. The plan also provides fifty-five policy actions and places specific target goals, complete with deadlines for meeting them. For instance, the province hopes to achieve electricity self-sufficiency by 2016, while ensuring that at least 93 percent of total electricity generation is from clean or renewable energy sources. The plan specifically rules out nuclear power as a source option. The BC Bioenergy Strategy complements the energy plan with a focus on the development of wood waste and other biomass resources for electricity generation.

A Green Energy Advisory Task Force was appointed in 2009 with a mandate to recommend further strategic actions that will be necessary to meet the goals of the energy plan, while also considering issues such as market opportunities for renewable electricity outside the provincial borders and the creation of new clean energy jobs. The task force issued their first report in April 2010. At the same time, the provincial legislative assembly passed the Clean Energy Act, which formalized several of the energy objectives and strategies included in both the energy plan and the Green Energy Advisory Task Force report. These include the goal to become a net exporter of electricity from clean or renewable sources and to reduce the expected increase in demand for electricity by at least 66 percent by 2020.

Under the BC Energy Plan, utilities are urged to develop new renewable sources of energy. While there is no formal renewable portfolio standard, the plan sets a voluntary goal for electricity distributers to meet any increase in demand a supply that includes at least 50 percent of clean electricity, as defined by the plan.

🌿 Green Business, Green Building, Green Jobs

Green Business

According to a February 2010 report from The GLOBE Foundation of Canada, green business is booming in British Columbia and will continue to grow into 2020. *British Columbia's Green Economy: Building a Strong Low-Carbon Future* presents an overview of the impact of the province's green economy for 2008 and offers a projection for the growth of green business into 2020. The survey included consideration of six key sectors within a green economy: clean and alternative energy, energy management and efficiency, green building, environmental protection, carbon finance and investment, and knowledge. For 2008, these six sectors contributed a total of C$15.3 billion to the provincial gross domestic product (GDP), accounting for about 10.2 percent of the GDP for that year. Clean and alternative energy was a leading sector, along with energy management and efficiency. These two sectors combined contributed C$6.1 billion. Using a range of economic growth scenarios, the survey projects that the provincial green economy could expand to C$27.4 billion by 2020.

The ICE Fund and the Pacific Institute for Climate Solutions

One initiative set to support the growth of the green economy is the Innovative Clean Energy Fund (ICE Fund). This initiative, which is part of the overall British Columbia Energy Plan, represents a commitment of C$25 million per year for the development of new sources of clean energy and technologies that support local economies. As of 2010, the ICE Fund has issued contributions of C$47 million toward thirty-four projects in communities throughout the province. The Pacific Institute for Climate Solutions was also established with support from the provincial government for the development of clean energy technologies that could translate into the growth in the green economy as well. The institute, which is based at the University of Victoria, represents a collaboration between British Columbia's four primary research universities and researchers from the private sector and government.

Green Jobs

The GLOBE Foundation's publication *British Columbia's Green Economy: Building a Strong Low-Carbon Future* included a survey of the number of jobs available in the green economy by both sector and job category. In

2008, the six key sectors of the green economy supported 117,160 direct full-time equivalent (FTE) jobs, representing 5.1 percent of total provincial employment. The number of direct and indirect jobs was 165,690. The environmental protection sector supported the most jobs with 32,700 direct FTE jobs, accounting for 28 percent of all green jobs in 2008. The energy management and efficiency sector was the second largest with 24,800 direct FTE jobs. When broken down by job categories (as defined by the North American Industry Classification System), the largest number of green economy jobs were related to wholesale trade. This was followed by professional, scientific, and technical services and transit and ground passenger transportation. Using a range of economic growth scenarios, the GLOBE Foundation survey projects that the total number of direct and indirect jobs in the provincial green economy could rise to 225,000 by 2020.

Jobs, Justice, Climate A number of government and labor organizations are actively involved in initiatives to expand the green economy job market. In September 2010, the British Columbia and Service Employees Union sponsored a two-day green economy conference entitled "Jobs, Justice, Climate—Building a Green Economy for BC." The conference was attended by more than one hundred labor leaders, activists, and environmental leaders. The conference has been considered a first step toward developing an action plan that will expand the job market in the green economy.

Green Building

In September 2008, a series of revisions, designed to encourage sustainable construction practices, were made to the general provincial building code by order of the minister of forests and range. These revisions, Ministerial Order 100, called for a new focus on energy efficiency in the design and construction of all buildings. A complementary BC Energy Efficiency Act was passed in 2008 that set specific energy efficiency standards for all equipment and appliances sold in the province (RSBC 1996 Chapter 114).

A number of private and government organizations have launched initiatives designed to further promote green building and energy efficiency standards in residential, commercial, and public buildings, including Built Green BC, the Light House Sustainable Building Centre, and the Community Action on Energy and Emissions (CAEE) initiative. In 2009, the CAEE published a revised *Energy Efficiency & Buildings: A Resource for BC's Local Governments* that outlines existing building regulations and provides a list of resources for local government officials as they strive to meet the provincial energy goals set by the *BC Energy Plan*.

The *Energy Efficient Buildings Strategy: More Action, Less Energy*, developed through the collaboration of several provincial ministries, further supports the BC Energy Plan by providing resources for communities to develop programs that reduce energy use and costs. The LiveSmart BC incentive program is a major part of the *Energy Efficient Buildings Strategy*. The program has already been very successful in encouraging and supporting families and business owners as they upgrade homes and businesses to be more energy efficient and self-sufficient. Launched in 2008, the LiveSmart BC program involves an investment of C$62 million through 2012. Meanwhile, a new study by the Columbia Institute, *This Green House: Building Fast Action For Climate Change and Green Jobs*, illustrated that homeowners can have a major impact on the province's greenhouse gas emissions and help create green job opportunities by retrofitting their homes with energy-efficient upgrades. According to the study, in 2008, heating, cooling, and electricity in buildings accounted for 28 percent of Canada's greenhouse gas emissions resulting from energy use. It also showed 20 jobs are created for every $1 million invested into retrofitting homes. The report encourages local municipalities to provide incentives and financing to remove the barriers from homeowners.

❧ The Grizzly Hunt: A Sustainable Practice or a Danger to the Bear Population?

Each year April 1 marks the opening of the trophy hunting season for grizzly bears in British Columbia's Great Bear Rainforest. There has been opposition to the hunt from the public and numerous conservation and environmental groups, due to the bear's status as a species of concern. However, the British Columbia Wildlife Branch has attempted to implement a strategy that will manage the grizzly population in a sustainable manner. This issue of the grizzly hunt divides the people of the province; although there are exceptions, in general, those who live in urban areas are opposed to the grizzly hunt, while those who live in rural areas support the hunt.

A report prepared by the David Suzuki Foundation, released in April 2010, noted that British Columbia may be home to as many as half of Canada's remaining grizzly bears. Known as a "keystone species," grizzlies are an essential part of maintaining a healthy ecosystem as they regulate prey species and spread seeds for many plant species. A 2008 government report estimated the grizzly bear population in the province at 16,014. While there is not complete agreement among biologists that this estimate is accurate, what is certain is that grizzly bears face numerous threats, such as habitat depletion, the effects of salmon population collapse and climate change, and human-caused mortalities. Between 1977 and 2009,

British Columbia may be home to as many as half of Canada's remaining grizzly bears. Known as a "keystone species," grizzlies are an essential part of maintaining a healthy ecosystem. © *Christopher Chapman/Alamy*

almost 11,000 bears were killed by humans, 87 percent of which were killed legally by hunters.

To address the management of the grizzly population, the British Columbia Wildlife Branch divided the province into 57 grizzly bear population units. Out of these, nine populations are so small that they are now listed as "threatened" by the government and are at risk of disappearing. In 1995, the BC government released the *Grizzly Bear Conservation Strategy*, which sought to regulate the number of bears that hunters kill each year and to establish grizzly bear management areas (GBMAs) that include no-hunting zones in the 57 population units. However, according to analysis by the David Suzuki Foundation, this strategy has not been adequately implemented.

The grizzly bear has been classified by the Ministry of Environment's Fish and Wildlife Branch as "big game" under the provincial *Wildlife Act*, which allows hunting of the bear on a "sustainable" basis. This means that the ministry can set limits on how many and where grizzly bears can be killed by hunters. However, studies have shown that grizzly bear hunting is contributing to an unsustainable level of grizzly bear mortality, rather than helping to sustain the populations. Between 2004 and 2008, in 20 out of the 57 population units, more bears were killed by hunting than the province's mortality rates allow. Combined with other human kills by wildlife management officials and by illegal poaching, mortality rates were exceeded in 36 areas between 2004 and 2008.

There is strong evidence that ending grizzly hunting would effectively reduce overall human-caused mortality to levels considered more sustainable by the government. For example, if hunting were not a factor in the Central Rockies GBPU, human-caused mortality would have fallen below the allowable mortality rate in 2004, 2007, and 2008. In some population units the mortality rate would even fall to zero.

The suggested solution to the problem of declining bear populations laid out in the David Suzuki Foundation report is to eliminate grizzly bear hunting in all parks and protected areas, and to establish a comprehensive network of core and benchmark no-hunting zones containing high-quality grizzly bear habitat. While this idea was established in the *British Columbia Grizzly Bear Conservation Strategy* through the establishment of GBMAs, the government has been slow to action and has only established three management areas since the strategy was published. Three management areas are obviously not enough, particularly when they are all concentrated on the coast and most grizzly bear mortality occurs in the province's interior regions.

At the opening of the April 2010 trophy hunting season, a network of animal and environmental protection groups worked together to condemn the season and call for the trophy hunt to be canceled. The coalition included the Humane Society International/ Canada, Pacific Wild, and Coastal First Nations. In total the network represents more than 20 million people worldwide. According to a 2009 poll, 78 percent of British Columbia residents are against the trophy hunt, particularly in the Great Bear Rainforest. Trophy hunting also jeopardizes the growing wildlife viewing industry, which is already more profitable than hunting. In March 2011, the David Suzuki Foundation launched an online lobbying campaign to renew its calls for the management areas. More than 300 grizzly bears were killed by humans in 2010, the majority due to legal trophy hunting.

BIBLIOGRAPHY

Books

Condon, Patrick M., and Jackie Teed. *Sustainability by Design: A Vision for a Region of 4 million: A Project of the Design Centre for Sustainability at the University of British Columbia.* Vancouver: Design Centre for Sustainability at the University of British Columbia, 2006.

Cashore, Benjamin William. *In Search of Sustainability: British Columbia Forest Policy in the 1990s.* Vancouver: UBC Press, 2001.

Howlett, Michael, et al. *British Columbia Politics and Government.* Toronto: Emond Montgomery, 2010.

Northeast British Columbia's Ultimate Potential for Conventional Natural Gas. Victoria: B.C. Ministry of Energy, Mines and Petroleum Resources, 2006.

Pacific Rim National Park Reserve of Canada Management Plan. Gatineau, Quebec: Parks Canada, 2010.

Web Sites

BC Bioenergy Strategy: Growing Our Natural Energy Advantage. Available from http://www.energyplan.gov.bc.ca/bioenergy

BC Energy Plan Report on Progress. British Columbia Ministry of Energy, Mines and Petroleum Resources. Available from http://www.energyplan.gov.bc.ca/report/BCEP_ReportOnProgress_web.pdf

British Columbia Climate Action for the 21st Century. Climate Action Secretariat, British Columbia Ministry of Environment. Available from http://www.env.gov.bc.ca/cas/pdfs/climate_action_21st_century.pdf

British Columbia Energy Plan: A Vision for Clean Energy Leadership. British Columbia Ministry of Energy, Mines, and Petroleum Resources. Available from http://www.energyplan.gov.bc.ca/default.htm

British Columbia Government and Service Employees Union. Available from http://www.bcgeu.ca/Green_economy_conference_a_success

British Columbia Greenhouse Gas Inventory Report 2008. British Columbia Ministry of Environment. Available from http://www.env.gov.bc.ca/cas/mitigation/ghg_inventory/pdf/pir-2008-full-report.pdf

British Columbia Ministry of Environment. Available from http://www.gov.bc.ca/env/

"British Columbia Organic Industry Overview." British Columbia Ministry of Agriculture and Lands. Available from http://www.agf.gov.bc.ca/organics/overview.htm

British Columbia's Green Economy: Building a Strong Low Carbon Future. Globe Foundation. Available from http://www.globe.ca/media/3887/bcge_report_feb_2010.pdf

"British Columbia To Develop Liquefied Natural Gas Industry." Office of the Premier. September 19, 2011. Available from http://www2.news.gov.bc.ca/news_releases_2009-2013/2011PREM0110-001179.htm

Canada: A New West Partnership. Accessed November 11, 2011. Available from http://www.newwestpartnership.ca/media

"Carbon-neutral B.C.: A first for North America." June 30, 2011.Available from http://www2.news.gov.bc.ca/news_releases_2009-2013/2011ENV0032-000805.htm

Center for Energy: British Columbia. Available from http://www.centreforenergy.com/FactsStats/MapsCanada/BC-EnergyMap.asp

Clean Energy Act (Bill 17-2010). Legislative Assembly of British Columbia. Available from http://www.leg.bc.ca/39th2nd/1st_read/gov17-1.htm

Climate Action Plan. British Columbia Ministry of Environment. Available from http://www.livesmartbc.ca/attachments/climateaction_plan_web.pdf

Climate Action Secretariat, British Columbia Ministry of Environment. Available from http://www.env.gov.bc.ca/cas

"Energy by the Numbers: British Columbia, Canada." Canadian Centre for Energy Information. September 2011. http://www.centreforenergy.com/Documents/AboutEnergy/ByTheNumbers/BC-bythenumbers.pdf

Connolly, Michelle; Jeff Gailus; and Faisal Moola. *Ensuring a Future for Canada's Grizzly Bears: A Report on the Sustainability of the Trophy Hunt in B. C.* The David Suzuki Foundation. Available from http://www.davidsuzuki.org/publications/downloads/2010/Ensuring-a-future-for-Canadas-grizzly-bears.pdf

Energy Efficiency Act [RSBC 1996] Chapter 114. British Columbia Laws. Available from http://www.bclaws.ca/EPLibraries/bclaws_new/document/ID/freeside/00_96114_01

Energy Efficient Buildings Strategy: More Action, Less. Government of British Columbia. Available from http://www.energyplan.gov.bc.ca/efficiency/PDF/EEBS-2008-Web.pdf

Forest and Range Practices Act. British Columbia Ministry of Forests and Range. Available from http://www.for.gov.bc.ca/code/

"Freshwater Sport Fishing in British Columbia." Prepared for Freshwater Fisheries Society of BC by GSGislason & Associates Ltd. October 2009. Available from http://www.gofishbc.com/docs/freshwater%20sport%20fishing%20in%20bc.pdf

Geist, Valerius, PhD. "Comments by Dr. Valerius Geist on the Report *Ensuring a Future for Canada's Grizzly Bears,* April 3, 2010, by the Suzuki Foundation." British Columbia Wildlife Federation. Available from http://www.bcwf.bc.ca/committees/wildlife/documents/ValGeistGrizzlyReportAReviewEdited.pdf

Green Energy Advisory Task Force Report. Government of British Columbia. Available from http://www.empr.gov.bc.ca/EAED/Documents/GreenEnergyAdvisoryTaskForce.pdf

"Grizzly Bear Conservation Strategy, June 1995." Government of British Columbia, Environmental Stewardship Division. Available from http://www.env.gov.bc.ca/wld/grzz/grst.html

Grow BC: A Guide to BC's Agriculture Resources. The British Columbia Agriculture in the Classroom Foundation. Available from http://www.aitc.ca/bc/uploads/growbc/1_intro.pdf

Indicators of Climate Change for British Columbia 2002. British Columbia Ministry of Water, Land and Air

Protection. Available from http://www.env.gov.bc.ca/cas/pdfs/indcc.pdf

Innovative Clean Energy Fund. Ministry of Small Business, Technology and Economic Development. Available from http://www.tted.gov.bc.ca/ICE-Fund/About/Pages/default.aspx

LiveSmart BC. Available from http://www.livesmartbc.ca

Ministerial Order No. M 100/2008: British Columbia Local Government Act. *British Columbia Codes 2006.* Available from http://www.bccodes.ca/Minister%20Order4.pdf

Opportunities to Explore: British Columbia Mining and Minerals 2009. British Columbia Ministry of Energy, Mines and Petroleum Resources. Available from http://www.empr.gov.bc.ca/Mining/investors/Documents/Opportunities_to_Explore%2811Sept2009%29.pdf

Pacific Institute for Climate Solutions. Available from http://www.pics.uvic.ca/index.php

Sullivan, Sean. "David Suzuki Calls on Premier to Create Grizzly Safe Haven." Global News. March 31, 2011. Available from http://www.globalnews.ca/david+suzuki+calls+on+premier+to+create+grizzly+safe+haven/216429/story.html

"The Forest Industry in B.C." Council of Forest Industries. Available from http://www.cofi.org/forest_industry_BC/default.htm

"This Green House: Building Fast Action For Climate Change and Green Jobs." The Columbia Institute. Available from http://www.columbiainstitute.ca/files/uploads/This_Green_House_Exec-summary.pdf

"Wildlife in British Columbia." Available from http://www.env.gov.bc.ca/fw/wildlife/

Manitoba

Manitoba is a Canadian prairie province known for its more than 110,000 lakes. The province's major industries include agriculture and energy, of which the province is a leader in producing hydroelectricity. Lake Manitoba and Lake Winnipeg are also vital to the province's economy, as the commercial fishing industry relies on these natural resources. Other major industries are transportation, manufacturing, mining, forestry, and tourism.

Climate

Manitoba is known for having some of the clearest skies in Canada year-round. Southern Manitoba has a fairly long frost-free season, consisting of between 120 and 140 days in the Red River Valley. It is also prone to high humidity in the summer months. There are three main climatic regions: the northern sections, which fall in the subarctic climate zone and have long, cold winters and brief, warm summers with little precipitation; the south, which is in the humid continental climate zone and has moderate precipitation; and the southwest, which, while also in the humid continental climate zone, tends to be drier, more prone to drought, is cold and windy in the winter, and is warm with moderate humidity in the summer.

In 2008, the government of Manitoba passed the Climate Change and Emissions Reductions Act. The act sets a target for reducing greenhouse gas emissions in the province of 6 percent less than Manitoba's total 1990 emissions by December 31, 2012. The province initiated a number of programs in order to begin efforts to meet this target, the majority of which are highlighted in the province's plan *Next Steps 2008: Action on Climate Change.* Some of these actions include expanding biofuel production and use, a coal-reduction strategy for Manitoba's last remaining coal-fired generating station, new building codes and standards, continuing to expand renewable power production, and creating a new Manitoba Sustainable Agriculture Practices Program.

The province also created a program called Community Led Emissions Reduction (CLER) in 2008 to encourage communities to take part in the reduction of greenhouse gas emissions. The four-year program was designed to provide communities with milestones and goals to work toward, as well as resources, tools, and funding. The importance of these programs is crucial, as the effects of climate change are already visible in the province. Northern communities are experiencing unpredictable winter conditions, polar bears are having fewer cubs and becoming thinner, and algae blooms on Lake Winnipeg are affecting water quality.

❧ Natural Resources, Water, and Agriculture

Natural Resources

There are remnants of the native prairie grasses in protected areas of Manitoba's central plains. Basswoods, cottonwoods, and oaks are common tree species there. Pelicans, beavers, raccoons, red foxes, and white-tailed deer are commonly found near Lake Manitoba; bison were once numerous but now exist only in small herds in protected areas. Some 27 species of waterfowl nest in southern Manitoba through the summer, and fall migrations bring thousands of ducks and geese. Polar bears and beluga whales are native to the Churchill area.

In 2010, there were 17 animal species listed as threatened or endangered. Endangered birds included the burrowing owl and the Eskimo curlew. There were no endangered mammals, but the polar bear, mule deer and woodland caribou were listed as threatened. Also in 2010, there were 10 plant species listed as threatened or endangered, including the western prairie fringed orchid and buffalo grass.

Manitoba's forest industry is the fifth largest manufacturing sector in the province. Northern

Manitoba's forests are dominated by pine, hemlock, and birch. As of 2003, Manitoba's forested area was 65 million acres (26.3 million ha), of which 37.6 million acres (15.2 million ha) was considered productive for timber. In 2008, the revenue of goods manufactured amounted to C$1.1 billion. The value of the forest industry's exports that same year came to C$472.8 million. The majority of exports go to the United States, followed by Europe and South America. The forest industry employs about 7,800 workers. Forestry also took on a greater role in the initiative to reduction of greenhouse gases with the creation of the Trees For Tomorrow program. The program called for planting five million trees in Manitoba over a five-year period, and in 2011 the province added a pledge of another one million trees for a total of six million. The program encourages tree planting on lands belonging to private owners, schools, municipalities, First Nations and more. Trees For Tomorrow provides landowners with a site inspection, development of a site plan, tree seedlings, overseeing of the planting, maintenance and follow-up survival assessments.

The mineral industry is Manitoba's second largest primary resource industry. In 2010, the combined value of mineral production for metals, industrial minerals, and petroleum totaled over C$2.5 billion. The province's mineral industry employs about 6,100 workers directly with another 18,000 indirectly. Base metals mined in the province include nickel (the province produces 20.1 percent of Canada's total), copper, zinc, and gold. Manitoba is the only province in Canada that produces the specialty minerals lithium, cesium, and tantalum. Industrial minerals such as dolomite, spodumene, silver, gypsum, salt, granite, limestone, peat, lime, sand, and gravel are also found in Manitoba.

Water

Manitoba is known as the land of 100,000 lakes, a legacy of enormous Lake Agassiz, which covered much of the province after the glaciers retreated. Lake Winnipeg, Lake Winnipegosis, and Lake Manitoba dominate the southern topography; Lake Winnipeg is the seventh-largest fresh-water lake in North America.

Manitoba is also home to extensive wetland areas in the southeastern, central, and northern areas of the province, which have accumulated peat deposits over time. Peat extraction industries operate in Manitoba bog sites, and much of the sphagnum peat moss that is created is exported to the United States for the horticulture industry. Peat harvesting in Canada has been widely debated when it comes to the issue of sustainability. According to the Canadian Sphagnum Peat Moss Association, a bog can be harvested for a period of between 15 and 50 years, because such small sections are taken each time. Peat harvesting companies

follow reclamation procedures to return the bog to its original state, minus the peat, to maintain wildlife habitats. The Manitoba government considers peat harvesting to be a growth industry.

Manitoba also has large areas of salt water wetlands that are influenced by the ebb and flow of sea water along Hudson Bay. These wetlands are important to nesting and migrating waterfowl, especially Canada and snow geese. Major rivers include the Red, Assiniboine, Nelson, Winnipeg, Hayes, Whiteshell, and Churchill Rivers.

The majority of commercial fishing activity occurs on Lake Manitoba and Lake Winnipeg, and generates more than C$50 million in economic activity each year. The majority of fish are exported out of the country. Pickerel (walleye), sauger, lake whitefish, northern pike, yellow perch, and lake trout are the most highly valued species harvested in Manitoba.

Agriculture

According to the 2008 Manitoba Department of Agriculture Census, the province was home to over 19,000 farms on a total of 19.1 million acres (7.7 million ha). The province's largest single crop is spring wheat, covering 3 million acres (1.2 million ha) or 25.7 percent of the province's crop land. Canola was the second largest crop accounting for 19.6 percent of crop land, followed by alfalfa, barley, and oats. Manitoba boasts the largest hog farms in Canada, with a reported 2.9 million pigs. Pigs are second in number to hens and chickens, and are followed by cattle, calves, and turkeys.

About 4 percent of Manitoba's farms reported organic production in 2006. The majority of these farms produced hay and field crops. Depending on their commodity mix, farms often have more than one organic status in the province. About 24 percent of these farms produced certified organic products, with almost 7 percent in transition to becoming certified.

⚘ Energy

Manitoba's key energy resources include hydropower, crude oil, geothermal, and wind. Approximately 9,600 people were employed in Manitoba's petroleum and utility industries in 2010, about 1.5 percent of the province's labor force.

Manitoba's current oil production is located in the southwest portion of the province along the northeastern flank of the Williston Basin, a sedimentary basin that also occupies portions of southern Saskatchewan, North Dakota, South Dakota, and Montana. Total production to May 2009 was 265 million barrels. In 2008, the province exported C$690 million worth of petroleum, mainly to the United States.

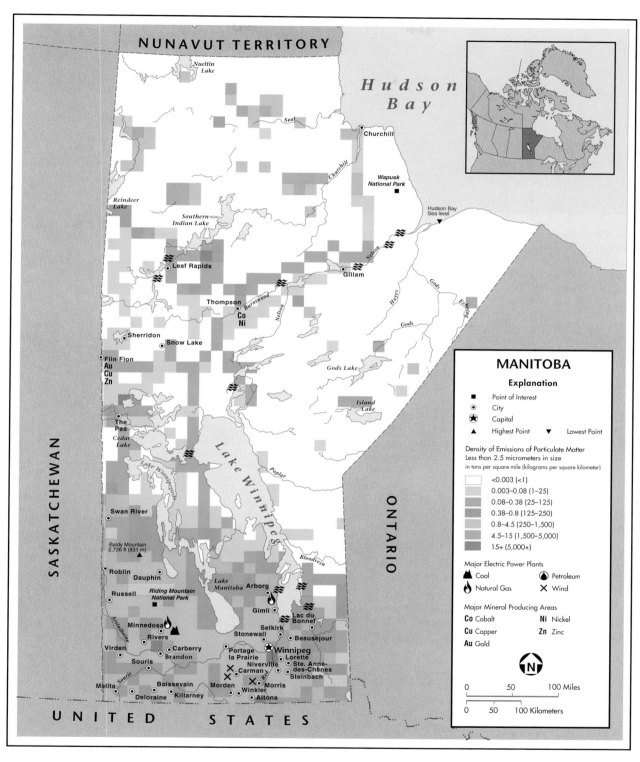

MANITOBA

Explanation

- ■ Point of Interest
- ⊙ City
- ★ Capital
- ▲ Highest Point   ▼ Lowest Point

Density of Emissions of Particulate Matter
Less than 2.5 micrometers in size
in tons per square mile (kilograms per square kilometer)

- <0.003 (<1)
- 0.003–0.08 (1–25)
- 0.08–0.38 (25–125)
- 0.38–0.8 (125–250)
- 0.8–4.5 (250–1,500)
- 4.5–15 (1,500–5,000)
- 15+ (5,000+)

Major Electric Power Plants
- ▲ Coal   ◉ Petroleum
- 🔥 Natural Gas   ✕ Wind

Major Mineral Producing Areas
- **Co** Cobalt   **Ni** Nickel
- **Cu** Copper   **Zn** Zinc
- **Au** Gold

0   50   100 Miles
0   50   100 Kilometers

SOURCES: *Energy Facts and Statistics.* Centre for Energy. Available from http://www.centreforenergy.com/FactsStats/MapsCanada; "Geographical Highlights." *The Canadian Encyclopedia.* Available from http://www.encyclopediecanadienne.ca/geoHighlights/canmap_geog_v1_eng.swf; "Highest Points by Province and Territory." *The Atlas of Canada.* Natural Resources Canada. Available from http://atlas.nrcan.gc.ca/site/english/learningresources/facts/faq.html#points; "Mining in Canada: Map." *Mining in Canada.* The Mining Association of Canada. Available from http://www.mining.ca/site/images/MapofCanada.pdf; "Particulate Matter < 2.5 Micrometers (PM2.5) Emission in 2007." *CAC Density Maps.* Environment Canada. Available from http://www.ec.gc.ca/inrp-npri/default.asp?lang=en&n=BD725B2A-1. © *2011 Cengage Learning.*

Manitoba also has large areas of salt water wetlands that are influenced by the ebb and flow of sea water along Hudson Bay. These wetlands are important to nesting and migrating waterfowl. © *All Canada Photos/Alamy*

Manitoba Hydro: Dominating Manitoba's Energy Sector

Manitoba has 14 hydroelectric generating stations, all owned and operated by Manitoba Hydro. The company serves 532,000 electric customers throughout Manitoba and 264,000 natural gas customers in various communities throughout southern Manitoba. The generating stations lie primarily on the Winnipeg, Saskatchewan, Laurie, and Nelson Rivers. The company also exports much of its electricity to neighboring provinces and the midwestern United States. During the 2009–10 year, export sales totaled C$427 million with 85 percent derived from the U.S. market and 15 percent from sales to Canadian markets. The company also purchases electricity from one of the largest wind farms in Canada, located near St. Léon, Manitoba. They have also negotiated a 27-year power purchase agreement to buy wind energy from a new 138-megawatt wind farm at St. Joseph, in southern Manitoba.

The province, which ranks first in Canada in energy efficiency, also has over 7,000 geothermal systems—many of which are residential installations. The province boasts several subdivisions that utilize geothermal heat pump technology, including a subdivision in Wawanesa, Manitoba.

Manitoba also leads other provinces in production and use of biodiesel fuel. Biodiesel fuel is produced from vegetable oilseed crops, animal fats, and wood pulp waste, which burns cleaner than diesel. Those in the Manitoba energy sector are exploring the use of pelletized grass, which utilizes switchgrass—a native perennial to Manitoba—as a renewable energy source. Continually improving technology, which allows for the combustion of the pelletized grass, creates new opportunity for renewable energy as well as for farmers looking to create new revenue streams.

Manitoba Provincial Profile

Physical Characteristics

Land area	213,729 square miles (553,556 sq km)
Freshwater area	36,387 square miles (94,242 sq km)
Highest point	Baldy Mountain 2,730 feet (832 m)
Forest lands (2011)	46.9 million acres (19.0 million ha)
Provincial parks (2011)	53

Energy Statistics

Total electricity generated (2009)	33.8 million megawatt hours
Hydroelectric energy generation (2009)	33.5 million megawatt hours
Wind energy generation (2009)	NA
Tidal energy generation (2009)	NA
Biomass energy capacity (2009)	NA
Crude oil reserves (2009)	52.8 million barrels (8.4 million cu m)
Natural gas reserves (2009)	NA
Natural gas liquids (2009)	NA

Pollution Statistics

Carbon output (2009)	1.6 million tons of CO_2 (1.5 million t)
Federal contaminated sites receiving funds (2008)	15
Particulate matter (less than 2.5 micrometers) emissions (2009)	52,593 tons per year (47,712 t/yr)

SOURCES: *Canada's Greenhouse Gas Emissions.* Environment Canada. Available from http://www.ec.gc.ca/ges-ghg/default. asp?lang=En&n=1357A041-1; *Canada Year Book, 2011.* Statistics Canada. Available from http://www.statcan.gc.ca/ pub/11-402-x/11-402-x2011000-eng.htm; *Energy Facts and Statistics.* Centre for Energy. Available from http:// www.centreforenergy.com/FactsStats/MapsCanada; *Federal Contaminated Sites.* Government of Canada. Available from http://www.federalcontaminatedsites.gc.ca/index-eng. aspx; "Forest Land by Province and Territory." Statistics Canada. Available from http://www40.statcan.gc.ca/l01/ cst01/envi34a-eng.htm; "Geographical Highlights." *The Canadian Encyclopedia.* Available from http://www. encyclopediecanadienne.ca/geoHighlights/canmap_geog_v1_ eng.swf; *National Pollutant Release Inventory.* Environment Canada. Available from http://ec.gc.ca/pdb/websol/emissions/ap/ ap_query_e.cfm

© *2011 Cengage Learning.*

❧ Green Business, Green Building, Green Jobs

Green Business

Manitoba has a number of incentives and rebates in place for businesses that wish to become more energy efficient. One example is the Green Energy Manufacturing Tax Credit. This refundable income tax credit is equal to 10 percent of the value of qualifying property produced in Manitoba and sold before 2019 for residential or commercial use. Qualifying property includes equipment

Manitoba has 14 hydroelectric generating stations, including the Seven Sisters power-generating station. © *Terrance Klassen/Alamy*

for wind power, solar energy, geothermal energy, and hydrogen fuel cells. In 2008, geothermal ground source heating systems were made eligible for the tax credit, and in 2009 the credit was expanded to include solar thermal heating equipment. Manitoba also has a number of incentives for businesses that replace their commercial appliances with more energy efficient machines.

Manitoba Hydro also offers rebates and loans to businesses in the province. Some of their programs include the New Buildings Program, where a business can design, build, and operate their new building to Power Smart standards; the Earth Power Program, which works to cut heating, cooling, and water heating costs with energy efficient and environmentally friendly geothermal heat pumps; and the Commercial Custom Measures program, which custom-designs electrical and natural gas systems for commercial buildings in order to provide the highest amount of energy savings.

Green Building

Manitoba introduced a Green Building Policy in April 2007. The policy makes sure that new, provincially-funded buildings are less costly to operate and maintain, use less energy, and produce fewer greenhouse gas emissions than conventional buildings. In order to ensure this, the policy requires the use of an integrated design process, minimum levels of energy efficiency, life-cycle costing of the building, a minimum certification of LEED Silver, and a preference for low or zero carbon renewable energy sources.

On the municipal level, Winnipeg has been working with Manitoba Hydro since 2002 in order to retrofit a number of buildings to improve their energy efficiency. As part of the city's Climate Change Action Plan, they have made improvements to the City Hall Complex and the Pan Am pool and weight room facilities. The City Hall Complex was certified under the Building Owners and Managers Association of Canada's "Go Green" Environmental Certification program in 2008.

Green Jobs

Manitoba's colleges offer a variety of programs to prepare students for green jobs. Red River College in Winnipeg offers courses in its Water and Wastewater School, where students can gain the knowledge and skills required to enter the field of water and wastewater treatment, or upgrade their abilities as a water treatment facility operator. The college also offers a concentration in Environmental Protection Technology under its Civil Engineering Technology Program. This option prepares students for careers in water supply and waste disposal, recycling and reuse, hydraulics, soil analysis, water and air quality, legislation and remediation, remote sensing, mapping and modeling, occupational health and safety, and environmental analysis.

The University of Manitoba's Natural Resources Institute offers students a master's in natural resource management and a doctorate in Natural Resources and Environmental Management. Students and faculty in the Institute research resource problems and issues such as natural resources policy, environmental and risk assessment, sustainable development, northern resources and native peoples, and environmental hazard management. Students and faculty also participate in community outreach programs involving city of Winnipeg waste management, the province of Manitoba water strategic plan, and the province's sustainable development initiatives.

The provincial power giant Manitoba Hydro has an Operating Technician Training Program, which prepares students for work in the hydroelectric field. Along with training associated with the Power Electrician Journeyman or the Industrial Mechanic Apprenticeship programs, students will receive training in operating Hydro and HVDC Converter Stations, including developing skills and techniques in control and regulation of all operating elements and auxiliaries used to generate and convert electrical energy in a power system. This will result in a dual certification as a Power Electrician/ Station Operator or an Industrial Mechanic/Station Operator.

⚜ Blue-Green Algae Blooms in Lake Winnipeg

As the sixth-largest freshwater lake in Canada, Manitoba's Lake Winnipeg accounts for the majority of the province's C$24 million-a-year fishing industry. However, this thriving industry has been threatened since the 1990s by blue-green algae blooms forming in the lake, depleting oxygen levels and threatening the lake's entire ecosystem.

What makes these algae blooms such a concern is that they produce toxins; blue-green algae that has

Blue-green algae bloom at Grand Beach on Lake Winnipeg.
© Terrance Klassen/Alamy

occurred in dugouts on farmland has been known to kill cattle. The algae occur when there is more phosphorus in the water than nitrogen. Only blue-green algae can supplement nitrogen, and therefore outcompetes other types of non-toxic algae. Because the algae produce toxins, it isn't consumed by zooplankton—tiny animals that are food for fish. The algae are therefore left to grow continually until they produce blooms that can grow to be hundreds of square miles. When the algae eventually die and begin to decay, the process, called eutrophication, uses up the oxygen in the water, causing the death of fish and other species.

Farms vs. Cities: Where Is the Phosphorus Coming From?

While the excess phosphorus entering Lake Winnipeg comes from both farms and city wastewater that is pumped into the lake's watershed (which covers more than 380,000 square miles), there has been some debate about which is the bigger culprit. The city of Winnipeg has come under scrutiny about how much their wastewater contributes to Lake Winnipeg's phosphorus levels. While the city is working on converting their wastewater treatment process to help lower phosphorus levels, city officials are concerned that the cost of upgrading all of the city's treatment plants would be too much. It would require an estimated C$300 million to upgrade the plants, which would result in higher water rates for residents. Considering that only about six percent of the phosphorus comes from the city of Winnipeg, officials are unsure if the transition would make enough of a difference to justify such a cost.

City officials also claim that agriculture may be more to blame for the phosphorus in Lake Winnipeg, and state that efforts to reduce nutrient levels should focus on that sector. Phosphorus enters the water from cow manure, which is additionally used to fertilize crops, adding even more of the nutrients to the run-off that ends up in Lake Winnipeg. While government reports state that agriculture in Manitoba is responsible for much of the phosphorus in Lake Winnipeg, farmers remain skeptical. They claim that they are not the root cause of Lake Winnipeg's algae problem because they take measures to keep phosphorus levels in check, such as giving livestock special feed to reduce the amount of phosphorus in their manure and rotating crops so that the land does not become over-fertilized.

As the finger-pointing continues between farmers and city officials about who is more to blame, it can safely be said that both of them are responsible for at least some the phosphorus that ends up in Lake Winnipeg, it also looks as though U.S. farms are to blame, as well. The Red River flows north from Minnesota and North Dakota into Lake Winnipeg, and carries with it run-off from farms along the way. The Lake Winnipeg Research Consortium states that about half of the phosphorus that ends up in the lake comes from these states, where agriculture is the biggest contributor.

Finding a Solution

Since the phosphorus arrives in Lake Winnipeg from a number of areas, the solution to the problem will have to come from a number of different directions. Wastewater services for the city of Winnipeg have begun upgrading their water treatment process in order to filter out nitrogen and phosphorus before the water is pumped back into the river system. They will be using a biological nutrient removal process, which involves growing a culture of bacteria that consumes the nitrogen and phosphorus. Once those nutrients are consumed, the bacteria are killed and the water can be discharged.

Both Manitoba and Minnesota have restricted phosphates in dish washing detergent and lawn fertilizers. Legislation has passed that encourages Manitoba farmers to use more buffer strips at the edges of their fields to slow erosion and runoff, though researchers say these won't necessarily prevent phosphorus from entering the watershed and ultimately Lake Winnipeg. Another factor in the increase of phosphorus is regular flooding that occurs in the watershed in both the United States and Canada. Phosphorus found in dozens of small dams that are used to ease downstream flooding and irrigate fields is absorbed by plants when it is reused. These dams could prove to be an integral part of the fight to lower nutrient levels in the watershed.

In September 2010, a Memorandum of Understanding was signed between Manitoba and the Canadian federal government to form the Lake Winnipeg Basin Initiative. The Initiative has five goals: to reduce blue-green algae blooms; to ensure fewer beach closings; to keep in place a sustainable fishery; to provide a clean lake for recreation; and restore the ecological integrity of the lake. The Canadian government has invested C\$17.7 million in the Initiative, which includes a comprehensive scientific research and monitoring program, governance initiatives, and support for community-based stewardship projects aimed at cleaning up the lake.

The gravity of the situation became clear when Dr. Peter Leavitt, who chairs research in environmental change and society at the University of Regina, released a five-year study of Lake Winnipeg in May 2011. The study, commissioned by the province, painted a picture of the challenges facing the lake, and identified clear benchmarks for returning the lake to health. Leavitt recommended reducing phosphorus levels by 50 percent in order to return it to pre-1990 conditions and to significantly reduce algae blooms. "Phosphorus levels in the lake are now worse than they were in Lake Erie when people were describing that lake as dead," Leavitt was quoted as saying in a release issued by the Manitoba government. "We're at a tipping point and if something isn't done now, the consequences will be dire." After the release of the report, Manitoba premier Greg Selinger pledged to launch an action plan to the necessary steps and return the lake to health.

BIBLIOGRAPHY

Books

Fosket, Jennifer. *Living Green*. Gabriola Island, BC: New Society Publishers, 2009.

Guide to the National Parks of Canada. Washington, DC: National Geographic, 2011.

The Importance of Nature to Canadians: The Economic Significance of Nature-Related Activities. Ottawa: Environment Canada, 2000.

Penziwol, Shelley *From Asessippi to Zed Lake: A Guide to Manitoba's Provincial Parks*. Winnipeg: Great Plains Publications, 2011.

Riding Mountain National Park of Canada and Riding Mountain Park East Gate Registration Complex National Historic Site of Canada Management Plan. Ottawa: Parks Canada, 2007.

Visser, Emily, and Luigi Ferrara. *Canada Innovates: Sustainable Building*. Toronto: Key Porter Books, 2008.

Wapusk National Park of Canada Management Plan. Ottawa: Parks Canada, 2007.

Web Sites

"Alternative and Renewable Energy." Manitoba Entrepreneurship, Training, and Trade. Available from http://www.gov.mb.ca/trade/globaltrade/environ/energy.html

C135. The Climate Change and Emissions Reductions Act. Manitoba Legislative Assembly. Available from http://web2.gov.mb.ca/laws/statutes/ccsm/c135e.php

Centre for Energy: Manitoba. Available from http://www.centreforenergy.com/FactsStats/MapsCanada/MB-EnergyMap.asp

Civil Engineering Technology. Red River College. Available from http://me.rrc.mb.ca/Catalogue/ProgramInfo.aspx?ProgCode=CIVCF-DP&RegionCode=WPG

Cleaning Up Lake Winnipeg. Environment Canada. Available from http://www.ec.gc.ca/doc/eau-water/winnipeg_e.html

"Community Led Emissions Reduction." Manitoba Local Government. Available from http://www.gov.mb.ca/ia/climate/index.html

Energy Efficiency. City of Winnipeg. Available from http://winnipeg.ca/Interhom/GreenSpace/EnergyEfficiency.stm

"Environmental Concerns." Canadian Sphagnum Peat Moss Association. Available from http://www.peatmoss.com/concern.php

Forestry Branch. Manitoba Department of Conservation. Available from http://www.gov.mb.ca/conservation/forestry/index.html

Green Energy Manufacturing Tax Credit. Manitoba Department of Entrepreneurship, Training and Trade. Available from http://www.gov.mb.ca/ctt/invest/busfacts/govt/manuf_taxc.html

Gunderson, Dan. "Farmers, scientists struggle with Red River phosphorus." MPR News. June 18, 2010. Available from http://minnesota.publicradio.org/display/web/2010/06/17/lake-winnipeg/

Gunderson, Dan. "Red River pollution threatening Lake Winnipeg." MPR News. June 17, 2010. Available from http://minnesota.publicradio.org/display/web/2010/06/17/lake-winnipeg/

Manitoba Agricultural Profile, 2006. Manitoba Agriculture, Food and Rural Initiatives. Available from http://www.gov.mb.ca/agriculture/statistics/census/mb_agricultural_profile.pdf

Manitoba Green Building Policy. Manitoba Department of Infrastructure and Transportation. Available from http://winnipeg.ca/Interhom/GreenSpace/EnergyEfficiency.stm

Manitoba Hydro. Available from http://www.hydro.mb.ca/index.shtml?WT.mc_id=2000

"Manitoba Oil Facts." Manitoba Department of Innovation, Energy and Mines. Available from http://www.gov.mb.ca/stem/petroleum/oilfacts/index.html

Natural Resources Institute. University of Manitoba. Available from http://www.umanitoba.ca/insti tutes/natural_resources/index.php

Next Steps 2008: Action on Climate Change. Province of Manitoba. Available from http://www.gov.mb.ca/ beyond_kyoto/

"Province Will Launch Action Plan To Save Lake Winnipeg: Selinger." Manitoba Government. May 31, 2011. Available from http://news.gov.mb.ca/ news/index.html?archive=2011-05-01&item=11618

"A Sea of Troubles: Lake Winnipeg in Crisis." CBC. Available from http://www.cbc.ca/manitoba/ features/lakewinnipeg/index.html

"Species at Risk." Manitoba Department of Conserva tion. Available from http://www.gov.mb.ca/ conservation/wildlife/sar/sarlist.html

"Trees For Tomorrow." Manitoba Forestry Branch. Available from http://www.gov.mb.ca/conserva-tion/forestry/t4t/index.html

W65. The Water Protection Act. Continuing Consolida-tion of the Statutes of Manitoba. Manitoba Legislative Assembly. Available from http://web2.gov.mb.ca/ laws/statutes/ccsm/w065e.php

Water and Wastewater School. Red River College. Available from http://me.rrc.mb.ca/Catalogue/ ProgramInfo.aspx?ProgCode=WATWP-NA&Re-gionCode=WPG

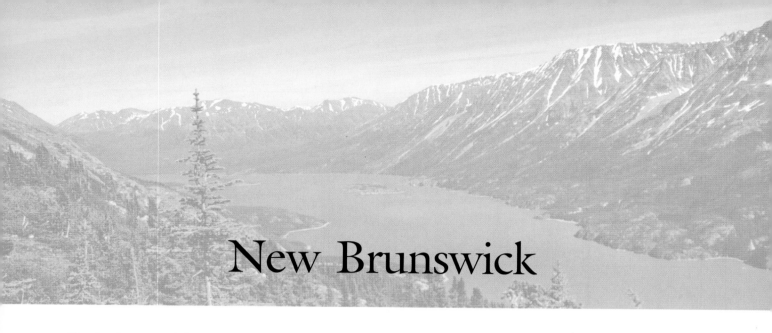

New Brunswick

The development of New Brunswick's green economy is based largely on plans that strengthen and improve the province's status as a major energy hub, where energy related companies, people, research, generation, distribution, and related activities and projects are located. But energy is only one point of the government's comprehensive development plan, which sets a goal for the province to reach self-sufficiency by 2026. Further developments in forestry industries and agriculture, and retaining the strength of the region's fishing industries are also important concerns for residents, businesses, and government alike.

Climate

The northern portion of the province has a continental climate featuring cold winters and warm summers. Temperatures along the northern coast are influenced by the cool waters of the Gulf of St. Lawrence. The southern region features a maritime climate that is cooler in the summer and mild in the winter, with coastal temperatures affected by the warmer waters of Northumberland Strait and the Bay of Fundy.

Climate Change According to a report from the New Brunswick Department of Environment, the effects of global climate change have already been noted throughout the province in a number of ways. There has been an increase in the frequency of winter thaws and in the intensity of rainstorms. In the north, winter snow pack has decreased by 25 percent since the 1970s, while in the south snowpack has decreased by nearly 50 percent. Since the early 1900s, the sea level has risen by about 11 inches (30 cm).

Recognizing the effects of greenhouse gas emissions on the climate, the province has initiated the *Climate Change Action Plan 2007–2012*. The plan outlines a series of policies and actions to be implemented to reach a set goal of reducing greenhouse gas emissions to 1990 levels by 2012 and by 10 percent below 1990 levels by 2020. The provincial economic development plan introduced in 2010, entitled *Our Action Plan to Be Self-Sufficient in New Brunswick*, will play a big role in the reduction of greenhouse gas emissions as well, since it hinges on the development of energy efficiency products and services, along with a push for greater use of renewable energy resources.

Natural Resources, Water, and Agriculture

Natural Resources

Forests and Parks About 85 percent of the province is covered in forest, with softwoods of spruce, balsam fir, pine, and cedar accounting for about 63 percent of forest species. Hardwoods include red and sugar maples, yellow and white birch, aspen, and beech. There are at least fourteen communities that are entirely dependent on forestry operations, with as many as 100 communities heavily dependent on forest industries, including sawmill and pulp and paper operations. According to the New Brunswick Forest Products Association's publication, *Forestry at a Glance*, forest industries accounted for about C$2.1 million each year, or 11.2 percent of the provincial GDP in 2006.

Further developments in forestry industries, particular those that involve a sustainable harvest for biomass energy sources, is a key factor in *Our Action Plan to Be Self-Sufficient in New Brunswick*, the economic development plan introduced in 2010. The plan set a goal for the province to be self-sufficient by 2026. Part of the plan includes exporting forest bio-products. A two-phase study completed by the Forest Products Association of Canada predicted that global demand for such product could reach more than $200 billion by 2015. But it also means further utilizing the province's forests for energy at home. There are multiple pulp and paper mills in New Brunswick that run on biomass energy. However, concerns remain that forestry areas should be limited to

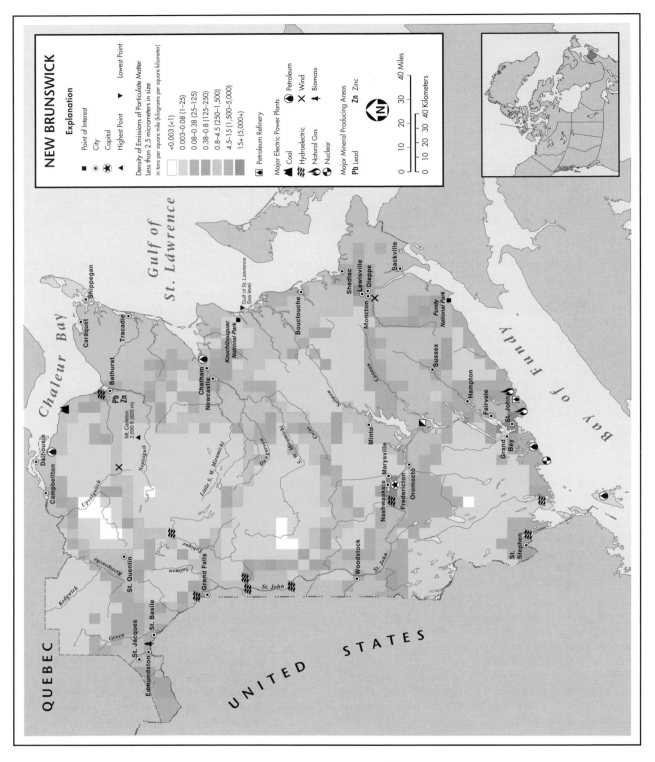

NEW BRUNSWICK

Explanation

■ Point of Interest
◉ City
✪ Capital
▲ Highest Point
▼ Lowest Point

Density of Emissions of Particulate Matter
Less than 2.5 micrometers in size
in tons per square mile (kilograms per square kilometer)

<0.003 (<1)
0.003–0.08 (1–25)
0.08–0.38 (25–125)
0.38–0.8 (125–250)
0.8–4.5 (250–1,500)
4.5–15 (1,500–5,000)
15+ (5,000+)

◉ Petroleum Refinery

Major Electric Power Plants
◆ Coal
⚡ Hydroelectric
⚙ Natural Gas
☢ Nuclear
◉ Petroleum
✕ Wind
▲ Biomass

Major Mineral Producing Areas
Pb Lead   **Zn** Zinc

0 10 20 30 40 Miles
0 10 20 30 40 Kilometers

SOURCES: *Energy Facts and Statistics.* Centre for Energy. Available from http://www.centreforenergy.com/FactsStats/MapsCanada; "Geographical Highlights." *The Canadian Encyclopedia.* Available from http://www.encyclopediecanadienne.ca/geoHighlights/cannmap_geog_v1_eng.swf; "Highest Points by Province and Territory." *The Atlas of Canada.* Natural Resources Canada. Available from http://atlas.nrcan.gc.ca/site/english/learningresources/facts/faq.html#points; "Mining in Canada: Map." *Mining in Canada.* The Mining Association of Canada. Available from http://www.mining.ca/site/images/MapofCanada.pdf; "Particulate Matter < 2.5 Micrometers (PM2.5) Emission in 2007." *CAC Density Maps.* Environment Canada. Available from http://www.ec.gc.ca/inrp-npri/default.asp?lang=en&n=BD725B2A-1. © 2011 Cengage Learning.

The Bay of Fundy. © *Danita Delimont/Alamy*

prevent overharvesting. To that end, New Brunswick was the first province to create a biomass policy with guidelines for how much of the Crown (public land) forests could be harvested.

The province is home to nine provincial parks and two national parks. Monte Carlton Provincial Park is home to more wildlife species that any other area in the province with at least one hundred species of birds, including grouse, owls, woodpeckers, ravens, and thrushes, and thirty species of mammals, including moose, red fox, lynx, porcupine, beaver, white-tailed deer, and red squirrel. Black bear, coyote, and bobcat can be found in parts of the province as well. Fundy National Park is home to the rare bird's-eye primrose, which is only found in this area of Canada. There are 31 threatened and endangered plant and animal species in New Brunswick, according to the Canadian Species at Risk Public Registry. Threatened and endangered animal species include the Canadian warbler, eastern meadowlark, least bittern and striped bass. Plant species include Gulf of St. Lawrence aster and Anticosti aster.

Minerals Mineral production in the province (including coal) increased in value from about C$906 million in 2005 to C$1.4 billion in 2006. The metals sector represents about two-thirds of mineral production, with zinc, lead, and copper the most valuable metals. New Brunswick mines also produce limestone, silica, dolomite, gypsum, and potash.

Water

Coastal Waters The province of New Brunswick is surrounded on three sides by the Baie des Chaleurs, the Gulf of St. Lawrence, Northumberland Strait, and the Bay of Fundy. The Gulf of St. Lawrence and the Bay of Fundy support a major commercial fishing industry for the province, with more than two thousand fishermen active in their waters. Commercial landings account for about C$200 million each year and more than 150 coastal communities rely heavily on fishing industries. Lobster and snow crab are among the most valuable catches. The aquaculture sector in New Brunswick ranks as the second largest in the country. Salmon farming represents nearly 95 percent of the sector's value. The primary commercial species produced in the province include Atlantic salmon, American oysters, rainbow and speckled trout, and blue mussels. Other species such as bay scallops, halibut, and sturgeon are growing in commercial potential.

New Brunswick Provincial Profile

Physical Characteristics

Land area	27,587 square miles (71,450 sq km)
Freshwater area	563 square miles (1,458 sq km)
Highest point	Mount Carleton 2,680 feet (817 m)
Forest lands (2011)	15.1 million acres (6.1 million ha)
Provincial parks (2011)	11

Energy Statistics

Total electricity generated (2009)	13.1 million megawatt hours
Hydroelectric energy generation (2009)	3.3 million megawatt hours
Wind energy generation (2009)	NA
Tidal energy generation (2009)	NA
Biomass energy capacity (2009)	38 megawatts
Crude oil reserves (2009)	NA
Natural gas reserves (2009)	NA
Natural gas liquids (2009)	NA

Pollution Statistics

Carbon output (2009)	11.1 million tons of CO_2 (10.0 million t)
Federal contaminated sites receiving funds (2008)	6
Particulate matter (less than 2.5 micrometers) emissions (2009)	27,273 tons per year (24,742 t/yr)

SOURCES: *Canada's Greenhouse Gas Emissions*. Environment Canada. Available from http://www.ec.gc.ca/ges-ghg/default. asp?lang=En&n=1357A041-1; *Canada Year Book, 2011*. Statistics Canada. Available from http://www.statcan.gc.ca/ pub/11-402-x/11-402-x2011000-eng.htm; *Energy Facts and Statistics*. Centre for Energy. Available from http:// www.centreforenergy.com/FactsStats/MapsCanada; *Federal Contaminated Sites*. Government of Canada. Available from http://www.federalcontaminatedsites.gc.ca/index-eng. aspx; "Forest Land by Province and Territory." Statistics Canada. Available from http://www40.statcan.gc.ca/l01/ cst01/envi34a-eng.htm; "Geographical Highlights." *The Canadian Encyclopedia*. Available from http://www. encyclopediecanadienne.ca/geoHighlights/canmap_geog_v1_ eng.swf; *National Pollutant Release Inventory*. Environment Canada. Available from http://ec.gc.ca/pdb/websol/emissions/ap/ ap_query_e.cfm

© 2011 Cengage Learning.

High tide overlooking the Flowerpot rocks in Fundy Bay. © GraÃ§a Victoria/ShutterStock.com

St. Lawrence. The other ports are Bayside, Dalhousie, and Miramichi.

The province has several coastal and inland wetlands, providing habitats for many bird and plant species. A large number of piping plover can be found along the shores of the Acadian Peninsula or nesting on the beaches of the Northumberland Strait.

Rivers, Lakes, and Wells Major rivers include the Miramichi, Nepisguit, Restigouche, and St. John. The Mactaquac, Grand Falls, and Beechwood hydroelectric generating stations are located along the St. John River. The Sisson and Tobique generating stations are found on the Tobique River and the Milltown station, the oldest in the province, is located on the St. Croix Rover. Hydroelectric power accounts for 22.5 percent of the province's total installed capacity.

The largest natural lake is Grand Lake, which is only 7 feet (2 m) above sea level, even though it is more than 43 miles (70 km) from the open sea. Several reservoirs have been formed behind dams on the St. John River.

There are more than 100,000 private wells in New Brunswick, supplying drinking water for about 300,000 residents.

Whale watching is a favorite activity on the Bay of Fundy, which is also famous for its unusual tides. Twice a day, with the rising tide of the Atlantic Ocean, nearly 110 billion tons (100 billion t) of water stream past the rocky headland in the Bay of Fundy. The tides rushing back to the Saint John River actually force the river to temporarily flow upstream at Reversing Falls. The eastern end of the Bay of Fundy has tides of nearly 50 feet (15 m), the highest in the world.

The province has five cargo ports. The Port of St. John is the busiest port in Eastern Canada, handling more than 30 million tons (27 million t) of cargo each year. Port of Belledune is located in Chaleur Bay in the Gulf of

Agriculture

Less than 20 percent of the total land area is suitable for agricultural land and only about one-third of that is used as cropland. Potatoes are by far the top commodity, accounting for about C$133 million in farm cash receipts (28 percent of total) in 2009. Floriculture and greenhouse sales came in at over C$26 million. Blueberries, barley, oats, and wheat are other primary crops. Poultry, beef, and hogs are significant products as well. Organic farms and produce are certified under national guidelines, and there are more than 60 farms and producers listed from New Brunswick in the Atlantic Canadian Organic Regional Network database. Organic farmers and residents also have the resource of the Falls Brook Centre, which is a sustainable community demonstration and training center in New Brunswick. The 400-acre (162-ha) site is certified organic and provides on-site programming to promote sustainability in a variety of areas, including agriculture.

Under *Our Action Plan to Be Self-Sufficient in New Brunswick*, the provincial economic development plan introduced in 2010, officials hope to revive the agricultural industry through the development of new value-added products and biofuel crops.

❧ Energy: A World-Class Energy Hub

Natural Gas and Oil

With a diverse mix of energy resources, the province of New Brunswick bills itself as a world-class energy hub. Natural gas is produced from the Dover field near Moncton and the McCully field near Sussex. The Maritimes and Northeast Pipeline in the south transports natural gas from the Sable Offshore Energy Project off the coast of Nova Scotia to markets in Atlantic Canada and the New England states of the United States. While the state has not produced crude oil since 1988, the Irving refinery in Saint John is the largest in Canada, producing 300,000 barrels of petroleum products per day. About 58 percent of these products are exported to the United States.

Electricity

The Point Lepreau nuclear power plant provides about 30 percent of the province's electricity. The plant, which opened in 1983, is operated by New Brunswick Power Nuclear Corporation, a subsidiary of the largest electric utility in Atlantic Canada, New Brunswick Power Corporation. The plant was taken offline in spring 2008 to refurbish the reactor with the goal of extending its operations until 2032. The refurbishment met several technical challenges that delayed its restart date from October 2009 to fall 2012. In the meantime, NB Power imported energy to replace the lost generating capacity from the offline nuclear plant. Officials anticipated the delay would cost an additional $1 billion in replacement fuel costs.

The coal-fired Grand Lake Generating Station was closed in March 2010, after the closing of the province's last operating coal mine at Salmon Harbour in December 2009.

Renewables

New Brunswick has begun to take advantage of its great potential for wind power. The Kent Hills farm, located southwest of Moncton, opened in 2008 as the first in the province. The Caribou Mountain Wind Farm near Bathurst became operational in 2009. In 2010, TransAlta (which operates the Kent Hills farm) announced plans for a Kent Hills 2 expansion, and had submitted proposals for a new Frosty Hollow Wind Farm near Sackville and the Stonehaven Wind Farm. Acciona Energy received approval for the construction of two wind farms in Aulac and Lamèque Island, but as of mid-2010, these projects were delayed as a result of the global recession. In August 2010, however, the company initiated construction plans for the Lamèque Island project. The 45 MW wind farm came online in May 2011 and features 30 turbines spread over 3,100 acres (1,255 ha), supplying energy to more than 8,000 homes.

The province has seven hydroelectric generating stations, accounting for about 22.5 percent of the province's total installed capacity. There are six thermal electric generating plants; one operating with coal, two operating with oil, and three operating with combustion turbines. As of 2010, the Canadian government has pledged up to C$9.8 million for the construction of the City of Saint John's Green Thermal Utility Project. The project is designed to deliver non-emitting and sustainable thermal energy for heating and cooling of existing buildings and new developments. The project is expected to be phased in over a period of up to ten years at an estimated cost of C$29.8 million. Federal funding is coming as part of the Green Infrastructure Fund. The remaining funds will be provided by the City of Saint John.

The province also has 38 megawatts of installed biomass-fired electricity.

Energy Goals

In 2007, the provincial government released a new comprehensive development plan with a stated goal for the province to reach self-sufficiency by 2026. *Our Action Plan to Be Self-Sufficient in New Brunswick* points to developments in energy efficiency and energy resources as one of the key factors in reaching that goal.

One step toward energy self-sufficiency is the Electricity Act of 2006 (OC 2006–274), which serves as a renewable portfolio standard that calls for the use of renewable energy sources to provide a minimum of 10 percent of the electricity sold by the standard service supplier in the province (i.e. NB Power) by 2016.

To support the development of renewable energy sources, the government introduced *The Community Energy Policy* in February 2010. The policy goal is to encourage development of locally owned and operated energy projects with fewer than 15 megawatts of generation. Such projects may be based on biomass, wind, solar, small hydro, or tidal power resources. As an incentive, selected projects will receive C$0.10 per kilowatt-hour for the renewable energy they produce. This feed-in tariff (FIT) will increase annually with the consumer price index beginning in 2011. As of August

2010, at least twelve groups showed an interest in developing energy projects.

The province continued its efforts to strengthen its energy plan with the finalization of a report from the New Brunswick Energy Commission, created by the government to survey the energy sector and provincial residents and establish recommendations for a ten-year plan. The commission released its final report in May 2011 with recommendations around five key objectives: "developing a plan for low- and stable-priced energy, ensuring the security of energy supplies, setting high standards of reliability in the generation and delivery of electricity, producing, distributing, and transmitting energy in an environmentally responsible manner, and strengthening and expanding the role of the independent energy and utility regulator." The commission made more than 50 recommendations to meet these objectives. Energy Minister Craig Leonard announced in September 2011 the government would release a formal energy policy by the end of 2011 that would address each of the 50 recommendations.

🍁 Green Business, Green Building, Green Jobs

Green Business

The development of New Brunswick's green economy is based largely on plans that strengthen and improve the province's status as a major energy hub, where energy related companies, people, research and development, generation, distribution, and related activities and projects are located. The development of renewable energy resources and energy efficiency products and services will play a major role in these plans, particularly as the economy is transformed to reach the overall provincial goal to become self-sufficient by 2026. This 2026 goal is outlined in *Our Action Plan to Be Self-Sufficient in New Brunswick*, which was published in 2007. The plan calls for the formation of an Energy Team to develop an energy investment strategy. This team includes members from the department for Alternative Energy and Market Development, which carries a mandate to undertake energy management initiatives that improve the security of supply, use, and diversity of energy resources to the benefit of the economy and the environment, and to foster the development of improved and expanded energy sources through infrastructure growth and ongoing regulatory reform.

Support for the green economy played a role in the 2010 provincial elections, which marked the first time that voters were able to cast a vote for members of the Green Party. Candidates for the Green Party campaigned on a green economy platform that included support for improved public transportation, the use of renewable energy, consumption of locally grown organic food, and rebuilding of the forest economy. The Greens gained 5 percent of the vote in the September 2010 elections, which was not enough to warrant seats in the assembly.

Green Building

The reduction of energy consumption and improvements in energy efficiency technologies and practices will play a major role in the provincial goal to become energy self-sufficient. To that end, the government initiated the *Province of New Brunswick Green Building Policy for New Construction & Major Renovation Projects*, which was published in 2010. Under this policy, building all new construction and major renovations for buildings with a floor area greater than 2,000 square meters must achieve a minimum of silver certification under the Canada Green Building Council Leadership in energy and Environmental Design program or a rating of three globes under the Green Globe Design for New Buildings and Retrofits program. Smaller buildings must meet the requirements outlined in the *Advanced Buildings Core Performance Guide Efficiency NB Edition*. This guide was developed by the New Buildings Institute Advanced Buildings Program and customized to address the issues of climate and available design best practices in the province of New Brunswick. It is the first such customized guide in Canada. The guide's recommendations will generally result in a building achieving energy savings of at least 20 to 30 percent beyond the performance of a building that meets the Model National Energy Code of Canada for Buildings 1997. Efficiency NB is the central resource organization for information and incentives regarding energy efficiency projects for residential, commercial, and industrial buildings throughout the province.

Green Jobs

Further developments in renewable energy sources and energy efficiency programs and services will undoubtedly lead to the creation of new jobs. To assist in workforce training efforts, Efficiency NB sponsors two-day Energy Efficient Renovations Workshops that focus on techniques to improve the energy efficiency of existing homes. New Brunswick Community College offers two-year programs in electrical engineering technology, with a focus on alternate energy systems, and environmental technology, with a focus on air, water, and soil analysis. Environmental studies majors at the University of New Brunswick benefit from programs sponsored through the university's Environment and Sustainable Development Research Center, including research internships and regularly scheduled educational events.

The City of Saint John's Green Thermal Utility Project, sponsored in part through the government of Canada's Green Infrastructure Fund, is expected to open a number of jobs over the ten-year period of construction and implementation. The Green Infrastructure Fund is part of the overall national economic stimulus plan to build communities and create new jobs.

The Atlantic Environmental Science Center located on the campus of the Université de Moncton houses the employees of several regional and national units of Environment Canada, including the Atlantic Laboratory for Environmental Testing, the Chief Information Branch, and the Enforcement Wildlife Division. There is a Canadian Wildlife Service office located in Sackville.

Sustainable Forest Management

In a province where forests cover 85 percent of the land and as many as eighty communities are heavily dependent on forest industries, it is no wonder that sustainable forest management is a concern for many. However, balancing the demands and desires of those benefitting economically from forest industries with those focused on environmental protection and conservation can be a difficult feat.

Public Concerns and Perceptions

Hoping to gain some insight into the concerns of the general population, the New Brunswick Department of Natural Resources sponsored a survey in 2007 on the issues of forest use and management. The results, published in *Public Views on Forest Management in New Brunswick: Report from a Provincial Survey*, indicated that about 44 percent of respondents viewed forests primarily as a place for the protection of water, air, and soil, while only about 17 percent ranked economic wealth and jobs as a primary value of provincial forests. Nearly all of the respondents agreed that it is important to maintain forests for future generations and 80 percent agreed that forests can be improved through management by humans. In addition, a little more than 67 percent of respondents agreed that forests should be managed to meet as many human needs as possible, but only 24 percent agreed that the primary function of forests was to provide products and services that are useful to humans.

Concerning forest management, more than 56 percent of respondents believed that the forest industries have too much control over forest management issues and nearly 57 percent believed that there were not enough protected areas throughout the province. However, when respondents were asked to note their familiarity with specific current forest policy initiatives, most indicated that they had never heard of four key initiatives, or had heard of them, but knew nothing about them. These were the Jaako Poyry report on wood supply, published in 2002; the vision document (*Our Shared Future*); forest management guidelines, and the First Nations forest harvest agreements.

Government Issues

To consider the needs of the forest industry and the role of the government in balancing both economic and environmental concerns, the province appointed a special Task Force on Forest Diversity and Wood Supply to consider the variety of viable management options. *Management Alternatives for New Brunswick's Public Forest* (also known as the Erdle report after the name of the task force chairman) was presented for review in August 2008, providing a number of recommendations for alternative management approaches, with a goal to maintain and improve the existing forests while also supporting and improving the forest industries on which so many residents rely. The report was presented to the public for review, with public hearing held in five cities and more than 600 comments submitted to the Department of Natural Resources. Based on the report and public feedback, the government presented its new management plan in January 2009.

Be... Sustainable in This Place: A Balanced Management Approach for New Brunswick's Crown Forest employs several of the alternatives suggested by the Erdle report. The plan calls for a decrease in overall conservation forest areas from 30 percent to between 23 and 25 percent. These areas are managed primarily for conservation purposes but allow some wood harvesting. That figure includes areas that are designated as protected areas (where no harvest is allowed). Under the plan protected areas will increase from 4 percent of the Crown forest areas to between 6 and 8 percent, and a goal is set to ensure that a minimum of 30 percent of all forest area consists of old growth trees. The designated plantation areas are expected to increase from a maximum of 25 percent to a maximum of 28 percent, with a wider variety of tree species added to these plantations. The plan is set to be fully implemented in 2012 and is designed to extend over 100 years.

Criticism and Praise

The plan has been received with mixed reviews. The Canadian Parks and Wilderness Society issued a statement of general disapproval, criticizing the decrease in conservation areas and the increase in plantations. The group argues that the proposed increase in protected areas is not nearly enough to conserve biodiversity in the province and has called for the government to establish a goal of more than 10 percent for protected areas. On the other side of the issue, a statement from the New Brunswick Forest Products Association marked approval for the plan, noting that it provides a balanced approach that will increase the yields of a wider variety of tree species in the long term, thus providing a more sustainable wood supply while also enhancing forest diversity and maintaining areas of long-lived species.

In response to some criticism, the government has pointed out that the plan is designed for a long-term approach. The supply of harvested wood will not increase in the short term, but will phase in over time as a wider variety of tree species are planted and maintained, with a 75 percent increase in wood supply predicted over the first fifty years. For 2009—10, the government invested more than C$25 million in silviculture operations on Crown land. While the government is committed to conservation efforts, it also considers the forest industries as a key growth sector in the overall provincial development plan to achieve self-sufficiency by 2026.

The discussion continued at a forestry summit in November 2010, which was attended by one hundred major stakeholders associated with forestry. A month later the government announced a series of actions that came out of the summit designed to strengthen and renew the forestry industry. These included creating separate task forces to set timber objectives for public and private lands, undertaking an innovation assessment to find new technologies and opportunities in the market, and reviewing the province's forest management approach, among other actions.

BIBLIOGRAPHY

Books

Ernst, Chloe. *Scenic Driving Atlantic Canada: Nova Scotia, New Brunswick, Prince Edward Island, Newfoundland, & Labrador*. Guilford, CT: GPP Travel, 2011.

Kouchibouguad National Park of Canada: Management Plan. Gatineau, Quebec: Parks Canada, 2010.

Matchar, Emily, and Karla Zimmerman. *Nova Scotia, New Brunswick & Prince Edward Island*, 2nd ed. London: Lonely Planet, 2011.

Soucoup, Dan. *Logging in New Brunswick: Lumber, Mills, and River Drives*. Halifax, N.S.: Nimbus Publishing Ltd., 2011.

Web Sites

"Acciona Energy Brings Lamèque Wind Power Project Online." Acciona Energy. May 6, 2011. Available from http://www.acciona-na.com/getattachment/21574cf6-da8a-49fa-b787-cfe22c05e123/

Arsenault, Mark. "Forest Plan Strikes a Balance." *Telegraph-Journal*. February 12, 2009. Available from http://telegraphjournal.canadaeast.com/rss/article/569608

Be . . . Sustainable in This Place: A Balanced Management Approach for New Brunswick's Crown Forest. Province of New Brunswick. Available from http://www.gnb.ca/0078/publications/BMAF-e.pdf

Caribou Mountain Wind Park: Chant Group. Available from http://www.chantgroup.com/index.php?option=com_content&view=article&id=104:caribou-mountain-wind-park-substation-and-collector-system-&catid=19:completed-power-projects&Itemid=38

Center for Energy: New Brunswick. Available from http://www.centreforenergy.com/FactsStats/MapsCanada/NB-EnergyMap.asp

The Community Energy Policy. New Brunswick Department of Energy. Available from http://www.gnb.ca/0085/Community/pdf/Community%20Energy%20Policy%20-%20English.pdf

"Community Energy Policy Improved; Strong Interest Shown." Province of New Brunswick. August 18, 2010. Available from http://www2.gnb.ca/content/gnb/en/news/news_release.2010.08.1441.html

Efficiency NB. Available from http://www.efficiencynb.ca/enb//home.jsp

Electricity Act (OC 2006–274). Available from http://www.gnb.ca/0062/PDF-regs/2006-58.pdf

"The Energy Hub." Province of New Brunswick. Available from http://www.gnb.ca/0085/Hubdef-e.asp

Environment and Sustainable Development Research Center, University of New Brunswick. Available from http://www.unb.ca/enviro/index.html

Fish Guide 2010. Province of New Brunswick. Available from http://www.gnb.ca/0078/publications/Fish-e.pdf

"Fundy National Park of Canada." Parks Canada. Available from http://www.pc.gc.ca/eng/pn-np/nb/fundy/index.aspx

"Government Announces Actions To Help Strengthen, Renew Forest Industry." Natural Resources of New Brunswick. Dec. 17, 2010. Available from http://www2.gnb.ca/content/gnb/en/news/news_release.2010.12.1899.html

"Government of Canada Supports Green Energy Infrastructure in New Brunswick." Infrastructure Canada. Available from http://www.buildingcanada-chantierscanada.gc.ca/media/news-nouvelles/2010/20100226saintjohn-eng.html

"Government Releases Long-Term Management Approach for Crown Forests." Communications New Brunswick. January 9, 2009. Available from http://www.gnb.ca/cnb/news/pre/2009e0087pr.htm

"Green Economy." Green Party of New Brunswick. Available from http://www.greenpartynb.ca/en/issues/green-economy

Kent Hills: TransAlta. Available from http://www.transalta.com/facilities/plants-operation/kent-hills

"Leonard Seeks Funds for Point Lepreau Mistakes." CBC News Canada. September 19, 2011. Available from http://www.cbc.ca/news/canada/new-brunswick/story/2011/09/19/nb-lepreau-wolsong-reactors-543.html

Management Alternatives for New Brunswick's Public Forest: Report of the New Brunswick Task Force on Forest Diversity and Wood Supply. New Brunswick Task Force on Forest Diversity and Wood Supply, Department of Natural Resources. Available from http://www.gnb.ca/0078/publications/Erdle Report-e.pdf

Martin, Gwen. "New Brunswick." *Evergreen.* Fall 2004. Available from http://evergreenmagazine.com/magazine/article/New_Brunswick.html

McHardie, Daniel. "N.B. Issues First-Ever Biomass Policy." CBC News Canada. November 5, 2008. Available from http://www.cbc.ca/news/canada/new-brunswick/story/2008/11/04/nb-biomass-policy.html

Morris, Chris. "N.B. Prepares New Energy Policy." Times & Transcript. September 28, 2011. Available from http://timestranscript.canadaeast.com/search/article/1443585

New Brunswick Agriculture Strategy. New Brunswick Department of Agriculture and Aquaculture. Available from http://www.gnb.ca/0168/NB-Agriculture-Strategy.pdf

"New Brunswick Climate: Two Personalities." Weather in Canada Observer. Available from http://www.weather-in-canada-observer.com/new-brunswick-climate.html

New Brunswick Energy Hub. Available from http://www.gnb.ca/0085/Hub-e.asp

New Brunswick Finfish Aquaculture Development Strategy 2010—2014. Province of New Brunswick. Available from http://www.gnb.ca/0168/FinfishStrategy2010-2014.pdf

New Brunswick Forestry at a Glance—2006. New Brunswick Forest Products Association. Available from http://nbforestry.com///uploads//Website_Assets/ForestryataGlance(E).pdf.

New Brunswick River Ice Manual. Environment Canada New Brunswick. Available from http://www.gnb.ca/0009/0369/0004/index-e.asp

"New Brunswick Science and Technology Centers." Environment Canada. Available http://www.ec.gc.ca/scitech/default.asp?lang=En&n=7CCADEA0-1

New Brunswick Shellfish Aquaculture Development Strategy 2010–2014. Province of New Brunswick.

Available from http://www.gnb.ca/0168/ShellfishStrategy2010-2014.pdf

New Brunswick Tourism and Parks. Available from http://www.tourismnewbrunswick.ca/Home/Destinations/Parks/ProvincialParks.aspx

"New Crown Forest Management Plan a Step Backwards for New Brunswick Environment and Industry." Canadian Parks and Wilderness Society. Available from http://cpawsnb.org/2009/01/new-crown-forest-management-pl.php

"Organic Production." New Brunswick Department of Agriculture and Aquaculture. Available from http://www.gnb.ca/0174/01740001-e.asp

"Organic Agriculture." Falls Brook Centre. Available from http://www.fallsbrookcentre.ca/programs/organic-agriculture

Our Action Plan to Be Self-Sufficient in New Brunswick. Province of New Brunswick. Available from http://www.nbliberal.ca/wp-content/themes/nbla/pdf/platform/report-E.pdf

"Port of Belledune Facilities." Business New Brunswick. Available from http://www.gnb.ca/0398/export_ex/info/shipping/marine/belledune/index-e.asp

"Port of St. John Facilities." Business New Brunswick. Available from http://www.gnb.ca/0398/export_ex/info/shipping/marine/saint_john/index-e.asp

A Practical Guide to the Importance of New Brunswick's Wetlands. Province of New Brunswick. Available from http://www.gnb.ca/0078/publications/wetland_guide-e.pdf

"Program Areas." New Brunswick Community College. Available from http://www.nbcc.ca/en/home/programs_and_courses/fulltimestudy/default.aspx#enviro

Province of New Brunswick Green Building Policy for New Construction & Major Renovation Projects. Province of New Brunswick. Available from http://www.gnb.ca/0099/pgbp-e.pdf

"Province Receives Final Report From Energy Commission." Government of New Brunswick. May 24, 2011. Available from http://www2.gnb.ca/content/gnb/en/news/news_release.2011.05.0566.html

Species at Risk in New Brunswick: Piping Plover. New Brunswick Department of Natural resources. Available from http://www.gnb.ca/0078/SpeciesAtRisk/pdf/plover.pdf

"Species at Risk Public Registry." Government of Canada. Available from http://www.registrelep.gc.ca/search/advSearchResults_e.cfm?

stype=species&lng=e&advkeywords=&op=1&lo-cid=8&taxid=0&desid=1,3,4&schid=0&

"Start Smart Prescriptive Path (Core Performance)." Efficiency NB. Available from http://www.efficien-cynb.ca/enb/3734/English

Stechyson, Natalie. "Forestry Embracing Bio-Products Trend." *Telegraph-Journal.* August 19, 2011. Available from http://nbbusinessjournal.canadaeast.com/front/article/1432996

2006 New Brunswick Mineral Industry Review. New Brunswick Department of Natural Resources. Available from http://www.gnb.ca/0078/minerals/PDF/Mineral_Industry_Review_Report.pdf

2008 Aquaculture Sector Overview. New Brunswick Department of Agriculture and Aquaculture. Available from http://www.gnb.ca/0168/30/ReviewAquaculture2008.pdf

Newfoundland and Labrador

Newfoundland and Labrador is the easternmost Canadian province. It features a wealth of natural resources in its forests and in its coastal waters. It is made up of two parts: the island of Newfoundland and Labrador, which is part of mainland Canada to the northwest of Newfoundland. The majority of the province's 500,000 residents live on Newfoundland. The province holds Canada's second largest conventional oil reserves and is home to about 2.5 million acres (1 million ha) of untapped offshore oil. However, the province is still in the process of weighing the environmental ramifications of drilling for the offshore oil. Meanwhile, it has great potential on the renewable energy front, with much of its electricity being generated by hydropower and with utilities exploring investments in wind power.

Climate

Newfoundland's climate can best be described as moderate and maritime. The island enjoys winters that are surprisingly mild by Canadian standards, though with a high rate of precipitation. Labrador, by comparison, has the cold winters and brief summers characteristic of the Canadian mid-North. Northern Labrador is classified as a polar tundra climate, while southern Labrador is considered to have a subarctic climate. St. John's is the windiest and foggiest city in Canada, while Churchill Falls receives the most snowfall. The northern lights, or aurora borealis, flicker over Labrador.

Taking Action Against Climate Change In 2005, the province's Department of Environment and Conservation released the *Newfoundland and Labrador Climate Change Action Plan*, and the plan was revised again in 2011. Newfoundland and Labrador could suffer from rising seas levels, increased shoreline erosion, thinning sea ice, more extreme weather events, and changes to the marine ecosystem that would affect important fish species. These actions could be especially damaging to the province, where 90 percent of the population lives near the shoreline. The province's 2005 plan to fight climate change complemented many of the Canadian government's ongoing initiatives in accordance with the Kyoto Protocol. The plan consisted of 40 actions divided under the categories Intergovernmental Relations, Government Operations, Transportation, Human Health, Ecosystem Health, Education, Municipalities, Industry, Buildings, Natural Resource Industries, Renewable Energy, and Sustainable Development. Some of the actions include establishing an energy use reduction target for provincial buildings, implementing climate change monitoring in provincial protected areas, and requiring that infrastructure projects receiving public funds meet a standard set of criteria with respect to climate change.

Under the Natural Resource Industries category, the majority of the actions related to the maritime and fisheries industry. Some of these actions included monitoring developments in climate change science, encouraging the development of new technologies in order to improve the energy efficiency of vessels and their equipment, and working towards regulations that will promote safety and efficiency of vessels. Along the lines of energy efficiency, the province also aimed to implement an energy plan to ensure that all energy sources are efficient and renewable.

In the 2011 update, additional goals were set, including developing flood risk maps to determine where rising waters would potentially damage coastal communities; monitoring and improving data on coastal erosion and precipitation changes; and raising awareness about climate change at the local level. Part of the plan also called for a residential rebate program and incentives for small to mid-sized businesses to improve the energy efficiency of homes and buildings. In the 2011 update, the provincial government also reaffirmed its commitment to reducing greenhouse gases to 10 percent below 1990 levels by 2020, and to 75–85 percent below 2001 levels by 2050.

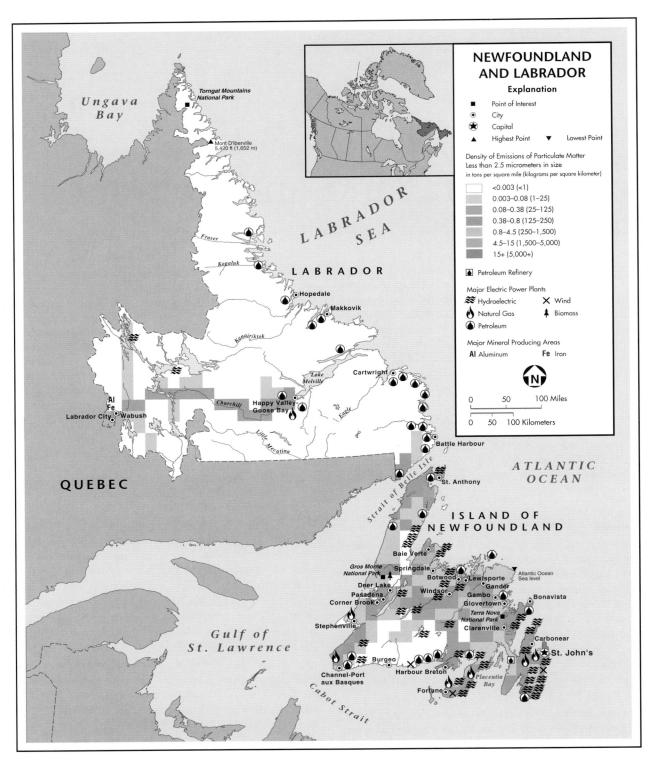

SOURCES: *Energy Facts and Statistics*. Centre for Energy. Available from http://www.centreforenergy.com/FactsStats/MapsCanada; "Geographical Highlights." *The Canadian Encyclopedia*. Available from http://www.encyclopediecanadienne.ca/geoHighlights/ canmap_geog_v1_eng.swf; "Highest Points by Province and Territory." *The Atlas of Canada*. Natural Resources Canada. Available from http://atlas.nrcan.gc.ca/site/english/learningresources/facts/faq.html#points; "Mining in Canada: Map." *Mining in Canada*. The Mining Association of Canada. Available from http://www.mining.ca/site/images/MapofCanada.pdf; "Particulate Matter < 2.5 Micrometers (PM2.5) Emission in 2007." *CAC Density Maps*. Environment Canada. Available from http://www.ec.gc.ca/inrp-npri/default.asp? lang=en&n=BD725B2A-1. © 2011 Cengage Learning.

⚜ Natural Resources, Water, and Agriculture

Natural Resources

Wildlife found in the province includes the largest migratory caribou herd, black bears, moose, snowshoe hare, arctic hare, beaver, fox, lynx, coyote, mink, muskrat, otter, red squirrel, weasel, marten, and the wolf, which is extinct on the island of Newfoundland, but still exists in Labrador. Bird species include willow ptarmigan, ruffed grouse, spruce grouse, Canada goose, mallard duck, and surf scoter.

As of 2010, there are 16 threatened or endangered species of plants and animals in Newfoundland and Labrador. Endangered and threatened animals include wolverine, woodland caribou, and American marten; plant species include Barren's willow, Long's braya, and Fernald's braya; and bird species include red crossbill, piping plover, ivory gull, and chimney swift.

Forestry Newfoundland and Labrador are home to the easternmost boreal forests in Canada. These forests are primary made up of coniferous trees mixed with hardwoods. Balsam Fir and Black Spruce are the dominant tree species found in the province, followed by White Spruce, White Fir, and Trembling Aspen. There are 32 provincial parks in Newfoundland and Labrador.

The lumber industry in Newfoundland and Labrador consists of more than 800 commercially licensed sawmills ranging in output size from a few thousand board feet per year to the largest one at approximately 50 million board feet. The majority of the province's lumber production—which is currently approaching 115 million board feet—is produced by a group of 11 larger mills that also recover pulp chips from their sawing residues. More than half of the lumber produced in the province is sold to markets in mainland Canada and in the United States, while a small amount finds its way to European markets. In 2009, the products coming out of the forest industry were worth about C $250 million, including paper and lumber.

Mining The province's mining industry has seen a sharp increase in value since 2004. In 2004, the value of mineral shipments was C$684 million, while the projected value of shipments for 2011 is C$4.7 billion. This jump in value is due to an increase in shipments and prices of iron ore from western Labrador, the opening of Voisey's Bay mine with its nickel and copper production, and the June 2011 opening of the Labrador iron mines near Schefferville. The mining industry was also projected to employ nearly 6,000 workers in 2011. Gold, copper, zinc, nickel, cobalt, iron ore, silver, and antimony are among the metal commodities mined in the province. Non-metal products such as slate, granite, and peat are exported to world markets. Aggregates for road building

and construction from the province's numerous quarries are supplied primarily to local markets, but there is increasing interest in supplying aggregates for export. In 2011 the province announced its intentions to create a minerals strategy, designed to balance the need for encouraging mining developments with the need to protect the environment.

Water

Some 22 species of whales, dolphins, and porpoises are found along the coastline-prominent species include humpback, fin, sperm, and minke whales; harbor porpoise; and saddleback dolphin.

Newfoundland and Labrador Provincial Profile	
Physical Characteristics	
Land area	144,353 square miles (373,873 sq km)
Freshwater area	12,100 square miles (31,339 sq km)
Highest point	Mount Caubvik 5,420 feet (1,652 m)
Forest lands (2011)	26.5 million acres (10.7 million ha)
Provincial parks (2011)	14
Energy Statistics	
Total electricity generated (2009)	38.4 million megawatt hours
Hydroelectric energy generation (2009)	36.2 million megawatt hours
Wind energy generation (2009)	NA
Tidal energy generation (2009)	NA
Biomass energy capacity (2009)	15 megawatts
Crude oil reserves (2009)	1.5 billion barrels (233.5 million cu m)
Natural gas reserves (2009)	NA
Natural gas liquids (2009)	NA
Pollution Statistics	
Carbon output (2009)	4.7 million tons of CO_2 (4.3 million t)
Federal contaminated sites receiving funds (2008)	12
Particulate matter (less than 2.5 micrometers) emissions (2009)	23,907 tons per year (21,688 t/yr)

SOURCES: *Canada's Greenhouse Gas Emissions*. Environment Canada. Available from http://www.ec.gc.ca/ges-ghg/default.asp?lang=En&n=1357A041-1; *Canada Year Book, 2011*. Statistics Canada. Available from http://www.statcan.gc.ca/pub/11-402-x/11-402-x2011000-eng.htm; *Energy Facts and Statistics*. Centre for Energy. Available from http://www.centreforenergy.com/FactsStats/MapsCanada; *Federal Contaminated Sites*. Government of Canada. Available from http://www.federalcontaminatedsites.gc.ca/index-eng.aspx; "Forest Land by Province and Territory." Statistics Canada. Available from http://www40.statcan.gc.ca/l01/cst01/envi34a-eng.htm; "Geographical Highlights." *The Canadian Encyclopedia*. Available from http://www.encyclopediecanadienne.ca/geoHighlights/canmap_geog_v1_eng.swf; *National Pollutant Release Inventory*. Environment Canada. Available from http://ec.gc.ca/pdb/websol/emissions/ap/ap_query_e.cfm

© 2011 Cengage Learning.

In 2009, the value of the commercial fish catch was more than C$400 million. Shellfish made up the highest landed volume, followed by pelagics (fish that live in the open sea, far from land) and groundfish. The majority of seafood exports go to the United States, followed by China, the United Kingdom, Japan, Denmark, and Russia. The majority of exports include snow crab and shrimp. In 2009, the commercial fishing industry employed over 22,000 workers.

In 1992, the Newfoundland and Labrador aquaculture industry faced a collapse of the cod stocks on the east coast. The government closed the fishery, and over 40,000 people lost their jobs. The cod stocks were overexploited and destructive fishing practices were used, leading to the collapse. Despite warnings and requests to reduce quotas, the government continued their practices because they were concerned that the loss of jobs would be too great. As a result of this short-term outlook, the marine ecosystem and the industry are still recovering. The industry's total export value for 2009 was C$92.1 million. Commercial fish farmed in the province include Atlantic Salmon, Steelhead Trout, and Blue Mussel. Approximately 655 individuals are currently employed in the aquaculture industry.

Agriculture

Newfoundland and Labrador's agriculture industry employs more than 6,200 people and has primary and value-added production worth over C$500 million. In 2006, the province had 558 farms over more than 89,000 acres. The largest crop in the province was alfalfa, rye, and tame hay, followed by fruits and berries, corn silage, and vegetables. Also in 2006, top livestock was cattle, followed by sheep and pigs.

In 2008, there were only two commercial farms in the province that had organic certification, both located in Portugal Cove outside of St. John's. While the organic movement has been slow to take off in Newfoundland and Labrador, word is getting out via the two organic farms—the Lien Farm and the Organic Farm—through a veggie co-op on the Organic Farm, produce from the farms becoming available at local grocery stores, organic produce being used in local restaurants more frequently, the start of a weekly farmer's market, the development of a local Atlantic Canadian Organic Regional Network (ACORN) chapter, and an organic workshop.

✤ Energy

Newfoundland and Labrador's energy resources include crude oil, hydropower, and wind power, from which the province also generates electricity, along with diesel and natural gas. In 2010, the mining, oil and utility sectors accounted for about 30 percent of Newfoundland and Labrador's gross domestic product, and the province received approximately C$2.1 billion in oil royalties. The energy and utilities workforce in Newfoundland and

Western Brook Pond Fjord of Newfoundland and Labrador.
© *sandra calderbank/ShutterStock.com*

Labrador totaled 3,100 employees in 2010, a drop of nearly half those employed in the sector in 2009. The province's energy exports include crude oil, refined petroleum products, and electricity. Newfoundland and Labrador rank second in conventional oil reserves in Canada, and third in conventional oil production.

Four oil projects—Hibernia, Terra Nova, White Rose, and North Amethyst—produced approximately 267,000 million barrels of oil a day in 2010. These projects, along with others in development, are all offshore and located in the undersea Jeanne d'Arc Basin. Onshore projects are located in western Newfoundland, with 0.28 million hectares that include onshore permits and one production lease. The province has another 1.02 million hectares of offshore area that is under exploration license, waiting to be developed.

Hydroelectricity and Renewable Energy

In 2009, Newfoundland and Labrador ranked third in hydroelectricity generation in Canada. Ten percent of Canada's hydroelectricity comes from the province, while 97 percent of the province's electricity comes from hydropower. Four utility companies—Newfoundland Power, Newfoundland and Labrador Hydro, Kruger Energy, and Algonquin Power—serve the energy needs of the province and provide hydroelectricity. The Churchill Falls Generating Station is one of the largest underground hydroelectric powerhouses in the world. The plant has 11 turbines with a rated capacity of 5428 MW. In 2008, the operation produced more than 34 terawatt hours (TWh) of clean electricity, with the majority of that energy sold to Hydro-Québec through a long-term power purchase arrangement set to expire in 2041.

As of 2010, the Lower Churchill Project was being developed, with two installations at Gull Island and Muskrat Falls. These installations would have a combined capacity of over 3000 MW and would significantly reduce carbon dioxide emissions every year from thermal, coal, and fossil fuel power generation—equivalent to the annual greenhouse gas emissions from 3.2 million automobiles. In November of 2010, it was announced that Nalcor, the corporation in charge of the Lower Churchill project, would be teaming up with Emera Energy of Nova Scotia for the project. Together they plan to funnel hydroelectric power from the Churchill River in Labrador through Newfoundland and into Nova Scotia. They are also discussing the possibility of exporting power to New Brunswick and the United States.

The province's utility companies are also involved in developing wind energy projects. Hydro currently has agreements to purchase energy produced by two 27-megawatt (MW) wind projects, which each consists of nine three-MW wind turbines. In 2008, Hydro purchased wind power from the first commercial wind development in Newfoundland, located in St. Lawrence. The Fermeuse wind site became operational in May 2009. These two wind developments have the potential to supply energy to approximately 14,000 homes, displace over 300,000 barrels of oil annually from the Holyrood Generating Station, and reduce sulphur and carbon dioxide emissions from the Holyrood plant by about 14 percent. In November 2010, it was also announced that power from the Lower Churchill project could also replace energy produced from the Holyrood plant, as well.

In 2007, the province released *Focusing Our Energy: Newfoundland and Labrador Energy Plan*. The plan's aim is to achieve six goals: Environmental Leadership, Energy Security, Sustainable Economic Development, Maximizing Electricity Export Value, Maximizing Long-Term Value of Oil and Gas, and Effective Governance. These goals formed a framework for developing the policy actions that are detailed in the report, and any actions that may be developed later. Some of the policy actions listed under the above goals include: leveraging nonrenewable oil and gas wealth into a renewable future by investing a significant portion of nonrenewable resource revenues in renewable energy infrastructure and development; developing and implementing a comprehensive petroleum resource marketing plan; positioning the province to take full advantage of Upper Churchill hydropower for provincial and export customers after its power contract expires; and by 2015, eliminating 1.4 million tons of GHG emissions per year, as well as all other pollutants from Holyrood, by building Lower Churchill and the Labrador–Island Transmission link.

✿ Green Business, Green Building, Green Jobs

Green Business and Green Jobs

In 2009, the Newfoundland and Labrador Federation of Labour released *Good Jobs, Green Jobs: Exploring Opportunities for Newfoundland and Labrador*, a discussion paper that was used by the Federation of Labour in stakeholder consultations across the province. The paper calls for the development of a green economy strategy for the province, similar to those from Alberta and Ontario's Green Energy and Green Economy Act. The report also discussed sectors in the province that would be targeted for green job and business growth. One such area was wind energy. The province already has contracts with Newfoundland and Labrador Hydro for 51 MW of energy, and both the island and mainland parts of the province have the potential for much more. The paper also discusses the province's potential for tidal and solar energy, and the continued development of a facility that produces peat fuel pellets in Stephenville.

Businesses have also been able to become more energy efficient through the province's Green Fund. The Green Fund is a program that uses C$25 million set aside for projects that reduce greenhouse gas emissions. Businesses are included in the project, which include the replacement of old outdoor lighting with more efficient LED lights in the Confederation Building Parking Lot in St. John's, and the installation of an integrated management system to reduce energy requirements in the Browning Harvey bottling facility's manufacturing process.

Newfoundland's colleges and universities also provide programs for students looking to enter clean energy jobs. Memorial University offers a Bachelor of Resource Management degree in Sustainable Resource Management. The program bridges scientific concerns about natural resources with policy development and management, and shares courses with other programs along with having fourteen courses of its own. The Marine Institute at Memorial University offers numerous programs focusing on the province's fisheries industry. One of these programs is the Marine Environmental Technologist degree. This program will prepare students to develop environmentally sound projects and to work to prevent and create responses to marine pollution or degradation.

The College of the North Atlantic offers an Environmental Technology cooperative education diploma program, which combines course and field work in chemical, biological, and engineering science focused on dealing with environmental pollution and sustainable development.

Green Building

The Newfoundland and Labrador Green Fund also has projects that support energy efficiency in homes and other buildings. One of their programs is with Exploits Pelletizing, Inc., which produces wood pellets for wood pellet stoves to heat homes. The provincial government has invested in a program that provides a 25 percent rebate to homeowners that purchase a wood pellet appliance. The production of wood pellets and their use in heating could divert up to 20 tons of waste and up to 4,400 tons of greenhouse gases per year.

The Green Fund has also supported a number of building projects. The group Choices for Youth is using the Green Fund in order to rebuild a portion of one of its buildings in order to make new apartments and program space that will be energy efficient. Greenhouse gas emissions should be reduced by 55 percent, with energy savings dropping by about C$7,400 per year. A major part of the Green Fund's commitment was to the promote energy efficiency in government buildings. To date, they have incorporated energy efficiency upgrades in five new government buildings, located in Clarenville, Corner Brook, and Grand Bank, Newfoundland. The building installed ground source heat pumps, which will divert more than 20,000 tons of greenhouse gases per year with all five buildings combined.

The Green Fund contributed more than C$900,000 to help a St. David's dairy farm afford an anaerobic digester and other equipment to process cow manure into bedding for the animals. The equipment also was expected to capture the methane gas released and turn it into energy, which significantly reduces the greenhouse gases emitted. The farm, New World Dairy, is the largest in Newfoundland.

❧ Offshore Oil and Gas Exploration: Worth the Risk?

Newfoundland and Labrador's offshore oil sector has been one of the province's most profitable industries. It produces nearly 270,000 barrels of oil per day, making up 10 percent of Canada's total oil production. While there have been attempts to plan natural gas projects, as of late 2010 the province was not producing any natural gas. Thirty-one percent of the province's government revenues were from the oil industry from 2009–2010. There are four oil-producing offshore projects in the province: Hibernia, Terra Nova, White Rose, and North Amethyst. Estimated oil reserves at each of these projects are 1.24 billion barrels at Hibernia, 419 million barrels at Terra Nova, and 283 million barrels discovered at White Rose. North Amethyst, a White Rose satellite expansion project, contains an additional 68 million barrels of oil. A fifth major project in the province, the Hebron project, contains an estimated 400–100 million barrels, and will begin production before the end of 2017.

The province's oil and gas industry is not only highly profitable, but also provides a multitude of jobs for the province. In the wake of the Gulf of Mexico's Deepwater Horizon oil spill in April 2010, questions were raised about the safety of deepwater offshore projects in Newfoundland and Labrador, and whether or not exploration for future projects should continue.

Hibernia is one of four oil projects in the province that produced approximately 267,000 barrels of oil a day in 2010. These projects, along with others in development, are all offshore and located in the undersea Jeanne d'Arc Basin. © All Canada Photos/Alamy

The fear that a blowout could occur at one of Newfoundland's oil rigs caused some politicians to call for a halt to drilling on Canada's deepest offshore well. Called the Lona O-55, the exploration well is situated in the Orphan Basin 1.5 miles underwater and owned by Chevron.

Questions were also raised after the Gulf of Mexico spill as to why an overall moratorium on drilling was not put in place in the province. The government and oil companies both stated that they went ahead with drilling the Lona O-55 because they were confident that they were doing everything possible to prepare for a similar situation. Natural Resources Minister Kathy Dunderdale stated that continuing exploration and drilling is vital to the province's economic future, and the risks of losing money and jobs were too great to halt drilling without more information. While the government did not halt drilling, they did appoint a Master Mariner Captain to conduct a review.

Newfoundlanders are no strangers to oil-related disasters. In 1982, the Ocean Ranger drilling platform sank, claiming 84 lives, and in 2009 a helicopter crashed killing 17 of 18 on board offshore workers and two crewmen. The purpose of the review was to investigate the Canada–Newfoundland and Labrador Offshore Petroleum Board (C-NLOPB). The board's purpose is to monitor the safety and environmental impact of offshore drilling. It's also supposed to get the most economically from the industry in terms of jobs and local business opportunity. After the Deepwater Horizon blowout, the board was faced with calls to impose a moratorium, like the U.S. government. They instead opted to begin drilling the Lona O-55 only 20 days after the Gulf of Mexico spill.

This decision led many to question the board's priorities and whether or not they are willing to take the time and money to adopt more aggressive safety measures while running the risk of driving away investment. The board has faced criticism in the past, particularly when more than a year after the helicopter crash, a judge finally ordered the board to revise its safety procedures for such flights. The board has also been accused of not properly assessing risks to marine life. The Newfoundland and Labrador Premier Danny Williams has defended the board, saying they did not have a conflict of interest, since unlike its U.S. counterpart, it doesn't collect royalties on oil production. However, the board does handle the leasing of exploration acreage, the maximization of production from the fields, and the management of industrial benefits that companies provide to the province. In November 2010, an inquiry into the helicopter crash reported that safety regulations for offshore operations need to be entirely rewritten. It also called for compliance to be more strongly enforced and that workers' safety needs to be of paramount importance. The report noted that the C-NLOPB needs to be more transparent with its information, and that it had been lax when it came to safety oversight in the past. The report recommends that an independent safety regulator should be put in place to enforce this and to improve oversight of worker safety.

It is understandable that there is a lot at stake in the province's oil industry. The offshore sector directly and indirectly employs about 13,000 workers, with about 100 local companies involved. Government revenues are at C $1.4 billion. The board has stated that even though it decided to keep drilling, it has stepped up its supervision of the project, requiring daily progress reports and performing inspections every three weeks. It has also argued that BP was not following best industry practices at the time of the blowout, and it will make sure that Chevron does.

Despite concerns over the C-NLOPB's interests and the risks involved, the Lona O-55 well was completed in August 2010. However, in August 2011, the board acknowledged the need for further review. At that time, it announced an independent review of a proposed drilling program, which was a planned exploration license at the Old Harry region. According to a media release from the board, the review's focus was to be "the potential environmental effects of the proposed drilling of a single exploration well." The board appointed a former cabinet minister of the New Brunswick legislature to conduct the review. C-NLOPB received more than 50 submissions calling for the environmental review from First Nations, fishing associations, municipalities, citizens, and environmental organizations.

BIBLIOGRAPHY

Books

Dearden, Philip, and Rick Rollins. *Parks and Protected Areas in Canada: Planning and Management.* 3rd ed. Don Mills, ON: Oxford University Press, 2009.

Ernst, Chloe. *Scenic Driving Atlantic Canada: Nova Scotia, New Brunswick, Prince Edward Island, Newfoundland, & Labrador.* Guilford, CT: GPP Travel, 2011.

Forbes Travel Guide: Canada. Chicago: Forbes Travel Guide, 2010.

Fosket, Jennifer. *Living Green.* Gabriola Island, BC: New Society Publishers, 2009.

The Importance of Nature to Canadians: The Economic Significance of Nature-Related Activities. Ottawa: Environment Canada, 2000.

Terra Nova National Park of Canada Management Plan. Ottawa: Parks Canada, 2009.

Torngat Mountains National Park Management Plan. Gatineau, Quebec: Parks Canada, 2010.

Visser, Emily, and Luigi Ferrara. *Canada Innovates: Sustainable Building.* Toronto: Key Porter Books, 2008.

Web Sites

"Atlantic Oil Spill Summit Needed: N.B. Minister." CBC. June 8, 2010. Available from http://www.cbc.ca/canada/new-brunswick/story/2010/06/08/nb-doucet-fisheries-oil-spill-summit-1044.html

Canada-Newfoundland and Labrador Offshore Petroleum Board. Available from http://www.cnlopb.nl.ca/

"Canadian Atlantic Fisheries Collapse." Greenpeace. Available from http://archive.greenpeace.org/comms/cbio/cancod.html

Chapter P-10. An Act Respecting Petroleum and Natural Gas. Newfoundland and Labrador Legislative Assembly. Available from http://www.assembly.nl.ca/legislation/sr/statutes/p10.htm

"Chevron in Canada: Atlantic Canada." Chevron Corporation. Available from http://www.chevron.ca/operations/exploration/atlantic.asp

"Chevron Nears End of Canada's Deepest Underwater Drilling Operation." *The Vancouver Sun.* August 20, 2010. Available from http://www.vancouversun.com/news/Chevron+nears+Canada+deepest+underwater+drilling+operation/3422787/story.html

Climate Change Action Plan 2005. Newfoundland and Labrador Department of Environment and Conservation. Available from http://www.env.gov.nl.ca/env/climate_change/govt_action/climatechange-planfinal.pdf

Climate Change Action Plan 2011: Charting Our Course. Newfoundland and Labrador Office of Climate Change, Energy Efficiency, and Emissions Trading. Available from http://www.exec.gov.nl.

ca/exec/cceeet/2011_climate_change_action_plan.
html

"C-NLOPB Announces Independent Review Of Proposed Drilling On Exploration License 1105 (Old Harry)." Canada-Newfoundland and Labrador Offshore Petroleum Board. August 25, 2011. Available from http://www.cnlopb.nl.ca/news/nr20110825.shtml

Crawford, Alison. "The Politics of Offshore Drilling." CBC. May 14, 2010. Available from http://www.cbc.ca/politics/insidepolitics/2010/05/the-politics-of-offshore-drilling.html

"Deep Drilling Starts off Newfoundland." CBC. May 10, 2010. Available from http://www.cbc.ca/canada/newfoundland-labrador/story/2010/05/10/nl-chevron-deepwell-510.html

"Department of Mines and Energy." Newfoundland and Labrador Department of Natural Resources. Available from http://www.geosurv.gov.nl.ca/minesen/mines_commodities/mining_overview.asp

"Environmental Technology (Co-op)." College of the North Atlantic. Available from http://www.cna.nl.ca/programscourses/2009-10/CNA%20Environmental%20Technology%20%28Co-op%29.pdf

Focusing Our Energy: Newfoundland and Labrador Energy Plan. Newfoundland and Labrador Department of Natural Resources. Available from http://www.nr.gov.nl.ca/energyplan/EnergyReport.pdf

Forestry Services Branch. Newfoundland and Labrador Department of Natural Resources. Available from http://www.nr.gov.nl.ca/forestry/

Good Jobs, Green Jobs: Exploring Opportunities for Newfoundland and Labrador. Newfoundland and Labrador Federation of Labour. Available from http://www.nlfl.nf.ca/issues-and-campaigns/green-jobs

"Innovative Technology To Promote Environmentally Friendly Farming Practices." *The Telegram.* April 21, 2010. Available from http://www.thetelegram.com/Arts—Life/Environment/2010-04-21/article-1449645/Innovative-technology-to-promote-environmentally-friendly-farming-practices/1

"Lower Churchill Project." Nalcor Energy. Available from http://www.nalcorenergy.com/lower-churchill-project.asp

McCarthy, Shaun, and Paul Waldie. "Perils and profit of offshore oil." *The Globe and Mail.* June 25, 2010. Available from http://www.theglobeandmail.com/report-on-business/industry-news/energy-and-resources/perils-and-profit-of-offshore-oil/article1618734/

"Mining in Newfoundland and Labrador November, 2011." Newfoundland and Labrador Department of Natural Resources. Available from http://www.nr.gov.nl.ca/nr/mines/Mining%20in%20NL,%20March%202011.pdf

"N.L. Calls For Offshore Drilling Review." The Expositor. July 2011. Available from http://www.brantfordexpositor.ca/ArticleDisplay.aspx?e=3172344&archive=true

"N.L., Emera Reach Lower Churchill Hydro Deal." CBC. November 17, 2010. Available from http://www.cbc.ca/canada/newfoundland-labrador/story/2010/11/17/nl-ns-lower-churchill-116.html#ixzz15YQcQVOb

"New Offshore Oil Safety Agency Needed: Inquiry." CBC. November 17, 2010. Available from http://www.cbc.ca/news/story/2010/11/17/helicopter-cougar-safety-report-117.html

"Newfoundland and Labrador." Centre for Energy. Available from http://www.centreforenergy.com/FactsStats/MapsCanada/NL-Energy Map.asp

"Newfoundland and Labrador Fishing Industry Highlights." Newfoundland and Labrador Department of Fisheries and Aquaculture. Available from http://www.fishaq.gov.nl.ca/stats/industry/fact_sheet_2009.pdf

Newfoundland and Labrador Green Fund. Available from http://www.env.gov.nl.ca/env/nlgf/index.html

Newfoundland and Labrador Hydro. Available from http://www.nlh.nl.ca/hydroweb/nlhydroweb.nsf/index.html

"Newfoundland and Labrador's Offshore Oil and Natural Gas Exploration and Production Industry: Contributing to a Strong Provincial Economy." Canadian Association of Petroleum Producers. Available from http://www.capp.ca/getdoc.aspx?DocID=176807

"Organics in Newfoundland and Labrador." CBC. Available from http://www.cbc.ca/nl/features/foodchain/organics.html

"Parks and Natural Areas." Newfoundland and Labrador Department of Natural Resources. Available from http://www.env.gov.nl.ca/env/parks/index.html

Statistics. Newfoundland and Labrador Department of Fisheries and Aquaculture. Available from http://www.fishaq.gov.nl.ca/stats/index.html

"Sustainable Resource Management." Memorial University. Available from http://www.swgc.mun.ca/resource/Pages/default.aspx

Northwest Territories

At first thought, the boreal and arctic lands of the Northwest Territories (NWT) may be one of the last spots that come to mind as an area with significant potential for economic growth. But with the discovery of diamonds in 1991 and major untapped gas reserves tucked beneath the Mackenzie Delta and the Beaufort Sea, the NWT has become a hotbed of activity for mining development projects that could prove to be a major boom for the region. Yet, such intense development may come at a high cost to the environment in a region that has already felt some of the effects of global climate change. An increase in industrial development and associated land use change could lead to significant increases in greenhouse gas emissions, consumption of fossil fuels. Further, since most resource-based industries either use water in their extraction and processing or change water cycling by significantly altering the landscape, increased industrial development in the Territories may also change the regions' water resources. As the local and federal governments have recognized the need to reduce energy consumption and promote the development of renewable energy sources, the government of the NWT is tackling the challenge of balancing economic gain with environmental protection and sustainability.

Climate

The Northwest Territories can be divided into three basic climate zones: arctic, subarctic, and boreal. While all three zones experience very cold winters, the southern boreal and subarctic regions have much more moderate summer temperatures. As in the Yukon, the varying amounts of daylight over the year are an important influence on climate and hydrological processes. In the northern Mackenzie River delta, there are 30 days in the winter when the sun does not rise at all and 57 days in summer when the sun does not set.

Climate Change Impact and Adaptation The effects of global climate change have already become a concern for the more than 43,000 residents in the NWT.

According to the *Northwest Territories Climate Change Impact and Adaptation Report* (published in 2008), rising temperatures have caused melting of the permafrost layer that underlies all areas of the NWT, which results in ground movement that weakens the foundation of roads and buildings. Furthermore, as permafrost patterns change, so will hydrological linkages among the different terrestrial landscape units, which will have water quality and quantity implications. Warmer winter temperatures have jeopardized the winter roads that are constructed on frozen lakes and rivers. The reduction of sea ice has led to a rise in sea levels and increased storm surges, which affect humans and wildlife alike in the northern coastal areas of the Territories.

Furthermore, the cold climate of the NWT translates into a need for greater energy consumption, which results in greenhouse gas emissions at levels that are higher than the national average. The territorial government estimates that greenhouse gas emissions are increasing by about 10 percent each year. Recognizing the need to take action, the government created the *Northwest Territories Greenhouse Gas Strategy 2007–2011*. The plan relied on educating residents and industrial leaders about climate change and encouraging them to reduce their greenhouse gas emissions levels. It also set a target for the government to reduce emissions from its own operations to 10 percent below 2001 levels by the year 2011. The government was on track to achieve those goals as of September 2011, and announced a new plan at that time with new goals for the coming years. The new strategy included goals of returning to 2005 emission levels by 2015. Because of the Territories' increase in mining, the territory government allowed for an increase of 66 percent over 2005 levels by 2020, with a return to 2005 levels by 2030. The plan is designed to allow for time to find and implement renewable energy resources, which will further reduce greenhouse gas emissions. In the report, the Northwest Territories government also considered implementing a cap-and-trade system, depending on potential partnerships with other provinces or territories.

The Snap Lake mine shown here is one of the first De Beers diamond mines outside of Africa. © *Tim Atherton 2000 Picture Desk Photos/newscom*

❧ Natural Resources, Water, and Agriculture

Natural Resources

The Canadian Taiga Forest covers about one-third of the Northwest Territories, accounting for about 28 percent of the Canadian taiga (boreal forest). Pine, aspen, birch, and poplar are among the most common tree species found in the taiga ecoregion. Woodland caribou, bison, marten, and black bear are among the mammal species found in the region, while bird species include the common raven, gray jay, fox sparrow, peregrine falcon, and bald eagle. Nahanni National Park, which covers part of the Taiga Plains and the Taiga Cordillera, was inscribed as the first UNESCO World Heritage Site in Canada in 1978. Wood Buffalo National Park, located primarily within the region known as the northern boreal plains, is the largest national park in Canada. It was established in 1922 to protect the free-roaming bison herds of the region and was inscribed as a UNESCO World Heritage Site in 1983.

While the timber industry is fairly small, the NWT forests may offer great potential in the development of a wood-based biomass energy industry. To that end, the government released the NWT Biomass Energy Strategy report in 2010, which identified biomass as an integral part of the overall renewable resources strategy for the territory. It identified the lack of timber harvesting as a unique opportunity for the territory to support a biomass effort. Trees could be harvested to produce pellets to burn for energy. According to the report, biomass energy also can be produced from the following sources: wood residue resulting from road building and maintenance, forest thinning for community protection, and forest fire burn areas; cardboard, paper, or construction and demolition waste; and fast-growing willow or poplar trees. Objectives in the report included educating residents and businesses about the potentials of biomass energy, promoting biomass as a heating option and promoting combined heat and power options. The report included twelve actions for creating a larger biomass impact in the Territories.

Canadian Diamonds In 1991, the discovery of diamonds in the Northwest Territories resulted in one of the largest land claim rushes in the history of Canada. The Australian-owned Ekati mine, which opened in 1998 near Lac de Gras, was the first diamond mine in Canada. Annual sales from the Ekati mine represent about 3 percent of the world's rough diamond supply by weight and 5 percent by value. The Diavik mine, located about 62 miles (100 km) southeast of the Ekati, opened in 2003, followed by the opening of the Snap Lake mine in 2008. The Snap Lake mine is one of the first De Beers diamond mines outside of Africa. NWT diamonds have gained a reputation for their high quality. Perhaps more important to buyers is that they are "clean" diamonds, in comparison to the "blood diamonds" from Africa that are considered illegal because revenues are used to finance terrorist activities. The three NWT mines produce about 15 percent of the world's rough diamonds.

Water

The Mighty Mackenzie The Mackenzie River is the longest river in Canada. It also represents the largest river basin in the nation and the second largest in North America (after the Mississippi). The major tributaries are the Slave, Peace, and Finlay Rivers. When combined with its tributaries, the total length of the Mackenzie River system is about 2,635 miles (4,241 km). The Mackenzie originates in Great Slave Lake, which is the second-largest lake in Canada and the deepest lake in North America. The region's commercial fishing industry is largely centered on this lake, with whitefish being the most profitable catch. Walleye, northern pike, and lack trout are some of the popular catches sought after by sports fishermen. Great Bear Lake to the north is the largest lake entirely within Canada.

Hydropower from six generating stations—Bluefish, Snare Rapids, Snare Falls, Snare Cascade, Snare Forks, and Taltson—provides more than 30 percent of the NWT total electric supply. The potential for hydroelectric power is much greater, however, leading the government to consider ways to promote further development of this renewable resource.

Water Resources Management Strategy

The government of the NWT has been working to create and implement a Water Resources Management Strategy, which will be one of the most forward-thinking strategies of its kind not only in Canada, but also in the world. The purpose of the strategy will be to manage water resources

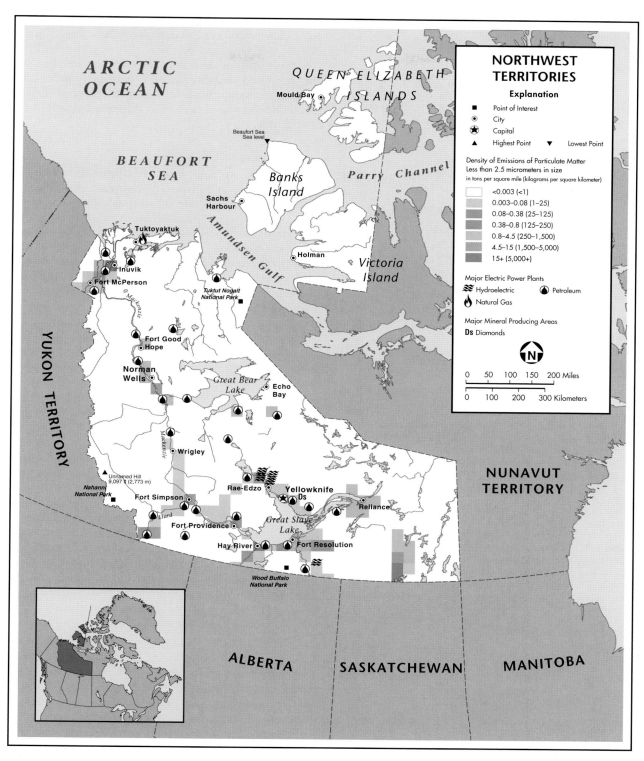

SOURCES: *Energy Facts and Statistics*. Centre for Energy. Available from http://www.centreforenergy.com/FactsStats/MapsCanada; "Geographical Highlights." *The Canadian Encyclopedia*. Available from http://www.encyclopediecanadienne.ca/geoHighlights/canmap_geog_v1_eng.swf; "Highest Points by Province and Territory." *The Atlas of Canada*. Natural Resources Canada. Available from http://atlas.nrcan.gc.ca/site/english/learningresources/facts/faq.html#points; "Mining in Canada: Map." *Mining in Canada*. The Mining Association of Canada. Available from http://www.mining.ca/site/images/MapofCanada.pdf; "Particulate Matter < 2.5 Micrometers (PM2.5) Emission in 2007." *CAC Density Maps*. Environment Canada. Available from http://www.ec.gc.ca/inrp-npri/default.asp?lang=en&n=BD725B2A-1. © 2011 Cengage Learning.

Northwest Territorial Profile

Physical Characteristics

Land area	456,792 square miles (1,183,086 sq km)
Freshwater area	62,943 square miles (163,022 sq km)
Highest point	Mount Nirvana (unofficial name) 9,098 feet (2,773 m)
Forest lands (2011)	70.1 million acres (28.4 million ha)
Territorial parks (2011)	43

Energy Statistics

Total electricity generated (2009)	NA
Hydroelectric energy generation (2009)	NA
Wind energy generation (2009)	NA
Tidal energy generation (2009)	NA
Biomass energy capacity (2009)	NA
Crude oil reserves (2009)	11.9 million barrels (1.9 million cu m)
Natural gas reserves (2009)	353.1 billion cubic feet (10.0 billion cu m)
Natural gas liquids (2009)	NA

Pollution Statistics

Carbon output (2009)	600,000 tons of CO_2 (500,000 t)
Federal contaminated sites receiving funds (2008)	15
Particulate matter (less than 2.5 micrometers) emissions (2009)	30,583 tons per year (27,744 t/yr)

SOURCES: *Canada's Greenhouse Gas Emissions*. Environment Canada. Available from http://www.ec.gc.ca/ges-ghg/default.asp?lang=En&n=1357A041-1; *Canada Year Book, 2011*. Statistics Canada. Available from http://www.statcan.gc.ca/pub/11-402-x/11-402-x2011000-eng.htm; *Energy Facts and Statistics*. Centre for Energy. Available from http://www.centreforenergy.com/FactsStats/MapsCanada; *Federal Contaminated Sites*. Government of Canada. Available from http://www.federalcontaminatedsites.gc.ca/index-eng.aspx; "Forest Land by Province and Territory." Statistics Canada. Available from http://www40.statcan.gc.ca/l01/cst01/envi34a-eng.htm; "Geographical Highlights." *The Canadian Encyclopedia*. Available from http://www.encyclopediecanadienne.ca/geoHighlights/canmap_geog_v1_eng.swf; *National Pollutant Release Inventory*. Environment Canada. Available from http://ec.gc.ca/pdb/websol/emissions/ap/ap_query_e.cfm

© 2011 Cengage Learning.

and issues, particularly when it comes to drinking water and environmental protection. The proposed strategy is based on the concept of integrated watershed management and the need to manage water resources in a comprehensive and systematic manner. Some of the issues that the strategy would address include land use planning, water related rights, transboundary water issues, and climate change.

Seal Hunting in the Beaufort Sea The Beaufort Sea of the Arctic Ocean lies to the north. The ringed seal, bearded seal, and harbor seal are all found in the in the waters of the Northwest Territories. Seal hunting is an extremely important part of the Inuit way of life, providing both food and clothing for this native group. While there are national laws that regulate trade of sealskins, seals are seen as a renewable resource that can be harvested responsibly and humanely under the federal marine mammals management programs. Beluga and bowhead whales can be found somewhat easily in the NWT waters.

Agriculture

A frigid climate is a major hindrance to traditional farming efforts in Northwest Territories. According to the national agricultural census, there were only thirty-two farms in the NWT in 2006, with forage crops among the most common. Some berries and herbs are also harvested for local use and sale, including strawberries, raspberries, and blueberries. Greenhouses are used in some communities to produce vegetables. In 2009, the Canadian government and the government of the Northwest Territories launched the Growing Forward program, designed to create a localized and competitive agriculture market in the territory. The agreement identified several programs to be initiated with producers in the region, including establishment of "market gardens" in 25 communities, a program to expand production in land-based agriculture and greenhouse operations, and establishment of a commercial game harvest program, among other programs.

Trapping & Hunting: Marten Furs and Wild Caribou

While a large portion of all meat and fish harvested is for local consumption, commercial wildlife production for meat and fur is one of the largest export-based industries in the area. Marten furs are among the most profitable trapping commodities. Other profitable small animal furs include muskrat, fox, beaver, mink, weasel, and squirrel. Wild caribou, reindeer, muskoxen, and bison are all harvested for food and skins. About 40 percent of all residents over the age of fifteen spend some time in trapping, fishing, and hunting activities.

⚜ Energy

Tapping the Potential for Oil and Gas in the Mackenzie Valley

The Norman Wells oil field in the central Mackenzie Valley is the most northerly producing oil field in Canada and one of the nation's largest. This field produces between five and six million barrels per year. The only other producing oil field in the territories is the Cameron Hills field southwest of Hay River. Combined production in 2010 was at more than 15,000 barrels per day.

Most of the natural gas reserves in the NWT lie beneath the Mackenzie Delta and the Beaufort Sea,

In the northern Mackenzie River delta there are thirty days in the winter when the sun does not rise at all and fifty-seven days in summer when the sun does not set. © *All Canada Photos/Alamy*

where discovered natural gas reserves are estimated at 16.2 trillion cubic feet. However, potential natural gas reserves have been estimated at more than four times that amount, at nearly 71 trillion cubic feet. To facilitate the shipment of natural gas from the region's primary Mackenzie Delta fields—Taglu, Nglintgak, and Parsons Lake—a new Mackenzie Gas Project pipeline has been proposed. The 743-mile (1,196-km) pipeline system could lead to a substantial increase in gas production for markets throughout Canada and into the United States. The demand for petroleum products has been increasing in the NWT by as much as 10 percent per year, primarily as a result of increased industrial development. More than half of the fuel used in the NWT is for transportation.

Building on the Potential for Hydroelectric Power

Forty-one percent of the region's total electricity supply comes from diesel-fired generating plants, but most of this sourced energy is used by the industrial sector. Residents are more likely to be linked to the hydroelectric power supply, with 77 percent of residential power coming from hydro sources. The Northwest Territories has six hydroelectric generating stations, providing about 32 percent of the total electrical supply. The potential for additional hydropower capacity is great. The region's six stations currently have a capacity of about 54.95 megawatts, but the potential for the region is estimated at 12,000 megawatts. In hopes of promoting the development of this renewable energy source, the government is working to implement a new *NWT Hydro Strategy* that could lead to greater energy independence, while also benefitting the environment through the reduction of greenhouse emissions. The government has also developed an *NWT Biomass Energy Strategy* to tap the region's potential for energy from wood. There are thirty-two diesel-fired thermal electric generating stations and two natural gas-fired stations in the NWT.

Energy for the Future

Published in 2007, *Energy for the Future: An Energy Plan for the Northwest Territories* provides a series of guidelines and basic principles for the development of energy policies and projects throughout the area. The plan focuses on the creation of energy efficiency programs, the reduction of energy consumption, and development of renewable energy sources that lead to greater energy independence. All energy initiatives are also aimed toward reducing energy costs and environmental impacts.

🌺 Green Business, Green Building, Green Jobs

Green Business & Green Jobs: Setting a Foundation

The economy of the Northwest Territories relies heavily on the mining industry, including gas, oil, and diamond production. Unfortunately, the continued development of this industry poses a significant challenge as local officials consider the ways to balance the need for development with the similarly pressing need to reduce energy consumption and protect the environment. While there are environmental jobs related to conservation and sustainable management efforts throughout the NWT, there is little else that might be considered as part of an official green economy. That may begin to change relatively soon, however, as the government has become more active in projects and strategies that promote the development of renewable energy. The *NWT Biomass Energy Strategy* and the *NWT Hydro Strategy* represent two major action plans that could lead to an increase in green business and green jobs. In the meantime, the government seems to be looking to build a new economy from a much more local level by encouraging residents and communities to embrace energy efficiency and sustainable living practices.

Green Building: Starting at Home

A major focus of the Northwest Territories government energy plan is the promotion of energy efficiency and renewable energy projects at residential, commercial, and industrial levels. The Alternative Energy Technologies Program is one initiative designed to assist residents and business owners in renovations of private and public buildings that lead to a reduction in energy consumption and/or a greater use of alternative energy sources. Funding for these projects is split into three categories. Through the Community Renewable Energy Fund, aboriginal and community governments may be eligible for funds covering up to 50 percent of total project costs for the installation of community-based alternative energy systems. The Medium Renewable Energy Fund provides up to one-third of project costs for commercial businesses. The Small Renewable Energy Fund offers one-third of the costs of funding for residential projects.

❧ The Mackenzie Gas Project

The Mackenzie Delta and the Beaufort Sea are believed to hold hidden resources that could prove to be extremely valuable, not only for the Northwest Territories, but for the nation as well. Discovered natural gas reserves in this region are estimated at about 16.2 trillion cubic feet. However, the potential natural gas reserves have been estimated at more than four times that amount, at nearly 71 trillion cubic feet. The proposed Mackenzie Gas Project represents a major effort to develop and facilitate the market for this vast reserve.

The project is sponsored by a coalition of companies led by Imperial Oil, including Shell Canada, Conoco-Phillips Canada, ExxonMobil Canada, Canada Properties, and the Aboriginal Pipeline Group. The latter organization represents the interests of the aboriginal people of the Northwest Territories. The project proposal includes plans to create three natural gas production facilities, a gathering pipeline system, a gas processing facility near Inuvik, a natural gas liquids pipeline from the Inuvik facility to Norman Wells, and a natural gas pipeline from the Inuvik facility into northwestern Alberta. The 743-mile (1,196-km) pipeline would run the entire length of the Mackenzie River and even further. It would be the biggest natural gas pipeline project in Canadian history and could lead to a major economic boom for the entire region, including increased tax revenues from the sale of natural gas and increased job opportunities in construction, operation, and other support occupations. However, optimism for the potential of this amazing project has been substantially tempered by concerns for the protection of the environment and the concerns of NWT residents.

The Impact on the Environment The proposed facilities will require a substantial increase in the consumption of petroleum products, which is already high within the Northwest Territories. The NWT government estimates that greenhouse gas emissions in the region are increasing by about 10 percent each year, just under normal development conditions. At a time when the federal and local governments are becoming more concerned over the issues of climate change, greenhouse gas emissions, and energy independence, such a massive fossil fuel-based development project seems to be directly opposed to the goals set for reducing energy consumption and improving energy efficiency.

The group Nature Canada has declared its concerns for the adverse effects on the land and wildlife of the Mackenzie River Valley, claiming that the project will cause major damage to the air, water, land, and wildlife surrounding the entire pipeline. The group asserts that construction of the pipeline will fragment habitats for caribou, bears, and wolves and cause permanent damage to important breeding and staging areas for millions of migratory birds. Construction will also require cutting of forest areas to develop the necessary infrastructure to support the project. Removing or changing surface vegetation is likely to lead to permafrost degradation and landscape change features, such as slumping, where the earth settles by sliding over itself. Such features could also damage pipelines and infrastructure. An additional concern is that the project will trigger an even greater rush in oil and gas development in the valley, leading to even greater environmental damage.

Economic Concerns

The Pembina Institute, a not-for-profit organization that provides policy research leadership and education on issues pertaining to climate change and green economics, has issued a report urging the Canadian government to consider the balance between corporate interests and resources owners, who are in this case the Canadian citizens. The oil and gas resources of the Northwest Territories are considered to be owned by all Canadian citizens and managed on their behalf by the government of Canada. The government is therefore responsible for ensuring fair compensation to the people for the use of these non-renewable resources. In *At a Crossroads: Achieving a Win-Win from Oil and Gas Developments in the Northwest Territories*, Pembina asserts that the royalty rate for oil and gas developments in the NWT is exceedingly low, which places corporate interests and profits ahead of the interests of the people. The group has urged the Canadian government to review and reform these royalty rates before the project moves forward.

Moving Forward

In December 2009, the Joint Review Panel for the Mackenzie Gas Project, which represents the Canadian Environmental Assessment Agency, issued a final report including more than 170 recommendations for the implementation and future monitoring and management of the project. The report concluded that, subject to full implementation of the panel's recommendations, there would be no significant adverse environmental, socioeconomic, or cultural effects as a result of the project. With the issue of this report, the project came under the review of the National Energy Board, an independent federal agency, which held a number of open hearings to consider the engineering, safety, and economic issues related to the project. The board approved the project in December 2010, but attached 264 conditions in the areas of engineering, safety and environmental protection that must be met by the partner companies. In 2011, the project saw several delays due to an extensive review process, and Shell Canada put its portion of the pipeline up for sale in July 2011 to get out of the project. The move prompted the other members of the consortium to ask the Canadian government for additional guarantees to ensure the pipeline becomes a reality. Consortium companies estimated another two years of development on the project before the four-year construction phase could begin.

BIBLIOGRAPHY

Books

Berkes, Fikret. *Breaking Ice: Renewable Resource and Ocean Management in the Canadian North.* Calgary: University of Calgary Press, 2005.

Dearden, Philip, and Rick Rollins. *Parks and Protected Areas in Canada: Planning and Management.* 3rd ed. Don Mills, ON: Oxford University Press, 2009.

Forbes Travel Guide: Canada. Chicago: Forbes Travel Guide, 2010.

Fosket, Jennifer. *Living Green.* Gabriola Island, BC: New Society Publishers, 2009.

Guide to the National Parks of Canada. Washington, DC: National Geographic, 2011.

Nahanni National Park Reserve of Canada Management Plan. Gatineau, Quebec: Parks Canada, 2010.

Wood Buffalo National Park Management Plan. Gatineau, Quebec: Parks Canada, 2010.

Web Sites

"Agriculture in the Northwest Territories." Agriculture and Agri-Food Canada. Available from http://www4.agr.gc.ca/AAFC-AAC/display-afficher.do?id=1198077564042&lang=eng

"Alternative Energies Technology Program." Government of the Northwest Territories Department of Environment and Natural Resources Available from http://www.enr.gov.nt.ca/_live/pages/wpPages/aetp.aspx

At a Crossroads: Achieving a Win-Win from Oil and Gas Developments in the Northwest Territories. The Pembina Institute. Available from http://pubs.pembina.org/reports/crossroads-nwt-oil-and-gas-revenue.pdf

"Canada: World Weather Information Service." World Meteorological Organization. Available from http://www.worldweather.org/056/m056.htm

"Canada's Diamond rush." *CBC News.* September 20, 2007. Available from http://www.cbc.ca/news/background/diamonds

Center for Energy: Northwest Territories. Available from http://www.centreforenergy.com/FactsStats/MapsCanada/NT-EnergyMap.asp

Ekati Diamond Mine. Available from http://www.bhpbilliton.com/bb/ourBusinesses/diamondsSpecialtyProducts/ekatiDiamondMine.jsp

Energy for the Future: An Energy Plan for the Northwest Territories. Government of the Northwest Territories. Available from http://www.iti.gov.nt.ca/Publications/2007/Energy/Energy%20for%20the%20Future.pdf

Government of the Northwest Territories: Industry, Tourism, Investment. Available from http://www.iti.gov.nt.ca

Government of the Northwest Territories Official Statement on Climate. Available from http://www.enr.gov.nt.ca/_live/documents/content/GNWT_Official_Statement_on_Climate_change.pdf

Growing Forward. Northwest Territories Industries, Tourism, and Investment. July 2009. Available from http://www.iti.gov.nt.ca/Publications/2010/furs-fishingagriculture/ITI_2290_Growing_Forward_Document_P6.pdf

Heiberg-Harrison, Nathalie. "New Greenhouse Targets Set For NWT." Northwest News Service. September 26, 2011. Available from http://nnsl.com/northern-news-services/stories/papers/sep26_11gg.html

Mackenzie Gas Project. Available from http://www.mackenziegasproject.com

Mackenzie Gas Project Office, Environment Canada. Available from http://www.ec.gc.ca/bpgm-mgpo/default.asp?lang=En&n=3A161B21-1

Nahanni National Park Reserve of Canada. Available from http://www.pc.gc.ca/pn-np/nt/nahanni/index.aspx

"National Energy Board Approves Mackenzie Gas Project." Canada National Energy Board. December 16, 2010. Available from https://www.neb-one.gc.ca/clf-nsi/rthnb/nwsrls/2010/nwsrls20-eng.html

Northern Voices, Northern Waters: Towards a Water Resources Management Strategy for the Northwest Territories. Government of Northwest Territories Department of Environment and Natural Resources. Available from http://www.enr.gov.nt.ca/_live/documents/content/Northern_Voices_Northern_Waters-Discussion_Paper.pdf

Northwest Territories Agriculture: State of the Industry 2000. Territorial Farmers Association. Available from http://www.farmnwt.com/State%20of%20the%20Industry%202000.pdf

Northwest Territories Biomass Energy Strategy. Northwest Territories Environment and Natural Resources.

January 2010. Available from http://www.enr.gov.nt.ca/_live/documents/content/NWT_Biomass_Energy_Strategy_2010.pdf

Northwest Territories Climate Change Impacts and Adaptation Report. Government of the Northwest Territories Department of Environment and Natural Resources. Available from http://www.enr.gov.nt.ca/_live/documents/content/NWT_Climate_Change_Impacts_and_Adaptation_Report.pdf

Northwest Territories Draft Hydro Strategy. Available from http://www.iti.gov.nt.ca/publications/2008/Energy/HYDROSTRATEGYSUMMARY.pdf

Northwest Territories Greenhouse Gas Strategy 2007–2011: A Strategy to Control Greenhouse Gas Emissions in the Northwest Territories. Government of the Northwest Territories Department of Environment and Natural Resources. Available from http://www.enr.gov.nt.ca/_live/documents/content/Greenhouse_Gas_Strategy_FINAL.pdf

Northwest Territories Power Corporation. Available from http://www.ntpc.com/index.html

Northwest Territories State of the Environment: Biodiversity 2010. Government of the Northwest Territories Department of Environment and Natural Resources. Available from http://www.enr.gov.nt.ca/_live/documents/content/2010_State_of_the_Environment_Biodiversity_Report.pdf

Northwest Territories State of the Environment Report Highlights 2009. Government of the Northwest Territories Department of Environment and Natural Resources. Available from http://www.enr.gov.nt.ca/_live/documents/content/NWT2009State_Enviro_ReportFINAL.pdf

"Northwest Territories Taiga." The Encyclopedia of the Earth. Available from http://www.eoearth.org/article/Northwest_Territories_taiga

"Our Wildlife." Government of the Northwest Territories Department of Environment and Natural Resources. Available from http://www.enr.gov.nt.ca/_live/pages/wpPages/Our_Wildlife.aspx

Penty, Rebecca. "N.W.T. Pushes Federal Government To Back Mackenzie Pipeline." *The Vancouver Sun.* July 18, 2011. Available from http://www.vancouversun.com/business/pushes+federal+government+back+Mackenzie+pipeline/5121776/story.html

"Take Action: Mackenzie Gas Project." Nature Canada. Available from http://www.naturecanada.ca/take_action_raise_voice_protect.asp

Wood Buffalo National Park of Canada. Available from http://www.pc.gc.ca/eng/pn-np/nt/woodbuffalo/index.aspx

Nova Scotia

Nova Scotia is Canada's second-smallest province, but is also the most populous province on Canada's Atlantic coast. The province is almost entirely surrounded by the Atlantic Ocean; nowhere in Nova Scotia is more than 42 miles (68 km) from the ocean. The province has traditionally had a resource-based economy, which has become diversified in recent years to incorporate an ever-growing offshore oil and gas industry, and more environmentally-friendly industries such as wind, hydro, tidal, and biomass energy. It has set ambitious standards for incorporating renewable energy into its portfolio in the near future, making it stand out among Canada's provinces. Nova Scotia's ComFIT (community feed-in tariff) program was North America's first-ever proposal to pay for community-owned tidal power plants.

Climate

Nova Scotia lies in the northern temperate zone and, although it is almost surrounded by water, the climate is classified modified continental rather than maritime. The temperature extremes of a continental climate, however, are moderated by the ocean. Because of cool currents of air and water from the Arctic alternating with warmer breezes from the Gulf Stream, extremes of summer and winter temperatures are not as evident as in central Canada. Average daily temperatures at the Halifax International Airport range from 21°F (-6°C) to 65°F (18.2°C) in July. The total average annual precipitation of 58.7 inches (149 cm) includes 107 inches (271 cm) of snowfall. Only on rare occasions does the temperature rise above 90°F (32°C) or fall below 14°F (-10°C) in winter. The frost-free season ranges from 120 days in northern Nova Scotia to 145 days in the Annapolis Valley.

In January 2009, Nova Scotia released *Toward a Greener Future: Nova Scotia's Climate Change Action Plan*. The plan has two goals—to reduce the province's greenhouse gas emissions (GHGs), and to prepare for the coming inevitable effects of climate change. The plan's target is to reduce GHG emissions by at least ten percent from 1990 levels by 2020. Nova Scotia plans to achieve this by imposing caps on emissions from Nova Scotia Power Inc. in 2010, 2015, and 2020. New air pollutant caps will also be put in place in 2015 and 2020. When it comes to transportation, the plan aims to compose Sustainable Transportation Strategy, make commercial trucks more efficient, provide incentives for consumers to use cars that use less fuel and cause less pollution, and enact regulations that will set fuel consumption and emissions standards for new vehicles. The plan also has nine actions devoted to adapting to the already inevitable effects of climate change, beginning with the creation of an Adaptation Fund for research and development. Such actions cannot be understated, as Nova Scotia is vulnerable to rising sea levels and an increase in strong storms due to its position at the end of the Atlantic hurricane track.

❧ Natural Resources, Water, and Agriculture

Natural Resources

Nova Scotia has more than 250 bird and mammal species. Deer, rabbit, pheasant, and ruffed grouse are prominent upland species, while beaver and waterfowl are common wetland species.

In 2010, there were 31 species of wildlife listed as at risk, and 24 species listed under the Nova Scotia Endangered Species Act. Mammal species include the American marten, Canada lynx, moose, and Gaspe shrew; bird species include piping plover, roseate tern, and harlequin duck; and plant species include pink coreopsis, thread-leaved sundew, and water-pennywort. The Atlantic whitefish and Blanding's turtle are also endangered.

Nova Scotia has 10.4 million acres (4.2 million ha) of forest. 1.5 million is owned by the province, 156,000 are

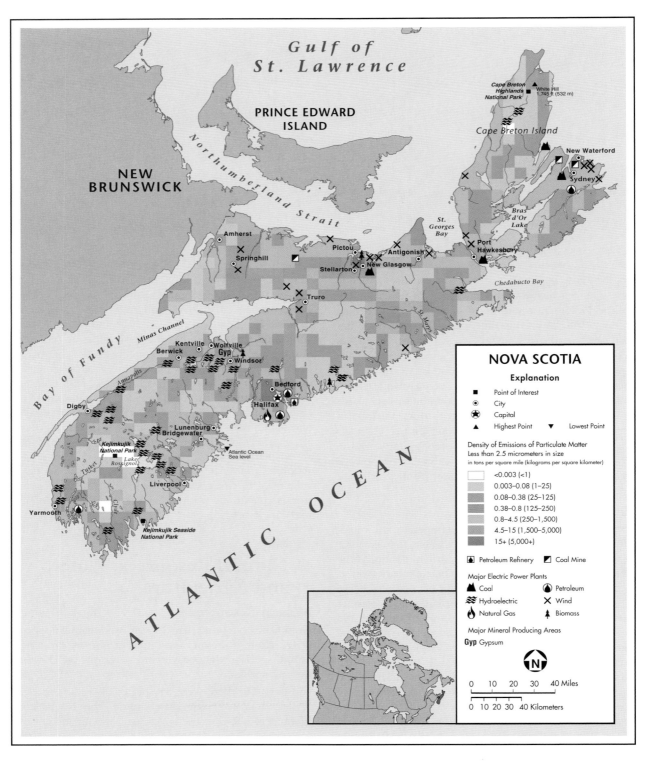

SOURCES: *Energy Facts and Statistics.* Centre for Energy. Available from http://www.centreforenergy.com/FactsStats/MapsCanada;
"Geographical Highlights." *The Canadian Encyclopedia.* Available from http://www.encyclopediecanadienne.ca/geoHighlights/
canmap_geog_v1_eng.swf; "Highest Points by Province and Territory." *The Atlas of Canada.* Natural Resources Canada. Available from
http://atlas.nrcan.gc.ca/site/english/learningresources/facts/faq.html#points; "Mining in Canada: Map." *Mining in Canada.* The Mining
Association of Canada. Available from http://www.mining.ca/site/images/MapofCanada.pdf; "Particulate Matter < 2.5 Micrometers
(PM2.5) Emission in 2007." *CAC Density Maps.* Environment Canada. Available from http://www.ec.gc.ca/inrp-npri/default.asp?
lang=en&n=BD725B2A-1. © 2011 Cengage Learning.

Nova Scotia Provincial Profile

Physical Characteristics

Land area	20,594 square miles (53,338 sq km)
Freshwater area	751 square miles (1,945 sq km)
Highest point	White Hill 1,745 feet (532 m)
Forest lands (2011)	10.5 million acres (4.2 million ha)
Provincial parks (2011)	125

Energy Statistics

Total electricity generated (2009)	11.6 million megawatt hours
Hydroelectric energy generation (2009)	1.1 million megawatt hours
Wind energy generation (2009)	100,000 megawatt hours
Tidal energy generation (2009)	30,000 megawatt hours
Biomass energy capacity (2009)	30.4 megawatts
Crude oil reserves (2009)	NA
Natural gas reserves (2009)	500.4 billion cubic feet (14.2 billion cu m)
Natural gas liquids (2009)	NA

Pollution Statistics

Carbon output (2009)	11.6 million tons of CO_2 (10.6 million t)
Federal contaminated sites receiving funds (2008)	29
Particulate matter (less than 2.5 micrometers) emissions (2009)	13,752 tons per year (12,476 t/yr)

SOURCES: *Canada's Greenhouse Gas Emissions*. Environment Canada. Available from http://www.ec.gc.ca/ges-ghg/default. asp?lang=En&n=1357A041-1; *Canada Year Book, 2011*. Statistics Canada. Available from http://www.statcan.gc.ca/pub/11-402-x/11-402-x2011000-eng.htm; *Energy Facts and Statistics*. Centre for Energy. Available from http://www.centreforenergy.com/FactsStats/MapsCanada; *Federal Contaminated Sites*. Government of Canada. Available from http://www.federalcontaminatedsites.gc.ca/index-eng. aspx; "Forest Land by Province and Territory." Statistics Canada. Available from http://www40.statcan.gc.ca/l01/cst01/envi34a-eng.htm; "Geographical Highlights." *The Canadian Encyclopedia*. Available from http://www. encyclopediecanadienne.ca/geoHighlights/canmap_geog_v1_eng.swf; *National Pollutant Release Inventory*. Environment Canada. Available from http://ec.gc.ca/pdb/websol/emissions/ap/ap_query_e.cfm

© 2011 Cengage Learning.

federal crown lands, 980,000 are owned by industry, and 2.8 million are privately owned. The province is covered mainly by softwood species, followed by mixed woods, and then hardwoods. Species of softwoods in the province include red and black spruce, balsam fir, white pine, eastern hemlock, eastern larch-tamarack, and red pine. Species of hardwoods include red maple, yellow birch, sugar maple, white birch, trembling and large tooth aspen, American beech, red oak, white ash, and grey birch. According to the *State of the Forest Report 1995–2005* from the Nova Scotia Department of Natural Resources, the total impact of the forest industry was C$700 million to the provincial GDP. The industry also employs 11,000 people and generates

exports of more than C$1billion or 17 percent of Nova Scotia export trade.

According to the Nova Scotia Department of Natural Resources, Nova Scotia is Canada's largest gypsum producer. The province also produces substantial amounts of crushed stone, salt, and coal. Minerals mined in smaller amounts include sand and gravel, limestone, anhydrite, peat, and metals. In 2006, total production value from the minerals industry was C$377 million, with a total impact on the provincial GDP of C$218.3 million.

Water

Nova Scotia's indented shoreline stretches 6,478 miles (10,424 km), while inland is a myriad of lakes and streams. The province is surrounded by three major bodies of water, the Gulf of Saint Lawrence to the north, the Bay of Fundy to the west, and the Atlantic Ocean to the south and east. Two major lakes include Bras d'Or Lake, a large body of salt water dominating the center of Cape Breton Island in the northeastern part of the province. Major rivers that drain into the lake include Baddeck River, Middle River, and Georges River. The largest freshwater lake in the province is Lake Rossignol, located in the southwestern part of the province, the modern shoreline of which was created in 1928 by the damming of the Mersey River.

Commercial and sports fishing are big business in Nova Scotia, ranking second in the province's major commodity groups under non-metallic minerals and fuels. In 2007, the province ranked first in value in fish landings, with a value of just under C$6 million. The fish with the highest quantities harvested were haddock, hake, herring, scallop, lobster, shrimp, and crab. Nova Scotia also had the highest value in fish exports as well, with over $950 million. Most of their exports go to the United States, Denmark, and Japan.

In December 2010, Nova Scotia introduced Water For Life, a new water plan. The strategy is a ten-year look at water issues facing the province and includes an integrated water management strategy, which takes a comprehensive look at all aspects of water usage, as well as human activities and their effect on the watersheds and ecosystems. Part of the integrated water management strategy involves creating a Nova Scotia Water Advisory Group to work with the provincial government. It also includes actions for protecting the water supply and increasing knowledge about the province's water resources.

Agriculture

In 2009, there were 3,795 farms in Nova Scotia, covering more than 995,000 acres of land. Crops in the province include corn for grain, barley, hay, wheat, oats, and corn. Top cattle are dairy and beef cows, and the province also has hog and sheep farms, and produces chickens, fowl, and turkey. Other crops in the province include potatoes,

Nova Scotia has about 3,795 farms covering more than 995,000 acres of land. The province also has 26 wind farms as of June 2011. © *Steve Winter/National Geographic/Getty Images*

honey, and mink pelts. Top fruits produced include apples, blueberries, and strawberries, while top vegetables include carrots, onions, and corn. The Annapolis Valley is referred to as the breadbasket of Nova Scotia. Nestled between the north and south mountains, the valley is home to many farms, markets, and vineyards that are popular destinations for anyone seeking farm fresh produce or a local wine. In addition to a wide range of fruits and vegetables, the Annapolis Valley is famous for its apples—a fact that is celebrated each spring in the four-day Apple Blossom Festival.

⚘ Energy

Nova Scotia's energy resources include natural gas, coal, wind, and hydropower. The province generates electricity from these sources as well as fuel oil. In 2008, provincial government revenues included $451.8 million in petroleum. Mining, oil and gas extraction, and utilities accounted for 5.4 percent of Nova Scotia's gross domestic product in the same year. Nova Scotia's energy workforce averaged 5,600 employees in 2010.

Oil and Gas Nova Scotia has worked with mainly offshore operations extracting oil and natural gas. The Sable Offshore Energy Project is underway, and the Deep Panuke natural gas project is forthcoming, with first production estimated for June 2012. Natural gas from the Sable project is pumped into the Maritimes and Northeast Pipeline, and most of it is shipped from there to the northeastern United States. The Sable project recently added a compression deck which should boost output by 25 percent and significantly increase overall project deliverability until 2016. The Deep Panuke project will be located about 109 miles (175 km) offshore of Nova Scotia, and the C$800 million project is expected to deliver between 200 million and 300 million cubic feet of natural gas per day. There are more than 630 billion cubic feet of natural gas available at Deep Panuke. The gas from Deep Panuke has been purchased by Repsol YPF, a Spanish oil and gas company.

The province began exploring onshore resources in only the past ten years, with a focus on gas, shale gas, and coal bed methane. The province has two production agreements for coalbed methane and one production lease for shale gas, and several companies are actively working on their exploration agreements by drilling wells and completing seismic programs.

The Royal Annapolis Tidal Generating Station is North America's only tidal power plant. © *Stephen Saks Photography/Alamy*

In 2009, the BEPCo Canada Company successfully bid for two offshore parcels for exploration. The combined potential resource in the two parcels is estimated to be from 3.3 to 10 trillion cubic feet of natural gas in place. As of late 2011, BEPCo Canada Co. was preparing to drill a deepwater well about 124 miles (200 km) south of Halifax.

The oil and gas industry's direct contribution to the Nova Scotia economy is up to C$990 million. The province has three petroleum-fired plants and one natural gas-fired plant that generate electricity.

Alternative Energy Sources Nova Scotia has energy projects in wind, hydro, biomass, and tidal power in place. The province had 26 wind farms as of June 2011, and could have as many as 300 or more by 2013. In a 2009 report commissioned by the Nova Scotia government, four renewable energy scenarios were presented, with the most favored involving a focus on wind energy and biomass energy. The report found that Nova Scotia residents overwhelmingly supported wind energy projects, and the outlook for biomass was generally positive, as long as trees were harvested in a way that is respectful of the environment.

Most of Nova Scotia's potential freshwater resources have already been developed for hydroelectricity. However, the Nova Scotia Department of Energy reviews those resources annually, from the perspectives of feasibility, economics, and the environment. The technology is constrained in the province due to its geography and the lack of a major river system to power a system. Therefore, most of the province's 32 hydro plants are small by utility standards, with the exception of the 230 megawatt plant at Wreck Cove, Victoria County. There are also two small privately owned hydro plants in Nova Scotia. In 2000, 8 percent of Nova Scotia's electricity was produced by hydro systems. Since the potential for hydro power is limited in the province, Nova Scotia has been looking outside of its borders for hydro power sources. The province is actively engaged in discussions to secure renewable hydro resources from the proposed Lower Churchill Falls development in Labrador. The hydroelectricity from Lower Churchill Falls could be available as early as 2015. However, it would require significant transmission infrastructure to have it delivered to Nova Scotia.

Nova Scotia's Bay of Fundy provides the province with tidal energy. Tidal energy is a form of hydropower that converts the energy of the tides into electricity. The technology used is called a tidal in-stream energy conversion (TISEC) device, which resembles an underwater windmill. Estimates suggest that tidal energy in the Bay of Fundy could produce up to 300 megawatts of energy, which is enough for about 100,000 homes.

Renewable Electricity Plan In April 2010, the government of Nova Scotia released *Renewable Electricity Plan: A Path to Good Jobs, Stable Prices, and a Cleaner Environment*. The plan has a target of reaching 25 percent renewable electricity by 2015, and 40 percent renewable electricity by 2020. This means that by 2020, the province will have the equivalent of 500,000 homes running on renewable power. To achieve this goal, the plan will split large and medium-sized projects evenly between Nova Scotia Power and independent producers; will establish a community-based feed-in tariff for community projects; will expand and enhance net-metering for individual projects and small businesses; and will incorporate biomass, tidal, and solar power to meet the targets.

Green Business, Green Building, Green Jobs

Green Business

In 2007, the Nova Scotia government passed the Environmental Goals and Sustainable Prosperity Act, which is comprised of 21 goals that recognize the critical link between the environment and the economy. Some goals commit to strategies that support stewardship of natural capital (land, water, wetlands, forests, minerals, parks and biodiversity), and other goals support clean air and water. Infrastructure related goals, such as the requirement for primary wastewater treatment, or the drinking water facility standards, link to built capital. All goals have a financial impact, such as the cost to the health care system of poor air quality or benefits that come from stewardship of our natural resources. As of 2011, the province had met and in some cases exceeded 10 of the 21 goals, and the act made strides in the areas of sustainability, including requiring all government buildings be built to LEED Silver status, and the adoption of a sustainable procurement policy, which requires businesses to consider environmental, social, and economic factors when making purchasing decisions. Also, earlier in 2011, the government created the C\$24 million provincial Clean Technology Fund designed to provide capital for local companies developing innovative green opportunities.

Nova Scotia offers a number of incentives for businesses that want to become more energy efficient and environmentally friendly. The province offers solar air and solar water heating rebates of up to 15 percent for businesses that install a system approved by Natural Resources Canada. The LEAF Program, through Canadian Manufacturers and Exporters (CME), offers manufacturing and export businesses funding of up to 75 percent for hiring a qualified consultant to carry out efficiency audits with an energy, productivity, or environmental focus.

Green Building

The government of Nova Scotia started the PerformancePlus: New Home Energy Efficiency Rebate Program in September 2010. The program provides rebates for homebuilders and new homeowners that build energy efficient homes in the province. For builders, rebate amounts increase based on the home's energy performance and range from C\$3,000 to C\$7,000. The higher the home's EnerGuide rating is, the more efficient the home will be.

In May 2010, the Conserve Nova Scotia program released the *Nova Scotia EnerGuide for Houses*, a guide to the province's rebates and incentives for retrofitting homes to be more energy efficient, or building new homes with sustainable features. One of the rebates available provides up to C\$1,250 for homes that install residential solar water heating systems.

Green Jobs

Nova Scotia Community College constructed the Centre for the Built Environment at their Waterfront Campus in Dartmouth. Finished in 2010, this state of the art teaching facility incorporates such things as solar panels, a solar hot water system, wind turbines, geothermal heating and cooling, and a green roof to reduce heating and cooling demands. With the Centre for the Built Environment as an example of green building, students also have the opportunity to receive a diploma in Natural Resources Environmental Technology, Energy Sustainability Engineering Technology, Environmental Engineering Technology—Water Resources, and to take part in a Residential Solar Hot Water workshop at the college.

Dalhousie University in Halifax offers a major in Environment, Sustainability and Society through its College of Sustainability. The College studies sustainability-based problems through a range of exciting lectures, seminars, and activities. Some of the College's strongest research areas lie in marine biology, climate change, and management with a focus on sustainability.

Saint Mary's University in Halifax offers a course in Green Chemistry, the design of chemical products and processes that reduce or eliminate the use and generation of hazardous substances. Also, Acadia University in Wolfville has a Renewable Energy seminar, which studies wind, solar, hydro, and geothermal energy and how governments, industries, and individuals are embracing these technologies. Along with this seminar, Acadia offers a major in Environmental and Sustainability Studies. The program offers two degree options—a Bachelor of Arts or a Bachelor in Recreation Management—with a choice of four concentration areas: Environmental Advocacy, Education & Activism; Sustainable Community Development; Innovation and Entrepreneurship for Sustainability; and Environmental Thought and Practice.

In the summer of 2010, Acadia University, the Nova Scotia Department of Environment, and Nova Scotia Community College developed the Nova Scotia Waste Resource Management Institute (WRMI). The Institute teaches students how to solve the many challenges associated with creating and maintaining composting operations, collecting organics, and developing backyard composting systems.

In another step in green job creation, it was announced in 2010 that the government of Nova Scotia was joining forces with Daewoo Shipbuilding and Marine Engineering, Ltd. (DSME) to establish a wind turbine tower and blade manufacturing facility at the site of a former railcar manufacturing company in Trenton. This new venture will create hundreds of new jobs, with 120 staff hired in the first year of operation.

Nova Scotia is using its development of renewable resources as a springboard for economic development and creation of sustainable jobs. Since 1990, Nova Scotia's economic growth was the slowest of all of Canada's provinces, and now it faces even greater challenges, such as a decline of more than 20,000 members in its workforce, mostly due to retirements. The province created *jobsHere: The Plan To Grow Our Economy* in 2010 as a strategy to jumpstart local employment. The government committed C\$200 million over three years to support initiatives, which include learning the right skills for good jobs, growing the economy through innovation, and helping businesses be more competitive globally.

❧ Biomass Energy in Nova Scotia: Sustainable or Detrimental?

There has been an ongoing debate about whether using biomass to create electricity would be a viable option to help Nova Scotia reach its requirement that 10 percent of the energy supply must come from renewable sources by

Sunset on the coast of Nova Scotia. © *gary yim/ShutterStock.com*

2013. Biomass energy involves burning wood waste such as bark, chips, and scrub logs in a steam boiler to generate electricity. In 2009, Nova Scotia Power and NewPage Port Hawkesbury paper mill presented a proposal for a biomass facility to the Nova Scotia Utility and Review Board (URB), which rejected it on the grounds that it didn't have the authority to approve an operational expense for an amount that would affect power rates for more than two decades. It also said there wasn't enough information to judge the value of the project.

In 2010, Nova Scotia Power and NewPage submitted a new proposal to the URB. The plan is to develop a 60-megawatt biomass facility that could produce three percent of the province's electricity, supplying up to 50,000 homes. The new proposal promises to create an additional 150 jobs and maintain the current mill jobs. The project plans to use "stem wood," which leaves tree stumps and branches on the forest floor in order to restore nutrients to the soil and to prevent carbon loss. The facility should eliminate the mill's need for oil and also provide energy to the province. However, many environmentalists remain concerned.

Despite protests from environmentalists, the plan was approved by the Nova Scotia URB in October 2010, but with conditions. The URB stated that any cost overruns that occur during construction or plant failures must be taken care of by the utility's shareholders, and not by customers. This is to protect customers from any costs to them that would be out of their control. NewPage estimates that construction of the facility will take 27 months, when the full implications of the project will finally be determined.

A Danger to Forests?

Environmental groups have been critical of the project, stating that it would encourage clear-cutting and require that too much of the forest be cut down. They are also worried that harvesting will occur in forested areas that are already listed as endangered. The project would require at least over 350,000 tons of wood per year. Despite a promise from Nova Scotia Power to hire a third-party auditor to make sure NewPage only uses stem wood, environmentalists claim there still isn't enough regulation in place to deter clear-cutting, or whole-tree harvesting, in private lots. They want a policy banning whole-tree harvesting completely. Currently, the Department of Natural Resources is working on standards for whole-tree harvesting; however, it would only apply to Crown-owned land, and still leaves privately owned land without any regulation. The fact that most wood lots are in small, private holdings makes it difficult to manage and regulate harvesting.

NewPage claims that they would only be using the equivalent of one percent of the land it manages for biomass energy, which represents only a small part of what they do. They have also maintained that they will adhere to government standards when extracting biomass from private woodlots. According to a 2009 report commissioned by the Nova Scotia government, if regulated properly, biomass could generate 15 percent of the province's renewable energy. However, environmentalists remain skeptical of NewPage's claims and of whether or not biomass would indeed be a sustainable source of energy.

NewPage threw a kink into the biomass plans, however, when it shut down its Port Tupper papermill operations and stopped harvesting there in August 2011. The company filed for Chapter 11 bankruptcy restructuring in September 2011, and agreed to sell the Port Tupper facility to pay down debts. Work had already begun on a C$208 million biomass facility for Nova Scotia Power in Point Tupper that was to use the wood waste from the papermill to produce biomass energy. The biomass facility was scheduled to come online in 2013, and was designed to create 60 MW of electricity for Nova Scotia Power. The power company intended to finish the biomass facility in spite of the NewPage closure.

BIBLIOGRAPHY

Books

Cape Breton Highlands National Park of Canada Management Plan. Gatineau, Quebec: Parks Canada, 2010.

Canso Islands and Grassy Island Fort National Historic Sites of Canada Management Plan. Ottawa: Parks Canada, 2009.

Ernst, Chloe. *Scenic Driving Atlantic Canada: Nova Scotia, New Brunswick, Prince Edward Island, Newfoundland, & Labrador.* Guilford, CT: GPP Travel, 2011.

Kejimkujik National Park of Canada Management Plan. Gatineau, Quebec: Parks Canada, 2010.

Matchar, Emily and Karla Zimmerman. *Nova Scotia, New Brunswick & Prince Edward Island,* 2nd ed. London: Lonely Planet, 2011.

Web Sites

2009 Agricultural Statistics. Nova Scotia Department of Agriculture. Available from http://www.gov.ns.ca/ agri/marketing/statistics/agriculture/nsstats2009. pdf

Adams, Michelle, and David Wheeler. *Stakeholder Consultation Process for: A Renewable Energy Strategy for Nova Scotia.* Dalhousie University. Available from http://www.gov.ns.ca/energy/resources/EM/ renewable/Wheeler-Renewable-Stakeholder-Consultation-Report.pdf

Bay of Fundy Tidal Energy: A Response to the Strategic Environmental Assessment. Nova Scotia Department of Energy. Available from http://www.gov.ns.ca/ energy/resources/EM/tidal/Tidal-SEA-Report-screen.pdf

"Biomass Energy Plan OK'd." CBC News. October 14, 2010. Available from http://www.cbc.ca/canada/ nova-scotia/story/2010/10/14/ns-biomass-approved.html?ref=rss

Centre for the Built Environment. Nova Scotia Community College. Available from http://www.nscc. ca/sites/CBE/

"Deep Panuke Start Date Changes Again." CBC News Canada. October 5, 2011. Available from http:// www.cbc.ca/news/canada/nova-scotia/story/ 2011/10/05/ns-encana-sbn-timeline.html

Economic Impact of the Mineral Industry in Nova Scotia. Nova Scotia Department of Natural Resources. Available from http://www.tmans.ca/MANS_files/ documents/local/Gardner-Pinfold%20report% 20May%202008.pdf

Environmental Goals and Sustainable Prosperity Act: Progress Report 2011. Nova Scotia Department of Environment. July 2011. Available from http://gov. ns.ca/nse/egspa/docs/EGSPA.2011.Annual. Report.pdf

"Fast Facts: Nova Scotia Fish Landings." Nova Scotia Fisheries and Aquaculture. Available from http:// www.gov.ns.ca/fish/marketing/statistics/ FastFacts_97-07.pdf

jobsHere: The Plan To Grow Our Economy. Government of Nova Scotia. November 2010. Available from http://www.gov.ns.ca/jobshere/docs/jobsHere-ThePlanToGrowOurEconomy.pdf

Linds, Jonathan. "Biomass Pros & Cons." *The Coast.* April 8, 2010. Available from http://www.thecoast. ca/halifax/biomass-pros-and-cons/Content? oid=1600303

"N.S. Biomass Energy Project Planned." CBC News. April 5, 2010. Available from http://www.cbc.ca/ canada/nova-scotia/story/2010/04/05/ns-biomass-newpage-power.html

Nova Scotia Department of Energy. Available from http://www.gov.ns.ca/energy/

Nova Scotia EnerGuide for Houses. Conserve Nova Scotia. Available from http://www.conservens.ca/ resources/energuide/EnerGuide-Rebate-Guide.pdf

"Nova Scotia Invests in Jobs, Green Economy." Government of Nova Scotia. March 5, 2010. Available from http://gov.ns.ca/news/smr/2010-03-05-trenton.asp

Parent, Mark. *Bill No. 146: Environmental Goals and Sustainable Prosperity Act.* Nova Scotia House of Assembly. April 12, 2007. Available from http://nslegislature.ca/legc/bills/60th_1st/1st_read/b146.htm

"PerformancePlus: New Home Energy Efficiency Rebate Program." Conserve Nova Scotia. Available from http://www.conservens.ca/performanceplus/

"New Page To Initiate Downtime at Port Hawkesbury Mill." NewPage Corporation. August 22, 2011. Available from http://investors.newpagecorp.com/index.php?s=43&item=199

Programs and Courses. Nova Scotia Community College. Available from http://www.nscc.ca/learning_programs/programs/default.aspx

Province of Nova Scotia Sustainable Procurement Policy. Nova Scotia Procurement Services. Available from https://www.gov.ns.ca/tenders/policy/pdf_files/procurementpolicy.pdf

Renewable Electricity Plan: A path to good jobs, stable prices, and a cleaner environment. 2010. Nova Scotia Department of Energy. Available from http://www.gov.ns.ca/energy/resources/EM/renewable/renewable-electricity-plan.pdf

Nova Scotia's Species at Risk: Conservation and Recovery. Available from http://www.speciesatrisk.ca/

"Sourcing Biomass." *Cape Breton Post.* September 14, 2011. Available from http://www.capebretonpost.com/Opinion/Editorial/2011-09-14/article-2747510/Sourcing-biomass/1

State of the Forest Report 1995–2005, Nova Scotia Forests in Transition. Nova Scotia Department of Natural Resources. Available from http://www.gov.ns.ca/natr/forestry/reports/State-Of-Forest-Report–April-2008.pdf

Toward a Greener Future: Nova Scotia's Climate Change Action Plan. Nova Scotia Department of Environment. Available from http://www.gov.ns.ca/energy/resources/spps/energy-strategy/Climate-Change-Action-Plan-2009.pdf

Water For Life: Nova Scotia's Water Resource Management Strategy. Nova Scotia Department of Environment. December 2010. Available from http://www.gov.ns.ca/nse/water.strategy/docs/WaterStrategy_Water.Resources.Management.Strategy.pdf

Nunavut

Nunavut, an Inuktitut word meaning "our land," was formerly a part of the Northwest Territories until 1999, when it became a separate territory. Nunavut is the largest political subdivision in Canada, with 18 percent of the total area of the country. Nunavut has a total area of 708,434 square miles (1.83 million sq km), making it both the least populous and the largest in geography of the provinces and territories of Canada. It has a mostly Inuit population of 29,474, spread over an area the size of Western Europe. Nunavut is also home to the north-ernmost permanently inhabited place in the world, Alert.

Climate

As in other northern provinces and territories, the varying amounts of daylight over the year are the strongest drivers of climatological and hydrological gradients in the region: between 20 and 24 hours of daylight in June and up to 24 hours of darkness in December. In January, the capital Iqaluit has only about 4.5 hours of daylight, but 20 hours of daylight in July. Average January temperatures range from -4°F (-20°C) along southern Baffin Island to -35°F (-37°C) along northern Ellesmere Island. Average July temperatures range from 50°F (10°C) along the southern mainland to 36°F (2°C) in the north; inland temperatures are warmer. Annual precipitation ranges from less than 3.9 inches (9.9 cm) around Ellesmere Island to 23.6 inches (59.9 cm) on southern Baffin Island. Most of Nunavut receives less than 11.8 inches (29.9 cm) of precipitation per year.

Taking Action for a Changing Climate In 2003, the territorial Department of Sustainable Development released the "Nunavut Climate Strategy." The report notes that over the last century the rise in temperature in some parts of Canada has been approximately 1°C, a rise that has never been recorded in such a short time span. Researchers are already seeing the effects of climate change in northern regions, such as the thinning of Arctic ice by nearly 40 percent over the last 30 years and extensive permafrost degradation. Native animals dependent on the cold climate will also be severely impacted as the changing weather patterns disrupt their habitats and activities. The report goes on to list the potential impacts that climate change will have on Nunavut, some of which include: the increase of temperatures by 41–45°F (5°–7°C), the disappearance of over one-half of the existing permafrost, flooding of low-lying coastal areas, loss of glaciers, introduction of new diseases, and loss of wildlife, fish, and plant species. Decreasing permafrost has additional consequences, as it threatens infrastructure and water resources by changing how water is stored and moved in the landscape.

The goals of Nunavut's Climate Change Strategy are to reduce greenhouse gas emissions, monitor climate change impacts, and develop adaptation strategies through 2013. These goals will be met by engaging government, non-government, industry, and the public in discussions about climate change and encouraging these sectors to take action. This will be accomplished by advancing knowledge of climate change through scientif-ic research and traditional Inuit institutions, and by identifying and implementing both long- and short-term actions to reduce greenhouse gas emissions and make use of more energy-efficient technologies. Actions taken will build upon and coordinate with existing legislation, policies, and initiatives of the government and specific actions taken to achieve the goals of the strategy will be contained in business plans. These business plans will be updated every three to five years in order to keep up with new technologies and funding.

❧ Natural Resources, Water, and Agriculture

Natural Resources

A short but intense summer produces many small but brilliant flowers in Nunavut, including purple saxifrage, sedge, louseworts, fireweed, and wintergreen. Other

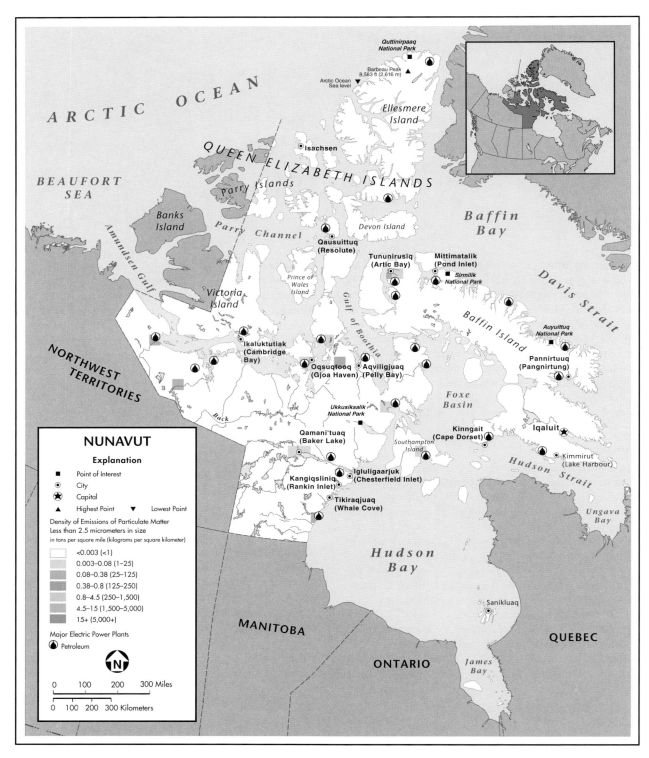

SOURCES: *Energy Facts and Statistics.* Centre for Energy. Available from http://www.centreforenergy.com/FactsStats/MapsCanada; "Geographical Highlights." *The Canadian Encyclopedia.* Available from http://www.encyclopediecanadienne.ca/geoHighlights/ canmap_geog_v1_eng.swf; "Highest Points by Province and Territory." *The Atlas of Canada.* Natural Resources Canada. Available from http://atlas.nrcan.gc.ca/site/english/learningresources/facts/faq.html#points; "Mining in Canada: Map." *Mining in Canada.* The Mining Association of Canada. Available from http://www.mining.ca/site/images/MapofCanada.pdf; "Particulate Matter < 2.5 Micrometers (PM2.5) Emission in 2007." *CAC Density Maps.* Environment Canada. Available from http://www.ec.gc.ca/inrp-npri/default.asp? lang=en&n=BD725B2A-1. © 2011 Cengage Learning.

Iceberg south of Devon Island, Nunavut. © *iStockPhoto.com/Murphy Shewchuk*

common flowers in the south include dandelions, chamomile daisies, harebells, and buttercups. About 200 species of flowers grow north of the tree line. The animal population in Nunavut includes mammals such as the caribou, musk ox, barren-ground grizzly bear, wolf, wolverine, fox, ermine, and hare. Caribou alone outnumber Nunavut's human population 25 to 1. Common marine mammals include seals, walruses, whales (including belugas, narwhals, bowhead whales, killer whales, blue whales, and sperm whales), and polar bears. Bird species include gyrfalcon, snowy and short-eared owl, rough-legged hawk, golden eagle, snow goose, goldeneye, and green-winged teal. Fish include lake trout, Arctic grayling, Arctic char, walleye, whitefish, and northern pike. Mosquitoes also breed in the shallow tundra lakes, and are an integral part of the regions food web.

In 2011, there were five animal species listed as endangered: Beluga whale (in the Eastern Hudson Bay), Eskimo curlew, ivory gull, red knot rufa, and Peary caribou. The beluga whale of Cumberland Sound were considered a threatened species, as were the peregrine falcon and Ross's gull. Only one plant species, a moss called Porsild's bryum, was considered to be threatened.

Nunavut boasts 20 parks and "special places," from Tupirvik Territorial Park in the north to the Thelon Wildlife Sanctuary in the south. The Thelon Wildlife Sanctuary covers 20,077 square miles (52,000 sq km) and was established in 1927 in order to conserve local muskox populations. Nunavut's parks not only offer sanctuary for native species, but provide campgrounds, hiking trails, and fishing spots for visitors so that they may learn more about the territory and its wildlife. Nunavut also has eight migratory bird sanctuaries and two national wildlife areas at Nirjutiqavvik and Polar Bear Pass.

Seal hunting and its associated activities contribute more than C$1 million to Nunavut's economy. A European Union (EU) seal ban enacted in 2010 may negatively impact revenues generated from the territory's seal hunt. Though the ban does not include trade from aboriginal groups, Nunavut's Inuit population fear the market will decline dramatically. The Tapiriit Kanatami, an organization representing Canada's Inuit seal hunters, appealed to the European General Court to revoke the ban. The court, however, sided with the EU in September 2011, upholding the ban due to issues of admissibility. Members of Tapiriit Kanatami said they would appeal the court ruling. Meanwhile, Nunavut is continuing to hone its own Sealing Strategy, which is designed to support the seal market and educate the public on the importance of sealing. Projects within the strategy include workshops, a

Nunavut Territorial Profile

Physical Characteristics

Land area	747,537 square miles (1,936,112 sq km)
Freshwater area	60,648 square miles (157,078 sq km)
Highest point	Barbeau Peak 8,583 feet (2,616 m)
Forest lands (2011)	2.0 million acres (0.8 million ha)
Territorial parks (2011)	36

Energy Statistics

Total electricity generated (2009)	NA
Hydroelectric energy generation (2009)	NA
Wind energy generation (2009)	NA
Tidal energy generation (2009)	NA
Biomass energy capacity (2009)	NA
Crude oil reserves (2009)	11.9 million barrels (1.9 million cu m)
Natural gas reserves (2009)	353.1 billion cubic feet (10.0 billion cu m)
Natural gas liquids (2009)	NA

Pollution Statistics

Carbon output (2009)	NA
Federal contaminated sites receiving funds (2008)	27
Particulate matter (less than 2.5 micrometers) emissions (2009)	787 tons per year (714 t/yr)

SOURCES: *Canada's Greenhouse Gas Emissions*. Environment Canada. Available from http://www.ec.gc.ca/ges-ghg/default.asp?lang=En&n=1357A041-1; *Canada Year Book, 2011*. Statistics Canada. Available from http://www.statcan.gc.ca/pub/11-402-x/11-402-x2011000-eng.htm; *Energy Facts and Statistics*. Centre for Energy. Available from http://www.centreforenergy.com/FactsStats/MapsCanada; *Federal Contaminated Sites*. Government of Canada. Available from http://www.federalcontaminatedsites.gc.ca/index-eng.aspx; "Forest Land by Province and Territory." Statistics Canada. Available from http://www40.statcan.gc.ca/l01/cst01/envi34a-eng.htm; "Geographical Highlights." *The Canadian Encyclopedia*. Available from http://www.encyclopediecanadienne.ca/geoHighlights/canmap_geog_v1_eng.swf; *National Pollutant Release Inventory*. Environment Canada. Available from http://ec.gc.ca/pdb/websol/emissions/ap/ap_query_e.cfm

© 2011 Cengage Learning.

fur development program, and public education via websites and promotional materials.

There is no forestry in Nunavut, as the territory lies nearly entirely north of the tree line (except for small areas of the south and west). As a result, firewood is in short supply.

When it comes to mining, Nunavut ranks in the top five of Canadian provinces and territories in exploration expenditures, with diamonds, gold, uranium, and base metals as the main exploration targets. The only mineral mined in the territory was gold until 2006, when the first diamond mine opened called the Jericho Diamond Project. Mineral exploration expenditure approached C$280 million in 2010, with plans for more mines to open in the near future. To continue Nunavut's position as a major mineral region, the government created *Parnautit: The Nunavut Mineral Exploration & Mining Strategy*, which details the region's framework for mineral exploration and mining.

In 2011, steelmaker ArcelorMittal and its partner Nunavut Iron Ore Acquisition, took control over the proposed Baffinland Iron Mines on Baffin Island in the northern part of Nunavut. The area is estimated to have potential for more than 780 million metric tons of iron ore. The companies will undergo an assessment and review process, which was expected to be completed in 2013 before mining could begin. However, logistics of mining the area will require ways to move massive amounts of ore out of the Arctic region.

Water: Glaciers and Ice Caps

The landscape of Nunavut has been shaped by ice sheets and glaciers, which carved out deep valleys and fjords, while the perenially frozen ground (permafrost) controls the storage and movement of water through this landscape. Today, glaciers and ice caps cover about 57,900 square miles (150,000 sq km) of Nunavut. However, in the twenty-first century, rising temperatures are leading to retreating sea ice, the alteration of the size and structure of the glaciers of Nunavut, and permafrost loss, which will alter hydrologic drainage patterns impacting freshwater and wetland sustainability.

Major mainland rivers include the Back and Coppermine, which flow north to the Arctic coast. The Thelon, Kazan, and Dubawnt rivers flow into Hudson Bay. Permafrost prevents runoff from draining into the ground, causing rivers and streams to flow rapidly after the spring thaw.

Sport fishing is a popular activity and is a source of income from tourism. In 2000, there were 662 active resident anglers in Nunavut. Principal species sought in Nunavut include Arctic char, Arctic grayling, and lake trout. Commercial fishing is a young industry but is already contributing to the territory's economic growth, estimated to contribute C$12 to C$14 million to the economy annually and provide more than 300 seasonal jobs. The highest growth has been seen in the offshore shrimp and turbot fisheries, a growing inshore fishery on south Baffin Island, and the maintenance of a sustainable harvest of wild char from lakes and rivers across the territory. In 2005, the landed value of turbot was C$23.6 million and C$2.9 million for shrimp. In 2004, the domestic use of Arctic char had a food replacement value of nearly C$4.4 million and commercial char sales were valued at C$1.2 million. Nunavut's largest fish processing facility is in Pangnirtung, with smaller operations in Iqaluit, Rankin Inlet, and Cambridge Bay, and several community facilities, such as those in Gjoa Haven, Chesterfield Inlet, and Whale Cove.

Agriculture

Nunavut did not have any farms as of 2001. Since 2004, the Nunavut Harvesters' Association has been working with the Canadian government through a program called Advancing Canadian Agriculture and Agri-Food (ACAAF) to explore new possibilities for establishing agricultural and agri-food industries in the region. Otherwise, Nunavut serves a specialized market for fish, shrimp, caribou, and muskox.

❧ Energy

The main source of energy produced in Nunavut is petroleum-fired thermal electricity. All of Nunavut's electricity, heating and transportation needs are met by imported fossil fuel. Two oil fields, seven gas fields, and seven oil and gas fields have been discovered in the Nunavut Arctic islands. Crude oil resources in Nunavut are estimated to be 322.9 million barrels, with an ultimate potential resource of 2,662 million barrels. The Brent Horn oil field was the only oil field that was operated from 1985 to 1996, producing 2.8 million barrels of oil. As there are no refineries in Nunavut, the oil was shipped by tanker to a refinery in Montreal every summer. Another oil field, the Balaena oil field, has reserves of 16.45 million barrels, but has not yet been produced.

Known natural gas resources in Nunavut are estimated at 16 trillion cubic feet, with an ultimate potential resource of 58.3 trillion cubic feet. The largest natural gas field in the Nunavut Arctic islands is Drake Point on Melville Island with 5.4 trillion cubic feet of reserves.

Due to the remoteness of the region, each community in Nunavut has their own individual electricity generation and distribution system; the territory does not rely on any kind of integrated grid. In 2009, Nunavut Power Corporation (also known as Qulliq Energy Corporation) operated 27 diesel plants which generated and distributed electricity to 25 communities. Overall, Nunavut's total installed capacity amounts to 54.3 megawatts, and electricity generation in Nunavut totaled 161 gigawatt-hours in 2009.

There is currently no hydrocarbon production in Nunavut.

Working Towards Wind and Hydroelectric Energy

Nunavut's Qulliq Energy Corporation (QEC), a government-owned company, is the territory's only generator, transmitter, and distributor of electrical energy. In recent years, the company has undertaken efforts to become more energy efficient by investing in alternative energy sources. Since 2006, QEC has been investigating sites and working towards making a hydroelectric facility.

QEC aims to finish its first hydroelectric generation facility, to help power the city of Iqaluit, by 2012. QEC will also continue investigating sites for more hydroelectric facilities in the future. QEC also has wind energy projects in Cambridge Bay, Kugluktuk, and Rankin Inlet. However, these projects have struggled due to lack of reliable suppliers and maintenance, as well as failing equipment due to extreme temperatures that the turbines were not designed to withstand. Despite setbacks, the company is still investigating the wind energy option and working on making it more economical.

Ikummatiit: An Energy Strategy for Nunavut

In 2007, the government of Nunavut published *Ikummatiit: The Government of Nunavut Energy Strategy*. The report focuses on four objectives that would guide the territory's actions on energy. The objectives are: Improve the security of the energy system by reducing reliance on fossil fuels and including clean, alternative energy and domestic energy sources; manage the cost of energy-based services by reducing the cost of providing energy and improving the efficiency of its use; reduce the impact on the environment by reducing energy-related emissions; and provide business and employment opportunities as the territory increases energy efficiency and uses renewable and domestic energy sources. The strategy addresses the fact that Nunavut is dependent on imported energy, despite its reserves, so there is a need to use energy more efficiently and to diversify energy sources. The strategy focuses on reaching an energy-efficiency target of a 20 percent reduction in energy consumption for the territory.

❧ Green Business, Green Building, Green Jobs

Green Business: Striving for Energy Efficiency

Many incentive programs are in development for Nunavut, but in the meantime businesses can take advantage of national programs, such as the ecoENERGY Retrofit Incentive for Energy. This program, begun in 2007, provides up to C$50,000 for businesses to reduce energy consumption and save energy in their industrial plants and buildings. For a building to qualify, it must be at least five years old and have been occupied for the last three years. A pre-project energy audit is required for each building by a qualified energy-efficiency evaluator, typically an experienced Professional Engineer or a Certified Engineering Technologist. Once a project proposal is accepted by the Canadian government, it must be completed within the following 18 months for Nunavut and other northern territories, and in 12 months for the remaining provinces.

In 2007, the government of Nunavut also introduced its Energy Efficiency Act, which restricts the sale of incandescent light bulbs due to their inefficiency. The government has been planning on extending the act to include more standards for electric and fuel appliances, introducing an "Arctic Star" logo to identify efficient products that are suitable for the Arctic.

Green Building

In an effort to make buildings more energy efficient, the government of Nunavut implemented the Nunavut Energy Management Program (NEMP). This self-funded program assists the government of Nunavut in entering into contracts with qualified energy management firms, who develop, finance, and execute retrofit strategies for government buildings. Measures taken include energy-efficient lighting, building automation systems, air sealing, insulation, operator training, and employee education. NEMP is made up of three smaller initiatives: the Nunavut Energy Retrofit Program (NERP), the Save 10 program, and the Facilities Energy Efficiency Review (FEER). NERP performs energy and water feasibility studies and provides building technology for the 518 government facilities being retrofitted; the Save 10 program is an educational initiative that trains building managers to operate the newly retrofitted facilities and to aid in reducing energy consumption in the workplace; and FEER oversees that new facilities meet all energy efficiency guidelines. When fully implemented, the NEMP could reduce energy expenses by 20 percent and save the territory C $2.8 million annually.

Nunavut also offers some incentives to residents who make their homes more energy efficient. One of these programs is the Homeowner Energy Efficiency Rebate Program, which provides qualified homeowners with up to C$1,000 in financial assistance (a 50% rebate of eligible costs) for energy efficient improvements that includes repairs to the purchase of energy efficient appliances. Lower-income homeowners can also take advantage of the Home Renovation Program, which has set aside funds to help low-income residents make their homes more energy efficient.

Green Jobs: Education for Conservation

Nunavut Arctic College offers an Environmental Technology Program that trains students for careers in resource development and management, fish and wildlife conservation, environmental protection, parks management, environmental assessment, waste management, environmental research, and environmental education. The college is also home to the Nunavut Research Institute, which opened its new headquarters in Iqaluit in February 2011. The Institute provides education and promotes knowledge of environmental issues and technologies not only to students at the college but to communities in Nunavut. One of the Institute's long-running projects has been their studies of the marine environment and climate in the Frobisher Bay area. The Institute also offers summer science camps for children ages 9 to 13. It operates out of its main location in Iqaluit, and has satellite offices in Arviat, Igloolik, Rankin Inlet, and Cambridge Bay.

Rankin Inlet opened its trade school in November 2010 and offers Nunavut-specific training programs geared toward future energy projects. The school also hosted a mine industry access program in 2011, helping local residents to become part of the mining industry.

Permafrost Melt: The Consequences of Climate Change on the Arctic

Permafrost is found beneath all of Nunavut's ground surface in either continuous or discontinuous coverage, some of which contains high amounts of ground ice. Permafrost is defined as soil or rock that remains below 0°C (32°F) throughout the year. Permafrost forms when the ground cools enough to form a frozen layer in the winter that persists through the following summer. Permafrost is covered by a layer of ground called the "active layer," which freezes and thaws with the changing seasons. The thickness of the permafrost and the active layer depend upon local climate, vegetation, and other soil properties. Naturally, as ground temperatures increase, the active layer thickens. Within the permafrost, almost all soil moisture is ground ice, which is an important aspect of permafrost terrain. Ground ice influences hydrologic processes, topography, vegetation, geomorphic processes, and the response of the landscape to environmental changes, so the loss of ground ice would have a profound impact on Arctic landscapes. Ground ice occurs in two forms: structure-forming ice, and as large bodies of almost pure ice. The differences between these two forms of ground ice are essential to construction and engineering, as projects need to be made to accommodate each type.

Due to the presence of permafrost throughout Nunavut, the melting of which due to the Arctic's warming temperatures would have a great impact on the entire territory. As temperatures rise, the permafrost will disappear, causing instability in soils that will have implications for the landscape, ecosystems, water resources and infrastructure. The region is already witnessing changes due to the warming climate along with permafrost melt and erosion. Residents have witnessed the presence of new bird species, such as sparrows, and extreme weather events such as hail and thunderstorms. Buildings have begun to buckle due to permafrost melt, and some residents have experienced water flowing up through their floors.

Erosion and landslide scarps are appearing upslope due to rising temperatures and loss of some permafrost which causes instability in soil. © *ZUMA Press/newscom*

In order to adapt to the effects on the land and infrastructure from permafrost melt, the Canada-Nunavut Climate Change Partnership was formed in 2009. Also known as Atuliquq (Inuktitut for "coming into force"), the project involves monitoring seven communities in the territory in order to help minimize damage from permafrost melt. The communities involved are: Iqaluit, Alert, Whale Cove, Kugluktuk, Cambridge Bay, Hall Beach, and Clyde River. The government of Nunavut, along with the Canadian Institute of Planners, is working to develop local climate change impact and adaptation plans in order to evaluate how best to deal with issues arising from permafrost melt and other effects of climate change. All of the communities involved face a rise in sea level by the year 2100, which could be as high as 20 inches (50 cm). However, the land will also rise somewhat due to an increase in the buoyancy of the peat soils and some isostatic rebound as permafrost melts beneath the active layer, making the sea-level rise not as significant as was first believed. Widespread permafrost degradation throughout the territories though, means that some communities may have to consider relocating much of their infrastructure as it would be adversely affected by erosion and land surface slumping caused from permafrost melt.

The Climate Change Partnership's preliminary plan for Cambridge Bay contained proposals for action that included establishing more accurate measuring and reporting methods for local ice to the community; providing satellite phones and other new forms of communication to hunters and trappers that they may report information on potential dangers to the community; increasing community awareness; and documenting elders' knowledge to better measure local ice conditions. Findings in Hall Beach showed that the erosion of the shoreline was one of the primary impacts of climate change in that community. Monitoring programs were recommended to record major storms, high waves, and

changes to sea ice. Community expansion on the coast was also discouraged, with feasibility studies recommended to look into expanding or even relocating the entire community. Another problem reported in Hall Beach and Clyde River was swaying power line poles. The poles tip in high winds because the permafrost that used to anchor them is now melting, and they are not held up as strongly. In 2010, researchers began working to measure and analyze permafrost melt in the capital city of Iqaluit. Researchers drilled holes in order to place sensors in the ground to measure exactly how fast the terrain is warming.

The project aims to finish plans for all seven communities by 2011. With temperatures rising more rapidly in the Arctic than anywhere else, causing centuries-old permafrost to melt and destabilize the landscape, it is essential that plans such as these be put into place, not only to save the infrastructure of the community, but also to learn more about what can be done to prevent adverse effects to the ecosystem.

BIBLIOGRAPHY

Books

Auyuittuq National Park Management Plan. Gatineau, Quebec: Parks Canada, 2010.

Berkes, Fikret. *Breaking Ice: Renewable Resource and Ocean Management in the Canadian North*. Calgary: University of Calgary Press, 2005.

Dearden, Philip, and Rick Rollins. *Parks and Protected Areas in Canada: Planning and Management*. 3rd ed. Don Mills, ON: Oxford University Press, 2009.

Forbes Travel Guide: Canada. Chicago: Forbes Travel Guide, 2010.

Fosket, Jennifer. *Living Green*. Gabriola Island, BC: New Society Publishers, 2009.

Quttinirpaaq National Park of Canada Management Plan. Ottawa: Parks Canada, 2009.

Web Sites

Arctic Climate Impact Assessment. Available from http://www.acia.uaf.edu/

Austin, Ian. "ArcelorMittal Moves Ahead With Bid For Arctic Miner." *The New York Times*. January 25, 2011. Available from http://dealbook.nytimes.com/2011/01/25/arcelormittal-moves-ahead-with-bid-for-arctic-miner/

Brennan, Marissa. "Partnership Helps Nunavut Communities Adapt to Climate Change." Natural Resources Canada. Available from http://www.nrcan-rncan.gc.ca/com/elements/issues/49/panpcn-eng.php?PHPSESSID=10d494274-c20acf22b9a9bbd962b7e33

"Climate Change in Nunavut." Government of Nunavut, Department of Environment. Available from http://

env.gov.nu.ca/sites/default/files/Climate%
20Change%20in%20Nunavut%20Backgrounder%
20Final.pdf

"Climate Change: Leading Practices by Provincial and
Territorial Governments in Canada." The Council of
the Federation. Available from http://www.coun
cilofthefederation.ca/pdfs/CCInventoryAug3_
EN.pdf

"Degrees of Variation: Climate Change in Nunavut."
Natural Resources Canada. Available from http://
adaptation.nrcan.gc.ca/posters/nu/nu_08_e.php

"Energy Facts & Statistics: Nunavut." Centre for Energy.
Available from http://www.centreforenergy.com/
FactsStats/MapsCanada/NU-EnergyMap.asp

"EU Seal Ban Challenge Rejected In Court." CBC News
Canada. Sept. 14, 2011. Available from http://
www.cbc.ca/news/canada/north/story/2011/
09/14/north-eu-seal-ban-challenge-rejected.html

"Energy Services: Saving Energy, Water, Money and Our
Environment." Government of Nunavut, Depart
ment of Community and Government Services.
Available from http://cgs.gov.nu.ca/en/energy-
services

"Find Energy Rebates in Your Province." *Canadian
Home Workshop*. Available from http://www.can
adianhomeworkshop.com/index.php?ci_i-
d=2833&la_id=1&page=4

"Geological Survey of Canada: Permafrost." Natural
Resources Canada. Available from http://gsc.nrcan.
gc.ca/permafrost/index_e.php

George, Jane. "Roll a Marble, Observe Climate Change
in Cambay." *Nunatsiaq Online*. Available from
http://www.nunatsiaqonline.ca/stories/article/
17119_Roll_a_marble_observe_climate_change_
in_Cambay/

*Ikummatiit: The Government of Nunavut Energy Strate-
gy*. Government of Nunavut. Available from http://
www.gov.nu.ca/documents/energy/energystrat
egy.pdf

The International Permafrost Association. Available from
http://ipa.arcticportal.org/

"lookUPnunavut." Government of Nunavut, Department of Economic Development and

Transportation. Available from http://www.loo-
kupnunavut.ca/index.html

"News Release: Trade School to Bring Training
Opportunities." Government of Nunavut. Available
from http://www.gov.nu.ca/news/2006/feb/
feb18.pdf

"Nunavut Climate Change Strategy." Government of
Nunavut, Department of Sustainable Development.
Available from http://www.gov.nu.ca/env/Cli
mate%20Change%20Full%20English%20low.pdf

Nunavut Department of Environment. Available from
http://env.gov.nu.ca/

Nunavut Harvesters Association. Available from http://
www.harvesters.nu.ca/

Nunavut Mineral Exploration, Mining, and Geoscience
Overview 2010. Nunavut Geoscience. August 2011.
Available from http://nunavutgeoscience.ca/geos
cience_e.html

Nunavut Parks. Available from http://www.nunavut
parks.com/

Rogers, Sarah. "Nunavut Opens Long-Awaited Trade
School." Nunatsiaq Online. November 19, 2010.
Available from http://www.nunatsiaqonline.ca/
stories/article/98789_nunavut_opens_long-awai-
ted_trades_school/

"Species at Risk Public Registry." Government of
Canada. Available from http://www.sararegistry.gc.
ca/default_e.cfm

"Trade In Seal Products." European Commission:
Environment. July 2011. Available from http://
ec.europa.eu/environment/biodiversity/animal_
welfare/seals/seal_hunting.htm

"Training Building Staff a Key Aspect of the Nunavut
Energy Management Program." Federal Buildings
Initiative Update, Natural Resources Canada. Avail
able from http://oee.nrcan.gc.ca/communities-
government/buildings/federal/fbi-update/issue17.
cfm?attr=8#bb

Zarate, Gabriel. "Scientists Scour Iqaluit for Permafrost
Melt." *Nunatsiaq Online*. Available from http://
www.nunatsiaqonline.ca/stories/article/
89789_scientists_scour_iqaluit_for_permafrost_
melt/

Ontario

Located in the east-central region of the country, Ontario is home to Ottawa, the national capital of Canada. The majority of the population is concentrated in the southern part of the province along Lake Ontario and Lake Erie. Ontario is Canada's leading province in manufacturing, and Toronto is the center of the country's financial services industry. Ontario's many rivers, including the Niagara River and Niagara Falls, have made the province a hub of hydroelectricity generation. The province's ambitious drive for a renewable-energy economy has caused some tension between the government and landowners in recent years however, with concerns over the reliability and safety of industrial wind turbines.

Climate

Ontario's climate is generally described as continental, but is heavily influenced by the presence of the Great Lakes, which interact to create three main climatic regions. Southwestern Ontario is described as having a moderate humid continental climate with warm, humid summers and cold winters. A more severe humid continental climate is found in central and eastern Ontario. Most of the province has a long cold winter, followed by a short spring and a long warm summer. Due to the presence of the Great Lakes, much of the province is prone to significant lake–effect snow in the winter. However, the eastern shores of Lake Huron and Lake Superior are subject to the most significant lake-effect snowfall. The northernmost regions of Ontario have a subarctic climate, with long, very cold winters and short summers with temperatures that range from cool to warm.

Battling Climate Change in Ontario Ontario's already varied climate could change drastically if measures are not taken to deal with the effects of global warming. Average temperatures are expected to rise as much as 5.4 to 14.4°F (3 to 8°C) in the next 100 years. This will cause an increase in severe weather events, such as storms, floods, droughts, and heat waves. Rising temperatures could change wildlife habitats, which would adversely affect species abundance and biodiversity. Higher temperatures also bring with them an increased risk of human diseases, and will cause the level of the Great Lakes to drop drastically, which would affect shipping and water supply.

Ontario released its *Climate Change Action Plan* in 2007. The main goals of the plan are to reduce greenhouse gas emissions to 6 percent below 1990 levels by 2014, 15 percent below 1990 levels by 2020, and 80 percent below 1990 levels by 2050. As of 2009, Ontario was 71 percent of the way towards its 2014 goal, and 56 percent of the way to its 2020 goal. The province is also preparing in the short term for the effects of climate change via the document *Climate Ready: Ontario's Adaptation Strategy and Action Plan*. This plan highlights five goals and more than 30 actions that will help the province adjust to and monitor the climate change situation through 2014. Examples of actions in the plan include amending the Ontario Building Code and conducting infrastructure vulnerability assessments, working with Public Health Units to educate the public on health hazards, and building adaptation plans into the Great Lakes agreements with other provinces and the United States.

🍁 Natural Resources, Water, and Agriculture

Ontario's Diverse Forests

According to Ontario's *Annual Report on Forest Management* for the fiscal year 2007–2008, forest product sales were estimated to be C\$15 billion and the industry employed about 168,000 people. Ontario's forests are made up of a variety of forest types across its different regions. The northernmost part of the province, known as the Hudson Bay Lowlands, is home to stunted tarmarack, black spruce, and white spruce. Forest covers less than 25 percent of land area in this region because it is mostly covered in wetlands.

South of the Hudson Bay Lowlands is the province's mixed-wood boreal forest. This is Ontario's largest forest region, featuring black and white spruce, jack pine, balsam fir, tamarack, eastern white cedar, poplars, and white birch.

The second-largest forest region in Ontario is the Great Lakes-St. Lawrence Forest, extending along the St. Lawrence River to Lake Huron and west of Lake Superior along the border with Minnesota. This region features eastern white pine, red pine, eastern hemlock, white cedar, yellow birch, sugar and red maples, basswood, and red oak. This is a transitional region, featuring species from the boreal forests and the deciduous forest. Many species of fungi, ferns, mosses, and shrubs are also found here.

The deciduous forest is Ontario's southernmost forest region, much of which is comprised of remnants of old-growth Carolinian forest. It is situated north of Lake Erie, and shares many tree and shrub species with the Great Lakes-St. Lawrence forest. It is also home to black walnut, butternut, tulip, magnolia, black gum, a variety of oaks, hickories, sassafras, and red bud. Because most of Canada's population resides in the south, much of the deciduous forest has been cleared for agriculture or infrastructure. Efforts in recent years have converted more than 321,000 acres (130,000 ha) of agricultural land back into forest.

In 1994, the Ontario government released a *Policy Framework for Sustainable Forests*. This framework serves as a guide for activities such as forest harvesting, the management of old-growth forests, and the conservation of non-timber products.

Wildlife Ontario is home to a wide variety of animal species. There are more than 80 mammal species, 400 bird species, 80 species of reptiles and amphibians, 20,000 invertebrates, 3,300 plant species, and 1,000 types of fungi and algae.

The Hudson Bay Lowlands is home to polar bear, arctic fox, snow goose, and the willow ptarmigan. South of the Lowlands, the Ontario Shield hosts eastern timber wolf, woodland caribou, moose, black bear, lynx, common loon, and the bay breasted warbler. The Mixedwood Plains, the province's southernmost eco-zone, serves as a habitat for white-tailed deer, southern flying squirrel, wild turkey, barred owl, spiny softshell turtle, and badger. Ring-billed gull, the Caspian tern, the Lake Erie watersnake, and the map turtle are found along Lake Erie. Hunters in Ontario can purchase licenses to hunt animals such as wild turkey, black bear, elk, moose, and deer.

More than 190 of Ontario's native species are at risk. "At risk" includes the classifications of extirpated, endangered, threatened, and special concern. Some of Ontario's endangered species include Butler's gartersnake, the barn owl, a subspecies of the American badger, and Blanchard's cricket frog.

Mining in Ontario Ontario is one of Canada's top producers of base metals, precious metals, and industrial minerals. Globally it is ranked in the top twenty in the production of each of the following: nickel, cobalt, platinum, copper, silver, and zinc.

In 2009, mineral production was valued at C$9.6 billion. Ontario is home to 27 metal mines that generated C$6.6 billion for the economy that same year. Ontario was the Canadian leader in exploration expenditures in 2009 with C$469 million and 336,000 active mining claim units.

Ontario is one of only a few areas that feature all the elements of the diamond industry, from mining to retailing. Located in Toronto, the Diamond Bourse of Canada provides a safe and credible venue for diamond dealers to buy and sell rough and polished stones. Located in Sudbury, the province's first diamond cutting and polishing facility opened in August of 2009. The facility cuts and polishes an estimated C$25 million worth of rough stones every year. These stones come from DeBeers Canada's Victor mine in the James Bay Lowlands.

Water

Four of the five Great Lakes surround Ontario, providing the longest fresh water beach in the world. The province is also bordered by Hudson Bay and James Bay in the north. The largest of the Great Lakes, Lake Superior, is also the world's largest body of fresh water. About 68,490 square miles (177,390 sq km), or one-sixth of Ontario's terrain, is covered by some 400,000 inland lakes and 37,000 miles (59,000 km) of rivers.

Flowing from Lake Erie into Lake Ontario, the short Niagara River is the site of Niagara Falls, located at the Ontario-New York border. The Falls drain some 800,000 gallons (3 million l) of water per second over its 187-foot (57-m) drop.

Agriculture

In 2006, Ontario was home to 57,211 farms. The majority of these farms produced grains and oilseeds, followed by beef cattle, hay, dairy, greenhouse and nursery, hogs, fruit, vegetables, poultry and eggs, and sheep and goats. According to cash receipts by commodity, the most profitable of Ontario's farm products were dairy, fruit, and vegetables.

There were 3,555 certified organic farms and 11,937 farms producing uncertified products in Ontario in 2006. Of the certified farms, 916 reported producing organic fruits, vegetables, or greenhouse products. Another 299 certified operations reported producing maple products. Uncertified operations produced organic hay, fruit, vegetables, greenhouse products, animals, and maple products.

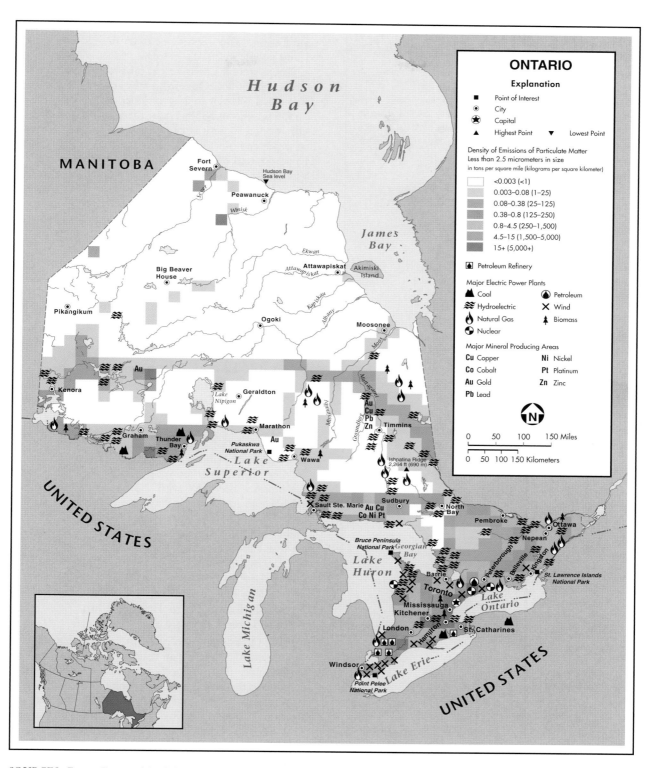

SOURCES: *Energy Facts and Statistics*. Centre for Energy. Available from http://www.centreforenergy.com/FactsStats/MapsCanada; "Geographical Highlights." *The Canadian Encyclopedia*. Available from http://www.encyclopediecanadienne.ca/geoHighlights/canmap_geog_v1_eng.swf; "Highest Points by Province and Territory." *The Atlas of Canada*. Natural Resources Canada. Available from http://atlas.nrcan.gc.ca/site/english/learningresources/facts/faq.html#points; "Mining in Canada: Map." *Mining in Canada*. The Mining Association of Canada. Available from http://www.mining.ca/site/images/MapofCanada.pdf; "Particulate Matter < 2.5 Micrometers (PM2.5) Emission in 2007." *CAC Density Maps*. Environment Canada. Available from http://www.ec.gc.ca/inrp-npri/default.asp?lang=en&n=BD725B2A-1. © 2011 Cengage Learning.

Ontario Provincial Profile

Physical Characteristics

Land area	354,342 square miles (917,742 sq km)
Freshwater area	61,257 square miles (158,655 sq km)
Highest point	Ishpatina Ridge 2,274 feet (693 m)
Forest lands (2011)	132.8 million acres (53.8 million ha)
Provincial parks (2011)	329

Energy Statistics

Total electricity generated (2009)	143.7 million megawatt hours
Hydroelectric energy generation (2009)	40.1 million megawatt hours
Wind energy generation (2009)	300,000 megawatt hours
Tidal energy generation (2009)	NA
Biomass energy capacity (2009)	165 megawatts
Crude oil reserves (2009)	10.3 million barrels (1.6 million cu m)
Natural gas reserves (2009)	685.7 billion cubic feet (19.4 billion cu m)
Natural gas liquids (2009)	NA

Pollution Statistics

Carbon output (2009)	49.4 million tons of CO_2 (44.8 million t)
Federal contaminated sites receiving funds (2008)	31
Particulate matter (less than 2.5 micrometers) emissions (2009)	261,875 tons per year (237,569 t/yr)

SOURCES: *Canada's Greenhouse Gas Emissions.* Environment Canada. Available from http://www.ec.gc.ca/ges-ghg/default. asp?lang=En&n=1357A041-1; *Canada Year Book, 2011.* Statistics Canada. Available from http://www.statcan.gc.ca/ pub/11-402-x/11-402-x2011000-eng.htm; *Energy Facts and Statistics.* Centre for Energy. Available from http:// www.centreforenergy.com/FactsStats/MapsCanada; *Federal Contaminated Sites.* Government of Canada. Available from http://www.federalcontaminatedsites.gc.ca/index-eng. aspx; "Forest Land by Province and Territory." Statistics Canada. Available from http://www40.statcan.gc.ca/l01/ cst01/envi34a-eng.htm; "Geographical Highlights." *The Canadian Encyclopedia.* Available from http://www. encyclopediecanadienne.ca/geoHighlights/canmap_geog_v1_ eng.swf; *National Pollutant Release Inventory.* Environment Canada. Available from http://ec.gc.ca/pdb/websol/emissions/ap/ ap_query_e.cfm

❧ Energy

Ontario's energy resources include crude oil, natural gas, hydropower, nuclear power, wind, biomass, and solar. Over 50 percent of the province's electricity is generated by nuclear power. There are three nuclear power plants in Ontario: Pickering Generating Station, Darlington Generating Station, and Bruce Power. Twenty-one percent of electricity is produced from hydropower, followed by coal, natural gas, and wind. In 2010, Ontario collected C$4.4 billion in revenue from its energy industry, almost all of which came from electricity generation and transmission. The energy sector employed more than 61,500 people in 2010.

There were 92 commercial oil and gas producers in Ontario in 2006. Ontario is the home of the first commercial oil well in North America, which was dug near Oil Springs in 1858. Today there are 1,045 active oil wells and 1,275 active natural gas wells, and 158 wells that produce both oil and natural gas. Of the gas wells, 513 are located offshore under Lake Erie. There are also 18 wells producing both oil and natural gas that are drilled horizontally beneath Lake Erie from onshore locations.

About 1 percent of the province's annual domestic consumption of crude oil and 2 percent of its annual domestic consumption of natural gas comes from Ontario's own reservoirs. In 2010, more than 528,000 barrels of conventional oil were produced with a reserve available of more than 10 million barrels. Ontario produced an estimated 22.6 million cubic feet of natural gas per day in 2010, with reserves of 685 billion cubic feet still available.

Renewable Energy Resources

In 2011, Ontario had an installed capacity of more than 1,630 megawatts of electricity from wind energy; which is 4.5 percent of Ontario's total installed capacity. The province, which had 36 wind farms as of July 2011, is home to four of Canada's largest wind farms. One of these is Prince Wind Farm, which boasts a capacity of 189 megawatts. Hydropower produces about 26 percent of Ontario's electricity with 200 hydropower facilities that have an installed capacity of 8,000 megawatts. Six percent of Ontario's energy is produced by biomass combustion, and the province offers both commercial and residential incentives for installing geothermal and solar energy systems. As of 2009, Ontario had 150 commercial solar projects with a capacity of 2 megawatts.

Ontario's Long-Term Energy Plan and the Green Energy Act

In 2007, Ontario released its Long-Term Energy Plan. It is a formalized, 20-year plan that forecasts and strategizes how to meet the province's electricity needs by 2030. Included in the plan is a goal to eliminate the use of coal as an energy source by 2014. In 2009, the Ontario government passed the Green Energy Act. The purpose of the Act is to encourage investment in renewable energy projects, to increase conservation, and to create green jobs and economic growth in the province. Some of the goals of the Act are to get Ontario running on a smart power grid, and streamlining the approvals process for renewable energy projects in order to guarantee new jobs and cleaner energy.

As of 2010, the use of coal in Ontario had already been reduced by 70 percent. Also that year, Ontario

Power Generation shut down two units each at its Lambton Generating Station and Nanticoke Generating Station. The province has a total of four coal-fired generation stations. In order to help consumers pay for their electricity as changes in the industry are made, the government also implemented the Ontario Clean Energy Benefit. The Ontario Clean Energy Benefit will give Ontario families, farms, and small businesses a 10 percent rebate on their bills for five years. This initiative will help families, small business owners, and Ontario farms that are feeling the effects of the rising costs of electricity.

🍁 Green Business, Green Building, Green Jobs

Green Business Incentives

Ontario offers a variety of incentive and rebate programs for businesses that wish to become more energy efficient. One program is the Energy Retrofit Incentive Program (ERIP), which offers grants to businesses that want to make their current buildings more energy efficient. These grants include up to C$240 per square meter of installed collector for solar water heating systems. Businesses have the option of following guidelines for predefined technologies, or creating their own customized retrofit based specifically on the level of efficiency improvement. The city of Toronto offers Sustainable Energy Funds that are zero interest loans to municipal, academic, social service, health care, and non-profit organizations for the installation of renewable energy systems that reduce greenhouse gas emissions. The loans range from C$50,000 to up to C$1 million per project for up to 49 percent of the total project cost.

Ontario also offers an incentive program to farms and businesses that wish to use biogas as an alternative energy source. The Ontario Biogas Systems Financial Assistance program was implemented in 2007 to fund up to C$400,000 to cover feasibility studies, construction, and implementation costs for biogas (anaerobic digester) systems.

Green Building

Ontario's 2006 Building Code introduced higher standards for energy efficiency for both houses and large buildings. Ontario was the first jurisdiction in Canada to mandate EnerGuide 80 levels for building projects. This means that all homes built after 2011 will have to meet the criteria for a rating of 80 using the EnerGuide system. This system measures a home's energy performance, and homes with a rating of 80 would represent a 35 percent increase in energy efficiency compared to homes built before 2006.

The Ontario Centre for Green Building Design and Development is an organization that works with the government and private builders to promote green building practices. As the Greater Toronto Chapter of the Canada Green Building Council, the Centre provides basic information about green building, current initiatives, and information about various incentive programs for building green. The organization also provides a Municipal Green Building Toolkit that is used to educate decision-makers on the essential components and procedures related to greening municipally owned buildings. It helps municipal decision makers identify and implement measures to increase the number of green buildings within their jurisdictions.

The Ontario Ministry of Energy offers numerous incentives and rebates for residents and businesses that wish to use alternative energy sources. For wind, solar, and hydro energy, the Ministry offers a Feed-in-Tariff program, which keeps renewable energy prices at a competitive level and offers long-term contracts to homeowners, business owners, and developers. For builders that install solar energy, the Ministry offers the Retail Sales Tax (RST) Rebate for Solar Energy Systems. This program returns the retail sales tax paid on solar energy systems to homeowners and builders who install or upgrade existing systems into residential buildings. There is also an RST Rebate available for wind, hydro, and geothermal energy.

Another program that Ontario offers to its residents is the Ontario Home Energy Savings Program (HESP). HESP reimburses 50 percent of the cost of a home energy audit up to C$150, and will pay up to C$5,000 for energy efficiency retrofits. It also offers up to C$750 to replace a wood-burning appliance.

Green Jobs

While Ontario's Green Energy Act has led to a climbing number of investments that have created new job opportunities for residents, many of these jobs require training. Institutions such as the Ontario Solar Academy are aiding in preparing the workforce for these renewable energy jobs. The Academy offers a 5-day Photovoltaic (PV) Design and Installation Course. The course covers fundamental knowledge and the design, installation, and evaluation of residential and commercial solar PV systems. Passing the final exam qualifies students for Ontario Solar Academy's "Solar Professional Certificate: Level One." The Academy also offers a 2-Day Advanced Solar PV Design and Electrical Code course. This course focuses on inverter string sizing, wire sizing, system design, and installations that follow local electrical code for residential and commercial solar PV systems.

Willis College in Ottawa offers a 31-week Wind Energy Technology program that prepares students for entry-level employment in the field. The University of Toronto also offers a minor in Sustainable Energy under

Ontario has 36 wind farms, four of which are among Canada's largest wind farms. © *Helen & Vlad Filatov/ShutterStock.com*

their Environmental Engineering program. The minor focuses on the sustainable use of energy, energy demand management, and public policy. The University of Toronto also houses a Sustainability Office that serves to make the campus more sustainable. The Sustainability Office also offers students the opportunity to propose research projects on sustainability, and to create their own independent studies.

❧ Ontario's Wind Farms: Healthy or Hazardous?

Part of Ontario's Green Energy Act and Long-Term Energy Plan are its ambitious goals to create 50,000 new jobs in the green energy sector and to eliminate the use of coal as an energy source. In order to meet these goals, the government has been working diligently to invest in a number of renewable energy projects. Despite the economic and environmental benefits that would occur from these projects, the government has found that not everyone is keen to move into a green energy economy so quickly.

Many of the province's wind energy projects have been met with opposition. Residents that are skeptical of the benefits of wind energy have protested projects; this has led to the projects' delay and even their cancellation. One canceled project involved eleven wind turbines that would have been located near Saugeen Shores on the Lake Huron coast. Enbridge, the company at the head of the project, stated that because the community insisted that the turbines be located at least 820 feet (250 m) away from property lines, it became too difficult for them to ultimately place all of the turbines. They had originally proposed locating the turbines 164 feet (50 m) from neighbor's property lines, and offered a compromise of about 400 feet (121 m) when they met with opposition. However, the residents insisted upon 820 feet (250 m), ultimately killing the project.

The Arguments against Wind Turbines

For those opposed to the installation of wind turbines, the reasons range from concerns for migratory bird populations, to property values, and even to human health. According to the group Wind Concerns Ontario, the presence of industrial wind turbines can lower property values, and are an unreliable and expensive source of energy. The group also claims that the noise and vibration from industrial wind turbines can cause adverse effects on human health, such as sleep deprivation, stress, headaches, and difficulty concentrating. They believe that there is a need for more long-term studies on the effects of wind turbines on human health before they should be installed, and that there should be clearer protocols for audible noise and low frequency sound around wind turbines. The group also cites dangers to wildlife, particularly migratory birds that may become injured or killed when coming into contact with a wind turbine, or that their migratory patterns may become disrupted.

Another concern from anti-wind energy groups is that the corporations backing these wind farms are only focused on profits and that their promises for more jobs are unfounded. They claim that the Green Energy Act has given unsustainable financial advantages to corporate wind developers who will therefore profit at the expense of property owners and taxpayers. Critics have loudly panned an agreement between the Ontario government and South Korea's Samsung, which allows the company to build wind and solar farms across Ontario along with four manufacturing plants. Residents are not only worried about the turbines themselves, but even some that are pro-wind energy are worried that this will give Samsung an unfair advantage over local wind producers. While the government has claimed that the deal could produce up to 15,000 jobs, concerns persist over the terms of the deal and the effects it could have on smaller energy firms.

Opponents to wind farms in Ontario claim that the noise and vibration from industrial wind turbines can cause adverse effects on human health, such as sleep deprivation, stress, headaches, and difficulty concentrating. © *Gordon Wood/Alamy*

Unfounded Concerns?

A lawsuit filed in January 2011 claimed that the Ontario government failed to consider how wind turbines affect human health. A resident of Prince Edward County filed the lawsuit, claiming that qualified medical experts were not consulted as they should have been before installing wind turbines. A rule had been put in place that turbines would be installed at a distance of around 1,800 feet (550 m) from any home; however, the plaintiffs complained that there was no certainty that this would be a safe distance. In response to the suit, Energy Minister Brad Duigan said that the province's chief medical officer stated there was no credible evidence that turbines are a health issue. Duigan made the point that continuing to burn coal would cause more respiratory illness than any issues that would come from wind turbines.

Researchers from wildlife groups have also found that the threat to wildlife is far less significant than other potential dangers, such as predators and collisions with

windows. However, it is less clear how habitat avoidance and displacement caused by the turbines will affect wildlife.

The province, however, put an indefinite moratorium on offshore wind projects in February 2011 to allow further research on issues that could arise from the wind turbines to be undertaken. That meant canceling at least one contract to provide energy to the province, and suspending other applications. The province had imposed a moratorium on offshore wind in the mid-2000s, but lifted it in 2008, saying the research conducted on environmental issues had been sufficient. Environmental minister John Wilkinson said in a statement issued by the government: "Offshore wind on freshwater lakes is a recent concept that requires a cautious approach until the science of environmental impact is clear. In contrast, the science concerning land-based wind is extensive." In September 2011 Trillium Wind Power Corp. filed a C\$2.25 billion lawsuit against the government relating to the moratorium, claiming the decision was politically motivated and had been made preceding an election to appease potential voters. Trillium was planning an offshore wind farm in the waters of Lake Ontario near Kingston that would produce up to 600 MW of power. Energy minister Brad Duguid called the lawsuit "offensive" in an interview with the *Toronto Star*.

The Fight Continues

The Ontario government continues to grapple with residents that oppose wind energy projects. While it has been noted that the majority of resistance in Canada is found in Ontario, the exact root of the opposition has not yet been determined, but is likely due to a lack of accurate information. Meanwhile, CBC Canada reported in October 2011 that two more wind projects were being developed northwest of Thunder Bay, the site of another project stopped by public outcry. The province also made changes to its Renewable Energy Approval requirements in January 2011 to provide additional time for residents to learn about projects and create greater buffer areas between proposed wind turbines and homes. The government is continuing to push for more renewable energy projects, including wind farms, in order to meet the ambitious goals for the Green Energy Act and to guarantee energy security for the province in the future.

BIBLIOGRAPHY

Books

Dearden, Philip, and Rick Rollins. *Parks and Protected Areas in Canada: Planning and Management*. 3rd ed. Don Mills, ON: Oxford University Press, 2009.

Forbes Travel Guide: Canada. Chicago: Forbes Travel Guide, 2010.

Fosket, Jennifer. *Living Green*. Gabriola Island, BC: New Society Publishers, 2009.

The Green Guide: Ontario . United Kingdom: Michelin, 2009.

Guide to the National Parks of Canada. Washington, DC: National Geographic, 2011.

Runtz, Michael W. P. *The Explorer's Guide to Algonquin Park*. Erin, ON: Boston Mills Press, 2008.

Sandilands, Allan P. *Birds of Ontario*. Vancouver: UBC Press, 2010.

Web Sites

Biogas Incentives. Ontario Ministry of Energy. Available from http://www.mei.gov.on.ca/en/energy/renewable/index.php?page=biogas_incentives

"Biomass Combustion." Ontario Ministry of Agriculture, Food, and Rural Affairs. Available from http://www.omafra.gov.on.ca/english/engineer/ge_bib/biomass.htm

Blackwell, Richard. "Ontario Stops Offshore Wind Power Development." *The Globe & Mail*. February 11, 2011. Available from http://www.theglobeandmail.com/report-on-business/industry-news/energy-and-resources/ontario-stops-offshore-wind-power-development/article1904138/

"The Building Code—Energy Efficiency and Barrier-Free Access." Ontario Ministry of Municipal Affairs and Housing. Available from http://www.mah.gov.on.ca/Page7154.aspx

"Climate Change." Ontario Ministry of the Environment. Available from http://www.ene.gov.on.ca/environment/en/category/climate_change/index.htm

Climate Change Action Plan Annual Report 2008–09. Ontario Ministry of the Environment. Available from http://www.ene.gov.on.ca/stdprodconsume/groups/lr/@ene/@resources/documents/resource/std01_079210.pdf

Climate Ready: Ontario's Adaptation Strategy and Action Plan 2011-2014. Ontario Ministry of the Environment. Available from http://www.ene.gov.on.ca/stdprodconsume/groups/lr/@ene/@resources/documents/resource/stdprod_085423.pdf

"Critics Pan Ont.'s Green Energy Deal with Samsung." CBC News. January 20, 2010. Available from http://www.cbc.ca/money/story/2010/01/20/samsung-deal-panned.html

"Crude Oil and Natural Gas Resources." Ontario Ministry of Natural Resources. Available from http://www.mnr.gov.on.ca/en/Business/OGSR/2ColumnSubPage/STEL02_167105.html

"Energy Facts & Statistics: Ontario." Centre For Energy. Available from http://www.centreforenergy.com/FactsStats/MapsCanada/ON-EnergyMap.asp

Green Energy Act Alliance. Available from http://www.greenenergyact.ca/

"Hunting in Ontario." Ontario Ministry of Natural Resources. Available from http://www.mnr.gov.on.ca/en/Business/FW/2ColumnSubPage/STEL02_168421.html

Jay, Paul. "Wind Resistance." CBC News In-Depth: Energy. March 7, 2007. Available from http://www.cbc.ca/news/background/energy/wind-resistance.html

"Nuclear Energy, Electricity Supply." Ontario Ministry of Energy. Available from http://www.mei.gov.on.ca/en/energy/electricity/?page=nuclear-electricity-supply

"Ontario Amends Renewable Energy Approval Regulation." Wind Concerns Ontario. January 7, 2011. Available from http://windconcernsontario.wordpress.com/2011/01/07/ontario-amends-renewable-energy-approval-regulation/

Ontario Centre for Green Building Design and Development. Available from http://www.greenbuildingontario.ca/

"Ontario Rules Out Offshore Wind Projects." Government of Ontario Newsroom. February 11, 2011. Available from http://news.ontario.ca/ene/en/2011/02/ontario-rules-out-offshore-wind-projects.html

Ontario Solar Academy. Available from http://solaracademy.com/ontario/

"Ontario Wind Farms Creating Huge Gusts of Opposition." Canada.com. September 2, 2006. Available from http://www.canada.com/city-guides/winnipeg/story.html?id=1393e10e-2e85-468f-86ef-a581e527060d

"Ontario Wind Turbines Challenged in Court." CBC News. January 24, 2011. Available from http://www.cbc.ca/canada/toronto/story/2011/01/24/wind-power-lawsuit.html

Ontario's Clean Energy Benefit. Ontario Ministry of Energy. Available from http://www.mei.gov.on.ca/en/energy/index.php?page=oceb

Ontario's Forests: Sustainability for Today and Tomorrow. Ministry of Natural Resources. Available from http://www.mnr.gov.on.ca/stdprodconsume/groups/lr/@mnr/@forests/documents/document/mnr_e000258.pdf

Ontario's Green Energy Act. Ontario Ministry of Energy. Available from http://www.mei.gov.on.ca/en/energy/gea/

Ontario's Long-Term Energy Plan. Ontario Ministry of Energy. Available from http://www.mei.gov.on.ca/en/pdf/MEI_LTEP_en.pdf

Spears, John. "Wind Power Firm Files $2.25 Billion Lawsuit." *Toronto Star.* September 28, 2011. Available from http://www.thestar.com/business/article/1061392–wind-power-firm-files-2-25-billion-lawsuit

"Summary of Agriculture Statistics for Ontario." Ontario Ministry of Agriculture, Food, and Rural Affairs. Available from http://www.omafra.gov.on.ca/english/stats/agriculture_summary.pdf

"Two New Wind Farms Planned Near Thunder Bay." CBC News Canada. October 11, 2011. Available from http://www.cbc.ca/news/canada/thunder-bay/story/2011/10/11/tby-gilead-wind-farms.html

University of Toronto Sustainability Office. Available from http://www.sustainability.utoronto.ca/Page4.aspx

"What Species Are at Risk in Ontario?" Ontario Ministry of Natural Resources. Available from http://www.mnr.gov.on.ca/en/Business/Species/2ColumnSubPage/STEL01_131230.html

Wind Concerns Ontario. Available from http://windconcernsontario.wordpress.com/

Wind Energy Technician. Willis College Ottawa. Available from http://ottawa.williscollege.com/wind_energy.php

"Wind Turbine Link to Ill Health Lacks Proof: Report." CBC News. May 20, 2010. Available from http://www.cbc.ca/health/story/2010/05/20/wind-turbines-health-ontario.html

Prince Edward Island

Prince Edward Island may be the smallest of the Canadian provinces, but it stands as a major center for green energy development as host to the Atlantic Wind Test Site and the Wind Energy Institute of Canada. These facilities are the cornerstone of the nation's wind energy research and development program, and the province itself has benefited greatly from the projects inspired by the facilities. As of 2010, the province had nine wind farms with a total capacity of 166 megawatts. As part of its overall energy strategy, the provincial government hopes to raise that capacity to 30 percent of its total energy needs by 2013. The energy strategy also looks toward further developments in biomass energy sources as a means of reducing its major dependency on imported fossil fuels to supply its energy needs. In related economic strategies, the government is looking toward new developments in the bioscience sector as one path to developing this industry.

Climate

With a location nearly halfway between the equator and the North Pole, and at the intersection of the Gulf Stream and Labrador Currents, the climate of Prince Edward Island experiences a wide range of seasonal influences. Winters are generally moderate, but there can be days and weeks of extreme cold as the northern winds sweep across the island. The winter can also feature short periods of warmer temperatures paired with heavy freezing rains. Summer temperatures are generally mild, with some dry spells. Most precipitation occurs in winter and spring.

Climate Change Strategy While Prince Edward Island has one of the lowest levels of greenhouse gas emissions in the nation, the effects of climate change have already been noted as serious. From 1990 to 2010, the province has experienced some of the warmest temperatures on record. Additionally, the sea level has risen by more than 11 inches (13 cm) since 1911. Officials have also noted that the frequency and severity of storm surges and hurricanes have increased considerable in recent years. In efforts to reduce the future effects of climate change, the provincial government has developed a plan to reduce greenhouse gas emissions while decreasing the province's dependence on the use of fossil fuels. Details of the plan are found in the 2008 publication of *Prince Edward Island and Climate Change: A Strategy for Reducing the Impacts of Global Warming*. This strategy sets forth a goal to reduce greenhouse gas emissions by 10 percent below 1990 levels by 2020 and by 75–85 percent below 2001 levels by 2050.

🍁 Natural Resources, Water, and Agriculture

Natural Resources: Forests and Wildlife

Prince Edward Island is considered to be part of the Acadian Forest region of Canada, but frequent clearing and replanting has changed the character of the forests, which now feature species different than those originally found on the island. The current forests consist primarily of young, small diameter trees, with common tree species that include red maple, polar, larch, white spruce, and balsam fir.

Some of the most common mammals on the island are beaver, mink, red fox, red squirrel, weasel, eastern coyote, muskrat, and raccoon, all of which contribute to the provincial fur trapping industry. Grey partridge, common snipe, snowshoe hare, and ring-necked pheasant are also found. Prince Edward Island is home to nine species of threatened or endangered animals, including the striped bass, Canada warbler, barn swallow, and common nighthawk.

Biomass Heat on Prince Edward Island Wood is harvested for both logs and fuel. Fuel wood and sawmill residue are used for biomass energy production, which accounts for about 10 percent of the total energy supply

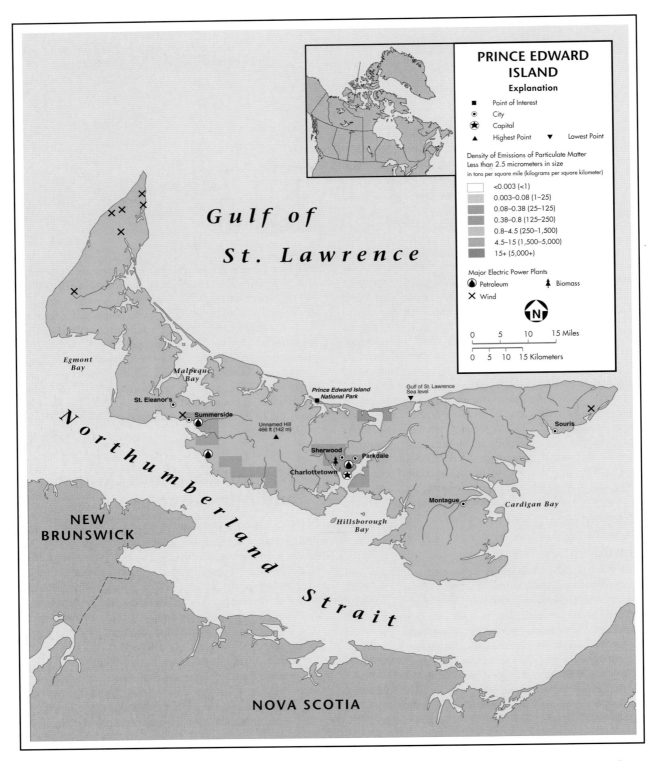

SOURCES: *Energy Facts and Statistics.* Centre for Energy. Available from http://www.centreforenergy.com/FactsStats/MapsCanada; "Geographical Highlights." *The Canadian Encyclopedia.* Available from http://www.encyclopediecanadienne.ca/geoHighlights/ canmap_geog_v1_eng.swf; "Highest Points by Province and Territory." *The Atlas of Canada.* Natural Resources Canada. Available from http://atlas.nrcan.gc.ca/site/english/learningresources/facts/faq.html#points; "Mining in Canada: Map." *Mining in Canada.* The Mining Association of Canada. Available from http://www.mining.ca/site/images/MapofCanada.pdf; "Particulate Matter < 2.5 Micrometers (PM2.5) Emission in 2007." *CAC Density Maps.* Environment Canada. Available from http://www.ec.gc.ca/inrp-npri/default.asp? lang=en&n=BD725B2A-1. © 2011 Cengage Learning.

Prince Edward Island National Park. *© All Canada Photos/Alamy*

of the province (municipal solid waste is also used as a biomass fuel source). Provincial authorities hope to increase the amount of energy, particularly biomass heat, that is produced through wood sources. To that end, the Environmental Advisory Council and the Public Forest Council of the Ministry of Environment, Energy and Forestry have combined efforts to develop a number of recommendations and strategies for expanding wood biomass production through responsible and sustainable forest management. These recommendations are outlined in the 2010 publication *Biomass Heat on Prince Edward Island: A Pathway Forward.*

Parks and Green Gables Prince Edward Island has twenty-five provincial parks, including eleven that are classified as camping parks. Prince Edward Island National Park is well known as the site of Green Gables, which is part of the national historic site celebrating the life of Lucy Maud Montgomery, the author of the *Anne of Green Gables* series of novels. The coastal park features sand dunes, beaches, sandstone cliffs, barrier islands, wetlands, and forest, all of which provide habitats for some of the 333 species of birds and waterfowl found on the island. Some common species include the great blue heron, piping plover, Canada goose, Atlantic brant, and mergansers.

Water

Prince Edward Island is located in the Gulf of St. Lawrence and separated from Nova Scotia and New Brunswick by the Northumberland Strait. There are many rivers and inland lakes, though most are quite small. Most notable among the rivers are the Cardigan,

Brudnell, and Montague Rivers, which are collectively known as The Three Rivers. The Three Rivers create three finger-like tidal estuaries as they flow into Cardigan Bay. The group of waterways was added to the list of Canadian Heritage Rivers in 2004 to honor the area as the site of the first French settlement on the island. The 28-mile (45-km) Hillsborough River system (also known as the East River) is the largest on the island; it was added to the Canadian Heritage list in 1997.

Prince Edward Island has four ports—Charlotte-town, Georgetown, Souris, and Summerside. The Port of Charlottetown is a deepwater commercial harbor that serves as the center of commerce for the province. Port of Summerside on Bedeque Bay is primarily a supply port for the island, but handles some exports of agricultural goods, particularly potatoes. The Port of Georgetown on Cardigan Bay is another deepwater harbor. The Port of Souris is a fishing station, a commercial shipping port, and an interprovincial ferry terminus.

Crustaceans and Carrageenan Fishing is a major commercial activity for the island province, with mollusks and crustaceans (particularly lobster) as the top species. Snow crab, groundfish, herring, cod, mackerel, giant bluefin tuna, and Malpeque Bay oysters are also important catches. Island blue mussels are cultivated in the province. Sports fishermen enjoy catches of brook trout, rainbow trout, white perch, rainbow smelt, and Atlantic salmon. Irish moss, a type of seaweed found along the coasts of the island, is harvested to produce the extract carrageenan, which is commonly used in processed foods.

The commercial fishing industry is struggling with the possibility that the Atlantic bluefin tuna may be listed

Prince Edward Island Provincial Profile	
Physical Characteristics	
Land area	2,185 square miles (5,659 sq km)
Freshwater area	NA
Highest point	Queen's County 466 feet (142 m)
Forest lands (2011)	700,000 acres (300,000 ha)
Provincial parks (2011)	29
Energy Statistics	
Total electricity generated (2009)	100,000 megawatt hours
Hydroelectric energy generation (2009)	NA
Wind energy generation (2009)	100,000 megawatt hours
Tidal energy generation (2009)	NA
Biomass energy capacity (2009)	1.2 megawatts
Crude oil reserves (2009)	NA
Natural gas reserves (2009)	NA
Natural gas liquids (2009)	NA
Pollution Statistics	
Carbon output (2009)	100,000 tons of CO_2 (90,700 t)
Federal contaminated sites receiving funds (2008)	8
Particulate matter (less than 2.5 micrometers) emissions (2009)	4,462 tons per year (4,048 t/yr)

SOURCES: *Canada's Greenhouse Gas Emissions*. Environment Canada. Available from http://www.ec.gc.ca/ges-ghg/default.asp?lang=En&n=1357A041-1; *Canada Year Book, 2011*. Statistics Canada. Available from http://www.statcan.gc.ca/pub/11-402-x/11-402-x2011000-eng.htm; *Energy Facts and Statistics*. Centre for Energy. Available from http://www.centreforenergy.com/FactsStats/MapsCanada; *Federal Contaminated Sites*. Government of Canada. Available from http://www.federalcontaminatedsites.gc.ca/index-eng.aspx; "Forest Land by Province and Territory." Statistics Canada. Available from http://www40.statcan.gc.ca/l01/cst01/envi34a-eng.htm; "Geographical Highlights." *The Canadian Encyclopedia*. Available from http://www.encyclopediecanadienne.ca/geoHighlights/canmap_geog_v1_eng.swf; *National Pollutant Release Inventory*. Environment Canada. Available from http://ec.gc.ca/pdb/websol/emissions/ap/ap_query_e.cfm

© 2011 Cengage Learning.

as an endangered species. In May 2011, the Committee on the Status of Endangered Wildlife in Canada (COSEWIC) recommended to the environment minister that the bluefin tuna be listed as endangered. The bluefin tuna is a high-value fish, some selling for thousands of dollars each. Total value to PEI commercial fishermen is estimated to be around C$5 million. Canada has a strict quota for the amount of Atlantic bluefin tuna that can be caught, and the quota was fulfilled in two days in 2010. Fishermen can only use a rod and reel to catch the fish.

Anoxic Waterways In the summer of 2010, at least fifteen PEI waterways were affected by a condition known as anoxia, a decrease in oxygen levels. The problem starts with an increase in the amount of nutrients added to the water through runoff from farming, logging, and septic systems. The nutrients cause excessive algae growth, turning the rivers green. As the algae dies and rots, oxygen is consumed from the water, leaving levels of oxygen so low that fish cannot survive. This problem can last for several weeks. A group of researchers from the provincial department of environment began monitoring the anoxic waterways very early in the process. While the problem can be solved by removing the algae from the waterways, this is an expensive and time consuming process. Researchers are instead focusing on the root of the problem, hoping to find ways to prevent undesirable runoff from entering the rivers to begin with.

Agriculture: Potatoes, Canola, and Tofu

Agriculture is an important activity on the island, with cash receipts of C$395.7 million reported in 2009. Potatoes are the single largest commodity. Grain and oilseed crops are grown in rotation with potato crops and include wheat, oats, barley, soybeans, and canola. About one-third of the soybean harvest is exported to Japan to produce tofu and miso. Blueberries, cranberries, and strawberries are popular berries. Apples are also produced. At least 35 percent of all island farms produce beef cattle. There are about 200 dairy farms on the island as well.

Organic farmers are certified through one of three certification bodies: the Organic Crop Improvement Association of PEI, the Maritime Certified Organic Growers Co-op Ltd., and Pro-Cert Organic. The PEI Certified Organic Producers Co-op is a group of 28 producers that are dedicated to helping the organics movement grow on the island. It was founded in 2002 with the goals of increasing organic production and educating islanders about organic food.

⚜ Energy

Fossil Fuels

Nearly 75 percent of the province's total energy supply is derived from petroleum products. With no natural gas or oil reserves of its own, the province relies heavily on imports to meet its energy needs.

Since 1944, there have been at least twenty exploratory wells drilled in search of natural gas. While two of these wells have found reserves, there are no current plans for development. There are substantial reserves of coal lying below the surface, but they are located too deep to be mined. There is some potential for coalbed methane production.

Electricity

More than 80 percent of the provincial supply of electricity is imported from oil and nuclear power facilities in New Brunswick via submarine cables from the mainland. However, as of 2011 the Point Lapreau Nuclear Plant remained offline after it was shut down in spring 2008 for refurbishment. Since then, the province has been paying extra for replacement energy. Eighteen percent of the total electrical supply comes from wind power, which is the province's most valuable renewable energy source. Ninety-six percent of the electricity produced solely on the island is generated by the island's nine wind farms, which have a total installed capacity of 166.6 megawatts. Maritime Electric operates two thermal electricity generating stations on the island, with a combination of fossil-fueled units and diesel-fired combustion turbines. A facility in Charlottetown produces thermal electric energy from woodwaste and municipal solid waste. There is also a small diesel-fired facility in the city of Summerside. The total installed capacity for thermal generation is 165 megawatts.

Renewables

Since the early 2000s, the provincial government has designed a number of strategies to promote the development and use of local renewable energy sources and ensure greater energy security and independence for the island. The details of these strategies are outlined in three primary documents released in 2008: *Prince Edward Island Energy Strategy, Prince Edward Island and Climate Change: A Strategy for Reducing the Impact of Global Warming,* and *Island Wind Energy: Securing Our Future: The 10 Point Plan.* In these documents, the provincial government has set a goal to substantially increase the installed capacity of wind power to 500 megawatts by 2013. The government took steps toward that goal in 2010 with the *Prince Edward Island Energy Accord.* In the five-year agreement, the government in partnership with its electric company, Maritime Electric Company Limited, negotiated revised rates with New Brunswick Power to reduce residents' rates by 14 percent. The accord also promised a 30 MW provincially owned wind farm that would help Prince Edward Island move closer to its goal of generating more than 30 percent its power with wind by 2013. The 2008 PEI energy strategy also calls for an increase in the amount of energy produced from biomass. As of 2008, about 10 percent of the energy in PEI was supplied from biomass, which includes fuel wood, sawmill residue, and municipal solid waste. The new goal set biomass at 20 percent of the total energy mix by 2018.

In 2009, the province launched an experiment with a small village in North Cape. The PEI Wind-Hydrogen Village is designed to exist completely off the energy grid, with wind power generating much of the energy needed. When the wind is not blowing, however, stored hydrogen supplies power to a back-up generator, which runs until the wind begins blowing again. The experiment showcases ways to combat the intermittent nature of wind power, while also creating opportunities for remote villages to generate their own power.

The Renewable Energy Act of 2004

The provincial renewable portfolio standard was set under the Renewable Energy Act of 2004, which called for utilities to provide at least 15 percent of their total electrical supply by renewable sources by 2010 (a goal that has been met) and at least 30 percent by 2013. A number of energy efficiency programs and incentives designed and implemented through the Office of Energy Efficiency (established in 2008) are expected to play an important role in reducing dependence on imported energy. The provincial government is also considering the establishment of renewable fuel standards, which would include the mandated use of E5 (a 5 percent ethanol blend) and B10 (10 percent biodiesel blend) by 2013. The mandate would call for the use of E10 and B20 by 2018.

⚜ Green Business, Green Building, Green Jobs

Green Business

Renewable energy and biosciences are noted as two of the four strategic sectors in the provincial economic development plan, *Island Prosperity: A Focus for Change.* In renewable energy, the primary focus is on the further development of wind energy. Details for expanding the industry are outlined in *Island Wind Energy—Securing Our Future: The 10 Point Plan.* The ten points include strategies to maximize both local energy security and economic benefits for residents, while also providing a means of generating revenue from green energy exports and opening opportunities for green energy developers and businesses.

Bioscience is already a growth sector of the island economy. The sector is generally divided into two focus clusters: technologies and products that are related to bioactive compounds and their application to human and animal health and nutrition, and bioproducts that convert biomass to value-added products such as energy and materials. The bioscience sector draws on the wealth of agricultural and marine resources available to the island. As of 2010, the bioscience sector includes more than twenty firms and eight research institutions employing more than seven hundred people. One of the most notable is the National Research Council's Institute for Nutrisciences and Health.

Plans to develop a green technology cluster, which will include subsectors in biofuels, solar and earth energy, fuel cells, and electric and hybrid vehicles, are also considered under the *Prince Edward Island Energy Strategy*.

Green Building: Energy Efficiency and Biomass Heating

Energy efficiency building strategies play an important part in the overall energy strategy. The PEI Office of Energy Efficiency (OEE) was established in 2008 with a specific mandate to provide programs, incentives, and advice for residents, business owners, and government agencies concerning ways to reduce energy use and maximize the energy efficiency of their homes and offices. Two primary programs sponsored by OEE are the Energy Smart Commercial and Institutional Buildings Retrofit Program and the Energy Efficiency Upgrades Program for Multi-Unit Residential Buildings. There are also loan and grant programs available for residents in single-family homes.

In October 2010, the Department of Environment, Energy and Forestry announced the launch of pilot projects involving the use of biomass heating systems at four provincial schools and one community hospital. The projects, which are expected to demonstrate the ease of use and energy efficiency of biomass as an alternative energy source, have been developed to further the efforts of both the energy and climate change strategies. The same month, the department announced the launch of the Business Energy Savings Program, a two-year awareness program designed to provide information and financial assistance for businesses making energy upgrades. This type of educational and outreach program is also part of the overall energy strategy.

Beginning in 2009, all government buildings and agencies were scheduled for inspection and completion of a full energy audit to determine potential measures to reduce energy use and increase energy efficiency. Facility managers of government buildings are expected to participate in energy management training programs.

Green Jobs

Employment in the renewable energy sector is relatively small, but stands to grow considerably as the provincial energy strategy unfolds. For instance, as of 2008, the bioscience sector provided 750 full-time equivalent jobs. One of the goals of the provincial economic development plan, *Island Prosperity: A Focus for Change*, is to increase employment to 2,000 full-time equivalent jobs.

❧ Prince Edward Island Wind Development

A Whirlwind of Development

The development of wind energy on Prince Edward Island began in 1980 with the launch of the Atlantic Wind Test Site and the Wind Energy Institute of Canada.

Darrieus wind turbine at Government of Canada windmill test site at North Cape on Prince Edward Island. © *Bill Brooks/Alamy*

These facilities, located at North Cape, serve as the cornerstone of the nation's wind energy research and development program. Drawing from initial projects that proved the island's potential for wind energy, the Prince Edward Island Energy Corporation (PEIEC) built the nation's first Atlantic commercial wind farm in 2001. This North Cape Wind Farms is adjacent to the Wind Energy Institute of Canada. Additional turbines were added in 2003 to bring the total capacity of the North Cape Facility to 10.56 megawatts, which is distributed by Maritime Electric Company, the main utility on PEI.

In 2007, PEIEC launched the Eastern Kings Wind Farm, with a total capacity of 30 megawatts. That same year, Suez Renewable Energy began operations at the Norway Wind Park and the West Cape Wind Farm, going online with total capacities of 9 megawatts and 19.8 megawatts respectively. Phase 2 of West Cape was launched by GDF Suez in 2009, adding 79.2 megawatts to the mix.

Canada's Windy City

The city of Summerside operates its own 12 megawatt wind farm. By purchasing additional power from the GDF Suez facility, Summerside gains nearly 48 percent of its supply of electricity from wind. In 2010, the city announced plans to install special battery systems in about one hundred test homes to consider ways to store some of the power generated during peak times for use as heat energy as needed. Financial incentives are being offered to residents who participate so they can install special furnaces or space heaters designed to work from the batteries.

As a result of these and other wind generating projects in the province, between 18 and 22 percent of the total electrical supply comes from wind power, with a total capacity of about 166.6 megawatts. The provincial government has already made plans to boost that percentage even higher within the next decade.

Securing Our Future: The 10 Point Plan

As part of an overall energy strategy initiated in 2008, the government developed a special wind energy plan entitled *Island Wind Energy—Securing Our Future: The 10 Point Plan*. The ten points include strategies to maximize both local energy security and economic benefits for residents, while also providing a means of generating revenue from green energy exports and opening opportunities for green energy developers and businesses. The provincial government has set a goal to substantially increase the installed capacity of wind power to 500 megawatts by 2013. This level of increased capacity could boost the sales of wind-generated electricity from 18 percent of total sales in 2008 to 30 percent by 2013.

But as of 2010, the 2013 target seemed a bit out of reach. In the wake of the recession, the PEI government has faced difficulties in attracting private developers with acceptable proposals. Several of those that have been considered thus far offered plans that would result in substantially higher power prices for a province that already has some of the highest utility costs in the nation. Authorities do not want residential consumers to be unduly burdened and fear that higher utility costs would be severely detrimental to businesses in the province. Provincial officials were also betting on the passage of cap-and-trade carbon-pricing policies as a chief support for wind development, but those policies have not come about. PEI's minister for Environment, Energy & Forestry, Richard Brown, whose term ended November 2011), stated in October 2010 that, if they had been enacted, carbon credits associated with wind power would have made wind farm development on PEI much more viable.

Even so, the government of PEI is still committed to the 500-megawatt goal, but has to consider an extended timeframe in order to ensure that all future developments are economically viable for the province. In the meantime, however, the Prince Edward Island Energy Accord, agreed to in November 2010, pushes the region forward with a provincially owned 30 MW wind farm.

Residential Concerns

While the development of the wind energy sector might be beneficial to local coffers, not everyone is in favor of building more turbines on the island. In February 2010, the city council of Eastern Kings took a community vote on a PEI Green Energy proposal to install twenty-eight new turbines near East Point. Of those residents present at the meeting, sixty-one said no and forty-five said yes. The vote was conducted by secret ballot and most residents were unwilling to speak to reporters following the vote, but at least one homeowner claimed to be concerned that the presence of wind turbines lowers property values. Some consider the noise produced by the wind turbines to be an unacceptable nuisance. One homeowner believes that more research needs to be done to determine the safest distance between wind turbines and residential homes. The city council sided with the majority vote in this case to reject the PEI Green Energy proposal.

BIBLIOGRAPHY
Books
Ernst, Chloe. *Scenic Driving Atlantic Canada: Nova Scotia, New Brunswick, Prince Edward Island, Newfoundland, & Labrador*. Guilford, CT: GPP Travel, 2011.

Forbes Travel Guide: Canada. Chicago: Forbes Travel Guide, 2010.

Matchar, Emily, and Karla Zimmerman. *Nova Scotia, New Brunswick & Prince Edward Island*. 2nd ed. London: Lonely Planet, 2011.

Rose, Alex. *Who Killed the Grand Banks?: The Untold Story Behind the Decimation of One of the World's Greatest Natural Resources*. Mississauga, ON: J. Wiley & Sons Canada, 2008.

Web Sites
"About PEI Certified Organic Producers Co-op." PEI Certified Organic Producers Co-op. Available from http://www.organicpei.com/content/page/coop_about/

"Anoxic rivers a growing problem for P.E.I." July 21, 2010. CBC News. Available from http://www.cbc.ca/canada/prince-edward-island/story/2010/07/21/pei-anoxic-rivers-584.html

Biomass Heat on Prince Edward Island: A Pathway Forward. Environmental Advisory Council–Public Forest Council Joint Working Group on Biomass Heat. Available from http://www.gov.pe.ca/photos/original/BioMassHeat.pdf

Blackwell, Richard. "Summerside stores the wind." October 13, 2010. *The Globe and Mail*. Available from http://www.theglobeandmail.com/report-on-business/industry-news/energy-and-resources/summerside-stores-the-wind/article1755871

Blackwell, Richard. "Why PEI's wind plan is dying." October 11, 2010. *The Globe and Mail*. Available from http://www.theglobeandmail.com/report-on-business/industry-news/energy-and-resources/why-peis-wind-plan-is-dying/article1752506

Center for Energy: Prince Edward Island. Available from http://www.centreforenergy.com/FactsStats/MapsCanada/PE-EnergyMap.asp

Charlottetown Harbour Authority Inc. Available from http://www.historiccharlottetownseaport.com/port-infrastructure

"Eastern P.E.I. says no to wind turbines." February 11, 2010. CBC News. Available from http://www.cbc.ca/money/story/2010/02/11/pei-eastern-kings-wind-vote-584.html

Energy Efficiency Initiative Designs and Achievable Potential for Prince Edward Island. Vermont Energy Investment Corporation. Available from http://www.gov.pe.ca/photos/original/eestudy08.pdf

Island Prosperity: A Focus for Change. Office of Biosciences and Economic Innovation. Available from http://islandprosperity.com/Island_Prosperity.pdf

Island Wind Energy— Securing Our Future: The 10 Point Plan. PEI Department of Environment, Energy and Forestry. Available from http://www.gov.pe.ca/photos/original/wind_energy.pdf

"P.E.I. Energy Accord Details Released." CBC News Canada. November 16, 2010. Available from http://www.cbc.ca/news/canada/prince-edward-island/story/2010/11/16/pei-new-details-energy-accord-584.html

"P.E.I. Makes Move Toward Hydrogen Future." CBC News Canada. May 20, 2009. Available from http://www.cbc.ca/news/canada/prince-edward-island/story/2009/05/20/pei-hydrogen-future.html

Prince Edward Island and Climate Change: A Strategy for Reducing the Impacts of Global Warming. PEI Department of Environment, Energy and Forestry. Available from http://www.gov.pe.ca/photos/original/env_globalstr.pdf

Prince Edward Island Department of Agriculture. Available from http://www.gov.pe.ca/af/agweb/index.php3?number=71208&lang=E

Prince Edward Island Department of Environment, Energy and Forestry. Available from http://www.gov.pe.ca/eef/index.php3?lang=E

Prince Edward Island Energy Accord. Prince Edward Island Department of Environment, Energy and Forestry. November 12, 2010. Available from http://www.gov.pe.ca/photos/original/eefeng-accord.pdf

Prince Edward Island Energy Strategy—Securing Our Future: Energy Efficiency and Conservation. PEI Department of Environment, Energy and Forestry. Available from http://www.gov.pe.ca/photos/original/env_snergystr.pdf

Prince Edward Island National Park. Available from http://www.pc.gc.ca/eng/pn-np/pe/pei-ipe/index.aspx

Prince Edward Island Office of Energy Efficiency. Available from http://www.gov.pe.ca/oee

"Prince Edwards Island's Forests." PEI Department of Environment, Energy and Forestry. Available from http://www.gov.pe.ca/eef/index.php3?number=1016534&lang=E

Renewable Energy Act (Ch. R-12.1) PEI Legislative Assembly. Available from http://www.gov.pe.ca/law/statutes/pdf/R-12-1.pdf

"Shipping Ports." The Government of Prince Edward Island. Available from http://www.gov.pe.ca/infopei/index.php3?number=13528&lang=E

36th Annual Statistical Review, 2009. PEI Statistics Bureau. Available from http://www.gov.pe.ca/photos/original/pt_annualreview.pdf

"The Three Rivers." The Canadian Heritage Rivers System. Available from http://www.chrs.ca/Rivers/ThreeRivers/ThreeRivers_e.htm

"Tuna Listing Would Be 'Nail In The Coffin.'" CBC News Canada. May 10, 2011. Available from http://www.cbc.ca/news/canada/prince-edward-island/story/2011/05/10/pei-tuna-endangered-fishermen-584.html

"Wildlife." PEI Department of Environment, Energy and Forestry. Available from http://www.gov.pe.ca/eef/index.php3?number=77981&lang=E

Wright, Teresa. "New Wind Farm For P.E.I.: Ghiz." *The Journal Pioneer.* September 27, 2011. Available from http://www.journalpioneer.com/Decision%20'11/Provincial%20election/2011-09-27/article-2760935/New-wind-farm-for-PEI-Ghiz/1

Quebec

The province of Quebec is already a leader in the development of sustainable and renewable energy. At least 97 percent of the electricity generated in Quebec is from hydroelectric power, accounting for 52 percent of the nation's hydroelectricity generation. As of 2010, Quebec had twelve wind farms, with about eighteen more in the works. The provincial energy strategy plays on the strength of wind and water, calling for major expansions in these sectors while also looking to further developments in biomass energy and energy efficiency technologies. At the same time, the provincial government is at work to promote sustainable development in other sectors, including forestry and nonfuel mineral exploration.

Climate

Southern Quebec has a humid continental climate with four distinct seasons, including hot summers and cold winters. Moving north, the winters become longer and colder while summers turn shorter and cooler. An arctic climate prevails in the far north. The northern and central coast experiences a temperate maritime climate. The most abundant precipitation occurs in the south, with very little in the north.

Climate Change The effects of global climate change have been a concern for Quebec for several years. According to the 2006–2012 climate change action plan, *Quebec and Climate Change: A Challenge for the Future*, average temperatures in the southern region of the province have risen by as much as 2.25°F (1.25°C) between 1960 and 2003. In the north, warmer temperatures since the 1990s have resulted in a significant increase in permafrost thaw. If the rate of warming continues, the province could experience greater weather extremes of drought or severe storms.

The climate action plan outlines twenty-six measures designed to reduce greenhouse gas emissions within the province and to adapt to the effects of climate change. These measures address a variety of issues, including energy consumption and efficiency, transportation, agriculture, and public health. The plan set a target goal to reduce greenhouse gas emissions by 6 percent below 1990 levels by 2012. As of 2010, the province was already at work to establish a 2013–2020 Climate Action Plan, with a new reduction target of 20 percent by 2020.

❧ Natural Resources, Water, and Agriculture

Natural Resources: Forests and Wildlife

More than 50 percent of the territory of Quebec is covered in forest. The boreal forest ecosystem of the north accounts for nearly 74 percent of the total and features species such as balsam fir, black and white spruce, jack pine, and larch. Hardwood forests can be found in the south, with common species that include sugar maple, yellow birch, beech, black cherry, and linden. The forests of Quebec account for 20 percent of total Canadian forests and 2 percent of the world's forests.

About 90 percent of the forests are publically owned (known as Crown Land) and 70 percent of the forest is classified as productive (commercial) forest. The forestry sector, including timber products, pulp and paper, and forest management activities, is a major economic sector, providing nearly 80,000 direct jobs.

The provincial forests serve as habitat for a diversity of wildlife that includes more than 650 vertebrate species and numerous invertebrates, with about 30,000 insect species. White-tailed deer, moose, and black bear are among the large mammals found in the province. Quebec is also home to one of the largest caribou herds in the world. There are more than 320 bird species in the province, including many migratory ducks and the Canada goose.

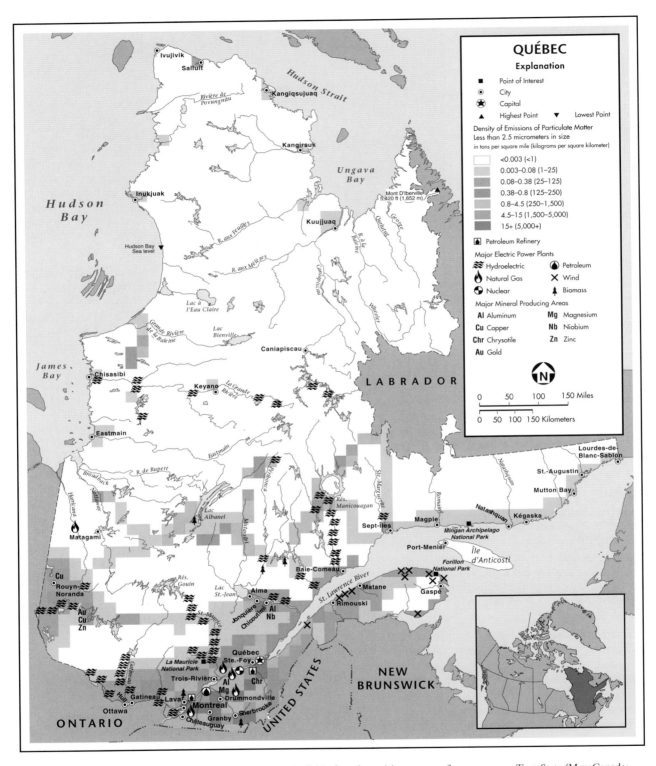

SOURCES: *Energy Facts and Statistics.* Centre for Energy. Available from http://www.centreforenergy.com/FactsStats/MapsCanada; "Geographical Highlights." *The Canadian Encyclopedia.* Available from http://www.encyclopediecanadienne.ca/geoHighlights/ canmap_geog_v1_eng.swf; "Highest Points by Province and Territory." *The Atlas of Canada.* Natural Resources Canada. Available from http://atlas.nrcan.gc.ca/site/english/learningresources/facts/faq.html#points; "Mining in Canada: Map." *Mining in Canada.* The Mining Association of Canada. Available from http://www.mining.ca/site/images/MapofCanada.pdf; "Particulate Matter < 2.5 Micrometers (PM2.5) Emission in 2007." *CAC Density Maps.* Environment Canada. Available from http://www.ec.gc.ca/inrp-npri/default.asp? lang=en&n=BD725B2A-1. © *2011 Cengage Learning.*

Quebec Provincial Profile

Physical Characteristics

Land area	527,079 square miles (1,365,128 sq km)
Freshwater area	68,312 square miles (176,927 sq km)
Highest point	Mont D'Iberville 5,417 feet (1,651 m)
Forest lands (2011)	181.3 million acres (73.4 million ha)
Provincial parks (2011)	101

Energy Statistics

Total electricity generated (2009)	193.8 million megawatt hours
Hydroelectric energy generation (2009)	187.9 million megawatt hours
Wind energy generation (2009)	500,000 megawatt hours
Tidal energy generation (2009)	NA
Biomass energy capacity (2009)	183.6 megawatts
Crude oil reserves (2009)	NA
Natural gas reserves (2009)	3.7 billion cubic feet (105 million cu m)
Natural gas liquids (2009)	NA

Pollution Statistics

Carbon output (2009)	19.6 million tons of CO_2 (17.8 million t)
Federal contaminated sites receiving funds (2008)	40
Particulate matter (less than 2.5 micrometers) emissions (2009)	205,330 tons per year (186,272 t/yr)

SOURCES: *Canada's Greenhouse Gas Emissions.* Environment Canada. Available from http://www.ec.gc.ca/ges-ghg/default.asp?lang=En&n=1357A041-1; *Canada Year Book, 2011.* Statistics Canada. Available from http://www.statcan.gc.ca/pub/11-402-x/11-402-x2011000-eng.htm; *Energy Facts and Statistics.* Centre for Energy. Available from http://www.centreforenergy.com/FactsStats/MapsCanada; *Federal Contaminated Sites.* Government of Canada. Available from http://www.federalcontaminatedsites.gc.ca/index-eng.aspx; "Forest Land by Province and Territory." Statistics Canada. Available from http://www40.statcan.gc.ca/l01/cst01/envi34a-eng.htm; "Geographical Highlights." *The Canadian Encyclopedia.* Available from http://www.encyclopediecanadienne.ca/geoHighlights/canmap_geog_v1_eng.swf; *National Pollutant Release Inventory.* Environment Canada. Available from http://ec.gc.ca/pdb/websol/emissions/ap/ap_query_e.cfm

© 2011 Cengage Learning.

Parks and UNESCO Sites A little more than 8 percent of the total land area of the province is protected, including twenty-three provincial parks (referred to as national parks by the provincial government) and three federal parks—Forillon, La Mauricie, and the Mingan Archipelago National Park Reserve. Miguasha, located on the Baie des Chaleurs, is a UNESCO World Heritage Site for the numerous fish and plant fossils found embedded in the sea cliffs. These fossils are considered to be more than 380 million years old. The province is also home to four UNESCO biosphere reserves under the UNESCO Man and the Biosphere Program. These areas are designated for conservation efforts that focus not only on the preservation of the natural environment, but also on the sustainable relationship between the people and the environment. The Quebec biosphere reserves are Mont-Saint-Hilaire, Charlevoix, Lac-Saint-Pierre, and Manicouagan-Uapishka.

Minerals Beneath the surface of Quebec lies a rich substratum of Precambrian rock that is noted for its wealth of gold, iron, copper, and nickel deposits. Along with these, more than thirty minerals are produced in the province, including zinc, silver, limestone, quartz, andlead. The province typically ranks within the top five in the nation for production of metallic substances and industrial minerals. In 2010, total mineral production in Quebec was valued at C$6.7 billion, ranking second in the nation after Ontario. That year, the most valuable mineral was gold, with a production value at more than C$1 billion. By weight, zinc was the most prominent, with production at about 201,627 metric tons. There are ongoing exploration projects in search of additional mineral deposits, which could include diamonds, lithium, and uranium. As of 2011, Quebec was also considering reopening an asbestos mine, despite the controversy surrounding that mineral. (Miners who have been exposed to high concentrations of asbestos fibers are at risk for developing mesothelioma, a type of lung cancer, and asbestosis, a pneumonia-like disease.) Although the European Union has banned the use and mining of asbestos, the Quebec project is under consideration because the mineral has some practical uses and the mine would like employ 35–500 workers.

Water: Rivers, Lakes, and Wetlands

Quebec's rivers and lakes cover about 12 percent of the total land area. The most dominant waterway is the Saint Lawrence River, which originates in Lake Ontario and flows into the Atlantic at the Gulf of St. Lawrence. The system of locks and canals that created the St. Lawrence Seaway (completed in 1959) provides a navigable link from the Atlantic Ocean to industrial centers around the Great Lakes. The St. Lawrence drains all of southern Quebec through numerous tributaries, including the Richelieu, Yamaska, Outaoais, Saint-Maurice, Saguenay, and Manicouagan. Quebec's many rivers serve as a major source of energy, since at least 97 percent of the electricity generated in Quebec is from hydroelectric power.

While Quebec has numerous lakes, most are relatively small. Lac Mistassini is the largest natural lake in the province. Other large lakes include L'eau Claire, Bienville, Saint-Jean, and Minto. Wetlands cover between 5 and 10 percent of Quebec. The northern most wetlands of the Taiga Shield consist of peatlands (bogs and fens), along with thousands of shallow lakes that were carved

Old city of Quebec with the St. Lawrence river in the background.   © Howard Sandler/ShutterStock.com

out by glaciers. These waters attract numerous migrating and nesting birds and ducks. The St. Lawrence lowlands and the Hudson Bay lowlands also feature marsh areas. Baie de l'Isle-Verte, Cap Tourmente, Lac Saint-François, and Lac Saint-Pierre are all listed as Ramsar Wetlands of International Importance.

Fishing and Trade Sport fishing in the lakes and rivers of the province is a popular recreational activity, with brook trout, lake trout, salmon, walleye, pike, and perch as the main catches. The protected copper redhorse is a fish that can only be found in the Richelieu River.

Commercial fishing along the coastal and maritime regions of the province is a major economic activity. There are sixty fishing harbors in the Quebec region, supporting thousands of jobs. Primary catches include snow crab, shrimp, lobster, groundfish (Atlantic and Greenland halibut and cod), and scallop. Seal hunting is still an important activity in the Magdalen Islands. There are approximately 160 aquaculture enterprises in the province as well. In the northern region, the native Cree and Inuit communities rely on fishing for subsistence.

There are fifty-one commercial ports in Quebec, the largest of which are at Montreal, Trois-Rivières, Quebec, Part Saguenay, and Sept-Iles. These are part of the national port system, deemed essential to domestic and international trade. Others serve local and regional economies.

Agriculture

At the 2006 agricultural census, Quebec ranked fourth in the nation for the number of farms, accounting for 13.4 percent of the national total. The total cash receipts from all farm and livestock production in 2010 was reported at C$7 billion, with total cash receipts of C$7.3 billion estimated in 2011. Sweet corn is the primary vegetable crop, while corn for grain and soybeans are also important. Quebec was first in the nation for the number of ewes, dairy cows, and pigs.

In 2006, about 7.6 percent of all of the farms in the province were certified for organic production. This represents 6.8 percent of the national total of organic farms. Quebec Vrai is the only certifying authority within the province. Requirements for organic certification are outlines in the Quebec Organic Reference Standards and the National Organic Program Regulations.

Agriculture and Agri-Food Canada sponsors four research centers in the province. The Horticulture Research and Development Center is located in Saint-

Jean-sur-Richelieu. Here, researchers focus on projects involving sustainable production, pest management, and preserving the quality of crops and horticulture once the products are harvested. Research substations in L'Acadie and Sante-Clotilde focus on mineral soil and muck soil horticulture research, while a Frelighsburg station maintains a variety of orchards for research purposes. The Food Research and Development Center in Saint-Hyacinthe works on developing better methods to preserve and process foods. Some research is also directed towards the nutritional and other health benefits of various food ingredients. The Dairy and Swine Research and Development Center in Lennoxville opened a new fully modernized, high tech section for dairy production research in 2010 to promote research in nutrition, physiology, immunology, and molecular biology related to the dairy industry. The dairy research program will also include projects that consider the environmental impact of dairy production. The Soils and Crops Research and Development Center in Quebec focuses on soil-water-air resources and management and the use of field crops in Eastern Canada.

The Institute for Research and Development for the Agri-Environment (IRDA) is a non-profit research corporation representing the cooperative efforts of government agencies and the Union of Agricultural Producers in promoting research for sustainable development in agriculture. The IRDA maintains five research centers in Quebec.

🍁 Energy

Oil and Natural Gas

While the province has no oil drilling operations of its own, there are three refineries producing a variety of products, including gasoline, lubricating oils, jet fuel, butane, and home heating oil. These three refineries represent 25 percent of the nation's total refining capacity. Natural gas production is low, but recent advances in technology for tight gas sands and gas shales have triggered renewed interest in exploration projects in the Utica Shale formation in the St. Lawrence lowlands of southern Quebec and northern New York and on Gaspé Peninsula.

First in Hydroelectricity

At least 97 percent of the electricity generated in Quebec is from hydroelectric power, marking the province as first in the nation for hydroelectric generation. A total of 52 percent of the nation's hydroelectricity is generated in Quebec. Hydro-Quebec, the province's wholly owned energy corporation, operates 60 hydroelectric generating stations with a total capacity of 34,503 megawatts, representing about 42 percent of the nation's total installed capacity for electricity. The Robert-Bourassa Generating Station with a capacity of 5,616 megawatts is the largest in the province. In 2011, a new Hydro-Quebec complex was under construction along the Romaine River. If completed on schedule, the complex will begin operation in 2020, and will consist of four generating stations with an annual generation of 8 terawatt hours. Another major project is the Eastmain-1-A/Sarcelle/Rupert Project, which includes a partial diversion of the Rupert River and the construction of two new powerhouses, two substations, and two transmission lines. When completed in 2012, the project will add an annual generation of 8.7 terawatt hours to the Hydro-Quebec total. As of 2011, the total hydroelectric generating capacity available in Quebec was estimated at about 47,330 megawatts.

First in Electricity

The province also ranks as first in the nation for overall electricity generation, accounting for a total of 34 percent of Canada's total generated electricity. This makes the province a major exporter of electricity. About 81 percent of electric exports go to the United States. In 2009, electricity exports were valued at C$1.5 billion. There are twenty-four petroleum-fired generating plants in the province and three natural-gas fired plants. There are four thermal electricity generating plants, with three gas turbine generating stations and a conventional oil-fired thermal generating station.

Quebec has one nuclear power plant, Gentilly-2, which provides nearly 3 percent of the provincial supply of electricity. The facility, which became operational in 1983, is undergoing a C$1.9 billion refurbishment that should be completed by 2012. Gentilly-1, a prototype, noncommercial reactor, was taken out of service in 1979.

Renewables

While hydropower reigns supreme in the province, there are also significant developments in other renewable energy sources. Quebec has twelve wind farms with a total of 499 turbines and a total installed capacity of 663.4 megawatts. As of 2010, about eighteen other wind farms were under construction or had signed power purchase agreements. The total combined capacity of these new projects is estimated at more than 2,300 megawatts. The province is also home to seven biomass electricity generating stations with a total installed capacity of 183.6 megawatts and a total generation of 193.8 terawatt hours.

Using Energy to Build the Quebec of Tomorrow

The government of Quebec has made plans that continue to build upon the strength of its energy sector to ensure the continued economic strength of the province, while also addressing issues of sustainability.

The 2006–2015 provincial energy strategy, *Using Energy to Build the Quebec of Tomorrow*, was released in 2006. The strategy outlines several policy actions geared toward meeting six primary objectives, including the need to strengthen its energy supply security and a plan to become a leader in sustainable energy development. The province has set a goal to implement new projects totaling 4,500 megawatts of hydroelectric power capacity and 4,000 megawatts of wind power capacity by 2015. The strategy also includes a number of energy efficiency goals, including a 20 percent reduction in government energy consumption. Considering Quebec's overwhelming strength in hydroelectricity, the provincial energy strategy is intrinsically linked to the *Hydro-Quebec Strategic Plan 2009–2013*, which outlines specific project plans for hydroelectric and wind development, along with a number of energy efficiency programs.

❧ Green Business, Green Building, Green Jobs

Green Business

The green economy is nothing new for Quebec. The province has been a national leader in sustainable energy production and technologies for several years and has implemented a number of plans and policies to support and create additional developments. In April 2006, the provincial assembly passed the Sustainable Development Act (Bill 118) to establish a common management framework that integrates sustainable development policies at all levels of government (provincial and municipal). The act provides a working definition for sustainable development and sets sixteen principles or categories for consideration, including environmental protection, economic efficiency, biodiversity preservation, and responsible production and consumption. To support research and development in sustainable technologies, the act also established a Quebec Green Fund, which is similar to the national Green Infrastructure Fund. In 2010, the provincial government approved the allocation of C$165 million from the Green Fund to support four new organic waste treatment projects in the Montreal region. These same projects also received C$150 million in support from the green Infrastructure Fund.

In 2008, the provincial government released *For a Green and Prosperous Quebec*, a six-year development strategy for the environmental and green technology industry. Under this plan, the government allocated C$282 million to support green business and green technology development and to increase the marketability of green industry products. One of the overall goals of the strategy is to make to expand the reach of the industry to international markets.

Green Jobs

According to data cited in *For a Green and Prosperous Quebec*, the environmental and green technology industry accounts for about 20 percent of all jobs within the province. The government hopes to see that percentage rise through implementation of the sustainable development strategy and the provincial energy strategy, *Using Energy to Build the Quebec of Tomorrow*. Recent studies indicate that the development of wind energy could provide a significant number of new jobs for the province. In *WindVision 2025: A Strategy for Quebec*, the Canadian Wind Energy Association (CanWEA) predicted that the addition of 8,000 megawatts of wind energy between 2016 and 2025 could create more than 9,800 jobs, along with more than 1,200 permanent jobs in operation and maintenance and 800 manufacturing jobs.

Green Building

As part of the 2006–2012 Climate Change Action Plan, the government of Quebec pledged to review existing building codes with the expectation of implementing revisions that will include energy efficiency and energy performance standards that would apply to all new buildings and homes within the province. However, green building practices have been adopted by a number of businesses and organizations. In 2003, the Mountain Equipment Co-op store in Montreal became the first retail building in Quebec to meet Natural Resources Canada's standards for above-average energy and environmental performance. As of 2010, there were at least twenty-six buildings certified under the Canada Green Building Council's Leadership in Energy and Environmental Design (LEED) program.

❧ The James Bay Project: Forty Years of Controversy

The James Bay Project initiated in 1971 by Hydro-Quebec (now the province's wholly owned energy corporation) and the government of Quebec was announced as the "project of the century." The two-phase project involved the diversion of the Eastmain, Opinaca, and Caniapiscau rivers to reservoirs on La Grande River to create an eight-station hydroelectric generating complex that now supplies more than 50 percent of the hydroelectric power of the nation. But this developmental project set in a then fairly remote area of the province sparked years of controversy between government officials, environmental groups, and most notably, the native Cree and Innu who lived in the area.

At the time the project was announced, the native Cree were neither informed nor consulted on the matter by the provincial government. When Cree leaders learned

James Bay electrical dam project. © *Megapress/Alamy*

that the project would include the flooding of large portions of wilderness areas that they had managed as primary hunting and fishing grounds for generations, they hoped to open discussions with the government in order to voice their concerns and consider modifications that would reduce the overall impact of the project on their culture and livelihoods. Initially, the government refused to enter into such negotiations, claiming that the land in question was provincial land and that the project would provide significant benefits to the native peoples. The Cree then initiated a series of legal battles against the provincial government in an effort to establish their rights to participate in the process that would affect the land that was so central to their existence. To do so, they had to legally establish that generations of responsible stewardship over the land in question, which included the freedom to hunt, fish, and trap on those lands, constituted a prima facie claim to rights in the territory.

For the Cree, there was more at stake than simply the right to hunt and fish or the right to claim ownership of the land. In this native culture, land is not owned by individuals or corporations, but is collectively managed by the community as a whole through principles that are based on a deep spiritual connection to both earth and animals. Hunting for the Cree is not simply a way to gain food, but is also the expression of a belief that the gifts of the earth are provided for the shared benefit of humanity, and come with a solemn responsibility to in turn protect the earth for the generations to come.

In 1973, a federal court ruled in favor of the Cree (and Innu), stating that they did appear to have an Indian title to the land. This forced the government to enter into negotiations with the people. While they did not expect to stop the project, the Cree argued for some technical modifications to the project and for shared rights in land use. The negotiations led to the signing of the James Bay and Northern Quebec Agreement (1975), which more firmly established certain property rights for the natives and provided a settlement of more than C$200 million

paid to the Cree. The Cree retained primary control over a portion of the lands designated as hunting territories.

The project moved forward, but brought a myriad of consequences. The massive flooding caused an increase in mercury levels in the waters as the underlying vegetation decayed, which in turned led to increased mercury accumulation in the local fish stock. Wildlife habitats and migration routes were destroyed, causing a significant disruption of the animal population on the Cree lands. And as Hydro-Quebec built new roads into the area, the population changed dramatically, creating a strain on the native culture through the introduction of alcoholism and other products and practices harmful to the community.

As the second phase of the project was set to begin in 1989, the Cree launched a massive campaign against it. Support for their cause came from an unlikely and unintended source. Power from Phase II was expected to be sold to four New England states, including New York. In 1992, then-governor Mario Cuomo of New York cancelled the contract with Hydro-Quebec in favor of other sources. The cancellation was the primary cause for suspension of work on the project, but negotiations persisted between the Cree and Hydro-Quebec. Agreements reached in 2002 (La Paix des Braves) and 2004, providing for shared revenues and greater Cree participation in management resources on traditional Cree lands, allowed for the completion of the project and opened the way for expansion projects on the Rupert and Romaine rivers.

These new projects come with new controversy. The non-profit francophone Rivers Foundation launched a campaign against developments on the Rupert River in 2004 and continues to support citizen protests against several hydroelectric projects in the province. The Rupert River project includes construction of a 768-megawatt powerhouse (Eastmain-1-A), near the existing Eastmain-1 powerhouse, and a 150-megawatt powerhouse, Sarcelle, at the outlet of Opinaca reservoir, as well as the, partial diversion of the Rivière Rupert. Controversy over the Romaine project has been growing since construction began in 2009. The electric transmission lines that are expected to be built for the Romaine project will run through the ancestral lands of the Innu of Uashat Mak Mani-Utenam. Throughout 2010, Innu leaders sought concessions from Hydro-Quebec for the use of land. Originally, Hydro-Quebec offered C$4 million in compensation, but the offer was rejected by Innu officials. In late 2010, Innu leaders threatened to initiate an international campaign against Hydro-Quebec if a deal could not be brokered. It seemed as if a major hurdle was cleared in January 2011, as the Innu band council reached an agreement in principle that would have included C$125 million in compensation from Hydro-Quebec and an agreement with the government for a stake in all future natural resources development on ancestral lands. However, the deal was rejected twice by the Innu population in referendums held in April and October 2011. At that time, it was unclear what course of action Innu leaders would take next.

An additional cause for concern was presented on Earth Day 2011, when the award-winning documentary *Chercher le Courant (Seeking the Current)* aired on the French-language branch of the CBC. The film by Alexis de Gheldere and Nicolas Boisclair portrays their 46-day canoe trip along the Romaine River. According to Gheldere, the original goal of the film was to document the ecosystems of the Romaine before it is changed by the four dams and resulting reservoirs. As the project progressed, a second goal developed: to question whether or not the power generated by the new plant would really be the most cost-effective way to meet regional energy needs. Throughout the course of the film, expert testimony is used to suggest that alternative energy sources, particularly wind power, may be better alternatives.

Officials from Hydro-Quebec had been made aware of the film's content earlier in the year, as the documentary made the rounds of various film festivals. An official statement from the company reiterated the advantages of hydroelectric power as a clean, reliable, and renewable source and states that alternative sources could not replace hydropower "for a variety of reasons related to economics, climate, and the environment."

BIBLIOGRAPHY

Books

Forbes Travel Guide: Canada. Chicago: Forbes Travel Guide, 2010.

Fostering Renewable Electricity Markets in North America. Montreal: Commission for Environmental Cooperation, 2007.

Lefebvre, Jean-Francois. *Énergies Renouvelables.* Quebec: Éditions MultiMondes, 2010 [French].

Torngat Mountains National Park Management Plan. Gatineau, Quebec: Parks Canada, 2010.

Saguenay–St. Lawrence Marine Park: Management Plan. Gatineau, Quebec: Parks Canada, 2010.

Web Sites

Blending the Environment with the Economy: 2006–2012 Climate Change Action Plan Fourth Annual Report. Quebec Ministry for Sustainable Development, Environment, and Parks. Available from http://www.mddep.gouv.qc.ca/changements/plan_action/bilans/bilan4-en.pdf

Canadian Press. "Innu warn of global fight against Hydro-Quebec." CBC News. November 2, 2010. Available from http://www.cbc.ca/canada/montreal/story/2010/11/02/innu-protest-hydro-project-in-quebec.html

"Census of Agriculture counts 30,675 farms in Quebec." Statistics Canada. Available from http://www.statcan.gc.ca/ca-ra2006/analysis-analyses/que-qc-eng.htm

Center for Energy: Quebec. Available from http://www.centreforenergy.com/FactsStats/MapsCanada/QC-EnergyMap.asp

Feit, Harvey A. *Hunting and the Quest for Power: The James Bay Cree and Whitemen in the 20th Century.* Available from http://arcticcircle.uconn.edu/HistoryCulture/Cree/Feit1

"Fisheries and Aquaculture." Fisheries and Oceans Canada, Quebec Region. Available from http://www.qc.dfo-mpo.gc.ca/peches-fisheries/index-eng.asp

"Focus on Wildlife in Quebec." Quebec Ministry of Natural Resources and Wildlife. Available from http://www.mrnf.gouv.qc.ca/english/international/wildlife.jsp

For a Green and Prosperous Quebec—Summary. Government of Quebec. Available from http://www.mdeie.gouv.qc.ca/fileadmin/sites/internet/documents/publications/pdf/ministere/quebec_vert_sommaire_en.pdf

"Forest Ecozones of Canada: Taiga Shield." Natural Resources Canada. Available from http://ecosys.cfl.scf.rncan.gc.ca/classification/classif10-eng.asp

"The Forests of Quebec: Vast and Fascinating." Quebec Ministry of Natural Resources and Wildlife. Available from http://www.mrnf.gouv.qc.ca/english/international/forests.jsp

"Hydro-Québec Sets the Record Straight Following the Release of *Chercher le Courant.*" Hydro-Quebec. January 23, 2011. Available from http://www.hydroquebec.com/media/en/index.html

Hydro-Quebec Strategic Plan 2009–2013. Hydro-Quebec. Available from http://www.hydroquebec.com/publications/en/strategic_plan/pdf/plan-strategique-2009-2013.pdf

The James Bay and Northern Quebec Agreement. Available from http://www.gcc.ca/pdf/LEG000000006.pdf

"The James Bay Project." *The Canadian Encyclopedia.* Available from http://www.thecanadianencyclopedia.com/index.cfm?PgNm=TCE&Params=A1ARTA0004099

"La Paix des Braves (Summary)." Prospectors and Developers Association of Canada. Available from http://www.pdac.ca/pdac/advocacy/aboriginal-affairs/la-paix-des-bravest.pdf

"LEED Projects: Quebec." Canada Green Building Council. Available from http://www.cagbc.org/leed/leed_projects/registered_projects/main110/

building_registrations.php?project_province=QC&-project_status=2

"List of Ports in Quebec." Transport Canada. Available from http://www.tc.gc.ca/eng/quebec/ports-menu-1338.htm

Mountain Equipment Co-op: Green Building in Montreal. Available from http://www.mec.ca/Main/content_text.jsp?FOLDER%3C%3Efolder_id=2534374302887085

Parcs Quebec. Available from http://www.sepaq.com/pq/index.dot?language_id=1

Quebec and Climate Change: A Challenge for the Future—2006–2012 Climate Change Action Plan. Quebec Ministry for Sustainable Development, Environment, and Parks. Available from http://www.mddep.gouv.qc.ca/changements/plan_action/2006-2012_en.pdf

Quebec Ministry of Natural Resources and Wildlife. Available from http://www.mrn.gouv.qc.ca/english/home.jsp

Quebec Organic Reference Standards. Conseil des appellations réservées et des termes valorisants (CARTV). Available from http://cartv.gouv.qc.ca/sites/documents/file/lois_reglements/quebec_organic_reference_standard_part3n.pdf

"Quebec Portal: Forest." Government of Quebec. Available from http://www.gouv.qc.ca/portail/quebec/pgs/commun/portrait/economie/ressourcesnaturelles/foret/?lang=en

"Quebec Portal: Quebec Mining." Government of Quebec. Available from http://www.gouv.qc.ca/portail/quebec/pgs/commun/portrait/economie/ressourcesnaturelles/quebecminier/?lang=en

"Quebec Portal: Wildlife." Government of Quebec. Available from http://www.gouv.qc.ca/portail/quebec/pgs/commun/portrait/geographie/climat/faune/?lang=en

"Quebec: The Best Place in the World for Mineral Exploration." Quebec Ministry of Natural Resources and Wildlife. Available from http://www.mrnf.gouv.qc.ca/english/international/mines.jsp

Quebec Vrai. Available from http://www.quebecvrai.org/about-us

"Romaine Complex." Hydro-Quebec. Available from http://www.hydroquebec.com/projects/romaine.html

Seeking the Current. Available from http://www.seekingthecurrent.com/?p=1

Sustainable Development Act (Bill 118, 2006, chapter 3). National Assembly of Quebec. Available from http://www2.publicationsduquebec.gouv.qc.ca/dynamicSearch/telecharge.php?type=5&file=2006C3A.PDF

"UNESCO Sites: World Heritage and Biosphere Reserves." Tourism Quebec. Available from http://www.bonjourquebec.com/qc-en/unesco0.html

Using Energy to Build the Quebec of Tomorrow: Quebec Energy Strategy 2006–2015. Government of Quebec. Available from http://www.mrnf.gouv.qc.ca/english/publications/energy/strategy/energy-strategy-2006-2015.pdf

"Wildlife Observation." Tourism Quebec. Available from http://www.bonjourquebec.com/qc-en/oiseaux0.html#onglet

WindVision 2025: A Strategy for Quebec. Canadian Wind Energy Association. Available from http://www.canwea.ca/pdf/canwea-quebec-windvision-e-web-final.pdf

Saskatchewan

The great wealth of natural resources found in Saskatchewan has placed the province as a major mineral, agricultural, and energy leader in both the nation and the world. Saskatchewan is the largest producer of potash in the world, accounting for 30 percent of worldwide production and containing about 50 percent of all potash reserves. The province is also one of the largest producers of high-grade uranium, most of which is exported for use in electricity generation. Saskatchewan accounts for more than 20 percent of worldwide production of high-grade uranium. With nearly half of Canada's total cultivated farmland, Saskatchewan is a major agricultural producer. Flaxseed production within the province accounts for 70 percent of the national total and 25 percent of world production. More than 95 percent of the lentils produced in Canada are grown in Saskatchewan, which provides 32 percent of the world's total lentil exports. In addition, Saskatchewan ranks as the second largest oil producer in Canada and the fifth largest oil producer in North America. However, the government faces a number of challenges in protecting the environment and moving toward a more sustainable economy. The potential for oil operations in the Athabasca oil sands is one of the hot topics for the twenty-first century, as is the need to reduce greenhouse gas emissions.

Climate

While the climate is generally characterized as continental, the province experiences a wide range of extremes, with bitterly cold winters in the north and scorching summer temperatures in the south. The variety of ecosystems across the province are also susceptible to severe climate events, such as droughts, floods, thunderstorms, blizzards, and tornados. Annual precipitation levels tend to decrease from north to south, with the prairie regions being among the driest.

According to a 2009 report from The Pembina Institute, greenhouse gas emissions in Saskatchewan in 2007 were three times higher per person than the Canadian average. In efforts to address this issue, the government passed the Management and Reduction of Greenhouse Gases Act (Bill 126) in 2010. The act established the authority of the government to adopt the federal target greenhouse gas reduction goal of 20 percent below 2006 levels by 2020 and created the necessary administrative framework to initiate strategies for achieving this goal. The act also established the Saskatchewan Technology Fund, through which large emitters will offer carbon compliance payments that will in turn be used to finance investments in low-emitting technologies and processes that reduce greenhouse gas emissions. The Climate Change Foundation was launched as a result of the act as well. This organization has a mandate to promote research and development of climate adaptation and mitigation technologies.

Natural Resources, Water, and Agriculture

Natural Resources: Forests

Forest covers 52 percent of the province, with about 37 percent of this total classified as commercial forest. The forests of the Taiga Shield ecosystem along the northern border of the province consist primarily of jack pine, white birch, and black spruce. The Boreal Shield to the south features these species, along with white spruce and trembling aspen. Further south, all of these species, along with balsam poplar, can be found in the Boreal Plain. The forest industries of softwood lumber, pulp, plywood, and engineered wood products have contributed more than C$1 billion annually to the provincial budget.

Parks and Wildlife There are thirty-four provincial parks, along with two national parks. Grasslands National Park is the only one in Canada that preserves a portion of the nation's natural mixed prairie grasslands. Bison were reintroduced to this park in 2005. As of 2010, the

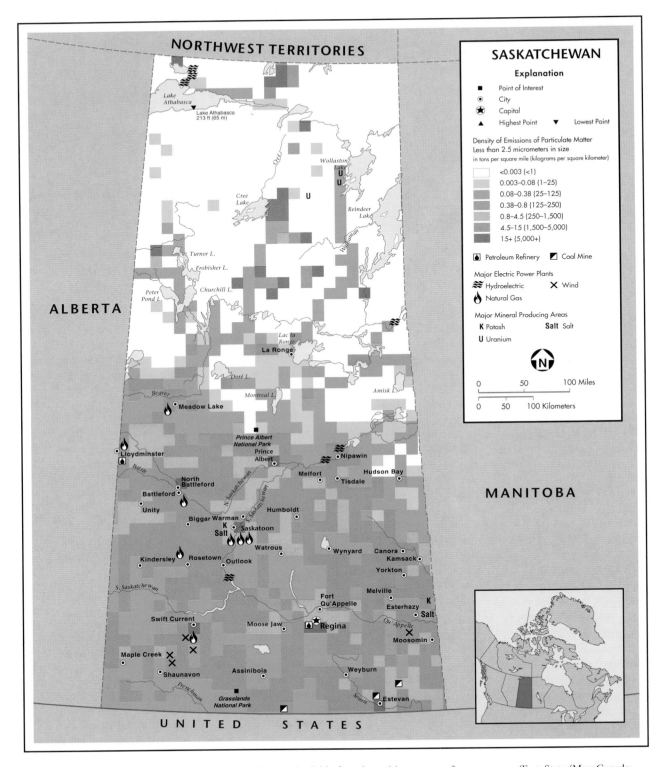

SOURCES: *Energy Facts and Statistics.* Centre for Energy. Available from http://www.centreforenergy.com/FactsStats/MapsCanada; "Geographical Highlights." *The Canadian Encyclopedia.* Available from http://www.encyclopediecanadienne.ca/geoHighlights/ canmap_geog_v1_eng.swf; "Highest Points by Province and Territory." *The Atlas of Canada.* Natural Resources Canada. Available from http://atlas.nrcan.gc.ca/site/english/learningresources/facts/faq.html#points; "Mining in Canada: Map." *Mining in Canada.* The Mining Association of Canada. Available from http://www.mining.ca/site/images/MapofCanada.pdf; "Particulate Matter < 2.5 Micrometers (PM2.5) Emission in 2007." *CAC Density Maps.* Environment Canada. Available from http://www.ec.gc.ca/inrp-npri/default.asp? lang=en&n=BD725B2A-1. © 2011 Cengage Learning.

Grasslands National Park is the only national park in Canada that preserves a portion of the nation's natural mixed prairie grasslands. © *Rolf Hicker Photography/Alamy*

resident herd had more than 150 animals. Visitors can also find wildlife species such as the black-footed ferret, black-tailed prairie dogs, mule deer, American badgers, swift fox, and coyotes. Bird species include the ferruginous hawk, long-billed curlew, loggerhead shrike, and common night hawk. Prince Albert National Park has the distinction of hosting the only fully protected white pelican nesting colony in Canada. It is also home to a large free-roaming herd of plains bison. Other wildlife residents include the timber wolf, woodland caribou, elk, moose, and black bear. As of 2011, there were 36 animal species listed as endangered or threatened in Saskatchewan, including the Canada warbler, great short-horned lizard, lake sturgeon, and woodland caribou. There were eight plant species listed as threatened or endangered, including western spiderwort, hairy prairie-clover, and small-flowered sand verbena.

Minerals Saskatchewan is the largest producer of potash in the world, accounting for 30 percent of worldwide production and containing about 50 percent of all potash reserves. The province is also one of the largest producers

of high-grade uranium (used to generate electricity), accounting for more than 21 percent of worldwide production. About 80 percent of the uranium produced in Saskatchewan is shipped to non-Canadian markets, to be used in nuclear power plants for the generation of electricity. The Fort à la Corne area is home to one of the world's largest kimberlite fields, which is now being explored for its potential value in diamond production. The salt produced in the province, primarily as a byproduct of potash operations, accounts for about 5 percent of the national production total. Other minerals produced in the province include gold, zinc, kaolin, silica sand, and bentonite.

Water: Rivers and Lakes

The name Saskatchewan is derived from a native Cree word meaning "swift-flowing river." The Saskatchewan River is formed by the confluence of the North Saskatchewan and the South Saskatchewan. This river cutting through the center of the state once served as a major transportation route for the fur trade. Now, two of the province's largest hydroelectric plants are located on the Saskatchewan. Other such facilities are found on the South Saskatchewan, the Churchill River, and the Athabasca River.

Saskatchewan boasts of having more than 100,000 lakes, with a majority of them found in the northern Canadian Shield. The largest lakes are Lake Athabasca, which is shared with Alberta, and Reindeer Lake, shared with Manitoba. Other larger inland lakes include Wollaston Lake, Cree Lake, and Lac la Ronge. One of the most unique lakes is Little Manitou, a saline lake fed by an underground spring which was reported to have healing qualities since the nineteenth century. The lake is now at the center of a popular tourist resort.

Fishing

A number of northern lakes support small commercial fishing operations. Overall, there are about seven hundred licensed fishing operations in the province employing about 1,500 people. Sport fishing is a far more popular pursuit with Arctic graying, goldeye, burbot, walleye, yellow perch, lake whitefish, and several species of trout among the popular catches. According to a 2006 report, sport fishing in the province contributed more than $156 million to the Saskatchewan economy.

Agriculture: Food for the Nation and the World

With nearly half of Canada's total cultivated farmland, Saskatchewan is a major agricultural producer for the nation and the world. Flaxseed production within the province accounts for 70 percent of the national total and 25 percent of world production. More than 95 percent of the lentils produced in Canada are grown in Saskatchewan, which provides 32 percent of the world's total

Saskatchewan Provincial Profile

Physical Characteristics

Land area	228,445 square miles (591,670 sq km)
Freshwater area	22,921 square miles (59,365 sq km)
Highest point	Cypress Hills 4,816 feet (1,468 m)
Forest lands (2011)	49.5 million acres (20.0 million ha)
Provincial parks (2011)	36

Energy Statistics

Total electricity generated (2009)	18.4 million megawatt hours
Hydroelectric energy generation (2009)	3 million megawatt hours
Wind energy generation (2009)	500,000 megawatt hours
Tidal energy generation (2009)	NA
Biomass energy capacity (2009)	NA
Crude oil reserves (2009)	958.6 million barrels (152.4 million cu m)
Natural gas reserves (2009)	2.8 trillion cubic feet (81.0 billion cu m)
Natural gas liquids (2009)	6.9 million barrels (1.1 million cu m)

Pollution Statistics

Carbon output (2009)	23.8 million tons of CO_2 (21.6 million t)
Federal contaminated sites receiving funds (2008)	5
Particulate matter (less than 2.5 micrometers) emissions (2009)	104,007 tons per year (94,354 t/yr)

SOURCES: *Canada's Greenhouse Gas Emissions*. Environment Canada. Available from http://www.ec.gc.ca/ges-ghg/default. asp?lang=En&n=1357A041-1; *Canada Year Book, 2011*. Statistics Canada. Available from http://www.statcan.gc.ca/ pub/11-402-x/11-402-x2011000-eng.htm; *Energy Facts and Statistics*. Centre for Energy. Available from http:// www.centreforenergy.com/FactsStats/MapsCanada; *Federal Contaminated Sites*. Government of Canada. Available from http://www.federalcontaminatedsites.gc.ca/index-eng. aspx; "Forest Land by Province and Territory." Statistics Canada. Available from http://www40.statcan.gc.ca/l01/ cst01/envi34a-eng.htm; "Geographical Highlights." *The Canadian Encyclopedia*. Available from http://www. encyclopediecanadienne.ca/geoHighlights/canmap_geog_v1_ eng.swf; *National Pollutant Release Inventory*. Environment Canada. Available from http://ec.gc.ca/pdb/websol/emissions/ap/ ap_query_e.cfm

© 2011 Cengage Learning.

lentil exports. Saskatchewan also accounts for 38 percent of the world's dry peas exports, representing more than 75 percent of total Canadian production. The province provides 45 percent of the nation's canola production and 80 percent of durum wheat. It is one of the largest producers of coriander, caraway, and green wild rice, and also provides significant quantities of beef and pork. The food and beverage industry in Saskatchewan is the largest manufacturing sector, accounting for about C$2 billion in annual sales.

There are more than 1,200 certified organic producers in the province, accounting for 35 percent of the nation's total organic production. The province is the leading Canadian exporter of organic grain and oilseed products, generating between C$50 and C$60 million annually in export sales. Organic producers may be certified by a number of agencies in Canada with assistance provided by Saskatchewan Agriculture.

⚜ Energy

Oil and Natural Gas

Saskatchewan ranks as the second largest oil producer in Canada and the fifth largest oil producer of all the American states and Canadian provinces. According to 2010 figures, crude oil reserves in Saskatchewan accounted for about 22.2 percent of the national total, while oil production accounted for 34.4 percent of the national total. The province ranks as the nation's third largest producer of natural gas, accounting for about 2.8 percent of total marketed production with 4.7 percent of total reserves.

There are two refineries in the province. The Consumers Co-op refinery in Regina produces gasoline and other petroleum products for sales at Federated Cooperative retail outlets in Western Canada. The Husky Energy refinery in Lloydminster primarily produces asphalt, with about 46 percent of production exported to the United States.

Saskatchewan was the first province in Canada to pass a law requiring a blend of ethanol in gasoline. The Ethanol Fuel Act, S. S. E-11.1 requires a blend of at least 7.5 percent ethanol. To support this program, the provincial government has established a grant program with funds assisting distributers and producers. This program is managed by Enterprise Saskatchewan and is set to continue through 2012. The annual ethanol production capacity for the province was estimated at 90 million gallons (340 million l) in 2010.

Bakken Shale

Since the early 2000s, a number of companies have been producing oil from the Bakken shale formation along the southern border of the province. The Bakken shale formation of the Williston Basin is a large shale play that covers parts of eastern Montana and western North Dakota in the United States and stretches into the Canadian provinces of Saskatchewan and Manitoba. In the oil and gas industry, the term "play" refers to a geographic region where an economic quantity of oil or gas is likely to be found. Shale is a type of sedimentary rock containing organic compounds that produce liquid hydrocarbons. According to a 2008 report from the U.S. Geological Survey (USGS), the Bakken Formation contains an estimated mean of 3.65 billion barrels of technically recoverable oil, meaning that the oil can be accessed using technologies that are currently available.

Mosaic potash mine, Colonsay, Saskatchewan. The province is the largest producer of potash in the world, accounting for 30 percent of worldwide production and containing about 50 percent of all potash reserves. © *All Canada Photos/Alamy*

More recent figures from the USGS indicate that the field could contain up to 4.3 billion barrels of recoverable oil. About 25 percent of the formation lies in Saskatchewan, but the amount of recoverable oil from this region is still uncertain. For the first half of 2010, provincial oil production from the Bakken play was estimated at 61,000 barrels per day.

Coal and Electricity

In 2010, there were three operating coal mines in the province, all located near the southern border. About 90 percent of the coal produced is used at electricity generating plants within the province, with the remainder exported to Ontario and Manitoba. There are three coal-fired thermal generation plants with a total capacity of 1,682 megawatts, accounting for about 43.5 percent of the province's total capacity. The largest is at Boundary Dam Power Station operated by SaskPower. In 2010, SaskPower announced that Unit 3 of the station would be refurbished to support a carbon capture and sequestration demonstration project. In 2010, 34.5 percent of Saskathewan's electricity was used for the production of potash, oil and gas, steel, mining, and chemicals. The percentage is expected to increase in the future. The province has seven natural gas-fired thermal generating plants with a total capacity of 1,113 megawatts.

Uranium

Saskatchewan is one of the world's largest producers of natural high-grade uranium (for electricity generation) and the only uranium-producing province in the nation. Production comes from three mines in the northcentral region—McArthur River, Rabbit Lake, and McClean Lake. In 2008, production from these mines accounted for about 21 percent of the total world production. Since

Saskatchewan has no nuclear generating facilities, all of the uranium is exported, with about 80 percent going to international markets.

Renewable Energy

There are seven hydroelectric generating stations in Saskatchewan with a total installed capacity of 853 megawatts. The largest facilities are located along the Saskatchewan River. As of 2010, the province also had four wind farms with a total capacity of 198 megawatts (MW) or 5 percent of the total capacity for the province. When the Centennial Wind Power Faculty opened in 2006, it was the largest capacity facility in the nation with 150 megawatts. It has since dropped to fourth in national rankings. The first phase of the C$69 million Red Lily Wind Project came online in February 2011, far ahead of schedule. The 26.4 MW wind farm, constructed by Algonquin Power & Utilities, features 16 turbines. The company also has secured the land rights for the second phase of the project, which will provide an additional 106 MW of generating capacity.

SaskPower is working on a biomass facility as well. It will be located at Meadow Lake and will use wood waste from the NorSask Forest Products mill to generate up to 36 MW of power for the province. The facility, called Meadow Lake Bioenergy Centre, is a collaboration between SaskPower, the provincial government, the First Nations Power Authority (FNPA), and the Meadow Lake Tribal Council (MLTC). In October 2011, SaskPower and MLTC began working on a 25-year purchasing agreement for the power generated by the facility. Meadow Lake Bioenergy Centre is expected to be online by 2014, and is projected to create 300 new jobs, including 25 permanent jobs.

The provincial government introduced the Saskatchewan Energy Strategy in 1995. The strategy's three main components address energy resource development, energy utilization, and energy utilities, and continue to provide structure for annual energy resource planning. The provincial Ministry for Energy and Resources, in its *Plan for 2010–11*, lists several key strategies, including modernization of energy and resource sector business and regulatory systems, support of innovation and research, structuring of the province's forest industry for sustainability and efficiency, ensuring sustainability of petroleum and mineral resources, and increasing Aboriginal participation in the resource industry.

🍁 Green Business, Green Building, Green Jobs

Green Business

In 2007, the government of Saskatchewan unveiled its Green Strategy, which is meant to serve as a framework for protecting the environment, addressing climate change, and promoting new developments in the green economy. In support of the strategy, the government created the Go Green Fund, which provides financial assistance for businesses working in or toward green industry. For instance, the Green Technology Commercialization Fund, which is part of the Go Green Fund, provides financial assistance to small and medium-sized businesses for the development and sale of green technologies. Organizations such as the Saskatchewan Environmental Industry and Managers Association are also working to promote the growth of the green economy.

Green Building

The Go Green Fund provides financial assistance for business owners, residents, and communities that are pursuing energy efficiency and conservation projects in buildings and homes. One of the programs sponsored under the program is the Energy Efficiency Rebate for New Homes, which provides financial incentives for residents building new homes under the specifications of the *Saskatchewan EnerGuide for House*, available through SaskEnergy. Also available from SaskEnergy is a geothermal rebate for homeowners who use the technology to power their homes.

The Saskatchewan chapter of the Canada Green Building Council is also active in supporting green building practices throughout the province. The chapter hosts an annual Building Saskatchewan Green Conference and Trade Show that serves as a major networking event for industry professionals. The Saskatchewan Forest Center was the province's first gold-level certified building under the Canada Green Building Council Leadership in Energy and Environmental Design (LEED) program.

Green Jobs

According to the 2009 *Environmental Industry Sector Labour Study* from the Saskatchewan Environmental Industry and Managers Association (SEIMA), about 2.7 percent of the total workforce, or 14,500 people, are involved in the environmental sector. The report indicates that there is an increasing demand for workers in environmental fields, but that there have also been challenges in recruiting new workers and providing training for what are often highly skilled positions. In one effort to address this challenge, SEIMA has partnered with the Saskatchewan Ministry of Advanced Education, Employment, and Labor to create the Saskatchewan Green Team, a program designed to provide opportunities for students to gain work experience and training in the environmental sector. The program provides subsidies for employers who provide employment opportunities for students ages 15 and older.

🍁 Development in the Athabasca Oil Sands

A potential new source of oil has some industry leaders optimistic that an economic boom is just about to start, but environmentalists are cautioning that mining operations in the Athabasca oil sands could lead to significant environmental problems, similar to those faced by neighboring Alberta.

The Athabasca oil sands lie along the border region with Alberta. Oil sands are a naturally occurring mixture of sand or clay, water, and tar-like bitumen, the latter of which can be extracted in a variety of methods. The oil sands found in Saskatchewan cover an estimated area of about 27,000 square miles (70,000 sq km) and may contain as much as 2.3 billion barrels of bitumen. However, while a number of developers are involved in exploration projects in the province, the sands in Saskatchewan lie too deep for the surface mining techniques currently used in Alberta. The deposits lying 606 feet (185 m) underground would require an extraction technique known as *in situ*, in which the bitumen is extracted underground before it is transported to the surface. Both techniques pose a number of environmental threats, including very high levels of greenhouse gas emissions. In situ mining could also lead to watershed contamination and significant disruptions in water use cycles.

Oilsands Quest Inc. has been the leading oil sands exploration and development firm in Saskatchewan since 2004, when the company acquired its first exploration permits in the northwest region. It was this company that made the first discovery of bitumen in what is now referred to as the Axe Lake Discovery. Since then, the company acquired five additional exploration licenses. In 2007, Oilsands Quest initiated a pre-commercialization study and launched a comprehensive baseline environmental study. In 2008, field testing began of recovery processes at the Axe Lake Discovery. In October 2009, bitumen was successfully mobilized. In early 2010, the company submitted plans and an application to the provincial government for a pilot project that could produce 30,000 barrels per day of commercial oil sands at Axe Lake. The plans were put on hold by the end of the year primarily due to difficulties in securing the necessary finances.

The delay comes as a welcome repose for environmental groups that have been raising flags of caution since production began in earnest in nearby Alberta. In 2009, the Saskatchewan Environmental Society, the Canadian Parks and Wilderness Society, and The Pembina Institute issued a joint report entitled *Carbon Copy: Preventing Oil Sands Fever in Saskatchewan*. The report takes a look at some of the damaging effects that oil sands mining has had in Alberta, in an effort to provide cautionary recommendations on measures that the

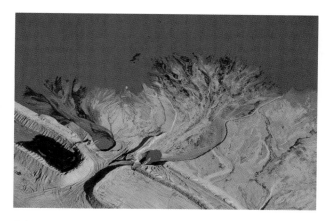

Athabasca oil sands in Fort McMurray, Saskatchewan. The oil sands found in Saskatchewan cover an estimated area of about 27,000 square miles (70,000 sq km). © *Alan Gignoux/Alamy*

Saskatchewan government should consider before allowing development to move forward. A significant increase in greenhouse gas emissions is noted as a primary consequence of oil sands mining operations. According to the report, in situ mining of oil sands creates three to five times more emissions per barrel than conventional oil production in North America. Saskatchewan is already noted as having greenhouse gas emissions that are three times higher per person than the Canadian average. Such a dramatic increase could have a serious affect on both air and water quality. The report also claims that an increase in acid rain over the northern lakes of Saskatchewan has already been noted, as nearly 70 percent of the sulphur dioxide and nitrogen oxides emitted by oil sand operations in Alberta have made their way into Saskatchewan.

In a section of recommendations, the report first outlines concerns related to public participation in the development process and calls upon the provincial government to undertake a major public consultation campaign to discern the wants and concerns of all citizens (including the First Nations and Metis people) before allowing any projects to move forward. Additional recommendations include the initiation of a comprehensive regional environmental assessment, the development of a regional land use plan, the establishment of greenhouse gas regulations that lean toward overall reductions, and the development of adequate monitoring systems for water resources and biodiversity.

In January 2011, the Saskatchewan *StarPhoenix* and the Regina *Leader-Post* published the results of a jointly sponsored poll by Sigma Analytics concerning the current level of public support for oil sands development projects in Saskatchewan. The results showed that 24.9 percent of respondents "strongly support" such developments. However, 23 percent were "opposed" or "strongly opposed" and more than 50 percent noted that they had some reservations about the projects. The survey included 612 respondents.

In the meantime, Oilsands Quest announced in September 2011 that it had agreed to sell property in Wallace Creek for an initial payment of C$40 million and another C$20 million at a later date in an effort to focus more on the Axe Lake discovery. The deal was set to go through in December 2011. The CEO of Oilsands Quest, Garth Wong, said in a released statement: "While Wallace Creek has shown considerable potential, it is not yet as well delineated as Axe Lake is and therefore considerably further away from commercial development." The Wallace Creek discovery required a different method of extraction, called steam assisted gravity drainage, and required further investment.

BIBLIOGRAPHY

Books

Berkes, Fikret. *Breaking Ice: Renewable Resource and Ocean Management in the Canadian North.* Calgary: University of Calgary Press, 2005.

Dearden, Philip, and Rick Rollins. *Parks and Protected Areas in Canada: Planning and Management.* 3rd ed. Don Mills, ON: Oxford University Press, 2009.

Forbes Travel Guide: Canada. Chicago: Forbes Travel Guide, 2010.

Fosket, Jennifer. *Living Green.* Gabriola Island, BC: New Society Publishers, 2009.

Guide to the National Parks of Canada. Washington, DC: National Geographic, 2011.

The Importance of Nature to Canadians: The Economic Significance of Nature-Related Activities. Ottawa: Environment Canada, 2000.

Prince Albert National Park Management Plan. Ottawa: Parks Canada, 2008.

Visser, Emily, and Luigi Ferrara. *Canada Innovates: Sustainable Building.* Toronto: Key Porter Books, 2008.

Web Sites

"Algonquin Power & Utilities Corp. Announces Commercial Operation of Phase 1 Red Lily Wind Project." Algonquin Power & Utilities Corp. February 28, 2011. Available from http://www.algonquinpower.com/newsroom/2011.asp#FEB28-2011

"Boundary Dam Integrated Carbon Capture and Storage Demonstration Project." SaskPower. Available http://www.saskpower.com/sustainable_growth/projects/carbon_capture_storage.shtml

Carbon Copy: Preventing Oil Sands Fever in Saskatchewan. The Pembina Institute. Available from http://pubs.pembina.org/reports/sask-carbon-copy-report.pdf

Center for Energy: Saskatchewan. Available from http://www.centreforenergy.com/FactsStats/Maps Canada/SK-EnergyMap.asp

Climate Change Saskatchewan. Available from http://www.climatechangesask.com/index.cfm

"Economic Evaluation of Saskatchewan's Commercial and Non-Outfitted Sport Fishing." Saskatchewan Ministry of Environment. December 2006. Available from http://www.environment.gov.sk.ca/adx/aspx/adxGetMedia.aspx?DocID=564,243,94,88, Documents&MediaID=227&Filename=Sask+Commercial+and+Non-Outfitted+Sport+Fishing.pdf&l=English

The Ethanol Fuel Act (Chapter E-11.1 Reg 1). The Legislative Assembly of Saskatchewan. Available from http://www.canlii.org/en/sk/laws/regu/rrs-c-e-11.1-reg-1/latest/part-1/rrs-c-e-11.1-reg-1-part-1.pdf

Field Guide to the Forest Ecosites of Saskatchewan's Provincial Forests. Saskatchewan Ministry of Environment, Available from http://www.environment.gov.sk.ca/adx/aspx/adxGetMedia.aspx?DocID=8734900c-f0b6-4f0d-9a63-d93326f466ce&MediaID=4081&Filename=Ecosites+of+Saskatchewan's+Provincial+Forests.pdf&l=English

"First Nations Renewable Power Project Moving Forward At Meadow Lake." SaskPower. October 3, 2011. Available from http://www.saskpower.com/news_publications/news_releases/?p=1217#more-1217

"Fishing." Saskatchewan Ministry of Environment. Available from http://www.environment.gov.sk.ca/fishing

"Go Green." Saskatchewan Ministry of Environment. Available from http://www.environment.gov.sk.ca/gogreen

Grasslands National Park of Canada Visitors Guide. Parks Canada Available from http://www.pc.gc.ca/pn-np/sk/grasslands/visit/visit6.aspx

Leighton, Jerry. "Bakken Formation: Will it fuel Canada's oil industry?" CBC News. June 27, 2008. available from http://www.cbc.ca/money/story/2008/05/23/f-langton-bakken.html

The Management and Reduction of Greenhouse Gases Act (Bill 126). Legislative Assembly of Saskatchewan. Available from http://www.legassembly.sk.ca/bills/pdfs/3_26/bill-126.pdf

Mineral Resources of Saskatchewan: Coal. Available from http://www.er.gov.sk.ca/default.aspx?DN=3549,3541,3538,3385,2936,Documents

Ministry of Energy and Resources. *Plan for 2010–11.* Available from http://www.finance.gov.sk.ca/PlanningAndReporting/2010-11/ERPlan1011.pdf

"Oilsands Quest To Sell Wallace Creek Assets." MarketWatch. September 27, 2011. Available from http://www.marketwatch.com/story/oilsands-quest-to-sell-wallace-creek-assets-2011-09-27-8000

"Oilsands Quest To Sell Wallace Creek, Focus on Developing Axe Lake." *The Canadian Press.* September 27, 2011. Available from http://www.canadianbusiness.com/article/47760–oilsands-quest-to-sell-wallace-creek-focus-on-developing-axe-lake

"Province Launches Green Energy Strategy." Government of Saskatchewan. April 12, 2007. Available from http://www.gov.sk.ca/news?newsId=57b440b5-31ff-402d-8a24-f243695e33ae

Roche, Pat. "Saskatchewan Bakken Field Going Strong." Daily Oil Bulletin. July 13, 2010. Available from http://www.albertasurfacerights.org/articles/?id=352

"Saskatchewan in Brief." Government of Saskatchewan. Available from http://www.gov.sk.ca/Default.aspx?DN=f80c0ebb-f1c6-497e-8bc0-30c215a5441f

"Saskatchewan EnerGuide for Houses." SaskEnergy. Available from http://www.saskenergy.com/saving_energy/energuide.asp

"Saskatchewan: Energy, Innovation, Opportunity." Saskatchewan Ministry of Energy and Resources. Available from http://www.er.gov.sk.ca/Energy.Innovation.Opportunity

Saskatchewan Energy Strategy, March 9, 1995. Available from http://www.gov.sk.ca/news?newsId=cad-da40a-00a1-4ee0-b6fa-7bd8810465d8

"Saskatchewan Green Team." Saskatchewan Environmental Industry and Managers Association. Available from http://seima.sk.ca/green_team

"Saskatchewan Lakes." Natural Resources Canada: The Atlas of Canada. Available from http://atlas.nrcan.gc.ca/auth/english/learningresources/facts/lakes.html/#saskatchewan

"Saskatchewan LEED Projects." Canada Green Building Council. Available from http://www.cagbc.org/leed/leed_projects/registered_projects.php?project_city=&project_province=SK&project_title=&building_type=&LEED_version=&project_status=2

"Saskatchewan Minerals: Minerals Industry." Saskatchewan Ministry of Energy and Resources. Available from http://www.er.gov.sk.ca/Minerals-Industry-Facts

"Saskatchewan Oil Sands." Oilsands Quest Inc. Available from http://www.oilsandsquest.com/our_projects/sask_oil_sands.html

"Saskatchewan River Basin." Partners for the Saskatch ewan River Basin. Available from http://www. saskriverbasin.ca/file/INTRO.pdf

"Saskatchewan's Ethanol Program." Enterprise Saskatch ewan. Available from http://www.saskethan olnow.ca/SaskEthanolProgram

"Saskatchewan's Forestry Sector." Saskatchewan Ministry of Energy and Resources. Available from http:// www.er.gov.sk.ca/forestry

Saskatchewan 2010/2011 Provincial Parks Guide. Saskat chewan Parks. Available from http://www.tpcs.gov. sk.ca/2010ParksGuide

"SaskPower Selects Carbon Capture Technology for Boundary Dam Project." Available from http:// www.gov.sk.ca/news?newsId=ffeaca54-7dda-41bc-989d-b0db37ad0dd3

Stewart, Jeanette. "Oilsands split Saskatchewan: poll." The StarPhoenix. January 4, 2011. Available from http://www.thestarphoenix.com/business/Oil sands+split+Saskatchewan+poll/4056119/ story.html

2010 Saskatchewan Anglers Guide. Saskatchewan Ministry of Environment. Available from http:// www.environment.gov.sk.ca/adx/aspx/adxGet Media.aspx?DocID=1741,243,94,88,Documents& MediaID=3318&Filename=2010+Anglers+Guide. pdf&l=English

"Transforming Saskatchewan's Electrical Future: Using Electricity More Efficiently." Canadian Centre for Policy Alternatives, November 2010. Available from http://www.policyalternatives.ca/newsroom/ updates/transforming-saskatchewans-electrical-future-using-electricity-more-efficiently

"Who Knew—Agriculture in Saskatchewan." Saskatch ewan Ministry of Agriculture. Available from http:// www.agriculture.gov.sk.ca/adx/aspx/adxGet Media.aspx?DocID=11034,4532,201,81,1,Docu ments&MediaID=6204&Filename=Who+Knew +-+Agriculture+in+Saskatchewan+-+Printer+ Friendly.pdf

"Wildlife Species at Risk in Saskatchewan." Saskatchewan Ministry of Environment. Available from http:// www.environment.gov.sk.ca/wildspeciesatrisk

Yukon

The Yukon, the smallest of Canada's three federal territories with a population of about 34,700, features spectacular natural vistas. Yukon is home to North America's second highest peak—Mount Logan—and many snow-melt lakes. Despite the long, cold winters, the long hours of sunshine during the short summer allow for hardy crops, such as vegetables, flowers, and fruit, to grow. The territory's main industry has historically been mining, with tourism coming in second. Due to the Yukon's pristine and untouched landscapes, ecotourism is a growing business in the territory.

Climate

The Yukon lies within a sub-arctic continental climate, which is strongly influenced by the extensive mountain ranges that dominate the territory's geography. Temperatures reach as high as 97°F (36.1°C) in the summer and as low as –76°F (–60°C) in the winter. The average frost free period ranges from 93 to 21 days, depending on the location due to the territory's varied geography. The region has long hours of daylight during the summer, which promotes rapid growth. This somewhat compensates for the cooler summer temperatures occurring north of 60° latitude. Average annual precipitation ranges from less than 8 inches (20 cm) to more than 16 inches (40 cm). The southwest region of the territory is where most agricultural production occurs, however it is subject to droughts between April and July which can cause problems for crop production. Climate and weather vary significantly throughout the Yukon in any given season due to the effects of large variations in altitude.

A Climate Change Action Plan for Yukon

According to the *Arctic Climate Impact Assessment* of 2004, winter temperatures in the Yukon rose by 5.4–7.2°F (3–4°C) between 1950 and 2000. Over the next 100 years, temperatures are predicted to rise another 7.2–12.6°F (4–7°C) if measures to curb climate change are not taken. Climate models predict increased winter precipitation, particularly in the far northern regions in the territory.

Overall there will also be an increase in storms, both winter and summer, with heavier snowfall, rainfall, and more thunder and lightning. These changes will lead to a number of adverse effects on the region. Permafrost, an important characteristic of the arctic ecosystem, could begin to melt, leading to instability in the terrain, change in water flowpaths, and erosion. Permafrost is particularly important to Yukon's infrastructure, in which many roads are constructed on ice during the winter. Climate change will also cause changes in the growing season, populations of caribou will drastically decline, and the agricultural and forestry sectors will be negatively impacted.

In order to address these issues, the Yukon government published a climate change strategy in 2006. This strategy outlines the government's role and goals for its response to climate change. In February of 2009, the Yukon government published the *Yukon Government Climate Change Action Plan*, which details 33 current and new initiatives that will help to advance the climate change strategy. The plan establishes four goals in order for the territory to mitigate the effects of climate change. The goals are to enhance the territory's knowledge of climate change, to then adapt to climate change, reduce greenhouse gas emissions, and finally, to take action in response to climate change. As part of the plan, the Yukon government capped greenhouse gas emissions in 2010, and has set a goal to reduce greenhouse gas emissions by 20 percent by 2015 and to become carbon neutral by 2020.

Yukon also partnered with the governments of Canada's two other territories, Nunavut and Northwest Territories, to create a document that focuses on practical climate change adaptation measures. *The Pan-Territorial Adaptation Strategy: Moving Forward on Climate Change Adaptation in Canada's North* was written in 2009 to recognize changes are coming in relation to climate change and to create a plan for managing the risks associated with that change across all the territories. The document includes six approaches for identifying and supporting current and future climate change action and adaptation. Those approaches include source funding, collaborating with other governments, supporting local communities, integrated adaptation, sharing of knowledge regarding climate change, and developing and sharing tools, technology, and innovation.

❧ Natural Resources, Water, and Agriculture

Natural Resources

The Yukon is home to woodland caribou, lynx, black bears, moose, gray wolves, golden eagles, and gyrfalcons. The only endangered species listed in the territory is the bowhead whale. Threatened species include the wood bison and the Anatum subspecies of the peregrine falcon. Species of special concern in the territory are the grizzly bear, polar bear, short-eared owl, the tundra subspecies of the peregrine falcon, and the Squanga whitefish. The *Yukon Wildlife Act* lists seven species as "specially protected." These species are elk, muskox, mule deer, cougar, gyrfalcon, peregrine falcon, and trumpeter swan. The Act states that no one may possess, hunt, or trap these species unless they are issued a special permit.

An estimated 6,000 to 7,000 grizzly bears inhabit the Yukon. The population is spread over the entire territory. Kluane National Park is home to the continent's most genetically diverse population of grizzly bears. Grizzly bears are hunted in the territory; however the harvest is directed at older male bears. Female bears with cubs and all cubs are protected from hunting.

The Yukon has rich areas of biodiversity, and the north coast is home to one-fifth of the world's arctic flora. The territory contains plants from three different regions: Beringia, the Western Cordilleran mountain ranges, and the boreal forest. Plant species native to Yukon include the Yukon, Kluane, and Scotter's draba, Ogilvie spring beauty, and Maclean's goldenweed. The territory lists one plant species—the Baikal Sedge—as threatened.

About 57 percent of the Yukon's land area is covered by forests, all of which is owned by the federal government. White spruce, black spruce, lodgepole pine, Alpine fir, aspen, and balsam poplar are the most common tree species. The territory's forest industry is made up of small operators who cut small volumes of timber for building materials, log homes, and fuel wood.

Mining in Yukon

Gold, lead, iron, copper, zinc, tungsten, molybdenum, coal, and nickel are mined in Yukon. Coal deposits are found in the northeastern and southeastern parts of the territory. Copper deposits are found in the southern half of the territory. Gold deposits are also found in the southern part of the territory, more notably in the southwest. In 2009, there were 135 active gold operations employing approximately 400 people. The gold produced from these operations was valued at C$48.23 million. Yukon is also home to one of the largest deposits of iron in the world, located in the Crest deposit. However, there isn't much exploration activity for iron currently going on in the territory. The Crest deposit is found in the northeastern part of the territory, with more occurrences found in the northwest. Yukon and the Northwest Territories together account for 20 percent of the world's tungsten deposits, and the Yukon also has significant zinc deposits in the southeast.

Yukon's Water Resources

Yukon's northern coast lies on the Beaufort Sea. Major rivers include the Yukon River and Mackenzie River. Most of the territory's area lies in the Yukon River's watershed. The southern part of Yukon has many large glacier-fed alpine lakes. The larger lakes include: Teslin Lake, Atlin Lake, Tagish Lake, Marsh Lake, Lake Laberge, Kusawa Lake, and Kluane Lake.

Apart from the Yukon River, the two main rivers that flow into the Mackenzie River in the Northwest Territories are the Liard River in the southeast and the Peel River and its tributaries in the northeast. The Yukon's freshwater rivers and lakes are monitored regularly to determine their water quality and to be sure that water quality guidelines are not being exceeded.

A small fishing industry operates in Dawson City to export salmon. Other commercial fisheries supply local consumers. Lake trout and lake whitefish are also harvested commercially. Overall, commercial fishing represents five percent of the territory's harvest.

According to Environment Yukon's 2005 sport fishing survey, in 2005 15,141 anglers held Yukon angling licenses. Fifty-three percent (8,018) were sold to Yukon residents, 21 percent to Canadians from outside Yukon, and 26 percent to non-Canadians. Anglers caught 275,000 fish that year, with arctic grayling, northern pike, and lake trout being the most widely caught species. Recreational fishing in the Yukon is a C$23 million-a-year industry.

Agriculture

Yukon has a small, but thriving, agricultural industry. Crops that grow well in the territory include grass hays, oats, potatoes, greenhouse vegetables, and flowers. As of 2007, there were 148 farms in the territory growing and producing items like forage, cheese, meats, vegetables, fresh produce, and bedding plants. Farmland was estimated to cover just over 25,000 acres (10,000 ha). Total gross farm receipts in 2005 totaled just more than C$4 million. In 2007, the territorial government set multiyear goals for increasing agriculture development and production from 2008 to 2012. Some of those goals

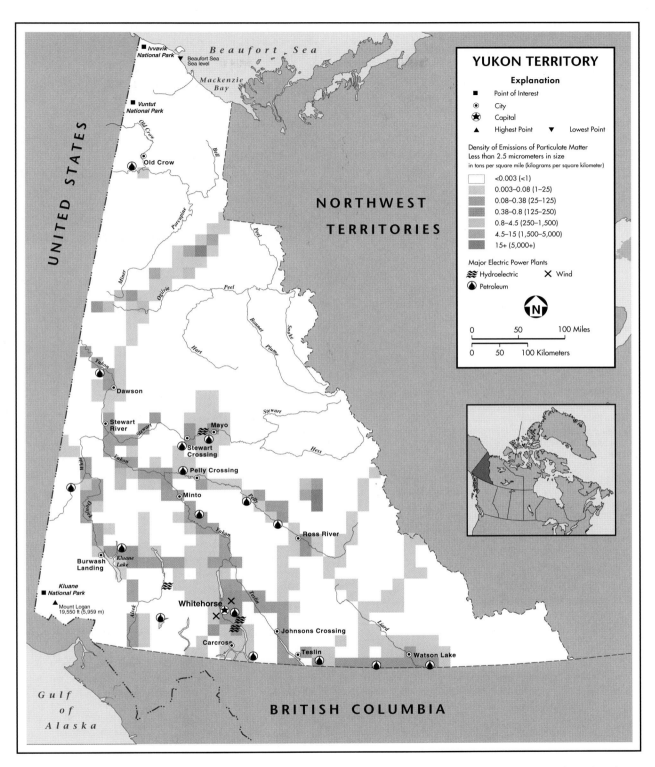

YUKON TERRITORY

Explanation

■ Point of Interest

◉ City

✪ Capital

▲ Highest Point   ▼ Lowest Point

Density of Emissions of Particulate Matter
Less than 2.5 micrometers in size
in tons per square mile (kilograms per square kilometer)

	<0.003 (<1)
	0.003–0.08 (1–25)
	0.08–0.38 (25–125)
	0.38–0.8 (125–250)
	0.8–4.5 (250–1,500)
	4.5–15 (1,500–5,000)
	15+ (5,000+)

Major Electric Power Plants

〰 Hydroelectric   ✕ Wind

◖ Petroleum

0   50   100 Miles

0   50   100 Kilometers

SOURCES: *Energy Facts and Statistics.* Centre for Energy. Available from http://www.centreforenergy.com/FactsStats/MapsCanada; "Geographical Highlights." *The Canadian Encyclopedia.* Available from http://www.encyclopediecanadienne.ca/geoHighlights/ canmap_geog_v1_eng.swf; "Highest Points by Province and Territory." *The Atlas of Canada.* Natural Resources Canada. Available from http://atlas.nrcan.gc.ca/site/english/learningresources/facts/faq.html#points; "Mining in Canada: Map." *Mining in Canada.* The Mining Association of Canada. Available from http://www.mining.ca/site/images/MapofCanada.pdf; "Particulate Matter < 2.5 Micrometers (PM2.5) Emission in 2007." *CAC Density Maps.* Environment Canada. Available from http://www.ec.gc.ca/inrp-npri/default.asp? lang=en&n=BD725B2A-1. © 2011 Cengage Learning.

Yukon Territorial Profile

Physical Characteristics

Land area	183,163 square miles (474,390 sq km)
Freshwater area	3,109 square miles (8,052 sq km)
Highest point	Mount Logan 19,551 feet (5,959 m)
Forest lands (2011)	19.5 million acres (7.9 million ha)
Territorial parks (2011)	7

Energy Statistics

Total electricity generated (2009)	NA
Hydroelectric energy generation (2009)	NA
Wind energy generation (2009)	NA
Tidal energy generation (2009)	NA
Biomass energy capacity (2009)	NA
Crude oil reserves (2009)	11.9 million barrels (1.9 million cu m)
Natural gas reserves (2009)	353.1 billion cubic feet (10.0 billion cu m)
Natural gas liquids (2009)	NA

Pollution Statistics

Carbon output (2009)	NA
Federal contaminated sites receiving funds (2008)	9
Particulate matter (less than 2.5 micrometers) emissions (2009)	27,428 tons per year (24,882 t/yr)

SOURCES: *Canada's Greenhouse Gas Emissions*. Environment Canada. Available from http://www.ec.gc.ca/ges-ghg/default. asp?lang=En&n=1357A041-1; *Canada Year Book, 2011*. Statistics Canada. Available from http://www.statcan.gc.ca/ pub/11-402-x/11-402-x2011000-eng.htm; *Energy Facts and Statistics*. Centre for Energy. Available from http:// www.centreforenergy.com/FactsStats/MapsCanada; *Federal Contaminated Sites*. Government of Canada. Available from http://www.federalcontaminatedsites.gc.ca/index-eng. aspx; "Forest Land by Province and Territory." Statistics Canada. Available from http://www40.statcan.gc.ca/l01/ cst01/envi34a-eng.htm; "Geographical Highlights." *The Canadian Encyclopedia*. Available from http://www. encyclopediecanadienne.ca/geoHighlights/canmap_geog_v1_ eng.swf; *National Pollutant Release Inventory*. Environment Canada. Available from http://ec.gc.ca/pdb/websol/emissions/ap/ ap_query_e.cfm

© 2011 Cengage Learning.

included expanding hay and feed production, increasing production and distribution channels for vegetables to meet local demand, and support education about and certification for organic operations.

⚜ Energy

Yukon has significant amounts of untapped natural gas and oil reserves. There are an estimated 900 million barrels of onshore crude oil resources, and an additional 4.5 billion barrels of offshore crude oil resources in the Beaufort Sea. Estimates for natural gas state that there are

Mount Logan, Yukon. © *Marc Muench/Alamy*

approximately 17 trillion cubic feet of onshore natural gas resources, with another 40 trillion cubic feet in the Beaufort Sea. Mining and gas extraction make up a significant portion of the territory's gross domestic product. Yukon received C$444,000 in oil and gas revenues in 2009. The territory is also being considered as home for 472 miles (760 km) of the Alaska Natural Gas Pipeline.

The territory's electricity is generated by hydro-power and natural gas. In 2009, there were four hydroelectric generating stations in Yukon: Fish Lake, Mayo, Whitehorse Rapids, and Aishihik. These stations have a production capacity of 76.7 MW of electricity, or 55 percent of Yukon's total installed capacity. The city of Whitehorse and the village of Mayo currently use low-grade geothermal energy in order to keep their water supplies from freezing during the winter months. There are numerous projects underway to further harness this renewable resource. Other sources of alternative energy that are used on a small-scale basis in Yukon include biomass, solar, and wind energy. The territorial government created a program called the Wind Prospecting Service for off-the-grid residents who wanted to explore wind as a source of energy. The program includes providing eligible residents a wind monitoring system to determine the energy potential for their site. In 2010, the first year of the program, two residents took part.

An Energy Strategy for Yukon

In 2009, the Government of Yukon published an energy strategy for the territory. The Energy Strategy for Yukon provides goals, strategies, and actions for efficiency and conservation to help guide the energy sector and government decisions. Specific goals of the strategy include increasing energy efficiency in the territory by 20 percent by 2020, increasing the supply of renewable energy by 20 percent by 2020, supporting strategic opportunities to replace imported diesel fuel with Yukon's own oil and gas resources, expand the territory's electrical transmission system, optimize the use of hydroelectricity, and to assess new and existing energy sources in the territory, such as biomass.

The government released an update in 2010, which highlighted forward progress in several key areas of the original report. These included improving the efficiency of the government's vehicle fleet and buildings, offering energy efficiency training and opportunities through the Yukon Housing Corporation, and supporting locally grown programs to reduce energy consumption from transportation. In June 2010, the government also adopted a green procurement policy, which affects all the goods and services purchased by the territorial government.

🍁 Green Business, Green Building, Green Jobs

Green Business, Green Jobs, and Green Training

The city of Whitehorse offers businesses, along with non-profit organizations and community groups, grants from their Environmental Fund for projects that will environmentally benefit the community. The projects must be aligned with one of the seven principles of the city's Strategic Sustainability Plan. For projects that are C$500 or less, the city may decide to fund 100 percent of the costs. For projects that are more than C$500, the city may provide 50 percent of the total cost.

Yukon College, located in Whitehorse, offers a number of programs that prepare students for environmentally or green-centered employment. The two-year Renewable Resources Management diploma program provides students with the knowledge, skills, and perspective to enable them to assist with the management of land, water, forest, fish, and wildlife resources in the north. It also prepares students for transfer to degree level programs in fields related to renewable resources management. Graduates of the program have found employment in lands and resource offices, fish and wildlife enforcement, environmental assessment, protected areas, fisheries, and private sector consulting firms.

Yukon College also offers a diploma in Northern Outdoor and Environmental Studies. This program focuses on environmental issues pertinent to northern systems. Some of these issues include resource depletion, wilderness fragmentation, loss of biodiversity, pollution, and global climate change. Students that complete the program often find work in education,

environmental policy or management, recreation, and tourism.

Green Building

Natural Resources Canada offers a number of commercial incentive programs for builders. The Commercial Building Incentive Program (CBIP) provides a funding incentive for buildings that are 25 percent more energy efficient than buildings that meet the Model National Energy Code for Buildings (the Model National Energy Code sets higher standards than the National Energy Code). Another program, C-2000, challenges participating builders to improve the energy efficiency potential of commercial office buildings through an integrated design process, energy modeling, the setting of energy efficiency and water conservation targets, and the use of low off-gassing finishing materials.

The Yukon Government also offers the Good Energy Rebate Program. Created in 2008, Good Energy was developed to be a comprehensive program. The program focuses on household appliances, heating appliances, and boat motors. The 2010/2011 version of the program added up to C$300 in rebates to residents that purchased an Energy Star-rated clothes washer, dishwasher, refrigerator, or freezer. Rebates went up to C$300 to C$600 for Energy Star-rated central heating units, up to C$600 for CSA-approved pellet stoves and EPA-approved woodstoves, and up to C$1,200 for CSA-approved solar water heating systems. During the 2009/2010 year, the program had 1,150 successful applicants that received rebates for 1,071 appliances, 211 heating appliances, and 106 boat motors. In total, the program for those years saved households approximately C$100,000 per year in electrical energy savings, and reduced carbon dioxide emissions by approximately 6,228 tons (5,650 t) per year.

🍁 Ecotourism: Protecting Yukon's Pristine Environment

The Yukon is a sparsely populated territory, which has resulted in much of its landscape remaining untouched. This has led to tourism becoming the territory's second most important industry. However, with the effects of climate change and disruption from mineral exploration looming over the land, the government of Yukon has taken measures to protect the land while retaining this vital industry.

As part of an effort to preserve the landscape, the Yukon is part of Leave No Trace, an international program that promotes the responsible use of wild lands. While Leave No Trace is not a set of strict rules or regulations, it educates the public with a checklist that travelers can follow when visiting Yukon's back country. Environment Yukon expanded upon this checklist in an informational booklet that they provide to wilderness tourists called *Into the Yukon Wilderness*. The seven items on the checklist are:

- Plan to leave no trace.
- Camp and travel on durable surfaces.
- Dispose of waste properly.
- Leave what you find.
- Minimize campfire impacts.
- Respect wildlife.
- Be considerate of others.

The booklet also discusses general wilderness safety, bear safety, fishing, hunting, and firearm usage and licenses, permits needed to transport wildlife parts and products, and access to developed and undeveloped First Nations land.

In 2009, Yukon Tourism and Culture published *Yukon Wilderness Tourism Best Management Practices for Heritage Resources*. This publication serves as a guide to provide wilderness tourists with up-to-date information about the protection of heritage resources, sites, and burials on the Yukon landscape. Since many of the resources in the territory are in remote areas that have not yet been surveyed, this guide engages the tourism industry in the protection of these resources. These best management practices are also essential because of the damage that wilderness tourism can cause to heritage sites if it goes on unchecked. Sites can be subjected to damage by the clearing of brush for campsites or subsurface disturbance from building cabins for guests. Heritage sites can also be subject to the looting of artifacts. The best management practices guide provides details for tourists and business owners on how to identify heritage sites and how to be careful not to disturb the land while camping, hiking, or building trails or lodges. The guide also provides detailed information on how to report newly discovered heritage sites or resources.

Climate Change and its Effects on Ecotourism

As the effects of a changing climate become more evident, visitors to the Yukon will have to be more careful of the changes in the landscape. Climate change could also affect the tourism industry in either positive or negative ways. While a warmer climate may mean more summer days for tourists, it could also cause heritage sites to become uncovered and vulnerable to destruction. Also, warmer air holds more moisture, which can produce more snow during the winter. The 2004 *Arctic Climate Impact Assessment* predicts that there will be more precipitation in the Yukon in both summer and winter, with overall heavier snowfall, rainfall, and an increase in storms. These changes could affect how and when many tourists travel to the Yukon, and also what adjustments would need to be made to the industry. There is also the issue of permafrost melting, which could cause instability

Sign for the Arctic Circle in the Yukon. © *Robert Harding Picture Library Ltd./Alamy*

in the land in many areas, which would be a danger to wilderness tourists and infrastructure in general. When it comes to hunting, shifting migrations could either bring in more hunters or cause a decline, and populations that are adversely effected by the changing climate may need to be protected.

Protecting the Landscape from Overdevelopment

Another concern for Yukon's ecotourism industry is the disruption to the land that can be caused by resource development, such as mining. In 2010, the Yukon Environmental and Socio-economic Assessment Board released an evaluation report of a case against a proposed exploration project in Tombstone Territorial Park. Canadian United Minerals, Inc. (CUMI) wanted to re-establish a camp to use heli-supported diamond and hydracore hydraulic drills, and mechanized trenching to search for minerals. Due to a clash between the development project and the area's physical, biological, archaeological, and cultural values, an assessment of the project and its possible impacts to the land was requested. When the area became a park, there were approximately 150 land claims in the area. All of the claimholders withdrew their claims after the establishment of the park except for CUMI.

Ultimately, the assessment recommended that the project could not proceed, as the problems it would cause could not be mitigated. The problems the project would cause are both social and environmental. The land has historically been used by First Nations groups, for guided hunting tours, and for ecotourism. The project would disrupt all of these activities and tourists would not be attracted to the area. Furthermore, exploration activities would disturb the environment. The use of snow machines would disrupt rare plant species and snow cover would be lost on the steep terrain. Migration routes for species such as Dall's sheep and caribou would be disrupted. Other species affected include moose, fish species in waterways near the project, and migrant bird species. Black bears and grizzly bears would also be disturbed and there would be an increase in bear-human contact, which poses a danger to both humans and bears. In September 2010, the Yukon government accepted the recommendation from the Yukon Environmental and Socio-economic Assessment Board and denied the mining company the ability to receive new exploration permits.

Ecotourism is a significant part of the territory's economy. Therefore, issues such as climate change and mineral exploration that both change and disturb the natural landscape pose a myriad of issues for the industry. The government of Yukon will have to work with these changes and with the mineral industry in order to continue to preserve their landscape and keep it safe for its many visitors.

BIBLIOGRAPHY

Books

Berkes, Fikret. *Breaking Ice: Renewable Resource and Ocean Management in the Canadian North.* Calgary: University of Calgary Press, 2005.

Dearden, Philip, and Rick Rollins. *Parks and Protected Areas in Canada: Planning and Management.* 3rd ed. Don Mills, ON: Oxford University Press, 2009.

Forbes Travel Guide: Canada. Chicago: Forbes Travel Guide, 2010.

Fosket, Jennifer. *Living Green.* Gabriola Island, BC: New Society Publishers, 2009.

Guide to the National Parks of Canada. Washington, DC: National Geographic, 2011.

Hart, E. J. *J. B. Harkin: Father of Canada's National Parks.* Edmonton: University of Alberta Press, 2010.

Howard, Roger. *The Arctic Gold Rush: the New Race for Tomorrow's Natural Resources.* London: Continuum, 2009.

The Importance of Nature to Canadians: The Economic Significance of Nature-Related Activities. Ottawa: Environment Canada, 2000.

Ivvavik Mountains National Park of Canada Management Plan. Inuvik, NWT: Parks Canada, 2007.

Visser, Emily, and Luigi Ferrara. *Canada Innovates: Sustainable Building.* Toronto: Key Porter Books, 2008.

Web Sites

Building Green and Beyond. Canada-Yukon Energy Solutions Centre. Yukon Development Corporation. Available from http://www.energy.gov.yk.ca/pdf/building_green_and_beyond.pdf

Designated Office Evaluation Report for Quartz Exploration at Tombstone Territorial Park 2010-0107. Yukon Environmental and Socio-economic Assessment Board. Available from http://www.cpawsyukon.org/peel-watershed/yesab-tombstone-report.pdf

Energy Strategy for Yukon. Department of Energy, Mines, and Resources. Government of Yukon. Available from http://www.energy.gov.yk.ca/pdf/energy_strategy.pdf

Energy Strategy for Yukon: Progress Report 2010. Department of Energy, Mines, and Resources. Government of Yukon. Available from http://www.energy.gov.yk.ca/pdf/EnergyStrategyProgressReport_2010_WEB.pdf

Environmental Fund. City of Whitehorse. Available from http://www.city.whitehorse.yk.ca/index.asp?Type=B_BASIC&SEC={D5FBD76B-5A72-4F1B-8104-95D55EA29D98}&DE=

Good Energy Rebate Eligibility Criteria: 2011-2012. Energy Solutions Center. Yukon Department of Energy, Mines, and Resources. Government of Yukon. Available from http://www.energy.gov.yk.ca/pdf/eligibility_criteria_2011__12.pdf

Government of Yukon Climate Change Strategy. Department of Environment. Government of Yukon. Available from http://www.environmentyukon.gov.yk.ca/pdf/ygclimatechangestrategy.pdf

Into the Yukon Wilderness. Department of Environment. Government of Yukon. Available from http://www.environmentyukon.gov.yk.ca/pdf/ityw.pdf

Minerals Branch. Department of Energy, Mines, and Resources. Government of Yukon. Available from http://www.emr.gov.yk.ca/mining/

Multi-Year Development Plan for Yukon Agriculture and Agri-Food: 2008-2012. Department of Energy, Mines, and Resources. Government of Yukon. December 2007. Available from http://www.emr.gov.yk.ca/agriculture/pdf/yukon_multi_year_development_plan.pdf

Northern Outdoor and Environmental Studies. Yukon College. Available from http://www.yukoncollege.yk.ca/programs/info/nes

Pan-Territorial Adaptation Strategy: Moving Forward on Climate Change Adaptation in Canada's North. Department of Environment. Government of Yukon. Available from http://www.anorthernvision.ca/documents/Pan-TerritorialAdaptationStrategyEN.pdf

Renewable Resources Management. Yukon College. Available from http://www.yukoncollege.yk.ca/programs/info/rrmt

Sport Fishing in Yukon 2005. Fisheries Management Section. Department of Environment. Government of Yukon. Available from http://www.environmen tyukon.gov.yk.ca/mapspublications/documents/fish_survey_report_2005.pdf

Status of Yukon Fisheries 2010. Fish and Wildlife Branch. Department of Environment. Government of Yukon. Available from http://www.environmen tyukon.gov.yk.ca/mapspublications/documents/status_yukon_fisheries2010.pdf

"Tombstone Park Mining Bid Denied." CBC News Canada. September 7, 2010. Available from http://www.cbc.ca/news/canada/north/story/2010/09/07/yukon-tombstone-park-mining.html

2009/2010 Good Energy Rebate Program. Energy Solu tions Centre. Department of Energy, Mines, and Resources. Government of Yukon. Available from http://www.energy.gov.yk.ca/pdf/good_energy_final_report_nov_10.pdf

"Wind Prospecting Service." Department of Energy, Mines, and Resources. Government of Yukon. Available from http://www.energy.gov.yk.ca/wind_prospecting_service.html

Ball, Matt, et al. *Yukon Agriculture 2008–2009 Interim Report*. Agriculture Branch. Department of Energy, Mines, and Resources. Government of Yukon. Available from http://www.emr.gov.yk.ca/agricul ture/pdf/soi2008_2009.pdf

"Yukon Climate." Department of Energy, Mines, and Resources. Government of Yukon. Available from http://www.emr.gov.yk.ca/agriculture/yukon_climate.html

"Yukon Energy Facts and Statistics." Centre for Energy. Available from http://www.centreforenergy.com/FactsStats/MapsCanada/YT-EnergyMap.asp

Yukon Energy Strategic Plan 2010–2012. Yukon Energy. Available from http://www.yukonenergy.ca/downloads/db/957_StratPlan2010_web.pdf

Yukon Exploration and Geology Overview 2009. Yukon Geological Survey. Department of Energy, Mines, and Resources. Government of Yukon. Available from http://www.geology.gov.yk.ca/pdf/YEG_overview_2009.pdf

Yukon Government Climate Change Action Plan. Department of Environment. Government of Yukon. Available from http://www.environmen tyukon.gov.yk.ca/pdf/YG_Climate_Change_Action_Plan.pdf

Yukon State of the Environment Interim Report 2007. Department of Environment. Government of Yukon. Available from http://www.environmen tyukon.gov.yk.ca/pdf/soe2007.pdf

Yukon Wilderness Tourism Best Management Practices for Heritage Resources. Department of Tourism and Culture. Government of Yukon. Available from http://www.tc.gov.yk.ca/publications/Wilderness_Tourism_BMP_for_Heritage_Resources.pdf

"Yukon Wildlife." Yukon Outfitters. Available from http://www.yukonoutfitters.net/ykwildlife.asp

Major Environmental Organizations and Advocacy Groups

AMERICAN BIRD CONSERVANCY

The American Bird Conservancy, like the Audubon Society, exists primarily to support bird conservation but broadly supports environmentalism and sustainability. Using education, advocacy and direct action, the ABC is the only U.S.-based organization that supports not just United States bird conservation, but species preservation throughout all of the Americas

> 1731 Connecticut Ave. NW, 3rd Floor
> Washington, DC 20009
> Phone: (202) 234-7181
> Phone: (888) 247-3624
> Fax: (202) 234-7182
> URL: www.abcbirds.org/

AMERICAN SOLAR ENERGY SOCIETY

The American Solar Energy Society (ASES) was established in 1954. ASES's stated goal is "to inspire an era of energy innovation and speed the transition to a sustainable energy economy." ASES offers education programs, sponsors research and conferences, and publishes a magazine, Solar Today.

> 4760 Walnut St., Suite 106
> Boulder, CO 80301
> Phone: (303) 443-3130
> Fax: (303) 443-3212
> E-mail: ases@ases.org
> URL: www.ases.org/

CANADA GREEN BUILDING COUNCIL (CaGBC)

The Canada Green Building Council (CaGBC) oversees the Leadership in Energy and Environmental Design (LEED Canada) program, which was launched by the U.S. Green Building Council in March 2000. LEED guidelines for practical and measurable green building design, construction,

operations, and maintenance solutions. The LEED rating system was developed by a committee made up of volunteers representing all areas of the building and construction industries. In addition to the LEED program, the CaGBC sponsors GREEN UP, a building performance program; Smart Growth, a program to help with development of policies for sustainable communities; and Living Building Challenge, a program that extends sustainable construction beyond LEED. In addition, the CaGBC has chapters in Alberta, the Atlantic provinces, British Columbia (Cascadia Chapter), Manitoba, Quebec, Saskatchewan, and two in Ontario (Ottawa and Toronto). The CaGBC also presents education programs aimed at career development for those engaged (or seeking employment) in green industries. Courses to prepare for LEED certification are presented in live webinars, workshops, and online courses , hosts meetings, and offers resource materials for K-12 classrooms, commercial real estate professionals, community development professionals, and others.

> CaGBC National Office
> 47 Clarence St., Suite 202
> Ottawa, ON, Canada K1N 9K1
> Phone: (613) 241-1184
> E-mail: info@cagbc.org
> URL: www.cagbc.org/

CANADIAN ENVIRONMENTAL LAW ASSOCIATION (CELA)

The Canadian Environmental Law Association (CELA) provides legal assistance to individuals and nonprofit groups who are confronting a pollution problem (or other issues relating to the environment). CELA operates as a specialty clinic with Legal Aid Ontario and helps those who lack the resources to challenge environmental violations through legal channels. CELA's Web site highlights some

of its groundbreaking cases, such as CELA's defense of Canada's first municipal bylaw outlawing the use of cosmetic pesticides; the Supreme Court of Canada found that municipalities have the right to regulate pesticide use.

> 130 Spadina St., Suite 301
> Toronto, ON, Canada M5V 2L4
> Phone: (416) 960-2284
> Fax: (416) 960-9392
> URL: www.cela.ca/

CANADIAN COUNCIL ON ECOLOGICAL AREAS (CCEA)

The Canadian Council on Ecological Areas (CCEA) was incorporated as a nonprofit organization in 1982 and was registered as a charitable organization in 1995. According to the CCEA Web site, its mission is "to facilitate and assist Canadians with the establishment and management of a comprehensive network of protected areas representative of Canada's terrestrial and aquatic ecological natural diversity."

> 3325 Rae St.
> Regina, SK, Canada S4S 1S5
> Phone: (819) 952-7935
> URL: www.ccea.org/

EARTHFIRST!

Earth First! was created in 1979. It is unique among environmental organizations, in that it functions as an activist advocacy organization, which employs tactics ranging from grassroots organizing and involvement in the legal process to civil disobedience. Earth First! calls itself a priority, not an organization. From the EarthFirst! Web site: " . . . Our direct actions in defense of the last wild places only seem radical compared to an entire paradigm of denial and control, where the individual is convinced they are powerless, and the organizations set up to protect the wilderness continue to bargain it away."

URL: www.earthfirst.org

EARTH LIBERATION FRONT

Earth Liberation Front (ELF) members are environmental activists. The organization is an independent environmentalist group, whose members are mostly anonymous. It promotes using acts of civil disobedience and economic sabotage to call attention to environmental issues. ELF maintains no office or press contacts.

URL: earth-liberation-front.org/

ECOLOGICAL SOCIETY OF AMERICA

The Ecological Society of America was established in 1915 during a meeting of the American Association for the Advancement of Science. It was founded to unify the science of ecology and to encourage communication among ecologists. The Society had more than 10,000 members worldwide as of 2011.

1990 M St., NW, Suite 700
Washington, DC 20036
Phone: (202) 833-8733
Fax: (202) 833-8775
URL: http://www.esa.org/

ECOLOGY ACTION

Ecology Action partners with local and state agencies, cities, counties and utilities to provide innovative environmental services that improve quality of life and contribute to a sustainable economy.

877 Cedar St., Suite 240
Santa Cruz, CA 95060
Phone: (831) 426-5925
Fax: (831) 425-1404
URL: www.ecoact.org

ENVIRONMENT CANADA

Environment Canada (EC), established in 1971, is the government agency dedicated to protecting the environment, conserving the country's natural heritage, and providing weather and meteorological information. The national government of Canada shares jurisdiction over environmental matters and EC works to coordinate with provincial and territorial governments to develop policies.

Inquiry Centre
10 Wellington, 23rd Floor
Gatineau, QC, Canada K1A 0H3
Phone: (819) 997-2800
Phone: (800) 66-6767 (toll-free from Canada only)
Fax: (819) 994-1412
E-mail: enviroinfo@ec.gc.ca
URL: www.ec.gc.ca/

ENVIRONMENTAL DEFENSE FUND

The Environmental Defense Fund (EDF) was founded in 1967 around the issue of the use of the pesticide DDT. Scientists and lawyers worked together to take legal action on behalf of the environment. This set the tone and mission for the EDF.

257 Park Ave. South
New York, NY 10010
Phone: (212) 505-2100
Fax: (212) 505-2375
URL: www.edf.org/

FOREST STEWARDSHIP COUNCIL

The Forest Stewardship Council (FSC) is an independent nongovernmental organization established in 1993 to promote the responsible management of the world's forests. Its International Center is located in Bonn, Germany, and it maintains a number of regional offices worldwide. Certification from the FSC is essential for a green retailer to have genuine "eco cred." With partners in more than 50 countries, the FSC helps and accredits companies, governments, and communities in forest management. FSC certification requires the operators to observe certain guidelines, which include prohibition of the conversion of natural forests or other habitat around the world; prohibition of both the use of highly hazardous pesticides and the cultivation of genetically modified trees (GMOs); respect for the rights of indigenous peoples; and consistent observance of these guidelines. Every FSC certified operation is visited at least annually; certification may be withdrawn if the operation is found to be noncompliant.

URL: http://www.fsc.org/

FRIENDS OF EARTH (FOE)

Founded in the 1960s, Friends of the Earth (FOE) supports a number of causes, primarily in the United States. With offices in Washington, DC, and San Francisco, California, and members in all 50 states, FOE urges policymakers to enact legislation to defend the environment.

Friends of the Earth DC
1100 15th St. NW, 11th Floor
Washington, DC 20005
Phone: (202) 783-7400
Fax: (202) 783-0444
Friends of the Earth CA
311 California St., Suite 510
San Francisco, CA 94104
Phone: (415) 544-0790
Fax: (415) 544-0796
URL: http://www.foe.org/

FRIENDS OF EARTH CANADA/LES AMI(E)S DE LA TERRE

Friends of the Earth (FOE) Canada began as a small group of volunteers in 1978. The organization seeks to represent environmental issues at the national, provincial, and local levels, through research, education and advocacy.

300-260 St. Patrick St.
Ottawa, ON, Canada K1N 5K5
Phone: (613) 241-0085
E-mail: foe@foecanada.org
URL: http://www.foecanada.org/

GREEN AMERICA (FORMERLY Co-Op AMERICA)

Green America, founded in 1982, was known as "Co-op America" until January 1, 2009. "Economic Action for a Just Planet" is the organization's slogan. It seeks to empower consumers by emphasizing economic initiatives to companies that produce products to do so in an environmentally responsible way. Green America approves business practices and companies may earn its green designation.

1612 K St NW, Suite 600
Washington, DC 20006
Phone: (800) 58-GREEN
URL: http://www.greenamerica.org/

GREEN COMMUNITIES CANADA

Green Communities formed as a network in 1995 and incorporated as the Green Communities Association, a membership organization, in 1996. In early 2005, the name was changed to Green Communities Canada to better reflect the national scope of the group's mission. Green Communities publishes a weekly online newsletter, *Green Communities News*, and sponsors conferences and meetings on environmental topics.

416 Chambers St., 2nd Floor
Peterborough, ON, Canada K9H 3V1
Phone: (705) 745-7479
URL: http://greencommunitiescanada.org/

GREENPEACE

Greenpeace began in 1971 when a group of activists staged a protest of nuclear tests off the coast of Alaska. Greenpeace has helped to stop whaling, nuclear testing, and has engaged in a successful campaign to protect Antarctica. Greenpeace had more than 2.5 million members worldwide as of 2011.

Greenpeace Supporter Care
702 H St., NW, Suite 300
Washington, DC 20001
URL: http://www.greenpeace.org/

INTERGOVERNMENTAL PANEL ON CLIMATE CHANGE

The Intergovernmental Panel on Climate Change (IPCC) is an independent nongovernmental international group of leading respected scientists. The organization's Web site states: "The IPCC was established to provide the decision-makers and others interested in climate change with an objective source of information about climate change. The IPCC does not conduct any research nor does it monitor climate related data or parameters. Its role is to assess on a comprehensive, objective, open and transparent basis the latest scientific, technical and socio-economic literature produced worldwide relevant to the understanding of the risk of human-induced climate change, its observed and projected impacts and options for adaptation and mitigation."

c/o World Meteorological Organization
7 bis Avenue de la Paix, C.P. 2300
CH-1211 Geneva 2, Switzerland
Phone: 41(22) 730-8208/54/84
Fax: (41-22) 730-8025/13
URL: www.ipcc.ch/

NATIONAL ASSOCIATION OF ENVIRONMENTAL PROFESSIONALS

Soon after the National Environmental Policy Act took effect on January 1, 1970, the National Association of Environmental Professionals was formed to provide a mechanism for professionals in the new field of environmental science to share information. NEPA connects those working in various jobs related to environmental technology, preservation, and other sectors. NEPA established the Council on Environmental Quality (CEQ) to assure the uniform application of NEPA provisions.

NAEP Headquarters
PO Box 460
Collingswood, NJ 08108
Phone: (856) 283-7816
Fax: (856) 210-1619
URL: www.naep.org/

NATIONAL AUDUBON SOCIETY

The National Audubon Society was founded in the late 1800s be George Bird Grinnell and named for John Audubon, the artist who created the well-known guide to North American birds. The Audubon Society's mission is "to conserve and restore natural ecosystems, focusing on birds, other wildlife, and their habitats for the benefit of humanity and the earth's biological diversity." The Audubon Society has chapters in more than 500 local chapters.

National Headquarters
225 Varick St.
New York, NY 10014

Phone: (212) 979-3000
URL: http://www.audubon.org/

NATIONAL GEOGRAPHIC SOCIETY

The National Geographic Society was established in 1888. It is one of the world's largest nonprofit scientific and educational institutions. Its interests include geography, archaeology, natural science, and environmental and historical conservation. National Geographic provides financial and technical support to expeditions and scientific fieldwork, geography education, and to programs that promote conservation.

PO Box 98199
Washington, DC 20090-8199
Phone: (800) 647-5463
URL: www.nationalgeographic.com

NATURAL RESOURCES CANADA

Natural Resources Canada (NRCan) is the successor to the Geological Survey of Canada (GSC), which was established on April 14, 1842. NRCan was established in 1994 to deal with natural resources issues for the benefit of all Canadians.

Natural Resources Canada
580 Booth St.
Ottawa, ON, Canada K1A 0E4
Phone: (613) 995-0947
URL: http://www.nrcan.gc.co/home

NATURAL RESOURCES DEFENSE COUNCIL (NRDC)

The Natural Resources Defense Council's Web site states that it "works to protect wildlife and wild places and to ensure a healthy environment for all life on earth." Hundreds of active lawyers and more than 1.2 million members work together to foster legislative change, especially aimed at preventing climate change and saving endangered species.

40 West 20th St.
New York, NY 10011
Phone: (212) 727-2700
Fax: (212) 727-1773
URL: http://www.nrdc.org

NATIONAL WILDLIFE FEDERATION

The National Wildlife Federation worked with state agencies to preserve animals and their habitats. With some 4 million members participating in grassroots efforts as of 2011, it is one of the largest organizations dedicated to wildlife issues. The organization was founded in 1936 by cartoonist Jay Darling with the support of President Franklin Delano Roosevelt.

11100 Wildlife Center Drive
Reston, VA 20190-5362
Phone: (800) 822-9919
URL: www.nwf.org

THE NATURE CONSERVANCY

The Nature Conservancy, founded in 1951, is dedicated itself to saving lands and waters. With over 117 million acres (6,879,684 ha) sustained, 5,000 miles (8,000 km) of rivers kept clean, and hundreds of marine conservation projects, the Nature Conservancy is one of the most successful and effective green organizations in existence. The science-based approach (they have 700 scientists on staff) is used in all conservation efforts around the world.

4245 North Fairfax Dr., Suite 100
Arlington, VA 22203-1606
URL: http://www.nature.org/

1% FOR THE PLANET

1% for the Planet collects contributions from corporations and then donates them to environmental organizations. In 2011, some 1,000 companies participated in the 1% for the Planet programs to contribute to environmental causes.

PO Box 650
Waitsfield, VT 05673
Phone: (802) 496-5408
Fax: (802) 496-6401
E-mail: info@onepercentfortheplanet.org
URL: www.onepercentfortheplanet.org/en/

SIERRA CLUB

The Sierra Club was first incorporated on May 28, 1892, in attorney Warren Olney's office in San Francisco. Those involved in its founding were John Muir, a group from the University of California led by J. Henry Senger, artist William Keith, and Stanford University president David Starr Jordan. The articles of incorporation stated the Sierra Club's purpose: "to explore, enjoy, and render accessible the mountain regions of the Pacific Coast; to publish authentic information concerning them," and "to enlist the support and cooperation of the people and government in preserving the forests and other natural features of the Sierra Nevada." The Sierra is one of the oldest conservation organizations in existence. As of 2011, the club had more than 1.3 million members. It has evolved to become a powerful force in influencing government and corporate policy in the United States. The Sierra Club spends an estimated $300,000 per year in lobbying.

National Headquarters
85 Second St., 2nd Floor
San Francisco, CA 94105
Phone: (415) 977-5500
Fax: (415) 977-5797
URL: http://www.sierraclub.org/

SIERRA CLUB CANADA

The Sierra Club Canada began in 1963 as local chapters of the U.S.-based Sierra Club. The national office opened in 1989 in Canada. In 1992, Sierra Club Canada incorporated as a national organization. As of 2011, there were five chapters—British Columbia Chapter, Prairie Chapter, Ontario Chapter, Quebec Chapter, and Atlantic Chapter. According to the organization's Web site, major program initiatives as of 2011 fell into the areas of health and environment, protecting biodiversity, atmosphere and energy, and sustainable economy.

> *412-1 Nicholas St.*
> *Ottawa, ON, Canada K1N 7B7*
> *Phone: (613) 241-4611*
> *Fax: (415) 977-5797*
> *E-mail: info@sierraclub.ca*
> *URL: http://www.sierraclub.ca/*

SUSTAINABLE COMMUNITIES ONLINE

Sustainable Communities Online was formerly known as the Sustainable Communities Network (SCN). CONCERN, Inc. and the Community Sustainability Resource Institute managed the SCN from 1993 to 2001; CONCERN has managed it since then. The initiatives and resources collected and presented on the organization's Web site are selected to help concerned citizens learn about opportunities to improve local communities and to make the community environment "healthier, safer, greener, more livable, and more prosperous."

> *c/o CONCERN, Inc.*
> *PO Box 5892*
> *Washington, DC 20016*
> *E-mail: concern@sustainable.org*
> *URL: www.sustainable.org*

UNITED STATES ENVIRONMENTAL PROTECTION AGENCY

The Environmental Protection Agency (EPA) was established on December 2, 1970, to address concerns about environmental pollution. President Richard M. Nixon created the agency to consolidate federal research, monitoring, standard-setting, and enforcement activities to ensure environmental protection. In carrying forth its mission "to protect human health and the environment," the EPA assumed responsibility for water quality (formerly handled by the Department of the Interior), for monitoring pesticides (formerly handled by the Department of Agriculture), for controlling solid waste and creating air quality regulations (formerly handled by the Department of Health, Education, and Welfare), and for control of radioactive materials (formerly handled by the Atomic Energy Commission). The EPA operates ten regional offices throughout the United States.

> *U.S. Environmental Protection Agency Headquarters*
> *Ariel Rios Building*
> *1200 Pennsylvania Ave., NW*
> *Washington, DC 20460*
> *Phone: (202) 272-0167*
> *URL: www.epa.org*

U.S. FISH AND WILDLIFE SERVICE (USFWS)

The U.S. Fish and Wildlife Service (USFWS), a bureau of the Department of the Interior established in 1940, operates eight regional offices throughout the country. In brief, the objectives of the USFWS are to support environmental stewardship, to guide conservation and management of the country's fish and wildlife resources, and to administer public programs to help citizens understand and appreciate fish and wildlife.

> *1849 C St., NW*
> *Washington, DC 20240*
> *Phone: (800) 344-WILD*
> *URL: www.fws.gov/*

U.S. GREEN BUILDING COUNCIL (USGBC)

The U.S. Green Building Council (USGBC) launched the Leadership in Energy and Environmental Design (LEED) program in March 2000. LEED guidelines for practical and measurable green building design, construction, operations, and maintenance solutions. The LEED rating system was developed by a committee made up of volunteers representing all areas of the building and construction industries. In addition to the LEED program, the USGBC presents education programs, hosts meetings, and offers resource materials for K-12 classrooms, commercial real estate professionals, community development professionals, and others.

> *2101 L St., NW, Suite 500*
> *Washington, DC 20037*
> *Phone: (202) 742-3792*
> *Phone: (800) 795-1747 (toll-free within U.S.)*
> *URL: www.usgbc.org/*

U.S. NATIONAL PARK SERVICE

The National Park Service (NPS) was created on August 25, 1916, by the National Park Service Organic Act. As of 2011, some 22,000 employees worked 58 national parks and approximately 340 other sites operated by the NPS. NPS is organized into four broad categories: Nature and Science, History and Culture, Education and Interpretation, and New and Information.

> *Office of Communications*
> *1849 C St., NW, Room 3310*
> *Washington, DC 20240*
> *Phone: (202) 208-6843*
> *URL: www.nps.gov*

WILDLIFE CONSERVATION SOCIETY

The Wildlife Conservation Society is dedicated to saving wildlife and their habitats. The organization's official statement reads: The Wildlife Conservation Society "saves wildlife and wild lands through careful science, international conservation, education, and the management of the world's largest system of urban wildlife parks."

> *Canada Headquarters*
> *720 Spadina Ave., Suite 600*
> *Toronto, ON, M5S 2T9*
> *Phone: (416) 850-9038*
> *E-mail: wcscanada@wcs.org*
> *United States Headquarters*
> *301 N. Willson Ave.*
> *Bozeman, MT 59715*
> *E-mail: wcsnorthamerica@wcs.org*
> *URL: www.wcs.org*

WORLD BUSINESS COUNCIL FOR SUSTAINABLE DEVELOPMENT

The World Business Council for Sustainable Development is an association of 200 leading companies from around the world. Its stated mission is "to provide business leadership as a catalyst for change toward sustainable development, and to support the business license to operate, innovate and grow in a world increasingly shaped by sustainable development issues."

> *Head Office*
> *4, chemin de Conches*
> *1231 Conches*
> *Geneva, Switzerland*
> *Phone: +41 (22) 839 3100*
> *Fax: 41 (22) 839 3131*
> *E-mail: info@wbcsd.org*
> *North America Office*
> *WBCSD U.S., Inc.*
> *1500 K St., NW, Suite 850*
> *Washington, DC 20005*
> *Phone: (202) 383-9505*
> *Fax: (202) 682-5150*
> *E-mail: info@wbcsd.org*
> *URL: www.wbcsd.org/*

WORLD WILDLIFE FUND

The logo of the World Wildlife Fund—a panda—is recognized by people around the world. Founded in 1961, the WWF has grown to have some 1.2 million members in the United States as of 2011. The WWF states on its Web site: "We are committed to reversing the degradation of our planet's natural environment and to building a future in which human needs are met in harmony with nature. We recognize the critical relevance of human numbers, poverty, and consumption patterns to meeting these goals." WWF hopes to "conserve 15 of the world's most ecologically important regions by 2020."

Headquarters
1250 24th St., NW
PO Box 97180
Washington, DC 20090-7180
Phone: (202) 293-4800
Fax: (415) 977-5797
URL: www.worldwildlife.org

WORLDWATCH INSTITUTE

Worldwatch was founded in 1974 by farmer and economist Lester Brown. It was the first independent research institute dedicated to monitoring and analyzing environmental concerns around the world. Worldwatch is recognized for its accessible, fact-based analysis of critical global issues. It publishes science-based analysis online; its reports are used by policymakers, private sector leaders, and citizens.

1776 Massachusetts Ave., NW
Washington, DC 20036
Phone: (202) 452-1999
URL: www.worldwatch.org

General Bibliography

BOOKS

Ahuja, S., ed. *Handbook of Water Purity and Quality*. New York: Academic Press, 2009.

Albright, Horace M., and Marian Albright Schenck. *Creating the National Park Service: The Missing Years*. Norman: University of Oklahoma Press, 1999.

Allenby, Braden R. *The Theory and Practice of Sustainable Engineering*. Upper Saddle River, NJ: Pearson Prentice Hall, 2012.

Archer, D. *The Long Thaw: How Humans Are Changing the Next 100,000 Years of Earth's Climate*. Princeton, NJ: Princeton University Press, 2009.

Athens, Lucia. *Building an Emerald City: A Guide to Creating Green Building Policies and Programs*. Washington, DC: Island Press, 2010.

Atlas of Global Conservation: Changes, Challenges, and Opportunities to Make a Difference. Berkeley: University of California Press, 2012.

Berkes, Fikret. *Breaking Ice: Renewable Resource and Ocean Management in the Canadian North*. Calgary: University of Calgary Press, 2005.

Boykoff, Maxwell T. *The New Carbon Economy: Constitution, Governance, and Contestation*. Malden, MA: John Wiley & Sons Inc., 2012.

Calkins, Meg. *The Sustainable Sites Handbook: A Complete Guide to the Principles, Strategies, and Best Practices for Sustainable Landscapes*. Hoboken, NJ: John Wiley & Sons Inc., 2011

Canada Innovates: Sustainable Building. Toronto: Key Porter Books, 2008.

Cashore, Benjamin William. *In Search of Sustainability: British Columbia Forest Policy in the 1990s*. Vancouver: UBC Press, 2001.

Cheek, Martin. *Clean Energy Nation: Freeing America from the Tyranny of Fossil Fuels*. New York: AMACOM, 2012.

Chiras, Daniel D. *The Homeowner's Guide to Renewable Energy*. Rev. ed. Gabriola, BC: New Society, 2011.

Condon, Patrick M., and Jackie Teed. *Sustainability by Design: A Vision for a Region of 4 Million*. Vancouver: Design Centre for Sustainability at the University of British Columbia, 2006.

Contaminants of Emerging Concern in the Environment: Ecological and Human Health Considerations. Washington, DC: American Chemical Society, 2010.

Dearden, Philip, and Rick Rollins. *Parks and Protected Areas in Canada: Planning and Management*. 3rd ed. Don Mills, ON: Oxford University Press, 2009.

DeLeon, Peter, and Jorge E. Rivera. *Voluntary Environmental Programs: A Policy Perspective*. Lanham, MD: Lexington Books, 2010.

DeSousa, Christopher A. *Brownfields Redevelopment and the Quest for Sustainability*. Boston: Elsevier, 2008.

Dilsaver, Lary M., ed. *America's National Park System: The Critical Documents*. Lanham, MD: Rowman & Littlefield, 1994.

Dolin, Eric Jay. *The Smithsonian Book of National Wildlife Refuges*. Washington, DC. Smithsonian Books, 2003.

Dorsey, Kurkpatrick. *The Dawn of Conservation Diplomacy: U.S.-Canadian Wildlife Protection Treaties in the Progressive Era*. Seattle, WA: University of Washington Press, 1998.

Eagan, Timothy. *The Big Burn: Teddy Roosevelt and the Fire that Saved America.* Boston, MA: Houghton Mifflin Harcourt, 2011.

Echaore-McDavid, Susan. *Career Opportunities in Agriculture, Food, and Natural Resources.* New York: Ferguson's, 2009.

Ernst, Chloe. *Scenic Driving Atlantic Canada: Nova Scotia, New Brunswick, Prince Edward Island, Newfoundland, & Labrador.* Guilford, CT: GPP Travel, 2011.

Everhart, William C. *The National Park Service.* Boulder, CO: Westview Press, 1983.

Fearn, E., ed. *State of the Wild 2010–2011: A Global Portrait.* Washington, DC: Island Press, 2010.

Feiden, Wayne. *Assessing Sustainability: A Guide for Local Governments.* Chicago: American Planning Association, 2011.

Forbes Travel Guide: Canada. Chicago: Forbes Travel Guide, 2010.

Fosket, Jennifer. *Living Green: Communities that Sustain.* Gabriola Island, BC: New Society Publishers, 2009.

Gevorkian, Peter. *Alternative Energy Systems in Building Design.* New York: McGraw-Hill, 2010.

Gunn, Angus M. *Unnatural Disasters: Case Studies of Human-Induced Environmental Catastrophes.* Westport, CT: Greenwood Press, 2003.

Hart, E. J. *J. B. Harkin: Father of Canada's National Parks.* Edmonton: University of Alberta Press, 2010.

Hoekstra, J. M., et al. *The Atlas of Global Conservation: Changes, Challenges, and Opportunities to Make a Difference.* Berkeley: University of California Press, 2010.

Howard, Roger. *The Arctic Gold Rush: The New Race for Tomorrow's Natural Resources.* London: Continuum, 2009.

Howlett, Michael, et al. *British Columbia Politics and Government.* Toronto: Emond Montgomery, 2010.

The Importance of Nature to Canadians: The Economic Significance of Nature-Related Activities. Ottawa: Environment Canada, 2000.

Ise, John. *Our National Park Policy: A Critical History.* Baltimore: Johns Hopkins Press, 1961.

Kemp, Roger L., and Carl J. Stephani. *Cities Going Green: A Handbook of Best Practices.* Jefferson, NC: McFarland, 2011.

Krosinsky, Cary, et al. *Evolutions in Sustainable Investment.* Hoboken, NJ: Wiley, 2012.

Luxton, Eleanor G. *Banff: Canada's First National Park.* 2nd ed. Banff, AB: Summerthought Publications, 2008.

Mackintosh, Barry. *The National Parks: Shaping the System.* Washington: National Park Service, 1991.

Matchar, Emily, and Karla Zimmerman. *Nova Scotia, New Brunswick & Prince Edward Island.* 2nd ed. London: Lonely Planet, 2011.

McClanahan, Tim R., and Joshua Cinner. *Adapting to a Changing Environment: Confronting the Consequences of Climate Change.* New York: Oxford University Press, 2011.

McKay, Kim, and Jenny Bonnin. *True Green: 100 Everyday Ways You Can Contribute to A Healthier Planet.* Washington, DC: National Geographic Society, 2006.

McKenzie-Mohr, Doug. *Social Marketing to Protect the Environment.* Thousand Oaks, CA: SAGE Publications, 2012.

Mills, Robin M. *The Myth of the Oil Crisis: Overcoming the Challenges of Depletion, Geopolitics, and Global Warming.* Westport, CT: Praeger, 2008.

National Geographic Guide to the National Parks of Canada. Washington, DC: National Geographic, 2011.

National Geographic Guide to National Parks of the United States. Amenia, NY: Grey House Publishing, 2012.

Neimark, Peninah, ed. *The Environmental Debate: A Documentary History, with Timeline, Glossary, and Appendices.* Washington, DC: National Geographic Society, 2011.

Nolon, John R. *Climate Change and Sustainable Development Law in a Nutshell.* St. Paul, MN: West, 2011.

Northeast British Columbia's Ultimate Potential for Conventional Natural Gas. Victoria: B.C. Ministry of Energy, Mines and Petroleum Resources, 2006.

Pearson, Richard G. *Driven to Extinction: The Impact of Climate Change on Biodiversity.* New York: Sterling, 2011.

Penziwol, Shelley. *From Asessippi to Zed Lake: A Guide to Manitoba's Provincial Parks.* Winnipeg: Great Plains Publications, 2011.

Regional Planning for a Sustainable America. New Brunswick, NJ: Rutgers University Press, 2011.

Repetto, Robert C. *America's Climate Problem: The Way Forward.* Washington, DC: Earthscan, 2011.

Rettie, Dwight F. *Our National Park System: Caring for America's Greatest Natural and Historic Treasures.* Urbana: University of Illinois Press, 1995.

Richardson, Lee. *The Oil Sands: Toward Sustainable Development.* Ottawa: Standing Committee on Natural Resources, 2007.

Ridenour, James M. *The National Parks Compromised: Pork Barrel Politics and America's Treasures.* Merrillville, IN: ICS Books, 1994.

Rose, Alex. *Who Killed the Grand Banks?: The Untold Story Behind the Decimation of One of the World's Greatest Natural Resources.* Mississauga, ON: J. Wiley & Sons Canada, 2008.

Rothman, Hal K. *Preserving Different Pasts: The American National Monuments.* Urbana: University of Illinois Press, 1989.

Runte, Alfred. *National Parks: The American Experience.* 3rd ed. Lincoln: University of Nebraska Press, 1997.

Sellars, Richard West. *Preserving Nature in the National Parks: A History.* New Haven: Yale University Press, 1997.

Shankland, Robert. *Steve Mather of the National Parks.* 3rd ed. New York: Alfred A. Knopf, 1976.

Shiell, Leslie. *Greater Savings Required: How Alberta Can Achieve Fiscal Sustainability from Its Resource Revenues.* Ottawa: C.D. Howe Institute, 2008.

Soucoup, Dan. *Logging in New Brunswick: Lumber, Mills, and River Drives.* Halifax, NS: Nimbus Publishing Ltd., 2011.

Stapilus, Randy. *The Water Gates: Water Rights, Water Wars in the 50 States.* Carlton, OR: Ridenbaugh Press, 2010.

Sundqvist, Goran, and Rolf Lidskog. *Governing the Air: The Dynamics of Science, Policy, and Citizen Interaction.* Cambridge, MA: MIT Press, 2012.

Swain, Donald C. *Wilderness Defender: Horace M. Albright and Conservation.* Chicago: University of Chicago Press, 1970.

Taylor, Dorceta. *The Environment and the People in American Cities, 1600s–1900s.* Durham, NC: Duke University Press, 2009.

Underwood, Deborah. *101 Ways to Save the Planet.* Chicago: Raintree, 2012.

Visser, Emily, and Luigi Ferrara. *Canada Innovates: Sustainable Building.* Toronto: Key Porter Books, 2008.

Wexler, Rex. *Greenpeace: How A Group of Journalists, Ecologists, and Visionaries Changed the World.* Emmaus, PA: Rodale, 2004.

Wirth, Conrad L. *Parks, Politics, and the People.* Norman: University of Oklahoma Press, 1980.

Wittig, Jennifer, et al. *The Great Lakes: An Environmental Atlas and Resource Book.* Toronto, ON: Great Lakes National Program Office, US Environmental Protection Agency, Government of Canada, 1995.

PERIODICALS

Alternatives Journal: Environmental Ideas and Action.

American Journal of Environmental Sciences.

Canadian Journal of Environmental Education (CJEE).

EcoHome Magazine.

Ecology.

Ecology Law Quarterly.

Eco-Structure: A Magazine of the American Institute of Architects.

Endangered Species Bulletin.

Environmental Sciences and Pollution Management.

Environmental Science and Technology.

Environments.

Ethics and the Environment.

GBD Magazine (Green Building and Design).

Global Environmental Politics.

GreenBuilder.

Journal of Environmental Economics and Management (JEEM).

Journal of Environmental Engineering.

Journal of Environmental Management.

National Wildlife Magazine.

Nature: International Weekly Journal of Science.

Science.

Scientific American.

Sierra.

Water Quality Research Journal of Canada.

World Watch.

WEB SITES

Adventures in Renewal Energy Technology: Canada. Available from http://www.re-energy.ca/

Agricultural Marketing Service. U.S. Department of Agriculture (USDA) National Organic Program. Available from http://www.ams.usda.gov/AMSv1.0/nop

Brundtland Report. Available from http://www.un-documents.net/wced-ocf.htm

Canadian Sustainability Indicators Network. Available from http://www.csin-rcid.ca

Center for Green Chemistry and Green Engineering, Yale University. Available from http://www.greenchemistry.yale.edu/

Community-Based Collaboratives Research Consortium. Available from http://www.cbcrc.org/

Ecosystem Management. Available from http://new.unep.org/ecosystemmanagement/

Environment Canada. Available from http://www.ec.gc.ca/

Environmental Justice, National Resources Defense Council. Available from http://www.nrdc.org/ej/default.asp

Forests Information Center. Available from http://www.unep-wcmc.org/forest/homepage.htm

Green Building Basics. Available from http://www.calrecycle.ca.gov/GreenBuilding/Basics.htm

Green Engineering, U.S. Environmental Protection Agency. Available from http://www.epa.gov/oppt/greenengineering/index.html

Greenaction. Available from http://www.greenaction.org/index.shtml

Gulf Restoration Network. Available from http://www.healthygulf.org/

National Atmospheric Deposition Program (NADP). Available from http://nadp.sws.uiuc.edu/NADP/

Nuclear Energy. Available from http://www.epa.gov/cleanenergy/energy-and-you/affect/nuclear.html

Pew Commission on Industrial Farm Animal Production. Available from http://www.ncifap.org/

Rand Corporation: Global Technology Revolution 2020. http://www.rand.org/pubs/monographs/MG475/

Renewal Energy Policy Project. Available from http://www.repp.org

Resources on U.S. Climate Change Research. Available from http://www.epa.gov/climatechange/index.html

Scorecard: The Pollution Information Site Available from http://www.scorecard.org/index.tcl

Soil Contamination. Available from http://www.epa.gov/superfund/students/wastsite/soilspil.htm

Superfund. Available from http://epa.gov/superfund/

Sustainable Consumption and Production Branch, United Nations Environmental Programme. Available from http://www.unep.fr/scp/publications/scpnet/

United Nations Environment Programme: Global Reporting Initiative (GRI). Available from http://www.globalreporting.org/Home

USAID: Environment. Available from http://www.usaid.gov/our_work/environment/

U.S. Environmental Protection Agency: Water Pollution Legal Aspects. Available from http://www.epa.gov/ebtpages/watewaterpollutionlegalaspects.html

U.S. National Oceanic and Atmospheric Administration (NOAA): Oil and Chemical Spills. Available from http://www.noaawatch.gov/themes/oilspill.php

Water Pollution. Available from http://www.epa.gov/ebtpages/watewaterpollution.html

General Index

Page numbers in boldface indicate the main essay for a topic. An italicized page number indicates a photo, illustration, chart, or other graphic.

Newfoundland and Labrador, 574–575
North Dakota, 358, 359
Northwest Territories, 580, 583
Nova Scotia, 591, *591*
Nunavut, 601
Ontario, 608
Oregon, 386
Pennsylvania, 396
Quebec, 623, 627, 628, *629*
Saskatchewan, 637
South Carolina, 416–417
South Dakota, 421, 425
Tennessee, 434, 435
Vermont, 464, 466, 469
Washington, 483, 486, 487
West Virginia, 496
Wisconsin, 508
Wyoming, 517, 518
Yukon, 646
Hydro-Quebec, 469, 627, 628–630

I

I-65 Clean Biofuel projects Corridor project, 161
Iberdrola Renewables, Inc., 350
IBEW (International Brotherhood of Electrical Workers), 281
ICCAC (Iowa Climate Change Advisory Council), 165
Iceberg, Nunavut, *599*
Idaho, **137–144**
 climate and climate change, 137
 energy, 140–141, 142
 green economy initiatives, 141–142
 natural resources, water, and agriculture, 137, *139*, 139–140, *142*, 142–143, 282
 state map and profile, *138*, 140*t*
Idaho Comprehensive Wildlife Conservation Strategy, 137
IECC. *See* International Energy Conservation Code (IECC) applications
Illinois, **145–153**
 climate and climate change, 145
 energy, 6–7, 145, 146, 148
 green economy initiatives, 148–149, *151*, 151–152
 natural resources, water, and agriculture, 145–146, 149–151, 239
 state map and profile, *147*, 148*t*
Illinois River, poultry litter contamination case, 57–58
Imprelis pesticide, 5
In situ extraction technique, 638, 639
Incentive programs for green economy initiatives
 Alabama, 23
 British Columbia, 549
 Georgia, 122
 Idaho, 141
 Iowa, 169

Kansas, 179, 180
Kentucky, 189
Manitoba, 556–557
Mississippi, 260
Nebraska, 289
Nevada, 297
New Brunswick, 565–566
New Mexico, 328
New York, 341
Nova Scotia, 592
Nunavut, 601–602
Ontario, 609
Prince Edward Island, 620, 621
Saskatchewan, 638
South Dakota, 426
Tennessee, 436
Virginia, 478–479
Yukon, 647
Indiana, **155–163**
 climate and climate change, 155
 energy, *159*, 159–161, *160*
 green economy initiatives, 160–161
 natural resources, water, and agriculture, 155–156, 158–159
 state map and profile, *157*, 158*t*
Innovative Clean Energy Fund (British Columbia), 548
Innu people, James Bay Project concerns (Quebec), 628, 629–630
Institute for Sustainable Energy, Environment, and Economy (ISEEE) (Alberta), 538
Institute of International Sustainable Development, 524
Integrated Risk Information System (IRIS), 9
International Brotherhood of Electrical Workers (IBEW), 281
International Coal Group, 190
International Energy Conservation Code (IECC) applications
 Alabama, 23
 Connecticut, 91
 Delaware, 100
 Idaho, 141
 Iowa, 171
 Kansas, 179
 Montana, 281
 Nebraska, 289
 New Hampshire, 308
 Tennessee, 436
 Texas, 447
 Vermont, 467
Interstate Renewable Energy Council (IREC), 8
Invasive Carp Research Program, 269
Invasive species
 Arkansas, 53–54
 Colorado, 79–80
 Florida, 112–113
 Hawaii, 128, 132
 Illinois, 145
 Michigan, 239
 Mississippi, 256, 258

Missouri, 269
Nebraska, 285
Ohio, 366, 368–369
Oregon, 384
 See also Asian carp threat
Invenergy, 350
Iowa, **165–174**
 climate and climate change, 165, 168
 energy, 168–171
 green economy initiatives, 170–171
 natural resources, water, and agriculture, 165, 166, 168, *168*, 171–172, *172*
 state map and profile, *168*, 169*t*
Iowa Climate Change Advisory Council (ICCAC), 165
Iowa Green Jobs Task Force, 171
Iowa Green Team, 170
Iowa Power Fund, 170–171
Iowa Workforce Development, 171
Iowa's Water & Land Legacy campaign, 171–172
IREC (Interstate Renewable Energy Council), 8
IRIS (Integrated Risk Information System), 9
Iron mining, Canada, 600, 644
Irrigation
 Arizona, 45, 48
 Florida, 112
 Kansas, 176, 178, 179–180
 United States, 4, *5*
 Washington, 486
Irrigation Non-Expansion Areas (Arizona), 48
ISEEE (Institute for Sustainable Energy, Environment, and Economy) (Alberta), 538
Isles, Inc., 319
Ivanpah Solar Electric Generating System (California), 66–67, 68

J

Jackson, Lisa, 1, 10
James Bay and Northern Quebec Agreement (Canada), 629
James Bay Project (Quebec), 628–630, *629*
Japan earthquake (2011), 6, 468
Jasper National Park (Canada), *527*
Jersey Fresh and Jersey Grown programs, 316
Jersey-Atlantic wind farm, *319*
JET (Jobs and Education for Texans) Fund, 447
Jewel Cave National Monument (South Dakota), 422
Jindal, Bobby, 198, 199
Jobs, Justice, Climate - Building a Green Economy for British Columbia (2010 conference), 549

Mount Washington Hotel
(New Hampshire), *306*
Mountain lion hunting, South
Dakota, 424
Mountain pine beetle infestation
British Columbia, 544
Canada, 527
Colorado, 74, 79–80
Wyoming, 514, *516*
Mountain Ridge Protection Act
(1983), 352
Mountaineer Wind Energy
(West Virginia), 497
Mountain-top coal mining, 7, 497,
497, 498–500
MPCA (Minnesota Pollution Control
Agency), 248
Mulroy, Patricia, 298, 299

N

Nahanni National Park (Northwest
Territories), 580
NAHBGreen (National Association of
Home Builders' Green Building
Program), 308–309
Nairn, Robert, 380
Nalcor Corporation (Newfoundland
and Labrador), 575
Nantucket Sound wind farm project,
223, 224, 229–230, *230*
Narragansett Bay, 406, 409–410
National Academy of Sciences (NAS),
2–3, 9
National Ambient Air Quality
Standard (NAAQS), 25
National Association of Home
Builders' Green Building Program
(NAHBGreen), 308–309
National Commission on the BP
Deepwater Horizon Oil Spill and
Offshore Drilling, 262
National Energy Board (Canada),
584
National Grid utility company, 229,
403, 408
National Mining Association, 499
National Oceanic and Atmospheric
Administration (NOAA), 199, 240,
406
National parks, forests, and recreation
areas
Alaska, 32
Arizona, 43
Arkansas, 53
California, 62
Canada, 526, *527*
Colorado, 74
Connecticut, 86
Delaware, 96
Florida, 106
Kentucky, 184
Louisiana, 194
Maine, 205, *206*

Maryland, 214
Minnesota, 245
Missouri, 266, *272*
Montana, 276
Nevada, 294
New Brunswick, 563
New Jersey, 314
New Mexico, 324
New York, 334
North Carolina, 346
North Dakota, 356, *361*, 362
Northwest Territories, 580
Ohio, 365–366
Pennsylvania, 394
Prince Edward Island, *617*
Quebec, 625
Saskatchewan, 633, 635, *635*
South Carolina, 414
South Dakota, 422
Utah, 452
Virginia, 474
Washington, 484
Wisconsin, 503
Wyoming, 514, 519–520
National Priorities List (NPL), 9
National Renewable Energy Labora-
tory (NREL), 77, 227
National Research Experimental
Reactor (Canada), 529
National Resources Defense Council
(NRDC), 290
National Water Management Center
(NWMC), 4
National Weather Center
(Oklahoma), 375, *376*
Natural gas consumption
Arizona, 45
Delaware, 98–99
Georgia, 120–121
Idaho, 140
Indiana, 159
Kansas, 178
Kentucky, 187
Maine, 206
Massachusetts, 227
Minnesota, 248–249
Mississippi, 259
Missouri, 269
Nebraska, 286
Nevada, 296
New Hampshire, 307
New Jersey, 317
New Mexico, 327
New York, 338
North Carolina, 349
North Dakota, 359
Oklahoma, 378
Ontario, 608
Oregon, 386
South Carolina, 416
South Dakota, 425
Utah, 455
Vermont, 466
Washington, 487
West Virginia, 494

Natural gas industry
Alabama, 22
Alberta, 537
Arkansas, 54–55, *55*, 56
British Columbia, 547
Canada, 528, 529
Colorado, 77
Kansas, 178
Louisiana, 197
Michigan, 236
Mississippi, 255, 259
Montana, 279
Nebraska, 286
New Brunswick, 565
New Jersey, 316–317
New Mexico, 327
Newfoundland and Labrador,
576–577
North Dakota, 359
Northwest Territories, 582–583,
584–585
Nova Scotia, 590–591
Nunavut, 601
Ohio, 370
Oklahoma, 378
Ontario, 608
Pennsylvania, *398*
Quebec, 627
Saskatchewan, 636
Texas, 445–446
United States, 7–8
Utah, 455
Virginia, 479–481, *480*
West Virginia, 494
Wyoming, 513, 518
Yukon, 646
Natural gas-fired power plants
Alberta, 537
Arkansas, 56
British Columbia, 548
California, 66
Colorado, 77
Delaware, 98
Florida, 109–110
Louisiana, 197
Maine, 206
Maryland, 216
Michigan, 236
Mississippi, 259
Nevada, 296
New Jersey, 317
New York, 338
Oklahoma, 378
Quebec, 627
Rhode Island, 407
South Carolina, 416
Texas, 446
Utah, 456
Virginia, 478
Wisconsin, 507
Yukon, 646
Natural resources
Alabama, 19
Alaska, 30, 32–33
Alberta, 533, 535–536, *536*